Principles of Marketing

openstax™

CONTENTS

19 | Sustainable Marketing: The New Paradigm   651

Preface

About OpenStax

OpenStax is part of Rice University, which is a 501(c)(3) nonprofit charitable corporation. As an educational initiative, it's our mission to transform learning so that education works for every student. Through our partnerships with philanthropic foundations and our alliance with other educational resource companies, we're breaking down the most common barriers to learning. Because we believe that everyone should and can have access to knowledge.

About OpenStax Resources

Customization

Principles of Marketing is licensed under a Creative Commons Attribution 4.0 International (CC BY) license, which means that you can distribute, remix, and build upon the content, as long as you provide attribution to OpenStax and its content contributors.

Because our books are openly licensed, you are free to use the entire book or select only the sections that are most relevant to the needs of your course. Feel free to remix the content by assigning your students certain chapters and sections in your syllabus, in the order that you prefer. You can even provide a direct link in your syllabus to the sections in the web view of your book.

Instructors also have the option of creating a customized version of their OpenStax book. Visit the Instructor Resources section of your book page on OpenStax.org for more information.

Art Attribution

In *Principles of Marketing*, art contains attribution to its title, creator or rights holder, host platform, and license within the caption. Because the art is openly licensed, anyone may reuse the art as long as they provide the same attribution to its original source.

Errata

All OpenStax textbooks undergo a rigorous review process. However, like any professional-grade textbook, errors sometimes occur. Writing style guides and other contextual frameworks also change frequently. Since our books are web-based, we can make updates periodically when deemed pedagogically necessary. If you have a correction to suggest, submit it through the link on your book page on openstax.org. Subject matter experts review all errata suggestions. OpenStax is committed to remaining transparent about all updates, so you will also find a list of past errata changes on your book page on openstax.org.

Format

You can access this textbook for free in web view or PDF through OpenStax.org, and for a low cost in print.

About *Principles of Marketing*

Summary

Principles of Marketing is targeted at the core marketing course for undergraduate business majors and minors. The book is designed for conceptual accessibility to students who are relatively early in their business curriculum (such as second-year students), yet it is also suitable for more advanced students. Due to the wide range of audiences and course approaches, the book is designed to be as flexible as possible. It provides a solid grounding in the core concepts and frameworks of marketing theory and analysis so that business students interested in a major or minor in marketing will also be prepared for more rigorous upper-level courses. Concepts are reinforced through detailed and realistic company and organization scenarios and examples from various industries and geographical locations. *Principles of Marketing* also includes a diverse array of organizations so that students can see themselves and relate to the key concepts discussed.

Pedagogical Foundation

Principles of Marketing emphasizes marketing concepts relevant to people working in a variety of business functions. To illuminate the meaningful applications and implications of marketing ideas, the book incorporates a modern approach, providing connections between topics, solutions, and real-world problems. This multifaceted framework drives the integration of concepts while maintaining a modular chapter structure. Theoretical and practical aspects are presented in a balanced manner. *Principles of Marketing* exposes students to a diverse range of for-profit and nonprofit organizations, industries, products, brands, and services.

Table of Contents

Employability, companies demonstrating ethical awareness, and marketing metrics are strong themes incorporated throughout most chapters.

While chapters are written to be independent, they do generally build on the understanding gained in the previous chapters. Please bear this in mind when considering alternate sequence coverage.

The table of contents (TOC) presents 19 chapter topics in the following sequence:

Unit 1	**Setting the Stage**
1	Marketing and Customer Value
2	Strategic Planning in Marketing
Unit 2	**Understanding the Marketplace**
3	Consumer Markets and Purchasing Behavior
4	Business Markets and Purchasing Behavior
5	Market Segmentation, Targeting, and Positioning
6	Marketing Research and Market Intelligence
7	Marketing in a Global Environment
8	Marketing in a Diverse Marketplace
Unit 3	**Product, Promotion, Price, and Place**
9	Products: Consumer Offerings
10	Maintaining a Competitive Edge with New Offerings
11	Services: The Intangible Product
12	Pricing Products and Services
13	Integrated Marketing Communications

Table 1

14	The Promotion Mix: Advertising and Public Relations
15	The Promotion Mix: Personal Selling and Sales Promotion
16	Direct, Online, Social Media, and Mobile Marketing
17	Distribution: Delivering Customer Value
18	Retailing and Wholesaling
19	Sustainable Marketing: The New Paradigm

Table 1

Coverage and Scope

The book is organized in a three-part structure.

Unit 1 (Setting the Stage) provides students with an overview of value as a driving concept and examines the strategic process that organizations should undergo to realize this for their customers.

Chapter 1 introduces students to the "basics" of marketing—what marketing is, the marketing mix and the 4P framework of marketing, customer relationship management, and how marketers go about determining consumer needs and wants. Featured company examples include Gatorade, Volkswagen, Zappos, TOMS, and Gexpro. Chapter 1 starts the ethical coverage found in every chapter and specifically examines the importance—and the dos and don'ts—of ethical marketing.

Chapter 2 explores marketing strategy, the purpose and structure of the marketing plan, and how results of the marketing strategy can be measured through marketing metrics. Featured company examples include Frito-Lay, Procter & Gamble, Emerson Electric, Apple, Everlane, and Starbucks.

Unit 2 (Understanding the Marketplace) provides students with analytical tools and frameworks to understand a broad range of customers (whether consumers or businesses), categorize them into target segments, and then gather data to make solid product decisions. The last two chapters in Unit 2 emphasize the challenges of expanding to international markets and reaching culturally and demographically diverse segments in domestic markets. (These nuances are properly explored more in-depth in elective, advanced courses.)

Chapter 3 focuses on consumer markets and buying behavior. Students glean an understanding of the types of consumer buying behavior, factors that influence that behavior, and the consumer purchasing decision process. Featured company examples include McDonald's, Zappos, PepsiCo, Patagonia, Birchbox, Abercrombie & Fitch, and Chipotle.

Chapter 4 focuses on the business-to-business (B2B) market. While there are similarities between consumer markets and B2B markets, there are also significant differences, including types of buyers and buying situations. Featured company examples include RingCentral, Office Depot, Barnes & Noble, Airbus, and Alibaba.com.

Chapter 5 explores how companies segment markets and select the target markets—those groups upon which companies will focus their marketing efforts. Featured company examples include Mattel Inc., McDonald's, Mercedes-Benz, and IKEA.

Chapter 6 focuses on the practice and process of marketing research and intelligence and their importance to an organization's success. In this chapter, students learn about how research is used as a tool to gather insights from customers and the industry. Featured company examples include LEGO, DuckDuckGo, and the Gallup Organization.

Chapter 7 introduces students to the global arena of marketing: the advantages and nuances of international trade, global trade, and marketing abroad. Featured global economic examples include the war between Russia and Ukraine, the global COVID-19 pandemic, increased prices of oil and other consumer goods, and the disruption of global supply chains.

Chapter 8 explores concepts that students must understand and apply correctly to successfully reach an ever-growing, diverse marketplace. Students will learn about diversity and inclusion marketing, multicultural and sociodemographic populations, cultural insights based on race and ethnicity, generational differences, and characteristics of specific communities that speak to their needs and preferences as consumers. Featured company examples include Procter & Gamble, PepsiCo, McDonald's, Target, Nike, and IKEA.

Unit 3 (Product, Promotion, Price, and Place) presents the standard 4P framework to organize, prioritize, and sequence marketing activities through the value chain.

Chapter 9 reviews the types of products, the product life cycle, branding a product, packaging a product, and the entire product experience. Students will learn how the product experience is developed and rolled out to the market. Featured company examples include Peloton, Netflix, Domino's Pizza, Starbucks, and Chipotle.

Chapter 10 introduces students to the manner in which companies acquire or maintain a competitive edge through offering new products. It explores the stages of the new product development process, factors that contribute to the success or failure of new products, and the stages in the consumer adoption process. Featured company examples include Swarovski, Taco Bell, Gillette, and Kentucky Fried Chicken.

Chapter 11 explores services—what's sometimes known as the "intangible product." It discusses how services are classified, their characteristics, and several related models, including the service profit chain model and the Gap Model of Service Quality. Featured company examples include Delta Air Lines, Zappos, Taco Bell, and the Ritz-Carlton.

Chapter 12 covers the pricing "P" of the marketing mix. It introduces students to the critical Cs of pricing and the five-step procedure for establishing pricing. Featured company examples include Amazon, GetUpside, Toyota, and IKEA.

Chapter 13 describes how companies utilize Integrated Marketing Communications (IMC) to fulfill their marketing goals and objectives. Students will learn about various IMC strategies through examples of companies like Peloton and the ups and downs of the fitness industry. Other featured company examples include TOMS and snack cake maker Little Debbie.

Chapter 14 introduces students to the promotion mix and its various elements. The focus of this chapter includes both successful and failed attempts at reaching the primary target markets. Communication, diversity, and social media are integral parts of this chapter. Featured company examples include Leo Burnett, GameStop, PepsiCo, and SeaWorld.

Chapter 15 delves into various sales strategies, as well as the steps in the selling process, while also reviewing the various methods of sales promotion used to create consumer demand. Featured company examples include Hilton, HelloFresh, and Cutco.

Chapter 16 explores the various digital and direct channels that marketers use to engage with customers, drive traffic to company websites, and turn shoppers into buyers. As consumers continue to spend more, marketers must embrace digital technologies to meet consumers where they are, whether it's on TikTok, Amazon, Instagram, or Gmail.

Chapter 17 explores the different types of distribution decisions that companies make when determining the best way to get products and services to customers. Consumer demand for the speedy delivery of everything from Nike sneakers to shave kits continues to increase. Featured company examples include Whole Foods, Netflix, Wayfair, and AstraZeneca.

Chapter 18 outlines the ever-changing importance of retailing and wholesaling. While retailing has seen a dramatic decrease in recent decades due to online shopping, students are introduced to up-and-coming retailers that may change this trend. Featured company examples include Walmart, AutoZone, QVC, and Costco.

Chapter 19 explores sustainable marketing and how it addresses the positive impact that companies can have on people and the environment. In addition, Chapter 19 explores how brands tackle sustainability and start from a place of purpose in their marketing. Featured company examples include Patagonia, Ben & Jerry's, and PepsiCo. (Designed as a supplemental chapter, Chapter 19 contains fewer review questions and features than do the other chapters in this title.)

Key In-Text Features to Drive Understanding

- **Marketing in Practice.** This feature box presents examples of challenges, managerial decisions, and the range of accepted marketing practices in real companies and industries. It may include a reference or link to an online resource (YouTube video, article, etc.).
- **Ethical Considerations.** Each chapter concludes with a section about common ethical issues pertaining to the chapter content, including an explanation of the importance of ethics in that particular context, common pitfalls, and a company-specific illustrative example.
- **Link to Learning.** Included multiple times in every chapter, this feature provides online resources and videos that are pertinent to students' deeper exploration of the topics. Link to Learning boxes allow students to connect easily to some of the most important thought leaders and concepts in the field.
- **Companies with a Conscience.** This feature box highlights a real company that is demonstrating the ethical practices introduced in the Ethical Marketing section.
- **Marketing Dashboard.** This feature box, included in six chapters, guides students through the process of applying the concepts in the chapter to analyzing and interpreting data (marketing metrics). The example solutions are visible to student within the feature for instant feedback.
- **Careers in Marketing.** This feature box, included in every chapter, has links to websites and videos that promote employability awareness, job exploration, and career opportunities in the marketing field.
- **Knowledge Checks.** Five multiple-choice questions are included at the end of all main chapter sections for student self-review at the point of learning. A student answer key is available at the end of the book.

Organizational and Reinforcement Materials to Support Learning

- **Learning Outcomes.** Every chapter section begins with a set of clear and concise student learning outcomes (LOs). These outcomes are designed to help the instructor decide what content to include or assign and can guide students on what they can expect to learn and be assessed on.
- **In the Spotlight.** Chapter openers include real-world marketing examples that explain the relevance of the topic for students.
- **Applied Marketing Knowledge.** This end-of-chapter feature includes five discussion questions that you can assign for students to apply their learned knowledge.
- **Critical Thinking Exercises.** This end-of-chapter feature presents four or five short-answer questions that challenge students' analytical thinking.
- **Building Your Personal Brand.** This end-of-chapter exercise guides students on how to build their personal brand in order to capture their professional identity, talents, and methods to differentiate themselves from others. This integrative feature will include activities such as building a LinkedIn profile, performing a personal SWOT analysis, etc.
- **What Do Marketers Do?** This end-of-chapter exercise asks students to interview an individual marketing practitioner as a method for investigating and understanding the various marketing jobs and careers. Suggested job titles and questions are provided.

- **Closing Company Case.** This is an in-depth case study of a real company that illustrates the chapter concepts and includes several discussion questions. It can be used as an in-class discussion prompt or as a written homework assignment. A sample answer or rubric is included in the Instructor's Manual.
- **Marketing Plan Exercise.** This running, end-of-chapter project, introduced in Chapter 1 and included in nine chapters, provides students with a downloadable template that they will use to fill out different sections as they move through the book. It is intended to be a multipart, semester-long exercise for which they will select a real company and product (service) to research and analyze.
- **Chapter Summary.** Designed to support both students and instructors, chapter summaries distill the information in the chapter down to key, concise points.
- **Company Names** are visually emphasized in red type in the text.
- **Key Terms.** Key terms are presented in bold text and are followed by an explanation in context. Definitions of key terms are also listed in the end-of-chapter glossary.

Answers to Questions in the Book

Sample solutions are provided for students and instructors at the end of each Marketing Dashboard feature. Answers to the Knowledge Checks are provided in the student answer key at the end of the book. The end-of-chapter Applied Marketing Knowledge discussion questions, Critical Thinking Exercises, and Closing Company Case review questions are intended for homework assignments or classroom discussion; thus, student-facing answers or solutions are not provided. Sample answers are provided in the Instructor Manual for instructors to share with students at their discretion, as is standard for such resources. Building Your Personal Brand, What Do Marketers Do?, and the Marketing Plan Exercise are integrative, open-ended assignments to which standard solutions are not available; students are expected to focus on their own business interests.

Additional Resources

Student and Instructor Resources

We've compiled additional resources for both students and instructors, including Getting Started Guides, an instructor's manual, a test bank, and image slides. Instructor resources require a verified instructor account, which you can apply for when you log in or create your account on OpenStax.org. Take advantage of these resources to supplement your OpenStax book.

Instructor's Manual. For each chapter, the Instructor's Manual includes a chapter overview, ideas for classroom activities, links to supplemental resources and examples, and discussion questions. The Instructor's Manual also contains sample answers to the end-of-chapter Applied Marketing Knowledge, Critical Thinking, and Closing Company Case discussion questions. Authored by Jaciel Keltgen, Minnesota State University, and Lauren Donovan, Delaware County Community College.

Lecture Slides. Using images, key terms, and examples, the lecture slides (in PowerPoint format) outline the main points of each chapter, providing a starting place for instructors to build their lectures. Authored by Debra Ellerbrook, Concordia University, Wisconsin.

Test Bank. The multiple-choice and short-answer questions in the test bank platform are correlated to learning outcomes (LOs) in the textbook, allowing instructors to customize tests to support a variety of course objectives. The test bank is available in Word format. Authored by Jaciel Keltgen, Minnesota State University, and Lauren M. Donovan, Delaware County Community College.

About the Authors

Senior Contributing Authors

Senior contributing authors: Maria Gomez Albrecht (left), Mark Green (center), Linda Hoffman (right).

Dr. Maria Gomez Albrecht, University of Texas at Dallas. Dr. Gomez Albrecht is an adjunct professor of marketing for executive education graduate programs at The University of Texas at Dallas. She is also a fractional chief marketing officer at Alonos Consulting, as well as the director of communications and project management for an international restaurant chain. She has a rich career background in academics and business practice, spanning over 20 countries and five different languages. Her specialties include strategic marketing and planning, brand management, multicultural marketing, loyalty and growth programs, project management, and product launches in domestic and international markets. She holds a PhD from Universidad Central de Nicaragua, a DBA from SMC University, and an MBA from Oral Roberts University. She is also a board officer and member of several academic and professional organizations such as Prospanica and the American Marketing Association.

Dr. Mark Green, Simpson College. Dr. Green is a professor of management at Simpson College. He teaches courses in management, marketing, digital marketing, international marketing, and entrepreneurship and innovation. He is coauthor of *Global Marketing* (10th Edition, Pearson, 2019). During the 2011–2012 academic year, he taught international marketing for the Consortium of Universities for International Studies (CUIS) in Paderno del Grappa, Italy. He directed Simpson's Semester in London program in 1997 and again in 2017. He holds a PhD in Russian linguistics from Cornell University, an MBA in marketing management from Syracuse University, and a BA in Russian literature from Lawrence University.

Linda Hoffman, Ivy Tech Community College. Linda Hoffman has over 20 years' experience teaching Principles of Marketing and other business management courses at Indiana Institute of Technology, Ivy Tech, and Concordia University. She has developed several online business courses for Ivy Tech Community College and Indiana Tech. She has authored and reviewed a variety of textbook chapters, supplements, and digital content. She holds a BS in business administration from Indiana Institute of Technology and an MS in adult education from Indiana University.

The authors wish to express their deep gratitude to Developmental Editor Stephanie Wall for her skillful editing and gracious shepherding of this manuscript.

Contributing Authors

Jacqueline Babb, Northwestern University

Lauren M. Donovan, Delaware County Community College

Debra Ellerbrook, Concordia University Wisconsin

Lisa S. Goolsby, Southern New Hampshire University

Jaciel Keltgen, Minnesota State University

Sarah M. Shepler, Ivy Tech Community College

Deborah Toomey, Northwest Missouri State University

Reviewers

Jacqueline Babb, Northwestern University

Diane Badame, University of Southern California

Dana Bailey, East Tennessee State University

Bryan Berndt, Rockland Community College

Lisa Cherivtch, Oakton Community College

Carol A. Decker, Johnson University

Beibei Dong, Lehigh University

Francis Dong, Catholic University (retired)

Debra Ellerbrook, Concordia University Wisconsin

Kevin Feldt, The University of Akron

Ignacio Godinez Puebla, The University of Texas at Tyler

Jaciel Keltgen, Minnesota State University

Keyah Levy, Simpson College

Ira Lovitch, Mount Saint Mary's University

Rajiv Mehta, New Jersey Institute of Technology

Monique Reece, University of Denver

Muhammed Saadiq, College of DuPage

Susan Schanne, Eastern Michigan University (retired)

Jere Smith, Southern New Hampshire University

Deborah Toomey, Northwest Missouri State University

Violet Zlatar-Christopher, California State University

Academic Integrity

Academic integrity builds trust, understanding, equity, and genuine learning. While students may encounter significant challenges in their courses and their lives, doing their own work and maintaining a high degree of authenticity will result in meaningful outcomes that will extend far beyond their college career. Faculty, administrators, resource providers, and students should work together to maintain a fair and positive experience.

We realize that students benefit when academic integrity ground rules are established early in the course. To that end, OpenStax has created an interactive to aid with academic integrity discussions in your course.

Approved | Ask Instructor | Not Approved

Your Original Work

Quoting & Crediting Another's Work

Checking Your Answers Online

Group Work

Reusing Past Original Work

Sharing Answers

Getting Others to Do Your Work

Posting Questions & Answers

Plagiarizing Work

Visit our academic integrity slider (https://openstax.org/r/interactive-image-defining). Click and drag icons along the continuum to align these practices with your institution and course policies. You may then include the graphic on your syllabus, present it in your first course meeting, or create a handout for students.

At OpenStax we are also developing resources supporting authentic learning experiences and assessment. Please visit this book's page for updates. For an in-depth review of academic integrity strategies.

Community Hubs

OpenStax partners with the Institute for the Study of Knowledge Management in Education (ISKME) to offer Community Hubs on OER Commons—a platform for instructors to share community-created resources that support OpenStax books, free of charge. Through our Community Hubs, instructors can upload their own materials or download resources to use in their own courses, including additional ancillaries, teaching material, multimedia, and relevant course content. We encourage instructors to join the hubs for the subjects most relevant to your teaching and research as an opportunity both to enrich your courses and to engage with other faculty.

Technology Partners

As allies in making high-quality learning materials accessible, our technology partners offer optional low-cost tools that are integrated with OpenStax books.

Unit 1
Setting the Stage

Unit Introduction

Welcome to *Principles of Marketing*! Some people may mistakenly believe that marketing skills can only be applied to marketing tasks, but the fact is that marketing isn't only for marketers. Studying marketing is essential in almost any career field, because it teaches you the basic principles that connect people, brands, and businesses.

This textbook is divided into three units:

- Unit 1: Setting the Stage
- Unit 2: Understanding the Marketplace
- Unit 3: Product, Promotion, Price, and Place

In this first section, we're going to set the stage for the remainder of this textbook, by first exploring marketing as a discipline and understanding the concept of customer value. Then we'll analyze the role of strategic planning in marketing, because strategy defines how you communicate that customer value to others.

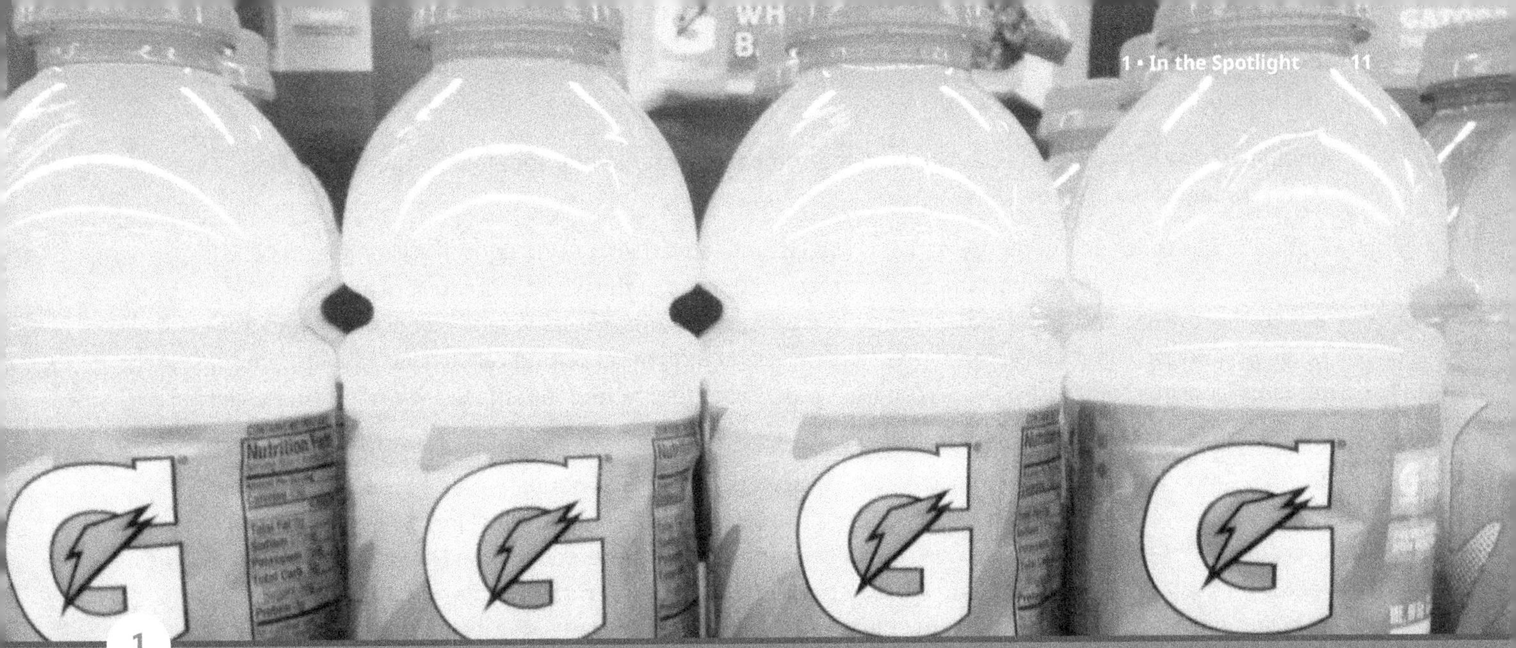

1 Marketing and Customer Value

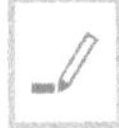

Figure 1.1 Gatorade remains a market-leading product due to parent company Pepsi's success with the marketing mix—product, price, place, and promotion. (credit: modification of work "Gatorade" by JeepersMedia/flickr, CC BY 2.0)

Chapter Outline

In the Spotlight

Since its launch in 1967, Gatorade has been a power player in the sports drink beverage category. Gatorade dominates the US sports drink market, garnering 67.7 percent of the market, followed distantly by the Coca-Cola Company's Powerade and BodyArmor brands at 13.7 percent and 9.3 percent, respectively.[1] The fact that Gatorade has maintained such a large market share demonstrates parent company PepsiCo's understanding of the marketing mix (i.e., product, price, place, and promotion), how to integrate these elements for its target market, and how to continually adapt its marketing mix to meet changing consumer demands.

First, let's consider its approach to the product itself. Gatorade managers saw the exercise boom coming as baby boomers began to age and wanted to be the performance and thirst quencher for everyone from kids to pros. The product, which was intended to replace electrolytes lost in sweat, was scientifically formulated first at the University of Florida and later at the Gatorade Sports Science Institute. But Gatorade didn't rest on its laurels when it comes to product innovation. For example, in order to lure back "lapsed" consumers with concerns over sugar, it launched Gatorade Zero, a thirst quencher without sugar. It also launched its G Series Performance, a new line of food and beverage products designed to provide fuel, fluid, and nutrients before, during, and after activity.[2]

In terms of pricing, Gatorade originally priced its product using a premium strategy because the product was unique. However, in order to retain its lead, the company subsequently adopted competitive pricing policies when competitors entered the market.[3]

Gatorade has continued to pump marketing dollars into advertising campaigns. For example, in 2020 it launched an iconic advertising campaign that featured some of the world's "greatest of all time (GOAT) athletes"— the NBA's Michael Jordan, tennis star Serena Williams, soccer legend Lionel Messi, and track star Usain Bolt. In the commercial, the sports stars appear at a mythical setting called "GOAT Camp," where student athletes (considered "future GOATS") can train with these stars.[4] Check out the GOAT camp commercial here.

Click to view content (https://openstax.org/books/principles-marketing/pages/1-in-the-spotlight)

In 2020 Gatorade launched an impactful digital strategy. When NBA games were canceled due to the pandemic, ESPN aired a 10-part documentary, "The Last Dance," about Michael Jordan's last year with the Chicago Bulls. Because Gatorade wasn't an official sponsor, it partnered with the NBA to stream 1998's Game 6 featuring the Jazz versus the Bulls in what would be superstar Jordan's last game with the Bulls. Gatorade sponsored a "watch party" keyed to the hashtag #Game6Live.[5] Review Gatorade's strategy on Twitter's Marketing website (https://openstax.org/r/gatoradegame6live), which outlines campaign results, opportunity, and steps taken.

Gatorade is an example of how one company built market dominance by creating the optimal integration of its marketing mix—product, price, place, and promotion—throughout a product's life cycle.

1.1   Marketing and the Marketing Process

Learning Outcomes

By the end of this section, you will be able to:
- **LO** 1 Define and describe marketing.
- **LO** 2 Describe the benefits of marketing to the organization, its interested parties, and society.
- **LO** 3 Explain the marketing process.

Marketing Defined

When you ask a group of people, "What's marketing?" most people will answer "advertising" or "selling." It's true that both of these functions are part of marketing, but marketing is also so much more. The American Marketing Association (AMA) defines marketing as "the activity, set of institutions, and processes for creating, communicating, delivering, and exchanging offerings that have value for customers, clients, partners, and society at large."[6] That's kind of a mouthful, so let's see if we can simplify it a bit.

At its most basic level, **marketing** is made up of every process involved in moving a product or service from the organization to the consumer. It includes discerning the needs of customers, developing products or services to meet those needs, identifying who is likely to purchase the products or services, promoting them, and moving them through the appropriate distribution channels to reach those customers. Marketing, quite simply, is about understanding what your customers want and using that understanding to drive the business.

Marketing can also be defined as the set of activities involved in identifying and anticipating customer needs and then attempting to satisfy those needs profitably.[7] But what does that really mean? Let's break down that definition:

- *Identifying customer needs.* This is typically where marketing research comes in. Methods of marketing research will be covered in a later chapter, but market research helps a company develop a detailed picture of its customers, including a clear understanding of their wants and needs.
- *Anticipating customer needs.* After analyzing the data collected, marketers can predict how products might be changed, adapted, or updated.
- *Satisfying customer needs.* If marketers have done their homework correctly and clearly understand their customers' needs, consumers will be pleased with their product purchase and will be more likely to make

additional purchases.

- *Profitably*. Profitability is a relatively simple term; it's when a company's revenue is greater than its expenses. In terms of marketing, the road to profitability means adding value to a product so that the price customers pay is greater than the cost of making the product.[8]

MARKETING IN PRACTICE

Reconciling Segmentation and Diversity

We live in a multicultural world where diversity, equity, inclusion, and belonging (DEIB) is no longer the "right" thing to do; rather, it's imperative. This is particularly true in marketing, because as the consumer population diversifies, brands have to authentically reflect a wide range of backgrounds and life experiences in order to effectively connect with consumers. Therefore, marketers must increasingly respect individual preferences, celebrate differences, and promote customization of products and services to meet customers' needs, wants, and preferences.

At the same time, to profitably produce and sell a viable product or service, marketers must identify potential customer groups and types with certain characteristics in common—i.e., market segmentation. Segmentation requires assigning individuals to predefined categories with predictable behaviors, based on standardized assumptions.

How does segmentation differ from stereotyping? How can segmentation support diversity?

Read the following articles to further explore these nuances:

- Chron: "Difference Between Stereotyping & Market Segmentation (https://openstax.org/r/stereotypingmarket)"
- Retail Dive: "Segmentation is dead (https://openstax.org/r/segmentationisdead)!"
- Spectrem Group Blog: "Why Segmentation Is OK in Market Research Not Life (https://openstax.org/r/whysegmentationok)"

Keep these questions in mind as you explore Unit 2 of this book, where you will learn more about Market Segmentation, Targeting, and Positioning before exploring the considerations of Marketing in a Diverse Marketplace.

How Marketing Benefits the Organization, Its Interested Parties, and Society

Before we go on, let's consider all the people and groups that an organization needs to consider and serve. **Interested parties** are those persons or entities that have an interest in the success or failure of a company. These parties can be categorized into two types: internal and external, as shown in Figure 1.2. You may see these people and groups referred to as "stakeholders" in business writing and other media.

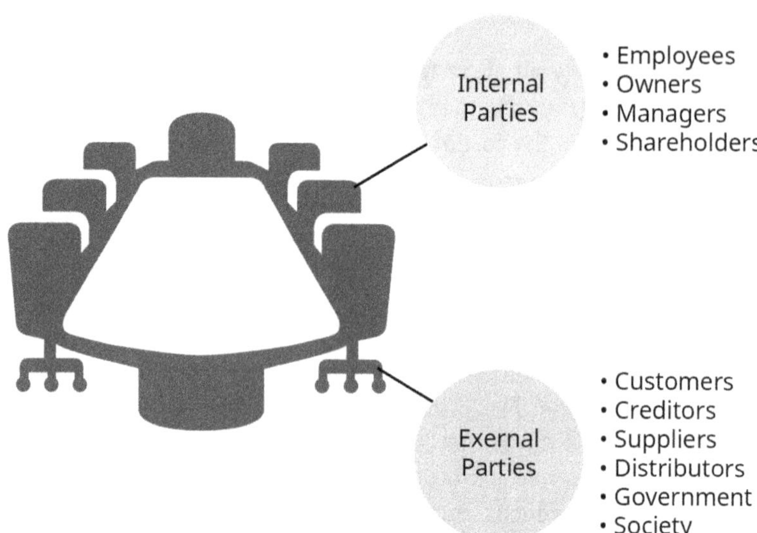

Figure 1.2 Types of Interested Parties (attribution: Copyright Rice University, OpenStax, under CC BY 4.0 license)

Internal interested parties are entities that reside within the organization and that affect—or are affected by—the actions of the company. These entities include employees, owners, managers, and investors (shareholders). When we think about marketing, marketers often tend to look outward. They build strategies to engage customers and show them what the company has to offer.

You might think that marketing would be primarily directed toward those outside the company, like customers, but marketing is also directed toward internal groups. **Internal marketing** involves promoting the objectives, products, and services of a company to its internal constituents—particularly employees.[9]

Think about a recent interaction you have had with a business employee. It could be the server who took your order at lunch or the sales associate at a big box store who showed you the features of the new laptop you were looking to purchase. Which interactions left you with a positive experience? Chances are that your evaluation of the experience is based on the interaction you had with the server or sales associate. That's a function and benefit of good internal marketing, employees who are motivated and empowered to deliver a satisfying customer experience.

External interested parties include those outside the company, such as customers, creditors, suppliers, distributors, and even society at large. External groups don't have a direct say in the company's decision-making process. However they are vital to the success of the company because companies can only succeed with the support of others.

How does marketing benefit external parties? First, consider what marketing does for consumers. It draws out their needs, creates new demand, locates untapped opportunities, and determines the possibilities of selling new products. Second, marketing creates form, time, place, and possession utilities for the company's goods and services. **Utility** refers to a product's usefulness to customers so that they are convinced enough to make a purchase. In other words, when you hear "utility" in marketing, think "usefulness to customers."

Marketing creates several different types of utility:

- **Form utility**. Form utility refers to how well an organization can increase the value of its product in the customer's eyes by making changes and altering its physical appearance.[10] For example, when you want a donut or a pastry, you don't want to buy the ingredients to make it; you want a donut in its final form so you can eat it. That's where the bakery and form utility come into play. The bakery combines flour, sugar, eggs, and other ingredients to make the cakes, donuts, and pastries that you purchase.
- **Time utility**. Marketing creates time utility when it makes products and services available to customers so that they can buy it when it is most convenient for them. Consider how many stores are open evenings, weekends, or even 24/7 to make it convenient for customers to shop there!

- **Place utility**. Marketing creates place utility when it makes goods or services physically available, convenient, and accessible to customers. Consider the ease a company like Uber Eats adds to your life when you're craving tacos in the middle of the night and you don't feel like getting dressed and driving to go get them. You can have your food delivered to you!
- **Possession utility**. Marketers facilitate possession utility by ensuring that a product is relatively easy to acquire. For example, many automobile manufacturers offer low (or sometimes no) interest rates on car loans to make it easy for you to walk out the door with a new set of car keys. Possession utility also encompasses the pride or satisfaction you get from owning a new product, such as a great-fitting pair of running shoes or a smartphone with all of the features you've been wanting.

Marketing's primary benefit to society is that it drives the consumer economy. Marketing leads to increased sales and revenue for a business which enables them to expand operations, create more internal jobs and external jobs for partners like suppliers. Marketing also contributes tax revenue to local, state, and federal governments, ultimately leading to overall economic growth.

The Marketing Process Defined

The **marketing process** refers to the series of steps that assist businesses in planning, analyzing, implementing, and adjusting their marketing strategy. Do an internet search for "steps in the marketing process," and you'll immediately see that some websites outline a 10-step process, whereas others propose a 4-step or 6-step process. For our purposes, we're going to use a 5-step process.

Steps in the Marketing Process

The 5-step process (see Figure 1.3) involves understanding the marketplace and customers, developing a marketing strategy, delivering value, growing customer relations, and capturing value from customers.[11]

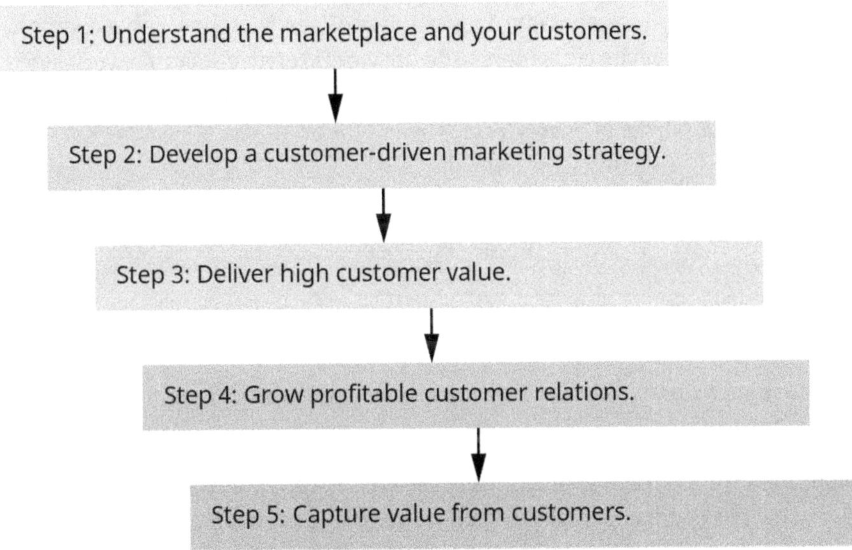

Figure 1.3 Steps in the Marketing Process (attribution: Copyright Rice University, OpenStax, under CC BY 4.0 license)

Step 1: Understand Both the Marketplace and Customers

Before you can start the marketing process, you need to have a good idea of what your marketplace looks like. This means answering some basic questions about your customers, like who they are, their income and purchasing power, and how much they're likely to spend (particularly on your products or services). If you decide to sell at lower prices in order to attain higher unit sales volume, your marketing strategy would look very different than if you decided to sell fewer products at a higher price.

Another way to approach this is to create separate brands and compete in both arenas. Consider Volkswagen. You might immediately think of the VW Beetle or the Jetta, but the company's brand portfolio extends beyond

VW passenger cars and SUVs. It's also the parent company for Audi, Bentley, Lamborghini, Porsche, and others, and these vehicles sell at very different price points than VW passenger cars.[12]

Step 2: Develop a Customer-Driven Marketing Strategy

Marketing strategy refers to a business's overall "game plan" to focus its limited resources in order to reach prospective customers and turn them into paying customers, hopefully for the long run.

It's said that there are two basic types of marketing strategy: a product-driven, "build-it-and-they-will-come" strategy and a customer-driven strategy, in which you analyze prospective consumers and then—and only then—create something that they want or need. We're going to focus on the latter strategy. What happens in a **customer-driven marketing strategy** is that the company shifts the focus from the product or service itself to its users. Customers' needs are the central focus and the point of beginning, not an afterthought. Your primary goal in a customer-driven marketing strategy is to determine what users want and/or need and then satisfy those users. Instead of being product-centric, it's about being customer-centric and developing a mutually beneficial relationship with customers.[13]

In a nutshell, it's about establishing a connection and a relationship. It's about understanding who your customers are, what their needs and wants are, and how you can best meet those needs and wants. It's about knowing your target market better than your competitors do and creating a strong **value proposition** for those users—a promise of value that communicates the benefits of your company's products or services. In short, it's what makes your product or service desirable to potential customers, helps them understand why they should buy it, how your company's product or service differs from those of its competitors, and how your offerings are superior to similar offerings from your competitors. [14]

Step 3: Deliver High Customer Value

Customers have myriad buying options and alternatives today. Given that, how can a company attract and—even more importantly—retain its customers? The answer is relatively simple: you give them value for their money. By definition, **customer value** is the ratio between the perceived benefits and costs incurred by the customer in acquiring your products or services.

The mathematical formula is simple:

$$\text{Value} = \frac{\text{Benefits}}{\text{Price}}$$

$$\left(V = B/P \right)$$

But "value" from the customer's perspective is a complex term, because we're really considering four different values types:

- Functional value: what the product "does" for the customer in terms of solving a particular want or need
- Monetary value: what the product actually costs relative to its perceived worth
- Social value: how much owning the product allows the customer to connect with others
- Psychological value: how much that product allows the customer to "feel better"[15]

Value is increased by boosting the benefits (in the form of product, place, or promotion) or minimizing the price.

Step 4: Grow Profitable Customer Relations

The bottom line is that profitable customer relationships are the "secret sauce" of any business. This step in the marketing process is where marketers acquire, keep, and grow customer relationships. Successful marketers know that acquiring customers is one of the hardest (not to mention one of the most expensive) elements of marketing. However, when you know clearly who those potential customers are, you can more effectively determine how to reach them, thus maximizing your marketing dollars.

It isn't enough to have a one-and-done sale. You want repeat buyers, so marketers need to remind customers about the company's products and/or services and how those products and services have met their needs and improved their lives so they make repeat purchases. Marketers need to consider how to reach customers about their offerings and make it easy and convenient for those customers to make continued purchases.

When customers have a positive relationship with a company or its products or services, they're more likely to become repeat buyers. Satisfied customers are also more likely to be interested in buying additional products or services from your company, and they tend to recommend products to others, further reducing the company's costs of getting new customers.[16]

Step 5: Capture Customer Value in the Form of Profits

The goal of successful customer relationship management (CRM) is creating high **customer equity**—the potential profits a company earns from its current and potential customers. It's a relatively simple concept: increasing customer loyalty results in higher customer equity.

Increasing customer equity is the goal of marketers because it's a bellwether for financial success. Think about it in simple terms: the higher a company's customer equity, the more profit the company generates, and the more valuable that company (and its products or services) becomes on the market.[17]

CAREERS IN MARKETING

Marketing Jobs

In every chapter of this book, you'll find this Careers in Marketing section. It's meant to outline various jobs so you can be well informed of all the things marketers do. These sections will outline various job roles, what you do day-to-day, qualifications needed, and sometimes even salary information.

If you've decided you want a job in marketing, it's important to know what kinds of jobs exist and what's expected in each role. Google and YouTube searches will bring you all kinds of information. It's recommended that you check out the insights from people in these roles and maybe even connect with them to ask them questions. Please do your homework, and determine what you like to do with your day, what you're good at, and how to build a network to find the right job for you.

Here are a handful of resources to get your thinking started:

- HubSpot: "How to Start Your Marketing Career When You Know Nothing About Marketing (https://openstax.org/r/careersblogstartyour)"
- Setup: "The Marketing Career Path: From Entry-Level to Chief Marketing Officer (https://openstax.org/r/themarketingcareerpath)"
- Coursera: "Your Guide to Landing an Entry-Level Marketing Job (https://openstax.org/r/articlesentrylevel)"
- Skillshare: "12 Entry-Level Marketing Jobs You Can Pursue Right Now (https://openstax.org/r/12entrylevel)"
- Indeed: "Entry Level Marketing Salary in the United States (https://openstax.org/r/marketingsalaries)"

Whatever job role you choose, marketing is a creative, interesting, and at times exciting role where you can make a real impact on people's lives. Enjoy!

Knowledge Check

It's time to check your knowledge on the concepts presented in this section. Refer to the Answer Key at the end of the book for feedback.

1. Coca-Cola's mission is to refresh the world, and to that end, it has ensured that you can buy a Coke product at numerous locations—vending machines, convenience stores, restaurant fountains, stadiums, etc. What type of utility has marketing created through this process?
    a. Form utility
    b. Time utility
    c. Place utility
    d. Possession utility

2. Which of the following provides the most complete definition of marketing?
    a. Marketing creates value.
    b. Marketing is made up of every process involved in moving a product or service from your organization to the consumer.
    c. Marketing includes distribution decisions.
    d. Marketing is about building relationships.

3. Which of the following is not an external interested party?
    a. Employees
    b. Customers
    c. Suppliers
    d. Society

4. The total potential profits a company earns from its current and potential customers is known as _______.
    a. customer equity
    b. the value proposition
    c. customer value
    d. the marketing process

5. At which step in the marketing process would the lifetime values to a company's customers be considered?
    a. Developing a customer-driven marketing strategy
    b. Delivering high customer value
    c. Growing profitable customer relations
    d. Capturing value from customers

1.2   The Marketing Mix and the 4Ps of Marketing

Learning Outcomes

By the end of this section, you will be able to:

LO 1 Define and describe the marketing mix.
LO 2 List and explain the 4Ps of marketing.

Marketing Mix Defined

Having a great product or service is just the first step in establishing a successful business or building a successful brand. The best product or service in the world won't translate to profits unless people know about it. How do you reach customers and help them connect with your product? That's the role of the marketing mix.

The **marketing mix** is commonly referred to as the tactics a company can use to promote its products or services in the market in order to influence consumers to buy. The marketing mix is also known as the 4Ps: product, price, place, and promotion (see Figure 1.4). Let's look more closely.

- The **product** is the good or service that the company provides.
- The **price** is what the consumer pays in exchange for the product.
- The **place** is where the product is purchased.
- **Promotion** is comprised of advertising, sales, and other communication efforts the company utilizes to attract the customer.

Figure 1.4 The Marketing Mix and the 4Ps of Marketing (attribution: Copyright Rice University, OpenStax, under CC BY 4.0 license)

The 4Ps of Marketing

To this point, we've been talking marketing in somewhat of an abstract manner. Instead of continuing with a theoretical discussion of the marketing mix and the 4Ps of marketing, we're going to approach these topics using an example of a product you probably already own—a backpack. Let's get started.

Product

Remember: product refers to a good or service that a company offers to its customers. Let's consider a product that many of you likely own as a college student: a backpack (see Figure 1.5).

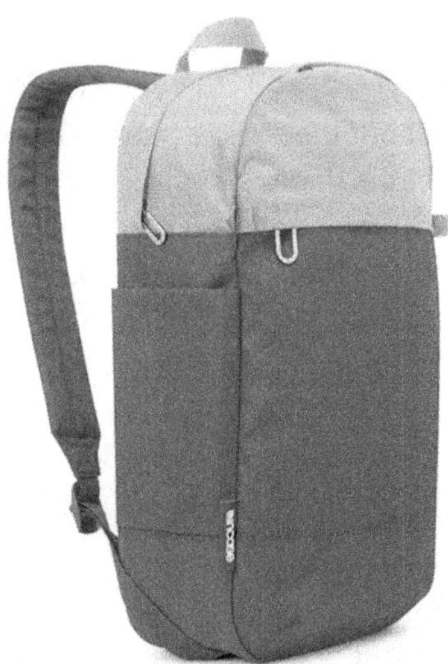

Figure 1.5 Marketing analyzes customer product needs to determine new product models or features that customers would value,

In terms of the first of the 4Ps, marketing analyzes the needs of consumers who buy backpacks and decides if they want more and/or different bags. For example, marketing will analyze what features consumers want in the bag. Do they want a water bottle pocket, padded shoulder straps, reflective tape, a padded laptop sleeve, or organizer pockets? Think about your own bag for a moment: Why did you buy this particular product? What features did it have that made it appealing to you?

Armed with market research knowledge, marketing then attempts to predict what types of backpacks different consumers will want and which of these consumers they will try to satisfy. For example, are you selling bags to adults for their children's use? Are you selling them to young adults who might want more (or different) graphics on the bag? Are you selling to adults who will use these bags for work or for school?

Marketing will then estimate how many of these consumers will purchase backpacks over the next several years and how many bags they'll likely purchase. Marketing will also estimate how many competitors will be producing backpacks, how many they'll produce, and what types.

Price

Price is the amount consumers pay for a product or service. There's a delicate balance here. On one hand, marketers must link the price to the product's real or perceived benefits while at the same time taking into consideration factors like production costs, seasonal and distributor discounts, and pricing product lines and different models within the line.

Marketers attempt to estimate how much consumers are willing to pay for the backpack and—perhaps more importantly—if the company can make a profit selling at that price. Pricing products or services can be both an art and a science. In the case of our backpack example, the company wants to determine two things:

- What's the minimum price that the company can charge for the backpack and still make a profit?
- What's the maximum price that the company can charge for the backpack without losing customers?

The "correct" answer usually lies somewhere in between those points on the price continuum.

Promotion

Promotion includes advertising, public relations, and many other promotional strategies, including television and print advertisements, internet and social media advertising, and trade shows. A company's promotional efforts must increase awareness of the product and articulate the reasons why customers should purchase their product. Remember: the goal of any promotional activity is to reach the "right" consumers at the right time and the right place.

In terms of our backpack example, marketing now needs to decide which kinds of promotional strategies should be used to tell potential customers about the company's backpacks. For instance, should you use TV advertisements to make customers aware of the backpack? If so, you'll want to run your commercials during programs that your target audience watches. For example, if you're selling backpacks to children (or trying to entice them to badger their parents to purchase them), children's cartoons may be the most cost-effective avenue to reach your target market. If your backpacks are designed for work or school, you'll likely decide to advertise on television programs that target younger adults.

LINK TO LEARNING

Netflix, JanSport, and *Stranger Things*

A real-world promotional example is the recent brand partnership between Netflix and JanSport, the backpack company. These two companies collaborated on a *Stranger Things*–branded backpack with the launch of the fourth season of *Stranger Things* in 2022. This collaboration created five Hawkins-inspired backpacks centered on various *Stranger Things* themes. Read more about this promotion and see the backpacks here (https://openstax.org/r/jansportxstranger).

Perhaps you'll decide to run magazine print ads. If so, you'll need to decide in which magazines you'll place the ads. Most magazines have a very specific readership demographic consisting of factors such as age, gender, and interests. If you're going to advertise those backpacks with print ads, you'll want to leverage readership demographics to ensure that your message is being seen by the right consumers—those who are most likely to buy your backpacks.[18]

What about internet advertising? **Internet advertising** (sometimes known as online advertising or digital advertising) is a promotional strategy in which the company utilizes the internet as a medium to deliver its marketing messages. If you're going to go the digital route, what types of internet advertising will you use? Search engine marketing? Email marketing? Social media ads? TikTok videos?

Place

Place considerations focus on how and where to deliver the product to the consumer most likely to buy it. Where did you buy your backpack? Did you buy it in a big box store, online, in an office products store, or perhaps even the school bookstore? Once again, through market research, marketers determine where potential customers will be and how to get the company's backpacks to them.

One important factor to note about the importance of place in the marketing mix is that it doesn't refer to the location of the company itself but rather to the location of the customers or potential customers. Place deals with strategies the marketer can employ to get those backpacks from their present location—a warehouse, for example—to the location of the customers.

Knowledge Check

It's time to check your knowledge on the concepts presented in this section. Refer to the Answer Key at the end of the book for feedback.

1. Which of the following is NOT one of the 4Ps of marketing?
    a. Product
    b. Price
    c. Place
    d. Positioning

2. Which of the 4Ps focuses on determining how much consumers would be willing to pay for a product or service?
    a. Product
    b. Price
    c. Place
    d. Promotion

3. Which of the 4Ps of marketing focuses on how and where to deliver the product to the consumer most likely to buy it?
    a. Product
    b. Price
    c. Place
    d. Promotion

4. DiJuan, a marketer for a soft drink company, ensures that his company's products are available in numerous locations—vending machines, convenience stores, restaurants, and supermarkets. Which element of the 4Ps is DiJuan addressing?
   a. Product
   b. Price
   c. Promotion
   d. Place

5. You're a marketer trying to determine which trade shows you might want to include in your marketing mix. Which element of the marketing mix would address this concern?
   a. Product
   b. Price
   c. Place
   d. Promotion

1.3 | Factors Comprising and Affecting the Marketing Environment

Learning Outcomes

By the end of this section, you will be able to:

- **LO** 1 Define and describe the marketing environment.
- **LO** 2 Explain the components of the marketing environment.
- **LO** 3 Identify and describe the internal factors of the marketing environment.
- **LO** 4 List and describe the components of the micro- and macroenvironments.

The Marketing Environment Defined

Organizations don't operate in a vacuum. They're not self-contained, self-sufficient machines; rather, they are complex systems that require interaction with facets of both their internal and external environments in order to survive and prosper. In this section, we're going to explore the internal and external factors that drive an organization's marketing activities.

The **marketing environment** is comprised of both the external and internal factors and forces that influence an organization's decision regarding its marketing activities. Some of these factors—internal factors— are within the control of the organization. Other factors—external factors—are outside the control of the organization. We'll explore these in more depth below.

To illustrate this concept of internal and external factors and forces, think about your body as an organization. Your body is composed of several internal organs and systems, like your heart, lungs, and digestive system. These organs and systems function both independently and yet interdependently to keep your body going. The same is true with a business. The systems of the business are the people and departments that make up the internal organization (such as marketing, accounting, human resources, etc.). And just like the human body, these systems function independently and interdependently.

At the same time, your body is exposed to external influences, like expectations from your family and friends, cultural or gender stereotypes, and family responsibilities, that influence decision-making in either a positive or negative way. The same is true of the marketing activities of a business. They're influenced by factors both from the macroenvironment and the microenvironment. Let's take a closer look at these factors.

The Components of the Marketing Environment

As we'll explore below, the internal environment is company-specific and includes the 5M framework and organizational culture. The external environment is subdivided into two components: the microenvironment (or task environment) and the macroenvironment (or broad environment), as illustrated in Figure 1.6

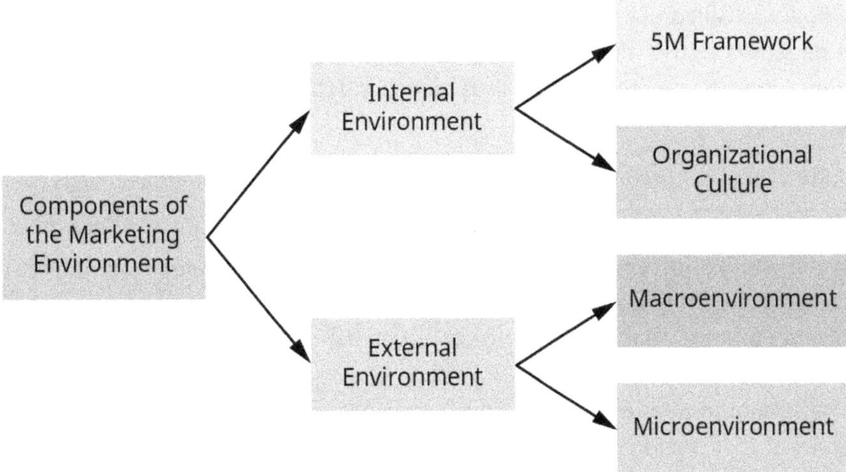

Figure 1.6 The Components of the Marketing Environment (attribution: Copyright Rice University, OpenStax, under CC BY 4.0 license)

Components of the Internal Environment

The internal environment in marketing refers to those elements *within* the organization that define the atmosphere within the company's structure. These factors include what's known as the 5Ms of marketing and organizational culture.

The **5Ms of marketing** (sometimes also called the 5M framework) is a marketing/management model that defines the elements of a marketing strategy that must be addressed in order to be successful. The five elements (sometimes known as the organization's assets) include minds, minutes, machinery, materials, and money.[19] Let's take a closer look at each of these factors:

- **Minds (Staffing):** This "M" might well be considered the most important factor because it's people who make sure the rest of the 5Ms are utilized in a productive manner to achieve the goals of the organization.[20]
- **Minutes (Time):** Time is another valuable asset. We've all heard the saying that time is money, and this is true within the marketing arena. For example, in formulating and implementing a new strategy, marketing needs to assess factors such as whether existing production processes are as efficient and effective as they can be, the length of time it takes the organization to introduce a new product to the market, and how responsive the organization is to competitive pressures.[21]
- **Machinery (Equipment):** Machinery consists of the equipment and/or physical assets used to process materials into finished or semifinished products.
- **Materials (Production):** Materials consist of the inputs needed to produce goods and services.
- **Money (Finance):** Perhaps second only to staffing, money is a very critical resource because it's used to acquire and/or hire other resources.

Organizational culture is comprised of the shared values, attitudes, expectations, norms, and practices that guide the actions of all within the company. Think about organizational culture as "the way we do things around here," and the culture can help or hinder an organization. For example, a good culture embodies positive traits that lead to improved performance and profit. On the other hand, a dysfunctional culture that's toxic and/or inefficient can hinder even the most successful organization.[22]

For an example of a positive organizational culture, consider Zappos, where happiness is at the core. Founder Tony Hsieh wrote a book on the topic and has said, "We're willing to give up short-term profits or revenue growth to make sure we have the best culture."[23] Hsieh was not afraid to put his money where his mouth was, either. In support of maintaining an outstanding company culture and a productive workforce, he instituted a policy that would pay new, unhappy employees $2,000 to quit following their four-week training period.[24]

By contrast, consider what a dysfunctional culture can do to an organization. During the summer of 2020, *The*

Ellen DeGeneres Show was called out for having a toxic work environment. Eleven employees spoke out publicly about the negative organizational culture. There were allegations of sexual misconduct, intimidation, and racism.[25] Ratings faltered as a result of the allegations, and DeGeneres ultimately decided to end her daytime talk show.

But how does organizational culture impact marketing? Here are three very tangible ways that your company's culture can make a positive impact on marketing:

- Branding and marketing efforts emanate from the organization's core values and culture and guide the organization's marketing message. Therefore, if your marketing message doesn't match the reality of the business, it's akin to that old adage of "putting lipstick on a pig."[26] You're talking the talk but not walking the walk.
- A strong culture strengthens your marketing message because it gives prospective customers a better idea of the values of your business, and customers who know what you believe and value are much more likely to do business with you. For example, research has demonstrated that 86 percent of buyers are willing to pay more for a positive customer service experience.[27] Once again, think about the culture at Zappos. One of the ways in which the company has developed a strong following of loyal customers is through its policy that call-center employees are empowered to do "whatever it takes" to make the customer happy. Call-center employees don't use scripts for calls, and there are literally no time limits on calls.[28]
- A strong organizational culture is also key in attracting and retaining employees. In his quest for a happier, more positive work environment, Hsieh implemented several policies at Zappos that he felt contributed to this environment, including a relaxed dress code, discounted food and drink, relaxation areas, and more.[29] TOMS (featured in Companies with a Conscience later in this chapter) is another excellent example of this.

Components of the External Environment

There are two elements within the external marketing environment: the microenvironment and the macroenvironment. Although the factors within these environments are not directly within the marketer's control, they still influence the decisions made by marketers. We'll first examine the factors in the microenvironment, as shown in Figure 1.7.

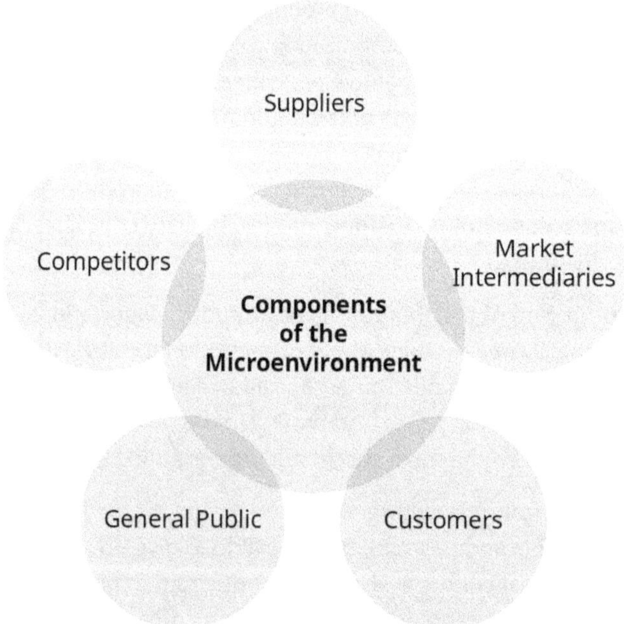

Figure 1.7 Components of the Microenvironment (attribution: Copyright Rice University, OpenStax, under CC BY 4.0 license)

The **microenvironment** consists of five predominant factors.

- **Suppliers.** Suppliers (sometimes also called *vendors*) are those partners from whom we receive the parts and products necessary for our business. Let's assume that your company produces microwave ovens. Some of your suppliers may be providers of transformers, the turntable, control panels, magnetrons, etc. As long as you have options in terms of the component suppliers, the bargaining power of each supplier is relatively weak. However, if two suppliers merge and decide to raise the price of the component the new entity supplies, that vendor now wields increased power.
- **Market Intermediaries.** Often, products are distributed by third-party sellers such as retailers, wholesalers, and others in the distribution channel. The reputation of these market intermediaries plays an important role in the marketing of the product or service, both positive and negative, so companies need to select and monitor market intermediaries on an ongoing basis. We'll learn more about the roles of these intermediaries in Distribution: Delivering Customer Value, but let's provide a couple of definitions and examples to help you better understand some of the parties in the distribution channel. **Retailers** (like Walmart or Target) purchase large quantities of goods from producers and then sell smaller quantities to end customers for personal use or consumption. **Wholesalers** purchase large quantities of products from producers and then sell to smaller businesses such as retail stores. A good example of a wholesaler is Gexpro, which sells electrical supplies for the construction industry.
- **Customers.** Understanding who your customers are will enable you to effectively reach them, whether online, locally in retail stores, or internationally.
- **Competitors.** Successful marketing strategies must be implemented after consideration of your competition. Knowing who your competition is and what they are and are not offering allows you to find the gap in the market. You want to be where the competition is not, at least in the sense of offering something unique to a targeted market.
- **General Public.** Because companies provide their offerings in communities that support them, they have an obligation to satisfy those communities. There's an old saying that "perception is reality," so marketers' actions must be evaluated through the perceptual lens of those communities, because the public's perception of you—your reputation—is essential to your success.[30]

Components of the Macroenvironment

Obviously, marketers can't ignore what's going on in the external environment. One of the tools used by companies to assess the environment in which they are operating is a **PESTLE analysis**. PESTLE is an acronym for political, economic, social, technological, legal, and environmental factors that provide marketers with a comprehensive view of the whole environment from multiple angles.[31] These **macroenvironment** factors can be used to understand current external influences so that marketers can more easily identify what might change in the future, mitigate the identified risks, and take advantage of competitive opportunities (see Figure 1.8).

Political Factors	Economic Factors	Social Factors	Technological Factors	Legal Factors	Environmental Factors
• New taxes • Fiscal policy • Trade tariffs	• Inflation rates • Interest rates • Foreign exchange rates • Economic growth patterns	• Demographics • Cultural trends • Population analytics	• Innovations in technology • Automation • Research and development • Technological awareness	• Consumer laws • Labor laws • Safety standards	• Climate • Geographical location • Stakeholder and consumer values

Figure 1.8 PESTLE Factors (attribution: Copyright Rice University, OpenStax, under CC BY 4.0 license)

Let's look at these factors more closely:

- **Political Factors.** These factors include environmental and trade restrictions, political stability, and business policy. For example, Tesla announced in late 2021 that it is moving its headquarters out of

California to Texas, following similar announcements by Hewlett Packard Enterprise (HPE) and Oracle, citing such things as lower housing costs and tax rates and fewer regulations, making it easier for companies to operate in Texas.

- **Economic Factors.** Economic factors play a huge role in terms of a company's prospects in a market. For example, economic factors affect pricing and can even influence the supply/demand curve for a product or service. For example, high inflation causes consumers to have less spending power, which translates into lower sales and revenue. In 2022, consumers experienced both product shortages and higher prices, blamed largely on COVID-19, Russia's war on Ukraine, and the availability of certain commodities, such as corn, sunflower oil, and wheat.[32]
- **Social Factors.** Social factors take in a wide swath of elements, such as cultural norms and expectations, health consciousness, population growth/decline, the age distribution of a population, and even career attitudes. Let's take one of these factors—age distribution—and examine how it impacts marketing. Baby boomers (born between 1946 and 1964) comprise approximately a quarter of the US population. It's largely as a result of this group's aging and retirement that active adult communities such as Del Webb and others have sprung up across the nation.[33]
- **Technological Factors.** These factors encompass the innovations and developments in technology that impact an organization's operations, as well as the rate of technological change. For example, look at one simple technological change with which we've all become comfortable in the public arena over the past decade or so: free WiFi. Starbucks was able to take advantage of this change and reposition its coffeehouses and differentiate itself from competitors by offering free WiFi.[34]
- **Legal Factors.** These factors include changes to legislation impacting employment, industry regulation, licenses and permits, and intellectual property.
- **Environmental Factors.** In the context of a PESTLE analysis, environmental factors refer to variables affecting the physical environment, like climate change, pollution, the scarcity of raw materials, and the growing concern over companies' carbon footprints.

Knowledge Check

It's time to check your knowledge on the concepts presented in this section. Refer to the Answer Key at the end of the book for feedback.

1. The extent to which the supply chain adds value to our marketing strategy is best addressed by our evaluation of which of the 5Ms?
   a. Materials
   b. Money
   c. Machinery
   d. Minutes

2. ________ consist of third-party sellers such as retailers, wholesalers, and other resellers in the distribution channel.
   a. Suppliers
   b. Market intermediaries
   c. Partners
   d. Customers

3. If you wanted to fill a gap in the marketplace, you would have to carefully consider ________ to see what is already available on the market.
   a. the competition
   b. the customers
   c. the public
   d. the resellers

4. Which of the domains of the macroenvironment are most likely to be responsible for cutting-edge innovations?
    a. Economic
    b. Technological
    c. Political and legal
    d. Social and cultural

5. You want to target a market more narrowly than simply using demographic data. You are also considering segmenting on people's attitudes and interests. Which domain of the macroenvironment is most likely to be a relevant data source for your decision-making?
    a. Economic factors
    b. Natural factors
    c. Political and legal factors
    d. Social factors

1.4 Evolution of the Marketing Concept

Learning Outcomes

By the end of this section, you will be able to:
    LO 1 Describe the production concept.
    LO 2 Define the product concept.
    LO 3 Discuss the selling concept.
    LO 4 Explain the marketing concept.
    LO 5 Summarize the societal marketing concept and its features.

The Evolution of Marketing

So now you've gotten the bird's-eye view of marketing as a practice, and you now know what marketing is. However, let's take a trip back through time to look at the evolution of marketing practices and how many of today's marketing strategies came to be. As you can see from Figure 1.9, and to use an old TV commercial tagline, you've come a long way, baby!

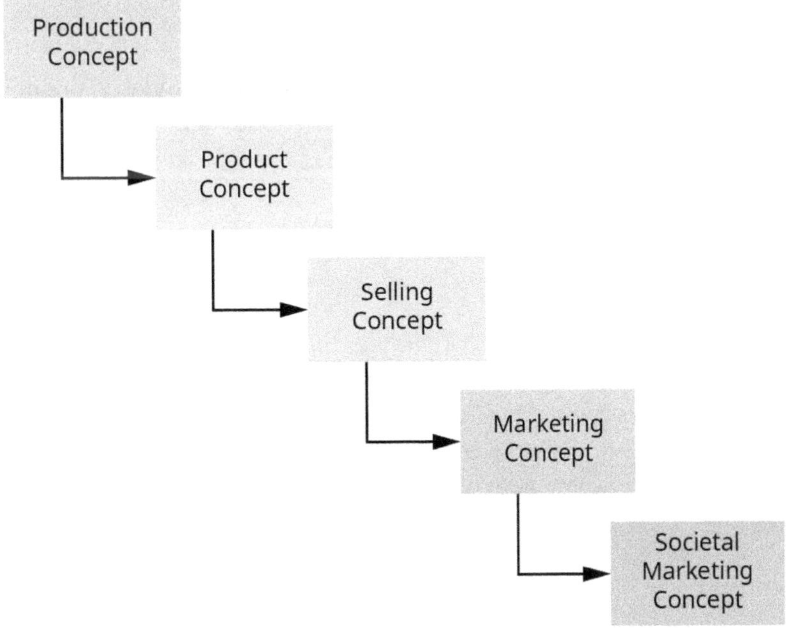

Figure 1.9 Evolution of Marketing (attribution: Copyright Rice University, OpenStax, under CC BY 4.0 license)

The Production Concept

In order to understand the production concept, it's important first to understand the history of technology and mass production. Spurred on by the use of steam power, the Industrial Revolution began in the United States by the middle of the 19th century. Although much of the population was still employed in agriculture, the expansion of commerce and industry drew millions of factory workers into cities and towns. Suddenly, an abundance of manufactured goods was available to households at a rate never experienced before.

The **production concept** assumed that consumers were mostly interested in product availability and price, not necessarily product features. As a result, companies concentrated on high production, low costs, and mass distribution. In other words, to use the oft-used line from the movie *Field of Dreams*, "If you build it, they will come." People were so hungry for mass-produced goods that companies didn't have to do a lot of sales or marketing. The production concept is thought to have lasted from just after the Civil War (1861–1865) until the 1920s.[35] For example, inventor Samuel Colt's company began mass -producing revolvers in 1835. The Waltham Watch Company (founded in 1850 in Waltham, MA) was the first to use division of labor to mass produce watches and clocks.

The Product Concept

From the 1920s until the 1950s, the **product concept** dominated. With product availability a thing of the past, consumers began to favor products that offered quality, performance, and/or innovative features. As a result, companies concentrated on making superior products and improving them over time. One of the problems with this type of thinking is that marketers may fall in love with a product (known as "marketing myopia") and may not realize what the market truly wants or needs. Consider the manner in which railroad marketers overlooked the growing competition from airlines, buses, and automobiles. In his book *Marketing Myopia*, author Theodore Levitt writes, "The railroads did not stop growing because the need for passenger and freight transportation declined. That grew. The railroads are in trouble today not because that need was filled by others (cars, trucks, airplanes and even telephones) but because it was not filled by the railroads themselves. They let others take customers away from them because they assumed themselves to be in the railroad business rather than in the transportation business."[36]

LINK TO LEARNING

The Reckoning

When American cars developed a reputation for not being reliable or dependable, this opened an opportunity for Toyota and other Japanese exporters in the late 1960s and 1970s. Learn more about this issue from David Halberstam's 1986 book *The Reckoning*. Read the *New York Times* 1986 review of this book (https://openstax.org/r/booksofthetimes).

The Sales Concept

By the 1950s, mass production had become the norm rather than the exception. Competition had increased over the years, and there was little unfulfilled demand in the marketplace. Marketing evolved from simply producing products that customers wanted to trying to persuade customers to buy through advertising and personal selling. The basic premise of the **sales concept** was that consumers and businesses need to be "coaxed" into buying, and the aim of companies was to sell what they made rather than make what consumers wanted.

The Marketing Concept

The **marketing concept** was built on the premise that an organization will achieve its goals when it satisfies the needs and wants of the consumer. As a result, firms began to focus on customer needs *before* developing products, rather than developing products and then trying to "sell" them to consumers. The marketing concept was also the start of relationship marketing— fostering long-term relationships with customers in order to ensure repeat sales and achieve stable relationships and reduced costs.

The Societal Marketing Concept

In a nutshell, the **societal marketing concept** is simple. Companies make good marketing decisions by considering not only consumers' wants and needs but additionally the balance between those wants and needs and the company's capabilities and society's long-term interests. The concept emphasizes the social responsibilities that companies bear. This means meeting consumers' and businesses' current needs while simultaneously being aware of the environmental impact of marketing decisions on future generations' ability to meet their needs.[37]

Knowledge Check

It's time to check your knowledge on the concepts presented in this section. Refer to the Answer Key at the end of the book for feedback.

1. The product concept focuses on ________.
   a. the quality of the product a company intends to sell
   b. the operations of manufacturing the product a company intends to sell
   c. the selling strategies a company will use to sell the product
   d. the needs of the customer

2. Which of the marketing eras or concepts is most closely related to sustainability and environmental consciousness?
   a. Production concept
   b. Marketing concept
   c. Societal marketing concept
   d. Sales concept

3. During which marketing era concept would companies not only produce products but also try to persuade customers through advertising and personal selling to purchase those products?
   a. Production concept
   b. Product concept
   c. Selling concept
   d. Marketing concept

4. Which of the following accurately represents the evolution of marketing?
   a. Production, product, sales, marketing, societal
   b. Product, sales, production, marketing, societal
   c. Marketing, production, sales, societal, product
   d. Societal, production, sales, marketing, product

5. During the societal marketing concept, ________.
   a. customers' wants and needs were first identified as essential
   b. trustfulness, honesty, and transparency became most important
   c. promotional efforts to move inventory were essential
   d. the customer was the focus

<table>
<tr><td>1.5</td><td>Determining Consumer Needs and Wants</td></tr>
</table>

Learning Outcomes

By the end of this section, you will be able to:
- **LO** 1 Explain how an organization identifies consumer needs and wants.
- **LO** 2 Describe the process through which an organization satisfies consumer needs and wants.

Identifying Consumer Needs and Wants

We've repeatedly mentioned satisfying customer needs. But understanding those needs and/or wants isn't always as simple as it sounds. For example, some customers have needs of which they're not fully aware; others can't articulate their needs, or the words require some degree of interpretation. Consider this: what does it mean when a customer asks for a "restful" hotel, an "attractive" bathing suit, or a "powerful" lawn mower?

Let's consider an example to illustrate this concept. A customer comes into your car dealership and indicates that she wants to purchase an inexpensive hybrid vehicle. That description is broad and subject to interpretation, so it's essential that the marketer probe further, because there are really five types of customers needs[38]

- **Stated Needs**. Stated needs are those that are clearly specified by the customer. It's what the customer requests. For example, you go into a big box store such as Best Buy and tell the sales associate that you "need a new phone."
- **Real Needs**. Real needs are one level above stated needs; they are more specific and define the parameters that are immediate to defining and fulfilling the need. In other words, real needs are what the stated needs actually mean. What are our phone buyer's real needs? Are they looking for a phone with long battery life, a high-resolution camera, or a lot of internal memory?
- **Unstated Needs**. Unstated needs are what the customer also expects but doesn't ask for. Once again, using our phone example, the consumer may expect but not express the desire for good service from the carrier and/or the big box store.
- **Delight Needs**. Delight needs are those that provide the "wow" factor. These needs, like unstated needs, can make some products more desirable than others if they meet those needs. Going back to our phone example, delight needs can be something like a phone case or other promotional gift.
- **Secret Needs**. Secret needs are those that a customer may not state or realize but can be one of the main reasons for choosing a particular product to fulfill the basic stated need. Do customers want a new cell phone as a status symbol but won't admit that status is important to them?

The bottom line is that responding only to a customer's stated need may not satisfy the customer. The marketer needs to understand what the customer really wants.

Satisfying Consumer Needs and Wants

You may be asking yourself at this point, "Does marketing satisfy needs, or does it create needs?" Some people feel that marketing creates needs and pressures consumers into buying unneeded products or services. However, marketing does not create needs; rather, it opens consumers' eyes to their wants, and it's up to marketers to understand those wants in order to guide consumers on the path to purchasing their products or services.[39] Marketing creates value, and value speaks to the satisfaction of customer needs and the benefits customers receive from the product. It's the customer, however, who ultimately determines how well the product fulfills their needs and how much value the product creates.

The challenge for the marketing team is to succinctly and compellingly articulate a value proposition that speaks directly to the benefits your product or service delivers.

The Value Proposition

A value proposition identifies the quantifiable benefits that customers can expect when they choose to purchase your company's product or service. A value proposition is, in effect, a promise from the company to the customer, and it can serve as a competitive differentiator to motivate customers to purchase your company's products or services. In other words, your value proposition should bring together in a brief, concise statement what your customer wants and/or needs and how your product or service will meet those wants and needs better than your competitors.[40]

That's a bit abstract, so we thought we'd include a few examples of some good value propositions:

- Bill Ragan Roofing: "Let us take the stress of roof repairs or a roof replacement off your shoulders."[41]
- Applied Educational Systems (AES): "Spend your time connecting with students, not planning and grading"[42]
- DuckDuckGo: "Tired of being tracked online? We can help."[43]
- HelloFresh: "Take the stress out of mealtime."[44]

The Exchange Process

Marketing facilitates what is known as the **exchange process**—the act of obtaining a desired product or service from an individual or business by providing in return something of value, as illustrated in Figure 1.10.

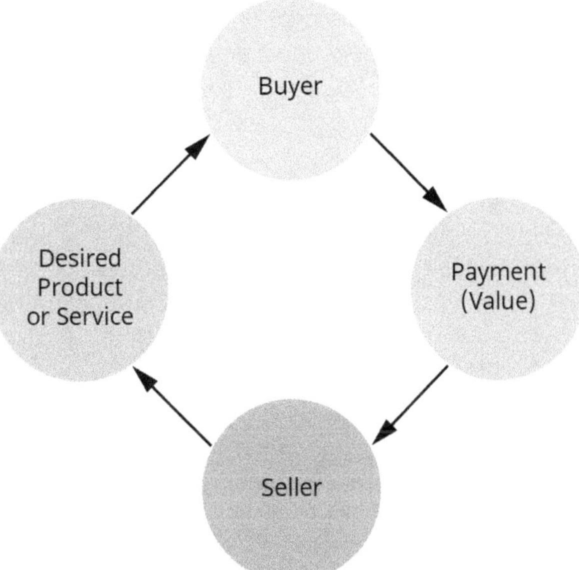

Figure 1.10 The Exchange Process (attribution: Copyright Rice University, OpenStax, under CC BY 4.0 license)

The **buyer** (or customer) initiates the exchange process. The buyer (who has a want or need) is the individual or business who is willing to pay money or provide other personal resources to satisfy this need or want. Let's simplify that definition with an example. When lunchtime rolls around and you're on campus or at your job, you're hungry; you have a need for food and drink. You go to the dining hall or a nearby restaurant to order lunch, and you're willing to pay money in exchange for your meal. Simple, right?

Keep in mind here, however, that there is a difference between a customer and a consumer. The **customer** is the individual or business that purchases the product or service. The **consumer** is the user of the product or service. To put this concept in simple terms, if a grandmother buys a toy for her grandson, she is the customer; her grandson (who will use the product) is the consumer. In the case of going out for lunch, you're both the customer and the consumer.

The **desired object** is the product or service itself. It may be a physical good, service, or experience that consumers expect will satisfy their wants and/or needs. Let's go back to our lunch example. The desired object is the meal. The **seller** is the individual or organization that supplies the need-satisfying product, service, or experience. Once again, in the lunch example, the seller would be the dining hall or the restaurant.

Inherent in the exchange process is what's known as **value**—the benefit to the customer or consumer relative to the cost in the exchange. In other words, value is the monetary worth of the benefits the customer receives in exchange for the product or service. Let's go back to our backpack example a few sections ago. You may really want that backpack because it keeps your "stuff" organized and it's lightweight (the benefits), but if the cost is too high, either in terms of the monetary cost or the time you'd have to spend going to the store to buy it, that backpack won't have value for you. No sale!

Knowledge Check

It's time to check your knowledge on the concepts presented in this section. Refer to the Answer Key at the end of the book for feedback.

1. _______ needs are those that provide the "wow" factor in a customer's purchase.
   a. Stated
   b. Real
   c. Unstated
   d. Delight

2. In the exchange process, the _______ is the individual who purchases the product or service, and the _______ is the individual who actually uses the product or service.
   a. buyer; seller
   b. buyer; customer
   c. customer; consumer
   d. consumer, customer

3. Which of the following terms refers to the promised value of a product or service?
   a. Valuation
   b. Value proposal
   c. Value assessment
   d. Value proposition

4. _______ is/are the benefit(s) to the customer or consumer relative to the cost of the product or service.
   a. Value
   b. The exchange process
   c. Stated needs
   d. Expectations

5. Which of the following best describes a satisfactory exchange process?
   a. One that allows the seller to incur the highest profit possible
   b. One that allows the buyer to pay the lowest price possible
   c. One that fairly addresses the needs of both the seller and buyer
   d. One that is most convenient without regard for either the seller or buyer

1.6 | Customer Relationship Management (CRM)

Learning Outcomes

By the end of this section, you will be able to:

- **LO 1** Define customer relationship management (CRM).
- **LO 2** Describe the impact of CRM on customer loyalty and retention.
- **LO 3** Explain how CRM builds customer equity.

The Impact of CRM on Customer Loyalty and Retention

In the final analysis, companies want to accomplish two things: improve customer service relationships and improve customer retention. It is typically easier and less expensive to retain a loyal customer than acquire a new one. One way to accomplish that is through **customer relationship management (CRM)**—the means through which companies track, manage, and analyze customer interactions.[45]

There are a number of CRM software systems available in the marketplace, and most accomplish the same thing. They basically track and work with data about customers. For example, they link and analyze customer contact information. They store and track contact with company representatives, such as phone calls, emails, live chat conversations, service requests, purchases, and returns. One good example of CRM software is Salesforce, which is the market leader for CRM software in North America, Western Europe, Latin America, and the Asia-Pacific region.[46]

There are many types of CRM software; however, most CRM software focuses primarily on one of the following major categories:

- **Operational.** Operational CRM software deals with three types of operations: marketing, sales, and service automation. Operational CRM software is intended to assist businesses in automating how they approach leads and potential customers in order to convert those potential customers into actual customers.[47]
- **Analytical.** Analytical CRM software is all about data management and analysis. The software is designed to collect, organize, and analyze the inputted data, providing management with insights needed to better understand market trends, understand customer needs and wants, and make data-driven strategic decisions.[48]
- **Collaborative.** No business functions on an island. When businesses share customer data with one another, they gain insights and additional perspectives on customer behavior that is mutually beneficial. This collaboration allows each business to obtain information that it would not otherwise have access to.[49]

Before we can explore how CRM impacts customer loyalty and retention, it's probably a good time for a few definitions. **Customer loyalty** is an ongoing positive relationship between a customer and a business. Customer loyalty is at the crux of repeat purchases of your product versus those of your competitors. One common way to accomplish this is to offer reward/loyalty cards. For example, you may have a frequent flyer card from an airline or a loyalty card from Starbucks or a retailer like Designer Shoe Warehouse (DSW), which rewards VIP customers with points for each purchase.

Customer retention is a closely related concept; it refers to a company's ability to transform new customers into returning customers. In its simplest terms, it's how you keep your customers coming back for more. The goal of customer retention is to reduce the number of customer defections, or those who buy your product at least once and then not again.

How does CRM impact customer loyalty and retention? Let's take a look at some of the ways CRM accomplishes this:

- **Leveraging Customer Data.** With CRM, a business can gather data on your existing customers and prospective customers so that their experience is a more positive one. For example, you can keep track of important dates such as customer birthdays or purchase anniversaries, and CRM software can send automatic emails to them with coupons or other incentives.[50]

- **Enhanced Customer Communications**. CRM software can be programmed to automatically send thank you notes to customers, send newsletters regarding new products, and send customer satisfaction surveys or polls so that you can glean more insight into your customers' levels of satisfaction with your product or service.[51]
- **Ascertaining Customer Needs.** Fostering customer loyalty begins with understanding what your customers want and need. An effective CRM program can track customers' purchase history, habits and preferences, and even web and email interaction. From this information, you can gain valuable insights that will aid you in developing targeted marketing strategies.[52]
- **Gathering Feedback.** We'd previously mentioned distributing customer surveys through use of your CRM software. This will provide you with valuable feedback not only about customers' perceptions of your product or service but also about their customer experiences. Have you ever received a message from Amazon after an online purchase, asking if you'd review the item you purchased? That's likely the result of an effective CRM system.[53]
- **Managing Customer Loyalty Programs.** CRM software can assist you in identifying prospective loyalty program members and track member rewards. Loyalty programs reward members for purchases and have been shown to increase customer retention. For example, according to research, approximately 84 percent of customers indicate that loyalty programs are an incentive to remain with a brand, and 66 percent report that their spending behavior is actually altered by the ability to earn rewards.[54]

The Role of CRM in Building Customer Equity

We have already talked about customer equity—the potential profit a company earns from all of its customers, both current and potential—and customer equity is a core CRM benchmark. CRM isn't a one-way communication street to customers. It's a two-way street that allows customers to define and consequently shape offerings in terms of their requirements. This paves the way for open, honest dialogue that can ultimately lead to benefits to customers, thus resulting in higher customer equity.

Knowledge Check

It's time to check your knowledge on the concepts presented in this section. Refer to the Answer Key at the end of the book for feedback.

1. Customer relationship management is accomplished by all of the following EXCEPT ________.
   a. establishing and tracking customer interactions
   b. finding ways of improving customer satisfaction from prior customer experiences
   c. communicating with customers in a personalized way
   d. offering the lowest price of all the companies on the market

2. What do you call the process of managing customer information in order to maximize brand loyalty?
   a. Marketing
   b. Customer relationship management
   c. Consumer retention management
   d. Branding

3. An ongoing positive relationship between a customer and a business is known as ________.
   a. customer equity
   b. customer loyalty
   c. customer retention
   d. customer lifetime value (CLV)

4. Which type of customer relationship management (CRM) system would pool data from outside companies and organizations in order to create even better experiences for their customers?
   a. Customer loyalty programs
   b. Operational CRM
   c. Analytical CRM
   d. Collaborative CRM

5. A program that offers discounts and special incentives designed to attract and retain customers is called a ________.
   a. customer loyalty program
   b. sweepstakes
   c. discount plan
   d. CRM software

1.7 | Ethical Marketing

Learning Outcomes

By the end of this section, you will be able to:
   LO 1 Define ethical marketing.
   LO 2 Describe the importance of ethical marketing.
   LO 3 Explain the dos and don'ts of ethical marketing.

Ethical Marketing Defined

As the term suggests, **ethical marketing** involves companies not only trying to market their products and services but considering how society will benefit from the introduction of those offerings. It's not so much a practice as it is a philosophy that tries to promote fairness, honesty, and a sense of responsibility in all of the marketing done by the company.

What are the principles of ethical marketing? According to Lapaas Digital, a digital marketing agency based in Delhi, India, some of those principles include the following:

- All marketing should be true.
- The privacy of the end user is most important.
- Marketing campaigns must adhere to the norms, standards, rules, and regulations set forth by the government and other lawmaking authorities.
- Marketing professionals must be transparent about what they are trying to convey and whom they are approaching to convey the same.[55]

The Importance of Ethical Marketing

Ethics are critical to a company's reputation, particularly when public opinion—particularly negative public opinion—can go viral in an instant, thanks to social media.

Ask yourself a question: how important are a company's ethics to you when you decide to purchase a product or service? According to new research by Mintel, 56 percent of US consumers stop buying from companies they believe are unethical. Perhaps even more importantly, approximately one-third of consumers are inclined to tell others when they perceive a brand to be taking actions that they perceive to be honest, fair, and responsible. Taking this one step further, 29 percent of them will share their support of ethical companies via social media.[56]

The Dos and Don'ts of Ethical Marketing

The data cited above presents a somewhat dire picture for companies that do not practice ethical marketing, so let's take a look at some of the dos and don'ts of ethical marketing.

First, the dos:

- *Ensure transparency.* Transparency is key, and marketers should attempt to provide the maximum amount of information to the consumer regarding the product, its usage, and safety concerns. For example, Southwest Airlines ran a clever marketing campaign entitled "Transfarency," promoting its philosophy that customers should be treated honestly and fares should actually stay low. The result? The campaign garnered nearly 5 million likes on Facebook alone.[57] How's that for earning the trust of potential customers?
- *Respect data privacy.* As we noted in our discussion of CRM above, marketers have the ability to collect vast amounts of data about consumers. Data privacy is the biggest concern for consumers in this data-driven world, so marketers must always respect data privacy. Consider the fallout experienced by Vizio (the TV manufacturer) when it was learned that its devices did not ask customers for permission to track and report viewing information. The amount of data being gathered and the fact that Vizio did not request permission from customers meant the company was potentially in violation of the Video Privacy Protection Act. The company was sued in a class action lawsuit.[58]
- *Prioritize the concerns of the consumer.* No matter how small the concern of your consumer is, a marketer's top priority should be to respond to those concerns in a prompt, meaningful way. How long do you expect to wait for a response to an email to a company regarding its product or service—a day, two days, a week? You might be surprised to learn that, according to research, 42 percent of consumers expect a response within 60 minutes and 32 percent expect a response within 30 minutes. That illustrates the importance of responding promptly in order to increase the chances of a positive customer experience.[59]

Now, the don'ts:

- *Don't overemphasize or exaggerate.* In marketing, this is sometimes referred to as "puffery." Of course, you want to convey the features and benefits of the product or service to the customer, but these need to be stated clearly and accurately. Don't promise something you can't deliver— doing so is unethical and not beneficial in the long run.
- *Don't make false or unverified claims.* One case illustrates the importance of honesty in advertising: Living Essentials, LLC, the makers of 5-Hour Energy shots, advertised its product as "doctor-recommended" and superior to traditional caffeine. Those claims were found to be misleading, and Living Essentials, LLC was ordered to pay $4.3 million in damages.[60]
- *Don't make false comparisons.* Not only shouldn't you make false or unverified claims about your own products or services, but you shouldn't do it to competitors' products either. As a matter of fact, companies can sue competitors for false advertising claims under the federal Lanham Act, alleging that they suffered lost sales or damage to their reputation as a result of the false statements by the competitor.[61]

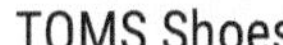

COMPANIES WITH A CONSCIENCE

TOMS Shoes

Figure 1.11 TOMS developed a marketing strategy with charitable giving in mind, in which the company shares products (such as shoes) or profits with those in need. (credit: "New Shoes Much :D" by Rob Ellis/flickr, CC BY 2.0)

TOMS (see Figure 1.11) was founded by Blake Mycoskie in 2006 after a trip to Argentina, where he saw how people were living in impoverished areas. Mycoskie decided to establish his company with giving in mind. He introduced what he calls the "One for One" concept: for every pair of TOMS shoes sold, the company donates another pair to a child in need. In a recent *Impact Report*, TOMS reported it had provided more than 95 million pairs of shoes to children in 82 countries.[62]

Emboldened by the success of the "One for One" concept, Mycoskie later expanded the model. For example, in 2011, the company introduced a line of eyewear and decided to use the same philanthropic principle but this time with a bit of a twist. Instead of donating glasses, TOMS donated a portion of the profits from each sale to save or restore the eyesight of those living in developing countries. To give you an idea of the success of this program, the company's website indicates that TOMS Eyewear has helped restore sight to more than 780,000 people.[63]

🗐 Chapter Summary

This chapter introduces the basic concepts of marketing, including adding value to a company's business. Marketing begins with strategy and relies on creating and delivering value to customers. It is crucial for marketers to understand exactly what customers value and determine how to deliver the value while also meeting company goals.

There are many activities involved in the marketing process, including creating products and services, advertising, selling, distributing, communicating, and building relationships. Marketers must also acknowledge the importance of employees, suppliers, and other partners involved in analyzing market opportunities. The most important aspect of creating value is understanding both the customer and the marketplace.

There are many tools marketers can rely upon as they develop strategies. The marketing mix—product, price, place, and promotion—has traditionally comprised the marketer's toolbelt. Understanding the marketing environment, or forces outside and within the control of marketers, forms the context of all marketing efforts. Consumers ultimately expect companies to be ethical, honest, and trustworthy. Marketers know success is contingent upon abiding by ethical, societal, and corporate governance standards.

🔑 Key Terms

5Ms of marketing   internal elements of a marketing plan that need to be resolved if the plan is successful

buyer   a person or institution that purchases goods or services

consumer   the final user of a purchased product or service

customer   a person who purchases a product or service

customer equity   total combined customer lifetime values of all the company's customers

customer loyalty   an ongoing positive relationship between a customer and a business

customer relationship management (CRM)   all strategies, techniques, tools, and technologies used by companies to develop, acquire, and retain customers

customer retention   the ability of a company to turn customers into repeat buyers and prevent them from switching to a competitor

customer value   the ratio of the perceived benefits relative to the costs incurred by the customer in acquiring the product or service

customer-driven marketing strategy   a marketing strategy that shifts the focus from the product or service to its users

delight needs   an added value that a customer might receive from a seller without prior expectation or request for the same

desired object   a physical good, service, or experience that consumers expect will satisfy their wants and/or needs

ethical marketing   process that emphasizes trustworthy, transparent, social, and culturally sensitive marketing policies

exchange process   the process of satisfying a need or want by giving something of value in exchange

external interested parties   a person or organization that does not have a direct relationship with a company but is affected by the operations of the business

form utility   the value given to a product by virtue of the fact that the materials and components that comprise it have been combined to make the finished product

interested parties   a group that has an interest in a company or organization and can either affect or be affected by it; often referred to as "stakeholders"

internal interested parties   those persons whose interest in a company comes through a direct relationship such as employment, ownership, or investment

internal marketing   the promotion of a company's objectives, products, and services to internal parties, such as employees, owners, managers, and shareholders

internet advertising   a set of tools for delivering promotional messages to people worldwide, using the internet as a global marketing platform

macroenvironment   the set of external factors and forces, not controlled by the company, that influence its operations

marketing   the activities a company undertakes to promote the buying or selling of a product or service

marketing concept   marketing philosophy that firms should analyze the needs of their customers and then make decisions to satisfy those needs better than the competition

marketing environment   all of the internal and external factors that drive and influence an organization's marketing activities

marketing mix   the set of actions or tactics that a company uses to promote its brand or product in the market

marketing process   the series of steps that assist businesses in planning, analyzing, implementing, and adjusting their marketing strategy

marketing strategy   a plan of action designed to promote or sell a product or service

microenvironment   those factors or elements in a firm's immediate environment that affect its performance and decision-making

organizational culture   beliefs and behaviors that determine how a company's employees and management interact and handle customer relationships

PESTLE analysis   a strategic framework used to assess the political, economic, social, technological, legal, and environmental factors affecting an organization

place   the geographical location in which the company sells its products and/or provides its services

place utility   making goods and/or services physically available or accessible to potential customers

possession utility   the amount of usefulness or perceived value from owning a product

price   the cost that consumers pay in order to acquire a product or service

product   anything that can be offered to a market that might satisfy a want or need

product concept   the orientation that consumers will favor those products that offer the most quality, performance, or innovative features

production concept   the orientation that consumers will always acquire products that are cheaper and more readily available

promotion   any type of marketing communication used to inform audiences of the relative merits or a product, service, or brand

real needs   the value the customer is going to derive from the stated good or service

retailers   companies that purchase large quantities of goods from producers and then sell smaller quantities to end customers for personal use or consumption

sales concept   orientation that analyzes buying and selling effects to place the focus primarily on generating sales transactions

secret needs   the needs that the consumer feels reluctant to admit

seller   the individual or organization that supplies the need-satisfying product, service, or experience

societal marketing concept   philosophy that a company should make marketing decisions by considering not only consumers' wants and the company's capabilities but also society's long-term interests

stated needs   those product or service needs that are clearly specified by the customer

suppliers   sometimes also called *vendors*, these are partners from whom we receive the parts and products necessary for our business

time utility   adding value to the consumer by having the product or service available when the consumer needs it

unstated needs   those needs that are not obvious but are expected by the customer

utility   how a product can be useful to customers in a way that convinces them to make a purchase

value   the difference between a customer's evaluation of the benefits and costs of one product when compared with others

value proposition   a promise of value to be delivered, communicated, and acknowledged

wholesalers   companies that purchase large quantities of products from producers and then sell to smaller businesses, such as retail stores

Applied Marketing Knowledge: Discussion Questions

1. Why is capturing customer lifetime value so important? Choose a retailer, and apply this concept as a way to explain, in part, its profitability and long-term viability in the marketplace.

2. The marketing mix has been compared to a toolbelt. In other words, successful marketers can devise an appropriate marketing mix by combining the right blend of tools: product, price, place, and promotion. Describe a recent product that you purchased on Amazon.com or some other online retailer (place), how you located it (promotion), and whether the price was competitive when compared to similar products.

3. Why do some marketers prefer to follow the 4Ps (product, price, place, and promotion) of marketing and others might prefer to follow the new pattern of the 5Ms (minds, minutes, machinery, materials, and money)?

4. A person can be a product. Please give an example of this.

5. According to the US Centers for Disease Control and Prevention, the birthrate is falling in communities around the world. In the United States, the birthrate fell by 4 percent in 2020, an all-time low. Describe why dwindling population is a demographic concern in the macroenvironment all businesses must contend with.

Critical Thinking Exercises

1. Your roommate in the dorm talks on his cell phone incessantly while you're trying to study. Since you're a broke college student and it's too cold to walk to the library, you decide to explore the marketplace for used noise-canceling headphones. How will you locate the best, most-affordable market offering to meet your needs? Describe how marketing messages may guide your steps in this process.

2. All consumers have needs and wants. You likely felt a state of deprivation this morning—hunger—and decided what you wanted to eat for breakfast. Do a bit of research to discover how your breakfast preference (want) compares to what a college student living in Osaka, Japan, might want to satisfy their need for sustenance.

3. Because relationships are so important in marketing, multiple tools have been developed to help manage customer relationships. Many technological advances assist marketers in their efforts. Promotional strategies include utilizing social media posts, websites, advertising, public relations, and sponsorships to communicate with the target audience. One of the most effective tools in planning/calendaring these promotional contacts or touch points is a Gantt chart. Do a bit of research on Gantt charts so you better understand this scheduling tool that also visually illustrates linkages between promotional activities and progress toward a marketing goal. List and discuss five benefits of using this CRM planning tool. Finally, in your research, did you discover an alternative method to visually depict a marketing project schedule?

4. In 2016, Amazon announced it was building its own logistics and shipping business in an effort to put the brakes on rising delivery costs. The overall goal was to deliver Amazon packages as well other packages from retailers and consumers in order to cut delivery costs in half. By 2021, Amazon was shipping 72 percent of its own packages as well as packages for Walmart and eBay. Read more about the effort (https://openstax.org/r/amazondeliveryfedex).

   With this new shipping venture in mind, answer the following questions:

   a. How is Amazon's decision to enter the logistics and shipping industry a move toward improving customer loyalty and equity?

    b. How will Amazon's new delivery service benefit Amazon?

    c. How do you predict Amazon's rivals in this distribution channel have responded?

5. Is it OK for companies to profile customers and predict their purchase behavior? Every time you, as a consumer, visit a website, your "cookies" are gathered and used to better understand your shopping behavior. Several years ago, Target's analysts developed an algorithm based upon Target customer buying behavior that predicted pregnancy. Those predicted to be pregnant—based upon the products they bought—were sent targeted marketing materials. The angry father of a high school student accused Target of erroneously sending his daughter a sales flyer for baby products. Supposedly, the daughter was pregnant. Read more about the incident (https://openstax.org/r/researchcompanyblog).

How do you feel about companies gathering intimate details about you for marketing purposes? Do you believe these companies develop a better relationship with you as a result? Despite being accurate, was Target's pregnancy-predicting algorithm ethical, invasive, or somewhere in between?

Building Your Personal Brand

Taking college courses is a huge step forward in your professional development. But there are additional activities that can also impact your self-awareness and provide credentials sought by employers. Campus career center directors, employers, and internship coordinators repeatedly stress the following suggestions for improving your employability.

1. Take free online courses through LinkedIn, Coursera, Google, or Microsoft. Completion of courses offers evidence of skill development. For instance, Google Analytics for Beginners, Advanced Google Analytics, and Fundamentals of Digital Marketing are all available for free since they boost online education linked to Google's technology products. Some courses even offer badges you can add to your LinkedIn profile, resume, and cover letters. You can find more information about these programs by reading these two articles from *The Report*, a source for trends on online education: [2022] 800+ Hours of Free LinkedIn Learning Courses with Free Certification (https://openstax.org/r/linkedinlearningfree) and [2022] 600+ Google Free Certificates and Badges (https://openstax.org/r/googlefreecertificates).

2. Join campus clubs and organizations where you can be part of a giving-back project, hone your project-management skills, or simply gain leadership experience. Employers value your initiative.

3. Keep up with current events—read newspapers, blogs, and other news sources that are pertinent to your field—because you'll need to carry on a conversation and because what we do requires a good sense of what's going on in the world.

4. Take advantage of campus services. Does your career center offer mock interviews? Will the staff help you develop a resume or edit one you've already written? Some colleges even offer short courses on etiquette.

5. Put together a list of possible references. Was your work in a particular course memorable? If so, ask your professor if they would refer you. Does your list of summer jobs indicate increasing responsibility or use of your education? Be certain that all of your references are on board; they must agree to give you an excellent reference and then should be kept in the loop about jobs you've applied for or, better yet, been offered.

6. Obtain a certification from HubSpot Academy, a well-known marketing website. Learn about the various certifications it offers by checking out its website (https://openstax.org/r/certificationoverview).

 What Do Marketers Do?

The American Marketing Association (AMA) has teamed up with the Digital Marketing Institute to offer specialized training within the marketing discipline. You can set yourself apart from other marketers with additional certifications. Are there other benefits you can take advantage of? Take a look at one of the 65 chapters located across the country. Is there one located in your city? Not only is membership a great way to volunteer, it's also an effective way to market yourself to potential employers. For instance, the Minnesota

Marketing Association (https://openstax.org/r/amaminnesota) welcomes students and professionals who are willing to help plan programs and organize mentorship programs. You can reach out to your state's AMA executive director and ask to interview them regarding student membership rates or opportunities for college students to interact with professional members. College students are also encouraged to enter an annual competition that demonstrates their marketing and business expertise before a panel of judges by providing innovative solutions to a real-world challenge.

You can also learn a lot by following AMA blogs where insights, ideas, and trends are discussed by knowledgeable professionals.

 ## Marketing Plan Exercise

MARKETING PLAN PROJECT—PART I

During this course, you will develop a marketing plan as part of a semester-long project. The marketing plan that you develop will build throughout the course over nine chapters of this textbook.

The purpose of Part I of this marketing plan project is twofold:

- To become familiar with the Marketing Plan Template
- To select a company or product for which you will be building the marketing plan throughout the semester

Instructions:

1. Download the Marketing Plan Template (https://openstax.org/r/marketingplantemp) and SAVE THIS DOCUMENT where you can easily access it again, because you will be completing additional sections of the plan throughout the course.
2. Select a company or product which will form the basis of your marketing plan. When selecting a company, please be sure to select a company or product that will (a) be of interest to you throughout the course and (b) have sufficient information available about the company on the internet for you to conduct research and make informed decisions in your marketing plan.
3. When selecting a company, please be sure NOT to choose a company that is so huge that it serves many diverse markets. For example, General Electric produces electrical and electronic equipment, aircraft engines, medical electronics; it also provides financial services and more. Procter & Gamble also has diverse product lines, including beauty, grooming, health care, fabric and home care, and feminine and family care. In the "real world," you would not prepare a single marketing plan for the entire company; instead, each division and/or product line would develop its own marketing plan. Therefore, if you want to use a large company, select a brand or product line for the purpose of your marketing plan.
4. On the Marketing Plan Template, add your name and course number to the header.
5. Complete the Company Profile Information on the Marketing Plan Template for the company you have selected.
6. Save the template with a new name using this naming convention: Course_First/LastName/Project Title. Example, MKTG101_JohnSmith_Marketing Plan.
7. Submit this document to your instructor as directed.

 ## Closing Company Case

Batdorf & Bronson

Coffee is a global drink loved by so many. From the simple espresso in Italy to the cinnamon added in Mexico, coffee is a global beverage. The origins of coffee date back to the ninth century. Legend has it that in a remote part of Ethiopia, a goat herder noticed his goats dancing about and full of energy. He realized they had eaten some nearby small red berries. Once the herder tried the berries, he too was dancing. The small red berries ushered in the discovery of coffee as a drink we cannot seem to get by without.

With a love for coffee and the thoughts of goats dancing in their heads, husband and wife Larry and Cherie Challain opened their first coffee bar—Dancing Goats in Olympia, Washington, in 1988. But as any coffee entrepreneur knows, a coffee bar is only as good as the coffee it serves. In a quest to serve the freshest coffee in the world, the duo acquired Batdorf & Bronson Coffee Roasters.

Roasting good coffee starts with finding the best coffee beans. The Challains know that to get good coffee beans, it is important to go to the source. By developing direct relationships with coffee farmers, Batdorf & Bronson is assured of the most sustainable and environmentally sourced beans in the industry.

For example, the Ethiopia Sidamo Guji is a grade 1 natural-processed bean grown on a privately held farm—Kayon Mountain. The farm is owned by Ato Esmael and his family. This organic-certified farm produces all-natural, sun-dried, and fully washed coffee. Sun drying means that once the beans are picked and washed, they are dried on raised beds for 12–20 days.

It has been over 30 years since the Challains served their first cup of coffee. Through their quest to improve the coffee experience for patrons and to elevate the growing experience, the Challains expanded their footprint. The duo knows that coffee beans are best served fresh. Freshness means being close to the source. The journey from the family farms to your cup is made easier through their additional roasting facility in Atlanta, Georgia. Being centrally located on the West and East Coasts means that beans can be roasted at either facility and be within a day's delivery of their own Dancing Goats coffee bars in Atlanta and Olympia as well as into the hands of their retail coffee partners across the country.

Both roasting facilities in Washington and Georgia can serve customers. Every Monday, orders are taken from the Dancing Goats retail partners. Batdorf & Bronson waits to receive orders on Monday before beginning roasting. For those who have not experienced the difference between freshly roasted coffee and all the rest— there is no comparison. Coffee is roasted on Tuesday, and retail partners receive their shipments on Wednesday.

Batdorf & Bronson is diligent about the roasting, brewing, and extraction process for all of its Dancing Goats Coffee Bars. It is equally concerned for its retail partners across the country. To provide the support needed by its small independent coffee bars, it provides instruction from its on-staff master baristas.

The experience of an adult coffee lover visiting a Batdorf & Bronson roasting facility is similar to that of a kid winning the golden ticket to the Willy Wonka Chocolate Factory. While your GPS is calculating the yards before turning into the parking lot, you can smell the coffee roasting. Upon entering the facility, you feel as though you are entering a sophisticated laboratory. Scales, thermometers, pristine roasting chambers, and carefully calibrated espresso machines are everywhere. Bags of green coffee beans are piled high and deep. The beans have recently arrived from the family farms located in coffee regions around the world.

To be a retail partner with Batdorf & Bronson means that you have a team behind you. It provides training for baristas, sample bags of new beans, and roast profile sheets describing the growing and harvesting process for the coffee you are serving your local community residents. Batdorf & Bronson is as diligent with every cup of coffee served to a customer as it is with every bean that is harvested and purchased for its roasting facilities. Because of this laser-like focus on quality, a cup of coffee brewed with Batdorf & Bronson beans is like no other coffee found at your typical coffee shop.

For customers who frequent the Dancing Goats Coffee Bars, they know the quality they can expect with their brewed coffee and espresso-based coffee drinks, and for that quality Dancing Goats is the go-to coffee of choice. For those who experience the Batdorf & Bronson difference at local coffee bars nationwide, the fresh taste and exceptional quality provide a reason to choose handcrafted, small-batch coffee shops over traditional "fast-food" coffee chains.[64]

To learn more about this coffee company, check its website here (https://openstax.org/r/dancinggoats).

Case Questions

1. Batdorf & Bronson is a coffee roasting facility. Dancing Goats Coffee Bars are retail stores. How does the ownership of a retail store help the supplier (Batdorf & Bronson) understand its customer?

2. Batdorf & Bronson has direct relationships with the family farms that grow the beans it buys, roasts, and distributes nationwide. How does this relationship with the coffee growers benefit its retail partners?

3. When Batdorf & Bronson provides a master barista to help train and educate retail partners, what is the value proposition it provides to the coffee bars that buy beans from it?

4. How is Batdorf & Bronson fulfilling the marketing concept?

References

1. Rachel Arthur, "Gatorade, Powerade & BodyArmor: How PepsiCo and Coca-Cola Are Playing in the Sports Drink Category," BeverageDaily, William Reed, updated March 25, 2021, https://www.beveragedaily.com/Article/2021/03/25/Gatorade-Powerade-BodyArmor-How-PepsiCo-and-Coca-Cola-are-playing-in-the-sports-drink-category.

2. Arthur, "Gatorade, Powerade & BodyArmor."

3. Darren Rovell, *First in Thirst: How Gatorade Turned the Science of Sweat into a Cultural Phenomenon* (New York: AMACOM, 2006).

4. Georgie Heath, "Tennis Legend Serena Williams Stars Alongside Lionel Messi, Michael Jordan and Usain Bolt in New Ad," NewsChain, Not a Newspaper, February 25, 2020, https://www.newschainonline.com/news/tennis-legend-serena-williams-stars-alongside-lionel-messi-michael-jordan-and-usain-bolt-in-new-ad-4408

5. "How Gatorade Ran It Back to '98 with #Game6Live," Marketing, Twitter, accessed May 7, 2022, https://marketing.twitter.com/en/success-stories/gatorade-game6live-twitter.

6. "Definitions of Marketing," American Marketing Association, last modified July 12, 2022, https://www.ama.org/the-definition-of-marketing-what-is-marketing/.

7. *Marketing and the 7Ps: A Brief Summary of Marketing and How It Works* (Maidenhead, UK: The Chartered Institute of Marketing, 2009), https://www.thensmc.com/sites/default/files/CIMpercent207Pspercent20Resource.PDF

8. "The Purpose of Marketing," Business, Tutor2u, updated March 22, 2021, https://www.tutor2u.net/business/reference/the-purpose-of-marketing.

9. "Internal Marketing: What It Is and Why You Need It," *Martyn Bassett Associates Blog*, Martyn Bassett Associates, March 4, 2021, https://www.mbassett.com/blog/internal-marketing.

10. Hitesh Bhasin, "What Is Form Utility? Definition, Meaning and Examples," Marketing91, February 1, 2020, https://www.marketing91.com/form-utility/.

11. "Marketing Process: 5 Steps of Marketing Process," iEduNote, last modified October 16, 2020, https://www.iedunote.com/marketing-process.

12. "Who Owns Volkswagen?," Lindsay Volkswagen of Dulles, last modified March 1, 2022, https://www.lindsayvolkswagen.com/who-owns-volkswagen/.

13. Ana Khlystova, "5 Steps to Creating a Customer-Driven Marketing Strategy," *HelpCrunch Blog*, HelpCrunch, July 2, 2019, https://helpcrunch.com/blog/customer-driven-marketing-strategy/.

14. "Value Proposition," Corporate Finance Institute, CFI Education, updated February 27, 2022, https://corporatefinanceinstitute.com/resources/knowledge/strategy/value-proposition/.

15. Mark Boedecker, "Value = Benefits/Cost," Direct from Midrex, Midrex Technologies, September 2020, https://www.midrex.com/commentary/value-benefits-cost/.

16. Melissa Traynor, "Building Profitable Customer Relationships," *Small Business Success Blog*, SCORE, June 27, 2019, https://sanluisobispo.score.org/blog/building-profitable-customer-relationships.

17. "What Is Customer Equity: Definitive Guide," Internet Marketing 101, SendPulse, updated August 27, 2021, https://sendpulse.com/support/glossary/customer-equity.

18. "Magazine Advertising: A Primer," Resources for Entrepreneurs, Gaebler Ventures, accessed January 4, 2022, https://www.gaebler.com/Magazine-Advertising.htm.

19. "How to Use the 5 M's of Marketing to Review Internal Resources," *Oxford College of Marketing Blog*, Oxford College of Marketing, last modified April 13, 2019, https://blog.oxfordcollegeofmarketing.com/2018/06/25/how-to-use-the-5-ms-of-marketing-to-review-internal-resources/.

20. Oxford College of Marketing, "Use the 5 M's."

21. Ibid.

22. Kellie Wong, "Organizational Culture: Definition, Importance, and Development," *Engage* (blog), Achievers, May 7, 2020, https://www.achievers.com/blog/organizational-culture-definition/.

23. Gustavo Razzetti, "How Zappos Designs Culture Using Core Values," *Culture Design Blog Posts*, Fearless Culture, December 9, 2019, https://www.fearlessculture.design/blog-posts/zappos-culture-design-canvas.

24. Katie Canales, "Tony Hsieh, the Late Former CEO of Zappos, Famously Pioneered the Concept of Paying New, Unhappy Employees $2,000 to Quit in Order to Maintain a Happy, Productive Workforce," Insider, November 30, 2020, https://www.businessinsider.com/zappos-tony-hsieh-paid-new-workers-to-quit-the-offer-2020-11

25. Krystie Lee Yandoli, "Ellen DeGeneres Is Ending Her TV Show after Allegations of Sexual Misconduct and a Toxic Workplace," BuzzFeed News, May 12, 2021, https://www.buzzfeednews.com/article/krystieyandoli/ellen-degeneres-show-ending.

26. Laura Click, "How a Strong Company Culture Dramatically Improves Your Marketing," Blue Kite, last modified October 13, 2016, https://flybluekite.com/successful-marketing-relies-well-defined-company-culture/.

27. Toma Kulbytė, "Key Customer Experience Statistics You Need to Know," *SuperOffice Blog*, SuperOffice, updated June 24, 2021, https://www.superoffice.com/blog/customer-experience-statistics/.

28. Bill Taylor, "Why Zappos Pays New Employees to Quit—and You Should Too," *Harvard Business Review*, May 19, 2008, https://hbr.org/2008/05/why-zappos-pays-new-employees.

29. Julianna Young, "7 Zappos Amenities That Boost Employee Happiness," *Zappos.com Culture Blog*, Zappos.com, June 12, 2019, https://www.zappos.com/about/stories/employee-happiness-amenities.

30. "The Impact of Micro and Macro Environment Factors on Marketing," *Oxford College of Marketing Blog*, Oxford College of Marketing, last modified November 8, 2021, https://blog.oxfordcollegeofmarketing.com/2014/11/04/the-impact-of-micro-and-macro-environment-factors-on-marketing/.

31. "What Is PESTLE Analysis? An Important Business Analysis Tool," PESTLE Analysis, last modified November 23, 2021, https://pestleanalysis.com/what-is-pestle-analysis/.

32. Megan Cerullo, "Product Shortages and Soaring Prices Reveal Fragility of US Supply Chain," CBS News, CBS Interactive, April 13, 2022, https://www.cbsnews.com/news/product-shortages-inflation-supply-chain-2022/.

33. Gregg Logan and Todd LaRue, "Marketing to Baby Boomers One More Time," *The Advisory*, May 30, 2019, https://www.rclco.com/publication/marketing-to-baby-boomers-one-more-time/.

34. Thomas Bush, "PESTLE Analysis: Technological Factors Affecting Business," PESTLE Analysis, July 11, 2016, https://pestleanalysis.com/technological-factors-affecting-business/.

35. "The Marketing Concept," OpExWorks.com Knowledge Base, OpExWorks Solutions, accessed May 7, 2022, http://www.opexworks.com/KBase/OpExWorks.com_Knowledge_Base.htm#Marketing_Management/The_Marketing_Concept.htm

36. Theodore Levitt, *Marketing Myopia* (Boston: Harvard Business Press, 2008).

37. "Societal Marketing Concept: Definition, Advantages, Examples," iEduNote, last modified June 13, 2021, https://www.iedunote.com/societal-marketing-concept.

38. "Needs: Meaning, Importance, Types & Example," MBA Skool, updated August 15, 2021, https://www.mbaskool.com/business-concepts/marketing-and-strategy-terms/1916-needs.html.

39. Jonathan R. Ferrer, "The Great Controversy: Does Marketing Create or Satisfy Needs?," LinkedIn, May 25, 2015, https://www.linkedin.com/pulse/great-controversy-does-marketing-create-satisfy-needs-r-ferrer-mba-5/.

40. "Value Proposition," Glossary, ProductPlan, last modified June 2, 2021, https://www.productplan.com/glossary/value-proposition/.

41. Bill Ragan Roofing Company (website), accessed July 18, 2022, https://www.billraganroofing.com/.

42. Ramona Sukhraj, "21 Value Proposition Examples That Every Marketer Can Learn From in 2021," *Newest Insights* (blog), IMPACT, June 3, 2021, https://www.impactplus.com/blog/value-proposition-examples.

43. Sukhraj, "21 Value Proposition Examples."

44. Ibid.

45. Wesley Chai, Tim Ehrens, and Karolina Kiwak, "CRM (Customer Relationship Management)," SearchCustomerExperience, TechTarget, September 25, 2020, https://www.techtarget.com/searchcustomerexperience/definition/CRM-customer-relationship-management.

46. "Salesforce Ranked #1 in CRM Market Share for Eighth Consecutive Year," News & Insights, Salesforce, December 16, 2021, https://www.salesforce.com/news/stories/salesforce-ranked-1-in-crm-market-share-for-eighth-consecutive-year/.

47. "A Brief on Three Types of CRM: Operational, Analytical, Collaborative," *OroCRM Blog*, Oro, April 1, 2020, https://oroinc.com/orocrm/blog/a-brief-on-three-types-of-crm-operational-analytical-collaborative/.

48. Oro, "Brief on Three Types."

49. Ibid.

50. "How CRM Can Help in Strengthening Customer Loyalty," *Commence CRM Blog*, Commence, July 26, 2020, https://commence.com/blog/2020/07/26/crm-strengthening-customer-loyalty/.

51. Commence, "How CRM Can Help."

52. Ibid.

53. Ibid.

54. Lindsey Peacock, "7 Innovative Customer Loyalty Programs to Keep Them Coming Back," *Ecommerce Marketing Blog*, Shopify, June 22, 2022, https://www.shopify.com/blog/loyalty-program.

55. "What Is Ethical Marketing? Complete Guide," Lapaas Digital, September 11, 2020, https://lapaas.com/ethical-marketing/.

56. "56percent of Americans Stop Buying from Brands They Believe Are Unethical," Mintel Press Office, Mintel, November 18, 2015, https://www.mintel.com/press-centre/social-and-lifestyle/56-of-americans-stop-buying-from-brands-they-believe-are-unethical.

57. "5 Brands That Used Transparency in Marketing and Won," *The Alida Journal* (blog), Alida, July 8, 2016, https://www.alida.com/the-alida-journal/5-brands-employed-transparency-marketing-and-won.

58. Eriq Gardner, "Vizio Can't Dodge Claims Its TVs Spy on Viewers," *The Hollywood Reporter*, July 26, 2017, https://www.hollywoodreporter.com/business/business-news/vizio-cant-dodge-claims-tvs-spy-viewers-1024438/.

59. "When Silence Is the Best Response on Social Media," Insights & News, BRG Communications, February 28, 2019, https://brgcommunications.com/when-silence-is-the-best-response-on-social-media/.

60. Ashley Lombardo, "5-Hour Energy Found Guilty of Misleading Advertising," MedTruth, April 25, 2017, https://medtruth.com/articles/news/5-hour-energy-misleading-advertising/.

61. Karl Kronenberger, "You Can Sue Your Competitor for False Advertising," News & Articles, Kronenberger Rosenfeld, September 20, 2018, https://krinternetlaw.com/news/article-detail/you-can-sue-your-competitor-for-false-advertising.

62. Arezou Naeini et al., "Case Study: How TOMS Shoes Made a Cause the Centre of Its Activities," *Business Today*, June 7, 2015, https://www.businesstoday.in/magazine/lbs-case-study/story/toms-shoes-shoes-for-free-cause-marketing-strategy-case-study-49364-2015-05-22.

63. TOMS Shoes, *TOMS Impact Report: 2019–2020*, 2021, https://www.toms.com/on/demandware.static/-/Library-Sites-toms-content-global/default/pdfs/TOMS_Impact_Report.pdf.

64. "Our History," Dancing Goats Coffee, https://www.dancinggoats.com/pages/our-history; Rachel Sanchez, "Two Names No More: Batdorf & Bronson Becomes Dancing Goats Coffee In Company Rebrand," Thurston Talk, March 24, 2022, https://www.dancinggoats.com/blogs/blog/two-names-no-more-batdorf-bronson-becomes-dancing-goats-coffee-in-company-rebrand-by-rebecca-sanchez; "Well-Known Olympia Coffee Business Changes Its Name," *The Olympian*, April 29, 2022, https://www.theolympian.com/

2

Strategic Planning in Marketing

Figure 2.1 A team of marketing strategists brainstorm to develop a strategic plan. (credit: modification of work "Design a Better Business Masterclass @ Zoku Amsterdam, October 2017" by Sebastiaan ter Burg/flickr, CC BY 2.0)

Chapter Outline

 # In the Spotlight

Frito-Lay, the producer of Doritos, Lay's, and Cheetos, is a $13 billion business division of PepsiCo.[1] If you're a snack food fan, you might have noticed how Frito-Lay seems to constantly come up with new flavors for its chips—dill pickle, Chesapeake Bay Crab Spice, Chile Limón, and more. You might picture nutritionists and scientists working in labs, trying recipe after recipe in order to come up with a winner. But Frito-Lay has a unique way of including customers in its strategic decision-making process.[2]

The company crowdsources its new flavors through a contest called "Do Us a Flavor," in which it asks customers to submit ideas for flavors they'd like Lay's to develop. The company then selects the three best entries and awards a cash prize to the winners.[3]

For example, Frito-Lay's "Turn Up the Flavor" contest resulted in three limited-time flavors inspired by three different music genres: hip-hop, pop, and rock. To pique interest in the content, Frito-Lay teamed up with singer/songwriter Bebe Rexha, who wrote the theme song for the campaign, and the company included a unique code for the new chip packets so that buyers could unlock Rexha's new tracks.[4]

Lay's Commercial

Check out the Lay's Turn Up the Flavor commercial with Bebe Rexha.

Click to view content (https://openstax.org/books/principles-marketing/pages/2-in-the-spotlight)

2.1 Developing a Strategic Plan

Learning Outcomes

By the end of this section, you will be able to:

- **LO** 1 Define strategic planning and list the steps in the strategic planning process.
- **LO** 2 Write an effective vision statement and mission statement.
- **LO** 3 Describe the role of company values.
- **LO** 4 Perform a gap analysis.
- **LO** 5 Write SMART objectives and goals.
- **LO** 6 Summarize ways to monitor progress of the strategic plan.

Strategic Planning Defined

Let's start with a simplified definition of strategy and then move on from there. Many if not most of you have watched a football game, either live or on TV. Perhaps you're a fan of a particular team or you'll watch the Super Bowl (perhaps just to see the commercials). Every football coach knows that you don't enter a game without a game plan—the process of taking plays out of the playbook and putting them into a game plan for a specific opponent. This isn't an easy task. The coaching staff has to consider the skills and experience of the players on the team as well as the strengths—and weaknesses—of the opposing team, and they will develop the plays that they feel will best neutralize the strengths of the opposing team while taking advantage of the strengths of their own players.

That football game plan is a great analogy for a business's overall **strategy**—the plans, actions, objectives, and goals that outline how the business is going to compete in its chosen markets given its portfolio of products or services. In marketing, a portfolio is a collection or listing of all the goods and services that a company sells to customers.

Distinctions are often made between corporate-level strategy, business-level strategy, and functional strategy, so let's briefly define them here. **Corporate-level strategy** covers the entire business in a complex organization where there are multiple businesses, divisions, or operating units (sometimes called **strategic business units**, or SBUs). Corporate-level strategies are formulated and implemented by upper management. **Business-level strategy** is the strategic plan created for a single business or operating unit, and these plans are generally developed by middle management to support the corporate-level strategy. Corporate-level and business-level strategies lead to the development of **functional strategy**, which is the plan to achieve the corporate- and business-level objectives in functional areas such as human resources, marketing, and production.

People say a picture is worth a thousand words, so take a look at how this breaks down in Figure 2.2.

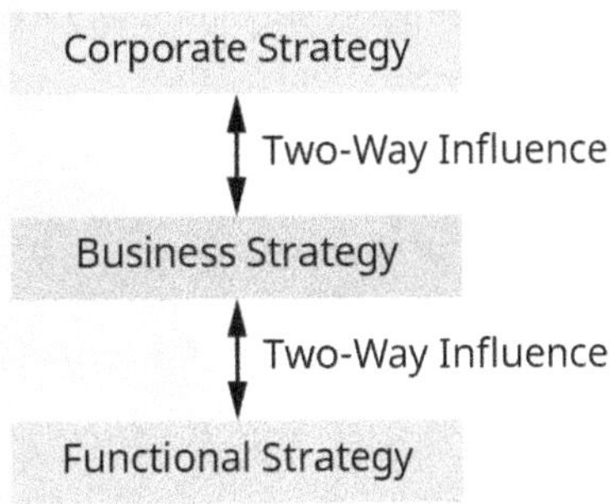

Figure 2.2 Different Levels of Strategy Required in Complex Organizations (attribution: Copyright Rice University, OpenStax, under CC BY 4.0 license)

Many organizations have only a single product line, market focus, or business, so they will require only a business-level strategy. However, with larger organizations, it can be important to break the overall business into smaller, more manageable strategic business units to maintain an overall focus on the business as a whole and pull the business-level strategies into a cohesive whole.

Consider, for example, Procter & Gamble. The producer of such diverse products as diapers, Tide detergent, and Oral-B toothpaste has five industry-based strategic business units—baby, feminine, and family care; beauty; health care; grooming; and fabric and home care, family care, and new ventures. Each of these SBUs has its own chief executive officer and functions essentially as a standalone business under the corporate "umbrella."[5]

When you consider the complexities of the diverse markets Procter & Gamble serves, this makes sense. Competing in the oral care market is vastly different than competing in baby products, so separate SBUs require separate strategic plans.

Steps in the Strategic Planning Process

There are many variations of the strategic planning process—almost as many as there are publications on strategic planning. For our purposes in this textbook, we're going to use the five-step process outlined in Figure 2.3. Keep in mind, however, that the process may be a little different for some organizations depending on the stage of their products in the product life cycle (which we'll learn more about in Products: Consumer Offerings), the maturity of the industry in which the business participates, how competitive the marketplace is, and other factors.

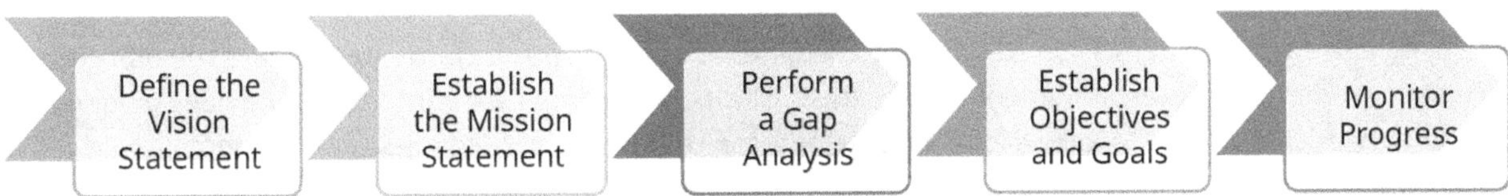

Figure 2.3 Steps in the Strategic Planning Process (attribution: Copyright Rice University, OpenStax, under CC BY 4.0 license)

These elements will all be defined in more detail in the sections that follow.

Step One: The Vision Statement: Where Do We See the Business Going?

The strategic planning process begins with a solid understanding of what the organization is trying to create—that is, its **vision statement**. A vision statement is forward-looking and is intended to create a mental image of what the organization wants to achieve in the longer term. Vision statements should be both inspirational and aspirational.

Let's look at some vision statements from companies with which you might be familiar so you'll see how this works:

- Amazon: "Our vision is to be earth's most customer-centric company; to build a place where people can come to find and discover anything they might want to buy online"[6]

- Volkswagen: "To make this world a mobile, sustainable place with access to all the citizens"[7]
- Fujitsu: "Understanding you better—serving you best"[8]

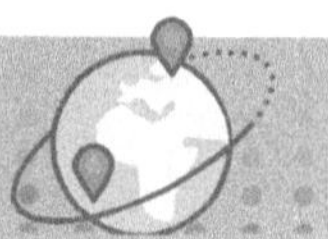

LINK TO LEARNING

Vision Statement

For more information on how to write a vision statement, take a look at this brief video from RapidStart Leadership.

Click to view content (https://openstax.org/books/principles-marketing/pages/2-1-developing-a-strategic-plan)

Step Two: The Mission Statement: Why Does the Business Exist?

Now that the vision statement is complete, it's time to tackle the mission statement, which quite simply answers the question, Why does the company exist? The **mission statement** of an organization sums up in one to three sentences what the company does, who it serves, and what differentiates it from its competitors. Whereas the vision statement provided the destination (i.e., Where is the business going?), the mission statement provides the guideposts for the business to get there.

Mission statements serve two purposes. First, a well-written mission statement helps employees remain focused on the aims of the business. Second, it encourages them to discover ways of moving toward increasing their productivity in order to achieve company goals. Mission statements aren't just for internal use, however. Prospective investors also often refer to a company's mission statement to see if their values align with those of the company. Once again, let's bring this definition to life by including a few mission statements from well-known companies:

- BMW: "The BMW Group is the world's leading provider of premium products and premium services for individual mobility"[9]
- Tesla: "To accelerate the advent of sustainable transport by bringing compelling mass-market electric cars to market as soon as possible"[10]
- Apple: "To bring the best personal computing products and support to students, educators, designers, scientists, engineers, businesspersons and consumers in over 140 countries around the world"[11]

There are also two types of mission statements: customer oriented or product oriented. What's the difference? A customer-oriented mission statement defines the business in terms of how it intends to provide solutions to customer needs. As examples, take a look at some of these customer-oriented mission statements:

- IKEA: "To offer a wide range of well-designed, functional home furnishing products at prices so low that as many people as possible will be able to afford them"[12]
- Netflix: "To entertain the world"[13]

The other type of mission statement is a product-oriented one. With a product-oriented mission statement, the focus is on the offering itself rather than the needs of customers. Again, look at a couple of examples of product-oriented mission statements so you can see the difference between these mission statements and the customer-oriented mission statements shown above:

- eBay: "To be the world's favorite destination for discovering great value and unique selection"[14]
- Genentech: "To develop drugs to address significant unmet medical needs"[15]

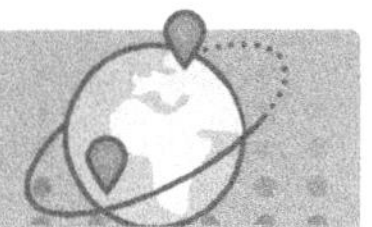

LINK TO LEARNING

Mission Statement

For more information on how to write an effective mission statement, check out this brief video from Bplans.

Click to view content (https://openstax.org/books/principles-marketing/pages/2-1-developing-a-strategic-plan)

Then watch this video from Entrepreneur.

Click to view content (https://openstax.org/books/principles-marketing/pages/2-1-developing-a-strategic-plan)

Step Three: Perform a Gap Analysis

Before we get into the specifics of how to perform a gap analysis, let's define it. Simply put, a **gap analysis** is an internal analysis of the company or organization to identify and review any inherent deficiencies that may hinder its ability to meet its goals. In other words, a gap analysis determines what factors in the organization may be causing it to underperform.

A gap analysis answers the following questions:

- Where are we now?
- Where would we like to be?
- What's stopping us from getting there?

A gap analysis as part of the strategic planning process is a way to determine where the "soft spots" are and where adjustments need to be made before setting a course of action.

There are four steps to completion of a gap analysis. Let's take a look:

- **Step 1: Identify the current state of the business, organization, or department.** Let's use an example of a company that wants to increase market share of its product line. To date, current growth is sluggish, averaging only 5 percent per year.[16]
- **Step 2: Identify where you want to be.** "Where you want to be" may be identified by using different terms—the desired state, the future target, or a stretch goal. It stands to reason that you'll want to consider your current state (from Step 1) and where you want to be in a reasonable time frame. Do you want to increase market share by 10 percent within the first year? Do you want to increase market share by 25 percent within the first three years? Because strategic plans often go out three to five years, your "where you want to be" can be lengthy as well.[17]
- **Step 3: Identify the gaps.** At this point in your gap analysis, you've identified where your organization current is and where it wants to be. Now it's time to identify how you're going to bridge that gap. This step involves figuring out what those gaps are. Is market share suffering because a new competitor introduced a similar but lower-priced product into the market? Is your pricing too high given production capabilities and costs? Has the advertising campaign introduced last year lost its sizzle, or worse yet, did your most recent advertising campaign flop?[18]
- **Step 4: Devise improvements to close the gaps.** It's time to determine the proper course of action to close the gap, keeping in mind the cost of implementation for each solution.[19] This is where the rubber hits the road, so to speak, because ideas are easy; it's the execution of those ideas that becomes challenging. An effective gap analysis not only identifies the problems (i.e., gaps) but also sets forth what needs to happen in specific terms to close those gaps. Will a new advertising campaign boost market share? Do we need to hire a new advertising agency? And what will a new advertising campaign cost? Are

there cost-cutting measures that can be taken to reduce manufacturing costs, thereby reducing the product's cost to consumers?

Step Four: Establish Objectives and Goals

With the mission and vision statement in place, along with a candid view of the organization through gap analysis, we can now define the goals and objectives for the organization. Goals and objectives are a critical part of every organization, particularly in the strategic planning process. When written effectively, these goals provide a sense of direction and a clearer focus. It's these goals that give the organization a target at which it can aim, so to speak.

But before we go further, let's differentiate between goals and objectives. Both terms refer to desired outcomes that the organization wants to achieve, but that's where the similarity ends. **Goals** are statements of desired outcomes that are expected to be achieved over a longer period of time, typically three to five years. Goals are broad statements of the desired results; they do not describe the methods that will be utilized in order to achieve those results. For example, common business goals may include increasing revenue or market share or reducing the company's carbon footprint.[20]

On the other hand, **objectives** are "action items." They are specific targets to be achieved within a shorter time frame, generally one year or less, in order to achieve the stated goal. Whereas goals describe the end result, objectives describe the actions or activities that need to take place in order to achieve the goal. For example, if your goal was to increase market share, the objective would likely be stated as something like "Increase market share to 6 percent by the end of the year."[21]

The goals and objectives of an organization define the key actions that allow it to execute its chosen strategy. However, in order to be effective, goals and objectives should be SMART— specific, measurable, attainable, realistic/relevant, and time-bound—as shown in Figure 2.4.

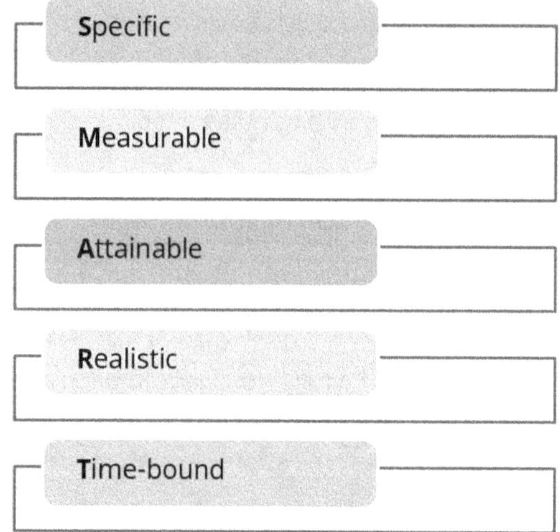

Figure 2.4 SMART Goals (attribution: Copyright Rice University, OpenStax, under CC BY 4.0 license)

- First, effective goals should be **specific**—there's the "S" in SMART goals. They should be clear and easy to understand. A specific goal answers questions like "What needs to be accomplished?" To illustrate this, imagine that you've decided to improve your grade point average. "Improve my GPA" is indeed a goal, but it's too vague to be a helpful goal. By how many points do you want to improve your GPA? To make your goal more meaningful (and specific), you might want to restate your goal as "Improve my current GPA from 2.8 to 3.5."
- Second, effective goals should be **measurable**—there's the "M" in SMART goals. Specificity is a solid start, but quantifying your goals makes it easier to track progress and see when you've achieved your goal. The bottom line is, you can't see results without knowing what they look like, and if you're not measuring anything, how will you know when and if you've accomplished it? Your original goal of "improve my GPA"

isn't measurable. How will you know when you've achieved your goal? When you've increased it by .1, .2, .5, or even a full point? By setting a goal to "improve my current GPA from 2.8 to 3.5 by the end of the semester," you've set a goal that's easily measurable—just look at your grades at the end of the semester!

- Third, effective goals should be **attainable**. There's actually some disagreement as to the name of this third element. Some marketing experts tout using "ambitious"; others suggest "achievable" or "actionable." For our purposes, we're going to stick with "attainable" because although goals should be a reach, establishing goals that aren't within reach can turn out to be an exercise in frustration. Let's go back to our GPA analogy. If it's mid-April and you're barely passing your current classes, you're just setting yourself up for failure.
- Fourth, effective goals should be **realistic**. Once again, there's actually some disagreement as to the name of this element; you may see it shown as "relevant" in other textbooks or articles. We're going to use "realistic" because the term reflects the balance between goals that are too easy and too hard. Taken in the context of a strategic plan, your goals must represent a substantial objective that you're willing and able to work toward, but there should be a reasonable chance that you can achieve it.[22] Getting back to our GPA analogy, if you've got Cs in all of your classes and it's already mid-April, improving your GPA to 3.5 by the end of the semester is probably not realistic.
- Finally, effective goals should be **time-bound**. Every goal should be grounded by a time frame within which the goal is to be achieved. Without a deadline, there is little sense of urgency to work to achieve the goal. Having a goal with a target date (like the end of the semester) gives you something to focus on and work toward and prevents everyday tasks from taking priority over your longer-term goals.

LINK TO LEARNING

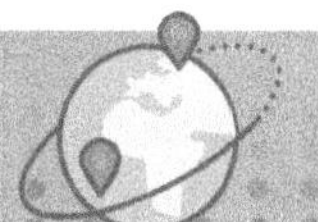

SMART Goals

For more information on establishing SMART Goals, check out this video from SMA Marketing.

Click to view content (https://openstax.org/books/principles-marketing/pages/2-1-developing-a-strategic-plan)

Monitor Progress

If you had decided to save money from each of your paychecks to eventually purchase a new car, you'd probably check the balance in your savings account on a regular basis to see how you're progressing toward your goal. The same is true in the strategic planning process. In order for goals and objectives to be effective, marketers need to monitor them on a continuous basis to determine if they're on track or if the goals and objectives need to be refined in response to unforeseen circumstances.

One way that marketers accomplish this is through the use of a marketing dashboard. Like the dashboard in your car, which tells you at a glance how much fuel you have, how fast you're going, and a host of other important information, a **marketing dashboard** summarizes important marketing metrics and key performance indicators (KPIs; to be covered later in this chapter) into easy-to-understand measurements.[23] This enables marketers to view ongoing progress so that they can be aware of potential problems before they actually become serious issues.

CAREERS IN MARKETING

Marketing Manager

Marketing manager jobs differ by company and industry, but in general it's a leadership position in charge of the marketing strategy at a company or for a product. Marketing managers often complete research, create pricing parameters, and work with other departments within the company such as finance, legal, advertising, promotion, and product development. Read this *Marketing Manager* article to learn more about (https://openstax.org/r/articlesmarketingmanager) the specifics of what a marketing manager does and the types of marketing manager that exist. It's commonly known that marketing managers need to be proficient in problem-solving. Read this article to learn why it's important (https://openstax.org/r/marketingproblemsolvingskill) and the specific skills you'll need.

There is growth potential in being a marketing manager. The US Bureau of Labor Statistics projects a 10 percent growth in the job role from 2021 to 2031, and you can read more about the job outlook here (https://openstax.org/r/advertisingpromotions).

Would you like to know more about the job role? Read this *Forbes* article to learn the top skills necessary, (https://openstax.org/r/educationbecomeamarketing) the typical path to this job, and degree requirements.

There are many types of jobs in marketing. You'll be introduced to several throughout this textbook. You'll also want to check out this list of 15 job titles and what the job role encompasses. (https://openstax.org/r/marketingjobtitle) Keep in mind that regardless of where you start in marketing, you have options as you move in your career journey. Many people move between marketing roles, and the skills you learn in each role will help you in other roles.

Knowledge Check

It's time to check your knowledge on the concepts presented in this section. Refer to the Answer Key at the end of the book for feedback.

1. Which of the following defines the reason why the business exists?
   a. Vision statement
   b. Mission statement
   c. Gap analysis
   d. Goals and objectives

2. Which of the following strategies covers the entire organization when the business includes multiple divisions or operating units?
   a. Functional strategy
   b. Strategic business unit strategy
   c. Corporate-level strategy
   d. Business-level strategy

3. What do you call the plans, actions, objectives, and goals that outline how a business will compete in its chosen markets?
   a. Mission statement
   b. Vision statement
   c. Gap analysis
   d. Strategy

4. Which of the following best describes a gap analysis?
    a. A statement that answers the question, Where do we see the business going?
    b. An internal analysis of the company to identify inherent deficiencies that may hinder its ability to meet its goals
    c. A statement that answers the question, Why does the business exist?
    d. A strategic plan created for a single business or operating unit

5. In "SMART goals," what does the "R" stand for?
    a. Relatable
    b. Rational
    c. Required
    d. Realistic

2.2 | The Role of Marketing in the Strategic Planning Process

Learning Outcomes

By the end of this section, you will be able to:
- **LO** 1 Explain the role of marketing in the strategic planning process.
- **LO** 2 Discuss the business portfolio and identify planning tools.
- **LO** 3 Describe a SWOT analysis.
- **LO** 4 List and describe marketing strategies based on analytics.

Explain the Role of Marketing in the Strategic Planning Process

To get a better idea of the importance of marketing in the strategic planning process, let's imagine that you're the owner of a manufacturing business that produces widgets. You've been able to recruit top engineering talent to design these widgets and source components from trusted, reliable vendors, and your manufacturing facility is efficient and can produce the widgets in a cost-effective manner. Sounds like a winning business, doesn't it?

Well, the only thing we've left out of the equation for success is customers, and without customers, the finest engineering staff and manufacturing facility in the world won't ring the bell in terms of profits or revenue. You need to determine who your customers are, what their needs and wants are, how you're going to reach them, and how you're going to persuade them to buy your widgets. That's where marketing comes into the strategic planning process, and that's why it plays a crucial role.

Marketing in the strategic planning process has several basic but critical functions:

- First, marketers assist the strategic planning team in executing a marketing philosophy throughout the strategic planning process.
- Second, marketers assist the organization in gathering and analyzing information necessary to examine the current situation (the first step in a gap analysis).
- Third, marketers are responsible for the identification of trends in the marketing environment and assessing the potential impact of those trends.[24]

Business Portfolio Definition

As noted above, many businesses have a single product or business unit. However, larger organizations such as Apple, Alphabet, General Electric, Meta, and Microsoft often have multiple diverse business units called strategic business units. Despite the fact that these SBUs report directly to the parent company's headquarters, they typically develop their own vision statements, mission statements, objectives, and goals, and the strategic planning for these SBUs is performed separately and apart from other SBUs within the organization.[25] When companies have multiple products or business units, these comprise the **business**

portfolio—the total group of product lines, services, and business units that the company possesses.

To give you a better sense of what a business portfolio entails, look at Figure 2.5, which illustrates the products and services of Microsoft and how each offering contributes to the overall strategic plan of the company.[26] Microsoft reported $168 billion in revenue in fiscal year 2021, and each of its product lines (or strategic business units) contributes to this revenue in differing amounts.[27] It's easy to see from this breakdown why each of these businesses under the Microsoft "umbrella" would have different strategic plans to execute within the markets they serve. You likely wouldn't have one overarching marketing or business strategy for all of these SBUs because the markets for Office, Gaming, LinkedIn, and the other SBUs are likely very different and would require different strategies to reach and retain customers.

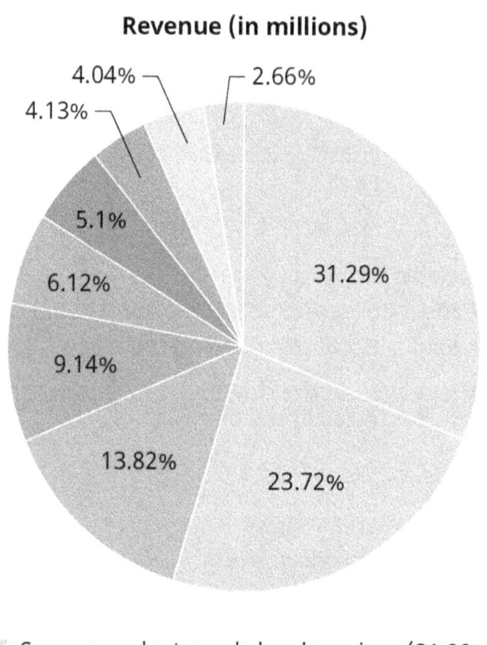

Figure 2.5 Composition of Microsoft Revenues (data source: *Microsoft Annual Report 2021*; attribution: Copyright Rice University, OpenStax, under CC BY 4.0 license)

Analyze and Design the Business Portfolio

There are many reasons why an organization would establish separate business units or product lines as it grows. For example, if the current product line is in a market where growth is limited, it may choose to branch out to other product lines or markets. Alternatively, an organization may choose to expand into other product lines to take advantage of emerging opportunities.

Emerson Electric, headquartered in St. Louis, Missouri, has five business segments: Network Power, Process Management, Industrial Automation, Climate Technologies, and Commercial and Residential Solutions (i.e., tools and storage). These business segments provide products as diverse as hardware and software technologies; motors; fluid control systems; heating and air-conditioning products and services; and tools, storage products, and appliances for residential, health care, and food services.[28] When you consider divisions as diverse as these, it should be readily evident why each is a separate division with separate strategies to compete in its respective marketplaces.

Conversely, a business may choose to expand in areas in which it already has experience and can use the power of its core competencies to establish sustainable competitive advantage with new products in existing markets.

There are a few tools that can help determine which course of action is best advised given the current circumstances of the organization, the marketplace, and other factors. Let's take a look at a few of them.

Boston Consulting Group (BCG) Matrix

The **BCG matrix** is a model developed by Boston Consulting Group that can be used to analyze a business's product lines or SBUs and make decisions about which to invest in in the future and which they should try to minimize further investment in or even eliminate. The bottom line is that no business has unlimited funds to invest in its product lines, and the BCG matrix is a useful model in determining how to allocate money in terms of marketing, research and development (R&D), etc. to that portfolio.

As shown in Figure 2.6, the BCG matrix considers both market share and market growth rate. The SBUs or products that have high market share in a high-growth market are called *stars* and are placed in the upper left quadrant. These are the opportunities that hold the most promise for the organization.

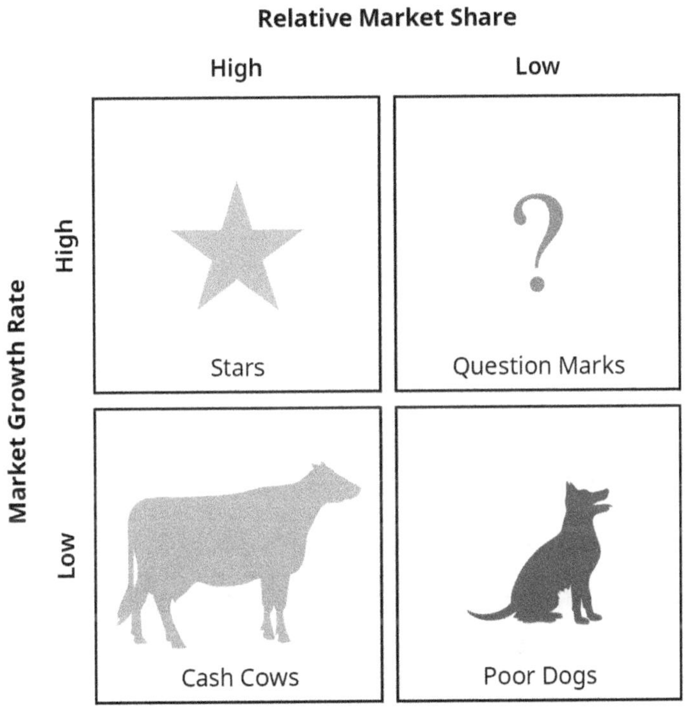

Figure 2.6 Boston Consulting Group (BCG) Matrix (attribution: Copyright Rice University, OpenStax, under CC BY 4.0 license)

Conversely, those SBUs or products that have low market share in a low-growth market are referred to as *dogs* and are placed in the lower right quadrant. These are prime candidates for divestiture or elimination because they have relatively low growth potential, and although the business has significant funds tied up in them, they bring in virtually nothing in terms of revenues. Divestiture could also provide needed capital to invest in your stars or question marks.

Cash cows, in the lower left quadrant, are an interesting breed, so to speak. A cash cow is an SBU or product that has high market share in a low-growth market. They're valuable to a business because they generate significant revenue that can fund other strategic initiatives or emerging opportunities. Incidentally, they're called cash cows because the thinking is to "milk" these products for profits.

Those SBUs or products that have a low market share in a high-growth market are called *question marks* (sometimes also called "problem children") and are placed in the upper left quadrant. Question marks are among the most complex decisions to be considered when developing a BCG matrix because a root cause analysis may be required in order to determine why these SBUs are, in fact, question marks. Obviously, with high-market growth, the market is strong, but there are one or more reasons why your organization hasn't been able to capitalize on it and gain market share. Does the product line need more investment in order to move into the "star" category? Is competition so strong in this market that additional funding in terms of advertising campaigns or other marketing tactics render them useless? Is the question mark just a trend in which you can expect high growth without a lot of market share for a short period of time?

Once you have categorized each of your SBUs or products on the BCG matrix, you'll have a crystal-clear vision of where each stands and can identify which you should prioritize and which need to be divested.

To better understand the BCG model, let's do a simplified matrix for Apple and some of its products (see Figure 2.7). Because Apple has so many products and services, we're showing only four hardware products in this matrix.

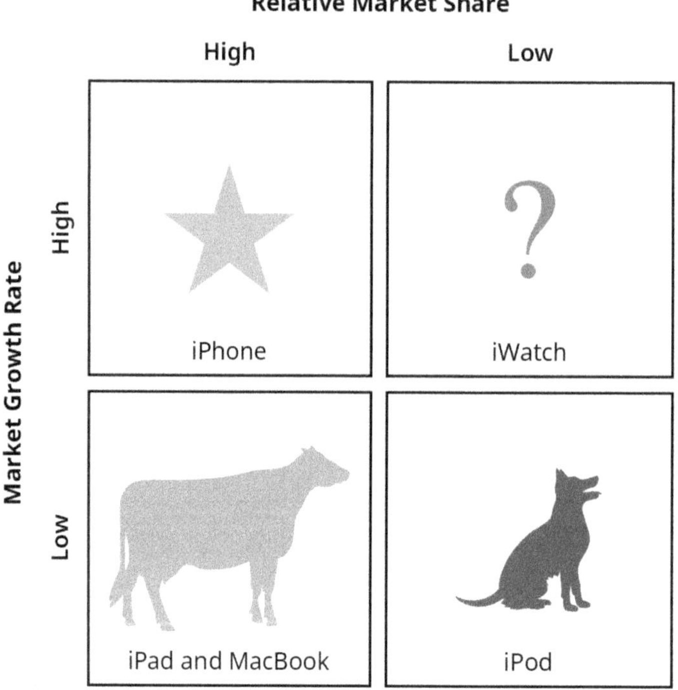

Figure 2.7 BCG Matrix of Apple's Portfolio (attribution: Copyright Rice University, OpenStax, under CC BY 4.0 license)

In this sample matrix, we're going to place the Apple iPhone in the star category. You'll recall from our discussion above that stars have relatively high market share in a growing market. Let's face it: the iPhone is the shining gem of Apple's portfolio. Even though Apple has diversified its product line, the iPhone is still responsible for 52 percent of the company's revenue, raking in an astounding $192 billion in 2021.[29]

Next, we're going to put the iPad and the MacBook in the cash cow category. Remember that the BCG matrix is built on two parameters—market share and market growth. Both the iPad and the MacBook have relatively high market share compared to competitors, but the market for these products is not growing much anymore.[30] The Apple iPad had a 31.5 percent share of the global tablet market during the first quarter (down from 38 percent in the previous quarter), and the MacBook still holds popularity, garnering 15.3 percent of the market share.[31] Both the iPad and the MacBook are well-established products that continue to generate substantial income for Apple, and these products require relatively little additional investment for them to remain profitable.

Let's move on to the question mark category. Remember that question marks have low market share in a high-growth market, and we're going to place the Apple iWatch in this category. The iWatch has the potential to become as big of a hit as the iPhone, but the jury is still out because there are too many unknowns in the market. Global sales of smartwatches increased by 13 percent in the first quarter of 2022, and the Apple iWatch continues to lead in market share.[32] However, Apple will need to analyze its iWatch vis-à-vis its other products to decide if it should continue to invest in the product.[33]

Finally, let's move on to the dog quadrant of the matrix. We're going to place the iPod in this category because market growth has slowed considerably as people use their phones to listen to music or podcasts. The iPod has experienced a shrinking market share as a result, and it wouldn't make sense for Apple to continue to invest in the iPod.[34] As a matter of fact, Apple announced in May 2022 that it would discontinue the iPod Touch, while the touch-screen model launched in 2007 will remain on sale until supplies run out.[35]

LINK TO LEARNING

BCG Matrix

Would you like to learn more about the BCG Matrix? Watch this brief video from Solve It Like a Marketer.

Click to view content (https://openstax.org/books/principles-marketing/pages/2-2-the-role-of-marketing-in-the-strategic-planning-process)

SWOT Analysis

SWOT is an acronym for a business's strengths, weaknesses, opportunities, and threats, and it is a useful aid for zeroing in on a feasible marketing strategy. The purpose of a **SWOT analysis** is really quite simple. Marketers want to identify the strengths and weaknesses in the organization's *internal* environment as well as the opportunities and threats that exist in the organization's *external* environment. It is generally presented in the format seen in Figure 2.8. You would complete the template with bullet points in each of the four quadrants.

Strengths	Weaknesses
Internal capabilities that may help a company reach its objectives	*Internal capabilities that may interfere with a company's ability to reach its objectives*
Examples: • Strong brand identity • Technological innovations • High market share in industry	Examples: • Outdated technology • Strong brand identity of competitors • High employee turnover
Opportunities	Threats
External factors that a company may be able to exploit for its advantage	*External factors that may create barriers or challenges to the company's performance*
Examples: • Competitor goes out of business • Low interest rates • Favorable exchange rates	Examples: • Rising interest rates • Pending legislation • Price war with competitor

Figure 2.8 Common SWOT Analysis Template (attribution: Copyright Rice University, OpenStax, under CC BY 4.0 license)

A SWOT analysis will aid in taking advantages of the organization's strengths and opportunities while avoiding (or at least minimizing) weaknesses and threats to its success. Realistically, some of the factors are in the control of the company (i.e., strengths and weaknesses), but other factors are outside the control of the company (i.e., opportunities and threats). Let's consider each of these in a little more detail.

Strengths can be factors such as patents or trademarks possessed by the company that hinder competitors in participating in the market; a better cost structure than competitors; a talented, innovative staff; or strong brand recognition in the market. Strengths are internal to the organization, and they're also positives. Questions to ask when developing this section may be: What do you do well? What unique resources you can draw on? Consider a company like Starbucks. If you were preparing a SWOT analysis for Starbucks, its strengths might include a strong brand image, solid financial performance, impressive growth in the number of stores, and an extensive international supply chain.[36]

Weaknesses are also factors within a company's internal environment, but these are hindrances to your success, so they're categorized as negatives. Weaknesses may be difficulty in accessing capital or funding, outdated technology, an unmotivated workforce, weak brand recognition, or high levels of debt. Let's go back to Starbucks. If you were preparing a SWOT analysis for Starbucks, some of its weaknesses may be high prices versus the competition and the imitability of its products.[37]

Now we'll switch over to external factors that affect the business. Opportunities are openings for something positive to happen if (and only if) you can capitalize on them. Opportunities can be moving into a new market segment that offers improved profits (like a snack food manufacturer moving into the health foods sector), competitors that have quality or delivery problems, or impending legislation that would favorably affect your organization if you're able to capitalize on it. Once again, let's go back to Starbucks. If you were preparing a SWOT analysis for Starbucks, some of its opportunities might be expansion in developing markets, a coffee subscription service similar to that offered by Panera Bread, and the introduction of new products and holiday flavors.[38]

Finally, threats are anything external to your organization that can negatively impact your business. These may include supply chain problems, ongoing staffing problems, new competitors entering the market, or impending legislation that would negatively impact your organization, like tariffs. If you were doing a SWOT analysis for Starbucks, you might identify threats such as competition with lower-cost coffee sellers, tightening discretionary spending due to inflation, or the rising price of coffee beans.[39]

LINK TO LEARNING

SWOT Analysis

Check out this video for a very simple example of a SWOT analysis.

Click to view content (https://openstax.org/books/principles-marketing/pages/2-2-the-role-of-marketing-in-the-strategic-planning-process)

When preparing a SWOT analysis, it is also helpful to compare elements by ranking strengths and weaknesses (internal factors) in terms of relative competitive importance. Marketers can also rank threats and opportunities (external factors) in terms of their likelihood and magnitude.[40]

Strategy

Earlier in this chapter, we pointed out the differences between corporate-level strategy, business-level strategy, and functional strategy. If you're a fan of movies like *Other People's Money* or *Wall Street*, you might think that corporate strategy focuses on hostile takeovers, mergers, and ruthless acquisitions.

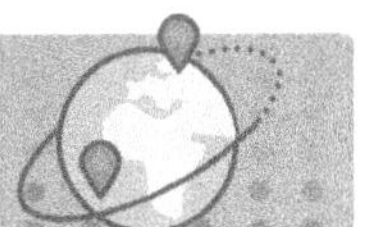

LINK TO LEARNING

Moneyball

The movie *Moneyball* is about a baseball general manager assembling a team by using computer analysis to hire new players. This is a great example of using analytics to inform strategy. Watch a clip of the movie here, where you see the analytics applied.

Click to view content (https://openstax.org/books/principles-marketing/pages/2-2-the-role-of-marketing-in-the-strategic-planning-process)

Market Penetration

When a company focuses on growing its market share in its existing markets, it is using what's known as a **market penetration strategy.** This approach generally entails significant expenditures in advertising and other marketing efforts in order to influence consumers' brand choice and create a brand reputation for the company, thereby increasing its market share.

In some mature industries (like soap, laundry detergent, or toothpaste), a market penetration strategy becomes a way of life because nearly all competitors are also engaged in intensive advertising and battle for market share. It becomes a way of life because companies fear that if they don't advertise as much as or more than their competitors, they will lose market share.

To give you an idea of how fierce the competition is with a market penetration strategy, consider Procter & Gamble, which spent $4.7 billion on advertising in 2020.[41]

Product Development

As noted above, a market penetration strategy focuses on existing products and existing markets. By contrast, a **product development strategy** involves the creation of new or improved products in order to drive growth in sales, revenue, and profit. Although the advertising expenditures involved with a market penetration strategy may be significant, they often pale compared to the expenditures involved in a product development strategy. This is because product development generally requires significant investment in R&D activities.[42]

The automobile industry provides a good illustration of the product development strategy. Car makers generally refresh their models every few years to encourage car owners to trade in their old vehicles and buy the redesigned cars with the latest tech features such as driver assist, Wi-Fi hotspots, and Apple CarPlay and Android Auto.[43] At the same time, all the manufacturers are spending billions of dollars developing new electric vehicle models to meet ambitious goals for phasing out gasoline-powered engines.

Another great example of a product development strategy is Tide laundry detergent. Tide has undergone more than 50 formulation changes over the past 40 years in an effort to continually improve its product's performance. The name always stays the same, but Tide has a "new and improved" formula with each new product release.[44]

If you doubt the power of a product development strategy, the next time you go to the grocery store or supermarket, just look at how many "new and improved" products are on the shelves!

Market Development

A **market development strategy** involves searching for new market segments and uses for a company's products. This strategy can involve the launch of its existing products into new markets or different geographical areas. In doing so, the company attempts to capitalize on the strength of the brand name it has developed in the existing markets and find new markets in which to compete.

Facebook is a great example of a market development strategy. It's difficult to remember when Facebook wasn't a household word, but Facebook started out as a small platform that enabled Harvard University students to compare headshots. The popularity of the platform spread to other college campuses, and eventually Facebook allowed nonstudents to join. It looks like the strategy worked—Facebook is now the largest social network in the world, with nearly 3 billion users![45]

To help you better understand these strategies, let's consider each one from the perspective of one company—Harley-Davidson. If Harley-Davidson were to adopt a market penetration strategy, the company would focus on selling more Harley-Davidson motorcycles in the US market. If the company were to adopt a product development strategy, it would begin selling a new product such as biker clothing for children under the Harley-Davidson brand in the US market. Harley-Davidson is currently pursuing a market development strategy, with plans to develop a new motorcycle to manufacture and sell in China. Harley-Davidson's diversification strategy might entail selling new products like children's biker clothing in China for the first time.

Product Diversification

A **product diversification strategy** is still another tool that companies can use to improve profitability and increase sales of new products. This strategy can be utilized at both the business level and the corporate level. At the business level, marketers would expand into a new segment of an industry in which the company is already operating.[46] For example, consider Apple. The company launched its revolutionary iPhone in 2007, but it didn't stop there. It has since diversified into tablets and other technology-related products.[47] At the corporate level, let's consider a dine-in restaurant that adds corporate catering and perhaps a fleet of food trucks—both businesses outside the scope of its existing business.

There are three types of diversification techniques, as shown in Figure 2.9.

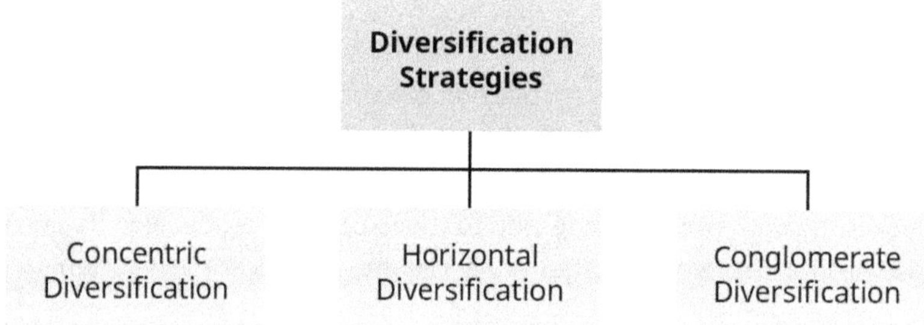

Figure 2.9 Types of Diversification Strategies (attribution: Copyright Rice University, OpenStax, under CC BY 4.0 license)

Let's look at each of these strategies in a little more detail.

The concept of **concentric diversification** revolves around the addition of similar products or services to an existing business.[48] If a picture is worth a thousand words, then an example has to be worth even more, particularly an example to which you can easily relate as a student. As you're reading this chapter, consider book publishers, like Harper Collins, Simon & Schuster, or Penguin/Random House. These book publishers don't only print the works of one author; rather, they have hundreds or perhaps thousands of authors' works in their arsenals. These publishers will publish print books, e-books (like the one you're reading right now), and audiobooks and may even sell the rights to some of the books for film and TV adaptations, allowing them to garner additional streams of revenue for one product.[49]

Conversely, the concept of **horizontal diversification** involves making available to existing customers new and perhaps even unrelated products or services so that you can garner a larger customer base.[50] For example, consider a company that produces dental hygiene products like toothbrushes and dental floss. In order to increase sales to existing customers, the company may decide to introduce into the market a line of oral irrigators or teeth whiteners. These products are new to the company, but they still serve the same customer base as its existing products.

Finally, conglomerate diversification takes horizontal diversification one step further. **Conglomerate diversification** involves the development and addition of new products or services that are significantly unrelated. You're not only introducing a new product, you're introducing a new product that is completely unrelated to your existing line of business.[51] Consider General Electric when looking for an example of conglomerate diversification. General Electric started out as a lighting business, but over the years, it has diversified into medical devices, household appliances, aircraft engines, financial services, and more. That's taking conglomerate diversification to a whole new level!

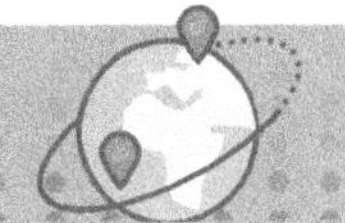

LINK TO LEARNING

Blue Ocean Strategy

Learn about market-creating strategies known as the Blue Ocean strategy from *Harvard Business Review*, where it uses Cirque du Soleil as an example.

Click to view content (https://openstax.org/books/principles-marketing/pages/2-2-the-role-of-marketing-in-the-strategic-planning-process)

Knowledge Check

It's time to check your knowledge on the concepts presented in this section. Refer to the Answer Key at the end of the book for feedback.

1. Marcus is preparing a SWOT analysis for the health club he owns. One of the factors he has identified is the fact that the health club is the only facility in the area that offers water aerobics classes. In terms of a SWOT analysis, how would this factor be characterized?
   a. Strength
   b. Weakness
   c. Opportunity
   d. Threat

2. What key metrics does the BCG matrix use to show the relative attractiveness of different offerings?
   a. Market share and market growth rate
   b. Market size and market share
   c. The ratio of dogs to cash cows in the product portfolio
   d. The potential for question marks to cross over and become stars

3. Hoffman Enterprises has a portfolio of businesses in a wide variety of unrelated industries. One of its strategic business units (SBUs) has high market share in a low-growth industry. How would this SBU be characterized in terms of the BCG matrix?
   a. Star
   b. Dog
   c. Cash cow
   d. Question mark

4. Sanjay is creating a SWOT analysis for the vegan restaurant he owns in a small college town. Until recently, there has been only one competitor in the vegan market, but that restaurant has recently closed temporarily due to health code violations. How would this development be characterized in terms of the SWOT analysis?
   a. Strength

   b. Weakness

   c. Opportunity

   d. Threat

5. Which strategy involves the creation of new or improved products to replace existing ones in order to improve a company's competitive position and sales?

   a. Market development

   b. Product diversification

   c. Horizontal diversification

   d. Product development

2.3 Purpose and Structure of the Marketing Plan

Learning Outcomes

By the end of this section, you will be able to:

  LO 1 Explain the purpose of a marketing plan.

  LO 2 List and discuss elements that should be included in a marketing plan.

Purpose and Structure of a Marketing Plan

A company's marketing plan (Figure 2.10) is without a doubt one of the most important planning tools in business. You might think that it's an activity that generates an impressive, colorful document that sits in a desk drawer until the next time it gets revised, but you'd be wrong.

If you're a new business seeking funding, the bank will want to see and understand your marketing plan before parting with funds. If you have an existing business that you want to grow, investors will likely go over your marketing plan with a fine-tooth comb to understand how additional funding will generate a positive return. Even if you're not seeking external funding, you still need a marketing plan to help you establish and achieve your sales and marketing goals in the most effective manner. That's because the marketing plan will set forth the specific actions that marketing team members need to take in order to reach target customers, build brand awareness, and of course, generate increased revenue.

If you like sports analogies, think about marketing plans as being akin to playbooks in football. A football playbook sets forth what needs to be done to win the game. The playbook breaks the team's strategy into actionable plays and defines who is responsible for what in order to win the game. That's exactly the purpose of a marketing plan as well!

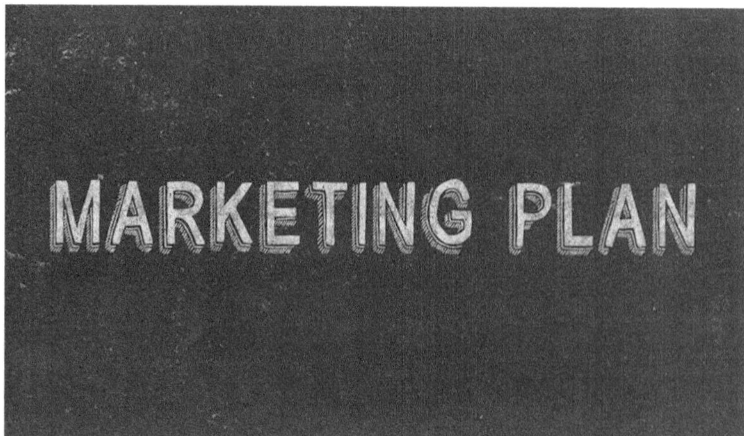

Figure 2.10 A marketing plan breaks a company's strategies into implementation steps and assigns responsibilities. (credit: "Marketing Plan Presentation Chalkboard Slide" by PLEXKITS/flickr, Public Domain)

Structure of a Marketing Plan

Do a quick Internet search on "structure of a marketing plan," and you'll get countless results. To make this even more confusing, there is little agreement within marketing about the precise structure of a marketing plan. Some marketing "experts" argue for 10 components, others for 5 or 6 components. For our purposes in this book, we're going to use a 12-element marketing plan comprising the elements shown in Figure 2.11, each of which will be discussed in detail.

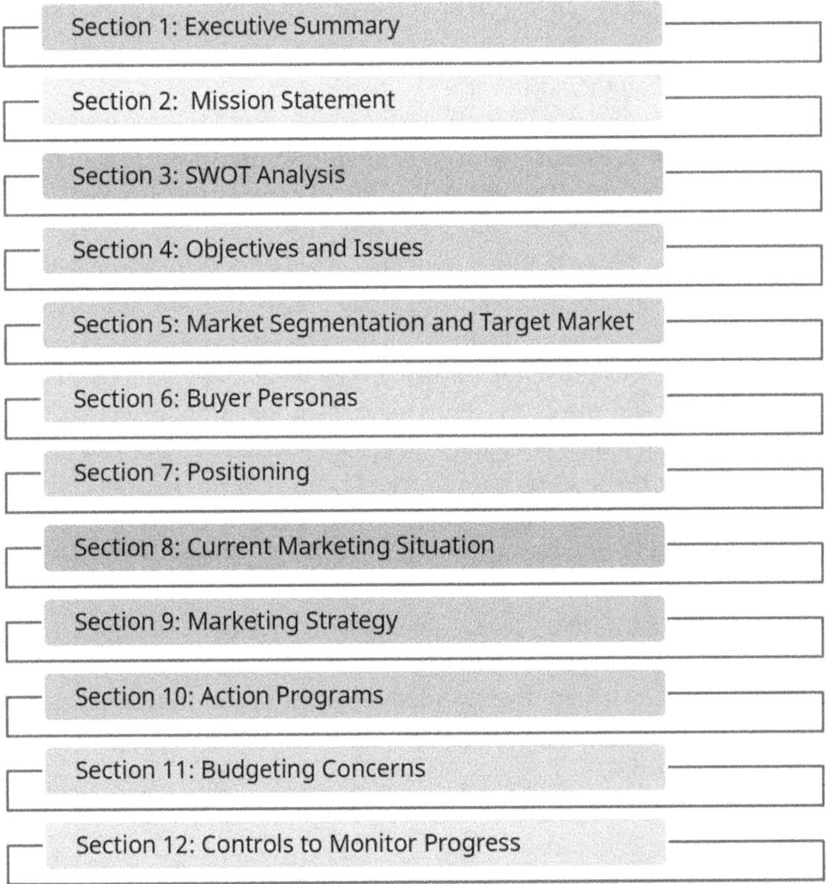

Figure 2.11 Elements of a Marketing Plan (attribution: Copyright Rice University, OpenStax, under CC BY 4.0 license)

If your professor has assigned the semester-long marketing plan template assignment, these next sections will provide you with excellent guidance for completing each of the sections. So let's dive right in.

Executive Summary

As the name suggests, the **executive summary** of your marketing plan provides those who will be reviewing your plan with a brief overview (usually one to two pages). It's going to give the reader a quick synopsis of the main parts of the plan—an overview of what your company has done, what it plans to do, and how it plans to do it.

Think of the executive summary as being an "elevator pitch" of the plan. If you're not familiar with elevator pitches, they're persuasive, concise introductions that provide the listener with the information they need to know within just a short period of time—usually the length of the average elevator ride.

The executive summary of your marketing plan should succinctly cover the main parts of the plan. It should contain information about the company, brand, products/services, the market itself, and the overall marketing direction of the company.

It's important to keep in mind that a marketing plan is typically written in sections separated by headings or subheadings. That's not the case with the executive summary. You'll write the executive summary as a series of paragraphs, and each paragraph will focus on a different section of the marketing plan.

Instead of talking about the executive summary strictly in abstract terms, let's see how this plays out in an example.

- **Introduction.** In this paragraph, you're going to provide the reader with an explanation of what they can expect. You're providing the context for the plan in order to make the subsequent parts of the plan easier to understand. In the introduction, briefly explain the plan, its purpose, and the key benefits to potential customers. Remember the KISS rule— **k**eep **it s**hort and **s**imple. Here's an example that might give some insight on what the introduction should look like:

  This marketing plan is presented for ABC Company, a manufacturer of electronic components for a variety of industries. We have developed a new product for the health care industry, and this marketing plan will demonstrate that ABC Company has a unique opportunity to expand into this dynamic, growing market.

- **Description of Company and Team.** In this paragraph, you're going to briefly describe your business. Be sure to include a succinct synopsis of the company's history, legal structure, and customer base. You'll also want to address a broad overview of sales figures. You will also list the key players involved in the business, including their positions within the company; their responsibilities, skills, and experience; and their role in achieving your marketing goals. This is particularly important if your company is seeking funding. The purpose of this section is twofold: (1) to convince lenders and/or investors to provide requested funds, and (2) to prove that you have the right team on board to capitalize on the opportunity you have defined. Once again, let's see how this section might appear on ABC Company's marketing plan. Please note that we've only listed two key members of the team for the sake of brevity, but you may include others:

  ABC Company was founded in 2002 and is based in Park City, Utah. The company produces electronic components for a variety of industries. When the company was founded, it produced electronic apparatuses primarily for the automotive industry. Its product line has expanded over the past 20+ years to include electronic apparatuses for the appliance and heating, ventilating, and cooling (HVAC) industries.

  Key Team Members:

  Khadija Simone, founder and CEO—Khadija has over 30 years of experience in the electronic apparatus industry, having managed divisions of two Fortune 500 companies before founding ABC Company. Khadija has a BS in electrical engineering from Purdue University and a master of business administration from the University of Chicago.

  Tanasha Turner, vice president of marketing—Tanasha has 20 years of sales and business development experience from working with several start-up companies that she helped grow into large businesses. She joined ABC Company in 2016 and has spearheaded the entry of the company into the appliance industry. Tanasha has a BA in marketing from the University of Pennsylvania and a master's in business marketing from California Coast University.

- **Description of Market Factors and Trends.** In this paragraph, you will set forth a brief description of the current marketplace and industry sectors within which you sell your products and/or services, the primary trends affecting and influencing them, and the innovations that are currently taking place within the market. Let's look at ABC Company's example:

  There are several large players in the electronic apparatus industry, including EAC Industries and Antwell Industries, as well as a few smaller companies that sell similar products to the automotive, appliance, and HVAC industries. The rapid pace of innovations in the industry is stimulating demand for newer and faster apparatuses. Digital technologies such as 5G mobile communication networks and 3D printing are expected to aid in the development of innovative electronic apparatuses.

- **Description of Products or Services Being Marketed.** In this paragraph, you will describe the key features and benefits of the new product being introduced in the marketing plan and outline its unique selling propositions to demonstrate how your company's products differ from or are superior to those of your competitors. You'll recall that ABC Company has developed a new product aimed at the health care industry, so this portion of its executive summary might look something like this:

    As noted above, ABC Company has created a new electronic apparatus for the health care industry. The success of this product would provide the company with an inroad to a new industry that uses the sophisticated technology developed by the company. This new product would provide the health care industry with improved efficiencies and cost savings vis-à-vis those that are offered by existing products on the market. Although there are similar products designed for other industries, there are currently no competitors for this type of product designed specifically for the health care industry.

- **Description of Customer Base and Related Marketing Activities.** In this paragraph, you will describe the key aspects of the target audience for your product and/or service. Where are you going to find your target customers? How will you reach them in terms of a promotional strategy? What methods do you intend to use in distributing your product or service? Let's look at how this paragraph might read in our hypothetical marketing plan:

    The target market for ABC Company's new product is large health care providers, including hospitals, research laboratories, and clinics. This marketing plan will outline its campaign to reach this target market through a combination of direct sales and social media marketing.

- **Financial Overview.** In this paragraph, you will define the key financial information related to both the short-term and long-term marketing activities set forth in the plan. If you are an existing company (like ABC Company), this might be as simple as highlighting sales growth over the last year and the anticipated marketing budget for the new product venture. Let's take a look at how this might look for ABC Company:

    ABC Company has experienced significant sales growth in the appliance and HVAC industries since the company's inception in 2002. Its sales revenue from these industries last year exceeded $23.4 million. Our marketing budget for the coming year in connection with entry into the health care industry is estimated to be $150,000.

- **Summary of Overall Objectives and Strategies.** In this final paragraph, you will briefly describe the plan's goals and the strategies the company will employ to achieve those goals. Remember that this executive summary is your marketing plan's "elevator pitch," so you'll want to conclude with a couple of sentences that entice the reader to continue to read your plan. Let's look at how this might play out for ABC's marketing plan:

    ABC Company has developed a marketing plan that will enable it to quickly make inroads into the health care industry and become the premier provider of electronic apparatuses to this growing market. We intend to use our experience and expertise in selling to the appliance and HVAC industries to showcase how this electronic apparatus can benefit the health care industry.

Mission Statement

The next section of your marketing plan will be the mission statement of your company. You'll recall from Section 2.1 that a mission statement is an action statement that clearly and concisely declares the purpose of the organization and how it serves its customers. It defines the what, why, and who of the organization. Once again, a picture (or in this case, an example) is worth a thousand words. Earlier in this chapter, we examined the mission statements of a couple of well-known businesses, so let's take a look at some mission statements for some other well-known companies:

- Pinterest: "Help people discover the things they love, and inspire them to go do those things in their daily lives"[52]
- Spotify: "To unlock the potential of human creativity by giving a million creative artists the opportunity to

live off their art and billions of fans the opportunity to enjoy and be inspired by it"[53]

- BBC: "To act in the public interest, serving all audiences through the provision of impartial, high-quality and distinctive output and services which inform, educate and entertain"[54]

Keep in mind that most mission statements are one to three sentences, almost never exceeding 150 words. You want to be succinct in letting people know what you do and who you do it for.

But how do you write a mission statement? You might start out by asking yourself four fundamental questions—what does the company do, how does it do it, who does it do it for, and why does it do what it does? The answers to these questions will likely give you enough information to synthesize and condense it into a meaningful mission statement. Remember that your mission statement should be more than just a meaningless string of "feel good" business jargon. It should be ambitious but realistic. It should be clear and concise. It should be focused on what the company does for its customers. Finally, it should keep employees focused on the organization's objectives.

SWOT Analysis

The next section in your marketing plan will include a SWOT analysis. We've covered the concept of a SWOT analysis in some detail earlier in this chapter, so we won't review it here. Suffice it to say that the SWOT analysis as part of your marketing plan is crucial in identifying key internal and external influences in your company's current position so that you can take advantage of the strengths and opportunities, mitigate the threats, and address your internal weaknesses.

Objectives and Issues

As noted earlier in this chapter, marketing plan objectives should be SMART—specific, measurable, actionable, realistic, and time-bound. Within your marketing plan, these objectives should be written in such a manner that they communicate precisely what needs to be achieved and who is responsible for each activity. For example, if you were writing this section of the marketing plan for ABC Company, an objective statement such as "Increase revenue by introducing a new product in the health care industry" would be too generic and not actionable. How much do you want to increase market share and during what time period? A better objective may be "Generate $1.7 million in sales in the health care industry by the end of the next fiscal year." Remember that writing specific goals and objectives can help you more clearly define and address the issues outlined in your marketing plan. You should also keep in mind that the marketing plan objectives aren't limited to just revenue. You may have objectives like increasing leads, in-store foot traffic, conversion rates, etc. Just make certain that each of these objectives is SMART.

Market Segmentation and Target Market

Essentially, what you will define in this section of the marketing plan is your target audience and your most likely buyers. We will cover market segmentation and targeting in more detail later in this textbook, but we'll give you a sneak peek into these concepts. Market segmentation is the process of dividing a target market into smaller, more defined categories of people or businesses with common needs and/or wants who are expected to respond similarly to a marketing action. Ultimately, the purpose of segmenting a market is to highlight the differences between groups of customers so that you can decide which group(s) upon which to focus your marketing efforts and resources—that's your target market.

Your marketing plan should include a description of the market for the product or service, the segments in this market, and how the plan will address the target market strategy.

Buyer Personas

The intricacies of buyer personas will also be covered in more detail in a later chapter, but your takeaway here is that a **buyer persona** is a semi-fictional representation of your "ideal customer" that helps you understand and relate to the audience to which you want to market your product and/or services. Buyer personas help marketers visualize the person to whom the company is selling so that marketing messages can be fine-tuned because brands that feel "human" to their target market usually succeed in building a rapport with them, improving the brand reputation for both existing and new customers.

This section of the marketing plan should address who your buyer personas are (and you can have several). These are one-page visual profiles outlining the demographics of your ideal customer, such as age, gender, motivations, and needs. For example, let's assume that your company sells outdoor apparel and hiking equipment. One of your buyer personas may be "On-the-go-Evan," a Gen Z male who enjoys being outside and participating in noncompetitive sports and relies on blog posts, influencers, and reviews to get unbiased information about the equipment he needs.[55]

Buyer personas aid marketers in bringing the target customer to life in a way that both inspires marketing strategies and prepares sales teams for conversations with customers that connect them in a meaningful way. How many buyer personas should you create? According to LinkedIn, although there isn't a "magic number," in most cases three to eight buyer personas are adequate.[56]

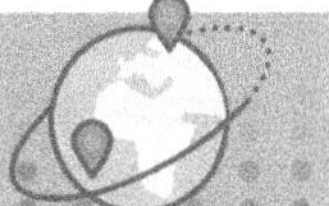

LINK TO LEARNING

Creating Buyer Personas

Creating buyer personas is an integral part of marketing, and it can be fun. For more information on steps to creating buyer personas, check out this tool from HubSpot that describes buyer personas (https://openstax.org/r/hubspotmakemypersona) and provides an interactive tool for creating them.

Positioning

Similarly, positioning will be covered in more depth in a later chapter. Remember that you first will have segmented the market by dividing it into distinct groups of customers and determined which customer group(s) you want to target. Positioning now defines where your product or service fits into the marketplace and why it is better than your competitors' products.

Product positioning is typically illustrated on a perceptual positioning map that uses two determinant attributes (those factors customers use in making their purchase decision) on the vertical and horizontal axes, and the marketer places his or her product offering on the map, along with those of the major competitors.

Once you've developed the map, you'll have a clearer idea of where your product or service stands in relation to the competition. The questions to address in your marketing plan might include the following:

- Do consumer attitudes toward your product or service match what you want them to think about it?
- Do consumer attitudes toward your competitors' products or services match what you perceive?
- Who are the competitors that consumers perceive as offering products or services that are close to yours?
- Are there holes or gaps in the map, indicating the potential for new offerings?

LINK TO LEARNING

Creating a Perceptual Positioning Map

See an example of a perceptual positioning map as applied to the fast-food industry.

Click to view content (https://openstax.org/books/principles-marketing/pages/2-3-purpose-and-structure-of-the-marketing-plan)

An important aspect of these maps is understanding how your products and your competition are perceived by customers, and this video shows you how to process and map this information.

Click to view content (https://openstax.org/books/principles-marketing/pages/2-3-purpose-and-structure-of-the-marketing-plan)

Check out this example using chocolate. If you're interested in using Excel data to create the map, watch this video example.

Click to view content (https://openstax.org/books/principles-marketing/pages/2-3-purpose-and-structure-of-the-marketing-plan)

Current Marketing Situation

This section of your marketing plan should provide the reader with a clear description of the current state of the marketplace, including your target market and the competitive environment. It should include a synopsis of the research into and analysis of your target market, your competitors, challenges in the marketplace, and the company's competitive differentiators. Some of the key items to address in the plan are as follows:

- **Market Description.** This isn't intended to be a comprehensive list, but this section should address things like statistics about the size of your target market; whether it is growing, shrinking, or staying the same; if it is changing; and why.[57]
- **Product Review.** The product review section of your marketing plan summarizes the main features of your company's products, including information about sales, price, and gross margins.
- **Competitive Analysis.** This section should include a discussion of your top competitors and how they fare in the marketplace vis-à-vis your company's products and/or services. This typically involves researching major competitors to glean insights into their products or services, sales, marketing tactics, product quality, pricing, market share, and distribution.

Marketing Strategy

Now let's get to the heart of the matter. This section of the marketing plan essentially sets forth the broad marketing strategy or game plan for achieving the objectives previously set forth in the plan. It should consist of specific strategies for target markets, positioning, the marketing mix (i.e., product, price, place, and promotion), and anticipated marketing expenditure levels.[58]

- **Product Strategy.** This is the "road map" that you'll use to develop your product(s) or features(s), including all tasks needed to achieve the objectives set forth in the marketing plan. The product strategy essentially outlines how the product(s) or service(s) will benefit the business, what problem it will solve, and the impact that it will make on customers and the business. It's only when this strategy has been set forth in straightforward terms that it can act as a baseline upon which you can measure success before, during, and after production.[59]
- **Pricing Strategy.** Pricing will be covered in a later chapter in this text, but be aware that pricing is one of the key components of any marketing plan. Not only will it determine how much revenue (profit) you will earn, but it will also play a key role in positioning your product in the minds of consumers. The "right" pricing strategy is one that conveys the message you want to get across to your target market in terms of quality and features vis-à-vis the competition because price is often what is used to determine the perceived (not actual) quality of the product or service. Some of the factors you'll want to consider in developing this section of your marketing plan are
  - setting a price that sends the right message in terms of quality and value in the minds of your target market,
  - setting a price that supports your promotion strategy (to be covered below), and
  - setting a price that maximizes profit.[60]

- **Promotion Strategy.** Your promotion strategy sets forth the tactics you intend to implement in your marketing plan in order to increase demand for your product(s) or service(s). List the methods you will use to gain awareness and interest in your product from those in your target audience. Methods of reaching potential consumers abound—company websites, social media networks, trade shows, and radio/television/website advertising. You'll want to list the advantages and disadvantages of each method and indicate why and how much it will cost to employ the method(s) you have selected.

- **Distribution Strategy.** Your distribution strategy describes how customers in your target market will purchase from you. Will they buy directly from your website, from a storefront, or through distributors or retailers? What are the costs involved in this type of distribution, and why do you believe your distribution strategy will enable you to get the right product into the hands of the right consumer at the right time?

Action Programs

You're getting to the end of the plan (finally). The marketing strategies outlined in the section above should now be translated into specific action programs that indicate what is to be done, when it is to be done, by whom it will be done, and the cost involved. The action program should list when activities will be started, reviewed, and completed.

Budgeting Concerns

The action plans outlined in the section above should enable you to make a supporting marketing budget that is essentially a projected profit-and-loss (P&L) statement. If you've previously taken an accounting course, you'll know that a P&L statement summarizes the revenues, costs, and expenses incurred during a specified period.

On the revenue side, this statement should indicate that forecasted number of units to be sold during the period outlined in the marketing plan and the average net price for revenues. On the expense side, this statement should indicate the cost of production, physical distribution, and marketing expenditures.[61]

Controls to Monitor Progress

Controls is the last section of the marketing plan. This section will outline the control methods that will be utilized to monitor the action programs outlined in the plan. The reason you'll want to monitor these metrics during the time period of the marketing plan is to see where things may have fallen outside the desired range, at which time you'll want to dig into the details, perform an analysis of the root cause of the problem(s), and make adjustments to get back on track.

LINK TO LEARNING

Marketing Plans

There are numerous online examples of marketing plans. To be a great marketer, it would be wise to review and study marketing plans and how they tell a unique company story. Here are several to check out:

- Shopify blog: "7 Inspiring Marketing Plan Examples (and How You Can Implement Them)" (https://openstax.org/r/blogmarktingplanexamples)
- University of Illinois (https://openstax.org/r/wpcontent2021marketingplan)
- Visit Baton Rouge (https://openstax.org/r/vbrmarketingplan)
- Bizfluent example for a generic restaurant (https://openstax.org/r/restaurantmarketingplan)

There's also a free marketing plan template available from HubSpot (https://openstax.org/r/marketingplantemplate).

Knowledge Check

It's time to check your knowledge on the concepts presented in this section. Refer to the Answer Key at the

end of the book for feedback.

1. In which section of the executive summary of a marketing plan would you describe the current marketplace and industry sectors within which you sell your products or services and the innovations currently taking place within the market?
   a. Description of products or services being marketed
   b. Description of customer base and related marketing activities
   c. Description of company and team
   d. Description of market factors and trends

2. In a SWOT analysis, which factors are internal to the organization?
   a. Strengths and opportunities
   b. Weaknesses and threats
   c. Strengths and weaknesses
   d. Opportunities and threats

3. What is a perceptual map, and how is it used?
   a. A perceptual map indicates the relative strength of competitors in the market segment.
   b. A perceptual map indicates the relative market share and market growth of a product portfolio.
   c. A perceptual map illustrates product positioning vis-à-vis the competitors.
   d. A perceptual map displays the product, pricing, promotion, and distribution strategy of the product or service.

4. In which section of the marketing plan would you identify key internal and external influences on the company's current position?
   a. Objectives and issues
   b. SWOT analysis
   c. Buyer personas
   d. Current marketing situation

5. In which section of the marketing plan would you include a competitive analysis and discussion of the company's top competitors?
   a. Positioning
   b. Target market
   c. Mission statement
   d. Current marketing situation

2.4   Marketing Plan Progress Using Metrics

Learning Outcomes

By the end of this section, you will be able to:
- **LO** 1 Define marketing metrics.
- **LO** 2 Explain key performance indicators (KPIs).
- **LO** 3 Provide examples of business objective KPIs.
- **LO** 4 Characterize sales/revenue generation KPIs.
- **LO** 5 Provide examples of market share KPIs.
- **LO** 6 Classify and discuss customer support KPIs.

Marketing Metrics Explained

There can be a lot of moving parts when running even a modest-sized organization. It is often helpful to focus on key measurable (quantifiable) values or variables that marketers aim to achieve within a specified period of time—known as **marketing metrics**. In the same way that a doctor measures height, weight, temperature, blood pressure, etc. to assess the health of a patient, a marketer uses marketing metrics to measure marketing performance.

Key Performance Indicators (KPIs) Explained

Have you ever pondered what life was like without the Internet? You can instantly type a term into a search engine, and within seconds, you'll have hundreds of thousands (or even millions) of results. It's estimated that, as of 2020, there was 40 zettabytes of data available on the Internet. (If you're curious, a zettabyte is approximately 1 trillion gigabytes).[62] That's both a blessing and a curse. There's so much information out there that sometimes it becomes difficult to focus on the information you really need.

The same is true with marketing metrics. On one hand, a marketer can examine virtually every single aspect of the customer journey, gleaning a fully detailed picture of what is going on in every stage; on the other hand, the sheer amount of data the metrics can yield can be overwhelming. Metrics tell us what is happening at any point in time without context as to why it is happening. That's why savvy marketers should have a solid understanding of metrics to draw out the full story. The way the marketer gets to the marketing metrics that yield the information that's needed is by identifying and maintaining a focus on the data that counts—the business's **key performance indicators (KPIs)**.

Although the terms *metrics* and *KPIs* are often used interchangeably, there is a subtle and very important difference. Metrics measure the performance of a particular process; KPIs are directly tied to business objectives and have targets and specific time frames for achieving those targets.[63] In a nutshell, think about KPIs as being a "scorecard" for company health.

Marketers typically establish goals and objectives related to KPIs, because it's an easy way to track progress. If the metrics remain within the forecasted range, marketers can focus on other more troubling elements of the SBU. On the other hand, when the metrics fall outside of the desired range, it's time to closely examine where the trolley is coming off the tracks, perform a root cause analysis, and make adjustments to get back on track.

The trend in marketing is to use real-time marketing dashboards that provide instant visibility of the metrics you've selected to track. It's a quick and easy overview of where you stand and how you're progressing toward your goals. It's also a huge time saver because instead of poring over spreadsheets and multipage reports to assess progress, a marketer can simply refer to the dashboard to obtain the information needed.[64]

LINK TO LEARNING

KPIs

For more information about marketing KPIs, take a look at this brief video from SMA Marketing about why marketing KPIs are vital for a business. Here are additional resources you may find helpful to learn about KPIs:

Click to view content (https://openstax.org/books/principles-marketing/pages/2-4-marketing-plan-progress-using-metrics)

- Toucan Toco: "The Most Important KPIs to Track for Improved Marketing Efficiency (https://openstax.org/r/themostimportantkpis)"
- Vital: "The 16 Marketing KPIs You Should Be Measuring (but Probably Aren't)" (https://openstax.org/r/16marketingkpistomeasure)
- HubSpot: "15 Key Performance Indicators to Help Improve Your Marketing" (https://openstax.org/r/marketingkey)

- Marketo Engage blog: "Prove Your Worth: 10 KPIs for Marketers (https://openstax.org/r/proveyourworth10kpis)"

Examples of Business Objective KPIs

There is a multitude of KPIs that marketers can choose to manage business objectives. The actual KPIs that are selected depend on the nature of the process, the type of information available, and the team. The important concept is to identify the "key" indicators that drive success. Instead of trying to develop information from a laundry list of 300 KPIs, it's preferable to identify a handful of the most useful KPIs that allow for the effective management of information. In other words, sometimes less is more, and instead of sifting through mountains of statistics (remember all those zettabytes of information on the Internet), you can choose from a small subset of measurements to review on a regular basis. Let's take a look at a few that you may wish to consider, as shown in Figure 2.12.

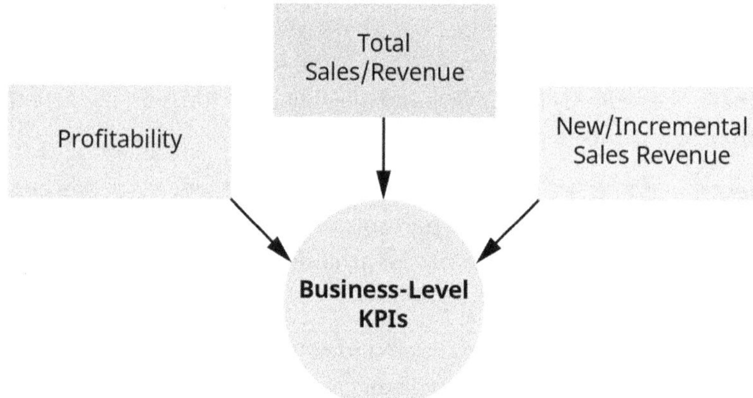

Figure 2.12 Business-Level KPIs (attribution: Copyright Rice University, OpenStax, under CC BY 4.0 license)

Total Sales/Revenue

Sales and revenue growth is a KPI that is used to determine whether sales and revenue are increasing or decreasing over a specified time period. It's calculated by dividing revenue generated during one time period by revenue generated over a subsequent time period, subtracting 1, and then multiplying by 100 to obtain a percentage.[65] Here is the formula:

$$\text{Sales versus Revenue} = \left(\frac{2022\,\text{Revenue}}{2021\,\text{Revenue}} - 1 \right) \times 100 = xx\%$$

For the sake of putting numbers to the formula so you can see how it actually works, let's assume that 2022 revenue was $1.8 billion, compared to $1.4 billion in 2021. If we populate the formula with these numbers, it looks like this:

$$\text{Sales versus Revenue} = \left(\frac{\$1.8\text{B}}{\$1.4\text{B}} \right) = 1.2857$$
$$1.2857 - 1 = 0.2857$$
$$0.2857 \times 100 = 28.57\% \;\text{Revenue Growth}$$

As a general rule, the metric would be used to suggest revenue growth over a year time span. However, for companies whose revenue is affected by seasonality (such as companies that produce snow blowers or bathing suits), it may make more sense to measure growth in revenue on a monthly or seasonal basis, as compared to the previous season.[66]

New/Incremental Sales Revenue

Marketers are also keenly interested in understanding how many new versus how many repeat customers a business has. The bottom line is that it's typically more expensive to acquire initial sales than repeat sales, and repeat customers (referrals) can serve as a powerful source of new customers. Accordingly, if the majority of sales are from return customers, that may point to a sign of weakness in a promotional program or other marketing activity.

Profitability

Gross margin as a percentage of sales is one of the most closely watched KPIs at most organizations. Gross margin is the percentage of sales revenue that the company can convert into gross profit, and it's generally a good measure of how efficiently the company generates gross profit from sales of products or services.

It stands to reason that if the gross margin of a product is negative, it's going to be difficult to make money at *any* level of sales. Thus, the higher the gross margin, all other elements being equal, the less sales are required to break even.

Examples of Sales/Revenue Generation KPIs

One of the most important metrics for any organization concerns sales/revenue. Let's look at some of the KPIs that can be helpful to marketers, as illustrated in Figure 2.13.

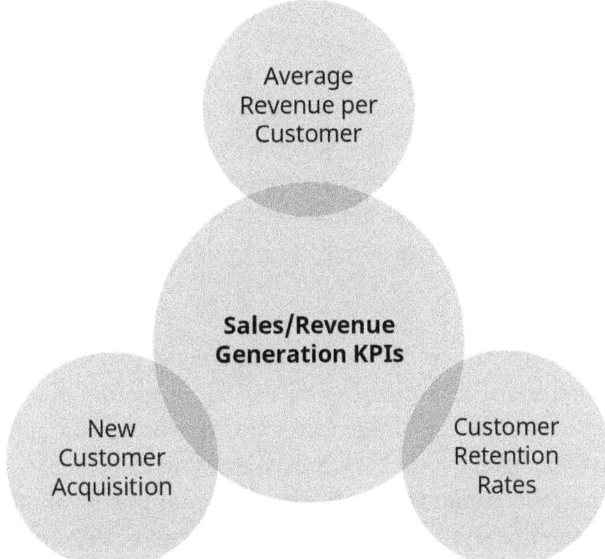

Figure 2.13 Sales/Revenue Generation KPIs (attribution: Copyright Rice University, OpenStax, under CC BY 4.0 license)

Average Revenue per Customer (ARPC)

This KPI measures the amount of money that a company expects to generate from an individual customer, and it's a relatively simple calculation: total revenue divided by the number of customers. Where this KPI comes in handy is that it assists the marketer in identifying trends among different time periods and segments of customers. A low ARPC score can point to a number of reasons: you're not targeting the right customer, or perhaps your product offering is priced too low. So marketers need to determine how to extract more revenue from the product—whether through different value add-on products or perhaps by targeting a more valuable customer base.[67]

New Customer Acquisition

As the term suggests, customer acquisition refers to bringing in new customers. It's the action of bringing customers down the "marketing funnel" from brand awareness to the purchase decision. Closely related to this KPI is customer acquisition cost (CAC)—in other words, the total cost of acquiring those customers, which is calculated by adding up the cost of sales and marketing efforts and then divided by the number of new customers acquired during a specific period.

Customer Retention Rates

As we pointed out above, it's cheaper to keep a customer than it is to find a new customer. The KPI for customer retention rates measures the percentage of customers in the current period who have purchased in the past. This KPI is particularly powerful when the product or service is subscription based, or requires a regular recurring purchase (e.g., cell phone monthly fee, electricity bill, etc.).

Examples of Market Share KPIs

Of course, it's important to track the sales/revenue KPIs mentioned above, but they don't tell the whole story. It's also important to track how the organization is faring in the marketplace compared to its competitors.

Let's consider a scenario to explain this further. Let's assume that your organization is in a highly competitive, fast-growing industry. Your marketing dashboard shows that your organization's sales increased 10 percent during the last fiscal year. On the surface, that might be a positive—who doesn't want sales to increase by 10 percent? However, with the right KPIs on your marketing dashboard, you might begin to see that all isn't as good as you initially surmised because the market in general grew at 20 percent during that same period and the sales of your major competitor grew 25 percent. That paints a different picture, doesn't it?

So, let's examine some market share KPIs that can paint a broader picture for marketers.

Market Share in Category

A company's market share in category (sometimes known as category share) is its sales as a percentage of all products in a category that the company sells. It is calculated by dividing the company's sales by the total sales in a category.[68] For most companies, market share is an important KPI because it easily translates into positive or negative performance. For example, increases in market share typically indicate that a company is doing more business, whereas declining market share suggests an undesirable outcome.[69]

Relative Market Share

Relative market share indexes a firm's or brand's market share against that of its leading competitor. It's more complicated that industry market share because it compares your organization to your rivals rather than to the industry as a whole.[70] How is it calculated? That's best explained using an example. Let's assume that you own an appliance store in town, one of a handful of stores in town that sell major appliances. Your sales bring in $1 million per year, for a 5 percent market share. Now imagine that the top appliance store in the area sells $1.5 million worth of major appliances a year, a 13 percent market share. To determine your relative market share compared to this competitor, divide your share by the competitor's:

$$5\% \div 13\% = 38\% \text{ Relative Market Share}$$

To get an even more in-depth picture, you can do the same for the smaller competitors in the market. This process would give you a slightly different perspective on market share growth. For example, in some competitive markets, a 5 percent share might make you one of the major players; however, in the example shown with the appliance stores, it appears that you're a long way from achieving the market share of your leading competitor.[71]

Examples of Customer Support KPIs

In a perfect world, companies would have products with zero defects and the same number of customer issues with those products. However, we all know we don't live in a perfect world, and zero defects and zero customer issues simply aren't a realistic expectation. There will be customer issues, and the key to retaining loyal clients is identifying and resolving those issues quickly. So let's look at some customer support KPIs that matter to marketers, as illustrated in Figure 2.14.

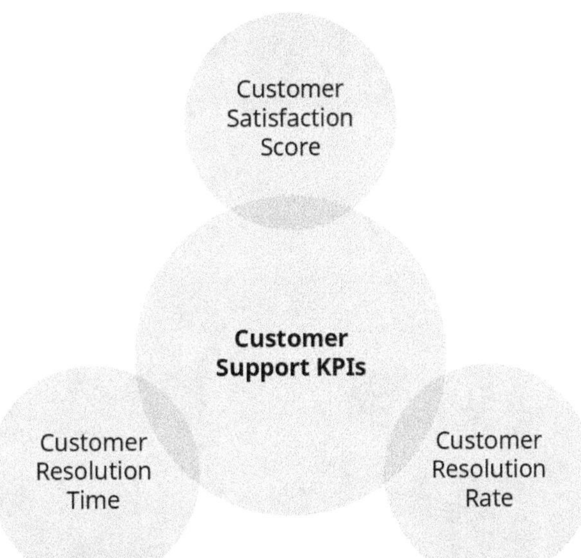

Figure 2.14 Customer Support KPIs (attribution: Copyright Rice University, OpenStax, under CC BY 4.0 license)

Customer Satisfaction Score

Customer satisfaction score (also known as CSAT) is the primary metric used to measure customer satisfaction. One way to measure CSAT is by sending out a customer satisfaction survey asking customers to rate their satisfaction on a scale of 1 to 5, with 1 being very unsatisfied and 5 being very satisfied. The calculation from that point is simple: take the number of satisfied customers (i.e., those who rated their satisfaction as either 4 or 5), divide that by the total number of responses, and finally multiple that number by 100. That formula will yield the percentage of customers who consider themselves satisfied—your CSAT score.[72]

Let's put some numbers to this formula to illustrate the point. Imagine that you've emailed a customer satisfaction survey to 15,000 customers and received 1,500 responses. Of those responses, 308 customers rated their satisfaction as "very satisfied," 447 rated their satisfaction as "satisfied," and the remaining 745 customers rated their satisfaction as "neutral," "dissatisfied," or "very dissatisfied." The calculation of the CSAT score would look like this:

$$(308 + 447) \div 1,500 = 50.33\%$$

Customer Resolution Rate

As we pointed out above, no matter how carefully you've planned and no matter how well you've trained your staff, things will inevitably go wrong with customers at some point. That's the harsh reality of dealing with customers. However, most (or at least many) customers will forgive a mistake if the organization acts quickly to resolve the problem to the best of its ability. Once again, the calculation for this KPI is relatively uncomplicated. To calculate customer resolution rate, subtract the number of unresolved cases from the total number of cases, and then divide the sum by the total number of cases. The fewer unresolved cases, the higher your customer resolution rate.[73]

Customer Resolution Time

Closely related to the customer resolution rate is customer resolution time because most customers expect immediate assistance. The longer it takes to resolve a customer issue, the less satisfied a customer will be. There are a couple of ways to calculate this. First, you could measure average resolution time by taking the sum of all case resolution durations and then dividing by the total number of customer cases. Alternatively, you could measure the first response time. This is the average time it takes from the time a customer reaches out for assistance and the length of time it takes for a customer service representative to respond.[74]

MARKETING IN PRACTICE

Classic Cleaners and Automated Reporting

Figure 2.15 Classic Cleaners wanted real-time data that would help it better understand its target customers and how it could use marketing to earn more business from them. (credit: "DSC_2665.JPG" by Banzai Hiroaki/flickr, CC BY 2.0)

Classic Cleaners is a provider of dry cleaning and laundry services based in Indianapolis, Indiana (see Figure 2.15). The company has 17 locations.[75] Like many businesses, Classic Cleaners always struggled with the question, What does my customer *really* want? The company wanted an easy solution to using real-time marketing to track and measure results and obtain insights that would aid it in making data-driven decisions.

Enter TBH Creative, which was hired by Classic Cleaners to transform its marketing efforts through automating reporting. TBH Creative worked with the company to set up a marketing dashboard to monitor statistics and analytics, complete an audit to determine which marketing efforts were effective, improve its website, and more.[76]

As Classic Cleaners' General Manager Steve Arnold stated, "We . . . wanted to start tracking our customers more thoroughly so we could identify who our target customers are, what types of messaging resonates with them, and how we could use marketing to earn more business from these customers."[77]

MARKETING DASHBOARD

Customer Lifetime Value (CLV)

Customers are not all the same. Some customers spend more money than others, while others are customers for long periods. As marketers, we want to know how much value to expect from customer groups to determine their value to the organization and how much we should be spending to attract and retain customers. **Customer lifetime value (CLV)** provides an estimate of how much a single customer is worth to a company over their customer life span. Unlike other marketing metrics, customer lifetime value is a forward-looking metric. Therefore, it is an estimate, not a guarantee.

Customer lifetime value is closely related to **customer acquisition cost**, which is the amount an organization invests in attracting a new customer. We want our customer lifetime value to exceed the customer acquisition cost to ensure that we are not spending more money to attract a customer than they are worth. However, we also know that customers have additional costs, such as our cost of goods sold or cost to serve. These costs must be calculated along with customer lifetime value to determine whether our customers are profitable. We also know that retaining current customers is important so that we are not continually investing in customer acquisition. To invest in existing customers, companies may introduce loyalty programs, increase customer experience, design positive user experiences, and/or connect with customers on social media.

A simple formula for customer lifetime value is:

$$\text{Customer Lifetime Value} = (\text{Annual Profit per Customer} \times \text{Average Number of Years Retained}) - \text{Customer Acquisition Cost}$$

The annual profit per customer considers the cost of goods sold and customer acquisition cost.

Give the customer lifetime value calculation a try for yourself. What is the customer lifetime value for each of the four segments in the example shown in Table 2.1?

Person	Annual Profit Per Customer	Average Number of Years Retained	Customer Acquisition Cost
Millennial parents	$10,000	12	$750
Millennial singles	$18,000	12	$750
Working moms	$22,000	8	$1,200
Gen Z emerging professionals	$34,000	2	$1,600

Table 2.1

Solution

Millennial parents: $119,250

Millennial singles: $215,250

Working moms: $174,800

Gen Z emerging professionals: $66,400

Which segment would you choose if you were tasked with starting a new campaign that maximized CLV?

Solution

Millennial singles have the highest CLV.

Let's suppose the customer experience team could increase the average number of years that the Gen Z segment retains from two to eight. Which segment would then have the highest CLV?

Solution

Gen Z would have the highest CLV at $270,400.

Knowledge Check

It's time to check your knowledge on the concepts presented in this section. Refer to the Answer Key at the end of the book for feedback.

1. What are key performance indicators (KPIs)?
   a. Industry economic forecasts gathered during external analysis
   b. A collection of all the detailed statistics we can find regarding firm performance
   c. A competitive analysis that allows a company to understand the strategic direction of competitors
   d. Specific variables that allow us to monitor the health/performance of the organization

2. How frequently should we monitor KPIs?
   a. Continuously
   b. Monthly when the financial statements are produced
   c. Annually when the yearly financial statements are produced
   d. When things just don't "feel" quite right

3. You've emailed a customer satisfaction survey to 20,000 customers and received 1,825 responses. Of those 1,825 responses, the ratings came back as:
   - 500 very satisfied
   - 300 satisfied
   - 1,025 neutral or dissatisfied or very dissatisfied

   What is the customer satisfaction score?

   a. 44 percent
   b. 27 percent
   c. 9 percent
   d. 11 percent

4. The observation is made that a single data point in isolation is not very useful. What can we do with a KPI data point to make it useful?
   a. Compare the KPI data point with a related goal/objective (forecast).
   b. Compare the KPI data point with our historical performance.
   c. Compare the KPI data point with industry averages.
   d. These are all useful things to do with a KPI data point.

5. Why is it important to track customer satisfaction?
   a. We don't need to; we already have their money.
   b. Customer referrals can be a powerful promotional tool.
   c. Customer acquisition can be expensive; repeat purchases can be much more profitable.
   d. Statements b and c are both correct.

2.5 | Ethical Issues in Developing a Marketing Strategy

Learning Outcomes

By the end of this section, you will be able to:
- **LO** 1 Explain the importance of ethical marketing.
- **LO** 2 Describe key ethical considerations in strategic planning.
- **LO** 3 Discuss examples of ethical companies.

The Importance of Ethical Marketing

Marketing ethics are essentially the moral guidelines that allow companies to scrutinize their marketing strategies and actions. It means that a marketer has an obligation to ensure that all marketing activities adhere to core ethical principles, such as integrity and honesty—both internally and externally.[78]

As we'll see below, ethical marketing is a crucial factor in an organization's overall growth over time, and it produces many benefits:

- **Customer Loyalty.** Every company wants customers who keep coming back to buy their products and services. Companies have learned over time that, with the adoption of common-sense ethics in marketing, they can more easily earn the trust of consumers.[79]
- **Improved Credibility.** Look beyond customers when considering this factor and think in terms of the respect and credibility an ethical company earns with its investors, competitors, and other parties.
- **Brand Enhancement.** Consumers, competitors, investors, and others have begun to look beyond product features and pursue brands that consider the three Ps of sustainability—people, planet, and profits.

Millennials and Generation Z: Purchases Follow Beliefs

During the American Industrial Revolution in the early 1900s, the United States saw the rise of iconic business enterprises like Ford, US Steel, J.P. Morgan, Union Pacific Railroad, and many others. Some (a few) gave generously to charitable causes. Others made their wealth using unscrupulous means, exploiting labor and using questionable business practices.

Corporate social responsibility (CSR) is the concept that a company should integrate social and environmental concerns into its business operations and practices. It didn't begin to take hold in the United States until the 1970s. In 1971, the Committee for Economic Development released a policy statement declaring the concept of a "social contract" between business and society, wherein the business has an obligation to constructively serve the needs of society.[80] This concept was further fueled in part by President George H. W. Bush's call for a "thousand points of light."[81] The bottom line is that CSR changed business as usual. Today, Fortune Global 500 firms spend approximately $20 billion on CSR initiatives each year, and companies take public positions on diversity, inclusion, education, and the environment.[82]

We are witnessing an evolution in consumer expectations as consumers begin to vote with their wallets. Millennials (those born between 1981 and 1996) and Generation Z (those born between 1997 and 2012) are now the biggest global generation, making up 65 percent of the world's population,[83] so it stands to reason that, as these generational cohorts enter their prime spending years, many companies have begun to focus their marketing efforts on this segment of the population. What marketers have discovered is that millennials and Zoomers (aka Gen Z) engage with brands differently than older generations like Generation X (born between 1965 and 1980) and the baby boomers (born between 1946 and 1964). They're more likely to steer clear of mass-market branded products in favor of smaller, eco-friendly brands. They are the most likely to make buying decisions on values and principles. For example, consider some statistics from a First Insight report that shows that 62 percent of both millennials and Zoomers are willing to spend more for sustainable products, compared with only 54 percent of Gen X and 39 percent of Baby Boomers.[84]

Nielsen, the information, data, and marketing firm, surveyed over 30,000 consumers in 60 countries to find out what influences and affects their buying habits. The results were somewhat amazing:

- 66 percent of global consumers are willing to pay more for sustainable products.[85]
- 73 percent (nearly three out of four) of millennials indicated that they would be willing to pay extra for sustainable goods.[86]

What implications does this have for marketing to these generations? The bottom line is that CSR is more than just a buzzword for these generational cohorts. To make an impact, companies need to use their resources to show—not just tell—these younger generations how business enterprises are making an impact through authenticity and transparency.

Key Ethical Considerations in Strategic Planning

It's no secret that the primary goal of marketers is to increase growth by creating and maintaining customers. However, sometimes pursuing that growth to satisfy shareholder goals to the exclusion of other groups (like customers) has led to high-profile ethical dilemmas. Let's consider a few:

According to a Gallup poll in 2021, approximately 6 percent of US adults report that they have used e-cigarettes within the past week[87] despite health warnings about vaping. The sale and distribution of e-cigarettes is banned or regulated in a growing number of countries much to the dismay of vaping aficionados. Where do you draw the line? Is vaping a matter of personal choice, or are people influenced by the marketing efforts of e-cigarette producers like Juul?

Consider the ethical implications behind this. Should e-cigarette manufacturers sell customers what they crave, or should they tailor their offerings based on what health experts say? Who gets to make that choice? Does the decision fall to the consumer, the producer, a public watchdog group, or the federal government?

Consider another ethical issue. During the first decade of the new millennium, Toyota vehicles experienced problems with unintended, uncontrolled acceleration that prompted over 6,200 complaints to the National Highway Traffic Safety Administration and were linked to more than 89 deaths over the next five years.[88] Early on, Toyota blamed driver error. Later, it issued recalls to address floor mats that pinned down accelerators in some cases. But the company hid a flawed gas pedal design and lied to regulators, Congress, and the public for years about the sudden acceleration problem, ultimately leading to a fine of $1.2 billion by the Justice Department, which contended that Toyota's efforts to conceal the problem and protect its "corporate image" led to a series of preventable fatalities. The settlement is being called the largest criminal penalty imposed on a car company in US history.[89]

Could these situations have been avoided with a stronger ethical focus and an eye toward the greater good? It all starts with the strategic planning process, which can be used to build "good" into the core of the organization.

Broader Participation

As pointed out in Marketing and Customer Value, an organization must consider all parties that it might impact, including investors, communities, governments, customers, employees, and suppliers. In the context of corporate social responsibility, this means that leaders of companies must create value for all of these groups while simultaneously producing a fair return for shareholders or owners.

Organizational and Individual Values

When considering organizational and individual values, the marketer needs to ask (and answer candidly) the following questions:

- Does the organization's mission reflect current activities that are focused on the triple bottom line?
- Does the organization's vision statement lead to outcomes that contain elements of social good?
- Do the organization's values reflect respect for one another, the community, and the environment?
- Are those values authentic, and do members of the organization live by them daily?

- Has the organization included goals and objectives that refer specifically to elements of social good?

These questions can help inform the organization's activities as it works through the strategic planning process. Thoughtful analysis and design at this stage can build strong organizations that not only deliver profits but also produce positive social outcomes for **all** parties.

▤ Chapter Summary

This chapter explores the topic of marketing strategy in more detail. Strategy starts with understanding where a company is, where it wants to go, what the operating environment looks like, and what tools it has to work with or could acquire. The foundation of who a company is is established based on the vision, mission, values, and goals and objectives of the organization.

The vast majority of organizations have a single product line or market focus. However, there are circumstances where a company may view its enterprise as consisting of a portfolio of products or operating units. In this chapter, we explore tools such as SWOT analysis and the BCG matrix that can help a company organize and analyze its portfolio.

We need to define a strategy for our organization whether we have one product or dozens. The strategy selected for each product line or business unit does not have to be the same. We explored strategies associated with market penetration, market development, product development, and diversification.

A well-known saying asserts, "If you fail to plan, you are planning to fail." This chapter explores the motivation for creating a formal marketing plan and the elements that should be included. The chapter also explores KPIs and the metrics required to organize, monitor, and manage an organization. The chapter finishes with a discussion of ethics, especially in terms of how authenticity, social justice, and doing business for good resonate with millennials and the Generation Z demographic.

⚷ Key Terms

BCG matrix   Boston Consulting Group's framework for analyzing an organization's strategic business units

business portfolio   the group of products, services, and business units that a company possesses

business-level strategy   outline of the actions and decisions a company plans to take to reach its goals and objectives

buyer persona   a semi-fictional representation of your ideal customers based on data and research

concentric diversification   the addition of similar products or services to an existing business

conglomerate diversification   the development and addition of new products or services that are significantly unrelated to a company's current offerings

corporate social responsibility (CSR)   the concept that a company should integrate social and environmental concerns into its business operations and practices

corporate-level strategy   strategy that establishes the overall value of a business through setting strategic goals and motivating employees to achieve them

customer acquisition cost   the amount an organization invests in attracting a new customer

customer lifetime value (CLV)   an estimate of how much a single customer is worth to a company over their customer life span

executive summary   a brief overview of a marketing plan

functional strategy   actions and goals assigned to business units that support the overall business strategy

gap analysis   an internal analysis of a company or organization to identify and review its inherent deficiencies that may hinder its ability to meet its goals

goals   the outcomes one intends to achieve

horizontal diversification   the development of new and perhaps even unrelated products or services to market to existing customers so that a company can garner a larger customer base

key performance indicators (KPIs)   quantifiable measure gauging a company's performance against a set of targets, objectives, or competitors

market development strategy   a growth strategy that identifies and develops new market segments for current products

market penetration strategy   a strategy used when a company focuses on growing its market share in its existing markets

marketing dashboard   summarizes important marketing metrics and key performance indicators into easy-to-understand measurements

marketing ethics   area of applied ethics dealing with the moral principles behind the operation and regulation of marketing

marketing metrics   what marketers use to monitor, record, and measure progress over time; are varied and can change from platform to platform

mission statement   action-based statement declaring the purpose of an organization

objectives   specific targets to be achieved within a specified period of time

product development strategy   complete process of delivering a new product or improving an existing one for customers

product diversification strategy   strategy to increase profitability and achieve higher sales volume through new products

product positioning   strategic exercise that defines where a product or service fits in the marketplace

strategic business unit   a relatively autonomous division of a large company that operates as an independent enterprise with responsibility for a particular range of products or activities

strategy   set of plans, actions, and goals that outlines how a business will compete

SWOT analysis   identification of internal strengths and weaknesses and external opportunities and threats impacting a business

vision statement   aspirational statement that articulates what an organization aims to achieve

Applied Marketing Knowledge: Discussion Questions

1. Your university annually evaluates the current and possible value of its strategic business units (SBUs). The university may examine its majors as SBUs, or it may examine each college, school, or division's performance while recruiting students. Use a Boston Consulting Group (BCG) matrix to examine the university's business portfolio—majors may be stars, cash cows, question marks, or dogs due to past and current enrollment in those majors. (Chances are good that underperforming "dog" majors will be phased out and financial support shifted from majors that serve as cash cows to fund growth of stars or question marks.) List two majors that fit into each of the growth-share matrix quadrants.

2. Why is perceived value important in price setting?

3. Personas are especially helpful as marketers consider the _______ for their products and are most commonly used when developing promotional materials.

4. What are SMART goals, and why are they important in strategic planning?

Critical Thinking Exercises

1. Like Clorox and Zoom, Peloton was poised to the seize market opportunities created by the COVID-19 pandemic and stay-home mandates ordered by cities and states. Research Peloton and construct a timeline of key Peloton events from 2020 through 2022. What key strategic decisions did Peloton make in the exercise-at-home market? (Be sure to include Peloton's summer 2021 decision to lower the price of its original bike by 20 percent.) What opportunities and challenges did Peloton face during the pandemic? How did consumer behavior change during the first year of COVID-19? How well did Peloton predict consumer demand for its exercise products? Now that you've seen the challenges a growth strategy presents, what do you see as the long-term business growth potential for Peloton?

2. Go to Clorox's website and review the company's primary products (https://openstax.org/r/clorox). Complete a SWOT matrix for Clorox that lists at least three strengths, weaknesses, opportunities, and threats. The first level in the SWOT has been provided for you below.

3. Disney is an example of a diversified company. Its success is based upon founder Walt Disney's artistic abilities and years of successful strategic planning. Answer the following questions:

A.   Why has it been important for Disney to identify new products and markets?
B.   How has Disney leveraged its strengths to pursue new opportunities?
C.   In addition to parks and resorts, list three products/services Disney has expanded into.
D.   In your opinion, is Disney an example of an ethical company that practices a double bottom line?

 ## Building Your Personal Brand

There are many brands that recognize the benefits of hiring brand ambassadors. Red Bull is one of these brands. Because college students constitute a major portion of its target market, Red Bull relies on student ambassadors (also called Marketeers) to interact with customers. According to Red Bull's Student Marketeer website, "student Marketeers are in direct contact with various consumers and customers, inviting product trial, helping establish Red Bull consumption in diverse occasions, supporting our sales teams, working with renowned athletes and of course ensuring an unforgettable brand experience for consumers at Red Bull events. Based on your skills, knowledge, experience and availability, your focus will be either on your campus or you'll cover the entire region on board the iconic Mini."[90]

Identify another brand that follows the strategy of welcoming brand ambassadors and express how finding this sort of part-time job might enhance your own brand.

 ## What Do Marketers Do?

Consider the city where you live. Why do you live there? Why have businesses chosen to locate there? Call your Chamber of Commerce and ask to speak to the chamber director or marketing director. Ask the following questions:

- Have you used strategic planning to explore growth opportunities?
- What are the strengths of our city that you express to Chamber members or businesses considering relocating here?
- Have there been any changes in politics, culture, ecology, or technology that offer opportunities to attract businesses to this community?
- Are there weaknesses or threats that our city must overcome to improve its growth and viability?
- How do college students contribute to the strengths of our city or overcome workforce threats?

 ## Marketing Plan Exercise

Complete the following information about the company and products/services you chose to focus on as you develop the marketing plan throughout the course. You may need to conduct research in order to obtain necessary information.

Instructions: Using the Marketing Plan Template file you created from the Marketing and Customer Value assignment, complete the following sections of your marketing plan:

- Executive Summary
- Mission Statement
- SWOT Analysis
- Marketing Goals and Objectives

Submit the marketing plan to your instructor for grading and feedback.

 ## Closing Company Case

Blue Zones

When adventurer Dan Buettner set off around the world, riding his bike and visiting far-off destinations, he put a way of living into motion. Through the study of various communities around the world, Dan discovered pockets where populations of older people seemed to be living longer than anywhere else on earth. There were five such places where people lived a very long time and were healthier than many of the world's people. Dan called these places "Blue Zones." The Blue Zones included Okinawa, Japan; Sardinia, Italy; Nicoya, Costa Rica; Ikaria, Greece, and Loma Linda, California.

The Blue Zone concept grew and developed through the work of Gianni Pes and Michel Poulain. They originally identified Sardinia as a part of the world where there was a high concentration of older men. As the two began mapping the regions of longevity, they highlighted the villages and termed the inner circle of them "Blue Zones."

"Dan and the team of demographers and researchers found that all blue zone areas share nine specific lifestyle habits that they call the Power 9."[91]

The Blue Zones became a New York Times best seller. Media attention followed, and soon there was increased interest in the lifestyles within the Blue Zones. People began to recognize the Blue Zones as the happiest places to live. Communities were looking for ways to emulate the lifestyles and successes of these regions and in turn boost their longevity.

Dan realized he had not only a business, but a mission. What would happen if Blue Zones were created around the world? What if every community became a Blue Zone and a happy and healthy place where people lived longer? Could chronic disease be eradicated? Would health care costs drop?

In 2009, Albert Lea, Minnesota, teamed up with Blue Zones by applying the same concepts seen in the other Blue Zone locations. The location was suffering a severe economic crisis and needed a strategy to get out of it.[92]

What do these communities get for signing on to be a structured Blue Zone? Lower obesity rates, smoking cessation, increased exercise among their populations, reduced health care expenses, and a happier and more productive community. The initiatives are incredibly effective at making changes in how people live, work, and play. The Blue Zones project is population health at work. Adopting Blue Zones is creating a culture and community of complete well-being—one in which the people have increased productivity due to less illness.

Creating these communities includes a phased in approach. Blue Zones starts with Phases I and II, which build the foundation. Through assessment and an understanding of current state and desired future state, the gaps and issues are identified. The plan is drawn, and then in Phase III there is a full transformation that includes the people, the places, and the policy. When the plan is fully accepted and implemented, people will enjoy longevity, lower health care costs, and the recognition that the community is a great place to live and work.

How does the Blue Zones process work for the communities that participate? The effort is a collaboration between the community and the Blue Zones team. Starting with a complete evaluation of the community, Blue Zones experts work with community leaders and residents to assess the current state of well-being. Understanding the challenges currently facing the community provides the team with the greatest opportunity to develop the opportunities that will transform the community.

The statistics speak for themselves. Now communities across the United States are working to find ways to combat the crippling effects of the nation's health care crisis. Blue Zones could be the answer. "The Blue Zones Project helped our community set amazing, aggressive, and achievable strategies that moved the Public Health agenda further in 10 months than what I could have expected in 10 years," said Lois Ahern, director of Freeborn County Health (retired), in Albert Lea.[93]

Case Questions

1. What is the mission and purpose of Blue Zones?

2. Marketers use strategies such as market penetration, market development, product development, and diversification. What is the optimal strategy for Blue Zones to pursue as it seeks to gain a foothold in the

United States?

3. What is the market segmentation and target market for Blue Zones?

4. Blue Zones works to create healthier communities. With this goal in mind, what are some of the KPIs Blue Zones might work to implement?

References

1. "About Us," Contact Frito-Lay, PepsiCo, accessed June 5, 2022, https://contact.pepsico.com/fritolay/about-us.
2. Werner Geyser, "10 of the Best Marketing Strategy Examples to Power Your Campaigns," Influencer Marketing Hub, updated August 1, 2022, https://influencermarketinghub.com/marketing-strategy-examples/.
3. Geyser, "Best Marketing Strategy Examples."
4. Ibid.
5. "Corporate Structure," Structure & Governance, Procter & Gamble, last modified March 24, 2020, https://us.pg.com/structure-and-governance/corporate-structure/.
6. Patrick Hull, "Be Visionary. Think Big," *Forbes*, December 19, 2012, https://www.forbes.com/sites/patrickhull/2012/12/19/be-visionary-think-big/.
7. "Analysis of Volkswagen Mission Statement & Vision Statement 2022," Visionary BusinessPerson, last modified August 22, 2022, https://visionarybusinessperson.com/volkswagen-mission-statement-vision-statement/.
8. "Corporate Vision," Fujitsu United States, accessed August 5, 2022, https://www.fujitsu.com/us/about/philosophy/vision/.
9. Barbara Farfan, "Mission Statements from the Automotive Industry," The Balance Small Business, Dotdash Meredith, updated November 20, 2019, https://www.thebalancesmb.com/auto-industry-mission-statements-4068550.
10. Gennaro Cuofano, "Tesla Mission Statement and Vision Statement Analysis 2022," FourWeekMBA, last modified May 21, 2022, https://fourweekmba.com/tesla-vision-statement-mission-statement/.
11. Christine Rowland, "Apple Inc.'s Mission Statement and Vision Statement (an Analysis)," Panmore Institute, updated May 9, 2022, https://panmore.com/apple-mission-statement-vision-statement.
12. "About Us," About IKEA, Inter IKEA Systems, updated June 12, 2022, https://about.ikea.com/en/about-us.
13. Anthony Rivera, "Netflix's Mission Statement & Vision Statement: A Strategic Analysis," Rancord Society, updated November 10, 2019, https://www.rancord.org/netflix-corporate-vision-statement-mission-statement-strategic-analysis.
14. "eBay Mission and Vision Analysis," Mission Statement, last modified January 27, 2021, https://mission-statement.com/ebay/.
15. Alessio Bresciani, "51 Mission Statement Examples from the World's Best Companies," Foresight & Strategy, AlessioBresciani.com, last modified April 11, 2022, https://alessiobresciani.com/foresight-strategy/51-mission-statement-examples-from-the-worlds-best-companies/.
16. Aman Kaur, "Conducting a Gap Analysis: A Four-Step Template," ClearPoint Strategy, Ascendant Strategy Management Group, last modified January 4, 2022, https://www.clearpointstrategy.com/gap-analysis-template/.
17. Kaur, "Conducting a Gap Analysis."
18. Kaur, "Conducting a Gap Analysis."
19. Kaur, "Conducting a Gap Analysis."
20. "Goals vs. Objectives: What's the Difference?," Indeed Career Guide, Indeed, updated July 1, 2022, https://www.indeed.com/career-advice/career-development/difference-between-goals-and-objectives.
21. Indeed, "Goals vs. Objectives."
22. Helen Sabell, "10 Steps for Effective Goal Setting: Set and Achieve Goals," The College for Adult Learning, updated March 15, 2021, https://collegeforadultlearning.edu.au/effective-goal-setting-set-and-achieve-goals/.
23. "Marketing Dashboard," Marketing Dictionary, Skyword, December 1, 2016, https://www.skyword.com/marketing-dictionary/marketing-dashboard/.
24. "The Role of Marketing in the Strategic Planning Process," Studopedia, accessed June 3, 2022, https://studopedia.org/7-101679.html.
25. "What Is the Strategic Business Unit? The Complete Guide," *AVADA Commerce Blog*, AVADA, May 12, 2022, https://blog.avada.io/resources/strategic-business-unit.html.
26. Microsoft, *Annual Report 2021*, October 2021, https://www.microsoft.com/investor/reports/ar21/index.html.

27. Microsoft, *Annual Report 2021*.

28. David Weedmark, "Emerson: Company Profile," The Balance Careers, Dotdash Meredith, updated May 30, 2019, https://www.thebalancecareers.com/emerson-company-profile-2071327.

29. David Curry, "Apple Statistics (2022)," App Data, Business of Apps, updated May 4, 2022, https://www.businessofapps.com/data/apple-statistics/.

30. "The BCG Matrix | Boston Matrix," Expert Program Management, last modified October 2, 2019, https://expertprogrammanagement.com/2011/04/bcg-matrix-boston-matrix/.

31. "Tablet Shipments Market Share by Vendor Worldwide from 2nd Quarter 2011 to 1st Quarter 2022," Statista, accessed June 27, 2022, https://www.statista.com/statistics/276635/market-share-held-by-tablet-vendors/.

32. William Gallagher, "Apple Watch Remains the Best Seller as Smartwatch Market Grows," AppleInsider, Quiller Media, June 1, 2022, https://appleinsider.com/articles/22/06/01/apple-watch-remains-the-best-seller-as-smartwatch-market-grows.

33. Gallagher, "Apple Watch."

34. Expert Program Management, "BCG Matrix | Boston Matrix."

35. Expert Program Management, "BCG Matrix | Boston Matrix."

36. S. K. Gupta, "Starbucks SWOT 2022: SWOT Analysis of Starbucks," Business Strategy Hub, updated January 24, 2022, https://bstrategyhub.com/swot-analysis-of-starbucks-starbucks-swot/.

37. Gupta, "Starbucks SWOT 2022."

38. Ibid.

39. Ibid.

40. Ibid.

41. "Procter & Gamble's Advertising Spending in the United States from 2009 to 2020," Statista, accessed June 5, 2022, https://www.statista.com/statistics/191998/ad-spending-of-procter-and-gamble-in-the-us/.

42. Charles W. L. Hill and Gareth R. Jones, *Essentials of Strategic Management*, 3rd ed. (Mason, OH: South-Western Cengage Learning, 2012).

43. Richard Daniels, "What Is Intensive Strategy? 3 Types of Intensive Strategies," Business Study Notes, updated August 7, 2020, https://www.businessstudynotes.com/finance/types-of-intensive-strategies/.

44. Hill and Jones, *Essentials of Strategic Management*.

45. Mark Hall, "Facebook," *Encyclopaedia Britannica*, updated November 9, 2021, https://www.britannica.com/topic/Facebook.

46. Gary Moorhouse, "Business Diversification Strategy: The Best Examples," *Latest News & Blog*, Shorts Chartered Accountants, August 9, 2021, https://blog.shorts.uk.com/business-diversification-strategy-examples.

47. "Product Diversification," Corporate Finance Institute, CFI Education, updated February 1, 2022, https://corporatefinanceinstitute.com/resources/knowledge/strategy/product-diversification/.

48. "Concentric Diversification: Examples, Strategy, Advantages and Disadvantages," *Harappa Blogs*, Harappa Learning, December 9, 2021, https://harappa.education/harappa-diaries/concentric-diversification-strategy/.

49. Harappa Learning, "Concentric Diversification."

50. "What Is Horizontal Diversification? Definition, Benefits and Examples," Indeed Career Guide, Indeed, March 15, 2021, https://www.indeed.com/career-advice/career-development/horizontal-diversification.

51. Conglomerate Diversification: Examples, Strategy, Meaning, Advantages and Disadvantages," *Harappa Blogs*, Harappa Learning, December 31, 2021, https://harappa.education/harappa-diaries/conglomerate-diversification/.

52. "Company," Pinterest Newsroom, Pinterest, accessed August 5, 2022, https://newsroom.pinterest.com/en/company; "Press," All about Pinterest, Pinterest, accessed August 5, 2022, https://about.pinterest.com/en/node/19/mailto%3Apress%40pinterest.com.

53. "16 of the Best Company Mission Statement Examples for Inspiration," *Biteable Blog*, Biteable, last modified April 5, 2022, https://biteable.com/blog/mission-statements/.

54. "Mission, Values and Public Purposes," About the BBC, BBC, accessed August 5, 2022, https://www.bbc.com/aboutthebbc/governance/mission.

55. Jonas Sickler and Patrick Lane, "9 Examples of Buyer Personas for B2B & B2C Brands," *SEO Blog*, Terakeet, June 12, 2020, https://terakeet.com/blog/buyer-persona-examples/.

56. Boz V., "How Many Personas Are Too Many?," LinkedIn, May 3, 2016, https://www.linkedin.com/pulse/how-many-personas-too-boz-zou/.

57. "Marketing Plan Current Situation Section," Resources for Entrepreneurs, Gaebler Ventures, accessed April 20, 2022, https://www.gaebler.com/Marketing-Plan-Current-Situation.htm.

58. "Marketing Plan: Contents of a Marketing Plan," iEduNote, last modified October 12, 2020, https://www.iedunote.com/marketing-plan.

59. Clint Fontanella, "The Straightforward Guide to Product Strategy," *The HubSpot Customer Service Blog*, HubSpot, updated March 17, 2022, https://blog.hubspot.com/service/product-strategy.

60. "How to Develop the Pricing Strategy for Your Marketing Plan," *PriceBeam Blog*, PriceBeam, February 7, 2017, https://blog.pricebeam.com/pricing-strategy-marketing-plan.

61. iEduNote, "Marketing Plan."

62. "A Community of 4.6 Billion," *Tech Blog*, Health IT, last modified September 20, 2021, https://healthit.com.au/how-big-is-the-internet-and-how-do-we-measure-it/.

63. Zoe Palmer, "KPIs vs. Marketing Metrics: What's the Difference?," Brand Chemistry, last modified August 25, 2020, https://www.brandchemistry.com.au/blog/kpis-vs-marketing-metrics.

64. "5 Benefits of Dashboards in the Marketing Industry," InfoCaptor BI, Rudrasoft, March 13, 2017, https://www.infocaptor.com/5-benefits-of-dashboards-in-the-marketing-industry.

65. "KPI of the Week: Revenue Growth," News & Publications, Porte Brown Accountants & Advisors, accessed June 5, 2022, https://www.portebrown.com/news/kpi-of-the-week-revenue-growth.

66. Porte Brown Accountants & Advisors, "KPI of the Week."

67. "What Is Average Revenue per User (ARPU) and How to Calculate It," Peel Insights, accessed June 4, 2022, https://www.peelinsights.com/post/what-is-average-revenue-per-user-and-how-to-calculate-it.

68. "Market Share," Encyclopedia Table of Contents, *Inc.*, updated February 6, 2020, https://www.inc.com/encyclopedia/market-share.html.

69. "Evaluating Market Share as a KPI," Insights, Ungerboeck, updated January 18, 2021, https://ungerboeck.com/resources/evaluating-market-share-as-a-kpi.

70. Fraser Sherman, "How Do You Calculate a Company's Relative Market Share?," Small Business, Chron.com, updated September 24, 2020, https://smallbusiness.chron.com/calculate-companys-relative-market-share-11401.html.

71. Sherman, "How Do You Calculate?"

72. "How to Measure Customer Satisfaction KPIs," Resource Center, GetFeedback, last modified January 20, 2022, https://www.getfeedback.com/resources/csat/how-to-measure-customer-satisfaction-kpis/.

73. Andrea Paul, "Top Metrics and Strategies for How to Measure Customer Service Performance," *Kustomer Blog*, Kustomer, last modified December 2, 2021, https://www.kustomer.com/blog/how-to-measure-customer-service-performance/.

74. Paul, "Top Metrics and Strategies."

75. "Locations," Classic Cleaners, accessed August 5, 2022, https://classiccleaners.com/locations/.

76. "Case Study: Company Tracks Performance with Marketing Reporting Dashboard," *Perspective, Tips, and Insights* (blog), TBH Creative, February 4, 2020, https://blog.tbhcreative.com/2020/02/case-study-marketing-reporting-dashboard.html.

77. TBH Creative, "Case Study."

78. Shivani, "Marketing Ethics: Meaning, Importance, and Examples," InviteReferrals, December 14, 2021, https://www.invitereferrals.com/blog/marketing-ethics/.

79. Shivani, "Marketing Ethics."

80. "Corporate Social Responsibility: A Brief History," Association of Corporate Citizenship Professionals, last modified April 21, 2022, https://accp.org/resources/csr-resources/accp-insights-blog/corporate-social-responsibility-brief-history/.

81. John Edelman, "George H. W. Bush's Impact on CSR," Insights, Edelman, December 5, 2018, https://www.edelman.com/insights/george-hw-bush-impact-csr.

82. Michael Ledecky, "Corporate Social Responsibility: Past, Present, and Future," *Resources to Engage Your Cause* (blog), EVERFI, last modified July 20, 2022, https://everfi.com/blog/community-engagement/csr-history/.

83. Submittable, "Millennials, Gen Z, and the Rising Demand for Corporate Social Responsibility," American Marketing Association, July 6, 2020, https://www.ama.org/2020/07/06/millennials-gen-z-and-the-rising-demand-for-corporate-social-responsibility/.

84. Submittable, "Millennials, Gen Z."

85. Ibid.

86. Ibid.

87. Zach Hrynowski and Megan Brenan, "What Percentage of Americans Vape?," Gallup News, Gallup, August 19, 2021, https://news.gallup.com/poll/267413/percentage-americans-vape.aspx.

88. Meagan Parrish, "The 2009 Toyota Accelerator Scandal That Wasn't What It Seemed," Manufacturing.net, Industrial Media, August 11, 2016, https://www.manufacturing.net/automotive/blog/13110434/the-2009-toyota-accelerator-scandal-that-wasnt-what-it-seemed.

89. Danielle Douglas and Michael A. Fletcher, "Toyota Reaches $1.2 Billion Settlement to End Probe of Accelerator Problems," *Washington Post*, March 19, 2014, https://www.washingtonpost.com/business/economy/toyota-reaches-12-billion-settlement-to-end-criminal-probe/2014/03/19/5738a3c4-af69-11e3-9627-c65021d6d572_story.html.

90. "Red Bull Student Marketeer," Red Bull Jobs, Red Bull, accessed June 4, 2022, https://jobs.redbull.com/us-en/microsite/student-marketeer.

91. "History of Blue Zones," Blue Zones, last modified April 30, 2021, https://www.bluezones.com/about/history/.

92. "Blue Zone Results: Albert Lea, MN," Blue Zones, last modified January 8, 2019, https://www.bluezones.com/blue-zones-results-albert-lea-mn/.

93. Blue Zones, "History of Blue Zones."

Unit 2

Understanding the Marketplace

Unit Introduction

Welcome to Unit 2 of *Principles of Marketing.* In Unit 1, the stage was set for studying marketing. Unit 2 discusses the analytical tools and frameworks to understand a broad range of customers (whether consumers or businesses) and categorize them into target markets. It then reviews marketing research techniques used to gather data and make sound marketing decisions. Finally, the last two chapters of this unit emphasize the challenges of expanding to international markets and reaching culturally and demographically diverse segments in domestic markets.

Consumer Markets and Purchasing Behavior

Figure 3.1 Understanding consumer purchasing decisions is important because it allows companies to better influence those behaviors. (credit: modification of work "Hong Kong Street Market" by Bernard Spragg. NZ/flickr, Public Domain)

Chapter Outline

In the Spotlight

There is no denying that COVID-19 affected the entire economy, but fast-food restaurants were particularly hard-hit when indoor dining was restricted. McDonald's quickly adapted during the pandemic by focusing on what it calls the 3 Ds: digital, delivery, and drive-through.

McDonald's had a strong position in terms of digital innovation even before the pandemic. It had installed self-order kiosks in its restaurants beginning in 2015 and launched its mobile app (Mobile Order & Pay) in 2017, allowing customers to browse the menu, find nearby restaurants, place their orders, and pay within the app. Digital sales exceeded $10 billion in 2020, nearly 20 percent of system-wide sales.

The company also tackled the efficiency of its drive-through lanes by investing in dynamic menu boards and cutting its menu items to its "core menu." As a result, McDonald's was able to shave 30 seconds from its drive-through time. That time savings enabled the company to serve 300 million additional drive-through customers.

The pandemic and the subsequent restrictions on indoor dining also led McDonald's to scale up its delivery platform and the number of restaurants that offer delivery. By ramping up the number of restaurants that offer delivery from 28,000 to 41,000 total restaurants, delivery sales more than tripled.

Focusing on the 3 Ds enabled McDonald's to weather the pandemic and create a faster, easier, and improved customer experience.[1]

3.1 Understanding Consumer Markets and Buying Behavior

Learning Outcomes

By the end of this section, you will be able to:
- **LO** 1 Define consumer buying behavior.
- **LO** 2 Explain the nature of the buyer's black box.
- **LO** 3 Describe how consumer behavior is characterized into types.

Consumer Markets and Consumer Buying Behavior Defined

How many buying decisions did you make today? Perhaps you stopped on the way to work or class to buy a soft drink or coffee, went to the grocery store on the way home to get bread or milk, or ordered something online. You likely make buying decisions nearly every day and probably don't give most of those decisions much thought. But the way you make those decisions is significant for marketers, because if they can understand *why* you buy what you buy and *when* you buy it, they can use that information to boost revenue.

Consumer buying behavior refers to the decisions and actions people undertake to buy products or services for personal use. In other words, it's the actions you take before buying a product or service, and as you will see, many factors influence that behavior. You and all other consumers combine to make up the **consumer market**.

The Buyer's Black Box

It stands to reason that the hundreds of millions of people who make up the global consumer market don't all buy the same products and services. Why do certain people prefer different items than others? The answer lies in the factors that influence consumer buying behavior. One model of consumer buying behavior is what's known as the **buyer's black box**, which is named as such because little is known about what goes on in the human mind. It's also known as the stimulus-response model.

As illustrated in the model shown in [Figure 3.2](#), consumer buying behavior is based on stimuli coming from a variety of sources—from marketers in terms of the **4Ps (product, price, promotion, and place)**, as well as from environmental stimuli, such as economic factors, legal/political factors, and technological and cultural factors.

These stimuli go into your "black box," which consists of two parts: buyer characteristics such as beliefs and attitudes, motives, perceptions, and values, and the buyer decision-making process, which is covered later in the chapter. Your response is the outcome of the thinking that takes place in that black box. What will you buy, where, when, how often, and how much?

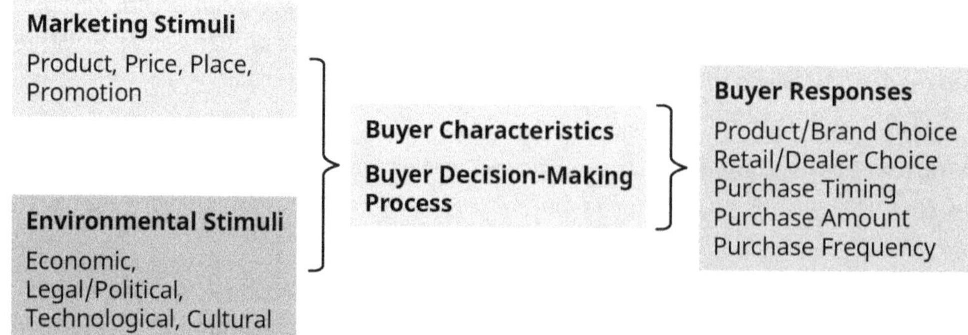

Figure 3.2 Stimulus-Response Model/Buyer's Black Box (attribution: Copyright Rice University, OpenStax, under CC BY 4.0 license)

Types of Consumer Buying Behavior

Buying behavior is not influenced solely by the external environment. It's also determined by your level of involvement in a purchase and the amount of risk involved in the purchase. There are four types of consumer buying behavior, as shown in Figure 3.3.

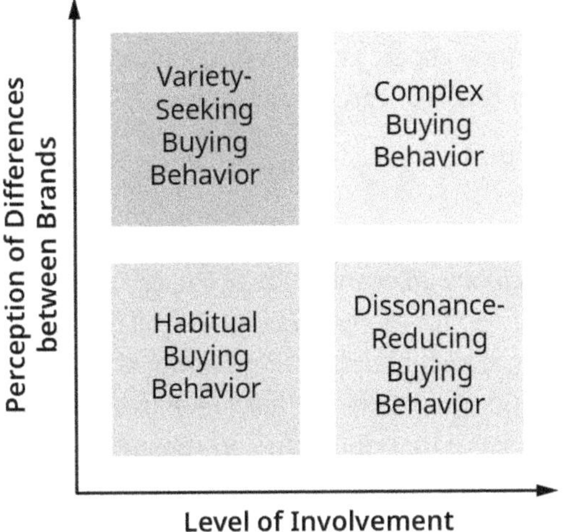

Figure 3.3 Types of Consumer Buying Behavior (attribution: Copyright Rice University, OpenStax, under CC BY 4.0 license)

Complex buying behavior occurs when you make a significant or expensive purchase, like buying a new car. Because you likely don't buy a new car frequently, you're highly involved in the buying decision, and you probably research different vehicles or talk with friends or family before reaching your decision. By that time, you're likely convinced that there's a significant difference among cars, and you've developed your own unique set of criteria that helps you decide on your purchase.

Dissonance-reducing buying behavior occurs when you're highly involved in a purchase but see little difference among brands. Let's say you're replacing the flooring in your kitchen with ceramic tile—another expensive, infrequent purchase. You might think that all brands of ceramic tile in a certain price range are "about the same," so you might shop around to see what's available, but you'll probably buy rather quickly, perhaps as a result of a good price or availability. However, after you've made your purchase, you may experience post-purchase dissonance (also known as buyer's remorse) when you notice some disadvantages of the tile you purchased or hear good things about a brand you didn't purchase.

Habitual buying behavior has low involvement in the purchase decision because it's often a repeat buy, and you don't perceive much brand differentiation. Perhaps you usually buy a certain brand of organic milk, but you don't have strong brand loyalty. If your regular brand isn't available at the store or another brand is on sale, you'll probably buy a different brand.

Variety-seeking buying behavior has the lowest customer involvement because brand switching is your norm. You may not be unhappy with your last purchase of tortilla chips, but you simply want to try something new. It's a matter of brand switching for the sake of variety rather than because of dissatisfaction with your previous purchase.

LINK TO LEARNING

The 4Ps and Consumer Behavior

Watch this short, humorous 4Ps video as a way to help you remember the concept. This video also includes several examples of target markets and how a marketer might respond.

Click to view content (https://openstax.org/books/principles-marketing/pages/3-1-understanding-consumer-markets-and-buying-behavior)

Consumer behavior is an important marketing topic, and depending on the marketing program at your institution, you may have the opportunity to take a consumer behavior course and learn more about the topics covered above. Studying consumer behavior is important in marketing because it will teach you how to best know your customer, an integral aspect to marketing a product or service. You can also watch this selfLearn-en video to get a stronger grasp of consumer behavior.

Click to view content (https://openstax.org/books/principles-marketing/pages/3-1-understanding-consumer-markets-and-buying-behavior)

As mentioned, environmental factors have an impact on consumer behavior. Can you think of a recent environmental influence that has had a significant impact? The coronavirus pandemic has probably been the most influential in recent years, and for many reasons! We still have a lot to learn about the impacts of the pandemic, and new information is being released daily about changing human behavior and the impact on marketing. For example, in this Google article, the author shares a cultural anthropologist's insights (https://openstax.org/r/thinkwithgoogle) for understanding consumer behavior and how it relates to three core needs all people experience—self-care, social connection, and identity—and how these needs correlate to recent YouTube video trends. Learn about how marketers can respond to this trend.

Continually trying to understand environmental influences will keep you on the cutting edge and ahead of the competition. It's a great practice to always be looking for the latest information so that you can shift your strategies as needed. Bain & Company is an example of one company that wanted to understand how the pandemic changed consumer behavior. The company ran a survey in 2021 to better understand the impact of the pandemic, and it found five trends from the data.

Click to view content (https://openstax.org/books/principles-marketing/pages/3-1-understanding-consumer-markets-and-buying-behavior)

A survey from Accenture (https://openstax.org/r/insightsstrategy), one of the top-ranked consulting firms in the world, found that the pandemic caused 50 percent of consumers to evaluate their purpose and what's important to them. Read more about the findings in this article.

Always be looking for information to be the best marketer you can be!

Knowledge Check

It's time to check your knowledge on the concepts presented in this section. Refer to the Answer Key at the end of the book for feedback.

1. You're considering buying a widescreen TV. You've researched different features, looked up and reviewed models on the Internet, and even asked a few friends for their recommendations. What type of buying behavior are you exhibiting?
   a. Dissonance-reducing buying behavior
   b. Variety-seeking buying behavior
   c. Complex buying behavior
   d. Habitual buying behavior

2. In the buyer's black box, external stimuli that are planned and created by the producer and/or seller are known as _______ stimuli.
   a. economic
   b. marketing
   c. technological
   d. social

3. Samantha sees a TV commercial announcing that a mattress she's been considering is on sale through the holiday weekend and makes plans to visit the store the next day in order to take advantage of the sale. In

terms of the buyer's black box, how would this TV commercial be characterized?
   a.   Product choice
   b.   Brand choice
   c.   Social stimuli
   d.   Purchase timing

4.   You're at the grocery store buying potato chips for a barbeque you're having this weekend. You normally buy Lay's potato chips, but you notice that Ruffles are on sale, so you pick up a few bags of Ruffles. What buying behavior have you displayed?
   a.   Dissonance-reducing buying behavior
   b.   Habitual buying behavior
   c.   Variety-seeking buying behavior
   d.   Complex buying behavior

5.   The decisions and actions people undertake to buy products or services for personal use are known as

   ________.
   a.   the consumer market
   b.   the buyer's black box
   c.   consumer buying behavior
   d.   complex buying behavior

3.2 | Factors That Influence Consumer Buying Behavior

Learning Outcomes

By the end of this section, you will be able to:
   LO 1 List and describe the cultural factors that influence consumer buying behavior.
   LO 2 Explain the social factors that impact consumer buying behavior.
   LO 3 Discuss the personal factors that influence consumer buying behavior.
   LO 4 Describe the psychological factors that influence consumer buying behavior.
   LO 5 Explain situational factors that impact consumer buying behavior.

Cultural Factors That Influence Consumer Buying Behavior

Why people buy isn't always a straightforward question. Think about the last time you bought a car, a bike, or other item. Why did you buy that specific make and model? Was it because its sleek style made you feel good about yourself? Perhaps you bought a particular brand because someone in your family bought the same brand. These are just a couple of examples of some of the factors that influence consumer buying behavior. Let's examine some others.

Cultural factors comprise a set of values or ideologies of a particular community or group of individuals. These can include culture, subcultures, social class, and gender as outlined in Figure 3.4.

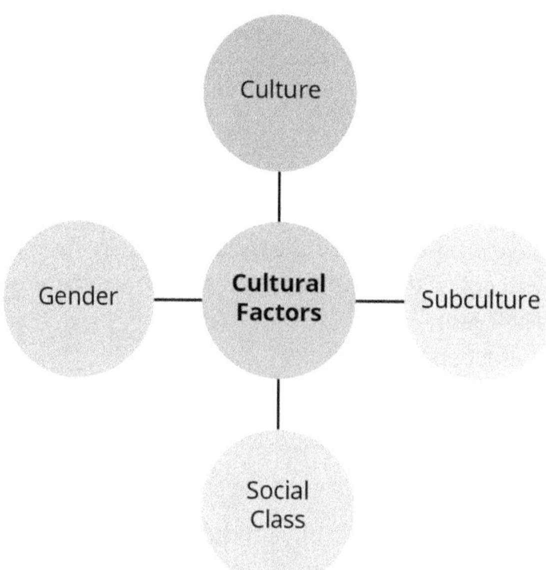

Figure 3.4 Cultural Factors Influencing Consumer Purchasing Behavior (attribution: Copyright Rice University, OpenStax, under CC BY 4.0 license)

Culture refers to the values, ideas, and **attitudes** that are learned and shared among members of a group. Human behavior is largely learned. When you were a child, you learned basic values, perceptions, wants, and behaviors from your family and other external influences like the schools and churches you attended. Consider how these values and attitudes have shaped your buying behavior. For example, in a traditional Hindu wedding in India, a bride may wear red lehenga to the wedding, whereas Christian brides typically wear white. In India, widows are expected to wear white, whereas widows in the United States and other parts of the world generally wear more somber colors to a funeral.[2]

A **subculture** is a group of people, such as environmentalists or bodybuilders, who share a set of values. Ethnic and racial groups share the language, food, and culture of their heritage. Other subcultures, like the biker culture, which revolves around a dedication to motorcycles, are united by shared experiences. The Amish subculture is known for its conservative beliefs and reluctance to adapt to modern technology. Think about what subculture(s) you may belong to and how they influence your buying behavior. For example, hip-hop music has long been associated with fashion, particularly sneakers. Run DMC's 1986 hit "My Adidas" led to the first endorsement deal between a fashion brand and a musical act, setting the stage for lucrative partnerships spanning the decades since—Master P with Converse, Jay-Z and 50 Cent with Reebok, Missy Elliott and Big Sean with Adidas, and Drake with Nike.

LINK TO LEARNING

Failures and Inspirations

Cultural factors play a major role in determining how best to market to consumers. There are numerous examples of company efforts that failed because they did not reflect an understanding of the culture in a particular market. Watch this CNBC video on why Starbucks failed in Australia and read this article about how Coca-Cola and PepsiCo failed (https://openstax.org/r/examplescompanyfailure) when they first moved into the Chinese market.

Click to view content (https://openstax.org/books/principles-marketing/pages/3-2-factors-that-influence-consumer-buying-behavior)

Also check out this CNBC video about why 7-Eleven failed in Indonesia.

Click to view content (https://openstax.org/books/principles-marketing/pages/3-2-factors-that-influence-consumer-buying-behavior)

Failures are always important because they come with learned knowledge, and if you understand the WHY behind the failure, the learning can lead to shifts in strategy and possible success. Read the inspiring story (https://openstax.org/r/inspiringstory) behind Run DMC's revolutionary market deal with Adidas and how it opened the door for current artists like 50 Cent, Jay-Z, and Puffy.

For more success stories, check out these videos about numerous companies that got it right (https://openstax.org/r/examplesofbrands). Examples include stories from Rihanna's Fenty beauty line, Adobe's "When I See Black" ad, Bumble's "Find Me on Bumble" campaign, and many more!

Your **social class** is also an important influence on your buying behavior. Sociologists base definitions of social class on several different factors, including income, occupation, and education. While there is disagreement on the number of social classes defined by income in the United States, many sociologists suggest five social classes: upper class, upper-middle class, lower-middle class, working class, and the economically disadvantaged.[3] Income is largely defined by disposable income (the money you have left to spend or save after taxes are deducted), but its influence goes beyond just dollars, euros, yen, etc. For example, a lower-middle-class individual might focus primarily on price when considering a product, whereas an upper-middle-class person might consider product quality and features before price. However, you also can be influenced by a social class to which you don't belong but by which you want to be accepted. Have you ever spent money you really didn't have on brand name running shoes or a designer purse because that's what your friends have?

Finally, your **gender** plays an important role in your buying behavior. People of different genders not only want different products as a result of their upbringing and socialization, but they approach shopping itself with different motives, perspectives, and considerations. While it's always dangerous to stereotype, those who identify as male typically follow a utilitarian, more logic-based approach when shopping. They want a quick, effortless shopping experience. Those who identify as female, on the other hand, make decisions on a more emotional level. Zappos considers these different motives and provides different layouts on their landing pages for different genders. While the "male" version focuses on providing clear navigation by product categories, the "female" version aims to sell on emotion.[4]

LINK TO LEARNING

Behind the Gender Differences

Gender differences lead to different buying behaviors. Read this article about one such example, Birchbox (https://openstax.org/r/men-vs-women), a hair care and skin care subscription service. For even more information, check out this article about the reasons for the differences (https://openstax.org/r/women-vs-men), which include purpose, experience, brain make-up, and more. Interesting reads!

You can also watch this Gaby Barrios TED Talk. Barrios is a marketing expert who speaks about how targeting consumers based on gender is bad for business.

Click to view content (https://openstax.org/books/principles-marketing/pages/3-2-factors-that-influence-consumer-buying-behavior)

This humorous video from The Checkout, a TV show about consumer affairs, discusses gender marketing packaging decisions and their impact on your wallet.

Click to view content (https://openstax.org/books/principles-marketing/pages/3-2-factors-that-influence-consumer-buying-behavior)

Another video about fashion brands focuses on how their parent companies leverage gender strategies.

Click to view content (https://openstax.org/books/principles-marketing/pages/3-2-factors-that-influence-consumer-buying-behavior)

CAREERS IN MARKETING

Women in Marketing

Let's look at gender from another angle—women advancing in marketing. Part of a series about jobs in marketing (https://openstax.org/r/gender-diversity), this article examines equity in the world of marketing. Findings include data on gender balance and inequality, and guidance on ways to improve.

For an inspirational moment, be sure to read these heartwarming stories about six mothers of great marketers (https://openstax.org/r/behindeverygoodmarketer).

Social Factors That Influence Consumer Buying Behavior

Social factors are those factors that are prevalent in the society where the consumer lives. Every society is composed of individuals who have different preferences and behaviors, and these individuals influence the personal preferences of others in the society. Humans are social individuals, and the influences of people's family, reference groups, and roles and status (refer to Figure 3.5) have a huge impact on their buying behavior.

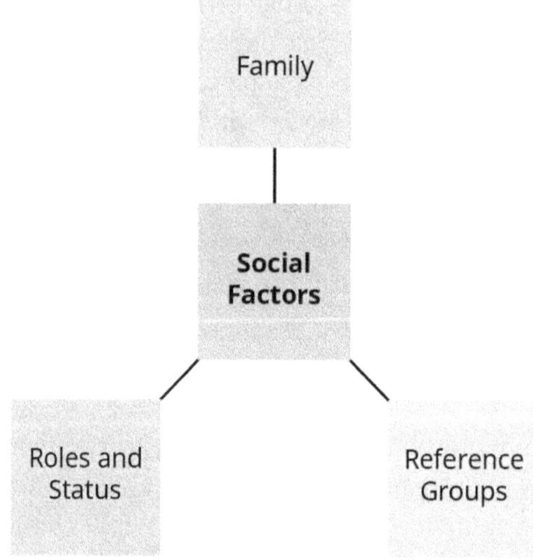

Figure 3.5 Social Factors Influencing Consumer Purchasing Behavior (attribution: Copyright Rice University, OpenStax, under CC BY 4.0 license)

Let's first consider the influence of **family**. It is generally believed that most people pass through two families: a family of orientation (i.e., the family to which you were born or with whom you grew up) and a family of procreation (the family formed through marriage or cohabitation, including your spouse, partner, and/or children). Consider first the family of orientation. When you were growing up, whether or not you recognized it, you likely developed some degree of buying behavior through watching adult members of your household and probably tend to buy the same products or services as you grow older. Was your father a die-hard Chevy driver? If so, the chances are good that you'll probably at least consider buying a Chevy, too. Now consider the influence that your spouse, partner, and/or children have on your buying behavior. You may want that Chevy pickup because that's what your father drove, but your spouse or partner may subtly (or perhaps not so subtly) sway you toward a Chevy crossover SUV because it's more practical with kids to transport to school, sports, and other activities.

Reference groups are those groups with which you like to be associated. These can be formal groups, such as members of a country club, church, or professional group, or informal groups of friends or acquaintances. These groups serve as role models and inspirations, and they influence what types of products you buy and which brands you choose. Reference groups are characterized by having opinion leaders—people who influence others. These opinion leaders aren't necessarily higher-income or better educated, but others view them as having more expertise in a particular area. For example, a teenage girl may look to the opinion leader in her reference group of friends for fashion guidance, or a college student might aspire to getting an advanced degree from the same university as an admired professor. Social media influencers also play a role here. Consider the influence that celebrities like Kendall Jenner (with more than 217 million Instagram followers)[5] or Leo Messi (with over 310 million Instagram followers)[6] have on individuals.

All people assume different **roles** and **status** depending upon the groups, clubs, family, or organizations to which they belong. For example, a working mother who is taking classes at the local community college assumes three roles at varying times—that of an employee, a mother, and a student. Her buying decisions will be influenced by each of these roles at different times. When she is shopping for clothing, her purchases may be influenced by any or all of these roles—professional attire for the office, casual clothes for classes, or yoga pants for home.

Personal Factors That Impact Consumer Buying Behavior

Personal factors, such as your occupation, age and life cycle stage, economic situation, lifestyle, and personality and self-concept also play a major role in your buying behavior (refer to Figure 3.6). Let's examine each of these in more detail.

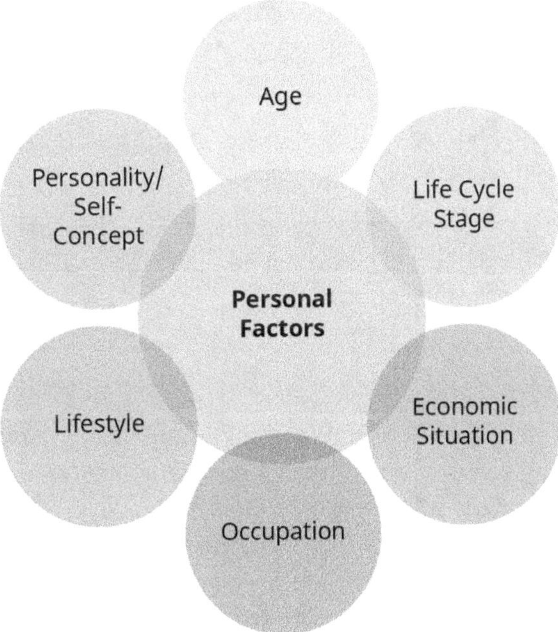

Figure 3.6 Personal Factors Influencing Consumer Purchasing Behavior (attribution: Copyright Rice University, OpenStax, under CC BY 4.0 license)

Age is a major factor that influences buying behavior because consumer needs and wants change with age. Your buying habits as a teenager or twentysomething are likely to be vastly different from your buying habits in middle age and beyond. Consider the four generational cohorts currently comprising the consumer market:

- Baby boomers (born between 1946 and 1964) are currently in their 60s and 70s. This generational cohort is approximately 70 million people strong in the United States and accounts for $2.6 trillion in buying power,[7] so you can imagine its impact on the consumer market. What types of products would you expect baby boomers to buy? Key categories for this group of buyers include pharmacy and health care products, household goods and appliances, wine, books (both digital and physical), cosmetics, and skin care products.[8]

- Generation X (born between 1965 and 1979/80) are currently in their 40s and 50s. This cohort is approximately 65 million strong[9] and generally has more spending power than younger generational cohorts because they're at or reaching the peak of their careers, and many Gen Xers are dual-income families.[10] This makes them an optimal target for higher-end brands and convenience-related goods, like made-to-order or prepared meals from the grocery store.

- Generation Y, also known as Millennials, (born between 1981 and 1994/96) are currently in their 20s and 30s. This cohort is the largest generation group in the United States, with an estimated population of 72 million.[11] One interesting aspect of Millennial buying is that they shop sustainably. They shop for brands that produce items with natural ingredients and ethical production lines and sustainable goods in every sector, such as food, household cleaning products, linens, and clothes.[12]

- Generation Z, also known as Zoomers, (born between 1997 and 2012) are currently in their teens to early 20s, and they are just starting to have an economic impact on the consumer market. Although over 67 million strong,[13] many Zoomers are still in school and living with their parents, and their discretionary spending is limited.

MARKETING IN PRACTICE

Marketing to the Ages

Knowing how to speak to your target market is critical. Knowing how to frame your message to a Baby Boomer versus a Gen Xer is what makes marketers successful. Want to know how to speak to each group? Check out these articles about marketing to different age demographics (https://openstax.org/r/marketingtodifferentage) and generational marketing (https://openstax.org/r/generationalmarketing).

Learn from real-world examples of how age-agnostic marketing (https://openstax.org/r/ageagnostic) can work.

Have you ever seen a commercial or advertisement that pulls on your heartstrings because it gets you reminiscing? Nostalgia is an impactful tool in marketing because it gives a feeling of meaning and comfort. Check out this online blog to learn more about the impact of nostalgia (https://openstax.org/r/examplesnostalgia) in marketing.

Likewise, your **life cycle stage** has a major influence on your buying habits. Consider the different buying choices you would make as a single person who is renting an apartment in an urban area versus the choices you would make as a homeowner in the suburbs with children. It should be noted, though, that age and life cycle stage can often be poor predictors of buying behavior. For example, some 40-year-olds are just starting their families, while others are sending their kids off to college. Still other 40-year-olds are single (or single again). Some 70-year-olds may fit the stereotype of a retired person with a fixed income; others are still active or perhaps still working, with plenty of disposable income.

Your **economic situation** (income) is a huge influence on your buying behavior. Higher income typically means higher disposable income, and that disposable income gives consumers more opportunity to spend on high-end products. Conversely, lower-income and middle-income consumers spend most of their income on basic needs such as groceries and clothing.

Your **occupation** is also a significant factor in your buying behavior because you tend to purchase things that are appropriate to your profession. For instance, a blue-collar worker is less likely to buy professional attire like business suits, whereas attorneys, accountants, and other white-collar workers may favor suits or business casual work clothes. There are even companies that specialize in work clothes for certain types of workers, such as health care professionals who buy scrubs or construction workers who buy steel-toed boots.

Your **lifestyle** reflects your attitudes and values. What do you consider to be your lifestyle? Do you strive to live an active, healthy lifestyle? If so, your purchasing decisions may focus on healthier food alternatives instead of fast food. Do you consider yourself to be a soccer parent? You may (perhaps reluctantly) forgo that sports car for a minivan in order to transport your kids to youth sporting events or other activities.

Your personality and self-concept are also important factors influencing your buying behavior. **Personality** is the characteristic patterns of thoughts, feelings, and behaviors that make a person unique. It's believed that personality arises from within the individual and remains fairly consistent throughout life.[14] Some examples of the many personality traits people might have include things like self-confidence, individualism, extroversion, introversion, aggression, or competitiveness. Your personality greatly influences what you buy as well as when and how you use or consume products and services.

Perhaps even more importantly, as consumers, people tend to buy not only products they need but also those products or services that they perceive as being consistent with their "self-concept." In other words, they generally want the products they buy to match or blend in with who they think they are.[15]

Psychological Factors That Influence Consumer Buying Behavior

Your buying choices are further influenced by several major psychological factors, including motivation, perception, learning, feelings, beliefs, and attitudes (refer to Figure 3.7).

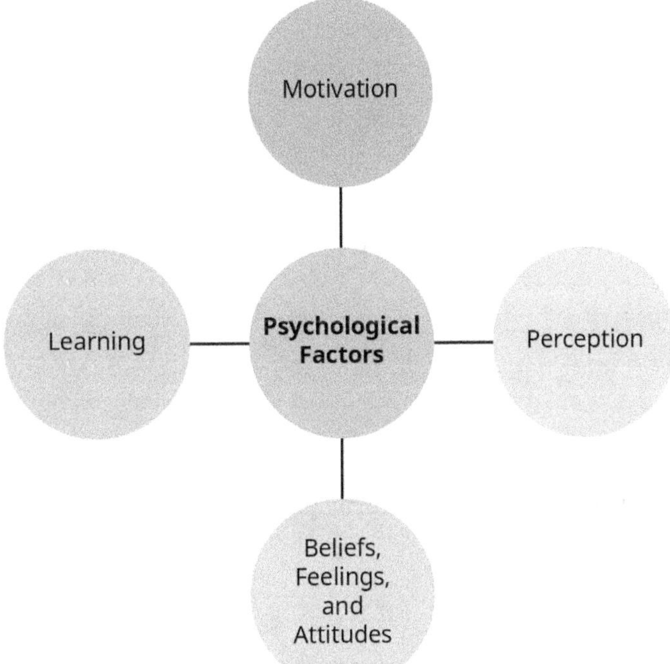

Figure 3.7 Psychological Factors Influencing Consumer Buying Behavior (attribution: Copyright Rice University, OpenStax, under CC BY 4.0 license)

Let's first consider how motivation affects your buying behavior. **Motivation** is the process that initiates, guides, and maintains goal-oriented behaviors. It's the driving force behind your actions. One of the most widely known motivation theories is **Maslow's hierarchy of needs** (see Figure 3.8).

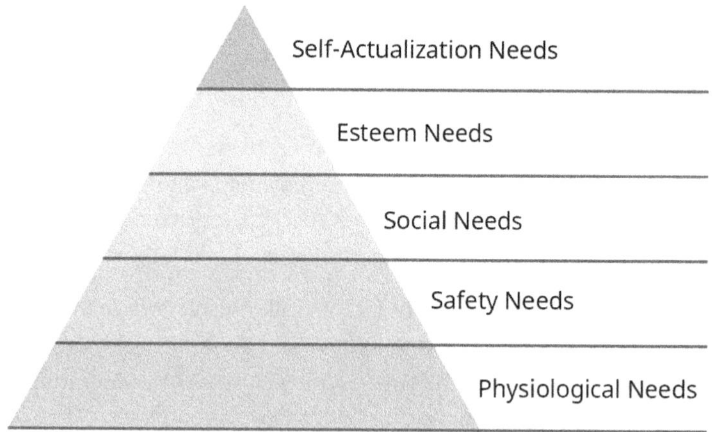

Figure 3.8 Maslow's Hierarchy of Needs (attribution: Copyright Rice University, OpenStax, under CC BY 4.0 license)

Abraham Maslow asserted that all individuals have five needs, arranged from the most basic lower-level deficiency needs to the highest-level growth needs. As Figure 3.8 shows, physiological needs are at the most basic level and include things like adequate food, water, and shelter. Think about how marketers may try to appeal to consumers based on physiological needs. For example, Snickers ran a very successful ad campaign based on the slogan "You're not you when you're hungry."

The second level is safety and security, the need to be safe from physical and psychological harm. Once again, consider just a few successful marketing campaigns that have focused on safety—"You're in Good Hands with Allstate" and Lysol's "Practice Healthy Habits" campaign with its tagline "What It Takes to Protect."

The third level is belonging, or social needs. This level includes things like the need for emotional attachments, friendship, love, or belonging to community or church groups.

Esteem, the fourth level, includes such needs as recognition from others, taking pride in your education or work, awards, and/or prestige.

The highest level is self-actualization, which involves self-development and seeking challenges. For example, Nike's "Find Your Greatness" campaign was intended to spark greatness in ordinary people, not just professional athletes.

LINK TO LEARNING

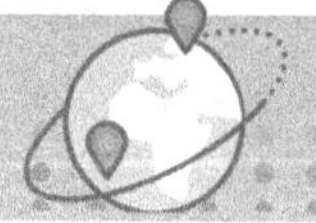

Examples of Maslow's Five Needs

Check out this Snickers' "You're not you when you're hungry" commercial, which appeals to basic human physiological needs.

Click to view content (https://openstax.org/books/principles-marketing/pages/3-2-factors-that-influence-consumer-buying-behavior)

This Lysol "What It Takes to Protect" commercial appeals to the human needs for safety and security.

Click to view content (https://openstax.org/books/principles-marketing/pages/3-2-factors-that-influence-consumer-buying-behavior)

Consider this public service announcement (PSA) from the Ad Council that is dedicated to fostering a more welcoming nation where everyone can belong. How does it appeal to the human need for community and belonging?

Click to view content (https://openstax.org/books/principles-marketing/pages/3-2-factors-that-influence-consumer-buying-behavior)

One awesome esteem level example to check out is this one from Dove. Dove launched a campaign to boost female self-esteem (https://openstax.org/r/doveself) and to celebrate female beauty in all shapes and sizes. The company also created "confidence-boosting boards" on Pinterest. The boards include self-esteem activities so girls and their parents can share words of encouragement.

Check out one of Nike's commercials from the "Find Your Greatness" campaign. How does it appeal to the human need for self-actualization?

Click to view content (https://openstax.org/books/principles-marketing/pages/3-2-factors-that-influence-consumer-buying-behavior)

Maslow asserted that people strive to satisfy their most basic needs before directing their behavior toward satisfying higher-level needs, so it stands to reason that consumer buying behavior would follow this model. For example, you'd first have to fulfill your needs for food and shelter before you might consider putting money away for retirement or purchasing a home security system.

LINK TO LEARNING

Maslow and Marketing

Understanding Maslow's hierarchy of needs will help you be an effective and impressive marketer. You're going to see this model in many of your business courses, not just marketing, so take the time to learn about it. Check out this brief video that may help you understand how to use Maslow's hierarchy of needs in marketing. Learn about why Maslow's hierarchy of needs matters.

Click to view content (https://openstax.org/books/principles-marketing/pages/3-2-factors-that-influence-consumer-buying-behavior)

Perception is the way in which people identify, organize, and interpret sensory information. It's another variable in consumer buying behavior because the perceptions you have about a business or its products or services have a dramatic effect on your buying behavior. What makes perception even more complex is that consumers can form different perceptions of the same stimulus because of three perceptual processes: selective attention, selective distortion, and selective retention. Let's take a closer look.

Every day, you're bombarded with marketing messages from TV commercials, magazine and newspaper ads, billboards, and social media ads. As of 2021, it was estimated that the average person encounters between 6,000 and 10,000 ads every single day.[16] It stands to reason that you can't possibly pay attention to all of the competing stimuli surrounding you, so you'll pay attention to only those stimuli that you consider relevant to your wants and needs at the time and screen out the rest. That's the process known as **selective attention**.

MARKETING IN PRACTICE

When Bombarding Backfires

Bombarding consumers with marketing messages can cause more harm than good. According to this article from Marketing Dive (https://openstax.org/r/studyadoverload), bombarding people with ads would negatively impact a brand. This article from the Advertising Association (https://openstax.org/r/newcredos) shares data that indicates bombardment and intrusiveness negatively impact perceptions of advertising.

How can you combat the issue? Quantcast outlines (https://openstax.org/r/bombardmentmight) ways to avoid ad bombardment.

CAREERS IN MARKETING

It's about Ability

Your personal brand will be a significant factor when it comes to finding a job. What does your personal brand say today? What is your marketing story? Is it what you want it to be? If not, what will you do to change it? The end-of-chapter content includes various ways to explore your personal brand to help you prepare for your job search.

How are you going to stand out among other candidates? What can you do with your résumé? According to Jason Shen's TED Talk, you should highlight your abilities and not your experience. He speaks to potential and how you can make yourself more attractive to potential employers by telling a story in a compelling way.

Click to view content (https://openstax.org/books/principles-marketing/pages/3-2-factors-that-influence-consumer-buying-behavior)

According to the American Marketing Association (AMA), you need to know yourself well. Self-knowledge will help you know the kind of work environment you perform best in and what kind of work you enjoy most. The AMA is a great place to learn how to stand out as a marketing job applicant (https://openstax.org/r/howtostandout), target companies, prepare your best résumé, and have a successful interview.

Check out these sources on how to stand out and ways you can beat the competition:

- Freemanleonard (https://openstax.org/r/marketersandcreat): "How Marketers and Creatives Can Stand Out in Today's Competitive Job Market"
- Recruiter.com (https://openstax.org/r/13triedandtrue): "13 Tried-and-True Creative Tactics Candidates Have Used to Stand Out in Interviews"
- Acadium (https://openstax.org/r/digitalmarketingcareer): "Launch Your Digital Marketing Career: How to Stand Out as a Candidate"
- Indeed (https://openstax.org/r/careeradvice): "8 Marketing Interview Questions to Expect"
- Entrepreneur (https://openstax.org/r/buildingyourbrand): "Building Your Brand Is How You Will Stand Out When Applying for a Job"
- Smart Insights (https://openstax.org/r/tacticstohelp): "7 Tactics to Help You Stand Out as a Marketer and Get Better Jobs"
- 24 Seven (https://openstax.org/r/10tipstoace): "10 Tips to Ace Your Next Marketing Job Interview"

If you want to go the extra mile in making yourself stand out, reach out to current marketers and ask them questions. You can find hundreds, even thousands, of current marketers on LinkedIn. Try targeting people from companies you're interested in or would like to learn more about. Look for specific people who are doing jobs that interest you. Going to an interview armed with information is incredibly powerful and will speak volumes to your interviewer. Be sure to find a way to work your completed research into the interview conversation because it will speak to your drive, curiosity, and ambition—all traits every interviewer wants to hear about. This will also be another way you can stand out from others interviewing for the job. Questions you could ask current marketers in preparation for an interview include (but by no means are limited to):

- What about you stood out in your interview process that made your current company hire you?

- Can you tell me about examples of people you've interviewed and why they stood out to you?
- How have candidates stood out when they spoke about their abilities in a job interview scenario?
- What are your thoughts on candidates sharing a college project with you as a way to demonstrate abilities?
- What advice do you have for me?

Be creative with your questions! Look online for other questions you could ask. Have fun!

Even the stimuli that people notice don't always come across in the way in which the marketers intended. **Selective distortion** is the tendency of people to interpret information in a way that fits their preconceived notions. This was demonstrated years ago when PepsiCo launched its Pepsi Challenge blind taste test commercials. Participants were presented with two colas in unmarked plastic cups and asked to taste both colas and choose the one they liked better. Then the tester would lift a small screen to reveal the brand the participants preferred. In TV commercials that aired for years, Pepsi showed the stunned reactions of loyal Coca-Cola drinkers who had chosen Pepsi over Coke in the test. One grandmother in a commercial said, "I can't believe it. I've never had a Pepsi in my life, but it must be better!"[17]

People also tend to forget much of what they learn and to retain information that supports their preconceived attitudes and beliefs. That's the power of **selective retention**, a bias by which you're more likely to remember messages that are closely related to your interests, values, and beliefs rather than those that are contrary to those values and beliefs.

Beliefs, feelings, and attitudes also play an important role in consumer buying behavior. **Beliefs** are consumer perceptions of how a product or brand performs relative to different attributes. These beliefs are generally formed through personal experience, advertising, and conversations with others, and they play a vital role because they can be either positive or negative. You can even hold both positive and negative beliefs about the same thing. For example, you may believe that coffee is good for you because it helps you focus and stay alert, but you may also worry about the effect of coffee on your health and the way it stains your teeth. Human beliefs aren't always accurate and can change according to the situation.

Consumer attitudes are a composite of a consumer's beliefs, feelings, and behavioral intentions toward a product or service (see Figure 3.9).

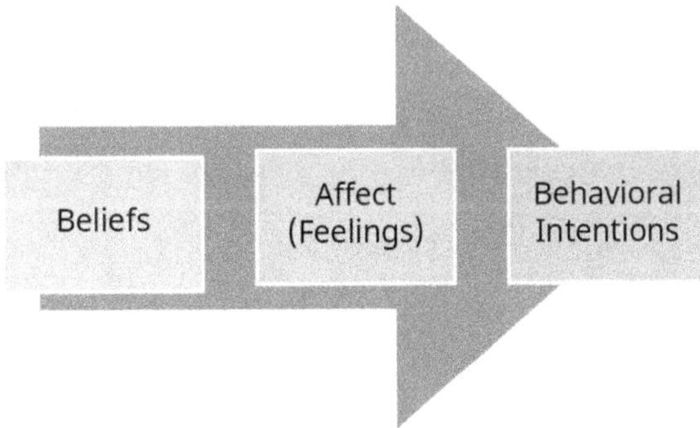

Figure 3.9 Components of Attitudes (attribution: Copyright Rice University, OpenStax, under CC BY 4.0 license)

We've already talked about beliefs, so let's focus for a moment on affect, or feeling. Consumers often have certain feelings toward brands, products, or services. Sometimes these feelings are based on people's beliefs, such as a vegetarian who can't stand the thought of eating a hamburger, but you may also have feelings that are relatively independent of your beliefs. For example, someone who has strong environmentalist beliefs may object to clearing forests to make way for a housing development but may have positive feelings toward Christmas trees because they subconsciously associate these trees with the experience that they had at Christmas as a child.

The behavioral intention aspect of an attitude is what you as a consumer plan to do—buy the brand or not buy the brand. As with affect, this is sometimes a logical consequence of your beliefs but may sometimes reflect other circumstances. Consider a consumer who doesn't particularly like a restaurant but will go there because it's an after-class gathering spot with her friends.[18]

Learning is still another important factor in consumer buying behavior. The fact is that consumer behavior is learned, and much of what you buy is based on your previous experiences with particular brands. This is commonly known as the Law of Effect, which asserts that, if an action is followed by a pleasant consequence, you're likely to repeat it; if the action is followed by an unpleasant consequence, you're less likely to repeat it. For example, let's say you buy an Apple iPhone. If your experience with the iPhone is positive, you'll probably be more inclined to buy another Apple product when you're looking for a tablet or wearable. On the other hand, if you've had a not-so-positive experience with your iPhone, you're likely to look at other brands when considering purchasing other devices.

MARKETING IN PRACTICE

Lessons in Psychology

Psychology is a big part of marketing. Insight into your customers' thinking will allow you to create marketing messages and stories that better speak to their needs. Learning, the process where customers acquire information they can apply to future purchases, is a foundational concept in marketing. Learn about the various types of learning and how they can impact marketing strategies from this Forbes article (https://openstax.org/r/becomeamindreader).

Situational Factors That Impact Consumer Buying Behavior

Situational factors influencing consumers are external (refer to Figure 3.10). These factors play an important role in how consumers experience a product and how these consumers' opinions are formed.

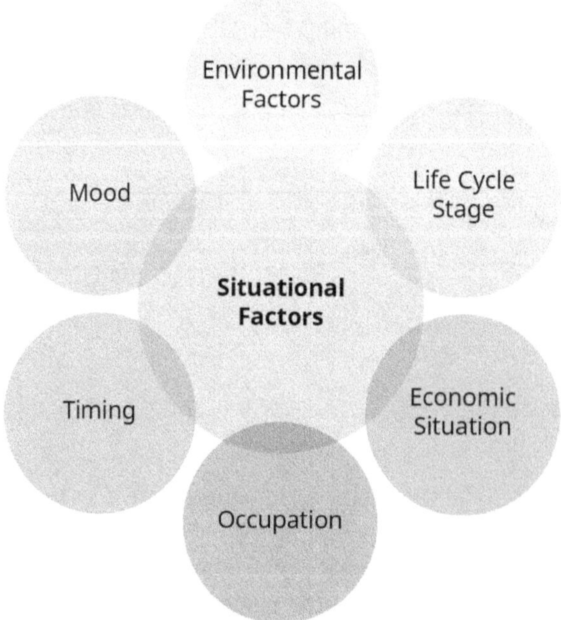

Figure 3.10 Situational Factors Influencing Consumer Buying Behavior (attribution: Copyright Rice University, OpenStax, under CC BY 4.0 license)

Environmental factors such as music, lighting, ambient noise, and even smells can either discourage or encourage a consumer's purchase decision. For example, researchers conducted a study on the effect of lighting on consumer purchases in a grocery store. They lit half the store with traditional fluorescent lighting and the other half of the building with LED lighting. Researchers conducted the study over 21 weeks and discovered that consumers bought 25 percent more products on the LED-lit side of the store.[19]

Spatial factors also play a role. The way a product is displayed may make it seem desirable, but a crowded store or a long line at the cash register can suddenly make that same product seem less desirable. Think about it: Have you ever seen a long line to check out at the cash register and put the product you intended to buy back on the shelf because it simply wasn't worth it to waste your time standing in line?

The Marketing in Practice feature box shows how sound and smell can affect consumers.

MARKETING IN PRACTICE

Abercrombie & Fitch

Figure 3.11 Psychological factors like smell and sound affect buying behavior, so Ambercrombie & Fitch utilizes fragrances and music as a way to attract customers. (credit: "Abercrombie & Fitch" by prayitnophotography/flickr, CC BY 2.0)

As consumers, people usually don't think twice about what a store smells or sounds like, the way it makes them feel or think, or what it makes them do. But Abercrombie & Fitch (A&F) thinks about it a lot (see Figure 3.11).

The company has its own line of men's fragrances called "Fierce," which is sprayed liberally in stores to give off what the company describes as a "lifestyle . . . packed with confidence and a bold, masculine attitude." A&F knows who it wants in its stores, and by associating its fragrance with its stores, it creates a self-fulfilling prophecy for its male clientele who, by wanting to smell like A&F, will be like the models and sales staff in the store.

A&F also plays loud club music throughout its stores, attracting young people who can withstand loud music longer, while older customers may run from it. It's just another way that A&F is enabling its stores to maintain a more youthful clientele and a "fresher" image.[20]

Watch this video on Abercrombie & Fitch's brand transformation for further insight on how A&F has positioned its retail brand Hollister as a global iconic teen brand and modernized the A&F brand to focus on young millennial consumers.

Click to view content (https://openstax.org/books/principles-marketing/pages/3-2-factors-that-influence-consumer-buying-behavior)

The social situation of shopping is another situational factor. Did you know that you're more likely to stop to look at certain products when you're in the company of a friend as opposed to a parent? The social aspect can even alter the price you're willing to pay. You might be more inclined to purchase a more expensive product when you're with a colleague or potential partner than you would if you're with a friend or spouse.[21]

The goal of your shopping trip is yet another situational factor. If you go to a store to look for a birthday present for your mother, your purpose is totally different than if you're casually shopping for a new pair of shoes. The reason for shopping dictates the kinds of products customers are willing to interact with at that time and may cause them to bypass certain products they would normally interact with on another shopping trip. This is even true at the grocery store. You'll interact with products differently if you're on your weekly shopping trip versus simply going into the store because you're out of milk.

Much like the purpose of your shopping trip, timing also influences your consumer behavior. If you're in a rush because it's Christmas Eve and you haven't bought a present for your best friend yet, you'll interact with fewer products than if you have hours to shop. Even if two people are looking for the same type of product, the one in a rush will probably end up with the most accessible product, whereas the leisurely consumer has time to weigh the price and quality of offerings.

Finally, your mood influences your buying behavior. Someone who is feeling sad or stressed interacts differently with products than a happy, relaxed shopper. The same can be said for someone who's fatigued versus someone who's full of energy.

MARKETING IN PRACTICE

Situational Factors

There are many examples where companies use situational factors in their marketing approaches. Here are several online sites and specific articles:

- Westin and the White Tea Signature Scent (https://openstax.org/r/transportedbyfragrance)
- The Aroma Trace (https://openstax.org/r/examplesofolfactory): "Best Examples of Olfactory Marketing in Companies"
- Sync Originals (https://openstax.org/r/musicpart): "10 Brands That Made Music Part of Their Marketing DNA"
- Omnify (https://openstax.org/r/lightingtechniques): "8 Simple Lighting Techniques That Boost Retail Sales"
- Science News (https://openstax.org/r/sciencedaily): "Does Background Noise Make Consumers Buy More Innovative Products?"
- Journal of the Academy of Marketing Science (https://openstax.org/r/springerlink): "Sounds Like a Healthy Retail Atmosphere Strategy: Effects of Ambient Music and Background Noise on Food Sales"

Knowledge Check

It's time to check your knowledge on the concepts presented in this section. Refer to the Answer Key at the end of the book for feedback.

1. You're at the shopping mall looking for a new pair of shoes when you smell the wonderful aroma of freshly baked pretzels. Before you know it, you've bought a giant pretzel with cheese sauce. What type of factors influenced your purchase?
   a. Psychological factors
   b. Social factors

   c. Situational factors

   d. Personal factors

2. Traditionally, in China, the bride's wedding gown is red because the color is associated with good luck, happiness, and prosperity. Which influence on consumer buying behavior does this illustrate?
   a. Culture
   b. Social class
   c. Lifestyle
   d. Personality

3. Jazmine purchases a wireless alarm system for her apartment. According to Maslow's hierarchy of needs, which level of needs does this purchase reflect?
   a. Physiological
   b. Safety/security
   c. Self-esteem
   d. Social

4. The tendency of people to interpret information in a way that supports what they already believe is known as ________.
   a. cognitive dissonance
   b. selective attention
   c. selective retention
   d. selective distortion

5. Attitudes are a composite of a consumer's beliefs, feelings about, and ________ toward a product or service.
   a. predispositions
   b. behavioral intentions
   c. preconceived notions
   d. attributions

3.3 | The Consumer Purchasing Decision Process

Learning Outcomes

By the end of this section, you will be able to:

LO 1 Explain the first stage in the consumer purchasing decision process.

LO 2 Summarize the second stage in the consumer purchasing decision process.

LO 3 Describe the third stage in the consumer purchasing decision process.

LO 4 Discuss the fourth stage in the consumer purchasing decision process.

LO 5 Explain the fifth and final stage in the consumer purchasing decision process.

Consumer Decision Process

This chapter has examined many of the factors that influence consumer buying behavior, but behind the visible act of making a purchase lies an important decision process that takes place before, during, and after the purchase of a product or service. Figure 3.12 shows the five stages of the **consumer decision process**.

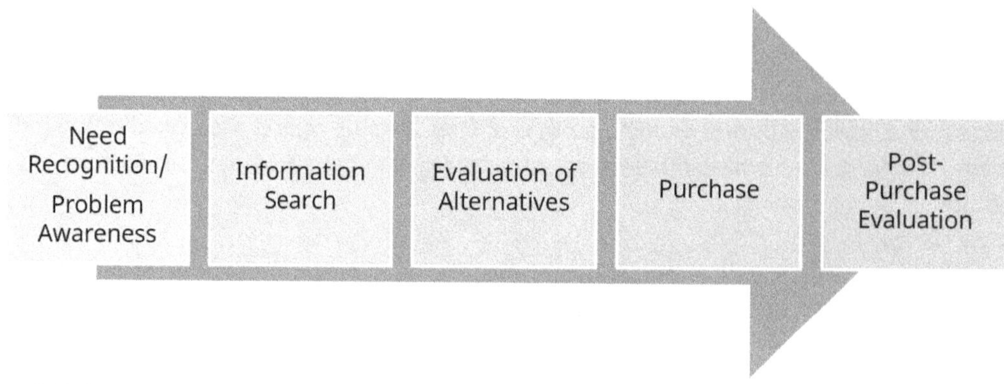

Figure 3.12 The Consumer Decision Process (attribution: Copyright Rice University, OpenStax, under CC BY 4.0 license)

A buyer passes through five stages of the consumer decision process when making choices about which products or services to buy. Let's examine each, starting at the beginning.

Stage 1: Need Recognition

The buying process starts when you sense a difference between your actual state and your desired state. This is referred to as problem awareness or need recognition. You might become aware of a need through internal stimuli (such as feeling hungry or thirsty when you're on a long road trip) or external stimuli (such as passing a bakery and smelling the wonderful aroma of cookies baking).

Sometimes recognizing the problem or need is easy. You've run out of toilet paper or milk. But other times recognizing the problem or issue is more complicated. For example, think about this first stage in terms of your decision to enroll in college. What was the stimulus that triggered your interest in attending college? Are you a working adult who has recognized that upward advancement in your company won't happen without possessing a college degree? Have you long aspired to be an entrepreneur, and you wanted to get some business and marketing courses under your belt so that you're better prepared for the challenges of entrepreneurship? Perhaps a career in marketing has been on your internal radar since high school, and you've decided to take the plunge and get your degree in marketing. Or perhaps, after graduating from high school, your parents gave you an ultimatum—either find a job or enroll in college.

Stage 2: Information Search

Now that you've identified the problem or need, you'll be inclined to search for more information. There are two different search states. The milder search state is called "heightened attention," in which you become more receptive to information about the product or service. The stronger search state is called "active information search," in which you might do some research about the product or service on the Internet (referred to as an internal search), ask friends and/or family members their opinions (what's known as an external search), or even visit stores to view and touch the product (called an experiential search).

Keep in mind, of course, that not all needs/problems identified in Stage 1 will require this second stage. If you've run out of bread or toilet paper, you're probably not going to do an information search; rather, you'll just go to the store to buy what you need, and your information search may be as simple as checking prices at the grocery store to see if your favorite brand is available or another brand is on sale. However, purchase decisions of more consequence will usually trigger an information search of some type.

Again, consider the process you went through in deciding which college to attend. What sources of information did you use to find out about the colleges or universities you considered attending? Did you look at their websites, talk with friends or family who attended that school, or perhaps even visit the campus and meet with an admissions counselor?

Stage 3: Evaluation of Alternatives

Consumers are said to view a product or service as a "bundle of product attributes," and you evaluate several attributes of a product or service in reaching your purchase decision. For example, if you're buying a smartphone, you'll consider factors such as battery life, speed, storage capacity, or price. If you're booking a hotel, you'll probably consider its location, cleanliness, free Wi-Fi, whether it has a free breakfast in the morning or a pool, and of course price.

What bundle of attributes did you use when evaluating your college alternatives? You may have considered factors such as location, size of the campus, whether the school had the program of study you wanted, if it had online learning, and cost.

Stage 4: Purchase Decision

This stage involves actually reaching a decision on the purchase of the product or service. One way people navigate all the information, evaluations, and choices in their purchase decision is to use **heuristics**—mental shortcuts or "rules of thumb." Heuristics are types of preexisting value judgments that people use to make decisions.

For example, do you believe that the more expensive product is always of higher quality than the lower-priced product? That's known as the price = quality heuristic. Brand loyalty is another heuristic people use in reaching their purchase decisions. For example, do you eat cereal? Do you always buy the same brand, or do you buy whatever's on sale or a brand for which you have a coupon? Country of origin is still another heuristic. Given a choice, do you prefer to buy products made in the United States versus products made in other countries?

How did you make your purchase decision to enroll in your college or university? What heuristics did you use?

Stage 5: Post-Purchase Evaluation

After purchasing the product or service, you'll experience either satisfaction or dissatisfaction. You may have second thoughts after making a purchase decision, and these doubts lead to **cognitive dissonance**, or buyer's remorse—tension caused by uncertainty about the correctness of your decision. This may lead you to search for additional information to confirm the wisdom of your decision in order to reduce that tension.

What determines if a consumer is very satisfied, somewhat satisfied, or dissatisfied with his or her purchase? Satisfaction is a function of the closeness between the buyer's expectations and the product's perceived performance. If the product's performance falls short of expectations, you'll be dissatisfied. If the product's performance meets your expectations, you'll be satisfied, and if the product's performance exceeds your expectations, you'll be very satisfied.

Think about the purchase decision you made when you decided to enroll in your college or university. Are you very satisfied, satisfied, or dissatisfied with your decision? Refer to Table 3.1 for a summary of the five stages of the consumer decision process.

Stage	Description
Stage 1: Need Recognition	The buying process actually starts when you sense a difference between your actual state and your desired state. This is referred to as problem awareness or need recognition. You might become aware of the need through internal stimuli (such as feeling hungry or thirsty when you're on a long road trip) or external stimuli (such as passing a bakery and smelling the wonderful aroma of cookies baking).
Stage 2: Information Search	Once the problem of need is identified, the next step is to search for more information that will help you make a choice. There are two different search states—heightened attention and active information search.

Table 3.1 Five Stages of the Consumer Decision Process

Stage	Description
Stage 3: Evaluation of Alternatives	This is the stage in the process where you'll evaluate several attributes of the product or service in making a decision on a purchase.
Stage 4: Purchase Decision	This stage involves actually reaching a decision on the purchase of the product or service.
Stage 5: Post-Purchase Evaluation	After purchasing the product or service, you'll now experience either satisfaction or dissatisfaction. You may have second thoughts after making the purchase decision, and these doubts lead to cognitive dissonance, or buyer's remorse. This may lead you to search for additional information to confirm the wisdom of your decision in order to reduce that tension.

Table 3.1 Five Stages of the Consumer Decision Process

CAREERS IN MARKETING

You Are Also a Consumer

Learn about the five stages of the consumer decision process in this video from Open Up (Upatras) Entrepreneurship and this article from Business Study Notes (https://openstax.org/r/stagesconsumerdecision).

Click to view content (https://openstax.org/books/principles-marketing/pages/3-3-the-consumer-purchasing-decision-process)

GWI, a company that researches global consumer thinking, published its 2022 consumer trends report (https://openstax.org/r/connectingthedots), which showed that consumers' needs and priorities have shifted. Read the report and see if you find the same results for yourself. Have your priorities and needs changed since the pandemic hit? What are the other factors influencing your needs assessment?

Several tools can help you with a personal needs assessment. Practice your marketing skills on yourself by trying this needs assessment worksheet (https://openstax.org/r/selfassessment). This personal awareness will help you in many ways, including finding the right job that best fits your interests and abilities. Also take a few assessments and compare your results to better identify jobs worth learning more about. There are several free career aptitude tests to try:

- 123 Career Test (https://openstax.org/r/careertest)
- Interest Assessment (https://openstax.org/r/interestassessment)
- Work Values Matcher (https://openstax.org/r/workvaluesmatcher)
- A Personality Color Test (https://openstax.org/r/personalitytest)

In addition to career aptitude tests, personality tests assess your skill level and your ability to succeed in a career. Try a few of these:

- Typology Central Jung Personality Test (https://openstax.org/r/typologycentral)
- Myers-Briggs Type Indicator (https://openstax.org/r/mbtipersonalitytype)

The Balance Careers site also provides a wealth of resources (https://openstax.org/r/freecareeraptitude) on additional aptitude, personality, talent, and preemployment tests. It's worth your time to dive into this information to help you identify which career might be your best fit.

Knowledge Check

It's time to check your knowledge on the concepts presented in this section. Refer to the Answer Key at the end of the book for feedback.

1. Janelle and her sister are planning a reception for their parents' 50th wedding anniversary. They have looked at several venues, comparing size, location and accommodations, photo opportunities, and parking. What stage in the consumer decision process model does this best illustrate?
   a. Need recognition
   b. Information search
   c. Evaluation of alternatives
   d. Purchase decision

2. Ra'Shana's car broke down on the way to work, and she realizes that she needs to quickly find a repair shop to take care of her vehicle. Which stage of the consumer decision process model does this represent?
   a. Need recognition
   b. Information search
   c. Evaluation of alternatives
   d. Purchase decision

3. Jason is considering buying a new laptop computer. He is researching different models based on factors like the processor, the hard drive capacity and speed, RAM, operating system, and price. He has also asked a few friends what they like and dislike about their laptops. Which stage of the consumer decision process model does this illustrate?
   a. Problem identification
   b. Evaluation of alternatives
   c. Information search
   d. Post-purchase evaluation

4. What is a heuristic?
   a. It is the mental conflict that occurs when a person's behaviors and beliefs do not align.
   b. It is a mental shortcut that allows people to solve problems and make judgments more quickly and efficiently.
   c. It is a function of the closeness between your expectations of a product or service and its actual performance.
   d. It is the process of assigning the cause of behavior to either internal or external characteristics.

5. Nathan and his husband have decided to purchase a new car. They have narrowed their list to a few models and visited a few dealerships to see the models and test-drive them. Which stage of the consumer decision process does this illustrate?
   a. Need recognition
   b. Information search
   c. Evaluation of alternatives
   d. Purchase decision

3.4 | Ethical Issues in Consumer Buying Behavior

Learning Outcomes

By the end of this section, you will be able to:

LO 1 Describe ethical issues related to consumer buying behavior.
LO 2 Identify the characteristics of an ethical consumer.

Ethical Issues in Consumer Buying Behavior

All purchase behavior is in some sense ethical, involving moral judgment. For example, a consumer is concerned about the abuse of human rights in a foreign country, so corporate involvement in that country may be a factor in the consumer's purchasing decisions. Similarly, consumers concerned about animal rights may consider whether a cosmetic product has been tested on animals. For example, in one 2017 survey, 32 percent of US cosmetics consumers reported that they would "very likely" stop purchasing their favorite brand if the manufacturer tested on animals.[22]

Ethical Consumerism

Economic theory suggests that consumers seek to maximize utility (the total satisfaction received from consuming a product or service) at the lowest cost possible, so it follows that firms that have higher costs of production will be driven out of the market. Recently, more and more firms have started using "ethical" labels as a means of **product differentiation**, a marketing strategy in which a brand identifies the one thing that makes it genuinely different from competitors and then leverages that notion in its branding and messaging. But what does this look like in action? Let's take a quick look at one popular brand that honed its differentiation strategy and succeeded as a result.

Like many fast-food chains, Chipotle (see Figure 3.13) focuses on the quality of its ingredients above all else. One of the brand's hallmarks is that it works with family farmers within a 130-mile radius of each of its locations and attempts whenever possible to source local and sustainably raised ingredients. Additionally, Chipotle eliminated genetically modified (GMO) foods from its menu, citing public concerns about the safety of genetically modified ingredients.[23]

Figure 3.13 Chipotle works with family farmers and has eliminated genetically modified foods as a way to differentiate itself in the market. (credit: "Chipotle" by JeepersMedia/flickr, CC BY 2.0)

MARKETING IN PRACTICE

Ethics and Corporations

Hundreds of companies are known for being ethical, including Patagonia (more information later in this chapter), TOMS, and Conscious Coffees, among others. Read about five examples of truly ethical companies (https://openstax.org/r/trulyethicalcompanies) and how they are working to make an impact in their markets.

Business Insider provides a list of the most ethical companies (https://openstax.org/r/themostethicalcompanies) in the world. Do any of the companies on this list surprise you? Are there companies missing that you think should be included?

What corporate ethical decisions are you aware of that have positively impacted a company's brand? Here are 10 examples (https://openstax.org/r/ethicaldecisionmaking) where companies made the ethical decision.

Many consumers research companies before making a purchasing decision. Is the ethical footprint of a company important to you? Does it impact where you purchase products and services? Why or why not?

Are You an Ethical Consumer?

At its most basic level, being an ethical consumer simply means choosing goods that are ethically sourced, produced, and distributed. Ethical consumerism has become something of a buzzword over the last decade, and organizations are taking notice of consumers' expectations in terms of social and environmental practices. Consider some statistics to better understand how consumers put ethical consumerism in practice:

- According to a Statista poll, 90 percent of US survey respondents indicated that they would boycott a brand if they discovered that the company was engaged in irresponsible business practices.[24]
- Research from Mintel, a market research firm, indicates that 56 percent of US consumers indicate that they would no longer do business with organizations they believe to be unethical.[25]
- A recent survey showed that consumers seek a match between their beliefs and those exemplified by the organization. According to the survey, an overwhelming 72 percent of respondents indicated that they purchase goods and services from companies with beliefs similar to theirs in terms of environmental preservation and child labor.[26]

By choosing brands that align with their values, consumers are voting with their pocketbooks. Modern consumers are more than willing to take their business elsewhere if they perceive a disconnect between their values and those of the organization, and they will likely share their sentiments on social media.

MARKETING IN PRACTICE

Consumer Ethics

Do consumers care about ethics when making a purchasing decision? You can find marketers on both sides of the fence on this hotly debated topic. Some studies show that consumers are interested in products that align with their values. Other studies show that consumers aren't interested. According to an article from *Kellogg Insight* (https://openstax.org/r/productisethical) (a publication from the Kellogg School of Management at Northwestern University), current research by Jacob Teeny, an assistant professor of marketing at Kellogg, suggests that consumers care.

This Jason Garman TEDx Talk focuses on ethical consumerism and the power of having a choice and a voice through purchasing decisions.

Click to view content (https://openstax.org/books/principles-marketing/pages/3-4-ethical-issues-in-consumer-buying-behavior)

Are you new to ethical shopping? Watch this video to learn the basics about shopping ethically. Also check out this article to learn specific reasons for being an ethical consumer (https://openstax.org/r/whyshopethically).

Click to view content (https://openstax.org/books/principles-marketing/pages/3-4-ethical-issues-in-consumer-buying-behavior)

This hotly debated topic is becoming a larger part of the conversation in marketing with the increase of eco-friendly products on the market. It's important in your marketing work that you're aware of the discussion, as it will help you to become a great marketer.

COMPANIES WITH A CONSCIENCE

Patagonia

Figure 3.14 Patagonia is known for its ethical leadership and environmental mission. (credit: "Trekkin!" by Pierce Martin/Zach Dischner/flickr, CC BY 2.0)

If you're looking for a company that's a leader in environmental and social responsibility on many fronts, look no further than Patagonia, a designer of outdoor clothing gear for the "silent sports"—climbing, surfing, skiing, snowboarding, fly fishing, and trail running (see Figure 3.14). Just start with Patagonia's mission statement: "Build the best product, cause no unnecessary harm, use business to inspire and implement solutions to the environmental crisis."

In addition to being fair-trade certified for all of its sewing production, the brand knows and publicly discloses all of its first-tier suppliers and is actively working to map out the rest down to the farm level for the raw materials used in its gear. Many consider Patagonia to be an outdoor brand, but it offers products in many categories, from sundresses to skinny jeans.[27]

A large portion of the company's products are made from recycled materials or raw organic cotton. Plastic soda bottles are made into fleece jackets, guayule plants are made into wetsuits, and they take back worn-out Patagonia products that consumers return to the store at no charge and then recycle them into their supply chain. Look no further if you want to be an ethical consumer![28]

Read more (https://openstax.org/r/supplychainenvironmental) about Patagonia's environmental responsibility program.

Chapter Summary

This chapter defined consumer markets and consumer buying behavior and discussed the buyer's black box, the concept that attempts to mark the pattern consumers follow when making a purchase decision. It also categorized consumer buying behavior into four types: complex buying behavior, dissonance-reducing buying behavior, habitual buying behavior, and variety-seeking buying behavior.

This chapter also looked at the cultural, social, personal, psychological, and situational factors that influence consumer behavior and scrutinized the stages of the consumer decision process. Finally, it examined the role of ethics in consumer buying behavior and discussed ethical consumerism.

Key Terms

4Ps the "marketing mix"—product, price, promotion, and place

attitudes a learned set of emotions, beliefs, and behaviors developed toward a particular brand, object, person, thing, or event

beliefs ideas that a person holds as being true

buyer's black box a model used in the study of the buying behavior of consumers

cognitive dissonance the mental conflict that occurs when a person's behaviors and beliefs do not align; also referred to as buyer's remorse

complex buying behavior the consumer buying behavior that occurs when the consumer is highly involved with the purchase and perceives significant differences between brands

consumer buying behavior the actions taken by consumers before buying a product or service

consumer decision process the process through which consumers become aware of and identify their needs, collect information on how to best solve those needs, evaluate alternative options, make a purchasing decision, and evaluate their purchase

consumer market a market where consumers purchase products and/or services for consumption

cultural factors a set of values or ideologies of a particular community or group of individuals that include culture, subcultures, social class, and gender

culture the pattern of learned and shared behavior and beliefs of a particular social, ethnic, or age group

dissonance-reducing buying behavior any activity aimed at decreasing the tension or feelings of discomfort and unease that accompany an unfamiliar purchase

economic situation a measure of a consumer's income and financial situation

environmental factors factors such as music, lighting, ambient noise, and smell that can either discourage or encourage a consumer's purchase decision

family a group of persons united by ties of marriage, blood, or adoption, or those who live in the same household

gender the socially constructed roles, behaviors, and norms of individuals, which vary between societies and over time

habitual buying behavior consumer buying decisions made out of "habit" and without much deliberation or product comparison

heuristics mental shortcuts that allow people to solve problems and make judgments quickly and efficiently

learning the acquisition of knowledge or skills through experience, study, or being taught

life cycle stages various stages in a human's life, including fetus, baby, childhood, adolescence, adulthood, and elderly

lifestyle the habits, attitudes, tastes, moral standards, economic level, etc. that together constitute the mode of living for an individual or group

Maslow's hierarchy of needs a theory of motivation by Abraham Maslow which states that five categories of human needs dictate an individual's behavior

motivation the process that initiates, guides, and maintains goal-oriented behaviors

occupation an activity or task with which one occupies oneself, usually the productive activity, service, trade, or craft for which one is regularly paid

perception   the manner in which sensory information is organized, interpreted, and consciously experienced

personality   the combination of characteristics or qualities that form an individual's distinctive character

product differentiation   a marketing strategy in which a brand identifies the one thing that makes it genuinely different from competitors

reference groups   groups that consumers compare themselves to or associate with

roles   the set of norms, values, behaviors, and personality characteristics attached to a status

selective attention   the process of directing one's awareness to relevant stimuli while ignoring irrelevant stimuli in the environment

selective distortion   a tendency of people to interpret information in a manner that supports what they already believe

selective retention   the tendency of people to retain only part of the information to which they are exposed

social class   a group of people within a society that possesses the same or similar socioeconomic status

social factors   factors that are prevalent in the society where a consumer lives

status   the relative social, professional, or other standing of an individual

subculture   a cultural group within a larger culture, often having beliefs or interests at variance with those in the larger culture

variety-seeking buying behavior   the buying tendencies of consumers who do not have a high involvement with a product when there are significant differences between brands

Applied Marketing Knowledge: Discussion Questions

1. What sort of purchasing behavior do you, as a student, exhibit? Do you stop by a convenience store and buy a soda on the way to class? This is convenience shopping behavior, and the business is located, conveniently, in your daily pathway. Do you sometimes buy a different beverage, perhaps an energy drink or a bottled iced tea? You're exhibiting variety-seeking behavior. When the time came for you to choose your college, what sort of shopping behavior did you engage in?

2. You belong to many membership groups. You might be a member of the college soccer team or sing in a choir. Right now, you likely aspire to join the group of college graduates. Why is it so important for marketers to know which groups consumers have joined or refer to when making purchases?

3. Businesses send you thousands of marketing messages each day through the radio, TV, Internet, billboards, and bus benches. You sort through these messages, perhaps unconsciously, and decide which ones to pay attention to. This is called selective attention. Which messages are most influential right now in your life as a student? Messages regarding your social life? Personal life? Psychological factors relating to your motivation to try a new product? Cultural factors such as gender-related products? A situational factor such as a flat tire? Where would you find an example of each message?

4. Provide a recent example of a purchase you made and describe your progress through the stages of the consumer decision process model.

5. You just locked your door and are heading out to get a haircut. How do these two needs—safety through the locked door and esteem through the haircut—fit with Maslow's hierarchy of needs? Why is this hierarchy helpful for marketers in understanding human needs and resulting buying behavior?

Critical Thinking Exercises

1. Research has shown that consumers' buying behavior changes over time, reflecting their age or stage of the family life cycle. Visit Salesfloor.com and read the summaries (https://openstax.org/r/shoppinghabits) this site offers on age-based shopping habits. Do you agree with research findings that despite being bombarded with digital content, Zoomers still prefer to stop in store? Do you research products thoroughly through search engines, reviews, and social media before purchasing? Explain why you agree

or disagree with this study's conclusions about generational buying behavior.

2. One way consumers evaluate alternatives is by identifying the "bundle of attributes" of a product or service. Assume that you're in the market for a new smartphone. What would that bundle of attributes look like? In other words, what attributes do you consider important, and how would you rank the importance of these features on a scale of 1 to 5, with 5 being the attribute of greatest importance and 1 being the attribute of lowest importance? Some attributes are already listed, but you can add your own attributes as well. Complete Table 3.2 with your rankings.

Attributes Considered	Importance of Attribute
Storage	
Battery Life	
Processing	
Price	
Ease of Use	
Durability	
Camera Quality	

Table 3.2 The Bundle of Attributes

3. Delve into McDonald's, a company mentioned at the beginning of this chapter. Does McDonald's have an environmental sustainability statement? If so, list evidence showing how McDonald's carries out this policy.

☼ Building Your Personal Brand

Knowing yourself well is essential to helping you identify your personal brand. How would you characterize your personal brand right now? Is it what you want it to be?

There are numerous free tools to help you gain self-awareness. The Careers in Marketing section earlier in this chapter lists numerous resources that you could try. Or you can try this short personality assessment (https://openstax.org/r/humanmetrics) that is similar to the Myers-Briggs Type Indicator. After you complete the assessment, your personality information will be revealed. You'll learn if you're extroverted or introverted, thinking or feeling, sensing or intuitive, and judging or perceiving. The results are shown as a four-letter acronym (for example, ENFP or ISTJ), and there are 16 possibilities that could arise.

Is the outcome a surprise to you, or is it as expected? Does it help explain some of your friendships, how you approach your studies, or the feelings you have? Keep your personality type in mind as you gain better understanding of yourself and others, and especially as you begin to develop and express your personal brand.

♟ What Do Marketers Do?

Have you ever wondered where analysts gather consumer behavior data and how they make sense of it? One way to find out is to ask someone who currently does this job. Using LinkedIn, conduct a search for data analysts in your geographic area and invite one or more to connect with you through the LinkedIn platform.

Once connected, send a message to each one telling them who you are and that you're a marketing student. Request a 15-minute phone conversation with them to ask them about their job. Come prepared to the phone conversation with a list of questions you want to ask. Be prepared to go off script and ask questions that come to mind on the spot. You can learn a lot about various marketing careers, and you can make great contacts by simply asking the right questions! What questions do you want to ask? You might consider some of the following:

- How did you get started in this area of marketing?
- Where do you collect data from, and how do you complete an analysis?
- What happens after you conduct an analysis?
- Do you help make marketing decisions based on your analysis?
- What areas of the company does your analysis impact?
- What specific courses did you take to prepare you for this job/career?

Closing Company Case

Wired Coffee Bar

Figure 3.15 Recognizing an opportunity to open a coffee shop in a small community where none existed, Wired Coffee Bar was launched. (credit: reproduced with permission of Wired Coffee Bar)

During high school and college, Lisa worked in an upscale retail boutique. On the mornings Lisa opened the store, she grew to love the deep, rich smell of the coffee that would permeate the air from the local gourmet food store across from the boutique. Her love for coffee only deepened as she experienced local cafés throughout her travels while in college. In the back of her mind, she glamorized opening her own café.

Throughout her early thirties, Lisa looked at locations, talked with coffee entrepreneurs, developed business feasibility studies, and dreamed of one day having her own place. One big problem was finding the right geographical area where a small, independent coffee shop would be successful.

After moving for the fifth time, Lisa realized the new, growing community where she now lived with her two small children lacked one important thing—good coffee. The town was rapidly expanding and was the fastest-growing community in the state of Tennessee. This might be the time and place to revisit the idea of a coffee shop.

Every feasibility study Lisa completed pointed to the need for strong community support. This new town had two important ingredients—college students and a burgeoning population. The area was abundant with many different church denominations; a few small, local colleges; and some new international businesses that had recently relocated to the community.

With no coffee shop in the town, Lisa believed her concept could be successful. Currently, if you wanted a coffee, the nearest place to grab a cup was a Starbucks, which was over 20 minutes away. Starbucks made specialty coffee mainstream, but it seemed that sitting down to enjoy a cup of coffee was becoming a thing of the past. As more and more people began grabbing their coffee from the drive-through, could a community coffee bar with a wide variety of seating options and complimentary Wi-Fi be successful?

Going forward with the idea, Lisa began to develop Wired Coffee Bar. Prior to opening, Lisa went to every local community event and provided free coffee for people to sample. Once the community had a taste of the coffee and an expectation for the opening, there was an eager clientele waiting in line on the first day of business. One customer even hugged Lisa to thank her for bringing coffee to the community.

The concept took off, and soon Lisa was a purveyor of fine coffee. Wired Coffee Bar was widely supported by the community. The local churches loved to meet for a coffee drink and connect with friends and neighbors. Throughout the day, business was conducted at the tables over a coffee, and into the evening hours college students gathered to study and talk with friends.

If you looked at the clientele throughout the day, you could see the "grab and go" customers who came every morning to get their mochas, lattes, and cappuccinos. Into the late-morning hours, the tables filled up with business meetings—builders and their new clients, PTA groups, pharmaceutical sales reps strategizing for the day and grabbing coffee for customers, and moms meeting for coffee before picking up kids at school. As the afternoon wore on, the seats would fill up with high school students meeting with tutors and friends to complete homework. The later evening hours had every seat filled with college students doing class projects or just "hanging out" with friends.

Wired Coffee Bar had a focused niche of coffee and community. The menu wasn't complex. It featured just coffee—hot, iced, and frozen. Wired also offered a variety of teas that could be served hot or iced. Along with the drink options, customers could choose from a selection of sweet or savory locally baked muffins, scones, quiche, cookies, and coffee cakes. But Wired was not a restaurant; they were a true coffee bar.

With a regular and steady customer base, Wired could see the busier times happening when school was in session, and then summers saw a lighter revenue stream as the college students left and the local families took summer vacations out of town. The coffee business definitely needed the local support to offset the vacation schedules of the college students.

Just as Wired Coffee Bar was hitting its stride, new coffee shops started to enter the once-dormant community. Each new coffee location offered a drive-through, something Wired Coffee Bar never wants to be—fast-food coffee. As Lisa looked at ways to create more business, provide good coffee, and differentiate from the masses, she wondered if her concept could survive the hustle and the need for quicker service and a less laid-back atmosphere.

For further resources, visit the company website (https://openstax.org/r/thewiredcoffeebar). They also have a Facebook page (https://openstax.org/r/facebookwiredcoffeebar) and an Instagram account (@getwiredcoffee (https://openstax.org/r/getwiredcoffee)).

Case Questions

1. What type of consumer buying behavior are consumers exhibiting when they are buying coffee?

2. Consumers are faced with many different influences when they are making purchasing decisions. What social influences have the greatest impact on the decision to purchase coffee from Wired Coffee Bar? What personal influences have the greatest impact?

3. What situational factors may influence consumers to purchase from Wired Coffee Bar versus Starbucks?

4. How might Wired Coffee Bar further differentiate itself from other coffee bars as consumers search for

alternatives in their buyer decision-making process?

References

1. Daniel Campos, "Committing to the Core: How McDonald's Innovated to Survive (and Thrive) During the COVID-19 Pandemic," Digital Innovation and Transformation (February 10, 2021), accessed August 04, 2021, https://digital.hbs.edu/platform-digit/submission/committing-to-the-core-how-mcdonalds-innovated-to-survive-and-thrive-during-the-covid-19-pandemic/.

2. MSG Management Study Guide. (n.d.), accessed August 4, 2021, https://www.managementstudyguide.com/cultural-factors-affecting-consumer-behaviour.htm.

3. "What Is Social Class?" (n.d.), accessed March 7, 2022, https://udel.edu/~cmarks/What%20is%20social%20class.htm.

4. Editor, "Women vs. Men—Gender Differences in Purchase Decision Making," zoovu Blog (July 16, 2019), accessed September 19, 2021, https://zoovu.com/blog/women-vs-men-gender-differences-in-purchase-decision-making/.

5. Kendall (@kendalljenner) • Instagram photos and videos (n.d.), accessed March 7, 2022, https://www.instagram.com/kendalljenner/.

6. Leo Messi (@leomessi) • Instagram photos and videos (n.d.), accessed March 7, 2022, https://www.instagram.com/leomessi/.

7. Statista Research Department, "US Population by Generation 2019," Statista (September 19, 2021), accessed March 7, 2022, https://www.statista.com/statistics/797321/us-population-by-generation/.

8. "The Online Shopping Habits of Today's Baby Boomers," SkuLocal (November 12, 2018), accessed June 13, 2022, https://www.skulocal.com/insights/the-online-shopping-habits-of-todays-baby-boomers/.

9. Statista Research Department, "US Population by Generation 2019," Statista (September 19, 2021).

10. *Consumer Insight: Generation X-fona.* (n.d.), accessed March 7, 2022, https://www.fona.com/wp content/uploads/2019/03/0319-FONA-Consumer-Insight_Gen-X.pdf.

11. Statista Research Department, "US Population by Generation 2019," Statista (September 19, 2021), accessed March 7, 2022, https://www.statista.com/statistics/797321/us-population-by-generation/.

12. Shannon Ciricillo, "What Are Millennials Buying: The Gen Y Shopping Guide, The Hub (July 7, 2019), accessed August 4, 2021, https://thehhub.com/2019/07/07/what-are-millennials-buying-the-gen-y-shopping-guide/.

13. Ibid.

14. Kendra Cherry, "What Is Personality?" verywellmind, accessed August 4, 2021, https://www.verywellmind.com/what-is-personality-2795416.

15. Sallie B. Middlebrook, "Personality and Related Characteristics That Affect Consumer Buying Behavior," ToughNickel (January 8, 2013), accessed March 7, 2022, https://toughnickel.com/industries/Buyer-Characteristics-and-Consumer-Behavior.

16. Sam Carr, "How Many Ads Do We See A Day? 2021 Daily Ad Exposure Revealed!" PPC Project (May 12, 2021), accessed August 4, 2021, https://ppcprotect.com/how-many-ads-do-we-see-a-day/.

17. Mithun Sridharan, "Selective Perception Marketing: How Can Big Data Help?" Think Insights (March 7, 2022), accessed June 13, 2022, https://thinkinsights.net/digital/selective-perception-marketing-big-data/.

18. Lars Perner, "Consumer Behavior: Attitudes," University of Southern California Marshall (n.d.), accessed March 7, 2022, https://www.consumerpsychologist.com/cb_Attitudes.html.

19. "How Grocery Store Lighting Impacts Customer Decisions," Stratus (May 13, 2021), accessed September 28, 2021, https://www.stratusunlimited.com/news/how-grocery-store-lighting-impacts-customer-decisions/.

20. Humayun Khan, "How Retailers Manipulate Sight, Smell, and Sound to Trigger Purchase Behavior in Consumers," *Shopify* Retail Blog (April 25, 2016), accessed June 13, 2022, https://www.shopify.com/retail/119926083-how-retailers-manipulate-sight-smell-and-sound-to-trigger-purchase-behavior-in-consumers.

21. Dana Severson, "Theories of Situational Factors That Influence Customers," Chron. (November 21, 2017), accessed August 4, 2021, https://smallbusiness.chron.com/theories-situational-factors-influence-customers-78765.html.

22. Statista Research Department, "Share of US Consumers Who Would Stop Purchasing from Cosmetics Companies That Test on Animals as of April 2017," Statista (April 26, 2017), accessed September 28, 2021, https://www.statista.com/statistics/753362/cosmetic-animal-testing-attitudes/.

23. Herosmyth Staff, "9 Perfect Brand Examples of Why It Pays to Differentiate," Herosmyth (February 24, 2020), accessed June 13, 2022, https://www.herosmyth.com/article/9-perfect-brand-examples-why-it-pays-differentiate.

24. Yaqub M., "20+ Fascinating Ethical Consumers Statistics Need to Know in 2022," Renolon (January 18, 2022), accessed March 7,

2022, https://www.renolon.com/ethical-consumers-statistics/.

25. Ibid.

26. Ibid.

27. Cory Baldwin, "Ethical, Sustainable Brands You Can Really Trust," Vox (August 22, 2017), accessed August 4, 2021, https://www.vox.com/2017/8/22/16171338/ethical-sustainable-fashion-brands-where-to-buy-sustainable-clothes.

28. Reasons We Love Patagonia. (n.d.). accessed August 4, 2021, from https://www.wearedore.com/photos/reasons-we-love-patagonia/.

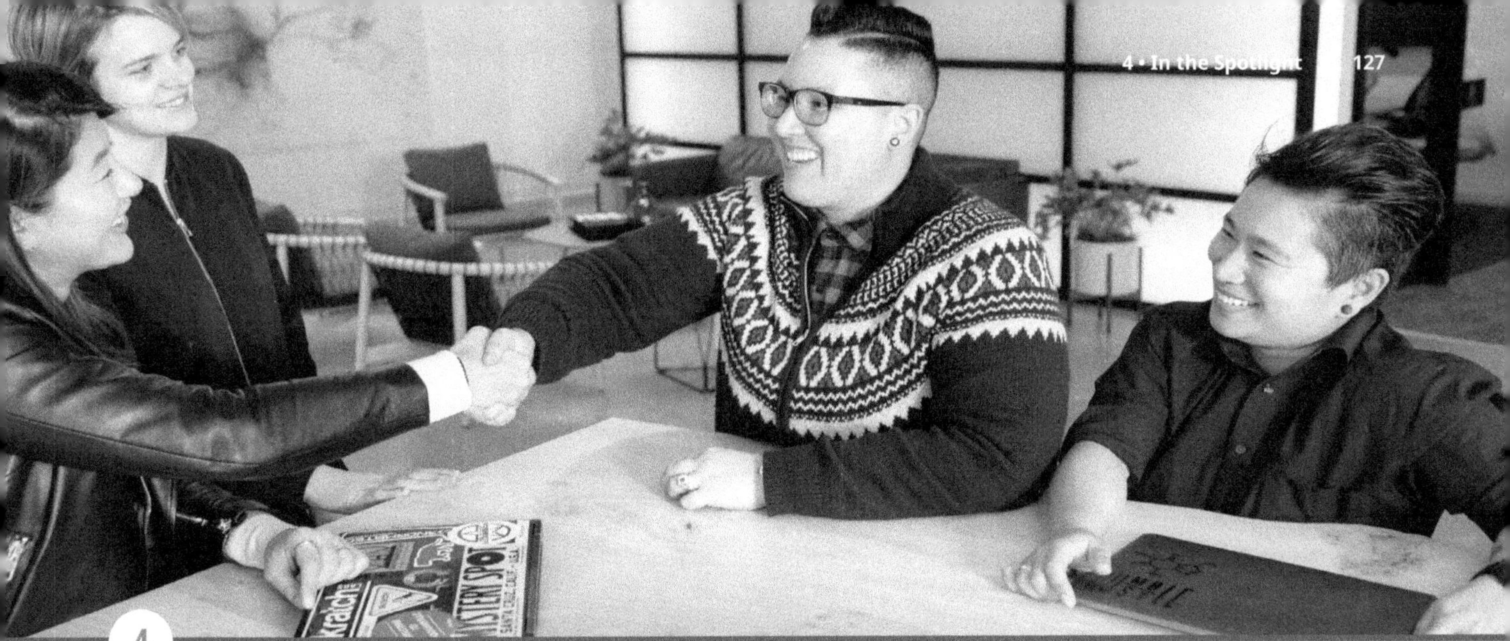

4 Business Markets and Purchasing Behavior

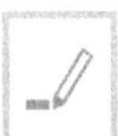

Figure 4.1 Business-to-business marketing is when one business sells products or provides services to another business, which involves building strong working relationships. (credit: "CC-BY-Mapbox-Uncharted-ERG_Mapbox-c086" by Mapbox Uncharted ERG/ flickr, CC BY 3.0 US)

Chapter Outline

In the Spotlight

Say hello to RingCentral, a company that provides businesses with cloud-based business communications solutions that include messaging, video meetings, phone, and an omnichannel cloud contact center. RingCentral, a business-to-business (B2B) company, partnered with Medallia, a customer feedback management software platform. Soon after implementing Medallia, RingCentral was able to obtain important insights about product innovation and was able to turn that feedback into product features and customer retention.

How did it do that? First, with direct access to customer feedback, the product teams at RingCentral can use that feedback to spur product feature innovations that meet customers' needs. Second, the company's sales and support teams were able to use that same customer feedback to tweak their training programs and support processes. The results? After rolling out the dashboards (visual displays of the information captured), the company's support team reached an average customer satisfaction (CSAT) score of 9/10 in two key market segments. "Without real time customer feedback and the opportunity to close the loop with the customer when the feedback is fresh, this score would have been much more difficult," said Chad Freeman, RingCentral's customer support director.[1]

LINK TO LEARNING

RingCentral

To learn more about RingCentral's business model, watch this video of Jim Cramer, from CNBC's show *Mad Money*, interviewing RingCentral's CEO.

Click to view content (https://openstax.org/books/principles-marketing/pages/4-in-the-spotlight)

4.1 | The Business-to-Business (B2B) Market

Learning Outcomes

By the end of this section, you will be able to:
- LO 1 Define the business-to-business (B2B) market.
- LO 2 Distinguish characteristics of the B2B market versus the business-to-consumer (B2C) market.

Business-to-business (B2B) is a marketing transaction or business conducted between businesses. It refers to businesses that sell products and/or services to other businesses, such as retailers or wholesalers, rather than to consumers. These transactions can include everything from materials used in manufacturing to office supplies or furniture and everything in between. B2B's "counterpart" is what's known as B2C, or business-to-consumer. The focus in B2C transactions is selling products, goods, and services to consumers for personal use.

Many businesses have both B2B and B2C components. For example, consider Office Depot. You may have stopped into an Office Depot store before the semester to stock up on pens, a ream of paper for your printer, or notebooks. That's a B2C transaction. However, a large law firm or an accounting firm might order hundreds of reams of copy paper, folders, and print cartridges from Office Depot. That's a B2B transaction.

Characteristics of the B2B Market

B2B markets differ from B2C markets in several ways (see Table 4.1). Let's take a closer look at each of these differences.

Business-to-Consumer Market (B2C)	Business-to-Business Market (B2B)
Buying decisions for individuals and/or households	Buying decisions for companies that serve consumers or other companies
Smaller purchases/many buyers	Larger purchases/fewer buyers
Direct demand	Derived demand
Shorter buying decision cycles	Longer, more complex buying decision cycles
More reliance on mass marketing	More reliance on personal selling
Many customers located throughout the world	Fewer customers, often geographically concentrated in areas based on cost, access, and availability of resources

Table 4.1 Differences between Consumer Markets/Buyers and Business-to-Business Markets/Buyers

- *Nature of the buying decision.* It may seem a little obvious, but it's important to remember that B2C buyers generally make buying decisions for themselves or their households, whereas B2B buyers make buying decisions for their companies, which serve either consumers or other companies. When you go grocery shopping, you're buying a loaf of bread, a gallon of milk, and a dozen eggs for yourself or your household. However, if you are buying food to be prepared and served at a large hospital or a university, the complexity and volume of that purchase will be far greater.
- *Fewer buyers, higher volume.* Another difference between the two markets is that B2B markets deal with fewer buyers, who purchase a much higher volume than the B2C market. For example, when Barnes & Noble sells textbooks to students, the potential market includes hundreds of thousands of students worldwide. These students purchase one or more textbooks for their semester's classes. However, Barnes & Noble is just one commercial buyer purchasing those hundreds of thousands of textbooks.
- *Direct demand versus derived demand.* Another difference between the two markets lies in the nature of the demand for products. B2C markets are driven by **direct demand**, the demand for goods and services for direct consumption purposes. By contrast, B2B markets are driven by what's known as **derived demand**, in that demand in the B2B market is dictated by the demand for consumer goods on the B2C market. For example, as more workers are working from their homes, the demand for computers has risen. As a result, you'll see derived demand in computer-related products, such as mice, monitors, printers, and so on.
- *Longer buying cycles.* As a general rule, the higher the dollar volume of the sale and the more complex the product, the longer it takes for the sale to be made. As a consumer in the B2C market, you might buy a desktop computer within a relatively short time after deciding that you need a new computer. In the B2B market, a hospital purchasing a magnetic resonance imaging (MRI) machine may well be spending millions of dollars, and the sale can take months or even years to accomplish. Not only will there be more people involved in the decision-making process, but the hospital needs to be concerned with many factors, such as safety, reliability, and post-purchase service. A lot of time and effort is typically required to "close the deal" with a big-ticket item like an MRI machine. We'll be examining the stages in the B2B buying process in depth later in this chapter, but the B2B buying process is typically longer and more complex, not only because of the involvement of different decision makers, but also because these decision makers must consider a wide range of factors when making high-volume or high-dollar purchases.
- *Reliance on personal selling.* Whereas B2C markets tend to rely more heavily on mass marketing, B2B markets typically are characterized by increased reliance on personal selling. Additionally, B2B purchasing is more likely to involve complex negotiations concerning price, delivery schedules, technical specifications, etc., so personal selling plays a vital role. Typically, because B2B buyers and sellers often need to work together to define problems and implement solutions, they focus on building long-term relationships rather than a one-and-done purchase. For example, it took nearly four years to negotiate the contract, but the Indian government and Airbus finally reached agreement on the purchase of 56 Airbus C295MW tactical transport aircraft from Airbus.[2]
- *Geographical concentration.* Finally, the scope of the market is different. In the B2C market, you have millions of potential customers dispersed throughout a region, a country, or perhaps the world. On the other hand, the B2B market is more concentrated. The B2B market has far fewer customers that are often geographically concentrated in areas based on cost, access, and availability of resources. Detroit (the heart of the US automotive industry) and Silicon Valley (home to many technology-based companies) are prime examples.

CAREERS IN MARKETING

B2B Jobs

If you're considering marketing for your job, B2B marketing is a career choice. Why would you want to go this path? Read this article from the author of *B2B Marketing Strategy* (https://openstax.org/r/b2bmarketingcareerchoice). If you're not entirely sure what a B2B marketer would do, read this article on HubSpot (https://openstax.org/r/b2bmarketing) to gain insight into the job role.

If you're still not quite clear on what B2B marketing is and how it differs from B2C, read this article from Business News Daily (https://openstax.org/r/5000whatisb2b) to gain more information. Get a sense for what the work looks like by using LinkedIn for B2B marketing (https://openstax.org/r/linkedinforb2b).

Knowledge Check

It's time to check your knowledge on the concepts presented in this section. Refer to the Answer Key at the end of the book for feedback.

1. The demand for smartphones and similar devices has created a demand for other needed components, such as touch-sensitive glass screens, microchips, and circuit boards. This is an example of _______ demand.
   a. direct
   b. irregular
   c. derived
   d. negative

2. Jason, a purchasing agent for an electronics firm, places an order with a supplier for diodes to be used in the manufacturing process. This is an example of a transaction in the _______ market.
   a. B2B
   b. B2C
   c. B2G
   d. C2C

3. Alejandro is a salesperson for a company that manufactures electrosurgical units. He calls on hospitals in his sales region to familiarize the buying centers in the hospitals with the benefits of his company's equipment. Which difference between B2B and B2C markets does this scenario illustrate?
   a. Longer, more complex buying decision cycles
   b. More rigid product standards
   c. More reliance on personal selling
   d. More reliance on mass marketing

4. Many of the world's high-tech companies are located in Silicon Valley, California, including the headquarters of more than 30 businesses in the Fortune 1000. Which difference between B2B and B2C markets does this illustrate?
   a. More reliance on personal selling
   b. Derived demand versus direct demand
   c. Fewer customers, often geographically concentrated in areas
   d. Larger purchases/fewer buyers than the B2C market

5. DaVonte has a home repair business. He goes to a home improvement store to purchase a large quantity

of lumber for his next repair project. While he is there, he picks up batteries for the smoke detector in his house. In this scenario, the lumber is a _______ purchase, and the batteries are a _______ purchase.

a. B2C; B2B

b. B2B; B2G

c. B2C; B2G

d. B2B; B2C

4.2 Buyers and Buying Situations in a B2B Market

Learning Outcomes

By the end of this section, you will be able to:

LO 1 Identify the types of buyers involved in the B2B market.

LO 2 Describe the types of buying situations that exist in the B2B market.

LO 3 List and describe the parties who participate in the B2B buying process.

Types of Buyers in the B2B Market

The B2B marketplace is populated by many different types of buyers, each with their own requirements, policies, and procedures. Some B2B buyers (known as *producers*) purchase goods in the B2B market so they can produce other goods to be sold to other businesses or consumers. Other B2B buyers (known as resellers) purchase goods in the B2B market so they can resell, rent, or lease those goods or services. Still other B2B customers, such as the government and nonprofit institutions such as the Wounded Warrior Project, the Salvation Army, churches, and charities, purchase goods to serve the public in some way.[3] These types of buyers are shown in Figure 4.2.

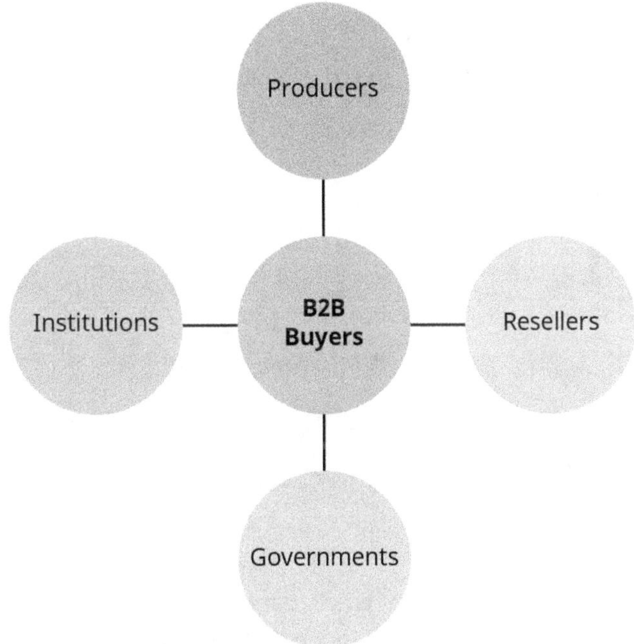

Figure 4.2 Types of Buyers (attribution: Copyright Rice University, OpenStax, under CC BY 4.0 license)

Producers are companies that purchase goods and services that are transformed into other products, and they include both manufacturers and service providers. For example, in one of its divisions, Emerson Electric produces electronic controls for the heating, ventilating, and air conditioning (HVAC) industry. Its buyers need to purchase capacitors, printed circuit boards, resistors, diodes, and dozens of other components in order to build those controls. Burger King needs beef patties, buns, lettuce, pickles, and other ingredients to make its sandwiches. Your local tattoo shop needs tattoo ink and needles. You've likely bought a smartphone. Imagine the dozens of components that go into the product's manufacturing—circuit boards, LCDs, speakers, microphones, batteries, etc. The producer needs to purchase these components from various vendors. This is a large market for B2B sellers, because producers don't typically buy in small quantities. For example, OSI supplies 45 million pounds of steak, salsa, beans, and other food products for Chipotle and has been supplying meat to McDonald's for over 50 years. From a marketing perspective, that's the kind of B2B relationship you want to pursue![4]

Resellers sell goods and services produced by other companies without any material change. These resellers include retailers, wholesalers, and brokers. This is a very important segment in the B2B market because these resellers typically buy in large volumes, so if marketers can convince these resellers to stock their organization's products, it can mean a significant uptick in sales. We'll learn more about retailers, wholesalers, and brokers in Distribution: Delivering Customer Value, when we talk about distribution, but some quick definitions may help here. **Retailers** are businesses that sell goods to consumers in relatively small quantities for personal consumption. Walmart and Target are two big retailers you're likely familiar with, but even the convenience store across from campus buys a variety of products, like candy, snacks, and soft drinks, from wholesalers to make them available for purchase—unaltered—by you. **Wholesalers**, on the other hand, typically purchase larger quantities from producers and then resell them to retailers. **Brokers** bring buyers and sellers together (for a commission, of course), and they may represent many producers of noncompeting products.

<table><tr><td>MARKETING IN PRACTICE</td></tr></table>

Alibaba

Figure 4.3 Alibaba.com, a leading platform for global wholesale trade, utilizes shipping containers to extend its reach to its millions of consumers and suppliers around the world. (credit: "Shotley Suffolk" by Martin Pettitt/flickr, CC BY 2.0)

Founded in 1999 by Jack Ma, Alibaba.com is an online B2B marketplace (see Figure 4.3). In this virtual marketplace, buyers and sellers have the ability to connect with one another and carry out purchase/sale transactions. Alibaba is sort of like a giant variety store for B2B buyers. The company has hundreds of millions of products in over 40 different categories, including machinery, consumer electronics, and apparel.[5]

Alibaba's B2B marketplace has millions of sellers, similar to eBay in the B2C market. The sheer number of sellers translates to millions of products to choose from, so B2B buyers can easily select the sellers and products that best suit their needs.

Many of Alibaba's suppliers are businesses that sell raw materials or manufactured goods, and the B2B buyers of these goods are typically retailers, wholesalers, sourcing agents, or manufacturers who source products for reselling for their own businesses (see Figure 4.3). Alibaba.com even has "Pay Later" options (backed by Kabbage Funding) so that buyers can purchase inventory, even if they don't have immediate funds available. This "Pay Later" option helps B2B buyers avoid more complicated financing options.[6]

For more information about Alibaba.com, watch this CNBC video.

Click to view content (https://openstax.org/books/principles-marketing/pages/4-2-buyers-and-buying-situations-in-a-b2b-market)

Trivia question for you: Who is the largest purchaser of goods and services in the world? If you answered the US government, you'd be correct.[7] **Government markets** make up the largest single business and organizational market in the United States. The US government buys everything you can imagine, from paper clips and staples to tanks, weapons, and jets. But it's not only products that governments purchase. They also enter into contracts with companies that provide services to citizens—everything from transportation to garbage collection and construction services.

You might be interested to know that there isn't one central department within the government that purchases all these products. Organizations that want to sell to the US government must first register with the System for Award Management and then consult with the General Services Administration (GSA), the agency that is charged with assisting hundreds of federal agencies that procure a vast array of routinely purchased products such as office supplies, vehicles, and information technology services. However, the savvy marketer knows that agencies don't buy products; people do. The agencies the GSA works with still have influence over what is purchased, so the marketer knows to contact each agency the organization wants to do business with and market its products to them.[8]

Institutions is a rather broad term for nonprofit organizations such as the Wounded Warrior Project and Ronald McDonald House Charities, charities, and churches, as well as educational institutions, hospitals, museums, nursing homes, and civic clubs. Like the government, these institutions often purchase large quantities of products and services. For example, a large nursing home buys food, beverages, linens, janitorial supplies, medications, and a host of other products and services to serve its residents. Similarly, a church may purchase candles, vestments, furniture, and much more.

A smart B2B marketer will carefully examine all of the markets mentioned above to determine if they represent significant potential opportunities, as well as looking at pursuing B2B opportunities abroad and online B2B markets.

Major Types of Buying Situations in the B2B Market

As a consumer, you face different types of buying situations every day. Some purchases you make are almost automatic and made with little forethought, such as when you stop for a cup of coffee on your way to work or class. Other buying decisions you make take more time and effort. The same is true in the B2B market. **Buy classes** refer to buying situations that are differentiated in terms of four characteristics: newness (i.e., how familiar or unfamiliar the product is to the B2B buyer), how many alternatives can/should be evaluated, how much uncertainty is involved in the buying situation, and how much information is required to make the buying decision.[9]

In the B2B market, there are four different types of buy classes. You can see the buy classes in Figure 4.4.

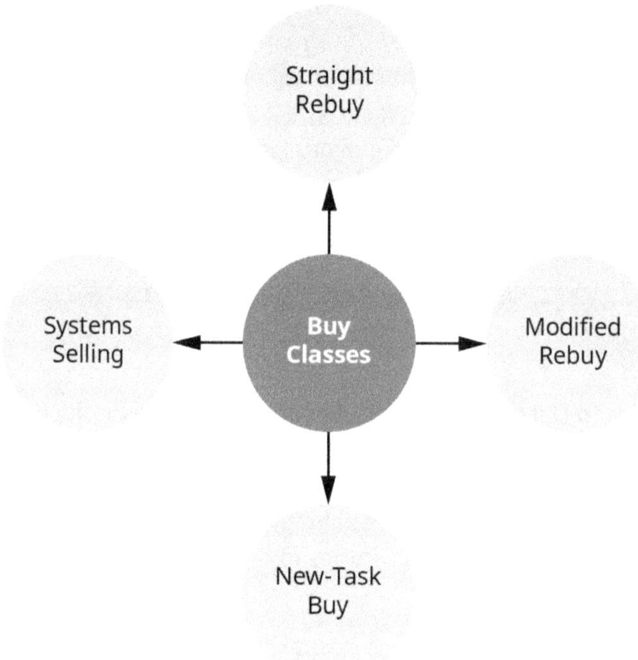

Figure 4.4 Types of Buy Classes in the B2B Market (attribution: Copyright Rice University, OpenStax, under CC BY 4.0 license)

Straight rebuys are the simplest buying situation for a B2B buyer. With a straight rebuy, the B2B buyer is making a routine purchase of a standard product or products with no modifications from a familiar supplier. An example of a straight rebuy would be a B2B buyer who orders copier paper, pens, and pencils from Office Depot or another local office supplier. That buyer has likely purchased these (or similar) products before, so the amount of effort involved in a straight rebuy is minimal beyond confirming that the order has been fulfilled.

In a **modified rebuy** situation, the B2B buyer is looking to purchase a similar product, but there are one or more significant differences from the previous purchase, such as new product specifications or a new supplier. Modified rebuy situations typically involve more effort on the part of the B2B buyer than straight rebuys because they have to consider product specifications, evaluate vendors, and negotiate new contracts. For example, let's consider a restaurateur who has changed the logo of the restaurant, necessitating buying new menus, coffee cups, and paper napkins. In essence, the same products are being purchased as before—menus, coffee cups and napkins—but the logo has changed. This might be the time for the restaurateur to look at different suppliers who may offer better pricing or cups in a different size and shape to better display the new logo. A modified rebuy situation involves more effort than a straight rebuy situation because the restaurateur is likely going to need to research product specifications, evaluate vendors, and possibly negotiate new contracts.

The **new-task buy** occurs when a B2B buyer buys a product or service for the first time. These buying situations are among the most difficult and time-consuming ones because typically the B2B buyer has no previous experience with the product, the service, or perhaps the vendors. This means that, instead of relying on past purchase orders or product specifications, the B2B buyer has to start from scratch and do considerable research in terms of product specifications, find out which firms supply the product, and obtain information on the quality, pricing, delivery, and customer service of each of these vendors. For example, if Whirlpool designs a new microwave oven, the B2B buyer will have to source new vendors to design an electronic control panel for this microwave.

Systems selling (sometimes called a solution sale) involves buying a complete solution to a problem or need rather than purchasing separate components from different vendors. For example, a B2B buyer may choose to purchase an entire human resource management system from one supplier rather than purchasing applicant and/or employee management software from one vendor, payroll software from another vendor, compensation and benefits management software from still another vendor, etc. and putting them together.[10]

Participants in the B2B Purchase Process

Think about how you make buying decisions in your household. You're likely the only decision maker involved in minor purchases, such as groceries or personal clothing. If you're buying a bigger-ticket item such as a new car or a flatscreen TV, you may involve other members of your household in the decision. That's typically not the case in B2B buying. The decision-making unit of a buying organization is referred to as the **buying center**, sometimes called a decision-making unit. Buying centers are comprised of all of the different people in the organization who have a stake in the B2B buying decision and have some degree of influence in the purchasing decision. The buying center can have one or more of the following roles, as shown in Figure 4.5.

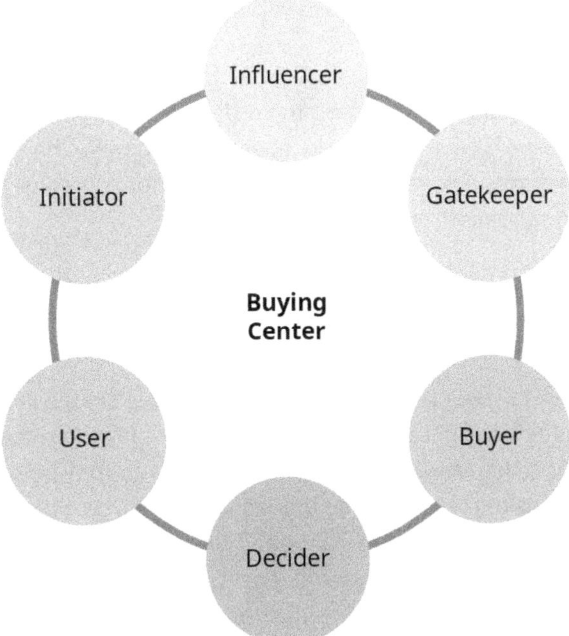

Figure 4.5 Individuals in the Buying Center (attribution: Copyright Rice University, OpenStax, under CC BY 4.0 license)

The **initiator** is typically the individual who first identifies a purchasing need within the organization. Initiators are the people within the buying center who start (or initiate) the buying process. For example, a machine operator might initiate a request for a particular tool or piece of equipment, or the payroll department may initiate a request for new payroll software. At other times, the need may be identified by senior management or the engineering department.

Influencers are those within the organization who help define specifications and/or provide information to be used in the evaluation process. Simply put, these are the people in the organization who **influence** the buying situation and provide information for strategically evaluating alternatives.[11] Influencers may not have a direct role in the purchasing decision, but they wield influence over the purchase. There are two categories of influencers. Business influencers typically focus on how the purchase impacts revenue, whereas technical influencers will generally focus on how the purchase will impact business processes and operations.

Gatekeepers filter information. The gatekeeper is the person the marketer has to negotiate their way through in order to reach the decision makers. Gatekeepers play a strategic role in the buying process, because they have the ability to allow only that information favorable to their opinion to flow to the decision makers. For example, an executive assistant might have control of the decision maker's appointment calendar and might tell the marketer, "There are no openings on the calendar at this time."

Buyers are those who have **authority** within the organization to select suppliers and negotiate and arrange the purchase terms. Buyers may also assist others within the organization to help shape product specifications, but their primary role is selecting vendors and negotiating the terms of the contract. They are also responsible for issuing purchase orders, following up, and keeping track of deliveries.

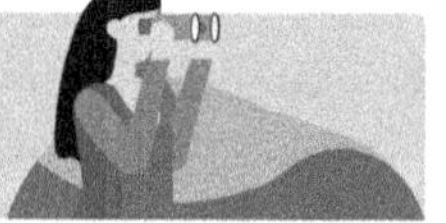

CAREERS IN MARKETING

Being a Buyer

Interested in learning more about what a buyer does on the job? Read this Indeed.com article (https://openstax.org/r/whatdoesabuyer) about the roles, responsibilities, salary, and education of a buyer. The article also includes steps to become a buyer. Also read this article from *The Princeton Review* on the life of a buyer (https://openstax.org/r/careers26buyer).

Deciders are the critical link for a marketer in getting the order, particularly in major purchases. These are the people within the organization who have the authority to select or approve the final suppliers. B2B buyers may be the deciders for routine purchases (i.e., straight rebuys), but in more complex purchases, decisions are often made higher up in the organization.

Users are those people within the organization who will actually use the product or service. These users may or may not be the initiators of the purchase proposal. However, depending on how complex the purchase is, they may help define product specifications.

It's important to note that not all of these parties may be involved in every buying decision, depending on the nature of the purchase, and sometimes people in the buying center play more than one role. For example, consider a medium-sized law firm that needs a new copier. The initiator may be an administrative assistant (who is also a user) who complains to their boss, the managing partner, that the copier is too slow and lacks features like auto-duplexing and the capacity to enlarge and reduce the size of documents. As such, the administrative assistant is also acting as a technical influencer, since they have firsthand knowledge of how a new copier with improved features would impact business processes. Since the managing partner in a law firm oversees the day-to-day operations, that person has the authority to direct the buyer to evaluate new copiers that would meet the specifications described by the administrative assistant and present an analysis of copiers. After evaluating the list provided by the buyer, the managing partner can make the final selection and thus act as the decider.

According to Tony Rutigliano and Brian Brim in their book *Strengths Based Selling*, "The days of a single economic decision maker are over in most companies and industries. Even some small businesses make decisions in groups."[12]

For example, a study in Germany found that 86% of procurement decisions at large- and medium-sized companies are made by groups of 2 to 20 people. In companies of less than 100 employees, there were typically 3 people involved, whereas in companies of 1,000 or more, there were as many as 34 people involved.[13] This illustrates the importance of the marketer (or salesperson) understanding the set of roles in the buying center, identifying the role(s) each individual plays, and developing an execution strategy to make the sale.

MARKETING IN PRACTICE

The Buyer Center

Watch this quick video of the buying center applied to a real-world example. It's a great way to gain insight into this process.

Click to view content (https://openstax.org/books/principles-marketing/pages/4-2-buyers-and-buying-situations-in-a-b2b-market)

Knowledge Check

It's time to check your knowledge on the concepts presented in this section. Refer to the Answer Key at the end of the book for feedback.

1. The largest business and organizational market in the United States is ________.
   a. producers
   b. institutions
   c. governments
   d. resellers

2. Jenae, a purchasing agent for an electronics firm, places an order with a local office supply company for several dozen reams of copy paper. He has ordered the same brand of paper from the company several times before. This is an example of ________.
   a. a straight rebuy
   b. a modified rebuy
   c. a new-task buy
   d. systems selling

3. Alejandro, the owner of a Mexican restaurant, decides to revise the restaurant's menu. He intends to use the same printing company but has to make several changes in the menu. What type of buying situation does this best illustrate?
   a. Systems selling
   b. Straight rebuy
   c. Modified rebuy
   d. New-task buy

4. The human resources manager submits a request to upper management for a new software package that will manage payroll, benefits, compliance, and information technology. Within the buying center, what role is illustrated by this scenario?
   a. Influencer
   b. Buyer
   c. Initiator
   d. Decider

5. Metro Corp. wants to acquire a new IT system, and Aliyah has been charged with selecting potential new vendors. Within the buying center, what is Aliyah's role?
   a. Gatekeeper
   b. Influencer
   c. Initiator

    d. Buyer

4.3 | Major Influences on B2B Buyer Behavior

Learning Outcomes

By the end of this section, you will be able to:

LO 1 List and describe the external influences on B2B buyer behavior.
LO 2 Explain the internal factors that influence B2B buyer behavior.
LO 3 Examine the individual factors that impact B2B buyer behavior.
LO 4 List and describe the interpersonal factors that influence B2B buyer behavior.
LO 5 Explain the conditional factors that impact B2B buyer behavior.

Think about it: B2B buyers are people just like you. They don't make buying decisions in a vacuum; rather, they are influenced by a number of different factors throughout the B2B buying process, just as consumers are influenced in making purchases for their own consumption. These factors can be grouped into five major categories: external factors, internal factors, individual factors, interpersonal factors, and conditional factors (as shown in Figure 4.6). Let's take a closer look.

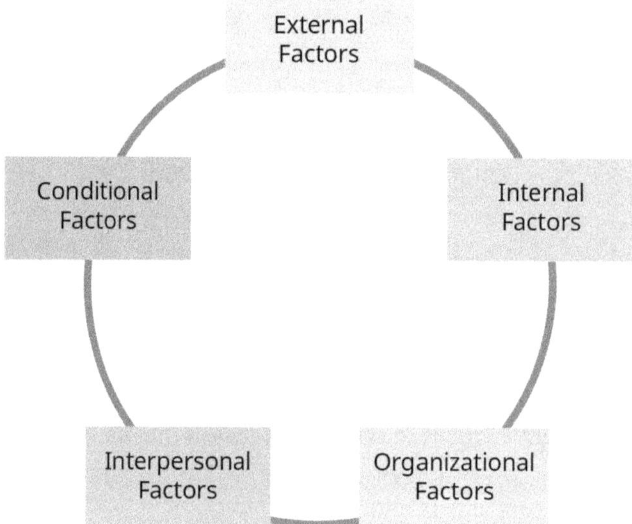

Figure 4.6 Influences on B2B Behavior (attribution: Copyright Rice University, OpenStax, under CC BY 4.0 license)

External Factors

External factors at work in the B2B buying decision can be economic conditions, the political/legal environment, competition, and the social environment.

First consider **economic factors**, such as the level of primary demand, the economic outlook, and the cost of money (i.e., interest rates). When the economy is strong, when unemployment is low, and when personal income is up, B2C demand increases, driving upward demand in the B2B market. Conversely, during economic recession, B2B buyers look for ways to cut costs, and buying is significantly reduced.

Political and legal factors also influence B2B buying decisions. These factors include the political system, the political situation, and government policies. Legal factors include laws, rules, and regulations, including tariffs (which are taxes on imported goods) and exchange rates (the value of one country's currency versus another.) To give you an idea of how such legal factors can negatively impact a firm, consider that, in 2018, after an expert panel found possibilities of health risks, the Indian government banned approximately 6,000 brands of medicine, dealing a blow to both domestic and foreign pharmaceutical firms.[14] It doesn't take much imagination to recognize the impact this policy had on these pharmaceutical firms.

Competition also affects B2B buying behavior. It stands to reason that, when a competitor changes its product offering and garners more market share, a business will want to respond by going on the defensive and changing its product offering as well, triggering one or more B2B buying situations. The fast-food industry is just one example of this. Wendy's was the first national fast-food chain to introduce salads in response to consumers' desires for healthier food options.[15] Shortly thereafter, many other competitors, including Arby's, McDonald's, Chick-fil-A, and Burger King, followed suit.

Finally, the **social environment** influences B2B buying behavior because each member of the class will likely approach the situation armed with different information, different perspectives, and perhaps different personal agendas. For example, the vice president of the marketing department may want to spend money on a new customer relationship management software package, whereas the vice president of the finance department may be more inclined to reserve capital and forego the purchase.

Internal Factors

Organizational factors are those factors internal to the organization that affect buying decisions. Every organization has certain **business objectives and goals**, and goods and services should be purchased according to these objectives. For example, if a company experiences a period of poor sales performance, management might slow down or halt major purchasing decisions until the financial performance of the company improves. Conversely, a company with a strong track record of sales may push for more strategic purchases to gain or maintain a competitive edge.

Consider how an organization's **technology** influences B2B buying behavior, particularly if the purchases must be compatible with the technology that is already in place in the organization. When purchasing a new product or service, decision makers are often reluctant to change the existing technology and go with something new.

Finally, **workforce skills** are as important as the decision makers and the products or services themselves since the workers are the ones who are going to use the new equipment or service and (hopefully) will make the most of it. Thus, new purchases must be compatible with the existing workforce skills, or employees must be offered training on the new technology.

Individual Factors

Just as with consumers, B2B buying decisions are influenced by the characteristics of the individuals in the buying center. Consider just one factor: age. FINN Partners compiled its B2B Buyer's Influence Report and discovered several interesting statistics. Millennials (i.e., those born between 1981 and 1995) are generally the most optimistic about purchase decisions. A whopping 83% are confident that they are paying a reasonable price, and 97% believed that the vendor would deliver as promised. This compares to only single digits for baby boomers (those born between 1946 and 1964).[16]

The B2B buyer's education also plays a role. A more educated buyer is assumed to select goods and services carefully and approach the buying decision rationally, whereas a buyer with less education may make the buying decision based on a hunch.

Job position typically conveys an individual's status within the organization. Those individuals involved in the buying decision who are higher up in the organization's hierarchy may have more influence than those with less formal authority within the organization.

Those involved in B2B buying decisions are, after all, human beings, so it stands to reason that personality will play a role. **Personality** refers to an individual's distinctive patterns of thinking, feeling, and behavior, and these factors will play a role in making buying decisions. Examples of the many personality traits that B2B buyers and consumers have include things like self-confidence, aggression, and competitiveness. For example, some risk-averse individuals may prefer to do business with a known supplier rather than a vendor they are not familiar with. Likewise, personal preferences play a role in the B2B buying situation. Some individuals in the buying center may favor products of a certain quality, brand, price point, and so on.

Interpersonal Factors

Business buying decisions are typically collective and follow procedures established by the organization. The buying center usually consists of several individuals with different formal or informal authority, status within the organization, and technical **expertise**.

If the buying situation involves a highly complex product or service, an individual with significant expertise will have and exert more influence in the buying decision. It's also important to note that some individuals in the buying center may have more influence than others, whether due to their position within the organization or their personal persuasiveness.

Finally, organizational politics and culture may also impact who the decision makers are and the degree of power or influence they exert on the decision process. Companies with a strong hierarchical structure may foster a tendency for decisions to be made at a higher level within the organization. This may be particularly true in international B2B transactions, which will be covered in more depth in Marketing in a Global Environment.

Conditional Factors

It stands to reason that the present financial condition of the organization will play a large role in the buying decision. If the organization is financially struggling and cash is in short supply, it may decide to make a purchase from suppliers who offer credit or may choose to purchase a less expensive product that is within its budget.

Likewise, availability of the product or service will play a significant role in the buying decision. An organization may choose to go with a supplier who can readily deliver the product or service within the time constraints of the project, even if the price is higher.

Knowledge Check

It's time to check your knowledge on the concepts presented in this section. Refer to the Answer Key at the end of the book for feedback.

1. Garrett's company is considering whether or not to purchase new manufacturing equipment that will lower its manufacturing cost significantly and improve its profit margins. Which factor appears to be influencing the B2B purchase?
   a. Workforce skills
   b. Personality
   c. Business objectives and goals
   d. Social environment

2. The local government has just passed an ordinance requiring manufacturing firms to reduce pollutants from their manufacturing processes. As a result, Shereace Manufacturing Company is investigating the purchase of pollution control equipment. What factor appears to be influencing the B2B purchase?
   a. Political and legal factors
   b. Economic factors
   c. Competition
   d. Workforce skills

3. Shane's company has been experiencing a downturn in sales, and cash is tight right now. This has caused Shane to look only at suppliers who offer credit to the company. Which factor appears to be influencing the B2B purchase?
   a. External factors
   b. Internal factors

   c.   Interpersonal factors
   d.   Conditional factors

4. Interest rates have gone up significantly in the past few months, prompting Johnson Manufacturing to reconsider purchasing a new building. Which factor appears to be at play in this B2B transaction?
   a.   Political and legal factors
   b.   Economic factors
   c.   Workforce skills
   d.   Competition

5. A worldwide shortage of microchips has prompted Vorderman Enterprises to use a new vendor who has higher prices but can deliver the product on time. Which factor appears to be at play in this B2B transaction?
   a.   External factors
   b.   Political and legal factors
   c.   Economic factors
   d.   Conditional factors

4.4 | Stages in the B2B Buying Process

Learning Outcomes

By the end of this section, you will be able to:
   LO 1 Explain and describe the stages in the B2B buying process.

The B2B Buying Process

The **B2B buying process**—the journey B2B buyers and the buying center take to complete a purchase—is significantly different and more complex than the consumer purchasing decision process. You'll recall from Consumer Markets and Purchasing Behavior. That the consumer buying decision encompasses five stages—need recognition or problem awareness, information search, evaluation of alternatives, purchase decision, and post-purchase evaluation. By contrast, the B2B process involves eight stages (shown in Figure 4.7). Let's take a closer look at each of these stages.

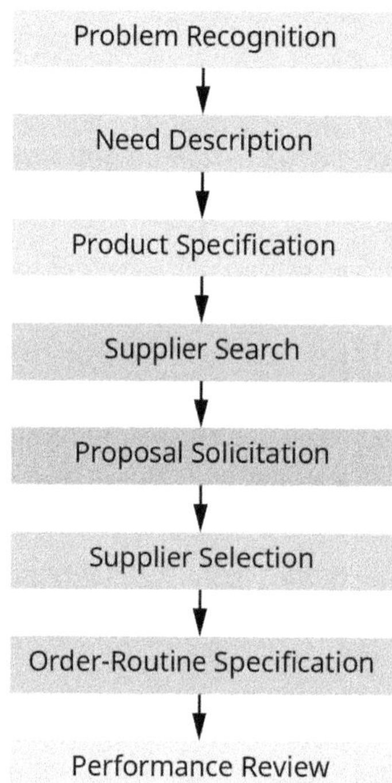

Figure 4.7 The Stages of the B2B Buying Process (attribution: Copyright Rice University, OpenStax, under CC BY 4.0 license)

Stage 1: Problem Recognition

Similar to the consumer purchasing decision process, the first stage in the B2B buying decision process begins when someone within the organization identifies a problem or a need that can be resolved through a purchase. For straight rebuy purchases, this stage may be as simple as the fact that the organization is running low on copier paper or toner. In a case like this, the B2B buyer simply places the order, and the process ends.

Modified rebuy purchases make the process more complex, as these may involve replacing outdated equipment, technological changes, or revising marketing brochures or advertisements. Now, instead of placing an order from an existing supplier for an already-purchased product, the B2B buyer has to follow through on more of the stages in the process.

New-task buying is the most complex. For example, your organization may decide that, due to the growth of the organization, it needs to purchase an accounting software system or a new piece of manufacturing equipment. In these cases, the B2B buying process will likely incorporate all of the steps listed in Figure 4.7.

Stage 2: Need Description

Next, the buying center will need to further define what needs to be purchased. This often involves collaboration among members of the buying center in terms of describing what is needed from a technical perspective, desired features, quantity, etc.

Consider a firm that is developing a new electronic control for an appliance. The components are many—a printed circuit board, capacitors, resistors, microprocessors, etc. Members of the buying center will be called upon to develop a **bill of materials**—a list of parts, items, assemblies, subassemblies, documents, drawings, and other materials required to create the control. Think of the bill of materials as the "recipe" used to create the finished product.

Stage 3: Product Specification

B2B buyers often develop **product specifications**, a blueprint that outlines the product to be built, how it will look, what features it will have, and how it will function. The product specification needs to be concise and readable for everyone in the buying center and yet contain sufficient technical data to provide the product team with the information it needs to develop the new product or feature.

Stage 4: Supplier Search

Now that you've established the technical specifications for the product, it's time to identify potential suppliers. This is where the experience of those in the buying center comes into play, as they attempt to determine which suppliers have the best quality, delivery, and price. Just like consumers in the "information search" stage of the consumer buying process, those in the buying center may look online to find suppliers, but there are many other resources available to B2B buyers, such as trade magazines, industry expert blogs, and webinars conducted by suppliers.

Stage 5: Proposal Solicitation

Once the list of potential vendors has been developed and whittled down, qualified vendors will be asked to submit proposals. If it's a relatively straightforward purchase, this proposal may be as easy as a vendor sending the buyer a catalog or providing the buyer with a link to the company's website. However, more complex purchases typically require the vendor to submit a detailed proposal outlining what the vendor can do to address the company's needs. This proposal will likely contain product specifications, timing, and—of course—pricing.

Stage 6: Supplier Selection

After reviewing the proposals from the various vendors, the buying center makes a choice. This stage in the B2B buying process involves a thorough review of the proposals submitted, with a critical eye tuned to factors such as supplier capabilities, reputation, warranties, price, etc. If the purchase requires a substantial financial outlay and/or is extremely complex, or if many proposals were solicited, the buying center may narrow down the list of vendors to just a few and invite them to meet (either in person or virtually) to further discuss the proposal and address any questions or concerns.

Stage 7: Order-Routine Specification

After selecting suppliers, the B2B buyer negotiates the details of the order. The critical items here are what is needed (i.e., the technical specifications), how much is needed (i.e., the quantity required), and when it is needed (i.e., the expected time of delivery). This stage will likely also include negotiation of things such as return policies, warranties, and other critical items involved with the purchase.

Stage 8: Performance Review

Just as consumers evaluate purchases after they have made them, and similar to the way that your employer may conduct a performance review to assess your job performance, the B2B buyer periodically reviews the performance of the selected supplier to assess if the product and the supplier meet expectations. For example, the B2B buyer may solicit product feedback from users and/or rate the supplier on different criteria such as quality, promptness of delivery, etc. As a result of the performance review, the B2B buyer may decide to continue, modify, or even end a supplier relationship.

Knowledge Check

It's time to check your knowledge on the concepts presented in this section. Refer to the Answer Key at the end of the book for feedback.

1. A blueprint that outlines the product the company will be building, what it is going to look like, and its specific requirements and functions is known as a ________.
   a. project scope
   b. bill of materials
   c. product specification

   d. participant matrix

2. Jackson has asked several qualified vendors to submit proposals. Which stage of the B2B buying process does this illustrate?
   a. Stage 2: Need description
   b. Stage 3: Product specification
   c. Stage 4: Supplier search
   d. Stage 5: Proposal solicitation

3. During which stage of the B2B buying process will members of the buying center be called upon to develop a bill of materials?
   a. Stage 1: Problem recognition
   b. Stage 2: Need description
   c. Stage 3: Product specification
   d. Stage 4: Supplier search

4. During which stage of the B2B buying process will the B2B buyer negotiate the order?
   a. Stage 4: Supplier search
   b. Stage 5: Proposal solicitation
   c. Stage 6: Supplier selection
   d. Stage 7: Order-routine specification

5. Donita has determined that the current payroll software system is no longer adequate to handle the growing number of employees in the company. Which stage of the B2B buying process does this illustrate?
   a. Stage 1: Problem recognition
   b. Stage 2: Need description
   c. Stage 5: Proposal solicitation
   d. Stage 8: Performance review

4.5 | Ethical Issues in B2B Marketing

Learning Outcomes

By the end of this section, you will be able to:
- **LO** 1 Discuss ethical issues pertaining to B2B marketing.
- **LO** 2 Explain the Foreign Corrupt Practices Act.
- **LO** 3 Provide an example of a company that displays ethics in B2B marketing.

Business Culture and Industry Practices

As we've seen above, there are several differences between B2C and B2B marketing. Consider purchasing, for example. Unlike B2C transactions, it is far more common in B2B transactions for vendors to offer "perks" such as free dinners, golf outings, and trips. In some foreign countries, B2B and government buyers not only expect these types of "perks" but also may demand bribes if you want to do business with them on their turf. This presents unique ethical challenges for B2B sellers and buyers. As a B2B seller, of course you want to make the sale, particularly if it's a large sale. On the other hand, you know that a reputation for ethical behavior, including honesty, transparency, and open communication, is critical to the success of your business and may even be the decisive factor in a B2B buyer's decision to buy from you instead of a competitor.

Bribes and "Grease Payments"

Transparency International, a watchdog group, annually ranks the likelihood of companies from the world's industrialized countries to bribe abroad. The index ranks 180 countries and territories by their perceived levels of public sector corruption on a sale of 1 to 100, in which 100 is perceived to be very clean and 0 is perceived to be highly corrupt.[17]

Which countries ranked in the bottom five for 2021? Let's take a look:

- South Sudan
- Syria
- Somalia
- Venezuela
- Yemen[18]

If you're curious, the United States ranked 25th in the world. And the least corrupt countries in 2021? That would be Denmark, Finland, and New Zealand, which tied for first place.[19]

LINK TO LEARNING

Fighting Corruption

For more information about Transparency International, including corruption wins, scandals, and predictions, check out this corruption perceptions index (https://openstax.org/r/encpi2021). You may also enjoy this TEDx Talks video about the power of corruption.

Click to view content (https://openstax.org/books/principles-marketing/pages/4-5-ethical-issues-in-b2b-marketing)

Let's consider how you would handle a scenario involving bribes. You're the plant manager in Taiwan for a US-based electronics company. You are expecting a critical shipment of diodes that are being imported into Taiwan from South Vietnam. Without the diodes, you will miss an important production deadline for a new—and potentially lucrative—customer. The shipment arrives in the Port of Taipei on a timely basis, but customs refuse to release the shipment, claiming that it needs to do further inspection, and it may be several days or even a couple of weeks before the shipment is released. However, an agent of customs advises you that in exchange for a "facilitation fee" of several hundred dollars, the process can be expedited. How do you handle this? Do you pay the "facilitation fee" (essentially a bribe, which is illegal according to the Foreign Corrupt Practices Act, covered below) and meet your customer's deadline, or do you refuse to pay the fee and miss your customer's deadline? How will missing that deadline impact your firm's relationship with the new customer?

Let's consider how you would handle still another similar scenario. You're the regional distribution manager for a US company, and you've been assigned to head up a new distribution facility in a South American country. At least two other competitors (both foreign corporations) are also trying to enter the same market, so you've been instructed to establish this facility as quickly as possible in order to beat the competition. However, government officials have advised you that it may take up to 10 months to obtain a building permit but that the time frame could be considerably shortened in exchange for the payment of an "expediting fee." These fees (essentially a bribe) are both illegal according to US law. However, your competitors are foreign firms not subject to US law, and paying such fees is neither illegal nor considered unethical. How will you handle this situation? Will you pay the fees in order to be first in the market, or will you let your competitors beat you to the market?

These are a couple of dilemmas faced by marketers in B2B situations.

LINK TO LEARNING

Corruption Scandals

Check out Transparency International's list of top corruption scandals (https://openstax.org/r/25corruptionscandals). Interesting read!

Price Fixing

Price fixing—an agreement among competitors (either written, verbal, or inferred from the parties' conduct) that affects prices or competitive terms—is prohibited by the Federal Trade Commission (FTC).[20] Keep in mind that, despite the term, price fixing isn't confined to an agreement to set the same price. Companies can also be involved in price fixing if they offer or withhold the same discounts or shipping terms or set a production amount or quota.

Price fixing is illegal because it's considered anticompetitive and hurts both consumers and businesses. Let's illustrate with a real-life example with a company you're likely familiar with—StarKist. In 2019, a San Francisco federal judge ordered the company to pay a fine in the amount of $100 million in connection with a canned tuna price-fixing conspiracy that involved StarKist, Bumble Bee Foods, and Chicken of the Sea, who regularly exchanged information about their sales and plans for pricing. The lawsuit alleged that, under the scheme, consumers were forced to pay more for canned tuna than they would have otherwise.[21]

LINK TO LEARNING

Tuna Price-Fixing Lawsuit

Learn more about the details of the price-fixing lawsuit from this short video on the Ring of Fire channel.

Click to view content (https://openstax.org/books/principles-marketing/pages/4-5-ethical-issues-in-b2b-marketing)

The Foreign Corrupt Practices Act

The **Foreign Corrupt Practices Act (FCPA)** was enacted in 1977. Its purpose is to prohibit the payment of bribes (sometimes called "facilitation fees") to foreign officials in order to obtain or retain business. The FCPA applies to prohibited conduct anywhere in the world and extends to publicly traded companies and their officers, directors, employees, stockholders, and agents.[22]

The Securities and Exchange Commission (SEC) and the Department of Justice work cooperatively to enforce the FCPA. Sanctions for violations can be significant, including both civil and criminal penalties. The SEC can bring civil enforcement actions against companies (along with their officers, directors, employees, stockholders, and agents) for violations or for bribery, and if found guilty under the act, the company may have to pay back its "ill-gotten gains" as well as paying prejudgment interest and civil penalties. For example, one of its most recent cases involved KT Corporation, a South Korean telecommunications company, in which the SEC alleged that the company had violated the books and records and internal accounting controls provisions of the FCPA by making improper payments to government officials in Korea and Vietnam.[23]

COMPANIES WITH A CONSCIENCE

Kforce

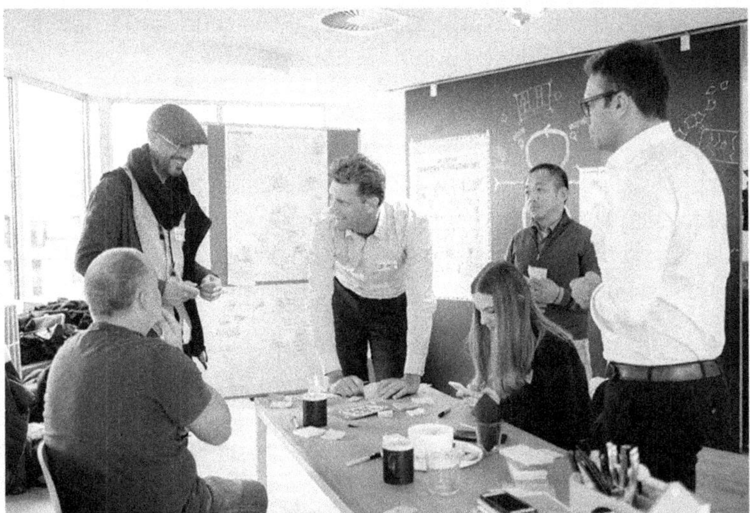

Figure 4.8 Giving to the community is continuing to grow as a priority for many companies, so they continually collaborate to develop ideas and initiatives within their mission statements or business plans. (credit: "Design a Better Business Masterclass @ Zoku Amsterdam, October 2017" by Sebastiaan ter Burg/flickr, CC BY 2.0)

Kforce is a B2B professional staffing and solutions firm that specializes in technology, finance, and accounting. Headquartered in Tampa, Florida, the company has over 50 offices nationwide and two national recruiting centers.[24]

The location of its corporate headquarters played a big role when Hurricane Irma struck South Florida and the Bahamas in 2017, because the hurricane's impact was felt on a personal level by the company. The hurricane, which struck Florida as a Category 4 storm, ripped off roofs, flooded coastal cities, and knocked out power for more than 6.8 million people.[25]

Instead of idly standing by or focusing solely on getting its business back up and running, Kforce decided to "make lemonade out of lemons" and have a positive impact on the community (see Figure 4.8). The company raised $1 million for the American Red Cross and sponsored private jet missions that flew essential supplies to the Bahamas. It also encouraged users to make donations for hurricane relief, generating several thousand additional dollars for the cause.[26]

But Kforce's philanthropy after Hurricane Irma wasn't a one-time deal. In 2021, the company expanded its "Day of Giving" campaign to a "Season of Impact" and encouraged employees to give their time and talents to nonprofit organizations of their choice. It also held a number of events such as a food drive and the Tampa Bay Heart Walk to benefit the American Heart Association.[27]

KForce does a lot for the community. Check out its website (https://openstax.org/r/kforcecorporate) to learn more about its corporate social responsibility programs.

Chapter Summary

In this chapter, we defined business-to-business (B2B) markets and buying behavior and explored the differences between business-to-consumer (B2C) and B2B markets. We discussed the types of buyers in B2B transactions—producers, resellers, governments, and institutions—and identified the different types of buy classes in the B2B market, as well as the roles of those in the buying center—the people within the organization who have varying influence on the purchase decision.

We examined the five major categories of influencing factors on B2B decisions: external factors, internal factors, organizational factors, interpersonal factors, and conditional factors. We also reviewed the eight stages of the B2B buying process: problem recognition, need description, product specification, supplier search, proposal solicitation, supplier selection, order-routine specification, and performance review. Finally, we explored some ethical issues with respect to the B2B buying process, including Transparency International's Corruption Perceptions Index and the Foreign Corrupt Practices Act (FCPA).

Key Terms

authority   the right to give orders, supervise the work of others, and make certain decisions

B2B buying process   encompasses 8 stages: problem recognition, need description, product specification, supplier search, proposal selection, supplier selection, order-routine specification, performance review

bill of materials   a comprehensive inventory of the raw materials, assemblies, subassemblies, parts, and components

brokers   individuals or businesses that bring buyers and sellers together, usually for a commission

business objectives and goals   achievable outcomes that provide a framework for achieving success

business-to-business (B2B)   a transaction or business conducted between one business and another

buy classes   buying situations that are distinguished on four characteristics: newness to decision makers, number of alternatives to be considered, uncertainty inherent in the buying situation, and the amount of information needed for making a buying decision

buyers   the people in the buying center who handle the paperwork of the actual purchase

buying center   groups of people within organizations who make purchasing decisions

competition   the rivalry between companies selling similar products and services with the goal of achieving revenue, profit and market share growth

deciders   the people in the buying center who ultimately determine any part of the entire buying decision

derived demand   market demand for a good or service that results from a demand for a related good or service

direct demand   the demand for a commodity for direct consumption purposes

economic factors   factors that affect the economy, such as interest rates, tax rates, laws, policies, wages, and government actions

expertise   expert skill or knowledge in a particular field

Foreign Corrupt Practices Act (FCPA)   a US statute that prohibits firms and individuals from paying bribes to foreign officials

gatekeepers   individuals in the buying center who control information and/or access to decision makers and influencers

government markets   purchases made by the governing bodies of nations, states, or communities

influence   the capacity to have an effect on the character, development, or behavior of someone or something

influencers   individuals whose views influence other members of the buying center in making the final decision

initiator   the person in the buying center who first suggests or thinks of the idea of buying the product or service

institutions   organizations, establishments, foundations, societies, or the like devoted to the promotion of a particular cause or program, especially one of a public, educational, or charitable character

modified rebuy   a buying situation in which an individual or organization buys goods that have been purchased previously but changes either the supplier or some element of the previous order

new-task buy   a complex B2B buying situation in which the organization buys a product or service for the first time

personality   the combination of characteristics or qualities that form an individual's distinctive character

political and legal factors   factors such as the political system, the political situation, and government policies that influence B2B buying decisions

producers   those individuals or businesses who buy raw goods to use in the creation of goods or services

product specifications   a document carrying essential information to keep teams on track when designing and developing a product

resellers   companies or individuals (merchants) that purchase goods or services with the intention of selling, leasing, or renting rather than consuming or using them

retailers   businesses that sell goods to consumers in relatively small quantities for personal consumption

social environment   the values, attitudes, beliefs, wants, and desires of the consuming public

straight rebuys   purchases in which the business customer buys the same goods from the same supplier in the same quantity at the same terms and requires minimal decision making

systems selling   selling a complete solution to a problem or need rather than one or more of the component parts

technology   applications of science, data, engineering, and information for business purposes

users   the people who consume or use the product or service

wholesalers   businesses that typically purchase larger quantities from producers and then resell them to retailers

workforce skills   also called employability skills, the basic skills a person must have to succeed in any workplace

Applied Marketing Knowledge: Discussion Questions

1. Go to the Tesla corporate website (https://openstax.org/r/tesla). Which market(s)—consumer, business, institutional, resellers, producers/suppliers—does Tesla serve? Why did Tesla decide to serve these markets? When reading Tesla's 2021 Impact Report (https://openstax.org/r/2021teslaimpactreport), what main goal does the company say it is "driven" by?

2. Manufacturers work with resellers primarily to move large amounts of inventory quickly, thus limiting stagnant inventory that can limit cash flow. Which two types of businesses historically have contributed to moving manufacturers' products to end consumers?

3. Visit your college's website, and look through academics, sports, organizations, and campus life. When looking at the photos, which items do you see depicted that are likely straight rebuys? Do you see sports uniforms, test tubes, musical instruments, computers, desks, library books? Which items are likely modified rebuys, new task situations, and systems selling?

4. What segmentation tools do you have at your disposal when marketing in a B2B setting? Are there challenges associated with using social media platforms in marketing to other businesses rather than individual consumers? If so, one of these challenges might be that members of the buying center are more experienced and less emotional purchasers. Can you identify additional challenges?

5. City, county, state, and federal governments are heavily engaged in the B2B market. List one product each governmental entity might purchase directly from a producer/supplier.

Critical Thinking Exercises

1. Compose a paragraph of 250–500 words using all of the following terms as they relate to B2B. The goal is

to prove you understand the meaning of each term.

Terms:

business markets

institutions

business culture

competitors

internal factors

gatekeeper

deciders

problem recognition

buying center

economic factors

personal selling

derived demand

product specifications

reseller

performance review

2. Explain the Foreign Corrupt Practices Act and why it is important as US businesses compete in the international marketplace.

3. Tesla is building a 10 million square-foot "Gigafactory" (https://openstax.org/r/teslagigafactory) in Nevada. While Tesla didn't rely on systems selling in building the manufacturing facility, the company did contract with many suppliers, such as Anning-Johnson (https://openstax.org/r/projecttesla), to provide vital elements such as decking. For Tesla, this was a new task situation. List the various phases Tesla went through to arrive at the construction and operation of this lithium-ion battery Gigafactory.

Building Your Personal Brand

Your personal brand is the skills and talents you bring to future employers or to your own business. Think about how businesses market to other businesses. How can you adopt some of those same marketing techniques and develop a plan to market yourself for an internship or employment?

Visit LinkedIn, and look at the profiles of a handful of marketing managers. Examine how each marketing manager depicts their brand within their profile. What do they say about themselves that's unique?

Now write a one-page summary of your brand.

 What Do Marketers Do?

Utilize LinkedIn to find brand managers in your geographic area, and invite one or more to connect with you. It's best to go beyond the suggested LinkedIn request message and be more inviting and clearer on why you are reaching out to them. Once linked, "interview" the professional by asking questions. A few questions to begin with might be: Was there a particular class in college that resonated with you and your career goals?

How did you find your first internship? Do you have suggestions that can help me improve my LinkedIn profile? Additional questions may explore their education, their experience, their career goals, and how they spend their days and weeks.

Closing Company Case

Corporate Medical Services

Corporate Medical Services (CMS) was established in Tennessee on October 1, 1995, with one person, one computer, and one client.[28] The company was started with the goal of providing Department of Transportation (DOT) customers with a resource to meet new drug testing requirements.

"The Federal Motor Carrier Safety Administration (FMCSA), along with the Department of Transportation (DOT), requires that persons subject to the commercial driver's license (CDL) requirements and their employers follow alcohol and drug testing rules."[29] These rules include procedures for testing, frequency of tests, and substances tested for. An employer who employs only themselves as a driver shall implement a random alcohol and controlled substances testing program of two or more covered employees in the random testing selection pool.

With a combination of technology and great customer service, the company grew steadily.

- 1995: CMS founded
- 1996: First office location established
- 1998: Nationwide 24/7 services offered
- 2001: Automated faxing of results
- 2001: New office location established due to growth of company
- 2004: Automated emailing of results
- 2008: Created in-house DotStop[i] consortium program
- 2009: Online results reporting made available
- 2010: Online scheduling of services made available
- 2012: Began providing management services for existing consortiums
- 2013: Introduced CMS's Sleep Express
- 2016: Began developing programs to automate DMV updates[30]

Today, CMS provides services to a wide variety of clients and industries across the United States and Canada. Clients include trucking, busing, firework manufacturers, schools, construction, hospital organizations, other third-party administrators, consortiums, and associations. In 2020, CMS reported over 100,000 drug screens and additional services for more than 2,500 companies.[31]

With stricter requirements coming to the industry, there is a tremendous need for drug and alcohol testing. Data reveals that there are 3.5 million truck drivers in the United States.[32] For just the trucking industry alone, the need for consortium services as well as company-sponsored drug and alcohol testing is increasing every year.

CMS prides itself as the concierge service provider in the industry. Figure 4.9 is a competitive analysis grid, and it outlines how CMS compares to its competitors based on the number of services they offer and the level of customer service provided. For example, DISA Global Solutions (DISA), Workforce QA, and FSS Solutions (FSS) are companies that provide a higher number of services than CMS but much lower customer service. CMS offers fewer services but the highest level of customer service. Notice that as companies offer more services, their level of customer service decreases.

Marketers use competitive analysis grids to understand how they compare to their competitors on the various metrics that are important in their industry. It is important for a company to grasp both its points of parity and

---

i DotStop is the brand name of a drug and alcohol testing consortium for trucking companies with 20 or fewer drivers.

points of differentiation compared to competitors.

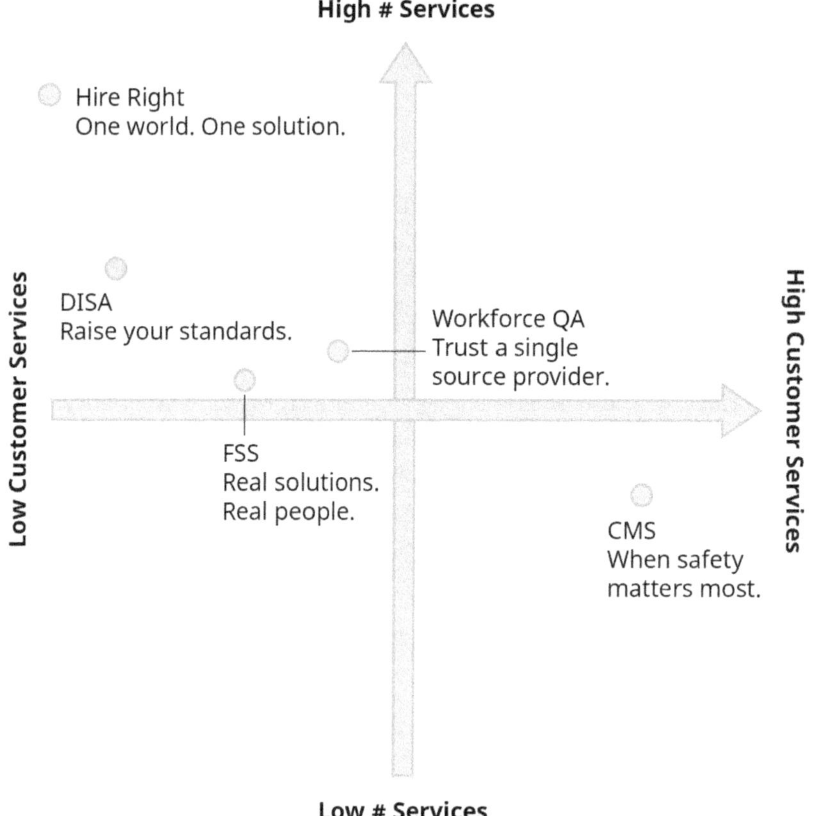

*As number of services provided increases, the level of customer service decreases.

Figure 4.9 Competitive Landscape (credit: reproduced with permission of Corporate Medical Services [CMS])

In choosing to differentiate their company based on service, CMS was promising customers an unrivaled experience when they needed drug or alcohol testing. Many times, the need for testing was the result of an emergency situation. Companies that relied on CMS for this service felt a level of comfort knowing they would be taken care of quickly and efficiently when they were in the most need.

Among the promises, CMS vowed the following:

1. Unrivaled Experience

"CMS has been helping companies manage the complexities of regulations and requirements for over 25 years. During that time, we have helped over 15,000 companies significantly reduce the hassle of managing their drug testing programs."

2. Concierge Level Personal Service

"Concierge level service is not a term frequently used in our industry, but we believe in it and actively demonstrate it to our clients daily. When you are miles from home and need support, it's what you want. It is always a good day at CMS, and we hope to make your day better by helping you in any way we can."

3. More Security, Less Hassle

"Dealing with governmental regulations and requirements is no easy task. We have developed processes, procedures, and performance benchmarks to deal with the complexity of this industry so that you don't have to. At the end of the day, you will be confident that your program is operating the way it should."

4. Respect

"We are here to serve our clients. To successfully accomplish that goal, we treat our staff, our clients, our vendors, and your donors with respect. In an industry where conversations can sometimes get tense, we handle every situation in a respectful and professional manner in order to mitigate any issues that may arise."

5. Speed of Technology

"Our systems and processes are designed to get you the results you need as quickly as possible, which is why no one is faster at reporting drug screens. Our system averages a 7-minute turnaround on negative reports, once released from the lab."

As CMS looked for growth, it began to work with industry trade associations. The trucking industry was growing rapidly. Industry leaders were continuing to expand their fleets, and new trucking companies were entering the market. Providing drug and alcohol testing was not something the companies wanted to think about—until it was a necessity. Corporate safety managers could be difficult to reach; however, with a narrow focus and significant industry knowledge, CMS was well positioned to network and provide critical information regarding the ever-changing government regulations.

CMS knew it needed to begin developing brand awareness and continue fostering relationships in the industry. When it was time to make the buying decision, CMS wanted to be in the top-of-mind consideration set. The company knew the buying cycle may be long for a corporate decision to change which provider they were using for testing. It was a process it was willing to wait for, and it was in it for the long haul.

Case Questions

1. Which characteristics of the B2B market are most evident for CMS?

2. If a trucking company wanted to buy services from CMS, what type of buying behavior would this be?

3. List and describe the major B2B buying influences prevalent for the CMS market segment.

4. List three ways Corporate Medical Services can become a leading contender in the supplier search stage of the B2B buying process.

References

1. "RingCentral Case Study," Medallia, accessed September 29, 2021, https://www.medallia.com/customers/ringcentral/.

2. Gastón Dubois, (2021, September 8). "Indian Government Approves Purchase of 56 Airbus C295MW for Its Air Force," Aviacionline.com, published August 9, 2021, https://www.aviacionline.com/2021/09/indian-government-approves-purchase-of-56-airbus-c295mw-for-its-air-force/.

3. "What Are the Four Types of B2B Markets?," IGW, accessed August 4, 2022, https://infographicworld.com/b2b-what-are-the-four-types-of-b2b-markets/.

4. Amy Lamare, "Meet the billionaire who supplies the burgers for McDonald's and Burger King," Celebrity Net Worth, published November 7, 2020, https://www.celebritynetworth.com/articles/billionaire-news/meet-the-billionaire-who-supplies-the-burgers-for-mcdonalds-and-burger-king/.

5. "How to Buy and Source from Alibaba," Alibaba.com Seller Central, published December 15, 2020, https://seller.alibaba.com/businessblogs/px65f6s8-how-to-buy-and-source-from-alibaba.

6. "How to Buy and Source from Alibaba," Alibaba.com Seller Central, published December 15, 2020, https://seller.alibaba.com/businessblogs/px65f6s8-how-to-buy-and-source-from-alibaba.

7. "Selling Greener Products and Services to the Federal Government," United States Environmental Protection Agency, last updated April 28, 2022, https://www.epa.gov/greenerproducts/selling-greener-products-and-services-federal-government.

8. "4.2 Types of B2B Buyers," University of Minnesota Libraries Publishing, accessed August 4, 2022, https://open.lib.umn.edu/principlesmarketing/chapter/4-2-types-of-b2b-buyers/.

9. "Buy Classes," Common Language Marketing Dictionary, accessed August 4, 2022, https://marketing-dictionary.org/b/buy-classes/.

10. "Systems Buying," Monash Business School, last updated February 2018, https://www.monash.edu/business/marketing/

marketing-dictionary/s/systems-buying.

11. "7 Different Members of the Buying Centre of an Organisation," Your Article Library, accessed September 29, 2021, https://www.yourarticlelibrary.com/organization/7-different-members-of-the-buying-centre-of-an-organisation/22538.

12. Marco Nink and John H. Fleming, "B2B Companies: Do You Know Who Your Customer Is?," Gallup.com, published November 11, 2014, https://news.gallup.com/businessjournal/179309/b2b-companies-know-customer.aspx.

13. Marco Nink and John H. Fleming, "B2B Companies: Do You Know Who Your Customer Is?," Gallup.com, published November 11, 2014, https://news.gallup.com/businessjournal/179309/b2b-companies-know-customer.aspx.

14. "Government bans hundreds of painkillers, creams, antibioticsm" Mint, accessed August 23, 2022, https://www.livemint.com/Companies/zDrBQAKhSFIuZtmyTHGJRO/Several-painkillers-creams-antibiotics-banned-by-governmen.html

15. Shirley Leung, "Wendy's Sees Green in Salad, So Rivals Begin to Follow Suit," The Wall Street Journal, published April 24, 2003, https://www.wsj.com/articles/SB105113127748655200.

16. "There's Intel to Be Gained Looking at B2B Buyers' by Generation," published January 28, 2020, https://www.finnpartners.com/news-insights/there-eys-intel-to-be-gained-looking-at-b2b-buyers-ey-by-generation/.

17. "Corruption Perceptions Index," Transparency International," accessed May 11, 2022, https://www.transparency.org/en/cpi/2021.

18. "Corruption Perceptions Index," Transparency International," accessed May 11, 2022, https://www.transparency.org/en/cpi/2021.

19. "Corruption Perceptions Index," Transparency International," accessed May 11, 2022, https://www.transparency.org/en/cpi/2021.

20. "Price Fixing," Federal Trade Commission, published December 15, 2017, https://www.ftc.gov/tips-advice/competition-guidance/guide-antitrust-laws/dealings-competitors/price-fixing.

21. "StarKist Price Fixing: StarKist to Pay $100M Fine in Tuna Price-Fixing Case," CBS News, updated September 11, 2019, https://www.cbsnews.com/news/starkist-price-fixing-starkist-to-pay-100m-fine-in-tuna-price-fixing-case/.

22. "Spotlight on Foreign Corrupt Practices Act," SEC Emblem, modified February 2, 2017, https://www.sec.gov/spotlight/foreign-corrupt-practices-act.shtml.

23. "SEC Enforcement Actions: FCPA Cases," SEC Emblem, modified June 6, 2022, https://www.sec.gov/enforce/sec-enforcement-actions-fcpa-cases.

24. "About Kforce," Kforce, accessed May 12, 2022, https://www.kforce.com/about-test/.

25. Chris Huber, "2017 Hurricane Irma: Facts, FAQs, and How to Help," World Vision, updated August 1, 2018, https://www.worldvision.org/disaster-relief-news-stories/2017-hurricane-irma-facts.

26. Brian Anderson, "3 Inspirational Examples of How B2B Brands Spread Cheer on #GivingTuesday," B2B Marketing Exchange, December 3, 2019, https://b2bmarketing.exchange/blog/3-inspirational-examples-of-how-b2b-brands-spread-cheer-on-givingtuesday/.

27. "Kforce Launches Season of Impact to Further Connect with Communities," Kforce, accessed January 27, 2022, https://www.kforce.com/press-releases/season-of-impact-2021/.

28. "CMS History," Corporate Medical Services, accessed May 12, 2022, https://corporatemedicalservices.com/our-company/cms-history/.

29. "CMS Executive Staff," Corporate Medical Services, accessed May 12, 2022, https://corporatemedicalservices.com/our-company/cms-executive-staff/.

30. "Drug & Alcohol Testing Program," FMCSA, accessed May 12, 2022, https://www.fmcsa.dot.gov/regulations/drug-alcohol-testing-program.

31. "CMS History," Corporate Medical Services, accessed May 12, 2022, https://corporatemedicalservices.com/our-company/cms-history/.

32. Stasha Smiljanic, "How Many Trucking Companies Are There in the United States," PolicyAdvice, accessed May 12, 2022, https://policyadvice.net/insurance/insights/how-many-trucking-companies-in-the-us.

Market Segmentation, Targeting, and Positioning

Figure 5.1 Market segmentation allows companies to focus their resources on their target markets—the markets where their marketing messages will best resonate. (credit: "3D Bullseye" by ccPixs.com/flickr, CC BY 3.0)

Chapter Outline

In the Spotlight

To begin this chapter, we are going to look at an example of a well-known company that successfully used market segmentation to appeal to a very specific consumer market as a way to revive one of its products.

Mattel Inc. is the producer of popular children's toys like Hot Wheels, Barbie, and Max Steel. Its action figure Max Steel was introduced in 1999 to only modest success in the United States, but it was enormously popular in South America, even outselling the company's top lines—Hot Wheels and Barbie. Nearly a decade later, marketers decided to revive the brand in the United States, hoping for a second chance at success.[1]

Mattel used a number of important market segmentation variables and market strategies to appeal to its target market. First, in terms of demographic variables, marketers recognized that the Max Steel figure typically appealed to boys (gender segmentation) between the ages of 6 and 11 (age segmentation), so they decided to focus on this segment by developing a website that included games, character biographies, and other features popular with boys in this age bracket.

Market research also revealed that its target audience was interested in superheroes and enjoyed watching videos and playing video games centered around these superheroes, so the company used psychographic and lifestyle segmentation to appeal to this segment.[2] For example, Mattel created a Disney Channel cartoon for Max Steel so that, months before the relaunch of the product in the United States, its target market was already familiar with the character and was more likely to buy (or pressure their parents to buy) the action figure. The result? Max Steel has become a minor superhero "staple" in toy aisles, cartoons, and movies.

5.1 | Market Segmentation and Consumer Markets

Learning Outcomes

By the end of this section, you will be able to:
- **LO** 1 Define market segmentation.
- **LO** 2 Describe the benefits of market segmentation.
- **LO** 3 Discuss methods of segmenting consumer markets.

Market Segmentation Defined

You may have heard the saying "You can't be all things to all people." That sums up the essence and purpose of **market segmentation**—the process of dividing a target market into smaller, more precisely defined groups of consumers or organizations who have common needs and are expected to respond similarly to a marketing action.

The Advantages of Market Segmentation to the Organization

It's estimated that the average person sees an astounding 4,000–10,000 advertising messages each day.[3] That's why it's critical to target the right market. Most marketers have limited advertising budgets, so using one marketing message to reach a broad audience may garner a few new customers, but it's likely to come at a high advertising cost.

Consider a company that makes woodworking tools for the professional or home hobbyist. The company would waste a lot of money placing ads in "general interest" magazines like *Reader's Digest* because the average reader likely has little interest in woodworking tools. A better bet would be placing ads in specialty magazines like *The Family Handyman* (published by the same company as *Reader's Digest*), *Wood Magazine*, or *Popular Woodworking*— publications aimed at professional woodworkers and hobbyists. Not only would it likely cost less to advertise in specialty magazines like these, but the ads would be more relevant to the company's desired customer base.

There are other benefits to market segmentation. Let's look at a few:

- **Improved Focus on the "Important" Customers.** Customers are not all alike. Some will love your product or service, while others will be indifferent. Instead of trying to appeal to everyone, market segmentation enables marketers to focus their efforts and resources on those customers who will likely result in revenue for the company.
- **Improved Product Development.** Market segmentation allows marketers to better understand what consumers want in a product or service, and that knowledge enables the marketer to make recommendations for refinements to existing products and services to meet those needs. This knowledge is equally important in terms of designing *new* products and services to meet the needs of the target market.
- **Improved Brand Loyalty.** When customers feel that your company's products or services are a good fit for them, they are more likely to stick with your brand and recommend it to others.[4]

Methods of Segmenting Consumer Markets

There are several different types of marketing segments you can create. We'll focus on four major types:

- Geographic segmentation: the "where"
- Demographic segmentation: the "who"
- Behavioral segmentation: the "how"
- Psychographic segmentation: the "why"

Let's first take a look at **geographic segmentation**, or dividing the market based on where your customers or potential customers live. There are several geographic parameters a marketer can use to focus their marketing efforts, including location, cultural preferences, climate, language, and population type and density (see Figure 5.2).

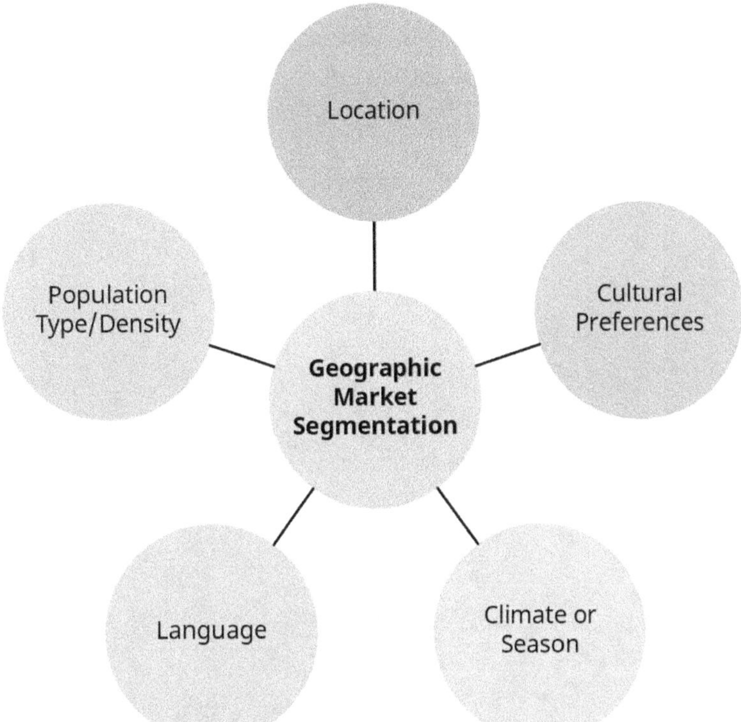

Figure 5.2 Geographic Market Segmentation (attribution: Copyright Rice University, OpenStax, under CC BY 4.0 license)

Let's explore each of these individually.

Segmenting the market on the basis of location can be as small as a county or zip code or as large as a country. Segmenting a market this way can also be used to identify a new geographic location into which the business may wish to expand.

Starbucks is a great example of a company that uses location segmentation. First, the company segments its markets according to global geographic segmentation—the Americas, China, and Asia Pacific and Europe, the Middle East, and Africa.[5] Each of these segments is then subject to sub-segmentation in order to cater to markets that share cultural preferences. For example, in China, where tea tends to be the beverage of choice, Starbucks offers a lengthy menu of tea-based drinks like Red Bean Green Tea Frappuccino and Black Tea Latte. In Taiwan, where consumers prefer creamy beverages, Starbucks offers Jeju Honey Peanut Latte and Happy Cheese White Mocha.[6]

Customers' choices and market behavior can also be influenced by their location in terms of climate or season. Segmenting the market this way also allows the marketer to present the most relevant information to the audience. There's not much of a need for snowmobiles during the summer, even in northern climates, and not much demand for convertibles in the middle of winter in those same northern climates. In the same manner, companies that sell beachwear are more likely to record increased sales during the summer and in warmer climates.

Language can be used to segment a market geographically. For instance, there are a number of different languages spoken in different regions and states in India. Therefore, it stands to reason that an advertisement in the Hindi language would miss the mark in states where Assamese or Telugu is spoken. These advertisements would need to be translated for people in different regions.[7] To give you an idea of the complexity of this, however, there are more than 19,500 languages or dialects spoken in India and 121 languages spoken by 10,000 people or more![8]

Finally, the marketer can segment the market on the basis of population type or density—in other words, whether the market is urban, suburban, or rural. Think about this in terms of a company that does home lawn treatments like fertilization, weed control, or grub control. That company would likely have more success targeting a suburban area where residents need extra yard care. It would be less successful in an urban area where residents have smaller yards or maybe no yards at all!

Demographic Segmentation: The "Who"

Now let's look at dividing a market on the basis of demographic segmentation (see Figure 5.3).

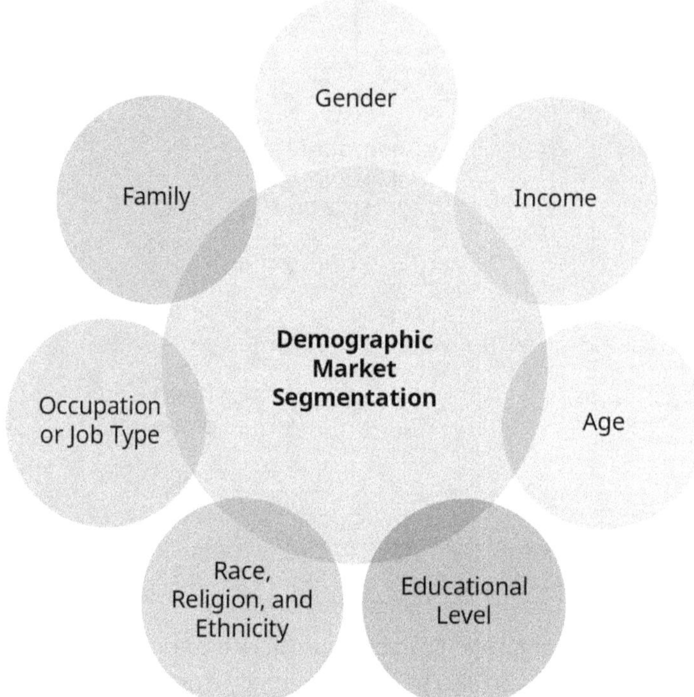

Figure 5.3 Demographic Market Segmentation (attribution: Copyright Rice University, OpenStax, under CC BY 4.0 license)

With **demographic segmentation**, the marketer will divide the market into smaller groups, generally on the basis of common demographic factors such as gender, income, age, educational level, race, religion, ethnicity, occupation or job type, and even family structure. These smaller segments enable marketers to focus their efforts and resources on those customers who will likely result in revenue for the company.

With gender segmentation, the market is divided into men and women. Those who identify as men and those who identify as women have different interests in terms of shopping for various products like apparel, shoes, and food. For example, look at the ad campaigns crafted toward women in fashion magazines such as *Vogue* or *Vanity Fair*. You'll likely see a different ad focus in magazines like *GQ* or *Men's Health*.

Income segmentation involves segmenting the market on the basis of monthly or yearly income. With income data, a company can determine how its potential consumer base spends money on both the high and low ends of the spectrum. Mercedes-Benz is a classic example of this as it markets different car models at different price points: A-Class vehicles starting in the low $30,000 range, C-Class in the $40,000–$55,000 range, E-Class in the $55,000–$72,000 range, and, finally, its S-Class vehicles, which are priced at $95,000 and up.[9]

Age is another common factor used to segment consumers. It's likely no surprise to you that our preferences change with age. The products that appeal to us as teens or young adults are likely not the same products that appeal to us when we're older. The age segmentation is threefold:

- **Age Range.** This type of segmentation represents a specific age group, such as children, teens, adults, and older adults. However, you also need to consider "perceived age" (i.e., how old you feel) versus "actual age" (i.e., your chronological age). Purchases tend to reflect our perceived age rather than our chronological age.
- **Life Cycle or Life Stage.** In the same way that our preferences change with age, they change with our life stage, and most people typically pass through many life stages, from childhood to adolescence to young adult, middle age, and older adult. This type of segmentation can be a little tricky, however, particularly in view of stereotypes and changing family dynamics. For instance, some teens or young adults may be parents, while middle-aged adults may be starting families, having second families, becoming empty nesters, or are single (or single again).
- **Generation Based.** This method of breakdown defines age by generation, such as baby boomers, millennials, and Generation X. Consumers within generations will differ slightly in age (for example, baby boomers were born between 1946 and 1964, and Gen Xers were born between 1965 and 1980[10]), but these generational cohorts still tend to share certain characteristics and ideas.

Education is another means through which marketers can segment a market, and it also affects the channels through which marketers reach the target market. For example, if you were going to open a bookstore in your hometown, you'd want to determine the average educational level in your community as part of your due diligence. Are most of your would-be customers elementary or middle school students? Their tastes in reading will be considerably different than if you live in a college town populated by a number of literary professors who prefer the classics.[11]

Race, ethnicity, and religion can be used to segment a market. It's always dangerous to stereotype, but consumers of different races, ethnicities, and religions have different preferences and needs. Consider a company like Zondervan, a leading bible publisher. It would make sense for the company to segment its market based upon religion because it offers products that complement the religious beliefs of a particular group. Likewise, IMAN Cosmetics is designed for women with darker skin tones, so its target market would likely be women of color.

Marketers can also segment the market based on occupation or job type. Focusing on a smaller segment of the market enables a company to make better use of its limited resources. For example, AllHeart is a producer of medical scrubs, nursing uniforms, shoes, and medical accessories, so it has segmented the market to focus on medical professionals. Another example can be found with Saf-Gard, a producer of safety shoes and work boots that meet or exceed safety standards. This company targets workers in the construction and farming industries.

Finally, a company can segment its market on the basis of family structure, marital status, whether there are children in the home, and the life stages of those in each family.

Behavioral Segmentation: The "How"

Behavioral segmentation divides consumers into market segments depending on their behavior patterns when interacting with a product or service (see Figure 5.4).

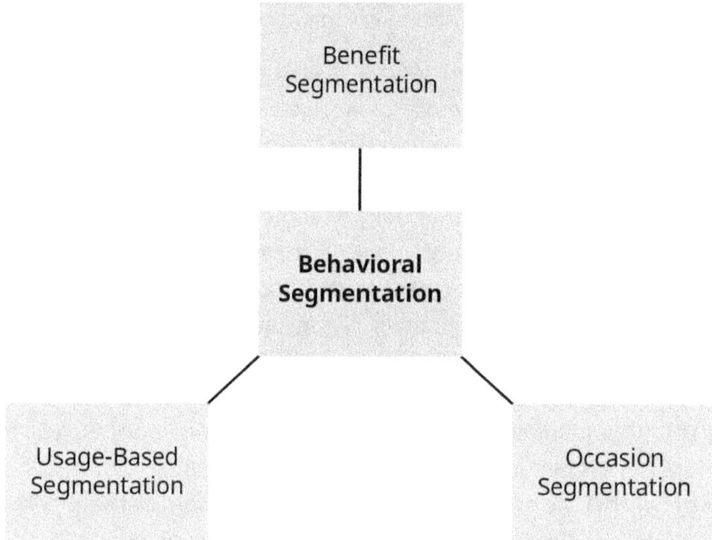

Figure 5.4 Behavioral Market Segmentation (attribution: Copyright Rice University, OpenStax, under CC BY 4.0 license)

The behavioral pattern benefit segmentation focuses on which benefits or features of a product or service are most applicable to the customer. Consider toothpaste. People who buy toothpaste may do so for a variety of reasons—sensitive teeth, tartar control, whitening, fresh breath, cavity prevention, etc. This means that two consumers may look identical in terms of their demographics but could have very different values regarding the benefits and features that are most important to them.

For example, Procter & Gamble markets various formulations of its Crest brand toothpaste, including Crest Kids, Gum Detoxify Deep Clean, Gum and Breath Purify Deep Clean, and more. Marketing messages sharing the toothpaste's benefits and differences are tailored for each formulation.[12]

Occasion segmentation divides consumers (or potential consumers) on the basis of the occasions when they make purchases or plan to buy. Occasion marketing is huge because marketers know that consumers will be purchasing certain items on certain occasions. Just look at the number of Internet or TV ads advertising chocolates, flowers, and jewelry in the weeks preceding Valentine's Day or the sudden appearance of PEEPS and chocolate bunnies before Easter.

Usage-based segmentation identifies various segments of users based on how much they use a product. Consumers are typically divided into groups of non-, light, medium, and heavy product users. As a general rule, companies target heavy users because, although heavy users may be a relatively small percentage of the market, they generally account for a high percentage of total buying. This is actually called the Pareto principle in marketing, which asserts that 80 percent of a company's revenue comes from the top 20 percent of repeat or loyal customers.[13]

LINK TO LEARNING

Pareto Principle

Regardless of which area of business you go into, the Pareto principle is a concept you will encounter often. It's a concept people adopt in their life and in management. Check out these resources to learn more:

- Simply Psychology article: Pareto Principle (The 80-20 Rule) (https://openstax.org/r/pareto-principle)
- Better Than Yesterday video: The Pareto Principle—80/20 Rule—Do More by Doing Less
  Click to view content (https://openstax.org/books/principles-marketing/pages/5-1-market-segmentation-and-consumer-markets)

- Fresh Books Blog article: How to Increase Productivity Using the Pareto Principle (https://openstax.org/r/waystoapplythe8020rule)
- HubSpot article: What Is the 80/20 Rule? How the Pareto Principles Will Supercharge Your Productivity (https://openstax.org/r/marketingparetoprinciple)

Psychographic segmentation breaks down consumer groups into segments that influence buying behaviors, such as lifestyle, personality variables, and values (see Figure 5.5).

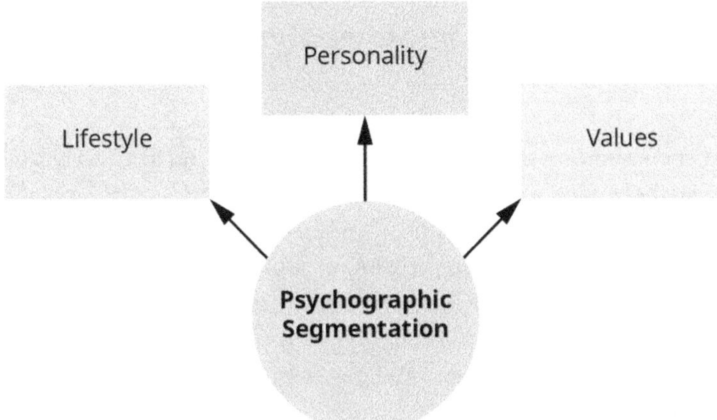

Figure 5.5 Psychographic Market Segmentation (attribution: Copyright Rice University, OpenStax, under CC BY 4.0 license)

A person's lifestyle provides insight on what they value, or how they spend their time and money. Marketers analyze three lifestyle dimensions, commonly called AIO (activities, interests, and opinions) variables:

- **Activities.** Activities focus on a person's daily routine and/or hobbies. For instance, if you're an urban dweller who rides your bike to work and works out regularly, your buying patterns are probably going to be vastly different from someone who drives to work and doesn't work out.
- **Interests.** Interests drive passions. What are your interests? Crypto investing? Gaming? Photography? That's important information to marketers because by identifying your interests (assuming you're a target consumer), they can more easily determine what marketing messages will appeal to you.
- **Opinions.** Opinions matter, and especially in the age of social media, opinions spread fast. Companies monitor social media sites to gain insight about consumers' opinions of their products or services and respond accordingly—and quickly! Companies such as PepsiCo and Mastercard continuously monitor 24/7 all social media postings about their companies, products, and competitors worldwide.

LINK TO LEARNING

Social Media Segmentation

There are a number of ways to segment social media markets. Read more about it on HubSpot: "8 Simple Ways to Segment Your Social Media Audience." (https://openstax.org/r/marketingsegmentsocialmedia) Understanding how social media influences market segmentation is critical. Read this article from Marketing Tech (https://openstax.org/r/marketingtechnews) to gain insight.

Marketers can also segment a market based on personality variables to create a group of people with similar personality traits because personality and purchasing habits are strongly related. To illustrate this, look at the fitness tool Mirror. This interactive home trainer has performed well in the market since its inception in 2018 because it targets those people who want to work out but can't find the time to go to the gym.

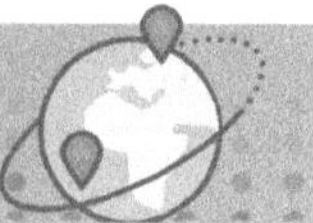

LINK TO LEARNING

Personality Segmentation

Harley-Davidson is another great example of a company that segments its market based on personality. Check out this video from Harley-Davidson as an example of how it is sending a message that resonates with motorcycle riders.

Click to view content (https://openstax.org/books/principles-marketing/pages/5-1-market-segmentation-and-consumer-markets)

Values are the principles and important things that influence the way you live and work. As one example, environmental concerns are becoming a value issue for consumers, and they are looking for products from companies that are better for the earth. Knowing this, IKEA has incorporated a furniture buyback and resale program in the United States. If you have a piece of IKEA furniture that's an oldie but still a goody and you want to retire it, IKEA will buy it back and help you pave the way toward sustainable living.[14] Another great example is Lululemon's Like New program. You can bring in any used Lululemon gear, trade it in at the store, get an eGift card for use at a Lululemon store, and 100 percent of the Like New profits are reinvested in the company's sustainability initiatives.[15]

In addition to the AIO model of psychographic segmentation, there is another model known as VALS (values, attitudes, and lifestyles) that segments consumers into eight different types (as shown in Figure 5.6).

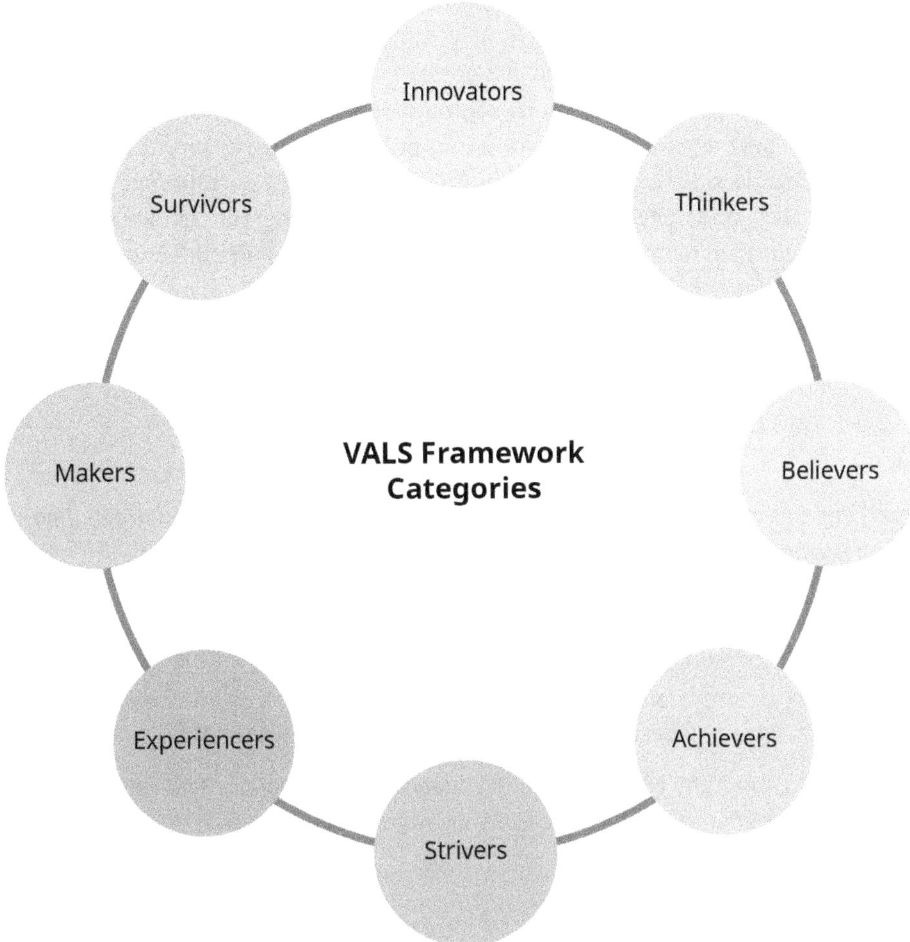

Figure 5.6 The VALS Framework (attribution: Copyright Rice University, OpenStax, under CC BY 4.0 license)

The premise of VALS is relatively simple: if you know what consumers are thinking, you will know which promotions or marketing messages will attract them to your product or service. And you can use the framework to determine what consumers are thinking by determining their values, attitudes, and lifestyles.[16]

Let's take a look at these eight consumer types:

- *Innovators* are characterized by high income and high resources. These innovators have definite individual tastes and preferences and are motivated to achieve the "finer things" in life.
- *Thinkers* are consumers who have resources and are motivated by their knowledge.
- *Believers* are subtly different from thinkers in that thinkers typically make their own decisions, whereas believers look to their peers for affirmation of their decisions. They have fewer resources than innovators or thinkers.
- *Achievers* tend to be high-resource consumers who want to excel, both at the workplace and within their families. They are likely to purchase brands that have stood the test of time in terms of their success in the marketplace.
- *Strivers* tend to be lower-resource consumers. They have similar values as achievers but lack the same level of resources.
- *Experiencers* have relatively high resources and want to experience "being different." The majority of experiencers are young adults.
- *Makers*, like experiencers, want self-expression, but they lack the resources to make that happen, so they tend to be more focused on building a better family than spending money.
- *Survivors* have the least number of resources and are the least likely to adopt innovative products. Survivors tend to be brand-loyal customers.[17]

Using Multiple Segmentation Bases

Keep in mind that a company doesn't have to use just one or two segmentation bases; it can use all of them or a mix of them, a process that's also known as **multi-segment marketing**. It's not uncommon for companies to develop products that compete against their own offerings as long as the new products offer different perceived benefits to consumers. For instance, Procter & Gamble sells several different types of laundry detergent, such as Tide, Gain, and Cheer. Each of these brands offers different benefits like all-temperature use, fresh scent, unscented, stain removal, or whitening. By having these different brands, P&G can appeal to multiple target markets.

CAREERS IN MARKETING

Market Research Analyst

What does a market research analyst do, you might ask? They study markets and data to determine potential new opportunities for a company. According to the Bureau of Labor Statistics (https://openstax.org/r/businessandfinancialmarket), the typical entry-level education required is a bachelor's degree, and there are about 741,000 jobs with an expected growth rate of 22 percent from 2020 to 2030. This article from Coursera, "What Is a Marketing Analyst? And How to Become One (https://openstax.org/r/articlesmarketinganalyst)," outlines job roles and responsibilities, compares this job to other types of analyst jobs, and describes steps for how to become a marketing analyst.

Watch this video to learn about the typical marketing analyst job description. And watch this video from a real digital marketing analyst at Accenture to learn what a typical day includes.

Click to view content (https://openstax.org/books/principles-marketing/pages/5-1-market-segmentation-and-consumer-markets)

Click to view content (https://openstax.org/books/principles-marketing/pages/5-1-market-segmentation-and-consumer-markets)

Knowledge Check

It's time to check your knowledge on the concepts presented in this section. Refer to the Answer Key at the end of the book for feedback.

1. In China, Starbucks offers tea-based drinks featuring regional ingredients. On what basis has Starbucks segmented its market?
   a. Demographic
   b. Behavioral
   c. Geographic
   d. Psychographic

2. A travel agency offers adventure trips like hut-to-hut camping in the mountains as well as quieter vacations in all-inclusive resorts. On what basis has the travel agency segmented its market?
   a. Psychographic
   b. Demographic
   c. Behavioral
   d. Geographic

3. Road Scholar is an American not-for-profit organization that provides educational travel programs geared primarily to older adults. On what basis has Road Scholar segmented the market?

    a. Geographic
    b. Psychographic
    c. Demographic
    d. Behavioral

4. Garnier offers a wide range of shampoos, including hydrating shampoo, smoothing shampoo, color-safe shampoo, volumizing shampoo, and more. On what basis has Garnier segmented the market?
    a. Geographic
    b. Psychographic
    c. Behavioral
    d. Demographic

5. Peloton's main products are Internet-connected stationary bikes and treadmills that enable subscribers to remotely participate in live classes via streaming media. This enables subscribers to have a "spin class" experience without going to the gym. On what basis has Peloton segmented the market?
    a. Demographic
    b. Behavioral
    c. Geographic
    d. Psychographic

5.2 | Segmentation of B2B Markets

Learning Outcomes

By the end of this section, you will be able to:
- **LO 1** Describe the challenges of segmenting B2B markets.
- **LO 2** Discuss the advantages of segmenting B2B markets.
- **LO 3** Explain methods of segmenting B2B markets.

Challenges of Segmenting B2B Markets

Just like its consumer market counterpart, business-to-business (B2B) market segmentation focuses on identifying unique market segments based on common characteristics. However, segmenting a B2B market is in many ways far more challenging than segmenting a consumer market because the motivations, processes, and considerations of B2B buyers are quite different from those of business-to-consumer (B2C) buyers. Let's take a closer look.

- **Challenge #1: Dealing with Highly Complex B2B Markets.** As discussed in Business Markets and Purchasing Behavior, decision-making in B2B markets is quite different from decision-making in B2C markets. In a B2C market, the consumer is often the only decision maker involved in making a purchase. That's not the case in B2B markets, where you're often dealing with a buying center—all the people in the organization who have varying influence on the B2B buy decision. You may also recall from this chapter that buying centers have a variety of members who play different roles, such as users, initiators, influencers, gatekeepers, decision-makers, etc. Accordingly, it can be difficult to identify precisely who the target buyer is.[18]
- **Challenge #2: Dealing with More Rational Buyers.** Although the view is somewhat controversial, it is said that B2B buyers are more "rational." Consumers tend to buy what they want and are more affected by emotions in buying decisions. Alternatively, B2B buyers typically buy what they need, and buying decisions are more deliberate, particularly in terms of price. Accordingly, in B2B markets, the marketer must determine the drivers of those needs.
- **Challenge #3: Complexity of B2B Products.** Just as the decision-making unit in a B2B transaction is more complex, so too are the B2B products themselves. When you make a major purchase, like a high-definition

TV, your choice is likely made on the basis of fairly simple criteria. You might evaluate things like screen size, resolution, and your budget. However, in the B2B market, even the simplest of products may have to be integrated into a larger system. For example, a new payroll system might have to be integrated into the company's human resources information system (HRIS). Another consideration with respect to the complexity of B2B products is that many B2B purchases are frequently tweaked to meet the company's detailed specifications, whereas consumer products are almost always standardized.[19]

Advantages of Segmenting B2B Markets

Market segmentation is a tried-and-true method that's been around since the 1950s, but there is still some confusion about how to use it in a B2B setting because it's not as clear-cut as other forms of market segmentation. How does a marketer target the characteristics of something impersonal like a business? Despite the challenges of segmenting B2B markets, it still plays a critical role. Let's examine some of the advantages.[20]

- **Improved Campaign Performance**. Similar to the previous example of a company using specialty magazines to reach the right target audience with the right message, B2B marketers can do the same. For example, Mailchimp, a marketing automation platform and email marketing service, examined user data to compare segmented marketing campaigns with non-segmented campaigns. The statistics based upon a comparison of 18 million email recipients were eye-opening. Campaigns directed toward defined market segments saw increases in a number of areas, including a 14.3 percent higher email open rate.[21]
- **Improved Customer Loyalty and Retention**. In our discussion of consumer market segmentation, we pointed out that market segmentation allows marketers to better understand what consumers are looking for in a product or service, and the same holds true with B2B market segmentation. The more marketers know about their customers' business objectives and challenges, the more they can attempt to meet their needs. That not only builds confidence in the brand but also ultimately leads to greater customer retention and loyalty.[22]
- **Assistance in Product Development**. By using market segmentation, a company can refine its products or services to better meet the needs of its B2B customers. For example, let's say your company's product is payroll software. Having better identified the needs of the target market, your company may be able to add new features and functionality to make it even more attractive for the target market and possibly add a new revenue stream by making the product useful for another market segment.
- **Improved Profitability**. Implementing a market segmentation strategy accomplishes three important goals. First, targeting the right B2B customers with the right message increases your company's competitiveness. Second, it enables the marketer to properly price products with the best price for its different customer segments. Third, it helps identify the best prices with which to target new customers and ensure that your organization's offerings are neither overpriced nor underpriced, thereby increasing profitability.[23]

Methods of Segmenting B2B Markets

How do you segment B2B markets? Just like with consumer markets, there is a variety of methods. Marketers can segment B2B markets based on firmographics, technographics, needs-based segmentation, value-based segmentation, and behavioral segmentation (see Figure 5.7). We will look at each of these in the following sections.

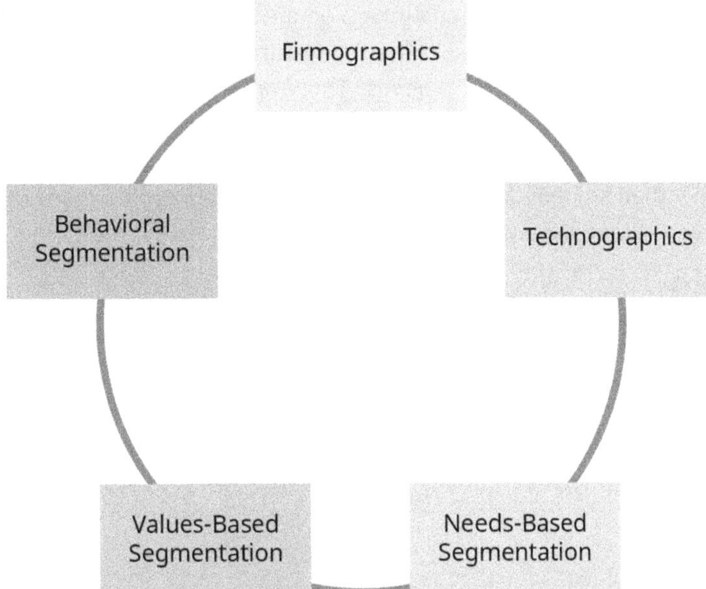

Figure 5.7 Methods of Segmenting B2B Markets (attribution: Copyright Rice University, OpenStax, under CC BY 4.0 license)

Firmographics

Where demographics are concerned with people, **firmographics** are concerned with companies. They are a grouping of B2B customers based on shared company attributes. There are five general categories of firmographics:

- **Industry.** What are the organization's primary activities? Once you've determined that piece of information, you can use market segmentation to group firms that are in a similar line of business.
- **Location.** The mantra in the real estate industry is that there are three things that matter: location, location, location. Just like with geographic segmentation in the B2C market, a marketer can choose a city, state, country or even a continent, depending on the line of business. For instance, depending on the cybersecurity challenges or threats faced by customers in different countries or regions, a cybersecurity firm may offer different cybersafety features in its software.[24]
- **Size.** Will your company target small and midsize operations or Fortune 500 companies? The needs of these organizations are vastly different. Firmographic size typically involves two components: revenue and number of employees.
- **Legal Structure.** In firmographics, legal structure denotes the legal status of a firm. For example, is the organization a sole proprietorship, a limited liability company, a corporation, or a nonprofit firm? Is it an independent business, a parent company, or a subsidiary of another business?[25] All of these factors are important to know in order to create targeted content.
- **Performance.** Customer segments can be broken down based on performance, such as market share, quarterly or annual sales figures, and growth and/or losses (both in employees and revenue).

Segmenting Customers Based on Technographics

Technographic segmentation is based on the various hardware and software technologies used by B2B customers. It allows the marketer to organize prospects by their technology ownership and usage and narrow the market to those prospects who want to invest in new technological solution in the future.[26]

Needs-Based Segmentation

Think about it: What's the point of marketing a product or a service to an organization that doesn't need it? **Needs-based segmentation** is the concept that a marketer should focus limited resources on those customers that need the product and have the ability to purchase it.

Needs-based segmentation clusters groups of customers on the basis of what they need or want when seeking a product. Does your company's product offer the features or benefits that the B2B buyer is seeking? Will the product meet the buyer's (or company's) needs? Those are the questions marketers need to answer when segmenting the B2B market based on needs. The late Theodore Levitt, an economist and a professor at Harvard Business School once said, "People don't want to buy a quarter-inch drill; they want a quarter-inch hole."[27] Accordingly, rather than segmenting a market based on firmographics, many marketers choose to segment it based on what is valued by decision influencers.

Value-Based Segmentation

Value-based segmentation (sometimes called tiering or profitability segmentation) groups customers according to the potential value they may bring to a business. It places potential customers with the same value level (or "transactional worth") into individual segments for target marketing. In its simplest terms, this approach is like the usage-based segmentation strategy of B2C markets. A marketer examines previous purchase data to determine how much a company buys, how frequently it buys, and the value of the purchases.[28]

Behavioral Segmentation

Behavioral segmentation considers the behavior of customers toward a company's products or services. We're not talking about two-way mirrors or covert operations here. This can be as simple as determining how the customer interacted with your company's website, what content they interacted with, and whether the customer opened your last marketing email. The marketer then segments customers on the basis of their interaction with the company and attempts to discern if customers within that segment have become more interested or less interested over time. Behavioral segmentation is often used together with value-based segmentation to identify which customers should be pursued to get greater value out of them.[29]

LINK TO LEARNING

The Importance of Segmentation

For more information on the importance of segmenting B2B customers, check out this video, The Importance of Segmenting Your Customers. This video is from B2B Business International Market Research, a market research company, and it speaks to the importance and value of knowing your customers.

Click to view content (https://openstax.org/books/principles-marketing/pages/5-2-segmentation-of-b2b-markets)

Knowledge Check

It's time to check your knowledge on the concepts presented in this section. Refer to the Answer Key at the end of the book for feedback.

1. Hoffman Enterprises, a manufacturer of electronic controls for appliances, has segmented its customers based upon the size of the company in terms of revenue and its geographic location. What method of segmenting B2B markets is Hoffman Enterprises using?
   a. Technographics
   b. Behavioral
   c. Firmographics
   d. Needs Based

2. Matias is a marketing manager for a company whose product integrates with customer relationship management (CRM) systems such as Salesforce. In order to segment the market, he researches which

companies currently use Salesforce as well as any other complementary or competing tools. On what basis is Matias segmenting the market?

   a. Technographics
   b. Value-based
   c. Behavioral
   d. Firmographics

3. Which form of B2B market segmentation differentiates customers according to their "transactional worth"?

   a. Behavioral
   b. Firmographics
   c. Value based
   d. Needs based

4. Which form of B2B market segmentation groups customers based on sets of characteristics such as industry, location, size, legal structure, and performance?

   a. Technographics
   b. Psychographics
   c. Firmographics
   d. Demographics

5. Which B2B market segmentation strategy clusters groups of customers on the basis of what features they normally look for in a product?

   a. Firmographics
   b. Behavioral
   c. Technographics
   d. Needs based

5.3 | Segmentation of International Markets

Learning Outcomes

By the end of this section, you will be able to:

   LO 1 Describe the challenges of segmenting international markets.
   LO 2 Discuss the advantages of segmenting international markets.
   LO 3 Explain methods of segmenting international markets.

Challenges of Segmenting International Markets

As we've outlined in this chapter, companies can't be all things to all people because buyers differ in terms of their needs, wants, and demands. Accordingly, just as with consumer markets and B2B markets, companies typically find it necessary to segment international markets.

That's not to say that segmenting international markets is easy; rather, the reverse is true: it adds a whole new set of complications, including differences in cultural, economic, and political environments in various countries. Additionally, because of those cultural, economic, and political differences, consumers in international markets tend to be more diverse in character than domestic markets. Moreover, the range of income levels and populations and the diversity of lifestyles in international markets tend to be significantly greater than in the domestic market.[30] Accordingly, a single marketing strategy for all segments is questionable at best.

Advantages of Segmenting International Markets

The advantages of segmenting international markets aren't all that different from the advantages of segmenting the consumer or B2B markets, but there are some subtle differences. A marketer in the United States may have a much easier time understanding the needs and wants of US consumers, but that may not be the case with international consumers. Segmenting the international market and conducting market research allows the marketer to have a better understanding of international customers. It also enables the marketer to identify similarities and differences across international markets, which may lead them to combine segments across countries or even regions.[31]

Methods of Segmenting International Markets

There are four primary methods of segmenting international markets, as shown in Figure 5.8.

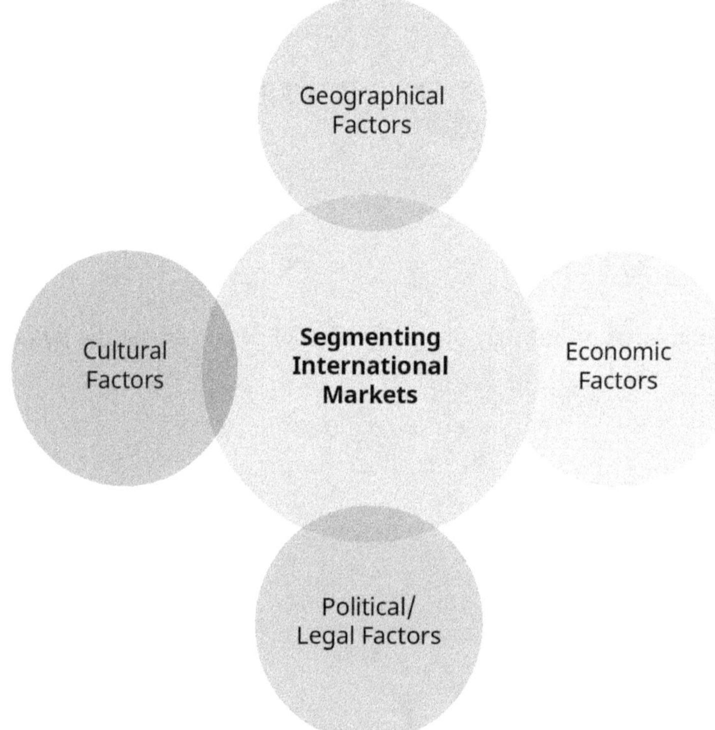

Figure 5.8 Segmenting International Markets (attribution: Copyright Rice University, OpenStax, under CC BY 4.0 license)

Geographic Segmentation

Just as with domestic markets, international markets can be segmented geographically. A company might segment by regions, such as Western Europe, the Middle East, Africa, Latin America, etc. Keep in mind, however, that although geographic segmentation groups countries by location, they may be very different from one another in other respects. For example, if you were to consider the countries included in a Western European region, you'd find that, both culturally and economically, the United Kingdom and Scotland are very similar, but both differ significantly from neighboring Ireland.[32] Similarly, people in West Africa tend to share similarities in dress, cuisine, and music, but these characteristics aren't shared extensively with groups outside of West Africa.[33]

In terms of geographic segmentation, marketers also need to consider the infrastructure of the country—the basic physical systems of the nation, such as roads, sewage treatment, communication, water treatment, electricity, etc. You may have the best product for the consumers in the international market segment, but if the infrastructure is such that you can't reasonably get the products to the consumers, that represents a restraining force that limits the opportunity.

Although the project is controversial, China has invested billions of dollars in an effort to strengthen its economy and global trade through its Belt and Road Initiative (BRI), a vast network of railways, energy pipelines, and highways through six economic corridors, both westward through former Soviet republics and southward to Pakistan, India, and Southeast Asia. In order to expand maritime trade traffic, China is investing in port development along the Indian Ocean, from Southeast Asia to East Africa and parts of Europe. The BRI spans a multitude of infrastructure projects intended to promote the flow of goods and foreign investment and is expected to impact more than 80 countries.[34]

Segmentation Based on Political and Legal Factors

As you've seen from our discussion of segmenting consumer markets, it's often done on the basis of factors such as age, gender, product usage, personality, etc. That's true as well in international markets, but the marketer needs to add still another dimension: country characteristics. These characteristics are typically political and legal factors, such as the type and stability of the government, how receptive the government is to foreign firms, monetary regulations, and how complex the bureaucracy of the nation is.[35] There are numerous other governmental policies that can interfere with international trade, such as tariffs (taxes imposed on imports), import quotas, currency controls, and local content requirements.

In 2022, in response to Russia's invasion of Ukraine, major sanctions have been put in place against Russia by the United States, the European Union, and the United Kingdom. For example, the United Kingdom imposed a 35 percent tax on some Russian imports, and several international companies like McDonald's, Coca-Cola, Starbucks and Marks & Spencer have either suspended operations in Russia or have withdrawn altogether. It doesn't take much to imagine the financial impact on Russia as a result of these sanctions.[36]

Segmentation Based on Economic Factors

Still another way to segment markets internationally is on the basis of economic factors—the level of economic development and the income levels of the population. This is often differentiated on the basis of whether the country is developing, developed, or underdeveloped. This classification is based on the nation's economic status (i.e., gross domestic product, gross national product, per capita income, degree of industrialization, and standard of living).

Developed countries typically have a high rate of industrialization and a relatively high level of individual income. Unemployment and poverty are typically low in developed nations, and citizens enjoy a relatively high standard of living, along with higher life expectancy.[37] It's likely in developed nations that companies will focus their international marketing efforts. According to the United Nations in 2020, 36 countries were classified as developed; interestingly enough, all of these countries were located in either North America, Europe, or "Developed Asia and Pacific."[38]

Developing countries, on the other hand, have a lower standard of living, a lower per capita income, and a slow rate of industrialization. Unemployment and poverty tend to be relatively high compared to developed countries, as are infant mortality rates.[39] The United Nations categorized 126 countries as developing, and all of these were located in either Africa, Asia, Latin America or the Caribbean.[40]

Underdeveloped countries are less developed economically than most other nations. These countries typically have little industry, and the standard of living is considerably lower than in developed or developing countries. Infrastructure may also be compromised in terms of roads, sewage treatment, water quality, etc. As a general rule, although there may be an attractive market for your company's product or service in an underdeveloped country, the challenges of getting the product into the customer's hands are often difficult to overcome.

Segmentation Based on Cultural Factors

Cultural factors, such as common language, religions, values, and attitudes, can also be used to segment a country or region. McDonald's uses a "think global, act local" strategy to help meet the cultural needs of various market segments. On one hand, it offers a standardized menu of offerings worldwide, like McNuggets and the McFlurry. On the other hand, it customizes other offerings on its menu to adapt to the cultural requirements of consumers. For example, in India, in order to appeal to vegetarian and non-beef-eating customers, McDonald's introduced the Maharaja Mac, which is made with a corn and cheese patty. The company also used the term "Maharaja" to appeal to India's history and liking of royalty and called it the "Social Burger" to suggest that it can be eaten quickly, giving people more time to spend with friends.[41]

McDonald's not only customizes its menu based on where it operates, but it also customizes its digital and TV advertisements depending on each country and consumer segment. For example, in Singapore, McDonald's ads attempted to appeal to consumers' love of nightlife by showing how McDonald's can enhance a night out, whereas in the United Kingdom, the company created cartoon ads focusing on Happy Meals to attract the large segment of children in the UK.[42]

Not to be outdone by McDonald's, Burger King also offers a wide variety of international menu items that aren't available in the United States. Did you know that there's a Spicy Shrimp Whopper available in Japan and a SufganiKing (Donut Burger) in Israel? In Norway, where there is one sauna for every two people, Burger King opened a fully operational spa complete with a 15-person sauna and media lounge where customers can enjoy their meals.[43]

One model that is particularly useful in assessing culture is social psychologist Geert Hofstede's cultural dimensions, originally published in the 1970s. Hofstede had studied IBM employees in over 50 countries and identified five dimensions that could be used to distinguish one culture from another.[44] Four of these dimensions directly affect marketing in different cultures:

- **Power Distance Index (PDI).** This dimension refers to how much power inequality exists within a culture and the degree to which people are accepting of this inequality. A high PDI score suggests that society accepts an unequal distribution of power, whereas a low PDI score means that power is shared and widely dispersed. If you're curious, the United States has a moderately low PDI score of 40 on a scale of 1 to 100, compared to a world average of 55.[45] This means that the United States is less accepting of hierarchy and authority than nations such as Malaysia, which has the highest power distance index in the world.[46] This cultural dimension plays an important role in marketing because, in countries where there is a high power distance index, marketers need to appeal to the leadership or the head of the family, whereas in low power distance index countries, it's more important to reach a broad range of "ordinary" people who will be the ultimate decision makers.
- **Individualism versus Collectivism (IDV).** This dimension refers to whether the culture emphasizes the needs and goals of the group as a whole or whether individual needs are paramount.[47] Think of individualism and collectivism as an "I" versus a "we" orientation. An individualistic society places emphasis on attaining personal goals, whereas a collectivist culture places emphasis on group goals and the well-being of the group. The United States has a very high individualism score of 91, compared to many Latin American countries such as Ecuador and Guatemala, which have single-digit individualism scores.[48] The implications for marketing are important here because for countries with high individualism, the marketing messages should emphasize how your products or services benefit them individually, such as by saving time and rewarding themselves. On the other hand, in countries with a low individualism ranking, it's more important to stress how buying your company's products will benefit the community as a whole.
- **Uncertainty Avoidance (UAI).** This dimension refers to the degree to which a society avoids risk or ambiguity. Societies with a high degree of uncertainty avoidance compensate for this uncertainty by establishing rules, policies, and procedures, whereas societies with low uncertainty avoidance more readily accept change. The UAI for the United States is 46, putting it into the moderate range compared to European nations like Italy (UAI of 75) and Poland (UAI of 93).[49] Let's consider how this affects marketing. Cultures with high uncertainty avoidance generally prefer to have product characteristics clearly spelled out, complete with product warranties and money-back guarantees. For example, if you want to market automobiles in that type of culture, it would be important to focus on the safety features of the car.

Conversely, cultures with low uncertainty avoidance are more accepting of trying something new.
- **Masculinity/Femininity (MAS).** This dimension refers to the degree to which gender-specific roles are valued in the society: Are "masculine" values such as achievement, ambition, and acquisition or "feminine" values such as quality of life and service to others valued more? In countries with a high masculinity ranking (e.g., Japan), men are intended to lead; women are supposed to follow. This is in direct contrast to countries with a low masculinity ranking (such as the United States and Canada), where women are treated equally to men and gender roles are more fluid. Societies with low masculinity would tend to respond negatively to gender-oriented promotion, so a neutral approach that appeals to both men and women would be more appropriate.[50] Consider how many brands in the United States focus on female empowerment and positive body image. That type of advertising would not appeal to a society with a masculine orientation.

Knowledge Check

It's time to check your knowledge on the concepts presented in this section. Refer to the Answer Key at the end of the book for feedback.

1. The Hofstede cultural dimension that assesses the degree to which a society avoids risk or ambiguity is known as ________.
   a. masculinity/femininity
   b. uncertainty avoidance
   c. power distance index
   d. individualism versus collectivism

2. Jamal's company is looking to expand into a market in West Africa, but Jamal wants to ensure that there are roads, bridges, nearby airports, and shipping terminals from which to distribute the product. Jamal is examining the country's ________.
   a. infrastructure
   b. governmental stability
   c. inflation and unemployment rates
   d. culture

3. Alexis is making a sales presentation in Japan, and she realizes suddenly realizes that she is the only woman in the meeting. This suggests that Japan has a high ________.
   a. degree of uncertainty avoidance
   b. individualism ranking
   c. power distance index
   d. masculinity ranking

4. Jose's firm is looking to market its products in Venezuela, but the marketing department is concerned about the current inflation rate in the country. This would be considered a(n) ________ factor.
   a. geographic
   b. political
   c. economic
   d. cultural

5. Which Hofstede cultural dimension assesses the degree to which gender-specific roles are valued in a society?
   a. Power distance index
   b. Masculinity/femininity
   c. Uncertainty avoidance

d.   Individualism versus collectivism

5.4 | Essential Factors in Effective Market Segmentation

Learning Outcomes

By the end of this section, you will be able to:

LO 1 List and describe the essential factors in effective market segmentation.

Essential Factors in Effective Market Segmentation

There's an acronym you can remember for the essential factors in effective and successful market segmentation—**ADAMS**. The acronym stands for five criteria:

- **A**ccessible
- **D**ifferentiable
- **A**ctionable
- **M**easurable
- **S**ubstantial

First, a market segment should be accessible. Can you reach consumers in that segment at an affordable cost, given the strengths and abilities of your marketing department? For example, if you discover that certain segments respond more effectively to outdoor advertising, social media campaigns, TV infomercials, or print ads, does your organization have the capabilities (and budget) to reach that segment?

Second, a market segment should be differentiable. In an ideal world, a market segment should be internally homogeneous (i.e., consumers within that segment have similar preferences and characteristics) but externally heterogeneous (i.e., different segments should be quite distinct and different from each other). You have to clearly define the differences between market segments so that the marketing programs directed at them can be implemented without overlap.

Third, a market segment should be actionable. Is it practical (or profitable) to execute a marketing strategy aimed at that segment? A market segment should be able to respond to a certain marketing strategy and have outcomes—e.g., awareness, interest, or purchase—that can be easily quantified.

Fourth, a market segment should be measurable. You should be able to accurately estimate the size of the market segment in terms of either sales value or number of customers so that you can decide whether, how, and to what extent you should focus your efforts on that segment.

Finally, a market segment should be substantial. It doesn't make sense to waste resources to market the product or service to a group too small to justify the expenditure of resources.[51]

Knowledge Check

It's time to check your knowledge on the concepts presented in this section. Refer to the Answer Key at the end of the book for feedback.

1. Mateus is a marketer for a consumer products company. His company is considering marketing a new breakfast drink, but Mateus wants to make certain that there is a sufficient number of consumers in his target audience to make the new product development process worthwhile. Which essential factor of market segmentation is he analyzing?
    a. Accessible
    b. Differentiable
    c. Actionable
    d. Measurable

2. Wall Enterprises is considering developing a new product for a market segment that has been identified by marketing research. However, based on the research, it appears that the market segment may be smaller than originally anticipated. Which essential factor of market segmentation does this reflect?
   a. Accessible
   b. Differentiable
   c. Substantial
   d. Actionable

3. Alma is analyzing the market segment she has identified for a new service to determine whether her firm can reach the consumers in that market within the constraints of her budget, given the resources of the firm. Which essential factor of market segmentation does this reflect?
   a. Accessible
   b. Actionable
   c. Substantial
   d. Measurable

4. Idris has been researching a potential market segment for his company's new product. He is concerned that, although the product holds considerable promise, the advertising campaign would be beyond the company's budget. Which essential factor of market segmentation appears to be lacking in Idris's analysis?
   a. Differentiable
   b. Substantial
   c. Measurable
   d. Accessible

5. Which essential factor in selecting a target market refers to the ability to accurately determine the size of the market in terms of either sales volume or number of customers?
   a. Actionable
   b. Differentiable
   c. Measurable
   d. Substantial

5.5 | Selecting Target Markets

Learning Outcomes

By the end of this section, you will be able to:
   LO 1 Define target market.
   LO 2 Explain target market strategies.

Target Markets Defined

Ultimately, the purpose of segmenting a market is to highlight the differences between groups of customers so that you can decide on which group(s) to focus your marketing efforts and resources—that's your **target market** (Figure 5.9).

Figure 5.9 Target marketing involves segmenting customer groups and focusing marketing resources on the segments that are most likely to purchase the product or service. (credit: "Three Arrows in the Centre of a Dart Board" by Marco Verch/flickr, CC BY 2.0)

Think of your target market in terms of focusing your marketing resources on segments that are more likely to buy from you. The bottom line is that target marketing is a more efficient, effective, and affordable way to reach customers and generate business. It's simply a subset of the total market.

Keep in mind that the target market isn't the same as the target audience. The target audience is narrower in that it refers to the group of consumers you expect to actually purchase the product. The audience may or may not overlap with the target market. For example, a children's toy may have a target market of boys between the ages of 6 and 12, but it's the boys' parents (who actually purchase the toy) who are the target audience. Let's take a look at how LEGO has mastered this concept.

MARKETING IN PRACTICE

LEGO

Figure 5.10 LEGO's segmentation strategy is to focus its marketing resources on parents who make the purchasing decisions and are interested in educating their children. (credit: "Lego" by Slack pics/flickr, CC BY 2.0)

You might think that children are the primary target market of toy manufacturers, but smart toy marketers know that they also have to market to parents because it's parents who actually buy the toys for their children. The marketers at LEGO (see Figure 5.10) seemed to have figured this out and have made the brand parent-approved by combining fun for children with an educational "twist."

LEGO brands its products not only as a creative outlet for children but also an opportunity to grow their interest in STEAM—a learning approach that incorporates science, technology, engineering, the arts, and mathematics. For example, one of its websites (https://openstax.org/r/educationlego) features education sets for children from preschool through middle school that promote learning through the toys. Another of its websites (https://openstax.org/r/aboutusdiscover) has an entire section of tips for playful parenting with LEGO bricks.[52] It also has websites for daily LEGO challenges and even daily build challenges and LEGO lessons for families at home.

Parents today want to buy their children toys that are safe and fun and that help them learn, and LEGO seems to have been able to win over the hearts (and money) of its target audience.

For more information about LEGO and STEAM, watch this video from Kansas City PBS.

Click to view content (https://openstax.org/books/principles-marketing/pages/5-5-selecting-target-markets)

Another important concept in target marketing is what's known as a **buyer persona**. A buyer persona is a semi-fictional representation of an ideal customer that helps marketers understand and relate to the target market. Buyer personas are intended to help marketers "visualize" those to whom they are selling so they can fine-tune their marketing messages.

Best Buy used personas in precisely this way. Its buyer personas are "Buzz" (the young tech enthusiast), "Barry" (the wealthy professional), "Ray" (the family man), and "Jill" (a soccer mom who is the main shopper for the household but usually avoids electronics stores).[53]

What's typically included in the buyer persona? Some examples include the following:

- **Name.** It may seem silly to include a made-up persona name like Best Buy did, but it's done so that the marketing team can more easily discuss their customers and plan how to reach them.
- **Age.** The age (or age range) of a persona allows for understanding generation-specific characteristics. As we pointed out in our earlier discussion of using age as a way to segment the market, consumers within the same age group tend to share characteristics and purchase preferences.
- **Interests.** The interests of the buyer persona describe things like hobbies or what they do in their spare time.
- **Media Usage.** What media platforms does the buyer persona use? Television, radio, the Internet? This is important because the marketer wants to know where to reach these "people" with their marketing messages.
- **Finances.** The income and other financial characteristics of the buyer personas help marketers glean insights as to what types of products or services will pique the interests of these buyer personas. These financial characteristics also assist in making decisions about price points and promotions that would be successful in reaching these customers.
- **Brand Affinities.** Do they like certain brands? If so, this can provide the marketer with valuable information about the type of content to which they best respond.[54]

LINK TO LEARNING

Importance of Buyer Personas

Customer personas are a tool to help marketers better understand their potential customers. Learn what a customer persona is and how to develop them from this brief Go Daddy video.

Click to view content (https://openstax.org/books/principles-marketing/pages/5-5-selecting-target-markets)
Also, check out this video from HubSpot's Stephen Higgins on how to use buyer personas to drive your marketing strategy.

Click to view content (https://openstax.org/books/principles-marketing/pages/5-5-selecting-target-markets)

Target Market Strategies

Thus far, we've discussed the how of segmenting a market and selecting target markets. At this point, it's up to the marketer whether the company will focus its efforts and resources on one or more of the identified segments or instead cater to the mass market. That choice is the determining factor in the company's marketing mix and its positioning plank. There are four generic target marketing strategies, as illustrated in Figure 5.11.

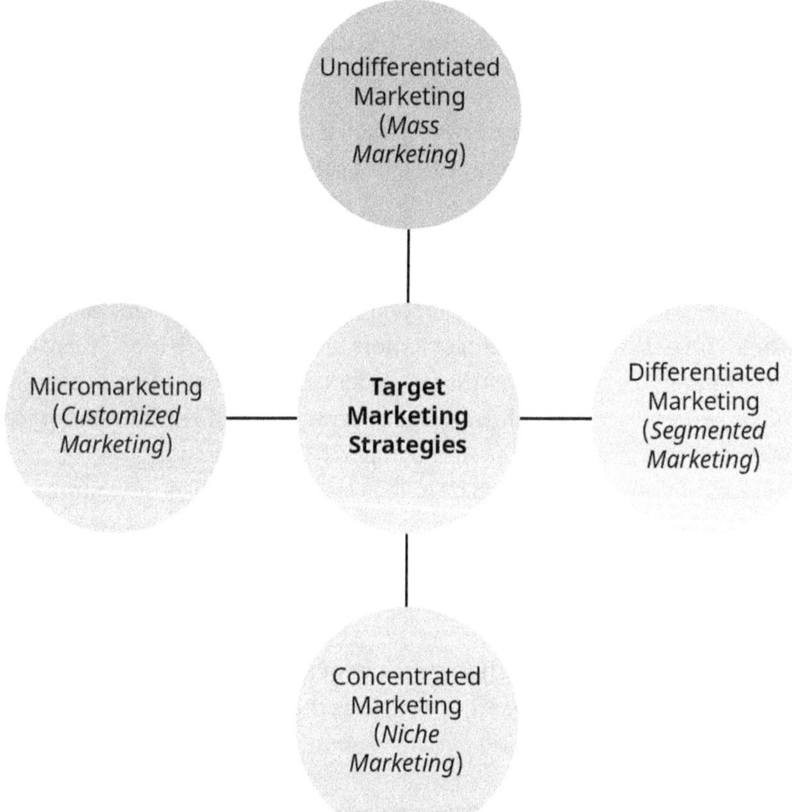

Figure 5.11 Target Marketing Strategies (attribution: Copyright Rice University, OpenStax, under CC BY 4.0 license)

Let's look at each of these strategies more closely.

Undifferentiated Marketing (Mass Marketing)

Sometimes there are no strong distinctions in customer characteristics. In cases like this, the costs involved in developing separate marketing mixes for separate target markets doesn't make financial sense. That's when a company may decide to use a single marketing mix for the entire market.

Let's imagine the entire market as one big apple pie. With undifferentiated marketing, the company doesn't take just one slice or perhaps a few slices of the pie—it takes the whole thing. The concept of **undifferentiated marketing** is quite simple. You want to reach as many people as possible and hope they'll jump on board with your product or service. Mass marketing is typically used when a brand has a product or service that has high market appeal, such as things that most (or maybe even all) people will always need or want. Consider a product that nearly everyone purchases, like soft drinks. Now think about all the advertising messages you get for a brand like Coca-Cola—you'll see TV commercials, magazine ads, billboards, banner ads in search engines, and the list goes on. That's the hallmark of mass marketing.

One of the biggest advantages of undifferentiated marketing is the scope and cost-efficiency of advertising on a much larger scale. Every single marketing message can be deployed across a variety of media channels and can potentially reach millions of consumers. This is where economies of scale come into play: with high-volume sales, production becomes less expensive because costs can be spread out over a larger amount of goods. That's a huge advantage compared to companies that produce products for smaller, more precisely targeted audiences. It's like buying in bulk at Sam's Club or Costco—because you buy so much of a product, the cost is lower. Companies that use undifferentiated marketing experience the same thing.[55]

Differentiated Marketing (Segmented Marketing)

Now let's take that same apple pie (the entire market), but instead of taking the whole thing, we're going to take only some of it. Perhaps we'll take just a few slices, or maybe we'll take more. It depends on how many target markets you want to serve. That's the premise of **differentiated marketing**.

This type of market targeting is one of the most common. A company identifies several target markets and designs separate, concentrated strategies for each. Separate brands are developed to serve each of the segments. Consider Nike, for example, which (like most apparel companies) offers different products for different segments. When Nike began its business, the founders were both competitive distance runners, so they targeted people like themselves as a segment of the running shoe market and the brand took off. However, in order to grow the business, Nike now focuses on three segments—women, young athletes, and runners.[56]

The automobile market is another good example of a clearly segmented market. Look around you on any given day, and you'll clearly see that people want different types of vehicles—small cars, big cars, SUVs, trucks, hybrids, and luxury cars. Many of the car makers like GM, Ford, Toyota, Honda, and others generally offer cars for most or all of the segments. For example, Honda's lineup includes models like the CR-V compact SUV, the Civic compact car, the midsize Honda Accord sedan, larger SUVs, and even a minivan.[57]

Concentrated Marketing (Niche Marketing)

Now we're going to take that same apple pie (remember, representing the entire market), and we're only going to take a single slice, and perhaps a small one at that. That's concentrated marketing.

Concentrated marketing doesn't mean that the company hasn't identified other target markets; it simply means that it chooses not to serve all of them. Some markets may not be attractive; other markets may not align with the company's business strengths. Therefore, the company focuses on just one target market with a single marketing mix. It channels all of its marketing efforts toward that specific segment with the aim of "owning" it over its competitors and creating strong brand loyalty.[58]

A good example of concentrated marketing is the eco-friendly cosmetics retailer LUSH. LUSH advocates for ethical buying and purity of handmade products and doesn't use animals in testing its products. As a matter of fact, at least half of its website is dedicated to fighting animal testing and overuse of plastic packaging and creating environmental awareness. The company also differentiates itself from its competitors with eco-friendly packaging and organic ingredients.[59]

This is a smart strategy for smaller companies or companies with limited resources that might be stretched thin if they attempt to compete in too many market segments. It has the added benefit that R&D and marketing can concentrate on understanding and meeting the needs of one group of customers rather than a diverse base of customers.

Micromarketing (Customized Marketing)

Micromarketing goes one step further than concentrated marketing and targets a specific group of individuals within a niche market based on specific information that has been collected about them.

For a good example of micromarketing, consider the real estate industry. A realtor may specialize in commercial sales or residential sales. Within the scope of residential sales, that realtor may drill down further and specialize in new construction, luxury properties, land and development, over-55 communities, or farms/ranches/equestrian properties.

Now let's assume that you're in the market for an expensive home in a particular area of the city. You'd likely contact a realtor who has developed a reputation in dealing with properties in a specific price range and knows the area where you'd like to move. That realtor is going to consider your specific needs and demands and will invest their efforts in finding a property that meets as many of your requirements as possible. That's micromarketing.

Stitch Fix is another good example of a company that uses micromarketing. Stitch Fix is an online personal styling service for men, women, and children that sends a selection of clothing and accessories to your door using a mix of machine learning, data, algorithms, and human stylists. The company uses "85 meaningful data points" about each customer, and based on those data points, it predicts clothing choices that the customer will want. If they doesn't like the product, they can just send it back with a prepaid, printable label within 30 days.[60] You can't get much more personalized than that!

Knowledge Check

It's time to check your knowledge on the concepts presented in this section. Refer to the Answer Key at the end of the book for feedback.

1. M&M's addresses people of all ages and appeals to everyone looking for sweets (that melt in your mouth, not in your hand). What target marketing strategy does M&M's use?
    a. Differentiated marketing
    b. Concentrated marketing
    c. Undifferentiated marketing
    d. Micromarketing

2. A ________ is a semi-fictional representation of your ideal customer that helps you understand and relate to the audience to which you want to market your product and/or services.
    a. buyer persona
    b. target market
    c. niche market
    d. brand affinity

3. Lefty's is a retail shop that makes specific products like left-handed scissors and left-handed notebooks for the population of left-handed people. What target marketing strategy does Lefty's use?
    a. Undifferentiated marketing
    b. Differentiated marketing
    c. Concentrated marketing
    d. Micromarketing

4. A running shoe company specializes in designing sustainable sneakers from recycled and renewable materials for athletes who care about the environment, as well as performance models of running shoes with less cushioning for runners who are concerned with speed. What target marketing strategy does the running company use?
   a. Concentrated marketing
   b. Undifferentiated marketing
   c. Differentiated marketing
   d. Micromarketing

5. 55places.com is a website for active adult "retirement" communities in the United States. It features unbiased information, current home sale listings, floor plans, photos, and third-party reviews. All the communities listed on the website are for residents who are age 55+. What target marketing strategy does the company use?
   a. Undifferentiated marketing
   b. Differentiated marketing
   c. Micromarketing
   d. Concentrated marketing

5.6 Product Positioning

Learning Outcomes

By the end of this section, you will be able to:
- **LO** 1 Define product positioning.
- **LO** 2 Explain approaches to product positioning.
- **LO** 3 Describe the positioning statement and perceptual maps.

Product Positioning Defined

So far, you've segmented the market by dividing the market into distinct groups of customers using the segmentation process and you've determined which customer group(s) you want to focus your marketing efforts on—the target marketing process. **Product positioning** is the process of deciding and communicating how an organization wants its market to think and feel about a product or service.

This third and final step is contained in what's known as the segmenting, targeting, and positioning model, the **STP model**. With the STP model, a company segments the market, selects the target market, and positions its products and services into the existing marketplace (see Figure 5.12). In their book *Positioning: The Battle for Your Mind*, marketing gurus Al Ries and Jack Trout write, "The basic approach of positioning is not to create something new and different, but to manipulate what's already up there in the mind."[61]

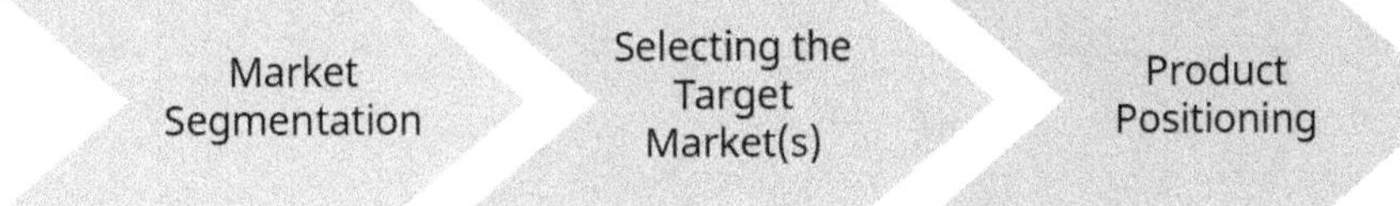

Figure 5.12 The STP Model (attribution: Copyright Rice University, OpenStax, under CC BY 4.0 license)

The STP model is helpful in identifying your most valuable customers and developing products and marketing messages that are targeted specifically toward those customers. This allows you to interact with each market segment in a more meaningful way by personalizing your messages (and hopefully selling more of your product!).

For example, Marriott International owns several different hotel chains that target specific consumer groups:

- Courtyard by Marriott focuses on over-the-road travelers who aren't looking for luxury and all the amenities; they just want a basic, clean hotel in which to stay during their trip.

- Ritz-Carlton hotels are by their nature more luxurious and target those travelers who don't mind paying a premium price for more luxury and amenities.
- Marriott ExecuStay hotels are aimed at professionals who need a longer-term place to stay (i.e., an extended stay hotel).

Since these target groups are seeking vastly different things from a hotel stay, Marriott tailors its marketing messages (and hotels) to appeal to the unique wants and needs of each specific group.[62]

As you can see, in this last step of the STP process, you want to first identify how you can most effectively position your product to target the customer segments that you've determined to be most valuable and then tailor the marketing mix that will be most effective in reaching them.

Approaches to Product Positioning

There are two main types of product positioning in marketing: head-to-head and differentiation. Let's take a look at both.

Head-to-Head Positioning

Head-to-head positioning focuses on comparison. It involves directly competing with competitors on similar product attributes in the same market. For instance, let's imagine that you have a small kiosk in a shopping mall where you serve freshly baked pretzels. If your kiosk makes different flavors of dough from scratch and your competitors use only processed frozen dough, you can set your pretzel business apart from your competitors in your customers' minds by emphasizing that selling point.

A classic example is when Avis (the car rental company) launched an advertising campaign that went head-to-head with Hertz, the market leader. Avis made a point of comparing itself to Hertz and made its position in the market a selling point using the slogan "When you're only No. 2, you try harder. Or else." This campaign positioned Avis as a direct competitor of Hertz and also did something unique: it highlighted its underdog status, turning it from a liability into an asset. The results? Prior to the ads, Avis was losing $3.2 million a year; after the ads, Avis improved its performance and earned $1.2 million. Remarkably, that was the first time in over a decade that Avis had been profitable.[63]

LINK TO LEARNING

Example of Head-to-Head Positioning

Another good example of head-to-head positioning is Wendy's, which launched an advertising campaign a few years ago saying that its beef is fresh, never frozen, versus its competitors, particularly McDonald's. Check out this Wendy's Super Bowl commercial from 2018 where it goes head-to-head with McDonald's.

Click to view content (https://openstax.org/books/principles-marketing/pages/5-6-product-positioning)

Differentiation Positioning

Differentiation positioning is all about emphasizing your product's or service's unique qualities vis-à-vis the competition. Similar to head-to-head positioning, you're going to focus on your offerings and attempt to convince customers to buy your products or services instead of those of the competition. However, dissimilar to head-to-head positioning, instead of competing in the same market, you'll attempt to identify new markets and seek out customers who may be interested in your offerings because of those unique qualities you've identified.[64] Common differentiation strategies are intended to draw consumers' attention to the value, quality, or uniqueness of your offering.

For instance, Curves, the largest women's fitness franchise in the world, succeeded by offering a fitness alternative to both home-based exercise routines and traditional health clubs. The experience of a Curves facility was entirely different from that of a typical health club. Instead of machines arranged in rows facing a TV, Curves arranged its machines in a circle to facilitate interaction among members. There were few (if any) mirrors and no men staring. The result was that Curves did not compete head-to-head with other health and exercise concepts; rather, it created new demand.[65]

Positioning Statements

In your other college courses, you may have heard terms such as *vision statement* and *mission statement*. We're going to add a third term to your vocabulary—*positioning statement*. Essentially, a **positioning statement** briefly describes your brand, product, service, and target market. Not only does it define how your brand meets the customer's needs, but it also tries to clarify why it does so better than your competition. It answers the question "What experience do you want your customers to have with this product or service?"

Templates for writing your positioning statement abound. Here are just a few examples:

- [Your brand] provides [your offering/benefit that makes you better than competitors] for [your customers] who [customer needs] because [the reason why your customers should believe you are better than competitors].[66]
- For [target audience], [brand name] is the [your market] that delivers [your points of differentiation] so they can [end benefit] because [your evidence].[67]

Now let's take a look at some examples of positioning statements for companies with which you're likely familiar so that you can see these templates in action:

- Amazon: "For consumers who want to purchase a wide range of products online with quick delivery, Amazon provides a one-stop online shopping site. Amazon sets itself apart from other online retailers with its customer obsession, passion for innovation, and commitment to operational excellence."[68]
- Apple: "For individuals who want the best personal computer or mobile device, Apple leads the technology with the most innovative products. Apple emphasizes technological research and advancement and takes an innovative approach to business best practices—it considers the impact our products and processes have on its customers and the planet."[69]
- McDonald's: "For individuals looking for a quick-service restaurant with an exceptional customer experience, McDonald's is a leader in the fast-food industry, with friendly service and consistency across thousands of convenient locations. McDonald's dedication to improving operations and customer satisfaction sets it apart from other fast-food restaurants."[70]
- Coca-Cola: "For individuals looking for high quality beverages, Coca-Cola offers a wide range of the most refreshing options—each creates a positive experience for customers when they enjoy a Coca-Cola brand drink. Unlike other beverage options, Coca-Cola products inspire happiness and make a positive difference in customers' lives, and the brand is intensely focused on the needs of consumers and customers."[71]

Perceptual Positioning Maps and How They Are Used

A **perceptual map** is a visual diagram that shows how the average target market consumer perceives your product versus those of your competitors.[72]

A perceptual map uses two determinant attributes on a graph. **Determinant attributes** are those attributes that a customer uses in making their purchase decision. In other words, what you do believe consumers' "hot buttons" are with respect to your product or service offering? You've got a vast array of determinant attributes to use. You could use price versus quality, sugar versus protein, or any number of other attributes. The bottom line is that these attributes should reflect what customers are looking for in the product or service.

Once you've established the determinant attributes, you plot your product offering onto the map. Let's imagine that your company is getting ready to introduce a new nutritional drink for seniors. You might start out with determinant attributes like high/low sugar and high/low protein (although you could use other determinant attributes like price, taste, etc.). Step one of your perceptual map might look something like Figure 5.13.

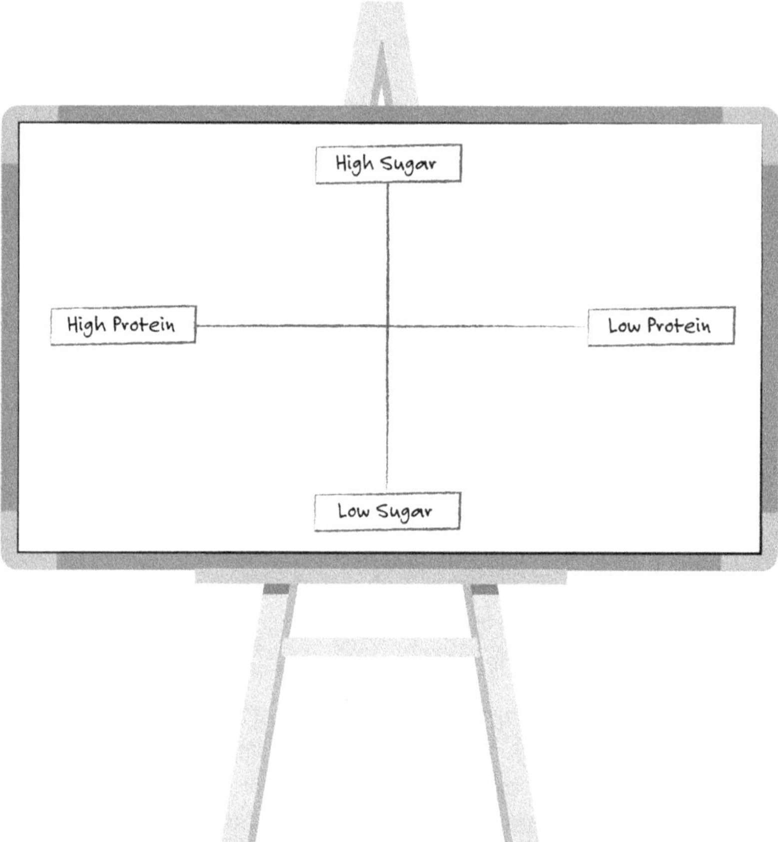

Figure 5.13 Perceptual Map Skeleton (attribution: Copyright Rice University, OpenStax, under CC BY 4.0 license)

Now it's time to map your offering as well as the competitors' offerings on the perceptual map. The simple combination of these two scores places the product offering onto the map. It's not necessary to list every single competitor on this perceptual map, but you should try for a list of at least 5 to 10 competitors.

Once you've mapped your competitors' offerings on the perceptual map, it may look something like Figure 5.14 (although you would have brand names in the circles instead of "Brand A," "Brand B," etc.).

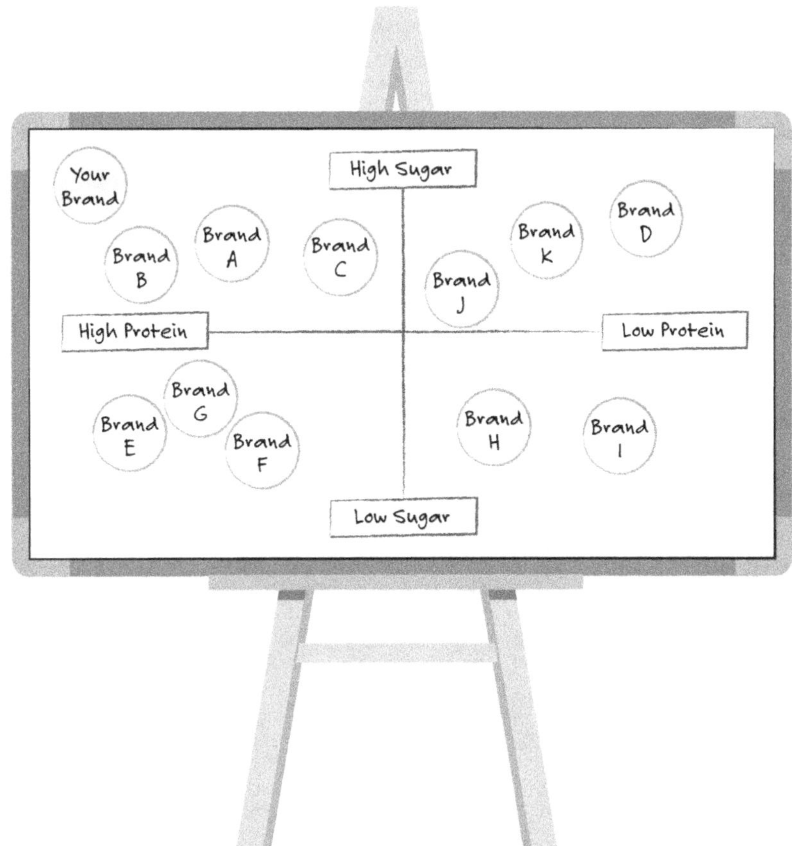

Figure 5.14 Sample Perceptual Map (attribution: Copyright Rice University, OpenStax, under CC BY 4.0 license)

Once you have developed the perceptual map, you will have a clearer idea of where your product or service offering stands vis-à-vis your competition. You will look at which brands occupy the same space as your offering (or a nearly identical space) based on consumer attitudes. Things to look for on your perceptual map include:

- Do consumer attitudes toward your offering align with what you want them to think about it?
- Do consumer attitudes toward your competitors' offerings align what you thought consumers would think about them?
- Look at the map closely and determine which of your competitors' offerings consumers perceive as being closest to your offering.
- Perceptual maps are also an opportunity to determine if there are any holes or gaps in the map. This may signal that there is potential for new offerings.[73]

Some other things to think about once you've completed your perceptual map:

- If consumer attitudes toward your offering aren't what you expected, it may be necessary to change your marketing actions to correct or modify these consumers' attitudes.
- Let's assume for a minute that consumers view your competitors' offerings as being very similar to yours. If this is the case, you may want to think about ways to make your offering stand out from the competition rather than going head-to-head with competitors.
- If there are gaps in the map that you think you can fill based on your company's capabilities, you may want to consider introducing a new offering or moving your offering into an unfilled position by modifying its features and attributes.[74]

Knowledge Check

It's time to check your knowledge on the concepts presented in this section. Refer to the Answer Key at the end of the book for feedback.

1. Which of the following BEST describes a positioning statement?
   a. It is a brief description of your offering, how it meets the needs of a consumer, and why it is superior to your competitor's offerings.
   b. It sets forth the group(s) of people with shared characteristics that you've identified as potential customers for your products.
   c. It defines where your offering fits in the marketplace and why it is better than competitors' offerings.
   d. It is a visual tool designed to demonstrate the perception of your offerings by the average target market consumer vis-à-vis your competitors' offerings.

2. The STP process is an acronym for _______.
   a. segmentation, targeting, and positioning
   b. screening, targeting, and promotion
   c. sampling, test marketing, and publicity
   d. segmentation, training, and promotion

3. Build-A-Bear put a twist on buying cuddly toys by providing consumers with the ability to modify and personalize their toys. What type of positioning strategy did Build-A-Bear use?
   a. Undifferentiated positioning
   b. Differentiated positioning
   c. Head-to-head positioning
   d. Niche positioning

4. When Artesha is on the road for her job and wants some fast food for lunch, she is looking for speed of service, value, and cleanliness of the restaurant. The factors would be referred to as _______.
   a. her buyer persona
   b. a perceptual map
   c. her determinant attributes
   d. a positioning statement

5. A visual technique designed to show how the average target market consumer perceives the positioning of competing products in the market place is known as _______.
   a. a positioning statement
   b. head-to-head positioning
   c. differentiation positioning
   d. a perceptual map

5.7 | Ethical Concerns and Target Marketing

Learning Outcomes

By the end of this section, you will be able to:
- **LO** 1 Discuss ethical implications of target market selection.
- **LO** 2 Provide an example of a company that displays ethics in target marketing.

Ethical Implications of Target Market Selection

To understand unethical target marketing, let's first review the notion of ethics in this realm. Ethics is the systematic study of morality—what people commonly refer to as "morals." The American Marketing Association (AMA) has a clear Statement of Ethics, and marketers are expected to conform to this ethical code. Before examining the issue of ethical target marketing, let's first review the general notion of ethics as it applies to marketing and other business disciplines.

Individuals and organizations choose to act morally—or immorally—when faced with a moral dilemma. The decision of whether to behave in a moral way or an immoral one has serious implications for oneself, for other individuals, and for society as a whole. The bottom line is that morally responsible, ethical marketers both sympathize with and empathize with consumers and their legitimate needs and wants. However, there are moral issues in terms of who is targeted and with what purpose. To illustrate these points, let's review some examples of target marketing tactics that can reasonably be construed to be immoral or unethical.

Ethnic and Racial Profiling

Earlier in this chapter, we used the example of a firm advertising woodworking equipment in specialty magazines rather than general interest magazines in order to stretch its limited advertising dollars. Do-it-yourselfers, amateur woodworkers, or hobbyists would be considered an **affinity audience** to the firm—that group of potential customers who have interests or hobbies in common. That's the positive aspect of target marketing.

However, there's a negative aspect to targeting affinity audiences as well. Over the past few years, Facebook has been criticized for potential discrimination on its ad platform by excluding users who have been classified into certain racial or ethnic affinity groups. As a matter of fact, Facebook was sued by the US Department of Housing and Urban Development because its algorithms allowed advertisers to purposely target their ads by race, gender, and religion, potentially violating federal laws that prevent discrimination in ads for jobs, housing, and credit.[75]

Facebook's algorithm and machine learning allowed advertisers to purposely target their ads by race, gender, and religion. In itself, trying to reach an affinity audience through advertising isn't illegal. The problem comes in because Facebook's platform allowed advertisers to exclude users based on that algorithm. For example, with Facebook's "ethnic affinity" marketing product, the company has the ability to exclude users by race or ethnicity.[76]

Children and Teens

According to Statista, there are approximately 73 million children in the United States between the ages of 0 and 17.[77] That's a huge target market that can be extraordinarily lucrative for a marketer. Accordingly, it makes sense to target this demographic because of its potential value.

However, there are inherent ethical issues involved in marketing to children, including distinguishing intent, gender stereotypes, violence, and obesity. Let's first consider distinguishing intent. According to the American Psychological Association (APA), children under the age of 7 or 8 can't discern the "persuasive intent" of advertising. In other words, they don't realize that the marketing message is made to sell something to them. Instead, children tend to accept the content at face value and believe that it's true, accurate, fair, and unbiased. This lack of distinguishing intent can potentially exploit children because it takes advantage of their inability to make sound, calculated decisions about a product or service based on the available information.[78]

Now let's consider gender stereotypes. At approximately age 2, children become conscious of the physical differences between boys and girls, and according to the Campaign for a Commercial-Free Childhood (CCFC), gender-stereotyped messages can interfere with that process. Consider the number of gender-stereotyped toys on the market today (or go to the toy section of any big-box store). For example, there are approximately 40,000 Disney Princess items on the market today, typically aimed at girls, whereas toys like Transformers are typically marketed to boys.[79]

Violence is still another ethical issue to consider. Research indicates that more than half of TV shows and even some commercials (particularly those for video games) contain violence, and the concern is that watching violence may desensitize youth to it and may even suggest to youngsters that violence is an effective way to settle conflicts.[80]

Another ethical issue is childhood obesity. According to the Centers for Disease Control and Prevention (CDC), childhood obesity has "more than tripled since the 1970s," and it's estimated that one in five school-aged children is obese.[81] Yet watch the commercials on children's TV shows, and you'll find that they are almost completely dominated by unhealthy food products like candy, sugary cereal, and snacks. To their credit, some forward-thinking companies have made it a practice not to advertise to children under 12 because of the association with childhood obesity. For instance, according to the Council of Better Business Bureaus, Brach's, Lemonhead, Ghirardelli, Jelly Belly, PEEPS, Mike and Ike, and Welch's Fruit Snacks avoid advertising to children under 12.[82]

Let's examine still another societal problem—vaping. According to recent studies, approximately four million students admit to vaping, an increase of over two million users. One of the major players in the industry is Juul, which has been criticized for targeting adolescents with colorful packaging; flavors like mint, crème, and mango; and a USB flash drive design that made the product small and easy to conceal in a backpack, pocket, or even a hoodie.[83] The problem has become so pervasive with young people that, in June of 2022, the US Food and Drug Administration was poised to issue an order removing Juul Labs vaping products from the market.[84]

Marketing to the Elderly

Older adults are also often exploited by target marketers. Older adults often have fixed incomes along with health problems, and this has made them a poplar target for products that give "assurances" of good health and affordability. The most common instances of bad ethics involve prescription drug targeting. Misleading statements about product efficacy are rampant, whether it's for a prominent drug manufacturer or a company that markets "natural" or "organic" products. The COVID-19 pandemic has seen this problem emerge in full force, with many brands touting a "cure-all" to alleviate the virus. The bottom line is that elderly audiences may make questionable purchasing decisions if they believe their health may be at risk as a result of not taking action.[85]

Low-Income Targeting

Low-income earners tend to be more susceptible to ads that promise a better way of life, such as high APR (annual percentage rate) credit cards and multilevel marketing schemes. Targeting low-income audiences can pose a threat to their safety and ultimately have dire legal ramifications.[86]

Low-income earners can also be wrongfully excluded from the market if companies curtail or fail to enable consumption of products because they "assume" the consumers cannot afford the product(s) at the specified price.

COMPANIES WITH A CONSCIENCE 

Subway

Figure 5.15 There are numerous ways to target markets, and Subway has chosen what many would call an ethical strategy because it focuses on offering families healthy options, unlike some of its competitors. (credit: "Mmm... Sammich" by jeffreyw/ flickr, CC BY 2.0)

We've just read about some of the ways that children are targeted in negative or unhealthy ways, so let's take a look at one company that tried to get it right, Subway (see Figure 5.15).

Back in 2014, Subway aligned itself with then–First Lady Michelle Obama's Let's Move! initiative. The company vowed to spend $41 million over a three-year period to promote a healthy-eating program aimed specifically toward children. The ad campaign bore the slogan "Playtime: Powered by Veggies."

But Subway didn't stop there. The company also teamed up with the Partnership for a Healthier America (PHA), a nonprofit organization that works with the private sector to help advance the goals of Mrs. Obama's Let's Move! initiative.

Suzanne Greco, vice president of operations for Subway, stated, "From a sign on each restaurant's door that says 'Playtime Powered by Veggies' to a video collaboration with Disney's The Muppets, [Subway] will build upon our ongoing efforts to create better choices for families."[87]

Watch this video on the partnership between Subway and the Let's Move! initiative.

Click to view content (https://openstax.org/books/principles-marketing/pages/5-7-ethical-concerns-and-target-marketing)

▣ Chapter Summary

In this chapter, market segmentation is defined and the differences between segmenting B2C, B2B, and international markets are explored. Segmentation, plus targeting and positioning, are the major elements of a customer-driven marketing strategy. Smart marketers know they can't reach and serve every buyer, so they approach the broader market with tools that help them identify, select, and position their products for consumers who are most likely to need the company's products and services.

Better understanding B2C or B2B markets also helps marketers better understand unmet needs, assisting in the development of new products and services. Targeted marketing, top-notch customer service, and new product developments that are based upon customer needs result in customer experiences that successfully reinforce brand loyalty.

⚷ Key Terms

ADAMS   the essential factors in effective market segmentation—accessible, differentiable, actionable, measurable, and substantial

affinity audience   a group of potential customers who have interests or hobbies in common

behavioral segmentation   method of grouping customers by their behavior patterns or interactions with a brand

buyer persona   semi-fictional representation of an organization's ideal customers based on data and research

concentrated marketing   marketing segmentation strategy in which the firm concentrates its efforts and resources on serving one segment of the market

demographic segmentation   grouping customers and potential customers together by focusing on certain traits such as age, gender, income, occupation, and family status

determinant attributes   those attributes of a product or service that consumers rely upon when making a purchase decision

differentiated marketing   marketing strategy that involves creating marketing campaigns that appeal to two or more different target audiences, demographics, or marketing segments

differentiation positioning   product/service positioning based on the differentiating characteristics or qualities that make an organization better than its competitors in the mind of the target audience

firmographics   a grouping of B2B customers based on shared company attributes; includes five categories: industry, location, size, legal structure, and performance

geographic segmentation   marketing strategy used to target products or services at people who live in or shop at a particular location

head-to-head positioning   directly competing with competitors on similar product attributes in the same market

market segmentation   the process of dividing a broad consumer or business market into subgroups based on shared characteristics

micromarketing   marketing strategy used on a targeted group of customers in a niche market

multi-segment marketing   marketing strategy in which the firm targets several different market segments simultaneously

needs-based segmentation   dividing the market up into smaller groups of people who have approximately the same needs

perceptual map   visual depiction of how target customers view and feel about a given brand or product

positioning statement   short description of an organization's target market(s) and the product(s) provided to them

product positioning   the process of deciding and communicating how an organization wants its market to think and feel about a product or service

psychographic segmentation   dividing consumers into subgroups based on shared psychological characteristics, including beliefs, motivations, and priorities

STP model   three-step marketing framework in which an organization segments the market, selects target market(s), and positions its products or services

target market   group of people with some shared characteristics that a company has identified as potential customers for its products

technographic segmentation   organizing B2B prospects by their technology ownership and usage

undifferentiated marketing   also called mass marketing, a strategy that entails creating one message for an entire audience

value-based segmentation   evaluating groups of customers in terms of the revenue they generate and the costs of establishing and maintaining relationships with them

Applied Marketing Knowledge: Discussion Questions

1. Somewhat like the cola wars of the 1980s, quick-service food chains are engaging in chicken wars. List and discuss at least two ways Chick-fil-A, Popeye's, and Slim Chickens have differentiated and positioned their products as they fight for customers.

2. Why would a local hair salon choose to use geographic segmentation variables and a narrow, concentrated marketing strategy rather than psychographic, demographic, or behavioral variables plus undifferentiated, differentiated, or micromarketing strategies? Might the salon be more successful at reaching its target audience by utilizing multi-segment marketing?

3. Describe the major elements of a positioning statement. Which words in the following Walt Disney World positioning statement—"For the young and young-at-heart, Walt Disney World is the theme park that best delivers on an immersive and magical experience because Walt Disney World, and only Walt Disney World, connects you to the characters and worlds you most desire"—illustrate what Disney World promises customers and why it delivers on this promise better than competitors in the entertainment industry?

4. Have you ever watched cartoons? If so, have you seen content that you would consider to be unethical targeting by advertisers? Common examples of ethical lapses include ethnic and racial profiling, promoting gender stereotypes, depicting violence, and encouraging child obesity.

Critical Thinking Exercises

1. Mountain Dew was introduced in 1940 and marketed as "moonshine," complete with Willy the Hillbilly proclaiming "It'll tickle yore innards!" Since PepsiCo acquired the brand in the 1960s, Mountain Dew has cycled through new looks, logos, slogans, packaging, flavors, and brand personalities now connected with speed and velocity rather than soda brewed in a whiskey still. Research Mountain Dew's history and consider this question: How has Mountain Dew steadily moved away from other competitors in the soft drink industry in its positioning efforts, and do you believe this movement has grown consumers' brand loyalty?

2. The three-step STP model has proven successful in stepping systematically through the target market selection process. How has your college proceeded from segmentation to targeting to effectively positioning? Offer examples of each step and develop a perceptual map showing how the average high school student may perceive your college's attributes versus its competitors'.

3. Why might candy companies such as Lemonhead, Ghirardelli, Jelly Belly, PEEPS, Mike and Ike, and Welch's Fruit Snacks make the pledge not to advertise to children under the age of 12? Does this decision also send a message to parents?

Building Your Personal Brand

There are numerous examples of successful personal brands. For good examples, read this article from the

Webflow blog where 18 of the best personal brand examples in 2022 are listed. (https://openstax.org/r/personalbrandingexamples) Using what you learned in this chapter about marketing to target markets and using the inspiration and knowledge gained from this article, write the opening page to your website. Keep in mind the things shared in the article on what made the personal brands stand out. And know your target market so you can craft a message that will appeal to them.

 ## What Do Marketers Do?

Utilize LinkedIn to find two sales managers in your geographic area and invite them to connect with you. Try using what you now know about segmentation, targeting, and positioning to consider industries you'd like to work in, where they might be located, and how you can make your resume appealing to them. Can you craft a compelling message that encourages sales managers to connect with you? Once linked, "interview" at least one sales professional and ask questions about what they enjoy most and least about their sales careers.

 ## Marketing Plan Exercise

Complete the following information about the company and products/services you chose to focus on as you develop the marketing plan throughout the course. You may need to conduct research in order to obtain necessary information.

Instructions: Using the Marketing Plan Template file you created from the Marketing and Customer Value assignment and expanded upon in Strategic Planning in Marketing, complete the following sections of your marketing plan:

- Market Segmentation
- Target Market
- Buyer Personas
- Positioning

Submit the marketing plan to your instructor for grading and feedback.

 ## Closing Company Case

Travelers Point Distillery

In early 2000, several friends got together to tell stories and drink bourbon. It was obvious that friends and stories come together with good bourbon. The best stories included the rich family history of Master Distiller Mel Lytton.

Dating back to the 1880s and into prohibition, Mel's great grandfather distilled bourbon in rural Virginia. Having grown up in a bourbon family, Mel not only had the ability to detect all the subtle flavors of a great bourbon, but he had the family recipe that had been passed down through the generations. And Mel knew how to distill it.

Mel had more stories than most. Having mastered the art of just about everything he set out to do, Mel was a stone mason, a blacksmith, and a carpenter skilled at woodworking. As Mel talked about the bourbon he was tasting and told stories of his family distilling in the mountains and backwoods of Virginia, an idea was born. The friends decided they would love to get into the business of distilling bourbon.

Bourbon is a truly American drink. It is generally aged in oak barrels and made with grain, primarily corn. Bourbon can range in price from thousands of dollars to $40–50 per bottle. In the early 1960s, Congress declared bourbon "America's Native Spirit."

While traditionally bourbon is mostly consumed by men, it is catching on with women too. In fact, bourbon is quickly gaining popularity among those 21 and over. "The Kentucky Bourbon Trail and the Kentucky Bourbon Trail Craft Tour have drawn more than 2.5 million visitors from all 50 states and 25 countries in the last five years and have become leading educational and tourism attractions."[88]

With the growth and popularity of bourbon drinking and collecting, it was clear that there was room in the industry for one more bourbon brand.

Mel's family recipe and his history of distilling made the group of friends confident in their ability to provide a craft or small-batch bourbon that would be equal to if not better than many currently available. They formed the company and found the perfect location to open the distillery—an old granary in the heart of America's farming country in Kirklin, Indiana. The community is uniquely located in the middle of the state with a major highway passing through the middle of the town. Kirklin truly is the crossroads of America.

With the original group of investors and a few additions, the business was formed. Mel began distilling the bourbon. It was put in barrels and up in the rack room to age. The label, the brand, and the distribution were in the works.

The group determined that some of the best things in life included bourbon and travels. In fact, many of the stories they told over a great glass of bourbon included their many collective travels around the world. The name for their new bourbon was decided—Travelers Point. It wouldn't be long before Travelers Point began marketing its bourbon.

As the company considered its branding and value proposition, the founders knew they wanted to have a unique story of production along with a price point that ranked with some of the premium bourbon brands currently on the market. Travelers Point bourbon would sell for around $45–60 per bottle. This would put it in the ranks of some of the sought-after brands with a following among die-hard bourbon drinkers.[89]

The difference in Travelers Point is obvious to discerning bourbon drinkers. The bourbon profile is unique, with deep caramel notes and a rich combination of oak and vanilla. Many bourbon drinkers enjoy the hunt for the perfect bourbon. Travelers Point has something special. Finding the market segment that is ready for a new bourbon with a long history will be critical to its marketing success.

For more information about Travelers Point Distillery, check out their website (https://openstax.org/r/travelerspointdistillery).

Case Questions

1. Based on the price point and branding for Travelers Point bourbon, what is the recommended method the company should use to segment its market?

2. Which target market strategy would you recommend for Travelers Point, and why?

3. What approach to brand positioning do you recommend for Travelers Point? Support your answer.

4. Develop a perceptual map of the bourbon brands currently selling for $40–60 per bottle.

References

1. Gregory Schmidt, "Mattel Is Reviving Max Steel Action Figure for a New Media Age," *New York Times*, January 27, 2013.

2. Sophia Chianese, "Market Segmentation: Mattel Case Study," LinkedIn, September 28, 2018, https://www.linkedin.com/pulse/market-segmentation-mattel-case-study-sophia-chianese/.

3. Jon Simpson, "Finding Brand Success in the Digital World," *Forbes*, August 25, 2017, https://www.forbes.com/sites/forbesagencycouncil/2017/08/25/finding-brand-success-in-the-digital-world/.

4. "What Are the Benefits of Market Segmentation?," Kadence International, last modified October 14, 2021, https://kadence.com/en-us/the-benefits-of-market-segmentation/.

5. Adam Jones, "Starbucks's Geographic Segment Update," Yahoo! Finance, Yahoo, January 20, 2015, https://finance.yahoo.com/news/starbucks-geographic-segment-173101323.html.

6. Cathy Jacobs, "What Is a Starbucks Menu Like around the World?," The Spruce Eats, updated September 17, 2020, https://www.thespruceeats.com/starbucks-menu-guide-766068.

7.   Jo Hartley, "Indian Languages: A Useful Guide to All the Languages Spoken in India," *Berlitz Blog*, Berlitz, October 31, 2021, https://www.berlitz.com/blog/indian-languages-spoken-list.

8.   "More Than 19,500 Mother Tongues Spoken in India: Census," *Indian Express*, July 1, 2018, https://indianexpress.com/article/india/more-than-19500-mother-tongues-spoken-in-india-census-5241056/.

9.   "2021 Mercedes-Benz Price List," Mercedes-Benz of Chandler, accessed October 20, 2021, https://www.mercedesbenzofchandler.com/manufacturer-information/mercedes-benz-price-list/.

10.   Michael T. Robinson, "The Generations: Which Generation are You?," CareerPlanner.com, updated October 21, 2017, https://www.careerplanner.com/Career-Articles/Generations.cfm.

11.   John Li, "Demographic Segmentation," PickFu, updated May 25, 2021, https://www.pickfu.com/demographic-segmentation.

12.   "A Toothpaste for Every Need," Crest US, Procter & Gamble, accessed July 2, 2022, https://crest.com/en-us/oral-care-products/toothpaste.

13.   Niyathi Rao, "The Pareto Principle (80:20 Rule) for Customer Success," *Customer Success Intelligence* (blog), SmartKarrot, March 17, 2021, https://www.smartkarrot.com/resources/blog/pareto-principle-80-20-rule-customer-success/.

14.   "Buy Back & Resell," IKEA, accessed November 30, 2021, https://www.ikea.com/us/en/customer-service/services/buyback-pubfeb6cc00.

15.   Lululemon Like New (website), Lululemon Athletica, accessed June 24, 2022, https://likenew.lululemon.com/.

16.   Hitesh Bhasin, "Vals: Values Attitude Lifestyle," Marketing91, January 30, 2020, https://www.marketing91.com/vals-values-attitude-lifestyle/.

17.   Ibid.

18.   "Market Segmentation Strategies: 3 Major Challenges B2B Enterprises Face and Ways to Tackle Them," Thoughts, Infiniti Research, December 12, 2018, https://www.infinitiresearch.com/thoughts/challenges-b2b-market-segmentation/.

19.   Paul Hague and Matthew Harrison, "Market Segmentation in B2B Markets," B2B International, last modified June 22, 2022, https://www.b2binternational.com/publications/b2b-segmentation-research/.

20.   "How Organizations Can Benefit from B2B Market Segmentation," *B2B Global Zone* (blog), Kompass International, May 4, 2021, https://www.solutions.kompass.com/blog/how-organizations-can-benefit-from-b2b-market-segmentation/.

21.   Kit Smith, "The Complete Guide to B2B Market Segmentation," Sopro, April 20, 2021, https://sopro.io/added-value/blog/b2b-market-segmentation-guide/.

22.   Rohit Roy, "How to Do Market Segmentation: 5 Most Effective Types of B2B Market Segmentation Strategies," Clodura, May 13, 2020, https://clodura.ai/blog/how-to-do-market-segmentation-5-most-effective-types-of-b2b-market-segmentation-strategies/.

23.   Emily Pribanic, "Benefits of Market Segmentation for Business," MarTech, TechFunnel, updated January 6, 2020, https://www.techfunnel.com/martech/benefits-of-market-segmentation-for-business/.

24.   Roy, "Market Segmentation."

25.   Roy, "Market Segmentation."

26.   Roy, "Market Segmentation."

27.   Mark Eardley, "B2B Customer Centricity: Why It's Vital for Needs-Based Segmentation," MarkLives.com, June 19, 2018, https://www.marklives.com/2018/06/b2b-customer-centricity-why-its-vital-for-needs-based-segmentation/.

28.   Roy, "Market Segmentation."

29.   Roy, "Market Segmentation."

30.   Yoram (Jerry) Wind and David R. Bell, "Market Segmentation," in *The Marketing Book*, ed. Michael J. Baker and Susan J. Hart, 6th ed. (Burlington, MA: Butterworth-Heinemann, 2008), 222–244, from https://faculty.wharton.upenn.edu/wp-content/uploads/2012/04/0702_Market_Segmentation.pdf.

31.   Wind and Bell, "Market Segmentation."

32.   Kenneth Fillmore, "Segmenting International Markets," *ZABANGA Marketing* (blog), updated June 4, 2022, https://www.zabanga.us/customer-relationships/segmenting-international-markets.html.

33.   Frank Jerry, reply to "How are the various African countries different from each other? What makes each of them unique?," Quora, April 25, 2014, https://www.quora.com/How-are-the-various-African-countries-different-from-each-other-What-makes-each-of-them-unique.

34.   Sonal Varma, Euben Paracuelles, and Craig Chan, "The Belt and Road Initiative: Globalization, China Style," Nomura Connects, Nomura Holdings, April 2018, https://www.nomuraconnects.com/focused-thinking-posts/the-belt-and-road-initiative-globalisation-china-style/.

35. "International Market Segmentation, Selection and Positioning," International Marketing, Hahu Zone, accessed June 24, 2022, https://hahuzone.com/international-market-segmentation-selection-and-positioning.

36. "What Are the Sanctions on Russia and Are They Hurting Its Economy?," BBC News, BBC, June 27, 2022, https://www.bbc.com/news/world-europe-60125659.

37. Ibid.

38. "Top 25 Developed and Developing Countries," Investopedia, Dotdash Meredith, updated May 27, 2022, https://www.investopedia.com/updates/top-developing-countries/.

39. Ibid.

40. Ibid.

41. Arianna and Virginia, "McDonald's International Market Communications Strategy," Global Marketing Professor, May 3, 2021, https://globalmarketingprofessor.com/mcdonalds-international-market-communications-strategy/.

42. Ibid.

43. Ian Burke, "From a 7-Patty Whopper to Burgers with Black Buns, Here Are 13 of the Wildest International Burger King Menu Items," Insider, August 18, 2019, https://www.insider.com/13-wild-burger-king-promotional-menu-items-not-in-us-2019-6.

44. "Hofstede's Cultural Dimensions: Understanding Different Countries," Career Skills, Mind Tools, accessed June 24, 2022, https://www.mindtools.com/pages/article/newLDR_66.htm.

45. "United States of America Business Etiquette, Culture, & Manners," International Business Etiquette and Manners for Global Travelers, International Business Center, accessed June 24, 2022, https://www.cyborlink.com/besite/us.htm.

46. Kate Sweetman, "In Asia, Power Gets in the Way," *Harvard Business Review*, April 10, 2012, https://hbr.org/2012/04/in-asia-power-gets-in-the-way.

47. Kendra Cherry, "What Is a Collectivist Culture? Individualism vs. Collectivism," Verywell Mind, Dotdash Meredith, February 23, 2022, https://www.verywellmind.com/what-are-collectivistic-cultures-2794962.

48. "Individualism," Geert Hofstede Cultural Dimensions, Clearly Cultural, accessed June 24, 2022, https://clearlycultural.com/geert-hofstede-cultural-dimensions/individualism/.

49. Mind Tools, "Hofstede's Cultural Dimensions."

50. Bert Markgraf, "How to Apply Hofstede's Classification Scheme in a Global Marketing Context," Small Business, Chron.com, last modified October 26, 2016, https://smallbusiness.chron.com/apply-hofstedes-classification-scheme-global-marketing-context-75008.html.

51. "5 Requirements for Effective Segmentation," *Commence CRM Blog*, Commence, February 18, 2021, https://commence.com/blog/2021/02/18/requirements-for-segmentation/.

52. Amanda Dodge, "How Lego Keeps Winning Fans Wherever It Goes," *ReferralCandy Blog*, ReferralCandy, February 9, 2017, https://www.referralcandy.com/blog/lego-marketing-strategy/.

53. Anne Gentle, "Best Buy's Personas Hit the Mainstream," JustWriteClick, September 29, 2005, https://justwriteclick.com/2005/09/29/best-buys-personas-hit-the-mainstream/.

54. "Examples of Buyer Personas for Any Business," Marketo Engage, Adobe, January 21, 2021, https://www.marketo.com/articles/buyer-persona-examples/.

55. Alexa Drake, "What Is Mass Marketing and How It's Effective," Learn Hub, G2, July 29, 2019, https://learn.g2.com/mass-marketing.

56. Ashley Lutz, "Nike Is Going after 3 Kinds of Customers," Insider, April 7, 2015, https://www.businessinsider.com/nike-is-going-after-3-kinds-of-customers-2015-4.

57. "Honda," Research & Reviews, Cars.com, accessed June 24, 2022, https://www.cars.com/research/honda/.

58. Smriti Chand, "Target Marketing: Four Generic Target Marketing Strategies," Your Article Library, last modified December 8, 2013, https://www.yourarticlelibrary.com/marketing/target-marketing-four-generic-target-marketing-strategies/13400.

59. Stevie Langford, "Market Targeting: Why It Pays to Differentiate," *Hurree's Marketing Blog*, Hurree, January 25, 2022, https://blog.hurree.co/blog/market-targeting.

60. Eric Lam, "What Every Marketer Can Learn from the Stitch Fix IPO," Medium, October 27, 2017, https://medium.com/@elam/what-every-marketer-can-learn-from-the-stitch-fix-ipo-54b208dd416c.

61. Al Ries and Jack Trout, *Positioning: The Battle for Your Mind* (New York: McGraw-Hill, 2001), 5.

62. "Explore Our Brands," Marriott Bonvoy, Marriott International, accessed February 23, 2022, https://www.marriott.com/marriott-brands.mi.

63. Seth Stevenson, "We're No. 2! We're No. 2!," Slate, August 12, 2013, https://slate.com/business/2013/08/hertz-vs-avis-advertising-wars-how-an-ad-firm-made-a-virtue-out-of-second-place.html.

64. Devra Gartenstein, "Two Types of Product Positioning," Bizfluent, Leaf Group, February 5, 2019, https://bizfluent.com/info-8352422-two-types-product-positioning.html.

65. Chan Kim and Renée Mauborgne, "Curves," Blue Ocean Strategy, Blue Ocean Global Network, last modified January 26, 2022, https://www.blueoceanstrategy.com/bos-moves/curves/.

66. Hannah Tow, "Awesome Brand Positioning Statement Examples (+Template)," Learn Hub, G2, April 30, 2019, https://learn.g2.com/positioning-statement-examples.

67. "Positioning Statement: 7 Examples and How to Write One," HelpCenter, Shark Byte, August 23, 2021, https://www.helpcenterapp.com/blog/how-to-write-positioning-statement-examples/.

68. Shark Byte, "Positioning Statement."

69. Shark Byte, "Positioning Statement."

70. Shark Byte, "Positioning Statement."

71. Meredith Hart, "12 Examples of Positioning Statements & How to Craft Your Own," HubSpot Blog, HubSpot, updated August 25, 2021, https://blog.hubspot.com/sales/positioning-statement.

72. "Understanding Perceptual Maps," Market Segmentation Study Guide, accessed March 23, 2022, https://www.segmentationstudyguide.com/understanding-perceptual-maps/perceptual-maps/.

73. Angela Hausman, "How to Build a Perceptual Map That Explodes Your ROI," MKT Maven, Hausman and Associates, October 16, 2020, https://www.hausmanmarketingletter.com/how-to-build-perceptual-map/.

74. Hausman, "Build a Perceptual Map."

75. Karen Hao, "Facebook's Ad-Serving Algorithm Discriminates by Gender and Race," MIT Technology Review, April 5, 2019, https://www.technologyreview.com/2019/04/05/1175/facebook-algorithm-discriminates-ai-bias/.

76. Safiya U. Noble and Sarah T. Roberts, "Targeting Race in Ads Is Nothing New, but the Stakes Are High," USA Today, November 12, 2016, https://www.usatoday.com/story/tech/columnist/2016/11/12/targeting-race-ads-nothing-new-but-stakes-high/93638386/.

77. "Number of Children in the United States in 2019, by Age Group," Statista, January 20, 2021, accessed October 21, 2021, https://www.statista.com/statistics/457786/number-of-children-in-the-us-by-age/.

78. "Exploitative Ethical Issues in Target Marketing," Paypervids, last modified November 10, 2017, https://www.paypervids.com/exploitative-ethical-issues-target-marketing/.

79. 14ideas, "Marketing to Kids: Is It an Issue?," Medium, April 19, 2017, https://medium.com/@14ideas/marketing-to-kids-is-it-an-issue-9df4b7085977.

80. Paula Giuffrida, "Letter: Time to Stop Violence on TV, Video Games," letter to the editor, Eagle-Tribune (North Andover, MA), April 22, 2022, https://www.eagletribune.com/opinion/letters_to_the_editor/letter-time-to-stop-violence-on-tv-video-games/article_42a1f22a-c19a-11ec-a152-9bab49ace2f0.html.

81. "Childhood Overweight & Obesity," Overweight & Obesity, Centers for Disease Control and Prevention, last reviewed April 1, 2022, https://www.cdc.gov/obesity/childhood/index.html.

82. 14ideas, "Marketing to Kids."

83. "Did Juul Target Teens, Knowing They'd Get Hooked?," WebMD, accessed June 24, 2022, https://www.webmd.com/connect-to-care/vaping/did-juul-target-young-people-smoking.

84. Ken Alltucker, "Report: Federal Ban on Popular Juul Products Forthcoming amid Youth Vaping Concerns," USA Today, June 22, 2022, https://www.usatoday.com/story/news/health/2022/06/22/fda-ban-juul-products-amid-youth-vaping-concerns-report-says/7701204001/.

85. "Ethical Target Advertising: Where Should Marketing Draw the Line?," Out of the Blue Blog, Blue Laser Digital, September 3, 2021, https://www.bluelaserdigital.com/ethical-target-advertising.

86. Blue Laser Digital, "Ethical Target Advertising."

87. Lynette Holloway, "First Lady, Subway Launch Healthy Eating Campaign for Kids," NewsOne, Interactive One, January 24, 2014, https://newsone.com/2848891/michelle-obama-subway/.

88. "Did You Know?," Kentucky Bourbon Trail, Kentucky Distillers' Association, accessed March 23, 2022, https://kybourbontrail.com/about/.

89. Travelers Point Distillery (website), accessed March 23, 2022, https://travelerspointdistillery.com/.

Marketing Research and Market Intelligence

Figure 6.1 Marketing research provides companies with data-driven insights that allow for deep understanding of their customers in order to develop products and services that meet those customers' needs. (credit: modification of work "Workshop: Biodiversity Data Mobilization - Day 3" by Maheva Bagard Laursen/GBIF/flickr, CC BY 2.0)

Chapter Outline

In the Spotlight

When you think of LEGO, you may imagine a child building a spaceship or castle, but LEGO wanted to learn more about how children are encouraged or discouraged to play with its bricks. In 2021, LEGO launched a research study of close to 7,000 parents and children aged 6 to 14 years old in seven countries to determine how gender stereotypes influence play in creative activities.

During this study, LEGO learned that girls are more open to bending gender roles than boys but that parents have learned to stereotype some careers as being gender-specific. Additionally, parents are more likely to encourage girls to play dress-up (83 percent for girls, 17 percent for boys), dance (81 percent for girls, 15 percent for boys), and bake (80 percent for girls, 20 percent for boys), while they suggest computer coding (71 percent for boys, 29 percent for girls) and sports for boys (76 percent for boys, 24 percent for girls). Due to these findings, LEGO initiated its "Ready for Girls" campaign.

The data compiled in this study allowed LEGO to take a step forward in helping to break down some gender norms when it comes to its product. On October 11, 2021, the International Day of the Girl, LEGO announced a new program to encourage girls to show their creativity. "Get the World Ready for Me" was launched with a 10-step guide to collect information about how girls are engaging with LEGO. Due to this program, LEGO has launched a campaign of stories about how girls are involved with imagination and creativity.

Through this campaign, LEGO identified a way to encourage girls to challenge worldwide views of gender norms (see Figure 6.2). The background necessary for this campaign was researched and used in a way that would help the company stand out. For LEGO and many other companies and organizations, research is its competitive advantage.[1]

Figure 6.2 Through the use of marketing research, LEGO was able to gain data-driven insights into gender stereotypes and launch a campaign that encouraged girls to challenge views on gender norms. (credit: "LEGO Shuttle Expedition and City Spaceport Comparison" by Adam Purves (S3ISOR)/flickr, CC BY 2.0)

6.1 | Marketing Research and Big Data

Learning Outcomes

By the end of this section, you will be able to:
- **LO** 1 Define marketing research.
- **LO** 2 Explain how marketing information provides an understanding of the customer and the marketplace.
- **LO** 3 Explain the role of big data and the marketing information system.

What Is Marketing Research?

Oftentimes people think of marketing as the process of communicating with a target market—sharing messages, products, and value with customers. However, marketers know that understanding customers, learning about their wants and needs, and developing a relationship with them is essential for success. Marketing research allows marketers to listen and assess the needs of the market, to understand what's missing and how to reduce those gaps from their customers, target markets, and prospective clients. Managers need marketing information in order to make data-driven decisions rather than make assumptions about consumers. In this chapter we're going to investigate the importance of marketing research, some strategies employed in the field, and how to complete the marketing research process.

Marketing research is the work to gather information and data about customers and markets. Let's look at the definition, why it's important, and the influx of big data.

Marketing Research Defined

According to the American Marketing Association (AMA), **marketing research** "is the function that links the consumer, customer, and public to the marketer through information."[2] Marketing research presents information gained through various sources as a resource for managers to make data-driven business decisions. Additionally, the AMA states that "marketing research specifies the information required to address these issues, designs the method for collecting information, manages and implements the data collection process, analyzes the results, and communicates the findings and their implications."[3]

The Importance of Marketing Information

Marketing information, also known as business intelligence, competitive intelligence, or marketing intelligence, is information about the market that helps to identify opportunities in the market. This information helps to determine a company's strengths and weaknesses while also evaluating the external environment's opportunities and threats. Ideas generated through analysis of marketing information support business decision-making from a long-term strategic approach to smaller issues at a tactical level.

Marketing information is essential for a company or organization to stay competitive and also meet the customer's needs. As referenced above, LEGO used marketing research to gather information about how children use its product but also how parents felt about opportunities for their children. Universities and colleges use information gathered through marketing research to build next year's recruitment materials by asking students their perceptions of the previous year's items. Additionally, a fast-food restaurant might conduct an analysis of the time of day each of its items are more likely to be purchased. Obvious to most, coffee would probably be an item more likely ordered earlier in the day. Other items might not be as evident but could require different preparation times. By accounting for when each of these items is most likely to be ordered, the restaurant can plan its inventory and schedule of employees more efficiently.

Big Data and the Marketing Information System (MIS)

The amount of data currently available is not only vast but is growing at an exponential level every day, which describes the concept of big data. **Big data** is the countless number of records that continues in an increasing capacity and at a faster rate. Because of the constantly changing landscape of data, it's difficult for companies to develop an approach for analyzing it. Big data is often described through the use of the three Vs: volume, velocity, and variety. The amount of data, or volume, is more than we have ever witnessed. Additionally, it is growing at a fast rate; the velocity is also ever increasing. We expect that the velocity of data will continue to surge exponentially as each day more users are contributing to the data available. Finally, there is the variety of data that is part of this enormous data set—because each user is contributing to the cache of data available, the diversity of data is just as unique as its creators.

LINK TO LEARNING

What Is Big Data?

Big data is massive amounts of data. But what does that mean? Think of all the data a smartphone generates with texts, searches, emails, photos, etc. Now consider how many smartphone users there are in the world. Watch this video and learn how much data is generated on the internet each day and how it can be classified through the three Vs concept.

Click to view content (https://openstax.org/books/principles-marketing/pages/6-1-marketing-research-and-big-data)

"Big data has become one of the most valuable assets held by enterprises, and virtually every large organization is making investments in big data initiatives."[4] This statement was based on a 2021 NewVantage Partners survey of senior C-level executives at Fortune 1000 companies regarding their perceptions of big data and their utilization of its resources. NewVantage Partners learned that many companies are already pursuing this data, with 96 percent reporting that their companies have already had success using big data and artificial intelligence programs. Additionally, 99 percent of the executives surveyed are pursuing either new or existing big data programs. Why are companies so keen to invest in this source? It is estimated that the world creates approximately 2.5 quintillion bytes of data daily. This vast accumulation of data can be collected through various methods, such as point-of-sale databases, connected devices through the Internet of Things (IoT), third-party marketing research firms, social media, location data from mobile devices, or surveys.[5] Tapping into the resource generators is helpful for companies to understand their customers, employees, or others.

So, who are these data generators? They are everyone, like you and your friends, who post content on social media, engage with web content through streaming services, and share stories through web applications. In addition, businesses are contributing to the massive amount of content available. Extra data (volume), at a faster rate (velocity), and from a more widely diverse set of people (variety) explain why it is called "big" data.[6] So how do businesses and individuals capitalize on this vast data world?

In order to be able to utilize and make the most of the availability of business data, businesses use a **marketing information system** to collect, analyze, and report interesting findings from internal and external data of the company. This system is an ever-changing database of content that is used to support the company or organization's marketing efforts. The marketing information system is the collection of data and requires actions taken by marketers to utilize the data saved.

CAREERS IN MARKETING

Market Research Analysts

Market research analysts are needed in numerous industries, and according to the US Bureau of Labor and Statistics (https://openstax.org/r/marketresearchanalysts), the job outlook has a much higher rate of growth than average. Read about the skills needed, typical pay, education requirements, and career outlook in this article (https://openstax.org/r/marketresearcher) and watch this video about the various types of jobs available as a market research analyst.

Click to view content (https://openstax.org/books/principles-marketing/pages/6-1-marketing-research-and-big-data)

Knowledge Check

It's time to check your knowledge on the concepts presented in this section. Refer to the Answer Key at the end of the book for feedback.

1. Anaya is collecting information from a variety of sources to make a decision on where to market her new line of designer scarves. Anaya is conducting ________.
   a. market intelligence
   b. big data
   c. management information system
   d. marketing research

2. The collection of data the company has gathered over time and used to make marketing decisions on a regular basis is called its ________.
   a. big data
   b. marketing information system
   c. marketing research
   d. survey data

3. Ryan and Christie are uploading their recent pictures to Instagram, tagging the photographer and the venue. What is this content adding to?
   a. Market intelligence

   b. Big data
   c. Management information system
   d. Marketing research

4. Which of the following is not a reason why marketing research is important for the success of a business?
   a. It provides a guarantee of customer satisfaction.
   b. It identifies opportunities in the market to explore.
   c. It helps to quantify customer perceptions.
   d. It uncovers weaknesses within a company.

5. Which of the following would not be considered marketing research?
   a. Analyzing the product purchases of current customers
   b. Measuring the number of reactions to a social media post
   c. Examining a competitor's database of information
   d. Surveying potential employees about why they are interested in working for a company

6.2 | Sources of Marketing Information

Learning Outcomes

By the end of this section, you will be able to:

LO 1 Identify sources of marketing information.
LO 2 Describe the different categories of marketing information.

Identify Sources of Marketing Information

Data, as mentioned in the first section of this chapter, comes from a variety of sources. In this section, we'll investigate the sources of important marketing information and how these resources can be accessed to meet the needs of the institution. Online resources such as company websites, journal databases, and e-commerce locations could provide valuable resources to someone opening a new business. For instance, if a new product is to be sold, some companies will review competitors' websites to glean information about comparable pricing before setting their price. The sources identified are closely aligned with the category of information and are described below.

Describe the Different Categories of Marketing Information

Marketing information can be derived from many sources. We will review three types in this section—internal data, external data, and competitive intelligence—and further explain other types of data in the next section. External and internal data both have unique qualities that make them essential for businesses to utilize. Additionally, competitive intelligence refer to specific types of data that must be examined to further the company or organization's continued success and effectiveness.

External Data and Databases

External data is data that originates from outside the organization. Examples of external data would be information gleaned from customers through a customer service survey or reviews of a competitor's website. Previously we learned about big data and the volume of information that is available daily. These data pieces would also be considered external data. Competitive and market intelligence is often gathered through these external sources of material. Data sources can include any interested parties of the business or a competitor's business, social media mentions, news articles, journal publications, and others. The only limitation of collecting external data is financial. Not all sources of information are free, and the time spent to collect these insights is also a valuable commodity as "time is money." Once external information is collected and available for those within the institution, it can be considered internal data.

Internal Data and Databases

Critical marketing intelligence can be data that already exists in the company's databases. This data is called **internal data** and gives the company a historic view of what has worked in the past as well as identifies times when the company did not meet its goals. Internal data includes sales, promotional effectiveness, pricing, product launch information, research and development, and logistics information. Examples of internal data include the percentage of coupons redeemed, the sales volume at specific prices, the highest-grossing motion picture for a production company, and even the most-missed question on last unit's marketing exam.

Businesses, organizations, nonprofits, and even colleges and universities use these types of data sources to make day-to-day and more comprehensive decisions. A **database** is a collection of related data. For instance, at the school you are currently attending, there are multiple databases—one for current students, one for alumni, and still another for faculty. Within each of these databases, there is information about that specific population. The current student database will be a list of all students who are enrolled in courses this term, with additional information such as what courses they are enrolled in, any past enrollments, grades earned, major, hometown, and academic advisor's name.

Competitive Intelligence

Marketing research can be conducted on every aspect of business and marketing. Understanding the competition and its strengths and weaknesses through an analysis of the industry and competing forces gives a company a competitive edge. **Competitive intelligence** is the collection of that information from the marketplace. A company's position must be examined to determine if it matches with the needs of the customers.

This competitive intelligence may be related to any of the marketing mix elements: product, price, distribution, or promotion. Checking prices of competitors' products to make sure a company's pricing is competitive, conducting a promotional audit to verify reach of the messages, or examining the competitive industry's distribution channels may allow the company to identify a new location, and all help to make the company more educated on future decisions. When in a competitive space, why do customers choose the competitor over the company's products? Marketing research can come in many forms and helps managers to make data-driven decisions. Once this data is collected, it becomes part of the business or organization's internal data cache.

Knowledge Check

It's time to check your knowledge on the concepts presented in this section. Refer to the Answer Key at the end of the book for feedback.

1. Which of the following is a source for external information?
   a. Sales receipts of your company's most popular product
   b. Employee salaries
   c. Comments received from a customer service survey
   d. Company's website content

2. Xin wants to determine the best price for a new product. What source of data would be the most appropriate to use?
   a. Price of a competitor's products
   b. Inventory expenses
   c. Journal articles
   d. Online news site

3. Which of the following is not a source of marketing information?
   a. Journal articles

    b. Social media posts
    c. Experiments
    d. Marketing information systems

4. Which of the following would be a good source of competitive intelligence?
    a. Experiments
    b. Product sales of a company's products
    c. Consumer responses to a poll on a company's new products
    d. Competitor's website

5. Critical data that already exists within a company's databases is called ________.
    a. big data
    b. internal data
    c. external data
    d. competitive data

6.3 | Steps in a Successful Marketing Research Plan

Learning Outcomes

By the end of this section, you will be able to:

LO 1 Identify and describe the steps in a marketing research plan.
LO 2 Discuss the different types of data research.
LO 3 Explain how data is analyzed.
LO 4 Discuss the importance of effective research reports.

Define the Problem

There are seven steps to a successful marketing research project (see Figure 6.3). Each step will be explained as we investigate how a marketing research project is conducted.

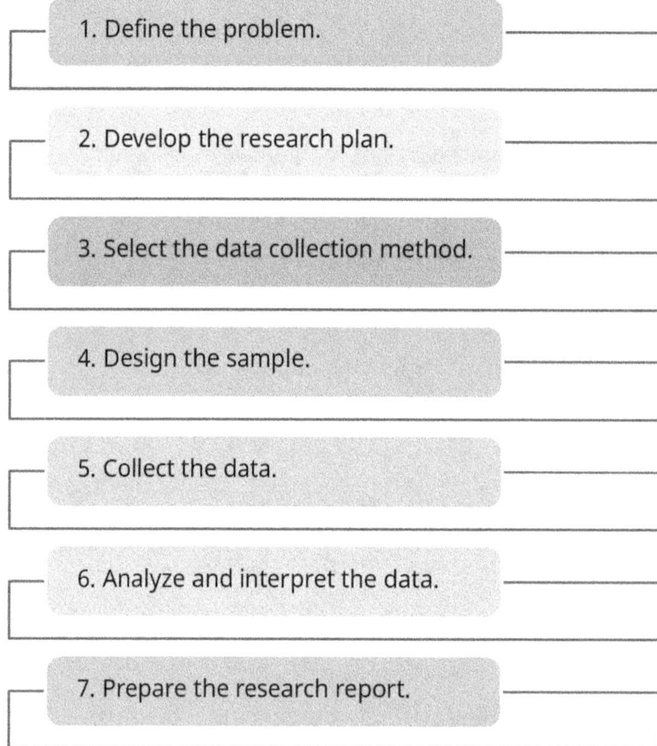

Figure 6.3 The Marketing Research Plan (attribution: Copyright Rice University, OpenStax, under CC BY 4.0 license)

The first step, defining the problem, is often a realization that more information is needed in order to make a data-driven decision. **Problem definition** is the realization that there is an issue that needs to be addressed. An entrepreneur may be interested in opening a small business but must first define the problem that is to be investigated. A marketing research problem in this example is to discover the needs of the community and also to identify a potentially successful business venture.

Many times, researchers define a research question or objectives in this first step. Objectives of this research study could include: identify a new business that would be successful in the community in question, determine the size and composition of a target market for the business venture, and collect any relevant primary and secondary data that would support such a venture. At this point, the definition of the problem may be "Why are cat owners not buying our new cat toy subscription service?"

Additionally, during this first step we would want to investigate our **target population** for research. This is similar to a target market, as it is the group that comprises the population of interest for the study. In order to have a successful research outcome, the researcher should start with an understanding of the problem in the current situational environment.

Develop the Research Plan

Step two is to develop the research plan. What type of research is necessary to meet the established objectives of the first step? How will this data be collected? Additionally, what is the time frame of the research and budget to consider? If you must have information in the next week, a different plan would be implemented than in a situation where several months were allowed. These are issues that a researcher should address in order to meet the needs identified.

Research is often classified as coming from one of two types of data: primary and secondary. **Primary data** is unique information that is collected by the specific researcher with the current project in mind. This type of research doesn't currently exist until it is pulled together for the project. Examples of primary data collection include survey, observation, experiment, or focus group data that is gathered for the current project.

Secondary data is any research that was completed for another purpose but can be used to help inform the research process. Secondary data comes in many forms and includes census data, journal articles, previously collected survey or focus group data of related topics, and compiled company data. Secondary data may be internal, such as the company's sales records for a previous quarter, or external, such as an industry report of all related product sales. **Syndicated data**, a type of external secondary data, is available through subscription services and is utilized by many marketers. As you can see in Table 6.1, primary and secondary data features are often opposite—the positive aspects of primary data are the negative side of secondary data.

	Strengths	Weaknesses
Primary Data	• Can be structured to be exactly what is needed • Under complete control of researchers • Timely, current data	• Expensive to implement • Takes time to compile • May not be generalizable beyond specific research question
Secondary Data	• Generally inexpensive or free • Can be accessed quickly • Available through a variety of sources	• May not match required parameters • Can be outdated • Same data accessible by competitors

Table 6.1 The Strengths and Weaknesses of Primary and Secondary Data

There are four research types that can be used: exploratory, descriptive, experimental, and ethnographic research designs (see Figure 6.4). Each type has specific formats of data that can be collected. **Qualitative research** can be shared through words, descriptions, and open-ended comments. Qualitative data gives context but cannot be reduced to a statistic. **Qualitative data** examples are categorical and include case studies, diary accounts, interviews, focus groups, and open-ended surveys. By comparison, **quantitative data** is data that can be reduced to number of responses. The number of responses to each answer on a multiple-choice question is quantitative data. Quantitative data is numerical and includes things like age, income, group size, and height.

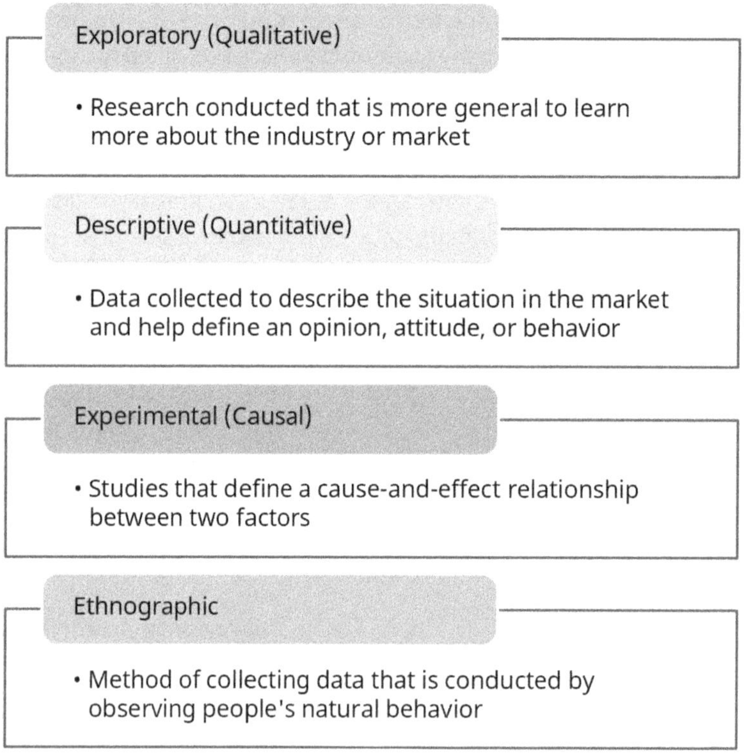

> **Exploratory (Qualitative)**
> - Research conducted that is more general to learn more about the industry or market

> **Descriptive (Quantitative)**
> - Data collected to describe the situation in the market and help define an opinion, attitude, or behavior

> **Experimental (Causal)**
> - Studies that define a cause-and-effect relationship between two factors

> **Ethnographic**
> - Method of collecting data that is conducted by observing people's natural behavior

Figure 6.4 Four Research Types (attribution: Copyright Rice University, OpenStax, under CC BY 4.0 license)

Exploratory research is usually used when additional general information in desired about a topic. When in the initial steps of a new project, understanding the landscape is essential, so exploratory research helps the researcher to learn more about the general nature of the industry. Exploratory research can be collected through focus groups, interviews, and review of secondary data. When examining an exploratory research design, the best use is when your company hopes to collect data that is generally qualitative in nature.[7]

For instance, if a company is considering a new service for registered users but is not quite sure how well the new service will be received or wants to gain clarity of exactly how customers may use a future service, the company can host a focus group. Focus groups and interviews will be examined later in the chapter. The insights collected during the focus group can assist the company when designing the service, help to inform promotional campaign options, and verify that the service is going to be a viable option for the company.

Descriptive research design takes a bigger step into collection of data through primary research complemented by secondary data. Descriptive research helps explain the market situation and define an "opinion, attitude, or behavior" of a group of consumers, employees, or other interested groups.[8] The most common method of deploying a descriptive research design is through the use of a survey. Several types of surveys will be defined later in this chapter. Descriptive data is quantitative in nature, meaning the data can be distilled into a statistic, such as in a table or chart.

Again, descriptive data is helpful in explaining the current situation. In the opening example of LEGO, the company wanted to describe the situation regarding children's use of its product. In order to gather a large group of opinions, a survey was created. The data that was collected through this survey allowed the company to measure the existing perceptions of parents so that alterations could be made to future plans for the company.

Experimental research, also known as **causal research**, helps to define a cause-and-effect relationship between two or more factors. This type of research goes beyond a correlation to determine which feature caused the reaction. Researchers generally use some type of experimental design to determine a causal relationship. An example is A/B testing, a situation where one group of research participants, group A, is exposed to one treatment and then compared to the group B participants, who experience a different situation. An example might be showing two different television commercials to a panel of consumers and then measuring the difference in perception of the product. Another example would be to have two separate packaging options available in different markets. This research would answer the question "Does one design sell better than the other?" Comparing that to the sales in each market would be part of a causal research study.[9]

The final method of collecting data is through an ethnographic design. **Ethnographic research** is conducted in the field by watching people interact in their natural environment. For marketing research, ethnographic designs help to identify how a product is used, what actions are included in a selection, or how the consumer interacts with the product.[10]

Examples of ethnographic research would be to observe how a consumer uses a particular product, such as baking soda. Although many people buy baking soda, its uses are vast. So are they using it as a refrigerator deodorizer, a toothpaste, to polish a belt buckle, or to use in baking a cake?

Select the Data Collection Method

Data collection is the systematic gathering of information that addresses the identified problem. What is the best method to do that? Picking the right method of collecting data requires that the researcher understand the target population and the design picked in the previous step. There is no perfect method; each method has both advantages and disadvantages, so it's essential that the researcher understand the target population of the research and the research objectives in order to pick the best option.

Sometimes the data desired is best collected by watching the actions of consumers. For instance, how many cars pass a specific billboard in a day? What website led a potential customer to the company's website? When are consumers most likely to use the snack vending machines at work? What time of day has the highest traffic on a social media post? What is the most streamed television program this week? **Observational research** is the collecting of data based on actions taken by those observed. Many data observations do not require the researched individuals to participate in the data collection effort to be highly valuable. Some observation requires an individual to watch and record the activities of the target population through **personal observations**.

Unobtrusive observation happens when those being observed aren't aware that they are being watched. An example of an unobtrusive observation would be to watch how shoppers interact with a new stuffed animal display by using a one-way mirror. Marketers can identify which products were handled more often while also determining which were ignored.

Other methods can use technology to collect the data instead. Instances of **mechanical observation** include the use of vehicle recorders, which count the number of vehicles that pass a specific location. Computers can also assess the number of shoppers who enter a store, the most popular entry point for train station commuters, or the peak time for cars to park in a parking garage.

When you want to get a more in-depth response from research participants, one method is to complete a **one-on-one interview**. One-on-one interviews allow the researcher to ask specific questions that match the respondent's unique perspective as well as follow-up questions that piggyback on responses already completed. An interview allows the researcher to have a deeper understanding of the needs of the respondent, which is another strength of this type of data collection. The downside of personal interviews it that a discussion can be very time-consuming and results in only one respondent's answers. Therefore, in order to get a large sample of respondents, the interview method may not be the most efficient method.

Taking the benefits of an interview and applying them to a small group of people is the design of a **focus group**. A focus group is a small number of people, usually 8 to 12, who meet the sample requirements. These individuals together are asked a series of questions where they are encouraged to build upon each other's responses, either by agreeing or disagreeing with the other group members. Focus groups are similar to interviews in that they allow the researcher, through a moderator, to get more detailed information from a small group of potential customers (see Figure 6.5).

LINK TO LEARNING

Focus Groups

Focus groups are a common method for gathering insights into consumer thinking and habits. Companies will use this information to develop or shift their initiatives. The best way to understand a focus group is to watch a few examples or explanations. TED-Ed has this video that explains how focus groups work.

Click to view content (https://openstax.org/books/principles-marketing/pages/6-3-steps-in-a-successful-marketing-research-plan)

You might be asking when it is best to use a focus group or a survey. Learn the differences, the pros and cons of each, and the specific types of questions you ask in both situations in this article (https://openstax.org/r/surveymonkey).

Preparing for a focus group is critical to success. It requires knowing the material and questions while also managing the group of people. Watch this video to learn more about how to prepare for a focus group and the types of things to be aware of.

Click to view content (https://openstax.org/books/principles-marketing/pages/6-3-steps-in-a-successful-marketing-research-plan)

One of the benefits of a focus group over individual interviews is that synergy can be generated when a participant builds on another's ideas. Additionally, for the same amount of time, a researcher can hear from multiple respondents instead of just one.[11] Of course, as with every method of data collection, there are downsides to a focus group as well. Focus groups have the potential to be overwhelmed by one or two aggressive personalities, and the format can discourage more reserved individuals from speaking up. Finally, like interviews, the responses in a focus group are qualitative in nature and are difficult to distill into an easy statistic or two.

Figure 6.5 A focus group is a research method for collecting customer data that involves a moderator asking questions of a small group of people who represent the target market. (credit: "Meeting" by UBC Learning Commons/flickr, CC BY 2.0)

Combining a variety of questions on one instrument is called a **survey** or **questionnaire**. Collecting primary data is commonly done through surveys due to their versatility. A survey allows the researcher to ask the same set of questions of a large group of respondents. Response rates of surveys are calculated by dividing the number of surveys completed by the total number attempted. Surveys are flexible and can collect a variety of quantitative and qualitative data. Questions can include simplified yes or no questions, select all that apply, questions that are on a scale, or a variety of open-ended types of questions. There are four types of surveys (see Table 6.2) we will cover, each with strengths and weaknesses defined.

	Strengths	Weaknesses
Mailed Surveys	• Ability to reach large population • Convenience of respondent	• Time delays • Expensive
Phone Surveys	• Respondent can ask questions • Collection in real time	• Time intensive • People don't answer calls from numbers they don't know
In-Person Surveys	• Respondent can ask questions • Follow-up questions can be asked based on answers	• Time intensive • People avoid talking with strangers
Electronic Surveys	• Less time intensive than other methods • Less expensive	• Identification as spam • Low response rate

Table 6.2 The Four Survey Method Options

Let's start off with **mailed surveys**—surveys that are sent to potential respondents through a mail service. Mailed surveys used to be more commonly used due to the ability to reach every household. In some instances, a mailed survey is still the best way to collect data. For example, every 10 years the United States conducts a census of its population (see Figure 6.6). The first step in that data collection is to send every household a survey through the US Postal Service (USPS). The benefit is that respondents can complete and return the survey at their convenience. The downside of mailed surveys are expense and timeliness of responses. A mailed survey requires postage, both when it is sent to the recipient and when it is returned. That, along with the cost of printing, paper, and both sending and return envelopes, adds up quickly. Additionally, physically mailing surveys takes time. One method of reducing cost is to send with bulk-rate postage, but that slows down the delivery of the survey. Also, because of the convenience to the respondent, completed surveys may be returned several weeks after being sent. Finally, some mailed survey data must be manually entered into the analysis software, which can cause delays or issues due to entry errors.

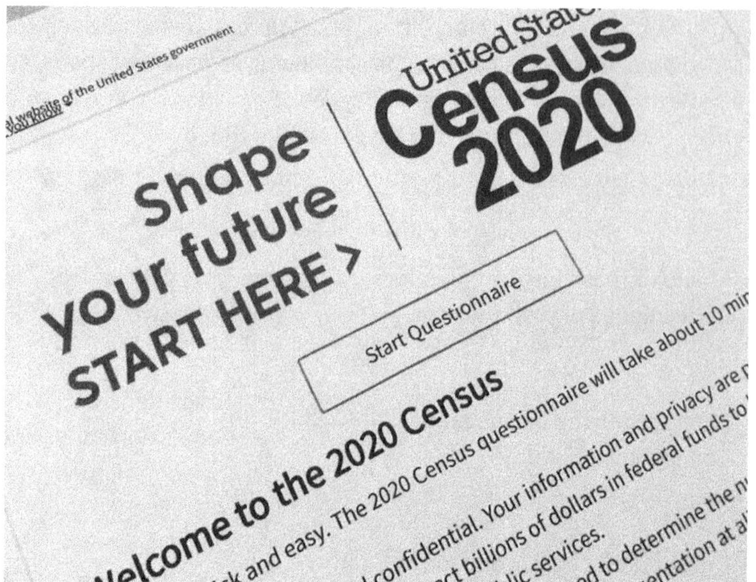

Figure 6.6 A mailed survey, like the US Census, is a research method for collecting customer data that utilizes the mail, which provides companies with a way to reach a large number of households. (credit: "Census" by KSRE Photo/flickr, CC BY 2.0)

Phone surveys are completed during a phone conversation with the respondent. Although the traditional phone survey requires a data collector to talk with the participant, current technology allows for computer-assisted voice surveys or surveys to be completed by asking the respondent to push a specific button for each potential answer. Phone surveys are time intensive but allow the respondent to ask questions and the surveyor to request additional information or clarification on a question if warranted. Phone surveys require the respondent to complete the survey simultaneously with the collector, which is a limitation as there are restrictions for when phone calls are allowed. According to Telephone Consumer Protection Act, approved by Congress in 1991, no calls can be made prior to 8:00 a.m. or after 9:00 p.m. in the recipient's time zone.[12] Many restrictions are outlined in this original legislation and have been added to since due to ever-changing technology.

In-person surveys are when the respondent and data collector are physically in the same location. In-person surveys allow the respondent to share specific information, ask questions of the surveyor, and follow up on previous answers. Surveys collected through this method can take place in a variety of ways: through door-to-door collection, in a public location, or at a person's workplace. Although in-person surveys are time intensive and require more labor to collect data than some other methods, in some cases it's the best way to collect the required data. In-person surveys conducted through a door-to-door method is the follow-up used for the census if respondents do not complete the mailed survey. One of the downsides of in-person surveys is the reluctance of potential respondents to stop their current activity and answer questions. Furthermore, people may not feel comfortable sharing private or personal information during a face-to-face conversation.

Electronic surveys are sent or collected through digital means and is an opportunity that can be added to any of the above methods as well as some new delivery options. Surveys can be sent through email, and respondents can either reply to the email or open a hyperlink to an online survey (see Figure 6.7). Additionally, a letter can be mailed that asks members of the survey sample to log in to a website rather than to return a mailed response. Many marketers now use links, QR codes, or electronic devices to easily connect to a survey. Digitally collected data has the benefit of being less time intensive and is often a more economical way to gather and input responses than more manual methods. A survey that could take months to collect through the mail can be completed within a week through digital means.

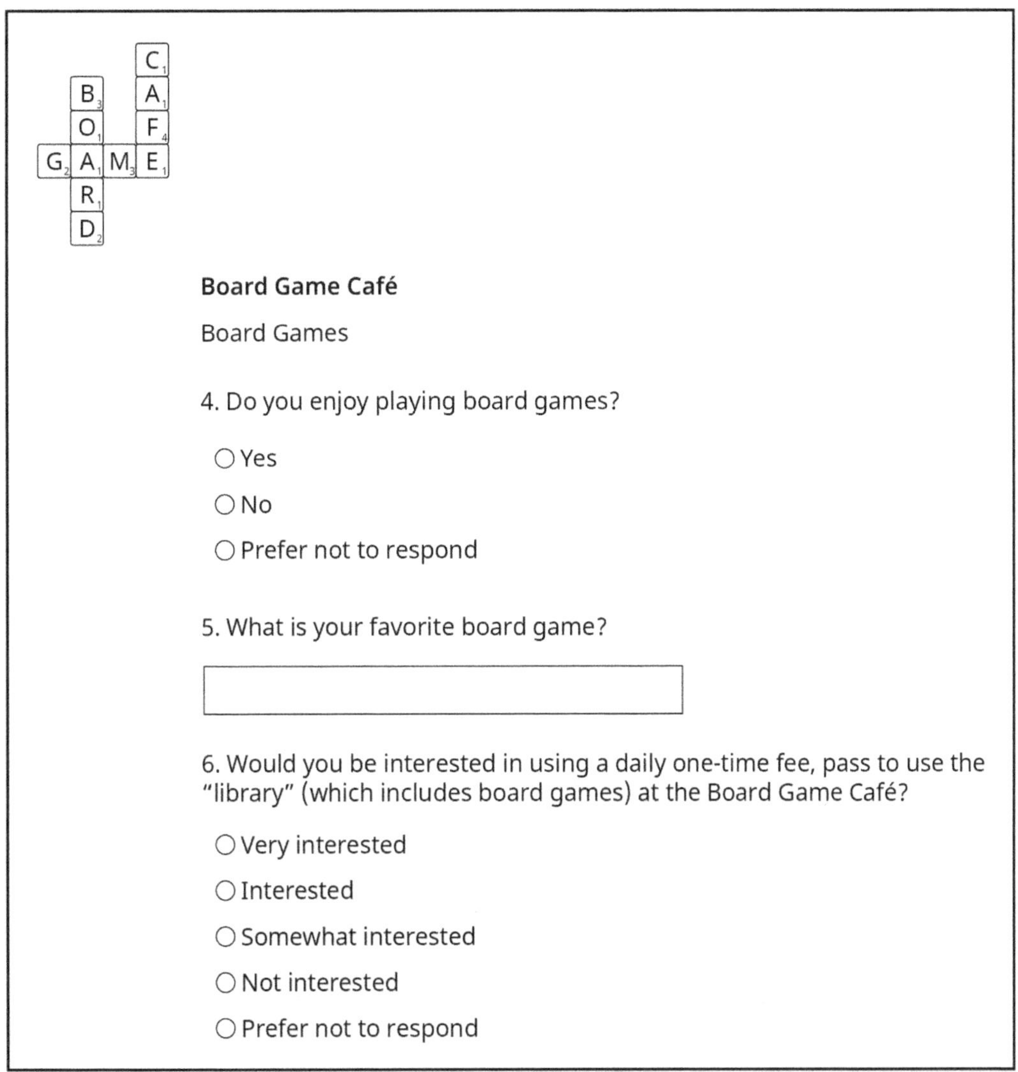

Figure 6.7 Online Survey Example (attribution: Copyright Rice University, OpenStax, under CC BY 4.0 license)

Design the Sample

Although you might want to include every possible person who matches your target market in your research, it's often not a feasible option, nor is it of value. If you did decide to include everyone, you would be completing a **census** of the population. Getting everyone to participate would be time-consuming and highly expensive, so instead marketers use a **sample**, whereby a portion of the whole is included in the research. It's similar to the samples you might receive at the grocery store or ice cream shop; it isn't a full serving, but it does give you a good taste of what the whole would be like.

So how do you know who should be included in the sample? Researchers identify parameters for their studies, called **sample frames**. A sample frame for one study may be college students who live on campus; for another study, it may be retired people in Dallas, Texas, or small-business owners who have fewer than 10 employees. The individual entities within the sampling frame would be considered a **sampling unit**. A sampling unit is each individual respondent that would be considered as matching the sample frame established by the research. If a researcher wants businesses to participate in a study, then businesses would be the sampling unit in that case.

The number of sampling units included in the research is the **sample size**. Many calculations can be conducted to indicate what the correct size of the sample should be. Issues to consider are the size of the population, the confidence level that the data represents the entire population, the ease of accessing the units in the frame, and the budget allocated for the research.

There are two main categories of samples: probability and nonprobability (see Figure 6.8). **Probability samples** are those in which every member of the sample has an identified likelihood of being selected. Several probability sample methods can be utilized. One probability sampling technique is called a **simple random sample**, where not only does every person have an identified likelihood of being selected to be in the sample, but every person also has an equal chance of exclusion. An example of a simple random sample would be to put the names of all members of a group into a hat and simply draw out a specific number to be included. You could say a raffle would be a good example of a simple random sample.

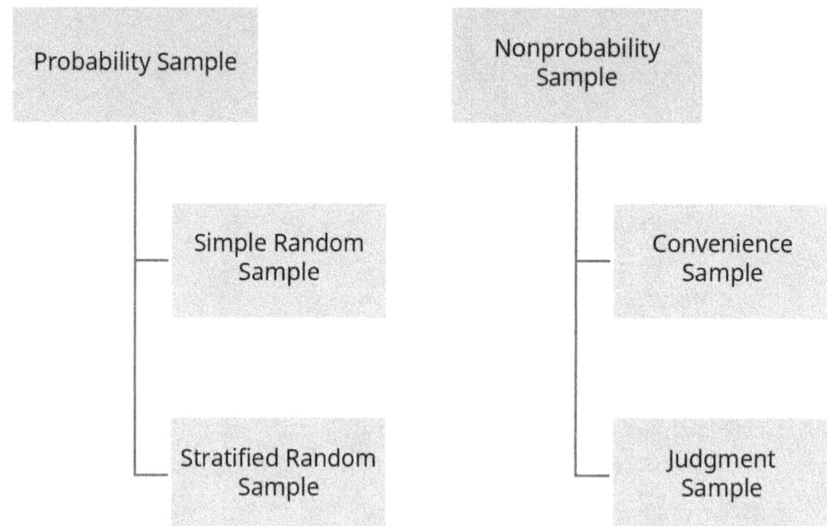

Figure 6.8 Type of Samples (attribution: Copyright Rice University, OpenStax, under CC BY 4.0 license)

Another probability sample type is a **stratified random sample**, where the population is divided into groups by category and then a random sample of each category is selected to participate. For instance, if you were conducting a study of college students from your school and wanted to make sure you had all grade levels included, you might take the names of all students and split them into different groups by grade level—freshman, sophomore, junior, and senior. Then, from those categories, you would draw names out of each of the pools, or strata.

A **nonprobability sample** is a situation in which each potential member of the sample has an unknown likelihood of being selected in the sample. Research findings that are from a nonprobability sample cannot be applied beyond the sample. Several examples of nonprobability sampling are available to researchers and include two that we will look at more closely: convenience sampling and judgment sampling.

The first nonprobability sampling technique is a **convenience sample**. Just like it sounds, a convenience sample is when the researcher finds a group through a nonscientific method by picking potential research participants in a convenient manner. An example might be to ask other students in a class you are taking to complete a survey that you are doing for a class assignment or passing out surveys at a basketball game or theater performance.

A **judgment sample** is a type of nonprobability sample that allows the researcher to determine if they believe the individual meets the criteria set for the sample frame to complete the research. For instance, you may be interested in researching mothers, so you sit outside a toy store and ask an individual who is carrying a baby to participate.

Collect the Data

Now that all the plans have been established, the instrument has been created, and the group of participants has been identified, it is time to start collecting data. As explained earlier in this chapter, data collection is the process of gathering information from a variety of sources that will satisfy the research objectives defined in step one. Data collection can be as simple as sending out an email with a survey link enclosed or as complex as an experiment with hundreds of consumers. The method of collection directly influences the length of this process. Conducting personal interviews or completing an experiment, as previously mentioned, can add weeks or months to the research process, whereas sending out an electronic survey may allow a researcher to collect the necessary data in a few days.[13]

Analyze and Interpret the Data

Once the data has been collected, the process of analyzing it may begin. **Data analysis** is the distillation of the information into a more understandable and actionable format. The analysis itself can take many forms, from the use of basic statistics to a more comprehensive data visualization process. First, let's discuss some basic statistics that can be used to represent data.

The first is the mean of quantitative data. A **mean** is often defined as the arithmetic average of values. The formula is:

$$\frac{Sum\ of\ Values}{Number\ of\ Values}$$

A common use of the mean calculation is with exam scores. Say, for example, you have earned the following scores on your marketing exams: 72, 85, 68, and 77. To find the mean, you would add up the four scores for a total of 302. Then, in order to generate a mean, that number needs to be divided by the number of exam scores included, which is 4. The mean would be 302 divided by 4, for a mean test score of 75.5. Understanding the mean can help to determine, with one number, the weight of a particular value.

Another commonly used statistic is median. The **median** is often referred to as the middle number. To generate a median, all the numeric answers are placed in order, and the middle number is the median. Median is a common statistic when identifying the income level of a specific geographic region.[14] For instance, the median household income for Albuquerque, New Mexico, between 2015 and 2019 was $52,911.[15] In this case, there are just as many people with an income above the amount as there are below.

Mode is another statistic that is used to represent data of all types, as it can be used with quantitative or qualitative data and represents the most frequent answer. Eye color, hair color, and vehicle color can all be presented with a mode statistic. Additionally, some researchers expand on the concept of mode and present the **frequency** of all responses, not just identifying the most common response. Data such as this can easily be presented in a frequency graph,[16] such as the one in Figure 6.9.

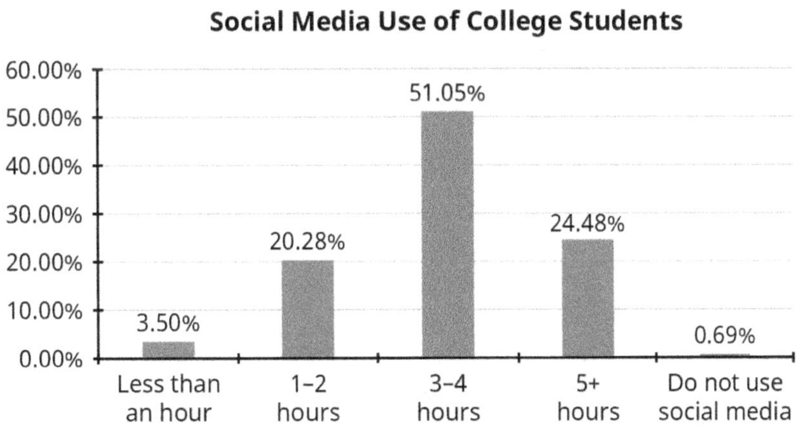

Social Media Use of College Students

Figure 6.9 Frequency Graph (attribution: Copyright Rice University, OpenStax, under CC BY 4.0 license)

Additionally, researchers use other analyses to represent the data rather than to present the entirety of each response. For example, maybe the relationship between two values is important to understand. In this case, the researcher may share the data as a **cross tabulation** (see Figure 6.10). Below is the same data as above regarding social media use cross tabulated with gender—as you can see, the data is more descriptive when you can distinguish between the gender identifiers and how much time is spent per day on social media.

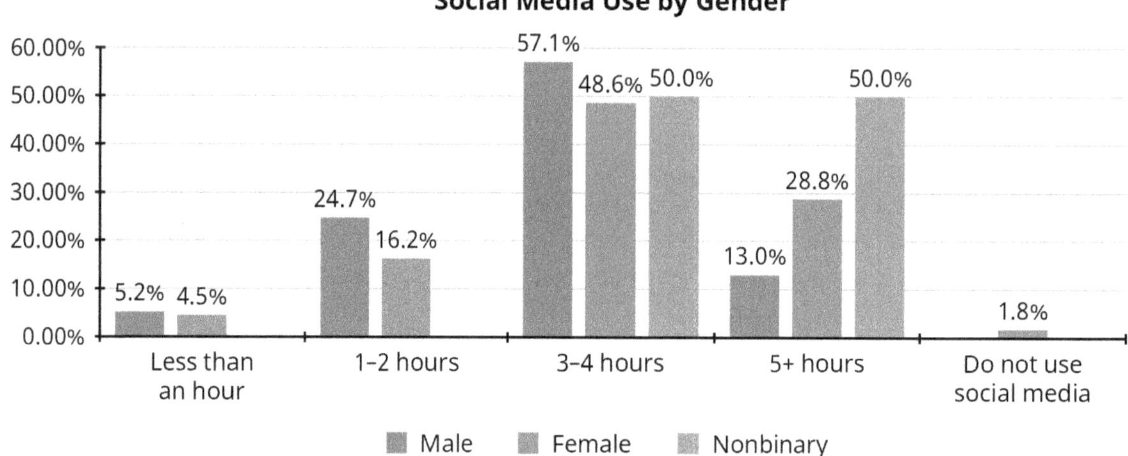

Figure 6.10 Cross Tabulation (attribution: Copyright Rice University, OpenStax, under CC BY 4.0 license)

Not all data can be presented in a graphical format due to the nature of the information. Sometimes with qualitative methods of data collection, the responses cannot be distilled into a simple statistic or graph. In that case, the use of quotations, otherwise known as **verbatims**, can be used. These are direct statements presented by the respondents. Often you will see a verbatim statement when reading a movie or book review. The critic's statements are used in part or in whole to represent their feelings about the newly released item.

LINK TO LEARNING

Infographics

As they say, a picture is worth a thousand words. For this reason, research results are often shown in a graphical format in which data can be taken in quickly, called an **infographic.**

Check out this infographic on what components make for a good infographic. (https://openstax.org/r/whatmakesgoodinfographic) As you can see, a good infographic needs four components: data, design, a story, and an ability to share it with others. Without all four pieces, it is not as valuable a resource as it could be. The ultimate infographic is represented as the intersection of all four.

Infographics are particularly advantageous online. Refer to this infographic on why they are beneficial to use online (https://openstax.org/r/infographicsbenefits).

Prepare the Research Report

The marketing research process concludes by sharing the generated data and makes recommendations for future actions. What starts as simple data must be interpreted into an analysis. All information gathered should be conveyed in order to make decisions for future marketing actions. One item that is often part of the final step is to discuss areas that may have been missed with the current project or any area of further study identified while completing it. Without the final step of the marketing research project, the first six steps are without value. It is only after the information is shared, through a formal presentation or report, that those recommendations can be implemented and improvements made. The first six steps are used to generate information, while the last is to initiate action. During this last step is also when an evaluation of the process is conducted. If this research were to be completed again, how would we do it differently? Did the right questions get answered with the survey questions posed to the respondents? Follow-up on some of these key questions can lead to additional research, a different study, or further analysis of data collected.

Methods of Quantifying Marketing Research

One of the ways of sharing information gained through marketing research is to **quantify the research**. Quantifying the research means to take a variety of data and compile into a quantity that is more easily understood. This is a simple process if you want to know how many people attended a basketball game, but if you want to quantify the number of students who made a positive comment on a questionnaire, it can be a little more complicated. Researchers have a variety of methods to collect and then share these different scores. Below are some of the most common types used in business.

Awareness

Is a customer aware of a product, brand, or company? What is meant by awareness? **Awareness** in the context of marketing research is when a consumer is familiar with the product, brand, or company. It does not assume that the consumer has tried the product or has purchased it. Consumers are just aware. That is a measure that many businesses find valuable. There are several ways to measure awareness. For instance, the first type of awareness is **unaided awareness**. This type of awareness is when no prompts for a product, brand, or company are given. If you were collecting information on fast-food restaurants, you might ask a respondent to list all the fast-food restaurants that serve a chicken sandwich. **Aided awareness** would be providing a list of products, brands, or companies and the respondent selects from the list. For instance, if you give a respondent a list of fast-food restaurants and ask them to mark all the locations with a chicken sandwich, you are collecting data through an aided method. Collecting these answers helps a company determine how the business location compares to those of its competitors.[17]

Customer Satisfaction (CSAT)

Have you ever been asked to complete a survey at the end of a purchase? Many businesses complete research on buying, returning, or other customer service processes. A **customer satisfaction score**, also known as CSAT, is a measure of how satisfied customers are with the product, brand, or service. A CSAT score is usually on a scale of 0 to 100 percent.[18] But what constitutes a "good" CSAT score? Although what is identified as good can vary by industry, normally anything in the range from 75 to 85 would be considered good. Of course, a number higher than 85 would be considered exceptional.[19]

Customer Acquisition Cost (CAC) and Customer Effort Score (CES)

Other metrics often used are a customer acquisition cost (CAC) and customer effort score (CES). How much does it cost a company to gain customers? That's the purpose of calculating the customer acquisition cost. To calculate the **customer acquisition cost**, a company would need to total all expenses that were accrued to gain new customers. This would include any advertising, public relations, social media postings, etc. When a total cost is determined, it is divided by the number of new customers gained through this campaign.

The final score to discuss is the **customer effort score**, also known as a CES. The CES is a "survey used to measure the ease of service experience with an organization."[20] Companies that are easy to work with have a better CES than a company that is notorious for being difficult. An example would be to ask a consumer about the ease of making a purchase online by incorporating a one-question survey after a purchase is confirmed. If a number of responses come back negative or slightly negative, the company will realize that it needs to investigate and develop a more user-friendly process.

Knowledge Check

It's time to check your knowledge on the concepts presented in this section. Refer to the Answer Key at the end of the book for feedback.

1. Sagar is completing a marketing research project and is at the stage where he must decide who will be sent the survey. What stage of the marketing research plan is Sagar currently on?

    a. Defining the problem

    b. Developing the research plan

    c. Selecting a data collection method

    d. Designing the sample

2. A strength of mailing a survey is that ________.

    a. you are able to send it to all households in an area

    b. it is inexpensive

    c. responses are automatically loaded into the software

    d. the data comes in quickly

3. Bartlett is considering the different types of data that can be pulled together for a research project. Currently they have collected journal articles, survey data, and syndicated data and completed a focus group. What type(s) of data have they collected?

    a. Primary data

    b. Secondary data

    c. Secondary and primary data

    d. Professional data

4. Which statistic can be used to show how many people responded to a survey question with "strongly agree"?

    a. Mean

    b. Median

    c. Mode

    d. Frequency

5. Why would a researcher want to use a cross tabulation?

    a. It shows how respondents answered two variables in relation to each other and can help determine patterns by different groups of respondents.

    b. By presenting the data in the form of a picture, the information is easier for the reader to understand.

    c. It is an easy way to see how often one answer is selected by the respondents.

    d. This analysis can used to present interview or focus group data.

6.4 Ethical Issues in Marketing Research

Learning Outcomes

By the end of this section, you will be able to:

    LO 1 Describe ethical issues relating to marketing research.

    LO 2 Discuss ways to avoid unethical research practices.

The Use of Deceptive Practices

In marketing research, there are many potential areas of ethical concern. Each day people share personal information on social media, through company databases, and on mobile devices. So how do companies make sure to remain ethical in decisions when it comes to this vast amount of research data? It is essential that marketers balance the benefits of having access to this data with the privacy of and concern for all people they can impact.

Too many times, we have heard about the lack of ethical decision-making when it comes to marketing research or personal data. Companies are hacked, share or sell personal information, or use promotion disguised as research. Each of these can be considered unethical.

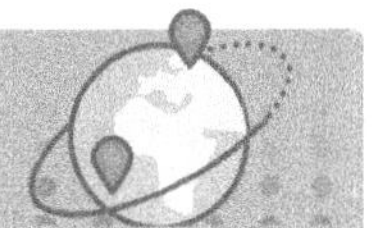

LINK TO LEARNING

The Insights Association

There is an organization devoted to the support and integrity of quality marketing research. This organization, called The Insights Association (IA), "protects and creates demand for the evolving insights and analytics industry by promoting the indisputable role of insights in driving business impact."[21] Having a solid understanding of ethical practices is critical for any marketing professional. Become familiar with terminology, responsibilities, enforcements, and sanctions of the IA's code of standards and ethics (https://openstax.org/r/codesofstandards).

First, let's look at some deceptive practices that might be conducted through research. The first is representing something as research when it is really an attempt to sell a product. This is called sugging. **Sugging** happens when an individual identifies themselves as a researcher, collects some data, and then uses the data to suggest specific purchases.[22] According to the Insights Association Code of Marketing Research Standards, researchers should always separate selling of products from the research process.[23]

Other deceptive research practices include using persuasive language to encourage a participant to select a particular answer, misrepresenting research data subjectively rather than objectively while presenting the results, and padding research data with fabricated answers in order to increase response rate or create a specific outcome.

Invasion of Privacy

Privacy is another concern when it comes to marketing research data. For researchers, **privacy** is maintaining the data of research participants discretely and holding confidentiality. Many participants are hesitant to give out identifying information for fear that the information will leak, be tied back to them personally, or be used to steal their identity. To help respondents overcome these concerns, researchers can identify the research as being either confidential or anonymous.

Confidential data is when respondents share their identifying information with the researcher, but the researcher does not share it beyond that point. In this situation, the research may need some identifier in order to match up previous information with the new content—for instance, a customer number or membership number. **Anonymous data** is when a respondent does not provide identifying information at all, so there is no chance of being identified. Researchers should always be careful with personal information, keeping it behind a firewall, behind a password-protected screen, or physically locked away.

Breaches of Confidentiality

One of the most important ethical considerations for marketing researchers is the concept of confidentiality of respondents' information. In order to have a rich data set of information, very personal information may be gathered. When a researcher uses that information in an unethical manner, it is a **breach of confidentiality**. Many research studies start with a statement of how the respondent's information will be used and how the researcher will maintain confidentiality. Companies may sell personal information, share contact information of the respondents, or tie specific answers to a respondent. These are all breaches of the confidentiality that researchers are held accountable for.[24]

Although we hear about how companies are utilizing customers' data unethically, many companies operate in an ethical manner. One example is the search engine DuckDuckGo. The search industry generates millions of pieces of user data daily; most of the providers of searches capitalize on this data by tracking and selling this information. Alternatively, DuckDuckGo has decided NOT to track its users. Instead, it has built its business model on the fact that no user information is stored—ever. Ethically, DuckDuckGo offers users private searches, tracker blocking, and site encryption. In an industry that is continuously collecting and selling personal search information, DuckDuckGo is the exception. There is no concern with being hacked because no data is collected.[25]

COMPANIES WITH A CONSCIENCE

Gallup

Figure 6.11 Due to ethical concerns around market research, companies like Gallup that specialize in market research must perform with high ethical standards in order to collect credible data so that their customers will value their work. (credit: "Survey" by EpicTop10.com/flickr, CC BY 2.0)

The Gallup Organization (https://openstax.org/r/gallup) is a market research firm that specializes in understanding market sentiment (see Figure 6.11). Every year among its numerous polls, Gallup completes an assessment of the honesty and ethical approach of different professions. In the 2021 survey, nursing was the top profession regarding these two measures.[26]

Gallup's research led additional findings about the state of ethics for businesses. "Ethical standards need to be at the core of an organization's purpose, brand and culture."[27] But what about Gallup's own ethical standards? Gallup is "a global analytics and advice firm that helps leaders and organizations solve their most pressing problems."[28] In order to be proficient and well-informed on the variety of topics Gallup investigates, it must hold itself and its employees to a high ethical standard.

Gallup completes multiple polls and research continuously. In order to meet the high standards of its public, Gallup must perform these practices in an ethical manner. Each step of the research process is completed with diligence and intention. For those reasons, Gallup is recognized for its ethically backed data. Gallup is a global leader in market insights and has locations in seven cities within the United States and an additional 27 locations internationally. According to Chuck Hagel, former Secretary of Defense of the United States, "Gallup is truly an island of independence—it possesses a credibility and trust that hardly any institution has. A reputation for impartial, fair, honest and superb work."[29]

Chapter Summary

In this chapter, we discovered the critical nature of marketing research on the success of a business. Big data, marketing intelligence, and marketing information systems were defined, and each was explained regarding its impact on the field of marketing research. Next, we learned about the seven steps of the marketing research process and how each step builds toward an actionable plan by management. The difference between secondary and primary data was clarified, and several sources of each were shared. Finally, ethical decision-making in research is essential as some very detailed information about consumers is collected.

Key Terms

aided awareness   when a product, brand, or company list is provided to select from to measure awareness

anonymous data   data in which the respondent is not identified

awareness   a consumer's familiarity with a product, brand, or company

big data   the countless number of records that continues in an increasing capacity and at a faster rate; often described as volume, velocity, and variety of data generated

breach of confidentiality   a situation where the researcher promises to hold private information but discloses it in an unethical manner without permission

causal research   studies that define a cause-and-effect relationship between two factors

census   when all potential target population members are included in the research

competitive intelligence   a collection of information about competitors from the marketplace

confidential data   data that is tied back to a respondent, but the respondent's personal information is not shared

convenience sample   a nonprobability sample type where potential respondents to the research are selected by convenience rather than through any scientific method

cross tabulation   an analysis of two variables and the frequency of each answer in relation to the other variable

customer acquisition cost   the total expenses a company spends to gain a new customer

customer effort score   a survey used to measure ease of service experience with an organization

customer satisfaction score   also known as a CES, a survey used to measure ease of service experience with an organization

data analysis   the distillation of information into a more understandable and actionable format

data collection   systematic gathering of information that addresses an identified problem

database   a collection of related data

descriptive research   data collected to describe the situation in the market and help define an opinion, attitude, or behavior

electronic surveys   surveys sent through digital means to respondents; respondents also reply to the survey digitally

ethnographic research   method of collecting data that is conducted by observing people's natural behavior

experimental research   studies that define a cause-and-effect relationship between two factors

exploratory research   research conducted that is more general to learn more about the industry or market

external data   data that originates from outside the organization

focus group   a small group, typically 8 to 12 people, who are asked several questions by a moderator and encouraged to build upon each other's responses

frequency   a report of the number of each answer received

in-person surveys   surveys conducted when the respondent and data collector are face-to-face

infographic   a representation of data in a variety of visual presentations

internal data   critical marketing intelligence that already exists in the company's records

judgment sample   a nonprobability sample type where the potential participants are selected based on a perceived match to the sample frame

mailed surveys   surveys sent to potential participants through a mail service, such as the US Postal Service

marketing information   also known as business intelligence, competitive intelligence, or marketing intelligence; information about the market that helps to identify opportunities available

marketing information system   a system used to collect, analyze, and report interesting findings from internal and external data of the company

marketing research   the function that links the consumer, customer, and public to the marketer through information

mean   an arithmetic average of values

mechanical observation   the use of electronic monitoring to record the actions of the observed

median   the middle number when all answers are organized from smallest to largest; if an even number of data, the mean of the two middle answers is the median

mode   the most common response

nonprobability sample   a situation which each member of the population has an unknown chance of being selected to be part of the sample

observational research   data collected by watching consumers and recording actions

one-on-one interview   an interview that happens on an individual level between researcher and respondent

personal observations   observations that are collected by human recorders

phone surveys   surveys conducted through the use of a telephone that can be completed through digital or human methods

primary data   unique information that is collected by the researcher with the current project in mind

privacy   maintaining the data of research participants discretely and holding confidentiality

probability sample   a sample in which everyone has a known chance of being included in the research

problem definition   the realization that there is an issue that needs to be addressed

qualitative data   data that cannot be distilled into number of responses, such as responses to an interview

qualitative research   data shared through words, descriptions, and open-ended comments

quantify the research   to take a variety of data and compile it into a quantity that is easily understood

quantitative data   data that can be reduced to number of responses, such as number of responses to each answer on a multiple-choice question

questionnaire   also known as a survey, a series of several questions that can collect a variety of qualitative and quantitative data; can be distributed through several different methods

sample   a portion of the entire population that is included in the research

sample frame   a parameter that defines who will be included in the sample and who would not be included

sample size   the number of respondents that are to be included in the research

sampling unit   each individual entities that is included in the sample

secondary data   any research that was completed, within the organization or outside of the organization, for another purpose

simple random sample   a type of probability sample where every entity has an equal chance of being selected

stratified random sample   a probability sample type where the population is divided into groups and then participants are selected from each stratum randomly

sugging   suggesting a purchase disguised as research

survey   also known as a questionnaire, a series of several questions that can collect a variety of qualitative and quantitative data; can be distributed through several different methods

syndicated data   a type of secondary data that is available through a subscription service

target population   the group of people that are of interest for a study

unaided awareness   when no prompts or lists of potential products, brands, or companies are given to test awareness

unobtrusive observation   a type of observation research where the observed is not aware they are being monitored

verbatims   exact quotations of responses to a qualitative question

Applied Marketing Knowledge: Discussion Questions

1. Why is it vital for companies to understand and use customer insights in gathering and managing marketing information?

2. Public policies and laws supporting ethics in marketing research have resulted in companies like Meta (formerly Facebook) being accused of intruding upon consumer privacy, misusing information gathered from users, and exploiting children. As a consumer, how do you feel about companies tracing your digital footprint? As a marketer, what value do you see in tracing consumers' online activities?

3. What are the seven steps necessary in designing a marketing research project?

4. List two reasons why quantitative research data is better utilized to measure a population's attitudes and potential responses to new product releases than qualitative data. List two reasons why qualitative data is most often collected to provide deeper insights into consumer behavior.

5. Research codes of conduct are published by the American Marketing Association, the American Association for Public Opinion Research, the Council of American Survey Research Organizations, and the Marketing Research Association in order to define standards of ethical behavior. List three overlapping areas these organizations have identified as important in regulating the marketing industry.

Critical Thinking Exercises

1. Draw a diagram depicting a marketing information system. Show how the marketing research process connects marketing managers with the marketing environment in order to collect information through internal records, marketing intelligence, and marketing research. Remember that the overall intent is first to assess information needs in order to reduce information gaps between the company and its customers, target markets, suppliers, and prospective clients. Amassing timely information allows firms to address these gaps, design the method for collecting information, manage and implement the data collection process, analyze the results, and disseminate results and their implications.

2. Conduct a survey of five college students via email, social media, telephone, or in person to learn more about the student demographic. Explain that you are collecting data for a classroom assignment only and will not identify them by name.
   Ask these questions:

   A. If you could adopt a rescue animal today, what would it be?
   B. What is the best pizza topping?
   C. Would you rather sneeze for an hour or have hiccups for an hour?
   D. Would you rather get $1 million right now or $10,000 per month for a lifetime?
   E. What is your least favorite food?

   2a. Summarize and report your results in a chart.
   2b. C and D are structurally different questions than A, B, and E. What is different between these questions?
   2c. Can your findings be applied to all college students? Why or why not?

3. The US Census gathers and disseminates detailed big data about US residents. Visit Explore Census Data (https://openstax.org/r/datacensus) and type your hometown into the search box. The results will include maps, web pages mentioning your hometown, and tables of information gathered by the decennial census as well as the American Community Survey. What method was used to collect this data? Do these tables represent probability or nonprobability samples? Why might these tables be important informational sources for marketers? Check out the table reporting age and sex. What is the median age? Does this statistic surprise you?

☀ Building Your Personal Brand

If you're a curious person, you may enjoy a career in data science, marketing research, or consumer insights. Businesses report that there is a growing need for data specialists—analysts, engineers, scientists, translators, and cybersecurity managers—to grasp the power of data insights to drive major business initiatives. Business professionals across organizations depend on analytical know-how to make informed decisions with real-time insights. Ongoing data evolution requires data scientists to learn and adopt new technology to accelerate organizational data strategies.

For budding professionals in the data science/consumer insights field, it's essential to have foundational knowledge in applied mathematics, statistics, data analytics and visualization, machine learning, computer science, or data engineering. These may be courses you wish to add to your upper-level academic work. You can also apply the resulting skill sets to your brand as you investigate internships and projects. Keep in mind that insights specialists must be able to communicate and present complex findings to cross-functional teams clearly and succinctly, driving data-driven decision-making from those findings.

Internal marketing departments generally rely on analysts to handle business intelligence and data scientists to aggregate company data. Read this article to better understand the role differences (https://openstax.org/r/marketinganalystsvsdatascientists) between a marketing analyst and a data scientist. Review the differences in salaries for marketing analysts and data scientists here (https://openstax.org/r/comparablysalaries).

Now build a chart summarizing the skills necessary for both roles and then identify which of those skills you feel you already possess and which of those you need to work on. For those skills that you need to develop, identify one or two steps you can take to add this to your personal brand.

 What Do Marketers Do?

Research is a part of many career paths for marketers and business personnel. Financial planners, human resource managers, logistics analysts, and marketing strategists all use research on a daily basis. Most businesses now rely upon customer loyalty and product/service ratings as they attempt to gain distinction among competitors. Many companies now ask consumers to rate their products and services. That rating is the next best thing to asking friends and family members for product suggestions. Customers want proof that products or services are reputable. Customer reviews are vital in providing personalized experience and insights to promote customer relationships.

Speak to a consumer insights specialist from a local advertising agency or a professor at your college or another university—especially one who specializes in big data analytics—about the importance of data in making marketing decisions. To find an insights specialist or professor, conduct a Google and/or LinkedIn search. Also check out this list of top marketing professors on Twitter (https://openstax.org/r/connectedmarketingprofessors).

In your interview, you might ask the following questions, but be sure to also include any questions you might have.

- What is big data, and how do firms gather it?
- How do companies I may be familiar with analyze and use data on a regular basis to inform marketing efforts?
- What are metrics, dashboards, and actionable goals?
- I understand that employee turnover is a major consideration in customer satisfaction these days. How does data analysis help companies measure employee satisfaction?
- Are there specific methods to gather information about customer satisfaction?
- I've received emails after making a purchase online, asking for my feedback. How seriously is this feedback taken?
- Can you give an example of how researchers may use primary and secondary data?

- Are there specific courses I should take if I'm interested in the data side of marketing?

 Marketing Plan Exercise

Complete the following information about the company and products/services you chose to focus on for this marketing plan exercise. You may need to conduct research to gather necessary information.

Instructions: Using the Marketing Plan Template file you created from Marketing and Consumer Value and expanded upon in Strategic Planning in Marketing and Market Segmentation, Targeting, and Positioning, complete the following section of your marketing plan: Current Market Situation/Situation Analysis.

Once complete, submit the marketing plan to your instructor for grading and feedback.

 Closing Company Case

Nordstrom

One day a customer walked into an upscale fashion retail store in Anchorage, Alaska, to return a set of tires. The store had a wide selection of shoes, clothes, and accessories, but no tires. However, the store that previously occupied the space did sell tires. After much discussion, a Nordstrom store manager made the return and accepted the tires. The story is legendary in customer service circles. It is also true.

A leading fashion retailer based in Seattle, Washington, Nordstrom prides itself on customer service and innovative methods of serving the customer. Founded in 1901, the company now operates 358 retail stores in the United States and Canada as well as online retail.[30]

Nordstrom has long been famous for its customer-centric mindset. The "Nordstrom way" has always been about serving customers according to their needs and making them feel good about the shopping experience. Part of the experience is focused on ease, selection, and convenience.

In 2020, Nordstrom saw tremendous growth in online sales. By integrating online and in-store sales, the company realized that 50 percent of customers who buy in store at Nordstrom have first had a digital experience with the retailer. Identifying trends between in-store sales and online sales has assisted Nordstrom in formulating a more customer-centric strategy.[31]

To better serve customers and increase sales, Nordstrom sales associates are key. Sales associates develop connections with the customer. With good questions and involvement in the customer experience, the sales associates determine consumer needs and wants. Understanding consumer needs and wants leads Nordstrom to craft an experience unparalleled in retail.[32]

Through careful study of the customer and the analytics available in online and in-person shopping patterns, Nordstrom has developed a more robust system that allows for seamless coordination between all Nordstrom properties. In developing a better customer experience, Nordstrom worked to really understand how customers live and behave.

From customer interactions, observation, online data, and careful marketing research, Nordstrom Local emerged. One key piece of information was that 35 percent of customers who place an online order first visited a store to help guide the purchase decision.[33] With Los Angeles and New York as the top markets, Nordstrom needed methods to connect with and help ease the purchase process for its customers in these locations.

One significant aspect of the purchase process was to make online ordering easier, allowing for quick in-store pickups and returns while also including a method of getting alterations when and where it was most convenient. The creation of Nordstrom Local was the answer. Through a Nordstrom Local, available in the top markets, the customer could get the Nordstrom experience—closer to home.

Nordstrom realized the more channels a customer could use, the more they would spend with the retailer. In fact, soon after opening Nordstrom Local, the company was able to determine that customers using the new locations spend 2.5 times the amount of all other customers. So how could the company better serve those customers and make transactions more profitable?

Part of the Nordstrom plan to connect the customer more fully with the "experience" included the ability to easily order online and pick up in-store—using Nordstrom Local made that possibility easier to achieve. Nordstrom Local also included tailors available at pickup, the exclusive Nordstrom Stylist who would travel to all stores within a local market area, easy returns and exchanges, and finally, Certified Gift-Wrapping Specialists to make special packages look styled for whatever the occasion.

Consumer insights help Nordstrom to provide curated merchandise for each store. When shopping at Nordstrom, you will find merchandise specific to the region and store location. Pop-up shops are a regular feature at Nordstrom. The pop-up allows for a preview of potential merchandise to meet the needs of the local market. A well-rounded plan to connect at every point of contact has allowed Nordstrom to create an experience unrivaled in the industry.

Case Questions

1. Nordstrom is legendary for providing the best customer experience. What are some of the ways Nordstrom has gathered marketing research from the consumer?

2. When Nordstrom analyzes the data found in its online sales platforms, what type of marketing research is it using?

3. In what ways has Nordstrom used data to enhance the customer experience?

4. Nordstrom realized a connection between online shopping and in-store shopping. It developed methods to capture the online customer and increase in-store sales. In what ways was Nordstrom able to understand customer shopping behaviors?

References

1. "Girls Are Ready to Overcome Gender Norms but Society Continues to Enforce Biases That Hamper Their Creative Potential," About Us, The LEGO Group, October 10, 2021, https://www.lego.com/en-us/aboutus/news/2021/september/lego-ready-for-girls-campaign/.

2. "Definitions of Marketing," American Marketing Association, last modified July 20, 2022, https://www.ama.org/the-definition-of-marketing-what-is-marketing/.

3. Ibid.

4. Mary K. Pratt, "How Big Data Collection Works: Process, Challenges, Techniques," Tech Accelerator, TechTarget, February 7, 2022, https://www.techtarget.com/searchdatamanagement/feature/Big-data-collection-processes-challenges-and-best-practices.

5. Ibid.

6. Rob Kitchin and Gavin McArdle, "What Makes Big Data, Big Data? Exploring the Ontological Characteristics of 26 Datasets," *Big Data & Society* 3, no. 1 (January–June 2016), https://doi.org/10.1177/2053951716631130.

7. Raimo Streefkerk, "Qualitative vs. Quantitative Research," Methodology, Scribbr, revised August 13, 2021, https://www.scribbr.com/methodology/qualitative-quantitative-research/.

8. "The 3 Types of Survey Research and When to Use Them," SurveyMonkey, Momentive, last modified May 4, 2021, https://www.surveymonkey.com/mp/3-types-survey-research/.

9. Ibid.

10. Ken Anderson, "Ethnographic Research: A Key to Strategy," *Harvard Business Review*, March 2009, 24, https://hbr.org/2009/03/ethnographic-research-a-key-to-strategy.

11. "Data Collection Methods: Definition, Examples and Sources," *Online Survey Software and Data Intelligence Blog*, QuestionPro, last modified July 21, 2022, https://www.questionpro.com/blog/data-collection-methods/.

12. "Restrictions on Telemarketing, Telephone Solicitation, and Facsimile Advertising," 47 C.F.R. 64.1200, 2021 comp., p. 486, sec.

(c)(1), https://www.govinfo.gov/content/pkg/CFR-2021-title47-vol3/pdf/CFR-2021-title47-vol3-sec64-1200.pdf.

13. Pritha Bhandari, "A Step-by-Step Guide to Data Collection," Methodology, Scribbr, revised August 13, 2021, https://www.scribbr.com/methodology/data-collection/.

14. Statistics.com, Glossary, s.v. "Median," accessed November 21, 2021, https://www.statistics.com/glossary/median/.

15. "Albuquerque City, New Mexico," QuickFacts, United States Census Bureau, accessed November 23, 2021, https://www.census.gov/quickfacts/fact/table/albuquerquecitynewmexico/PST040219.

16. Statistics.com, Glossary, s.v. "Mode," accessed November 21, 2021, https://www.statistics.com/glossary/mode/; Statistics.com, Glossary, s.v. "Frequency Distribution," accessed November 21, 2021, https://www.statistics.com/glossary/frequency-distribution/.

17. "Unaided vs. Aided Brand Awareness Survey Questions: What Do They Tell You?," SurveyMonkey, Momentive, last modified April 9, 2021, https://www.surveymonkey.com/mp/unaided-vs-aided-brand-awareness-survey-questions/.

18. "What Is CSAT and How Do You Measure It?," Experience Management, Qualtrics, last modified August 10, 2022, https://www.qualtrics.com/experience-management/customer/what-is-csat/.

19. Dom Nicastro, "What Is Customer Satisfaction Score (CSAT)?," CMSWire, Simpler Media Group, September 20, 2021, https://www.cmswire.com/customer-experience/what-is-customer-satisfaction-score-csat/.

20. "Customer Effort Score (CES): Examples, Definition, and Calculations," *Online Survey Software and Data Intelligence Blog*, QuestionPro, last modified December 16, 2021, https://www.questionpro.com/blog/customer-effort-score/.

21. "IA Code of Standards & Ethics," (2021). Insights Association, November 2021, https://www.insightsassociation.org/Tools-Resources/Codes-of-Standards.

22. Terry Masters, "Ethical Considerations of Marketing Research," Chron.com, Hearst, March 1, 2019, https://smallbusiness.chron.com/ethical-considerations-marketing-research-43621.html.

23. Insights Association, "IA Code."

24. Masters, "Ethical Considerations."

25. DuckDuckGo (website), accessed November 20, 2021, https://duckduckgo.com/.

26. Lydia Saad, "Military Brass, Judges among Professions at New Image Lows," News, Gallup, January 12, 2022, https://news.gallup.com/poll/388649/military-brass-judges-among-professions-new-image-lows.aspx.

27. Ghassan Khoury and Maria Semykoz, "The New Frontier of Business Ethics," Workplace, Gallup, February 6, 2019, https://www.gallup.com/workplace/246197/new-frontier-business-ethics.aspx.

28. "About," Gallup, last modified June 1, 2022, https://www.gallup.com/corporate/212381/who-we-are.aspx.

29. Ibid.

30. Ken Worzel, "Market Strategy: Q&A with Ken Worzel," Press Releases, Nordstrom, accessed March 30, 2022, https://press.nordstrom.com/news-releases/news-release-details/local-market-strategy-qa-ken-worzel.

31. "Nordstrom to Host Virtual Investor Event on February 4," Press Releases, Nordstrom, January 21, 2021, https://press.nordstrom.com/news-releases/news-release-details/nordstrom-host-virtual-investor-event-february-4.

32. "Celebrating Our 120th Anniversary with WWD and Footwear News," Press Releases, Nordstrom, accessed June 11, 2022, https://press.nordstrom.com/news-releases/news-release-details/celebrating-our-120th-anniversary-wwd-and-footwear-news.

33. Christian Conte, "Nordstrom Customer Service Tales Not Just Legend," *Jacksonville Business Journal*, September 7, 2012, https://www.bizjournals.com/jacksonville/blog/retail_radar/2012/09/nordstrom-tales-of-legendary-customer.html.

7

Marketing in a Global Environment

Figure 7.1 International marketing opportunities can be advantageous for many companies if they are aware of global differences and potential challenges. (credit: modification of work "world-map-background1_0" by bmnnetwork/flickr, CC BY 2.0)

Chapter Outline

7.1 The Global Market and Advantages of International Trade
7.2 Assessment of Global Markets for Opportunities
7.3 Entering the Global Arena
7.4 Marketing in a Global Environment
7.5 Ethical Issues in the Global Marketplace

In the Spotlight

Starbucks is no stranger to the global marketplace. In 2020, the Seattle-based coffee company had over 30,000 stores in 80 countries.[1] Each fall, Starbucks's United States–based fans anticipate the release of the Pumpkin Spice Latte (or PSL, as it has come to be known). But what about other countries?

In 2021, the Starbucks Pumpkin Spice Latte was made available in stores across Europe, the Middle East, and Africa.[2] But the advertisements and the specific Pumpkin Spice Latte formula were modified from what you see in the United States because they were specifically crafted for each of the company's global markets. For example, in Portugal, the iced version of the Pumpkin Spice Latte is more popular, so it is marketed more heavily than the hot latte.[3]

Starbucks has seen its share of failures when expanding into global markets. In 2000, the company opened its first coffee shop in Australia. However, the company failed to allow the Australians to "develop an appetite for the Starbucks brand."[4] Asking locals to pay a premium for a brand that wasn't already ingrained in their culture didn't go over well. In the first seven years, the company reported losses of over $105 million and closures of 61 Australian stores.[5] Since then, Starbucks has changed its marketing strategy in Australia to focus on tourists rather than locals, and the result has been slower than desired.

The company has learned from its failures and successes across the globe. For example, in 2018, Starbucks opened its Starbucks Reserve Roastery in Milan, Italy. You might be surprised when visiting the Roastery as you can't order a Frappuccino, but instead, you can order wood-fired pizza and cocktails. The company promotes its Milan location as a cup of coffee and an experience. "Milan Roastery is the crown jewel of Starbucks global retail footprint—a place where Italian customers can come to discover the art and science of coffee in a breath-taking environment."[6]

Global markets vary by many factors. Look at our coffee example. Something as seemingly basic as coffee is perceived very differently across the globe, and marketers must be keenly aware of how to appeal to each market.

7.1 | The Global Market and Advantages of International Trade

Learning Outcomes

By the end of this section, you will be able to:

LO 1 Define global market opportunities.
LO 2 Explain why international trade is advantageous to business.
LO 3 Discuss the challenges of international trade.

Global Market Opportunities Defined

For some, the thought of expanding business operations into the global market is new, exciting, and fun. For others, it may seem daunting or impossible. At some point, most if not all companies will decide if and how they will expand into global markets based on global market opportunities. **Global market opportunities** simply refer to conditions that are favorable for a company to expand outside its home country market. These conditions include internal factors, such as the company's ability and knowledge, as well as external factors, such as market growth, customer demand, and regulations or trade barriers within the industry.

Many companies have a presence in the global marketplace at some level. Consider a small Etsy shop that sells custom-printed T-shirts. While the T-shirts may be printed in the United States (maybe even in someone's garage), the T-shirts may be purchased in foreign markets, such as China. While Etsy is a small-scale example, larger companies may have a greater presence in the global marketplace. Consider that Nike, founded in 1964, now sells its products in 170 countries that serve more than 30 major sports and consumer lifestyles.[7] While there are considerable risks to entering global markets, there are numerous advantages as well.

Advantages to International Trade

There are several advantages to international trade, including increased revenues, decreased competition, faster growth, diversification of risk, and the ability to more easily find buyers of excess inventory. Let's look at each of these in more detail.

Increased Revenues

One of the most obvious advantages to international trade is an increase in revenue. Recall that revenue is the money earned from business operations, so the more countries in which a product or service is available, the more revenue will be generated.

Decreased Competition

A US-based company may have a great deal of competition. Consider the automobile industry. In the United States, most households own at least one vehicle. Competition in this industry is rather fierce, and it would be difficult for a new company to enter the market. However, in developing countries where automobiles are not as prevalent or infrastructure is still in development, competition for automobile buyers could be much lower.

Alternatively, fiercer automobile competition in some countries may force competitors to leave the market or choose not to enter at all. China is the world's largest vehicle market in terms of both sales and manufacturing output.[8] As such, carmakers around the world continue to vie for the Chinese automobile market share. However, the market is mainly dominated by its domestic automakers, making international competition difficult.[9]

For example, the Hongguang Mini EV, a battery electric microcar manufactured by China-based SAIC-GM-Wuling, has been a top EV seller since 2020.[10] In an effort to take market share, Ford has set the "groundwork to accelerate a refresh of the company's product portfolio in China by launching three new vehicles offered only in China."[11]

Faster Growth

For companies with a growth strategy, international expansion may be a viable option to achieve these goals. This is particularly true when the home country's market is saturated or experiencing slow or no growth. A market becomes saturated when there is enough capacity in the industry to meet all of consumer demand or when consumer demand begins to decrease. Either instance may make the international market an attractive opportunity for a business.

In addition to the growth of the company, as firms decide to expand into global markets, the international market will also experience growth. For example, when Amazon expanded its global operations to include a fulfillment center in Poland, the company had to hire employees to fulfill those orders. As of 2022, the Poland fulfillment center employed 25,000 people.[12] These individuals use their paychecks to purchase goods and services within their economy, causing the economy to grow. As new companies enter these markets, individuals are given the opportunity to consume a wider selection of goods and services and to move into higher standards of living.

Diversification of Risk

Risk refers to any situation or condition that leads a company to decreased profits or even failure.[13] Have you ever heard the saying "Don't put all your eggs in one basket"? It refers to putting all of your effort in one area and risking great loss. It's a reminder of how international expansion can help diversify business risk. Rather than focusing on one product or one market, companies are able to spread their risk across various markets. Additionally, while one country may be experiencing a recession and causing sales for a company to decline, another country may be experiencing a boom, which would likely result in an increase in sales for that same company. With operations in multiple countries, a company can potentially balance the up and down markets. A downturn in one or a few markets will not cause the company to fail completely because the demand in other markets may be growing.

Disposal of Surplus Goods

A final major advantage to international trade is the ability to dispose of surplus goods. For example, prior to each Super Bowl, the NFL makes clothing for both teams that states each is the winner so that supply is available immediately after the game. However, only the winning team's clothing is sold after the game. Rather than the losing team's clothing going to the landfills, it is donated to other countries, decreasing the waste of the unsold product.[14] Do not confuse the disposal of surplus goods with the concept of *dumping*, an illegal practice that will be discussed later in the chapter.

Challenges to International Trade

While there are numerous advantages to international trade, there are also challenges. Those challenges are discussed in more detail in the following sections.

Understanding the Business Environment

Regardless of where a business is located, its success depends largely on management's understanding of the business landscape. The **business landscape** refers to all internal and external factors of the business, its industry, and its environment. Companies that intend to expand internationally often make the grave mistake of assuming the landscape of a new market is the same of that in the home country, a concept known as **ethnocentrism**. In most instances, this causes companies to stumble or even fail. Understanding the nuances, expectations, and regulations in international markets is one element that drives success.

Understanding the Target Country's Business Politics

Politics, laws, and industry relationships shape the environment of businesses both locally and abroad. The way business is conducted varies greatly from country to country, and businesspeople must not only be aware of these differences but must also have the ability to adapt to the local business politics.

Differences in Regulations and Marketing

Remember, there is no one-size-fits-all marketing campaign. You can imagine how this notion is amplified when thinking about marketing in various countries. Marketers must be in tune with their target markets to succeed. Additionally, marketing is perceived differently in various cultures, and it is important to understand how cultural differences influence consumer behavior.

For example, in the United States, it is not uncommon to see a plethora of advertisements for prescription medications targeting the general public. Most other countries do not regularly advertise prescriptions to the public but rather to the doctors prescribing those medications. In fact, the United States and New Zealand are the only countries where this type of marketing is allowed.[15] Each international market requires marketers to adapt or create new marketing strategies, which can vary considerably with each of the marketing mix elements—product, price, place, and promotion.

Cultural Differences

Local culture has an impact on marketing campaigns. It's common for marketers and other businesspeople to find it challenging to understand the differences between their own culture and the target market. Cultural sensitivity can help to alleviate these challenges when preparing marketing campaigns for other countries and cultures. **Cultural sensitivity** is the awareness and appreciation of and the ability to adapt to a cultural, ethnic, racial, or other group other than one's own.[16] By increasing cultural sensitivity, marketers can better create marketing campaigns that truly encompass the target market.

Two examples of companies not readily prepared come from Nivea and Gucci. In 2017, Nivea launched a social media campaigned stating "White Is Purity." The phrase was perceived by the public as being racially insensitive. To make matters worse, the slogan was then used by white supremacists in their propaganda.[17] While the company apologized and removed the campaign, these marketers should never have let the campaign leave the idea room. In 2019, luxury fashion designer Gucci introduced a balaclava knit jumper that had material that went up and around the mouth. The advertisement for this clothing featured a White woman modeling the sweater with bright red lipstick. Many critics noted its similarity to blackface. The company immediately pulled the $890 sweater from stores.[18]

LINK TO LEARNING

Gucci

Read more about the balaclava polo jumper from Italian designer Gucci (https://openstax.org/r/gucciwithdrawsjumper), the public commentary, and Gucci's official response. Also check out the details behind the Nivea "White Is Purity" ad (https://openstax.org/r/niveaadonline) and the uproar from consumers.

Cultural differences are an important factor in the marketing of a product, but these differences are also critical with business practices. Suppose you are meeting with a business partner in another country. Do you know if there is a gift-giving expectation? You may be aware that there are ethical concerns and sometimes prohibitions with gift giving in the United States, but in other countries it would be unprofessional to attend a meeting without a gift. For example, in Japan, it is customary to bring a small gift with an initial sales call.[19] In the United States, some companies won't allow employees to accept gifts.

Using another US example, it is not unusual to "get right down to business" when meeting with others. Conversely, it may take several meetings of developing rapport with Japanese businesspeople before business is ever discussed. In addition, it's commonplace in Japan for people to not shake hands (see Figure 7.2) but rather bow to one another.[20]

Figure 7.2 Understanding cultural differences is important in marketing products and in business practice; for example, shaking hands is not globally accepted. (credit: "CC-BY-Mapbox-Uncharted-ERG_Mapbox-b053" by Mapbox Uncharted ERG/flickr, CC BY 3.0)

LINK TO LEARNING

Cultural Sensitivity

There are many ways you can begin to be more culturally sensitive. The first step is awareness. Read this short article (https://openstax.org/r/fiveways) on five ways to improve your cultural awareness. Also check out this video to learn how to develop cultural competency as a skill.

Click to view content (https://openstax.org/books/principles-marketing/pages/7-1-the-global-market-and-advantages-of-international-trade)

Knowledge Check

It's time to check your knowledge on the concepts presented in this section. Refer to the Answer Key at the end of the book for feedback.

1. When conditions are favorable for a company to expand globally, the company is experiencing _______.
   a. global market opportunities
   b. international trade
   c. growth
   d. increased sales

2. Which of the following is NOT an advantage of international trade?
   a. Increased sales
   b. Growth
   c. Cultural barriers

   d. Diversification of risk

3. Being aware of and appreciating variations in culture is known as _______.
   a. cultural sensitivity
   b. cultural barriers
   c. cultural differences
   d. marketing regulations

4. Ashia is planning a business dinner with her new clients in Chile. She has never visited Chile before and is not familiar with their customs. Which of the following would you NOT advise Ashia to do?
   a. Tell Ashia she should consider talking with a colleague who has traveled to Chile before.
   b. Tell Ashia to study some of the most important Chilean customs so as not to embarrass herself or offend her dinner guest.
   c. Tell Ashia that if she is in doubt, she should follow her dinner guests' lead on what is appropriate.
   d. Tell Ashia not to worry about it because the Chilean businesspeople should adapt to her customs because her customs are the best ones to follow.

5. Which of the following is true regarding business politics?
   a. They do not vary from culture to culture.
   b. Business politics can vary greatly across cultures, and businesspeople should decide what is within their own ethical compass before deciding to conduct international business.
   c. Business ethics are the same across every culture.
   d. When conducting business in a foreign market, you should always do what is asked of you, even if it's unethical or illegal in your home country.

7.2 | Assessment of Global Markets for Opportunities

Learning Outcomes

By the end of this section, you will be able to:
   LO 1 Identify the different ways marketers can assess opportunity in global markets.
   LO 2 Discuss effective methods of analyzing global opportunities.

Internal Assessment for Global Readiness

According to Douglas Quackenbos and his coauthors in their *Harvard Business Review* article "Does Your Company Have What It Takes to Go Global," "external factors only set the stage for an international opportunity."[21] In other words, even though a global market may represent an opportunity for the company, the organization also must be prepared internally to expand. The factors external to the organization—a country's economy, for example—is only half of the equation. Company leaders must do a thorough internal assessment of their organization to determine if it has what it will take to expand globally. Managers and marketers who will be working directly in the international market should have fully assessed the other countries' regulations, business landscape, and cultural differences, for example.

Harvard Business Review has a published list of the seven common characteristics found with companies that have been successful in international expansion.[22] The list includes attitude, aptitude, magnitude, latitude, rectitude, exactitude, and fortitude, each of which is defined in Table 7.1.

Characteristic	Definition
Attitude	Global expansion is a priority.
Aptitude	The company has the knowledge and skills to expand.
Magnitude	The scope of expansion is aligned with capabilities.
Latitude	The company has the ability to adapt.
Rectitude	The company has the legal and ethical flexibility to adapt to foreign markets.
Exactitude	Corporate culture aligns with flexibility and ambiguity of expansion.
Fortitude	There is a commitment to long-term expansion despite setbacks.

Table 7.1 Seven Characteristics of Firms That Win Globally

Economic Infrastructure

Economic infrastructure refers to the facilities of an economy that benefit the production and distribution of goods and services.[23] Infrastructure includes anything that would be required to produce and/or transport goods and services—for example, roads, railways, and high-speed Internet. Imagine that you are starting a lemon tree farm. You would not plan your farm in Michigan, where the temperatures often fall below freezing, because that would wipe out your lemon crops. Or imagine starting an online company where you sell art, but you live in a location where your Internet access is spotty and unreliable. Infrastructure considerations are critical in business needs evaluation.

Consumer Income and Purchasing Power

There are three types of income for you to be aware of:

- **Consumer income**, the amount of money a household or individual earns. Consumer income is often defined as the amount of money a household has to spend.
- **Disposable income**, the income available after taxes are paid.
- **Discretionary income**, the money available once consumers have paid taxes and living expenses such as, rent, food, heat, groceries, etc. This income is the predominant type of income that interests marketers because it's the money consumers typically have the most flexibility with.

Marketers evaluate discretionary and disposable income differently. It depends on the type of product or service they offer. For example, consider the impact of inflation. With inflation, the cost of goods and services increases but individual income does not also increase, meaning things cost more but there isn't additional income to cover the additional cost. When this happens, consumers purchase fewer items and prioritize their spending differently because with the increase in the cost of necessities, there is less discretionary income to spend. As a result, consumers will cut back on nonessential items. Due to this, marketers of luxury goods are concerned with discretionary income, while marketers of packaged consumer goods are concerned with disposable income.

Companies are also impacted by inflation. Just as it costs consumers more to purchase the same goods and services during inflation, inflation will increase the cost of production for companies to create the same number of products. Companies have various tactics on addressing environmental influences like inflation. One way in which companies of consumer-packaged goods avoid increasing prices during inflation is to decrease the size of products while not increasing the price, a practice known as shrinkflation. For example, Procter & Gamble's Charmin ultra-soft toilet paper 18-count mega package was decreased in 2022 from 264 double-ply sheets per roll to 244 two-ply sheets, yet the price either remained the same or was slightly increased.[24] Often with shrinkflation, consumers don't notice that a package is smaller, and they focus on their ability to get as much as they can for the price.

Purchasing Power

Purchasing power is defined as how many goods can be purchased with one unit of currency. As you can imagine, purchasing power varies greatly across the globe and is of great importance when deciding whether to expand into foreign markets. For example, in a country where consumers have very little income and poor purchasing power, it would be difficult to sell expensive, nonessential goods. Consumers simply would not have the money to purchase them.

Currency Exchange Rates

Marketers and other business executives must understand foreign exchange rates and how fluctuations can affect marketing strategies.[25] An **exchange rate** is the rate at which one country's currency can be exchanged for that of another country. Because currency exchange rates fluctuate daily, the prices of goods and services in global markets will also fluctuate.[26] In turn, fluctuations in prices of goods and services will have an impact on the purchasing power of consumers and even larger effects on economic indicators such as jobs and inflation.

Suppose that in 1997, your US-based family imported British pantry items from the UK in order to create and export its own brand of barbecue sauce for sale in the UK. In 1997, it took $1.64 to buy 1 British pound (£).[27] So, $1.00 was worth £0.61 in British currency (1/1.6).[28] In this situation, the dollar is relatively weak compared to the British pound. One British pound would go a long way toward paying for that barbecue sauce.

Fast-forward 25 years. For the majority of 2021, it only took $1.37 to buy £1.00. So, $1.00 would buy £0.73 worth of British goods in 2021 (1/1.37). As you can see, the dollar had strengthened relative to the pound (which is the same as saying the pound had weakened relative to the dollar). This means that, by 2021, your dollar would buy more in terms of paying for British imports; conversely, consumers in the UK would have to pay more for your barbecue sauce!

LINK TO LEARNING

Exchange Rates

Exchange-Rates.org is a great resource (https://openstax.org/r/exchangeratesorg) for comparing exchange rates between hundreds of countries. Try it out by indicating countries in the From and To fields and check out the currency value between countries.

Analyzing Governmental Actions

Just as every economy in the world operates differently, so does each country's government. Businesses are greatly influenced by politics in every country (some more than others). Therefore, understanding how governmental actions impact the ability to be successful in a global market is imperative.

Political Stability

A country's political stability can impact nearly every facet of the country. Most notably, political stability has been linked to economic conditions in various countries. When there is increased political stability, the country's economy tends to stabilize or grow.[29] This is of keen interest to marketers as they consider new foreign markets to enter. As a country's stability increases, the opportunities to gain early entry into these markets grows. Conversely, many companies choose to avoid entering markets that lack political stability, not only because of the shaky economy but also because of potential changes in leadership, laws, and regulations.

Consider Russia's invasion of Ukraine in early 2022. In response, many companies pulled their operations out of Russia in a show of support for Ukraine. McDonald's, which opened its first Russian location in 1990, was one of the first global companies to cease operations there. The company stated that the activities of the Putin government were not consistent with McDonald's values, but also that the turbulent operating environment made it untenable to continue operations there.[30]

Trade Regulations

In an effort to promote (or inhibit) trade with other countries, governments often have some level of trade regulations. These regulations can be within industries or with specific nations or groups of nations. The common trade regulations surrounding imports and exports around the world include tariffs, quotas, trade blocs, and embargoes. Additionally, countries have specific regulations for foreign companies hoping to establish business within their markets.

Tariffs are taxes that governments impose on imports coming into the country. Tariffs can be imposed as a percentage (most common) or dollar amount. Tariffs are generally used by governments to bring more money into a country. Japan, for example, has one of the lowest tariffs in the world at 2.5 percent for nonagricultural products.[31] Conversely, the East African nation of Seychelles once had a much higher tariff rate, averaging well over 50 percent prior to joining the World Trade Organization (WTO) in 2015.[32] After joining the WTO, tariffs were reduced to under 25 percent.[33]

Quotas are maximum allowable units to be imported into or exported out of a specific country. Quotas are often used by a country to protect a domestic industry. For example, if the US government limited the number of Japanese automobiles to 2 million imports per year, this would cause lower sales of imported vehicles and, in turn, higher sales of domestically produced vehicles.[34]

Embargoes are bans on trading a product with a specific country and are imposed between countries that have different political ideologies. The United States, for example, has embargoes against Cuba, Iran, North Korea, and Syria that prohibit all transactions with these countries without a license.[35]

Trade blocs are intergovernmental agreements that remove barriers of trade within regions of the world. There are currently 10 major trade blocs in the world.[36] The United States-Mexico-Canada Agreement (USMCA) and the EU27 are two prominent examples. The USMCA allows free trade among Canada, the United States, and Mexico.

There are a variety of examples of the sorts of approaches countries will take with trade regulations. For example, companies may impose strict laws and regulations on who can own the factors of production. In some instances, there are issues with corrupt governments requiring bribes and kickbacks.

Transparency International publishes an annual survey called the Corruption Perceptions Index (CPI). Marketers use this survey for insights into country dynamics and can evaluate market viability of their product or service offering. This guide helps company leadership determine how much work they may have in understanding a country's way of operating and what kind of work it would take to make their product or service successful.

LINK TO LEARNING

CPI

The Corruption Perceptions Index (CPI) is an interesting and interactive tool where you can select specific countries to find their CPI rating. One hundred eighty countries are each rated on a scale of 0 to 100, where 100 indicates very clean and 0 means highly corrupt. Interact with the index here (https://openstax.org/r/transparencyencpi) and learn more about the CPI rating scale and assessment by watching this video (https://openstax.org/r/howcpiscores).

If you'd like to learn more about the Transparency International organization and its work, check out this brief summary of its 2021 annual report (https://openstax.org/r/publicationsannualreport).

Analyzing Sociocultural Factors

While the economic and political factors of a foreign market will determine a firm's ability to *enter* a market, the sociocultural factors may be most important in determining whether goods and services will be *successful* in a market. **Sociocultural factors** include values, behaviors, culture, lifestyle, and language that shape a person's or group's way of living. As you can imagine, there are hundreds of cultures around the world, and every culture within a country has its own nuances, preferences, and even ways of conducting business. Marketers who want enter foreign markets must have a deep understanding of these factors to establish effective marketing strategies.

Lifestyles

The way a person or group lives is known as their **lifestyle**. Each person has their own unique lifestyle, while cultures and families share similar traits within their collective lifestyles. Marketers must get to know their consumers to understand their buying behavior and how their lifestyles affect it.

In 2009, toy manufacturer Mattel Inc. opened a huge, three-story, Barbie-inspired flagship store in Shanghai, China. What marketers failed to do before making this market-entry decision was to study the lifestyles of Chinese consumers. In China, the culture stresses educational toys and playtime that builds skills; Barbie was neither of those. The store closed after only two years.[37]

Marketers must also be careful to avoid stereotypes of other cultures and countries. **Stereotypes** are oversimplified perceptions, images, or ideas of a person or groups.[38] While they can be negative or positive, they are overgeneralized perceptions about an entire group or people. Companies sometimes learn the hard way to avoid stereotypes.

For example, in 2014, Delta Air Lines, a major US passenger airline carrier (see Figure 7.3), made a big stereotype blunder with its social media marketing. The company sent out a congratulatory tweet to the US team for its win over the Ghanaian team in the World Cup in which it used a photo of a giraffe to represent Ghana.[39] Unfortunately, Delta marketers failed to realize that there is not one wild giraffe in Ghana; this is a frequent stereotype about the entire continent of Africa. In fact, there are over 50 countries in Africa, but only around 20 have naturally wild giraffes.[40] The Twitter market caught on to this error quickly and proceeded to tease Delta for its stereotype mistake.

Figure 7.3 Marketing based on stereotypes can lead to big mistakes, such as when a social media post by Delta Air Lines incorrectly assumed that Ghana was home to wild giraffes, resulting in the market openly teasing the company on Twitter for its blunder. (credit: "Phuket 2018" by un.cloned/flickr, CC BY 2.0)

Law and Politics

Laws and politics have a large impact on a country's economy and, in turn, how products will (or even can) be marketed. Political and legal decisions made within a country's system surrounding tariffs, labor laws, the environment, and even an expectation of bribery can impact a business's decisions. Even politics between two countries can have a big impact on decisions made by marketers.

In 2019, President Donald Trump increased the tariffs on Chinese goods to 25 percent. Several companies subsequently opted to pull their production facilities out of China. For example, Apple and Dell moved some of their production to Vietnam and other parts of Asia to avoid these tariffs.[41]

Education

Education impacts a consumer's product and service choices. Generally speaking, the more educated an individual is, the more discretion they use when purchasing products.[42] In other words, that person will spend more time researching various products before deciding which to purchase. Levels of education also effect an individual's choices in magazines, television shows, and other entertainment.[43] Therefore, platforms, messages, and even specific words marketers choose for the promotion mix will depend on the level of education that the target market holds. Is the market tech savvy? If not, using technical words and messages may confuse a consumer who doesn't understand the message.

Technology

The availability of technology within an international market will have several impacts on marketing efforts. First, the ability for consumers to access and use technology will directly impact the goods and services that are being marketed. Second, the company's access to technology to produce goods and services within the country will also be impacted.

For example, Uganda has the second-youngest population in the world.[44] It is also ranks among the poorest countries in the world.[45] Because of this, someone may make the mistake of thinking that Uganda would not be a market to enter with technology, but this is far from true. While many citizens of Uganda live without electricity or running water, the country's population of 45.74 million is estimated to own around 16 million cell phones, but only around 1 million homes have electric lights.[46] Due to the young population seeking to be more connected with others, the people of Uganda prioritize and are heavily reliant on their cell phones (see Figure 7.4).

But if there is limited electricity, how do Ugandans charge their cell phones? It has certainly been a challenge for many who have to share solar power with neighbors or travel to a nearby village that has electricity. However, the use of portable charging solutions has become more widespread. One company, Charge Ko Technologies, has turned this into an opportunity and created various portable charging solutions, including solar backpacks and energy generation through bicycle usage.[47] While some impoverished Ugandan consumers may not be able to afford these products, the company is hopeful that the wealthier will purchase enough to help bring the price down over time.

Figure 7.4 Cell phone use is widespread in Uganda because people prioritize connecting with other people, resulting in portable charging stations because electricity is a limited resource. (credit: Sarah Shepler, photographer)

Conducting a Cross-Cultural Analysis

When the Walt Disney Company decided to open Disneyland Hong Kong in 2005, the company struggled to gain momentum with its Chinese target market. Among other blunders, such as its high admission price, the company assumed that its Chinese market would love the Disney brand as much as Americans do. The company failed to realize that, unlike Americans, the Chinese did not grow up with the Disney brands and characters. Imagine walking into a fantasy theme park with characters you had never heard of or seen before. Unlike Americans, the Chinese do not view Disney characters as cultural icons. The fantasy aspect of the brand and park was another issue Disney faced. Its closest competitor, Ocean Park, provided visitors with real animals, educational material, and thrilling rides. The Asian market, which values education, found Disney's high ticket prices with little educational value to be wasteful when the park initially opened.[48]

Values

Cultural values are often unspoken. They include the aesthetics, socialization, and religious aspects woven throughout a culture. Consider the Disney example. Marketers stumbled with truly understanding the Chinese consumer culture when opening Disney Hong Kong by assuming that Chinese values were similar to those of Americans.

Customs and Cultural Symbols

Like other cultural values, customs are often unspoken. **Customs** consist of mannerisms or behaviors that are considered characteristics within a social system.[49] For example, in Spain, the afternoon siesta is a cultural custom. The siesta is an afternoon nap taken after the midday meal. Businesses will close for extended lunch breaks to allow employees to take their afternoon siesta.[50] If you are considering opening a business in Barcelona, you should expect to do the same!

Cultural symbols are physical representations of a culture's language, values, and traditions. They include items such as flags, gestures, holiday decorations, and many others. For example, in China, the national animal is the giant panda, and it has significant cultural importance as a symbol.[51] Similarly, the maple leaf is symbolic of Canada[52] (see Figure 7.5).

Figure 7.5 Cultural symbols, like the Canadian maple leaf, are physical representations of a culture's language(s), values, and traditions. (credit: "Vancouver B.C. - Canadian Flag 'Maple Leaf'" by David Paul Ohmer/flickr, CC BY 2.0)

Language, Idioms, and Nuances

It may seem obvious, but even language differences play a large role in the marketer's job as products and services are rolled out in international markets. Brands and product names may have one meaning in the home country and a completely different meaning in another language. For example, Nestlé had problems when rolling out its Gerber baby food in France because "Gerber" translates to "puke" in French. For obvious reasons, this didn't appeal to French parents choosing food for their infants.[53]

Nuances are words, phrases, or beliefs that vary slightly from one culture to another and can cause miscommunication in translation. For example, UK citizens use the word "jelly" to describe what people in the United States would call "Jell-O," and they use the word "biscuit" for "cookie."[54]

Idioms are phrases used in a culture that mean something completely different. For example, if you hear someone say "break a leg" in the United States, it would mean "good luck." However, using this idiom in another culture may leave the other person quite confused or even offended, thinking it was meant literally to go break their leg.[55] In Spanish-speaking cultures, the popular idiom "a lot of noise and no walnuts (mucho ruido y pocas nueces)" means "all talk and no action," but it would have no meaning in the United States.[56]

However, even idioms can become problematic within and across languages and cultures. In 2022, Lizzo, a world-renowned pop star, issued an apology and a rerelease of a song because she had used a culturally insensitive word that she was unaware of at the time of recording.[57]

CAREERS IN MARKETING

Global Marketing Manager

With the increase in companies doing business internationally, global marketing managers' job roles are becoming more important. Global marketing managers work to understand what international markets need, the competition, rules and regulations, and local cultures and values. They then use this information to develop global marketing strategies that appeal to the local market. Learn more about this role from these sources:

- Noodle article: "How to Become a Global Marketing Manager (https://openstax.org/r/managercareerguide)"
- Marketing Business Network video: "What Is Global Marketing?"
  Click to view content (https://openstax.org/books/principles-marketing/pages/7-2-assessment-of-global-markets-for-opportunities)
- Learn.org: "What's the Job Description of a Global Marketing Professional (https://openstax.org/r/whatsthejobdescription)?"

Knowledge Check

It's time to check your knowledge on the concepts presented in this section. Refer to the Answer Key at the end of the book for feedback.

1. During the Russian invasion of Ukraine in 2022, the Russian ruble's value decreased to less than one United States penny. This conversion from ruble to dollar is known as the ________.
   a. exchange rate
   b. business landscape
   c. purchasing power
   d. consumer income

2. Generally speaking, when a country's political stability improves, so does its ________.
   a. international business
   b. purchasing power
   c. economy
   d. consumer income

3. The assumption that all Chinese individuals are extremely gifted in mathematics is known as a ________.
   a. stereotype
   b. lifestyle
   c. culture
   d. sociocultural factor

4. During the Russian invasion of Ukraine in 2022, United States President Joe Biden halted all imports of Russian oil. This action is known as a(n) ________.
   a. tariff
   b. quota
   c. trade bloc
   d. embargo

5. The United States, Canada, and Mexico are part of a trade bloc known as ________.

a. ASEAN
b. USMCA
c. tariffs
d. embargoes

7.3 | Entering the Global Arena

Learning Outcomes

By the end of this section, you will be able to:
- **LO** 1 List the strategies used in global competition.
- **LO** 2 Discuss the different forms of global competition.

Ways in Which an Organization Can Enter the Global Arena

After a company has decided to enter the global marketplace, managers must determine which method of international involvement is best for the company's strategic goals. These methods include exporting, franchising, licensing, joint ventures, strategic alliances, and direct foreign investment (see Figure 7.6). Each method represents a different level of involvement. Let's look at each of these in more detail.

| Exporting | Franchising | Licensing | Joint Ventures | Strategic Alliances | Direct Foreign Investment |

Figure 7.6 Global Market Methods for Entering a Marketplace (attribution: Copyright Rice University, OpenStax, under CC BY 4.0 license)

Exporting

The most basic and least involved method to enter global markets is through exporting. **Exporting** is when a company makes a product or service in one country and sells it in others. Many companies choose this method of entry into global markets because it requires the least amount of m risk and allows the firm's managers to learn the ins and outs of international business. For example, in the UK's East Midlands, the county of Northampton is home to Alfred Sargent & Sons, Church's, John Lobb, and other shoemakers. An increased emphasis on exporting allowed these dying businesses to see new life because people in other countries wanted a piece of traditional "English cobbling."[58]

Franchising

Franchising is a business strategy in which the owner (the franchisor) allows another person or entity (the franchisee) to operate a business using the franchisor's products, branding, and knowledge in exchange for a fee.[59] Over 90 percent of the McDonald's around the world are franchises owned by independent local businesspeople.[60] The cost to franchise a business varies. A person interested in opening a McDonald's franchise will need $500,000 in liquid assets and $45,000 for a franchise fee and should expect to spend between $1.3 million and $2.3 million over time.[61] On the other hand, franchising the exercise brand Jazzercise requires a one-time initial fee of $1,250 and liability insurance.[62]

Franchising rules and commitment vary by company for both home-based and international markets.

Licensing

Licensing is a contract in which one organization permits another to use its name, brand, or trademark on its own items. While licensing and franchising might seem similar, franchising involves all business operations, whereas licensing applies to a specific aspect (usually trademarked) of the business.[63] Licensing agreements allow the company to enter other markets without as high of a financial risk. However, with little business involvement in licensing by the licensee (the company licensing its brand), strong business relationships are critical in order to reduce the risk of the licensor damaging the brand's reputation. With licensing, the licensee loses brand control. Licensing is common in the fashion industry, where well-known apparel brands such as Armani license their names to companies that make eyeglass frames, fragrances, and watches.

Joint Venture

A **joint venture** is a business arrangement whereby two or more companies create one single enterprise or project. The joint venture can last for any length of time but typically is not permanent. The advantage of a joint venture is that the two companies share all the risks associated with the venture.[64] In 2012, Kellogg's and Wilmar International Limited announced a joint venture. Kellogg's wanted to expand its presence in the Chinese market. Creating a joint venture with Wilmar International provided the company with an extensive distribution network. Both companies benefited from this venture: Wilmar International through its financial incentives and Kellogg's with a way to penetrate the market.[65]

Strategic Alliance

A **strategic alliance** occurs when two companies from different countries agree to invest resources in a mutually beneficial way. For example, Microsoft relies heavily on alliances when entering new markets as a way to optimize the knowledge and market identification of local companies. Uber and Spotify entered into a strategic alliance to allow Uber riders to connect to their Spotify account and stream music while catching a ride.[66]

Direct Foreign Investment

The most involved and riskiest way for a business to get involved in the international arena is through direct foreign investment. **Foreign direct investment (FDI)** involves establishing operations within a foreign country. Consider automobile manufacturers. Nearly all producers have made significant investments in manufacturing outside of their home countries. For example, Tesla invested in a Shanghai factory to produce electric vehicles (EVs), and in 2022, the company announced it is "taking steps to ramp up output in order to double its original planned annual target to 1 million cars."[67]

Forms of Global Competition

Global competition can come from international firms, multinational firms, and transnational firms. Let's look at each to better understand their impact.

Any firm that operates on a global level is classified as an **international firm** regardless of the intensity of the involvement. International firms can further be classified as either multinational firms or transnational firms. Often, this classification depends on the business structure and products or services offered.

The most common characteristic of a multinational firm is its centralized business structure. Consider Amazon, whose headquarters are located in Seattle, Washington.[68] Amazon operates in over 50 countries across the globe.[69] However, the majority of all major decisions are made at its headquarters, making it a multinational firm.

Let's look at McDonald's again. The company's franchise strategy relies heavily on the brand name and similar core menu items across the globe. However, the company also allows for local responsiveness by allowing local menu items to be included in the menu. For this reason, McDonald's is often referred to as a **transnational firm**, one that allows for a higher degree of localization.[70]

Knowledge Check

It's time to check your knowledge on the concepts presented in this section. Refer to the Answer Key at the end of the book for feedback.

1. Janai is considering opening a McDonald's in her home country of Nicaragua. Which type of market entry strategy would she use?
   a. Franchise

   b. Joint venture
   c. Strategic alliance
   d. Exporting

2. Imagine you are interested in entering the global marketplace. Which would be the easiest way for you to begin?
   a. Franchising
   b. Strategic alliance
   c. Exporting
   d. Joint venture

3. Ryana owns a T-shirt company in Japan. With her T-shirts, she applies Disney characters and pays Disney royalties based on each shirt sold and an agreement the two companies entered into. Which of the following is Ryana most likely involved in?
   a. Licensing
   b. Unethical behavior
   c. Trademark fraud
   d. Franchising

4. A company wants to expand into a particular global market, but local firms are better equipped to handle some business processes, such as logistics. Additionally, it is particularly difficult to enter this market. Which of the following would you recommend to the expanding company?
   a. Franchising
   b. Exporting
   c. Licensing
   d. Joint venture

5. After being hired at ABC Corporation, you realize that all decisions for each facility in the world are made at the headquarters you work at in Pensacola, Florida. Which type of firm best describes the one you are working at?
   a. Exporting firm
   b. International firm
   c. Transnational firm
   d. Importing firm

7.4 | Marketing in a Global Environment

Learning Outcomes

By the end of this section, you will be able to:
   LO 1 Describe how marketing strategies are adapted for a global marketplace.
   LO 2 Summarize how global strategies affect the 4Ps of marketing.

Adapting Marketing Strategies for the Global Marketplace

Until this point, we've mostly been learning about the bigger-picture decisions that a company must make when deciding whether to enter the global marketplace. Once these company-wide decisions are made, marketing managers must determine the most effective way to market their products in the new markets. They must determine if completely new products or existing products will be offered in the new market. Additionally, they must determine if the other marketing mix variables must be adapted to the local market.

A **standardized global marketing strategy** is one in which a company uses the same marketing strategy in all markets. Coca-Cola primarily uses a standardized marketing strategy in all markets. The brand, brand name, and iconic cursive writing in white on red background can be seen all over the world. The advantage that Coca-Cola has in this strategy is that the company can spread the cost of marketing over all the regions in which it operates.[71]

Adapted Global Marketing

Conversely, a company may not find success in a one-size-fits-all marketing strategy. In this case, the company may choose an **adapted global marketing strategy**, one in which marketing strategies differ among global markets. If a company chose an adapted global marketing strategy, there would be high marketing costs associated with each of the markets in which the company conducted business. Netflix, for example, offers different content (movies and shows) in each of its markets based on the customer demands in each country.[72]

The 4Ps of Marketing in a Global Environment

Now that the company has chosen either a standardized or adapted marketing strategy for its global operations, it's time to consider each of the 4Ps of global marketing—product, price, place, and promotion.

Product

Companies entering new foreign markets have three choices surrounding the product. They include straight product extension, product adaptation, and product invention. Each has its own advantages and disadvantages and levels of risk. Let's take a look:

- **Straight Product Extension**
  A **straight product extension** is a strategy that entails maintaining the same product for both home and foreign markets. As you can imagine, this is the easiest product strategy and has the same advantages as a standardized marketing strategy. Some products are globally known and need no modifications in order to sell them.

- **Product Adaptation**
  Product adaptation is when companies modify products to align with the local culture. For example, Nike manufactures different styles of shoes based on the local culture's preferences, such as the Nike Air Zoom, a high-intensity interval training (HIIT) shoe that was released in Australia.[73] This particular shoe is not available in the United States and looks quite different than other performance shoes offered in the United States.[74]

  Consider another well-known company: McDonald's has around 38,000 franchises globally. However, not all global markets have the same tastes as what you might expect in the United States. In fact, it often goes beyond taste preferences and into religious and cultural norms. For example, there are over 160 of the Golden Arches in India, but none of them sell pork or beef, and they even keep separate kitchens for vegetarian and meat preparations. The company announced it would be opening vegetarian-only restaurants to better serve the Indian markets.[75]

- **Product Invention**
  The most involved product strategy used in global marketing is that of product invention. **Product invention** consists of creating entirely new products for a global market. Consider the earlier example of the Ugandan market. Because less than half of the population has access to electricity, there is a potential for companies to invent new products, such as cooling systems, that do not require electricity.[76]

LINK TO LEARNING

7-Eleven and Product Adaptation

There a numerous examples of product adaptation across markets. Check out this video on how 7-Eleven differs between American and Japanese markets.

Click to view content (https://openstax.org/books/principles-marketing/pages/7-4-marketing-in-a-global-environment)

Price

When pricing a product in a foreign market, there are other factors to evaluate in addition to home country considerations. Tariffs, the local economy, shipping, and other factors need to be considered because these will all have an impact on earnings and profit.

Do you know in which country it is the most expensive to purchase a car? You might be surprised to hear it is Singapore. The small island country doesn't have a lot of room to accommodate everyone having an automobile, so the government has imposed high import taxes and yearly fees to keep the number of automobiles down.[77]

Place: Distribution Channels

When marketers are considering distribution channels in foreign markets, they may find themselves with limited options compared to their home country. In the United States, for example, most companies find themselves with many choices of wholesalers, retailers, and supply chains. However, in more remote areas of the world and developing countries, those options can be limited. Consider again our Uganda example. Most retailers, particularly outside the capital city of Kampala, are "mom-and-pop" stores. Additionally, there are few transportation routes, and the ones that do exist consist mostly of dirt roads and a few highways. Unlike the United States, it is rare to see tractor trailers (semis) carrying containers of goods from one location to another. Instead, taxis, motorbikes, and foot traffic are the main modes for product transportation.

It is imperative that marketers consider the whole channel when making distribution decisions. The **whole channel** refers to the design of the international channels that incorporates all members, including the manufacturing, retailer, and wholesaler sites as well as transportation.[78]

Have you seen the movie *Captain Phillips* starring Tom Hanks? The movie was loosely based on the true story of the Maersk Alabama container ship that was hijacked by Somali pirates off the coast of Somalia. Yes, pirates exist, and when they are able to capture large cargo ships, they can loot a lot of valuable cargo.[79] While many large vessels avoid pirate territory when considering the whole channel, pirates still exist today and are often waiting at sea to steal millions of dollars' worth of goods.

Promotion

Just as marketing managers must determine whether to adapt their product to new markets, they must also determine the best course of action for the promotion strategy. Nearly all promotion strategies will need to adapt to some degree in different markets, even if it is a simple product expansion.

Consider Coca-Cola, whose brand name remains unchanged. However, in some countries, the slogan is slightly tweaked to have a more local meaning, but with the same underlying promotional message. Refer to Table 7.2 for some of the Coca-Cola slogans used around the world.[80]

Country	Slogan
India	Always the Real Thing
United States	Real Magic
New Zealand	Real Magic
Spain	Siente El Sabor (Feel the Flavor)
Hungary	Kóstold meg az érzést (Taste the Flavor)
Indonesia	Rasakan Keajaiban (Real Magic or Feel the Magic)

Table 7.2 Coca-Cola Slogans

Knowledge Check

It's time to check your knowledge on the concepts presented in this section. Refer to the Answer Key at the end of the book for feedback.

1. A company that uses the same marketing strategy in all markets is most likely utilizing which of the following?
   a. Standardized
   b. Adapted
   c. Invention
   d. Modified

2. Which of the following is correct regarding the promotion strategy of global markets?
   a. All promotion strategies should remain the same across markets.
   b. Promotion strategies of global markets should deviate only slightly from the home market.
   c. Promotion strategies should reflect the market, some to different degrees.
   d. Promotion strategies of global markets should always be completely different from the home market.

3. Which of the following Coca-Cola slogans is used in New Zealand?
   a. "Real Magic"
   b. "Always the Real Thing"
   c. "Feel the Flavor"
   d. "Feel the Magic"

4. Which of the following is part of the whole channel?
   a. Promotions
   b. Communications
   c. Price
   d. Distribution channel members

5. Which country has the highest automobile prices?
   a. China
   b. Singapore
   c. United States

   d.   Canada

7.5 | Ethical Issues in the Global Marketplace

Learning Outcomes

By the end of this section, you will be able to:

- **LO 1** Identify ethical issues facing global organizations.
- **LO 2** Provide an example of a company that displays ethics in the global marketplace.

Identifying Ethical Issues in the Marketplace

As with all business decisions, there are ethical matters to consider when entering into the global marketplace.

Outsourcing

Outsourcing refers to a business moving some of its operations to a foreign country for the purpose of saving money and time or to increase volume and quality. WhatsApp, an encrypted communication app owned by Meta Platforms (formerly Facebook), has been used globally for several years. Based out of California, the company realized that it would have difficulty growing if it did not outsource. In 2012, the company began utilizing Russian companies for a small fraction of what it would have had to pay within the United States.[81] While outsourcing has its advantages, many will argue that outsourcing eliminates jobs in the home country.

Work Standards and Conditions

Unlike most developed countries, those countries still developing often have much lower standards for working conditions. This has been a topic of hot debate for many years in the United States and around the world as companies have moved some or all of their operations to countries with lower standards. In Xinjiang, China, more than half a million people from ethnic minority groups are forced to pick cotton for the fashion industry.[82] Well-known companies such as Nike, Apple, and Levi's have come under the same scrutiny in more recent years. While cheaper production costs will provide the company with more profits, more often than not, lower standards, working conditions, and otherwise unethical behavior will put them under a microscope. Alternately, many companies and experts will argue that even the worst of working conditions have a positive impact on developing nations.[83]

Workplace Diversity and Equal Opportunity

In recent decades, many countries have passed regulations to include and promote diversity in the workplace.[84] However, in other countries, diversity and equal opportunity remain human rights issues. Having a diverse workforce has numerous benefits, particularly in those companies expanding globally. Companies committed to diversity have increased chances of success in the global market; diversity often breeds an increase in ideas and cultural intelligence and creates a more agile workforce.[85]

Additionally, marketers must also be considerate of diversity within their marketing strategies. Alienating underrepresented groups of people within a target market might not only cost sales but also backfire in terms of representation. Procter & Gamble has utilized its many marketing platforms to not only include diversity but also to shed light on societal struggles of people of many racial identities in its target markets. The company has also extended diversity into its hiring practices to "mirror the US population."[86]

Child Labor

The use of child labor is seen by most Americans as unethical. The United Nations (UN) has implemented many treaties that establish human rights for children within member nations.[87] However, each country has its own standards for child labor and the minimum age at which a child can work.

Bribery and Corruption

Bribery and corruption may seem like a thing from the past, but in fact, both are still quite prevalent in both developed and developing nations. Nearly all countries have laws against bribery and corruption, but in many areas that are politically unstable, doing business means bribing officials. When a company decides to expand into international markets, the managers and marketers must decide to what degree they are willing to participate in practices that would otherwise be deemed illegal or unethical in the home country. The Foreign Corrupt Practices Act of 1977 "was enacted for the purpose of making it unlawful for certain classes of persons and entities to make payments to foreign government officials to assist in obtaining or retaining business."[88]

Dumping is a practice in which a company manufactures a very large of number of goods and exports them to a foreign market and the product is offered at an extremely low price to the consumer market. This often drives out all competition in the market. Once competition is driven out, the company then raises the price of the product, essentially creating a monopoly on the product. The United States and other countries have laws strictly prohibiting the practice of dumping, and many impose fines against those companies attempting to practice dumping.

LINK TO LEARNING

Free and Fair Trade

As a marketer, it's important to be aware of ethical practices. Learn more about the United States Department of Commerce and how it promotes free and fair trade (https://openstax.org/r/howdumpingandunfair).

COMPANIES WITH A CONSCIENCE

Kao Corporation

Figure 7.7 Global companies are also interested in ethical business practices; for example, Kao, a Tokyo-based company, and Costco, a US-based company, partnered to develop foldable containers for repeated product use. (credit: "Costco-Ribboncutting-21" by Baltimore County Government/flickr, Public Domain)

Founded in 1887 in Tokyo, Japan, Kao is a "16-time Ethisphere World's Most Ethical Companies honoree and [it has] been honored every year since Ethisphere started recognizing companies."[89] The company's strategies aim for zero waste when producing its cleaning and health and beauty products. Using leftover materials, Kao developed Bio IOS, a sustainable ingredient in its cleaning products. Its product development process encourages consumers to use refill packs to reduce waste.[90]

In 2022, Kao and Costco teamed up to begin testing foldable containers that allow for repeated use as packing materials in a Kanagawa Prefecture Costco warehouse (see Figure 7.7).[91] To read more about this initiative and to see the packaging, visit the Kao website (https://openstax.org/r/newssustainability).

The company has plans to expand the use of these reusable packing materials into other warehouses and hopefully further into the industry. Kao prides itself on the innovation of societal and environmentally friendly products as well as practicing gender equality and universal product design.[92]

Chapter Summary

As outlined in this chapter, transportation, technological developments, and business landscape and cultural considerations go hand in hand with globalization. Marketers must develop competitive marketing strategies in a realm far different than they're accustomed to. Decisions have expanded to encompass complex international considerations. Once a company has decided to enter an international marketplace, it must decide how best to make that entry. Some companies decide to export products, some determine a joint venture is the best approach, and others elect to invest in building manufacturing facilities. Each offers differing levels of investment, control, and potential profit. An additional and vital concern is whether the company will standardize its product offerings or shift products to adapt to cultural differences. In any event, successful businesses select their marketing partners and intermediaries carefully as they aim to add value global customers want.

Key Terms

adapted global marketing strategy   a strategy in which a company utilizes different marketing strategies in different global markets

business landscape   everything internal and external to the business, its industry, and its environment

consumer income   the amount of money a household or individual earns

cultural sensitivity   awareness and appreciation of and the ability to adapt to a cultural, ethnic, racial, or another group other than one's own

cultural symbols   physical representations of a culture's language, values, and traditions

cultural values   unspoken aesthetics, socialization, and religious aspects woven throughout a culture

customs   mannerisms or behaviors that are considered characteristics within a social system

discretionary income   the money individuals and households are left with after paying taxes and other living expenses, such as food and shelter

disposable income   the money individuals and households are left with after paying taxes

dumping   the practice in which a company manufactures a very large of number of goods and exports them to a foreign market to see cheaply

economic infrastructure   the physical facilities of an economy that benefit product and distribution

embargoes   trading bans on a product with a specific country; imposed between countries that have different political ideologies

ethnocentrism   an assumption that the business landscape or culture of an international market is the same as the home country or personal culture

exchange rate   the rate at which one country's currency can be exchanged for that of another country

exporting   when a firm makes a product or service in one country and sells it in others

foreign direct investment (FDI)   the process of establishing operations within a foreign country

franchising   a business strategy in which the owner (the franchisor) allows another person or entity (the franchisee) to operate a business using the franchisor's products, branding, and knowledge in exchange for a fee

global market opportunities   conditions that are favorable for a company to expand into the global marketplace

international firm   a company that operates on a global level regardless of intensity of involvement

joint venture   a business arrangement whereby two or more companies create a single enterprise or project

licensing   a contract in which one organization permits another to use its name brand or trademark on its own items

lifestyle   the way a person or group lives

outsourcing   the process of moving some of a business's operations to a foreign country for the purpose of saving money and time or to increase volume and quality

product adaptation   when companies modify products to align with the local culture

product invention   when companies create entirely new products for a global market

purchasing power   the goods that can be purchased with one unit of currency

quotas   maximum allowable units (usually in currency) to be imported into or exported out of a specific country

risk   any situation or condition that leads a company to decreased profits or even failure

sociocultural factors   values, behaviors, culture, lifestyle, and language that shape a person's or group's way of living

standardized global marketing strategy   a strategy in which a company uses the same marketing strategy in all markets

stereotypes   oversimplified images, perceptions, or ideas of a person or group

straight product extension   a strategy that entails maintaining the same product for both the home and foreign markets

strategic alliance   when two companies from different countries agree to invest resources in a mutually beneficial way

tariffs   taxes that governments impose on imports into the country

trade blocs   intergovernmental agreements that remove barriers to trade within regions of the world

transnational firm   a company that allows for a higher degree of localization

whole channel   the design of the international channels that incorporates all members, including the manufacturing, retailer, and wholesaler sites as well as transportation

Applied Marketing Knowledge: Discussion Questions

1. Why do most global organizations envision the world as a huge market without borders?

2. Describe the differences between exporting products, forming joint ventures, and licensing products.

3. What factors do companies consider when determining a foreign country's market attractiveness?

4. Adding value to the delivery network is tricky and complex for international sellers. With whom do these sellers usually partner to move products seamlessly through distribution channels?

Critical Thinking Exercises

1. Marketers must consider the global marketing environment when determining strategy. In addition to the international trade system, economic environment, and cultural norms, what other environmental factor is a critical consideration? Use an example to illustrate the importance of this environmental factor.

2. Thousands of businesses must strike a balance between standardizing marketing practices on a global scale versus adapting products to local markets. List two companies within the same industry, such as Toyota and Volkswagen, that approach their global marketing strategy using product standardization or adaptation. Then check global sales to help determine which approach is most effective.

3. Procter & Gamble makes dozens of laundry detergents and adapts these products to market preferences around the world. Two of these brands include Ariel and Mif. Why might European markets prefer Ariel's formulation and Russian markets demand Mif? Build a list of three reasons why Western Europe and Eastern Europe may differ in their laundry detergent preferences.

4. You are working on a marketing campaign for the Japanese division of Malley's Chocolates. You have created a pitch to top executives for a commercial featuring a Japanese husband surprising his wife in her bedroom on Valentine's Day with a small box of chocolates containing four candies. Would this be a good idea for a commercial? Why or why not?

Building Your Personal Brand

There are ways to build skills that will help you in international markets. Consider the items shared in this chapter and consider what you might do to enhance your skills. Then write a one-to-two-page document outlining a plan for what you will do to improve your skills. Be specific and include a timeline. You might also want to meet with international business instructors to help identify areas to include.

Here are several things to consider:

- Does your campus offer courses or workshops in diversity? Many diversity training opportunities also offer a certificate of completion that you can include in your resume.
- Is there a foreign language requirement at your university? If so, this education plus a study abroad experience will reinforce your language skills, business etiquette, and exposure to cultural realities. Satisfying college requirements can also work in your favor.
- Political science courses offer credits toward graduation that also may extend to the political realities of foreign countries or regions, enhancing your awareness of business practices, economic conditions, and historical underpinnings.

 ## What Do Marketers Do?

Part of the International Trade Administration, Export Assistance Centers (found in the United States, Europe, the Middle East, Africa, and Asia) help US-based businesses plan, develop, and execute international strategies to succeed in today's global marketplace through the. Find the center nearest to you (https://openstax.org/r/uscommercialservice) and conduct a short interview with an export counselor there to learn more about their job. To learn more about global market opportunities through the International Trade Administration, watch the short video "Discover Global Markets."

Click to view content (https://openstax.org/books/principles-marketing/pages/7-what-do-marketers-do)

Here are some questions to ask:

- What services does the center offer?
- What is an "initial market check"?
- Does the center provide customized market research?
- Does the International Trade Administration work with US consulates and embassies?
- Are there training or networking events to attend where I can network and learn more?
- How does the export center help companies located in rural areas successfully export products?
- What training did you complete to qualify for your position?

 ## Closing Company Case

Timmy Global Health

Founded in 1997 by Dr. Charles (Chuck) Dietzen, Timmy Global Health has a mission to empower communities to address health disparities in a sustainable way. For over two decades, Timmy has supported care sites across four countries in Latin America and Africa: Guatemala, Ecuador, the Dominican Republic, and Nigeria. Since its founding, it has served 100,000+ patients through medical service trips and local follow-up care. The most enduring legacy is the trusting relationships it has built with local communities.

With a vision to build a healthier world through a community of global health leaders, Timmy has been active at more than 18 colleges and universities throughout the United States. For two decades Timmy organized to provide medical clinics and much-needed supplies to people in underserved areas. All who went on the medical service trips learned the mission of health care firsthand by tending to those who most needed the care and resources.

Dr. Chuck founded Timmy Global Health in Greenwood, Indiana. His reputation as a physician and his connection to schools and community health leaders was a primary driver for his development of the organization near the area where he lived and worked. However, it was the spirit of giving and the generosity that Hoosiers (Indiana natives) are known for that solidified his decision to have the organization headquartered in Greenwood.

Through the years, Dr. Chuck provided his vision and numerous resources to Timmy Global Health. Dr. Chuck was the biggest fundraiser and the visionary behind many of the programs and global community connections. Having traveled to over 30 countries himself, he knew the challenges and the opportunities around the globe.

When Dr. Chuck founded Timmy Global Health, his idea was to have an organization that was self-sustaining. With good leadership at the helm, the possibilities were endless for the work that could be conducted throughout the world. Timmy needed good leaders who had a passion for the underserved and a willingness to work in various capacities. It would take individuals who were interested in mission over profit.

Over the years, Timmy saw many challenges to the model of service. Good leadership was difficult to find, and over its path from infancy to maturity, Timmy had its share of both good leadership and poor leadership. As a nonprofit, it was fundamental that the organization always continue to raise money, spend conservatively, and hire people who were service minded. Through the work it did around the globe, Timmy was also dependent on workers in-country who could liaise with Timmy's partner organizations.

Each country Timmy worked with had a different political and economic system that required a network of individuals with a working knowledge of the country. Understanding and working around operational disparities was a job requirement for those who worked for Timmy Global Health. Moving medicine, supplies, and people to meet the needs of the underserved required a different set of resources in each country.

Timmy's mission was challenged in late 2019 when the COVID-19 pandemic disrupted its global network. Forced to shut down its mission trips and still work to support global health issues, the organization created an updated service model with a way to empower communities to achieve their stated health goals.

The organization had to streamline operations. It realized remote work was at the core of what it did. To that end, the organization sold its headquarters building, downsized its staff, and focused on building up its financial reserves. Continuing to work with its partners in the countries it serves, Timmy was able to pay for the salaries of local doctors, buy essential medications and supplies, provide personal protective equipment to clinic staff and patients, pay for the transport of patients, train community health workers, and even start new programs.

Looking toward the future, the organization is still exploring models of remote work that can lead to better utilization of resources. Technology is allowing for continued connection with the in-country partners. College chapters are continuing to raise money and awareness and provide local health care support for underserved communities in their own local areas. Timmy is looking to add more college chapters in the United States and abroad.[93]

The COVID-19 pandemic proved that global health care affects us all. As our world and how we work together changes, it is important to have fluid plans to address how we operate. How we care for each other may change, but the ability to do so should remain.

Read more about Timmy Global Health on its website (https://openstax.org/r/timmyglobalhealth), Facebook page (https://openstax.org/r/timmyglobalhealthfb), or Instagram account (https://openstax.org/r/timmyglobalhealthinsta).

Case Questions

1. To provide for the needs of underserved people in communities around the globe, Timmy Global Health faced many challenges. What are some of the most pressing challenges in the global landscape?

2. What are some of the global issues that have impacted Timmy Global Health and the work it does?

3. Marketers often have to adapt to international markets. What are some of the adaptations most prevalent for the work Timmy Global Health is doing?

4. Ethical issues are always a concern for any company. When working internationally, ethics can be a challenge since practices in a home country may be very different than in a foreign country. What are some ethical issues that may pose difficulties for Timmy Global Health?

References

1. "Company Timeline," Starbucks Stories & News, Starbucks, January 24, 2019, https://stories.starbucks.com/press/2019/company-timeline/.

2. "'Tis the #PSL Season Again!," Starbucks Stories & News, Starbucks, August 27, 2021, https://stories.starbucks.com/emea/stories/2021/tis-the-psl-season-again/.

3. Ash Read, "Everything You Need to Know about Global Marketing Strategy," *Ecommerce Marketing Blog*, Sumo, updated January 21, 2020, https://sumo.com/stories/global-marketing-strategy.

4. Ashley Turner, "Why There Are Almost No Starbucks in Australia," CNBC, July 25, 2018, https://www.cnbc.com/2018/07/20/starbucks-australia-coffee-failure.html.

5. Turner, "No Starbucks in Australia."

6. Starbucks Arrives in Milan: Roastery Honors Italian Espresso Culture, Design and Craft," Starbucks Stories & News, Starbucks, September 5, 2018, https://stories.starbucks.com/press/2018/starbucks-arrives-in-milan-italy-roastery/.

7. "Number 2: We Are Global," *Nike, Inc.: A Growth Company*, Nike, n.d., https://media.corporate-ir.net/media_files/IROL/10/100529/nike-gs09/global.html.

8. "Automotive Industry," China: Country Commercial Guide, International Trade Administration, January 4, 2022, https://www.trade.gov/country-commercial-guides/china-automotive-industry.

9. "Chinese Car Market: How Automakers Compete for First Place," Daxue Consulting, August 2, 2020, https://daxueconsulting.com/chinese-automakers-compete-for-first-place/.

10. Wikipedia, s.v. "Wuling Hongguang Mini EV," last modified August 28, 2022, 02:48, https://en.wikipedia.org/wiki/Wuling_Hongguang_Mini_EV.

11. "Ford China Sells 125,000 Vehicles in First Quarter, Accelerating Localization and Delivery of Ford+ Growth Plan," Ford Media Center, Ford Motor Company, April 14, 2022, https://media.ford.com/content/fordmedia/fap/cn/en/news/2022/04/14/ford-china-sales.html.

12. "Amazon Creates 25,000 Permanent Roles and Keeps Growing in Poland," Amazon News, Amazon.com, https://www.aboutamazon.eu/news/press-lounge/amazon-creates-25-000-permanent-roles-and-keeps-growing-in-poland.

13. Will Kenton, "What Is Business Risk? Definition, Factors, and Examples," Investopedia, Dotdash Meredith, updated March 25, 2022, https://www.investopedia.com/terms/b/businessrisk.asp.

14. Jordan Mendoza, "What Happens to the Super Bowl 56 Championship Gear Made for the Cincinnati Bengals?," *USA Today*, February 14, 2022, https://www.usatoday.com/story/sports/nfl/super-bowl/2022/02/14/super-bowl-bengals-losing-gear/6638847001/.

15. "Do Not Get Sold on Drug Advertising," Harvard Health Publishing, Harvard Medical School, February 14, 2017, https://www.health.harvard.edu/medications/do-not-get-sold-on-drug-advertising.

16. *APA Dictionary of Psychology*, s.v. "cultural sensitivity," accessed August 30, 2022, https://dictionary.apa.org/cultural-sensitivity.

17. "This Cinco de Mayo, Don't Be a Jerk: 6 Valuable Lessons from Culturally Insensitive Ad Campaigns of Recent Months," Ideas, Thunderfoot, May 5, 2017, https://teamthunderfoot.com/ideas/valuable-lessons-culturally-insensitive-ad-campaigns/.

18. Niamh O, "10 Brands and Businesses That Got Their Marketing Horribly Wrong," TopMBA, QS Quacquarelli Symonds, updated April 15, 2021, https://www.topmba.com/mba-programs/specializations/marketing/10-brands-and-businesses-got-their-marketing-horribly-wrong.

19. "Guide to Gift Giving around the World," *GlobeSmart Blog*, GlobeSmart, last modified April 7, 2020, https://www.globesmart.com/blog/guide-to-gift-giving-around-the-world/.

20. "Business Etiquette in Japan," The City of Yokohama Europe Representative Office, last modified August 17, 2020, https://yokohama-city.de/en/business-etiquette-japan/.

21. Douglas Quackenbos et al., "Does Your Company Have What It Takes to Go Global?," *Harvard Business Review*, April 11, 2016, https://hbr.org/2016/04/does-your-company-have-what-it-takes-to-go-global.

22. Quackenbos et al., "Does Your Company?"

23. *Module 1: Introduction to Infrastructure Economics*, NPTEL, accessed February 3, 2022, https://nptel.ac.in/content/storage2/courses/109106089/module%201.pdf.

24. CNNWire, "Toilet Paper Roll Slimming Down? Products May Continue to Shrink in Size, Quantity amid Inflation," ABC11 Raleigh-Durham, NC, ABC, March 9, 2022, https://abc11.com/inflation-high-prices-consumer-products-shrinkflation/11635527/.

25. "What You Should Know before Going Global," *Small Business Management in the 21st Century* (Washington, DC: Saylor Academy, 2012), https://saylordotorg.github.io/text_small-business-management-in-the-21st-century/s19-02-what-you-should-know-before-go.html.

26. Saylor Academy, "What You Should Know."

27. "USD to GBP Historical Exchange Rates," OFX, USForex, last modified June 30, 2022, https://www.ofx.com/en-us/forex-news/historical-exchange-rates/usd/gbp/.

28. Financial Management Service, *Treasury Reporting Rates of Exchange 1997* (Washington, DC: US Department of the Treasury, 1997), https://www.govinfo.gov/content/pkg/GOVPUB-T63_100-df6e98d19bcf6ba2d231a10f6c9d5260/pdf/GOVPUB-T63_100-df6e98d19bcf6ba2d231a10f6c9d5260.pdf.

29. Mădălina Radu, "Political Stability: A Condition for Sustainable Growth in Romania?," *Procedia Economics and Finance* 30 (2015): 751–757, https://doi.org/10.1016/S2212-5671(15)01324-6.

30. Bill Chappell, "McDonald's Is Leaving Russia, after More Than 30 Years," NPR, May 16, 2022, https://www.npr.org/2022/05/16/1099079032/mcdonalds-leaving-russia.

31. "Trade Regulations of Japan," Guide and Resources, HKTDC Research, May 10, 2022, https://research.hktdc.com/en/article/MzM0NTcxMjg4.

32. "Seychelles Joins the World Trade Organization and Reduces Tariffs," Simplified Trade Solutions, April 7, 2015, https://simplifiedtradesolutions.com/seychelles-joins-the-world-trade-organization-and-reduces-tariffs/.

33. Simplified Trade Solutions, "Seychelles."

34. "Effect of Import Quotas," Glossary Terms, Economics Help, accessed August 30, 2022, https://www.economicshelp.org/blog/glossary/effect-of-import-quotas/.

35. "Embargoed and Sanctioned Countries," Office of Trade Compliance, University of Pittsburgh, last modified March 8, 2021, https://www.tradecompliance.pitt.edu/embargoed-and-sanctioned-countries.

36. "10 Major Regional Trading Blocs in the World," *Export Genius Blog*, Export Genius, March 30, 2018, https://www.exportgenius.in/blog/10-major-regional-trading-blocs-of-the-world-236.php.

37. Andrew Seale, "Seven Epic Cases of Companies That Failed Internationally," Touchpoint by Firmex, Firmex, https://www.firmex.com/resources/blog/seven-epic-fails-by-businesses-that-tried-expanding-into-foreign-markets/.

38. Saul McLeod, "Stereotypes," Simply Psychology, Simply Scholar, updated 2017, https://www.simplypsychology.org/katz-braly.html.

39. Zoe Kelland and Erica Sánchez, "Debunking 15 Common Myths and Misconceptions about Africa," Global Citizen, Global Poverty Project, January 12, 2018, https://www.globalcitizen.org/en/content/africans-are-all-poor-and-15-other-myths/.

40. Benjamin Elisha Sawe, "Where Do Giraffes Live?," WorldAtlas, Valnet, July 25, 2018, https://www.worldatlas.com/articles/where-do-giraffes-live.html.

41. Yun Li, "More Than 50 Companies Reportedly Pull Production out of China due to Trade War," CNBC, July 18, 2019, https://www.cnbc.com/2019/07/18/more-than-50-companies-reportedly-pull-production-out-of-china-due-to-trade-war.html.

42. Abhijeet Pratap, "Effect of Demographic Factors on Consumer Behavior: Age, Sex, Income and Education," Notesmatic, updated December 27, 2021, https://notesmatic.com/effect-of-demographic-factors-on-consumer-behavior-age-sex-income-and-education/.

43. Anna Engelbertink and Schevaa van Hullebusch, "The Effects of Education and Income on Consumers' Motivation to Read Online Hotel Reviews," *Research in Hospitality Management* 2, no. 1–2 (2013): 57–61, https://doi.org/10.1080/22243534.2013.11828292.

44. Jennifer Long, "Technology in Uganda Sees Profitable Growth," *Borgen Magazine*, August 17, 2020, https://www.borgenmagazine.com/technology-in-uganda/.

45. Moses Owori, "Poverty in Uganda: National and Regional Data and Trends," Resources, Development Initiatives, October 2, 2020, https://devinit.org/resources/poverty-uganda-national-and-regional-data-and-trends/.

46. Laura Gray, "Does Uganda Have More Mobile Phones Than Light Bulbs?," BBC News, BBC, March 25, 2016, https://www.bbc.com/news/magazine-35883649.

47. Geoffrey Mutabazi, "Ugandan Startup Finds Innovative Solutions for Mobile Charging," interview by Paul Ndiho, *Africa 54 Interviews*, VOA News, Voice of America, April 27, 2022, https://www.voanews.com/a/uganda-company-charging/6575561.html.

48. "Hong Kong Disneyland Faces Tough Competition," NBC News, NBC Universal, September 10, 2006, https://www.nbcnews.com/id/wbna14774923.

49. Ashley Crossman, "The Importance Customs in Society," ThoughtCo., Dotdash Meredith, updated November 5, 2019, https://www.thoughtco.com/custom-definition-3026171.

50. "A Brief History of the Spanish Siesta," *All about Barcelona Tourism* (blog), BCN Exclusive Private Tours, July 29, 2018, https://barcelonaexclusiveprivatetours.com/blog/a-brief-history-of-the-spanish-siesta.

51. John Spacey, "21 Examples of Cultural Symbols," Simplicable Guide, Simplicable, July 5, 2020, https://simplicable.com/en/cultural-symbols.

52. Spacey, "21 Examples."

53. Thomas Metcalf, "Marketing Blunders & Global Culture," Small Business, Chron.com, last modified November 21, 2017, https://smallbusiness.chron.com/marketing-blunders-global-culture-64855.html.

54. "11 Foods That Have Different Names in the UK and the US," Bayswater, Eurocentres, September 13, 2016, https://www.eurocentres.com/blog/11-foods-different-names-uk-us.

55. "English Idioms," Resources for Learning English, EF Education First, accessed August 30, 2022, https://www.ef.edu/english-resources/english-idioms/.

56. "10 Fascinating Idioms in Different Languages," *TakeLessons Blog*, TakeLessons, May 13, 2016, https://takelessons.com/blog/idioms-in-different-languages-z14.

57. Sian Cain, "Lizzo Removes 'Harmful' Ableist Slur from New Song Grrrls after Criticism," *Guardian*, June 13, 2022, https://www.theguardian.com/music/2022/jun/14/lizzo-removes-harmful-ableist-slur-from-new-song-grrrls-after-criticism.

58. Laura Dixon, "Northampton's Traditional Shoemaking Revival," *Wall Street Journal*, March 6, 2014, https://www.wsj.com/articles/SB10001424052702304675504579391241012877548.

59. Adam Hayes, "Franchise," Investopedia, Dotdash Meredith, updated September 4, 2021, https://www.investopedia.com/terms/f/franchise.asp.

60. "Franchising Overview," Corporate, McDonald's, accessed August 30, 2022, https://corporate.mcdonalds.com/corpmcd/franchising-overview.html.

61. Lxi Lisa Goetz, "The Cost of Buying a McDonald's Franchise (MCD)," Investopedia, Dotdash Meredith, updated June 7, 2021, https://www.investopedia.com/articles/insights/072516/cost-buying-mcdonalds-franchise-mcd.asp.

62. "Details," Fitness Franchise: Dance Workout Instructor, Jazzercize, accessed August 30, 2022, https://www.jazzercise.com/Teach/Details.

63. Sally Lauckner, "Franchising vs. Licensing: What's the Difference?," Small Business, NerdWallet, October 22, 2020, https://www.nerdwallet.com/article/small-business/franchising-vs-licensing.

64. Wex, s.v. "joint venture," updated July 2021, https://www.law.cornell.edu/wex/joint_venture.

65. Kacey Culliney, "Kellogg Strikes Cereal and Snack Joint Venture with Chinese Monopoly Wilmar," BakeryandSnacks, William Reed, updated September 25, 2012, https://www.bakeryandsnacks.com/Article/2012/09/24/Kellogg-Wilmar-joint-venture-China.

66. "Strategic Alliance: Meaning, Examples and Types," *Harappa Blogs*, Harappa Learning, December 20, 2021, https://harappa.education/harappa-diaries/strategic-alliance-meaning-examples-and-types/.

67. "Tesla Said Readying Its China Factory for Even Greater Volumes," Bloomberg, June 23, 2022, https://www.bloomberg.com/news/articles/2022-06-23/tesla-said-readying-its-china-factory-for-even-greater-volumes.

68. Tommy Unger, "Amazon Corporate Headquarters," Maps and Buildings for Amazon & Microsoft, https://campusbuilding.com/b/amazon-corporate-headquarters/.

69. Dan Alaimo, "Amazon Dominates International Marketplace Reach," Retail Dive, Industry Dive, September 10, 2018, https://www.retaildive.com/news/amazon-dominates-international-marketplace-reach/531926/.

70. Shahil Usman, "McDonald's & Its Transnational Business Strategy," LinkedIn, April 4, 2020, https://www.linkedin.com/pulse/mcdonalds-its-transnational-business-strategy-shahil-usman.

71. "Global Marketing Strategy Guide: Tips and Examples," *Translator's Blog*, Tomedes, January 27, 2021, https://www.tomedes.com/translator-hub/global-marketing.

72. Tomedes, "Global Marketing Strategy Guide."

73. "Nike Zoom Running Shoes," Nike AU, Nike, accessed August 30, 2022, https://www.nike.com/au/w/zoom-air-running-

shoes-37v7jz8y8c6zy7ok.

74. "High Intensity Interval Training," Nike.com, Nike, accessed August 30, 2022, https://www.nike.com/w/hiit-9q3qg.

75. "McDonald's to Beef Up in India with Meatless Menu," CBS News, CBS Interactive, September 5, 2012, https://www.cbsnews.com/news/mcdonalds-to-beef-up-in-india-with-meatless-menu/.

76. "Access to Electricity (% of Population) – Uganda," World Bank Open Data, World Bank Group, accessed August 30, 2022, https://data.worldbank.org/indicator/EG.ELC.ACCS.ZS?locations=UG.

77. "Top 10 Most Expensive Countries to Buy Cars," *ezFEED* (blog), ezAUTO.MY, September 14, 2020, https://ezauto.my/blog/2020/09/14/top-10-most-expensive-countries-to-buy-cars/.

78. "Whole Channel View," The Definition, accessed August 30, 2022, https://the-definition.com/term/whole-channel-view.

79. Brian Beckcom, "Captain Phillips and the Truth about What Happened," *Blog & News*, VB Attorneys, October 30, 2017, https://www.vbattorneys.com/blog/maersk-alabama-and-somali-pirates-suit.

80. Wikipedia, s.v. "List of Coca-Cola slogans," last modified July 7, 2022, 05:41, https://en.wikipedia.org/wiki/List_of_Coca-Cola_slogans.

81. "Why Do Companies Outsource? Lessons Learned and Outsourcing Examples," *Our Blog*, NIX United, August 24, 2020, https://nix-united.com/blog/outsourcing-who-does-it-and-why/.

82. Helen Davidson, "Xinjiang: More Than Half a Million Forced to Pick Cotton, Report Suggests," *Guardian*, December 15, 2020, https://www.theguardian.com/world/2020/dec/15/xinjiang-china-more-than-half-a-million-forced-to-pick-cotton-report-finds.

83. Christopher Blattman and Stefan Dercon, "Everything We Knew about Sweatshops Was Wrong," *New York Times*, April 27, 2017, https://www.nytimes.com/2017/04/27/opinion/do-sweatshops-lift-workers-out-of-poverty.html.

84. Erika C. Collins, "Global Diversity and International Employment," in *The Employment Law Review*, ed. Erika C. Collins, 11th ed. (London: Law Business Research, 2020), 19–28.

85. Tina Yazdi, "5 Reasons Why International Success and Diversity Are Inseparable," Amplitude, November 16, 2017, https://amplitude.com/blog/why-diversity-and-international-success-are-inseparable.

86. Gillian Oakenfull, "Marketing with Cultural Intelligence for Growth and Good," *Forbes*, April 7, 2021, https://www.forbes.com/sites/gillianoakenfull/2021/04/07/pg-brands-lead-with-cultural-intelligence/.

87. "Child Labor and the Law," Child Labor Facts, GoodWeave, accessed August 30, 2022, https://goodweave.org/the-issue/laws/.

88. "Foreign Corrupt Practices Act," Fraud Section (FRD), US Department of Justice, last modified February 3, 2017, https://www.justice.gov/criminal-fraud/foreign-corrupt-practices-act.

89. "Past World's Most Ethical Companies," World's Most Ethical Companies, Ethisphere, last modified February 18, 2022, https://worldsmostethicalcompanies.com/past-honorees/.

90. Nikola Gemeš, "44 of the World's Most Ethical Companies (Updated 2022)," *GreenCitizen Blog*, GreenCitizen, April 10, 2022, https://greencitizen.com/blog/ethical-companies/.

91. "Kao and Costco Test the Introduction of Foldable Containers as Reusable Packing Material," News Release, Kao, July 28, 2022, https://www.kao.com/global/en/news/sustainability/2022/20220728-001/.

92. Gemeš, "World's Most Ethical Companies."

93. Timmy Global Health, https://www.timmyglobalhealth.org/; "Timmy Global Health Responds to COVID-19," Timmy Global Health Blog, https://www.timmyglobalhealth.org/blog/timmy-global-health-responds-to-covid-19; "Wrestling at Its Finest—21st Annual Timmy Takedown," EinPresswire.com, September 22, 2022, https://www.einnews.com/pr_news/592255251/wrestling-at-its-finest-21st-annual-timmy-takedown;

8

Marketing in a Diverse Marketplace

Figure 8.1 Diversity marketing is an adaptation strategy in which companies tailor their marketing mix (price, product, place, and promotion) to meet the preferences of targeted populations. (credit: modification of work "Diversity Quilt" by OregonDOT/flickr, CC BY 2.0)

Chapter Outline

In the Spotlight

Multinational consumer goods corporation Procter & Gamble is a good example of a company that understands the significance and impact of marketing in a diverse marketplace. P&G has a long history of reaching out to consumers from different sociocultural communities. In 1961, the company became one of the first major manufacturers in the United States to air a TV commercial in Spanish aimed at Hispanic consumers on a Spanish-language channel (later known as Univisión).[1]

After the Civil Rights Act was signed in 1964 and the Equal Employment Opportunity Commission (EEOC) was formed in 1965, P&G proactively launched its own affirmative action plans across all its business units. P&G instituted the changes even before the EEOC was fully functional. That same year, P&G also conducted product research with Hispanic consumers in Miami, focusing on the scent used in its Secret deodorant line. This commitment to diversity in business practices has remained strong through the years.

P&G continues to demonstrate how to embrace diversity marketing, not just through actions, but through core beliefs and values. The company debuted its "Widen the Screen" campaign in 2021 during the National Association for the Advancement of Colored People (NAACP) Image Awards. The commercial has several short episodes developed by a team of Black creators. Its message is intended to challenge stereotypes and negative attitudes toward the Black community. In a special TV interview, influencer and daytime TV celebrity

Oprah Winfrey strongly praised the campaign's creative opportunities, since Black creators account for only 6 percent of all films made.[2] These types of initiatives are evidence that P&G remains steadfast in its support of cultural and societal values, as well as expanding marketing's horizons to be more inclusive.

Diversity in marketing is often shortsightedly thought of as simply featuring people, objects, or situations linked to various cultural or sociodemographic groups in marketing efforts. These are important components, but diversity marketing goes much deeper than that. In a 2021 keynote presentation about advancing diversity in advertising and business, P&G Chief Brand Officer Marc Pritchard emphasized that the company's commitment to consumers extends to race, ethnicity, and gender representation equal to the American population.[3]

Pritchard added that true and complete inclusion calls for having equitable representation throughout the entire business, including up and down the company's supply chain. This means that even subcontracted agencies, production crews, and media companies that P&G works with reflect the market's diverse demographics. P&G is a diversity marketing champion because it believes in the accurate representation of all people in advertising and communications, regardless of cultural or social group, to build a better society.

P&G's value-creating strategies and purposeful actions embody the concepts of this chapter. Marketing in a diverse marketplace is about understanding why and how to meet consumers' diversity-based needs, while achieving corporate objectives and driving business sustainability at the same time. P&G's campaign "Widen the Screen" invites viewers to widen their perspectives and appreciate the full picture of Black people's lives through a series of diverse everyday situations.

Click to view content (https://openstax.org/books/principles-marketing/pages/8-in-the-spotlight)

8.1 | Strategic Marketing: Standardization versus Adaptation

Learning Outcomes

By the end of this section, you will be able to:
- **LO** 1 Define marketing standardization.
- **LO** 2 Define marketing adaptation.
- **LO** 3 Explain when to use diversity marketing as an adaptation strategy.

Standardization Strategy Defined

To meet the marketplace's demands, companies must carefully formulate competitive strategies based on internal and external conditions. These strategies must balance the capabilities of the organization's business activities, such as marketing, sales, operations, customer service, finance, and human resources management, with multiple environmental factors in the market. Among these are competition, globalization, technology, culture, and changes in consumer demographics and behavior. Companies can choose between two types of strategic approaches, standardization or adaptation, depending on these internal and external variables.

Standardization is the process of purposefully applying identical or consistent guidelines to achieve uniformity. It is not limited to goods and services. Ideas, experiences, data, manufacturing processes, metrics, and operating practices within a business can also be standardized.

A standardized strategy is expressed through the sameness of an offering's features, packaging, pricing, messaging, or advertising to consumers in the marketplace. Companies adopt this strategy for several reasons. These include increasing sales, reducing costs, maximizing efficiencies, improving competitiveness, and gaining a larger customer base.

Think about Apple products. The company standardizes its iPhone, iPad, and Mac computers worldwide. Anywhere you go, Apple devices look and work the same. Only the devices' power source is changed, because of power voltage differences in different parts of the world. Standardization allows Apple to streamline production, speed up market launches, and increase device recognition around the globe.

Adaptation Strategy Defined

Adaptation is the process of adjusting a company's work efforts, goods, or services in response to specific needs, tastes, or expectations from different groups of consumers. An adaptation strategy typically involves two steps. The first is identifying the modifications required to increase an offering's appeal among a targeted audience. The second is implementing the changes based on the organization's abilities and resources. Both of these tasks are crucial to determine the strategy's viability.

Why do companies consider modifying products when doing so generally entails additional costs? The reason is that adaptations are useful to create unique market offerings, generate interest, or provide a competitive differentiation. In other words, this strategy is advisable when the outcome of the change results in reduced risks to the business. Companies can also adapt an existing product, instead of creating a new one, to reduce costs associated with producing new goods. For example, Ford Motor Company adapts the D4 automobile platform for chassis design and engine configuration to its Ford and Lincoln models to save money and offer cars at competitive price points.

Sometimes businesses need adaptation strategies because of market disruptions caused by socioeconomic issues, natural disasters, or health concerns like the COVID-19 pandemic. Zoom, the video conferencing company, was forced to adjust its practices at lightning speed to meet the unexpected demand uptick caused by the pandemic. In only five months (December 2019 to April 2020), Zoom's customer base grew from 10 million to 300 million users.[4] Zoom's adaptation strategy included new data centers, extended partnerships, price and service changes, and platform updates to serve all types of customers.

Diversity Marketing as an Adaptation Strategy

In marketing, an adaptation strategy translates into tailoring the **marketing mix**—product, price, place, and promotion—to suit the preferences of targeted populations. Adaptation strategies are often associated with entering a foreign country.

McDonald's is a good example of a company that adapts its marketing mix to be locally relevant to diverse global consumers. McDonald's introduced the McVeggie and the McAloo in India (see Figure 8.2), the Bai Shrimp Filet-O and the Bai Teriyaki Chicken Filet-O in Japan, poutine fries in Canada, the Picanha ClubHouse Burger in Brazil, and the Bubblegum Squash McFlurry in New Zealand. Besides adjusting the menu (product), McDonald's also aligns advertisements (promotion) and services with local expectations (price and place), while delivering a consistent customer experience from one country to another.

Figure 8.2 McDonald's McAloo Tiki Burger in India is an example of how one company adjusted its marketing mix to meet local preferences. (credit: "McAloo Tiki" by igb, CC BY 2.0)

This strategy is not limited to marketing in different parts of the globe. Companies can adjust any element of the marketing mix when expanding their market share within a region or a single country. This decision, however, should not be taken lightly. Adapting marketing efforts can be costly, time consuming, and disruptive to the business. Plus, unexpected changes in a product's message can be confusing to existing customers.

Marketing adaptation is clearly an option to grow the marketplace. When this strategy is based on a population's cultural or demographic differences, it is diversity marketing. Here is a good example from Nike. The "Nike by You" (see Figure 8.3) shoe-designing service enables the company to expand its appeal to different population segments. By allowing consumers to change the footwear's colors and materials, Nike delivers products adapted to audiences' ethnic and social preferences.[5]

Figure 8.3 The Nike by You shoe campaign is a shoe-customization product that lets consumers design their shoes to meet their individual preferences. (credit: "SSL10007" by cagbay/flickr, CC BY 2.0)

LINK TO LEARNING

Nike and Diversity

To prepare for a marketing career, learning from companies that are known for their diversity campaigns will help you with your future campaigns. According to eMarketer data (https://openstax.org/r/nikeleadsconsumer), Nike is a company with one of the highest levels of diversity in its advertising. Here are a few examples supporting information about Nike's diversity and inclusion campaigns:

- Emmy-winning You Can't Stop Us
  Click to view content (https://openstax.org/books/principles-marketing/pages/8-1-strategic-marketing-standardization-versus-adaptation)
- You Can't Be Stopped campaign (https://openstax.org/r/nikeyoucantbestopped)
- Nike Unlimited You commercial
  Click to view content (https://openstax.org/books/principles-marketing/pages/8-1-strategic-marketing-standardization-versus-adaptation)
- Nike By You (https://openstax.org/r/nikebyyou)
- Nike Diversity, Equity, and Inclusion strategy (https://openstax.org/r/diversityequityinclusion)

There are other companies that are also known for their diversity and inclusion strategies. Read about some of them in this HubSpot article (https://openstax.org/r/inclusivemarketingcampaigns).

Diversity marketing is an effective response to consumers' cultural or demographic diversity in a market. Why is it an adaptation strategy? Because diversity marketing involves changing a product or service to match the needs, wants, and demands of a population's subgroup of consumers.

Knowledge Check

It's time to check your knowledge on the concepts presented in this section. Refer to the Answer Key at the end of the book for feedback.

1. Choosing between standardization and adaption strategies includes ________.
    a. balancing internal capabilities, like operations, with external forces, like competition
    b. assessing only external forces, like technology, and consumer demographic changes
    c. adjusting only a company's resources, assets, and conditions to the market
    d. assessing and reducing the company's consumer base to be more effective

2. Which of the following is NOT a reason to implement a standardized marketing strategy?
    a. To increase sales and reduce costs
    b. To maximize a company's manufacturing or production efficiencies
    c. To improve competitiveness and increase customer base
    d. To increase flexibility with constrained standards

3. A marketing adaptation strategy involves ________.
    a. adjusting a company's efforts and the marketing mix to increase appeal
    b. responding to targeted consumers' specific needs, tastes, or expectations
    c. implementing company changes based on organizational abilities and resources
    d. All of these statements are correct.

4. Adaptations are useful for all the following EXCEPT ________.
    a. creating a unique market product
    b. generating interest for a service
    c. reducing production costs
    d. providing a competitive differentiation

5. An adaptation strategy to expand into culturally or demographically diverse markets can benefit a company by ________.
    a. reducing business disruptions
    b. increasing the customer base
    c. speeding up the execution time
    d. shifting the marketing focus solely to the company

8.2 Diversity and Inclusion Marketing

Learning Outcomes

By the end of this section, you will be able to:
- **LO** 1 Define diversity marketing, multicultural marketing, and sociodemographic marketing.
- **LO** 2 Explain why diversity marketing is needed in today's marketplace.
- **LO** 3 Explain the importance of diversity in market research.
- **LO** 4 List the factors that impact diversity marketing.

Diversity Marketing Defined

As you read in the previous section, **diversity marketing** is a strategic approach that involves identifying diverse subsegments of the population within a market and creating intentional marketing efforts to reach wider audiences. This last piece is key. It has an element of inclusion because it purposefully incorporates identity-specific consumers that have been overlooked or pushed to the margins of society such as some ethnic minorities, people with disabilities, elderly adults, low-income persons, and other groups. **Marginalized consumers** are often excluded in mainstream advertising, translating into missed business opportunities. Diversity marketing is a strategy for marketers to include them.

Diversity marketing is more than just an awareness of minority identities, underrepresented communities, or racial distinctions. It is about being culturally responsive, meaning having an actionable understanding of diverse consumers' interests and preferences based on shared cultural and sociodemographic characteristics. Consider the five key parameters most often used to describe diversity: cultural, racial, and ethnic; gender and sexual identity; generational; religion; and disability.[6] Culture, race, and ethnicity are part of the cultural aspect, while the others are part of the sociodemographic aspect. Because of the broad scope of diversity marketing, as seen in Figure 8.4, this strategy can help marketers reach larger market audiences. Diversity marketing can also influence consumers' mindsets and generate positive attention.

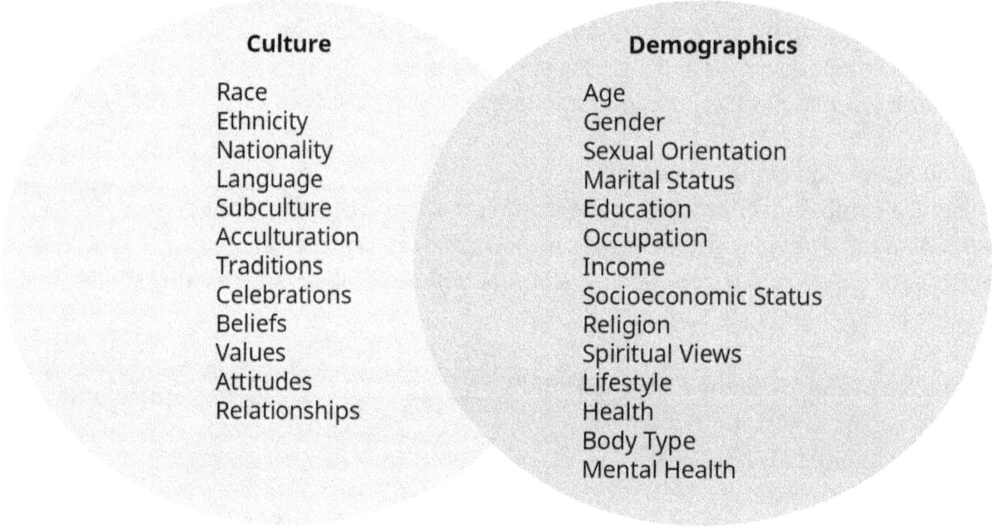

Culture

Race
Ethnicity
Nationality
Language
Subculture
Acculturation
Traditions
Celebrations
Beliefs
Values
Attitudes
Relationships

Demographics

Age
Gender
Sexual Orientation
Marital Status
Education
Occupation
Income
Socioeconomic Status
Religion
Spiritual Views
Lifestyle
Health
Body Type
Mental Health

Figure 8.4 Diversity Marketing Dimensions (attribution: Copyright Rice University, OpenStax, under CC BY 4.0 license)

Importance of Diversity Marketing

The idea of marketing driven by consumer diversity is very relevant and meaningful, because today's marketplace is changing dramatically. This evolution is happening not only in the United States but also around the globe. For marketers, this means that generalizing buyers, households, or communities anywhere in the world is a shortsighted perspective, because it limits business growth and commercial possibilities. Plus, oversimplifying population segments can also adversely affect a company's reputation by shifting the public's opinion in a negative way. The consequences can hurt sales, lead to missed opportunities, and undermine competitive status. This makes it essential to align markets and diversity marketing goals.

Even though "one size fits all consumers" type of tactics worked in past decades, that is no longer the case. Failure to recognize diversity marketing as an essential component of any marketing plan in these changing times is definitely a business blunder. In a study conducted by Adobe in 2019 among 2,000+ consumers, results showed that 61 percent of participants believed that diversity in marketing campaigns was important, and at least 38 percent were also said to be more inclined to trust brands that showed good diversity in advertisements.[7] Inclusion and diversity marketing are vital to a company's success in any market.

What It Means to Businesses

Leading the marketing strategy with a diversity-driven intention can increase customer satisfaction and build stronger brand loyalty. Top Design Firms surveyed hundreds of consumers in late 2020 and found that 67 percent would consider making repeat purchases from companies committed to diversity in marketing campaigns.[8]

Another report confirmed that these observations are not restricted to specific populations. Market analysis by Heat agency found that high diversity scores for brands translated into a whopping 83 percent higher preference by consumers.[9] Besides improving brand sentiment overall, studies show that companies that build emotional ties through diversity marketing programs generate more revenue, increase stock price performance, and enhance brand perceptions.[10]

What It Means to Consumers

Diversity marketing is important on a personal level because of what it implies. Companies that prioritize this strategy clearly demonstrate a higher level of understanding, value, and respect for all individuals in society. The conscientious inclusion of racially, ethnically, culturally, and socially distinct groups in marketing efforts suggests a genuine desire to communicate and engage with everyone.

Acknowledging consumers' differences and adopting tactics to meet each group's needs and preferences also validates individuals' importance in the market. From a consumer standpoint, the application of diversity and inclusion measures in a company's marketing practices shows a universal recognition and appreciation for people.

Factors Impacting Diversity Marketing

As shown in Figure 8.4, diversity marketing is based on a variety of cultural and sociodemographic consumer characteristics. Marketers have to be mindful of these distinctions so marketing communication campaigns launched are sensitive to the audiences they are attempting to serve. After all, cultural and sociodemographic factors can greatly influence consumers' motivations, reactions, and decisions. Other related variables, such as behavioral and personal, can shape buyers' consumption levels and their receptiveness to marketing messages. Given the impact of these factors, for companies to be successful in any market, the focus of diversity marketing has to be **customer centric** rather than **company centric**. Being customer centric is when a company targets customers first regarding any decisions about its goods, services, or experiences, while company centric is when a company focuses decisions from the perspective of the organization. Building a proper sociocultural conscience in marketing starts with good research.

Market Research

Market research is essential for developing successful marketing strategies because it leads to consumer insights. It also identifies potential communication gaps. This means that diversity must be treated as a market research factor to learn about multidimensional audiences. Leveraging consumer diversity in the research process has several benefits. For instance, it provides the information needed to better understand people's cultural or social differences. This is useful for companies to avoid wrong assumptions and avert public mishaps.

To do good research, marketers do not have to belong to or identify with a specific consumer group. However, understanding how ethnic and sociocultural differences impact buyers' decisions and actions requires **diversity marketing intelligence (DMiQ)**. Diversity marketing intelligence refers to the capability of identifying, accepting, and valuing the diversity of consumers within a market and using this knowledge to tailor the marketing mix accordingly.

In early 2018, Tarte Cosmetics introduced to the market its highly anticipated Shape Tape Foundation. The launch featured 15 shades of makeup, almost all light tones. However, the product was not well received. Loyal customers were furious because of the lack of shades for people with darker skin. Tarte Cosmetics was accused of being a whitewashed brand and even making deeper skin-toned people feel inadequate.[11] The company quickly apologized for alienating customers and changed its product and marketing communication.

LINK TO LEARNING

Fenty Beauty

Rihanna did more than just lend her name to the brand Fenty Beauty—she also developed products that increased diversity in the beauty business with its 40-shade foundation range and a wide range of sizes, making $100 million in sales the first 40 days! The company has been criticized for use of child labor by some of its suppliers, and has made what its founder described as careless choices during a fashion show. But it remains known for continuing to reflect a more inclusive approach to beauty and clothing products. Read more about Fenty Beauty from this Latana article (https://openstax.org/r/buildbrandawareness) or this article from *Newsweek* (https://openstax.org/r/rihannafentybeauty).

When diversity marketing efforts fall short, as the Tarte Cosmetics case shows, it is often the result of racially or socially charged insensitivities and missteps. The outcome can have costly repercussions for companies. In 2017, PepsiCo (see Figure 8.5) received heavy backlash for its "Live for Now Moments Anthem" campaign featuring Kendall Jenner. The commercial was criticized for trivializing the Black Lives Matter (BLM) movement and undermining protesters' real-life hardships in pursuit of peace and justice.[12] It was described as insensitive and offensive.

LINK TO LEARNING

Live for Now Moments Anthem

Evaluating successful campaigns and failures is important in the learning process. Find as many opportunities as you can to learn from failures. Start by watching Live for Now Moments for an example of a campaign that failed because it was offensive and missed the mark.

Click to view content (https://openstax.org/books/principles-marketing/pages/8-2-diversity-and-inclusion-marketing)

PepsiCo defended its position as not intending to be socially disrespectful. However, PepsiCo withdrew the commercial, estimated to have cost $5 million to produce, and widely apologized to the market and to Jenner.[13] A final lesson here is that when diversity marketing efforts are done correctly—as Fenty Beauty did—it can boost brand awareness, consumer engagement, and sales.

Figure 8.5 The PepsiCo commercial "Live for Now Moments Anthem" was an expensive lesson for the company—a failed campaign that was criticized for making light of a culture's real-life hardships. (credit: "Pepsi" by Mike Mozart, JeepersMedia/flickr, CC BY 2.0)

Race and Ethnicity

Two out of every five individuals in the United States—over 40 percent of the population—identify racially or ethnically as other than non-Hispanic White.[14] Researchers expect this trend to keep growing in the coming decades, and as consumer diversity increases, cultural identification becomes even more important. Race, ethnicity, and culture give meaning to one another. This makes it critical for marketers to pay attention to how multiracial or multiethnic consumers identify culturally. Having a **multicultural identity** means that a person has been exposed to various cultures and self-identifies as being part of more than one racial or ethnic community or various social groups.[15] We will focus on four key multicultural identity segments of the American population: Hispanic, Black, Asian, and Native American/Alaska Native.

Being multicultural can take many forms. Multicultural individuals may speak multiple languages or have different sets of friends in each culture. From a marketing perspective, multicultural consumers may have different responses to brands or products depending on their multicultural affiliation.[16] Why is this significant? Because marketers must consider the effects of multiculturalism on the marketplace when developing the marketing mix. Race and ethnicity are clearly linked to diversity marketing.

Modelo Especial is a good example. Modelo Especial is a Mexican beer that has successfully capitalized on its heritage to target the Hispanic population while also appealing to the general market. Marketed by Constellation Brands, the beer has had strong sales in the United States since the 1990s.[17] In 2019, Hispanic consumers captured close to 70 percent of the brand's national sales, but Hispanic people are only about half of the customer base.[18] Over the course of several decades, various aspects of Hispanic culture have been widely embraced in the United States. Have you heard of artists like Jennifer Lopez, Pitbull, Bad Bunny, and J Balvin? The marketing team at Constellations Brands attributes the brand's mainstream appeal not only to connecting well with Hispanic consumers but also to the openness of millennial and Gen Z consumers to different cultures and lifestyles.

Sociodemographics

In marketing, **sociodemographics** describes the combination of social and demographic factors that characterize specific consumer groups in the market. These factors are mostly quantifiable, meaning they can be measured or verified to a certain extent. Though race and ethnicity are cultural factors, sometimes they are included in market research as sociodemographic parameters. This is done to increase the generalization of consumer findings and to uncover potential areas of concern linked to social issues.[19]

Sociodemographic variables typically consist of gender and sexual orientation, age or generation, family structure, religion, education level, and income. The latter two are also frequently associated with socioeconomic status. Disability is another variable that can be treated as a demographic factor. Figure 8.4 offers a more comprehensive list of diversity marketing's sociodemographic factors.

Just like with multicultural consumers, segmenting buyers based on shared sociodemographic factors allows companies to tailor goods or services to match the needs and preferences of this diverse group. This enables marketers to develop the right marketing mix—as well as create effective advertising content—to influence distinct consumers. Here is how Disney uses family structure as a sociodemographic factor to segment and target social media users. Disney on Ice is a music and skating show that brings the magic of Disney to ice rinks around the country. People with small children are more likely to consider family entertainment activities, so Disney on Ice targets these consumers on Facebook with tailored family-oriented ads.

Multicultural Marketing Defined

Multicultural marketing is a strategic approach to intentionally target audiences based on different racial, ethnic, and cultural identities and backgrounds. It focuses on relevant, value-rich, and culturally authentic communication tailored to multicultural consumers.

You are probably asking, Is multicultural marketing the same thing as diversity marketing? After all, both are often used interchangeably. The answer is no; they are not the same thing. Diversity marketing is an inclusive approach that results in reaching a wider portion of the entire market. Multicultural marketing is a *subcategory* of diversity marketing that is aimed at multicultural individuals.

Multicultural Populations

Racial and ethnic diversity continue to grow every day around the world. In the United States, in particular, demographers predict a majority–minority population shift by the mid-2040s, as Figure 8.6 shows. In other words, the bulk of American consumers will identify as multicultural, meaning racially and ethnically diverse people of color.

This projection has enormous marketing implications for companies and nonprofit organizations. As the marketplace becomes even more racially and ethnically diverse, marketing efforts must be aligned to the needs and expectations of multicultural groups to be effective.

Let's take a closer look at these key multicultural segments of the American population:

- **The Hispanic population** is the largest multicultural group in the nation and makes up about 19 percent of the total population. According to data-driven marketing company Claritas, the Hispanic population is one of the fastest-growing groups, with over 63 million individuals, and is also responsible for 59 percent of the country's population growth between 2010 and 2021.[20] Plus, by 2026, business strategists believe that nearly two out of every three consumers in the United States will belong to this ethnic group.[21] With a median age of 29, this group also has the youngest population in the country.
- **The Black population** is also a growing segment with 46.9 million individuals—or 14.2 percent of the total population—according to the 2020 US Census. This group is made up of three different subethnicities: individuals who identify as Black alone (single race), or as Black Hispanic, or as Black with another race such as White or Native American (multiracial). The Black population in general has the second youngest median age. In fact, almost 60 percent of this group were millennials or younger (under the age of 38) in 2019 based on findings from the American Community Survey.[22]
- **The Asian population** accounts for 7.2 percent of the American population with 24 million individuals from combined subethnicities as reported by the 2020 Census. Like Black people, Asian people also self-classify as either single race, Asian Hispanic, or multiracial individuals. Communities often included as part of the Asian multiracial composition are Native Hawaiians and Pacific Islanders. Asians' three classifications combined experienced the fastest population growth of all multicultural segments in the

nation between 2000 and 2019.[23] The Asian population has a median age of 34 and is expected to reach around 35 million individuals by 2040.[24]

- The **Native American/Alaska Native population** represents 1.1 percent of the population in the United States with 3.7 million individuals identifying as single race Native people. During the 2020 Census, these Native groups were combined with other races and ethnicities, boosting the number to 9.7 million people, or about 2.9 percent of the total population.[25]

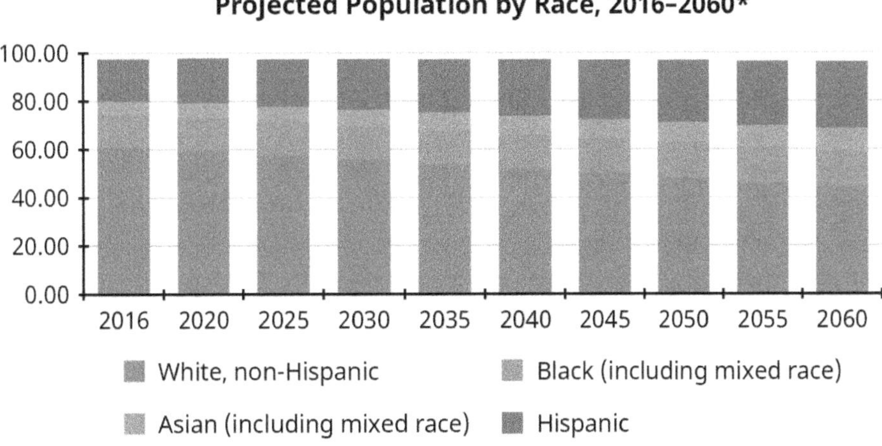

Figure 8.6 US Population Projections from 2016 to 2060 by Race and Ethnicity (data source: US Census Bureau; attribution: Copyright Rice University, OpenStax, under CC BY 4.0 license)

Sociodemographic Marketing Defined

Sociodemographic marketing is a strategic approach to intentionally target audiences based on shared social and demographic characteristics. Sounds familiar? Like multicultural marketing, sociodemographic marketing also focuses on relevant and authentic communications with consumers. Both strategies help business and organizations align their products and services with audiences' needs, preferences, and expectations.

In a 2019 study, nearly 3,000 consumers were asked to consider ads with sociodemographic attributes like gender identity, sexual orientation, age, socioeconomic status, and physical ability. Results showed 64 percent of consumers taking some sort of action after seeing an ad with sociodemographic diversity.[26]

You might be wondering, Is sociodemographic marketing the same thing as diversity marketing then? The answer is no. Again, as with multicultural marketing, sociodemographic marketing includes underrepresented and overlooked consumers in a large population. Sociodemographic marketing is another *subcategory* of diversity marketing.

Sociodemographic Populations

While all sociodemographic consumer groups are important, the following are essential segments of sociodemographic marketing:

- **LGBTQIA+ population**. LGBTQIA+ stands for lesbian, gay, bisexual, transsexual, queer/questioning, intersex, asexual, and other sexual identities. About 5.6 percent of American adults—roughly 14.4 million individuals—identify as LGBTQIA+ according to a 2020 survey.[27] In general, LGBTQIA+ consumers spend more at retail stores than other groups and have a higher percentage of online purchases compared to non-LGBTQIA+ households. Not only is this segment part of diversity marketing, but the LGBTQIA+ community is very diverse too.
- **Generational population**. Consumers are grouped into age clusters based on birth year. These populations include 21.7 million Traditionalist or Silent Generation (born between 1928 and 1945), 70.6 million baby boomers (born between 1946 and 1964), 65 million Generation X (born between 1965 and

1980), 72.2 million Generation Y or millennials (born between 1981 and1996), 67 million Generation Z or Zoomers (born between 1997 and 2009), and 27.6 million Generation Alpha (born between 2010 and 2025) according to 2020 US Census data.[28] Every generation is unique and has different historical references, challenges, interests, and technological experiences that impact these consumers' preferences and appeals.

- **Socioeconomically disadvantaged population**. These individuals tend to come from low-income households, experience financial insecurity, and have less access to education. In the United States, the estimated number of people living in poverty was over 34 million individuals in 2019.[29] The majority of disadvantaged consumers are located either in poor rural areas or inner-city communities that lack social resources and infrastructure to reduce poverty.[30] Marketers must be careful targeting these consumers to avoid negative repercussions from the market.
- **Consumers with disabilities**. This group represents an estimated 61 million Americans. About one in four adults lives with some type of disability.[31] Disability is a classification derived from an impairment related to mobility, learning, intellectual, or other types of functions. This group is also considered very diverse because disabilities span cultural, social, and demographic factors. Consumers with disabilities have been traditionally underrepresented in marketing efforts, though studies show they are one of the largest sociodemographic market opportunities after baby boomers and other segments.[32]

CAREERS IN MARKETING

Multicultural Marketing Director

With the growing opportunities for multicultural marketing, demand is growing for multicultural marketing directors. If this job opportunity interests you, do your research on what type of skills are desired by hiring managers. To get you started, read this article about the 7 Must Have Qualities in a Multicultural Marketing Director (https://openstax.org/r/7musthavequalities). You can also learn directly from marketing executives in this article about how marketers can foster diverse cultures (https://openstax.org/r/20topmarketershowfoster) and who is getting hired and promoted in this area. The best way to learn is to follow others doing the work. Expand your network to include diverse and inclusive leaders. Start by checking out this list of 59 female marketing and growth influencers (https://openstax.org/r/femalemarketingandgrowth).

As you're building a portfolio of skills for the job market, remember to continue to develop your soft skills. Why, you might ask? Read this article: 7 Soft Skills You Need to Achieve Career Growth (https://openstax.org/r/marketingsoftskills).

Knowledge Check

It's time to check your knowledge on the concepts presented in this section. Refer to the Answer Key at the end of the book for feedback.

1. Diversity marketing is a strategic approach that includes ________.
   a. identifying different subsegments of consumers
   b. creating advertisements to connect with specific consumers
   c. consumers that share cultural and sociodemographic characteristics
   d. All of these statements are true.

2. Which of the following is true regarding why diversity marketing is important?
   a. Today's marketplace is changing dramatically everywhere.
   b. Buyers, households, and communities are staying the same.

   c. Consumers don't believe that diversity in advertising is important.
   d. Diversity marketing has no impact on brand loyalty.

3. For companies to be successful in any market, the focus of diversity marketing should be ________.
   a. company centric
   b. brand centric
   c. consumer centric
   d. industry centric

4. Diversity in market research is a good idea because it can ________.
   a. help companies win over people from different population segments
   b. provide information to better understand cultural and social differences
   c. reduce wrong assumptions and avert public relations missteps
   d. All of these statements are true.

5. Which is not an example of a diversity marketing consumer segment?
   a. Multicultural segments like Hispanic, Black, and Asian people
   b. Sociodemographic segments like tech-savvy and digital natives
   c. Multicultural segments like American Indian and Alaskan Native people
   d. Sociodemographic segments like Gen Xers, Zoomers, and consumers with disabilities

8.3 | Multicultural Marketing

Learning Outcomes

By the end of this section, you will be able to:
   LO 1 Define culture.
   LO 2 Explain the difference between tangible and intangible cultural objectives.
   LO 3 List the main elements through which culture is expressed.
   LO 4 Describe Hofstede's cultural dimensions.

What Is Culture?

You have already read about corporate culture in Marketing and Customer Value and cultural factors influencing buying behavior in Consumer Markets and Purchasing Behavior. Let's explore culture in more detail. After all, learning about culture is the first step to understand why the concept is a fundamental component of multicultural marketing and how it connects with diversity marketing.

Culture refers to the social norms, beliefs, behaviors, and accomplishments that characterize a particular set of individuals. Culture also encompasses shared customs, arts, language, foods, and knowledge. In essence, it is a snapshot of a society's accepted way of living at a given place or time. Figure 8.7 provides a more extensive view of the things that represent it. As you can see, culture clearly influences many aspects of life.

The term originates from the Latin word *cultura*, which is associated with nurturing, growing, and cultivating.[33] This explanation makes sense because some cultural aspects are taught or passed down from one generation to the next. Think of it as planting a seed—not a physical one, but a seed of inner values. Culture is also fostered through community socialization. The outcome of these shared learnings leads to the continued growth of a group's cultural identity and its idiosyncrasies.

To be effective in an increasingly diverse marketplace, marketers need to recognize the profound role that culture plays in consumers' behaviors and purchasing decisions. That is why multicultural insights are so important to diversity marketing.

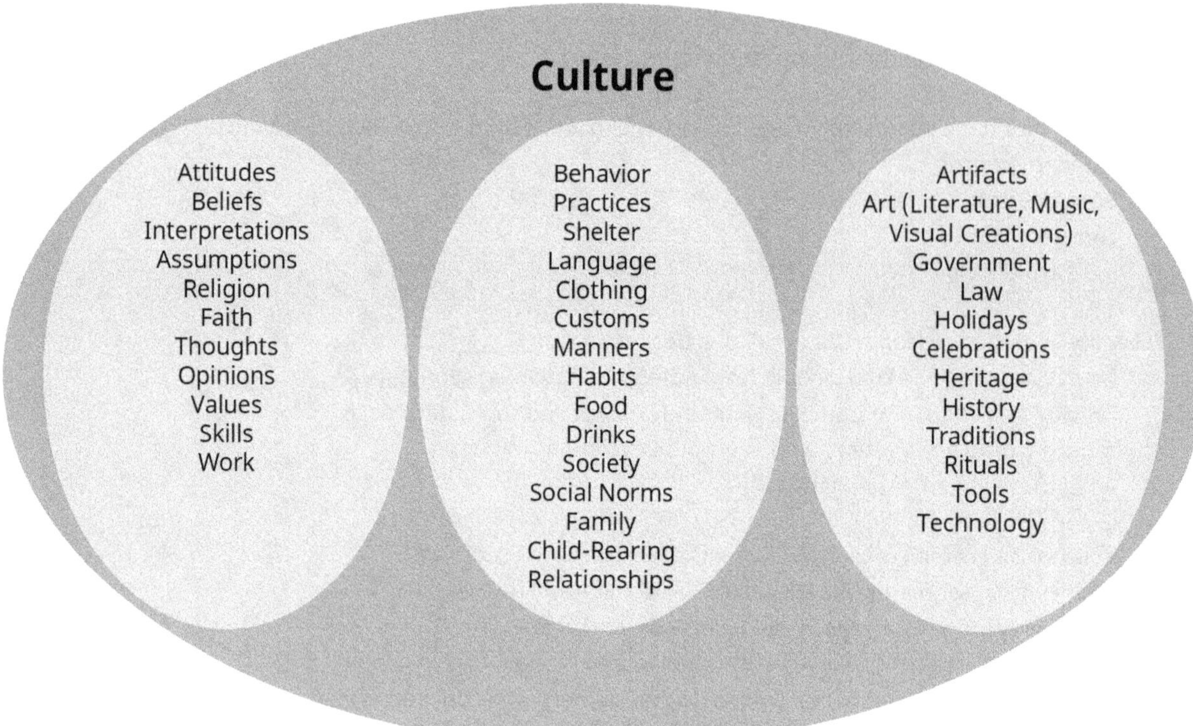

Figure 8.7 What Is Culture? (attribution: Copyright Rice University, OpenStax, under CC BY 4.0 license)

Tangible versus Intangible Culture

Culture is both tangible and intangible. This means that it can be seen, but it can also be concealed. Anthropologist Edward T. Hall describes it as an iceberg with external and internal surfaces.[34] As Figure 8.8 depicts, some elements of culture are readily visible, like the tip of the iceberg. Traditions, music, languages, artifacts, clothing, and literature are just a few aspects that are easy to recognize. They are tangible and external. In other words, they are the conscious part of culture.

Other aspects of culture are like the bottom part of the iceberg. Did you know that 90 percent of an iceberg's mass is hidden below the waterline? Thought processes, assumptions, skills, beliefs, and interpretations are more difficult to observe. Can you see a person's thoughts? Can you understand a person's worldviews without asking? These things happen out of sight, making them the subconscious part of culture. Intangible and internal aspects are just like the larger portion of the iceberg in the sense that they are often beneath the surface.

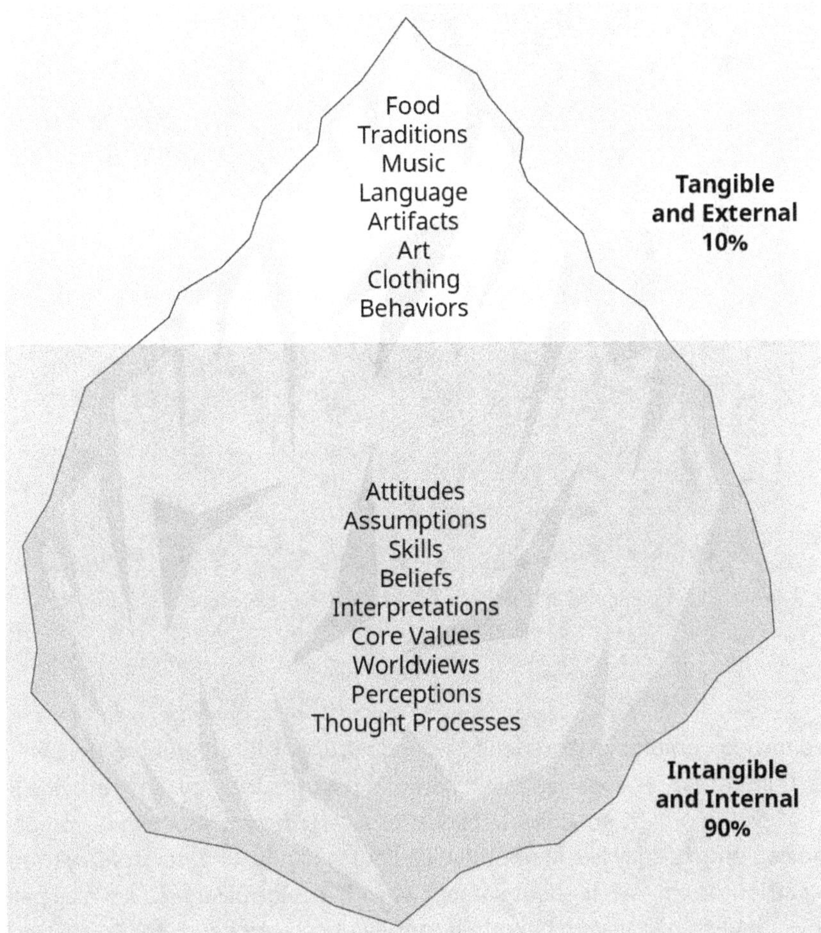

Figure 8.8 The Cultural Iceberg (attribution: Copyright Rice University, OpenStax, under CC BY 4.0 license)

The iceberg analogy gives us a valuable lesson about cultural insights. Connecting with multicultural consumers requires understanding not only those elements of culture that can be observed but also those that are deep-seated in a specific community.

The "Texican Whopper" campaign from Burger King (see Figure 8.9) makes this point clear. Burger King was forced to revise the ads that featured a tiny Mexican wrestler dressed in a poncho-style Mexican flag standing next to a tall American cowboy. Some Spanish-speaking customers thought the campaign was funny. However, others were offended. Insights about the distaste for stereotypes and the high respect for the flag as a national symbol could have prevented this situation. It could have also saved Burger King money because the campaign had to be redone.

Figure 8.9 Burger King's "Texican Whopper" campaign was a failure because the marketers lacked an understanding of the unseeable elements, or the internal and intangible aspects, of Mexican culture. (credit: "Burger King" by Mike Mozart, JeepersMedia/ flickr, CC BY 2.0)

Main Expressions of Culture

Culture is expressed through emotional experiences, symbols, linguistic communication, values and attitudes, and other practices. Cultural expressions are a vital part of a person's identity. They provide insights about what an individual believes in or why an individual behaves a certain way. How would you perceive somebody waving an American flag on a holiday like Memorial Day, Fourth of July, or Veteran's Day? You would probably think the person is patriotic, right? What about somebody with a colorful sugar skull face painting on Día de Los Muertos? Or how about someone with beautifully henna-decorated hands for Diwali? Visible manifestations of culture empower people to be comfortable with personal thoughts and feelings. Visible symbols also help people to be accepted in a given community by showing solidarity.

Symbols

Symbols are essential expressions of culture that represent a group's ideologies, values, and actions. They include things such as objects, ceremonial artifacts, designs, colors, and ideas. Printed characters, words, signs, and logos can be symbols too. Even punctuation marks, or emoticons, symbolize facial expressions or people's feelings. Marketers must be careful when using symbols because they can have different representations or meanings among different cultures. For instance, the emoticon :) symbolizes happiness in the United States. However, in Japan the emoticon for happiness looks more like this (^_^) or has a triangle-shaped mouth instead of a parenthesis.[35]

In the United States, the rainbow flag and its variations are symbols of the LGBTQIA+ community. Yet, for people who emigrated from Peru or have family in the Andes, the rainbow flag symbolizes the reign of the Inca empire.[36] As you can see in Figure 8.10, both flags are alike but not identical (the Andean rainbow flag has two blue stripes). Despite the similarities, the rainbow flag as a symbol has different meanings to both groups.

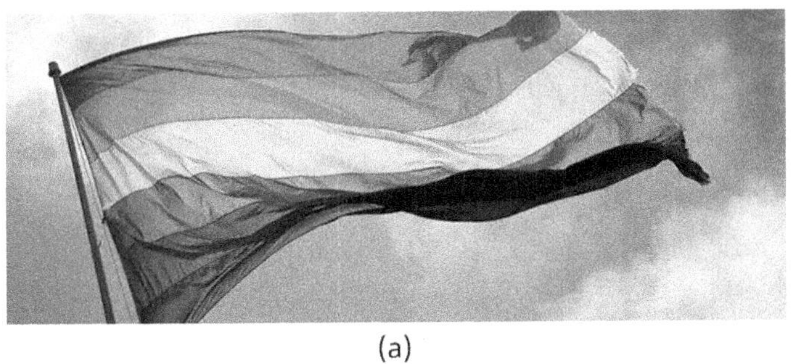
(a)

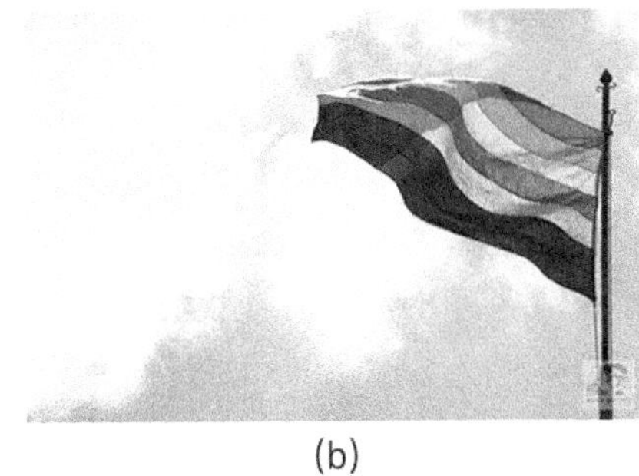
(b)

Figure 8.10 Marketers need to be aware of what symbols mean to different groups so that they can be sure the messages they share are interpreted as intended. (credit: "Rainbow Flag" by Dave/flickr, CC BY 2.0; "Cusco-Peru" by Paulo Guereta/flickr, CC BY 2.0)

Language

Like symbols, language is an important part of culture. Language communicates personal identity. It also shapes how people perceive the world around them. Have you heard of 9Lives? It is a popular brand of cat food in the United States owned by the J.M. Smucker Company. The brand's name comes from the popular expression that cats have nine lives. However, did you know that in Spanish and Portuguese, the expression is that cats only have seven lives? For these multicultural consumers, such language differences can influence their perceptions of the product.

Language takes verbal and nonverbal forms; it can be spoken, signed, or written. In fact, there were 7,139 living languages reported around the world in 2021, with 23 of them in particular adding up to a combined number of speakers totaling over half the globe's population.[37] The top 15 languages in Figure 8.11 are based on the number of native- and second-language speakers in the world. Language is a main expression of culture because it provides insights to connect with audiences.

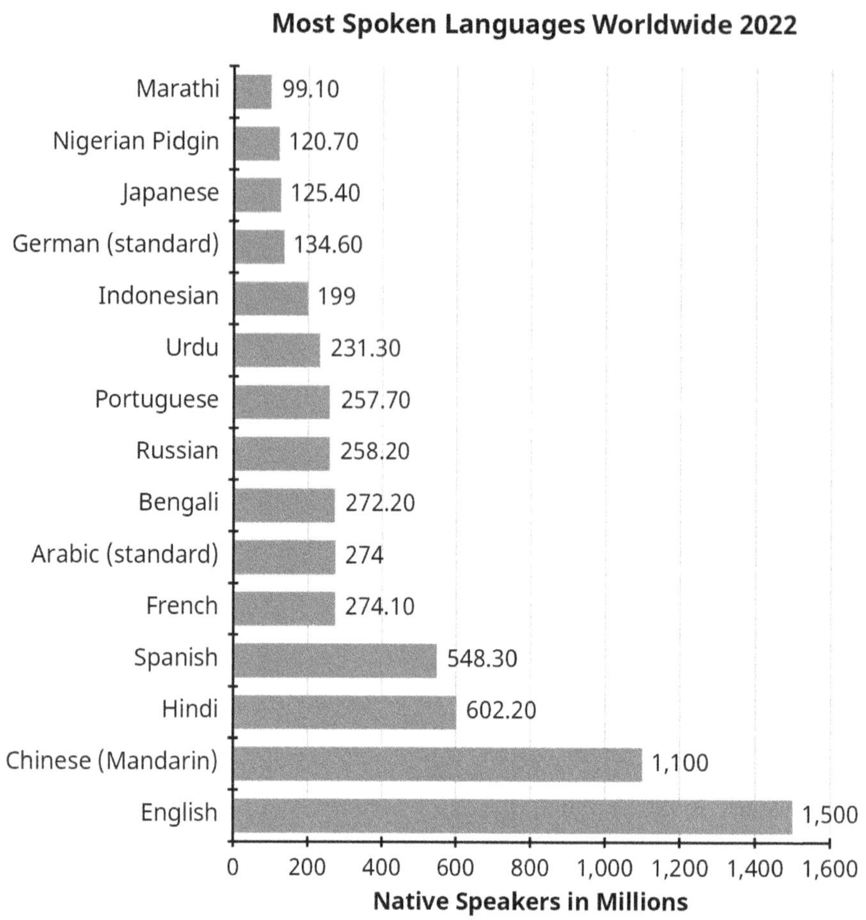

Most Spoken Languages Worldwide 2022

Figure 8.11 The Languages Most Spoken around the World (data source: Ethnologue, 2022; attribution: Copyright Rice University, OpenStax, under CC BY 4.0 license)

As you have read, consumer diversity in the marketplace is growing. That is why it is imperative for marketers to conduct language research with targeted populations to avoid miscommunication or lost opportunities. This means that even within cultural groups, there are speech regionalisms and slang terms that can affect the success of marketing campaigns.[38]

The Hispanic population has multiple subethnicities that prove this point. Let's say that an automotive tire company wants to market its product to Hispanic consumers throughout the United States. The company could create several ad variations using words for *tire* that are popular among the subgroups. It could use the word *gomas* for Puerto Rican consumers in New York, *llantas* for Mexican buyers in Texas, *neumáticos* for Chilean clients in California, or *ruedas* for Cuban shoppers in Florida. The challenge for the company would be to decide if the effort and expense associated with creating multiple ads are justified. It should also consider if the words have other meanings among the subgroups. For example, for Puerto Ricans *ruedas* are thin wheels, not something associated with car tires.

Values and Attitudes

Values are cultural indicators of a society's standards for goodness and justice. They are described as basic beliefs that guide behavior and give meaning to actions and attitudes. Dutch social psychologist and diversity thinker Geert Hofstede created a survey to uncover how national culture reflects a society's values.[39] Hofstede summarized the survey's findings into the following dimensions:

- **Individualism versus Collectivism.** Culture is classified as either individualistic or collectivistic. In the United States, non-Hispanic White people and individuals of European descent tend to have an individualistic view. Individualism places a higher value on personal accomplishments and individual experiences. Hispanic, Black, and Asian people lean toward a collectivistic view.[40] Collectivism values achieving group or family goals above those of individuals. The level of individualism versus collectivism, however, varies within multicultural segments, so it is important not to make assumptions.

- **High versus Low Power Distance.** In addition to their basic function, products can also serve to display an individual's power or position in society. Think about flip phones and smartphones. Cost-wise, the traditional flip phones are a lot less expensive in general. Yet, smartphone ownership is on the rise. This is due not only to the additional capabilities of smartphones, but also to the fact that their ownership is seen as a symbol of social status. Hispanic and Black people also use smartphones more than other groups for online access to health information and educational content.[41]
- **Masculinity versus Femininity.** Gender can strongly impact the creative concept and messaging behind marketing promotions, ads, and social media. American society in general is masculine oriented, with Black men having a stronger view of masculinity than non-Hispanic White and Hispanic counterparts.[42] Achievement, power, and strength are considered masculine traits. For this reason, the message of many ads in the United States is about product performance and functionality. Some Asian groups such as Japanese and Chinese are also masculine oriented. However, other Asian subgroups are considered more feminine oriented.[43] For these consumers, visual ads that emphasize quality of life, people, and relationships would have a higher appeal.
- **Uncertainty Avoidance.** A high dislike for ambiguity and the unknown is not just an individual trait; it is a characteristic of societies in general. Cultures that do not tolerate uncertainty well seek safety and rules to reduce anxiety. These cultures also embrace technology to feel safer, which might explain why Hispanic people are such quick adopters of it. Black and Asian people also tend to avoid uncertainty and high risks more than non-Hispanic White people.[44]
- **Long-Term versus Short-Term Orientation.** This dimension describes how individuals believe and behave in society. It is also based on links to the past and challenges in the future. Cultures with long-term orientation value perseverance, orderliness, thriftiness, and having a sense of shame. Asian people overall rate extremely high in the long-term orientation.[45] Short-term cultures, on the other hand, focus more on personal steadiness, happiness, and stability. The challenge for marketers is to balance orientations to successfully reach diverse audiences and influence consumption.
- **Indulgence versus Restraint.** Societies that prioritize satisfaction, leading a happy life, and savoring leisure activities with family and friends are described as indulgent. On the other hand, societies that favor living according to strict traditional norms and curbing life's enjoyment are seen as restrained.

How Culture Influences Diversity Marketing

Identifying multicultural population segments and engaging them with intentional efforts is at the core of multicultural marketing. However, this requires having cultural insights because culture influences consumers' decision-making processes and purchasing behaviors. The lack of cultural insights can spell disaster when marketing to this audience.

Let's look at some cultural perspectives about living experiences, outlook, and community involvement. Living in the present moment and sharing situations with loved ones is an important goal to 42 percent of Hispanic people in comparison to only 23 percent of non-Hispanic White people.[46] Based on this insight, marketers targeting Hispanic consumers should create advertisements that feature meaningful messages and friendly people sharing a profound experience instead of simply showing the features of a product or service.

Hispanic, Black, and Asian consumers overall are more optimistic than non-Hispanic White consumers. In a study about their financial outlook, multicultural consumers were twice as optimistic as non-Hispanic White consumers about reaching economic success in their lifetime. As collectivistic-oriented cultures, they also think more about family and community when making financial decisions. Plus, when it comes to community, Hispanic and Black consumers believe more can be achieved by working together than non-Hispanic White consumers.[47]

These insights suggest that expressions of culture and elements like confidence, hope, and teamwork are crucial for implementing multicultural marketing campaigns. As you read earlier, multicultural marketing is a subcategory of diversity marketing. This means that culture has a significant impact on diversity marketing as well.

Knowledge Check

It's time to check your knowledge on the concepts presented in this section. Refer to the Answer Key at the end of the book for feedback.

1. Culture is described as which of the following?
   a. Social norms, beliefs, and accomplishments of particular individuals
   b. Elements taught or passed down from one generation to the next
   c. Something that influences consumers' decision-making processes and purchasing behaviors
   d. All of these

2. Which of the following are not examples of tangible or external expressions of culture?
   a. Actions and behaviors
   b. Traditions and customs
   c. Values and attitudes
   d. Music and visual arts

3. Marketers must be careful when using symbols as cultural expressions because ________.
   a. there are too many to choose from among different cultures
   b. they can have different meanings among different cultures
   c. they can have similar meanings among different cultures
   d. they are verbal and nonverbal forms of communication

4. An advertisement that appeals to personal accomplishments, independence, and assertiveness is an example of which of Hofstede's cultural dimensions?
   a. High power distance
   b. Masculinity
   c. Individualism
   d. Long-term orientation

5. An advertisement that is visually appealing and emphasizes quality of life, people, and relationships is an example of which of Hofstede's cultural dimensions?
   a. Femininity
   b. Masculinity
   c. Uncertainty avoidance
   d. Short-term orientation

8.4 Marketing to Hispanic, Black, and Asian Consumers

Learning Outcomes

By the end of this section, you will be able to:
   - **LO** 1 Describe the Hispanic, Black, and Asian identities.
   - **LO** 2 Define acculturation.
   - **LO** 3 Explain how identity-related characteristics and factors connect Hispanic, Black, and Asian consumers.
   - **LO** 4 Describe how to market to Hispanic, Black, and Asian consumers.

Hispanic, Black, and Asian Consumer Identities

The United States is a mixture of nationalities, backgrounds, cultures, and identities. This mixture has been shaped through many decades of immigration from people across many lands and by their interactions with their new environments. The US population is often referred to as consisting of majority and minority groups. The majority consists of non-Hispanic White people. The minority consists of other races, ethnicities, and communities. From a marketing standpoint, companies have historically treated the majority segment as the mainstream market. Conversely, the minority segment has been treated as a subgroup of consumers, or the multicultural market.

As you read earlier in the chapter, the demographics of the United States continue to change, and the majority segment will cease to exist in the future. The country is expected to become a "plurality nation" by 2050. This means that no group will have a *sizeable* majority. The non-Hispanic White population is projected to remain the largest single group.[48] However, the majority position will be lost in terms of population percentage. Check out Figure 8.6 again to compare the overarching segments.

Hispanic Identity

Let's examine the data from the 2020 US Census to better understand Hispanic consumers. The Hispanic population reached over 63 million people in 2020. Is this number significant? Yes, because it means that one out of every five people in the United States is Hispanic or of Hispanic descent. This is a 23 percent growth since the previous census! In fact, the Hispanic population has grown significantly in the last four decades. The Hispanic population is projected to reach almost 100 million individuals by 2050.

Hispanic people are not a uniform group or single ethnicity. On the contrary, the Hispanic population in the United States is very diverse. Hispanic people originate from 20 different countries, as shown in Figure 8.12, and can belong to any race. An overwhelming 83 percent of the Hispanic population belongs to just five subethnicities. These subgroups are Mexican (62.2 percent), Puerto Rican (9.5 percent), Cuban (3.9 percent), Salvadoran (3.9 percent), and Dominican (3.5 percent).[49] The rest of the population is made up of the other 15 Hispanic subethnicities.

You are probably familiar with the terms *Hispanic*, *Latino/Latina*, and *Latinx*. They are often used interchangeably but can have different meanings. *Hispanic* is a language-based term that describes individuals from a Spanish-speaking country. *Latino/Latina* is a location-based term that identifies gendered individuals whose families originate in Latin America regardless of the language they speak. For example, a person from Spain is considered Hispanic because of language but not Latino because of location. A person from Brazil is considered Latino/Latina because of location but not Hispanic because of language (Brazilians speak Portuguese). Unlike *Latino/Latina*, the term *Latinx* is gender neutral. While *Latinx* has picked up momentum among some groups, many Hispanic people dislike the word or find it offensive.

Hispanic	Hispanic/Latino	Latino
• Spain	• Argentina • Bolivia • Chile • Colombia • Costa Rica • Cuba • Dominican Republic • Ecuador • El Salvador • Guatemala • Honduras • Mexico • Nicaragua • Panama • Paraguay • Peru • Puerto Rico • Uruguay • Venezuela	• Belize • Brazil • French Guiana • Guyana • Haiti • Suriname

Figure 8.12 Hispanic People and Latinos in the United States by Country of Origin (attribution: Copyright Rice University, OpenStax, under CC BY 4.0 license)

Many cultures integrate traditions in their lives as the generations progress. Hispanic people demonstrate this same movement of traditions, from their countries and cultures of origin into their family practices in the United States. Why is that? It has to do with identity. Identity is a person's self-image. **Cultural identity**, in particular, is how a person identifies with a given culture, ethnicity, or social group. It is a sense of belonging that influences personal thinking and actions.

For the majority of Hispanic people, identity is strongly linked to heritage or to their family's country of origin.[50] Customs and social practices are strong components as well. To increase its connection with these consumers, Target (see Figure 8.13) appealed to the Hispanic identity with its *sobremesa* commercial. The *sobremesa* is the additional time spent at the dinner table with friends and family after a big meal for relaxing or having meaningful conversations. This Hispanic tradition does not have a direct translation in terms of American culture. Target created the hashtag *#SinTraducción* for the campaign, which means "without translation" to further emphasize this. Target also used "There will always be a part of you that simply doesn't translate" as the slogan for social media outreach. The commercial is part of the retailer's first campaign ever aimed directly at Hispanic millennials.

Figure 8.13 Target created the *sobremesa* commercial as a way to appeal to the Hispanic identity. (credit: "Target" by Mike Mozart, JeepersMedia/flickr, CC BY 2.0)

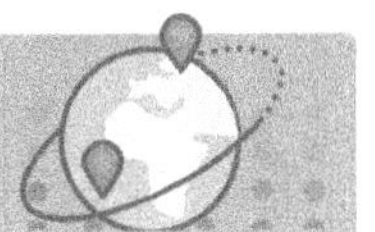

LINK TO LEARNING

Target "Sobremesa" Commercial

Target's "Sobremesa" commercial shows an entire Hispanic family sitting at the table clearly *after* the meal has ended to share desserts and enjoy fun conversation as a group.

Click to view content (https://openstax.org/books/principles-marketing/pages/8-4-marketing-to-hispanic-black-and-asian-consumers)

Black Identity

Black people are the second largest multicultural group in the United States after Hispanic people. Let's consider the statistics from the 2020 US Census again. The Black population shows growth at 46.8 million people in 2020 versus 38.9 million people a decade earlier. Black consumers make up 14.2 percent of the country's total inhabitants. Another key point is that individuals who identify as Black in combination with another race have increased 88.7 percent since the last census. This "in combination" trend is not unique to the Black community; the "in combination" identification accounted for the majority of the changes in all the racial categories.[51]

This multicultural segment shows a couple of other interesting changes that impact consumer and consumption behaviors. For example, Black consumers are forecasted to account for 15–17 percent of the total population growth in the nation over the next decade. Black people have also had the largest change in education level in recent years. Since the 2010 census, the percentage of Black people with an undergraduate degree has increased by more than 55 percent. [52]

While Black people account for 14.2 percent of the population, this segment makes up just under 10 percent of spending on goods and services. This is because Black workers earn a lower median income than other demographics. However, this inequity in spending and wealth is showing signs of moving toward a better balance. The growing Black population is estimated by management consulting firm McKinsey to represent over $300 billion per year in unmet demand.[53]

A 2019 survey by the Pew Research Center shows that nearly 75 percent of Black people believe that race is at the center of their identity.[54] Race is deeply tied to how people perceive themselves. When it comes to defining the Black identity further, the community is also facing a unique challenge. There is a growing argument in the United States over differences between Black people who emigrated from Africa and those who did not. The debate is caused by the ancestral link to slavery that many American-born Black people have but immigrants do not. Plus, Black people can also have other subethnicities such as Black Hispanic and multiracial (White, Asian, or Native American). While the subethnicities may not be physically visible, marketers need to be aware that identity differences can be significant among the Black population.

These multicultural consumers also feel relatively well connected to the broader Black community and prioritize social activities that offer support to the group as a whole. To show solidarity with the BLM movement, popular ice cream brand Ben & Jerry's (see Figure 8.14) named one of its flavors "Justice ReMix'd" to raise awareness of racism and criminal justice reform. The company worked with the Advancement Project national office to advocate for social change and civil rights. Ben & Jerry's also enacted a multipoint corporate plan challenging other companies to champion the cause and join the conversation about racial inequalities.

Figure 8.14 Ben & Jerry's created a new flavor of ice cream as a way to connect with the Black Lives Matter movement and raise awareness around racism and criminal justice reform. (credit: "Peace, Love & Ice Cream" by Rob Olivera/flickr, CC BY 2.0)

Asian Identity

The Asian population in the United States has also increased since the last census. This growth has been fueled largely by foreign-born individuals. There were 19.9 million people in 2020 who identified as single-race Asians. This number is up from 14.7 million a decade earlier. There were also 4.1 million people in 2020 who identified primarily as Asian "in combination" with another race. In fact, this combination of single race and mixed race increased a whopping 55.5 percent from 2010 to 2020, making it one of the fastest-growing demographic segments.[55] Overall, the Asian population in the United States is 24 million individuals, which is 7.2 percent of the total country's inhabitants. The US Census Bureau projects this multicultural community to more than double by 2060.

Like the Hispanic population, the Asian population is very diverse too. Figure 8.15 shows the 22 different subethnicities that make up these multicultural consumers. Did you know that six of these origin groups account for 85 percent of the total Asian American community? These groups derive from the Asian continent and the Indian subcontinent. These origin groups are Chinese (24 percent), Indian (21 percent), Filipino (19 percent), Vietnamese (10 percent), Korean (9 percent), and Japanese (7 percent).[56] The remainder of the Asian people come from Native Hawaiian, Pacific Islander, and other subgroups.

Figure 8.15 Groups of Origin for the Asian Population in the United States (attribution: Copyright Rice University, OpenStax, under CC BY 4.0 license)

The geographic distribution of this population is worth noting. There are over 9.8 million Asian people living in the western region of the country. This is nearly half the entire Asian population! Plus, almost one-third of Asian consumers live in California alone, making Asians one of the state's largest population segments. The southern states have the second largest Asian population with 5.3 million individuals. Overall, Asian people are projected to be the largest source of immigrants by 2055, accounting for 36 percent of all immigration, followed by Hispanic people at 34 percent.[57]

As an immigrant group, Asian people have the fastest adoption rate of the English language. Almost 75 percent of Asian households speak English, and nearly two-thirds of American-born Asians speak English only. Asian people are also more likely than the average American household to live in a multigenerational setting.[58] Because of their diversity and unique characteristics, it is difficult to narrow it down to a uniform Asian identity. This poses a challenge for marketers. Creating generalized messages for Asian people or having a "one size fits all" marketing approach is unwise. Plus, making assumptions about consumers' purchasing behaviors as a singular market can be very tricky, if not inadvisable, because there is not a sole Asian cultural identity.

A 2019 survey about race found that 56 percent of Asian people said race was a key part of their identity.[59] Using this insight, Nike created two different—but very effective—commercials targeting different subsegments of Asian consumers. Nike's "The Great Chase" is inspired by the longtime Chinese tradition of gifting money in little red envelopes.

LINK TO LEARNING

Nike

Check out the "Great Chase" commercial and compare it to the upbeat "Da Da Ding" commercial featuring Indian women practicing many types of sports.

Click to view content (https://openstax.org/books/principles-marketing/pages/8-4-marketing-to-hispanic-black-and-asian-consumers)
Click to view content (https://openstax.org/books/principles-marketing/pages/8-4-marketing-to-hispanic-black-and-asian-consumers)

The Acculturation Spectrum

People who immigrate to the United States from another country will probably experience some personal level of acculturation. Even American-born multicultural individuals whose families speak another language at home besides English may also experience acculturation. **Acculturation** is the process by which a person's family cultural patterns change because of direct and constant contact with a different culture.[60] Acculturation can happen in various degrees. The spectrum ranges from complete adoption to total rejection of the new culture. Individuals that simultaneously merge both cultures in daily life are considered bicultural.

Hispanic and Asian consumers can experience various degrees of acculturation. This depends on birthplace, immigration status, community connections, and personal comfort level. For instance, a person born in the United States to immigrant parents is more likely to be acculturated than unacculturated. For marketers, being aware of acculturation levels is important because they play a significant role in how these multicultural consumers respond to marketing messages. Here is another example. Hispanic people in general think of language as a tool to preserve the culture. As a result, unacculturated Hispanic consumers are more likely than acculturated consumers to support a brand that advertises to them in the Spanish language. This effort is seen as a sign of respect and appreciation.[61]

Identity-Connecting Characteristics and Factors

The Hispanic, Black, and Asian populations each have a general set of cultural characteristics based on their multicultural identities. Being aware of each segment's personal characteristics helps marketers create effective marketing promotions and advertisements. In addition to internal characteristics, these consumers are also influenced by external factors such as social circumstances and market behaviors. Let's explore characteristics and factors in more detail.

Hispanic Consumers

Hispanic consumers in general are optimistic, family-oriented, warmhearted, and hospitable.[62] The culture's energy and liveliness are visible through elements like music, food, decor, and language. Hispanic people place a high value on relationships and social interactions. Have you noticed that some commercials aimed at Hispanic consumers show people in close proximity, touching, or hugging? Physical contact is important to this multicultural segment. It is seen as a way to build trust and group harmony. Did you notice it in Target's *sobremesa* commercial?

Hispanic consumers support brands that demonstrate cultural authenticity, transparency, and honesty. After all, openness and having meaningful connections are at the heart of these consumers' values. In terms of factors, the concept of product quality and service quality is deeply desirable to Hispanic consumers. Have you heard of Hispanic actress Jessica Alba? Alba, who is of Mexican descent, founded The Honest Company (see Figure 8.16) in 2012 with the mission of formulating safe, high-quality personal and beauty products for the family. Other factors that influence Hispanic consumers include companies' pledges to sustainability and social responsibility. Indeed, these are growing concerns that shape this community's purchasing behaviors.

Figure 8.16 Hispanic consumers support products that demonstrate the qualities that are important to them—optimistic, family-oriented, warmhearted, and hospitable—which is why the Honest Company's message of safe products for the family resonates. (credit: "A Few of My Favorite Fhings: Honest Company" by Abi Porter/flickr, CC BY 2.0)

Black Consumers

Two noteworthy characteristics of Black consumers in general are determination and self-expression. As you read earlier in the chapter, race is a key component of the Black identity. The social, educational, and economic struggles that Black people have faced because of racial discrimination and injustice have made these consumers highly determined to pursue their dreams regardless of the obstacles encountered. Self-expression is also a significant cultural trait. It is a way to show personal pride in one's identity. Among Black consumers, self-expression is typically conveyed through fashion, music, sports, and the arts.

Like Hispanic consumers, Black people are optimistic and resilient. Strong community bonds, observance of religious practices, and deep commitments to social activism are factors closely linked to Black consumers' identities. The opportunity to raise a collective voice about key issues is a fueling factor too. In 2020, Beats by Dre launched the "You Love Me" campaign (see Figure 8.17).

Figure 8.17 Beats Electronics, founded by Black rapper Dr. Dre, launched its "You Love Me" campaign in 2020. (credit: "Beats by Dr Dre" by Mike Mozart, JeepersMedia/flickr, CC BY 2.0)

LINK TO LEARNING

Beats by Dr. Dre

Beats is a leading manufacturer of audio products cofounded by Black rapper Dr. Dre. The two-minute commercial plays on the audio pun and challenges viewers to emotionally listen by asking the question "You love Black culture, but do you love me?"

Click to view content (https://openstax.org/books/principles-marketing/pages/8-4-marketing-to-hispanic-black-and-asian-consumers)

Asian Consumers

Asian cultures are steeped in rich traditions and customs. Asian consumers are very proud of their heritage, and at the same time, they identify well with the American culture. Asian people share this **cultural duality** characteristic with Hispanic people. Cultural duality is not the same thing as acculturation. Cultural duality happens when an individual's cultures overlap with each other and the person feels a sense of belonging to both simultaneously. Did you know that almost 50 percent of Asian consumers in the United States watch TV in both English and in an Asian language?[63] This helps them stay current with American culture while keeping connected with their native culture.

Shared societal values are a trait that influence people's behaviors. One of these is collectivism. Think about Hofstede's cultural dimensions, individualism versus collectivism in particular. Collectivism places more emphasis on group activities than on individual ones. Overall, Asian societies are collectivistic, though the degree of collectivism varies among the populations' countries of origin.[64] Cultural celebrations are also a factor linked to identity. Instacart, Target, Wells Fargo, and Toyota are just a few companies marketing to Asian consumers in the United States using traditional festivities like Diwali and Lunar New Year to appeal to the group's collectivism.

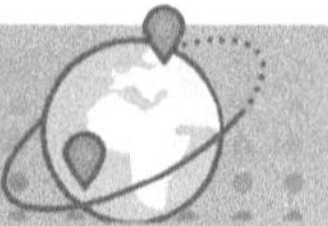

LINK TO LEARNING

Asian Celebrations

Two examples posted on social media platforms are Wells Fargo's Happy Lunar New Year on Instagram (https://openstax.org/r/wellsfargoinsta) and Toyota's Diwali tweet on Twitter (https://openstax.org/r/toyotastatus).

Marketing to Hispanic, Black, and Asian Consumers

As you have seen, marketing to each of these multicultural segments is unique. Marketers must do the research and understand the demographics, cultures, identities, and group characteristics of these targeted consumers. It is also equally important to recognize that none of these elements are static. They are dynamic and interact with one another.

Being successful with multicultural marketing, and ultimately with diversity marketing, includes many factors. Success also requires connecting with each consumer segment on a personal and intimate level. This inevitably means that marketers must recognize the similarities and differences between the cultural identities that shape daily life experiences in the United States.

In the upcoming decades, the meaning of the terms *minority* and *majority* segments are going to wane in significance. Groups that have been historically classified as the minority market are going to grow, while the group historically classified as the majority is going to shrink in size. This is setting the stage for a future of a "plurality nation," further emphasizing the importance of multicultural trends and diversity marketing.

Knowledge Check

It's time to check your knowledge on the concepts presented in this section. Refer to the Answer Key at the end of the book for feedback.

1. Which of the following is the largest segment of multicultural consumers in the United States?
    a. Asian population
    b. Black population
    c. Hispanic population
    d. Native American and Alaskan Native population

2. Which ethnic term can be used for a person from Puerto Rico or of Puerto Rican descent?
    a. Only Hispanic
    b. Both Hispanic and Latino/Latina
    c. Only Latino/Latina
    d. None of these terms are correct.

3. Acculturation is the process by which a person's family cultural patterns change because of direct and constant contact with _______.
    a. their home culture
    b. a different culture
    c. many cultures simultaneously
    d. a high degree of global travel

4. When it comes to cultural identity, which of the following do the overwhelming majority of Black people believe is a major contributor and attribute?
    a. Cultural duality and relationships
    b. Education and income level
    c. Immigration status and conventionality
    d. Race and community

5. Effectively marketing to Hispanic, Black, and Asian consumers requires _______ with each multicultural demographic and understanding _______.
    a. connecting; segmentation
    b. surveying; advertising
    c. using influencers; social media
    d. using culturally relevant idioms; fun advertising

8.5 Marketing to Sociodemographic Groups

Learning Outcomes

By the end of this section, you will be able to:
- **LO** 1 Define sociodemographic marketing.
- **LO** 2 Explain how to market to the LGBTQIA+ community.
- **LO** 3 Explain how to market based on generational differences.
- **LO** 4 Explain how to market to consumers with disabilities.
- **LO** 5 Describe how sociodemographic trends will impact future marketing.

Sociodemographic Marketing

As defined earlier in the chapter, sociodemographics is the combination of two distinct factors—social and demographic—within a given population. This combination results in a set of quantifiable variables for narrowing down customers in a large market. Social variables can be quite literally *anything* with which people identify. In other words, social variables are associated with identity. Because of that, they can include racial and ethnic identities too. Social variables are broad and can feel loosely defined. However, it is this unstructured nature that often provides important insights for marketers. Demographic variables, on the other hand, are more specific or have precise descriptions. These include things like gender, age or generation, religion, marital status, income, employment, education, political affiliation, disability, and more.

As you have already read, sociodemographic marketing is a subcategory of diversity marketing (refer back to Figure 8.4). It intentionally targets certain audiences with attractive advertising and promotions based on shared social and demographic variables. Overlaying these two factors has several worthwhile benefits for marketers. One of them, for instance, is that it makes it easier to detect market trends and shopping patterns based on a large number of consumers with variables in common. Such findings are indispensable for marketers to gauge the financial and emotional impact of their marketing efforts.

Another benefit is that sociodemographic marketing creates valuable opportunities for reaching historically underrepresented individuals or underserved communities. This outreach is significant because it demonstrates companies' commitments toward a more diverse and inclusive market. Sociodemographic marketing also enables marketers to adapt products, services, and messaging to be more effective for both businesses and consumers.

Marketing to the LGBTQIA+ Community

The LGBTQIA+ population is composed of consumers who express a diversity of gender identities, preferences, and sexual orientations. The acronym stands for lesbian, gay, bisexual, transgender, queer/questioning, intersex, and asexual. The plus sign (+) represents other sexual identities as well as allies who are not LGBTQIA+ members but support the community's cause. The acronym has evolved over the decades to become more inclusive and capture diverse relationships, expressions, and identities.

The LGBTQIA+ community in the United States is growing. In 2012, only 3.5 percent of Americans self-identified as LGBTQIA+. American analytics company Gallup shows this number increasing to 5.6 percent in 2020 (see Figure 8.18). Did you know that one in six adults in Generation Z (born between 1997 and 2012) identifies as LGBTQIA+?[65] This indicates a growth trend reaching toward 16 percent in the future as other generations age out.

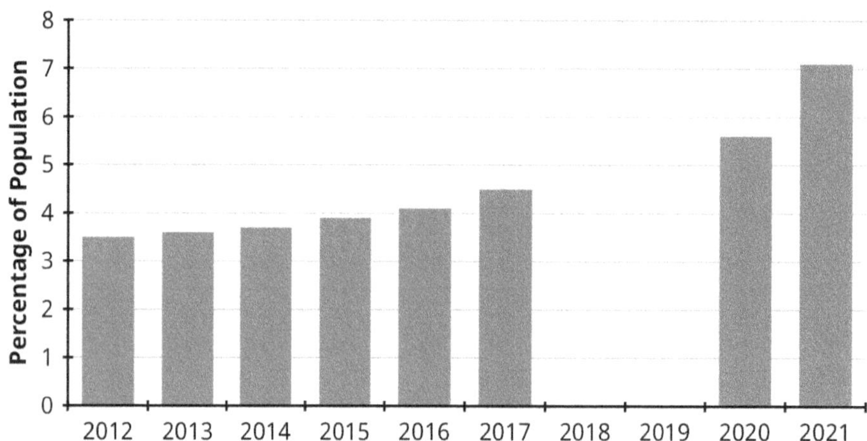

Figure 8.18 Americans' Self-Identification as LGBTQIA+ (data source: Gallup [survey data not available for 2018–2019]; attribution Copyright Rice University, OpenStax, under CC BY 4.0 license)

You might be wondering what is driving this growth. Some of it is attributed to greater confidence in both societal acceptance and in the ability to find support within the LGBTQIA+ community itself. Sociologists and psychologists have known for a long time that a sense of belonging, whether to a family or a social group, is essential for normal and optimal human functioning. Therefore, the growth of the LGBTQIA+ community is also partly the result of this human need to belong. Plus, it is driven by a political and sociological need to be represented and treated fairly as well.

For marketers, focusing on the societal experience around belonging (acceptance, welcoming, support, and inclusion) is key for reaching the growing number of LGBTQIA+ consumers. Global furniture giant IKEA (see Figure 8.19) understands this very well. In 2021, IKEA promoted the #ProgressIsMade campaign in the United States during the entire month of June. The campaign featured rainbow-themed products like carrying bags and an audio speaker cover. IKEA donated up to $50,000 in proceeds from these limited-edition products to LGBTQIA+ nonprofit organization GLSEN. In Canada, IKEA displayed at select stores 10 different love seats as concept art inspired by Pride flags to increase its support for inclusion during Pride month.

Figure 8.19 IKEA's #ProgressIsMade campaign in the United States focused on the societal experience of belonging for LGBTQ+ consumers. (credit: "IKEA" by Rob Olivera/flickr, CC BY 2.0)

LINK TO LEARNING

IKEA Loveseats

Learn more about the IKEA love seat collection and see the designs by reading these articles:

- Insider (https://openstax.org/r/ikeadesigned10loveseats)
- Newswire (https://openstax.org/r/representationwithloveseats)
- NBC News (https://openstax.org/r/ikeadebutspride)
- Muse by Clio (https://openstax.org/r/ikeamade10special)

What can marketers do to be more successful in advertising to LGBTQIA+ consumers? Consider the following steps. First, review the company's values and have an open and honest conversation with leadership about authentic support of the LGBTQIA+ community. After all, genuine care and inclusiveness are the base for all marketing efforts. Second, establish guidelines on how to speak with and about the LGBTQIA+ community. This means the words, tone, imagery, and core messaging of marketing communications. Third, find experts to provide advice and insights into the community. This reduces the possibility of unknowingly offending this consumer segment. Plus, using group members for brainstorming and evaluation is extremely helpful too. Fourth, test and verify that products, services, and messaging are perceived as designed.

Marketing to the Generations

Age is a frequently used demographic statistic for segmenting populations. Age is also expressed or compared in terms of generational groups. This approach enables marketers to capture a larger number of consumers by grouping them into defined categories.

You read earlier in the chapter about these categories: Silent Generation, baby boomers, Generation X, millennials, Generation Z, and Generation Alpha. Figure 8.20 shows these generations based on their percentage among the American population. Think about this. A member of Generation Alpha (people born between 2010 and 2025) is born every *nine seconds* in the United States. This generation is expected to account for 2 billion individuals worldwide by 2025![66] Grouping consumers into generational segments helps maximize marketing efforts and reach a larger portion of the total market.

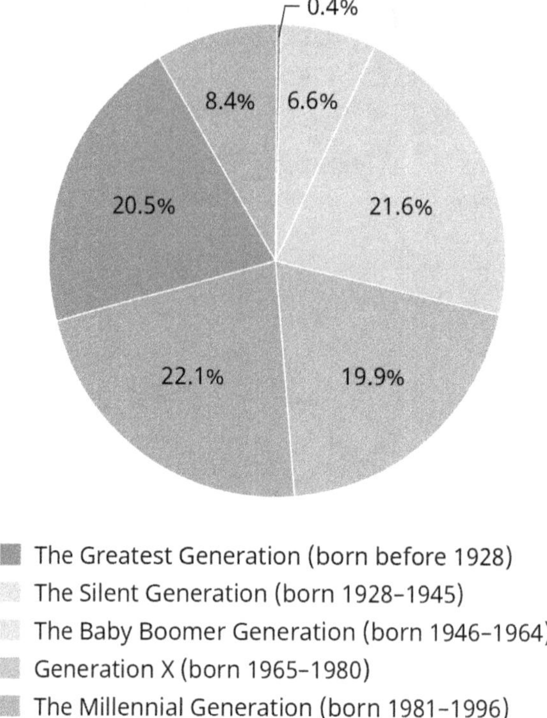

Figure 8.20 Distribution of Generations in the United States (data source: Statista; attribution: Copyright Rice University, OpenStax, under CC BY 4.0 license)

It is crucial for marketers to keep in mind that each generation has unique life experiences built on social, economic, and political dynamics associated with their formative years. These experiences influence each generation's views and values, which subsequently impact their behaviors as consumers. Let's consider Generation Z and Generation Alpha again. Members of both generations are highly technologically literate. They have also been directly impacted by the COVID-19 pandemic's aftermath in terms of remote learning and reduced face-to-face interactions. Consequently, this "lockdown generation" has spent more time engaged with social media and virtual environments. Marketers need to consider how such situations will influence these generations' shopping behaviors and consumption patterns.

There are many factors that can be combined with a generational view of consumers. One of the more useful for marketers to keep in mind is economic influence. Figure 8.21 shows the wealth distribution by generation in the United States as of 2020. This chart tells a significant story.

Until 2008, the Silent Generation and earlier generations controlled a relatively equal amount of wealth. Two primary factors gradually shrunk the amount of wealth of these consumers: natural mortality and the 2008 recession. Conversely, the wealth of baby boomers grew. In fact, many have said that the Boomer Generation is the wealthiest generation to have ever lived. Generation X's wealth started to grow in 2015, but the ability of this generation to build riches has slowed down compared to preceding generations. Millennials' wealth building appears to be even slower (see Figure 8.22).

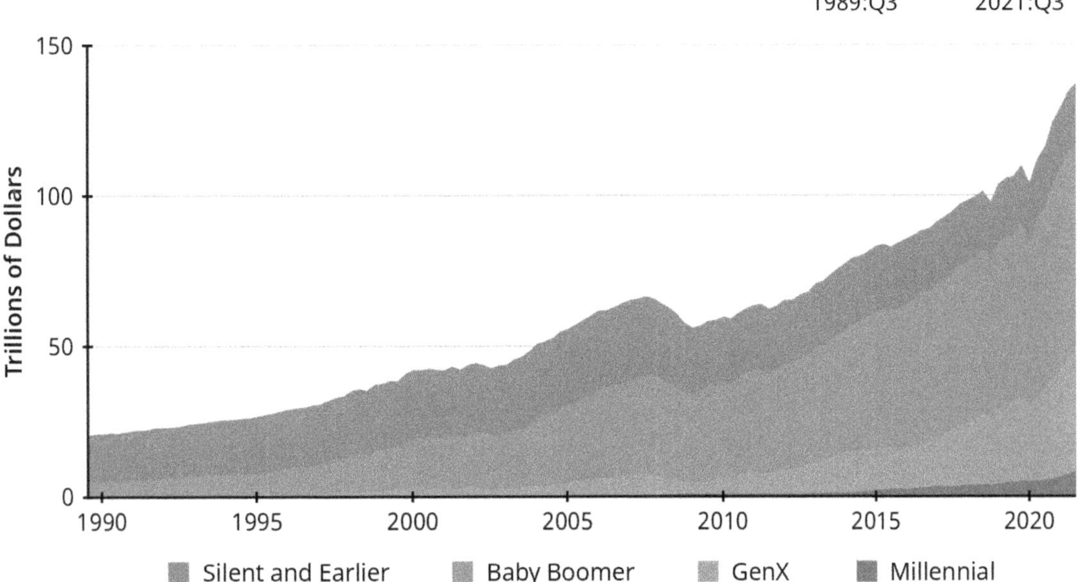

Figure 8.21 Wealth Distribution by Generation (data source: Board of Governors of the Federal Reserve System/federalreserve.gov, Survey of Consumer Finances and Financial Accounts; attribution: Copyright Rice University, OpenStax, under CC BY 4.0 license)

What does this mean? Wealth and income level play a role in people's spending decisions, so marketers need to understand how it is shaped by generational groups. Here are some steps to consider to be more successful in advertising to consumers based on their generations. First, use deeper and more extensive combinations of sociodemographic variables. Grouping by generation alone is likely not enough. Adding another variable such as income, education, or social markers may prove useful. Second, use focus groups and individuals who fit the target group to provide direct input and ideas. Third, consider adapting the marketing communication to fit the norms of each generation. Fourth, test and verify that products, services, and messaging are perceived as designed.

Marketing to Consumers with Disabilities

Americans with disabilities make up a much larger segment of the market than you might realize. There are approximately 61 million Americans with disabilities. That number is over 18 percent of the total population of the United States. When the word *disability* is used, many people usually visualize a mobility difficulty like having trouble walking or climbing stairs. However, as seen in Figure 8.22, functional mobility makes up less than a third of the different types of disabilities. Other forms include cognitive or neurological, autonomous living, and sensory related. This makes consumers with disabilities a very diverse group too.

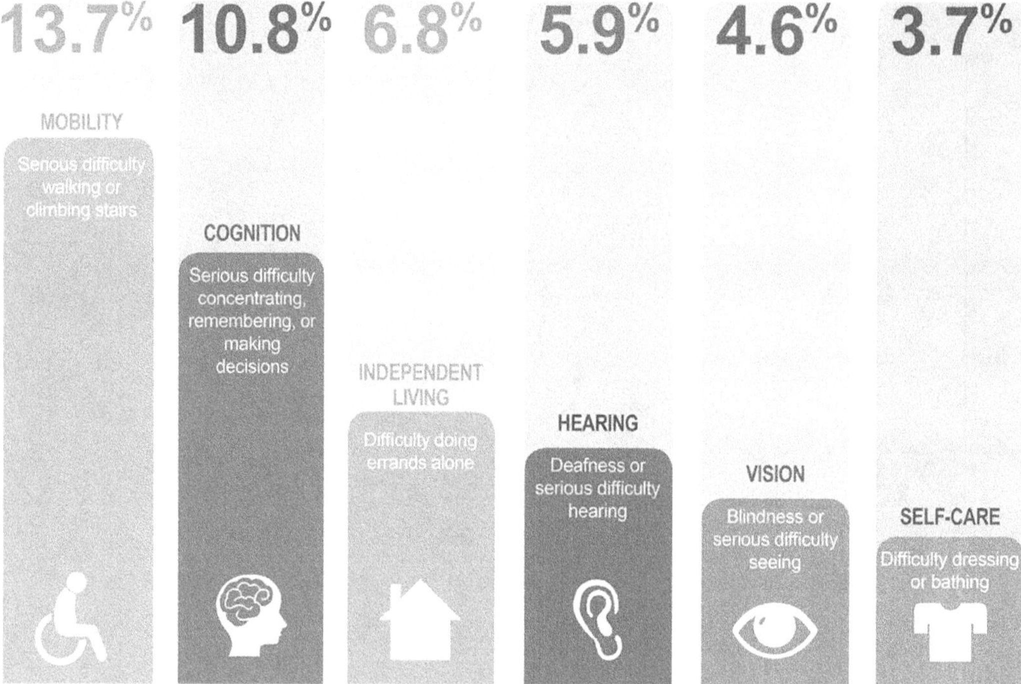

Figure 8.22 Percentage of Adults with a Functional Disability (credit: "Percentage of adults with functional disabilities" by Centers for Disease and Control and Prevention/CDC.gov, Public Domain)

Disability is more frequent in adults over the age of 65 and in women. Among racial and ethnic segments, it is more common in non-Hispanic, Native American, and Alaskan Native people. Adults living with a disability are also more likely to be obese, smoke, have heart disease, and have diabetes.[67] While disabilities are very often important and impactful aspects of people's lives, people with disabilities have many defining characteristics, goals, needs, and identities.

How can marketers best reach consumers with disabilities? By using an approach that ensures the company's efforts express humanity, authenticity, and inclusivity. Let's look at a couple of examples. In January 2019, a picture from a bridal boutique's window display went viral due to its powerful inclusivity message. The display showed a mannequin in a wheelchair dressed in a wedding gown. In February 2022, Hispanic model Sofia Jirau made history as the first person with Down syndrome to become a model for Victoria's Secret. These examples demonstrate that people with disabilities are not only part of our social fabric but also are an integral part of the overall market.

Other suggestions for marketers consist of ensuring that disabilities are properly represented. This means consulting or hiring individuals who have a disability rather than using actors or models who do not. Marketers also need to keep in mind how disabilities affect marketing communications. In other words, think about closed captioning on videos or the use of alternative text on images for websites. The types of disabilities are diverse, so marketing initiatives have to be diverse as well. That is what makes sociodemographic marketing a subset of diversity marketing.

Developing Sociodemographic Trends and Their Future Impact

Discovering sociodemographic trends takes an enormous amount of study. To do an effective job, marketing researchers are constantly working with a multitude of variables. They set parameters, collect data, analyze it, and come up with ideas based on results. This work is done repeatedly over time. It is precisely the extended time frame that enables marketing researchers to see market patterns surface. Let's check out some current trends that will have a future impact for companies and marketers in general.

Population Stagnation

The population has been growing around the world at historically unprecedented rates for many years now.

Yet, there are several sources claiming that it will decline globally around the middle of the 21st century.[68] The United States has already been in a relatively steady population growth decline—or population stagnation—according to trends from the US Census Bureau. In fact, the American growth rate has slowed to its lowest point in over 120 years. If this trend continues, the United States will see its first net population decrease in the next couple of years.[69]

Marketers need to consider the sociodemographic factors that are contributing to this trend: births, deaths, and international migration. No doubt COVID-19 has impacted the death rate, which was already being fueled by the growth deceleration from years earlier. Figure 8.23 illustrates the population changes in the United States through 2021 based on some of these factors. The rapid percent change in 2020 and 2021 is probably due to the pandemic's effect.

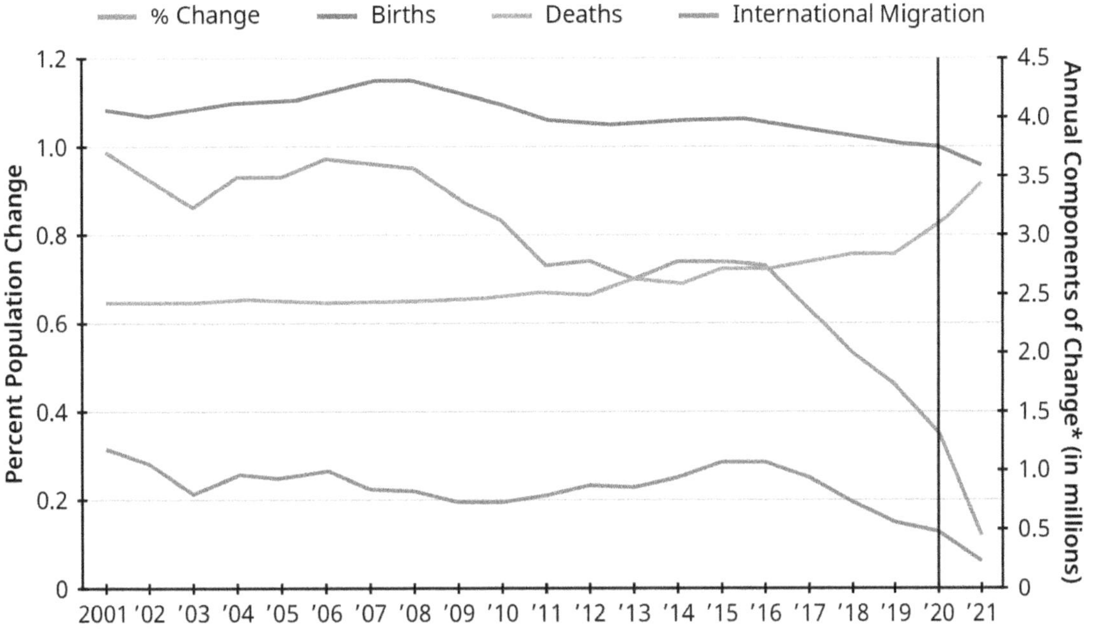

Figure 8.23 Population Change and the Components of Change: 2001–2021 (data source: United States Census Bureau/census.gov; attribution: Copyright Rice University, OpenStax, under CC BY 4.0 license)

Consumer Spending Dominated by Baby Boomers

While this is not a new trend, it is certainly one that will continue through the 2030s as the baby boomer population ages out. The American Association for Retired Persons (AARP) reports that American workers over 65 years of age have a median income of $78,000 per year, while workers under age 65 have a median income that is only $55,000.[70] Keep in mind that this statistic is about individuals who are actively working, meaning not yet retired. Couple it with the wealth accumulation information you read about earlier. The baby boomer population certainly exerts outsized economic and purchasing influence, making this an important current and future market segment.

Understanding sociodemographic trends such as population growth and decline as well as market consumption based on generational groups is crucial for marketers to create relevant and effective marketing campaigns in the growing age of marketplace diversity.

Knowledge Check

It's time to check your knowledge on the concepts presented in this section. Refer to the Answer Key at the end of the book for feedback.

1. Sociodemographic marketing is a subcategory of diversity marketing, and it targets audiences based on
   ________.

   a.   psychological distinguishing factors
   b.   political affiliation
   c.   geographical and governmental boundaries
   d.   shared social and demographic variables

2. Which of the following is a key marketing approach for reaching the LGBTQIA+ audience?
   a.   Focus on the societal experience around belonging.
   b.   Build empirical value differences in products and services.
   c.   Compare mainstream market adoption levels for new technology.
   d.   Use a personal argument as a persuasive purchasing strategy.

3. Which of the following is a useful step to improve a marketer's ability to reach a generational target audience?
   a.   Use deeper and more extensive combinations of sociodemographic variables.
   b.   Add variables such as income, education, or social markers.
   c.   Use focus groups to provide direct input and deeper insights and ideas.
   d.   All of these are useful steps.

4. When marketing specifically to consumers with disabilities, you can express inclusivity in advertising by using _______.
   a.   all individuals, even those who do not have a disability
   b.   impersonal and abstract images
   c.   individuals who have a disability
   d.   only nonvisual advertising media

5. Which of the following is an emerging sociodemographic trend that will impact future marketing?
   a.   Rapid population growth in the United States
   b.   Consumer spending dominated by baby boomers
   c.   Redistribution of economic wealth
   d.   Hemispherical global migration caused by global warming

8.6 | Ethical Issues in Diversity Marketing

Learning Outcomes

By the end of this section, you will be able to:

LO 1 Identify the ethical issues related to diversity marketing.
LO 2 Discuss how to address different consumer values to reduce issues in marketing.

Ethical Considerations in Marketing

The issues related to business ethics reside within society's definitions and standards. Like with many topics, what is considered ethical business behavior or an accepted practice today can change tomorrow based on context. In other words, business ethics do not remain fixed. Ethical standards transform and adapt in conjunction with changes in the business environment.

Consider the following scenario. Let's say you are visiting the doctor for your annual checkup. How would you feel if the doctor walked into the exam room smoking a cigarette? Most people would have a negative reaction to this. In most places in the United States, it is against city ordinances to smoke indoors in public places unless it is a designated smoking area. These ordinances are enforced because the government recognizes that smoking is a health hazard. If your doctor walked into the exam room with a cigarette, it would pose several ethical concerns. However, did you know that until the 1950s, doctors approved of smoking and even appeared in cigarette ads? By the mid-1960s, the medical field developed clarity around the hazards of smoking, and norms were changed in society and in advertising. Figure 8.24 shows an advertisement making this point.

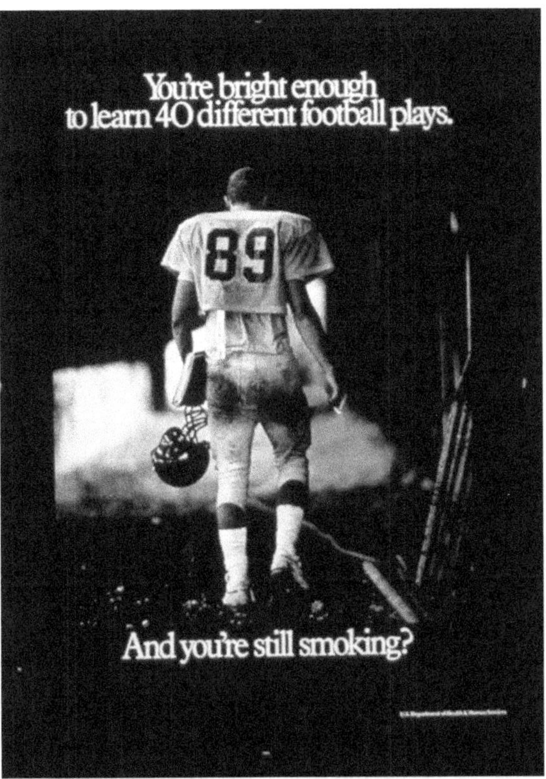

Figure 8.24 Evolving ethical standards impact marketing campaigns by requiring companies to transform their messages to meet new societal norms, as exemplified by modern anti-smoking advertisements. (credit: "You're Bright Enough to Learn 40 Different Football Plays" by NIH National Library of Medicine, CDC/nlm.nih.gov, Public Domain 1.0)

Where do business ethics come from? Ethics originate from the need and desire to promote both fair and equitable competition in the market. Ethics are supported by legislation such as the Sherman Antitrust Act from the US Department of Justice. Ethical considerations in diversity marketing have a similar background. They are linked to companies' fair and equitable outreach and representation of diverse audiences in the market. These include multicultural and sociodemographic consumer segments in particular.

Business ethics shape companies' and employees' work behaviors, corporate activities, and marketing efforts. This implies that ethics are inseparable from a company's brand. Why? Because a brand is essentially what a business stands for and what it represents. Consumers associate certain characteristics and traits with a company's brand. These expectations, in turn, influence purchasing actions. For this reason, marketers need to take great care in creating an accurate reflection of the company's ethics that are also culturally and socially sound.

Ethics are often contextual, so it is important to recognize that values and behaviors vary by culture, identity, and other demographic variables. This means it is imperative to truly understand targeted segments as thoroughly as possible. It is common for marketers to research things like buying patterns, consumption sentiment, desired features, and media efficacy. However, to succeed in a diverse marketplace, research must extend deeper. It needs to be ethically based on target segments' cultural sensitivities and social issues. Economic fairness, political viewpoints, differences in technological access, legal protections, and environmental risks should also be considered in ethical marketing research.

Ethical Issues in Diversity Marketing

One of marketing's primary functions is to reflect an organization's business ethics and values to the marketplace and to consumers. This must be done in an active and intentional manner. Marketers have a responsibility to ensure that efforts and communications are honest, balanced, and authentic to the company and to the marketing profession. Creating awareness of cultural and social issues that impact ethical practices is also a key function of diversity marketing.

Cultural and Social Values

How messages are perceived and decoded in advertising is the most publicly visible representation of a company's ethics, values, and overall business culture. Marketers need to ensure that advertising campaigns do not reinforce harmful stereotypes and unconscious biases. This is not easy to do because, after all, cultural and social beliefs are deeply seated. This explains why some biases are unconscious.

Stereotypes and unconscious biases are evident in every facet of life. In fact, everybody has them. Cultural stereotypes and social biases are common in advertising. Let's explore some situations. Asian people share many cultural values and characteristics. As you have read, the Asian population in the United States is comprised of 22 different countries of origin. Red is considered a lucky color by most Asian people. When advertising to Chinese consumers, it is typical to see the color red used prominently. However, assuming that all Asian consumers feel the same about this color is stereotyping. For Japanese people, green symbolizes youth and vital energy; yellow is associated with vitality and light for Korean people.[71]

You may have seen ads that suggest that only boys or men play football or maybe that only girls and women cook. These types of ads perpetuate gender stereotypes. That's why campaigns like Procter & Gamble's groundbreaking 2014 "Like a Girl" campaign challenged people's stereotypes with its ads about what it means to do things as a female. Here is yet another example. Radio advertisers could ignore baby boomers in favor of millennials and Generation Z consumers. This bias is driven by the incorrect assumption that baby boomers are not active radio listeners, which is not true. Stereotypes and biases can cost companies a lot of money in negative publicity and lost opportunities. From an ethical perspective, biases can have unintended discriminatory results among diverse consumer segments.

Diversity Representation

Diversity marketing is about reaching a larger portion of the total market by including diverse population segments such as multicultural and sociodemographic audiences. Representation matters for a growing number of consumers. While trying to be inclusive, marketers need to steer clear of tokenism. **Tokenism** happens when an individual from either a minority group or an underrepresented community is included in ads or marketing communications to prevent criticism. Tokenism is a symbolic act that gives the appearance of representation. However, it is not a genuine desire to portray consumer diversity.

When it comes to ethical considerations such as advertisements' diversity balance, the focus is on ensuring positive associations. This inclusive balance is not limited to just people. It also applies to terms, phrases, and other forms of communication. For instance, the misuse of words or incorrect translations can inadvertently convey a lack of sensitivity to multicultural or sociodemographic consumers. Marketers may offend without intending to do so. As an example, as you read earlier in the chapter, some terms can be disliked by ethnic consumers.

Marketers need to intentionally consider every characteristic, factor, and set of values that shape diversity and inclusivity. These need to be weighed against the perceptions of each consumer segment. Doing a thorough job of research, design, and review goes a long way to ensuring a fair and equitable representation of all consumer segments.

COMPANIES WITH A CONSCIENCE

Culturally Sensitive and Socially Inclusive Marketing

Multinational industry leaders like Coca-Cola, Google, Adidas, Unilever, AT&T, Marriott International, and Microsoft are just a few of the companies that, like P&G, are focusing their marketing efforts on being more culturally sensitive and socially inclusive. Even niche players, partnerships, and private companies such as Bumble, Fenty Beauty, and ThirdLove are also championing diversity as a core value through equal cultural and sociodemographic representation rather than just chasing a trend in marketing.[72]

Consider Coca-Cola's long history of advertisements and promotions, for example. In the early 1970s, Coca Cola released the "Hilltop" commercial (also known as "I'd Like to Buy the World a Coke"), which showed people from different races and cultures bonding over the beverage. In 2011, the company launched the groundbreaking campaign "Share a Coke" in Australia to connect with consumers in a personal way while influencing product purchases. The campaign went viral and became a global success.[73]

For the 2014 Super Bowl and the Winter Olympics in Sochi, Russia, Coca-Cola launched the "America Is Beautiful" campaign.[74] Recognizing the growth of multicultural consumers in the United States, the campaign's commercial featured seven young bilingual American women singing in different languages. It also showed culturally diverse consumers from all walks of life. Although the campaign was subject to severe criticism and sparked outrage and boycotts by some people, Coca-Cola was applauded by others for its commitment to a more inclusive marketing communication. That is what diversity marketing is all about.

Chapter Summary

Marketing reflects an organization's ethics and values as it communicates, especially with current and prospective customers. Marketers have learned to adjust over time to changes in the marketplace, especially as technology, the environment, politics, culture, and demographics have evolved and altered customer needs, wants, and demands. This chapter introduces concepts primarily concerned with culture and diversity and the need for businesses to focus more on customer individuality than on customer commonality. Research shows that companies that build emotional ties through diversity generate more revenue, increase stock price performance, and enhance brand perceptions.

Marketers must be constantly aware of demographic trends, especially in multicultural identities, generational differences, consumers with disabilities, and changes in spending. Ethics, too, transform and adapt to the business environment. Ethical norms not only promote fair and equitable competition, they also set standards for brand stewardship and social responsibility.

Finally, the focus of many successful marketers today is to rely on marketing intelligence to guide them toward establishing and maintaining positive customer associations across population characteristics.

Key Terms

acculturation   the process by which a person's family cultural patterns change because of direct and constant contact with a different culture

adaptation   the process of adjusting a company's work efforts, goods, or services in response to specific needs, tastes, or expectations—whether real or perceived—from different groups of consumers

Asian population   third largest multicultural group in the United States; made up of 22 different subethnicities from the Asian continent, Hawaii, and islands of the Pacific; can belong to a single race or mixed races

Black population   second largest multicultural group in the United States; made up of three different subethnicities: single race, Black Hispanic, or Black mixed with another race (White or Native American)

company centric   a company's approach to focusing decisions and execution from the perspective of the organization rather than the customers

consumers with disabilities   sociodemographic group living with some type of disability related to mobility, learning, intellectual, or other types of functions; a very diverse group because disabilities span cultural, social, and demographic factors

cultural duality   characteristic of a multicultural individual for whom cultures overlap with each other and the person feels a sense of belonging to both at the same time

cultural identity   how a person identifies with a given culture, ethnicity, or social group, which instills a sense of belonging that influences personal thinking and actions

culture   objective and subjective elements like social norms, beliefs, behaviors, accomplishments, customs, arts, language, foods, and skills that characterize a particular group of individuals' way of life

customer centric   a company's focus on putting targeted customers first regarding any decisions about its goods, services, or experiences to create satisfaction and strengthen loyalty

diversity marketing   a strategic approach that involves identifying different subsegments of the population—*based on shared cultural and sociodemographic characteristics*—and creating intentional marketing efforts to connect with these consumer groups

diversity marketing intelligence (DMiQ)   the capability of identifying, accepting, and valuing the diverseness of consumers within a market and using this knowledge to tailor the marketing mix accordingly

generational population   sociodemographic category based on birth year clusters that includes Lost Generation (1883–1900), Greatest Generation (1901–1927), Traditionalist/Silent Generation (1928–1945), baby boomers (1946–1964), Generation X (1965–1980), millennials/Generation Y (1981–1996), Zoomers/Generation Z (1997–2009), and Generation Alpha (2010–2024)

Hispanic population   largest multicultural group in the United States; made up of diverse subethnicities and races originating from 20 different Spanish-speaking countries in North America, Central America, the Caribbean, South America, and Europe

LGBTQIA+ population   community composed of individuals who express a diversity of genders, preferences, and sexual orientations that include lesbian, gay, bisexual, transsexual, queer/questioning, intersex, asexual, and other sexual identities

marginalized consumers   populations of consumers that have been pushed to the margins of society and are often excluded in mainstream advertising

marketing mix   the four key elements—product, price, place, and promotion—that shape the development and execution of marketing objectives to reach a target market

multicultural identity   having an affinity with multiple racial or ethnic groups that a person has been exposed to and self-categorizing as being part of more than one of them

multicultural marketing   a subcategory of diversity marketing aimed at intentionally targeting audiences based on different racial, ethnic, and cultural identities and backgrounds

Native American, Alaska Native population   multicultural group of individuals of a single race and mixed races who are native to the United States and its territories including American Indians, Alaska Natives, Native Hawaiians, and American Samoans

sociodemographic marketing   a subcategory of diversity marketing aimed at intentionally targeting audiences based on shared social and demographic characteristics such as gender and sexual orientation, age or generation, family structure, religion, education, income level, and disability

sociodemographics   the combination of social and demographic factors that characterize specific consumer groups in the market

socioeconomically disadvantaged population   disadvantaged community that lacks social resources and infrastructure to reduce poverty; members tend to be in low-income households, experience financial insecurity, and have less access to education

standardization   the process of purposefully applying identical or consistent guidelines to goods or services to achieve uniformity

tokenism   the practice of including an individual from either a minority group or an underrepresented community in marketing efforts simply as a symbol

Applied Marketing Knowledge: Discussion Questions

1. The Special Olympics offers businesses the opportunity to sponsor local, regional, national, and international events. Using what you have learned from this chapter, list three reasons why companies such as Procter & Gamble, Toyota, Coca-Cola, United Airlines, Microsoft, and the NFL would choose to spend millions of marketing dollars to partner with Special Olympics.

2. The United States is moving swiftly to a "plurality nation" status, according to the US Census Bureau. Identify two major multicultural trends that have and will continue to impact market segmentation.

3. Student Services on your campus likely has a diversity and inclusion staff that encourages an expansive range of cultural perspectives, experiences, voices, and methods for taking action on campus. How does your college or university market diversity and inclusion services to prospective students through its website?

4. Market fragmentation is the concept that all markets are increasingly diverse and comprised of smaller segments of consumers that respond differently to marketing messages. Media, too, has splintered, and in addition to having access to information provided by newspapers, magazines, TV, and radio, consumers now have access to millions of informational sources. However, severe fragmentation of both consumers and ways to communicate with them poses many challenges in marketing efficiency and branding. Why?

5. DMiQ reveals that baby boomers offer the best marketing opportunities for firms. Which sociodemographic group offers the next best marketing opportunity by sheer size of the segment?

Critical Thinking Exercises

1. Like Nike's marketing adaptation with "Nike by You," other retailers offer customers individualized products. For instance, you can design your own jeans (https://openstax.org/r/makeyourownjeans) online. Brainstorm five other products that may lend themselves to customized offerings that express cultural or sociodemographic differences.

2. Diversity marketing intelligence (DMiQ) refers to the capability of identifying, accepting, and valuing the diversity of consumers within a market and using this knowledge to tailor the marketing mix accordingly. Thus, capturing insights about consumers' heritage, experience, lifestyle, beliefs, or living situations helps explain the nuances and idiosyncrasies associated with diversity. These insights helped identify that the LGBTQIA+ community generally spends more money online and at retail stores. Additionally, the research firm Out Now estimates the LGBTQIA+ community spends more than $211 billion on travel. How can the travel industry employ DMiQ to derive more value from this group that enjoys travel and is willing to pay for it?

3. Research has shown that members of the baby boomer generation possess the most wealth in the United States and are responsible for 70 percent of annual spending on prescriptions and medical supplies. Are there any ethical considerations in developing marketing messages to this large and older segment of society that doesn't want to be pigeonholed as "elderly"?

Building Your Personal Brand

Students who are building their résumés have always been encouraged to set themselves apart from the competition for internships, jobs, and volunteer experiences. In other words, focus on what makes you stand out from other job seekers. If you are bilingual, why not prepare your résumé, blog, or LinkedIn profile in both languages? Are you especially knowledgeable in a particular area such as designing alternate reality games? Do you collect comic books or baseball trading cards? All of these interests, collections, and abilities not only have the potential to create a dialogue with potential employers, but they also highlight your heritage, lifestyle, or singularity to your advantage.

What Do Marketers Do?

Relatively few recent marketing graduates think about entering the nonprofit arena. Some of the key positions in nonprofits include marketing director, event coordinator, director of development, communications specialist, and volunteer coordinator.

There are many nonprofit organizations operating in the United States that strive to serve multicultural groups and sociodemographic communities. Some have purposeful objectives like equitable rights and inclusivity. Some national examples include Advancement Project, American Civil Liberties Union (ACLU), Asian Americans Advancing Justice (AAJC), Equal Justice Initiative (EJI), Human Rights Campaign Foundation, League of United Latin American Citizens (LULAC), National Association for the Advancement of Colored People (NAACP), National Immigration Law Center, National Organization on Disability, National Urban League, Prospanica, The Asian American Foundation (TAAF), The PhD Project, and The Trevor Project.

Contact a local nonprofit organization and interview an employee filling one of the above-mentioned roles. Questions may include:

- What drew you to this organization?
- What is its mission?
- What groups or communities does it serve?
- Does the position require specific training?
- How many volunteers do you have, and what are their responsibilities and time commitments?

Finally, consider whether volunteering for this organization may fulfill you, add to your résumé, and/or bring you in contact with future employees, colleagues, and friends.

 ## Closing Company Case

Lineout

If 50 is the new 30, most 50-year-olds want to look 30. Consumers in their twenties want to look like their favorite Hollywood star or Instagram influencer. New methods, procedures, and products are flooding the market to appeal to the market demand for better skin, reduced facial wrinkles, and improved appearance. A big part of the market for skin care products is dermal fillers. According to Fortune Business Insights, the global dermal fillers market is projected to grow from $3.07 billion in 2021 to $6.28 billion in 2028 at a compound annual growth rate (CAGR) of 10.8 percent in the forecast period, 2021–2028.[75]

Noninvasive and minimally invasive procedures for smoother and younger-looking skin are rising in popularity among many different demographic groups. Through facial fillers or digitally enhanced photographs, many people are looking to improve their look. While most consumers may not have the money or the willingness to undergo surgical cosmetic procedures, many are very willing to take an alternate route—receive an injection that may last 3, 6, or 12 months and provide the appearance of younger-looking, smoother, line-free skin.[76]

Looking to break into the market of dermal fillers and provide excellence in the injection experience and outcome, Lineout jumped into the market. The company didn't want to be a typical medical spa with a wide breadth of services. Instead, it was looking to be a boutique provider of an in-demand service done with excellence and provided through a vast network of boutique locations nationwide.

Like the nail salon that only does nails, Lineout is a boutique that focuses only on facial fillers. The boutique experience with niche specialization was lacking in the industry. To provide facial injections with precision and only do the best for its clients, Lineout had a business model that could break into the market and be replicated throughout the country.

While most medical spas market primarily to middle-aged women, Lineout realized the market was much bigger and much more diverse than most medical spas recognized. Consumers of various ages, genders, and ethnicities were seeking facial fillers. Many of the medical spas were set up to cater to the female market. With feminine-sounding names, pink pastels, and soft floral graphics, the marketing was all focused toward this one demographic.

Lineout purposefully structured its business to meet the needs of a more diverse market. With simple graphics, a bright color palette, and marketing promotion through various channels, Lineout was able to tap a broader market.

The male audience skewed older.[77] To meet the needs of men who were wanting facial fillers, Lineout promotions included male-themed blogs, promotions through barbershops, and digital advertising with business and sports teams. For men "in the know," *lineout* is a rugby term. Rugged men saw Lineout as a product for them as they stepped into the facial filler's market.

On the opposite spectrum, young women had much different needs for facial fillers. Younger women primarily wanted lips that looked like the Kardashians and "line"-free foreheads, similar to what they were seeing from favorite celebrities and Instagram influencers. Media choices for women in their late teens and early twenties were primarily focused on TikTok and Instagram along with some select YouTube channels and reality shows. Lineout was able to connect with this audience by targeting messaging specific to the bigger, beautiful lip craze.

And finally, the biggest and most obvious market was middle-aged women who made facial fillers part of their skin care. Getting facial fillers for this demographic was as regular as a teeth cleaning or appointment with a hairstylist. Without hesitation, this market signed up for regular appointments and memberships that provided discounts for frequent and regularly scheduled sessions.

Lineout counted this demographic as its bread and butter. Demand from this market segment is highest, and this consumer group is also the most discerning. Without all the traditional services offered by medical spas, Lineout had to ensure that the level of skill and the overall results were superior to other services in the market. To reach this market, Lineout created specific blogs to address the stated concerns and needs. Lineout used Facebook and select digital channels to court the older women seeking facial filler services.

While the marketing for each demographic is a bit different, the services and the experience are similar for each of the company's market segments. Men want specific things from their facial fillers, young women want something different, and middle-aged women are even more precise. Lineout provides for each diverse need while maintaining its niche focus of only doing facial fillers.

Learn more about the company from the Lineout website (https://openstax.org/r/lineoutaesthetics) and Instagram feed (https://openstax.org/r/instagramlineoutaesthetics).

Case Questions

1. How does Lineout adapt its marketing for each of the diverse markets it serves?

2. The trend in noninvasive cosmetic procedures grows every year. What are some of the factors that have impacted the demand for facial fillers?

3. What are the factors Lineout is considering when looking at how it changes its marketing to meet the needs of its different consumer markets?

4. The various consumer groups Lineout is serving have different and unique concerns. What are some of the factors that have created the concerns?

References

1.   Procter & Gamble, *A Common Goal Drives Our Aspirations: P&G and the Hispanic Community*, n.d., https://www.pg.com/images/company/who_we_are/diversity/multi/Hispanic%20Corporate%20Brochure%20-%20English.pdf.

2.   OWN, "OWN and P&G Present: Widen the Screen—A Fuller View of Black Life," May 20, 2021, YouTube video, 1:06, https://youtu.be/J11Vfgha6uc.

3.   Jack Myers, "P&G's Marc Pritchard Sets Diversity Priorities and Goals for Ad Community," MediaVillage, October 6, 2021, https://www.mediavillage.com/article/pgs-marc-pritchard-sets-diversity-priorities-and-goals-for-ad-community/.

4.   Jason Nazar, "13 Leadership Lessons from Zoom Founder and CEO Eric Yuan," *Entrepreneur*, April 21, 2021, https://www.entrepreneur.com/article/368550.

5.   Masaaki Kotabe and Kristiaan Helsen, *Global Marketing Management*, 8th ed. (Hoboken, NJ: Wiley, 2020), 252.

6.   Helen Eboh Cletus et al., "Prospects and Challenges of Workplace Diversity in Modern Day Organizations: A Critical Review," *Holistica* 9, no. 2 (August 2018): 35–52, https://doi.org/10.2478/hjbpa-2018-0011.

7.   Sonia Thompson, "Data Shows Consumers Want Diversity in Marketing: Why Many Brands Struggle to Get It Right and How to Fix," *Forbes*, February 5, 2020, https://www.forbes.com/sites/soniathompson/2020/02/05/data-shows-consumers-want-diversity-in-marketing-why-many-brands-struggle-to-get-it-right-and-how-to-fix/.

8.   Shelby Jordan, "Why Is Diversity Marketing Important?," Top Design Firms, November 11, 2020, https://topdesignfirms.com/web-design/blog/diversity-marketing.

9.   Robert Williams, "Study: Diversity in Ads Correlates to Gains in Revenue, Brand Perception," Marketing Dive, Industry Dive, October 2, 2019, https://www.marketingdive.com/news/study-diversity-in-ads-correlates-to-gains-in-revenue-brand-perception/564153/.

10.   "The Heat™ Test: Measuring DEI Effectiveness in Advertising," Deloitte Digital, Deloitte, last modified August 12, 2022, https://www.deloittedigital.com/us/en/offerings/customer-led-marketing/advertising--marketing-and-commerce/heat-test.html.

11.   Louis Baragona, "Fans Are Furious after Tarte Unveiled Its New Foundations That Cater Almost Entirely to White People," Insider, January 18, 2018, https://www.insider.com/tarte-cosmetics-shape-tape-foundation-range-2018-1.

12. Alexander Smith, "Pepsi Pulls Controversial Kendall Jenner Ad after Outcry," NBC News, NBC Universal, April 5, 2017, https://www.nbcnews.com/news/nbcblk/pepsi-ad-kendall-jenner-echoes-black-lives-matter-sparks-anger-n742811.

13. Char Adams, "How Many Millions Could Pepsi's Pulled Kendall Jenner Ad Cost the Company?," *Essence*, updated October 26, 2020, https://www.essence.com/culture/kendall-jenner-pepsi-commercial-company-cost/.

14. Abby Budiman, "Americans Are More Positive about the Long-Term Rise in US Racial and Ethnic Diversity Than in 2016," Pew Research Center, October 1, 2020, https://www.pewresearch.org/fact-tank/2020/10/01/americans-are-more-positive-about-the-long-term-rise-in-u-s-racial-and-ethnic-diversity-than-in-2016/.

15. Andre Anugerah Pekerti and David Clinton Thomas, "n-Culturals: Modeling the Multicultural Identity," *Cross Cultural & Strategic Management* 23, no. 1 (2016): 101–127, https://doi.org/10.1108/CCSM-06-2014-0063.

16. Eva Kipnis et al., "Consumer Multicultural Identity Affiliation: Reassessing Identity Segmentation in Multicultural Markets," *Journal of Business Research* 98 (May 2019): 126–141, https://doi.org/10.1016/j.jbusres.2018.11.056.

17. Canadiuga Wine Company, "Amendment No. 2 to Form S-3 Registration Statement under the Securities Act of 1933," All SEC Filings, Constellation Brands, November 8, 1994, https://ir.cbrands.com/sec-filings/all-sec-filings?form_type=&year=1994##document-2239-0000950131-94-001692-2.

18. Alexia Elejalde-Ruiz, "Chicago, Long a Miller Stronghold, Has a New Top-Selling Beer: Modelo Especial Captures the City's Sales Crown," *Chicago Tribune*, September 5, 2019, https://www.chicagotribune.com/business/ct-biz-modelo-especial-growth-chicago-20190905-dq3xaw3npzdendkjsgtteyzvsy-story.html.

19. Annette Flanagin, Tracy Frey, and Stacy L. Christiansen, "Updated Guidance on the Reporting of Race and Ethnicity in Medical and Science Journals," *JAMA* 326, no. 7 (August 17, 2021): 621–627, https://doi.org/10.1001/jama.2021.13304.

20. Claritas, *The 2021 Hispanic Market Report: The New American Mainstream*, 2021, https://www2.claritas.com/2021-Hispanic-Market-Report-Website.

21. Claritas, "Claritas Projects Hispanic Consumers Will Account for 67% of Total US Population Growth in the Next Five Years," GlobeNewswire, September 20, 2021, https://www.globenewswire.com/en/news-release/2021/09/20/2299985/0/en/Claritas-Projects-Hispanic-Consumers-Will-Account-for-67-of-Total-U-S-Population-Growth-in-the-Next-Five-Years.html.

22. Christine Tamir, "The Growing Diversity of Black America," Pew Research Center, March 25, 2021, https://www.pewresearch.org/social-trends/2021/03/25/the-growing-diversity-of-black-america/.

23. Abby Budiman and Neil G. Ruiz, "Asian Americans Are the Fastest-Growing Racial or Ethnic Group in the US," Pew Research Center, April 9, 2021, https://www.pewresearch.org/fact-tank/2021/04/09/asian-americans-are-the-fastest-growing-racial-or-ethnic-group-in-the-u-s/.

24. Abby Budiman and Neil G. Ruiz, "Key facts about Asian Americans, a Diverse and Growing Population," Pew Research Center, April 29, 2021, https://www.pewresearch.org/fact-tank/2021/04/29/key-facts-about-asian-americans/.

25. Tim Henderson, "Census Prompts Push for More Indigenous School Lessons," *Stateline* (blog), The Pew Charitable Trusts, October 19, 2021, https://www.pewtrusts.org/en/research-and-analysis/blogs/stateline/2021/10/19/census-prompts-push-for-more-indigenous-school-lessons.

26. Victoria Petrock, "Consumers Expect Brands to Be Inclusive," Insider Intelligence, November 25, 2020, https://www.emarketer.com/content/consumers-expect-brands-inclusive.

27. Jeffrey M. Jones, "LGBT Identification Rises to 5.6% in Latest US Estimate," Gallup, February 24, 2021, https://news.gallup.com/poll/329708/lgbt-identification-rises-latest-estimate.aspx.

28. Michael Dimock, "Defining Generations: Where Millennials End and Generation Z Begins," Pew Research Center, January 17, 2019, https://www.pewresearch.org/fact-tank/2019/01/17/where-millennials-end-and-generation-z-begins/.

29. Jessica Semega et al., *Income and Poverty in the United States: 2019*, Report No. P60-270 (Washington, DC: United States Census Bureau, September 2020), https://www.census.gov/library/publications/2020/demo/p60-270.html.

30. "New Index Ranks America's 100 Most Disadvantaged Communities," Affecting Change to Prevent & Alleviate Poverty, Poverty Solution at the University of Michigan, January 30, 2020, https://poverty.umich.edu/2020/01/30/new-index-ranks-americas-100-most-disadvantaged-communities/.

31. "Disability Impacts All of Us," infographic, Disability and Health Promotion, Centers for Disease Control and Prevention, last reviewed September 16, 2020, https://www.cdc.gov/ncbddd/disabilityandhealth/infographic-disability-impacts-all.html.

32. National Business & Disability Council, "Disabilities in the United States," infographic, The Viscardi Center, July 15, 2015, https://www.viscardicenter.org/wp-content/uploads/2016/09/2015_NBDC_MAP_InfoGraphic_Disabilities_in_the_United_States_market_07.15.15.pdf.

33. Merriam-Webster, s.v. "culture (*n.*)," accessed October 30, 2021, https://www.merriam-webster.com/dictionary/culture.

34. Mayra Rodriguez Ruiz and Neusa Olinda Varela Spínola, "Improving the Intercultural Communicative Competence of English Language Students," *Journal of Intercultural Communication*, no. 49 (March 2019), https://immi.se/oldwebsite/nr49/ruiz.html.

35. University of Alberta, "Culture Is Key to Interpreting Facial Emotions," ScienceDaily, April 5, 2007, https://www.sciencedaily.com/releases/2007/04/070404162321.htm.

36. Pavlína Springerová and Zdeňka Picková, "Aspects Determining the Auto-identification of Native Communities in Contemporary Peru," *Ethnologia Actualis* 18, no. 1 (June 2018): 68–92, https://doi.org/10.2478/eas-2018-0010.

37. David M. Eberhard, Gary F. Simons, and Charles D. Fennig, eds., "How Many Languages Are There in the World?," in *Ethnologue: Languages of the World*, 25th ed. (Dallas, TX: SIL International), accessed October 30, 2021, https://www.ethnologue.com/guides/how-many-languages.

38. Julie Otto, "Connecting with Hispanics in South Florida," Sun Sentinel Media Group, August 22, 2018, https://www.sunsentinelmediagroup.com/blog/connecting-with-hispanics-in-south-florida/.

39. "Geert Hofstede," People, The British Library, accessed October 30, 2021, https://www.bl.uk/people/geert-hofstede.

40. Heather M. Coon and Markus Kemmelmeier, "Cultural Orientations in the United States: (Re)Examining Differences among Ethnic Groups," *Journal of Cross-Cultural Psychology* 32, no. 3 (May 2001), 348–364, https://doi.org/10.1177/0022022101032003006.

41. Monica Anderson, "Racial and Ethnic Differences in How People Use Mobile Technology," Pew Research Center, April 30, 2015, https://www.pewresearch.org/fact-tank/2015/04/30/racial-and-ethnic-differences-in-how-people-use-mobile-technology/.

42. Juliana Menasce Horowitz, "Americans' Views on Masculinity Differ by Party, Gender and Race," Pew Research Center, January 23, 2019, https://www.pewresearch.org/fact-tank/2019/01/23/americans-views-on-masculinity-differ-by-party-gender-and-race/.

43. "Country Comparison," Hofstede Insights, last modified June 21, 2021, https://www.hofstede-insights.com/country-comparison/china,japan,south-korea,vietnam/.

44. Geert Hofstede, Gert Jan Hofstede, and Michael Minkov, *Cultures and Organizations: Software of the Mind*, 3rd ed. (New York: McGraw-Hill, 2010).

45. "Working with Cultural Differences," Our Thinking, Change Factory, accessed October 30, 2021, https://www.changefactory.com.au/our-thinking/articles/working-with-cultural-differences/.

46. Opal Tomashevska, "6 Key Differences Drive Multicultural Consumer Behavior," CCUL Headlines, Carolinas Credit Union League, November 13, 2018, https://www.carolinasleague.org/news/426658/6-key-differences-drive-multicultural-consumer-behavior.htm.

47. Tomashevska, "6 Key Differences."

48. "US Census Bureau Projections Show a Slower Growing, Older, More Diverse Nation a Half Century from Now," Newsroom, United States Census Bureau, December 12, 2012, https://www.census.gov/newsroom/releases/archives/population/cb12-243.html.

49. Luis Noe-Bustamante, "Key Facts about US Hispanics and Their Diverse Heritage," Pew Research Center, September 16, 2019, https://www.pewresearch.org/fact-tank/2019/09/16/key-facts-about-u-s-hispanics/.

50. Paul Taylor et al., "When Labels Don't Fit: Hispanics and Their Views of Identity," Pew Research Center, April 4, 2012, https://www.pewresearch.org/hispanic/2012/04/04/when-labels-dont-fit-hispanics-and-their-views-of-identity/.

51. Nicholas Jones et al., "Improved Race and Ethnicity Measures Reveal US Population Is Much More Multiracial," America Counts: Stories behind the Numbers, United States Census Bureau, https://www.census.gov/library/stories/2021/08/improved-race-ethnicity-measures-reveal-united-states-population-much-more-multiracial.html.

52. Christine Tamir, "Key Findings about Black America," Pew Research Center, March 25, 2021, https://www.pewresearch.org/fact-tank/2021/03/25/key-findings-about-black-america/.

53. Michael Chui et al., "A \$300 Billion Opportunity: Serving the Emerging Black American Consumer," *McKinsey Quarterly*, August 6, 2021, https://www.mckinsey.com/featured-insights/diversity-and-inclusion/a-300-billion-dollar-opportunity-serving-the-emerging-black-american-consumer.

54. Amanda Barroso, "Most Black Adults Say Race Is Central to Their Identity and Feel Connected to a Broader Black Community," Pew Research Center, February 5, 2020, https://www.pewresearch.org/fact-tank/2020/02/05/most-black-adults-say-race-is-central-to-their-identity-and-feel-connected-to-a-broader-black-community/.

55. Jones et al., "Race and Ethnicity Measures."

56. Budiman and Ruiz, "Key Facts."

57. Budiman and Ruiz, "Key Facts."

58. Budiman and Ruiz, "Key Facts."

59. Barroso, "Most Black Adults."

60. Maria Gomez Albrecht, "The Effect of Bicultural Acculturation among Hispanic Consumers' Attitudes and Its Implications for Mobile Advertising" (PhD diss., Swiss Management Center University, 2020), unpublished.

61. Gomez Albrecht, "Effect of Bicultural Acculturation."

62. Pew Hispanic Center, "Life Satisfaction, Priorities and Values," in *Between Two Worlds: How Young Latinos Come of Age in America* (Washington, DC: Pew Research Center, December 2009), https://www.pewresearch.org/hispanic/2009/12/11/vii-life-satisfaction-priorities-and-values/.

63. Nielsen, *Asian-Americans: Culturally Diverse and Expanding Their Footprint; The Asian-American Consumer 2016 Report*, May 2016, https://www.nielsen.com/insights/2016/asian-americans-culturally-diverse-and-expanding-their-footprint/.

64. Kathleen Y. Kawamura, "Body Image among Asian Americans," in *Encyclopedia of Body Image and Human Appearance*, ed. Thomas F. Cash (Waltham, MA: Academic Press, 2012), 2:95–102.

65. Jones, "LGBT Identification."

66. "What Is Generation Alpha?," *Casey Connects* (blog), The Annie E. Casey Foundation, November 4, 2020, https://www.aecf.org/blog/what-is-generation-alpha.

67. Centers for Disease Control and Prevention, "Disability Impacts All."

68. *The Lancet*, "World Population Likely to Shrink after Mid-century, Forecasting Major Shifts in Global Population and Economic Power," ScienceDaily, July 15, 2020, https://www.sciencedaily.com/releases/2020/07/200715150444.htm.

69. Luke Rogers, "US Population Grew 0.1% in 2021, Slowest Rate since Founding of the Nation," America Counts: Stories behind the Numbers, United States Census Bureau, December 21, 2021, https://www.census.gov/library/stories/2021/12/us-population-grew-in-2021-slowest-rate-since-founding-of-the-nation.html.

70. AARP, "More Americans Working Past 65," April 22, 2019. https://www.aarp.org/work/employers/americans-working-past-65/#:~:text=The%20%2478%2C000%20average%20earnings%20for,in%201962%2C%20the%20report%20says.

71. Jacob Olesen, "Color Meanings in Japan," Color Meanings, last modified February 7, 2022, https://www.color-meanings.com/color-meanings-japan/; Meong Jin Shin et al., "Colour Preferences for Traditional Korean Colours," *Journal of the International Colour Association* 9 (2012): 48–59, https://www.aic-color.org/resources/Documents/jaic_v9_05.pdf.

72. Nadra Nittle, "Brands Once Used Elitism to Market Themselves. Now Inclusion Sells," The Goods by Vox, Vox Media, December 7, 2018, https://www.vox.com/the-goods/2018/12/7/18129445/brands-inclusion-fenty-third-love-victorias-secret.

73. "What Was the 'Share a Coke' Campaign?," Coca-Cola Australia, Coca-Cola, September 2, 2019, https://www.coca-colacompany.com/au/faqs/what-was-the-share-a-coke-campaign.

74. Patrick Kevin Day, "Coca-Cola Super Bowl Ad Stirs Controversy," *Los Angeles Times*, February 3, 2014, https://www.latimes.com/entertainment/tv/showtracker/la-et-st-coca-cola-super-bowl-ad-stirs-controversy-20140203-story.html.

75. "Dermal Fillers Market Size, Growth and Revenue Analysis," Fortune Business Insights, accessed September 26, 2021, https://www.fortunebusinessinsights.com/industry-reports/dermal-fillers-market-100939.

76. "From Extreme to Mainstream: The Future of Aesthetics Injectables," McKinsey & Company Our Insights, December 20, 2021, https://www.mckinsey.com/industries/life-sciences/our-insights/from-extreme-to-mainstream-the-future-of-aesthetics-injectables

77. GQ Staff, "Are Dermal Fillers Getting Popular Among Men Today?" GQ Grooming, September 28, 2021, https://www.gqmiddleeast.com/gq-partnership/why-are-men-getting-dermal-fillers-now#

Unit 3

Product, Promotion, Price, and Place

Unit Introduction

In this last unit, we will be exploring next-level marketing concepts. We will look at product marketing, services marketing, pricing, integrated marketing communications, the promotion mix, social media marketing, distribution, retailing and wholesaling, and sustainability.

Enjoy the topics and their corresponding examples!

9

Products: Consumer Offerings

Figure 9.1 Marketing strategies define and support the product life cycle and brand, such as Peloton's approach to bundling fitness products and online classes. (credit: modification of work "Woman Riding Exercise Bike" by onthegosports.com.au/ SportsFanaticAustralia/flickr, CC BY 2.0)

Chapter Outline

In the Spotlight

Peloton, producer of high-end home fitness equipment and streaming fitness classes, has taken advantage of the tech boom to bundle its products and service for a recurring revenue source. Peloton is known for its expensive at-home fitness bikes and treadmills aimed at a high-end target audience. Once a customer purchases a bike for $1,500–$2,600 and/or a treadmill for $3,500,[1] most fitness companies would not expect additional revenue from a customer for several years.

But Peloton sees itself as a technology company that facilitates service. Peloton CEO John Foley has said that "we see ourself more akin to an Apple, a Tesla, or a Nest or a GoPro—where it's a consumer product that has a foundation of sexy hardware technology and sexy software technology."[2] In the case of Peloton, that sexy software technology comes in the form of streaming workout classes including cycling, strength, boot camp, yoga, and meditation taught by charismatic instructors who have become social media influencers. The price tag for Peloton customers is a recurring $39 monthly fee for all access on top of the cost of the product.

Peloton customers are purchasing more than a one-time durable good. Instead, they are buying a networked effect in which they are connected to fitness instructors and one another. Hailed the new form of competitive advantage, networked effects bring customers closer to the brand through personal connections between the brand and customers and between customers. Once a customer is a loyal part of the network, the cost to switch brands in terms of habit and lifestyle is high. As a result, loyal customers are less likely to brand switch and are less price sensitive.

While product bundling isn't a new concept—think about a value meal at a restaurant that includes a sandwich, fries, and a beverage—the product-service bundle is an emerging trend among technology companies. It provides recurring revenue for the brand while bringing the customer into a more intimate customer experience, leading to brand loyalty. Typically, the service fees ultimately provide more revenue per customer than the one-time product purchase in this model. The recurring revenue model makes the product facilitate the service exchange, blurring the traditional product-service lines.

What examples come to mind when you think of product-service bundles? Do you have a prediction for how this trend may shape product development in the future?

9.1   Products, Services, and Experiences

Learning Outcomes

By the end of this section, you will be able to:

- **LO** 1 Differentiate between products, services, and experiences.
- **LO** 2 Describe how consumer and business/industrial products are classified.
- **LO** 3 Identify the four levels of a product.

Products and Services Defined

When a customer makes a purchase, they expect value from that exchange. Think about what you ate for breakfast today. You paid money to receive a product that satisfied your hunger. Is that all the value you received? Perhaps not. If you ate eggs, bacon, and coffee at a restaurant, you had both a product and a service experience. Maybe someone at the restaurant handed you a menu, took your order, brought your food, refilled your coffee, cleaned up dishes, and collected payment for your meal. The eggs, bacon, and coffee were the product, while the acts of the restaurant staff were a service. And the summation of it all was the product–service experience.

Products are tangible items that are part of an exchange between a buyer and seller. Products can be seen, touched, owned, and stored. For example, the computer or tablet you're using to read this textbook is a product. You may have visited a store to see and touch the product before purchasing to ensure it met your needs. Post-purchase, the computer or tablet is yours to own and store for later use as you please. The tangible nature of the product allows the consumer to possess it.

Services are intangible solutions that are also an exchange between buyer and seller. Unlike products, services cannot be touched, owned, or stored for later use. For example, a college course on marketing is a service. Students cannot own the course; they cannot store it for later, nor will they have a tangible object representing the course. Another defining feature of a service is the customer is typically a part of the service experience. Imagine buying tickets to your favorite band in concert. You will have to attend the concert to realize the full benefit of the service experience.

While a computer is a true product and a marketing class is a true service, many exchanges between buyer and seller fall somewhere in the middle of the product–service continuum (see Figure 9.2). Think back to the restaurant breakfast at the top of this section; restaurants are a prime example of an exchange that includes products and services. Marketers are typically working with an offering that falls on the product–service continuum. This means that they need to understand how to influence consumer behavior in the search for products and services.

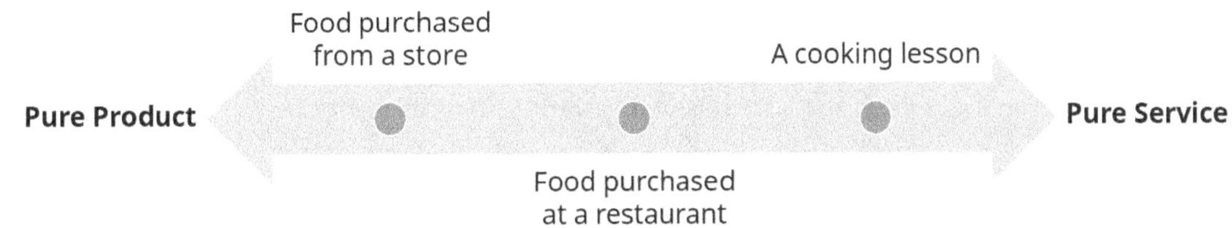

Figure 9.2 The Product–Service Continuum (attribution: Copyright Rice University, OpenStax, under CC BY 4.0 license)

Customer Experience

Customer experience (CX) is the overarching impression that customers have of a brand. Therefore, each touchpoint with a product or service becomes a part of the customer experience. A strong customer experience integrates technology, marketing, sales, and customer service to deliver a strong brand perception.

For example, if you have ever visited an Apple Store, you probably have experienced one of the most lauded customer experiences there is. From the moment you walk in, you are surrounded by products and transported into a world of technology. Each touchpoint, from the check-in on an iPad to the latest products that are available for use, reinforces the brand through customer experience. Brands with strong customer experience tend to have more loyal customers who become brand advocates.

MARKETING IN PRACTICE

Netflix

Netflix has perfected the customer experience (see Figure 9.3). Using technology as a driver, Netflix predicts its customers' viewing preferences using an algorithm, removing friction from the user experience and making the brand an essential part of its customers' lives. Netflix's use of personalization is common among companies that excel in customer experience. The customer is at the center of the experience that is entirely tailored to them.

Figure 9.3 The Netflix brand is known for perfecting the streaming business by optimizing usage data to create an individualized and customized user experience. (credit: "Netflix Logo on the PC Monitor, Photographed through a Magnifying Glass" by Marco Verch/flickr, CC BY 2.0)

Once users enter the Netflix website, they see an experience that makes their viewing opportunity seamless and flexible. Netflix lets the user know right away that it streams thousands of movies and television shows on various devices. The sign-up involves three easy steps, and then the customer is brought into a viewing world built around them.

The Netflix algorithm analyzes viewing habits based on a variety of factors, including:

- Viewing history
- Genre or category
- Time of day watched
- How long the user watched
- Devices currently streaming
- Rating history for similar content
- Other Netflix users with similar preferences on the platform[3]

As the algorithm learns more about the viewer, the customer experience improves, becoming essential to customers' lives and building brand loyalty.

Classifications of Consumer and Business Products

Product managers classify products first by whether they are consumer products or industrial products. This classification is essential because businesses typically make product purchase decisions to create a consumer good. Meanwhile, consumers are buying products for their personal use. Therefore, this distinction impacts how product managers design, market, and sell products.

Consumer products are classified into four main categories (see Table 9.1):

1. **Convenience products** are products that consumers can purchase easily, quickly, and without a lot of thoughtful decision-making. Convenience product purchases may be habitual in that the consumer buys the same brand each time. In addition, they are typically lower-priced and have wide distribution, so they are easily accessible to consumers. Frozen waffles, bar soap, milk, and bathroom cleaners are examples of convenience products.
2. **Shopping products** require more thought from the consumer. Consumers may research and shop around for shopping products, seeking the best quality or price. Shopping products are typically available at a few retail stores and online, and they may be priced higher than convenience products. Exercise equipment, technology, clothing, and airline tickets are shopping products.
3. **Specialty products** have unique qualities that consumers will make an extra effort to seek out. The product's unique nature typically means that the consumer will not comparison shop and will spend a significant amount of time and money to procure the product. Luxury cars, rare breeds of saltwater fish, fine art, and jewelry are examples of specialty products.
4. **Unsought products** are consumer goods that a buyer doesn't anticipate purchasing. As a result, the consumer is often not aware of the product or does not think it is needed. A flat tire that needs repairing, a roof damaged in a storm that needs to be replaced, and funeral services are examples of unsought products.

Type of Product	Price	Consumer Decision-Making Process	Distribution
Convenience	Low	This is a habitual/automatic purchase process that involves little comparison shopping.	Widespread distribution at several retail outlets
Shopping	Low-Mid	There is time spent on the consumer decision-making process and comparison shopping for price and quality.	Selective distribution at retail outlets that match customer and brand type
Specialty	High	Having a specific brand or product in mind means little comparison shopping. Typically, this is a special purchase with a lot of planning.	Exclusive distribution at one or a select few retail outlets
Unsought	Variable	The consumer is unaware or uninterested, so they exert little thought or comparison shopping.	Variable distribution depends on the product

Table 9.1 Types of Products

Classifications of Business and Industrial Products

Businesses purchase products to aid in manufacturing or creating consumer products or services. For example, if you have ever been to a doughnut shop, you might think about how the bakers produce a doughnut. The bakers have probably purchased baking equipment, ingredients for the doughnuts, boxes to package the doughnuts, and a service to make deliveries. Business and industrial products are classified as follows:

1. **Raw materials** are the products that a business needs to purchase in order to make a consumer good, such as flour, sugar, and yeast in our doughnut example.
2. **Manufactured materials and parts** are products used to create the product. For example, large baking sheets are manufactured materials specific to a bakery and purchased to enable product creation.
3. **Capital items** are assets that are valuable to the business and have tangible value. For example, our bakery's large ovens would be considered a capital item.
4. **Supplies and services** are goods and services that are typically disposed of and do not contain a tangible value. For example, the bakery's boxes are part of its supplies to package doughnuts.

The Three Levels of Product

In marketing, we often say that consumers do not make rational decisions—this consumer decision-making process ties directly to how we think about products. Therefore, product marketers should ask themselves, "What's the problem the consumer is trying to solve?" The answer to this question gets to the root of the core product. The **core product** is what your customer is actually buying: convenience, ego, ease, flexibility, etc. For example, if you have ever purchased single-use plastic water bottles, you were likely purchasing a core product of convenience.

The second level of a product is the **actual product**: a toaster, a waffle, or a sports car, for example. The actual product includes the product features, brand, level of quality, packaging, and design.

The third level of a product is the **augmented product**: warranties, customer service, product support, etc. The augmented product is the unseen aspects of the product essential to its service to you. For example, Butterball launches a turkey talk-line that provides tips on cooking the perfect Thanksgiving turkey each Thanksgiving. So if you have turkey roasting questions, the talk-line is ready and waiting to answer your questions in this augmented product. A hotel might provide concierge services to obtain tickets to events or limousine service, dry cleaning services, recommendations for local restaurants, etc. All of these would be augmented services. (see Figure 9.4).

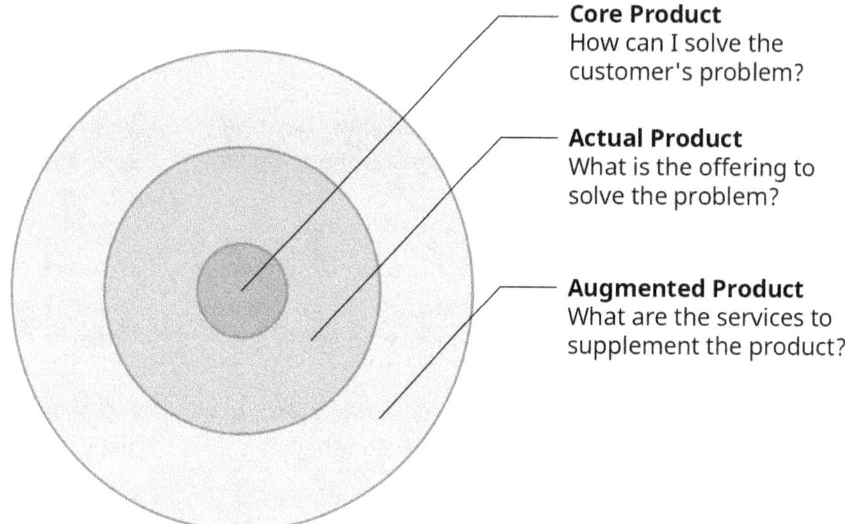

Figure 9.4 Three Levels of a Product (attribution: Copyright Rice University, OpenStax, under CC BY 4.0 license)

CAREERS IN MARKETING

Product Marketer

A product marketer, also sometimes known as a product marketing manager, promotes a product and its features to a target market. Learn more about this job role through this article from HubSpot (https://openstax.org/r/productmarketingmanager), including a job description, necessary qualifications, and job responsibilities. Also, check out this video from a Google employee about being a product marketer.

Click to view content (https://openstax.org/books/principles-marketing/pages/9-1-products-services-and-experiences)

If this job interests you, check out this article from Indeed (https://openstax.org/r/whatdoesaproductmarketingmanagerdo) that outlines more details, including the typical salary, necessary skills, and education requirements. Or refer to this guide on how to take the next step and get a job in product marketing (https://openstax.org/r/theultimateguidetogettingajobinproductmarketing).

Lastly, to start preparing for a job in this role, check out this mock interview for the product marketing manager role.

Click to view content (https://openstax.org/books/principles-marketing/pages/9-1-products-services-and-experiences)

Knowledge Check

It's time to check your knowledge on the concepts presented in this section. Refer to the Answer Key at the end of the book for feedback.

1. Which of the following is the best example of a pure service?
    a. Haircut
    b. Meal at a restaurant
    c. Frozen waffles

    d. Sports car

2. Jorge visited his favorite retailer to find that the store had transformed into a space with product demonstrations, product trials, and technology, which improved his overall perception of the brand. This is called a(n) _______
    a. product
    b. service
    c. experience
    d. advertisement

3. A package of gum at the checkout of a grocery store is considered a(n) _______ product.
    a. convenience
    b. shopping
    c. specialty
    d. unsought

4. Potbelly Sandwich Shops use paper bags to hold customers' sandwiches. What type of industrial product is the bag?
    a. Raw materials
    b. Manufactured materials and parts
    c. Capital items
    d. Supplies and services

5. At the beginning of this chapter, we learned about the Peloton brand. Peloton users use not only the physical bike also but online classes with an instructor to stay fit within their own homes. This need represents the _______ product.
    a. core
    b. actual
    c. augmented
    d. valued

9.2 | Product Items, Product Lines, and Product Mixes

Learning Outcomes

By the end of this section, you will be able to:
- **LO** 1 Define product items, product lines, and product mixes.
- **LO** 2 Describe product line length and depth.
- **LO** 3 Discuss product line filling and product line stretching.

Product Line Length and Depth

Companies typically sell many products, some of which are singular and some of which are part of a larger category of offerings. So let's start with a **product item**, a particular good that a company sells. For example, Domino's Pizza sells its original hand-tossed pizza as a product item on its menu.

A company will also sell a product item as a part of a broader **product line**. A product line is a set of products that are similar or complementary. For example, Domino's sells crunchy thin, handmade pan, Brooklyn style, and gluten-free crust along with its hand-tossed pizza crust as a part of a product line.

A **product mix** contains all the products that a company sells. In addition to pizza, Domino's sells salads, sandwiches, appetizers, pasta, desserts, and beverages. These products make up the product mix for Domino's

(Figure 9.5).

There are benefits to brands in organizing into product lines and mixes. For example, if you have ever added a chocolate lava cake to your Domino's order, you know firsthand that products within a mix are easily cross-sold. You may have also seen a commercial where Domino's promotes its product mix, creating efficiencies in its media advertising spend. In addition, breadth of products provides some assurance that competitors will not compete in the same space. Finally, you may have noticed that some appetizers and desserts are packaged in the same box, creating supply efficiencies.

On the flip side, if product offerings are too similar, they may cannibalize (or steal from) the original product, resulting in lower profitability. For example, if Domino's had 30 types of pizzas, the stores might have to stock extra ingredients to make those pizzas, but Domino's might not sell more pizzas as a whole because the product line offerings are too similar.

Figure 9.5 A product item, like a pizza from Domino's Pizza, is part of a company's product mix—all of the products it sells. (credit: "Saki's Pizza" by thepizzareview/flickr, CC BY 2.0; modification of work "Salad" by Jackie L Chan/flickr, CC BY 2.0; "Pasta with Homemade Baguette" by Stacy Spensley/flickr, CC BY 2.0; "Mmm... I Want Everything on Mine" by jeffreyw/flickr, CC BY 2.0; modification of work "Chocolate Fudge Brownies" by startcooking kathy & amandine/flickr, CC BY 2.0; modification of work "Fast Food Chicken Nuggets" by Walt Stoneburner/flickr, CC BY 2.0)

Product Line Depth and Product Mix Width

Product line depth refers to the number of products in the line. Using our previous example, Domino's carries five products in the pizza product line. Meanwhile, the **product mix width** refers to the number of product lines a brand carries. Domino's offers seven product lines within its product mix (pizza, salads, sandwiches, appetizers, pasta, desserts, and beverages).

The product line depth and product mix width allow a company to diversify its offerings to maximize customer loyalty and mitigate risk. For example, if a customer enjoys Domino's Pizza, they may extend their order to include one of the other offerings in the product mix. On the flip side, if a customer has a bad experience with the pizza, they might try chicken or pasta instead next time. However, it is essential to note that too many offerings can cannibalize one another and drive up the cost of goods sold because of the variations that each product requires.

Product Line Filling and Product Line Stretching

One of the reasons for an ample product line is to leave no room for competitors to solve a customer's need. Companies use a **product line filling** strategy when they add products to the product line to ensure that competitors do not enter their market. If you wonder why Domino's has so many pizza toppings, consider that it might be product line filling at work.

On the other hand, it might make more sense for a company to add product lines. The addition of product lines is a practice called **product line stretching**. There are three main ways to stretch a product line:

1. **Stretching Downward.** A brand introduces a product line that is less expensive than its current offering. This may open a new target market or change a brand's positioning in a competitive market. However, it is essential to consider whether stretching down might shift the brand's perception or take share from other product lines. Tesla introduced its Model 3 following its more expensive Model S, following the stretching downward strategy.[4]
2. **Stretching Upward.** A brand introduces a product line that is more expensive than its current offering. This may increase profitability or reposition the brand. First, however, it is essential to determine whether the brand has equity in the upward market. Godiva introduced its gold collection to stretch its product line upward.
3. **Stretching Up and Down.** A brand can stretch up and down simultaneously. While this has the potential for great rewards, it also introduces a fair amount of risk. Dell utilizes a strategy to stretch up and down with its everyday access laptops, creator laptops, and all the way up to its immersive gaming laptops.

Suppose Domino's wanted to join the wood-fired pizza trend. It could employ an upward product line stretching strategy to introduce Domino's to a more upscale market that appreciates wood-fired pizza.

Knowledge Check

It's time to check your knowledge on the concepts presented in this section. Refer to the Answer Key at the end of the book for feedback.

1. Oreo's selection of flavors would be considered a ________.
   a. product
   b. product line
   c. product mix
   d. product category

2. A product mix contains ________.
   a. a mix of the company's most popular products
   b. a singular product
   c. all the products that a company sells
   d. a group of similar products

3. If Domino's were to add a Chicago-style stuffed pizza to its menu, this would represent an expansion of the ________ of its pizza offerings.
   a. product line depth
   b. product mix width
   c. product items
   d. product differentiation

4. Product line depth refers to ________.
   a. product characteristics
   b. the number of product lines
   c. product assortment
   d. the number of products in the product line

5. Which of the following is a benefit of product line filling?
   a. Less money spent on research and development
   b. Protection against competitors

c.   Creates a product line assortment
d.   Stretches the product line

9.3 | The Product Life Cycle

Learning Outcomes

By the end of this section, you will be able to:
LO 1 Define the product life cycle.
LO 2 List and describe the stages of the product life cycle.

The Product Life Cycle

Have you ever wondered what happens after a new product launch? Is the product successful right away, or does it need a little help from marketing to realize its potential? Then, as the product matures, does it stay on the shelf, or does it have a natural endpoint? The **product life cycle** (see Figure 9.6) maps the stages a product goes through, tracking its sales and profitability.

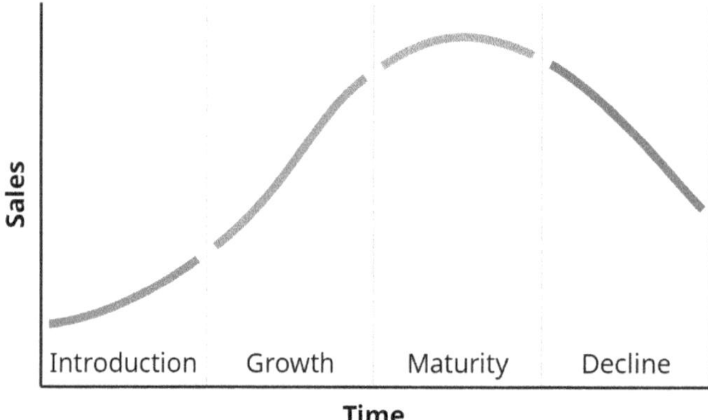

Figure 9.6 The Product Life Cycle (attribution: Copyright Rice University, OpenStax, under CC BY 4.0 license)

The Product Life Cycle Stages

The product life cycle begins in the **introduction stage**. This is when consumer awareness is building and sales are starting to grow. The marketing investment is high as brands invest heavily in advertising and sales promotion to encourage trial. Profitability is low due to costs to launch and scale a new product. What products can you think of that are in the introduction stage of the product life cycle?

Once a product catches on in the marketplace, it enters the **growth stage** of the product life cycle. The growth stage is characterized by increasing sales and the potential for copycat brands to enter the market once they see revenue and profitability. In addition, products require less marketing and distribution investments during the growth stage, making them more profitable. However, a brand can decide to invest in product improvements and distribution, which may decrease profitability in the short term in exchange for long-term gain. When hoverboards were new to the market, they experienced explosive growth that quickly tapered off.

The product enters the **maturity stage** when sales growth slows and profitability levels taper off. The maturity stage is typically the longest stage of the product life cycle, with products remaining in this stage for years or even decades. Profitability may remain if the brand has a solid competitive advantage or decline if too many competitors enter the market. Marketing investment can increase at this stage if the brand has a rival, and product modification can alter the product to meet consumers' needs. Yet often a brand will retain a low level of marketing during the maturity stage to remind consumers of its benefits. Kraft Macaroni & Cheese is an example of a product that has a solid place in the market and has stabilized as a mature product.

Eventually, most products enter the **decline stage**. The decline stage is characterized by a significant decrease in sales and profitability. Sometimes the decline occurs because the market has changed: technology has evolved, consumer tastes have shifted, or the need that the product satisfies is no longer relevant. Other times, the product is pushed out by rising costs or competitors. Many companies report their earnings quarterly and do not want to keep an unprofitable brand in their portfolio. As a result, companies typically try to divest a product in the decline stage. Another company may pick up the brand, invest in it, and bring the product back to a growth or maturity stage. Apple's iPod entered the decline stage when the popular iPhone was introduced, bringing a host of features plus music.

It is important to note that products do not always travel through the product life cycle at a linear rate, nor do they all travel through all product life cycle stages. For example, a product can be introduced and never gain traction, so it goes directly from introduction to decline. Or a product might gain popularity rapidly during the growth stage and then meet a quick decline. This phenomenon occurs when products are fads.

Knowledge Check

It's time to check your knowledge on the concepts presented in this section. Refer to the Answer Key at the end of the book for feedback.

1. Which of the following is NOT a stage of the product life cycle?
   a. Introduction
   b. Growth
   c. Maturity
   d. Profitability

2. Which criterion does the product life cycle use?
   a. Sales
   b. Profitability
   c. A and B
   d. None of these are correct.

3. Which stage of the product life cycle is characterized by a rapid increase in sales?
   a. Introduction
   b. Growth
   c. Maturity
   d. Decline

4. Which stage of the product life cycle is characterized by stable sales and profitability?
   a. Introduction
   b. Growth
   c. Maturity
   d. Decline

5. Which of the following is a reason that brands may not follow the product life cycle sequentially?
   a. Brands can grow rapidly.
   b. Brands can skip the product life cycle all together.
   c. Brands can be a fad.
   d. Brands can skip to maturity right away.

9.4 | Marketing Strategies at Each Stage of the Product Life Cycle

Learning Outcomes

By the end of this section, you will be able to:

LO 1 Discuss marketing strategies in the introduction stage of the product life cycle.
LO 2 Classify marketing strategies used in the growth stage of the product life cycle.
LO 3 Characterize marketing strategies used in the maturity stage of the product life cycle.
LO 4 Identify marketing strategies used in the decline stage of the product life cycle.

Marketing Strategies in the Introduction Stage

The introduction stage is characterized by awareness-building to encourage trial. There is a significant investment in marketing activities at this stage to make the shift from early adopters to a broader audience, and pricing is a means of enticing trial.

A **rapid skimming strategy** sets a high price along with extensive advertising and sales promotion to establish the product in the marketplace. This strategy allows a product to gain share quickly and fend off potential competitors. Technology innovations typically use a rapid skimming strategy to attract early adopters who are willing to pay a higher price.

In contrast, a slow skimming strategy may be utilized when there is not an anticipated influx of competitors. The **slow skimming strategy** sets high prices with low advertising and sales promotion investment. For example, we may see a rapid skimming strategy for the new model of a truck or SUV in the automobile market because competition is high and the barrier to entry is low. On the other hand, the Tesla brand used a slow skimming strategy in its initial launch with a high-priced offering making it exclusive.

A **rapid penetration pricing strategy** is appropriate when volume sales will increase market share quickly, and a lower-priced strategy is employed. Rapid penetration pricing strategies encourage customers to try a product and switch to a new brand. This strategy works well with product categories with many competitors and price-sensitive customers. For example, Old Navy used a rapid penetration pricing strategy when it opened its stores in 1994 with an $8 jeans promotion under the assumption that if customers tried its jeans, they would be hooked and become brand advocates.

In contrast, a **slow penetration pricing strategy** establishes low prices and low promotion to capture share more slowly in a market that typically does not readily react to promotion. Products that do not have a lot of brand equity and are necessities do not respond to promotion readily and are appropriate for a slow penetration pricing strategy. For example, if a store brand of butter were to establish an everyday low price without the use of promotion, it would be adopting a slow penetration pricing strategy.

Marketing Strategies in the Growth Stage

The growth stage is characterized by growing sales and increasing competition in the marketplace. Investment in product and place is essential at the growth stage to maximize market share and scale quickly.

Brands may improve product quality or add new features in the growth stage based on early lessons from the introduction stage and to fend off competitors. Products with a first-mover advantage may find competitors who replicate their products entering the market, so product improvement is essential. For example, OXO is a brand that uses universal design to innovate products to make them easier to use. This continuous product improvement makes it a leader in the kitchenware market.

Once a product becomes mainstream in the growth stage, expanding distribution channels can increase market share. While expanded distribution adds expense, it also brings the product to more customers in various settings. For example, Chicago-based Home Run Inn Pizza was so famous in the restaurant format that it expanded to grocery stores to increase share.

Finally, brands use promotion to shift their message from awareness to preference. The shift from a niche market to a mass market typically involves an advertising investment. In 2021, TikTok moved from awareness to preference, and its promotion followed suit, reminding users why they enjoy using the platform.

Marketing Strategies in the Maturity Stage

Stability characterizes the maturity stage: profits, customers, and pricing. While this sounds like good news, brands must defend their market share from increasing product replication and product innovation from competitors.

Products in the maturity stage may engage in **market modification**, an extension of the product to new customers. For example, Cheerios adopted a market modification strategy when it positioned its cereal to the aging baby boomer demographic as a heart-healthy breakfast. This strategy opened a new market for Cheerios to increase its market share.

Products in the maturity stage may also engage in **product modification**, altering products to fit the market. Modifications may be made to the function of the product, the quality of the product, and/or the style of the product. For example, Chobani modified its yogurt product in 2015 by altering the container, allowing the customer to flip toppings into yogurt, and changing the functionality of the yogurt and topping product.[5]

Marketing Strategies in the Decline Stage

The decline stage of the product life cycle is characterized by declining sales and profitability. The product is at the end of its life cycle and is no longer sustainable or a good investment. Brands reduce to a core set of activities and set out to divest the brand asset.

A brand might **divest** a product to protect the rest of its portfolio, either by selling the brand or discontinuing it. For example, the Coca-Cola brand divested New Coke in 2002 after 17 years on the market in various forms.[6] The product was taken off the shelves because it was unsuccessful in the marketplace.

A brand might also choose to **harvest** an unsuccessful product. Harvesting involves reducing all unnecessary expenses to retain any remaining revenue. In addition, harvesting allows the brand to invest cash in its more profitable products. Typically, products do not reemerge after harvesting and more often are divested over time. Technology products, such as smartphones, are often harvested as their up-to-date replacements hit the market. Refurbished products may be sold at a discount or used for parts for new models.

Knowledge Check

It's time to check your knowledge on the concepts presented in this section. Refer to the Answer Key at the end of the book for feedback.

1. Mohammad's Shoe Company is expanding distribution for its most popular shoe line. The shoe line is in the _______ stage of the product life cycle.
   a. introduction
   b. growth
   c. maturity
   d. decline

2. Jia has established a rapid skimming strategy for her ice cream shop. The ice cream shop is in the _______ stage of the product life cycle.
   a. introduction
   b. growth
   c. maturity
   d. decline

3. Carlos has ceased all nonessential spending for his computer repair business. The computer repair

business is in the _______ stage of the product life cycle.
   a. introduction
   b. growth
   c. maturity
   d. decline

4. LaToya has found a new market for her restaurant by expanding to catering. The restaurant is in the _______ stage of the product life cycle.
   a. introduction
   b. growth
   c. maturity
   d. decline

5. Jamie's legal business has had some early success and decided to add estate planning to its business portfolio. The legal business is in the _______ stage of the product life cycle.
   a. introduction
   b. growth
   c. maturity
   d. decline

9.5 Branding and Brand Development

Learning Outcomes

By the end of this section, you will be able to:
   LO 1 Define branding and discuss its benefits.
   LO 2 Discuss ways in which an organization can build strong brands.

Branding

A **brand** is an intangible asset with tangible value. We cannot see, touch, or put a brand on a balance sheet. Rather, a brand is a feeling that is made up of the organization's promotion efforts along with consumer meaning. The value of a brand is challenging to measure, but it is often the most valuable part of a company.

Think about the Harley-Davidson brand (see Figure 9.7). What images and feelings does it evoke? Those images and feelings are its brand, and companies spend a lot of resources developing and nurturing their brands. The brand is the reason that customers purchase and advocate. A brand is the feeling associated with a product or service that gives it currency in the marketplace. The brand is the essence of the product or service and must be reinforced at every touchpoint. The marketing team at Harley-Davidson knows this all too well. Brand is Harley's business, and the company knows that every product, every promotion, and every event must reinforce the brand, which will build value over time to become a significant asset.

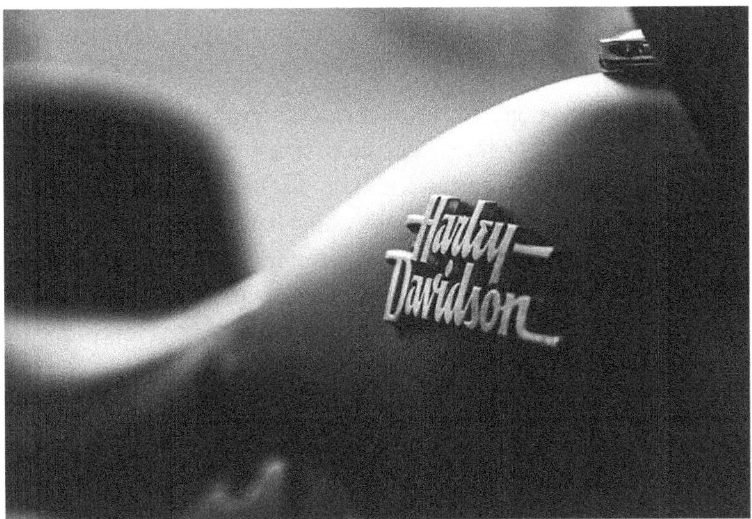

Figure 9.7 A brand like Harley-Davidson is an intangible and valuable asset whose tangible value to a company is created by an organization's promotional efforts. (credit: "Harley Davidson" by informedmag.com/flickr, CC BY 2.0)

Branding is the process of developing a brand. Successful brands engage their customers on a personal level, connecting to their emotions and needs. Some of the assets of a brand, such as the brand name, brand mark, or brand positioning, can be influential in creating a feeling about a brand.

LINK TO LEARNING

Logos

Visit the Harley-Davidson website (https://openstax.org/r/harleydavidson) for more logo examples. While looking at the logos, think about its name. What emotions are associated with the brand name and mark? While marketing teams can influence how a brand is seen in the marketplace, consumers often define the brand.

Did you know that the colors used in logos have meaning? This website shares a handful of stories (https://openstax.org/r/webfxlogocolors) behind the colors of famous logos.

Brands are created experiences that are shared among most loyal customers. Harley-Davidson customers experience the brand together through events and organized rides, creating brand meaning and contributing to the overall feeling.

Benefits of Branding

The central benefit of branding is establishing a connection with customers that encourages them to purchase the brand, creating a financial return. But you may be wondering how companies can measure the impact of their brand. **Brand value** is the financial asset associated with a brand. Brand valuation occurs when a company is sold and becomes a part of the financial transaction, along with the assets and liabilities on the company's financial statements. There is no singular measure of brand value, so the valuation process is subjective and may be based on brand visibility, customer loyalty, and perception of the brand, along with financial measures such as revenue.

Brand equity is the additional value that a brand has over a substitute. If a consumer will pay more for one similar product over another because of the brand, that difference represents its brand equity. For example, Tide, owned by Procter & Gamble, is the market leader in the laundry space.[7] While its product may not differ significantly from its competitors, Tide demands a higher price because of its brand equity. The brand equity measure is the amount that a brand with equity can charge over its counterparts. Take a moment and look up the price of Tide and a few competitors. What does that tell you about Tide's brand equity?

Kevin Lane Keller developed the brand equity model to illustrate how brands can develop equity. He postulated that if a brand could develop positive associations, it could charge more than its competitors. The model begins with defining a brand through its identity. Brands should answer the question, Who are you and how do you solve the consumers' needs? The next level of the model determines a brand's meaning. On one hand, how well does the brand perform, and on the other, how does it meet consumers' social and psychological needs? The third level of the framework is about feelings and thoughts. In other words, What do consumers think of your brand and what judgements do they make about it? Finally, the top of the pyramid examines brand resonance, or how much connection, engagement, or loyalty the brand has with its consumers.[8]

LINK TO LEARNING

Keller's Brand Equity Model

Keller's brand equity model is a prevailing framework that scholars use to think about the concept of brand equity. Check out this article (https://openstax.org/r/kellerbrandequitymodel) to learn more about the model and how you could apply it to a brand.

Building Strong Brands

If a brand is a combination of the efforts made by the marketing team and how consumers think, feel, and act, then there is some room for the marketing team to build a strong brand. A strong brand is resonant in the minds of consumers and solves their problems.

Building a strong brand begins with **brand positioning**, or the way the brand signals emotions in consumers' minds. Brands can position themselves based on an attribute—one aspect of the product or service. For example, Taco Bell has positioned itself as the option for late-night cravings. This singular aspect defines its positioning. The problem with positioning based on an attribute is that it is easily replicable by competitors.

The second method of positioning is benefiting the consumer—how the product or service solves the consumer's problem. For example, the Eggo brand's positioning is convenience. The brand solves the consumer's morning rush issue by providing a convenient breakfast solution. The benefits positioning works well for convenience products.

Lastly, a brand can position itself based on values. Values-based positioning is the most robust brand positioning because it links to a consumer's personal beliefs. For example, Ford uses the language "Built Ford Tough" in its advertising to connect to American values of hard work and determination. Ford's strategy is particularly effective because brands can connect to consumers' sense of self and how they show up to the world.

A product's **brand name** also clues consumers in to feelings, thoughts, and attitudes. Therefore, marketing teams spend a lot of time selecting brand names that evoke a feeling harmonious with the brand. A strong brand name also helps consumers see the benefit of the brand. For example, a favorite of many, Kellogg's Frosted Mini-Wheats, tells the consumer that they are eating something made of wheat with a touch of sugar.

A brand name should also translate effectively into a variety of languages. Finally, a brand name should be unique to that product. For example, we all know that the brand Pop-Tarts is a toaster pastry that pops out of a toaster. This is a distinctive element of the Pop-Tarts brand that is exemplified by its name.

Brands use **trademarks (service marks)** to ensure that they are protected under the law. According to the United States Patent and Trademark Office, a trademark can be any "word, phrase, symbol, design or a combination of these things that identified your goods and services."[9] Brands can trademark their names, logos, packaging, or even specific colors that represent the brand. This ensures that competitors do not replicate a known brand and cause confusion among customers. You will know that a brand is trademarked if you see a "TM" or "R" near the name or logo. Take a peek in your pantry to view trademarks on food packaging.

Brands can be owned in one of four ways: national brand, private brand, licensed brand, or co-brand. Each has its unique set of advantages and disadvantages, which will be discussed in this section.

National brands are the name brands that sell a product or service under its corporate name and identity. Brands like Heinz, Smartwater, and Morton's Salt are examples of name brands. Brand equity commands higher prices, so national brands typically charge higher prices than their private brand counterparts. National brands often pay for premium retail space, making them a convenient choice for shoppers. However, price-sensitive shoppers may be turned off by the higher prices of national brands.

Private-label brands are store brands that are similar products to a national brand and labeled privately. If you have shopped at a Walgreens, you may have seen its private-label brand of products that begin with the prefix *Wal-*. A McKinsey study indicates that price accounted for 45 percent of brand switchers from national to private brands, while lack of availability was a secondary reason.[10] The same study suggests that customers can develop loyalty to private-label brands. However, the private-label brand must create a point of differentiation relevant to the target audience in the same way that a national brand would.

Licensed brands provide the likeness of their brand as a fee for use. If you wear eyeglasses, you likely have a licensed brand name on your eyeglasses frame. Brands like Tiffany & Co., Kate Spade, and Tommy Hilfiger do not produce eyeglasses frames. Rather, they license their brand to manufacturers like Luxottica, an Italian eyewear company that makes the product with the licensed brand name. Licensing a brand is a quick way to gain recognition and benefit from the brand's equity. On the other hand, licensing fees can be costly and ultimately reduce profitability for manufacturers.

Finally, two or more brands may collaborate to **co-brand**; a product. Co-branding brings the equity of each brand together for greater value. For example, Doritos and Taco Bell developed Doritos Locos Tacos, a co-branded line of tacos that feature Doritos as the shell and Taco Bell ingredients as the toppings. In this case, the two brands had a similar target audience and could benefit from the awareness and equity of the other. However, co-branding necessitates a revenue split, which could impact financial results for each brand. Table 9.2 lists the advantages and

Brand Type	Advantages	Disadvantages
National brands	Well-known by consumers; OK to charge more	Some consumers unwilling to pay more than for private-label brands
Private brands	Attract price-sensitive customers	More difficult to build brand equity
Licensed brands	Gain brand recognition and benefit from brand equity	Expensive licensing fees
Co-brands	Benefit from the equity of both brands	Revenue split between two or more brands

Table 9.2 Types of Brands: Advantages and Disadvantages

MARKETING IN PRACTICE

Trader Joe's

Most of us do not love our weekly grocery shopping trip. Aisles upon aisles of boxes, cans, and cartons lining shelves create monotony in shopping for the food that nourishes us. We have trudged through supermarkets, pilling items into our carts uninspired—until Trader Joe's entered the scene.

Trader Joe's has taken the drudgery of grocery shopping and created a customer experience. Using the tenets of the Blue Ocean Strategy, Trader Joe's removed the costly parts of the traditional grocery store such as a large footprint and overwhelming stock that do not add to the customer experience. And it added Hawaiian shirts, friendly employees, interesting food selections, and a much smaller store. The result is a true neighborhood store that is so popular that Trader Joe's fan groups have popped up all over the Internet, and the cult brand has continued growth since its inception.

So what's the magic in creating an experience out of what used to be a chore? Trader Joe's looked at the customer experience from beginning to end to determine what its shopper values and what can go by the wayside.

Trader Joe's prioritized building its culture through empowering its "crew members." Employees at Trader Joe's are interviewed for enthusiasm and cross-trained throughout the store's operations.[11] Crew members are Trader Joe's fans themselves and are known for giving recommendations to customers and are empowered to connect with the customers, adding to the neighborhood feel of the store. The food at Trader Joe's is interesting to the shopper, much of it convenient and ready to eat. Trader Joe's leverages social media to put its food front and center with recipes and easy-to-prepare pairings. Trader Joe's thinks about the in-store experience and stocks about 10 percent of the food of a normal supermarket,[12] making choices easier on the customer.

LINK TO LEARNING

Interbrand's Best Global Brands

Interbrand ranks the best global brands annually. Take a look at the Interbrand website to see which brands make the top 100 (https://openstax.org/r/interbrandbestbrands) and consider what attributes led them to the top of the list.

Knowledge Check

It's time to check your knowledge on the concepts presented in this section. Refer to the Answer Key at the end of the book for feedback.

1. Which of the following is a benefit of a brand?
   a. Consumers always choose name brands.
   b. Brands can command higher prices.
   c. Shareholders demand strong brands.
   d. Every company must have a brand.

2. Which of the following describes the financial asset associated with a brand?
   a. Brand price

   b. Brand name
   c. Brand equity
   d. Brand value

3. Which of the following is NOT a means of brand positioning?
   a. Value
   b. Benefits
   c. Brand equity
   d. Attributes

4. The Whole Foods 365 brand is an example of a ________.
   a. national brand
   b. private brand
   c. licensed brand
   d. co-brand

5. Uber and Spotify teamed up to bring custom playlists to Uber rides. This is an example of a ________.
   a. national brand
   b. private brand
   c. licensed brand
   d. co-brand

9.6 | Forms of Brand Development, Brand Loyalty, and Brand Metrics

Learning Outcomes

By the end of this section, you will be able to:
- **LO 1** Identify branding strategies.
- **LO 2** Describe degrees of brand loyalty.
- **LO 3** Discuss metrics that can be used to measure brand strength and value.

Brand Development

New products can be added to a brand at any time. There are a few ways to add products that are classified on two measures: new/existing brand name and new/existing product category (see Figure 9.8).

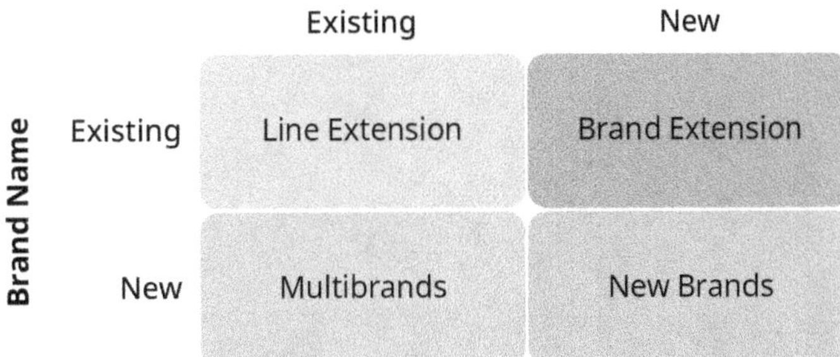

Figure 9.8 Brand Development Matrix (attribution: Copyright Rice University, OpenStax, under CC BY 4.0 license)

Line extensions create new opportunities for an existing product and brand to serve customers. For example, the Oreo brand adds flavors to its product line for holidays. These line extensions provide the existing brand with an extension of its current product. As a result, a line extension may sell more products to already-aware and interested customers without many risks. However, sometimes brands may overextend their product lines and products may be too similar, failing to increase sales.

Brand extensions leverage the brand name to new product categories. For example, Starbucks developed a line of bottled coffees under its corporate brand name. A brand extension uses awareness and equity in the brand to gain instant recognition and affinity for the new product, which may increase sales rapidly. However, if the new product is inferior to the brand's known quality, the entire brand portfolio may be at risk.

Multibrands are new brand names within a company's existing product category. For example, Nabisco manufactures various cookies within a product line but is marketed with different brand names. In this case, Chips Ahoy, Oreo, and Teddy Grahams all have brand equity on their own and do not need the benefit of the Nabisco brand. Each of these brands has a significant market share, so there is a benefit to retaining a multibranding approach. However, a multibranding approach does not work when the products have a small market share or fail to gain favorable retail shelf space to encourage sales.

New brands are an entirely different entity from the parent company. A new brand strategy can be effective if the new product or service is markedly different from the existing offering and benefits from its own branding. For example, the Starbucks brand owns Ethos Water. Ethos is in a beverage category other than Starbucks's primary offering and retains its name. A new brand strategy works well when the new brand is distinct from the parent brand and has a defined target market and positioning; however, a marketing strategy for a new brand can be expensive to maintain over time.

Brand Loyalty Levels

As you can see, brands spend time and resources to gain loyal customers. Loyal customers are the holy grail of marketing because they will purchase your brand and advocate for the brand to others. Loyal customers become instant word of mouth, spreading the positive attributes of a brand. However, not all customers are intensely loyal to one brand. Instead, customers fit into one of four loyalty categories (see Figure 9.9).

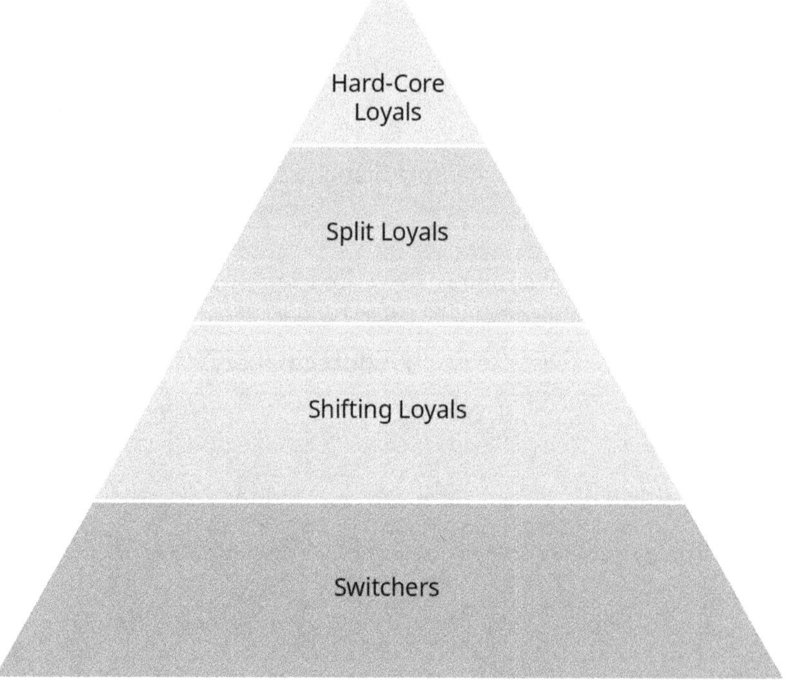

Figure 9.9 Loyalty Categories (attribution: Copyright Rice University, OpenStax, under CC BY 4.0 license)

Switchers are customers who continually change their purchasing behaviors. Switchers may be motivated by price, convenience, or innovation. Therefore, it is essential to develop a product or service that meets the switching consumers' needs to retain them as customers. For example, a switcher might purchase the lowest-price laundry detergent each time they are at the store.

Shifting loyals are customers who are loyal to one product or service for a time, then turn their loyalty to a different product or service for the second period. Brands can expect that shifting loyal customers will move back and forth between products and services. For example, a shifting loyal might purchase a Toyota followed by a Honda, then turn their loyalty back to Toyota for a third purchase.

Split loyals are customers who have a consideration set of two to three products or services in the category. The split loyal is willing to buy this select set of brands on any occasion without hard-core loyalty to any in the group. However, brands can convert split loyals into hard-core loyals with product/service consistency, loyalty programs, and marketing efforts. For example, customers may have loyalty to Gap, Banana Republic, and J.Crew for workwear.

Hard-core loyals are the customers that every brand wants. They are tried-and-true customers who will generally only purchase one brand in a category. For example, when purchasing from a catalog, they tend to make a purchase with less concern about price. In addition, hard-core loyals often tell friends and family about their purchases, extending word-of-mouth marketing for the brand. Brands need to retain hard-core loyal customers. For example, Dunkin' knows that loyalty is essential to its business, so it rewards its loyal customers with free food and coffee through its DD Perks program.

Metrics to Measure Brand Effectiveness

Brand sentiment is challenging to measure. Unlike sales or revenue, sentiment is not easily quantifiable. However, brands must measure their effectiveness because organizations invest heavily in building brands. There are three ways to quantify a brand's impact: brand lift, brand engagement, and brand preference.

Brand lift measures perception over time. To determine whether the campaign improved perceptions, brands can survey customers and noncustomers about their perception of a brand pre-campaign and again post-campaign. Keep in mind that positive perception doesn't necessarily mean that people will make a purchase; it simply indicates a positive affect toward the brand.

Brand engagement measures how deeply the customer identifies emotionally with a brand. Deeply engaged customers typically make more purchases, advocate for the brand, and become loyal customers. Social media metrics, time spent on site, subscriptions, and bounce rate are ways to measure brand engagement.

Brand preference measures consumer behavior by determining the degree to which a brand is preferred over others in the category. Brand preference is the most accurate of the three measures in predicting sales, as its focus is on behavior over attitudes. Marketing research is the best way to assess brand preference.

MARKETING DASHBOARD

Profit Margins

Profit margins are a widely used financial measure to determine the profitability of a business, considering the cost to manufacture and sell a product or service and measuring how much of every dollar in sales or services your company keeps from its earnings. **Cost of goods sold**, or COGS, describes expenses directly attributable to the product or service. It is important to deduct COGS from profitability to fully understand how much direct costs impact profitability. However, expenses don't end once manufacturing costs are considered. Companies pay for overhead, such as office space, trucks, and warehouses. They also account for depreciation on their assets, pay taxes, and incur costs for employee salaries. All of these expenses chip away at profitability. Profit margin calculates profitability after expenses.

There are two types of profit margin on an income statement: gross profit and net profit.

Gross profit margin equates to net sales minus the cost of goods sold. The gross margin shows the amount of profit made before deducting selling, general, and administrative (SG&A) costs. The formula for gross profit margin is

$$\text{Gross Profit Margin} = \frac{(\text{Net Sales} - \text{COGS})}{\text{Net Sales}} \times 100$$

The calculation is expressed as a percentage.

Net profit margin takes the calculation one step further. It deducts all expenses from profitability, including administrative, sales, amortization, debt payments, taxes, income, and asset depreciation. This provides a more accurate look at profitability because it considers all the costs associated with producing and selling the product or service. The formula for net profit margin is

$$\text{Net Profit Margin} = \frac{(\text{Revenue} - \text{COGS} - \text{Other Taxes \& Expenses})}{\text{Revenue}} \times 100$$

The calculation is expressed as a percentage.

Suppose your sandwich shop is interested in its profit margins for a single order. Look at the chart and calculate the gross and net profit margins.

Total revenue	$6.25
COGS	$3.50
Administrative, sales	$0.75
Taxes, depreciation, debt payments, amortization	$0.50

Table 9.3

Solution

Gross profit margin: 44%

Net profit margin: 24%

Which measure is more accurate?

Solution

Net profit margin considers all expenses, so it is a more accurate measure than gross profit margin that only considers COGS.

Your business partner, Priya, wants to decrease the revenue of a single order to $5.50. How will that impact your profit margins?

Solution

Profitability per order will decrease if revenue decreases unless COGS or other expenses are reduced in turn.

Knowledge Check

It's time to check your knowledge on the concepts presented in this section. Refer to the Answer Key at the end of the book for feedback.

1. Domino's Pizza recently added sandwiches to its menu. This is an example of a ________.
    a. line extension

   b. brand extension
   c. multibrand
   d. new brand

2. The North Face adds a new parka to its line of North Face–branded winter coats. This is an example of a
   ________.
   a. line extension
   b. brand extension
   c. multibrand
   d. new brand

3. Bethany purchases a different bar soap every time she shops based on what is on sale. Bethany can be
   considered a ________.
   a. switcher
   b. shifting loyal
   c. split loyal
   d. hard-core loyal

4. Jorge only purchases Apple computers and will not accept a substitute. Jorge can be considered a ________.
   a. switcher
   b. shifting loyal
   c. split loyal
   d. hard-core loyal

5. Which of the following brand metrics measures intended behavior?
   a. Brand lift
   b. Brand engagement
   c. Brand preference
   d. Brand equity

9.7 Creating Value through Packaging and Labeling

Learning Outcomes

By the end of this section, you will be able to:

LO 1 Describe how an organization creates value through packaging and labeling.
LO 2 Explain how packaging is used as a marketing tool.

Creating Value through Packaging and Labeling

If you have ever purchased from Apple, you know the power of sleek packaging. Apple is known for its simple white design packaging with metallic logos. Products are visually appealing in their packages, and unboxing an Apple product feels like an experience. Apple's packaging is as innovative as its products, which brings us to an important lesson in packaging. The package and label must represent the brand effectively (see Figure 9.10). While not one of the 4Ps of marketing, packaging is an important element of the marketing mix based on its close tie to the product. Packaging is also a critical shopper marketing tool as related to place. And, certainly, effective packaging can be its own form of promotion.

Figure 9.10 Product packaging can be a powerful promotional tool because of its close product connection, as demonstrated by Apple packaging. (credit: "iPad Pro & Apple Pencil" by Brett Jordan/flickr, CC BY 2.0)

A package essentially serves as a container for the product. It has a functional purpose to protect the product from harm. Package designers are first and foremost concerned with protecting the product and secondarily with designing an appealing package and label that piques interest on store shelves and online retailers' websites.

There are a variety of benefits to effective packaging and labeling. The first is that consumers see packaging before seeing a product. This provides a sensory experience that can influence a purchase. Colors, fonts, and logos can appeal to the eye, while packaging material can appeal to the sense of touch. These clues give a customer a sense of what to expect inside the package.

Additionally, the package reflects the brand, cuing the customer in to the brand feeling. For example, LaCroix is flavored carbonated water sold in brightly colored cans. The cans, as seen below, attempt to make the customer feel the excitement of opening a tasty carbonated beverage (see Figure 9.11).

Figure 9.11 The LaCroix can is a product container that reflects the brand and creates a feeling of fun and excitement for the customer. (credit: "Grapefruit La Croix + Flowers" by www.quotecatalog.com/quotes/inspirational/flickr, CC BY 2.0)

The functional benefits of packaging are numerous. First, a package serves to store the product to protect it from harm in transit from manufacturer to customer. Items such as foam and cardboard shield the product from damage and keep it clean. Second, packaging can also serve as convenience and safety for customers to carry items and store them in the home. For example, Tide Pods are sold in a plastic container with a child-locked lid. This packaging is convenient for customers to safely store the pods in their home.

Third, packaging can aid in the product's usability or become a part of the product experience itself. For example, drinkable yogurt is sold in small bottles. The bottles become part of the product experience when a consumer takes a sip of the yogurt. Fourth, packaging and labeling can aid in a brand's compliance with the law. For example, the Federal Trade Commission Act of 1914 stipulates that false, misleading, or deceptive labels or packaging may be upheld as unfair competition.[13] Thus, packaging and labeling allow a brand to be clear, accurate, and transparent in communication with customers.

Packaging can also have perceptual benefits to customers as they seek to associate with brands. Brand packaging containing logos might indicate status of the customer or signal the customer's values pertaining to quality. Tiffany & Co. is known for its "little blue box," a package that indicates status and a quality product inside (see Figure 9.12). The blue color of the box is a copyrighted by Tiffany as part of its brand's intellectual property.[14]

Figure 9.12 Known for its distinctive shade of blue, Tiffany's little blue box shares the company's brand value with consumers via a perceptual connection. (credit: "Tiffany & Co - Boxes" by ajay_suresh/flickr, CC BY 2.0)

Packaging Used as a Marketing Tool

Packaging can be used to differentiate a brand, either through design or functionality. For example, beautifully designed packages, such as Tiffany's little blue box, differentiate the brand through its status. Meanwhile, functional packaging, such as potato chip bags filled with air, serves as differentiation to deliver uncrushed chips.

Packaging can also create a customer experience. Unboxing a product can contribute to the positive emotions associated with a brand. Artisans who sell goods on Etsy understand packaging as a contributor to customer experience. Artisans will often take special care to package goods beautifully with a handwritten note of gratitude. Personalization and packaging make Etsy customers feel involved in an experience.

Packaging can display the value of a product. A well-designed, attractive package demonstrates value instead of a package that frustrates a consumer. For example, American Girl dolls are packaged in a box with a window to show the doll's face and serve as a keepsake for the owner. The packaging is so popular that some collectors purchase the package without a doll.

Knowledge Check

It's time to check your knowledge on the concepts presented in this section. Refer to the Answer Key at the end of the book for feedback.

1. How can a brand capture attention with packaging?
   a. Location in store
   b. Supply chain
   c. Colors, fonts, and logos
   d. Printing the price on the package

2. Which of the following functional benefits of packaging is at play when the package becomes a part of the product?
   a. Storage
   b. Convenience
   c. Safety
   d. Usability

3. Which of the following functional benefits of packaging is at play when the package protects the customer from personal harm?
   a. Storage
   b. Convenience
   c. Safety
   d. Usability

4. Maria purchased a Louis Vuitton purse for her mom because of the dust cover that protects the purse from wear and tear. This is an example of packaging used as a marketing tool for ________.
   a. brand differentiation
   b. creating customer experience
   c. displaying value
   d. encouraging people to purchase

5. The brand team at a technology company created product packaging that was enjoyable to unbox. This is an example of packaging used as a marketing tool for ________.
   a. brand differentiation
   b. creating customer experience
   c. displaying value
   d. encouraging people to purchase

9.8 Environmental Concerns Regarding Packaging

Learning Outcomes

By the end of this section, you will be able to:
   LO 1 Describe environmental concerns with respect to product packaging.
   LO 2 Discuss strategies that are being used to address environmental concerns.

Environmental Concerns in Product Packaging

Consumers are increasingly concerned about the environmental impact of packaging and its contribution to waste. A study by McKinsey indicates that more than half of US consumers are highly concerned about the impact of product packaging. While it is not a top criterion for purchase, product packaging is a consideration among consumers. Furthermore, consumers are willing to purchase products that have green packaging, such as recycled plastics and fiber-based substitutes.[15]

Groceries are typically packaged in glass, cardboard, plastic, and metal cans. Single-serve plastics are a concern when used for groceries, as they cannot be recycled. Electronics and other fragile products may be packaged with cardboard and foam, which can find their way into landfills. In addition to the energy used to manufacture the product, packaging adds to the environmental burden. Discarded product packaging can be found in landfills, as street litter, and in water sources, harming the environment. Creation of product packaging depletes critical resources, such as trees, and adds to air pollution.

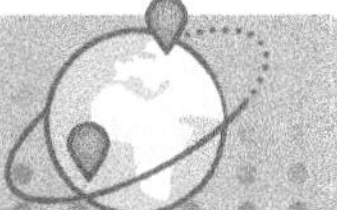

LINK TO LEARNING

How Much Plastic Floats in the Great Pacific Garbage Patch?

Check out this website that describes the impact (https://openstax.org/r/theoceancleanup) of the Great Pacific Garbage Patch. Think about the impact that packaging has on the environment and what you can do to reduce your personal plastic waste.

Companies are innovating on packaging to make it sustainable. As you may see at a restaurant like Chipotle, brands are adopting more fiber-based packaging and compostable, and recyclable options (see Figure 9.13).

Figure 9.13 Chipotle's commitement to the environment through sustainable packaging and reuse is a strong part of its brand. (credit: "Quesadilla Steak Burrito + Carnitas Bowl" by punctuated/flickr, CC BY 2.0)

Companies are also looking at ways to reduce packaging to only its necessary components. Boxed Water Is Better has adopted a cardboard box for its water that is 75 percent paper and 100 percent recyclable (see Figure 9.14). The packaging is free of BPA and other chemicals. The paper is ethically sourced and shipped flat to reduce the amount of space in a truck, further reducing the company's carbon footprint.[16]

Figure 9.14 Boxed Water Is Better makes sustainable packaging decisions in order to be environmentally responsible. (credit: "Boxed Water, Complete with an Expiry Date. Meanwhile, There's a Drought in California" by Schill/flickr, CC BY 2.0)

Cradle-to-cradle packaging design takes the waste out of the life cycle of a package. The package is designed to be something that can be reused or 100 percent recycled. It is meant to imitate nature's processes by being regenerative. A cradle-to-cradle approach uses renewable energy and keeps parts of the biological world within the biological world. In a similar way, some consumer goods flow in a technical cycle, so that the material resources can be generated into new products (see Figure 9.15).

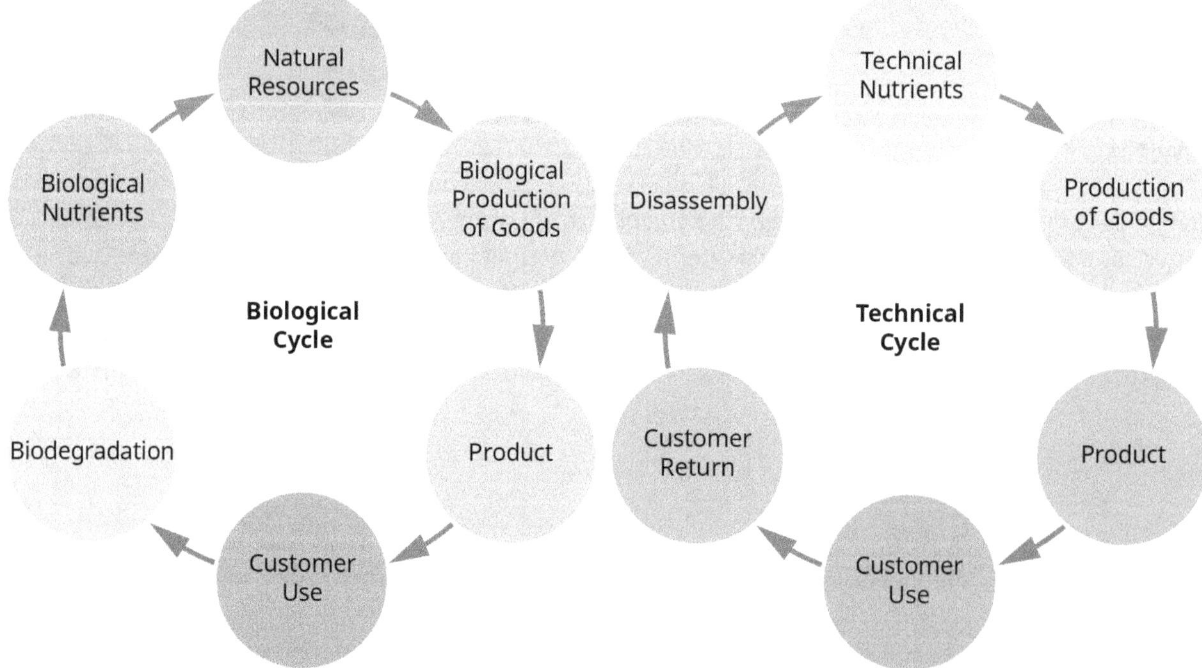

Figure 9.15 The Cradle-to-Cradle Approach (attribution: Copyright Rice University, OpenStax, under CC BY 4.0 license)

E-commerce introduces an additional challenge: How can companies sustainably ship single products to a customer? Companies must consider protecting the item, efficiency, cost, and sustainability in their e-commerce packaging. Companies can reduce packaging and use recycled or recyclable materials in their packaging. Additionally, companies can provide return-ready packaging so packages that need to be returned to the manufacturer are the same packages that arrive with the product.

Knowledge Check

It's time to check your knowledge on the concepts presented in this section. Refer to the Answer Key at the end of the book for feedback.

1. Which of the following is not a type of grocery product packaging?
   a. Paper
   b. Plastic
   c. Metal
   d. Wood

2. Which of the following is not part of the technical cycle?
   a. Product
   b. Use
   c. Disassembly
   d. Natural resources

3. Which of the following is a trend in sustainable packaging?
   a. Increasing the amount of packaging
   b. Using boxes
   c. Using only necessary resources
   d. Using plastic

4. Where can discarded packaging be found?
   a. Water sources
   b. Landfills
   c. On the ground
   d. All of these are correct.

5. Which part of the cradle-to-cradle approach is regenerative?
   a. Production
   b. Product
   c. Use
   d. Biodegradation

9.9 Ethical Issues in Packaging

Learning Outcomes

By the end of this section, you will be able to:
- **LO** 1 Explain ethical issues with respect to product packaging.
- **LO** 2 Discuss product safety and ethical packaging trends.

The Importance of Ethics in Product Packaging

In addition to concerns about sustainability, marketing professionals must be mindful of ethical concerns regarding packaging. Remember, a consumer can see the package on the store shelf, not the product inside.

The customer is seeking guidance, explanation, and assurance of a product's quality from the packaging. The package must not mislead customers about the size, quality, ingredients, or health claims. The graphics on a package must also properly represent the product inside. For example, a package might display a photo of a product that is larger or more substantial than the product inside, leading the consumer to erroneously believe that the product matches the photo.

Product packaging should be effective in protecting the product. Therefore, brands have a responsibility beyond sustainability to design packaging that ensures that the product survives transport from the manufacturer, to the wholesaler, to the retailer, and finally home with the customer. Think about the last time you purchased eggs at the grocery store. The eggs are quite fragile, but they are packaged in such a way that minimizes damage as the container travels from the farm to your home. It would be unethical for a brand to reduce packaging to save money and leave the consumer with a damaged product.

Additionally, product packaging informs the customer of important safety issues. For example, a package with small parts might have a warning that it is a choking hazard for children under the age of three.

Companies must consider groups beyond their customers. Government, advocacy groups, and NGOs may influence ethical packaging. Some experts predict that ethical packaging will become a legal mandate, so brands have an incentive to think about packaging today and prepare for a more sustainable future.

Chapter Summary

Products are the consumer offering. They are the reason that the customer is making a value exchange. Products and services differ but are inextricably linked through experiences. Consumer products are classified in four ways based on consumer behavior, price, and distribution. Meanwhile, business and industrial products are classified by materials, parts, capital items, and supplies/services.

Products are often not the only offering for a company. Rather, products are sold in product lines and mixes to maximize consumer choice and profitability. Companies may stretch or fill their product lines to appeal to new customers or create new options for existing offerings. A product lives through a product life cycle, including introduction, growth, maturity, and decline, all of which consider revenue and growth. Marketing decisions are often made based on where a product is in the product life cycle. Companies may use levers such as product innovation, pricing, and promotion to encourage purchase.

Ultimately, products become part of a brand. A brand is a feeling that is evoked and a reason that consumers might make a purchase. Brand equity is an intangible asset with tangible value for a company, so it must be protected. Brands position themselves in consumers' minds to capture brand equity. Developing a brand can occur through extension or creating a new offering. Consumers have varying degrees of brand loyalty, which can be measured through preference, lift, and engagement.

Packages are more than containers for products, they are also an extension of the brand. They are useful in brand identity, differentiation, and customer experience. Packaging and labeling also serve functional benefits such as storage, convenience, protection, safety, usability, and legality. Brands should be mindful that packaging has an environmental impact. Brands are continually innovating their packaging designs to meet sustainability expectations.

Key Terms

actual product   product available for purchase

augmented product   product having unseen aspects essential to customers

brand   an intangible asset with tangible value; made up of promotion efforts and customer meaning

brand engagement   measure of how deeply the customer identifies emotionally with a brand

brand equity   the additional value that a brand has over a substitute

brand extensions   products that leverage the brand name to new product categories

brand lift   measure of customer and noncustomer perception of a product over time

brand name   the official name of a brand

brand positioning   the way a brand signals emotions in consumers' minds

brand preference   measure of the degree to which a brand is preferred over others in the category

brand value   the financial asset associated with a brand

branding   the process of developing a brand

capital items   assets valuable to a business that also have tangible value

co-brand   to bring the equity of two brands together for greater value

convenience products   products that consumers can purchase easily, quickly, and without a lot of thoughtful decision-making

core product   product solution that the customer is actually buying: convenience, ego, ease, flexibility, etc.

cost of goods sold   expenses directly attributable to the product or service

cradle-to-cradle packaging design   product design that eliminates waste from the life cycle of package

customer experience   the overarching impression that customers have of a brand

decline stage   part of the product life cycle characterized by a significant decrease in sales and profitability

divest   to sell a brand or discontinue a product to protect a portfolio

gross profit margin   comparison of profit before expenses to total revenue

growth stage   part of the product life cycle characterized by increasing sales; stage when copycat brands may enter the market

hard-core loyals   tried-and-true customers who will generally only purchase one brand in a category

harvest   to reduce all unnecessary expenses to retain any remaining revenue

introduction stage   part of the product life cycle when consumer awareness is building and sales are starting to grow

licensed brands   brands that provide the likeness of their brand as a fee for use

line extensions   products that create new opportunities for an existing product and brand

manufactured materials and parts   products used to create a product

market modification   an extension of a product to new customers

maturity stage   part of the product life cycle when sales growth slows and profitability levels off

multibrands   new brand names within a company's existing product category

national brands   name brands that sell a product or service under its corporate name and identity

net profit margin   calculation that deducts all expenses from profitability

new brands   an entirely different brand entity from a parent company

private-label brands   store brands that are similar products to a national brand and labeled privately

product item   a particular good that a company sells

product life cycle   the stages a product goes through, tracking its sales and profitability

product line   a set of products that are similar or complementary

product line depth   the number of products in a line

product line filling   products added to a product line to keep competitors from entering the market

product line stretching   addition of product lines

product mix   all the products a company sells

product mix width   the number of product lines a brand carries

product modification   alteration of products to fit the market

products   tangible items that are part of an exchange between a buyer and a seller

profit margins   a widely used financial measure to determine the profitability of a business; considers costs to manufacture and sell a product or service

rapid penetration pricing strategy   strategy that sets a lower-price strategy; appropriate when volume sales will increase market share quickly

rapid skimming strategy   strategy that sets a high price along with extensive advertising and sales promotion to establish a product in the marketplace

raw materials   products that a business needs to purchase in order to make a consumer good

services   intangible solutions that are an exchange between buyer and seller

shifting loyals   customers who are loyal to one product or service for a time, then turn their loyalty to a different product or service at another time

shopping products   products that require more thought from the consumer as they seek the best quality or price

slow penetration pricing strategy   strategy that sets low prices and little promotion to capture market share slowly in a market not susceptible to promotion

slow skimming strategy   strategy that sets high prices with low advertising and sales promotion investment

specialty products   products that have unique qualities that consumers will make an extra effort to seek out

split loyals   customers who have a consideration set of two or three products or services in a category

supplies and services   goods and services that are typically disposed of and do not contain a tangible value

switchers   customers who continually change their purchasing behaviors

trademarks (service marks)   symbols that show legal ownership of a brand name or brand mark

unsought products   consumer goods that a buyer doesn't anticipate purchasing

Applied Marketing Knowledge: Discussion Questions

1. Think of a product that you have used recently. What are the core, actual, and augmented products?

2. How would you promote a shopping product differently than a specialty product?

3. Look at the Oreo product line. Why are there so many products? What purpose does this variety serve?

4. Consider the Sears brand. Which stage of the product life cycle is Sears currently in? What do you recommend it do to change this stage?

5. Discuss a brand to which you are loyal. Why are you loyal to the brand? How does the brand contribute to your loyalty?

6. Would you consider yourself a switcher, shifting loyal, split loyal, or hard-core loyal for your favorite brand? Why?

7. Look at the Apple brand packaging in this chapter. How does this packaging meet the criteria that we discuss in the chapter?

8. Review Boxed Water Is Better's website (https://openstax.org/r/boxedwaterisbetter). How do the website and packaging address environmental concerns?

9. Discuss a brand's packaging. How could the brand reduce its packaging or introduce recyclable packaging?

10. Why are safety statements important on packaging? What might you add to product safety statements?

Critical Thinking Exercises

1. Brainstorm purchases that you have made this week. Classify each into convenience products, shopping products, specialty products, or unsought products.

2. Explain the product life cycle. How and why might it change based on certain criteria?

3. Examine the package of a product that you have in your pantry at home. Determine how the packaging aligns with the brand, protects the product, and displays value.

Building Your Personal Brand

Can you honestly say that you "own" who you are? Do your habits and mannerisms belong to you? Are you comfortable in your skin?

In her TED Talk, Harvard professor Amy Cuddy discusses how body language impacts how others perceive you. Our nonverbals give others a perception about who we are and how we are feeling. Our body language conveys dominance, much like animals do to show their power. Our posture and the space that we take up signals confidence. But sometimes we take cues from others. If our conversation partner is showing dominance, our body language might shrink in response. It turns out that posing for dominance changes the way we think and act. So use body language to your advantage next time you are trying to make an impression.[17]

Watch Amy Cuddy's video "Your Body Language May Shape Who You Are" and develop a perspective on how you can use body language to develop your personal brand. Specifically, write a 1-to-2-page document outlining what you will start doing and what you will stop doing, and explain why. Your professor might even enjoy seeing a photo of your "power pose."

Click to view content (https://openstax.org/books/principles-marketing/pages/9-building-your-personal-brand)

What Do Marketers Do?

A product manager is the keeper of a brand. Their job is to develop the product strategy—the what, where, when, and how much of a product. Then, a product manager coordinates a cross-functional team of professionals from marketing, development, finance, legal, operations, manufacturing, supply chain, and more to bring the product to market successfully and shepherd the product through its life cycle. Product managers understand how strategy underpins a product's success in the market and serves as a path to grow the brand.

Interview a product manager to determine the following:

1. What is their philosophy on successful product management from launch through the product life cycle?
2. What does their job entail? Who are the key members of their product ecosystem?
3. What is the career path that led them to this role?

Product managers can be found at companies of all sizes, including both B2B and B2C. You can use your network on LinkedIn or your professor to source an interviewee.

 ## Marketing Plan Exercise

Complete the following information about the company and products/services you chose to focus on as you develop the marketing plan throughout the course. You may need to conduct research in order to obtain necessary information.

Instructions: Using the Marketing Plan Template file you created from the Marketing and Customer Value assignment and expanded upon in Strategic Planning in Marketing, Market Segmentation, Targeting, and Positioning, and Marketing Research and Market Intelligence, complete the following section of your marketing plan:

• Marketing Strategy: Product

Submit the marketing plan to your instructor for grading and feedback.

 ## Closing Company Case

Ramblewood

In 2018, husband and wife duo Zach and Riley McDonald began getting a flood of requests to help with events. Each of them individually had significant talents. They were great foodies, and they understood good food both in taste and in presentation. Their combined skill for aesthetics in design, display, color, and texture was remarkable. And they were both gifted at bringing everything together and staging it all like a flawlessly produced Broadway show.

When the idea to create a business doing event planning started to become a reality, both were employed full-time while also tending to their young family. To say their plates were full was an understatement. However, after helping with a few events, the duo realized they had a passion for event planning, and they both really enjoyed working with people, helping others to bring their dreams to reality.

Figure 9.16 Ramblewood's unique value proposition is that it is a one-stop shop for the various components involved in hosting an

Zach and Riley were both very involved in their community, and they were often guests at events around town. They noticed a lack of coordination between all the moving event components—planning, floral design, event rentals, decor, and catering. Was there a marketplace need to coordinate an event from beginning to end?

After putting together a few events for friends and acquaintances, they received rave reviews. Requests started pouring in for their services. With a keen eye for every detail and methodical oversight for all facets of an event, the Ramblewood team had a unique niche in its market. And with a robust start, Ramblewood came to life.

Ramblewood had a compelling value proposition in that it was a one-stop-shop for all event components. It was not uncommon for an event host to research, interview, and coordinate with musicians, furniture and linen rentals, caterers, florists, bakers, digital designers, and printers. Ramblewood would do it all and coordinate it seamlessly to take some of the stress off the work of an event.

While weddings might be the primary event market, Ramblewood had a strong following with corporations, family reunions, baby showers, bridal showers, and birthday parties. No event was too big or small for Ramblewood. If clients wanted to host an event to flawlessly match a vision, Ramblewood could make it a reality.

With over a decade of art and design experience, Zach and Riley were able to sit down with their clients and hear about their dreams and visions to bring them to reality. The team had a special skill for looking at creative ways to stretch the budgets and create focal points that would make an experience unforgettable.

As the business was getting off the ground, Zach and Riley wondered how to scale and still create the unique experience expected by every event. However, they were worried that quick growth might damage their unique brand. The two wanted to maintain the integrity of the brand. Every event deserved to have the same attention to detail and beauty they had built in to their very first event.

Zach and Riley quickly realized that every event they managed was in fact their "calling card." Guests who attended Ramblewood events talked about the experience. Guests discussed the beauty of the flowers, the exceptional food, the layout and decor, and most importantly, how well the event flowed. Each event had elements that created "oohs" and "ahs" that prompted the question, Who created this event? Marketing through word of mouth and social media seemed to be creating the growth engine Zach and Riley were seeking.

The essence of the Ramblewood brand was to create the vision and develop a magical experience for every guest in attendance. "From small intimate home parties or dinners, to large upscale corporate events, we love them all. We love hearing what the event is about and who it is for and then custom building your event into a true lasting experience"[18] was Ramblewood's mission.

After four years of unforgettable events, the duo chose to extend their brand with an upscale gourmet grocery market to deliver event elements in one location. Market customers could stop in and take a little bit of Ramblewood home. Ramblewood created RMarket—a place for a few magical moments available for everyone, including napkins, flowers, food, decor, and dishes.

The small company Zach and Riley launched was growing rapidly, and its brand was associated with the best events in the South. Growth was coming with the addition of its gourmet food market, and the two were looking for the next steps for their business. [19]

To learn more about Ramblewood, visit its website (https://openstax.org/r/ramblewoodco).

1. Ramblewood provides many benefits to its customers. What are the four levels of product provided by Ramblewood?

2. Products are tangible items offered for exchange between a buyer and seller. Services are intangible solutions that are also an exchange between buyer and seller. Ramblewood provides event planning. As part of its "offering," it also supplies flowers, decor, and food. Where does the Ramblewood offering fall on the product–service continuum?

3. Ramblewood was able to capitalize on positive word of mouth to build its business at the introduction stage. As it entered the growth phase, it incorporated some marketing strategies used by many companies. What did Ramblewood do to fuel growth?

4. Brands are built in the hearts and minds of the customers. Successful brands engage customers on a personal level, connecting to their emotions and needs. Name some of the strategies Ramblewood uses to create its brand.

References

1. "Compare Bikes: Which One Is Right for You?," Peloton, accessed February 1, 2022, https://www.onepeloton.com/bikes/compare; "Tread Specs: Take a Closer Look," Peloton, accessed February 1, 2022, https://www.onepeloton.com/tread/specs.

2. Marco Iansiti and Karim R. Lakhani, *Competing in the Age of AI: Strategy and Leadership When Algorithms and Networks Run the World* (Boston: Harvard Business Review Press, 2020).

3. Erica Schneider, "How Netflix Creates Immersive Experiences with Exceptional Design and UX," *All Things Data-Driven Marketing* (blog), CXL, August 27, 2021, https://cxl.com/blog/netflix-design/.

4. John A. Davis, *Competitive Success: How Branding Adds Value* (Hoboken, NJ: John Wiley, 2010), 76.

5. Roberto A. Ferdman, "Goodbye, Good Old Greek Yogurt," *Washington Post*, December 18, 2015, https://www.washingtonpost.com/news/wonk/wp/2015/12/18/goodbye-good-old-greek-yogurt/.

6. Kieran Fogarty et al., "New Coke," *Encyclopaedia Britannica*, August 13, 2018, https://www.britannica.com/topic/New-Coke.

7. "Sales of the Leading Liquid Laundry Detergent Brands of the United States in 2018," Statista, accessed May 19, 2022, https://www.statista.com/statistics/188716/top-liquid-laundry-detergent-brands-in-the-united-states/.

8. Kevin Lane Keller and Vanitha Swaminathan, *Strategic Brand Management: Building, Measuring, and Managing Brand Equity*, 5th ed. (Hoboken, NJ: Pearson, 2020).

9. "What Is a Trademark?," United States Patent and Trademark Office, last modified June 13, 2022, https://www.uspto.gov/trademarks/basics/what-trademark.

10. Steven Begley and Angus McOuat, "Turning Private Labels into Powerhouse Brands," Retail Insights, McKinsey & Company, October 30, 2020, https://www.mckinsey.com/industries/retail/our-insights/turning-private-labels-into-powerhouse-brands.

11. Mark Mallinger and Gerry Rossy, "The Trader Joe's Experience," *Graziadio Business Review* 10, no. 2 (2007), https://gbr.pepperdine.edu/2010/08/the-trader-joes-experience/.

12. Drew Wilkinson, "How Trader Joe's Makes the Experience Its Competitive Advantage," *Customer Service Blog*, Fonolo, updated November 17, 2021, https://fonolo.com/blog/2019/03/how-trader-joes-makes-customer-experience-its-competitive-advantage/.

13. "Federal Trade Commission Act," *Encyclopaedia Britannica*, August 16, 2017, https://www.britannica.com/event/Federal-Trade-Commission-Act.

14. "Tiffany Blue," Tiffany & Co. Newsroom, Tiffany & Co., last modified December 14, 2020, https://press.tiffany.com/our-story/tiffany-blue/.

15. David Feber et al., "Sustainability in Packaging: Inside the Minds of US Consumers," Insights on Paper, Forest Products & Packaging, McKinsey & Company, October 21, 2020, https://www.mckinsey.com/industries/paper-forest-products-and-packaging/our-insights/sustainability-in-packaging-inside-the-minds-of-us-consumers.

16. "Is Boxed Water Really Better?," Boxed Water, accessed December 10, 2021, https://boxedwaterisbetter.com/pages/how-we-compare.

17. Amy Cuddy, "Your Body Language May Shape Who You Are," filmed June 28, 2012, in Edinburgh, Scotland, TEDGlobal 2012 video, 20:46, https://www.ted.com/talks/amy_cuddy_your_body_language_may_shape_who_you_are.

18. http://www.ramblewoodco.com/events

19. "Wedding Specialists: Ramblewood," *CityScope Magazine,* https://cityscopemag.com/city-scope/wedding-specialists-ramblewood/

Maintaining a Competitive Edge with New Offerings

Figure 10.1 A new product's success is dependent on the product development cycle and why consumers adopt new products. New product development involves a process of stages. (credit: "Chandelier" by Drew Coffman/flickr, CC BY 2.0)

Chapter Outline

In the Spotlight

Swarovski, a well-known company that specializes in crystal cutting, developed a campaign around diversity and acceptance a few years ago in an effort to reach worldwide customers. One such campaign that was launched during the holiday season in China focused on the Advent calendar despite the fact that the observance of Advent is primarily a Western tradition. If you're not familiar with Advent calendars, they're a type of calendar that counts down the days from December 1 to December 25, Christmas day. On each day in December, you open a pouch or flap on the calendar where a small candy or toy is included. Swarovski took the concept to a whole new level.

The Swarovski Advent calendar retailed for $458 and contained 25 individual compartments with Swarovski crystals. You might be thinking that the price is a little high, but think again—the market supported the price, and the calendars sold out quickly. While the physical Advent calendars took off in the market, so did the digital version. With the digital calendar, users would play interactive games, earn game cards, and then swap the cards with other people. After they collected seven unique cards, they could turn them in to Swarovski for a gift.

Later in this chapter, we're going to explore some measurement metrics for determining the success of new product launches, but one immediate indicator that a product launch was successful is a quick sellout. For Swarovski, the fact that their Advent calendar sold out so quickly is a testament to the successful product launch.[1]

10.1 New Products from a Customer's Perspective

Learning Outcomes

By the end of this section, you will be able to:

- **LO** 1 Define a new product.
- **LO** 2 Explain "newness" from the perspective of the customer.
- **LO** 3 Explain the risks and rewards of developing new products.

New Product Defined

You've probably watched at least one episode of the popular television show *Shark Tank*, where budding entrepreneurs pitch their business plans to a panel of investors in return for funding. To date, over 1,000 sales pitches have been made on the show—some forgettable, others memorable—and some pitches have resulted in wildly successful businesses. Some of *Shark Tank*'s most successful products include the Squatty Potty (over $200 million in sales since appearing on *Shark Tank*), Bombas Socks (over $225 million), and Scrub Daddy (over $330 million).[2]

LINK TO LEARNING

Shark Tank

You will learn a lot about new products and their development by watching *Shark Tank*. You can watch the episodes online here (https://openstax.org/r/sharktank). Interested in learning which *Shark Tank* products have been most successful? Check out these stories:

- **Shark Tank Tales:** "12 Most Successful Shark Tank Products" (https://openstax.org/r/bestsellingsharktank)
- **Good Housekeeping:** "Top 42 Gifts That Got Their Start on Shark Tank" (https://openstax.org/r/homeproducts)
- **Entrepreneur:** "Shark Tank" (https://openstax.org/r/sharktanktopic)
- **Vulture:** "Shark Tank Contestant Who Pitched Face Masks in 2009 Has No Regrets" (https://openstax.org/r/sharktankirina)
- **Looper:** "The Most Expensive Deals on Shark Tank" (https://openstax.org/r/themostexpensivedeals)
- **Hustle Story:** "21 Most Famous Shark Tank Failures in 2022" (https://openstax.org/r/the21mostfamoussharktank)
- **Failory:** "Shark Tank: 7 Products That Failed & Their 3 Biggest Mistakes" (https://openstax.org/r/sharktankfailures)
- **Bplans:** "5 Lessons Shark Tank Can Teach You About Pitching to Angel Investors" (https://openstax.org/r/5sharktanklessons)

Perhaps you've got an idea for a new product that's going to take the world by storm. If so, this chapter will be especially relevant for you. We're going to explore everything about new products in this chapter: the stages of new product development, what facets of those new products contribute to their success or failure, how consumers adopt new products, and more.

You would think that a "new product" would be an easy definition, but the term can mean different things. In fact, there are five different categories of new products (see Figure 10.2), each one unique.

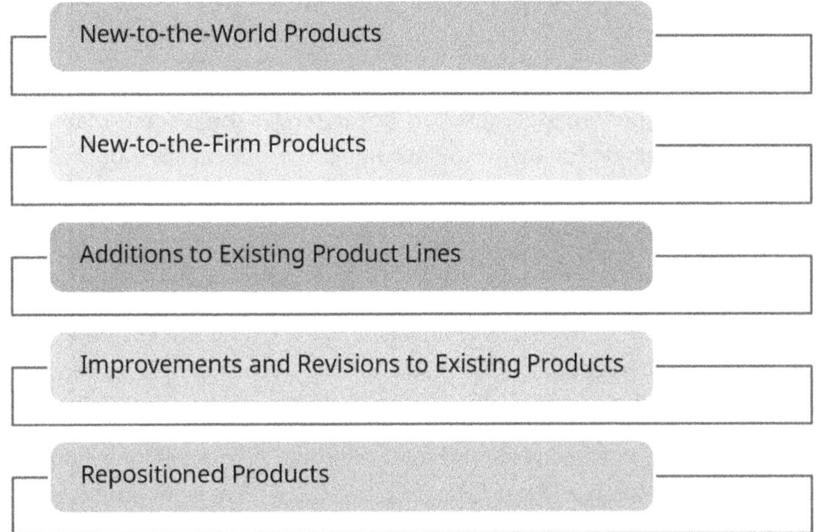

Figure 10.2 Categories of New Products (attribution: Copyright Rice University, OpenStax, under CC BY 4.0 license)

Let's look at these new product categories in more detail.

- **New-to-the-World Products**: New-to-the-world products essentially are new inventions that create new markets. Some examples from products recently introduced include biomagnetic ear stickers for weight loss, cat self-groomers, and portable blenders.[3]
- **New-to-the-Firm Products**: These are products that are new to a company but not to the world. It's likely that marketers have seen a gap in the market and their product line and attempted to fill that void by adding a "me-too" type of product to their product line. For example, Nature Valley originally only made granola cereal but later introduced granola bars that could be eaten "on the go."[4] There's a perfect example of a company that saw a gap in the market and added a product that wasn't new to the world, but it certainly was new to Nature Valley.
- **Additions to Existing Product Lines**: Recall that a product line is a group of related products marketed under a single brand. Additions to existing product lines are simple product line extensions, designed to "flesh out" the product line. During its 130+ years in business, Coca-Cola has launched a number of product line extensions. The next time you're in a supermarket, look on the shelves in the soft drink aisle. You'll likely see a number of different flavors and styles of Coca-Cola varieties, such as Coca-Cola Cherry, Coca-Cola Cherry Vanilla, Coca-Cola Vanilla, Coca-Cola Zero, and more.[5]
- **Improvements and Revisions to Existing Products**: This is when existing products are improved. Think about how many times you've seen "new and improved" on the packaging of a product that you've been using for a while, like laundry detergent. As a concrete example, Meta (formerly Facebook) released its Oculus Quest 2 VR (virtual reality) headset and controllers late in 2021, which was simply an updated version of its original Oculus Quest.[6]

LINK TO LEARNING

Oculus Quest 2

Are you new to VR and would like to see what you can do with the Oculus Quest 2 device? Check out this short video where Meta Quest uses YouTube to market the features and benefits of using the Oculus 2. Meta Quest also provides tons of videos about how you can use the Oculus 2 in fitness, gaming, social experiences, and space exploration. Check out those Meta Quest videos here. (https://openstax.org/r/metaquestvr)

Click to view content (https://openstax.org/books/principles-marketing/pages/10-1-new-products-from-a-customers-perspective)

- **Repositioned Products**: Another reminder: product positioning is the process that defines how your product is different from others on the market.[7] Repositioned products are those that are retargeted for a new use or application. For example, Bayer repositioned its aspirin from treating headaches, fever, and inflammation to also safeguarding against heart attacks.[8]

Customer Perceptions of Newness

Just as there are different ways to categorize new products, there are different customer perceptions of newness. The difference in these perceptions is the result of how much change they cause in a consumer's existing habits. Newness can be categorized three ways:

- **Discontinuous Innovation:** Sometimes referred to as radical or disruptive innovations, discontinuous innovations consist of new-to-the-world products that are so different from products currently existing in the market that they require a significant change in consumer behavior when adopted. For example, think about how cell phones have changed the way we communicate today. Older cell phones did one thing—make and receive phone calls. With a smartphone, you can still make phone calls, but you can also listen to music, send and receive emails, surf the Internet, conduct online banking, and get driving directions, to name just a few. Consider how learning to operate all the features on your smartphone required you to change your behavior.[9]
- **Continuous Innovation:** This is the other end of the spectrum from discontinuous innovation. With continuous innovation, the existing product undergoes marginal changes and doesn't alter customer habits. For example, when Sony introduced new TVs that promised sharper, brighter TV pictures, the picture quality was better, but as a consumer, it didn't require you to change your TV viewing habits.[10]
- **Dynamically Continuous Innovation:** With dynamically continuous innovation, some changes in consumer habits are necessary, but the changes aren't as large or small as you see with the two other types of innovation. For example, manual and even electric typewriters have gone the way of the dinosaur since the advent of PCs, but the keyboard layout remained the same, so little change was required with consumer habits.

Risks and Rewards of Developing New Products

We started this chapter with a discussion of *Shark Tank* and some of the products that have been successful in the market as a result of the television show. However, not all products are successful, and there are both risks and rewards when developing new products.

Rewards of Developing New Products

You have probably heard the saying "No risk, no reward," and nothing could be truer in terms of new product development. However, a company's ability to maintain its competitive edge in the market requires a delicate balance between the necessity and the challenges of new product development.

We've already looked at Swarovski's successful product launch of its Advent calendar, but let's consider a few other examples to show you just how rewarding a well-executed product launch can be. Instagram, the social networking platform that allows users to share photos and videos, was first released in October 2010, and it quickly racked up 25,000 users in one day. The company now boasts that it has more than 1 billion (that's with a "b") monthly active users. Instagram succeeded by introducing bold features in its platform, from video editing features to interactive features like face filters and polling.[11]

And, of course, we can't talk about successful product launches without mentioning Apple, whose original iPhone was one of the most successful product launches in history—racking up 1 million units sold within just 74 days of its launch.[12]

Keeping the success of these products in mind, let's look at the reasons why products succeed.

- **Targeting New Markets:** New product development gives businesses the opportunity to expand into new markets, providing an opportunity to connect with different target markets. This creates the added benefit of growing their customer base. For example, research from the Centers for Disease Control and Prevention (CDC) indicated that Americans were reporting symptoms of anxiety and depression since COVID-19 came about, so PepsiCo launched two new drinks that claim to support relaxation—Driftwell and Soulboost.[13]

- **Increasing Market Share:** Think about market share as a pizza, and every company that participates in the market has a slice (obviously some slices are bigger than others). As the market grows, a company needs to expand with it in order to keep its share of that pizza, but it can also increase its market share—and take another slice or two of pizza—through new product development.

- **Increasing Revenue Stream:** Revenue streams are all the ways a company can generate cash from the sale of its products or services. New products and/or services will create additional revenue streams that will generate extra income for the business, perhaps spurring even more new product development. For example, Apple generates revenue streams by developing new hardware products such as the Apple Watch and AirPods wireless headphones, and the company enjoys recurring revenues from services such as iCloud, Apple Music, and Apple TV+.

Risks of Developing New Products

Developing new products has many unforeseen issues and surprises, so it should come as no surprise to you that there are some significant risks associated with these efforts.

- **Lack of Differentiation:** There can be many problems with the design of a product, including insufficient differentiation from competitors' products. Perhaps the product or service did not solve enough problems or did not solve them sufficiently, or the product incompletely addresses the needs of the target market.

  For example, in 2021 Apple discontinued its HomePod smart speaker, which was not perceived as being sufficiently different from Amazon's Echo despite offering high-quality music playback.

- **Financial Feasibility:** New product development is expensive and can be financially risky for companies. It's important that a financial feasibility study is conducted in the earliest stages of new product development to determine whether it's worth launching the product or service in the context of sales and revenues.

  Financial feasibility is the primary reason why pharmaceutical companies typically don't invest large amounts of money in developing a new drug if the market for the drug is small. Novartis was the exception to this rule. The company developed a drug that treats children under the age of two suffering from spinal muscular atrophy (SMA). According to the Cleveland Clinic, only 1 in 10,000 children suffer from this rare genetic mutation, but Novartis went ahead and developed the drug anyway.[14] With a price tag of $2,125,000 for a one-dose treatment, it's the most expensive drug the world has ever seen.[15] You may be asking yourself, Is it worth it? Just ask the parents of a child suffering from SMA.

- **Technical Feasibility:** Technical feasibility studies are equally important as a financial feasibility study. Does the organization have the technical resources to meet capacity? Can the technical team convert the idea into a working product or service?

  For example, while Taco Bell's Doritos Loco Taco was in development, the team wasn't sure it was technically possible to coat a taco shell with the iconic Doritos flavoring. Its research and development (R&D) department spent approximately two years developing over 40 prototype taco shells before it found the right combination of crunch, seasoning, and flavor.[16]

- **Poor Timing:** Author Joshua Harris once wrote, "The right thing at the wrong time is the wrong thing." This couldn't be truer when it comes to new product development. You may have developed the best product or service, but if it's introduced to the market at the wrong time, it's likely to fail. The product development process can take a year or longer, and imagine the market changes that can take place during that time. A new competitor may enter the market before you do, consumer preferences and needs can change, legislative or environmental regulations can change, or the economy can go south before you're ready to launch.

The situation with in-home COVID-19 testing kits is a perfect example of poor timing. By the time the US government made these kits widely available to the public, the need for these tests had greatly diminished because the majority of the population had already been vaccinated.

Knowledge Check

It's time to check your knowledge on the concepts presented in this section. Refer to the Answer Key at the end of the book for feedback.

1. Many years ago, liquid soap was introduced in place of traditional bar soaps. This innovation changed an intrinsic feature of the product, but it's used for the same purpose. This is an example of _______.
   a. discontinuous innovation
   b. continuous innovation
   c. dynamically continuous innovation
   d. noncontinuous innovation

2. Coca-Cola, a behemoth in the soft drink market, decides that it is going to develop and market Coca-Cola popsicles. What type of new product would this constitute?
   a. New-to-the-world
   b. New-to-the-firm
   c. Improvements and revision to existing products
   d. Repositioned product

3. Saundra went to the grocery store and purchased the same laundry detergent she's been buying for years, but she noticed that the packaging had been changed and the label indicated that the laundry detergent was "new and improved." What category of new products would the laundry detergent likely fall under?
   a. New-to-the-world products
   b. New-to-the-firm products
   c. Repositioned products
   d. Improvements and revisions to existing products

4. Hoffman Enterprises has introduced a new product to the market that has undergone only marginal changes and doesn't alter consumer use habits. What type of product has Hoffman Enterprises introduced?
   a. Discontinuous innovation
   b. Continuous innovation
   c. Intermittent innovation
   d. Dynamically continuous innovation

5. Sources through which a business earns income from the sales of goods or services are known as _______.
   a. capital gains
   b. incremental income
   c. profits
   d. revenue streams

10.2 Stages of the New Product Development Process

Learning Outcomes

By the end of this section, you will be able to:
- **LO** 1 Identify the stages of the new product development process.
- **LO** 2 Define and describe the important factors of each stage of development.

The New Product Development Process

The new product development process involves activities where a company thinks of a new product concept and introduces a new product offering. New product development usually follows a process divided into stages (see Figure 10.3).

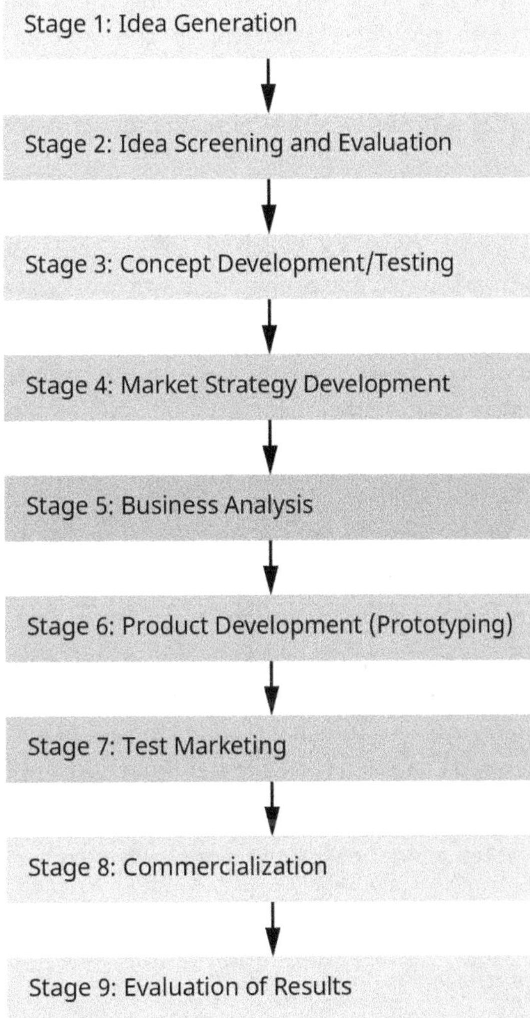

Figure 10.3 Stages in the New Product Development Process (attribution: Copyright Rice University, OpenStax, under CC BY 4.0 license)

Stage 1: Idea Generation. With idea generation, you are working to create as many ideas as you can. The purpose of this stage is to focus on the products that are more likely to turn a profit so you can reduce the product development expense later in the process and develop profitable products.[17]

Instead of looking at the new product development process in abstract terms, let's discuss a potential product idea and follow it through all the steps of the process. Imagine that you're a marketer for a food processing company, and you believe there is a gap in the market for a high-protein freeze-dried yogurt powder that can be added to juice to make a nutritious, low-fat, fruit-flavored smoothie. This is what's known as a **product idea**—a new product that a company could potentially offer to the market. This idea may have been generated by **internal sources** such as research and development (R&D), market research, or employees who are not part of R&D. On the other hand, the idea may have come from **external sources** such as customers, suppliers, distributors, or even competitors.

Stage 2: Idea Screening and Evaluation. This is the process of filtering through the ideas brought to the table by your team, picking the ones that are most likely to turn a profit, and dropping the less favorable ones. For example, with our high-protein freeze-dried yogurt powder, the team would create numerous product concepts that they then sift through to reach the best idea.

Stage 3: Concept Development and Testing. In this stage, a product idea can be turned into several **product concepts**—the perception of a new idea or innovation. The product team will consider *who* will use the product (e.g., children, athletes, or adults), *what* benefits the product will provide (e.g., meal replacement, a snack, nutrition, or energy), and *when* consumers would typically consume the product (e.g., for breakfast, as a midmorning or afternoon snack, or after a workout or exercise).

For example, your product team may come up with the following product concepts for our yogurt powder:

1. The yogurt powder would be marketed as an instant, on-the-go breakfast drink.
2. The yogurt powder would be marketed as a high-protein snack that is more nutritious than plain juice or milk.
3. The yogurt powder would be marketed to adults or athletes who work out and want to replenish the body's loss of protein during exercise.

It's important to develop these product concepts because each concept defines the product's competition. For example, Concept #1 would compete against other breakfast foods such as cereal, breakfast bars, toast, and bacon and eggs. Concept #2 would compete against juice, soft drinks, and plain milk. Concept #3 would compete against protein shakes.

Once you've developed your product concept, it's time to test that concept with consumers in what you believe to be your target market. This is what's known as **concept testing**. Concept testing is a market research method in which customers are presented with a description of a product or service.

Let's assume that the product concept we've chosen is the instant, on-the-go breakfast drink. Customers in the target market would be presented with a description of the product that may read something like: "Our product is a high-protein powdered yogurt mixture that is added to juice to make an instant breakfast smoothie that provides nutrition, good taste, and convenience. The product will be offered in individual packages, six to a box, priced at $3.49 per box."

Potential customers will then be asked a series of screening or qualifying questions, such as:

- To what extent do you like or dislike this product?
- How appealing are the attributes of the product?
- How likely would you be to purchase this product?

Quite often, these (and other) questions are scored using a five-point Likert Scale. For example, the last question might be scored on the basis of these five options: definitely would purchase; likely would purchase; may or may not purchase; unlikely to purchase; and definitely would not purchase. The answers to these questions suggest if the product will likely be successful in the market or not. If the answers are generally positive, the product concept will move to the next stage; if the answers are less than positive, the product concept will likely be rejected.

Stage 4: Market Strategy Development. Once concept testing has been completed and the decision has been made to proceed further, it's time for the product team to develop a preliminary marketing strategy plan. This plan will address the target market for the product. It will outline product positioning, pricing, distribution, promotion, budget, and both short- and long-term goals for sales, market share, and profit.

Stage 5: Business Analysis. Armed with the preliminary marketing strategy plan, the company now needs to assess the new product's business appeal. For example, the company will want to know if sales will be sufficient for the company to make the desired profit. The company will need to understand the costs involved in the new product development in terms of research and development, manufacturing, and marketing.

There are a couple of different analyses that can be done:

- Payback: This simply refers to the time frame within which the company can expect to recover the investment it made in the product development process.
- Break-even analysis: This analysis determines how many units must be sold before the company recoups its costs and starts making a profit.

These analyses are performed so that management can now determine if anticipated profits from the sale of the breakfast drink mix will satisfy company objectives. If the answer is yes, the product concept moves on to the next stage, product development. If the answer is no, the product concept is shelved.

Stage 6: Product Development. Remember that, until now, our product concept has existed only as words or perhaps a drawing. If our breakfast drink mix has passed the business analysis test, it will now move into the product development stage, and engineering will develop a physical version of the product, called a **prototype**.[18]

It's important to note that sometimes the company realizes in this stage that the product concept simply can't be translated into a commercially feasible product. For example, through market research, Maxwell House determined that consumers wanted a coffee that was "bold, vigorous, and deep tasting." However, after working with coffee blends for four months, the company determined that it was too expensive to commercially produce the formula, so Maxwell House changed the blend to meet its targeted manufacturing cost. Unfortunately, the taste of the new blend didn't meet consumers' expectations, and the new product flopped.[19]

The prototype is then put through functional and customer tests to see how well it perform. For example, at carpet manufacturer Shaw Industries, temporary employees are paid to walk on carpet samples for eight hours a day to see how the carpet holds up.[20] At Gillette, volunteers come to work unshaven so they can use certain razors, shaving cream, or aftershave and complete questionnaires. (The "motto" of this group is "We bleed so you'll get a good shave at home.")[21]

Stage 7: Test-Marketing. If the product team is satisfied with how the prototype performs functionally, the product concept is then test-marketed to determine its viability before it's launched on a large scale. Typically, the product is introduced in a limited number of stores or in a few geographic regions in order to gauge customer acceptance. There are several methods of consumer-goods marketing testing, but we'll just cover a few here:

- **Sales-Wave Research**: This is the least costly method of test-marketing. With this method, consumers are initially allowed to try the product at no cost. They are then reoffered the product (or a competitor's product) at a reduced price a number of times (i.e., sales waves). The point of this research is to see how many consumers select the new product and record their reported levels of satisfaction with the product.[22]
- **Controlled Test-Marketing**: In this type of test-marketing, the company arranges for a certain number of stores to carry the new product. The new product is delivered to the store, and marketers manage shelf position in the store, pricing, point-of-purchase displays, and more. The company then measures sales results through the scanners at checkout.
- **Test-Marketing**: Of course, the best (but also the most expensive) way to test a product concept is with a full-blown market test. The company will select a few representative cities (markets that closely resemble

the target customers) and introduce the product with a full advertising and promotional campaign. In essence, the company is measuring the success of the new product on a smaller scale before launching it on a national or even global scale. Curious to know the top cities to test-market a national product? They are Nashville, Tennessee; Cincinnati, Ohio; Indianapolis, Indiana; Charleston, South Carolina; and Jacksonville, Florida.[23]

- **Simulated Test-Markets**: With this method, consumers are exposed to simulated market situations in order to gauge their reactions. Marketers interview consumers in two stages: concept stage and after use. The concept stage interviews provide the marketer with information about the product's appeal and trial rate, whereas the post-usage interviews determine consumers' likelihood of purchasing the product again.
- **Crowdsourcing**: Crowdsourcing is the practice of using the input of a large group of people. This form of market testing would be particularly useful if your product includes mobile apps, web apps, or websites. The product team would choose a crowdsource testing platform, test the product, analyze the results, and tweak the product accordingly.[24]

Stage 8: Commercialization. In this stage, the company launches the product, complete with full-scale production, distribution, advertising, and sales promotion. The cost of launching a new product varies depending on the product itself, the industry, and the competition.

Stage 9: Evaluation of Results. As we've pointed out with the marketing metrics features in this textbook, you can't fix what you don't measure, so it's important after commercialization for the company to review the marketing performance of the new product. Is the new product accepted by consumers? Is there sufficiently high demand, sales, and profits? Are there competitors who are introducing a similar new product in the market? Depending on the answers to these questions, savvy marketers will closely monitor the performance of the new product and make changes as needed in both the marketing plan and the marketing mix strategy.[25]

CAREERS IN MARKETING

Product Development as a Career

Most companies have product manager (PM) as a job role. In this job, you manage the product creation or further development. Check out this summary of what a product developer position (https://openstax.org/r/productdeveloperjobs) entails, including average salaries.

This article from Stanford online (https://openstax.org/r/whatyouneed) outlines what you need to know to have a career in product management. ZipRecruiter also outlines skills and training needed (https://openstax.org/r/whatishowtobecome) for this job role.

Many companies post job descriptions to help you prepare. Here are a few for the product manager job role:

- Google PM (https://openstax.org/r/careersgoogle)
- Facebook (Meta) PM (https://openstax.org/r/productmanagement)
- Twitter PM (https://openstax.org/r/twitterproductmanager)
- Amazon PM (https://openstax.org/r/projectprogram)

If you're interested in learning more about the product manager job role and career, read here about the typical path you can expect (https://openstax.org/r/productmanagercareerpath).

Knowledge Check

It's time to check your knowledge on the concepts presented in this section. Refer to the Answer Key at the

end of the book for feedback.

1. A physical version of the product concept that is developed during the new product development process is called a _______.
   a. mock-up
   b. model
   c. prototype
   d. precedent

2. You've gathered customers in the target market and presented them with a description of the product concept you have selected. This process is known as _______.
   a. prototyping
   b. concept testing
   c. test-marketing
   d. crowdsourcing

3. At what stage in the new product development process would you launch the product, complete with full-scale production, distribution, advertising, and sales promotion?
   a. Test-marketing
   b. Product development
   c. Business analysis
   d. Commercialization

4. The least costly method of test-marketing is known as _______.
   a. controlled test-marketing
   b. sales-wave research
   c. simulated test-marketing
   d. crowdsourcing

5. What is the first stage in the new product development process?
   a. Idea screening and evaluation
   b. Market strategy development
   c. Commercialization
   d. Idea generation

10.3 | The Use of Metrics in Evaluating New Products

Learning Outcomes

By the end of this section, you will be able to:
- **LO** 1 Explain the importance of establishing new product metrics.
- **LO** 2 Describe metrics used to evaluate the success or failure of new products.

The Importance of Establishing New Product Metrics

There are few marketing activities that are as difficult to manage as new product development. Not only does a company have to juggle multiple tasks like new features and innovative technologies against factors like cost, risk, and time to market, but it has to ensure that it's making the most efficient use of its limited resources on new products that will meet both its short-term and long-term strategic goals. In this section we're going to review product development metrics that can measure the success (or failure) of your new product launch.

Product metrics are quantifiable data that a business tracks and analyzes to determine how successful its new product(s) are. One way that companies accomplish this is by using key performance indicators (KPIs). KPIs are target metrics set by a company as a way to measure if the product is delivering on expectations. An example of a KPI could be targeted new customers per month or revenue growth.

LINK TO LEARNING

KPIs

If you haven't already heard the term KPI, and you plan on working at a business, it will become a part of your language. No matter what job role you hold in a company, KPIs are important to understand. Learn more about KPIs from there resources:

- KPI.org: "What Is A Key Performance Indicator (KPI)? (https://openstax.org/r/kpibasics)"
- HubSpot: "How to Choose the Right KPIs for Your Business" (https://openstax.org/r/choosingkpis)
- Toucan Toco: "The Most Important KPIs to Track for Improved Marketing Efficiency" (https://openstax.org/r/mostimportantkpis)
- The Marketing Journal: "5 Marketing KPIs You Cannot Measure but Should Care About" (https://openstax.org/r/marketingjournal)
- Virtual Strategist Video: "How to Develop Key Performance Indicators"
  Click to view content (https://openstax.org/books/principles-marketing/pages/10-3-the-use-of-metrics-in-evaluating-new-products)

Specific Metrics Used to Evaluate New Products

There are any number of metrics you can use to measure the success of a new product. For our purposes, we're going to focus on just a few of the more common KPIs (see Figure 10.4).

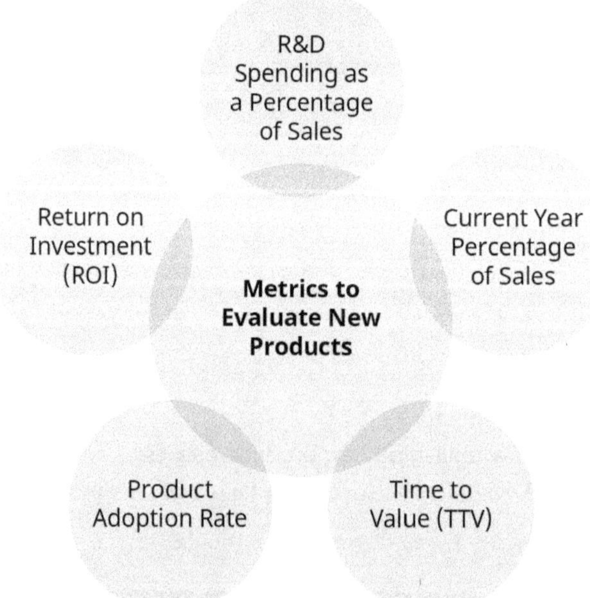

Figure 10.4 Metrics to Evaluate New Products (attribution: Copyright Rice University, OpenStax, under CC BY 4.0 license)

- **Research and Development Spending as a Percentage of Sales:** This metric is used to compare the effectiveness of R&D expenditures between companies in the same industry. It's important to use companies within the same industry because R&D numbers vary widely based upon the industry. For example, pharmaceutical and software companies tend to spend considerable dollars on R&D, whereas consumer product companies generally spend less. The percentage is calculated as R&D dollars spent divided by total sales.

- **Current Year Percentage of Sales:** This method calculates cost of goods sold, inventory, cash, and other financial line items as a percentage of sales and then applies that percentage to future sales estimates. It's a "quick and dirty" way to estimate the product's future value.[26]
- **Time to Value (TTV):** Time to value refers to how long it takes new users to recognize your product's value (sometimes referred to as the "aha!" moment in marketing). Obviously, the sooner this occurs, the better, although time to value varies widely depending upon the product itself.[27] For example, if you purchase a new book for your Kindle, it's a matter of seconds before the book is available to you. On the other hand, if you subscribe to a magazine, it may be days or weeks before you see your first issue.
- **Product Adoption Rate:** When launching a new product, this metric is almost always at or near the top of the product team's list of KPIs to track. Product adoption (or user adoption) is the process by which people learn about a product and start using its features to meet their needs.[28] The formula for calculating the adoption rate: divide the number of new users by the total number of users.
- **Return on Investment (ROI):** This is a metric formula used to evaluate the profitability, or overall value, of an investment. In marketing, you can use ROI to measure the profitability of a new product launch. To calculate the marketing ROI, you would take the sales from that product, subtract the marketing costs, divide by the marketing costs, and multiply by 100.[29]
  For example, if sales grew by $100,000 as a result of the new product launch, but the cost of the marketing campaign was $20,000, the ROI would be:

$$\text{Return on Investment (ROI)} = \frac{(\text{Sales} - \text{Costs})}{\text{Costs}} \times 100$$

$$\text{Return on Investment (ROI)} = \frac{(\$100,000 - \$20,000)}{\$20,000} \times 100 = 400\%$$

Knowledge Check

It's time to check your knowledge on the concepts presented in this section. Refer to the Answer Key at the end of the book for feedback.

1. Data measurements that businesses use to evaluate the success of new products are called ________.
    a. ROI
    b. product adoption rates
    c. R&D
    d. product metrics

2. Which method calculates cost of goods sold, inventory, cash, and other financial line items as a percentage of sales and then applies that percentage to future sales estimates?
    a. Product adoption rate
    b. Current year percentage of sales
    c. Time to value (TTV)
    d. Revenue growth rate

3. To calculate this metric, the return of the investment is divided by its cost.
    a. Time to value (TTV)
    b. R&D spending as a percentage of sales
    c. ROI
    d. Revenue growth rate

4. This metric measures how long it takes new users to recognize the value of a new product.

   a. Product adoption rate

   b. ROI

   c. Time to value (TTV)

   d. Revenue growth rate

5. Which of the following metrics would likely NOT be used to evaluate the effectiveness of new products?

   a. R&D spending as a percentage of sales

   b. Time to value (TTV)

   c. Return on investment (ROI)

   d. Annual recurring revenue (ARR)

10.4 Factors Contributing to the Success or Failure of New Products

Learning Outcomes

By the end of this section, you will be able to:

LO 1 Identify and discuss factors that contribute to the success of a new product.

LO 2 Identify and discuss factors that contribute to the failure of a new product.

What Factors Contribute to the Success of New Products?

The story about how the Dollar Shave Club was started is more than just urban legend. Founders Mark Levin and Michael Dubin met at a party and commiserated about how expensive razor blades were. After that party, using their own money and investments from start-up incubator Science Inc., they launched their website that sold razor blades much more cheaply starting in April 2011. These founders seized an opportunity based on several insights: that prices for blades charged by market leader Gillette were perceived as too high; that most men do not want to shop in stores for shaving supplies; and lastly, that the move to online/subscription boxes was gaining traction. Five years later, the company was bought by Unilever for an astounding $1 billion.[30]

LINK TO LEARNING

Direct-to-Customer Sales

Watch this viral video of the founders speaking about the virtues of direct-to-customer sales. It's funny and informative. Check it out!

Click to view content (https://openstax.org/books/principles-marketing/pages/10-4-factors-contributing-to-the-success-or-failure-of-new-products)

Instant, phenomenal, new product success is what every marketer wants to achieve when launching a new product. But the reality is quite different. When you look objectively at new product introduction success or failure, significant differences emerge between successful and unsuccessful product launches. There's a similar pattern or a recipe for success. Figure 10.5 outlines the key factors that strongly influence new product success.

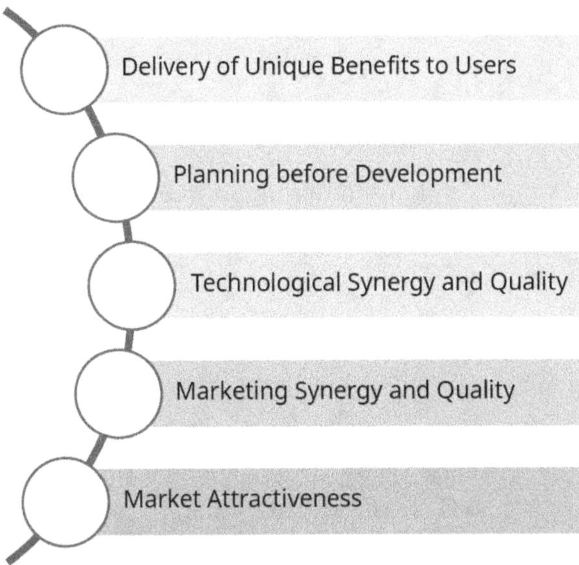

Figure 10.5 Factors Contributing to the Success of a New Product Launch (attribution: Copyright Rice University, OpenStax, under CC BY 4.0 license)

Let's explore each of these factors:

- **Delivering Unique Benefits to Users:** The product itself—in terms of its design, features, and benefits to customers—is the often the bellwether of new product success. Are you introducing a "me too" product vis-à-vis the competition, or does the new product deliver unique benefits to the consumer? It probably comes as no surprise that innovative products typically fare better than those that have few elements of differentiation. As a matter of fact, research has shown that innovative products that offer unique benefits versus the competition have five times the success rate of products with fewer elements of differentiation.[31]

- **Planning before Development:** This would seem almost intuitive, but unfortunately, many companies fail to plan properly before developing a new product. Remember the old phrase "If you fail to plan, you plan to fail." The "rule of thumb" in successful new product development is to thoroughly define the product before development gets underway. This means defining the target market, the product concept, customer needs and wants, and product requirements. Numbers don't lie. Research has demonstrated that new products in which predevelopment activities were well-defined and executed had a success rate of 75 percent versus just over 31 percent for products in which those predevelopment activities were lacking.[32]

- **Technological Synergy and Quality: Technological synergy** is when a new product is built on the firm's existing technological resources. The bottom line is that new products that have a strong fit between the project needs and the company's existing technological and production resources are typically much more successful in the marketplace. The further away the product strays from the company's current technology, the less likely it is that the product will be successful.[33]

- **Marketing Synergy and Quality:** Like technological synergy, marketing synergy is also an important factor in new product success. **Marketing synergy** examines the fit between the needs of the new product development project and the company's sales, advertising resources, customer service capabilities, distribution, and marketing research. The closer the fit, the more successful the product will likely be in the marketplace. As a matter of fact, according to research, new products in which marketing synergy existed were 2.3 times more likely to be successful than products where marketing synergy was lacking.[34]

- **Market Attractiveness:** Market attractiveness is a measure of potential value and considers factors like short- and long-term profit, market growth rate, how much competition currently exists in the market, the cost of entry into the market, and how much the product satisfies the needs of customers in the target market.[35]

Kentucky Fried Chicken (KFC)

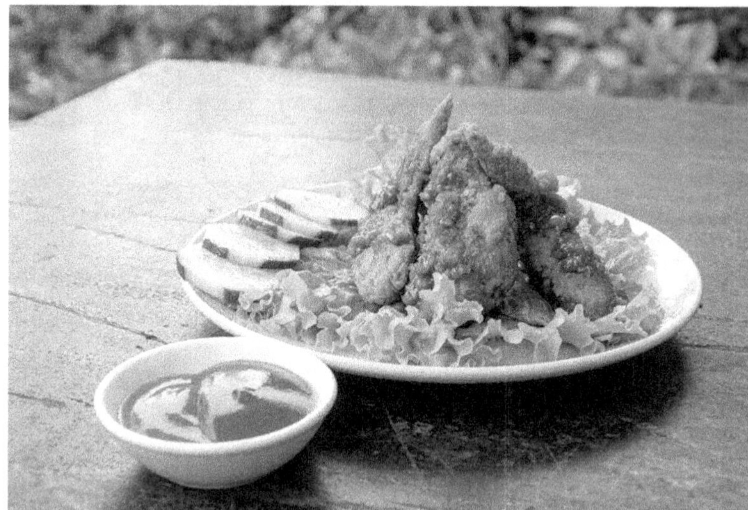

Figure 10.6 To address falling sales in the latter part of the year, KFC developed a new product that appeals to customers during the holiday season. (credit: "Food Photo of Fried Chicken Wings with Cucumber Slices and Lettuce on a Wooden Table with Tomato Ketchup and Chili Sauce" by Marco Verch/flickr, CC BY 2.0)

If you were to ask people what they eat during the holiday season, you'd probably get answers like turkey or ham. It's not likely that many of them will say fried chicken (see Figure 10.6). That's less than ideal for Kentucky Fried Chicken (KFC) because despite the fact that consumer spending typically spikes during the last six weeks of the year, KFC's sales typically falter.

Fortunately, savvy marketers at KFC came up with a new product designed to remind consumers of KFC during the holiday season: the KFC 11 Herbs and Spices Firelog that, when ignited, makes your house smell like fried chicken.[36] The idea behind this new product was twofold. First, a home's fireplace usually plays an important role in the holiday season. Second (and perhaps more importantly for KFC), hopefully the smell of fried chicken makes people want to *eat* fried chicken!

Some of KFC's promotional efforts involved discussions on TV talk shows and magazines. From these initiatives came 5,000 user-generated social posts and the logs being sold out in three hours![37] How's that for a successful product launch?

What Causes New Products to Fail?

We've just examined the factors that are favorable to the success of a new product, but what about the reverse? Those failure rates we mentioned in the previous section aren't to be taken lightly.

Statistics on New Product Failure

So, you've made it through all the stages of new product development, and you think your troubles are over. Think again! Just because something is new, improved, or changed doesn't guarantee that consumers will accept it or even hear about it. Every person reacts differently in how they hear about innovation, how they understand it, and whether they accept it.

Harvard Business School professor Clayton Christensen has been quoted as suggesting that approximately 30,000 new products are launched each year, and 95 percent of them fail. A study by the Product Development and Management Association found that new product failure rates varied among industries, ranging from 35 percent for health care products to 49 percent for consumer goods. Although those numbers are significantly lower than that proposed by Professor Christensen, the message remains the same: successful product launches shouldn't be taken for granted.[38]

What causes new products to fail? The reasons are likely different from one product to the next, but certain key factors appear to contribute heavily to the failure (see Figure 10.7).

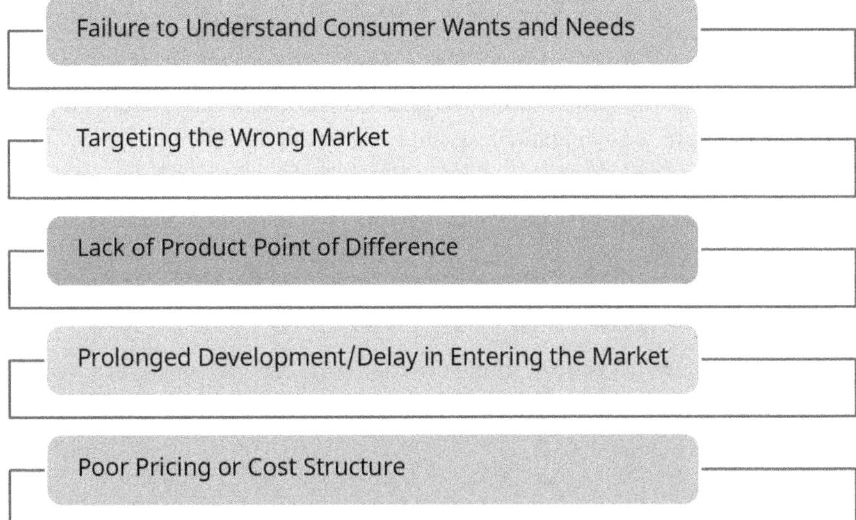

Figure 10.7 Contributing Factors to the Failure of a New Product (attribution: Copyright Rice University, OpenStax, under CC BY 4.0 license)

Let's review each of these factors more closely.

- **Failure to Understand Consumer Needs and Wants:** Let's illustrate this with a real-life scenario that some of you may recall: Google Glass "smart glasses," which were like eyeglasses with smartphone capabilities (i.e., wearable technology). When Google announced the product in 2013, it issued a statement of principle reading, "We think technology should work for you — to be there when you need it and get out of your way when you don't." However, sales were disappointing despite the company's usual market hype, and it quickly became clear that consumers didn't want or need the product. There were other devices with longer battery life, faster processors, and better cameras, and most had lower prices. Google discontinued the product's development in 2015.[39]
- **Targeting the Wrong Market:** It doesn't matter how incredible your technology is or how phenomenal you think your product is. If you can't reach the right people in the right market at the right time to buy your product, it's likely going to fail. Even Microsoft fell prey to this mistake. The company decided to challenge the Apple iPod and launched Zune in 2006. The product failed, and Microsoft later admitted that it was just chasing Apple, and its product gave consumers little incentive to switch from the iPod to Zune.[40]
- **Lack of Product Point of Difference:** This could also be referred to as a lack of product uniqueness. If a new product doesn't satisfy a unique need of consumers, it's unlikely to dislodge existing brands that are available. The bottom line is that, to succeed in the market, a product has to either satisfy a new function or satisfy an existing function in new ways. For example, Google launched Google+, its own social media site, in 2011 to compete with Facebook. However, Google+ was unable to distinguish itself from Facebook, and the site never garnered the market share Google anticipated. The company shut down personal accounts in 2019.[41]
- **Prolonged Development/Delayed Market Entry:** You've probably heard the idiom that "time is money," and this is especially true in new product development. If a company takes too long to launch a product, it often spells doom for the product launch. By the time the product hits the market, the economy may have taken a downturn, consumer needs may have changed, or new competitors may have entered the market.

That's what happened to Amazon when it introduced its Fire Phone after four years of development. CEO Jeff Bezos had said at the time, "Our job is to build the greatest device we know how to build, and then customers will choose. The other job we have is to be patient."[42] Apparently, that patience didn't pay off, because by the time the phone was introduced to the market in 2014, Apple and Android already had several generations of smartphones on the market. Amazon ceased production of the Fire Phone just a year later and discontinued sales soon thereafter. Sometimes, timing is everything!

- **Poor Pricing or Cost Structure:** Unfortunately, many new products suffer from a poor pricing or cost structure. Perhaps the company designed the product with a number of innovative features to try to bring "something new and different" to the market, but the inclusion of all those features made the product more costly to produce. You may be keeping your fingers crossed that the market will be willing to pay more for that "new and improved" product, but the reality is that this may not be the case.

Knowledge Check

It's time to check your knowledge on the concepts presented in this section. Refer to the Answer Key at the end of the book for feedback.

1. The degree to which a new product is built on the firm's existing technological resources is known as _______.
    a. market attractiveness
    b. marketing synergy
    c. technological synergy
    d. cost-benefit analysis

2. A study by the Product Development and Management Association found that new product failure rates varied among industries, ranging from 35 percent for ________ to 49 percent for ________.
    a. health care products; consumer goods
    b. consumer goods; pharmaceuticals
    c. consumer goods; technology products
    d. technology products; health care products

3. Graham, a marketer for ABC Corporation, was concerned about the new product launch because R&D was months behind in development and the economy appeared to be heading toward a recession. Which factor contributing to the failure of new products is Graham's concern?
    a. Lack of product differentiation
    b. Prolonged development/delayed market entry
    c. Targeting the wrong market
    d. Failure to understand customer needs/wants

4. Your company has added so many features to the new product you're launching that the price point when it hits the market is going to be significantly higher than originally anticipated. Which factor contributing to the failure of new products is at play here?
    a. Lack of product differentiation
    b. Prolonged development/delayed market entry
    c. Targeting the wrong market
    d. Poor pricing or cost structure

5. The FurZapper, which removes pet hair from laundry in the washing machine, was introduced on *Shark Tank* and became an immediate hit. It garnered over 5,000 five-star reviews on Amazon because customers were amazed at how much pet hair it trapped in the washer. Which factor contributing to the success of new products is likely at play here?

a. Delivering unique benefits to users
b. Technology synergy
c. Planning before development
d. Market attractiveness

10.5 | Stages in the Consumer Adoption Process for New Products

Learning Outcomes

By the end of this section, you will be able to:

LO 1 Describe the stages in the adoption process for new products.
LO 2 Identify and define new product adopter categories.

Stages in the Adoption Process

Consumers go through five stages in the process of adopting a new product (see Figure 10.8).

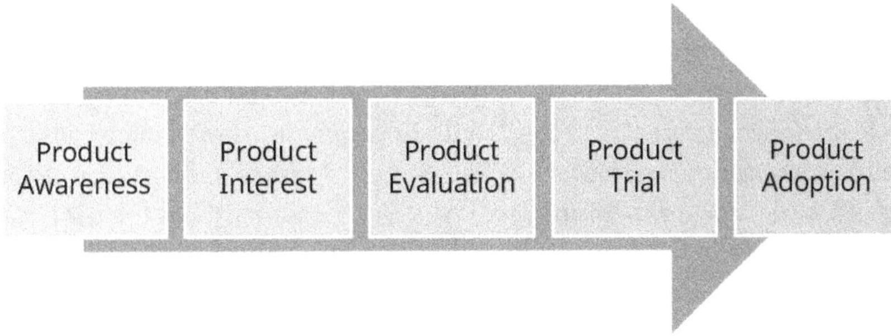

Figure 10.8 Stages in the Consumer Adoption Process (attribution: Copyright Rice University, OpenStax, under CC BY 4.0 license)

Let's look at each of these stages in the **consumer adoption process** (often referred to as the "hierarchy of effects model") in some detail.

- **Stage 1: Product Awareness**. The first stage in the consumer adoption process is simply creating awareness that the product is available, so the company develops a successful marketing strategy to make customers cognizant of the new product. This strategy might include creating a strong presence for the product in social media, for example. The goal here is to reach as many customers as possible at a relatively low cost. Let's assume for a minute that you're watching a football game on Saturday afternoon, and you see a television commercial for a mouthwash that whitens your teeth while you rinse. You're now aware of the product, thanks to that commercial!
- **Stage 2: Product Interest**. In this stage, consumers are aware of the product, and it has piqued their interest. The company should guide consumers by providing easily accessible information on the product, such as a website, blog posts, tutorials, or instructional videos. Let's go back to our mouthwash example. You're intrigued with the concept that a mouthwash can whiten your teeth, so you call your brother who's a dentist to ask if he's familiar with the product and what he has to say about it. That's product interest.
- **Stage 3: Product Evaluation**. Before they buy it, consumers will typically examine, compare, and evaluate the product. They haven't purchased it yet, and they often look to social media channels, such as online reviews and recommendations, to see how other consumers feel about the product or service. Think about it: How many times have you viewed customer reviews on Amazon prior to purchasing a product? In our example of the mouthwash, you might do an Internet search to read reviews of the product before you actually purchase it. That's product evaluation.
- **Stage 4: Product Trial**. This is the stage in the consumer adoption process where the consumer actually tries the product out. It might be a free sample in a retail store or a "100 percent money-back guarantee" trial purchase of an online product. This is also the stage in which marketers are hoping that the product will deliver on consumer expectations.

- **Stage 5: Product Adoption**. When consumers enter this phase, they're ready to buy, whether it's online or in a retail store. As a marketer, hopefully you've made the acquisition and payment process as seamless as possible so that your customers can easily obtain your product.

It should be noted that there are five characteristics of innovation, and each affects the rate of adoption differently. This is also known as the process of **diffusion of innovation**—the process through which new products are adopted (or not) by customers. Let's take a look:

- **Relative Advantage**: How much is the new product "better than" what it replaces? This is, of course, based entirely on a consumer's perception, but as a general rule, the easier it is to recognize the advantages of using the product, the more quickly it will be adopted.
- **Compatibility**: This is the level at which the innovation fits into a specific society due to economic, lifestyle, and cultural reasons. For example, PCs were very compatible with middle-class lifestyles, so the product was quickly adopted. On the other hand, the diffusion of birth control in parts of the world is not compatible with social mores due to religious beliefs and cultural values.
- **Complexity**: How difficult is the new product for the adopter to understand and use? If the difficulty level is too high, it is less likely that adoption/diffusion will take place. Think about your own experiences: Have you ever returned a product because it was too complicated to use?
- **Divisibility**: Divisibility is the ability to give the product a "test run" before putting down your hard-earned cash. For example, in no small part due to the COVID-19 pandemic, some online car sellers like Carvana and Shift, as well as some car dealerships, have adopted touchless test drives. The car is brought to the shopper's home, it's wiped down with disinfectant, and the consumer takes the car for a test drive alone while the delivery person waits.[43]
- **Communicability**: You may know your product is great, but you need to be able to effectively communicate to your audience. Communicability is the ability to effectively communicate the benefits and results of using the product, and when those benefits and results are both observable and describable to others. Let's imagine for a moment that you've purchased an expensive Peloton bike to get in shape after the new year. Would you continue to use it if you didn't see the desired results? Perhaps even more importantly in terms of communicability, would you be willing to share your results with others if those results weren't favorable?

It was first thought that diffusion was a one-step process: from mass media (i.e., advertising) to the individual. Marketers now recognize that it is a two-step process, and the second step is **personal influence**—that is, communication between individuals in which individuals can affect the purchasing decision of others because of their authority, knowledge, or position. For example, Kylie Jenner is a powerful social media influencer with over 250 million followers on Instagram.[44]

New Product Adopter Categories

Consumers adopt new products at their own speed. Some want to have the "latest and the greatest" as soon as it is available. If you doubt that, just look at the lines around any Apple store on the day of a new product release. Others tend to wait a while before buying. Scholar and professor of sociology at The Ohio State University Everett Rogers is credited with introducing the diffusion of innovation theory in 1962, in which he explained how a product or idea gains momentum and spreads through a population or society. In his theory, he identified five adopter categories (see Figure 10.9).[45]

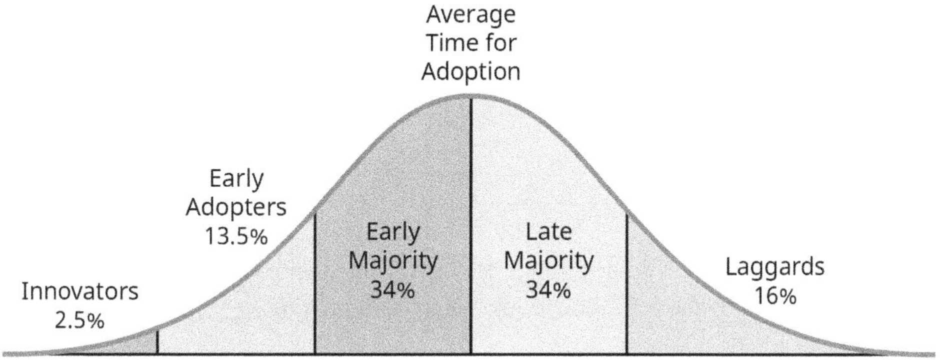

Figure 10.9 Categories of Adopters of New Products (attribution: Copyright Rice University, OpenStax, under CC BY 4.0 license)

Let's look at each of these categories in a little more depth.

- **Innovators**: Innovators are the risk-takers in the market. As a general rule, they have higher-than-average income and are typically well-educated. They enjoy the "rush" of taking risk but are also willing to accept the consequences of failure. It's the innovators who buy new products as soon as they hit the market.
- **Early Adopters**: Early adopters are actually the best target market for new innovations. These people tend to be well-educated "opinion leaders" with neighbors and friends, and their product advice is generally accepted more readily than product advice provided by innovators.
- **Early Majority**: The early majority typically look to the innovators and early adopters to determine if the new product meets expectations because they don't want to take the risk of being the first to adopt the new product, but they do accept innovation before the "average person." This group of consumers is typically above average in terms of education and income but also tend to be "followers" in their social group.
- **Late Majority**: Consumers in the late majority category are typically slow to catch on to the popularity of new services, products, ideas, or solutions. About 34 percent of the population will buy a new product only after about half of the population does. They're not interested in the "bells and whistles" (i.e., functionality and benefits) of the "latest model" and want simple, cost-effective products that focus on specific uses. As a general rule, their income and education are limited, and they're typically unwilling to take a chance with a new product unless the majority of consumers has already adopted the innovation.[46]
- **Laggards**: Laggards are more in tune with the past than the future, and they're leery of new ideas. By the time they adopt a product, there's probably already a new version or innovation taking its place.

Knowledge Check

It's time to check your knowledge on the concepts presented in this section. Refer to the Answer Key at the end of the book for feedback.

1. Garrett is the type of consumer who has to have the absolute "latest and greatest" technology products on the market. He is often the very first of his group of friends to acquire the newest smartphone or other gadget. Garrett would be considered a(n) _______.
   a. early adopter
   b. laggard
   c. late majority
   d. innovator

2. What is the first stage in the consumer adoption process?
   a. Product awareness
   b. Product evaluation
   c. Product trial
   d. Product interest

3. The extent to which the beneficial results of using a new product are observable or describable to others is referred to as ________.
    a. divisibility
    b. product awareness
    c. marketing synergy
    d. communicability

4. Bob refuses to get "on board" with smartphones. He insists on having a landline in his apartment. In terms of the new product adopter categories, Bob would be considered a(n) ________.
    a. early adopter
    b. innovator
    c. laggard
    d. late adopter

5. Which group of consumers tends to be unwilling to take a chance on a new product or innovation until the majority of consumers has already adopted the product?
    a. Innovators
    b. Early majority
    c. Laggards
    d. Late majority

10.6 Ethical Considerations in New Product Development

Learning Outcomes

By the end of this section, you will be able to:

LO 1 Discuss violations of patents, trademarks, and/or copyrights.
LO 2 Describe ways to exercise due care in product development.

Violations of Patents, Trademarks, and/or Copyrights

Before we proceed with a discussion of the areas of concern with respect to patents, trademarks, and copyrights in new product development, it would probably be helpful to have some definitions. **Patents** secure the right to exclude others from making, using, or offering for sale the invention you've developed. As a general rule, US patents last 20 years from when the application is filed with the US Patent Office. **Copyrights** are original works of authorship that include software, songs, television shows, and motion pictures. **Trademarks** are words or symbols legally registered or established by use as representing a company or product. Collectively, these terms are referred to as **intellectual property (IP)**.

You may think that intellectual property infringements are uncommon or, at least, limited to new product development by smaller companies, but nothing could be further from the truth. Patent lawsuits and ever-increasing scrutiny for anticompetitive behavior have cost "Big Tech" companies like Apple, Microsoft, and Google hundreds of millions of dollars.

For example, in March 2021, a jury ruled against Apple for patent infringement and ordered it to pay over $300 million to Personalized Media Communications LLC. That same year, a judge ruled that Google had infringed on five patents owned by Sonos, and if the ruling is upheld, it may result in the ban of imports of products like Google Home and Pixel smartphones.[47]

Intellectual property infringement can have serious consequences in terms of both monetary fines and, of course, the reputation of the company. Penalties can include civil damages, lost profits, injunctions, payment of the other damaged party's attorneys' fees, and even felony charges with prison time.[48]

Methods of Exercising Due Care During Product Development

Intellectual property rights add immense value to a company's assets. Imagine having a product team invest time, energy, and money developing and then launching a new product only to discover that the company's intellectual property rights aren't protected or—worse yet—that the product team has infringed on another company's intellectual property rights. That's why it's important in the product development stage to do three things:

- **Conduct a Trademark Search:** It's critical to know whether anyone else is already using the mark *before* time and resources are invested into developing a name and market recognition. For example, Takeda Pharmaceuticals was required to change the name of its antidepressant drug Brintellix to Trintellix because of consumer confusion between Brintellix and an anti-blood-clotting drug named Brilinta.[49]
- **File a Trademark Application:** Filing a trademark application provides the company with a bona fide statement of intention to use the mark within six months of the application.
- **Conduct a Patent Search:** If the product relates to a technological or scientific invention, the company should also conduct a patent search. As noted above, the patent excludes others from making, using, or selling a claimed invention for 20 years.[50]

Another issue that you may hear a lot about is the control or lack of control users have over their personal data. Companies that collect personal data have to carefully (and ethically) consider what information is embedded in systems design, how much data is really needed from users, where that data will be stored, and when and how it will be disposed of after use.[51]

COMPANIES WITH A CONSCIENCE

Meta

Figure 10.10 Meta is taking steps to better address ethical issues regarding users' personal data. (credit: "The Art of Facebook" by mkhmarketing.wordpress.com/about/flickr, CC BY 2.0)

Meta (formerly Facebook) has come under fire for several reasons recently, including a scandal that involved a whistleblower (see Figure 10.10). This person revealed that the tech giant "chooses profits over safety" when they released internal research and documents and testified before the United States Senate.[52]

However, the company took steps to ensure ethics in its new product development by hiring Zvika Krieger to its Responsible Innovation Team (RIT). Although the team had been in existence for some time, it's growing in size with the emergence of new ethical issues. Krieger's role focused on ethical issues in both the engineering and the design processes. For example, the RIT was involved in the decision to disallow filtering dating app results by race.

The RIT focused on the design and development stage of product development with the specific role of identifying ethical issues. Krieger departed Meta, and the RIT was dissolved in 2022; most members moved into other areas of the company, where they may be able to influence decisions more directly.

Chapter Summary

In this chapter we discussed the different forms of innovation as applied to new product development. The rewards of this development can include means to target a new market, to increase market share, and to increase revenue streams. Included in the risks are financial and technical feasibility and a lack of differentiation from existing products. There are seven stages to developing new products that include idea generation, idea screening and evaluation, concept development and testing, marketing strategy development, business analysis, product development, and test-marketing. The stages are followed by commercialization and evaluation of results.

Metrics are used to evaluate such things as R&D spending as a percentage of sales, return on investment (ROI), the percentage of sales due to the new product release, and other key concepts.

New products succeed when there is synergy and quality of technology and marketing and when the product delivers benefits to users. By contrast, failure can be due to targeting the wrong market and misunderstanding consumer needs/wants. The adoption process was discussed and includes different categories of consumers.

Key Terms

additions to existing product lines   product line extensions that involve changes to styles or flavors

business analysis   the fifth step in the new product development process, in which a potential new product is evaluated

commercialization   the eighth step in the new product development process, in which the product is launched with full-scale production, distribution, advertising, and sales promotion

communicability   the ability to communicate to the audience the benefits of using a particular product or service

concept development and testing   the third step in the new product development process, in which a product concept is developed into a detailed idea

concept testing   market research method in which customers are presented with a description of a product or service

consumer adoption process   stages consumers go through in adopting a new product

continuous innovation   category of "newness" in which the existing product undergoes only marginal changes that do not alter consumer habits

copyrights   original works of authorship that include software, songs, television shows, and motion pictures

crowdsourcing   using the input of a large group of people for market testing

diffusion of innovation   theory about how products gain momentum and spread through a population or society

discontinuous innovation   new-to-the-world products that require a significant change in consumer behavior when adopted

divisibility   the ability of a consumer to give a product a "test run" before purchasing it

dynamically continuous innovation   changes to a product or service that require little change to consumer habits

early adopters   consumers who are willing to try new products typically before others but not as early as innovators

early majority   consumers who are initially reluctant to risk trying a new product but accept innovation

evaluation of results   the ninth and final step in the new product development process, in which a company evaluates product launch performance based on predetermined metrics

external sources   in product development, sources of ideas for new products or services from those outside the organization

idea generation   the first step in the new product development process, in which many new ideas for a product are developed

idea screening and evaluation   the second step in the new product development process, in which ideas are filtered to those most likely to turn a profit

improvements and revisions to existing products   improvements to existing products that fine tune or perfect them

innovators   consumers who are the first to take a risk and buy new products as soon as they are available

intellectual property   collective term used to describe patents, copyrights, and trademarks

internal sources   in product development, sources of ideas for new products or services from those inside the organization

laggards   consumers who are skeptical of new ideas and are reluctant to try new products

late majority   consumers who are slow to catch on to the popularity of new services, products, ideas, or solutions

market attractiveness   the measure of potential value; considers factors like short- and long-term profit, market growth rate, how much competition currently exists in the market, the cost of entry into the market, and how much the product satisfies the needs of customers in the target market

market strategy development   the fourth step in the new product development process, in which a preliminary marketing strategy is developed

marketing synergy   the fit between the needs of the new product development project and the company's marketing capabilities

new-to-the-firm products   products that are new to a company but not to the world

new-to-the-world products   new product inventions that create new markets

patents   the right to exclude others from making, using, or offering for sale an invention

personal influence   communication between individuals in which individuals can affect the purchasing decision of others because of their authority, knowledge, or position

product adoption   the fifth stage in the consumer adoption process, also known as user adoption, in which people learn about a product and start using its features

product awareness   the first stage in the consumer adoption process, in which a company creates awareness that the product is available

product concepts   perceptions of a new idea or innovation

product development   the sixth step in the new product development process, in which a potential new product undergoes development; may include the creation of a prototype

product evaluation   the third stage in the consumer adoption process, in which consumers examine, compare, and evaluate the product prior to purchase

product idea   concept of a new product that a company could potentially offer to the market

product interest   stage in the consumer adoption process in which the product has piqued the consumer's interest

product metrics   quantifiable data that a business tracks and analyzes to determine how successful its new products are

product trial   the fourth stage in the consumer adoption process, in which the consumer tries the product out

prototype   in new product development, the creation of a physical version of the product

repositioned products   products that are retargeted for a new use

return on investment (ROI)   a metric formula used to evaluate the profitability of an investment and, in marketing, the measurement of the profitability of a new product launch

revenue streams   all the ways in which a company can generate cash flow from the sale of its products or services

technological synergy   the extent to which a new product is built on the firm's existing technological resources

test-marketing   the seventh step in the new product development process, in which a product concept is test-marketed to determine its viability before launch to market

trademarks   words or symbols legally registered or established by use as representing a company or product

Applied Marketing Knowledge: Discussion Questions

1. Explain the differences in:
   a. Continuous innovation
   b. Dynamically continuous innovation
   c. Discontinuous innovation

2. List the stages of new product development.

3. Consider new product adopter categories and answer the following questions.
   a. Do you believe that consumers are always in the same category? For example, once a laggard, always a laggard? Can someone be a laggard in one category and an early majority in another?
   b. What impact do these categories have on new product development?
   c. Can you think of a time or product category where marketing would want to push more consumers into one category?

Critical Thinking Exercises

1. From a consumer perspective, what motivates you to try a new product? What new products have you tried in the last year? Did you continue to purchase them after the initial trial?

2. Idea generation is the first step in new product development. Where do those ideas come from? Do all the ideas that are suggested make it to the prototype stage? Explain your answers.

3. Success and failure are always possible outcomes of new product development. Describe two factors that may lead to success and two factors that may lead to failure of a new product.

4. Ethical considerations of new product development include avoiding violations of patents, trademarks, and/or copyrights. How can marketing and R&D departments work to make sure that they do not violate these standing rights?

Building Your Personal Brand

Review this Ascent article by Aaron Weber (https://openstax.org/r/the5psofpersonalbranding) and pay attention to his explanation of the 5 Ps for building your personal brand. Write two paragraphs on what you feel your personal brand is today. Is it what you want it to be? Interview three colleagues, classmates, or family members and ask them to describe how they see your brand. Add a paragraph to your write-up describing their assessment.

Add another paragraph discussing your brand assessment compared to those you interviewed. Is it the same or different? Include changes you would like to make and the impact it would have on your personal brand.

What Do Marketers Do?

Using an online networking platform—for example, LinkedIn—network and connect with someone in product development. Explain that you have a college project and that you'd like to interview them. There are hundreds of product development professionals, and you will quickly find that professionals in this field love to talk about their products and ideas.

Use the following questions as a guide to dig deeper into their job responsibilities.

1. Could you please outline your career and how you got started on this path?
2. Please outline for me your current job responsibilities.
3. Do you specialize in a particular product concept (food, fashion, etc.)?
4. How do you interact with and support your team or clients in this role?

5. What product have you worked on that you are most proud of or excited about?
6. What product did you work on that failed? What did you learn in that process?
7. What advice can you offer me if I choose to pursue product development as my career path?

As always, follow up with any questions that you have, being respectful of their time, and be sure to thank them for their information and help!

 ## Closing Company Case

Maintaining a Competitive Edge with New Offerings—Ember

Every morning, millions of Americans wake up and prepare a cup of coffee. But as they sit down to drink it, the deluge of interruptions begins. Once the interruptions begin, that delicious dark roast often goes cold. Within the United States there are approximately 150 million coffee drinkers.[53] Throughout the day, people pour a cup of coffee, a cup of tea, or a variety of other hot drinks, only to be distracted and come back to a cold beverage. Many hot beverage drinkers have transitioned to the insulated travel mug where the drink stays hot for a while, but it too eventually gets cold.

Back in 2009, Clay Alexander was eating his breakfast. By the time he took his last bite, his scrambled eggs were cold. Alexander began experimenting with dinner plates that could stay hot and keep food at the same temperature throughout the meal. Then, one day as he was drinking coffee, he realized that using the same the technology with a coffee mug would be a transformative experience. In playing with the technology, he developed the Ember mug. (Watch this video for more information on the Ember mug development story.)

Click to view content (https://openstax.org/books/principles-marketing/pages/10-closing-company-case)

Alexander's first version of the Ember mug looked like something from *Weird Science*. The prototype mug was not sleek or stylish and definitely was not easy to clean. But as he carried his early version of the Ember mug to work and around town, curious commuters began to ask questions. Alexander was raising awareness and piquing the interest of potential new consumers. Through his interactions, he knew that there was definitely interest in a product that could keep beverages at a constant temperature for a long period of time.

This new innovation was a juncture of cutting-edge digital technology and the low-tech coffee mug. Using technology to warm the cup and keep a hot beverage at a constant temperature, Ember transformed the common mug. The Ember mug was able to keep hot beverages at a constant temperature for hours.

Creating the new product required hours of development. Building the product meant developing, testing, creating more prototypes, more testing, and running a business analysis. The new product was great. There was nothing like it on the market. But would customers buy it? A new entrant in the market often comes with a high price tag. All the hours, months, and years of development are coupled with the high cost of creating brand awareness.

The biggest question with the Ember mug was, How would the customer respond? Innovators are the first to purchase new market entry products, and they typically look for and buy new products before the rest of the market. And for this product, that market would probably include the coffee connoisseur and die-hard coffee drinkers. As with any new product, the biggest obstacle would be creating awareness and connecting with consumers about the benefits of the Ember mug.

Alexander knew that consumers were already attached to their smartphones, so he incorporated the Ember technology into something they already used. Consumers could control the temperature of their Ember mug beverages through the Ember app on their smart phones. With dozens of settings to create and keep the perfect temperature, Ember technology was easy and very customizable.

Getting the product to market meant getting it right and easily educating the consumer on the benefits of the Ember mug. The Ember mug incorporates smart LEDs to indicate when the mug has the beverage at the perfect temperature. Using a built-in battery, the Ember mug can work all day if placed on its charging coaster or upward of two hours without the coaster after being fully charged. The Ember mug also comes with auto-sleep technology to know when to turn off as well as built-in temperature controls for the variable preferences of consumers.

Figure 10.11 Product innovation focused on keeping coffee warm for long periods of time. (credit: "coffepour.jpg" by Eric McGregor/flickr, CC BY 2.0)

Initially the Ember was only available for sale on the company's website; however, as brand awareness increased and consumer demand picked up, the Ember could be purchased through both online and in-store retailers. The mug can now be purchased at Amazon, Best Buy, Costco, Starbucks, and several other locations.[54]

Ember has been featured in leading publications such as *Forbes*, *Fast Company*, and *People* as well as broadcast and digital media including *Today*. With many positive reviews, excellent public relations, and organic word of mouth from customers, the Ember mug saw positive growth. Since the introduction of the original 10-ounce mug, Ember added a 14-ounce version as well as a travel mug and plenty of added charging options.

Case Questions

1. How did the Ember mug redefine the coffee-drinking experience?

2. What was the first step Alexander needed to do in developing the Ember mug?

3. What three things helped drive sales of the Ember mug?

4. How would you describe the first customers of the Ember mug?

References

1. "December Holiday Campaigns That Caught Our Eye," AgencyChina, January 9, 2018, https://agencychina.com/blog/december-holiday-campaigns-that-caught-our-eye/.

2. "12 Most Successful Shark Tank Products," Shark Tank Tales, accessed January 8, 2022, https://sharktanktales.com/best-selling-most-successful-shark-tank-products/.

3. Nicole Martins Ferreira, "15 Best New Products You Need to Know About," Oberlo, October 26, 2020, https://www.oberlo.com/blog/new-products.

4. "About Us," Nature Valley, accessed June 12, 2022, https://www.naturevalley.com/about-us.

5. Desirae Odjick, "Product Line Extensions: What They Are, Examples, and Tips for Forming Your Strategy," Shopify Blog, June 24, 2021, https://www.shopify.com/blog/product-line-extensions.

6. "Oculus Quest 2: Our Most Advanced New All-in-One VR Headset," Meta, accessed January 18, 2022, https://www.oculus.com/quest-2/.

7. Maximilian Claessens, "Categories of New Products—What Is a New Product?" Marketing-Insider, September 18, 2016, https://marketing-insider.eu/categories-of-new-products/.

8. Ian Mullaney, "Teaching Old Drugs New Tricks: Why Companies Reposition Medicines," *The Conversation*, February 12, 2012, https://theconversation.com/teaching-old-drugs-new-tricks-why-companies-reposition-medicines-4621.

9. Katrina Grant, "How Have Cell Phones Changed Communication?" Techwalla, accessed January 18, 2022, https://www.techwalla.com/articles/how-have-cell-phones-changed-communication.

10. Kishore Shenoy, "Difference between Continuous Innovations and Discontinuous Innovations," LinkedIn, March 18, 2018, https://www.linkedin.com/pulse/difference-between-continuous-innovations-kishore-shenoy-ranjal/.

11. Frederik Bussler, "10 Successful Product Launches to Inspire Product Innovation," Commerce.AI, accessed June 12, 2022, https://www.commerce.ai/blog/10-successful-product-launches-to-inspire-product-innovation.

12. Bussler.

13. Ellen Byron, "Companies Target a New Market: The Stressed Out," *The Wall Street Journal*, July 10, 2021, https://www.wsj.com/articles/companies-target-a-new-market-the-stressed-out-11625889712.

14. "Spinal Muscular Atrophy (SMA)," Cleveland Clinic, accessed June 12, 2022, https://my.clevelandclinic.org/health/diseases/14505-spinal-muscular-atrophy-sma#:~:text=How%20common%20is%20spinal%20muscular,of%206%2C000%20to%2010%2C000%20children.

15. John Cumbers, "Why Some Drugs Cost $2.1 Million per Dose and How One Company Plans to Change This," *Forbes*, December 16, 2021, https://www.forbes.com/sites/johncumbers/2021/12/16/why-some-drugs-cost-21-million-per-dose-and-how-one-company-plans-to-change-this/?sh=58a0f9898953.

16. Caitlyn Hitt, "The Well-Seasoned History of Taco Bell's Doritos Locos Taco," Thrillist. August 11, 2020, https://www.thrillist.com/news/nation/history-of-taco-bell-doritos-locos-tacos.

17. Maximilian Claessens, "The New Product Development Process (NPD)—8 Steps," Marketing-Insider, January 31, 2022, https://marketing-insider.eu/new-product-development-process/.

18. "Managing the Development Process Development to Commercialization," Zabanga Marketing, June 3, 2022, https://www.zabanga.us/sales-force/anaging-the-development-process-development-to-commercialization.html.

19. "Managing the Development Process."

20. "Managing the Development Process."

21. "Many Marketers Are Now Using New Simulated Marketing Technologies," Zabanga Marketing, accessed July 26, 2022, https://www.zabanga.us/customer-relationships/objective-4-sia.html.

22. "Consumer Goods Market Testing," Zabanga Marketing, accessed May 6, 2022, https://www.zabanga.us/sales-force/consumergoods-market-testing.html.

23. Christopher Pliny, "Top U.S. Microcosm Cities to Test Market a National Product," SmallBusiness.com, August 28, 2014, https://smallbusiness.com/product-development/best-u-s-cities-to-test-market-a-national-product/.

24. Marvin Burman, "5 Ways Product Managers Can Use Crowdsourcing Effectively," Applause, May 30, 2017, https://www.applause.com/blog/examples-of-crowdsourcing.

25. Lindsay Kolowich Cox, "How to Launch a Product, According to HubSpot's Product Marketers," HubSpot Blog, August 24, 2021, https://blog.hubspot.com/marketing/product-launch-checklist#:~:text=Launching%20a%20product%20can%20cost,you're%20hoping%20to%20achieve.

26. Jay Fuchs, "The Percent of Sales Method: What It Is and How to Use It," HubSpot Blog, May 5, 2020, from https://blog.hubspot.com/sales/percent-of-sales-method.

27. Katryna Balboni, "11 Essential Product Metrics for Measuring Product-Led Growth," Appcues Blog, accessed January 8, 2022, https://www.appcues.com/blog/product-led-growth-metrics.

28. "What Is Product Adoption & How Do You Measure It Properly?" Heap, accessed January 8, 2022, https://heap.io/topics/what-is-product-adoption-how-do-you-measure-it-properly.

29. Jason Fernando, "Return on Investment (ROI): How to Calculate It and What It Means," Investopedia, June 30, 2022, https://www.investopedia.com/terms/r/returnoninvestment.asp.

30. Joe Lazauskas, "How Storytelling Turned Dollar Shave Club into a Billion Dollar-Brand," *Marketing Insights* (blog), Convince & Convert, accessed January 18, 2022, https://www.convinceandconvert.com/content-marketing/storytelling-turned-dollar-shave-club-into-a-billion-dollar-brand/.

31. Robert G. Cooper, "From Experience: The Invisible Success Factors in Product Innovation," *Journal of Product Innovation*

Management 16 (1999), 115–133, https://dep.ufmg.br/old/disciplinas/epd836/artigo03.pdf.

32. Robert Cooper and Elko J. Kleinschmidt, "Success Factors for New-Product Development," in *Wiley International Encyclopedia of Marketing*, eds. Jagdish N. Sheth and Naresh K. Malhotra (John Wiley & Sons Ltd., 2010), https://www.researchgate.net/publication/227992240_Success_Factors_for_New-Product_Development.

33. "What Makes Products Successful?" Magnetic, accessed May 6, 2022, https://fluxx.uk.com/2015/11/what-makes-products-successful.

34. Robert G. Cooper and Elko J. Kleinschmidt, *New Products: The Key Factors in Success* (Chicago: American Marketing Association, 1990).

35. Cooper and Kleinschmidt.

36. Conor Bond, "5 Product Launch Examples That Are Worth Studying (+ Tips for Success)," Crayon Competitive Intelligence Blog, July 16, 2021, https://www.crayon.co/blog/5-examples-of-great-product-launches.

37. Bond.

38. Kurt Schroeder, "Why So Many New Products Fail (and It's Not the Product)," The Business Journals, March 14, 2017, https://www.bizjournals.com/bizjournals/how-to/marketing/2017/03/why-so-many-new-products-fail-and-it-s-not-the.html#:~:text=A%20study%20by%20the%20Product,to%20be%20taken%20for%20granted.

39. Justin Burton Weidner, "How and Why Google Glass Failed," Investopedia, August 8, 2021, https://www.investopedia.com/articles/investing/052115/how-why-google-glass-failed.asp.

40. Jared Shaffer, "11 Reasons New Products Fail," UserVoice, accessed January 8, 2022, https://www.uservoice.com/blog/why-products-fail.

41. Michael B. Sauter, Evan Comen, Thomas C. Frohlich, and Samuel Stebbins, "When Product Launches Go Awry: 50 Worst Product Flops of all Time," *USA Today*, July 11, 2018, https://www.usatoday.com/story/money/2018/07/11/50-worst-product-flops-of-all-time/36734837/.

42. Victor Luckerson, "4 Reasons Amazon's Fire Phone Was a Flop," *Time*, October 4, 2014, https://time.com/3536969/amazon-fire-phone-bust/.

43. Philip Reed, "The New World of Car-Buying: Remote Negotiation, Home Delivery and No-Touch Test Drives," MarketWatch, April 14, 2020, https://www.marketwatch.com/story/the-new-world-of-car-buying-remote-negotiation-home-delivery-and-no-touch-test-drives-2020-04-14.

44. "9 of the biggest social media influencers on Instagram," Digital Marketing Institute, September 19, 2021, https://digitalmarketinginstitute.com/blog/9-of-the-biggest-social-media-influencers-on-instagram#:~:text=A%20social%20media%20influencer%20is,company's%20arsenal%20when%20done%20right.

45. "Diffusion of Innovation," Corporate Finance Institute, April 24, 2021, https://corporatefinanceinstitute.com/resources/knowledge/other/diffusion-of-innovation/.

46. Charlie Wells, "Forget Early Adopters: These People Are Happy to Be Late," *The Wall Street Journal*, January 26, 2016, https://www.wsj.com/articles/forget-early-adopters-these-people-are-happy-to-be-late-1453827437.

47. Hannah Towey, "Big Tech Giants Apple and Google Are Losing Legal Battles Over Patents Amid a Recent Litigation Surge, Risking Hundreds of Millions in Potential Costs," *Business Insider*, August 16, 2021, https://www.businessinsider.com/big-tech-apple-google-optis-sonos-legal-battles-over-patents-2021-8.

48. Adam Uzialko, "Tips to Avoid Intellectual Property Infringement," *Business News Daily*, June 29, 2022, https://www.businessnewsdaily.com/6043-intellectual-property-tips.html.

49. "Brintellix (Vortioxetine) Renamed Trintellix (Vortioxetine) in U.S. to Avoid Name Confusion," Takeda, May 16, 2016, from https://www.takeda.com/newsroom/newsreleases/2016/brintellix-vortioxetine-renamed-trintellix-vortioxetine-in-u.s.-to-avoid-name-confusion/.

50. Sanford E. Warren Jr., "Protect Assets and Limit Liability: Three Things to Consider When Launching a New Product," *IRMI Update*, International Risk Management Institute Inc., April 2011, https://www.irmi.com/articles/expert-commentary/three-things-to-consider-when-launching-a-new-product.

51. Michael Huth, "Rethinking Product Development and Usage to Make a Tech Business Ethical," Nasdaq, February 10, 2021, https://www.nasdaq.com/articles/rethinking-product-development-and-usage-to-make-a-tech-business-ethical-2021-02-10.

52. Brian McHugh, "Facebook Under Fire as Whistleblower Reveals Harmful Practices," Marist Circle, October 25, 2021, https://www.maristcircle.com/citynational-news/2021/10/25/facebook-whistleblower-reveals-harmful-practices.

53. "Coffee Statistics 2022," E-Imports, accessed July 24, 2022, https://www.e-importz.com/coffee-statistics.php

54. "Find an Ember Retailer Near You," Ember, accessed July 24, 2022, https://ember.com/pages/retailers

11

Services: The Intangible Product

Figure 11.1 Services are intangible, nonphysical products, such as childcare, and they make up the majority of the US GDP. (credit: "DSC_1551" by Josh Ward/flickr, CC BY 2.0)

Chapter Outline

11.1 Classification of Services
11.2 The Service-Profit Chain Model and the Service Marketing Triangle
11.3 The Gap Model of Service Quality
11.4 Ethical Considerations in Providing Services

 **In the Spotlight**

Services are acts a consumer is willing to pay for, and there are hundreds of different types. One such service is day care. According to the US Chamber of Commerce, 88 percent of two-parent families and 83 percent of single-parent families relied on non-parental care prior to the COVID-19 pandemic and spent approximately $42 million on early care and education.[1]

Sara Bullock, who has a background in early childhood education and four children of her own, owned a childcare business in Maryland for more than 10 years. When her husband was required to move to Tennessee for his job, she closed her business and started a new childcare business using a different business model. She changed it from a conventional daycare center to a "drop-in" center, allowing parents to bring in their children for short periods of time (anywhere from one to seven hours) without requiring them to make a monthly commitment. That was the birth of MeTime Drop-In Child Care. The concept has been so successful that Bullock has already begun plans to open a second location.[2]

11.1 | Classification of Services

Learning Outcomes

By the end of this section, you will be able to:
- **LO** 1 Define services.
- **LO** 2 List the classification of services.
- **LO** 3 Describe the characteristics of services.

Services Defined

You may have heard that the United States' economy is primarily considered a service economy. But do you know why this is? Figure 11.2 provides the answer. It outlines the percentage each industry contributed to the gross domestic product (GDP) in 2020.[3] (A quick refresher from your economics course: the GDP is a measure of the total monetary value of all finished goods and services generated within a country's borders during a specified period of time.) Which industries are the largest contributor to the GDP? Service industries. (Note that this figure does not include smaller industries such as utilities, or mining and agriculture.) When you total the service industries, they make up a whopping 67 percent of GDP versus only 10.8 percent for manufacturing.

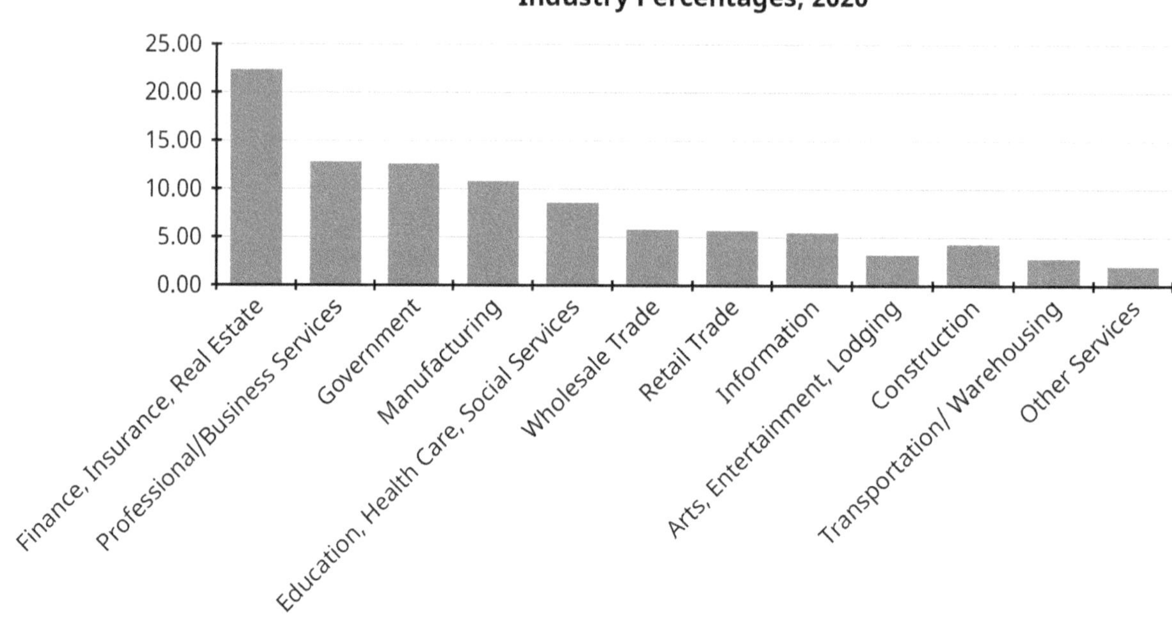

Figure 11.2 Percentages Added by Industry to the US GDP in 2020 (data source: BEA; US Department of Commerce; attribution: Copyright Rice University, OpenStax, under CC BY 4.0 license)

In a nutshell, **services** are the nonphysical, intangible economic activities. On the other hand, physical goods are the things we can touch or handle, commonly called tangibles. Do you realize that, as you read this textbook, you're participating in the services sector of the economy? That's because education is considered part of the service sector. The service sector also includes things like banking, medical treatment, transportation, insurance, and many more categories. Based on the fact that the majority of contributions to the GDP in the United States are services, and more than half of the country's workforce is employed in producing "intangibles," it's critical to understand this important sector from a marketing perspective.

Consider the challenges to marketers when selling services as opposed to products. A consumer can't touch or see the service before they purchase, so it's difficult to examine or evaluate benefits. Think about it: you can't take a service out for a test drive the way you might if you were buying a new car. Yet it's just as crucial for organizations that provide services to build brand awareness and brand loyalty.

Classification of Services

Services are classified as people-based services or equipment-based services. And within those classifications, there are subcategories (see Figure 11.3).

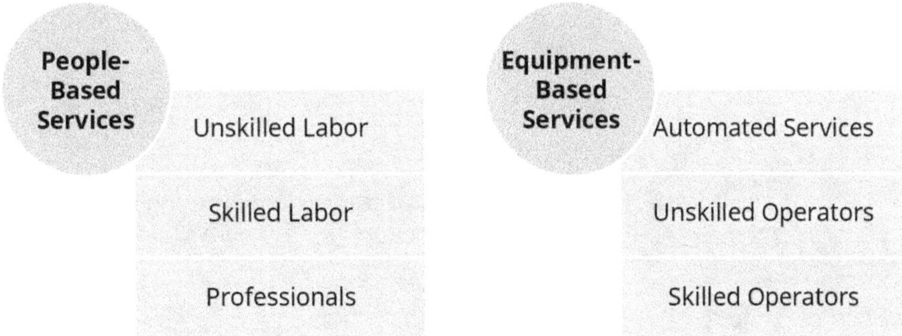

Figure 11.3 Services Classifications (attribution: Copyright Rice University, OpenStax, under CC BY 4.0 license)

People-Based Services

People-based services are when people primarily deliver the service, rather than equipment or machinery (see Figure 11.4 for examples). It's the individuals delivering the service, and the knowledge and skills that they possess, that add value and allow the service to be performed. People-based services can be broken down further into these subcategories:

- services provided by unskilled labor: parking lot attendants, babysitters, and janitors
- services provided by skilled labor: plumbers, caterers, and hairstylists
- services provided by professionals: doctors, attorneys, college professors, and accountants

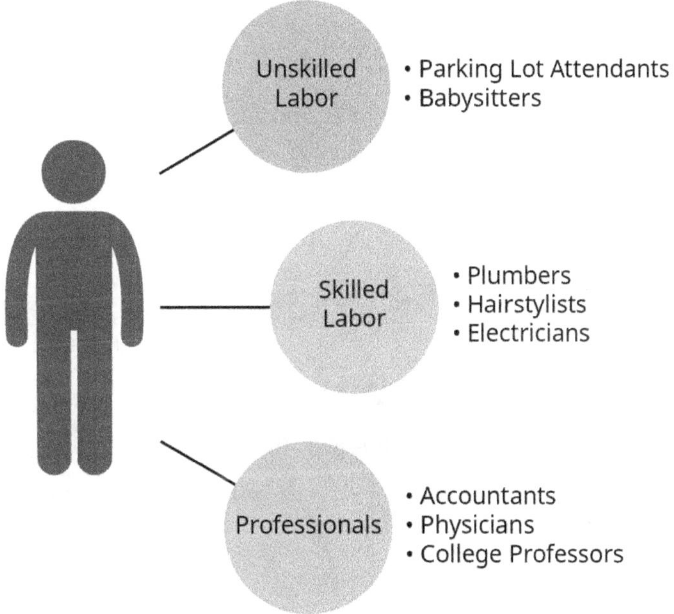

Figure 11.4 People-Based Services (attribution: Copyright Rice University, OpenStax, under CC BY 4.0 license)

Equipment-Based Services

Equipment-based service firms utilize equipment, machinery, and other forms of technology to perform service tasks (see Figure 11.5). Similar to people-based services, equipment-based services can be further broken down into subcategories:

- automated services: car washes and parking meters
- equipment-based services operated by relatively unskilled operators: dry-cleaning equipment

- equipment-based services operated by skilled operators: X-ray machines and ultrasound equipment

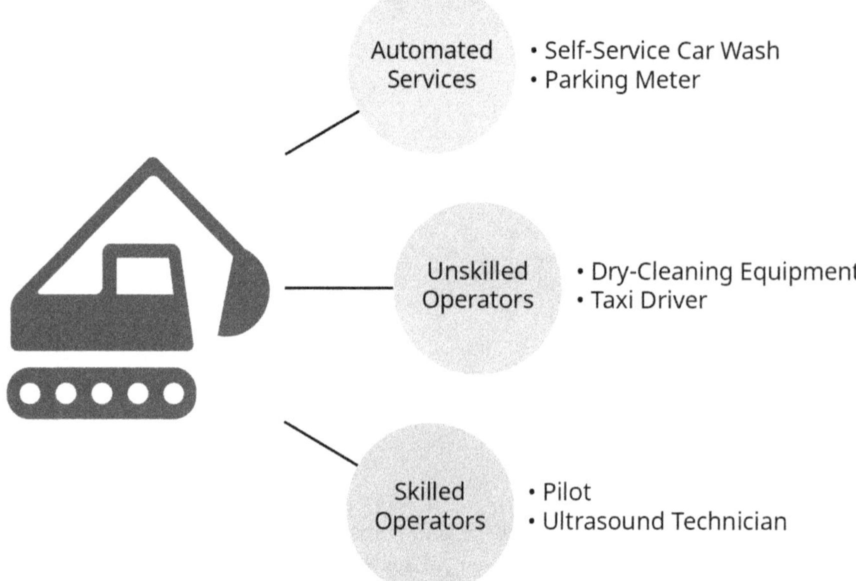

Figure 11.5 Equipment-Based Services (attribution: Copyright Rice University, OpenStax, under CC BY 4.0 license)

There is another way to categorize services, according to well-known author and professor Christopher Lovelock (1940–2008). He proposed four broad categories of services:

- people processing: services toward people's bodies
- possession processing: services toward possessions
- mental stimulus processing: services toward people's mind
- information processing: services toward intangible assets[4]

In Figure 11.6, the categories are defined on a two-dimensional matrix, wherein one of the dimensions is the direct recipient of the service and the other is the nature of the service act.[5]

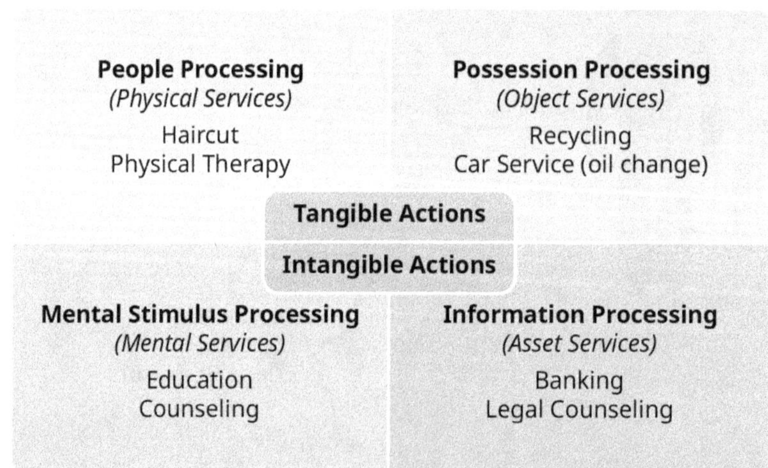

Figure 11.6 Lovelock's Categories of Service (attribution: Copyright Rice University, OpenStax, under CC BY 4.0 license)

LINK TO LEARNING

Lovelock

If you plan to continue toward a marketing degree, you'll want to familiarize yourself with Christopher Lovelock's work. You can run a search on Amazon.com for his books or a search in your browser for articles and more information. Start by reading his Wikipedia page (https://openstax.org/r/christopherlovelock) to learn about his academic background and achievements.

Let's look at each of these categories in more depth. The first two categories (people processing and possession processing) involve tangible actions directed toward a person's physical body or property, whereas mental stimulus processing and information processing involve intangible actions directed toward a person's mind or information. We'll expand on this in the following sections.

People Processing

In **people processing** services, the customer is a direct recipient of the service, and the production and consumption of the service are simultaneous. Consider examples of services where you must be present in the service facility in order to interact with the service provider and receive the service, such as barbershops or hair salons, physical therapists' offices, or restaurants.

Possession Processing

The difference between people processing and **possession processing** is that the service is directed toward the customer's physical possessions. In other words, production and consumption are separate. Your only involvement is dropping off the item that requires service or repair and explaining the problem. For example, once you have taken your car in for an oil change, you do not need to be physically at the location for the oil change to occur. Similarly, once you've dropped your clothes off at the dry cleaner's, you don't need to be physically present when the cleaning process is performed. These services are tangible because the direct recipient is one of your possessions rather than you as a person.

Mental Stimulus Processing

In its simplest explanation, **mental stimulus processing** is when the services interact with your mind rather than your body. Time and mental effort are required from the customer to receive this type of service. What you're doing right now—reading this textbook—is a prime example of mental stimulus processing. Other examples include psychotherapy or counseling services. The key here is that services rendered in this category are intangible.

Information Processing

Information processing is the most intangible form of service, although it can be transformed into a tangible service output like reports, books, letters, DVDs, etc. Some examples of information processing services are things like meeting with your financial advisor regarding investment advice, legal services, and banking.[6]

LINK TO LEARNING

Service Industry Stats and a Changing Industry

If you'd like more insight into service industries, check out the US Bureau of Labor Statistics website (https://openstax.org/r/blsgov). It categorizes industries and provides interesting statistics on employment.

Companies are launching new services every day. Think about it—services like Uber didn't exist 20 years ago. As a marketer, understanding services and their business models is critical. Start here and read about on-demand service companies (https://openstax.org/r/serviceindustries) and how services—and apps—are changing the industry. And also check out this article about the top 15 service businesses for 2022 (https://openstax.org/r/articlesmallbusiness).

Characteristics of Services

As outlined in Figure 11.2, service industries contribute the major percentage of the US GDP. It's important to understand that this shift from the manufacturing sector to the service sector isn't limited to the United States. Increasingly, the world economy is being characterized as a service economy. Looking at economic history, we can see a natural evolution in developing countries from the agricultural industry to the service sector as the mainstay of the economy. That's why it's critical for marketers to understand the characteristics of services.

As we pointed out above, some services come from physical products, such as getting a haircut or having your income tax return prepared by a professional. But other services are completely intangible. When you rent a hotel room, travel on an airplane, visit your doctor, attend a professional sporting event, or get advice from a lawyer or an accountant, you're buying a service, so a marketer needs to consider the characteristics of services in order to get the right marketing messages to the right target market (see Figure 11.7).

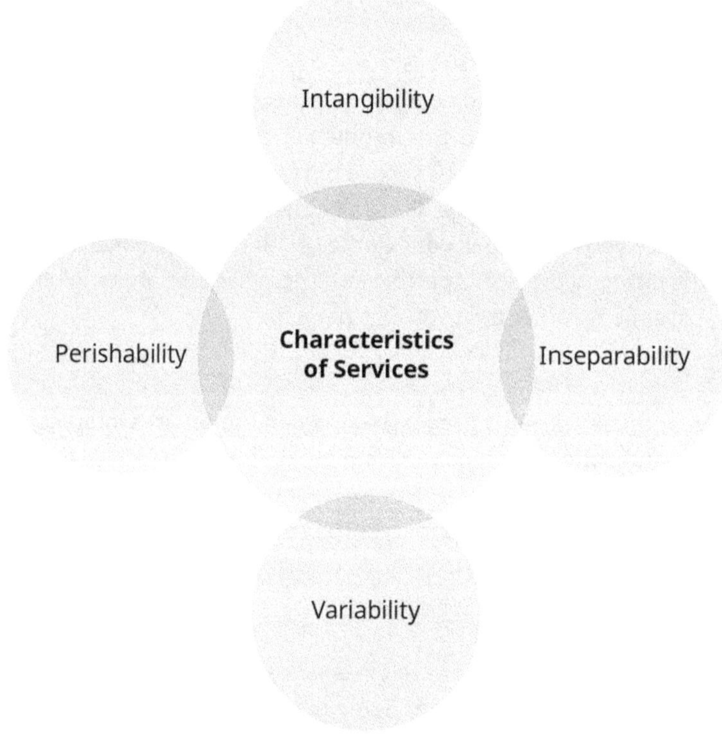

Figure 11.7 Characteristics of Services (attribution: Copyright Rice University, OpenStax, under CC BY 4.0 license)

Service Intangibility

By their very nature, services are **intangible**. This means they can't be seen, tasted, felt, smelled, or heard before they are purchased. Consider the last time you purchased automobile insurance for your car. Other than the physical policy the company sends you (the only tangible asset), what you've paid for is completely intangible—it's the company's promise to pay claims against the policy.

Intangible services have a number of implications in marketing. The very fact that there's nothing to touch, hear, smell, and so on typically increases the level of uncertainty that a consumer faces when choosing between services offered by your organization or those of competitors. Intangible services can seldom be tried out, inspected, or even given a "test drive" by a customer. Customers have to rely on the word of the marketers in order to assess what they're actually going to get in return for what they've paid. In effect, they are buying a promise.

Savvy marketers reduce this uncertainty by creating physical "evidence" that allows the consumer to picture the service before it is purchased. For example, a hair salon may have imaging software that predicts how you would look with different hairstyles or colors. Companies like Zenni and Eyebuydirect have a virtual mirror that allows you to "try on eyeglasses" and see how the selected frames look on your face before you purchase.[7]

Service Inseparability

The order of production and consumption between a physical product and a service differs. Think about a box of Girl Scout cookies, a physical good or product. The cookies were produced, stored, sold, and finally consumed. That's not the way it works with services. Like goods, services are sold, but they are produced and consumed simultaneously. They can't be separated from the service providers, whether they are people or equipment.[8] For example, try to get money out of your bank on a weekend or evening without an ATM, or try to get a haircut without the physical presence of your stylist. That's the concept of **service inseparability**—you can't separate the delivery of the service from the presence of the customer. In other words, the service provider is physically connected to the service and is evaluated on the basis of their communication skills, language, demeanor, personal hygiene, and clothing.

The impact to the marketer in these services—in which the service provider and customer must both be present—is how service providers (sometimes called frontline employees) conduct themselves in the presence of the customer because it may determine the likelihood of repeat business.[9] There are also other marketing implications with this concept, such as customer cooperation and participation, not to mention the influence from other customers who may be present.

Service Variability

Have you ever gone to a restaurant and had stellar customer service? You were seated promptly by a cheerful hostess; the busser filled up your water glass and refilled it several times during the evening; the waitstaff was attentive but not to the point of being annoying; and your dirty dishes were cleared promptly. But perhaps the next time you visit the same restaurant, your experience isn't quite as amazing. The hostess isn't as cheerful, and it takes her several minutes to seat you. It takes a while for someone to refill your water glass. The waitstaff isn't nearly as attentive as they were during your first visit. What went wrong?

Perhaps what you've experienced is what's known as **service variability**—the quality of the service depends on who provides it, when it is provided, and how it is provided. For example, Delta Air Lines prides itself on improving peoples' lives and exceeding customer expectations.[10] However, because services are provided by humans who have human experiences where they may not be feeling well or they are having a bad day, the service may be variable between employees. One Delta employee may be cheerful and efficient, while another lags due to their energy and state of mind.

This is a challenge to marketers because products generally have little variability: each unit is built to certain specifications. For example, if you buy an Apple iPad Pro and your classmate purchases the same model, it's likely that the two iPads will be virtually identical. The case color may be different, but otherwise they are the same. That's not the case with a service, where there will undoubtedly be variations in the quality of the service depending on who offers the service, when it is offered, and at which location. Service-based companies need to rely on standardizing processes to the extent possible, frequent audits, customer surveys, and most importantly, customer feedback.

Service Perishability

Unlike most goods, services can't be produced and stored for later use or sale. Services are, in effect, performances by the service provider. That's the concept of **service perishability**. Did you miss tonight's concert because of traffic? Too bad, because a ticket for tonight's concert can't be used for tomorrow night's performance. Hotel rooms that are not occupied, airline seats that are not purchased, and unused gym memberships cannot be reclaimed.[11] Because these items can't be stored for later use, they are considered a perishable service. This is particularly important for marketers because the perishability factor and the fluctuating demand poses special problems in capacity planning, scheduling, product planning, and pricing.[12]

One way that marketers deal with this problem is by manipulating demand. Consider how many restaurants offer "happy hours" with discounted food and drinks during the late afternoon or early evening. Restaurants do this because this time is typically the period where there is a lull before the start of the dinner rush.

CAREERS IN MARKETING

Salaries

You might be curious about the salaries of marketing jobs. There are numerous online resources that provide guides, but the best step to take is to check out popular sites like Monster, Indeed, and LinkedIn to view current job positions. They may not all include the salary, but most will include salary ranges. The following is a list of a few of resources to get you started.

- Monster: "High-Paying Marketing Jobs" (https://openstax.org/r/highpayingmarketingjobs)
- Acadium: "How Much Do Marketers Make? Marketing Job Salaries in 2022" (https://openstax.org/r/marketingjobsalaries)
- All Business Schools: "Marketing Manager Salaries and Job Outlook" (https://openstax.org/r/allbusinessschools)
- Indeed: "Entry Level Marketing Salary in United States" (https://openstax.org/r/entrylevelmarketing)

Knowledge Check

It's time to check your knowledge on the concepts presented in this section. Refer to the Answer Key at the end of the book for feedback.

1. You purchased an airline ticket to go on vacation, but on the way to the airport, you get a flat tire and miss your flight. Which characteristic of service does this example illustrate?
   a. Service variability
   b. Service inseparability
   c. Service perishability
   d. Service intangibility

2. You go to a new hairstylist, and he suggests that you add highlights to your hair, cut off a few inches, and add some layers. You're hesitant to do so because you can't imagine what you're going to look like with your new hairstyle. What characteristic of service does this example illustrate?
   a. Service intangibility
   b. Service variability
   c. Service perishability
   d. Service inseparability

3. You go to the spa to get a massage, but your regular massage therapist is off for the day. The massage therapist to whom you're assigned does an adequate job, but they don't have the same technique as your regular massage therapist. What characteristic of service does this example illustrate?

    a. Service inseparability
    b. Service perishability
    c. Service variability
    d. Service intangibility

4. You go to your Certified Public Accountant (CPA) to have your tax return prepared and filed for the year. How would this service be characterized in terms of classifications of services?
    a. People-based services: unskilled labor
    b. Equipment-based services: unskilled operator
    c. People-based services: professionals
    d. Equipment-based services: skilled operator

5. You're headed to lunch with friends at a downtown restaurant. Because there is no restaurant parking lot, you have to park on the street and feed the parking meter or risk getting a parking ticket. How would the service provided to you by the parking meter be classified?
    a. Equipment-based services: unskilled operator
    b. People-based services: professionals
    c. People-based services: skilled labor
    d. Equipment-based services: automated service

11.2 | The Service-Profit Chain Model and the Service Marketing Triangle

Learning Outcomes

By the end of this section, you will be able to:
    LO 1 Define and explain the purpose of the service-profit chain model.
    LO 2 Describe the steps in the service-profit chain model.
    LO 3 Explain the Services Marketing Triangle.

Definition and Purpose of the Service-Profit Chain Model

Just like goods-producing businesses, service firms use marketing to position themselves in selected markets. These businesses position themselves in the market through marketing mix activities (i.e., product, price, place, and promotion). However, because of the inherent differences between services and tangible products, different marketing approaches may be required. Consider a product like a laptop or smartphone. The products are fairly standardized, so they can be produced and shipped to retailers and then sit on shelves in the store until purchased by a consumer. However, if you're a service business, it takes the interaction of the frontline employee and the customer to literally create the service. The interaction between the employee and customer is important in creating the value of that service.

The **service-profit chain model**, created by a group of Harvard researchers in the 1990s, establishes relationships between profitability, employee satisfaction, loyalty, and productivity. The concept is reasonably simple: happy workers make happy customers who keep coming back and tell their friends. The model itself is a little more complicated and states the following:

- Internal service quality (the support received by frontline employees from the rest of the organization) leads to employee satisfaction.
- Employee satisfaction results in employee loyalty, productivity, and the willingness to go that "extra mile" for the customer, which creates value.
- Value contributes to customer satisfaction, resulting in customer loyalty.
- Customer loyalty translates to profitability and growth for the organization.

Perhaps the most critical aspect of this model is that all of these points link together, are equally important, and depend on one another. There are no shortcuts to increasing profitability. Didn't quite follow that? Refer to Figure 11.8 for a visual depiction.

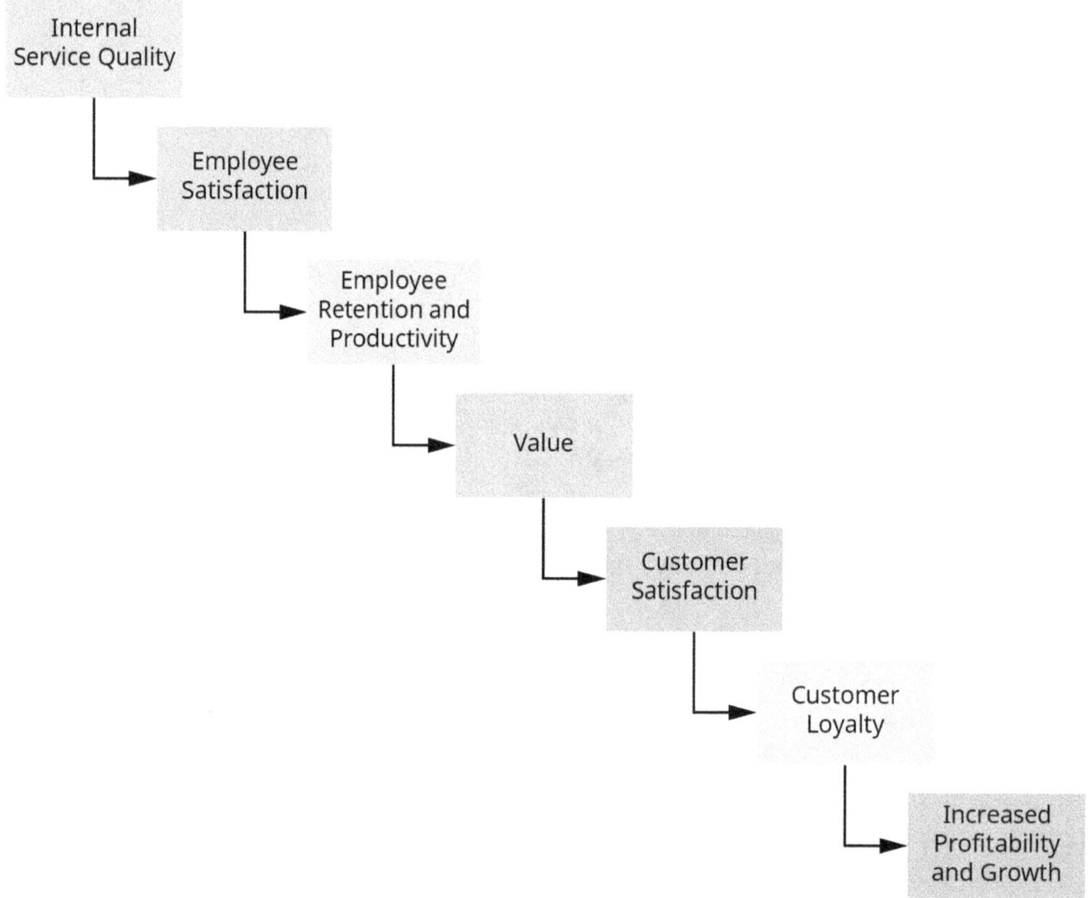

Figure 11.8 The Service-Profit Chain Model (attribution: Copyright Rice University, OpenStax, under CC BY 4.0 license)

Steps in the Service-Profit Chain Model

The service-profit chain model connects the interworkings and relationships between the different parts of a business. It impacts employee satisfaction and retention, customer satisfaction, customer loyalty, and profitability. Let's take a closer look.

Internal Service Quality

Internal service quality refers to the perceived satisfaction frontline employees experience when they are supported by effective policies and service from the organization. If you've ever worked in a restaurant, you'll be familiar with the terms "back of house" and "front of house." Front-of-house employees are "guest-facing" roles like hosts/hostesses and servers—those who intentionally interact with the customer. Back-of-house employees like bussers, dishwashers, and cooks typically don't have direct interaction with the customer. Rather, it's their work that supports the front-of-house employees. Even if your server may is friendly, attentive, and efficient, if your silverware is dirty or your steak isn't prepared as ordered, the overall dining experience is going to be less than optimal. In addition to the customer dissatisfaction, server/employee satisfaction will also suffer due to the lack of support from the back-of-house staff.

Consider another example. Your flight was delayed, and it took forever to get your luggage and rental car. By the time you get to your hotel, you're tired and cranky, and you just want to check in and get some rest. The front desk clerk is cordial and efficient. However, your room isn't available because the housekeeping staff hasn't cleaned the room yet. Who gets the brunt of your anger? Imagine the lack of job satisfaction on the part of the front desk clerk who's tried to do everything right and was thwarted by the lack of support from housekeeping.

One of the ways that this problem can be alleviated within an organization is to create an employee feedback loop in which frontline employees can communicate problems that hurt productivity, satisfaction, and loyalty. The feedback loop is a critical element because, as consultant Sidney Yoshida reports in his study "The Iceberg of Ignorance," 4 percent of an organization's frontline problems are known by top management, 9 percent are known by middle management, 74 percent are known by supervisors, and 100 percent are known by employees.[13]

Employee Satisfaction

Employee satisfaction is the level of happiness or contentment employees have with their jobs and work environment. It's often the direct result of company policies and support services that empower employees to deliver quality products and services. If employees are satisfied with the company's policies, it's easier to facilitate a happy attitude that helps consumers have pleasurable experiences with the organization.

For several years, Zappos has made Fortune's list of "100 Best Companies to Work For." The late CEO Tony Hsieh focused so much on the happiness of his team and customers that he wrote a series of books about it, including *Delivering Happiness: A Path to Profits, Passion, and Purpose*. He recognized that the only person-to-person contact a customer would have with an online retailer would be with customer service personnel, so he encouraged his employees to go above and beyond for the customer.[14]

Employee Retention and Productivity

Employee turnover is one of the most frustrating and recurring problems that organizations face. Turnover is costly regardless of whether it's involuntary (such as termination due to poor performance) or voluntary (such as employee-decided resignation or retirement). The conservative estimate from the Society of Human Resource Management (SHRM) is that it costs six to nine months of an employee's annual salary to replace that person.[15] That's why **employee retention**—keeping employees motivated so that they choose to remain with the company—is so critical.

The good news is that employee satisfaction is inversely related to employee turnover. In other words, an increase in employee satisfaction brings about a decrease in employee turnover. Perhaps even more importantly, studies have shown that low turnover leads to an increase in organizational **productivity** (the efficiency and output of employees) and performance. For example, some time ago, Taco Bell discovered that its restaurants with high employee retention had twice as many sales as other stores and had 55 percent higher profits than restaurants with high turnover. In response to these findings, the company enhanced its internal service quality by giving employees more latitude for on-the-job decision-making.[16]

LINK TO LEARNING

The Great Resignation

You may be aware of the Great Resignation, in which employees are leaving their jobs in large numbers. Because of the cost to hire, train, and retain employees, employee retention is a major concern for organizations. There are many reasons why this is happening, and there are ways companies can improve to help them retain their employees. Read these articles from the Pew Research Center (https://openstax.org/r/majorityofworkers), Forbes (https://openstax.org/r/workersarequitting), and Mashable (https://openstax.org/r/2022greatresignation) about this shift in employee thinking.

There are corporate strategies companies can take to counteract this resignation trend. Learn about these strategies from LinkedIn (https://openstax.org/r/talentengagement) and Family Business (https://openstax.org/r/familybusinessmagazine).

External Service Value Proposition

Customer value is also known as **external value proposition**. It's the promise of value that a customer expects a business to deliver.[17]

Think about your last haircut. Why did you choose to get your hair cut at that particular salon versus a competitor? Certainly, the quality of the haircut itself was important, but the customer value you experienced from your stylist played a role. What else factored into your experience? How about the other behind-the-scenes employees who made it easy for you to book an appointment or who checked you in efficiently, the person who kept the salon clean and attractive, and the person who made it easy for you to pay and perhaps book another appointment when you were leaving?

That's why employees (both frontline and behind the scenes) play a major role in ensuring customer value. Satisfied, motivated employees generally (and genuinely) care about the company and the services it provides and can convey this to consumers in an honest, positive manner.[18]

Customer Satisfaction

The next two steps (customer satisfaction and customer loyalty) in the service-profit chain model are related and directly linked. A dissatisfied customer will not be loyal and will likely not do business with the company in the future. Conversely, **customer loyalty**—the ongoing positive relationship between a customer and business—is a result of **customer satisfaction**—or the measure of how happy customers are with the company's products, services, and capabilities.

The greater the satisfaction from a customer, the more likely they will return. Additionally, satisfied customers often serve as unofficial "ambassadors" of the company and will spread the word about their positive experience.[19]

Customer Loyalty

The definition of customer loyalty is when a person goes to the same company for subsequent services, even if that service is more expensive than those of the competitor. The customer makes a deliberate choice to do repeat business with a company with which they have had positive experiences, resulting in growth and higher profits for the company.[20]

Profit and Growth

In terms of the service-profit chain model, profit isn't the goal; it's the result. The formula is really quite simple:

- Happy employees result in happy customers.
- Happy customers mean repeat business and spreading the word about your organization.
- Repeat (and new) business mean profit and growth for the organization.

The key is to keep employees happy because it leads to company profits.

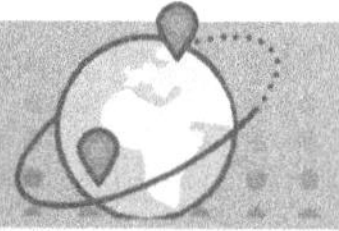

LINK TO LEARNING

Putting the Service-Profit Chain to Work

Learn from this *Harvard Business Review* article (https://openstax.org/r/puttingtheservice) about the connectivity of the service-profit chain links.

Interested in understanding how the model works in other industries? Read this *Hospitality News and Business* (https://openstax.org/r/serviceprofitchain) article about why the service profit chain is important in the hospitality industry.

Ritz-Carlton

Figure 11.9 The Ritz-Carlton Hotel directly impacts its service-profit model by empowering its employees to provide a positive experience for customers. (credit: "Cannes" by Fred Romero/flickr, CC BY 2.0)

Employee empowerment is one of those buzzwords that has become popular over the last few decades. It's defined as the ways in which an organization provides its employees with some autonomy and freedom to make decisions and have some control in their day-to-day activities. For example, a supermarket may empower its cashiers to match competitors' ads without approval from a manager for up to a certain dollar amount.

If you were the owner of a business, how much latitude would you give your employees in helping customers? A lot? A little? None? The Ritz-Carlton, considered a gold standard for hospitality (see Figure 11.9), allows its employees to spend up to $2,000 to solve customer problems without manager approval.[21]

You might be shaking your head right now, trying to understand this. Two thousand dollars seems like a lot of money to be left to the discretion of employees, doesn't it? But you may not realize that the average Ritz-Carlton customer will spend approximately a quarter of a million dollars with the hotel chain over their lifetime. When you consider that the customer lifetime value (CLV) of a Ritz-Carlton guest is $250,000, that $2,000 doesn't seem hard to believe, does it?[22]

For more information about Ritz-Carlton and its commitment to customer service, watch this brief video with Ritz-Carlton founder Horst Schulze and Yahoo! Finance where he discusses the importance of and value in caring for customers.

Click to view content (https://openstax.org/books/principles-marketing/pages/11-2-the-service-profit-chain-model-and-the-service-marketing-triangle)

The Service Marketing Triangle

The **Service Marketing Triangle** is a visual image of a model that speaks to the importance of people in a company's ability to keep its service promises (see Figure 11.10). It might help to imagine the Service Marketing Triangle as a three-legged stool. Take out one of the legs, and the stool won't stand for long. That's the premise and the importance of the Service Marketing Triangle—all three aspects must be achieved or exceeded for the customer to be delighted.

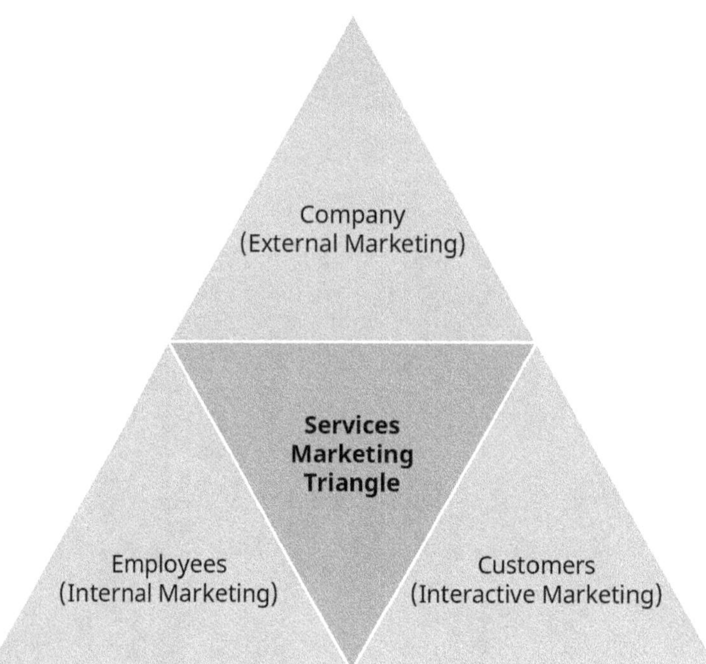

Figure 11.10 The Services Marketing Triangle (attribution: Copyright Rice University, OpenStax, under CC BY 4.0 license)

External Service Marketing—Making Promises

External service marketing refers to the promotion of an organization's services in an external environment where the company promotes its services to customers through various traditional techniques like pricing, advertising, direct marketing, public relations, and personal selling. These marketing techniques are intended to achieve multiple aims, such as creating and increasing awareness, setting price expectations, and setting expectations for the level of service to be delivered.[23]

Internal Service Marketing—Enabling Promises

In a service business, employees are seen as "internal customers." As you've seen from the discussion on the service-profit chain model, if a company wants to better serve its customers, it has to start with satisfying its employees so that they're committed to delivering the best service possible to external customers. That's the essence of internal service marketing.

Internal service marketing is the process of motivating employees to deliver customer value and ensure customer satisfaction by acting as a team. While that is obviously true for frontline employees who interact with the customer, it is equally applied to all employees, including those behind-the-scenes employees who support the frontline employees. In other words, all employees of an organization need to be empowered so they can deliver great customer service.

Key components of internal service marketing include motivating employees, training them in customer satisfaction techniques, ongoing communication of company goals and objectives, and (of course) good pay and working conditions.[24]

Interactive Service Marketing—Keeping Promises

Interactive service marketing is the communication between the service provider and the customer, called a **service encounter**. The service encounter is where external marketing promises are either upheld, exceeded, or broken by employees.

Interactive service marketing is critical because it sets short-term and long-term customer satisfaction. In its simplest terms, when a customer is happy in the short term, they are more likely to be happy over the long term.[25]

Let's review the elements of the Service Marketing Triangle with an example of a fine-dining restaurant in a major metropolitan area. The three "parties" involved in the Service Marketing Triangle are the owner of the restaurant, the restaurant employees, and the diners. As part of *internal marketing*, the owner may offer training to servers about the pairing of certain dishes on the menu with wines offered by the restaurant or hold a "huddle" at the beginning of each shift to train servers about daily specials and wine pairings. As part of *external marketing*, diners might be lured to the restaurant through the restaurant's Facebook page, which touts its extensive list of wines and the fact that servers are experienced in recommending wines to enhance the flavor of the menu items. Finally, as part of interactive marketing, servers are encouraged to give diners full descriptions of all menu items and daily specials and recommend which wines to pair with their food choices, leading to a more satisfying dining experience.[26]

LINK TO LEARNING

Service Marketing Triangle

Check out this brief video about the Service Marketing Triangle model to gain a better understanding.

Click to view content (https://openstax.org/books/principles-marketing/pages/11-2-the-service-profit-chain-model-and-the-service-marketing-triangle)

Knowledge Check

It's time to check your knowledge on the concepts presented in this section. Refer to the Answer Key at the end of the book for feedback.

1. According to the service-profit chain model, what drives organizational profitability and growth?
   a. Internal service quality
   b. Employee satisfaction
   c. Customer loyalty
   d. Value

2. The extent to which employees are happy or content with their work environment is known as which of the following in the service-profit chain model?
   a. Employee satisfaction
   b. Internal service quality
   c. External value proposition
   d. Customer loyalty

3. Which two steps in the service-profit chain model are related and directly linked?
   a. Internal service quality and value
   b. Value and customer satisfaction
   c. Customer satisfaction and customer loyalty
   d. Internal service quality and increased productivity and growth

4. In the Service Marketing Triangle, _______ occurs when employees and customers associate and communicate.
   a. internal marketing
   b. external marketing
   c. interactive marketing
   d. customer satisfaction

5. In the service-profit chain model, there is a(n) _______ relationship between employee satisfaction and employee turnover.
   a. behavioral
   b. equivalent
   c. parallel
   d. inverse

11.3 | The Gap Model of Service Quality

Learning Outcomes

By the end of this section, you will be able to:
   LO 1 Describe the Gap Model of Service Quality.
   LO 2 List and describe the dimensions of service quality.

Dimensions of Service Quality

While we're still on the subject of customer satisfaction, let's take a look at still another model that aids marketers in better understanding customer satisfaction: the **Gap Model of Service Quality** (sometimes also known as the Customer Service Gap Model or the Five-Gap Model), first proposed in 1985. The importance of this model is that it demonstrates that customer satisfaction is essentially a function of perception. In other words, if the service provided meets or exceeds customers' expectations, they will be satisfied; if not, they will be dissatisfied, likely as a result of one of the customer service gaps presented below.[27]

According to the model (see Figure 11.11), there are five major gaps or potential inconsistencies organizations encounter in seeking to meet customers' expectations of the customer experience.[28]

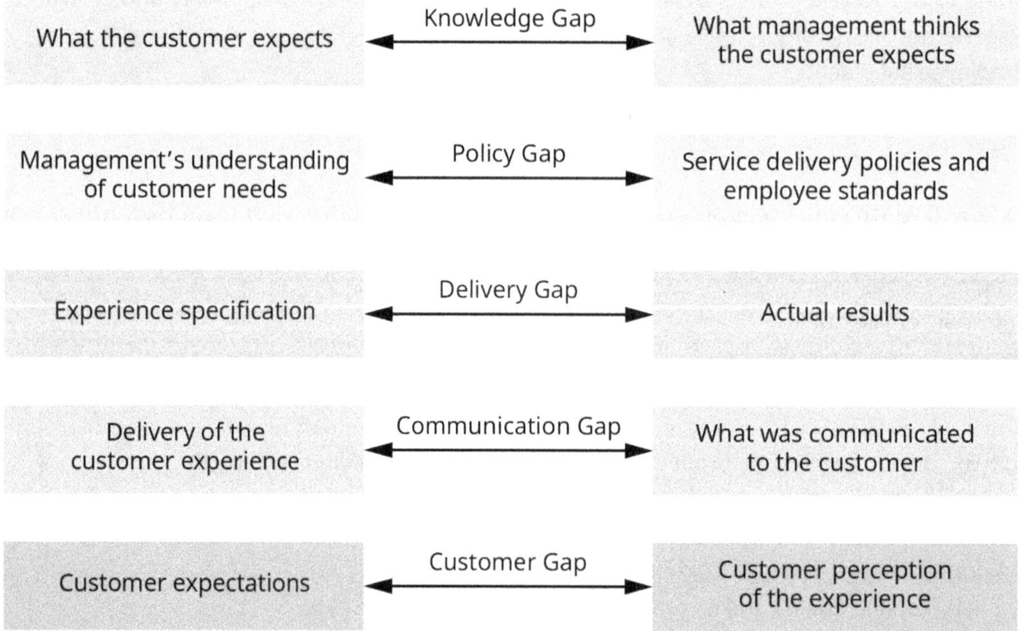

Figure 11.11 Gap Model of Service Quality (attribution: Copyright Rice University, OpenStax, under CC BY 4.0 license)

The gaps are:

- Gap 1—knowledge gap: the difference between customer expectations and what managers *think* they expect
- Gap 2—policy gap: the difference between management's understanding of the customer's needs and how they translate that understanding into service delivery policies and standards for employees
- Gap 3—delivery gap: the difference between the experience specification and the actual results of the

service
- Gap 4—communication gap: the difference between the delivery of the customer experience and what is communicated to the customer
- Gap 5—customer gap: the difference between the customer's expectations of the service or experience and their perception of the experience

Let's look at each one of these gaps in a little more detail.

Gap 1: The Knowledge Gap

The **knowledge gap** is the difference between what customers expect and what the company *thinks* they expect.[29] The bottom line here is that the company doesn't know exactly what customers want. This could be due to a variety of factors—lack of communication between frontline employees and management, inadequate market research, or simply a failure to listen to customer feedback, including complaints. For example, a hotel manager may think that guests want a hot breakfast instead of a continental breakfast, but the reality is that guests are more concerned with the cleanliness of their rooms or the speed of the Internet service at the hotel than they are with breakfast.

Gap 2: The Policy Gap

The **policy gap** reflects the difference between management's perception of the customer's needs and the translation of that understanding into its service delivery policies and standards. Typically, management has an accurate understanding of what the customer wants, but performance standards haven't been established that ensure the appropriate employee behaviors are displayed.[30] Using the hotel example again, assume that a number of customers have complained that the phone rings innumerable times before it is answered. Management wants to address this issue, so it establishes a policy that phones must be answered "quickly." What's your interpretation of the word *quickly*—two rings, four rings, six rings? Specificity here is the key.

Gap 3: The Delivery Gap

The **delivery gap** is the difference between service standards and policies and the actual delivery of the service. In this situation, frontline service workers *know* what to do to delight the customer; they simply aren't doing it. For instance, management may have established a policy that the front desk phones get answered on or before the second ring, but the front desk employees are allowing phones to ring much longer before answering. This gap may arise due to improper training, lack of capability on the part of employees, unwillingness to meet the established service standards, or staff shortages.

Southwest Airlines is a great example of this. According to its website, the mission of the company is "dedication to the highest quality of Customer Service delivered with a sense of warmth, friendliness, individual pride and Company Spirit."[31] The company doesn't "overhype" its service, so there is no delivery gap—the difference between the experience specification and the actual delivery of its service. This is demonstrated by the fact that, compared to other airlines, Southwest has the greatest customer service rating, earning a 33.9 percent excellence rating.[32]

Gap 4: The Communication Gap

If marketers are doing an effective job in terms of their promotion efforts, the customer is likely to be highly influenced by that promotion. The problem now becomes, the company had better deliver. The **communication gap** is the difference between the delivery of the service and what is communicated to the customer. In other words, what did the company promise versus what did it deliver?

For example, if your coffee shop asserts in its advertising and on its menu that its food is gluten-free, and it isn't, customer expectations won't be met. Failure to deliver on a promise hurts the company's credibility. Former US President Donald Trump wrote, "A brand is two words: the 'promise' you telegraph, and the 'experience' you deliver."[33]

Gap 5: The Customer Gap

The **customer gap** is the difference between the customer's expectations of the service or experience and their perception of the experience itself. In an ideal world, the customer's expectations would be nearly identical to their perception, but customer perception is totally subjective and has been shaped by word of mouth, their personal needs, and their own past experiences. The problem here is that each individual perceives their world through their own eyes, and everyone perceives reality differently. In other words, while reality is a fixed factor, perception of reality is a variable.

LINK TO LEARNING

Understanding the Gap Model

Watch this video and learn more about quality of service and the gap model from Jochen Wirtz, a well-known marketing author.

Click to view content (https://openstax.org/books/principles-marketing/pages/11-3-the-gap-model-of-service-quality)

Also check out this article from Indeed about the GAP Model of Service Quality (https://openstax.org/r/careerdevelopmentgapmodel), with examples.

The RATER Model

In their book *Delivering Quality Service,* researchers Valerie Zeithaml, A. Parasuraman, and Leonard Berry identified five dimensions of service that customers use when evaluating service quality. Their research pointed to the fact that these five dimensions result in service excellence and lead to higher customer loyalty. This model is sometimes known as the **RATER framework of service quality**.[34] Refer to Figure 11.12 for a visual representation of the RATER framework.

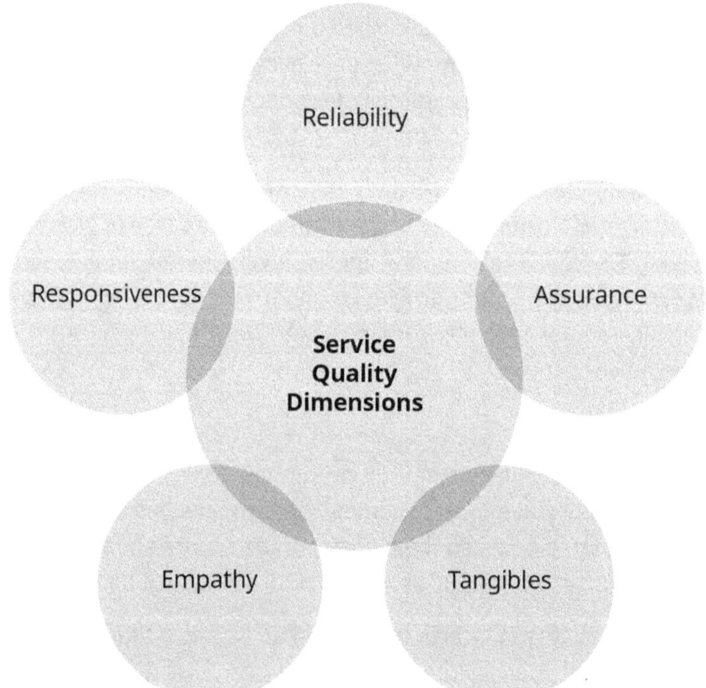

Figure 11.12 The RATER Framework of Service Quality (attribution: Copyright Rice University, OpenStax, under CC BY 4.0 license)

Let's explore each of these dimensions (represented by the acronym RATER) in some detail:

Reliability

R, for **reliability**, depicts the organization's capability to provide accurate, dependable, and on-time service.[35] Consistency is critical. Companies that provide on-time, error-free service to customers tend to have repeat customers. Research has shown that service reliability is three times more important to customers than the latest equipment or flashy uniforms.[36] The bottom line when it comes to service reliability and quality is: Do you deliver as promised?

Assurance

A, for **assurance**, is the degree to which the organization inspires trust in its customers. For example, when you take your sick pet to a veterinarian or have your income tax return prepared (or any other service, for that matter), you expect the service provider to be an expert in the service they're delivering. Research has shown that communicating this expertise to customers is important. If customers aren't aware of that expertise, they often have less confidence in that provider, which can lead to a low assessment of that provider's service.[37]

Does your organization inspire confidence in its service providers? Whether you're a hairstylist, a physical therapist, a tattoo artist, or any number of other service professions, it's important to communicate your expertise *before* you do the work. For example, a plumber's business card may contain the words "licensed, bonded, and insured." Hairstylists generally display their state licenses in their work space. Doctors often have framed diplomas in the office from medical school, residencies, and fellowships. These are all ways in which these service providers communicate their competencies. Communicating these competencies to customers helps shape expectations and influence assessments in advance of the service.[38]

Tangibles

When we talk about **tangibles** in the RATER model, we're focusing on factors such as the physical appearance of both the physical facility and employees. Does your organization present itself professionally? This is one of the factors in the RATER metric that is hard to define because it takes into account customers' perceptions, and different customers may respond in different, subjective ways to the environment created.

Let's imagine that you're taking that special someone out for a romantic or special-occasion dinner at a fine-dining restaurant. What tangibles contribute to that experience? You may expect a knowledgeable, uniformed staff; soft lighting and background music; an appealing menu; and clean restrooms. All of these tangibles will factor into your overall perception of the quality of service you receive.

Another good example of tangibles in terms of the RATER model is the Mayo Clinic in Rochester, Minnesota, where tangibles include Warhol prints on the wall, Chihuly sculptures hanging from the ceiling, and a professionally attired staff that projects a sense of caring and expertise. There are 500 original pieces of art from 70 US artists on display throughout the hospital.[39]

Customer perception isn't the only challenge marketers face in terms of tangibles. It's also the fact that, done right, customers may not even notice and point out the tangibles unless their feedback is negative. That's why listening and acting on customer complaints is critical in improving an organization's tangibles and promoting a strong customer service image.[40]

Empathy

Empathy in terms of the RATER model means focusing on customers attentively to ensure that they receive caring and distinguished service. It isn't enough to be efficient and thorough in delivering service to customers—it's also about service providers "connecting" with customers during delivery of the service and making them feel valued.

You may have heard the old saying that it's not *what* was said, it's *how* it was said. The same is true of providing service. For example, let's go back to the example of that special dinner in the fine-dining restaurant. Imagine that you accidently spill your beverage all over the table. A busser is called to clean the spill, change the tablecloth, and provide you with new silverware and napkins. That busser may have taken care of those tasks effectively and efficiently but didn't make eye contact, smile, or ask you if you needed anything else. In this hypothetical situation, the busser's tasks were performed fully, but you didn't feel that they cared about your predicament.[41]

Responsiveness

A service staff's desire to treat customers with respect and provide satisfactory and quick service speaks to their **responsiveness**. This dimension focuses on promptness and willingness. Accordingly, the organization has to ensure that customers are getting quick service, without delay, and with an effort that makes customers believe the company genuinely wants to help them.[42]

Responsiveness is directly in line with the amount of time that customers wait for an answer or a solution. Have you ever called an organization with a service question and had to play "20 Questions" with the company's automated phone system? You know the drill—press 1 for option A, press 2 for option B, press 3 for option C, etc. The chances are that your patience evaporated after about the fourth telephone prompt and you were left screaming "Representative" into your phone. That's a classic example of a company that needs to focus on its responsiveness if it wants to generate customer loyalty.

LINK TO LEARNING

Applying the RATER Model to Real-World Companies

Check out this video about Disney guest service and the RATER model.

Click to view content (https://openstax.org/books/principles-marketing/pages/11-3-the-gap-model-of-service-quality)

Also look at this article that applies the RATER model (https://openstax.org/r/ratermodel) to Amazon, Thermomix, Apple, and a bank.

Knowledge Check

It's time to check your knowledge on the concepts presented in this section. Refer to the Answer Key at the end of the book for feedback.

1. Which gap in the Gap Model of Service Quality represents the difference between what customers expect and what the company thinks they expect?
   a. Communication gap
   b. Customer gap
   c. Knowledge gap
   d. Policy gap

2. Management in a hotel perceives that the biggest problem in customer service is the length of time that it takes to check in guests, so they have established a policy that check-in will take no more than 5 minutes. Which gap in the Gap Model of Service Quality does this action illustrate?
   a. Policy gap
   b. Delivery gap
   c. Communication gap
   d. Customer gap

3. In the Gap Model of Service Quality, which dimension is the difference between the customer's expectation of the service and their perception of the experience?

   a. Communication gap
   b. Delivery gap
   c. Customer gap
   d. Knowledge gap

4. The acronym RATER in the RATER framework of service quality stands for which dimensions of service quality that result in service excellence and lead to higher customer loyalty?
   a. Responsibility, accuracy, tangibles, empathy, and responsiveness
   b. Risk, acceptance, transparency, earnings, and revenue
   c. Reliability, assurance, tangibles, empathy, and responsiveness
   d. Revenue, appreciation, trust, efficiency, and responsibility

5. Which dimension in the RATER model represents the physical facilities, employees' appearance, equipment, machinery, and information systems?
   a. Assurance
   b. Responsiveness
   c. Transparency
   d. Tangibles

11.4 | Ethical Considerations in Providing Services

Learning Outcomes

By the end of this section, you will be able to:
- **LO 1** Describe the ethical considerations in providing services to customers.
- **LO 2** Discuss how ethics contribute to customer satisfaction.

How Do Ethics Contribute to Customer Satisfaction?

In 2019, AT&T ran a series of TV commercials featuring a variety of professionals who don't quite "make the grade." These commercials included a surgeon who has "almost" been reinstated and a tax professional who will get your taxes into an "okay" place when his audit is over. The catchphrase is each of these commercials was "Just OK is not OK." The same is true of an organization's ethical culture. Do you want your ethical culture to be "just OK"?

In this chapter, we've been talking about the importance of building customer loyalty, which drives profitability and growth. But what about the link between ethics and customer loyalty? Ethics are becoming central to consumers, employees, and a company's reputation (and hence its ability to gain customer loyalty). New research from Mintel, a market intelligence agency, reveals that over half of US consumers stop buying from companies they perceive to be unethical.[43] Talk about a wake-up call!

Service Excellence through Ethics

Obviously, ethics matter. But how do you ensure that those ethics are instilled and demonstrated by your employees, particularly those frontline employees who interact directly with the customer? The National Ethics Association (NEA) has two suggestions. First, within your ethics program, make customer service a core component. Second, promote values and ethics, and include them within the rules for your frontline workers along with the consequences if they aren't followed.[44]

According to the NEA, steps can include the following:

- Identifying customer service behaviors that are unethical, like lying to customers or failing to display sensitivity to customers with problems.
- Training employees on an ongoing basis in desired behaviors.

- Ensuring customers know that promises aren't empty words but rather a commitment to their satisfaction.
- Monitoring interactions between frontline employees and customers to spot ethical gaps, especially in times of high stress and work volume.
- Leading by example. It's not enough to just "talk the talk" when it comes to ethical behavior within the organization; managers also need to "walk the talk." It's important to "walk the talk" of ethical behavior as a model for employees when dealing with customers' complaints and problems.[45]

Royal Caribbean Group is another company that takes its ethical behavior seriously. It has a Code of Business Conduct and Ethics decree that connects its core values (fairness, integrity, honesty, and trustworthiness) to all of its actions. Chairman and CEO Richard Fain reaffirms its commitment to integrity and an ethical culture and states, "Simply complying with the law is not enough; we need to be ABC (Above and Beyond Compliance)."[46] Beyond just words, however, the company has established an ethics hotline managed by The Network, a leading third-party hotline provider. Through the use of this ethics hotline, employees can anonymously report their concerns about ethics violations 24 hours a day, 7 days a week, by either telephone or the Internet.[47]

LINK TO LEARNING

Royal Caribbean

Read more about Royal Caribbean's Code of Business Conduct and Ethics on its website (https://openstax.org/r/2019cleanfinal).

Also, read this article on the potential ethical issues (https://openstax.org/r/potentialethicalissues) specific to service marketing.

COMPANIES WITH A CONSCIENCE

Nasco Gulf

Figure 11.13 Ethics are becoming increasingly more important to customers and the services they use, so companies like Nasco Gulf, an insurance company, are focusing more on trust as a way to develop long-term loyalty. (credit: "WOCinTech Stock - 81" by WOCinTechChat.com/flickr, CC BY 2.0)

You may not be familiar with Nasco Gulf, a leading insurance agent in Dubai, but the company stands out in its Customer Service Code of Conduct (see Figure 11.13). The "customer service mission is to provide customers with timely, responsive service with integrity, simplicity, and a passion for excellence while meeting or exceeding the customer's expectations."[48]

The principles upon which Nasco serves its customers are trust, understanding, and resolve. The following is from its Customer Service Fundamental Principles:

- "Trust—I work hard to gain and maintain customer trust in us . . .
- Understand—I understand our customers and their needs . . .
- Resolve—I solve our customer's problems, even if the solution is difficult"[49]

Nasco lists its values on its website for all to see. The company outlines that its word is good, it is a bold partner, it works to earn loyalty, and it focuses on what matters. For more information about Nasco Gulf, visit the Nasco Gulf website. (https://openstax.org/r/nascogulf)

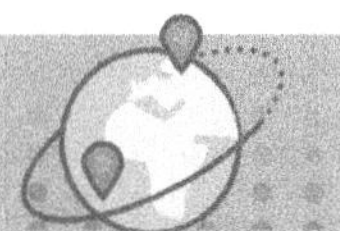

LINK TO LEARNING

When It Goes Wrong

We have all heard the stories where companies poorly handled a customer issue, and you can easily find numerous videos where customers have recorded a company's poor customer service. Here are a few articles that share some of the more well-known stories:

- CBS News (https://openstax.org/r/shockingviralvideos)
- RingCentral (https://openstax.org/r/badcustomerservice)
- Forbes (https://openstax.org/r/unethicalmarketing)

▣ Chapter Summary

In this chapter, we explore services. One of the first concepts is that services are intangible, meaning that they cannot be felt, tasted, heard, or smelled before purchase. Customer satisfaction is dependent upon many factors, the first one being the communication of what can be expected by the customer and the actual customer experience. It can be considered a communication gap when customer expectations and experiences do not match. This gap is the first point in the Gap Model of Service Quality. The second point is based on the perception of service received versus customer expectations. Other issues covered in this model are service quality, knowledge, and policies.

Service goes a long way in building customer satisfaction and loyalty; without returning customers, a business is doomed to struggle and fail.

Employees are responsible for a sizable amount of what goes into satisfaction at the customer level. One of the key points is employee satisfaction and retention. A more engaged, happier employee delivers a higher level of customer service. This is an additional point that employers are measuring. The act of internal service marketing is a concept that many have not experienced. This covers the activities that the company engages in to keep employees involved with delivering the desired level of service.

External service marketing is the act of promoting or selling services to the customer. This is a well-known concept both inside and outside the company.

Services can be further examined with the understanding of the following concepts: Services are inseparable; they are produced and consumed at the same time. They are intangible, which means that they cannot be touched, felt, heard, tasted, or smelled before purchase. They are perishable, so they cannot be stored in inventory for future use or sale. They are variable, meaning that the service depends on who provides them, as well as when, where, and how. These concepts help to explain the complexities of marketing services and satisfying the consumer.

⚷ Key Terms

assurance   in terms of the RATER model, the degree to which an organization inspires trust in its customers

communication gap   in the Gap Model of Service Quality, the variance between what is communicated to the customer and their actual experience

customer gap   in the Gap Model of Service Quality, the variance between the customer's expectations and their perception of the service

customer loyalty   an ongoing positive relationship between a customer and a business that drives repeat purchases

customer satisfaction   a measurement that determines how happy customers are with a company's products, services, and capabilities

delivery gap   in the Gap Model of Service Quality, the difference between the experience specification and the actual delivery of the service

empathy   in terms of the RATER model, focusing on customers attentively to assure they receive caring and distinguished service

employee retention   an organization's ability to retain its employees and stop employees from leaving

employee satisfaction   the level of happiness and contentment employees have about their jobs and the work environment

equipment-based services   when machinery or equipment plays the primary role in the service delivery

external service marketing   the action of promoting or selling services to customers and potential customers

external value proposition   the value companies promise to deliver to customers post-purchase

GAP Model of Service Quality   theoretical marketing model that helps to identify the gaps between the perceived service and the expected service

information processing   intangible actions directed at a customer's assets, such as insurance or consulting

intangible   unable to be seen, tasted, felt, smelled, or heard

interactive service marketing   the communication between the service provider and the customer; also called a **service encounter**

internal service marketing   satisfying employees to motivate them to work as a team to satisfy customers

internal service quality   the perceived level of satisfaction an employee experiences with services offered by internal service providers

knowledge gap   in the GAP Model of Service Quality, the difference between what customers expect and what managers think they expect

mental stimulus processing   situation in which the services interact with the customer's mind rather than the body

people processing   services in which the customer is the direct recipient of the service and production and consumption are simultaneous

people-based services   tasks in which people, rather than equipment or machinery, play a major role in the delivery of the service

policy gap   in the GAP Model of Service Quality, the difference between managers understanding customer needs and being able to turn that into service delivery practices

possession processing   services in which the service is directed toward the customer's physical possessions

productivity   the efficiency and output of employees

RATER framework of service quality   theoretical model that focuses on the five dimensions of service excellence: reliability, assurance, tangibles, empathy, and responsiveness

reliability   in terms of the RATER model, the organization's capability to produce an accurate, dependable, and on-time service

responsiveness   in terms of the RATER model, promptness and willingness to provide satisfactory and quick service

service encounter   a consumer's direct contact with a service provider

service inseparability   concept where services must be produced and consumed concurrently

Service Marketing Triangle   a visual representation of a strategic model that outlines the importance of people in a company's ability to keep its service promises

service perishability   concept that states services cannot be stored in inventory for future use or sale

service variability   concept that states the quality of the service depends on who, when, where, and how it is provided

service-profit chain model   model that establishes relationships between profitability, employee satisfaction, loyalty, and productivity

services   nonphysical, intangible economic activities

tangibles   in terms of the RATER model, the physical appearance of both the facility and its employees

Applied Marketing Knowledge: Discussion Questions

1. Review this *Houston Chronicle* article about the eight elements of service marketing (https://openstax.org/r/8elementsservicemarketing). Pick two different service-oriented organizations and describe each of these eight elements as they relate to the service each company offers. Conduct additional research if needed to address these eight elements.

2. Take the information that you have learned about internal and external marketing and describe two instances where as a student you have noticed excellent and poor marketing strategies. Are they internal or external, and why did you feel the way you did about them?

3. Consider service variability instances where you were a customer and noticed exceptional service and poor service. For each instance, answer the following questions:
   a. Were you surprised?

   b. What specifically made you notice?

   c. Had you had this experience before with this company or another company?

   d. What response did you have? For instance, did you compliment? Tip? Complain? Do nothing? And why?

   e. If you were the company owner, what kind of training program would you develop to address the poor service you experienced? What might you implement as a reward for exceptional service? Why?

4. Analyze the differences between internal and external marketing.

   a. Define both terms.

   b. Consider and list the positive impact that both internal and external marketing can have on an organization.

Critical Thinking Exercises

1. Agree or disagree with the following statement: I tip for service based solely on the amount of the bill, not on things like quality of service, timing, etc. Discuss or make a list of the reasons why you agree or disagree.

2. Nordstrom's reputation was built upon its value proposition of superior service. The company has maintained a high level of service over the years. Research other retailers that have a similar service-oriented value proposition. It could be a car company, restaurant, clothing store, etc. In looking at the changing demographics, do you believe that this level of service will continue to be perceived as value? If not, what will take its place?

3. Have you ever experienced service that was so poor that you did not return? Compare your views with someone that you know. Is this a common service issue?

Building Your Personal Brand

"Communication is the act or process of using words, sounds, signs, or behaviors to express or exchange information or to express your ideas, thoughts, feelings, etc., to someone else."[50] What type of communicator are you? Analytical? Intuitive? Functional? Personal? Research communication styles and describe which best describes you. Outline a plan on how you might communicate with those who adhere to a different style. To get started, try this free communication style assessment (https://openstax.org/r/communicationstyles). There are also other assessments available online, so try a few and see and see if there are any differences.

Keep in mind that communication also includes nonverbal signs such as our facial expressions and body language. How does your body position change when communicating a happy story versus a sad story? Try this body language self-assessment (https://openstax.org/r/scienceofpeople).

A large percentage of our personal brand comes from how we communicate with others. Think about the people you admire; odds are they communicate in a way that you understand and relate to. Work on becoming comfortable in your style and recognizing the styles of others. If you do this, others will be comfortable with you, and they will remember you. Often, a key component to a promotion is being noticed and remembered for the personal brand you exhibit.

What Do Marketers Do?

Considering that "70% of small businesses are operated and owned by a single person," the question arises: Who is doing the marketing?[51]

Find at least two small service businesses, one that you know to be successful and one that might be hanging on by a thread (hair salons, dry cleaners, mechanics, party planners, florists, etc.). Call and see if you can arrange a time, either on the phone or in person, to ask questions about their marketing efforts. You might want to do a bit of homework before you do. Here are questions that will help you gather information:

1. Do they consider what they do to promote their business as marketing?
2. Do they have someone who helps them?
3. Do they have a website or Facebook page?
4. What are the main activities that they do to market their business?
5. Do they have a formal business plan? A budget?
6. How do they figure out what their budget should look like?
7. Are there efforts that they consider successful and anything that seriously did not work?
8. Do they respond to the marketing of their competitors?

Of course, there are additional questions that you can ask as time permits. The idea here is to get a good look at what the challenges are to marketing a small business. Is this something that you see yourself doing—perhaps even as a business of your own?

 Closing Company Case

Adventist Health Castle

Adventist Health Castle in Kailua, Hawaii, is an award-winning hospital focused on serving the mind, body, and spirit of its patients. The 300 physicians provide services to the entire island of Oahu, following the mission to "care for the community and share God's love."[52]

Adventist Health Castle offers programs in wellness and lifestyle, cutting-edge weight-loss procedures, and advanced imaging techniques. All programs come with a patient-focused approach with compassion and dedication from its health team. The mission statement of "transforming the health experience of our community by improving health, enhancing interactions and making care more accessible" is accomplished through "integrity, compassion, respect, and excellence."[53] In 2017, it won the Malcolm Baldrige National Quality Award, an award that recognizes the excellent patient care the staff provides to the community.

Adventist Health Castle is proud of its Wellness and Lifestyle Medicine center because of the variety of health education and lifestyle resources it provides for the community. It offers classes, events, and services to the public for a small fee or often for free. Check out more here (https://openstax.org/r/adventisthealth) about the medical services it offers.

Health systems are a product of the community they serve, and Adventist Health Castle is no exception. To help with its cause, it developed a community needs assessment to understand the concerns and needs of the populations within its service area. From that work, it has developed numerous programs and events, including diabetes care classes and improved access to health services. It also added ENT, cardiology, and dental services to its Rural Health Clinic in Laie. With this addition of the new Rural Health Clinic, Adventist's system served 2,432 unique patients in its first year.[54]

With its work, Adventist Health Castle expanded access to classes to include a center in Kaneohe. Multiple locations allow the health system to extend its reach to the community with more classes and events. And it's working! Through a postcard mailing, Adventist received a positive response to class enrollment.

Another initiative created around better access to care included having physician practices add more office hours to include evenings and weekends. Through this effort, Adventist has been able to engage with more patients and coordinate care better for the populations it serves.

With this work, the community has seen many positive outcomes including increased overall health due to the greater availability of healthy center resources. Serving a community means adapting to the needs of the community and meeting the populations where they are most vulnerable.

Case Questions

1. Adventist Health Castle is a health system operating to serve the population of Oahu. How would you classify its services?

2. When community members choose to take a class on diabetes management, they are learning about diabetes from a clinical nurse instructor. The instructor informs the participants of the health risks associated with unhealthy lifestyle choices. Different clinical nurse instructors teach the classes each time. Depending on who teaches the course, the participants may learn the risks of a sedentary lifestyle. This is an example of which service characteristic?

3. Adventist Health Castle realized that access to health services was an important need in its community. To provide for that need, it developed a multidisciplinary clinic to serve rural communities. It immediately started seeing and treating patients. How does this fit into the service-profit chain?

4. When Adventist Health Castle added more hours to physician practices, what dimension of service quality was it addressing be

References

1. Andrea Forstadt, "10 Service-Based Business Ideas," US Chamber of Commerce, April 2, 2021, https://www.uschamber.com/co/start/business-ideas/service-based-business-ideas.

2. "Success Story: MeTime Drop-In Child Care," Pathway Lending, March 26, 2018, https://www.pathwaylending.org/news-and-blog/success-story-metime/.

3. "Percentage Added to U.S. GDP by Industry 2020," Stastista, June 3, 2021, https://www.statista.com/statistics/248004/percentage-added-to-the-us-gdp-by-industry/.

4. Richa Saxena, "SM: Session3: Service Classification, Characteristics and Triangle," *The Awakener* (blog), November 26, 2015, http://richaprof.blogspot.com/2015/11/sm-session3-service-classification.html.

5. Rakesh Panchal, "Service Marketing: Four Categories of Services," *My View: M-bullshit* (blog), April 7, 2014, http://misbullshit.blogspot.com/2014/04/service-marketing-four-categories-of.html.

6. Ibid.

7. Jake, "These 21 Alternatives to Warby Parker Also Let You Try-On Prescription Eyeglasses at Home in 2022," Modern Fellows, July 28, 2022, https://www.modernfellows.com/alternatives-to-warby-parker/.

8. "4 Characteristics of Service," iEduNote, accessed November 11, 2021, https://www.iedunote.com/service-characteristics.

9. Ibid.

10. Delta Airlines, "Delta Airlines Mission & Vision Analysis," accessed June 15, 2022, https://mission-statement.com/delta-airlines/.

11. "4 Characteristics of Service," iEduNote, accessed November 11, 2021, https://www.iedunote.com/service-characteristics.

12. S. R. Rao, "Implications of Unique Features of Services," Citeman, December 14, 2007, https://www.citeman.com/2519-implications-of-unique-features-of-services.html.

13. John Ryder, "Why the Iceberg of Ignorance Is Still Relevant and How to Melt It," *Hive* (blog), June 26, 2019, https://www.hive.hr/blog/iceberg-of-ignorance/.

14. Will Schmidt, "5 Lessons from Zappos on Employee Happiness," Classy, accessed October 14, 2021, https://medium.com/classy-blog/5-lessons-from-zappos-on-employee-happiness-10e3889b7ba

15. iGrad Author, "The Cost of Replacing an Employee and the Role of Financial Wellness," *The Well* (blog), Enrich Financial Wellness, accessed May 22, 2022, https://www.enrich.org/blog/The-true-cost-of-employee-turnover-financial-wellness-enrich#:~:text.

16. Nkem Anigbogu, "Understanding the Service-Profit Chain," LinkedIn, March 13, 2018, https://www.linkedin.com/pulse/understanding-service-profit-chain-nkem-anigbogu/.

17. Basha Coleman, "How to Write a Great Value Proposition [5 Top Examples + Template]," HubSpot, March 10, 2022, https://blog.hubspot.com/marketing/write-value-proposition.

18. P. Mulder, "Service Profit Chain," Toolshero, October 5, 2018, https://www.toolshero.com/strategy/service-profit-chain/.

19. Ibid.

20. Ibid.

21. Adam Toporek. "The Ritz-Carlton's Famous $2,000 Rule," Customers That Stick, September 12, 2017, https://customersthatstick.com/blog/customer-loyalty/the-ritz-carltons-famous-2000-rule/.

22. Ibid.

23. "Services Marketing Triangle," Expert Program Management, accessed November 11, 2021, https://expertprogrammanagement.com/2018/03/services-marketing-triangle/.

24. Ibid.

25. Ibid.

26. Anam Ahmed, "What Is a Service Marketing Triangle?" *Chron.*, March 8, 2021, https://smallbusiness.chron.com/service-marketing-triangle-61170.html.

27. "What Is the GAP Model of Service Quality? (With Examples)," Indeed Career Guide, November 23, 2021, https://www.indeed.com/career-advice/career-development/gap-model.

28. Ibid.

29. Ibid.

30. Ibid.

31. Sean Peek, "What Your Business Can Learn from Southwest Airlines," Business.com, August 2, 2022, https://www.business.com/articles/southwest-airlines-great-customer-service/.

32. Ibid.

33. Donald Trump, "A brand is two words: The 'promise' you telegraph, and the 'experience' you deliver," Minimalist Quotes, accessed February 27, 2022, https://minimalistquotes.com/donald-trump-quote-18890/.

34. Arlen, C. (2018, July 2). The 5 service dimensions all customers care about. Retrieved November 11, 2021, from https://www.serviceperformance.com/the-5-service-dimensions-all-customers-care-about/.

35. Ibid.

36. Ibid.

37. Ibid.

38. Ibid.

39. Mary Carole McCauley, "New Hopkins Hospital Takes an Artful Approach to Health Care," *Baltimore Sun*, April 26, 2012, https://www.baltimoresun.com/health/bs-xpm-2012-04-27-bs-hs-hopkins-art-20120427-41-story.html.

40. "Measuring Customer Service Quality with the RATER Framework," Simplesat, accessed November 11, 2021, https://www.simplesat.io/measuring-customer-service-quality-rater-framework/.

41. Ibid.

42. M. M. Kobiruzzaman, "Five Dimensions of Service Quality—Servqual Model of Service Quality," Newsmoor, September 15, 2020, https://newsmoor.com/servqual-model-five-key-service-dimensions-servqual-gaps-reasons/.

43. "56% of Americans Stop Buying from Brands They Believe Are Unethical," Mintel, November 18, 2015, https://www.mintel.com/press-centre/social-and-lifestyle/56-of-americans-stop-buying-from-brands-they-believe-are-unethical.

44. National Ethics Association, "Customer Service Ethics: Beware the Dark Side," December 2, 2011, https://www.ethics.net/articles/customer-service-ethics-beware-the-dark-side.

45. Ibid.

46. Royal Caribbean Cruises Ltd., *Code of Business Conduct and Ethics*, 2019, https://www.rclinvestor.com/content/uploads/2019/09/COBE_Eng-2019_Clean_Final.pdf.

47. Chief Executive Office [username], "Royal Caribbean Ethics Hotline," Ship Happens forum, September 29, 2014, http://www.inozemstvo-posao.com/smf_1-1-2_install/index.php?topic=9533.0.

48. Nasco Gulf, *Customer Service Code of Conduct*, accessed November 11, 2021, http://www.nascogulf.com/Content/uploads/NASCO_Customer_Service_Code_of_Conduct_-_V1.pdf.

49. Ibid.

50. *Merriam-Webster*, "communication," accessed March 8, 2022, https://www.merriam-webster.com/dictionary/communication.

51. Deyan Georgiev, "Small Business Statistics [Guide to Success in 2022]," Review42, May 12, 2022, https://review42.com/resources/small-business-statistics/.

52. "Home page," Adventist Health Castle, https://www.adventisthealth.org/castle.

53. "About Us: Mission, Vision, and Values," Adventist Health Castle, accessed May 5, 2022, https://www.adventisthealth.org/castle/about-us/mission-vision-values

54. Adventist Health Castle, *2019 Community Health Plan Update*, 2019, https://www.adventisthealth.org/documents/community-benefit/2019-chp-update-ar/Castle_2019_Community-Health-Plan-Update-Annual-Report.pdf.

12

Pricing Products and Services

Figure 12.1 Price is one of the marketing mix elements and a factor that impacts customer decisions. (credit: modification of work "Thrift Shop Helps Consumers, Community" by W. Wayne Marlow/USAGHumphreys/flickr, CC BY 2.0)

Chapter Outline

In the Spotlight

In February 2005, Amazon launched Amazon Prime, which offered unlimited two-day delivery for millions of items.[1] At a time when consumers were accustomed to paying high shipping fees and experiencing slow service, the membership service—$79 per year—offered a new alternative. It was a first-of-its-kind pricing structure that has sparked many companies to do the same. Today's subscription services cover everything from toilet paper to dog toys. Amazon Prime is still arguably the most prevalent subscription service in history. In 2021, Amazon reported its Amazon Prime members had reached 200 million worldwide.[2]

The membership, according to a public letter from Jeff Bezos, executive chair of the Amazon board, "takes the effort out of ordering; no minimum purchase and no consolidating orders. Two-day shipping becomes an everyday experience rather than an occasional indulgence."[3]

Since its first offering in 2005, Amazon has raised its prices only three times—in 2014 to $99 a year, in 2018 to $119, and most recently to $139/year.[4] While rumbles in the market suggested that these price increases might drive away customers, Amazon has proven this was not the case. The price increases through the years also included new benefits—Amazon Prime video, Prime Pantry, Prime Reading, and many others. The company demonstrates that consumers are, in fact, willing to pay higher prices—so long as they can perceive value that is added to the increase in price.

12.1 | Pricing and Its Role in the Marketing Mix

Learning Outcomes

By the end of this section, you will be able to:

- **LO** 1 Define pricing.
- **LO** 2 Explain pricing and its role in the marketing mix.
- **LO** 3 Explain the psychology of pricing.

Pricing Defined

Anytime anything is sold, a price is involved. Recall that during the exchange process, a seller is offering something of value to a buyer in exchange for also something of value. This value to the seller is often referred to as price. The practice of pricing is not a new concept. Some of the oldest records of prices ever discovered were found on clay tablets with symbols in Uruk, located in modern-day Iraq. The records are written receipts of exchanges of sheep, beer, and barley and date back to 3300 BCE![5]

You may recall that price is one of the 4Ps of marketing, or one element in the marketing mix. Once a product has been developed, marketers must determine at which price the product or service will be offered to the target market. Today, pricing is one of the more difficult decisions that marketers must make in the marketing mix because it directly impacts the perception of value from the customer as well as the company's bottom line. Poor decisions in pricing can have immediate and catastrophic effects on profits that are difficult for companies to recover from. Price decisions must be linked to a product or service's real and perceived value while also considering competition, supply costs, and when discounts should be offered.

Simply put, **price** refers to the exchange of something of value between a buyer and a seller. The price determines how much revenue the company will earn and drives the financial health of the organization. However, marketers cannot simply price products and services based on the expected revenue of the organization. The price must be set so that the buyer sees value in the product offering and the price they will pay for it. In other words, marketers must put the perception of value in the product's price at the forefront while also considering the financial impact to the organization.

While price is what is referred to when discussing most goods and services, price can take on many terms depending on the exchange that is taking place. In higher education, you are paying tuition—the price—in exchange for your education. If you need an attorney, you are likely going to pay a fee—the price—for services rendered. When you are traveling and have to pay a toll, it is the price you pay for using the road or bridge. Regardless of the exact terminology used, pricing of goods and services have the same basic elements.

Elements of Pricing

While a marketer is determining the price of goods and services, they must keep in mind that pricing must benefit both parties involved in the exchange process: the seller (company) and the buyer (customer). Both parties must see value in the product process through pricing for the exchange process to be successful. We'll first discuss how price is an indicator of value to the buyer and then turn our attention to the seller.

Price as an Indicator of Value

When a buyer purchases a product or service, they seek to satisfy a need through the purchase. The customer will, consciously or not, use several criteria to determine the amount they are willing to spend to satisfy that need. These criteria ultimately lead to the value that the customer sees in the product.

The price-value equation is a subjective assessment by a consumer about what they deem as a value. The price-value equation states that as a customer's expectations are met at what they consider an acceptable price, value is realized. Value is related to the quality and price of the product, and the formula is

$$Value = \frac{Quality}{Price}$$

For example, if a consumer purchases a high-end designer Chanel handbag for $11,000, they might equate the value to a beautiful, high-end, well-made handbag that will last for many years. They may also subconsciously believe the bag will portray a certain social status while carrying it. For them, there is value and quality in the product, and they are willing to pay the high price.

Consider another example: you are in the middle of fixing dinner, and you realize you don't have enough milk for the dish you are preparing. There is a convenience store just a block away from your house and a grocery store five miles away. If you send your partner to walk to the closer convenience store, they will pay more for the milk than if they were to drive the extra five miles to the grocery store, which would be less expensive. With the higher-priced item at the convenience store, you are paying for the convenience. The value in this scenario is in the time saved even at a higher price.

With these two examples, the perceived benefits are directly related the price-value equation. Perceived benefits can include status, convenience, brand, quality, etc. and can vary from buyer to buyer or even situation to situation.

Perceived costs can also include a host of criteria in addition to the price printed on the price tag. Let's return to the milk purchase example. If the situation were different—say you were not in the middle of cooking dinner—would your decision change? Perhaps. You will still consider other factors before making the decision. How long does it take for you to drive that extra five miles? Is the grocery store known for having long lines during the time you will be shopping? Do you need other items you can only get at that store? Does the store carry the brand of milk you prefer? These are only a few of the many considerations you make before you decide to make the purchase. These are all perceived costs and are weighed against the perceived benefits the buyer considers when determining value.

MARKETING IN PRACTICE

Upside

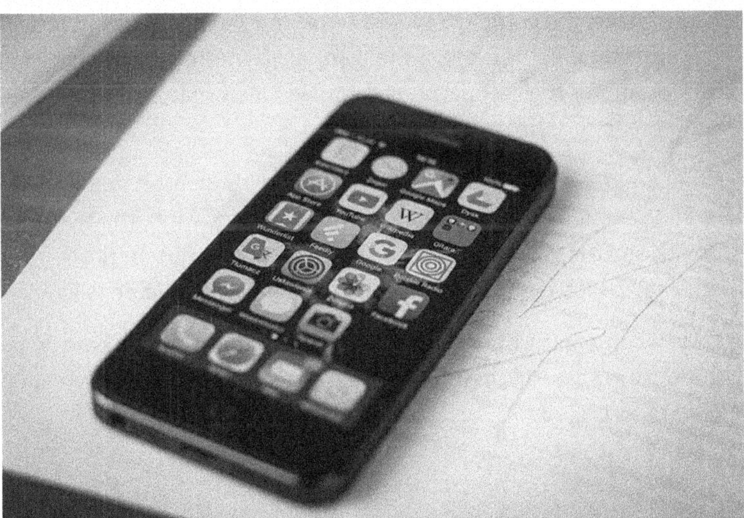

Figure 12.2 Upside is an app that benefits both customers and businesses by playing on the psychological effects of pricing. (credit: "iPhone Home Screen" by freestocks.org/flickr, Public Domain)

Founded in 2016, Upside is an app that promotes itself as saving customers money on purchases at gas stations as well as helping local brick-and-mortar businesses earn more profit. Here's how it works: Upside links to gas stations, restaurants, and grocery stores within a specified mile-radius of the user. The user chooses to claim an offer on the app and has four hours to upload the receipt. The linked businesses are those that have contracted with Upside to drive business to their establishment. Once redeemed, cash is deposited into the user's account and can be cashed out for gift cards or to a PayPal account.

Upside is banking on the value equation as well as psychological factors of pricing to attract both buyers and sellers. Gas prices, for example, are relatively unchanged from station to station in a small geographical area. If the user is able to get 25 cents cash back per gallon on their fill-up, they may swap convenience of the closer station with that of getting a cash reward at a station a few miles away. If the buyer chooses the station with cash back over one without, the seller (gas station) also finds value in a one-time or new customer.

For more information about Upside, visit the app's website (https://openstax.org/r/getupside).

Price in the Marketing Mix

Recall that the marketing mix elements include product, price, promotion, and place. Marketers create value through the maximization of benefits within an acceptable price point using the marketing mix elements. Price, however, is the only element of the marketing mix that directly produces revenue for the company. The other elements are considered costs to organization. Another way to think of price as differing from the other elements is to understand the price not only creates perceived value for the customer but also harvests monetary value for the company. Because price is the revenue-generating element of the marketing mix, it is vital that marketers set the right price both to match buyer perceptions and to maximize company profits. Profit is determined by subtracting total expenses from total revenue.

The Profit Equation

Recall that the goal of any for-profit company is make a profit. The price marketers set for goods and services offered will have a direct impact on the company's profit-making ability. Therefore, it is imperative that the price set is one that achieves value not only for the buyer but also for the company. Certainly, buyers would prefer a lower price—or even free—for goods and services. It's simply not feasible for a company to give its products and services away for free; the company would cease to exist very quickly, which does not serve either the company or the buyer well. Rather, it is in the company's interest to set prices that create value for the buyer and profit maximization for the company, as this gives the organization the best chance of continuing to create value in the long term.

So what is the best price that creates value for the seller? In short, it's the one that creates value for the buyer and simultaneously generating the maximum profit. If a price is set too high, the buyer may refuse to purchase because they do not see the value; in turn, the company loses out on profit. Alternatively, if the price is set too low, the company may be losing out on profits when a buyer would be willing to pay a higher price.

Profit is the financial gain of a company, or the difference between the amount earned and the amount spent in buying, operating, or producing something. It is the difference between total revenue and total costs and is calculated with the profit equation.

$$\text{Profit} = \text{Total Revenue} - \text{Total Costs}$$

Let's look at this formula more closely.

- **Total revenue** is the money generated from normal business operations. It is calculated by the sales price of a product times the quantity of units sold. For example, a company selling wireless earbuds for $19.99 that sold 5,000 units in one period has revenues of $99,950.
- **Total costs** of a company are the costs of sales and operating expenses. It is all expenses related to operating the business that are directly related to producing a good or service and that are indirectly

related to producing goods and services. In other words, it includes items such as building leases, employee salaries, and electricity as well as direct costs in producing the product, such as component parts and equipment.

Total costs can be categorized as either fixed or variable. **Fixed costs** are those expenses that do not change regardless of the number of units sold. For example, if the company selling wireless earbuds makes one unit or one million units, the company still has to pay the mortgage for the building it is occupying; the mortgage payment does not increase or decrease based on the number of units produced. Alternatively, **variable costs** do change based on the number of units produced. In the wireless earbud example, the company would spend more per unit if it ordered fewer units. If it ordered a higher quantity of units, the unit price would decrease.

In determining profit, the total costs include both the fixed and variable costs. The formula is

$$\text{Total Costs} = \text{Fixed Costs} + \text{Variable Costs}$$

When setting prices, the marketer must determine how much profit can be made from the sale of goods and services. However, as mentioned earlier, profit is not the only deciding factor in price. Much research has been done on how psychology also effects the perception of pricing.

The Psychology of Pricing

From a marketer's standpoint, these are all factors that must be considered when setting price. In addition to the value perceived by the buyer, the marketer must also understand other psychological factors that influence the buyer's perception of price. Several psychological pricing examples are discussed next.

Price Anchoring

When Steve Jobs introduced the Apple iPad during a Keynote in 2010, he showed off the high-resolution screen and talked about its revolutionary features. "What should we price it at?" he asked. "If you listen to the pundits, we're going to price it at under $1,000, which is code for $999." He put a giant $999 on the screen. He finally went on: "I am thrilled to announce to you that iPad pricing starts not at $999, but at just $499." The screen then showed the $999 price being crushed with the $499 price.[6] The crowd went wild!

The concept of **price anchoring** relies on the first piece of information that a buyer sees. This acts as an anchor, or a frame of reference for what the buyer expects a price to be. Steve Jobs used this concept in his introduction of the iPad. The anchor price he quoted was $999. This immediately made buyers believe the product should be priced around $999. However, when Jobs showed the actual price, starting at $499, the buyers immediately believed, psychologically, that it was a great deal. Viewers did not know what the worth of the iPad was; they just believed they were saving nearly $500 by having the initial anchor of $999.

Artificial Time Constraints

Marketers—particularly retailers—often use the psychological strategy of **artificial time constraints**. These trigger a sense of urgency in the buyer; if they don't buy today, they'll miss out on a great deal. Whereas a consumer may have been on the fence about spending money, these artificial time constraints act as a catalyst for consumers to spend money right now. And there is a lot of power in artificial constraints: consumers are afraid of missing out and don't want to later regret not buying. But consumers can often find the same prices many times throughout the year because retailers use this tactic frequently.

Price Appearance

A study on the effects of auditory representation in pricing showed that buyers believed $1,555.83 was a very complicated price and difficult to comprehend quickly. The study further outlined that a price of $1,555 (no cents) was *better* but that buyers were able to more easily and quickly comprehend a price of $1555 (no commas) and thus more likely to pause and consider the product.[7]

If you've ever gone to a fancy restaurant, you may have noticed the prices on the menu are in a small font and don't have zeros at the end. The price will be listed as $29 instead of $29.00. Psychologically, longer prices appear to be more expensive because they take longer to read. This effect is augmented by the use of a dollar sign. Similarly, the use of prices with multiple syllables seems more expensive because consumers pronounce the prices in their head. In short, the longer it takes to read and pronounce, the more impact the buyer believes it has on their wallet,[8] which is explained by **price appearance**.[9]

Price Gouging

Price gouging is when companies or individuals take advantage of a situation, typically an emergency or natural disaster, and charge exceptionally high prices for products or services. In some states, like New York, it's illegal for businesses to price gouge during a state of emergency.[10] In fact, New York was the first state to enact a price gouging law. In 1978, when there was a shortage of oil for heating in the winter and the lives of young and elderly people were threatened, the state created a law where companies could not sell goods or services at excessive prices.[11]

Can you think of recent examples where price gouging was a potential concern? During the COVID-19 pandemic, several states posted on their government websites lists of items that couldn't be subject to price gouging. Currently, the US Department of Justice provides a list of items that can't be hoarded or subject to price gouging due to COVID-19 precautions, including masks and other personal protective equipment (PPE), respirators, ventilators, and medical gowns.[12] There have been other instances where price gouging was an issue. According to AccuWeather, "some of the most rampant examples of price gouging came during the most destructive storms in recent years, such as Hurricane Katrina, Hurricane Sandy, Hurricane Harvey, and Hurricane Irma."[13] After Hurricane Katrina, a hotel manager boosted room prices and was sentence to five years in jail.[14]

CAREERS IN MARKETING

Pricing Analyst

A pricing analyst studies the market and analyzes data to determine the best pricing for products. This article from Zippia provides helpful information about (https://openstax.org/r/pricinganalystjobs) the job role, including qualifications, career paths, salary, education, resume templates, and online courses to improve skills. Indeed.com also provides a thorough job description (https://openstax.org/r/descriptionpricinganalyst) that outlines top duties and qualifications.

The best way to understand the core of any job is to learn from people who have done the job. Watch this video from a pricing analyst where he discusses his career.

Click to view content (https://openstax.org/books/principles-marketing/pages/12-1-pricing-and-its-role-in-the-marketing-mix)
Also check out this article on what makes a great pricing analyst (https://openstax.org/r/whatmakesagreat). Some people wonder how a pricing analyst and a data analyst differ. Learn the answer to that question in this article (https://openstax.org/r/interviewquery).

Once you've determined this may be the career for you, prepare for an interview by watching this video.

Click to view content (https://openstax.org/books/principles-marketing/pages/12-1-pricing-and-its-role-in-the-marketing-mix)

Knowledge Check

It's time to check your knowledge on the concepts presented in this section. Refer to the Answer Key at the end of the book for feedback.

1. You receive an email from your favorite clothing store. It is having a one-day sale where everything is 50 percent off. The retailer is using a form of psychology known as _______.
    a. artificial time constraint
    b. price appearance
    c. profit
    d. fixed costs

2. Which of the following best describes the profit equation?
    a. Profit = Fixed Costs – Variable Costs
    b. Profit = Total Costs – Total Revenue
    c. Profit = Total Revenue – Total Costs
    d. Profit = Fixed Costs + Variable Costs

3. Marquis has decided to purchase a new kitchen table. He looks at various brands online and decides to purchase one that is $500 more than the others because it is a brand his parents had when he was growing up and they offer free delivery. These factors indicate Marquis has perceived _______ in the higher-priced table.
    a. value
    b. artificial time constraints
    c. costs
    d. profit

4. Kilee sees an advertisement for a new computer. The advertisement portrays an initial price of $699 that has a large red "X" through it with a new price of $499. The advertisement is utilizing which pricing concept?
    a. Artificial time constraints
    b. Price appearance
    c. Price gouging
    d. Price anchoring

5. The perception of a buyer's value includes which of the following?
    a. Profit a company can expect from sales
    b. Perceived benefits less the perceived costs associated with a purchase
    c. Revenue expected from a sale
    d. Costs of manufacturing the product

12.2 | The Five Critical Cs of Pricing

Learning Outcomes

By the end of this section, you will be able to:
    LO 1 List the five critical Cs of pricing.
    LO 2 Characterize the five critical Cs of pricing.

Cost

What should you charge for a product or service? As you've probably discovered by now, pricing is not something that marketers approach without a lot of research. Using the five critical Cs of pricing can help to determine the *best* price—one that provides optimal value to the buyer and profit maximization for the company. Figure 12.3 illustrates the five critical Cs to consider when pricing: cost, customers, channels of distribution, competition, and compatibility.

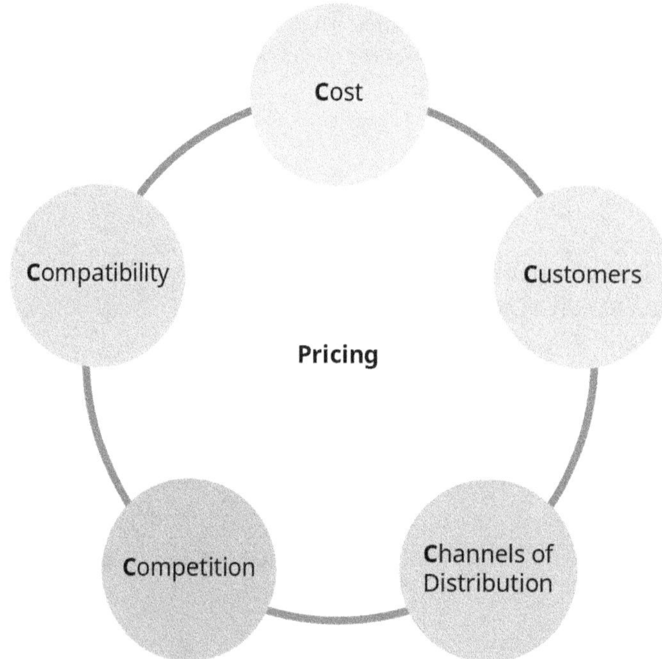

Figure 12.3 The Five Critical Cs of Pricing (attribution: Copyright Rice University, OpenStax, under CC BY 4.0 license)

Cost is the most obvious element of the pricing decisions. As we've already discussed, you must know the cost of doing business—both fixed and variable—before you can set an adequate price. However, cost alone cannot be the only basis on which a pricing decision made. After all, buyers never know (and don't care) how much it costs a business to produce its goods and services.

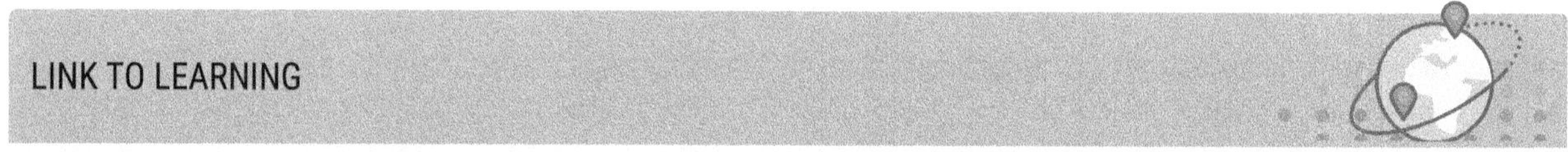

LINK TO LEARNING

The Five Critical Cs of Pricing

Scale Finance has provided an excellent article (https://openstax.org/r/the5criticalcs) that may help you get your mind around the five Cs of pricing.

Customers

Customers are another key element to pricing decisions, as you've learned already in this chapter. Marketers must determine not only what customers expect a product or service to be priced at but also what those customers are willing to pay. Toyota manufactures cars and markets them toward the middle class. Through research, it has determined what its target market is willing and able to pay for a particular vehicle. Alternatively, Lexus, which is marketed as more of a luxury car, has a higher price point and is marketed to a different market than that of Toyota.

Channels of Distribution

Many products are sold through channels of distribution—intermediaries who move products from manufacturer to end users. Intermediaries affect the prices of products because they also need to maximize their profits. Therefore, pricing decisions must consider profits, expenses, and the value they are adding to the product or service.

IKEA began as a mail-order catalog in 1953 in Älmhult, Sweden. Today, it is a global home furnishings brand that focuses on sustainability.[15] Its distribution channel consists of the manufacturer, dealer, wholesaler, and retailer. Each of these channel members are in business to make a profit. Therefore, the price strategy that

IKEA utilizes must help to ensure that each member is financially satisfied while making a profit itself and keeping the price that is of value to the end user. If any of the channel members (or the end user) does not find value in the price set by IKEA, the entire channel becomes weak and unsustainable.

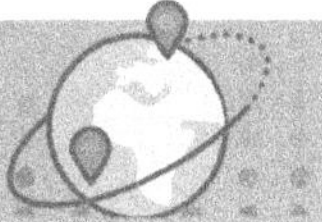

LINK TO LEARNING

IKEA

IKEA is a very interesting company to study when you are learning about marketing and business. As this blog examines (https://openstax.org/r/marketingstrategyin), it has 1,600 suppliers for manufacturing products that deliver to 186 global stores. That's a complex—and successful—system!

The MBA Skool website (https://openstax.org/r/marketingmixservices) provides an explanation of the IKEA marketing strategy and the four Ps, including IKEA's distribution model.

The Contact Pigeon blog outlines (https://openstax.org/r/contactpigeon) IKEA's strategy that made it the successful company it is today.

Competition

Every company and product faces competition. Even the most unique products are competing for buyer dollars. Buyers' perception of one product in comparison to that of alternatives has an important impact on pricing decisions. Gazelle Bikes is a top-tier manufacturer of bicycles. The bikes offered by Gazelle have a starting price point of $1,499.[16] One of Gazelle's competitors, Giant, has a starting price point of $1,720.[17] For bicycle enthusiasts, these price points are important when comparing one brand with another; an enthusiast who comes across a new brand of bicycles with a starting price of just $200 would not position it with Gazelle and Giant bicycles.

Compatibility

Panama City Beach has been one of the most popular spring break destinations of college students for decades. In fact, it is considered the "Spring Break Capital of the World."[18] It is well-known for its late-night parties, concerts, and celebrity sightings. Hotels and clubs along the beach of Panama City drive their marketing efforts toward this segment of the market: college-aged spring break–goers. The prices they set for the weeks of spring break are compatible with both this segment of the market's ability to pay and the businesses' profitability. Conversely, hotels in areas of Florida that are more family-friendly set prices that are considered a value for families and promote the hotels toward families rather than college-aged partygoers.

Pricing decisions are not made in a vacuum. When marketers set a price for a good or service, it must be consistent with the other marketing objectives. Imagine if McDonald's starting offering a $20.00 ribeye steak. This decision would be inconsistent with the marketing of the company's low-priced fast food, would be confusing to customers, and thus would not be successful.[19]

MARKETING IN PRACTICE

The Five Cs of Pricing

The five Cs of pricing has long been a standard for marketing practitioners. However, some practitioners also consider another area when determining price: context. Context refers to a more complex strategy of pricing where marketers set—and change—prices according to variables external to the company. For example, an ice cream truck in the US Midwest would arguably have more traffic during the peak summer hours and less during the colder winter months. The owner of the ice cream truck would change their prices to best fit the context (in this case, weather). The product (ice cream) remains the same regardless of the price, but the price is changed to fit the context of the situation. The appropriateness of using this strategy depends on several factors, including the product category, market size, and other nuances of the industry.

Knowledge Check

It's time to check your knowledge on the concepts presented in this section. Refer to the Answer Key at the end of the book for feedback.

1. Which of the critical Cs of pricing includes taking into the consideration the value of the product to retailers and suppliers?
   a. Cost
   b. Competition
   c. Channels of distribution
   d. Customers

2. Amir is the head of marketing and is explaining to colleagues that the company's new boutique bed and breakfast near the ocean should not be priced similarly to the local Super 8 motel. Amir explains that the new bed and breakfast is of the highest quality, has posh amenities, and is therefore being marketed to upper- and upper-middle-class couples. Amir is explaining which of the critical Cs of pricing?
   a. Cost
   b. Competition
   c. Customer
   d. Compatibility

3. Kevin is a marketing intern at a large corporation. They are tasked with presenting a price for a new service the company will be offering. Which of the following would you recommend Kevin do first?
   a. Analyze the critical Cs of pricing
   b. Choose a pricing strategy
   c. Create an advertisement
   d. Ask his friends what price they would be willing to pay

4. Which of the following statements is false with regard to pricing?
   a. Customers are interested in the price of the product, not the cost to a company.
   b. Cost only includes the materials needed to produce a product.
   c. If cost is not considered in pricing, the company will likely be unsuccessful.
   d. Costs include both variable and fixed costs.

5. Which of the following is not a critical C of pricing?
   a. Customers
   b. Cost
   c. Competition
   d. Commitment

12.3 | The Five-Step Procedure for Establishing Pricing Policy

Learning Outcomes

By the end of this section, you will be able to:
- **LO** 1 List the five-step procedure for establishing pricing policy.
- **LO** 2 Describe ways to determine the pricing objective.
- **LO** 3 Identify ways to estimate demand.
- **LO** 4 List ways to estimate costs.
- **LO** 5 Explain how to analyze the external environment.
- **LO** 6 Discuss selecting pricing strategies or tactics.

Determine Pricing Objectives

Whether a product is new to the market or established, marketers face the challenge of setting prices. Recall that the main objective for pricing is for the buyer to perceive value in the product while the company maximizes profits. Marketers often use a five-step approach for establishing pricing policies (see Figure 12.4).

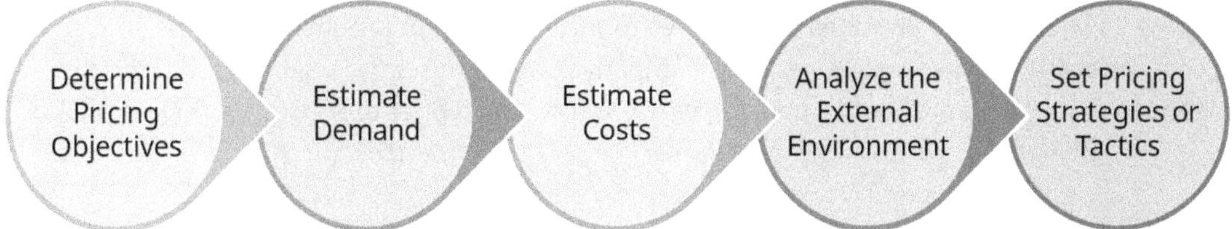

Figure 12.4 The Five-Step Process for Establishing Pricing Policies (attribution: Copyright Rice University, OpenStax, under CC BY 4.0 license)

During the first step in establishing pricing policies, the marketing team will set the pricing objectives (see Table 12.1). The most common pricing objectives are based on customer value, cost, sales orientation, market share, target return, competition, and being customer-driven. It is not uncommon for more than one objective to be set within the company. Let's take a look at each of the pricing objectives in more detail.

Objective	Description
Customer value	Based on a product's added value
Cost	Based on the cost to produce a product
Sales orientation	Developed to boost sales volume(s) of a product
Market share	Focused on increasing market share
Target return	Focused on a specific profit at a specific time
Competition	Developed based on competitors' prices
Customer driven	Focus on what the customer is willing to pay

Table 12.1 Pricing Objectives

Customer Value–Based Objective

As you've already learned, it's essential to have a deep understanding of the value a product will provide for customers. Before Jim Semick and his team launched GoToMeeting, a conferencing app, they developed the pricing of $49 "all you can meet flat-rate pricing." This pricing was unique to the industry, and Semick stated that they determined this pricing structure based on dozens of interviews with potential customers. From these interviews, the GoToMeeting team discovered key areas that would provide value to customers not only through the product itself, but also through the flat-rate price structure that was easy to understand.[20] Semick utilized the **customer value–based objective**, one in which the company has a good understanding of the value-added benefits of a product and sets its price accordingly.

Cost-Based Objective

A fairly simple way to price products and services is using the **cost-based objective**. This pricing objective sets prices based on the costs of doing business, which were explained earlier in the chapter. The biggest pitfall of utilizing this pricing objective is that it might not align well with the customer's value perception. Remember, customers don't know (or care) what the cost of doing business is, so long as they receive value in their purchase. Therefore, marketers run the risk of overpricing the product. Marketers using this objective also run the risk of pricing their products too low and failing to maximize profits.

Consider the manufacturing of a smartphone. Assume the total cost to the manufacturer to produce one smartphone is $3,000. This cost includes all expenses to the company for producing this one smartphone (product costs, variable and fixed expenses). The company chooses to set the selling price of this smartphone to include these costs plus a profit of 10 percent, which sets the final price at $3,300 $(3,000 + 10\% \times 3,000)$.[21]

Sales-Oriented Objective

A company may wish to seek a boost in sales volume of a product. In this case, marketers would choose the **sales-oriented objective**. The goal of a sales-oriented objective is to increase the volume, or units sold, of a product against the company's sales over a period of time. This objective is achieved by raising or lowering prices to increase sales. An increase in sales assumes a direct impact on profits, thus maximizing profits. Consider the smartphone manufacturer again. Executives have set a sales goal of 1,000 units within the first quarter. Marketers may choose to lower the price of the smartphone to meet the goal. So perhaps the company changes the price from $3,300 to $3,100 for a short period of time until the sales goal is reached. Note that it is still covering the cost to manufacture the product and still making some profit.

Market Share–Oriented Objective

A **market share–oriented objective** is one in which the company's pricing objective is to set prices based on those of the competition. This strategy involves comparing similar products being offered in the market and pricing at, below, or above those prices depending on the products offering. The cell phone market is one example of an industry that leans on market share orientation. The biggest suppliers of cell phones—Apple, Google, and Samsung —take their pricing cues from one another and are priced very similarly.[22]

Target Return Objective

A **target return objective** is one in which marketers calculate the price so that it returns a specific profit in a given period of time. Let's assume that a company has invested $1 million into a new product. Company executives wish to recuperate 10 percent of those costs in year one of sales. If it costs the company $2 to manufacture one unit of product and marketers estimate that it will sell 50,000 products in the first year, marketers know they will need to price the product high enough that it will yield the desired results. The obvious drawback to this objective is that much of the decision is based on estimations of units sold in a given time frame.

Competition Objective

A **competition-based objective**, as its name suggests, is when a company sets its prices according to the prices of its competitors. Amazon uses this pricing objective often with some of its most popular products.

Using data intelligence, the company gathers the prices of products of its competitors and sets its prices just below the price set by competitors.[23]

Customer-Driven Objective

Some companies choose to set prices based on **customer-driven objectives**—that is, what the customer is willing to pay for a product or service. Auctions, e-trades, and bids are common examples of customer-driven objectives. eBay, for example, allows a company (or individual) to place an item for sale on its website. Often, the interested buyer will bid on the item, thus stating what they are willing to pay. The highest bidder is then able to buy the product.

Estimate Demand

After setting the pricing objectives, marketers will estimate the product or services demand. **Demand** is an economic term that refers to the buyer's desire and willingness to purchase a product or service at various prices. All other factors being consistent, an increase in price will result in a decrease in demand. The demand curve is a visual representation to understand demand.

Understanding the Demand Curve

The **demand curve** is a graph that shows how the demand for a product or service varies with the change in price. As you can see from Figure 12.5, the price (p) is located on the vertical axis and the quantity (q) demanded is located on the horizontal axis. As the price of a product increases, the demand of the product decreases.

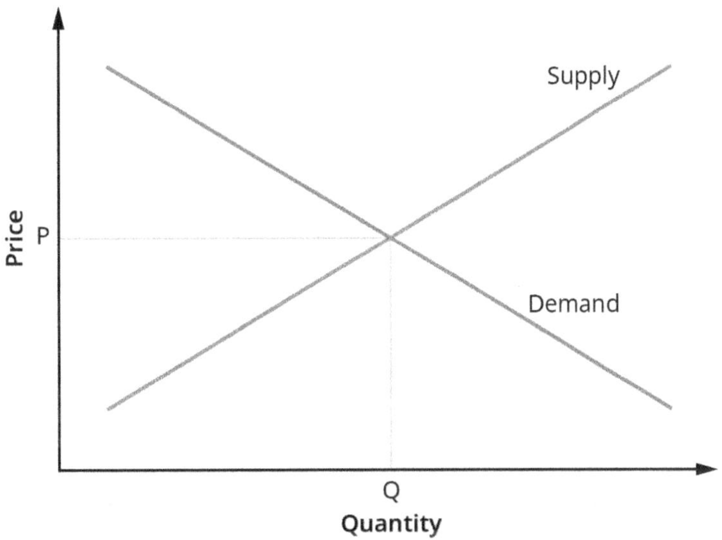

Figure 12.5 Demand Curve (attribution: Copyright Rice University, OpenStax, under CC BY 4.0 license)

The relationship between price and demand shown in the figure above is contingent on certain conditions remaining constant. Such conditions include substitute goods, personal income, and consumer tastes, which are discussed further below. Changes in these conditions can cause a change in demand that might not follow this basic concept of the demand curve.

The Demand Curve for Prestige Products

One pricing strategy that negates the demand curve is prestige pricing. **Prestige pricing** is a strategy that marketers use to set high prices knowing that demand will increase with higher prices because the higher price increases the perceived value of the product. Prestige pricing is closely tied to brand image and appeals to buyers who see value in elevated status. Consider these brands of shoes. The Adidas Yeezy Boost 750 costs around $76 to produce but sometimes sells for over $1,000, while the D Rose 5 Boost costs around $43 and sells for around $100. So why the large price difference? The Yeezy Boost 750 pricing strategy is that of prestige pricing. The allure and exclusivity of the Yeezy Boost 750 allowed the company to price the shoes at a much higher price.[24]

LINK TO LEARNING

Prestige Pricing

In this article, HubSpot explores (https://openstax.org/r/prestigepricing) the pros and cons to prestige pricing and things to consider when implementing this strategy. Included are several prestige pricing examples such as the Adidas Yeezy Boost and the D Rose 5 Boost, diamonds, cars, AirPods, and T-shirts.

Demand Elasticity

What will be the impact of demand for a product if the price is changed? If the product is discounted, will demand increase? If the price goes up, will demand decrease? The concept of demand elasticity helps marketers answer these questions. In short, **demand elasticity** is a measure of the change in the quantity demanded in relation to the change in its price. Mathematically, it is derived from the percent change in quantity demanded divided by the percent change in price. If you have been considering buying a new home, would the prices of homes sway your decision? Perhaps so. Home prices are considered elastic because the price has a huge impact on the demand for new homes. Additionally, there are many options for housing, including apartments, roommates, living with relatives, condos, etc.[25]

As a second example, consider gasoline. Since we need gasoline to get to work, school, the grocery store, and meetups with friends, it is considered relatively inelastic. There are very few substitutes for gasoline. Because gasoline has inelastic demand, the price may fluctuate considerably, but the demand for gasoline remains relatively the same. Consider the higher gas prices of 2022, averaging over $5.00/gallon across the United States and even higher globally. Even though the prices have risen, the demand for gasoline has not changed because people still must travel to work and other essential places.[26]

In summary, if a product is determined to be inelastic, the demanded quantity does not change with a change in price. Conversely, if the product is elastic, the demanded quantity will change with a change in price. You might be asking: What makes a product elastic or inelastic? There are several factors that will help determine how elastic a product or service will be.

Factors in Demand Elasticity

When determining the demand elasticity of products and services, there are several factors to keep in mind. These include substitutes, the effect of income, time, and cross-elasticity of demand (see Figure 12.6). Let's explore each of these in depth.

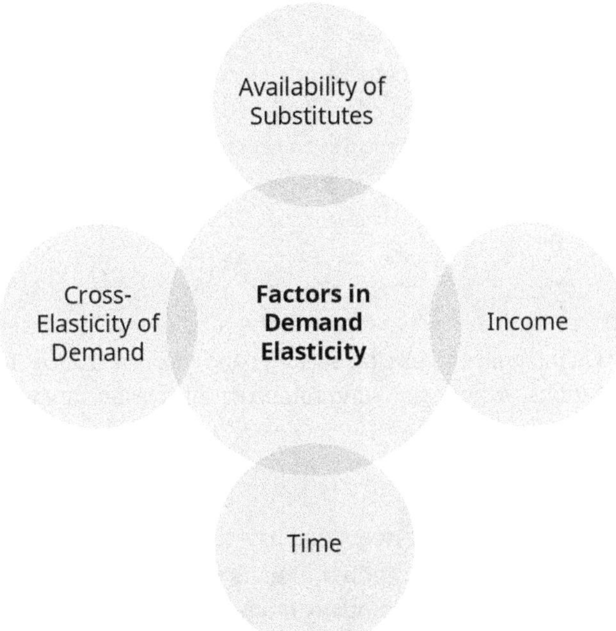

Figure 12.6 Factors in Demand Elasticity (attribution: Copyright Rice University, OpenStax, under CC BY 4.0 license)

Availability of Substitutes

Substitutes are products and services that are similar to the one being offered. If a buyer can easily choose a different product when the prices change, the demand will be more elastic. For example, if you are at the grocery store to buy English muffins but the store is out, you can easily choose to purchase bagels instead. Conversely, if there are relatively few or no alternatives, demand will be more inelastic. Consider the generic need for gasoline. It is fairly inelastic. The availability of substitutes for car travel is inconvenient. However, the demand for gasoline at specific gas stations is considered elastic because buyers can choose the gas station they prefer based on price. If two gas stations are located within a convenient geographic region to the buyer, they will choose the station that has lower prices.

Income

Buyers have limited money to spend on their needs and must make decisions on how the purchase of goods and services will impact their total income. The **income effect** is the way in which buyers see the change in price affecting their real income. Generally, an increase in price indicates that the buyer will have less money left over to spend; therefore, they will choose to buy less of a product, decreasing demand. The opposite is also true: the lower a price, the more money buyers have to buy more of the product, thus increasing demand. Consider the 8.6 percent inflation that the United States saw between May 2021 and May 2022. Because inflation is a general rise in prices, consumers noticed that their purchases of goods and services caused their real income to decline. In other words, consumers had less money to spend on products and ultimately chose to purchase less of those products.

Time

When the price of a good or service is changed, it takes time for buyers to adjust to the change in price. The time factor of price elasticity indicates that the product's elasticity of demand is dependent upon the time it takes buyers to adjust to the new prices. For example, if there is a sharp decrease in the price of automobiles, buyers would not immediately go out and buy a new vehicle. Rather, it would take some time to save money for a down payment, secure a loan, and generally go through the buying process. Therefore, the demand for automobiles would increase, but over time rather than immediately.

Cross-Elasticity of Demand

What happens when one of two similar products has a price increase or decrease? If the price of coffee increases, it would be expected that the demand of tea (a substitute product) would also increase. Buyers see the price increase and look for lower-priced substitutes to replace the higher-priced item. The **cross-elasticity of demand** measures the amount demanded of one good when the price for a similar good or service changes.[27]

Estimate Costs

The next step in determining a pricing policy is to estimate the total cost of producing a product or service. Recall that maximizing profits is the goal of a pricing strategy and marketers must factor the cost of doing business into pricing considerations. When estimating total costs, it is important to divide costs into fixed and variable costs.

Fixed and Variable Costs

As mentioned earlier in this chapter, costs are categorized as either fixed or variable. Fixed costs are those expenses that do not change regardless of the number of units sold. Consider the example used earlier in the chapter of manufacturing a smartphone. If the company manufacturers 1,000 or 100,000 smartphones, the company must pay the same amount for its lease on the property the plant is located on. The lease payment does not change based on the number of units produced. Alternatively, variable costs do change based on the number of units produced. In this same example, the amount manufacturing spends is dependent on the number of smartphones produced.

Analyze the External Environment

The fourth step in determining prices is to analyze the external environment. The external environment is comprised of factors outside of the organization that impact marketing decisions. While marketers cannot directly change these factors, they should be aware of how they might impact pricing decisions.

One way to remember the factors of the external environment is through the acronym PESTLE: political, economic, social, technological, legal, and environmental.[28] Questions to consider in a PESTLE analysis when analyzing the external environment as it relates to pricing are included in Table 12.2.

Factors	Question	Example
Political	What is the current political situation as it relates to the market?	A price cap on certain pharmaceuticals would limit the price a company could charge.
Economic	What is the current economic climate?	During inflation or deflation, prices may need to increase or decrease.
Social	How is culture changing or shaping the industry?	During the latter months of the year, the Indian market purchases more vehicles than at other times of the year.
Technological	What technologies are trending?	If technology for a product is becoming obsolete, a decrease in price may be necessary.

Table 12.2 PESTLE Factors

Factors	Question	Example
Legal	What current legislation is impacting the industry?	A new vehicle emission law may require new technology, thus increasing the price of vehicles.
Environmental	What are the environmental concerns of the product?	A highly toxic product or process may need to have a higher price to properly and safely dispose of byproducts.

Table 12.2 PESTLE Factors

LINK TO LEARNING

PESTLE Analysis

There are hundreds of online resources that discuss PESTLE. Here are a few to start with:

- The Corporate Finance Institute provides a PESTLE walk-through (https://openstax.org/r/corporatefinanceinstitute).
- The Oxford College of Marketing outlines the advantages and disadvantages of a PESTLE analysis (https://openstax.org/r/oxfordcollegeofmarketing).
- Business-to-you provides a video, sample analysis, and a full list of PESTLE factors (https://openstax.org/r/scanningtheenvironment).

Competitors' Costs, Prices, and Products

It probably seems obvious by now that analyzing the competition is key in setting prices. Marketers must constantly analyze both current and potential competition in the market to understand how their products will measure up to that of the competition. If a competitor is planning to introduce a nearly identical product to one that your organization already has on the market—but at a much lower price—you will need to consider how that will affect your sales as well as analyze how it is offering such a lower price. Should you lower your price? Consider changing suppliers for lowered costs? Take a cut in profits to stay competitive? All of these questions, and more, will help you as a marketer determine what pricing strategy should be used.

Stage in the Product Life Cycle

How long a product—and its substitutes—have been in the market will have an impact on the marketer's choice of pricing strategies. Recall that the product life cycle consists of four stages: introduction, growth, maturity, and decline. During the introduction stage, marketers must choose pricing strategies wisely to capture the intended market and begin recuperating research and development costs. As a product moves through the other stages of the life cycle, prices may need to be changed in order to stay relevant to consumers.

Status of the Economy

As you can imagine, the state of the economy at any given time will have an impact on the buyer's ability to purchase products as well as their willingness to spend. Economic factors that marketers should specifically be aware of when considering demand for products include employment, inflation, interest rates, and consumer confidence.[29]

One of the main factors that influences consumer demand is the employment rate. The **unemployment rate** is a measure of the number of people who are not employed but are actively seeking work in a given period—usually one month. When buyers are employed and receiving steady income, they are more likely to use discretionary income. **Discretionary income** is the money left over after all taxes and necessities—such as food and housing—are paid. When discretionary income decreases, demand for nonessential items also decreases.

Inflation is an economic measure of the rate of rising prices of goods and services in an economy. When inflation incurs, prices for most goods and services rise. Therefore, the amount of discretionary income a buyer has decreases, and demand for nonessential goods and services also decreases. Consider the high inflation in the United States economy from 2021 to 2022, which was 8.6 percent as of May 2022.[30] The rate of inflation is currently the highest that it has been since 1981. Because of the higher price of goods and services within the economy, consumers are spending more of their earned income on necessities such as food and shelter. This, in turn, causes them to purchase fewer nonessential items such as vacations, toys, and the like. Inflation also impacts pensions and other retirement accounts, so as inflation rises considerably, people are even less likely to spend their discretionary income and more likely to save anything left over after essentials for future use.[31]

Even consumers who do not have a deep understanding of the economy have some degree of optimism regarding the overall state of the economy. This is known as **consumer confidence**—it measures how optimistic consumers are about the economy and their own finances.[32] When consumers have little optimism in the economy, they are more likely to save their discretionary income rather than spend it.

The overall status of the economy—both current and future—is important for marketers to be aware of as it has a direct impact on the ability and willingness of buyers to spend money. Choosing pricing strategies that are aligned with the health of economy will have a greater chance of success.

Select Pricing Strategies or Tactics

After gathering all the data explained in previous steps, marketers are ready to set specific pricing strategies or tactics. The strategies and tactics chosen for a product or service should align with the other marketing mix elements, create value for the customer, and maximize profits for the company. In the next section, we will discuss specific strategies and tactics and how to optimize each.

Knowledge Check

It's time to check your knowledge on the concepts presented in this section. Refer to the Answer Key at the end of the book for feedback.

1. Sam is explaining to her friend Beth that prices for video conferencing software is increasing because more people are working from home. This relationship can be described by _______.
   a. prestige pricing
   b. customer-driven pricing
   c. the demand curve
   d. the income effect

2. Each month you pay your rent. It is $800 and does not change based on the number of hours you work. This is known as a _______.
   a. variable cost
   b. fixed cost
   c. changing cost
   d. profit

3. Decreases in prices are most often associated with which stage of the product life cycle?
   a. Introduction

  b. Growth
  c. Maturity
  d. Decline

4. Adding fixed costs to variable costs yields which of the following?
  a. Total costs
  b. Profit
  c. Value
  d. Inflation

5. When the price of a product increases and the demand for its substitute product increases, this is explained by ________.
  a. elasticity
  b. inelasticity
  c. a change in income
  d. cross-elasticity of demand

12.4 | Pricing Strategies for New Products

Learning Outcomes

By the end of this section, you will be able to:

LO 1 List the pricing strategies for new products.

LO 2 Explain each pricing strategy for new products.

Price Skimming

When a new product is introduced to the market, marketers often use one of three pricing strategies. Remember that when a company introduces a new product to the market, a good deal of financial resources have already been used even before the first unit is sold. Therefore, it is important for marketers to choose an appropriate price that both appeals to buyers and helps to recuperate the costs of research and development so that the company can begin to maximize profits more quickly.

Price skimming is a new-product strategy in which marketers choose to initially set a high price for a product or service and lower it over time. The goal of price skimming is to attract the segment of the market that is willing to pay the highest possible price for the product. Once achieved, the price is lowered to attract another segment of the market and so on. The term *skimming* comes from the skimming the cream, layer by layer, from raw milk—or in this case, each segment of customers.

Innovative technology often uses price skimming. For example, when Sony launched the PlayStation 3, it was set at a fairly high price of $599. With little competition and a well-established brand, it was successful. Each year thereafter, it lowered the price—and gained new customers—until it eventually reached a price of $299.[33]

Market Penetration Pricing

The opposite of price skimming is **penetration pricing**. The penetration pricing strategy is one in which the new product or service is set at the lowest price possible. This strategy's objective is to penetrate the market, or gain as many customers in all segments as possible from the beginning of the product life cycle.

In the late 1990s, Netflix introduced its movie rental service. For a monthly subscription fee, users could rent four movies at a time with no return date. The low initial price targeted the most segments of the market and allowed customers to try the new service with little effort or financial impact.

Break-Even Pricing

Break-even pricing is a pricing strategy in which marketers choose a price that will cover all of the costs of manufacturing. The break-even point is when the number of units produced equals the revenue for the product. The break-even point will produce zero profit but will cover all associated costs.

The break-even formula is calculated by dividing the total fixed costs by the production unit price minus variable unit costs. The break-even point in units will tell a marketer exactly how many units must be sold in order to start making a profit.

$$\text{Break Even} = \frac{\text{Fixed Costs}}{(\text{Unit Price} - \text{Variable Unit Costs})}$$

Let's look at an example. Assume you are opening a new gourmet cookie shop and you have estimated your projected costs. You'd like to know how many units you must sell in order to break even and then start making a profit. Let's assume your fixed costs are $20,000. This includes rent, deliveries, ingredients, and new signage. You have estimated your variable costs to be $1.50 per unit, or cookie. You plan to charge $2.00 per cookie. How many units must you sell to break even? Using the formula above, you find that you must sell 40,000 cookies in order to break even.

$$\text{Break Even} = \frac{\$20,000}{(\$2.00 - \$1.50)}$$

$$\text{Break Even} = \frac{\$20,000}{(\$0.50)}$$

$$= 40,000 \text{ Units}$$

Knowledge Check

It's time to check your knowledge on the concepts presented in this section. Refer to the Answer Key at the end of the book for feedback.

1. Luis is planning to introduce a new product to the market. Their aim is to gain as much of the market share as possible in the early introduction stage, so they are thinking of setting an initially low price. Which pricing strategy is Luis using?
   a. Break-even analysis
   b. Price skimming
   c. Penetration pricing
   d. Psychological pricing

2. Alexandra is working on the pricing strategy for her new food truck items. She is interested in knowing how many hamburgers she will need to sell in order to break even. Which formula should she use?
   a. Fixed Costs + Variable Costs
   b. Fixed Costs − Variable Costs
   c. Fixed Costs/(Unit Price + Variable Unit Cost)
   d. Fixed Costs/(Unit Price − Variable Unit Cost)

3. Tomas is selling his bottled sodas for $2.00 each at the vendor fair. His fixed costs are $100. He estimates that his variable costs are $0.25 per bottle. How many bottles of soda must Tomas sell to break even?
   a. 57
   b. 2
   c. Less than 1
   d. 25

4. Which of the following is true of price skimming?
   a. It captures the most market share in the introduction stage of a product.

    b. It is setting an initially high price of a product.

    c. It is setting an initially low price of a product.

    d. It determines break-even units.

5. David hopes to capture as much of the market as possible with the company's new product. Which pricing strategy should David use?

    a. Price skimming

    b. Cost-based pricing

    c. Psychological pricing

    d. Penetration pricing

12.5 | Pricing Strategies and Tactics for Existing Products

Learning Outcomes

By the end of this section, you will be able to:

LO 1 List the pricing strategies and tactics for existing products.

LO 2 Provide examples of each pricing strategy and tactic.

Product Line Pricing

More often than not, marketers must make pricing decisions on existing products rather than new products. As products go through the product life cycle, price changes will likely need to occur to maintain value for customers and continue to maximize profits. Some common strategies and tactics for existing products are discussed next.

Many large companies offer multiple products and product lines in their product mix. One strategy for pricing products is to price products in a product line the same or similar. For example, Unilever is the manufacturer of many brands that you've likely heard of: Dove, Axe, and Hellman's to name a few. Within its host of products, Unilever has divided its products into price categories; higher priced items have a higher perception of value and so on. (Recall that a product line is a group of related products differentiated by features and price.) Unilever sets a higher price for some of its product lines and lower price points for others in order to capture various target markets, known as **product line pricing** (see Figure 12.7).

Figure 12.7 Companies utilize pricing strategies like product line pricing to appeal to various target markets through multiple products. (credit: "d2590-1" by Stephen Ausmus/USDA/flickr, CC BY 2.0)

Captive Product Pricing

Assume you need to purchase a new printer for your home computer. Once you buy the printer, you're also going to need to purchase what? That's right, ink. Captive product pricing uses a strategy that requires both a core product and a captive product. In the above example, the core product is the printer and the captive product is the ink. When you are shopping for the printer, you are likely to take into consideration the price you will have to pay for ink as well. Marketers may price the printer at a very reasonable price, knowing it will catch your attention and thus make the price of the ink seem less expensive. Captive product pricing maximizes profits by intentionally pricing both the core and captive products at a level that will increase the perceived value to consumers.

Bundle Pricing

Bundle pricing is another popular pricing strategy that marketers use to promote purchasing multiple products at once. Consider when you go to the drive-through at your favorite fast-food establishment. Ever notice that it is cheaper or nearly so to purchase a "meal" than each item individually? Have you ever gone to the drive-through intending to get a cheeseburger but feel compelled to get the value meal instead because it only costs a little more? This strategy is used to prod customers to purchase (and spend) more than they may have otherwise.

Psychological Pricing (Odd/Even Pricing)

One popular form of psychological pricing is odd-even pricing. Similar to price appearance discussed earlier in this chapter, **odd-even pricing** banks on human motivation to lure in customers. The "odd" in this pricing tactic refers to the odd number at the end of a price, such as $19.95. Psychologically, the odd number in the price equates to value; the product is not $20.00, it is still in the "teens" at $19.95. Conversely, the "even" in the tactic utilizes even numbers at the end of the price, often zero, as in $50.00. This pricing tactic leads buyers to believe that the product is of higher quality because it is a nice, even number. Luxury items are often priced using the "even" side of odd-even pricing.

Ever wonder how odd-even pricing got its start? Decades ago, retailers began using this pricing strategy not to lure customers but rather to force cashiers to open their cash register drawers to make change—and thus record the sale. Over time, consumer psychologists studied the impact of odd-even pricing on consumption and found it to work!

Economy Pricing

When you are grocery shopping, are you surprised to see that name-brand products are priced much higher than store brands even though the product is essentially the same? Does the name brand really cost that much more to produce? Well, yes and no. Brand-name items spend considerably more on advertising than store brands. In order to recoup those costs (and based on the fact that name brands have a higher value perception to buyers), companies set prices higher for name brands. **Economy pricing**, on the other hand, is a tactic in which store brand prices are set much lower than their name-brand competitors. The focus on these products is selling in high volume by lowering prices and minimizing advertising costs.

Another example of economy pricing is used in the airline industry. Allegiant Air strives to offer no-frills air travel that is priced considerably lower than its competitors. But you have to get your seats fast at the lowest prices because the price increases as seats fill up. Oh, and if you want to travel with any luggage, you'll need to pay extra; Allegiant charges for any luggage other than one personal item.

Knowledge Check

It's time to check your knowledge on the concepts presented in this section. Refer to the Answer Key at the end of the book for feedback.

1. You are considering purchasing cable for your new apartment. You would really like to add HBO to your

cable plan, so you can watch some of the shows all of your friends are talking about. You can purchase basic cable for $49.99 per month and add HBO for an additional $12.99 month as a standalone addition. Alternatively, you can choose a package that includes HBO for $59.99. Obviously, you will choose the less expensive package. The cable company is using which of the following pricing tactics?

    a. Product line pricing

    b. Odd-even pricing

    c. Bundle pricing

    d. Economy pricing

2. Finley was tasked with setting the price of a new coffee maker that would utilize coffee pods instead of traditional coffee filters. Because customers would have to buy the pods in order to utilize the product, Finley should consider which pricing tactic?

    a. Captive pricing

    b. Odd-even pricing

    c. Bundle pricing

    d. Economy pricing

3. Thames is shopping for a new pair of jeans. He notices that one brand is priced at $49.99 and another is priced at $50.00. He immediately chooses the pair priced at $50.00 because he believes they are of better quality. Which pricing tactic was used to help Thames make his decision?

    a. Odd-even pricing

    b. Captive pricing

    c. Bundle pricing

    d. Economy pricing

4. Which of the following is NOT considered a pricing tactic for existing products?

    a. Odd-even pricing

    b. Price skimming

    c. Bundle pricing

    d. Captive pricing

5. Daphne often buys store or generic brand items at the grocery store because they are so much cheaper than name-brand items. Which pricing tactic is generally used for store or generic brands?

    a. Bundle pricing

    b. Cost-based pricing

    c. Psychological pricing

    d. Economy pricing

12.6 | Ethical Considerations in Pricing

Learning Outcomes

By the end of this section, you will be able to:

    LO 1 Identify ethical issues related to the pricing of products and services.

    LO 2 Describe the different types of unethical practices.

Price Fixing

Recall that *ethics* is defined as behaviors based on values and beliefs of right and wrong. In marketing, unethical behavior can have catastrophic consequences. If a customer's trust is broken with a product, their likelihood of continuing to do business with that company dramatically decreases. Companies practicing unethical behavior run the risk of not only losing customers and profits, but also facing legal consequences. Let's explore some unethical (illegal) practices as they relate to pricing.

Price fixing occurs when two or more competitors agree to set prices at a specific level. The practice of price fixing force customers to pay higher prices than normal with no substitute alternatives. Consumers who purchased or leased certain automobiles were part of a class-action lawsuit involving several automobile manufactures. The brands, including Audi, BMW, Buick, Chevrolet, and many others agreed to pay into the settlement after being accused of conspiring together to artificially inflate the prices of various auto parts.[34]

Deceptive/Illegal Price Advertising

Deceptive price advertising is an unethical pricing practice in which the advertised price of a product is misleading to consumers. For example, let's assume a company advertised a product with a "suggested retail price" of $9.99 but is offering the same product for the "low price of only $4.99." If the same product is actually priced in a market in the same country for $9.99, it is not considered deceptive. However, if the product is not priced at $9.99 in any other market, it is considered deceptive.

Say you sell hats for a price of $29.99, but sales are sluggish. You decided to offer your hats "buy one get one free," but just before the sale starts, you raise the price of one hat to $59.99. Is this deceptive price advertising? Yes. This is not a bargain for consumers and is considered deceptive according to the Federal Trade Commission (FTC).

Predatory Pricing

Another unethical (and usually illegal) pricing strategy is that of predatory pricing. **Predatory pricing** occurs when a company prices goods or services so low that other companies cannot compete. Predatory pricing often entails a company selling products below its cost with the intent of driving out competition and creating a monopoly situation. Once competition is eliminated, the company will often increase the prices exponentially—not only to recuperate losses from the lower prices, but also to make more profit. Under various antitrust laws, this practice is illegal when it seeks to drive out competition and makes a market susceptible to monopolies.[35] In 2000, Walmart was accused by the Wisconsin Department of Agriculture, Trade, and Consumer Protection of predatory pricing practices. The complaint stated that the company was selling staple goods such as butter and milk below cost with a goal to drive out competition and create a monopoly.[36] In short, predatory pricing undermines the free market where supply and demand sets prices.

Price Discrimination

Price discrimination is a pricing strategy that charges different prices to customers based on what the seller believes it can get the customer to agree to. This pricing strategy is not illegal so long as it does not cause specific economic harm. But marketers should be wary of using this price tactic, as it could lead to disloyal customers if they feel they are not getting the best price.

Monopoly Gouging

Monopoly gouging is when a seller increases the prices of goods and services that are not considered fair or competitive. If there are no or very few substitutes, a company may be enticed to force buyers to pay a much higher price, leaving them no options. When there are very few competitors in a market, such as utilities, the industry is highly regulated by the government. For example, your electric company cannot choose to randomly increase prices to increase profits; it must follow a regulated process when increasing prices.

During the winter of 2020–2021, Texas experienced much colder and snowier conditions than usual. Millions were left without power, and dozens lost their lives. As hotels began to fill up, prices skyrocketed. A Super 8 motel was shown on Hotels.com at nearly $400/night, exponentially higher than in ordinary times. Identifying price gouging is a bit more complicated than it seems. While basic economics would expect higher demand to equal higher prices, the practice of price gouging is not only unethical but also illegal in many states when a disaster is announced.[37]

COMPANIES WITH A CONSCIENCE

Warby Parker

Warby Parker sought to find a solution to the problem of expensive eyeglasses—a medical necessity for many people. The company stated that "the eyewear industry [was] dominated by a single company that has been able to keep prices artificially high while reaping huge profits from consumer who have no other options."[38] Warby Parker set out to change the way in which glasses were offered to consumers. The company's direct-to-consumer approach and a uniform pricing strategy have made waves in the eyewear industry.

All of Warby Parker's eyeglasses are not only priced lower than its competitors, but all of its eyeglasses are priced the same: $95. The average cost of eyewear was $263, making it difficult for some consumers to afford the needed glasses and making it difficult for people to distinguish the value between a $200 pair of glasses and a $400 pair of glasses.[39]

The company bypassed traditional supply chains and began making glasses in-house. It also talked directly to customers to understand the needs of the market and, in turn, is able to offer prescription eyeglasses at a fraction of the cost. In addition, it saw a global problem: too many people need glasses but cannot afford them. That's why the company donates one pair of glasses for every pair sold.

Chapter Summary

In this chapter, we explored the process of setting pricing for products and services and the importance of pricing to the profitability of a business. We defined fixed and variable costs and how they factor into the break-even equation in initial pricing decisions. Commonly used pricing objectives were defined as cost based, sales oriented, market share, and target return. These objectives are used to set a clear pricing strategy for both products and services.

The new-product pricing strategies of price skimming and penetration pricing were defined, explaining common practices used based on the product type and placement in the market. The psychology of pricing based on consumer buying habits was identified and defined. Techniques include odd-even pricing, prestige pricing, and artificial time constraints.

The final concept we covered was ethics in pricing and how the consumer can identify unethical and/or illegal pricing practices. Price fixing, deceptive/illegal pricing in advertising, price discrimination, and monopoly/price gouging were discussed as practices that are used in an effort to increase profits.

Key Terms

artificial time constraints   pricing strategy that creates a sense of urgency in buyers' minds

break-even pricing   pricing strategy in which marketers choose a price that will cover all the costs of manufacturing

bundle pricing   pricing strategy that promotes purchasing multiple items at once; used to prod customers to purchase (and spend) more than they may have otherwise

competition-based objective   product pricing based on the prices of a company's competitors

consumer confidence   an economic indicator that measures the degree of optimism that consumers have regarding the overall state of the country's economy and their own financial situations

cost-based objective   product pricing based on the costs of doing business

cross-elasticity of demand   the change in price of one good or service as a similar good or service's price changes

customer value–based objective   product pricing based on a company's understanding of the value-added benefits of a product

customer-driven objective   product pricing based on what a customer is willing to pay for a product or service

deceptive price advertising   an unethical pricing practice in which the advertised price of a product is misleading to consumers

demand   a buyer's ability and willingness to purchase a specific product or service

demand curve   a graph that illustrates the relationship between demand and price

demand elasticity   measure of the change in the quantity demanded in relation to the change in its price

discretionary income   a household's money that is left over after all taxes and necessities are paid

economy pricing   setting a price much lower than competitors to sell high volumes of a product

fixed costs   costs of doing business that do not change based on number of units produced

income effect   the perception buyers have of how price changes will affect their income

inflation   an economic measure of the rate of rising prices of goods and services in an economy

market share–oriented objective   setting prices at, below, or above competitors in an effort to increase market share

monopoly gouging   when a seller increases the prices of goods and services that are not considered fair or competitive

odd-even pricing   psychological pricing strategy that uses prices that end with odd or even numbers to attract customers

penetration pricing   new product or service strategy that sets the lowest price possible in order to reach the majority of the market in the introduction stage

predatory pricing   when a company prices goods or services so low that other companies cannot compete

prestige pricing   a strategy marketers use to set high prices knowing that demand will increase with higher prices because the higher price increases the perceived value of the product

price   the exchange of something of value between a buyer and seller

price anchoring   a frame of reference for a buyer to set an expectation of a price

price appearance   the way in which a customer perceives a price based on how it is visually represented

price discrimination   selling goods and services at different prices to different customers

price fixing   two or more companies agreeing to set certain prices in the market

price gouging   when companies take advantage of a situation, typically an emergency or natural disaster, and charge exceptionally high prices for products or services

price skimming   pricing strategy in which a company initially sets a high price for a product or service and lowers it over time as new segments of the market are reached

product line pricing   setting a higher price for some product lines and lower price points for others in order to capture various target markets

profit   the financial gain of a company

sales-oriented objective   setting prices based on the goal of increasing the volume of sales

substitutes   products and services that are similar to the one being offered

target return objective   setting prices so they return a specific profit during a given period of time

total costs   total expenses of doing business

total revenue   the money generated from normal business operations

unemployment rate   measure of the number of people not employed in an economy during a given period of time

variable costs   costs that vary based on the number of units produced

Applied Marketing Knowledge: Discussion Questions

1. Choose a mass retailer such as Walmart or Target and look at its weekly advertisement. You can do this online, in the store, or with a physical flyer. Identify and analyze the pricing strategies used. Apply what you have learned to how you personally respond to those strategies.

2. Consider what products the penetration-price strategy and the price-skimming strategy work for. What are the advantages and disadvantages of these strategies?

3. Analyze the role pricing plays in strategic marketing.

4. Discuss with your family and friends what you have learned about pricing. Ask them how they respond to odd-even pricing, prestige pricing, and artificial time constraints. Note generational differences and possibly how family traditions can skew the answers.

Critical Thinking Exercises

1. Compose a 150–200-word paragraph using all the following terms as they relate to pricing. The goal is to prove you understand the meaning of each term.

   Terms to include:

   - Unemployment
   - Inflation
   - Discretionary income
   - Consumer confidence

2. Describe a break-even point and provide a mathematical example.

3. Pick one product that you would find at a grocery store, a mass merchandiser, and a convenience store.

Now go to each of these stores and check the price of the product you selected. Note if the product is on sale or listed at its regular price.

Are the prices consistent? Is one store higher or lower across the board? What would compel a consumer to pay higher prices for products when they can purchase them at a lower price?

 Building Your Personal Brand

One of the most important tasks you have in establishing your personal brand is how you are going to communicate your skill level and experience to others. Let's start by developing a 30-second elevator pitch about yourself. An elevator pitch is what you would say about yourself if you were in an elevator with someone and only had the time between floors to share your message. What is the most important thing you would want to share about yourself and your personal brand if you were in an elevator with a hiring manager at company you want to work for? Things to consider covering include a quick introduction, your unique value or skill that would want to make them hire you, and something engaging about yourself to help them remember you.

 What Do Marketers Do?

Using LinkedIn, find a pricing analyst. Reach out to them, introduce yourself, and let them know that you're a student wanting to know more about their job role. Then schedule an interview. Questions you may want to ask include:

- What is your background and education, and what brought you to this job?
- What do you feel are the pros and cons of this job role?
- Share with me what a typical day, week, and year look like in this job role.
- How has COVID-19 impacted your work?
- What advice do you have for someone interested in pursuing this job?

 Marketing Plan Exercise

Complete the following information about the company and products/services you chose to focus on as you develop the marketing plan throughout the course. You may need to conduct research in order to obtain necessary information.

Instructions: Using the Marketing Plan Template file you created from the Marketing and Customer Value assignment and expanded upon in Strategic Planning in Marketing, Market Segmentation, Targeting, and Positioning, Marketing Research and Market Intelligence, and Products: Consumer Offerings, complete the following section of your marketing plan:

- Marketing Strategy: Pricing

Submit the marketing plan to your instructor for grading and feedback.

 Closing Company Case

Naked Wines

Buying a good bottle of wine can be hit or miss. A consumer can pay a lot and not enjoy the wine or pay a little and really love the wine. As with any product, there are fixed costs and variable costs included in the price of a bottle of wine. Some of those expenses include the costs of production, the raw materials including grapes, barrels, bottles, utilities, and labor. Other costs include administrative overhead, sales, and marketing costs.[40]

Of course, distribution must be factored into the price of a bottle of wine. With an indirect distribution channel, wine often passes from the winemaker to a distributor, a wholesaler, and then a retailer. Macroenvironmental factors such as nature can affect pricing by affecting the grape supply, which will also add to the overall cost.

In addition to the obvious cost factors, there are psychological factors such as branding, exclusivity, and rating points. Wine rating points are awarded to wines based on input from industry experts and wine critics. Bottles with higher ratings points can generally command a higher price. In addition, a bottle with greater notoriety and awards will also be able to sell for significantly more than more obscure wines or those just starting out.

Breaking into the wine-making business can be incredibly challenging. All business start-ups face steep hurdles in the beginning stages. Wine making may well have more sunk costs than a typical start-up. With grapes taking years to grow and reach their peak and the labor for harvesting, juicing, and fermenting, entering the wine-making business can quickly burn through start-up cash. [41]

Getting money from a bank to start a business means business plans, initial investment, proven experience, and endless paperwork that takes up valuable time that could be spent tending the grapes. And making a name for yourself in the wine industry can take years. How do you get consumers to choose and buy your wine from the thousands of labels available?

Enter Naked Wines (https://openstax.org/r/nakedwines). The company was founded as a way to help small, independent winemakers break into the wine business. Started in 2008, Naked Wines had a mission to give consumers great wines at significantly reduced prices and help winemakers get the funding needed to start their business. [42]

Naked Wines thought it could break into the wine business by allowing consumers to join as investors. When a customer buys from Naked Wines, they become an investor. Each month investors purchase wine at a reduced cost from Naked Wines, which in turn invests in the winemakers it represents.

While the pricing is an advantage, being invested in the winemakers is a bigger advantage. Each month, investors get to choose which wines are delivered to them. The wines are carefully curated based on their wine preference profile along with the ratings they provide to the winemakers on previous purchases.

The Naked Wines business model allows the winemakers to have access to funding and market research, while the investors have access to great wines. As Naked Wines continues to grow from an initial start in the United Kingdom to operations in the United States, it continues to add winemakers and investors. Small winemakers who would otherwise not have had an opportunity to grow their business have found success and community through Naked Wines.

Case Questions

1. What are the psychological factors that affect the pricing of wine?

2. Name the five critical Cs of pricing evident in the Naked Wines pricing model.

3. What elements of the external environment are most evident in the pricing of a bottle of wine?

4. How might you best define the pricing strategy for Naked Wines?

References

1. George Hatch, "What You Need to Know about Amazon Prime: 2005–Today," *Pattern Blog*, Pattern, August 20, 2020, https://pattern.com/blog/amazon-prime-a-timeline-from-2005-to-2020/.

2. Parkev Tatevosian, "Amazon Reaches 200 Million Prime Members: Here's Why That's a Big Deal," The Motley Fool, April 27, 2021, https://www.fool.com/investing/2021/04/27/amazon-reaches-200-million-prime-member-milestone/.

3. Hatch, "What You Need."

4. Anisha Sekar and Tommy Tindall, "What Is Amazon Prime? The Benefits, the Cost and Whether It's Worth It," NerdWallet, June 28, 2022, https://www.nerdwallet.com/article/finance/amazon-prime-benefits-cost-worth.

5. Charles Fishman, "Which Price Is Right?," *Fast Company*, February 28, 2003, https://www.fastcompany.com/46061/which-price-right.

6. Steve Jobs, "2010 Apple iPad Keynote," Apple Soldier, January 28, 2010, YouTube video, 1:32:35, https://www.youtube.com/

watch?v=lTNbKCAFHJo&t=4453s.

7. Keith S. Coulter, Pilsik Choi, and Kent B. Monroe, "Comma n' Cents in Pricing: The Effects of Auditory Representation Encoding on Price Magnitude Perceptions," *Journal of Consumer Psychology* 22, no. 3 (July 2012): 395–407, https://doi.org/10.1016/j.jcps.2011.11.005.

8. Eric Yu, "What Is Psychological Pricing? 4 Strategies, Examples, and Tactics," Price Intelligently, ProfitWell, updated June 28, 2021, https://www.priceintelligently.com/blog/bid/181764/psychological-pricing-strategy-where-s-your-head-at.

9. Yu, "What Is Psychological Pricing?"

10. "Price Gouging Is Illegal," NYC Department of Consumer and Worker Protection, City of New York, accessed May 31, 2022, https://www1.nyc.gov/site/dca/media/Face-Masks-in-Short-Supply-Due-to-COVID-19.page.

11. Christopher E. Ondeck et al., "State Price Gouging Laws and Price Controls: A Historical View on a Questionable Objective," *The National Law Review*, September 18, 2020, https://www.natlawreview.com/article/state-price-gouging-laws-and-price-controls-historical-view-questionable-objective.

12. "Combating Price Gouging & Hoarding," Coronavirus Response, United States Department of Justice, updated March 23, 2022, https://www.justice.gov/coronavirus/combatingpricegouginghoarding.

13. Mark Puleo, "The History of Price Gouging amid US Disasters and How Different States Fight against It," AccuWeather, last modified July 1, 2019, https://www.accuweather.com/en/weather-news/the-history-of-price-gouging-amid-us-disasters-and-how-different-states-fight-against-it/344793.

14. Puleo, "History of Price Gouging."

15. "This Is IKEA," IKEA, accessed June 1, 2022, https://www.ikea.com/us/en/this-is-ikea/.

16. "eBikes," Gazelle Bikes, Royal Dutch Gazelle, accessed June 11, 2022, https://www.gazellebikes.com/en-us/ebikes.

17. "Full Suspension Mountain Bikes," Liv Cycling, accessed June 11, 2022, https://www.liv-cycling.com/us/bikes/mountain-bikes/full-suspension.

18. Panama City Beach Spring Break (website), CMG, accessed June 11, 2022, https://www.pcbeachspringbreak.com.

19. "The 5 Critical Cs of Pricing," Scale Finance, accessed May 30, 2022, https://scalefinance.com/the-5-critical-cs-of-pricing/.

20. Jim Semick, "SaaS Pricing: How to Price Software Products," Pragmatic Institute, May 20, 2015, https://www.pragmaticinstitute.com/resources/articles/product/how-to-price-saas-products/.

21. Hitesh Bhasin, "Cost-Based Pricing: Definition, Types, Examples, Advantages and Disadvantages," Marketing91, August 30, 2021, https://www.marketing91.com/cost-based-pricing/.

22. Patrick Campbell, "What Is Market-Based Pricing: Advantages & Disadvantage (+Examples)," Recur, ProfitWell, February 19, 2020, https://www.profitwell.com/recur/all/market-based-pricing.

23. "Competitive Pricing: Definition, Advantages & Disadvantages," *Prisync Blog*, Prisync, October 18, 2018, https://prisync.com/blog/competitive-pricing-advantages-vs-disadvantages/.

24. Jay Fuchs, "A Crash Course on Prestige Pricing (with Real-Life Examples)," *The HubSpot Sales Blog*, HubSpot, last modified October 15, 2021, https://blog.hubspot.com/sales/prestige-pricing.

25. Mary Hall, "Elasticity vs. Inelasticity of Demand: What's the Difference?," Investopedia, Dotdash Meredith, updated June 30, 2022, https://www.investopedia.com/ask/answers/012915/what-difference-between-inelasticity-and-elasticity-demand.asp.

26. Eliana Eitches and Vera Crain, "Using Gasoline Data to Explain Inelasticity," *Beyond the Numbers* 5, no. 5 (March 2016), https://www.bls.gov/opub/btn/volume-5/using-gasoline-data-to-explain-inelasticity.htm.

27. Adam Hayes, "Cross Price Elasticity: Definition, Formula for Calculation, and Example," Investopedia, Dotdash Meredith, updated July 31, 2022, https://www.investopedia.com/terms/c/cross-elasticity-demand.asp.

28. Francis Joseph Aguilar, *Scanning the Business Environment* (New York: Macmillan, 1967).

29. J. B. Maverick, "Which Economic Factors Most Affect the Demand for Consumer Goods?," Investopedia, Dotdash Meredith, updated March 17, 2022, https://www.investopedia.com/ask/answers/042815/which-economic-factors-most-affect-demand-consumer-goods.asp.

30. "Historical Inflation Rates: 1914–2022," US Inflation Calculator, CoinNews Media Group, last modified May 11, 2022, https://www.usinflationcalculator.com/inflation/historical-inflation-rates/.

31. Kimberly Amadeo, "How Inflation Impacts Your Life," The Balance, Dotdash Meredith, updated December 31, 2021, https://www.thebalance.com/inflation-impact-on-economy-3306102.

32. "US Consumer Confidence," The Conference Board, updated August 30, 2022, https://www.conference-board.org/data/consumerconfidence.cfm.

33. Bharath Sivakumar, "Price Skimming: Definition, Strategy, & Examples," Feedough, July 17, 2021, https://www.feedough.com/price-skimming-definition-examples/.

34. "Auto Parts Price-Fixing 4th Round Class Action Settlement," Top Class Actions, October 16, 2019, https://topclassactions.com/lawsuit-settlements/closed-settlements/926433-auto-parts-price-fixing-4th-round-class-action-settlement/.

35. Will Kenton, "Predatory Pricing," Investopedia, Dotdash Meredith, updated January 30, 2022, https://www.investopedia.com/terms/p/predatory-pricing.asp.

36. Stacy Mitchell, "Wal-Mart Charged with Predatory Pricing," Institute for Local Self-Reliance, November 1, 2000, https://ilsr.org/walmart-charged-predatory-pricing/.

37. Natalie B. Compton, "Texas Hotel Prices Skyrocketed after Power Outages. Here's What to Know about Price Gouging," *Washington Post*, February 17, 2021, https://www.washingtonpost.com/travel/tips/texas-hotel-storm-price-gouging/.

38. "History," Warby Parker, accessed May 30, 2022, https://www.warbyparker.com/history.

39. Knowledge@Wharton, "The Consumer Psychology behind Warby Parker's $95 Pricing for Eyeglasses," *Time*, May 23, 2013, https://business.time.com/2013/05/23/the-consumer-psychology-behind-warby-parkers-95-pricing-for-eyeglasses/.

40. "10 Tips for Getting into the Wine Business," Napa Valley Wine Academy, https://napavalleywineacademy.com/10-tips-for-getting-into-the-wine-business/

41. Kerana Todorov, "Farming for Labor Day: Winemakers Discuss the Challenging 2022 Harvest," Wine Business, September 23, 2022, https://www.winebusiness.com/news/article/262997

42. https://us.nakedwines.com/content/about/about-us

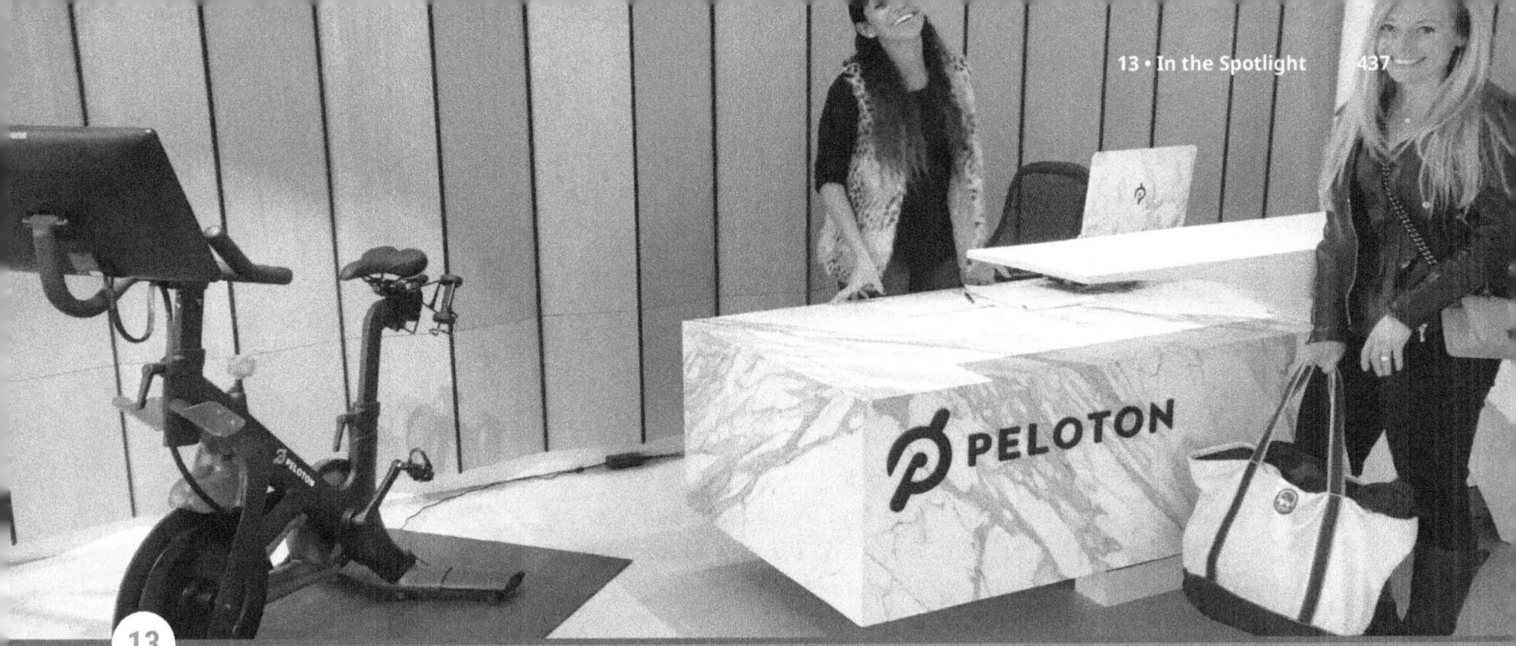

13 Integrated Marketing Communications

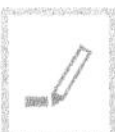

Figure 13.1 Peloton uses an integrated marketing strategy to reach consumers through multiple channels. (credit: modification of work "Going Backstage at Peloton HQ" by Jurvetson/flickr, CC BY 2.0)

Chapter Outline

In the Spotlight

Peloton started in 2012 with a group of ambitious people and the mission to "use technology and design to connect the world through fitness, empowering people to be the best version of themselves anywhere, anytime."[1] In 2019, Peloton, still a relatively new company, released a holiday television ad that put it front and center in a very controversial spot. The ad opens with a mother and daughter walking down a set of stairs to open Christmas presents. You can see the snow outside through the windows of the house. At the bottom of the stairs is her husband waiting with a Christmas gift.

"A PELOTON?!?" she shrieks—but it isn't immediately clear if she is happy with the gift. The commercial progresses with the mother documenting her fitness journey. She rides after work. She rides early in the morning. She rides through the seasons as you watch them change through the windows of the house.

The audience watches as she records her fitness journey on her Peloton. Toward the end of the ad, a Peloton instructor gives the young mother a name in a workout class by saying "Let's go, Grace from Boston!" As the commercial comes to an end, Grace shares her journey with her husband. It turns out she was talking to him the whole time.

"A year ago, I didn't realize how much this would change me," she says, now a true believer. After her year-long journey and her new "fit" state, Grace thanks her husband for the gift and how it transformed her.

Consumers immediately took to social media to accuse Peloton of promoting a negative body image, economic privilege, and archaic marital relationships. The controversial ad sparked a significant spike in social media engagement. The brand and the ad were widely publicized in the media. The ad and the controversy definitely produced significant brand awareness and an intense interest in the benefits of using a Peloton.

Once the controversy died down, Peloton was a well-known brand name. And with the lockdowns that came with the COVID-19 pandemic, consumers around the world were seeking options for in-home exercise. Peloton was poised to become the market leader with a reputation as a premier means of in-home workouts.

Much of Peloton's success is a result of its robust integrated marketing strategy. Consumers learn about Peloton through a variety of methods: YouTube ads, television commercials, mall kiosks, social media posts, and web content. Though the organization does its best to develop its promotional messages, its best marketing strategy is the excellent word of mouth and rave reviews from all its loyal and satisfied customers. Using multiple avenues for reaching customers is known as an integrated marketing communication strategy, the core concept that you'll learn more about in this chapter.

Throughout 2020 and into 2021, during the height of the pandemic, Peloton experienced a 172 percent increase in sales.[2] But quick growth can create other problems. As Peloton's popularity exploded during the COVID-19 pandemic, management issues began to surface. In February of 2022, Peloton saw a 73 percent drop in its stock price, which led to the ousting of founding partner and CEO John Foley. Marketing communications can bring much-needed brand awareness, but it's been said that great marketing can quickly kill a bad company. What is next for the twice-named "CNBC Disrupter 50 Company"?[3]

13.1   The Promotion Mix and Its Elements

Learning Outcomes

By the end of this section, you will be able to:

- LO 1 Define the promotion mix and explain its importance.
- LO 2 List and describe the elements of the promotion mix.

What Is the Promotion Mix?

We are all consumers, and we have all been the target of promotional campaigns. To connect with consumers of a target market, companies conduct extensive market research so that they may better understand the consumer. When companies understand the consumer, they can better structure a message to appeal to the consumer and also find the best channels for reaching the customer.

The created messages aim to get consumers' attention. Sometimes they create awareness of a new event, a new product, a new idea, or a place to visit. Sometimes they are asking consumers to make a purchase. Marketing promotion is all around us.

According to the marketing firm Yankelovich Inc., the average digitally connected person is exposed to around 5,000 ads per day.[4] Among the biggest promotional spenders in the United States is Disney.[5] Disney produces ads for everything from its movies and toys to its vacation clubs and theme parks. While we should be flattered that these companies are thinking of us and trying to figure out how to reach us and what messages they should send, many consumers are busy trying to figure out how to shut out the messages.

When you sit down to watch television, you are typically exposed to ads that a company believes that you will respond to based on the research it has done about the audience watching the show you tuned in to watch. During your time scrolling through your news feed on Facebook, you are being served ads that correspond to your Internet search history and even products you may have mentioned while your phone was on and your news feed open. Digital advertising relies heavily on algorithms of your search history and site visits.

As recipients of these marketing messages, many consumers believe that marketing is only advertising or sales. However, advertising and sales are simply two options in a marketer's arsenal of communication tools used to connect with the target market. Developing a marketing communications strategy is something marketers should only do after they have developed the rest of the marketing mix.

In fact, marketers have a wide variety of strategies to use from the overall promotional mix (see Figure 13.2). Most companies choose to use a combination of the promotional mix methods to create an integrated marketing communication message that reaches the customer in many different ways. When the messaging is integrated, the consumer receives the same message no matter which method of promotion is chosen. If the consumer is watching the news and hears a story about the company or product, public relations has impacted them. If they then scroll through their social media accounts at the end of the day and they see an ad for the same product, advertising has impacted them. When they sort through their email and have a message from the company, they have received a direct marketing communication.

No longer does promotion need to rely heavily on just one method of marketing communication. Marketers can be much more targeted and more cost-effective in the promotional methods they choose. Using a combination of methods to send the same message allows the marketer to be more strategic in their messaging and in their budgeting.

The best products are nothing until the consumer knows about them. Without good promotion, the best products are just secrets. We all have things we want to say, and on any given day we make phone calls, create Instagram posts, upload TikTok videos, send emails, shoot off text messages, and talk face-to-face with people. And just like us, marketers also have things to say. Usually, they want to tell consumers about their new brand extension of Reese's, a trade-in allowance for a new Toyota Camry that just hit the car lot, or even a buy-one-get-one-free promotion for your Starbucks latte. How marketers decide to say and send the message is the promotion mix.

The **promotion mix** is the set of strategies marketers use to communicate with their customers. With combined strategies, the promotion mix creates a powerful method of connecting with the customer and conveying all the other marketing mix elements for a holistic marketing approach. The promotion mix allows marketers to reach customers in many different ways, ensuring that the message is seen, heard, and understood. After determining and defining the target market, creating a good product, selecting a pricing strategy and optimal price, and deciding on the distribution method, the marketer is ready to communicate with the customer.

Messages sent by multiple methods provide a better opportunity for consumers to see and hear the message and make the connection back to the company. When a message is only sent by one method, the potential for interference, noise, and avoidance is more likely to occur. Marketers use a multichannel approach to send an integrated message.

Figure 13.2 The Promotional Mix (attribution: Copyright Rice University, OpenStax, under CC BY 4.0 license)

Promotion Mix Defined

The full set of strategies that combine to make up the promotion mix include advertising, sales promotion, personal selling, public relations, direct marketing, and Internet/digital marketing. Each of these methods is intended to produce different results when used. Combining the elements creates an overall integrated message designed to reach consumers at various points in their path to purchase. Marketers call this integrated messaging integrated marketing communications.

The Importance of the Promotion Mix

Of all the marketing mix variables, the promotion mix can be further divided into different message channels that allow for connection and communication with the customer. When the promotion connects with the customer, it is the moment when all the marketing activities come together. When the messaging and method of delivery reach the customer and create the desired result, the marketing has achieved its purpose.

The strategies in the promotion mix provide the marketer with an arsenal of methods to achieve their marketing objectives, such as increasing sales or introducing a new product. However, consumers are bombarded with marketing messages throughout the day, and these are combined with the business of everyday life events like news, music, work, chores, family, and friends. With this busy pace and activity, the consumer is very difficult to reach. For the busy consumer, one communication method alone is not likely to cut through the clutter and noise to reach them and make an impact. Marketers must combine the various communication elements to connect with the customer and meet the communication objective.

Elements of the Promotion Mix

When analyzed individually, each of the **promotional mix elements** is powerful. They each have a part to play in the overall success of a company. When combined and carefully executed, they create powerful brands with legions of loyal fans and followers—the consumers. What do each of these promotional mix elements do, and how do they contribute to the whole process of connecting with the consumer?

Advertising

Advertising is a multibillion-dollar industry. According to Statista, in 2020 alone, worldwide advertising spending reached \$586 billion.[6] **Advertising** is paid, nonpersonal communication from an identified source that allows for creative messaging about all aspects of a product, service, idea, person, or place. Consumers are able to quickly point to advertising as a form of promotion. It is perhaps the element of the promotional mix that we are most familiar with and the one we have been most exposed to throughout every phase of our lives.

From our very first commercial showing how much fun it is to build with LEGO to imagery of a toddler walking the Disney streets with a costumed princess and Cinderella's castle in the foreground, we know what advertising looks like. And while advertising can take many forms, it is important to note that advertising consists of carefully designed messaging from the company to the consumer. Advertising is meant to produce a response in the viewer. And advertising is all about what the company wants to tell us.

Advertising can be the pop-up window while we are doing a Google search. It can be the Chick-fil-A billboard we pass every day on our way to work. Advertising can be the trailer we watch before our movie starts. And advertising can be the fun Doritos spots we look forward to during the annual Super Bowl.

While advertising can be a costly means of communication with the customer, it is relatively inexpensive based on the number of people reached. When NBC priced the 2021 Super Bowl at $6 million for a 30-second spot, with a record 96 million viewers, the price averaged out to around $0.06 per person reached.[7]

Advertising is effective based on the **frequency** with which it is usually viewed. And because of the media, the advertising message can usually be repeated many times, depending on the budget. Due to its repeatability, production costs have a better return on investment (ROI) the more an ad is used, and the recall of the ad increases significantly.

Sales Promotion

Most consumers love a **sales promotion**. It creates a feeling of excitement and often includes a bit of a gaming experience into the purchase decision. Marketers value the benefits of sales promotions because the results are immediate and they have a wide variety of options when using this promotional mix element. A sales promotion is a method for a marketer to induce sales in the short term. Sales promotion is not a long-term strategy but is geared toward specific calls to action, typically aimed at getting the consumer to buy something immediately or enter a sweepstakes or contest (see Figure 13.3).

Figure 13.3 Sales discounts are a promotional mix element that marketers use to appeal to customers and to deliver short-term sales for the company. (credit: "Sales Promotion at a Shop Window in Munich" by Henning Schlottmann/Wikimedia Commons, CC BY 4.0)

Using sales promotions can be an effective method of getting the consumer to try a product or buy more of a product, or it can be a way to quickly deplete an inventory to make way for new products.

While sales promotions have many tactics that the marketer can employ, several commonly used examples of sales promotion include the following:

- **Buy One Get One (BOGO).** When Domino's Pizza offers the customer a free pizza when they buy a medium one-topping pizza, this BOGO deal is used to get an immediate increase in sales for Domino's pizza. Consumers may buy Domino's over other pizza brands because they can get more pizza for their money.

- **Enter to Win**. PepsiCo needed to gain traction with the millennial audience. It needed to boost the Lay's brand of potato chips and compete with new flavorful organic chips that were getting market share in the category once dominated by Lay's. To generate new interest in its brand, Lay's launched a campaign for consumers to create a new flavor. New flavors could be entered, Lay's would create samples, and the winner of the new chip flavor would win $1 million.
- **Coupons**. This method of promotion has come a long way with the use of technology. While consumers are still able to "clip" coupons and redeem them at the point of sale to receive savings on the products they are buying, many companies are making coupons available through mobile apps and discount codes to apply at the point of sale through an e-commerce store. Using coupons is a great method of inducing trial of a new product and increasing market share.

For National Ice Cream Day (see Figure 13.4), Cumberland Farms wanted to increase the sales of its house brand of ice cream, Ultimate Scoop.[8] It offered consumers a digital coupon for $1 off a pint of the ice cream. Cumberland Farms' existing customers received their coupon via text message, and new customers could text in to get the coupon.

Figure 13.4 Cumberland Farms used a coupon promotional strategy as a way to increase the price of its ice cream. (credit: "Ice Cream Cone" by Sean MacEntee/flickr, CC BY 2.0)

- **Rebates**. Companies offer rebates to induce purchase and generally to receive something in return besides the sale. When a rebate is offered for the purchase of an Energy Star–certified product, the consumer gets a designated dollar amount off the price of the product, and in turn they must submit the proof of purchase along with identifying information about themselves.

Personal Selling

Personal selling is one of the most expensive forms of promotion because it is a one-on-one, person-to-person form of communicating with the customer. The role of the salesperson is to inform and persuade the customer. This is usually done in what is termed an exchange situation. The salesperson is exchanging knowledge and something of value, while the customer is exchanging money for the item of value. Personal selling is ideal for products that can be customized, are complex, and have a relatively high price point.

Typically, personal selling is most often used in business-to-business (B2B) markets. Business buyers have longer buying cycles, more complex buying situations, and larger budgets. The pharmaceutical industry is well-known for using personal selling. Company representatives must have a high degree of training and knowledge about the products they are selling to physicians and hospitals. It is also very common to have a sales force to sell equipment and machinery to manufacturing plants. Businesses rely on the knowledge and service of the sales force selling them products.

In the business-to-consumer (B2C) market, personal selling is used for items that cost more or items that have a high degree of variation. We find sales representatives when we buy automobiles, home improvement products, and insurance. The job of the sales representative is to determine our needs and provide solutions that fill those needs.

When compared to advertising, which has a very general message directed to a very large audience, personal selling is an individualized message for one or several people within the buying group. When evaluating the costs of personal selling, it is typically hundreds to thousands of dollars per person reached.

The process of personal selling can be time-consuming. The process of selling and the tasks of the sales force can be complex. The sales professional is tasked with prospecting to identify the right customers and then qualifying them to make certain they are a good fit for the product.

It is not uncommon to hear people say, "You talk a good game. You could sell to anyone." In reality, salespeople do not want to talk people into a product. A good sales force only wants to sell to customers who want and need the product. The best sales force knows that when the customer is a good fit, they will bring repeat business and good word of mouth.

While some salespeople have a natural inclination for selling, others are highly skilled with the technical knowledge of the products they are selling. Understanding customers, the buying situation, and the product being sold are a few of the skills needed to master the art of selling. Good sales professionals know that the real work of the sale is to service the needs of the client long after the sale has been made.

Public Relations

Public relations is a nonpaid, nonpersonal form of promotion. Because it is nonpaid, it has a high degree of credibility and is beneficial because a typically credible, non-biased third party is the messenger. While there are many tactics that marketers might use for public relations, some of the most commonly used include press releases, press conferences, events, and annual reports.

Many of the other promotional tools focus specifically on communication with the customer. By contrast, public relations includes efforts to work with the community where it operates, media, government officials, educators, and potential investors.

When Nordstrom opened its flagship store in Manhattan, it unlocked the doors a few days early for a VIP celebration that included Vogue's editor, Anna Wintour, along with actresses, models, and designers. Some of the noted attendees included Zoe Saldana, Katie Holmes, Olivia Wilde, Karlie Kloss, Joan Smalls, Winnie Harlow, Tory Burch, Tommy Hilfiger, and Stacey Bendet of Alice + Olivia. Guests formed long lines around the store in an attempt to access the party.[9]

TOMS shoes has long been a leader in cause marketing (see Figure 13.5). When you buy from TOMS, one-third of the profits go to Grassroot Good.[10] TOMS' annual report highlights the people the company helps and how it helps them. Investors and any interested parties receive the annual report that details the work TOMS does right along with the profits it is making.

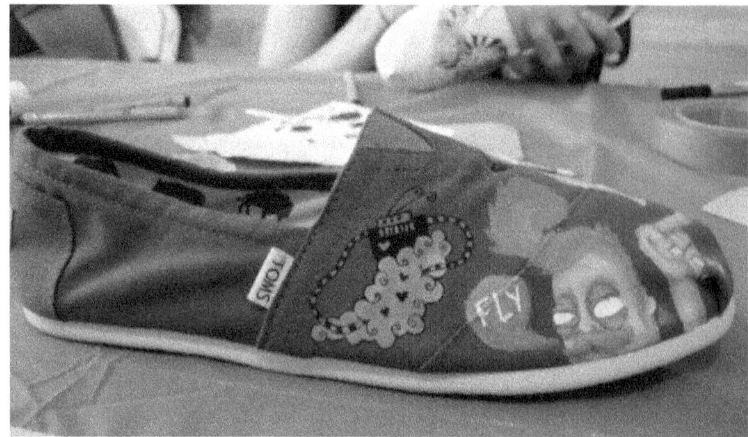

Figure 13.5 TOMS Shoes has effectively utilized a cause strategy, which has led to positive public relations with customers. (credit: "Toms Shoes at OhNo!Doom" by OhNo!Doom Collective/flickr, CC BY 2.0)

When celebrities wind up in the news, it is public relations, and it works to keep their name before the public and their fans. So the headline that hits the front page of the *New York Times* or is a leading story on the NBC nightly news both create publicity for the celebrity. Businesses also use publicity. A business might have a product as part of a movie, such as BMW vehicles showing up in 37 of the highest-grossing movies of 2018.[11]

Public relations can also include crisis communication when negative issues occur. One of the biggest public relations issues happened in 1982 to Tylenol. A malicious person or persons in the Chicago area tampered with a few bottles of Tylenol Extra Strength capsules by replacing the actual capsules with cyanide-laced capsules. Consumers who unwittingly bought the Tylenol ended up dead. Johnson & Johnson, the maker of Tylenol, was facing issues that could easily have destroyed its business. The issue was the leading story for every news outlet.

Johnson & Johnson faced the issue head-on and made the bold move to have Tylenol removed from all shelves. The recall resulted in the removal of 30 million products from store shelves.[12] In the end Tylenol was a hero and won the trust of a nation.

Direct Marketing

Direct marketing allows for direct communication with the customer. Messages can be tailored to specific market segments and even personalized toward individual consumers. Early tactics of direct marketing included telephone and mail; however, technology has allowed for new methods of connecting with the customer to include text messaging and email marketing.

In 2019, the Data & Marketing Association (DMA) reported that the direct mail industry was valued at $44.2 billion.[13] It's the second largest channel for ad spend in the United States, and it continues to grow. Transformed by technology, direct marketing is finding new methods to connect with the customer. Most connection includes a call to action that provides for immediate feedback on the effectiveness of the method.

Internet/Digital Marketing

Internet/digital marketing includes uses of technology to reach customers at many different points of interaction. Marketers have at their disposal a variety of methods to reach their customers and brand products. Some of the tools include websites, landing pages, social media pages, widgets, and customer relationship management (CRM) systems. All the digital properties work together to drive traffic to the branded properties and engage the consumers.

Digital marketing is geared toward very specific market segments and is primarily interactive. Think of digital marketing as the mechanism that produces the immediate interaction with the customer and produces some type of feedback. Digital is considered two-way communication between the company and the customer. During the early stages of launching the SPANX brand, Sara Blakely primarily used digital marketing with a heaving emphasis on social media.[14] She involved her women friends who were in her target market demographic and had them post about the brand through their social media.

By contrast, Internet marketing is sending a message to a mass audience. The Internet is used to for digital marketing and includes websites and digital ads as well as the two-way communication of social media. Other forms of digital marketing include mobile technology such as SMS and mobile apps.

When a consumer completes a Google search for shoes and then jumps to Facebook to scroll their feed and are served shoe ads from Nordstrom, Macy's, and Steve Madden, they have been targeted by these shoe companies. The targeting, immediacy, and changeability of the messaging makes digital a quick and efficient method of reaching consumers. Digital promotional tools are extremely effective and can cut through the clutter and reach the consumer when they are in the demand phase of the buying process and have signaled an intent to purchase.

According to a 2020 chief marketing officer (CMO) survey from Gartner, two-thirds of promotional budgets are being spent on digital.[15] Because of the tremendous analytics available, marketers are able to assess the effectiveness immediately. Messages can be tested for effectiveness and quickly changed if they are not producing results. It is very difficult to get the same quick feedback with any of the other forms of promotion. Through careful tracking and robust customer relationship management (CRM) systems, marketers are quickly able to promote products, increase brand awareness, and move consumers down the sales funnel to instantly purchase through online e-commerce sites.

Utilizing mobile app technology, marketers are able to push promotions to customers while segmenting them by their behaviors and simultaneously filling their CRM with insights and analytics that can help drive promotions and sales.

CAREERS IN MARKETING

Integrated Marketing Career

An integrated marketing communications (IMC) professional builds and manages campaigns that integrate all the facets of marketing—advertising, public relations, digital campaigns, sales, etc. If you're interested in this job role, check out this article to learn about the qualifications, experience, and salary (https://openstax.org/r/requirementsintegrated). You can also refer to programs offered by educational organizations that specialize in integrated marketing. A few examples of those educational organizations include San Diego State University (https://openstax.org/r/businesssdsuedu), Marist (https://openstax.org/r/integratedmarketingcomm), Northwestern (https://openstax.org/r/imcprofessionalinfo), and Eastern Michigan University, to name a few. Check out this list for the Best Marketing Communication Colleges according to Best Accredited Colleges (https://openstax.org/r/bestaccreditedcolleges).

Additional resources to explore include the following video:

- IMC Careers from Northwestern's IMC director
  Click to view content (https://openstax.org/books/principles-marketing/pages/13-1-the-promotion-mix-and-its-elements)
- Introduction to IMC geared toward marketing management students
  Click to view content (https://openstax.org/books/principles-marketing/pages/13-1-the-promotion-mix-and-its-elements)
- Evolution of IMC from Marist College
  Click to view content (https://openstax.org/books/principles-marketing/pages/13-1-the-promotion-mix-and-its-elements)

Knowledge Check

It's time to check your knowledge on the concepts presented in this section. Refer to the Answer Key at the end of the book for feedback.

1. The goal of an integrated marketing communications (IMC) program is to _______.
   a. have all of a company's marketing and promotional activities project a consistent image and message to its target market
   b. control all facets of a product's distribution
   c. communicate with customers only through television commercials
   d. have complete control over all facets of the marketing mix

2. One of the promotional mix methods is advertising. Advertising may be defined as any _______.
   a. communications about a good, service, or company
   b. paid forms of nonpersonal communication about a good, service, or company
   c. communication that moves the product from the wholesaler to the retailer
   d. communication from a company sales representative to a company buyer

3. If you have a new brand and you want to reach a large consumer audience, which promotional mix element would probably be used?
   a. Sales promotion
   b. Personal selling
   c. Advertising
   d. Public relations

4. Dunkin' includes coupons in its print magazine advertisements. This is an example of _______.
   a. sales promotion
   b. public relations
   c. personal selling
   d. Internet/digital promotion

5. When a singer who is voted off *The Voice* television series appears on *Today* to discuss the experience, it is an example of _______.
   a. advertising
   b. public relations
   c. sales promotion
   d. direct marketing

13.2 | The Communication Process

Learning Outcomes

By the end of this section, you will be able to:
   LO 1 Describe the communication process.
   LO 2 Identify and discuss each element of the communication process.

Communication Process Defined

At first glance, the communication process seems simple. However, a deeper look shows the complexity and issues that are involved with communicating. When choosing how to send a message to the consumer, it is important to understand how the communication process works. All forms of marketing promotion are methods of communicating from the company to the consumer. No matter which method of promotion you use, the elements of the communication process are important to recognize and consider.

Understanding how communication flows helps the marketer to create better messaging, better media, and a response system that facilitates the communication objective. Sending and receiving a message are only two small parts of the complex system that marketers work with when trying to send promotional messages to consumers.

Within the complex system of communicating are the variables of the sender, encoding, messaging, media, the receiver, decoding, and the feedback loop—all while contending with constant noise. Out of all the elements of the communication process, only the sender, the encoding, the message, and the media are in the marketer's control. All of the other elements are outside of what marketing can control. Marketers must understand all of the other aspects of the communication process to mitigate the unknown and meet the campaign objectives.

When we consider communication, we are simply transmitting information. On the granular level, the communication process is how the message gets created, sent, and received. The elements of the communication process are consistent no matter what the message is or how you choose to send it. However, the variation in messaging, medium, and receiver all affect the encoding process and the feedback loop (see Figure 13.6).

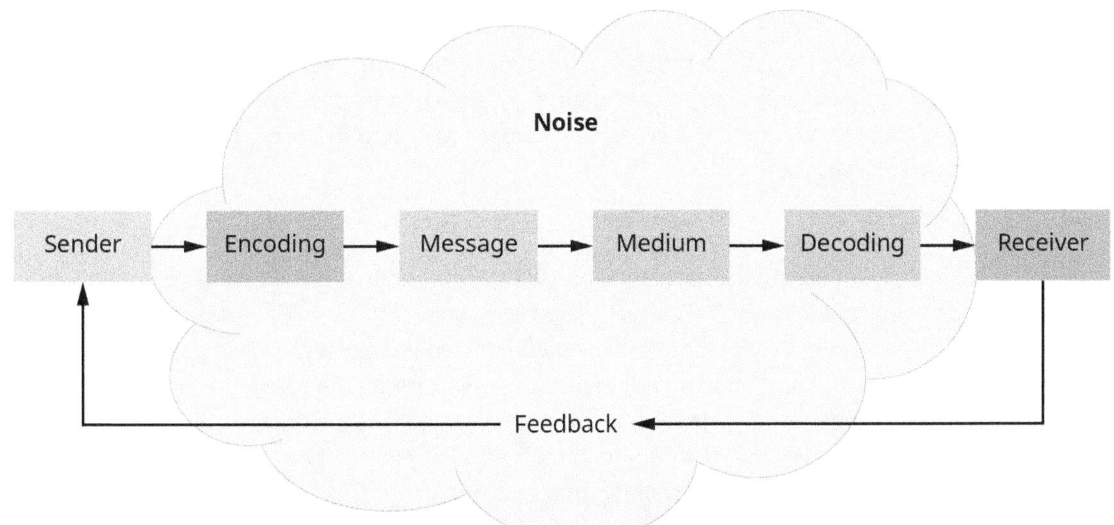

Figure 13.6 The Communication Process (attribution: Copyright Rice University, OpenStax, under CC BY 4.0 license)

The Elements of the Communication Process

In order for communication to happen, it must go through a process. Both personal and professional communication are comprised of several elements that occur in order for the exchange of information to take place. For communication to happen, there must be a sender of the message and a receiver of the message. Between the sender and the receiver is the message itself as well as the channel by which the message is sent. All the variables in between include the elements that are uncontrollable and, if not managed well, can cause issues. These elements include the encoding and decoding of the message as well as the noise that gets in the way and the feedback that helps us gauge the success or failure of the message.

The Sender

The **sender** is the source of the message. This can be the company, the marketer, or the hired talent for a commercial. For example, when PepsiCo signed a multiyear contract with Beyoncé to be a brand ambassador, Pepsi made Beyoncé the sender of its messaging.[16]

Encoding

How the message gets developed is the creative process marketers go through to put meaning behind the information they want to share with their customer. The process of creating the message is known as **encoding**. The process of putting the thoughts and ideas into words or symbols is encoding. Encoding could be writing a press release, developing a tag line, writing ad copy, creating a jingle, or designing a brand symbol. How a marketer chooses to encode the message should be dependent on the characteristics of the audience.

The Message

From the encoding process, a message is developed. For marketers, the goal is to have the message reflect the value the product provides to the consumer. When Nike tells its customers to "Just Do It," it has created a message. Dove's "Real Beauty" campaign created a message that beauty comes in many different forms.

The Medium

Once the marketer has the message developed, they need to send it. The **medium** is how the message is delivered. The message could be sent through the television in the form of an advertisement or a news story. The message could travel to the customer through an email directly in the customer's inbox. Or the message could be a salesperson describing why the new Ford Broncos are safe and dependable.

The Receiver

In marketing, the customer is generally the **receiver**. However, messaging can also be delivered to groups and organizations. When Comcast develops its annual report and sends it to its group of investors, the investors are the receivers of the message. If Chick-fil-A creates a billboard saying to "Eat More Chicken," the travelers passing the billboard are the receivers.

Decoding

Decoding is the process of unpacking the message and giving it meaning. It is the receiver's understanding of the message that has been sent. Many things affect the process of decoding, some of which include the receiver's knowledge and experience. To create the most effective messages and delivery, the marketer needs to have extensive research about and understanding of the receiver. When the consumer hears the message "Red Bull gives you wiings," the company (sender) wants to convey that the product will give the customer (receiver) the energy to do whatever they want to do. If the receiver believes that they can actually fly after drinking Red Bull, there was an error in the decoding process.

Feedback

The **feedback loop** tells the sender if the receiver understood the message as they were intending it when they encoded the message. Feedback is the checkpoint on a specific call to action. It can be a return email, a click to a website, or a purchase using a coupon. When the feedback loop is complete, the marketer has data regarding the communication process.

Personal selling has the richest method of feedback. If the salesperson is in front of the receiver and can hear their voice when they respond and can see their body language, they have a complete understanding of whether the encoding was effective when the decoding takes place. If the marketer sends a coupon to a consumer via a mobile app and the consumer redeems the coupon at the point of purchase, the redemption is the feedback loop for the sales promotion.

Noise

In the communication process, many elements are outside of the marketer's control. The biggest factor that can be a point of conflict for the marketer is the **noise** that interferes with the receiver's ability to get the message, decode it, and provide feedback. All the elements that get in the way of the receiver getting the message are noise. Noise can be the distractions that happen while the ad plays during an episode of *Seal Team*—things such as getting a snack, talking to a family member or friend, or surfing channels just as the ad is playing. Noise can be the other thousands of messages targeting the same receiver and vying for their attention.

The marketer's job is to understand the various sources of noise and work to create encoding and mediums that will help to reduce the interference. It is typically believed that because of all the noise that exists, the receiver must be exposed to the message on average 7–10 times before they take action toward the message.

Knowledge Check

It's time to check your knowledge on the concepts presented in this section. Refer to the Answer Key at the end of the book for feedback.

1. When a message is created and the company chooses to have a celebrity as the spokesperson, what does the celebrity represent in the communication process?
   a. Sender
   b. Feedback loop
   c. Medium
   d. Noise

2. Which of the following is considered noise in the communication process?
   a. The sender sings a jingle.
   b. A special news bulletin interrupts a paid ad.
   c. The consumer calls the 800 telephone number displayed in the advertisement.
   d. The consumer clips the coupon from a mailer.

3. A popular form of communicating is through television advertisements. Which element of the communication process is the television advertisement?
   a. Noise
   b. Sender
   c. Medium
   d. Feedback loop

4. Putting thoughts, ideas, or information together in symbolic form is called _______.
   a. encoding
   b. noise
   c. decoding
   d. sender

5. The Tennessee Department of Tourist Development purchased and ad in *Southern Living*. The ad encouraged people to choose the state of Tennessee for summer vacations. Along with beautiful, scenic photos of Tennessee, the ad includes the tagline "Tennessee sounds good to me." In this print ad, the source of the advertising message is _______.
   a. the Tennessee Department of Tourist Development
   b. *Southern Living* magazine
   c. the people in the scenic pictures
   d. readers of the magazine

13.3   Integrated Marketing Communications

Learning Outcomes

By the end of this section, you will be able to:
- **LO** 1 Define integrated marketing communications (IMC).
- **LO** 2 Discuss why IMC is important in marketing.

Integrated Marketing Communications (IMC) Defined

Now that you are familiar with the various forms of marketing promotions, how do you use them? Because consumers are all different—no matter how they fit into your target market—it is important to reach them through a combined approach, using a variety of the methods in the marketing promotion mix.

The method of using various forms of the promotional mix to send the same message to the target audience is called **integrated marketing communications**.

Importance of IMC in Marketing

If a group of friends is planning to go out to dinner, as the group organizer you may find it best to text some friends and call others. The message is the same: "Let's meet for dinner at Chipotle at 6:00 p.m." The methods of communication are different depending on the traits and characteristics of the group. This works similarly in marketing. Marketers have many forms of communicating through the various methods available in the promotional mix. However, it is important to send the same message in different ways to reach different customers within the target market. And consumers need to hear the same message many times and in many different forms.

Benefits of IMC

Benefits of an integrated marketing campaign are many. As a marketer seeks to create awareness, stimulate demand, or even encourage product trial, they are continuously seeking methods of cutting through the clutter and noise and trying to reach their intended audience—the customer. When using one method, they may reach a few customers; when using two or more methods, the odds begin to increase; and when using all of their available promotional mix methods to reach the consumer with a consistent message, marketing becomes more effective. The benefits of the integrated approach are significant.

Better Results

Without an integrated approach, the marketing message and methods of delivery will be disjointed. Different members of the marketing team may be sending very different messages to the consumer. The consumer will then be confused as to what they should do. Think of it as a bike with all the pieces lying on the sidewalk—the bike doesn't work very well. However, when the pieces all come together to form the bike, it glides smoothly along the sidewalk. It is the same when the message comes together.

When Taco Bell (see Figure 13.7) wants to tell the consumer that the Grilled Steak Burrito is only available for a limited time, it can send the message many different ways. The consumer soon knows the Grilled Steak Burrito is only available for a limited time. They have received the same message through ads on television and radio, an email, a photo and reminder on Instagram, and a billboard on their way to work. After receiving the same message in many different ways, the consumer realizes there is some urgency in getting to Taco Bell to try the new Grilled Steak Burrito. When the customer is in physical proximity to their local Taco Bell, apps such as RetailMeNot can send push notifications to customers when they pass the location. The offer can include BOGO or other promotions to convince the customer the time to purchase a Grilled Steak Burrito meal is now.

Figure 13.7 Taco Bell effectively utilized an IMC strategy to tell customers that its Grilled Steak Burrito was available for a limited time. (credit: "Taco Bell" by JeepersMedia/flickr, CC BY 2.0)

Increased Efficiency

Having streamlined communication channels all working toward a unified goal reduces waste and increases productivity. The marketing effort should not create divergent messaging. Through integrated marketing communications, the creation of a clear and simple message allows the marketing team to focus on the single message while each team member uses their skills to push the message through their unique specialization, be it public relations or advertising. Everyone comes together through a shared goal.

Improved Brand Awareness

You can tell a small child to brush their teeth multiple times, and chances are good it still won't happen. But when a parent tells the child to brush their teeth, the dentist provides them with a toothbrush and tells them to brush their teeth, and Elmo shows them the importance of brushing their teeth, soon the child understands that it is a good idea to brush their teeth. The same thing happens when Southwest Airlines publishes all of its fares and fees on its website, broadcasts ads on television and radio, send emails to its Southwest Rapid Rewards customers, and advertises on its mobile app (see Figure 13.8).

Figure 13.8 An IMC strategy in which the consumer hears product or service benefits through multiple channels, as utilized by Southwest Airlines, allows a company to increase brand awareness. (credit: "Waikiki IMG_2379" by John Martinez Pavliga/flickr, CC BY 2.0)

Repeated Success

Through the use of an integrated approach, marketers are finding repeated success. Success is generally based on the metrics chosen for the campaign objectives. Typically, marketers are concerned with objectives such as return on investment, cost per impression, cost per lead, and customer lifetime value. With a truly integrated campaign, you will see the objectives remain the same while the execution strategies change across the various promotional methods.

Customer Satisfaction

When customers know the brand promise and they hear it repeated often with increased company connection, customers are more educated and have more realistic expectations. The combination of connection and knowledge leads to increased customer satisfaction.

Knowledge Check

It's time to check your knowledge on the concepts presented in this section. Refer to the Answer Key at the end of the book for feedback.

1. British Airways used the James Bond movie *Die Another Day* to show that James Bond flies first class. The airline also ran ads with the slogan "Save your moneypennys, fly like Bond," which referenced one of the main characters in the film. The airline also posted ads where consumers were watching the movie. This an example of ________.
   a. the marketing mix
   b. distribution
   c. integrated marketing communications
   d. advertising

2. The goal of integrated marketing communications is to ________.
   a. have all marketing and promotional activities project a consistent unified image
   b. gain control of the distribution process
   c. use only paid methods of promotion
   d. develop a competitive pricing structure

3. When Sally is able to quickly recall the Taco Bell ad and think about purchasing a Grilled Steak Burrito from Taco Bell when she is hungry, it indicates which of the following benefits of an integrated marketing communications approach?
   a. Increased efficiency
   b. Customer satisfaction
   c. Improved brand awareness
   d. Expense

4. Tina knows that when she goes to Walgreens, she can use coupons and her reward points. She is thrilled with the way she saves money at Walgreens, and she is happy to be able to use so many of the great promotional opportunities. She tells many of her family and friends about her savings and her experience. Which of the following integrated marketing communications benefits is Tina demonstrating?
   a. Better results
   b. Increased efficiency
   c. Improved brand awareness
   d. Customer satisfaction

5. When a marketer uses multiple promotional methods to send a consistent message to the consumer, they are demonstrating the use of _______.
   a. advertising
   b. public relations
   c. integrated marketing communications
   d. personal selling

13.4 | Steps in the IMC Planning Process

Learning Outcomes

By the end of this section, you will be able to:

- **LO 1** List the steps in the IMC planning process.
- **LO 2** Summarize the details of each step in IMC planning.

Identify the Target Audience

All successful IMC campaigns start with a good foundation and a carefully written and executed plan. Every step in the marketing process should be driven by research; the same is true for the IMC planning process (see Figure 13.9).

Figure 13.9 The IMC Planning Process (attribution: Copyright Rice University, OpenStax, under CC BY 4.0 license)

Understanding the audience is integral to creating an effective IMC campaign. Using a variety of tools, marketers are able to identify the target audience. The more that is known about the target audience, the higher the likelihood is of making sure the message is coded correctly and the right medium for effective encoding and reduced noise is chosen.

Marketers employ many tools to understand the target audience. Both primary and secondary marketing research can provide significant insights. A clear understanding of the consumer allows the marketer to create messages that resonate with the needs and wants of the target audience.

Determine the Marketing Communications Objectives

Marketing campaigns must start with clear objectives. Objectives define what needs to be done, and they help to keep the strategy and tactics clearly aligned. Good objectives will help marketers create cohesive messaging across all the promotional mix methods. Objectives need to be simple, and they should be written in such a way that they provide opportunity for analysis. If done correctly, marketers should be able to analyze if the messaging and the medium are working. When creating objectives, follow the SMART guidelines: simple, measurable, actionable, realistic, and time-bound.

The 5A Framework

The **5A framework** is the map of the customer's needs. Through the 5A framework (see Figure 13.10), marketers create messaging that moves the customer through the funnel, or customer journey with the brand. The 5As provide the marketer with clear steps on the role of the messaging at each step of the framework.

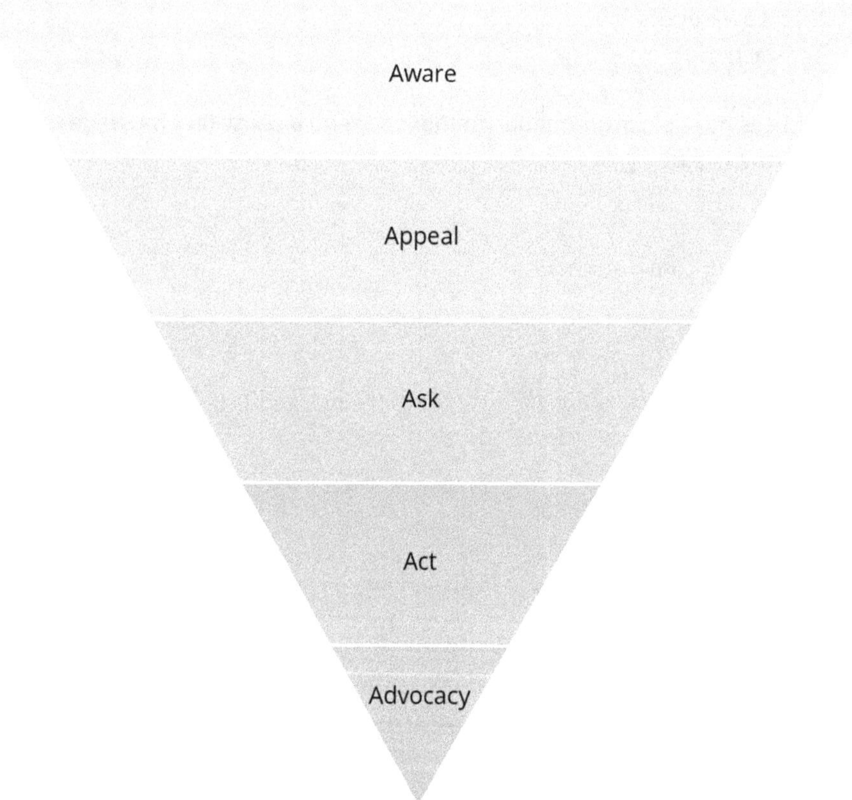

Figure 13.10 The 5A Framework (attribution: Copyright Rice University, OpenStax, under CC BY 4.0 license)

Let's look at the five steps of the 5A framework in more detail:

- **Aware:** The first stage in the customer journey with any product is to be aware that the product exists. It is difficult for a product to be desired by the customer if they don't know about it.
  When Angel Johnson launched her activewear company ICONI, she needed to stand out from more popular and well-funded activewear brands. As a Black woman–owned business, Angel wanted to appeal to other women, many of whom needed different types of activewear. Angel found success in creating awareness through running ads on Amazon, where customers could easily find and purchase her products.[17]

- **Appeal:** After becoming aware that a product exists, the consumer must gain some understanding of what the product can do for them. If the benefits are favorable for the consumer, they may put it in their consideration set of things that appeal to them.

- **Ask:** After the appeal stage, the consumer may become motivated to actively seek out information about the product. When the consumer asks the company about the product, they have opened the channels of communication. This is part of the feedback loop. Methods of asking include the consumer engaging online through a chatbot or a contact form or by calling a listed phone number.
- **Act:** Further down the customer journey funnel, if the customer has received information and they feel it is favorable, then they will act. The action can be to either purchase the product or not purchase the product. Either form of action must be evaluated by the marketing team. The marketer can determine if the messaging created a favorable or unfavorable reaction and then modify the messaging for the segment that acted not to buy the product.
- **Advocacy:** At the bottom of the funnel is the marketer's holy grail—the consumer becomes a loyal customer. The marketer can begin to calculate lifetime value, but most importantly the consumer becomes an advocate for the product. Through their advocacy, the consumer provides positive word of mouth and encourages purchase by other consumers.

Design the Message

A key element of integrated marketing communications is creating the message. Messages are designed to fulfill the established objectives. Depending upon the objective and the desired action of the consumer, the marketer may create the message to meet the various stages in the customer journey and have a call to action.

The biggest part of the message design is the content of the message. To move the consumer to the point where they act, marketers have at their disposal various forms of appeal. The appeal is the approach used to attract the attention of the target audience or to persuade it to take action.

Create the Message Content

When creating the message, the marketer has to consider not only the stage of the customer journey, but the product's features and benefits as well. Other factors to consider in the message content include the media and the traits and characteristics of the target market. All of the segmentation bases should be considered when creating the appeal.

Rational Appeals

When Toyota advertises the features of alternative-fuel vehicles and tells the consumer how those features benefit them, it is creating a rational appeal (see Figure 13.11). **Rational appeals** prompt the consumer to make the choice for the product because of all the ways they will benefit from using it.

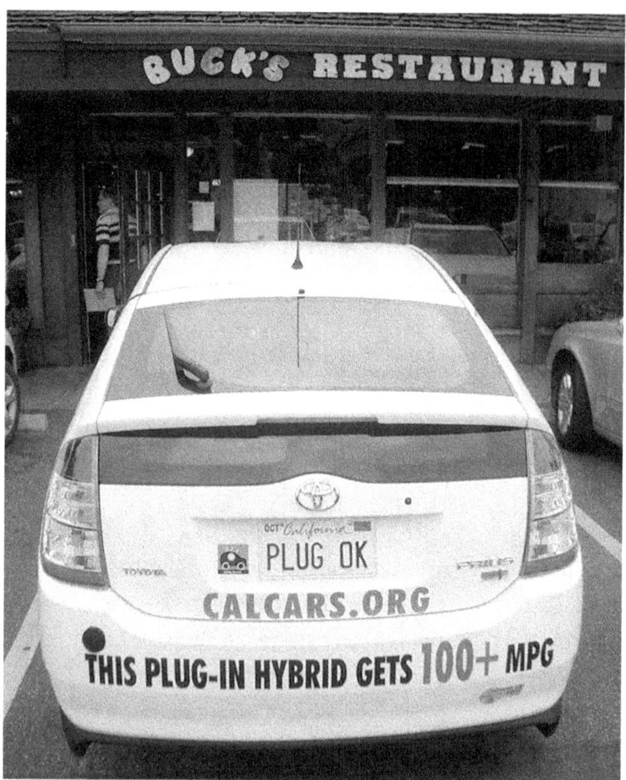

Figure 13.11 IMC messages that appeal to a consumer's rational side, like Toyota's alternative fuel vehicle, speak to the benefits the consumer will see from using the product or service. (credit: "Another Breakfast at Buck's" by Jurvetson/flickr, CC BY 2.0)

Emotional Appeals

Consumers have a wide variety of emotions. Advertising messages can play to all those emotions. A few of the typical **emotional appeals** include happiness, fear, trust, sadness, anger, and guilt. It can be quite effective to create fear if the customer doesn't purchase the product. Some examples of common fear appeals include skin care products and the fear of the effects of aging on skin. Vitamins and supplements use the fear of being unhealthy. And automobiles promote the fear of not being safe in a crash unless you drive a certain brand with a good crash-test rating.

LINK TO LEARNING

Happiness Campaign

Coca-Cola (see Figure 13.12) wanted to associate drinking a Coke with being happy and created a whole campaign on the emotion of happiness. Everything in the campaign was focused on drinking Coke and choosing to be happy. They created the #choosehappiness hashtag to be used in their social and digital promotions. Consumers would include their pictures drinking a Coke with friends and add #choosehappiness. Check out this commercial from the campaign.

Click to view content (https://openstax.org/books/principles-marketing/pages/13-4-steps-in-the-imc-planning-process)

Figure 13.12 IMC messages that speak to a consumer's emotional side, like Coca-Cola's "Happiness" campaign, influence purchasing behavior by playing to the wide variety of emotions that consumers have. (credit: "Coca Cola" by JeepersMedia/flickr, CC BY 2.0)

Public health campaigns often rely on **fear appeals** (see Figure 13.13). If you continue a behavior there may well be negative consequences, which can arouse fear in the consumer. These campaigns seek to change behavior through fear. Fear appeals can be very effective in some circumstances.

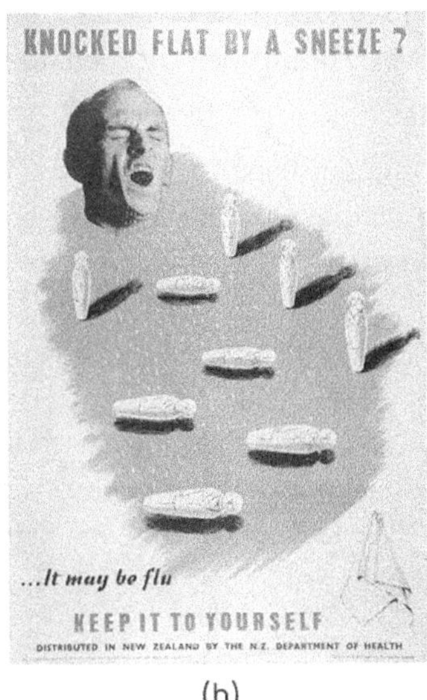

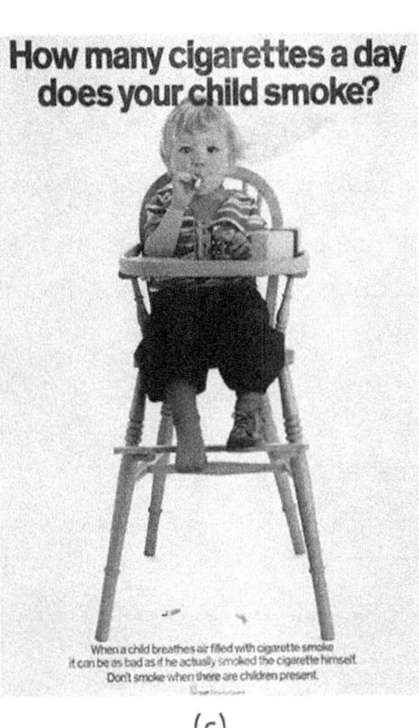

(a)   (b)   (c)

Figure 13.13 IMC messages that speak to consumers' fears create a sense of panic that if message isn't heeded, something bad may happen. (credit: "Cancer Take Warning" by Archives New Zealand's health poster collection, transferred by the Department of Health/ Railways Studios/Archives New Zealand/flickr, CC BY 2.0; "Knocked Flat by a Sneeze" by Archives New Zealand's health poster collection, transferred by the Department of Health/Archives New Zealand/flickr, CC BY 2.0; "How Many Cigarettes a Day Does Your Child Smoke?" by Archives New Zealand's health poster collection, transferred by the Department of Health/Archives New Zealand/ flickr, CC BY 2.0)

Moral Appeals

A **moral appeal** pushes the consumer to want the product because of a sense of morality or social good (see Figure 13.14). The messaging may encourage the consumer to do the "right thing." If they don't do what is being asked of them, the situation will get worse.

Figure 13.14 Messages based on morals encourage consumers to do what is considered right. (credit: "Beer Bottle Chained with Handcuffs and Don't Drink and Drive Text" by Marco Verch/flickr, CC BY 2.0)

Message Structure

Promotional messages generally have common elements, which include a slogan, the text or content, and the graphics. The graphics can include photos and brand identification. Messages can tell stories with words or lead the audience to their own conclusion based on the graphics.

When Apple first promoted its iPod, the company used the imagery of a very colorful background, a completely black silhouette, and the stark contrast of the all-white iPod with white headphones. The graphic alone conveyed the message that the iPod would allow consumers to "jam" to their own tunes through this new device.

Message Format

The format of the message depends largely on the media being used to send the message. For example, a television ad combines sight and sound, while radio is reliant only on sound. The same is true for print, billboards, and various digital campaigns. Formatting the message needs to take into consideration the target market as well as the medium of the message.

Determine the Budget

Promotional budgets are determined based on many variables. In developing the promotional budget, it is important to consider where the consumer is in their journey. Additional considerations include the current level of brand awareness for the product, accessibility of the target market, creation of the promotion, and specific media under consideration. There are several commonly used methods of creating promotional budgets.

- **Objective and Task:** This is perhaps the best method but is often used the least. With objective and task, the marketer determines the objectives of the IMC campaign and what tasks need to be done in order to complete the objectives. The tasks are priced, and the level of reach (number of consumers who will see the message) and the frequency (the number of times the consumer will see the message) are estimated. Based on the tasks necessary to achieve the campaign objectives, the budget is established.
- **Top Down:** With a top-down budgeting approach, the IMC campaign budget is issued from the operating budget based on input from the executives responsible for setting the budgets. While this method takes into consideration the overall organization, it pays little heed to the needs of the specific campaign.
- **Percent of Sales:** While personal selling is one of the methods included in the promotional mix, it is not the only method. A percent-of-sales approach attributes sales to all the functions of marketing. Generally, an organization may provide an arbitrary percent of overall sales as the total budget for the marketing promotions. Because many issues affect the sale of a product, it is difficult to make sales the only

determinant of the marketing activities and the promotional methods.

- **Affordable:** The affordable method allocates only the amount of money the company can provide to a marketing budget. This method does not create a mindset of growth within the organization. A robust marketing strategy is focused on the growth of the organization. Affordable only provides for what is left over after all the other expenses have been allocated.
- **Competitive Parity:** If you were to look at the advertising budgets of competitors in the same industry, you might very likely see that they are spending similar amounts on a very similar promotional mix. Companies of every size closely monitor the promotional activities of their competitors. With the competitive parity method of budgeting, the allocations essentially mirror whatever the closest competitor is spending on promotions. This method of budgeting doesn't allow for increased market share.

Develop Strategies and Tactics

The promotional strategies include the promotional methods the marketer chooses in order to achieve the objectives. Within the promotional methods, the tactics are the specifics the marketer must use to achieve the objectives. For example, if Panera Bread wants a 10 percent increase in brand awareness for its decorated Christmas sugar cookies from November 26 to December 30, it may choose to use the following strategy and corresponding tactics:

A strategy might be to create an Internet/digital messaging campaign focused on creating awareness with a message to try the Panera Christmas sugar cookies for a limited time. The tactics might then be developed as follows:

- Develop push ads through the Panera Bread mobile app
- Publish pop-up banner ads through Google
- Post campaign messages in Instagram
- Post campaign messages in Facebook

Select the Promotional Tools

The marketer must decide on the mix of promotional tools based on the established marketing objectives. Choosing the mix of promotional methods is also primarily dependent on the consumer and how best to reach them.

When Timmy Global Health, a not-for-profit organization, wanted to do an end-of-year fundraising ask, it chose to reach its donor base through direct mail. The organization chose an email campaign for the segment of its market that is responsive to email and has an email address in the CRM system. For a small segment of its market, those who are older and not responsive to digital marketing, it chose to do a direct mail campaign with a postcard mailed through the US Postal Service.[18]

LINK TO LEARNING

Direct Mail Examples

There are hundreds of examples where companies have used direct mail campaigns in their promotional mix. Check out some of the best as referenced in this article (https://openstax.org/r/bestdirectmail).

Designing the Promotion

In considering the target market and the message to send, the marketer must think of the desired response. Three important issues arise in the design of the promotion: what to say (message), how to say it (creative), and who should say it (source). This leads the marketer to the overall message strategy, which will look at the appeal as it relates to the brand positioning. A marketer will consider the following in designing a promotion:

- **Message Strategy:** A good **message strategy** must tie the brand to the target audience. What will appeal to them? What action do you want them to take? How does the brand positioning need to be portrayed? The marketer may choose to highlight how the product compares to the competition (points of parity), or the marketer may choose to focus on how the product is different (points of difference). In doing so, it is important to showcase the product or service through the value it will bring to the target market. Ultimately, the customer wants to know "What's in it for me?"
- **Creative Strategy:** Through a **creative strategy**, the marketer is able to translate their message into words, images, and sounds. If the message and the creative do not match up, the communication objectives may miss their mark. The creative strategy helps the marketer cut through the clutter and get the attention of the target audience. A properly done creative strategy serves as the guiding principles to develop good content.
- **Communication Channel:** Think of the **communication channel** as the delivery mechanism, taking the message from the company to the consumer. Determining which channel is generally guided by the audience, the message, and the creative strategy. Channels can be nonpersonal or personal. The channel options are as varied as the consumers themselves.
  Personal communication channels can include social networks like friends, family, and neighbors. They can also include paid or unpaid experts and even the company's own sales force. Nonpersonal communication channels include everything from television and radio to billboards and direct mail.

In designing the promotion, the marketer can mix and match the message, creative, and communication strategies until they have the right combination to execute on their objectives and connect with the target market.

For example, when World Food Championships wanted to reach home cooks, professional chefs, and aspiring chefs to participate in its Food Sport events, it enticed them with the opportunity for a big payout in winnings. And it created a connection with them through smaller local qualifying events. When the winners of smaller events received a Golden Ticket to compete, they were instantly excited. Then they realized the competition would allow them to meet with even bigger food celebrities and increase their chances of television fame (see Figure 13.15).

Figure 13.15 Designing a promotion involves developing a strategy around message, creativity, and communication—an approach that was effectively implemented by the World Food Championships when it wanted to reach a wider variety of cooks. (credit: "Cookin' with Gas (Oh Wait, That's Induction...)" by Shrie Bradford Spangler/flickr, CC BY 2.0)

Scheduling the Promotion

Knowing when to promote and how often to promote is a critical juncture in the promotional process. For scheduling purposes, it is important to understand the complexity of the message and the medium or channel for delivery. If the average of 5,000 promotional messages a day is correct, the consumer will need to see a message many times in order to become aware and act. To move them down through the customer journey, the message has to cut through the clutter and stick.

Reach is the number of consumers who will be exposed to the promotional message at any given time. Frequency is the number of times the consumer will be exposed to the message. Using the combination of reach times frequency, the marketer is able to determine the promotional schedule. Marketers typically work to create promotional schedules that optimize the exposure to the target market. Once again, we see that having extensive knowledge of the target market is critical to creating effective campaigns. There are three promotional schedules a marketer may consider:

- **Continuous:** With a **continuous promotional schedule**, the marketer will conduct the promotion year-round on a very regular schedule. Consumers will continuously see the ads.
- **Flighting**: Through a **flighting promotional schedule**, the marketer will run a period of heavy promotions and then go for a period of time without any promotional messaging. The idea is to give the target market a break and avoid potential wear-out of the message.
- **Pulsing:** If you see promotions on a regular basis and then suddenly you see them a lot during certain seasons, the sender is using a **pulsing schedule**.

For example, let's consider the television commercial for MyPillow. Throughout a broadcast, the MyPillow commercial plays two or three times. The commercial plays every night on one broadcast station. However, during holiday seasons, the commercial plays more often. The commercial is often accompanied by a special code. With the code, viewers can receive a discount on the pillows. The viewer gets a discount, and MyPillow receives analytics to determine if its budget for this commercial television time is effective. In this example,

MyPillow is utilizing a pulsing schedule for its promotional efforts.

Evaluate and Measure the Objectives

Before starting a promotional campaign, marketers must establish objectives. Including measurable and time-bound objectives is important. The marketer must evaluate the campaign on a continual basis to ensure that every element in the campaign is working to achieve the objective. Measuring and evaluating the campaign on a continual basis allows the marketer to evaluate the elements and make changes. Typically, objectives also have financial accountability. Changing elements of a campaign avoids overspending on components that are not working to meet the objectives.

Some common **key performance indicators (KPIs)** for evaluating promotional campaigns include the following:

- return on investment
- cost per lead
- cost per sale
- conversion
- engagement

Digital promotional campaigns allow marketers to track many analytics in real time and have the ability to make changes to the campaign in real time. The advantages of digital media include a host of valuable analytics, such as the following:

- website traffic
- page views
- bounce rate
- conversion rate
- impressions
- cost per click

MARKETING DASHBOARD

ROCI

IMC is centered on data-driven decision-making to drive organizational value. So it's no surprise that the founder of IMC, Don Schultz, determined a way to measure IMC campaigns. Schultz calls this metric **return on customer investment (ROCI)**. ROCI is a marginal analysis that shows the efficiency of marketing communications spending. We often think of effectiveness as the key measure of a campaign's success. But equally important is the efficiency of how we spend resources. We should consider how hard our resource works for us.

We should also be concerned about how well our investment does in the short term and the long term. After all, we are trying to build financial returns for our organizations. ROCI looks at short- and long-term value by considering the change in profitability and value during the period and overall.

IMC considers all aspects of the marketing communications relationship, not just a single campaign. The ROCI metric looks at how revenue grows over time and not just in response to one action.

The formula for ROCI is as follows:

$$\text{ROCI} = \text{Profit from Customer in Current Period} + \frac{\text{Change in the Customer's Value in Period}}{\text{Customer's Value at the Beginning of the Period}}$$

Let's say we own an ice cream shop and we are interested in the efficiency of our recent IMC campaign. So, we decide to conduct an ROCI calculation for an average customer using the following data. What is the ROCI?

Profit from the customer in the current period	$38.00
Change in customer's value in the current period	$10.00
Customer's value at the beginning of the period	$21.00

Table 13.1

Solution
$38.48

Last period, the ROCI was $37.50. What factors might impact the change from the previous period to this period?

Solution
ROCI considers all aspects of the IMC relationship, so as the relationship grows, the ROCI does as well.

What is the value of the ROCI calculation?

Solution
It determines the marketing communication campaigns that yield the most profitable customers.

LINK TO LEARNING

Don Schultz

Hear from Dr. Schultz directly about IMC trends in this video.

Click to view content (https://openstax.org/books/principles-marketing/pages/13-4-steps-in-the-imc-planning-process)

Knowledge Check

It's time to check your knowledge on the concepts presented in this section. Refer to the Answer Key at the end of the book for feedback.

1. The first step in the IMC planning process is ________.
   a. determine the objectives
   b. determine the budget
   c. identify the target audience
   d. select the promotional tools

2. According to the 5A framework, when Jennifer uses the Panera Bread coupon sent through a text message to her mobile device, which stage of the customer journey is she in?
   a. Advocacy
   b. Aware

    c. Appeal

    d. Act

3. When advertising is scheduled to run constantly without variation, this is referred to as _______.

    a. flighting

    b. continuity

    c. reach

    d. pulsing

4. When Nestlé shows an advertisement that has children coming down the stairs on Christmas morning to the smell of freshly baked Nestlé Tollhouse chocolate chip cookies, this is an example of which method of message appeal?

    a. Rational

    b. Emotional

    c. Fear

    d. Moral

5. The CFO for Wendy's tells the CMO that after doing the annual budget, there is only $700,000 left for marketing promotions. Which form of budgeting is Wendy's using?

    a. Objective and task

    b. Competitive parity

    c. Affordable

    d. Percent of sales

13.5 | Ethical Issues in Marketing Communication

Learning Outcomes

By the end of this section, you will be able to:

    LO 1 Identify ethical issues with respect to marketing communications.

    LO 2 Discuss ways to maintain and foster ethical marketing communications.

Socially Responsible Marketing Communications

While some argue that marketing makes people buy things they don't want, marketing cannot *make* someone buy something. The adage "buyer beware" still holds true. And while there are stories of rogue marketers not holding to the American Marketing Association (AMA) code of ethics, ultimately marketers want lifetime customers. The lifetime customer is easier to educate, more agreeable, and generally a good word-of-mouth testament for the company. It is difficult to get and keep customers without ethical marketing.

Marketers look to self-regulation as the first line of defense. It is in the marketer's best interest to always maintain a code of ethics in order to serve their customers and grow their organization. Good brands are always built on trust.

After self-regulation, there is regulation by trade associations, followed by federal regulation. The federal agencies with oversight for marketing promotions include the following:

- **Federal Trade Commission (FTC).** The FTC maintains oversight of commercial speech, unfair methods of competition, and deceptive advertising.
- **Federal Communications Commission (FCC).** The FCC regulates broadcast communication and has jurisdiction over the radio, television, and telephone sectors.
- **Food and Drug Administration (FDA).** This organization has authority over labeling, packaging, branding, ingredients lists, and advertising of packaged foods, pharmaceutical products, and cosmetics.

- **CAN-SPAM Act.** This regulation monitors commercial email practices and is one of the prominent regulations that affect many marketers across industries.

Companies have realized that when they are socially responsible, it benefits many of their customers, their communities, the environment, and their shareholders. Customers have come to expect more from the companies they purchase from, and they want to support companies that "do good." When companies support and sponsor programs and charities that are important to their customers, their customers in turn support them.

In 2021, Subaru celebrated 14 years of its Share the Love event.[19] To celebrate this event, it debuted a national ad campaign highlighting the people, places, and pets that have been impacted by its social responsibility. Charities supported by Subaru include the American Society for the Prevention of Cruelty to Animals (ASPCA), Make-A-Wish Foundation, Meals on Wheels America, and the National Park Foundation. In its advertising, Subaru also showcases some of the local charities—selected by Subaru retailers—that benefit from the Subaru Share the Love event, as well as the impact of the automaker's work with Feeding America to help address food insecurity.[20]

Maintaining and Fostering Ethical Marketing Communications

Ethical marketing communications includes avoiding activities that could mislead consumers—communication such as withholding information, making misleading claims, and misstating information. In an effort to make products be all that a consumer would want from them, marketers can easily go down the slippery slope that leads to ethical missteps. To make sure marketing communication doesn't follow any of the common unethical practices, it is important to be aware of two of the most used and violated ethical issues:

- **Puffery** is when marketers exaggerate at extreme levels. For example, a marketer may say that a product is "10x stronger than the competition." This is an unethical statement unless the marketer can support this claim through independent research from a third-party firm. Using general terms such as "awesome," "fabulous," and "best" are all acceptable, but making specific statements crosses the ethics threshold.
- **Paid sponsorship** is when a person promoting a product is paid by the company to make an endorsement. We've all seen the political ads describing who has paid for the ad and who has endorsed the ad. When we see a television commercial and it has a Ford truck driving over rugged terrain and we hear "Built Ford Tough," we are certain the ad was paid for and sponsored by the Ford Motor Company. However, if we scroll through Instagram and we see one of our favorite Instagram accounts using the new Babyliss Pro Titanium Flat Iron for their styling hair, and they are extolling its many great features, we cannot be sure if this Instagram account simply really likes the flat iron or if they are a paid influencer. Paid influencers must disclose their relationship to the brand so the consumer is notified that the endorsement of the product is a business arrangement. Disclosing paid sponsorship is a big issue, particularly for advertorials, native advertising, paid links, influencer marketing, affiliate marketing, and any "pay for play" content.

COMPANIES WITH A CONSCIENCE

Farmer Direct Organic

This group of farmers in Canada and the United States banded together to provide better food and better prices. The mission of Farmer Direct Organic is not only to grow better food but to change the way consumers think about food and how they eat. The farmers who participate in the cooperative are focused on quality and transparency. All of their food is 100 percent organic and 100 percent farmer owned.

Through its Facebook and Pinterest accounts, Farmer Direct Organic showcases the family farms that grow the food it sells. Consumers can purchase Farmer Direct Organic at Fresh Market and Whole Foods locations throughout North America. In keeping with its mission to help consumers eat better food, the company shares recipes and serving suggestions on social media and the organization's website.

With a vision of a "food future that is good for you, for your family, for farmers, and for the planet," Farmer Direct Organic carefully monitors the food that bears its brand, and it has an unwavering commitment to pesticide monitoring, transparency, and traceability from the store back to the farm that grew the food that is now on your table.[21]

Chapter Summary

After the marketer has facilitated all the other marketing mix variables, they are ready to communicate with their intended target audience. Marketers have a set of promotional methods for communicating. This chapter explores the various methods of communication along with modeling the communication process.

Throughout the chapter we explore the various promotional methods: advertising, personal selling, sales promotion, public relations, direct marketing, and internet and digital marketing. The communication process has multiple steps: sender, receivers, message, medium, encoding, decoding, feedback, and noise. To get messages through the process, it is important for the marketer to have an extensive understanding of the intended target audience.

To reach the target audience and build value for an organization, the marketer typically sends a consistent message through multiple promotional methods; this is called integrated marketing communications (IMC).

Key Terms

5A framework   map of the consumer's various need states as they find out about a product and finally decide to purchase

advertising   a paid form of nonpersonal communication about a product, service, or idea

buy one get one (BOGO)   promotion strategy in which consumers are offered the opportunity to buy one product at regular price and get a second item free

communication channel   delivery mechanism that takes the message from the company to the consumer

continuous promotional schedule   process of conducting promotions year-round on a regular schedule

coupons   sales promotion strategy that works to induce a consumer to buy a product based on a price reduction

creative strategy   method of translating a message into words, images, and sounds

decoding   method of transforming and interpreting a message

direct marketing   method of promotion that directly connects with the customer and generally requires a response or transaction

emotional appeals   advertising messages that appeal to human emotions

encoding   process of putting ideas and thoughts into a transmittable form

enter to win   promotion strategy where consumers must complete entry requirements for a chance to win something of value from a company

fear appeals   campaigns that seek to change behavior through fear

feedback loop   notification that the message has been received between the sender and the receiver

flighting promotion schedule   process of running a period of heavy promotions and then going for a period of time without any promotional messaging

frequency   number of times the target market is exposed to a promotion

integrated marketing communications   development and execution of multiple promotional methods that include a coordinated message

Internet/digital marketing   promotional method that utilizes the Internet and digital technology such as text messaging, phone applications, and social media to reach consumers

key performance indicators (KPIs)   methods of evaluating promotional campaigns

medium   various methods of communicating with a target audience; may include broadcast, print, outdoor, and other forms

message strategy   method of developing a message based on how the message will best tie the brand to the target market

moral appeal   information communicated to the consumer to appeal to their sense of right and wrong

noise   unplanned distractions that interfere with the communication between a sender and a receiver

paid sponsorship   when a person promoting a product is paid by the company to make the endorsement

personal selling   one-to-one communication between the seller and the buyer; used to inform and persuade the buyer

promotion mix   tactics marketers use to communicate with the customer

promotional mix elements   tactics to communicate with the customer including advertising, sales promotion, personal selling, public relations, and direct marketing

public relations   nonpaid, nonpersonal communication

puffery   providing unrealistic and unsubstantiated claims about a product

pulsing schedule   process of running steady promotions followed by a period of heavy promotions

rational appeals   information communicated to the consumer based on how they will benefit

rebates   sales promotion strategy in which consumers must provide key information to a company in exchange for dollars off the product

receiver   intended message recipient

return on customer investment (ROCI)   a marginal analysis that shows the efficiency of marketing communication spending

sales promotion   promotion that creates an incentive to purchase; provides for a fairly immediate increase in sales in the short term

sender   source of a message; can be an organization or person

Applied Marketing Knowledge: Discussion Questions

1. Evaluate the skills that are required to be successful in a personal-selling position. What are they, and why do you believe they would be important?

2. Consider the communication process discussed in this chapter. Explain the process as you understand each step. Where do you believe the biggest challenges are from a marketing perspective?

3. Explain the ethical issues involved in the messaging that marketers create. How can they make sure that they are not crossing the line when it comes to these issues?

4. Identify some of the benefits and the pitfalls of paid sponsorships. Occasionally an issue hits the news about something that had a blowback effect on the company that sponsored a team, event, and/or product.

Critical Thinking Exercises

1. Compose a 150–200-word paragraph using all the following terms as they relate to integrated marketing communications. The goal is to prove you understand the meaning of each term.

   Terms:

   - advertising
   - digital marketing
   - frequency
   - reach
   - feedback loop
   - sales promotion

2. Several companies come to mind when we think about great integrated marketing communications; Target and Gap are two of those. Consider other companies that have campaigns that you recognize in any form of marketing that truly stand out. What makes them memorable?

3. Socially responsible marketing campaigns such as the Subaru one mentioned are becoming more visible over time. Identify two to three other campaigns that you have seen. What do they use as a motivator? Is it to give to a cause, to buy a product or service that they sell based on the fact that they make a donation in your name, or is it simply an informative campaign?

Building Your Personal Brand

One of the key ways that you can build your personal brand is by association. The following is a list of marketing associations. Research each of these to determine which organization(s) are most congruent with your goals. Many of these organizations have local chapters that you can join, where you can attend a function, or that you can simply use to gather additional information. These are great ways to network with other marketing professionals, organizations, and industry leaders. From this association you can continue to develop a network of peers that you can gather information, experiences, and ideas from.

- American Advertising Federation (AAF) is a leading professional organization that includes members across all disciplines and career levels in advertising.
- American Marketing Association (AMA) is the largest marketing association in North America with more than 30,000 members globally.
- Association of National Advertisers (ANA) is a leading marketing and advertising organization.
- Association of International Product Marketing and Management (AIPMM) is a membership-based professional organization for product managers, brand managers, and more.
- Association of Network Marketing Professionals (ANMP) is the premier association uniting network marketing professionals worldwide.
- Legal Marketing Association (LMA) is the universal voice of the legal marketing and business development profession.
- Social Media Association (SMA) informs, inspires, and empowers business through social, digital, and future media.
- Society for Marketing Professional Services (SMPS) is for marketing and business development professionals in the architecture, engineering, and construction industry.

What Do Marketers Do?

Using the same list of marketing associations above, contact the one that interests you the most and ask if it is possible to speak with a member. Explain that you are a student and you would like to interview someone in the field. Before the interview, consider what information you would like to leave the interview with. Below is a list to get you started, but be sure to add anything else that the list does not contain and be prepared to ask follow-up questions for clarity.

1. Tell me about yourself. What is your education, how long have you held this position, and how did you get here?
2. Can you outline your current job?
3. What does your typical day look like?
4. What do you like best and least?
5. What is the biggest challenge of this position?
6. What does a career path look like from where you are now?

Marketing Plan Exercise

Complete the following information about the company and products/services you chose to focus on as you develop the marketing plan throughout the course. You may need to conduct research in order to obtain necessary information.

Instructions: Using the Marketing Plan Template file you created from the Marketing and Customer Value assignment and expanded upon in Strategic Planning in Marketing, Market Segmentation, Targeting, and Positioning, Marketing Research and Market Intelligence, Products: Consumer Offerings, and Pricing Products and Services, complete the following section of your marketing plan:

- Marketing Strategy: Promotion

Submit the marketing plan to your instructor for grading and feedback.

 Closing Company Case

Little Debbie

Part of your childhood nostalgia may include the Little Debbie Oatmeal Creme Pie, Nutty Buddy, or Swiss Roll. These much-loved products are from the family bakery known as McKee Foods. The company was founded in 1934 by O. D. and Ruth McKee. The company started out as Jack's Cookie Company, a small bakery in Chattanooga, Tennessee, that was bought by the couple to provide convenient snacks for school lunches.

Prior to McKee Foods, bakery or snack cake items were not individually wrapped and sold in a multipack carton. The snack cake brand was named Little Debbie after the founders' granddaughter. Her image is still the famous logo on all packaging. Back in the 1960s, a carton of 12 cakes and cookies had a suggested retail price of 49 cents.

Among the company's brands are Little Debbie, Sunbelt Bakery, Drake's Cakes, and Fieldstone Bakery. The largest brand is Little Debbie, with a wide range of favorites from Apple Fruit Pies to Zebra Cakes. Little Debbie offers seasonal items in rotation, such as Christmas Tree Cakes. Distribution extends to all 50 states, Mexico, and Canada.

The Little Debbie brand of products is widely available in grocery stores, convenience stores, and vending machines. The company has many best-selling products that are pantry mainstays in households throughout the markets they serve. Because the company is such an American icon, the products evoke a sense of nostalgia in many consumers. One such product: Christmas Tree Cakes. Debuting in 1985, the beloved product can be found on shelves to celebrate Christmas and is widely anticipated by consumers around the start of the Thanksgiving season. It is one of the best-selling holiday treats.

For the 2021 holiday season, Little Debbie launched a new Christmas treat, Christmas Tree Cake Ice Cream. To create this new confection, Little Debbie partnered with Hudsonville Ice Cream, a Michigan-based company that has been in business for over 90 years. The new product launched with a great deal of media attention. Public relations were in full swing with articles in newspapers across the country as well as trial of the product on live news broadcasts. Additional headlines appeared in digital media outlets to amplify the message that this new treat was available in stores for the holidays "while supplies last."[22]

Little Debbie featured the product in its social media with release information on all of its channels starting in October, well ahead of the holiday selling season. The company has a robust social media presence with over two million fans on Facebook, 85,000 followers on Instagram, and 200,000 followers on Twitter. The likes, shares, and positive comments had social media buzzing in anticipation of this new product.[23]

Case Questions

1. When Little Debbie creates its message about the Christmas Tree Cake Ice Cream, what is an example of the encoding?

2. Because this promotion was largely dependent on public relations and publicity, what is the potential noise that may interfere with the media?

3. How did Little Debbie integrate its communication for the introduction of the Christmas Tree Cake Ice Cream?

4. What type of appeal is Little Debbie using for the launch of the Little Debbie Christmas Tree Cake Ice Cream?

 References

1. "The Peloton Story," Peloton, accessed June 30, 2022, https://www.onepeloton.com/company.

2. Jordan Valinsky, "Peloton Sales Surge 172% as Pandemic Bolsters Home Fitness Industry," CNN Business, Cable News Network, September 11, 2020, https://www.cnn.com/2020/09/11/business/peloton-stock-earnings/index.html.

3. Ian Thomas, "The Fall of Peloton's John Foley and the Stock Market's Big Founder Problem," CNBC, updated February 14, 2022, https://www.cnbc.com/2022/02/12/the-fall-of-pelotons-john-foley-and-the-markets-big-founder-problem.html.

4. Sheree Johnson, "New Research Sheds Light on Daily Ad Exposures," SJ Insights, September 29, 2014, https://sjinsights.net/2014/09/29/new-research-sheds-light-on-daily-ad-exposures/.

5. "Largest Advertisers in the United States in 2020," Statista, accessed June 15, 2022, https://www.statista.com/statistics/275446/ad-spending-of-leading-advertisers-in-the-us/.

6. "Advertising Media Owners Revenue Worldwide from 2012 to 2026," Statista, accessed June 21, 2022, https://www.statista.com/statistics/236943/global-advertising-spending/.

7. Brian Steinberg, "NBC Seeks Record $6 Million for Super Bowl Commercials (Exclusive)," *Variety*, June 16, 2021, https://variety.com/2021/tv/news/super-bowl-commercials-price-record-1234998593/.

8. Isabelle Gustafson, "Cumberland Farms Offers National Ice Cream Day Discount," CStore Decisions, WTWH Media, July 16, 2020, https://cstoredecisions.com/2020/07/16/cumberland-farms-offers-national-ice-cream-day-discount/.

9. Tessa Trudeau, "Hello, New York! Nordstrom's New Manhattan Store," Nordstrom, accessed June 15, 2022, https://www.nordstrom.com/browse/style-guide/fashion-news/events/nordstrom-opens-new-manhattan-store.

10. "Impact Overview," TOMS, accessed June 15, 2022, https://www.toms.com/us/impact.html.

11. Ben Stewart and Maude Campbell, "Most Famous Movie Cars of All Time," *Popular Mechanics*, March 22, 2022, https://www.popularmechanics.com/cars/g625/top-10-movie-cars-of-all-time/.

12. Judith Rehak, "Tylenol Made a Hero of Johnson & Johnson: The Recall That Started Them All," *New York Times*, March 23, 2002, https://www.nytimes.com/2002/03/23/your-money/IHT-tylenol-made-a-hero-of-johnson-johnson-the-recall-that-started.html.

13. Andrew Robinson, "What Is the Response Rate from Direct Mail Campaigns?," DMA: Data & Marketing Association, May 21, 2021, https://dma.org.uk/article/what-is-the-response-rate-from-direct-mail-campaigns.

14. Clare O'Connor, "How Spanx Became a Billion-Dollar Business without Advertising," *Forbes*, March 12, 2012, https://www.forbes.com/sites/clareoconnor/2012/03/12/how-spanx-became-a-billion-dollar-business-without-advertising/.

15. Rama Ramaswami, "Gartner CMO Spend Survey 2020–2021: Technology and Digital Channels Withstand Budget Cuts," Marketing Insights, Gartner, August 17, 2020, https://www.gartner.com/en/marketing/insights/articles/gartner-cmo-2020-2021-tech-digital-channels-withstand-budget-cuts.

16. Meghan Casserly, "Beyoncé's $50 Million Pepsi Deal Takes Creative Cues from Jay Z," *Forbes*, December 10, 2012, https://www.forbes.com/sites/meghancasserly/2012/12/10/beyonce-knowles-50-million-pepsi-deal-takes-creative-cues-from-jay-z/.

17. Matt Miller, "Angel Johnson's Gym Mishap Turned into the Thriving Activewear Brand ICONI," Amazon Ads, Amazon, March 28, 2022, https://advertising.amazon.com/en-us/blog/iconi-by-angel-johnson-and-the-black-business-accelerator/.

18. https://www.timmyglobalhealth.org/; https://www.shoutoutstudio.com/timmy-global-health/

19. "Share the Love," Subaru of America, last modified May 26, 2022, https://www.subaru.com/our-commitment/share-the-love.html.

20. Subaru of America, "Subaru Share the Love Event Returns for Fourteenth Consecutive Year," News Releases, Cision, October 18, 2021, https://www.prnewswire.com/news-releases/subaru-share-the-love-event-returns-for-fourteenth-consecutive-year-301402491.html.

21. "About Farmer Direct Organic," Farmer Direct Organic, accessed June 21, 2022, https://fdorganic.com/pages/about.

22. Chrissy Callahan, "Little Debbie Is Turning Its Famous Christmas Tree Cakes into Ice Cream," Today, NBC Universal, https://www.today.com/food/little-debbie-christmas-tree-cakes-are-now-ice-cream-flavor-t234396.

23. "This Is McKee;" McKee: A Family Bakery, https://mckeefoods.com/1/this-is-mckee; "Our History," McKee: A Family Bakery, https://mckeefoods.com/105/our-history; "Who We Are," Little Debbie, https://www.littledebbie.com/6/who-we-are

14

The Promotion Mix: Advertising and Public Relations

Figure 14.1 Advertising is a form of promotion and can be presented in many channels; one example is the billboards in Times Square in New York City. (credit: modification of work "Times Square, NYC" by MK Feeney/flickr, CC BY 2.0)

Chapter Outline

In the Spotlight

Leo Burnett was a journalist for the *Peoria Times* in Illinois when he decided to start his own advertising firm with the same name in 1935.[1] His strategies were fairly simple: to utilize models who looked like ordinary people instead of Hollywood stars. His motto: "What helps people, helps business." That strategy paid off big for Philip Morris with the introduction of the iconic—albeit now considered unethical—Marlboro Man. In 1952, the ageless Tony the Tiger cartoon icon for Kellogg's Frosted Flakes was also born from the Leo Burnett ad agency. Other notable companies that have utilized the Leo Burnett ad agency include Procter & Gamble, McDonald's, and Fiat, to name just a few.

Today, the company has offices around the globe, and it still prides itself on aligning brands with human values. According the company, "Leo Burnett was built on a simple belief. That the most creative, most effective and most powerful work has people at its core—their needs, wants, dreams and hopes. It's a belief that can be seen in action in everything we make."[2]

In July of 2021, Leo Burnett London released a new advertisement for McDonald's—"Fancy a McDonald's?"—that showcases one of life's simpler pleasures: laughter. It featured a television advertisement with no dialogue, just some friends and family enjoying time together.[3] The advertisements, a big success, ultimately highlight Leo Burnett's ability to reach a multitude of audiences across cultures and generations.[4]

LINK TO LEARNING

Leo Burnett

There is a lot to learn from the Leo Burnett advertising agency. Check out the agency's website (https://openstax.org/r/leoburnett) to see the various kinds of campaigns the company has worked on. Be sure to check out the News section to read about several campaigns.

Interested in the campaigns mentioned in this section? Check out these websites:

- Fancy a McDonald's laughter commercial
  Click to view content (https://openstax.org/books/principles-marketing/pages/14-in-the-spotlight)
- Kellogg's discussion about the Tony the Tiger campaign (https://openstax.org/r/nutritionhowdidyoucome)
- Food nonfiction's history of Tony the Tiger (https://openstax.org/r/foodnonfiction)
- Video on the history of Tony the Tiger
  Click to view content (https://openstax.org/books/principles-marketing/pages/14-in-the-spotlight)

14.1 | Advertising in the Promotion Mix

Learning Outcomes

By the end of this section, you will be able to:
LO 1 Define advertising and provide examples.
LO 2 Discuss the importance of advertising in the promotion mix.

Advertising and its Importance in the Promotion Mix

Marketers utilize a variety of ways—or media channels—to promote the organization's offerings. Regardless of the media channel used, marketers must be consistent in the communication they send to customers.

Advertising is paid communication messages that identify a brand or organization and is intended to reach a large number of recipients. The most traditional media that are used for advertising include newspapers, magazines, television, radio, Internet, and billboards (see Figure 14.2). The increase in the availability and use of the Internet and other technology has also led organizations to advertise on mobile phones, through email, on social media, and on other digital devices.

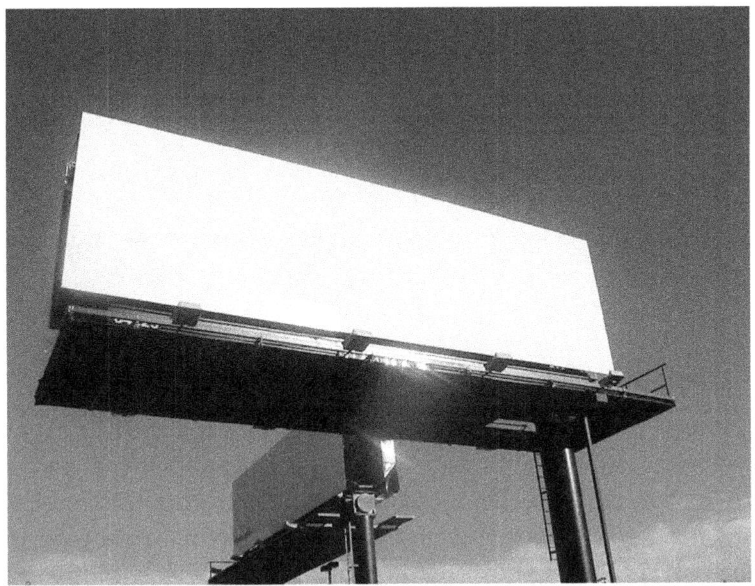

Figure 14.2 Billboards are one channel for advertising. (credit: "March04 015" by Lord Jim/flickr, CC BY 2.0)

Like every promotion mix element and media channel, advertising has its own advantages and disadvantages. Advertising is fairly expensive, so the cost to the organization is high. However, advertising reaches a large audience with one ad, so the cost per exposure is relatively low. For example, just one 30-second commercial during the 2021 Super Bowl cost companies around $6 million.[5] But with 96.4 million viewers, the cost per exposure (assuming every viewer sees the commercial) is only around 6 cents per viewer. Because advertising is nonpersonal and reaches a large audience, the message can get distorted from the marketer's intention to that of the audience. For this reason, it is difficult to quickly change the message if it is misunderstood, and it also difficult to capture how well the message was received.

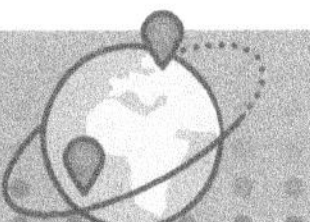

LINK TO LEARNING

Cost of Super Bowl Commercials over Time

Super Bowl ads have a large following, and the expense has increased each year. Check out this article from *The Sporting News* (https://openstax.org/r/superbowlcommercials) that compares the cost of commercials from 1967 to 2022.

Product Advertisements

Product advertisements are those that promote a specific product within the organization's product mix. These advertisements focus on a singular product and intend to bring brand awareness to a product or to differentiate the brand from competitors. In 2013, PepsiCo created a print ad showing a can of Pepsi wearing a Coca-Cola cape, wishing the audience a Happy Halloween. In 2020, Coca-Cola used the same advertisement to counteract the original ad by stating: "Everyone wants to be a hero!" Both are examples of product advertisements, cheekily comparing two fiercely competing brands.[6]

LINK TO LEARNING

Pepsi versus Coke

Brands roasting one another through advertisements is not something that PepsiCo invented. It's been done many times. To see the Pepsi versus Coke campaigns as well as other big brands roasting their competitors, check out this Bulldog article (https://openstax.org/r/5brandsroasted).

Institutional Advertisements

Unlike product advertisements that focus on one product or brand in an organization's product mix, **institutional advertisements** focus on the organization. This differs also from public relations—discussed next—in that it is a paid form of communication. The goal of institutional advertising is to create a positive image or support for the entire organization. Institutional ads also have the advantage of creating a positive impact by attracting potential candidates and increasing employee engagement within the organization. At the start of the COVID-19 pandemic, many companies stepped up to help mitigate the effects the pandemic had on the country. Early on, Anheuser-Busch switched some of its operations from distilling beer to making hand sanitizer. In April 2020, just one month after the pandemic hit the United States, the company had already delivered over 500,000 bottle of hand sanitizer.[7] The company utilized both print and television advertisements to communicate its philanthropic efforts to consumers. It wasn't trying to sell the public a Budweiser, but rather was using the ads to help bolster its image to consumers.

Importance of Advertising

While there has been a major increase in commercial-free television and the ability to skip ads in multiple media platforms, advertising still remains an important part of the promotion mix. Advertising assists in consumer awareness—making sure the audience is aware of a product or service and its benefits. Advertising also helps to retain customers through reminders and can show audiences that a business aligns with their values. However, with the increase in society's reluctance to believe what they see in advertisements, it is more important than ever that marketers ensure they are sending the right message at the right time.

Knowledge Check

It's time to check your knowledge on the concepts presented in this section. Refer to the Answer Key at the end of the book for feedback.

1. Promoting a product in a television commercial aligns with which of the promotion mix elements?
   a. Advertising
   b. Public affairs
   c. Social media
   d. Institutional advertising

2. You see a television advertisement from Ford thanking frontline heroes during the pandemic. Which term best describes this advertisement?
   a. Product advertising
   b. Public relations
   c. Institutional advertising
   d. Press relations

3. As a new marketer in a firm, you are asked to provide the advantages of using advertising in an upcoming promotion strategy. Which of the following would be included in your list of advantages?

   a.   Advertising's per-exposure cost is an advantage.
   b.   Advertising is nonpaid, so it does not cost the company.
   c.   Advertising's message is easy to change.
   d.   Advertising's effectiveness is easy to capture early.

4.   Breana sees an advertisement that compares Colgate toothpaste with that of Crest. She decides to change her toothpaste brand based on this new information. Which term best describes what Breana was exposed to?
   a.   Institutional advertisement
   b.   Public relations
   c.   Social media
   d.   Product advertisement

5.   Which of the following is a false statement about advertising?
   a.   It is still as important to the promotion mix as other elements.
   b.   It is the least costly of all promotion mix elements.
   c.   It should always be a well-thought-out strategy.
   d.   It assists in consumer awareness and brand loyalty.

14.2 | Major Decisions in Developing an Advertising Plan

Learning Outcomes

By the end of this section, you will be able to:
   LO 1 List the steps involved in developing an advertising plan.
   LO 2 Describe the details involved in each step of advertising development.
   LO 3 Discuss methods for assessing and evaluating the advertising program.

Major Advertising Decisions in an Advertising Plan

As with any successful plan, certain decisions need to be made while creating an advertising plan. Advertising is expensive and should have specific objectives with clear communication to the audience to ensure the right message is being sent at the right time with the biggest impact. These steps include choosing the objective(s), choosing a push or pull strategy, establishing a budget, developing the strategy, executing the program, and assessing the impact (see Figure 14.3).

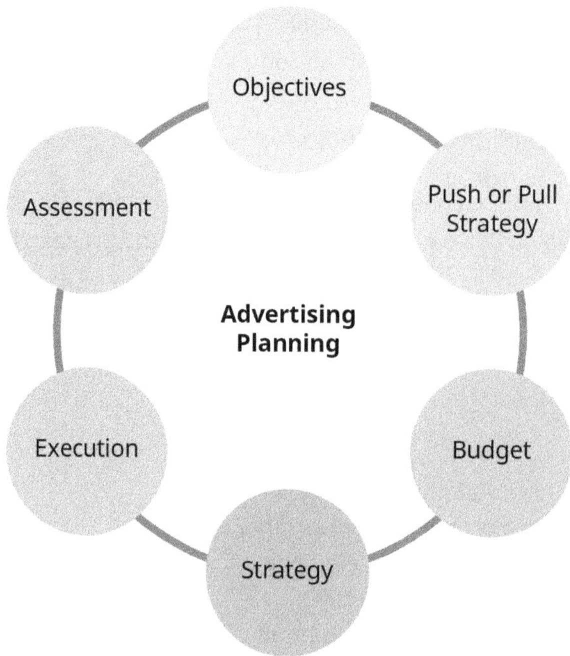

Figure 14.3 Decisions in an Advertising Plan (attribution: Copyright Rice University, OpenStax, under CC BY 4.0 license)

Establishing Advertising Objectives

The aim of advertising is to communicate something to an audience. The objectives of such communication can vary depending on the goals of the advertisement. Some common objectives of advertising include information, persuasion, comparisons, and reminders. Let's explore each of these types of advertising objectives in more detail.

Informative Advertising

Informative advertising is most often used as a new product is being introduced in the market. The goal of **informative advertising** is to bring awareness to a product through educational communication to increase demand for the product. A new product can only be successful if people know it exists and why.

Specific messages of informative advertising will vary depending on the product or service. A simple teaser of a new product is effective for some products, while for others, more detailed information may be necessary so the audience understands the product. For example, when the newest iPhone is about to be launched, Apple often uses a short and simple advertisement with only a photo of the phone and its available date. For an existing brand such as Apple, this works well because consumers are already familiar with the product's brand. Conversely, when a brand-new product is brought to market that consumers may not be aware of, more information may be necessary in the message.

Persuasive Advertising

The goal of **persuasive advertising** is to convince consumers to purchase by highlighting the benefits of a product or service being advertised. Whereas informative advertising often uses facts and figures to introduce a product, persuasive advertising often focuses more on the emotions of the audience. For example, when an automobile company advertises a brand of its SUV, it might include a scene with a family and focus on the safety of the vehicle (see Figure 14.4). This is an attempt to showcase the benefits of the automobile to the consumer on an emotional level.

Figure 14.4 Car advertisements are a form of persuasion intended to appeal to consumers' emotions by highlighting the product or service benefits to the consumer. (credit: "Audi Q5 Vs BMW X3 Vs Land Rover Freelander 2 - Comparison - NRMA New Cars" by The NRMA/flickr, CC BY 2.0)

Comparative Advertising

Comparative advertising's aim is to showcase the benefits and values of one product over its competitors. Wendy's, a fast-food burger establishment known for its "fresh never frozen" beef, has long used comparative advertising to showcase its freshness over competitors, particularly McDonald's—its biggest competitor. The marketing team at Wendy's often uses humorous advertisements to compare its food with competitors, and in recent years, the company has become known for its humorous social media posts.

Reminder Advertising

Reminder advertising is aimed at bringing a product back into the forefront of the consumer's mind. Typically, reminder advertising is used during the maturation stage of the product life cycle. For any well-established brand, most advertisements are considered reminder advertisements—unless the brand is introducing a new product or a change to an existing product. McDonald's 2021 advertisements that remind consumers to get their friends fries if they say they don't want them is an example of reminder advertising, as the company is not introducing a new product but rather reminding audiences that McDonald's is there as a choice in fast food.[8]

Push Strategy versus Pull Strategy

After choosing an objective for the advertising plan, marketers must determine whether a push or pull strategy will be most effective. A **push strategy** is aimed at pushing the brand in front of an audience. Often a push strategy will utilize multiple forms of advertising media so that the product or service is in front of the consumer at multiple times. Common push strategies involve sending postcards or emails and placing ads in print and television media.

Conversely, a **pull strategy** is intended to bring audiences to the product. For example, if a company is launching a new game app, the company may choose to advertise in another game app. The interested consumer would then click on the advertisement and be pulled into the new product (app).

LINK TO LEARNING

GameStop

GameStop is a great example of a company with push and pull strategies. Check out its website for examples (https://openstax.org/r/gamestopdeals).

Establishing the Advertising Budget

The next step in the advertising decision process is establishing an advertising budget. There are several approaches to this decision, but it is important to keep in mind that the advertising budget is just one component of the overall promotion budget. Table 14.1 outlines the most common approaches to budgeting.

Budget Approach	Definition
Percent of sales	Budgets are set as a percentage of prior years' sales or predicted future sales.
All you can afford	Budgets are set after all other necessary expenditures have been covered in the organizational budget.
Return on investment (ROI)	Budgets are set based on the expected return, in dollars, an advertising campaign will produce.
Competitive parity	Budgets are set based on predications of what competitors will spend.
Objective and task	Budgets are set based on the objectives set for activities planned.

Table 14.1 Advertising Plan Budget

Companies often use previous year (or period) data to set objectives for the current or future years. Marketing budgets can use the same approach. The **percentage-of-sales approach** utilizes prior years' sales or predicted year's sales and sets a percentage of those sales aside for advertising. This is a simple way to budget, particularly in stable markets. However, it is somewhat backward of what you have learned thus far in marketing: instead of advertising creating sales, it assumes sales creates advertisements.

Some companies choose to budget their advertising dollars after all other organizational budgeting is complete. The **all-you-can-afford approach** to budgeting ensures everything else in the organization is budgeted for and then sets aside the remaining funds for advertising. This is a practical and simple approach, but it can often lead to budgets that have less money than desired for much-needed advertising.

Unlike other approaches to budgeting, the return-on-investment (ROI) approach views advertising as an investment rather than a cost. The idea behind the **return-on-investment (ROI) approach** is that for every dollar spent on advertising, a return of that dollar—plus some—is expected. The disadvantage to this approach is the difficulty in determining exactly which ad, media, or campaign is specifically contributing to the return.

The **competitive-parity approach** relies on setting budgets based on the expected budgets of competitors. This approach works well in stable markets where competition is well established. However, with this approach, marketers are setting rather important budgetary decisions based on competition and can lose sight of internal objectives.

The final common approach to budgeting for advertising is the objective and task approach. The **objective-and-task approach** is budgeting based on the objectives set previously for the advertising plan. This approach does not consider previous sales or expected competitor budgets. However, marketers must be aware that this approach can lead to overspending when other factors are not considered.

Developing the Advertising Strategy

After marketers and other company executives set a budget for the advertising plan, it is time to work toward the advertising strategy. In this stage of planning, marketers will create the message and choose the appropriate media.

Creating the Advertising Message

Creating the advertising message can be a difficult task for marketers, particularly in the current climate of media. The advertising message is the visual or auditory information that is used in an advertisement to inform or persuade the audience regarding the product, service, or organization. Messages are usually broken down into five areas: the headline, subheading, copy, images, and call to action.[9] See Table 14.2. Each area must be consistent with one another and with the overall strategy of the advertising plan and the company's values and mission.

Message Component	Purpose	Example
Headline	Grabs the attention of the target audience	Buy One Get One Free! (BOGO)
Subheading	Clarifies the headline or provides attention details	Buy a couch, get a matching recliner free
Copy	Answers any immediate questions of the audience	Add a stylish yet comfortable look to your living room with our new rich brown couch and recliner in soft chenille fabric, built to last for generations
Image(s)	Visuals to enhance the message	An image of a family sitting on a new couch and recliner watching television
Call to action	Tells the audience what they need to do now that they have seen the advertisement	Come to our showroom today to select your couch!

Table 14.2 Advertising Message Components

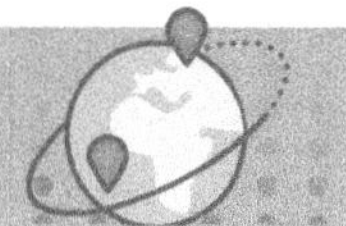

LINK TO LEARNING

Advertising Messages

There are numerous examples of the message components listed in Table 14.2. Check out these articles discussing ways each of these can be successful:

- Live About article: "Buy One Get One Free (BOGO) Sales Events (https://openstax.org/r/buyonegetone)"
- Ecwid article: "5 Effective "Buy One, Get One Free" Promotions for an Online Store (https://openstax.org/r/5-typesofbogof)"
- Drip article: "Limited-Time Offers: 10 Creative Ways to Drive More Online Sales (https://openstax.org/r/limitedtimeoffers)"
- HubSpot article: "50 Call-to-Action Examples You Can't Help But Click (https://openstax.org/r/

calltoaction)"

Selecting Advertising Media

Once the message is determined, the marketer will select which advertising media is appropriate for the message. The selection of advertising media will often be determined based on reach, frequency, impact, and engagement that the marketer is hoping for.

Reach refers to the estimated number of potential customers that can be reached with an advertising campaign. **Frequency** refers to how many times someone is exposed to an advertisement in a given time period or how many times an advertisement is shown in a time period.

Impact refers to how quickly members of the audience receive an advertising message. The form of media that is used will help to determine the impact of the message. For example, a direct mailing may take longer to be received by the audience than a Facebook advertisement. Finally, **engagement** refers to any interaction with advertising content. This becomes particularly important in digital marketing. The number of times members of an audience click on an Internet ad would measure the engagement of that particular advertisement. Clearly, the more engagement, the more likely a consumer is to make a purchase. Keep in mind that engagement can also be negative—such as a "dislike" or negative comment on a social media advertisement.

There are trade-offs between reach and frequency. It seems obvious that marketers would want an advertising campaign to reach the greatest number of people possible with one advertisement. But is one exposure enough to call a person to purchase the product? Often, potential consumers need to be exposed to a message more than once before they will make a purchase. Therefore, the marketer must decide whether reaching the most people or reaching the same people the most is more beneficial to the advertising strategy.

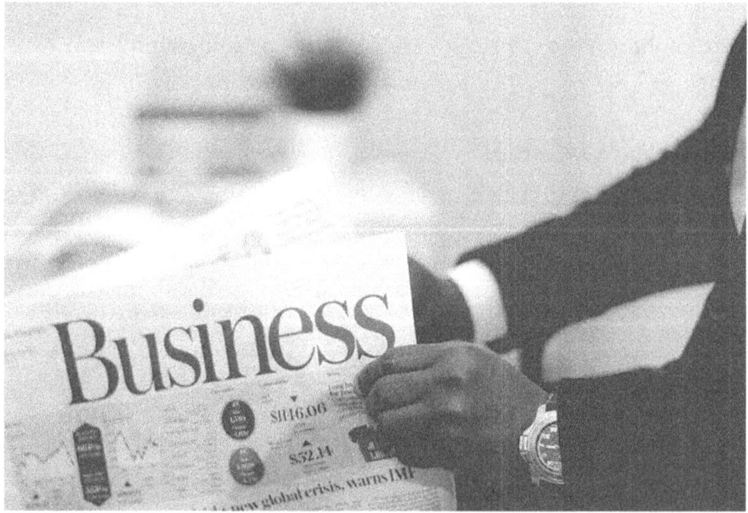

Figure 14.5 Newspapers are a form of print media advertisement. (credit: "Business Newspaper" by bestpicko.com/flickr, CC BY 2.0)

Different Media Alternatives

As you learned earlier in this chapter, there are different forms of advertising media that marketers will choose from. Most marketing strategies do not focus on only one media but rather on a mix of media that are most likely to reach the target audience. Print media includes magazines, newspapers, brochures, and fliers (see Figure 14.5). Broadcast media includes radio and television.

Outdoor advertising is a very economical option because it has such a large reach. Banners, flags, wraps, events, billboards, and even automobiles are types of outdoor advertising. Most companies have shifted their budgets away from some of these more traditional media and moved to digital media. Digital media is any advertising done via the Internet, mobile phones, and other devices other than television and radio (Kindles, iPads, etc.).

LINK TO LEARNING

Car and Social Media Advertising

Have you ever seen a car drive by advertising a company or service? There are companies that will pay you to advertise on your car. Read more about three companies (https://openstax.org/r/getpaidtoadvertise) that will pay you to put their advertisement on your car.

Check out these thought leader articles on social media marketing trends in 2022 (https://openstax.org/r/digitalagencynetwork) from Digital Agency Network. And learn about the value and impact of social listening (https://openstax.org/r/whatissocial) here.

Each media has its own advantages and disadvantages and best uses. When marketers decide on media to be used, they must consider the product or service, the target market, and any budgetary constraints. For example, a product that is primarily targeted toward senior citizens would be best advertised through traditional media, while millennials are more likely to see advertisements in digital form.

Executing the Advertising Program

At this stage in the advertising plan, marketers are almost ready to release their advertisements to the chosen media. However, before doing so, most marketers will choose to test their advertising to a small group of the target audience to ensure all the messaging is clear and concise.

Pretesting the Advertising

Pretesting advertising involves research that predicts the performance of an advertisement before it airs. The three most common types of pretesting are portfolio tests, jury tests, and theater tests.

Portfolio tests consist of respondents browsing through various versions of an advertisement and then being asked to recall certain details from each. Respondents are chosen from the target audience, and those advertisements most recalled by participants are chosen to air for the entire target audience.

Similarly, **jury tests** are a form of pretesting in which the respondents discuss the advertisements most likely to induce a purchase.

Theater tests utilize a sample of the target audience as well. In this form of pretesting, the audience is shown advertisements—usually television ads—in the context that they would be shown to the entire target market.

Assessing and Evaluating the Advertising Program

After pretests are completed, it is time for the marketers to make any necessary changes and disseminate the ads to the target audiences through the chosen media. But the advertising planning does not end there. Once advertisement messages have been out, marketers then must assess and evaluate the programs. Even the best-planned and best-tested programs can still be failures.

Post-testing the Advertising

Post-testing simply refers to testing the effectiveness of a campaign after it has launched. Marketers have several ways in which they can post-test the advertising campaign.

Aided recall is a type of advertising posttest that uses cues to assist a sample audience in recalling brands and products in an advertisement.

The opposite of aided recall, **unaided recall** does not use any cues or prompts to test the recollection of the advertisement message. The respondent is typically asked open-ended questions to gauge information retained from the advertising message.

Attitude tests investigate the attitudes of a sample target audience toward a product or service. Often, the attitude test will ask the respondent to compare the advertised product with a competing product.

An **inquiry test** is a type of advertising posttest that runs two or more similar ads on a limited scale and determines which of the ads are most recalled by and effective for respondents.

Another form of advertising posttest is the sales test. The **sales test** determines how many sales will be made based on a test market. This test can be done as either a pretest or a posttest. As a pretest, it is used as an estimate or prediction of future sales that the advertisement will attract. As a posttest, it measures the actual sales that can be linked to the advertisement.

Knowledge Check

It's time to check your knowledge on the concepts presented in this section. Refer to the Answer Key at the end of the book for feedback.

1. Daved is a marketer looking to see how successful his new marketing campaign was. Which of the following would you suggest to Daved?
   a. Posttest
   b. Pretest
   c. Jury test
   d. Portfolio test

2. As a marketer in charge of a new advertising campaign, what is the first step you will utilize in planning?
   a. Determine a budget
   b. Decide on a push or pull strategy
   c. State the objectives
   d. Execute the plan

3. If the target market for a product or service is millennials, which advertising media would you most likely choose?
   a. Digital media
   b. Outdoor advertising
   c. Newspapers
   d. Billboards

4. Jamal is trying to explain the difference between reach and frequency to his classmates. Which of the following best describes *reach*?
   a. Interactions with an advertisement
   b. Estimated number of times a potential customer will see an advertisement
   c. How quickly the audience will be reached with an advertisement
   d. Estimated number of potential customers to see an advertisement

5. Which of the following is the final step in the advertising plan?
   a. Assessment
   b. Strategy
   c. Budgeting

    d. Execution

14.3 | The Use of Metrics to Measure Advertising Campaign Effectiveness

Learning Outcomes

By the end of this section, you will be able to:

LO 1 List the key performance indicators (KPIs) for measuring the effectiveness of an advertising campaign.

LO 2 Describe how each KPI is measured.

Key Metrics in Measuring Success

The most well-planned advertising campaigns are only effective if they bring about some result. Marketers use performance metrics to determine the effectiveness of a campaign.

Key performance indicators (KPIs) are indicators that measure how an advertising campaign is achieving certain goals or objectives. There are several KPIs marketers choose to measure to determine the impact of an advertising campaign. These metrics help marketers make changes to campaigns in order to meet the goals and objectives set forth.

Brand Recognition

Brand recognition refers to the ability of a campaign audience to recognize and identify a specific brand. It measures the extent to which an audience can identify a brand with only a logo or photo. Depending on the advertising media used, marketers will choose the most appropriate metric to measure brand recognition. There are also numerous brand-tracking software programs that will gather this data for marketers.

Brand Awareness

While brand recognition and brand awareness sound very similar, there is a distinct difference. **Brand awareness** takes recognition a step further to determine if audiences can recall information about the brand. Awareness often seeks to determine the emotions and impressions that a campaign has raised with specific advertisements.

Impressions (Ad Views)

During an advertising campaign, marketers are also interested in quantifying how many times an advertisement appears in a chosen medium, known as **impressions**. To calculate impressions, you need to first determine the rating of the advertisement. The rating is simply a percentage of the target audience that is reached with an advertisement. This data is often gathered by outside firms, such as Nielsen, a long-time marketing research firm.

The following is the accepted impressions formula:

$$\text{Impressions} = \text{Rating} \times \text{Target Population} \times \text{Number of Ads Run}$$

Let's assume that one of your television advertisements ran 2 times this week. Your target audience is 1 million people. You discover that your ad has a rating of 30 percent, or 0.30. Using the impressions formula

$$\text{Impressions} = 0.30 \times 1{,}000{,}000 \times 2 = 600{,}000 \text{ Impressions}$$

LINK TO LEARNING

Nielsen

If you're going to be a marketer, you're going to need to know Nielsen Company, a "global leader in audience measurement, data and analytics, shaping the future of media."[10] To better understand what the Nielsen Company is about, read this Investopedia article. (https://openstax.org/r/investopedia)

Check out Nielsen's 2022 Global Annual Marketing Report (https://openstax.org/r/annualmarketingreport) about current trends.

Conversion Rate

A **conversion rate** refers to the percentage of an audience that has completed a desired action. The formula for conversion rate is

$$\text{Conversion Rate} = \frac{(\text{Number of Converts})}{(\text{Audience Size})} \times 100\%$$

For example, a web page advertisement may be attempting to get a viewer to click on the advertisement.

The conversion rate, then, would be the percentage of those viewers who clicked on the advertisement. Using our example of the web page advertisement, let's assume that our audience size 500,000 and the number of converts (that is, the number of viewers who click the ad) is 100,000. Our conversion rate would be

$$\text{Conversion Rate} = \left(\frac{100{,}000}{500{,}000} \right) \times 100\% = 0.020, \text{ or } 2.0\%$$

While industry averages can vary, generally a conversion rate somewhere between 2 percent and 5 percent for traditional marketing and above 10% for digital marketing is considered effective.[11]

Return on Ad Spend (ROAS)

Marketers are also often interested in calculating the return on advertising spending. **Return on ad spend (ROAS)** is a metric that measures the amount of revenue earned for every dollar spending on advertising. Unlike the other metrics discussed, ROAS utilizes the revenue from advertising. To calculate ROAS, you will simply divide the revenue for a given period by the advertising dollars in the period. The ROAS formula is

$$\text{ROAS} = \frac{\text{Revenue}}{\text{Advertising Dollars}}$$

Let's assume your company spent $1,000 on an online campaign in a given month. The revenue generated from this campaign was $5,000. Your ROAS for this campaign in this period would be $5, or a 5:1 ratio:

$$\text{ROAS} = \frac{\$5{,}000}{\$1{,}000} = \$5$$

In other words, for every $1 spent on advertisement, your company generated $5 in revenue.

Knowledge Check

It's time to check your knowledge on the concepts presented in this section. Refer to the Answer Key at the end of the book for feedback.

1. Ally is a new marketer trying to determine the return on ad spend that her first marketing campaign netted. She spent $500 on a Facebook advertisement, and the ad brought in $20 of revenue. Which of the following would be the return on ad spend (ROAS)?

a. $25
b. 5:1
c. 10,000
d. $2.50

2. You show your friend the Adidas logo and ask them which brand it identifies. This is an example of

_______.

a. brand impression
b. brand awareness
c. brand recognition
d. conversion rate

3. Coco is trying to determine if the most recent ad she created and launched has been effective at increasing revenue. Which of the following metrics would you recommend Coco use?
a. ROAS
b. Impressions
c. Brand awareness
d. Brand recognition

4. Indicators that measure the effectiveness of an advertising campaign are known as _______.
a. KMAs
b. Recalls
c. ROIs
d. KPIs

5. Liam is interested in the ratings of a recent television advertisement. They are interested in calculating the impressions of this ad. Liam knows that the target population of this ad is 500,000, and the ad runs three times. Which information is Liam missing to calculate impressions?
a. Converts
b. Rating
c. Conversion rate
d. Number of weeks the ad ran

MARKETING DASHBOARD

Measuring the Impact of Advertising

When marketing professionals purchase advertising, they are primarily interested in who will see it. Advertising is dependent on views, as it is not direct response like search or email marketing. Therefore, marketing professionals are looking for the biggest bang for their buck. This is where cost per thousand (CPM) comes in. The "M" in cost per thousand represents the Latin term *mille*. CPM is the cost to advertise to 1,000 people.

An advertisement's cost per thousand depends on a variety of factors. One such factor is how targeted an ad is to a given audience. Targetability increases the cost per thousand. Another factor is whether the media is digital or traditional. Traditional media (television, radio, print, and outdoor) have a higher CPM than digital advertising. Niche media may have higher CPM than mass media.

There are some legitimate criticisms of CPM. First, an ad view does not indicate an intent to purchase. It simply means that a prospective customer saw the ad. We have no way of knowing whether the ad was persuasive or changed behavior. CPM does not allow us to track behavior. Next, ad views may be duplicative or not properly targeted, potentially wasting the impression. For example, if you see an ad for the same running shoe three times and you're not a runner, the brand wasted three impressions on you because you have no intent to purchase. Finally, ads may not run or load as intended, wasting advertising dollars on a failed impression.

$$CPM = \frac{(Campaign\ Cost)}{(Impressions)} \times 1{,}000$$

Let's revisit our ice cream shop from Integrated Marketing Communications**. We decided to run an advertising campaign in the local newspaper. We paid $1,000 for 2,000 impressions. What is our CPM?**

Solution

$500

Last period, we acquired 15 customers from our advertising campaign with an average customer lifetime value of $50. Did our advertising campaign have a profitable result in the last period?

Solution

No. We spent $1,000 on advertising and gained $750 in revenue.

Let's say we decide to reallocate our $1,000 advertising spend on a more targeted campaign. Do you expect that our CPM will increase or decrease?

Solution

CPM will most likely increase because targeted media typically has a higher CPM.

14.4 | Public Relations and Its Role in the Promotion Mix

Learning Outcomes

By the end of this section, you will be able to:

- **LO** 1 Define public relations and discuss its role in the promotion mix.
- **LO** 2 List and describe the tools of public relations.

Public Relations Defined

With today's ever-changing media landscape, maintaining a positive image with the public is of utmost importance. This is where public relations becomes an important tool in the promotion mix. **Public relations** is about creating and maintaining a favorable public image. Unlike other tools in the promotion mix, public relations is not paid for; it is earned media. The result of public relations is called **publicity**.

There are two sides to public relations. The first is considered the "fun" side, where marketers get to share stories of all the great things an organization is doing. This helps to promote the brand's image in a positive, feel-good way. The other side of public relations is damage control. This is when something negative happens within an organization and marketers must perform crisis communication—that is, addressing issues that could negatively impact the reputation of a brand. Consider in 2017, amid the height of Black Lives Matter protests, when PepsiCo aired a commercial featuring Kendall Jenner calming an angry crowd by simply handing a police officer a can of Pepsi.[12] Activists slammed Pepsi for trivializing such an important issue. Originally, Pepsi released a statement supporting its advertisement, but public backlash soon changed that position, and the company issued an apology, saying it had "missed the mark" with its intentions.

CAREERS IN MARKETING

Public Relations

A public relations professional is someone who shares information on behalf of a company. There are various types of public relation jobs, and knowing the types of skills you should have to get the job is important. Read this article to learn about the various types of jobs and the necessary (https://openstax.org/r/masterclass) skills needed.

Read this article from *Harvard Business Review* to gain insight (https://openstax.org/r/therightcareer) into whether a job in public relations is right for you. And learn from this expert guide on how to get a job in public relations (https://openstax.org/r/may18anexpertguide). Want to learn about what a day looks like for a public relations professional? Check out this video from a public relations professional about what a day in the life of a real-world public relations professional looks like.

Click to view content (https://openstax.org/books/principles-marketing/pages/14-4-public-relations-and-its-role-in-the-promotion-mix)

The Role of Public Relations in the Promotion Mix

In many organizations, public relations has been an afterthought or a sidebar to marketing, something used only when a crisis has occurred. However, public relations is more important than ever as the public seeks brands that have values aligned with their own and are not hesitant to boycott those who don't. In fact, according to a 2017 survey, 86 percent of consumers say that authenticity is a key factor when deciding which companies and brands they will support.[13] For example, in the past several years, the public has become more aware and vocal about the use of Photoshop in advertisements. In fact, many celebrities have spoken out about their own photos being Photoshopped in media and the unauthenticity it translates to the public. Similarly, companies such as CVS, Dove, and Target have stopped—or limited—the use of model editing to challenge unrealistic beauty standards.

The Tools of Public Relations

In an age of information access and sharing, companies can no longer afford to hide behind their mistakes, nor can they afford to miss opportunities to boast about their good deeds. Marketers need to be keenly aware of how the organization's image is portrayed publicly—to all interested parties. There are several tools that marketers should use to positively impact this image. While the goal of public relations and publicity is to promote positive images to the public, marketers must use public relations to minimize the impact of negative publicity as well.

Consider CNN's *Blackfish*, which aired in 2013. The documentary shed light on the consequences of keeping orcas in captivity, forcing them to perform for sightseers at sea parks. It takes a deep dive into the lives of these captive marine mammals and how sometimes such animals can be deadly, as was witnessed at SeaWorld in 2014.[14] The results of the negative publicity created by the documentary caused SeaWorld's park attendance, as well as its market value, to drop.[15]

LINK TO LEARNING

Examples of Bad Publicity

Watch the *Blackfish* official trailer and see for yourself the message behind this documentary, and read here about the impact (https://openstax.org/r/worldanimalprotection) this negative publicity had on SeaWorld.

Click to view content (https://openstax.org/books/principles-marketing/pages/14-4-public-relations-and-its-role-in-the-promotion-mix)

You can find numerous examples of bad publicity on the Internet. Check out this article that identifies (https://openstax.org/r/mediatoolkit) many from companies such as Easy Jet, Tinder, and Tesla.

Press Relations

Press relations entails establishing and maintaining positive relationships with those in the media, such as newspapers and television. Press relations are controlled internally by the marketing team and often include the marketer sending press releases and other stories that help to maintain a positive image of the brand. Although press relations are controlled internally, it is up to the media whether the stories will be disseminated to the public. Consider your local news station that covers a story of a local bakery raising money for charity. The bakery owner or marketer has most likely sent the news station a press release of the upcoming event. The local news station will decide if it will or will not cover the story in its newscast. The more positive relationships the bakery team has with the local news station, the more likely it is to receive media coverage.

Public Affairs

Another important tool of public relations is **public affairs**—efforts to influence public policy and engage with public officials and trade associations. Public affairs often align with noncorporate entities, such as nonprofits and government agencies. However, for-profit organizations are becoming more and more involved in public affairs. Organizational leaders and marketers often share their economic impact with legislators to help policy makers amend or set new policies. For example, when Walmart plans to open a new store, the executives often reach out to local legislators to explain the goodwill and positive impact on the local economy. They continue conversations with local politicians to show they are "good citizens" of the community and help to impact local (as well as state and federal) legislation.[16]

Lobbying

Very similar to public affairs, **lobbying** involves the intention of influencing public policy and law. Lobbying is a way for companies to influence legislation in their favor. Lobbying is a large part of the political system in the United States, and many companies and industry associations contribute massive amounts of money to influence politicians. Lobbying has come under a lot of scrutiny over the years as companies continue to grow and have larger resources to influence laws and legislation in their favor as opposed to favoring the individual or the greater society.[17]

For example, in 2020, the National Association of Realtors was the top lobbying association in the United States, followed by the US Chamber of Commerce, Pharmaceutical Research and Manufacturers of America, and the American Hospital Association. Together, these associations spent over $200 million lobbying to impact local, state, and federal legislation.[18]

Events

Organizations are increasingly sponsoring or hosting special events to show support for various causes. Such events are also a way to showcase the company, products/services, and/or brands to the public. Often, companies use special events to show the public that their values and ideals are part of their business model. For example, Kroger has sponsored and volunteered for the Susan G. Komen Central Indiana Race for a Cure for many years. With one of its division offices located in Indianapolis, Indiana, the company has been covered by media for its involvement in the local chapter of the Breast Cancer Foundation.[19] The events not only provide a much-needed community service but also generate positive publicity for the company.

Digital Media/Social Media Marketing

Social and digital media have become important tools for marketing managers, and the use of these platforms is advantageous in public relations as much as in advertising. The biggest advantages to using digital tools in public relations and publicity is that they can reach a larger audience in a short time, are fairly inexpensive in comparison to other mediums, and allow for real-time communication.

The San Francisco Batkid took social media by storm when the campaign was rolled out by Make-A-Wish Foundation. A boy fighting leukemia wished to be Batman, and the campaign went viral with the hashtag #SFBatman. People everywhere took time to volunteer and take part in the boy's dream.

LINK TO LEARNING

#SFBatman

Check the #SFBatkid Twitter hashtag here (https://openstax.org/r/hashtagsfbatkid) to see the Batkid's journey, watch the trailer to a movie telling his story, and watch a video showcasing the public relations campaign.

Click to view content (https://openstax.org/books/principles-marketing/pages/14-4-public-relations-and-its-role-in-the-promotion-mix)

Click to view content (https://openstax.org/books/principles-marketing/pages/14-4-public-relations-and-its-role-in-the-promotion-mix)

Knowledge Check

It's time to check your knowledge on the concepts presented in this section. Refer to the Answer Key at the end of the book for feedback.

1. What is a promotion mix element that is earned rather than paid for?
   a. Public relations
   b. Advertising
   c. Television advertisements
   d. Web page advertisements

2. Which of the following is a way companies attempt to influence public policy and law?
   a. Press relations
   b. Events
   c. Lobbying
   d. Publicity

3. Mikel does not have a lot of money for marketing his new business. But he wants to raise awareness of his company and decides to commit to handing out free water at a local 5K run. Which of the following is Mikel participating in?
   a. Events
   b. Lobbying
   c. Press relations
   d. Public affairs

4. As a marketer, you are responsible for creating and maintaining positive relationships with the press.

Which part of public relations are you responsible for?
a. Lobbying
b. Publicity
c. Public affairs
d. Press relations

5. As a new business owner, Michaela is attempting to sway local leaders to give the business a tax cut for the first year of operation. She invites all the local officials to a public meeting, where she presents the anticipated economic impact of her business. Michaela is engaged in which public relations tool?
a. Press relations
b. Public affairs
c. Lobbying
d. Events

14.5 | The Advantages and Disadvantages of Public Relations

Learning Outcomes

By the end of this section, you will be able to:
LO 1 Discuss the advantages of public relations.
LO 2 Discuss the disadvantages of public relations.

Advantages of Public Relations

From a business perspective, the greatest advantage to public relations is that of cost; public relations is not a paid form of promotion. However, there are other advantages that accompany a well-thought-out public relations strategy.

Increasing Brand Credibility

Because public relations are unpaid and come from an objective source—news media—they are perceived as much more credible than paid forms of advertising. In fact, it is the most credible and persuasive form of promotion. Most consumers value the opinions of news media and opinion leaders over that of a company's best advertising.

Increasing Sales and Leads

Another advantage of public relations is that of sales and leads. Again, because public relations is considered a more credible source of information, various tools in public relations can help to increase sales and leads for the organization. Imagine you are attending an event that is raising money for the local animal shelter because you are a huge animal advocate. You see signs that an organization unfamiliar to you is the lead sponsor. While you may never have heard of this organization, let alone considered buying from this company in the past, the fact that it is helping raising money for the local animal shelter sways your decision to do business with them. For example, let's look at Campfire Treats, which makes dog treats. This company was one of the first in its industry to embrace the Better Chicken Commitment (BCC) to ensure better treatment of chickens.[20] The company has gained industry publicity and is becoming popular with pet owners that embrace more humane animal treatment.[21]

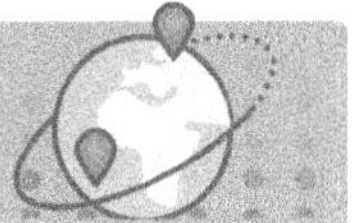

LINK TO LEARNING

Pet Food Industry.com

Check out this Pet Food Industry.com article (https://openstax.org/r/petfoodindustry) to learn more about Campfire Treats and its commitment to BCC. If you're interested in learning more about the product, check out this video review from Top Dog Tips or this article from Groovy Goldendoodles (https://openstax.org/r/groovygoldendoodles).

Click to view content (https://openstax.org/books/principles-marketing/pages/14-5-the-advantages-and-disadvantages-of-public-relations)

Positive Brand Image

Because consumers are more likely to patronize organizations whose values align with their own, public relations has the distinct opportunity to provide a positive brand image to audiences. When organizations are authentic in their own values, it translates to increased loyalty and brand equity.

Cost-Effectiveness

As you've already learned, public relations is not a paid tool in the promotion mix. A really good brand or company story can be picked up by several media outlets, exposing the promotion to a large audience. Considered the Ice Bucket Challenge that went viral in 2015. The challenge was first promoted by Pat Quinn and Pete Frates as a way for the public to better understand how Lou Gehrig's disease (amyotrophic lateral sclerosis [ALS]) affects those with the disease. The challenge raised over $115 million worldwide for the disease and was an extremely cost-effective (and fun) way to raise funds when it went viral on social media.[22]

Disadvantages of Public Relations

While public relations is a cost-effective way to potentially reach a large audience, it does come with its own set of challenges, including no direct control, lack of guaranteed results, and a difficulty in evaluating effectiveness.

No Direct Control

Unlike other tools in the promotion mix, marketers have no direct control over public relations. In other words, the media controls how the organization is portrayed, when—or if—the coverage will appear, and where it will be placed. This is why press relations is such an integral part of the public relations strategy.[23]

Lack of Guaranteed Results

Proficient marketers will spend time crafting the perfect press release, curating photographs, and getting just the right message to the media. They can even have excellent relationships with media personnel, but it is ultimately the decision of the media if it will publish a story. A story that is buried deep in a newspaper's pages or a blur during a news program may not create the results marketers intended.

Difficulty of Evaluating Effectiveness

Public relation activities can be difficult to measure. A marketer can observe media mentions and stories, but the impact they have on the audience can be difficult to determine. Other tools in the promotion mix can be targeted to the audience of interest, but public relations is not. As such, marketers should consider paying keen attention to areas such as website traffic and social media mentions or shares to determine who is seeing the press and what they are saying about it.

Knowledge Check

It's time to check your knowledge on the concepts presented in this section. Refer to the Answer Key at the end of the book for feedback.

1. After watching a TikTok, you learn that Thinx—a company that produces period underwear—has donated over $25,000 in period and other products to Afghan women who have recently fled their country. Because of this, you decide to purchase Thinx products. Which advantage of public relations has been achieved in this scenario?
   a. Increased sales and leads
   b. Lack of direct control
   c. Guaranteed results
   d. Direct control

2. Public relations has all the following advantages except ________.
   a. increased brand credibility
   b. increased brand image
   c. direct control
   d. increased sales and leads

3. When Story Land, a children's museum in New Hampshire, reopened, it utilized public relations. Numerous local television stations picked up and reported the story, providing free marketing to potential customers. The company bet on the positive virality of its press release, which worked in its favor. Which of the following disadvantages explains why Story Land "bet on the positive virality"?
   a. No direct control
   b. Increased brand recognition
   c. Increased sales
   d. Guarantee of results

4. Which of the following is a true statement concerning public relations?
   a. Public relations is more expensive than advertising.
   b. Public relations has more of a guarantee of positive results than other forms of promotion.
   c. Public relations has the most message control of the various forms of promotion.
   d. Public relations is free but has no guarantee of results.

5. When Taco Bell was hit with a lawsuit that claimed its seasoned beef was only 35 percent beef, the company utilized social media to show its ingredients, a campaign that was wildly successful. Which of the following was Taco Bell hoping for?
   a. Guaranteed results
   b. Improved brand image
   c. Direct control of the message
   d. Increase sales and leads

14.6 | Ethical Concerns in Advertising and Public Relations

Learning Outcomes

By the end of this section, you will be able to:
   LO 1 Illustrate ethical issues with respect to advertising.
   LO 2 Illustrate ethical issues with respect to public relations.

Ethical Issues Related to Advertising

Marketers must be keenly aware of not only the legal implications of advertising, but also the ethical ramifications. The Federal Trade Commission (FTC) has a number of laws that help to protect consumers against false claims in advertisements. The watchdog group Truth in Advertising is an independent, nonprofit organization that "empower[s] consumers to protect themselves and one another against false advertising and deceptive marketing."[24]

Truth in Advertising

Every year, Americans spend billions of dollars on health-related products, such as supplements, exercise programs, and nonprescription medication. Unfortunately, many of the advertisements claim that these—and many other—products will perform in a way that has not been proven. Not only can such claims be very harmful to individuals, but they can also get companies in big trouble.

In 2021, Subway was put in the spotlight by its own franchisees for its "Eat Fresh" slogan. The franchisees claimed that the slogan was misleading and that Subway's ingredients were often days or weeks old when they arrived at the stores and that the meat was laden with chemicals.[25]

Advertising to Children

Marketers must be keenly aware of how they advertise to children. Children are exposed to advertising just as often as adults. It is estimated that children view more than 40,000 commercials per year.[26] However, children and youth do not understand how to decipher those advertisements that are trying to get them to want something. For products that are harmful to, not meant for, or illegal to sell to children, marketers need to steer clear of advertising to children.

The vape company Juul found itself in hot water in 2019 when it was accused of marketing to teens. The company advertised its product—intended for adults only—on websites such as Nickelodeon, the Cartoon Network, and Seventeen, all sites directed toward youth.[27]

Advertising Harmful Products

When organizations run advertisements for potentially harmful products, they can be held legally liable for the claims and for any harm caused by the product. Even if the company is not held legally liable, the reputation of the business can be damaged.[28]

Have you ever noticed in a prescription drug commercial, there is considerable time spent on the side effects of the medication? Or that at the bottom of the screen there is a disclosure that the actor is not an actual patient? These are all required by the Federal Food, Drug, and Cosmetic Act (FFDCA), the Food and Drug Administration (FDA), and the FTC to adhere to truth in advertising expectations.

Ethical Issues Related to Public Relations

Similar to being truthful in advertising, marketers must also be aware of how they are disseminating information via public relations. Again, with the increase in social media and the Internet in general, it is much easier for consumers to find information regarding companies. In addition, it is much more commonplace for consumers to call out companies that are being unethical or dishonest. It is much easier for organizations to be honest and transparent up front than try to dig themselves out of a public relations nightmare.

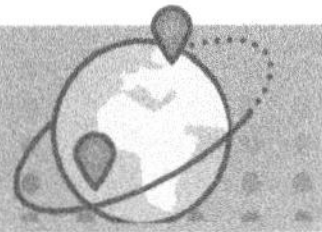

LINK TO LEARNING

IKEA

The start of the COVID-19 pandemic required the entire world to shift its perspective. This was true for marketers as well. Many companies changed their marketing strategies from selling goods and services to creating feelings of goodwill and solidarity. IKEA, the Swedish furniture manufacturer, was no exception. In a marketing campaign launched early in the pandemic, the company offered six ways to build a furniture fort, giving the public ways to cope with being quarantined. The campaign earned a nod in *AdWeek*'s most notable advertisements.[29] Read more about the campaign, and see the forts, here. (https://openstax.org/r/ikeafurnitureforts)

Transparency

An important part of managing public relations is to disseminate information to the public. It can be a very effective way of gaining loyalty and interest in the brand. The more transparent a company is to its target market, the more trust consumers have in the brand.

Whole Foods, known for offering natural foods, faced scrutiny over its mislabeling of genetically engineered foods. The company's top priority became that of transparency, and it requires every product sold as non-GMO to go through a verification process.[30]

Selective Truth Telling

Selective truth telling is a practice in which a person or organization tells a portion of the truth but omits other portions of the truth. Particularly in the face of scrutiny, marketers have always had to decide how much of the truth should be provided in order to satisfy the public but also protect the organization. In more recent years, many organizations have been increasingly telling the whole truth upfront, to avoid being called out later.

Verifying Facts and Information

Fact-checking in a process to verify facts on an issue. Marketers must do their best to present information that is valid to their target. This should be done before the information gets released to the public. In a society of "fake news," consumers are more skeptical than ever when it comes to information. Obviously, presenting information that is not factual will lead to decreased trust from the public.

COMPANIES WITH A CONSCIENCE

TOMS

In 2006, Blake Mycoskie founded TOMS shoes (see Figure 14.6), the name of which comes from the word "tomorrow." TOMS is committed to its One for One model: for every item purchased, an item is donated to those in need.[31] Since its inception, TOMS has also committed one-third of its profits to grassroots movements.[32]

Figure 14.6 TOMS is an example of a company that built a company, product, and mission focused on giving. (credit: "Spring" by molltiply/flickr, CC BY 2.0)

TOMS remains transparent, and the company's behavior is aligned with its values. In every advertising campaign launched, TOMS' philanthropic mission is consistently reinforced to the public. As a result, it's nearly impossible for anyone to think of TOMS as anything but aligned completely with its mission, whether one is visiting the company's website, viewing print media, or looking at the company's social media.[33]

Chapter Summary

In this chapter, we discuss the importance of advertising and public relations in the promotional mix. Major decisions that need to be made in order to successfully build a strong advertising campaign include establishing objectives, creating an advertising budget, developing a strategy, executing the campaign, assessing and evaluating the program, and post-testing the advertising. The use of metrics to measure the success provide key information to marketers and include brand recognition and/or awareness, ad views, conversion rates, and return on ad spend.

The advantages and disadvantages of public relations as it impacts the promotion mix were discussed, along with related ethical issues. The tools used to carry out public relations and publicity were explained.

Key Terms

advertising   paid communication messages that identify a brand or organization and are intended to reach a large number of recipients

aided recall   a type of advertising posttest that uses cues to assist a sample audience in recalling brands and products in an advertisement

all-you-can-afford approach   advertising budget approach that ensures everything else in the organization is budgeted for and then sets aside the remaining funds for advertising

attitude tests   a type of advertising posttest that investigates the attitudes of a sample target audience toward a product or service

brand awareness   metric used to determine if audiences can recall information about a brand

brand recognition   the ability of a campaign audience to recognize and identify a specific brand

comparative advertising   type of advertising that showcases the benefits and values of one product as compared to its competitors

competitive-parity approach   advertising budget strategy that relies on setting budgets based on the expected budgets of competitors

conversion rate   the percentage of an audience that has completed a desired action

engagement   any interaction with advertising content

frequency   how many times someone is exposed to an advertisement in a given time period or how many times an advertisement is shown in a time period

impact   how quickly members of the audience receive an advertising message

impressions   quantifying how many times an advertisement appears in a medium

informative advertising   a type of advertising intended to raise awareness of a product through educational communication to increase demand of the product

inquiry test   a type of advertising posttest that runs two or more similar ads on a limited scale and determines which of the ads are most recalled by and effective for respondents

institutional advertisements   advertisements intended to create a positive image or support for an entire organization

jury tests   a form of pretesting in which the respondents discuss the advertisements that are most likely to induce a purchase

key performance indicators (KPIs)   indicators (metrics) that measure how an advertising campaign is achieving certain goals or objectives

lobbying   networking and other efforts that have the intention of influencing public policy and law

objective-and-task approach   advertising budget strategy that is based on the objectives set previously for the advertising plan

percentage-of-sales approach   advertising budget strategy that utilizes prior years' sales or predicted year's sales and sets a percentage of those sales aside for advertising

persuasive advertising   a type of advertising that aims to highlight the benefits of a product or service being advertised

portfolio tests   a type of advertising pretest that consists of respondents browsing through various versions of an advertisement and then being asked to recall certain details from each

press relations   efforts to establish and maintain positive relationships with those in the media by sending press releases and other stories that help to maintain a positive image of the brand

pretesting advertising   research that predicts the performance of an advertisement before it airs

product advertisements   advertisements that promote a specific product within the organization's product mix

public affairs   efforts to influence public policy and engage with public officials and trade associations

public relations   any actions that help to create and maintain a favorable public image

publicity   notice or attention given by the media

pull strategy   advertising strategy intended to bring audiences to the product

push strategy   advertising strategy aimed at pushing the brand in front of an audience

reach   the estimated number of potential customers you can reach with an advertising campaign

reminder advertising   advertising aimed at bringing a product back into the forefront of the consumer's mind

return on ad spend (ROAS)   metric that measures the amount of revenue earned for every dollar spent on advertising

return-on-investment (ROI) approach   advertising budget strategy that focuses on every dollar spent on advertising; a return of that dollar—plus some—is expected

sales test   a type of posttest in advertising that determines how many sales will be made based on a test market

theater tests   a form of advertising pretest in which the audience is shown advertisements—usually television ads—in the context that they would be shown to the entire market

unaided recall   a type of advertising posttest that does not use any cues or prompts to test the recollection of the advertisement message

Applied Marketing Knowledge: Discussion Questions

1. List the objectives of advertising.

2. Explain the five approaches to creating a marketing budget.

3. List the tools used for public relations and explain how each of these are used.

4. List the tools used for publicity and explain how each is used.

Critical Thinking Exercises

1. Explain the key metrics used to measure the success of an advertising campaign.

2. List the advantages and disadvantages of public relations.

3. Provide examples of ethical issues related to advertising and include ways to avoid them.

4. Provide examples of ethical issues related to public relations and include the ways to avoid them.

Building Your Personal Brand

The act of building a personal brand requires a commitment that comes with having a well-developed and clear path. One of the many tools that a person can use to set and review their progress is the GOOD framework from Quantum Workplace (https://openstax.org/r/quantumworkplace). This framework can be used to set goals, identify obstacles and opportunities, and make decisions. As with any strategic goal-setting framework, the important thing to remember is that it should be used organically, allowing for the shifts that come with growth and development.

The framework includes the following parts:

- Goals: What goals are you setting? What needs to be done to achieve them?
- Obstacles: What is standing in your way? Can you work around or remove the obstacles?
- Opportunities: What can you pursue for learning and development to move you forward?
- Decisions: What decisions do you have to make to reach your goals? What will you do more of? What will you do less of?

This framework can be utilized on a personal and professional basis. The idea is to monitor and review throughout the year to determine whether you are on track, have the need to reassess, have achieved your goals, or need to create new ones.

 ## What Do Marketers Do?

Send a message to your college or university marketing department asking for a time to talk to the marketing manager about their job for your class. These positions vary greatly based on how many functions they outsource. Use the following questions as a guide to dig deeper into their process and responsibilities.

1. Please share with me your employment history and how you got to where you are today.
2. Can you summarize your job responsibilities?
3. Is the organizational structure of the company you work for private, nonprofit, or state?
4. Can you share with me what functions, if any, are outsourced (for example, website design, website maintenance, graphic design, or printing of materials)? How long have you been outsourcing these functions?
5. How many employees report to you, and what is person's role?
6. What challenges do you face with the structure you currently have in place?

Feel free to add any questions you might have. Thank them for their time. From this interview you should be able to gain more insight into how different areas of marketing are handled within a given organization's marketing department.

 ## Closing Company Case

Peloton

If you have ever taken a class at your local gym, you know the excitement of the camaraderie and competition that takes place when you are in a class of like-minded individuals all sharing the same goal and passion for performance. Former Barnes & Noble e-commerce executive John Foley liked riding his stationary bike but wanted to bring the gym class experience to his at-home riding sessions. And in 2012, the idea for Peloton was born.[34]

Hailed as "Netflix for Fitness," Peloton introduced its first bike in 2013. The company had slow and steady growth. With several rounds of funding, the start-up took off and began to take hold among consumers who enjoyed the rigorous workouts provided by trainers through the built-in bike video screens and subscription service to the various "rides."[35]

For Christmas 2019, Peloton debuted what turned out to be a significant ad for the young brand. Featuring a husband buying a Peloton for his wife, the ad took viewers through the mind and thoughts of the wife while she rode her bike and seemingly got more "in shape." Viewer outrage kicked up as some viewers believed the ad depicted a husband body-shaming his wife with the gift of exercise for the holidays. Check out the Peloton Christmas Commercial from 2019.

[Click to view content (https://openstax.org/books/principles-marketing/pages/14-closing-company-case)](https://openstax.org/books/principles-marketing/pages/14-closing-company-case)
While the ad may have sparked some controversy, it did one thing successfully—it got people talking about Peloton. The ads allowed the viewer to glimpse the life of a Peloton user—it showed the fun method of the

video courses, the use of the bike no matter what the weather outside, and the potential transformation of the Peloton user.

The other element of the ad's storyline is that it sparked a parody ad produced by Maximum Effort, a film production and digital marketing agency.[36] The agency was founded by the actor Ryan Reynolds, and the parody ad featured a voice-over by Reynolds himself. Although the ad was for Aviation Gin, a brand owned by Reynolds, the ad featured the "wife" from the Peloton Christmas ad. The parody ad did three things—kept people talking about Peloton, created a memorable story for Aviation Gin, and connected Reynolds and the Peloton brand.[37]

Click to view content (https://openstax.org/books/principles-marketing/pages/14-closing-company-case)

As Peloton began to take off in the United States, the country literally came to a screeching halt. In January 2020, the COVID-19 pandemic hit the country. Within months, citizens everywhere were quarantined, with gyms, restaurants, travel, businesses—everything—shut down. What started as 14 days to slow the spread turned into months. Remote work and learning became the norm, and people started to feel restless cooped up in their homes.

As the pandemic surged, so did Peloton. It picked up the fitness gauntlet, and in 2020, for the first quarter ever, the company turned a profit with a 172 percent increase in sales, stock up 220 percent, and over 1 million subscriptions. The new challenge for the organization was in the fulfillment of orders.

During the pandemic of 2019–2021, Peloton became a household name. It was the topic of discussion on the Fox News show *The Five*. Hosts Greg Gutfeld and Dana Perino regularly discussed the joy they got from using their Peloton bikes. Consumers everywhere were "riding out" the pandemic on a Peloton.

Even as sales surged and Peloton became a household name, it was being woven into the fabric of the American culture, such as on the '90s hit show *Sex and the City*. With the aging of the show's stars, the demographic of viewers was prime for a reboot. And so, in late 2021, the show's stars reprised their famous roles and *And Just Like That* debuted.

The show premiered on HBO to a record audience.

Per HBO Max, the *Sex and the City* revival starring Sarah Jessica Parker, Cynthia Nixon and Kristin Davis had a strong 24-hour performance that ranks as the most viewed series premiere of a new HBO or HBO Max series on the streaming service. Overall, the *AJLT* opener ranks in the Top 10 of all HBO Max's movies and series debuts, including both HBO and Max originals, trailing just some of the tentpole Warner Bros. movies that launched on the platform.[38]

> However, the huge debut marked a significant moment for Peloton. In the first episode, one of the major stars of the show, Mr. Big, dropped dead of a heart attack after a spin on his Peloton. Throughout the episode, the love affair Mr. Big has with his bike and his appreciation for the instructor provide the major plotline to the show. This led to the question, How would the character's death affect Peloton?

Product placement has always been a significant public relations initiative of consumer product companies. The *James Bond* franchise traditionally partners with well-known brands for placement in the movies and use by the popular cultural icon. The use of real products helps connect the consumer to the movie. It is usually a boon to the brand, and the movie benefits from the more realistic quality the product adds to the movie.

In the case of Peloton and Mr. Big, Peloton did not pay for the placement, but they did agree to the brand's use in the show. According to a spokesperson for the company, the plotline was a complete surprise.[39] So how does the show recover from "death by Peloton"?

Enter a new parody advertisement developed by Ryan Reynolds and Maximum Effort. When Reynolds created the ad for Aviation Gin that poked a little fun at Peloton and its "body-shaming" commercial, the actor became connected with the marketing arm of Peloton. It was time for a new parody. In this go-around, the focus would be on Peloton and Mr. Big. Actor Chris Noth, who played Mr. Big in the television show *Sex and the City* and the reboot *And Just Like That*, agreed to appear in the ad. Less than 48 hours after the show debut and the death of Mr. Big, Noth made an appearance in a Peloton ad, which shows him very much still alive. The big win all around is for Peloton and its significant increase in brand awareness.

The response from Peloton to the death of the main character Mr. Big on *And Just Like That* was to create an advertisement showing him very much alive—a clever approach and certainly an effort that gained Peloton brand recognition. Watch his death on the television show, and watch the commercial response here.

Click to view content (https://openstax.org/books/principles-marketing/pages/14-closing-company-case)
Click to view content (https://openstax.org/books/principles-marketing/pages/14-closing-company-case)

Case Questions

1. How did Peloton reach audiences with its message about the advantages of at-home exercise on its bike and corresponding trainer subscription services?

2. How was Peloton able to discern the effectiveness of its advertising when it debuted the 2019 commercial that was dubbed "body-shaming"?

3. What are some of the ways Peloton has generated brand awareness through publicity?

4. Peloton became the subject of the first episode of the show *And Just Like That*, a reboot of the hit show *Sex and the City*. What are the advantages and disadvantages to the product placement of Peloton in the show's premiere episode?

References

1. Leo Burnett (website), accessed July 7, 2022, https://leoburnett.com/.

2. Leo Burnett.

3. Andrew Long, "'Fancy a McDonald's?' Serves Up Life's Simple Pleasures: A Q&A with Andrew Long, Creative Director, Leo Burnett London," Leo Burnett, October 15, 2021, https://leoburnett.com/news/fancy-a-mcdonalds-serves-up-lifes-simple-pleasures-a-qa-with-andrew-long-creative-director-leo-burnett-london.

4. Leo Burnett.

5. Brian Steinberg, "NBC Seeks Record $6 Million for Super Bowl Commercials (Exclusive)," *Variety*, June 16, 2021, https://variety.com/2021/tv/news/super-bowl-commercials-price-record-1234998593/.

6. Roger Riddell, "Coke Fan's Halloween Response to Pepsi Ad Goes Viral," Food Dive, Industry Dive, November 4, 2013, https://www.fooddive.com/news/coke-fans-halloween-response-to-pepsi-ad-goes-viral/190208/.

7. "Anheuser-Busch Delivering More Than 5000,000 Bottles of Hand Sanitizer for COVID-19 Relief Efforts," Newsroom, Anheuser-Busch, updated May 29, 2020, https://www.anheuser-busch.com/newsroom/2020/04/anheuser-busch-delivering-hand-sanitizer-for-covid-19-relief-eff/.

8. Rebecca Riserbato, "The Beginner's Guide to Reminder Advertising," *The HubSpot Marketing Blog*, HubSpot, updated June 11, 2021, https://blog.hubspot.com/marketing/reminder-advertising.

9. "What Is an Advertising Message: Guide," Internet Marketing 101, SendPulse, updated August 22, 2022, https://sendpulse.com/support/glossary/advertising-message.

10. "About Nielsen," Nielsen Overview, https://www.nielsen.com/about-us/about/#:~:text=Nielsen%20is%20a%20global%20leader,trusted%20intelligence%20that%20fuels%20action.

11. "Conversion Rate of Online Shoppers in the United States from 4th Quarter 2020 to 4th Quarter 2021, by Device," Statista, accessed July 8, 2022, https://www.statista.com/statistics/234884/us-online-shopper-conversion-rate-by-device/.

12. Business Insider, "People Are Outraged by This Pepsi Ad Starring Kendall Jenner," April 5, 2017, YouTube video, 01:32, https://www.youtube.com/watch?v=_4CCkUVXHBQ.

13. "Stackla Survey Finds Authenticity Drives Brand Affinity and Consumer-Created Content Influences Purchases," *Nosto Newsroom* (blog), Nosto, November 9, 2017, https://stackla.com/resources/reports/the-consumer-content-report-influence-in-the-digital-age/.

14. Wikipedia, s.v. "Tilikum (orca)," last modified July 20, 23:09, https://en.wikipedia.org/wiki/Tilikum_(orca).

15. "7 Companies Hurt by Bad Publicity," MarketWatch, August 18, 2014, https://www.marketwatch.com/story/7-companies-hurt-by-bad-publicity-2014-08-18.

16. "Three Examples of Successful Public Affairs Strategy," Quorum, last modified August 2, 2022, https://www.quorum.us/blog/examples-successful-public-affairs-strategy/.

17. Jake Frankenfield, "Which Industry Spends the Most on Lobbying?," Investopedia, Dotdash Meredith, updated June 02, 2022, https://www.investopedia.com/investing/which-industry-spends-most-lobbying-antm-so/.

18. "Top Lobbying Spenders in the United States in 2020," Statista, accessed June 17, 2022, https://www.statista.com/statistics/257344/top-lobbying-spenders-in-the-us/.

19. "Susan G. Komen Names Kroger Central Division Outstanding Volunteer Group of the Year," Susan G. Komen Central Indiana, Susan G. Komen, July 28, 2016, https://komencentralindiana.org/wp-content/uploads/2013/09/2016-Kroger-national-award-PR-final.pdf.

20. Alyssa Hardt, "Campfire Treats Embraces the Better Chicken Commitment," Petfood Industry, WATT Global Media, December 1, 2021, https://www.petfoodindustry.com/articles/10847-campfire-treats-adopts-the-better-chicken-commitment.

21. "Campfire Treats Adopts the Better Chicken Commitment to Raise the Bar for Farm Animal Welfare," Pets+, November 19, 2021, https://petsplusmag.com/campfire-treats-adopts-the-better-chicken-commitment-to-raise-the-bar-for-farm-animal-welfare/.

22. "Understanding the Impact of the Ice Bucket Challenge on the ALS Association's Finances," The ALS Association, June 5, 2019, https://www.als.org/blog/understanding-impact-ice-bucket-challenge-als-associations-finances.

23. "Pros and Cons of Public Relations," The Lonely Entrepreneur, October 30, 2017, https://lonelyentrepreneur.com/entrepreneur-public-relations-2/.

24. "About," Truth in Advertising, last modified February 28, 2022, https://truthinadvertising.org/about/.

25. Mura Dominko, "Subway's 'Eat Fresh' Slogan Is Alarmingly Misleading, Operators Say," Eat This, Not That!, Galvanized Media, April 27, 2021, https://www.eatthis.com/news-subway-eat-fresh-slogan-alarmingly-misleading/.

26. Brian L. Wilcox et al., *Report of the APA Task Force on Advertising and Children* (American Psychological Association, February 20, 2004), https://www.apa.org/pubs/reports/advertising-children.

27. Julia Belluz, "The Vape Company Juul Said It Doesn't Target Teens. Its Early Ads Tell a Different Story," Vox, January 25, 2019, https://www.vox.com/2019/1/25/18194953/vape-juul-e-cigarette-marketing.

28. Scott Thompson, "The Advertisement of Harmful Products," Small Business, Chron.com, last modified October 26, 2016, https://smallbusiness.chron.com/advertisement-harmful-products-65363.html.

29. Sara Spary, "Ikea's Quarantine Campaign Offers 6 Ways to Make Furniture Forts," *Adweek*, May 13, 2020, https://www.adweek.com/brand-marketing/ikeas-quarantine-campaign-offers-6-ways-to-make-furniture-forts/.

30. Jonha Richman, "5 Examples of Companies Succeeding through Transparency," *Entrepreneur*, May 27, 2016, https://www.entrepreneur.com/article/274636.

31. Blake Mycoskie, "Trendsetter: TOMS Founder Blake Mycoskie on Starting a Movement," interview by Katie Morell, October 5, 2011, https://www.americanexpress.com/en-us/business/trends-and-insights/articles/trendsetter-toms-founder-blake-mycoskie-on-starting-a-movement/.

32. "Wear Good," TOMS, accessed July 8, 2022, https://www.toms.com/us/impact.html.

33. Dan Shewan, "Ethical Marketing: 5 Examples of Companies with a Conscience," *The WordStream Blog*, WordStream, updated May 20, 2022, https://www.wordstream.com/blog/ws/2017/09/20/ethical-marketing.

34. Jordan Valinsky, "Peloton Sales Surge 172% as Pandemic Bolsters Home Fitness Industry," CNN Business, Cable News Network, September 11, 2020, https://www.cnn.com/2020/09/11/business/peloton-stock-earnings/index.html.

35. Valinsky, "Peloton Sales Surge."

36. David Griner, "Ryan Reynolds on How His Peloton Ad Collaboration Came Together in 48 Hours," *Adweek*, December 13, 2021, https://www.adweek.com/convergent-tv/ryan-reynolds-on-how-his-peloton-ad-collaboration-came-together-in-48-hours/.

37. David Griner, "How Ryan Reynolds Pulled Off Aviation Gin's Peloton Parody, Capping His Year of Genius Ads," *Adweek*, December 13, 2019, https://www.adweek.com/creativity/how-ryan-reynolds-pulled-off-aviation-gins-peloton-parody-capping-his-year-of-genius-ads/.

38. Joseph Pisani and Megan Graham, "Peloton: Don't Blame Us for What Happened in 'And Just Like That . . .' (Spoilers Ahead)," *Wall Street Journal*, December 10, 2021, https://www.wsj.com/articles/peloton-dont-blame-us-for-what-happened-in-and-just-like-that-spoilers-ahead-11639097331.

39. Alexandra Del Rosario and Nellie Andreeva, "'And Just Like That . . .' Delivers HBO Max's Strongest Series Debut; 'The Sex Lives of

College Girls' Peaks in Viewers with Finale," *Deadline*, December 10, 2021, https://deadline.com/2021/12/and-just-like-that-hbo-max-strongest-series-debut-the-sex-lives-of-college-girls-peaks-viewers-finale-1234889116/.

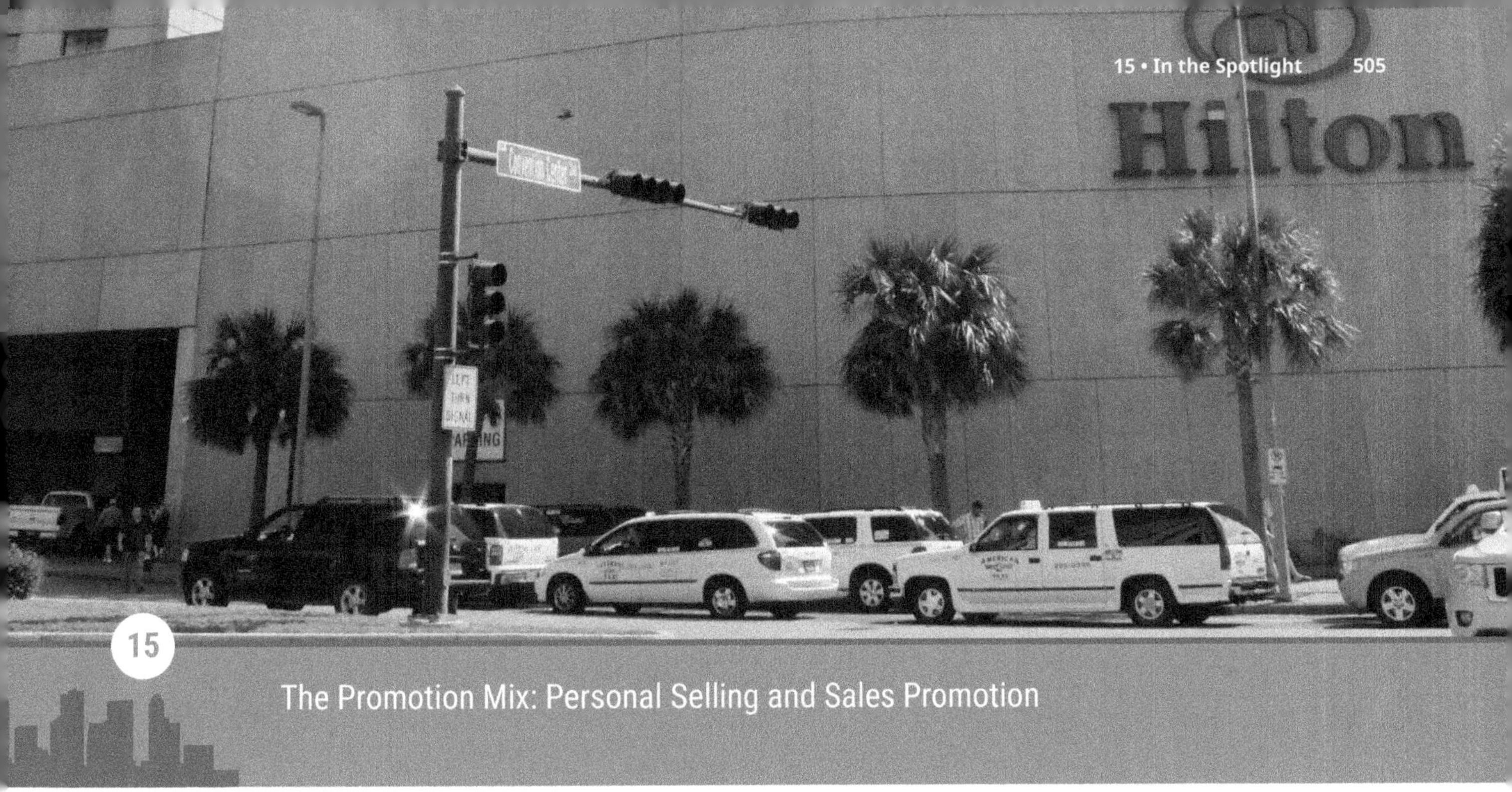

15 The Promotion Mix: Personal Selling and Sales Promotion

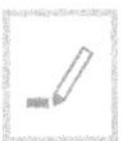

Figure 15.1 Hilton Hotel utilizes a personal selling process with its HGV product. (credit: modification of work "Hilton Hotel @ Riverwalk Shopping Mall" by Thank You (22.5 Millions+) views/flickr, CC BY 2.0)

Chapter Outline

In the Spotlight

Since 1919, when Conrad Hilton bought his first hotel, Hilton Hotels and Resorts has been providing a good night's sleep to travelers around the world. With over 6,800 hotels within its portfolio (including several sub-brands), Hilton has a hotel to meet the needs of just about any traveler. Hampton Inn is a beloved brand for road-weary business travelers as well as families. The Conrad is one of the luxury brands for Hilton. And DoubleTree is another favorite brand for business travelers, known for the gooey, warm chocolate chip cookies presented at check-in. To reward travelers, Hilton offers several tiers of Hilton rewards: Silver, Gold, and Diamond. Reward members are able to trade their points for various perks, including free nights. During off-peak travel, Hilton offers a variety of sales promotions; for example, one program it offers is 3X points on every stay for three nights or more.

Consumers who travel often are able to increase their points through certain purchases and promotions that Hilton will offer to spur more travel. Hilton also connects with customers through Hilton Grand Vacations (HGV). HGV is a time-share within the Hilton portfolio of properties and rooms. When customers join HGV, they are buying ownership in the exclusive club properties.

To increase the sale of the HGV properties, Hilton runs promotions to sign Hilton customers for a tour of a new property and a presentation about the benefits of ownership. In exchange for participating in a tour of HGV properties, customers are offered incentives, such as three nights and four days of a Hilton hotel stay for a discounted price. In exchange for the discounted rooms, customers agree to a tour and to sit through a sales presentation.

HGV sales professionals are typically real estate agents who understand how to structure vacation rental properties and time-share sales. Every sales professional selling the HGV properties is well-versed in the cost of vacations, how to structure real estate deals, and the benefits of being a member of HGV. Once a customer agrees to the tour and the sales presentation, the sales representative is tasked with making sure the decision makers are present, and when possible, the goal is to have customers make their decision before the tour is over. These strategies have been very effective at generating continuous streams of income from HGV members.

15.1   Personal Selling and Its Role in the Promotion Mix

Learning Outcomes

By the end of this section, you will be able to:
  - **LO** 1 Define personal selling.
  - **LO** 2 Discuss the role of personal selling in the promotion mix.

Personal Selling Defined

Personal selling is the one-on-one interaction between a company representative (salesperson) and the buyer (customer or prospect). The interaction is intended for the salesperson to uncover the needs and wants of the prospect and discuss how the product or service will help to satisfy the customer's needs and wants. The salesperson works to develop a relationship with the prospect with the intention of having them buy the company's product and become a customer.

The Role of Personal Selling in the Promotion Mix

The promotion mix includes the marketer's tactics for communicating with consumers. Determining how to use the promotion mix is dependent on the goals and objectives of the overall marketing strategy as well as the nature of the product, the market segments being targeted, and the message the marketer wishes to send.

Generally, marketers will use a combination of the promotion mix tactics to create an integrated approach to connecting with customers. Out of all the promotion mix strategies, personal selling is the strategy that connects directly with the customer in a one-on-one setting and focuses on building relationships. Personal selling is ideal if the product is more complex in nature, higher in price, and customizable according to a customer's needs.

Relationship Selling

Relationship selling is a method of personal selling used to better understand the needs and wants of the buyer. If the product is relatively high in price and has some customizable attributes, the salesperson will strive to become a trusted advisor to the customer. This allows the salesperson to develop a relationship that will create trust and ultimately fit the best product with the customer to fulfill their needs and wants and solve a problem they are having that put them in the market for the product. TalEx, a fast-growing human resource company, works with its clients to find the right talent for open positions at a variety of companies. Sales representatives for TalEx work as trusted advisors to collaborate with clients to help find the right staffing solutions for growing companies.

When to Use Personal Selling

Personal selling is best utilized as a promotional strategy when the products are higher in price, variable in nature, and require some explanation or education. Hilton Grand Vacations (HGV) employs real estate agents to sell club memberships. Due to the variety of membership purchase levels, the explanation and education of how to use the membership, and the higher price of the time-share vacations, the sales force spends time educating clients about the product. Typically, personal selling is used for products that are also in the introductory stage of the product life cycle and for products that require significant follow-up after the sale. Business-to-business (B2B) strategies are largely reliant on personal selling as a primary promotional strategy.

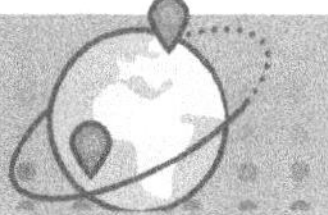

LINK TO LEARNING

Personal Selling

Watch this video to learn more about personal selling. Learn when personal selling is most relevant, the cons, and what types of products it is most suited for.

Click to view content (https://openstax.org/books/principles-marketing/pages/15-1-personal-selling-and-its-role-in-the-promotion-mix)

Watch this personal selling role-play to gain insight into a sales call situation, and read this guide for the advantages, the disadvantages, the process, the strategies, and examples of personal selling (https://openstax.org/r/salespersonalselling).

Click to view content (https://openstax.org/books/principles-marketing/pages/15-1-personal-selling-and-its-role-in-the-promotion-mix)

Knowledge Check

It's time to check your knowledge on the concepts presented in this section. Refer to the Answer Key at the end of the book for feedback.

1. Companies typically use personal selling as the promotional strategy of choice when which of these is true?
   a. The product is higher in price.
   b. The product requires the sales professional to spend significant time educating the customer.
   c. The product has a lot of variation.
   d. All of these statements are true.

2. Personal selling is ________.
   a. unpaid advertising to consumers
   b. a method of increasing sales in the short term
   c. one-on-one interaction between a sales professional and a potential buyer/customer
   d. used for handling routine purchases

3. If a company has a higher-priced product that requires some variation according to the customer's needs and wants, which method of promotion is best?
   a. Direct marketing
   b. Personal selling
   c. Advertising
   d. Public relations

4. Which of the following is NOT a reason for personal selling to be used?
   a. When the product is complicated
   b. When the product has a lot of competition
   c. When the product needs to be demonstrated

d.   When the product is highly technical

5.   Jasmine works for a Honda dealership. Jasmine has spent considerable time listening to a potential customer talk about what features they are looking for in a new car. Jasmine is able to identify the best Honda automobile to meet the needs of the customer. What feature of sales is Jasmine demonstrating?
    a.   One-on-one interaction
    b.   Meeting the needs and wants
    c.   Personal communication
    d.   All of these features are correct.

15.2 Classifications of Salespeople Involved in Personal Selling

Learning Outcomes

By the end of this section, you will be able to:
    LO 1 List the various roles involved in personal selling.
    LO 2 Describe the differences between the various personal selling roles.

Order Takers

Within the role of personal selling, there are various types of selling functions. Many organizations utilize more than one type of personal selling. Various sales personnel within an organization may fulfill several of the roles. The type of personal selling is dependent on the nature of the product as well as the customer.

In many sales situations, the salesperson is responsible for prospecting to find new customers as well as working to match the right products with the customer needs and wants. However, some organizations have sales personnel that are only responsible for taking orders from customers, called **order takers**. They work to identify the customer and find the right product fit. Within the role of the order taker, there are typically two different types of order takers, inside and outside.

Inside Order Takers

An **inside order taker** is the person who talks with a customer when they walk into the business to place an order, or they are the one who is answering the phone, responding to an online inquiry, or responding to an email to accept customer orders as they are placed. Often the inside order taker may have to answer questions or discuss details of the product order. Their role is to serve as the liaison between the customer and the company. They make sure the right product is ordered according to the requests of the customers.

Restaurants typically replenish inventory on a weekly basis. When a sandwich shop calls its supplier to order more paper products and cleaning supplies, it calls the inside order taker. For some businesses, the inside order taker may be referred to as an inbound customer service agent. In this case, the inside order taker will make sure they have the order submitted correctly and will typically communicate about any out-of-stock products or any variation of the typical order.

Another type of inside order taker is in the business-to-consumer (B2C) market, where a consumer will shop at a store and pick a product. An example of this would be the cashier at Walmart or other retail outlet. When the consumer is ready to pay for the product, and if they choose to check out with a cashier rather than the self-checkout option, they are checking out with the inside order taker. In the role of inside order taker, the cashier carefully scans each of the products and completes the sale. For online retailers, the inside order taker is the one making sure the products ordered from the online shopper are in stock and available for fulfillment. They may contact the customer if the product is unavailable or if there are questions about the order.

Outside Order Takers

Outside order takers work with customers who routinely buy products, and their role is to take in and process those orders. The outside order taker is not required to persuade a customer to purchase, but rather they are a resource for the customer in fulfilling orders. In addition, they are a resource to their customer and may offer insight and advice on inventory patterns and expected delivery times.

Your neighborhood hair salon is a good example of a business that relies on an outside order taker. Hair salons typically have both a supply of the products they use on their customers and a supply of products they sell to their customers for home use. The beauty products sales force consists of multiple sales roles. However, the outside order taker routinely checks in with the salon owner and will fill out the order sheets to replenish product stock that is low.

Order Getters

The role of the **order getter** is critically important to the revenue of many businesses. The order getter is responsible for finding customers and persuading them to purchase. They might also be responsible for increasing orders from current customers. The order getter is typically well versed in their products and has superior knowledge about the industry. Additionally, successful order getters are often viewed as a trusted advisor by the customers they serve. Many businesses rely heavily on the order getter to work with them to solve their problems through the products they represent.

The order getter must be able to listen to the customer and respond with solutions that will be mutually beneficial to both companies. In the role of the order getter, it is not uncommon to work with a customer for a year or more before ever making a sale. iSalus is a perfect example of this. In an effort to get the company's cutting-edge patient engagement software into health systems, the sales force must identify the decision makers within the health system as well as work with those who will be using the software. Educating and engaging with a variety of teams within the health system, as well as waiting on budget approvals, can take anywhere from 6 to 18 months. Laying the foundation can be a lengthy process but can be very rewarding when everything comes together and the sale is made.

Support Personnel

A typical sales force includes various **support personnel** that help facilitate the sales process. Support personnel can take on many functions in the process of making the sale, including marketing, prospecting, setting appointments, educating customers, building goodwill, checking inventory and order status, as well as providing service after the sale. There are two primary types of support personnel utilized in the sales process: missionary salespeople and technical specialists.

Missionary Salespeople

Missionary salespeople are often employed by manufacturing firms to represent the company and call on retailers in an effort to inform or persuade them to buy the firm's products. In some cases, they may also be referred to as a detailer. It is the job of the missionary salesperson to inform customers about new products and promotional specials and to encourage new orders and reorders. Missionary salespeople are most common with manufacturing, pharmaceutical, and software companies. A salesperson for McKesson Corporation's pharmaceutical products will work with physicians in their territory. Typically, they meet with the physicians, provide education on new products, leave samples, and connect with the physician's practice on a regular basis to keep the company's products in use.

Technical Specialists

A **technical specialist** serves as an assistant to a firm's existing customers. Their role is to advise on many aspects of the product, such as technical specifications, application, design, and installation. As the name implies, this job is highly technical and often requires formal training. Many people in the role of the technical specialist have backgrounds in science or engineering. The types of products and the applications for the products determine the need for and training of the technical specialist.

Team Selling

Many of today's customers and products are complex. The more expensive and high-tech the product, the more important it is to have a team of people to assist the client in making sure the product meets their needs and wants. Team selling is a sales approach that can improve the likelihood of a good experience that meets or exceeds the customer's expectations. **Team selling** involves the lead salesperson bringing in other functional support people from within the organization. Other functions that are often involved include finance, engineering, and accounting. These various functions can assist with the skills and knowledge to address specific customer problems or issues and work through objections or special circumstances that may be required to make the sale. Bringing extra skills and knowledge to the situation can make for a better product fit and a good outcome whereby the client sees the company and products as invaluable.

CAREERS IN MARKETING

Personal Selling

Personal selling is a technique used by sales professionals to make a connection and possible sale with customers. There are several techniques and tips for personal selling, and you can read about them in this Indeed article (https://openstax.org/r/careerdevelopmentpersonalselling).

There are many types of sales jobs. If a career in sales interests you, spend time learning about the different kinds of sales jobs and how they differ. Start by reading this article to learn about the things to consider (https://openstax.org/r/typesofsalesjobs) in a sales job, types of sales job titles, and job types. Read this article from Indeed about all the various (https://openstax.org/r/findingajob) types of sales jobs to explore.

There is a lot to explore when learning about sales jobs. Check out these resources to learn more:

- Indeed: "10 Sales Skills Reps Should Have (https://openstax.org/r/salesskillsforreps)"
- ResumeGenius: "Top 12 Sales Skills for Your Resume + Examples (https://openstax.org/r/resumehelp)"
- Brainshark: "17 Sales Skills All Reps Need (https://openstax.org/r/keysalesskills)"
- LiveAbout: "Important Sales Skills That Employers Value (https://openstax.org/r/salesskillslist)"
- HubSpot: "How to Understand & Thrive in Digital Sales" (https://openstax.org/r/salesdigitalsales)
- HubSpot: "The Best Sales Job Boards for Finding or Filling a Sales Job (https://openstax.org/r/searchforsalesjobs)"

A career in sales can be fast-paced, exhilarating, and competitive. If sales interests you, be sure to do your homework so that you're sure to find a position and industry you're passionate about.

Knowledge Check

It's time to check your knowledge on the concepts presented in this section. Refer to the Answer Key at the end of the book for feedback.

1. The practice of using call centers, where employees receive calls from customers and provide service by taking orders and answering queries, is called ________.
   a. customer response marketing
   b. guerilla marketing
   c. reactive marketing
   d. inside order taking

2. The management of Javier's Bicycles has an approach where the call center makes appointments and the

sales professionals go out to meet with the potential customers and discuss the various products available. This is an example of _______.
   a. inside order takers
   b. team selling
   c. technical specialists
   d. internal marketing

3. Special-Lite makes industrial doors for many commercial applications. Once the sales professional meets with the customer to discuss the products they wish to buy, the sale moves into production, and a special person within the company is assigned to make sure the doors meet the requirements specified in the blueprints. This person is a(n) _______.
   a. order getter
   b. order taker
   c. technical specialist
   d. telemarketer

4. Pfizer uses sales professionals to visit with physician offices and inform the physicians of the new medications and the uses for the medications and to encourage them to prescribe the new medications to their patients. This form of sales professional is often called _______?
   a. technical specialist
   b. order taker
   c. order getter
   d. missionary sales

5. 84 Lumber has personnel who work to set appointments and check inventory levels. What type of person does this for the sales force?
   a. Support personnel
   b. Missionary sales
   c. Technical specialist
   d. Order getter

15.3 | Steps in the Personal Selling Process

Learning Outcomes

By the end of this section, you will be able to:
   LO 1 List the steps in the personal selling process.
   LO 2 Describe each step in the personal selling process.

Step 1: Prospecting and Qualifying

The **selling process** is a seven-step process (see Figure 15.2) used for selling a product. The process can be multifaceted, lengthy, and complex, depending on the product and the prospect. While all salespeople are different, generally most sales professionals go through the same selling process.

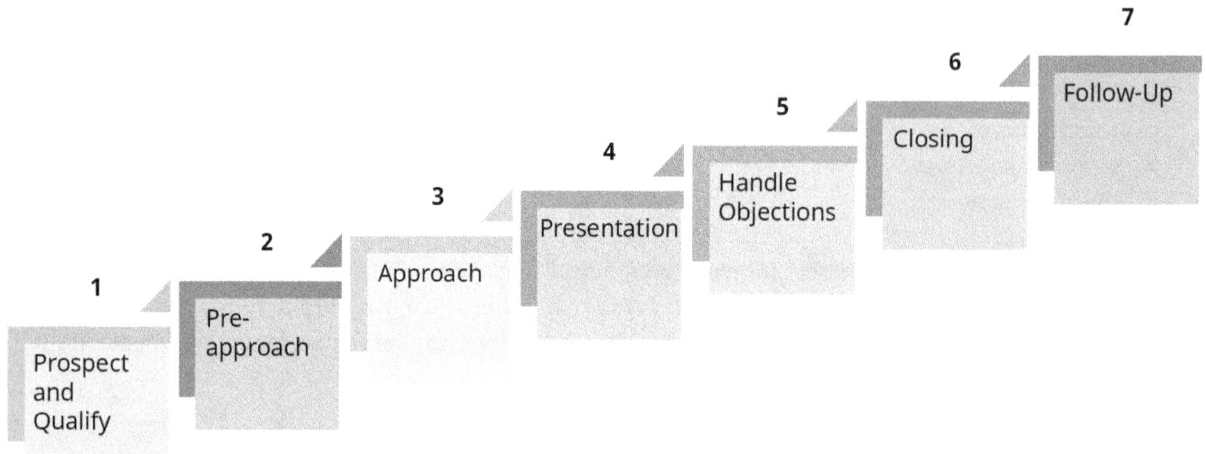

Figure 15.2 Steps in the Selling Process (attribution: Copyright Rice University, OpenStax, under CC BY 4.0 license)

The first step in the sales process is to find, or **prospect** for, strong potential customers. In prospecting, sales professionals will work to create and develop a database of potential customers, called **sales leads** through lead generation. Getting the names and contact information for the database is the act of prospecting. Each business or company has its own methods of prospecting and qualifying. For some companies, the process is rigorous and lengthy; for others, it can be nothing more than a quick phone conversation.

There are many methods of lead generation. Utilizing digital strategies is one example. Many companies may prospect leads through a digital advertising campaign that triggers potential customers to sign up for information about a product. Other forms of prospecting can include meeting potential customers at trade shows, use of a referral program, or purchasing a list of customers from a third-party company that meets the criteria for the target market.

Once the sales professional has a database of leads, the next step is **qualification** of those leads. Not all names in a database may be the right candidates for a company's products. There are many reasons why a candidate may not be a good fit for a company's products. For example, some leads may have recently purchased a competitor's product, and others may not be in a financial position to afford the product. The sales professional wants to reduce the list to include only the leads who are a good fit and are more likely to be receptive to purchasing the company's products. Qualification may also include making sure the contact has the authority to make the purchasing decision.

You might be asking yourself how a salesperson or company tracks these leads and keeps all the various communication touch points organized. They typically have two software tools to help them: **sales force automation** (SFA) and **customer relationship management** (CRM) software. SFAs are used to acquire a customer, and CRMs are used to retain and manage customers after the sale.[1]

According to Salesforce, a company known for one of the most popular CRMs on the market, CRM software "is a technology for managing all your company's relationships and interactions with customers and potential customers. The goal is simple: Improve business relationships to grow your business."[2]

LINK TO LEARNING

Difference between CRMs and SFA

Check out this short article from SelectHub (https://openstax.org/r/sfavscrm) that outlines in more detail the difference between CRMs and SFAs.

Step 2: Pre-approach

The **pre-approach stage** can best be described as a thorough analysis or research of the potential candidate. It is in the pre-approach stage that the sales professional will conduct a very detailed study of the prospect, which will often include information about specific product needs, what current brands they might be using, brand awareness, who the decision makers are, and general knowledge of personal interests and financial standing. The research findings are meant to help the sales professional to find out needs and wants as well as the best way to approach the prospect for the sales presentation.

Some of the research that sales professionals seek to review as part of their investigation may include interviews with other clients, financial reports, credit histories, and any sources of public information. Most companies with a sales force and sales process will use robust customer relationship management (CRM) databases to collect, filter, and track prospects through the stages of the sales process. Information that is uncovered during the pre-approach will be added to prospect records in the CRM system.

Step 3: Approach

Information gathered in the pre-approach helps the sales professional during the **approach** phase. Utilizing the insights they have gathered about the prospect, the sales professional seeks to contact the prospect to build rapport and gather more information on the needs and wants of the prospect. During this phase, it is very important for the sales professional to create a positive impression, ask the right questions, and begin building a relationship with the prospect.

A soft approach is generally the best strategy, as the goal is to build the relationship and not necessarily push product. Hard-sell tactics are often rebuffed during this early contact with the prospect. Ideally the role of the salesperson in this early stage is to ask questions and listen. It is through listening intently to the prospect that the salesperson can detect the fit for the product and ultimately the best way to sell the product. Information gathered during the approach will often be used in the presentation stage.

Step 4: Presentation

Once the prospect has made it through the approach stage, the sales professional is ready to present the product to the prospect. During the **presentation** stage, the goal is to showcase the features about the product that will be of most benefit to the prospect based on the needs uncovered during the pre-approach and approach stages. Often the presentation may include education on the aspects of the product that the prospect will find most beneficial to solve their problems. This is the time for the sales professional to highlight the benefits of the product and answer questions the prospect might have. For example, college admissions departments work with students to showcase the best of the university in an attempt to persuade them to enroll. Part of the presentation process includes tours of the campus, meetings with current students, attending classes, and experiencing campus life.

The best sales professionals are good listeners. Good listening strategies work to build rapport and create winning strategies. When you listen carefully to your prospects, they will tell you exactly how to sell to them. Using information provided by the prospect, a good sales professional will be able to turn it into a winning sale. Several methods of sale presentation include a stimulus-response format, formula selling, a need/satisfaction format, adaptive selling, and consultative selling.

Stimulus-Response Format

When a salesperson has done the research and they understand many of the issues that might be presented by the customer, they are able to provide a stimulus, and the customer provides a response. The skilled salesperson is able to counter every response with a new stimulus. The goal is to sell based on the response from the customer. To be effective, the salesperson must follow a script, which has been developed based on the pre-identified needs and wants of the customer.

Formula Selling Format

Advertising has typically been dependent on the customer going through a specific set of actions before responding. One of the most common consumer response models is the **AIDA model**, which encompasses attention, interest, desire, and action. Marketers often look to the AIDA model when putting together advertising campaigns. The AIDA model is also used for **formula selling**. The goal is for the salesperson to take the customer through the various stages of response until they get to the purchase of the product. The skilled sales professional will make sure they are providing stimuli and responses for each of the stages of AIDA.

Need/Satisfaction Format

The **need/satisfaction format** of selling is an approach where the sales professional opens the sales presentation by probing the potential customer with questions in an effort to uncover their needs. The sales presentation is then tailored to the customer by showing how the product/service will satisfy the customer needs.

For example, the owner of a busy café may be met with a question about scheduling from a salesperson who sells scheduling software. The salesperson may start with a question such as "This café is so busy; is it difficult to schedule your staff?" Once the café owner talks about the challenges of scheduling, the salesperson now has information they need to custom tailor the sales presentation about scheduling software to the specific needs identified by the café owner.

Adaptive Selling

Adaptive selling is one of the most customer-centric sales methods available to the sales professional. Using the **adaptive selling** approach requires the sales professional to adapt their selling strategy and even the product to meet the needs and solve the problems of the customer. To fully utilize this approach requires that the sales professional rapidly customize their approach to meet the needs of different customers. Many sales professionals are taking advantage of the big data that is now readily available to better target customers. Armed with data about what is going on in the market, the salesperson can now adapt their presentation with real time information.

Consultative Selling

Perhaps this method was best exemplified in the movie *Miracle on 34th Street.* In the movie, the Macy's Santa Claus suggests a location, other than Macy's, where a mother can get a toy for her son. **Consultative selling** makes the sales professional a consultant who develops a relationship with the customer and takes on an advisory role to help the customer solve their problems. Generally, the problem will get solved through purchase of the product, but it can also be solved in various other ways. The sales professional becomes the anchor to helping the potential customer solve their problems.

Step 5: Handling Objections

Preparation during the qualification, pre-approach, and approach stages of the sale process, provide the sales professional with the information they will need to handle objections. In many situations, seasoned sales professionals are able to successfully present the product and answer questions without having objections. Good research on the customer and an understanding of how the product will help them and solve their problems allow the sales professional to avoid objections. However, when the customer does present an objection, the skilled sales professional will need to be agile at handling them.

Typically, strategies for handling objections include listening, restating the question, and responding with additional questions. Price is generally always voiced as an objection. Knowing the common objections and having a strategy to handle them prior to the presentation will help advance to the close stage.

Step 6: Closing

Asking for the order is perhaps the hardest step in the sales process for many sales professionals. Up to the point of the close, the sales professional has spent a tremendous amount of time and energy with the prospect. Much of the work of the sales professional has been around building a relationship with the prospect. Asking for the order is a source of tremendous fear for many sales professionals because this is the point where all of their work could unravel. What if the customer says no? Then what?

Many sales professionals fear the possibility of rejection. They also consider that they may get the timing wrong. However, if the sales professional has prepared, they know that asking for the order is the point where they make the prospect a customer. One way to eliminate the guesswork of timing is to do a trial close by talking about things such as financial terms or delivery of the product. The customer's response to the trial close questions will alert the sales professional to the prospect's readiness to purchase.

Step 7: Follow-Up

After the order is placed, the real work begins. Upon closing a sale and signing the prospect as a customer, the sales professional is now tasked with onboarding the customer and ensuring that everything progresses smoothly with the sale of the product. Because it is much more lucrative for a company to keep current customers happy than to go out and prospect for new customers, the follow-up is a major step in creating lifetime customer value (LCV). Most salespeople would rather maintain their current clients than search for new clients. The follow-up after the sale is a critical step in getting repeat business, customer referrals, and upsells during the next order cycle.

Knowledge Check

It's time to check your knowledge on the concepts presented in this section. Refer to the Answer Key at the end of the book for feedback.

1. Lucia works for ABC Home Centers. The company sells roofing and windows to customers looking to make home improvements. Lucia's main job with the company is to identify people who might be in the market for home improvement products. As part of Lucia's job, she calls people to see if they would be interested in finding out more about ABC's products. What stage of the sales process is Lucia doing?
   a. Closing
   b. Handling objections
   c. Presentation
   d. Prospecting and qualifying

2. Tony likes everything about the products from Supreme Restaurant Equipment. He is just about ready to purchase, but he has some questions about the payment methods and financing. At what stage of the selling process does the sales professional deal with Tony's questions?
   a. Handling objections
   b. Closing
   c. Pre-approach
   d. Qualifying

3. Shakira has been working with a customer for quite some time. She has a good rapport with the customer, and the customer often asks her a lot of questions regarding other matters in the industry. When Shakira is ready to work with the customer for an order, she talks with them about the pros and cons as well as other companies' products that might be a good fit. What type of selling approach is Shakira using?
   a. Adaptive
   b. Hard sell
   c. Stimulus-response

    d. Consultative

4. "Besides you, are there other decision makers that buy apparel?" This is a question that you might ask during what stage of the sales call?
   a. Pre-approach
   b. Close
   c. Approach
   d. Handling objections

5. Keith is with his prospect, and he is out on a test drive for the new Ford F-150. He is telling the prospect about the safety features of the truck. What stage of the selling process is Keith in?
   a. Approach
   b. Close
   c. Presentation
   d. Handling objections

15.4 | Management of the Sales Force

Learning Outcomes

By the end of this section, you will be able to:

- **LO** 1 Identify the issues involved in managing a sales force.
- **LO** 2 List the various ways a sales force can be structured.
- **LO** 3 Describe the tasks involved in sales force recruitment and selection.
- **LO** 4 Discuss key metrics that can be used to assess sales performance.
- **LO** 5 Describe the tasks involved in supervising and evaluating a sales force.
- **LO** 6 Summarize the metrics that can be used for sales force performance evaluation.

Issues Involved in Managing a Sales Force

A sales force can be the lifeblood of an organization's revenue cycle, so it's important that they are incentivized to produce new clients, maintain current clients, and generate revenue for the organization. Proper management of the sales force includes setting goals, motivating, incentivizing, supporting, and monitoring.

Typical issues specific to sales include motivating and challenging the sales force. A sales force is always under pressure to meet sales targets, often linked to revenue goals, so a manger needs to constantly be working with their sales team to keep them motivated and hit the targets.

Finding the right person for the job is an important role for a sales manager. Sales managers often look for recent college graduates to fill sales positions. In addition, sales managers may look for someone already experienced in sales and then train them for the specific industry and products. Whatever set of skills a company might be looking for, finding the right mix of professionals can be challenging.

Sales Force Management Defined

Sales force management includes a very wide range of responsibilities. There are many tasks involved in sales force management, including the process of hiring, training, and motivating sales staff, as well as coordinating activities and implementing a sales strategy designed to increase sales revenue.

Setting Sales Force Objectives

For the sales force to be effective, they must understand what is expected of them. Establishing a clear set of objectives conveys to the sales force the expectation and how they will be evaluated. Sales force objectives can be set for the entire sales force as well as individual sales professionals. Objectives are usually set based on revenue goals, and they should be clearly established with measurement metrics and a time frame for completion. Typical sales force objectives include a mix of generating new customers and working with current customers.

Serving Existing Customers

Much of the work of a sales professional is around serving the existing customer. It is important to keep customers satisfied. Most organizations rely heavily on existing customers to provide good reviews, customer referrals, repeat purchases, and upsell of existing products. Sales professionals are expected to continue developing and building the relationship with existing customers to ensure they are satisfied. This can include checking on inventory, dealing with supply issues, and educating on product application. Objectives may include how often the sales professional is expected to keep in contact with the existing customer.

Developing New Customers

Growth is a key driver of most organizations, and growth comes through new sales to existing customers and also through sales to new customers. A sales force objective of obtaining a certain number of new customers is common. The sales force must have a lead pipeline of prospective customers they are constantly working to turn into customers.

Increasing Market Share and Profit

Additional methods for companies to grow include obtaining more market share as well as more profitable sales. When there are sales objectives for market share, they usually focus on an increase in the proportion of the firm's sales as compared to the total number of products the firm sells overall in the industry.

Enhancing Customer Satisfaction

An important element of obtaining new customers as well as getting additional sales from existing customers is keeping customers satisfied. Satisfaction can mean good reviews, referral business, and lifetime customers. Objectives for customer satisfaction usually involve the sales force working with customers and obtaining reviews and endorsements.

Designing the Sales Force Strategy and Structure

There are many ways to design and develop a sales force. Careful thought to the customer is usually the best practice for establishing the right structure. Other factors in determining the best structure involve the company and its products. Sometimes organizations utilize all of the methods to structure the sales force.

For example, Pfizer has a neuroscience product and structures its sales force by product, customer type/size, and geography. The Pfizer pharmaceutical sales representative for the neuroscience product calls on neurologists, represents only one or two products so that they are an expert on the efficacy and uses, and has a very tight geographical territory, usually focused on a few zip codes depending on the number of neurological medical practices in a given area.

Territorial Sales Force Structure

Setting up a sales force territory is typically done based on the number of prospects and customers as well as the size of the customer and the potential revenue from the typical sale. The goal is to make the territories equitable for all of the sales force. Geographic territories are typical and take into consideration the amount of time spent in the field and how large the coverage area may be for the sales force.

Product Sales Force Structure

Firms typically want the sales force to be knowledge experts on the products they represent. It is common for a company to provide the sales force with a portfolio of products and to include continuous training on all aspects of the products they sell. In order to provide the best resources, companies create structure around product portfolios and have their sales force structured according to the products they sell. For example, in wine distribution, some sales representatives work with restaurants, the "on-premise" segment. Other sales reps would serve retail outlets, including supermarkets and independent wine shops.

Customer (Market) Sales Force Structure

In addition to knowledge of the products, the sales force needs to be knowledgeable about the customers and the industries they serve. Many companies structure their sales force according to the industry or customers. A company that sells products within the restaurant industry may be structured according to quick service, fast fresh, food truck, and fine dining.

Determining the Size of the Sales Force

Investing in a sales force is significant for any company. Sales professionals must be properly incentivized, and the pay and benefits packages can be quite high for experienced and well-trained employees. Companies must determine the number of potential customers as well as the time to nurture prospects into customers. The size of the sales force must be considered in relation to the complexity of the product, the profit margins on sales, and the size and number of customers in the markets served.

Recruiting and Selecting Salespeople

Hiring and training a sales force is a significant process and cost for companies. The sales manager must have a set of skill requirements and product knowledge that the right candidate must have in order to fill the available roles. There is significant agreement that good salespeople all possess the traits of self-motivation, time management, optimism, empathy, and the ability to network. Many salespeople make themselves valuable based on the network of contacts they are able to maintain.

Most recruiting starts with a job description detailing the requirements and the necessary skills that are needed to do the job. Finding the right candidates often starts through listing available job openings on many of the digital job boards, such as Indeed, CareerBuilder, and LinkedIn. Executive recruiting firms can also be instrumental in finding and matching the right job candidates.

Training Salespeople

Training of the sales force is a significant effort for most companies. Many organizations have a formal training program and spend considerable time and resources to keep the sales force knowledgeable on the products and industries served. Areas of training include sales strategies and how to sell, the products being sold, the industries served, and the company itself.

The best training programs are a combination of classroom activities and in-the-field training. Companies typically have their own training programs. New hires will spend a couple of weeks to a few months in training before they are given their own accounts and territories. Training, however, is not only for the newly hired sales professionals. Most companies have continuous training requirements for their sales force. Training for existing employees often includes company processes, information on products, and enhancing sales skills. Most top-performing sales teams spend time training with company managers as well as other sales professionals.[3]

Compensating Salespeople

Compensation of the sales force is typically focused on providing a fair wage as well as incentivizing and motivating. Many organizations combine a variety of compensation methods to meet both individual goals and the overarching organizational goals.

Commission Only

Using a **commission**-only compensation structure provides for the motivation and incentive to make sales. Seasoned sales professionals typically enjoy a higher commission or commission-only structure. They are confident in their ability to sell the products and want to recognize the significant compensation enjoyed by a high commission structure on the sales they make.

The advantages of a commission-only compensation structure are that the company is not burdened with the expense of the sales force, as it only pays the sales professional if they have made a sale. This structure provides incentive and motivation for the sales professional to make sales and work hard.

The disadvantages of this structure include potential burnout of the sales force as well as a possible situation where the sales force uses aggressive practices to make sales.

Salary Only

When an organization uses the sales force more as trusted, it tends to provide a salary structure. Using salary-only compensation provides for stability of the sales force and the inclination of the sales professional to spend significant time with the customers and prospects.

A new salesperson at a car dealership might start on salary for a few months while learning the business. Later, after gaining product knowledge, developing a prospect list, and gaining the trust of the veteran sales staff, that person might switch to commission only.

The advantages of the salary-only structure are that it gives the organization control over the sales expense and is easy to administer. There are, however, a few disadvantages. One of the major disadvantages is that there is no incentive or motivation to make a sale. Another major disadvantage is that when sales decline, the expenses remain the same.

Salary and Commission

Many organizations utilize a combination of salary and commission. This allows for control of the sales force and the activities while still providing the sales force with incentives and motivation.

The major advantage to the combination structure is that it provides a certain amount of financial stability for the sales force while also incentivizing them to make sales. A disadvantage to the organization is that it is difficult to administer, and it makes the selling expense less predictable.

Salary and Individual Bonus

Another form of compensation is a base salary plus individual bonuses upon meeting goals and objectives. The advantages are control over the selling expense and incentive to meet goals and objectives established for the sales force. The disadvantage is primarily in the administration of the structure to make sure the bonus is sufficient to provide motivation and incentive and to keep track of the bonus structure.

Salary, Commission, and Bonus

This is the most complex of all of the compensation methods, as it combines all elements: a base salary, commission based on sales, and bonus based on goal targets. The advantages for the employee are the security from the salary combined with an incentive through the commission and bonus. There are two levels of incentive and motivation to keep the sales force engaged and actively working on making sales. The disadvantages include the complexity of managing the structure and tracking commissions and bonuses.

Supervising and Evaluating the Sales Force

While most sales professionals are self-motivated, they still require supervision, and this will include methods of evaluation to make sure the predetermined objectives have been met. Sales managers are tasked with developing the objectives and goals as well as monitoring and evaluating the success of the sales effort. There are a number of methods used to supervise and evaluate.

Quantitative assessments focus on the items that can be measured. They are less subjective and allow the sales manager to focus on the goals and objectives set for the sales force. A quantitative assessment may include a scale to rank activities of the sales force. For example, Paychex may evaluate the sales force based on how many leads they have acquired in a given month, the number of meetings with prospects, and the number of communication touch points with existing clients.

Another key element of evaluation includes the behavioral aspects of selling. Behavioral evaluations tend to be subjective in nature; however, they can be very helpful in identifying the right actions for the sales force to be effective at selling. Typically, a sales manager may accompany a sales professional for a day. The goal of the sales manager is to see how the sales professional handles their day, communicates with clients, answers questions, and conducts follow-up activities.

Useful Metrics to Assess Sales Performance

There are many metrics utilized by sales managers to gauge the performance of the sales force. The metrics should align with the goals and objectives of the organization and the sales function. Ideally, sales managers rely on metrics to provide the sales force with clear targets to work toward.

Sales Metrics

Sales metrics include data that serve to measure the individual performance of the sales professional, the team as a whole, and the company's sales performance over a period of time. Sales managers use the data to measure and evaluate areas that are doing well and those that need improvement.

Most sales teams have found that a few key metrics are instrumental in evaluating the overall success of the sales efforts. Every activity of the sales force needs to work toward making the sale. Metrics for sales productivity look to gauge the effectiveness of the efforts. Some typical productivity metrics include

- percentage of time spent on selling activities;
- percentage of time spent updating the CRM;
- percentage of lead follow-up; and
- percentage of leads generated.

Time is of the essence in connecting with "warm" leads, or potential customers who have expressed interest in the product. **Lead response time** measures evaluate the responsiveness of the sales force to the leads generated. Most sales programs seek an acceptable time frame for response. Some examples include

- time to contact a new lead;
- time to respond to a customer question;
- time to prepare a new prospect presentation; and
- time to create a proposal.

The **opportunity win rate** is a good measure to gauge the effectiveness of the sales force. It is important to know how many leads the sales force is given and how many leads become prospects. Knowing the opportunity win rate will help to determine where the sales force might need extended training on closing sales; it will also help to determine how many leads are needed in order to convert to clients.

Knowledge Check

It's time to check your knowledge on the concepts presented in this section. Refer to the Answer Key at the end of the book for feedback.

1. Lev is the sales manager for John Paul Mitchell Systems. He is responsible for the North American sales division. Lev is currently reviewing the total number of salons and looking to estimate the size of his sales force. What sales force management function is Lev performing?
   a. Setting sales goals
   b. Looking at territories
   c. Estimating the number of sales professionals he will need
   d. Writing job descriptions

2. Part of Malika's job with H2O Pool Supplies is to identify potential new customers. She is required to spend 20% of her time working to bring in new customers. What type of objective is Malika working toward?
   a. Serving existing customers
   b. Increasing profits
   c. Enhancing customer satisfaction
   d. Developing new customers

3. Terra Cotta Landscape Supply is currently developing a two-day session for all sales professionals within the organization. During this two-day meeting, the sales professionals will be learning about new products and applications for their clients. This is an example of what element of managing a sales force?
   a. Compensating
   b. Training
   c. Recruiting
   d. Evaluating

4. Johnny has worked for Nestlé for 15 years. He is paid based on the sales he makes. What type of compensation is Johnny most likely making?
   a. Base salary
   b. Bonus
   c. Commission
   d. Salary and commission

5. Ranee is concerned with making sure she has a set number of appointments with customers each week. Ranee is most likely being evaluated based on what?
   a. Percent of time spent on selling activities
   b. Percent of time spent generating leads
   c. Time it takes her to develop a proposal
   d. Percent of time working in the CRM

15.5 | Sales Promotion and Its Role in the Promotion Mix

Learning Outcomes

By the end of this section, you will be able to:

LO 1 Define sales promotion.
LO 2 Discuss the importance of sales promotion in the promotion mix.

Sales Promotion

Sales promotion is a promotional strategy focused on inducing sales in the short term. Of all the promotional activities, sales promotion is solely focused on a direct call to action to buy something. Sales promotion can be targeted to intermediaries through a push strategy or directly to consumers through a pull strategy. Marketers often use sales promotion in tandem with other promotional strategies. When McDonald's advertises, for example, "Free fries on Friday when you purchase a menu item through the app," it is using advertising along with sales promotion to induce consumers to use the app and to increase sales on Fridays.

When products are at the introductory stage of the product life cycle, sales promotion can be effective at inducing trial of a product. The greater the competition, the more a sales promotion strategy becomes important for getting consumers to switch or try a new or different product. Product manufacturers often use sales promotion in-store to set apart the brand or product at the time of purchase. As you walk past the cheese aisle at the grocery store, you might see Sargento offering a buy-one-get-one (BOGO) deal. This is a sales promotion geared toward getting the customer to buy more of Sargento or possibly try Sargento for the first time.

Importance of Sales Promotion in the Promotion Mix

Many of the strategies in the promotion mix are informative in nature. However, when other strategies are combined with sales promotion, there is a direct and immediate call to action to purchase the product. Companies needing to create sales in the short term will benefit from sales promotion. Utilizing sales promotion is a very effective strategy for generating trial of a product in the introductory stages of the product life cycle (PLC).

Spreading of Information

Sales promotion is very effective at spreading information about new products and product modifications. Creating awareness of the brand to new markets and customers is another effective use of sales promotion.

When MyPillow has an advertorial during Fox News and provides a code for a reduced price of its renowned pillows, the advertorial serves to tell new customers about the products as well as provide an incentive to purchase the product immediately.

Stimulation of Demand

One of the key elements to good sales promotion is that it stimulates sales in the short term. Sales promotion gives customers an immediate incentive to purchase a product.

Sonic Drive-In (see Figure 15.3) offers half-price drinks and slushes every day from 2:00 to 4:00 as a "happy hour" special. The use of this sales promotion tactic does two things: first, it incentivizes consumers to buy drinks, and second, it provides sales during the slow times of the day.

Figure 15.3 Sonic Drive-In uses a half-price sales promotion to stimulate sales during slow times of the day. (credit: "Sonic Drive In and Eat In Restaurant, Bristol CT 5/2014" by Mike Mozart, JeepersMedia/flickr, CC BY 2.0)

Customer Satisfaction

Today's customer is presented with thousands of messages. Companies are driven to get noticed, increase sales, and keep their customers satisfied. Sales promotions are one method a company may use to increase customer satisfaction. A survey from RetailMeNot "showed that coupons can affect brain chemistry and can make customers happier." The research concluded that an online shopper who received a $10 coupon was 11% happier and had 38% higher oxytocin levels than those who didn't get a discount.[4] Providing the occasional discount can chemically make a customer happier, resulting in a more satisfied customer, who may spend more in the future and may become a loyal shopper.[5]

Stabilization of Sales Volume

Sales promotion can also be used to help stabilize sales volume. Because sales promotion works to incentivize purchase of a product in the short term, companies often use this promotional tactic to drive sales and meet targets. Typical sales promotion tactics used to increase sales include buy-one-get-one-half-off and other specific discounts that are available when used by a certain time. The time element provides the company with the target for the sale, and the customer is provided with an incentive to purchase by a certain time.

MARKETING DASHBOARD

Cost of Customer Acquisition

We often think about profitability based on the difference between what we spend to create a product or service and the amount a customer pays for that product or service. However, we have to remember that there are costs to acquiring customers. In this chapter, you learned about two promotional activities that create costs to reach customers: sales and sales promotion.

Within the sales process, an organization pays a salesperson salary and/or commission to make sales. This is an example of a cost to acquire a customer. As you can imagine, we want our cost to acquire to stay low. For example, if we sold multimillion-dollar airplanes, it would be reasonable to spend thousands of dollars on a salesperson to make that sale. However, if we were selling several-hundred-dollar televisions, our cost to acquire a customer must be much lower.

Sales promotion is another promotional expense. For example, if a pizza brand provides samples at Costco, this might encourage a customer to purchase pizza. And if that customer keeps buying pizza, the cost of the pizza sample was worth it for the value that the customer will bring over the life of the relationship. Other categories of promotional costs include advertising, public relations, social media, search, and direct marketing.

The formula for cost of acquisition is the total cost of marketing activities divided by number of customers acquired.

$$\text{Cost of Acquistion} = \frac{\text{Total Cost of Marketing Activities}}{\text{Number of Customers Acquired}}$$

In this formula, you will see an assumption that all customers are worth the same amount, but as savvy marketers, we know that this is untrue. This is why we need to use a variety of marketing metrics when evaluating campaigns.

Give the cost of acquisition calculation a try for yourself. What is the cost of acquisition in the example provided below?

Type of Promotion	Expense	Yield
Television Advertising	$1,250,000	400,000 customers
Catalog Mailing	$750,000	250,000 customers
Search Engine Marketing	$550,000	90,000 customers
Outdoor Activation	$1,500,000	70,000 customers

Table 15.1

Type of Promotion	Expense	Yield
Ad Agency Fees	$600,000	0 customers
TOTAL	$4,650,000	810,000 customers

Table 15.1

Solution

$$\$5.74 \text{ per customer}$$

Formula:

$$\$4,650,000 / 810,000$$

What additional information do you need to determine whether the cost of acquisition is appropriate for the product or service?

Solution

The price of the product/service, total sales, expenses, and margins associated with the product or service

Let's suppose that this example is for a national bookseller. The bookseller has an average profit per customer of $90 over the customer's lifetime. Would the cost per acquisition that you calculated provide a good value for the bookseller? Why or why not?

Solution

Yes. It is worth it to spend $5.74 to acquire a customer worth $90 on average over the lifespan of the relationship;

$$\$90 > \$5.74$$

Knowledge Check

It's time to check your knowledge on the concepts presented in this section. Refer to the Answer Key at the end of the book for feedback.

1. The retail store Ann Taylor is offering 75% off if you order online today and sign up to receive the newsletter. This is an example of what promotional mix strategy?
    a. Advertising
    b. Personal selling
    c. Public relations
    d. Sales promotion

2. When Starbucks has a happy hour special from 2:00 to 4:00 and drinks are half price, what is the purpose of the sales promotion?
    a. Lose money
    b. Stimulate demand
    c. Spread information
    d. Increase customer satisfaction

3. Rolex calls itself the "Official Timekeeper" of the Wimbledon and Australian Open tennis championships, by virtue of its sponsorships of the marquee events. What is the most likely objective for Rolex's sponsorship deal with these events?

   a. Lose money
   b. Stimulate demand
   c. Spread information
   d. Increase customer satisfaction

4. Sales promotion consists of a collection of incentive tools designed to do what for the product?
   a. Stimulate demand
   b. Create brand awareness
   c. Provide free publicity
   d. Inform

5. Sally loves to receive her coupons from American Eagle. She typically looks in her email every day to see what promotions the company will be sending. The American Eagle sales promotions are helping to accomplish which important task?
   a. Increased customer satisfaction
   b. Providing information
   c. Increasing brand awareness
   d. Developing junk mail

15.6 | Main Types of Sales Promotion

Learning Outcomes

By the end of this section, you will be able to:

LO 1 Discuss the primary types of consumer-oriented sales promotion.
LO 2 Discuss the primary types of trade-oriented sales promotion.

Consumer-Oriented Sales Promotion

Sales promotion can be categorized in two ways. The first category of sales promotion is consumer-oriented, which focuses on the consumer pulling the product through the marketing channels. The second category is trade-oriented, which is intended to push the product through the channel to the consumer.

Consumer-oriented sales promotion provides the customer with an immediate inducement to purchase a product. The goal is to have the consumer seek out the product and "pull it" through the marketing channel. There are many common forms of consumer-oriented sales promotion.

Coupons

The goal of **coupons** is to reduce the price of the product and prompt the consumer to make an immediate purchase. The major goal is to increase sales quickly, attract repeat purchases, or try new versions of a product. Consumers using coupons recognize the savings when they relinquish the coupon at the time of purchase. Coupons come in many different forms, including printed, digital, and mobile. Because a coupon has to be redeemed to obtain the reward, manufacturers can determine the effectiveness of the coupon offer and the method of delivery.

The company HelloFresh sends a direct mail piece with a coupon for 16 free meals. When consumers sign up for the home delivery meal plan, this is a great example of how a coupon might be used to create brand awareness and acquire new customers. The direct mail might also include a code to use online for digital application of the offer.

Samples

Samples are most often used to induce trial of a new product. This tactic can be very effective to increase sales volume during the early stages of the product life cycle and to help with better distribution. Samples can be given out in stores, at events, or through the mail. This is an expensive form of sales promotion but can be highly effective at inducing purchase. Costco regularly has samples within its aisles and at the immediate point of sale as consumers are shopping. Another example is from the 2022 SXSW conference in Austin, Texas, when Creminelli Fine Meats distributed free mini packs of salami to showcase the company's line of "charcuterie-grade snacking" products. The makers of White Claw Hard Seltzer were corporate sponsors of the event; conference-goers were treated to free samples of new flavors, such as Passion Fruit.[6]

Premiums

Premiums are items offered free or at a minimum cost alongside the purchase of a product. Some of the most famous premiums include the McDonald's Happy Meal toys and Cracker Jack ("The more you eat the more you want") with a prize inside.[7] Premiums are very good for attracting new buyers and providing an incentive for customer loyalty. The use of the Happy Meal toy created significant customer loyalty among consumers who wanted to collect all the toys in a series.

Contests

Contests make consumers use their skills to compete for prizes. Using contests allows customers to engage with products and become invested in the process of trying to win something of value. Companies often use contests in coordination with other sales promotion tactics, such as coupons. Doritos regularly includes a contest as part of its advertising. Pepperidge Farm challenged consumers to #GoForTheHandful and create an Instagram duet with pro basketball player Boban Marjanović. The goal was to see if consumers could hold more Goldfish crackers in their tiny hands compared to the large hands of the pro basketball player. Winners were treated to Goldfish for a year and the title of Official Goldfish Spokeshand.[8] Contests are based on analytical or creative skills.

Sweepstakes

Where contests are based on skill, **sweepstakes** are based on chance. Companies use sweepstakes in order to increase sales volume in the short term. Sweepstakes ask contestants to submit their names for inclusion in a drawing for prizes. Publishers Clearing House conducts one of the most well-known sweepstakes. The company ultimately wants consumers to order magazines; however, the purchase of a magazine is not necessary to enter and win the $1 million cash prize. However, Publishers Clearing House is able to add to its mailing list when consumers enter to win.

Loyalty Programs

Loyalty programs have increased in popularity. Most of today's loyalty programs are tied to a mobile app. The attractiveness of loyalty programs is that when consumers spend, they get points toward something free. For example, Wired Coffee Bar offers consumers $5 off of a product in-store when they spend $50.

Point-of-Purchase Displays

Point-of-purchase displays have been a hallmark in store aisles for decades. The point-of-purchase display allows manufacturers to showcase their products in a way that stands out from all the other products in the store. Companies typically utilize the point-of-purchase promotion method for new products that are being introduced to the market. Some common forms of point-of-purchase presentations include outdoor signs, window displays, countertop containers, display racks, and self-serve cartons. The key to good point-of-purchase is having a display that attracts customers and enhances the brand image of the product being offered.

Rebates

Rebates provide some type of reimbursement of the cost of a product when the consumer completes certain information about the time, place, and price of the product purchased. Typically, the consumer must submit the rebate form by a certain date and must include receipts or bar codes from the purchase. Rebates usually induce the consumer to buy the product as it is being offered at a perceived cheaper price. Consumers often fail to submit the required materials to receive the rebate, as they might see the process as too laborious.

MARKETING IN PRACTICE

Domino's

Figure 15.4 Companies will often use national days for sales-oriented promotions, like Domino's does on National Pizza Day. (credit: "Domino's Pizza delivery bikes" by Erica Fischer/flickr, CC BY 2.0)

Companies use sales promotion to generate more sales and to promote their brands. Setting up special days for certain products and causes can help bring focus and attention as well as boost sales or donations in the short term. For example, days such as National Coffee Day, National Pet Adoption Day, and National Pizza Day put a spotlight on the product or cause and can work to create a news story, which helps to generate consumer interest.

During National Pizza Day, companies selling pizza will run various promotions geared toward selling more pizza and getting consumers across the country to eat pizza. While Domino's Pizza regularly runs discounts and promotions, most of them are "deals" that consumers can use on a regular basis (see Figure 15.4). Pizza delivery companies regularly utilize sales promotion strategies as a way to deal with the highly competitive nature of the pizza delivery industry.

For National Pizza Day 2022, Domino's, a company known for fast pizza delivery, ran an unusual sales promotion offering cash back if consumers picked up their pizza instead of having it delivered. For a limited time, Domino's, the world's largest pizza chain, offered to give consumers back $3 when they opted to pick up their pizza instead of having it delivered. "The $3 coupon was redeemable the following week on another carryout order of $5 or more before tax and gratuity."[9]

Trade-Oriented Sales Promotion

Trade-oriented sales promotion is focused on the channel intermediaries: the wholesalers and retailers. The goal is for the intermediary to be incentivized to push the product to the consumer.

Allowances and Discounts

Manufacturers provide the retailers or wholesalers with allowances to pass along in the form of price breaks to the end customer. For example, Ford Motor Company might offer a $3,000 trade-in allowance for the new F-150. This is an incentive to come into the dealership and buy the F-150.[10] The dealer has the allowance from Ford and is able to pass the savings to the consumer as an incentive to come in and buy a new truck.

Cooperative Advertising

Advertising can be expensive for retailers. Typically, they advertise products they have in stock in an effort to induce consumers to come in and make a purchase. **Cooperative advertising** is a way for manufacturers to help with the cost of the advertising, in exchange for the retailer to advertise the products produced by the manufacturer. When supermarket chain Publix advertises Boar's Head meats and cheeses, Publix is using cooperative advertising from Boar's Head to run the ads featuring Boar's Head products.

Cash Bonuses

Some manufacturers provide bonus cash as an incentive for the retail sales associates to push the manufacturers' products. Bonuses can be given to the sales associate who sells the most or to the store that is the highest sales producer. It is then up to the store to determine how best to use the cash bonus.

Credit Terms

One way for manufacturers to help the retailers and wholesalers who sell their products is to provide them with favorable **credit terms**. Often these terms allow the wholesaler or retailer to sell the products long before actually having to pay for the product.

Dealer Conferences

When companies have dealers who distribute their products, they want to incentivize the dealer sales force to sell the product. Additionally, the dealer conferences are a good method of training and educating dealers to work with customers and ultimately sell the product to them.

Push Incentives

Push incentives work to create demand for a product through discounts that retailers pass on to customers. In the mobile phone industry, Apple may provide a discount on phones through one of its retail partners in an effort to encourage buyers to choose the iPhone through the distributor. Push strategies focus on selling directly to the customer. Typical tactics include point-of-sale displays and direct approaches from the retail store sales professionals to the customers.

Knowledge Check

It's time to check your knowledge on the concepts presented in this section. Refer to the Answer Key at the end of the book for feedback.

1. _______ are certificates that entitle the bearer to a stated saving on the purchase of a specific product.
   a. Samples
   b. Coupons
   c. Rebates
   d. Premiums

2. Which of the following consumer promotion tools offers a free amount of a product or service delivered door-to-door, sent in the mail, picked up in a store, attached to another product, or featured in an advertising offer?
   a. Coupons
   b. Rebates

   c. Premiums
   d. Samples

3. Which of the following allows consumers to do things in order to have a chance of winning?
   a. Coupons
   b. Sweepstakes
   c. Contests
   d. Rebates

4. Which of the following is an example of a trade promotion?
   a. Allowances and discounts
   b. Coupons
   c. Loyalty programs
   d. Premiums

5. Which of the following elements of the marketing communications mix consists of a collection of incentive tools, mostly short term, designed to stimulate quicker or greater purchase of particular products or services by consumers or the trade?
   a. Advertising
   b. Personal selling
   c. Public relations
   d. Sales promotion

15.7 | Ethical Issues in Personal Selling and Sales Promotion

Learning Outcomes

By the end of this section, you will be able to:
- **LO** 1 Discuss the ethical issues that may arise in personal selling.
- **LO** 2 Discuss the ethical issues that may arise in sales promotion.

Ethical Issues in Personal Selling

The goal of sales is to create customer loyalty and repeat purchases. Developing the relationship with the customer is best done through honesty and integrity. Sales should always be conducted with a long-term goal of developing a lifetime customer and not just one sale.

However, with sales goals as the driving force behind the sales activities, the sales force can be pressured into practices that might be counter to building customer loyalty. Without proper regulation and a code of ethics, sales efforts can run afoul of ethical rules. Good sales managers seek to have control features built in to prevent the temptation to have a climate of dishonesty.

Ethical issues that can arise within the sales function of a company include dishonest claims about a product, slanderous comments about the competition, padding of company expense accounts and/or misuse of the expense account, artificially inflating sales data to meet goals and bonuses, and bribes and kickbacks.

Sales professionals are typically self-starters who are out in the field working with their customers. In a sales role, companies provide the sales professionals expense accounts and credit cards as a way to work with and build relationships with clients. Without close supervision and company policies and guidelines, the sales professional can be tempted to participate in unethical practices. If a code of conduct is not present, it is often hard to resist the temptations. Some of the most common practices and temptations include misuse of the company credit card, inflating sales to reach goals, and receiving kickbacks.

Misuse of Company Credit Cards or Expense Accounts

Misuse of company credit cards and expense accounts can happen with any employee, but given the solitary nature of the sales professional, it is typically prone to happen more often with them. Because the work of the sales professional is fairly independent from the rest of the organization, it can create situations where there isn't enough accountability. Misuse can happen through double billing, padding the expense account, or overcharging for expensed items.

To handle issues of expense misuse, it is best to have policies and procedures in place along with a record of accounting for expenses and providing receipts for all expensed items.

Inflating Sales Data

Because sales professionals are often given sales targets and expectations to meet the targets, they are at risk for finding methods of inflating their sales numbers to meet the targets. If the sales professional gets behind or feels pressure to meet goals, it can be appealing to find methods of showing goal achievement. The method of inflating sales can also be termed channel stuffing. This practice happens when a company forces more products through the distribution channel than the channel is actually capable of selling.

When the sales organization calculates the sales targets based on shipments of products, the method of channel stuffing helps to meet the targets in the short term. However, long-term sales targets are adversely affected, especially if the channel partners return the products.

An example of how this might happen can be explained through a company that sells over-the-counter medicines. If it has products with an expiration date in a few months, it may ship all of the products with the near-term expiration date. When the products don't sell within the expiration time frame, the products are shipped back for a return. The sales in the short term where high, and the targets were met. However, in the long-term, the company is faced with a large shipment of returned product.

In 2016, in an effort to meet sales goals and targets, Wells Fargo employees created millions of fraudulent savings and checking accounts for clients without their consent. Regulatory agencies such as the Consumer Financial Protection Bureau (CFPB) penalized the company and fined it $185 million for the illegal activity.[11]

Accepting Kickbacks

Another unethical practice is when sales professionals accept **kickbacks**. There are many forms of kickbacks. Companies that deal internationally are often at the biggest risk for kickbacks, as it is common practice in some countries. Sales professionals that have long-term relationships can be tempted to take advantage of the situation, particularly if both sides profit from the scheme. There are many types of kickback schemes. Primarily a kickback scheme involves two people who work together to change the pricing structure, and in turn they both generally pocket some profit from the sale. Under the 1977 Foreign Corrupt Practices Act (FCPA), it is unlawful to pay or promise to pay another person for the purpose of retaining their business.

COMPANIES WITH A CONSCIENCE

Tentree

Figure 15.5 Tentree runs consumer-oriented promotions in which it plants 10 trees for every purchase made. (credit: "Tree Near Barkisland" by Tim Green/flickr, CC BY 2.0)

Tentree is a sustainable clothing brand. Like many online stores and clothing brands, it regularly runs promotions, including a percent off of the purchase price when you sign up for their newsletter. But along with the typical consumer-oriented promotions, Tentree also plants 10 trees for every purchase (see Figure 15.5).

According to Tentree's Facebook page, "We believe that big change starts small. Small as in bringing your reusable tote to the grocery store, getting your coffee refilled in a thermos, and choosing to wear sustainably made T-shirts. These small choices add up (trust us, we've done the math), and we're here to celebrate each and every one of them. By planting 10 trees for every purchase, we hope to make big change accessible to everybody and show the lasting impact that one small choice can have."[12]

So far, the company has planted over 81 million trees. The clothing it manufactures and sells is designed to have a very small environmental impact. And consumers are incentivized to purchase from Tentree because for every item purchased, the company plants 10 trees. Tentree has a goal that customers are pushing to reach—1 billion trees planted by 2030.[13] Its earth-first philosophy is at the heart of every garment it sells.

Ethical Issues in Sales Promotions

When it comes to sales promotions, many ethical issues can arise. One of the most well-known issues with sales promotion happened with a popular McDonald's game (see Figure 15.6). For years, McDonald's ran its Monopoly game as a method to increase the consumer purchase of meals along with Monopoly game pieces that could net customers winnings from the fast-food giant. Not only was the game popular with customers, but it did exactly what the sales promotion was supposed to do: it increased sales. Unfortunately, the head of security for the company that ran the promotion and printed the game pieces took out all the winning game pieces in a scam worth $24 million.[14]

Figure 15.6 McDonald's Monopoly game was an effective consumer-oriented promotion that resulted in a $24 million scam. (credit: "McDonald's Monopoly 2014" by Mike Mozart, JeepersMedia/flickr, CC BY 2.0)

Hidden Fees

One of the most common issues with ethics in sales promotion is in **hidden fees** that might be tacked on to the promotion. The travel and hospitality industry can be an example of the hidden fees often found in the fine print for the unwary customer looking for a "deal." An airline might have advertised prices, but upon booking, the traveler may realize the baggage and airport fees make the price higher than other advertised rates. This can also be a common practice with hotels and resorts. The advertised price may look appealing, and the sales promotion may seem like a good deal, but by the time resort fees are tacked on to the price, the promotional discount isn't as attractive.

Ambiguous Terms and Conditions

Legal documents have long been considered tricky to maneuver. A company may provide the terms and conditions and a link to click or simply acknowledge that you have read through the 15,000-word document for understanding. But does anybody really read the documents? Do consumers really understand what they are reading and agreeing to? Most likely, the legal jargon has gone unread, and the customer is typically unaware of what they have agreed to. However, it is in the best interest of the company to look out for the best interests of their customers. If the end goal is long-term customer satisfaction, all of the work of the company should be around making sure the customer is satisfied. Providing **ambiguous terms and conditions** does nothing to really protect the customer relationship.

📖 Chapter Summary

This chapter covers personal selling and promotions, both integral components of marketing. Personal selling is defined as communication between a buyer and a seller and can be customized based on the product or service. Much of personal selling is enhanced when the salesperson engages in relationship development to build loyalty.

Personal selling involves inside and outside order takers and their primary responsibility to create a relationship with the buyer. Consider inside order takers as the clerks employed by a company to assist the customer and complete the final sale. Outside order takers are out making calls on customers and delivering inventory. Order getters are the highly trained salespeople, and missionary salespeople are the ones that facilitate experiences such as samples in the store. A technical salesperson is one that has extensive product knowledge that they use to present a product.

Personal selling is broken down into steps, It begins with identifying a qualified customer or prospecting; from this point leads are identified. This is then followed by an approach, a presentation, handling objections, closing, and asking for the order. There are many components involved in each step based on the product/service, customer, timing, and ability of the salesperson to close the sale. The final step is the follow-up.

Sales force management was covered, including the definition, purpose, and construction of compensation packages. Assessment of performance, using sales performance metrics for quantitative assessment, and qualitative goals are important functions of sale management.

The final section discusses promotion, which is a form of marketing communication that is used to inform target audiences of a good, service, brand, or issue. Considered a basic element of the marketing mix, promotion includes various tactics that encourage purchase. Examples include coupons, sweepstakes, rebates, premiums, special packaging, cause-related marketing, and licensing. Loyalty programs are increasingly used to build customer loyalty and repeat sales while at the same time generating valuable consumer information.

Additional incentives include push incentives, which cover a marketer's effort and expenditure to influence channel members stocking and promotional efforts. Pull incentives, on the other hand, cover a marketer's effort and expenditure to influence consumer and customer demand and preference for the marketer products, using advertising, coupons, and other forms of promotion.

Finally, ethical issues with personal selling and promotions were discussed. Fraud and misuse of funds for sales personnel can be closely monitored using software developed to track this information. With promotions, hidden fees, which are one-time add-ons that may not be fully disclosed to the consumer, will carry additional unfair costs. Where contracts are concerned, ambiguous terms and conditions are considered problematic, and customers as well as marketers should be aware and avoid these issues.

🔑 Key Terms

adaptive selling   an approach to personal selling in which selling behaviors are altered during the sales interaction or across customer interactions, based on information about the nature of the selling situation

AIDA model   the model consumers go through when becoming interested in a product. First the product must grab their attention, then they gain interest, they have a desire for the product, and they act to acquire the product

ambiguous terms and conditions   when a contract is unclear and misleading

approach   the stage of the sales process where the salesperson makes the initial approach to introduce the product to the customer

commission   the compensation paid to salespeople based on a fixed formula related to the salesperson's activity or performance

consultative selling   focuses on the expertise of a salesperson with problem solving

contest   a marketing or consumer sales promotion technique that involves collection, matching, or use of skill to complete a project or activity with the goal of a prize or reward for the player

cooperative advertising   an approach to paying for local advertising or retail advertising whereby the details are handled by a local retail store but is partly or fully paid for by a national manufacturer whose product is featured in the ad

coupon   a printed certificate entitling the bearer to a stated price reduction or special value on a specific product

credit terms   credit terms of the agreement between the buyer and seller with length of time and payments to be made

customer relationship management   the process sales personnel undertake to work with the customer to build the relationship and move into the role of a trusted advisor

formula selling   an approach in which the sales presentation is designed to move the customer through the stages in the decision-making process, such as get the customer's attention, develop interest, build desire, and secure action

hidden fees   also called undisclosed fees and are fees that are not made known to the buyer

inside order taker   a salesclerk or order clerk that is employed for a company that address questions and complete the final sale

kickbacks   illegal payment for preferential or improper service

lead response time   the activity of evaluating factors through data analytics, demographics, buyer behavior, competitor analysis, and economics

loyalty programs   a form of promotion focused on repeat purchases and frequently attached to a sales receipt, punch card, or stamp card

missionary salespeople   individuals who have the power to influence the customer to purchase a product or service

need/satisfaction format   a type of customized sales presentation in which the salesperson first identifies the prospective customer's needs and then tries to offer a solution that satisfies those needs

opportunity win rate   the number of sales closed divided by the total number of opportunities created; calculates another opportunity to track sales

order getters   highly trained salespeople who know their products, services involved, and competition across the street

order takers   sales personnel that are responsible for taking orders from customers by identifying the customer and finding the right product fit

outside order takers   salespeople out in the trenches, visiting customers and delivering inventory to retailers and wholesalers

personal selling   communication between a buyer and seller. The primary responsibility is to build a relationship with the buyer.

point-of-purchase displays   displays that allow manufacturers to showcase their products in a way that stands out from all the other products in the store

pre-approach stage   the stage of the sales process where the salesperson will work to understand the needs of the customer and begin working with them to become a customer

premiums   a promotional tool that is often defined in three forms: merchandise offered at a lower price or free; an item of value, other than the product; souvenir merchandise

presentation   the stage of the sales process where the salesperson showcases the features about a product that will be of most benefit to the prospect based on the needs uncovered during the pre-approach and approach stages

prospect   a potential qualified customer who has the willingness, financial capacity, authority, and eligibility to buy the salesperson's offering

qualification   the process the salesperson undertakes to make sure the sales lead is a good fit for the product they are selling

quantitative assessments   numbers driven and based on inputs and outputs of the sales cycle

rebates   a form of promotion that rewards consumers for sending information to the company

relationship selling   a method of personal selling used to better understand the needs and wants of the buyer

sales force automation   a software tool that helps organizations acquire customers

sales leads   a database of potential customers that sales professionals work to create and develop through lead generation

sales promotion   a short-term way of enticing the consumer to purchase a product or service

samples   providing consumers with a free sample of a product is a form of promotion

selling process   includes all of the steps the salesperson will implement as they work with the buyer to become a customer

support personnel   fulfill the responsibilities that assist the sales team in supporting the customer and completing the sale

sweepstakes   a marketing or consumer sales promotion that involves the offering of prizes to participants, where winners are selected by chance and no consideration is required

team selling   the practice of involving a group of people familiar with the viewpoints and concerns of a customer's key decision makers to sell and service a major account

technical specialist   a salesperson who has extensive product knowledge and uses this knowledge as the focal aspect of the sales presentation

Applied Marketing Knowledge: Discussion Questions

1. Consider which of the sales positions you have engaged with in the last month. Would they be inside or outside order takers, order getter, missionary, technical, or a team? In what circumstances did you have this experience?

2. Explain in detail what happens in each of the steps in personal selling process.
   a. Prospecting and Qualifying
   b. Pre-approach
   c. Approach
   d. Presentation
   e. Handling Objections
   f. Closing: Asking for the Order
   g. Follow-Up

3. Partner with a fellow student, and practice the personal selling process. Take turns being the buyer and then the seller.

4. Define sales promotion and discuss its importance in the promotion mix.

Critical Thinking Exercises

1. Compose a paragraph (150–200 words) using all of the following terms as they relate to personal selling. The goal is to prove you understand the meaning of each term.

   Terms:

   Order takers
   Inside order takers
   Outside order takers
   Order getters
   Support personnel
   Missionary salespeople
   Technical specialists
   Team selling

2. Consider the promotions that you have participated in. List them and the product that they were used to promote. Did you buy the product based on the promotion? If you did, what was the selling point? If you did not, where did it miss the mark? Pick a product that you are familiar with, and create a promotion aimed at the consumer.

3. Identify a time you've read about or were personally involved in an unethical sales experience.

 Building Your Personal Brand

Consider the concept of personal selling, and apply it to yourself. What information would you need? How would you go about crafting your message? First, gather the facts that you would like someone to know about you, and create a list. Next, craft the basic "elevator pitch" introduction (that is, you only have an elevator ride to tell someone your unique value). What would that pitch include?

Next, make a list of the situations where you might need an introduction (sales pitch) that is longer and contains more detail. Consider a job interview (much of this information should be on your resume), joining a club or professional organization, or volunteering. Each of these situations calls for slightly different information.

Create several different personal selling scripts for yourself, and have someone you know read them and provide feedback. Consider their feedback, and revise as you see fit. If requested, submit your scripts to your instructor.

 What Do Marketers Do?

We are surrounded by personal selling encounters: cell phone, insurance, services in a bank, restaurant, and the list goes on. Pick a service that you would like to learn more about. Now find a person that holds the job of personally selling that service/product. Reach out to them; you can call, walk into a business, or make an appointment, any way that you choose. Introduce yourself, and tell them you are a student and would like to ask some questions.

1. Start with simple information. What does the job entail?
2. How did they get the job? How long have they been doing personal selling?
3. Do they enjoy what they do? What are the best parts and the worst parts of the job?
4. Do they think that there are skills that are needed to do the job well? If they do, what are they?
5. Can they discuss the compensation structure (they might hesitate, but explain you do not need specifics, just general information)?
6. Do they have the opportunity to move up into management if they would like?

Add any additional questions, or ask for clarification of something that you do not understand. End with thanking them for their time.

This exercise should provide you with firsthand information about this job; you can always choose another person that is in a totally different service/product category to compare the details of the job.

Closing Company Case

Cutco

In 1949, Cutco began manufacturing knives in Olean, New York. At the time, Cutco was making products for Wear-Ever Aluminum, a division of Alcoa. In 1982, the company went through a management buyout that made it a private company. The Cutco name was derived from the time under Alcoa, when it existed as the Cooking Utensil Company.

For the past 70 years, Cutco has been a family business that prides itself on being made in America.[15] The company has a deep-rooted commitment to providing American jobs. Through quality of craftsmanship, the

Cutco products are an American staple in many kitchens, and they are the reliable cookware of choice for many home cooks.

Through its commitment to service and quality, Cutco has one of the leading guarantees in the industry. All Cutco products are backed by The Forever Guarantee. No matter how the consumer acquired the product—self purchase or gift—the products come with a lifetime performance guarantee, which includes free sharpening. If at any time the customer is not satisfied with the performance, Cutco will correct or replace the product. Because Cutco relies on lifetime customers and word-of-mouth referrals, its primary responsibility is to customer satisfaction.[16]

While Cutco has 15 retail stores in the United States, it has long relied on its sales force through Vector Marketing. For years, Vector has hired and mentored a mostly collegiate sales force. In fact, 85 percent of the Vector sales force is comprised of college students.

Vector Marketing is a single-level direct sales company, and it sells only Cutco. The relationship between Vector and Cutco dates back to 1985. Early in the 1980s, Vector Marketing was an independent seller of Cutco. Because of Vector's success, Cutco bought it to replicate the success it was having with Cutco's product.[17]

The Vector Marketing home office is in Olean, New York—by its parent, Cutco. It also operates 250 independent locations throughout the United States, Canada, and Puerto Rico. However, during its busy summer months, when students everywhere are working to earn money for college, Vector Marketing has over 300 temporary locations.

Because of the weekly pay, flexible schedules, and superior sales training, tens of thousands of college students have experienced the joy of cutting a penny with the kitchen shears or slicing through a piece of extra-thick rope courtesy of the sharp Cutco blades. Hundreds of thousands of family kitchens across North America have watched the sales demonstration, asked good questions, provided referrals, and purchased a set of Cutco knives and kitchen accessories.

Vector Marketing works hard to recruit, educate, train, and incentivize its sales force. The hardworking Vector Marketing sales representatives know that up for grabs is a total of $40,000 to full-time undergraduate students who sell the most—the top 50 students get this award every summer. Vector also gives a guaranteed base pay and even pays the student for the appointment, regardless of whether they make the sale. The company doesn't want a reputation for high-pressure sales although they do pay commissions. Vector Marketing and Cutco realize only satisfied customers are repeat and referral customers.

When the Vector Marketing sales representative calls to set up the appointment, they courteously ask about when the customer can view the Cutco presentation. When you are in the presentation, the sales representative will go through a carefully scripted and rehearsed presentation, which will take you through the features and the related customer benefits afforded with ownership of your Cutco blades.

Throughout the presentation, the potential customer is asked if they have questions and, further, what they think of the various Cutco knives and accessories they have been shown. At the end of the presentation, the potential customer is intentionally asked which pieces they are going to buy, and they are encouraged to make the purchase by being offered an additional incentive Cutco tool as a gift with purchase.

Most of the prescreened customers have come to the Vector Marketing representative by way of a close friend or family member. Not only is Cutco an undisputed superior product with a lifetime guarantee, but the quality of the link from the customer back to the sales representative helps to solidify the sale. Saying no is very difficult. Almost all objections have already been eradicated.

After the presentation is over, the order has been placed, and the sales representative is closing up the meeting, they ask for 10 referrals. All good sales representatives know that the best customer is a word-of-mouth referral.

Check out the Cutco website (https://openstax.org/r/cutco) and the Vector Marketing website (https://openstax.org/r/vectormarketing).

Case Questions

1. How would you classify the type of sales force utilized by Cutco?

2. What is the presentation style utilized in selling Cutco?

3. Describe the compensation structure for the Vector Marketing Cutco sales force.

4. Explain how the Vector Marketing sales team develops relationships with its customers?

References

1. "Sales Force Automation Technology and CRM: What's the Difference?," *Sales Blog & Field Sales Management*, ForceManager, last modified February 4, 2021, https://www.forcemanager.com/blog/sfa-vs-crm-how-to-decide/.

2. "CRM 101: What Is CRM?," Salesforce, accessed June 25, 2022, https://www.salesforce.com/crm/what-is-crm/.

3. Julie Thomas, "What Companies That Grew in 2020 Realize about Sales Training," *Forbes*, January 8, 2021, https://www.forbes.com/sites/forbesbusinessdevelopmentcouncil/2021/01/08/what-companies-that-grew-in-2020-realize-about-sales-training.

4. Roger Dooley, "Coupons: Better Than Kissing," *Forbes*, December 21, 2012, https://www.forbes.com/sites/rogerdooley/2012/12/21/coupons-kissing.

5. Min-Jee Hwang, "How to Use Pricing and Promotions to Improve Customer Satisfaction," *Wiser Retail Strategies* (blog), Wiser, July 13, 2017, https://blog.wiser.com/how-to-use-pricing-and-promotions-to-improve-customer-satisfaction/.

6. Olivia Cruz, "Creminelli Works with Keep Austin Fed for an Upgraded Snack Experience," News, SXSW Conference & Festivals, February 22, 2022, https://www.sxsw.com/news/2022/creminelli-works-with-keep-austin-fed-for-an-upgraded-snack-experience/.

7. Tom Huddleston Jr., "How the 'McMillions' Scammers Rigged McDonald's Monopoly Game and Stole $24 Million," Make It, CNBC, February 9, 2020, https://www.cnbc.com/2020/02/07/how-mcmillions-scam-rigged-the-mcdonalds-monopoly-game.html.

8. Jessica Miller, "9 Examples of Brands Crushing Social Media Contests in 2021," ShortStack, Pancake Laboratories, June 22, 2021, https://www.shortstack.com/blog/9-examples-of-brands-crushing-social-media-contests-in-2021/.

9. Amanda Breen, "It's National Pizza Day. Grab the Hottest Deals from Domino's, Papa John's, Pizza Hut and More," *Entrepreneur*, February 9, 2022, https://www.entrepreneur.com/article/417720.

10. "2022 F-150 Pricing and Incentives," Ford, accessed May 10, 2022, https://www.ford.com/trucks/f150/pricing-and-incentives/.

11. "Wells Fargo Agrees to Pay $3 Billion to Resolve Criminal and Civil Investigations into Sales Practices Involving the Opening of Millions of Accounts without Customer Authorization," Office of Public Affairs, United States Department of Justice, February 21, 2020, https://www.justice.gov/opa/pr/wells-fargo-agrees-pay-3-billion-resolve-criminal-and-civil-investigations-sales-practices.

12. "About," Tentree, accessed June 25, 2022, https://www.tentree.com/pages/about.

13. Tentree, "Tentree Pledges to Plant One Billion Trees by 2030 in Support of 1t.org," News Releases, Cision, January 22, 2021, https://www.newswire.ca/news-releases/tentree-pledges-to-plant-one-billion-trees-by-2030-in-support-of-1t-org-819565992.html.

14. Huddleston, "How the 'McMillions' Scammers."

15. "American-Made Knives. Guaranteed Forever," Cutco Corporation, https://www.cutco.com/products/american-made.jsp

16. Ibid.

17. "Who We Are," Vector Marketing Corporation, https://www.vectormarketing.com/who-we-are/#:~:text=Vector%20Marketing%20is%20a%20single,independent%20sellers%20of%20CUTCO%C2%AE.

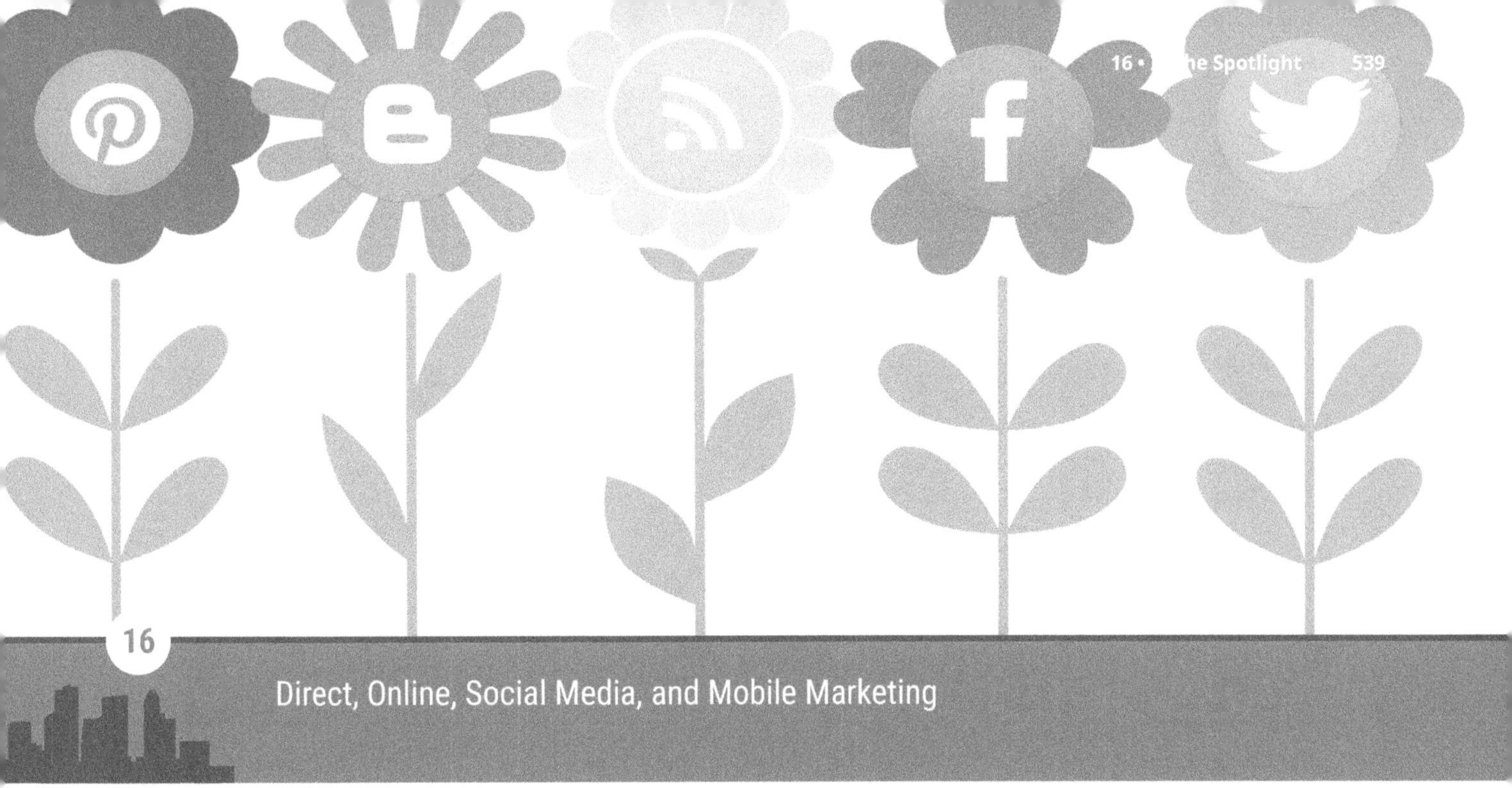

Direct, Online, Social Media, and Mobile Marketing

Figure 16.1 Social media marketing through Pinterest, Twitter, and other platforms is one way to reach consumers. (credit: "Growing Social Media" by mkhmarketing.wordpress.com/about/flickr, CC BY 2.0)

Chapter Outline

16.1 Traditional Direct Marketing
16.2 Social Media and Mobile Marketing
16.3 Metrics Used to Evaluate the Success of Online Marketing
16.4 Ethical Issues in Digital Marketing and Social Media

In the Spotlight

When Dominik Richter, Thomas Griesel, and Jessica Nilsson launched meal-kit provider HelloFresh in October 2011, they did what many successful entrepreneurs seek to do: disrupt a market. While the idea of not having to plan and shop for dinner meals seems enticing for consumers, changing consumer behavior is a challenging task.

HelloFresh needed to convince consumers to stop planning and shopping for meals the way they've always done it. The founders recognized that they needed the right combination of traditional direct and online direct marketing tools to persuade consumers to make a hard pivot.

It starts with the HelloFresh website (https://openstax.org/r/mealkitdelivery), which offers a beautifully designed, user-friendly experience that makes customizing meals, scheduling delivery, and placing orders easy and secure. HelloFresh also uses social media to drive visitors to respond to a variety of calls to action. For example, website visitors are presented with a variety of offers aimed at persuading them to try HelloFresh, including free shipping, surprise gifts, and free meals.

HelloFresh also recognizes the power of direct mail by sending offers similar to those presented on its website and social media to targeted consumers at home via the US Postal Service. It's clear that there is integration between HelloFresh's digital messaging and its direct mail pieces.

HelloFresh has certainly reaped the rewards of an excellent direct and online direct marketing strategy. In 2021, HelloFresh led the market with more than 7.2 million subscribers.[1]

Check out these additional resources about Hello Fresh:

- Hello Fresh Instagram (https://openstax.org/r/instagramhellofresh)
- Hello Fresh Twitter (https://openstax.org/r/twitterhellofresh)
- Hello Fresh LinkedIn (https://openstax.org/r/linkedincompanyhellofresh)
- Consumer Affairs Reviews (https://openstax.org/r/foodhellofresh)
- Taste of Home Review (https://openstax.org/r/articlehellofreshmeal)

16.1 | Traditional Direct Marketing

Learning Outcomes

By the end of this section, you will be able to:

> **LO** 1 List and describe the various forms of traditional direct marketing.
> **LO** 2 Explain how the digital age has impacted direct marketing.

Forms of Traditional Direct Marketing

Direct marketing involves using communication tools to engage directly with individual consumers for the ultimate purpose of calling them to take some marketing action (see Figure 16.2). That action can be a consumer visiting a website or calling a phone number. Ultimately, the goal is to motivate the consumer to make a purchase. If you've received a catalog in the mail or caught yourself watching an entire infomercial about the newest kitchen gadget or gym equipment, you've experienced traditional direct marketing as a consumer.

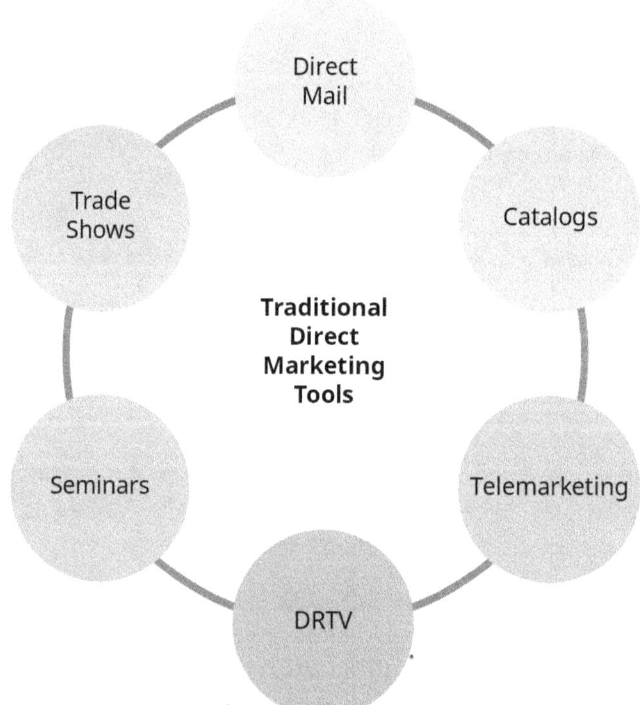

Figure 16.2 Types of Direct Marketing (attribution: Copyright Rice University, OpenStax, under CC BY 4.0 license)

Direct-Mail Marketing

Direct mail arrives in people's homes every day and is typically delivered by the US Postal Service. When marketers use **direct-mail marketing**, they communicate promotional messages and offers directly to people's homes or places of business. Examples of direct-mail marketing include postcards featuring an offer, discount, or coupon code. Seasonal catalogs and glossy look books that present the latest fashions are additional examples.

Like all forms of direct marketing, direct mail is designed to call the consumer to take an action, whether it's to visit a website, scan a QR code, or call a phone number. It also is highly targeted in that companies can send mail based on demographic characteristics such as age, income, zip code, and buying behavior.

Direct mail has some key advantages over other forms of promotion. First, as consumers are inundated with digital messages, direct mail offers the opportunity to stand out and capture attention. Even mostly digital-facing companies like Warby Parker (see Figure 16.3) and Casper (mattresses) have added direct mail to their promotion portfolios in an attempt to stand out from other brands.

Figure 16.3 Warby Parker utilizes direct marketing as a way to reach consumers. (credit: "Warby Parker Sunglasses" by Christopher Fields/flickr, CC BY 2.0)

Direct mail also reaches an entire household of people. This is an important advantage for product categories where household members typically discuss and decide on a product together.

Finally, direct mail has the characteristic of lingering. Other forms of promotion, such as advertising and email marketing, don't have as long a life span as direct mail. According to RetailWire, the average life span of a direct mail piece is 17 days, which means that a household may review that message repeatedly over the life of the mail piece.[2]

The major disadvantage of direct mail is that many consumers consider it to be junk and throw it out without every reading the offer. Also, mail can take time to land in homes. Although the US Postal Service offers speedier delivery options, these come at an increased cost.

Catalog Marketing

Catalog marketing, also known as direct mail order, dates back to the 19th century and is one of the oldest forms of promotion. Catalogs typically include a variety of products that are often vividly displayed in a high-gloss magazine-like format.

Companies such as Lands' End and IKEA have long used catalogs to entice consumers to call the phone number or visit the website displayed on the catalog. The call to action is precisely what makes catalog marketing direct marketing. Consumers are presented with vivid product images and an offer such as free delivery or 20 percent off if the consumer responds to the call to action.

According to a 2020 article published in *Harvard Business Review*, catalogs are making a comeback. Consumers report being excited to receive a catalog. In fact, response rates for catalogs have jumped 170 percent over the last decade.[3]

Unlike emails and advertisements, catalogs remain in consumer homes long after they arrive. Companies like Target and Amazon have used catalog marketing to connect with customers and present featured products across the seasons.

Telemarketing

Telemarketing is a form of direct marketing that involves a company representative placing or answering customer calls for the purpose of guiding a consumer toward making a purchase. During the calls, the representative or agent typically communicates offers to potential customers. Like other forms of direct marketing, the goal is to motivate the consumer to take some action, such as making a purchase or setting up a follow-up appointment.

Telemarketing can be outbound or inbound. With outbound telemarketing, a company representative contacts the prospective customer directly by phone. With inbound telemarketing, demand for the product or service is generated through other channels such as advertising, email, or direct mail. In response to messages delivered through these channels, the customer is motivated to contact the company directly regarding the product or service.

Companies that manage large volumes of calls typically use a **call center**, which is a centralized space where agents answer inbound calls and place outbound calls. The call center serves as the centralized location where customer information is collected or confirmed and then the customer is directed to the right product or service representative. With the explosion in the use of smartphones to search the web, consumers can direct dial from any web page that presents a phone number for contacting the company. Many inbound calls are routed to agents who are located offshore in India and other countries.

Car dealerships often use telemarketing in combination with online direct marketing tools to connect with buyers who show interest in a vehicle listed in the dealership's online inventory. The dealership website may invite consumers to complete a form, after which a sales representative will call the consumer to set up a test drive appointment or answer questions about availability.

Telemarketing can be effective in cases where the consumer expects a phone call. The explosion of unsolicited phone calls from telemarketers, however, has led to a rise in regulation around this direct marketing tool. In 2003, the US government created the National Do Not Call Registry, which bans unsolicited telemarketing calls.[4] Consumers must opt in and give permission to be called by a company. Businesses that do not comply with the law face a hefty fine for violations.

Direct-Response TV (DRTV)

Direct-response television marketing is a type of direct marketing that is designed to compel viewers to take some immediate action, such as calling a phone number or visiting a website presented during a television commercial. The commercials typically involve a persuasive demonstration of a product, after which consumers are provided with a toll-free number or a website to order. The television stations QVC and HSN are excellent examples of DRTV, selling everything from apparel to appliances.

LINK TO LEARNING

DRTV in Action

This movie clip from the film *Joy* starring Jennifer Lawrence as real-life entrepreneur Joy Mangano shows DRTV in action.

Click to view content (https://openstax.org/books/principles-marketing/pages/16-1-traditional-direct-marketing)

DRTV commercials often run 60 or 120 seconds but can be shorter. DRTV commercials that run for 30 minutes or longer are called infomercials. Dollar Shave Club has garnered 27 million views of its famous direct-response television commercial featuring founder Michael Dubin hilariously identifying all the problems with traditional shave products (see Figure 16.4). The commercial features the website domain several times and a clear call to action to the consumer to visit the site to learn more.

Figure 16.4 DRTV marketing compels consumers to take action and is used by the Dollar Shave Club, QVC, and HSN. (credit: "Shave of the Day, 08/21/09" by Dharion/flickr, CC BY 2.0)

Infomercials often feature a spokesperson promoting the benefits of a product. In many cases, there is a persuasive demonstration of the product, and viewers are called to "act now." Some of the most well-remembered infomercial products include the Snuggie, Magic Bullet, and Proactiv. A carefully executed commercial coupled with the right product can generate billions of dollars for companies. Proactiv, for example, which was rebranded as Alchemee in 2022, generated $1 billion in sales in 2020 from its famous acne skin-care line.[5]

Because it offers the advantage of capturing customers in real time and because it's easy to measure, DRTV continues to be an effective direct marketing tool.

Seminars

Seminars allow companies to share their expertise and knowledge related to a topic, issue, or industry. These can be done in person or virtually and are a great tactic for developing trust and building relationships with consumers. They have additional advantages that include building greater brand awareness and introducing new products or services, and they may ultimately lead to increased sales.

Trade Shows

Trade shows are exhibition events that provide companies the opportunity to present themselves and their products and services to industry peers. Trade shows are suited for the business-to-business (B2B) market and are sponsored and hosted by industry trade organizations. They are an excellent way for industry professionals to network and grow their businesses. They are also wildly popular. For example, one of the most popular trade shows, Consumer Electronics Show, or CES, attracts thousands of companies that showcase their latest technology. This trade show serves as an intersection for industry professionals in the health, gaming, and automotive spaces, and participants include tech companies such as Google, Microsoft, and E3, among others.

Companies that participate in trade shows can benefit in the following ways. First, trade shows allow company representatives to visit with existing customers to grow current sales and further solidify their partnership. They also give companies a chance to connect with and present to new buyers.

Every year, MailCon brings together marketing professionals, brands, and agencies to discuss the latest trends in email technology, strategy, and automation. Major brands like Wayfair, Girl Scouts of the USA, Ford Motor Company, and A&E Networks gather to network and learn about advancements in the email marketing space.[6]

LINK TO LEARNING

Digital Marketing

Digital marketing reaches customers where they are at—online. HubSpot answers some of the most common questions it gets about digital marketing in this article (https://openstax.org/r/marketingwhatisdigitalmarketing).

How Has the Digital Age Impacted Marketing?

The digital age has changed the way marketers engage with customers and build relationships. While the traditional channels of print, television, and radio certainly present advantages, the digital age has created opportunities for marketers to engage with consumers in a highly personalized and interactive way.

Online Direct Marketing Defined

While traditional forms of direct marketing center on engaging directly with consumers through channels like mail and television, **online direct marketing** uses a rich collection of digital tools to target individual consumers with an offer that requests a response or action. The online direct marketing tools covered in this section include website marketing, email marketing, content marketing, online video marketing, blogs, and online forums.

LendingTree is a great example of a fintech (financial tech) company disrupting the traditional banking industry. LendingTree has revolutionized the way consumers and banks participate in the lending process. It excels at matching consumers searching for financing with banks looking for qualified customers. It is LendingTree's digital marketing tools that make this matching process possible.

A consumer who searches the web and lands on LendingTree's website is invited to compare quotes and plans that are tailored to their age, income level, and location by filling out an online form. LendingTree then displays consumer-relevant plans and quotes based on their demographics and follows up with an email inviting consumers to view offers from financial institutions. If the customer is a Gmail user, consumers may then see digital ads later on sites like YouTube and in their Gmail inbox.

Direct Meets Digital: The Evolution of Direct Marketing with Technology

The explosion in internet usage and online shopping coupled with the evolution of digital technologies has resulted in the emergence of online direct marketing. While traditional forms of direct marketing remain important for engaging with consumers, the channel has evolved as technology has evolved. With 3.5 billion smartphone users worldwide, marketers recognize the value in engaging with consumers through mobile devices. In the United States alone, 65.6 percent of Americans report that they check smartphones 160 times a day.[7]

In response to the explosion in smartphones and internet usage, online direct marketing is getting a larger share of advertising spend. In 2020, advertisers spent $139.8 billion on digital marketing, and that number is expected to grow to $200 billion by 2025.[8]

Forms of Online Direct Marketing

There are several online direct marketing tools that can be used (see Figure 16.5). Let's take a look at each tool in the following section.

Figure 16.5 Online Direct Marketing Tools (attribution: Copyright Rice University, OpenStax, under CC BY 4.0 license)

Website Marketing

Website marketing is the promotion of a website that results in driving traffic or visitors to the site to learn more about the product or company or to make a purchase. The purpose of website marketing is to attract online shoppers who may be interested in a company's product or service offering.

Developing a website is one of the most important steps a company can take to establish a digital presence online. Websites serve a variety of purposes. Some are designed to nurture consumers and guide them toward making a purchase while others are designed to facilitate transactions. For example, car manufacturers like Toyota and Honda use their websites to deliver details and options related to their product lines. Consumers can use interactive tools to change out features and colors based on their preferences; however, consumers would likely visit a dealership to make the actual purchase.

Amazon.com is designed to allow third-party sellers to share product details, reviews, and product comparisons. Its purpose is to facilitate a purchase transaction in which the consumer buys something directly from the site. Shopify has recently emerged as the "anti-Amazon" by offering sellers more than a dozen services ranging from e-commerce websites to inventory management and payment processing.

There are still other websites whose purpose is not transactional but that are designed to build community and engagement among customers. Bleacher Report's website offers sports articles, game scores, and live sports streaming. Fans are invited to comment and engage with one another regarding the latest sports news. The website also offers the option of signing up for its newsletter delivered to consumers' email inboxes. Whether it's to communicate information, facilitate a transaction, or build a community, websites should be designed with a positive user experience (UX) in mind.

Email Marketing

Email marketing is a type of direct marketing that is highly personal and designed to build relationships with consumers. Marketers use email to communicate promotions about products and share relevant content. It offers the advantage of connecting companies with highly targeted consumers at a much lower cost than other channels. Email usage statistics are also impressive, making this channel attractive as an online direct marketing tool.

Email boasts over 4 billion daily users; 99 percent of people report checking their email on a daily basis.[9] Given the low cost and high usage rate, email marketing can be a profitable way to connect with customers. Marketers generally send two types of emails: transactional emails and marketing emails. A transactional email is a type of email that is sent to customers following a commercial transaction, such as a purchase or a return. When online shoppers purchase athletic apparel from Dick's Sporting Goods, they receive an email confirmation confirming the order.

Marketing emails are promotional in nature and typically involve a marketing offer. Old Navy sends marketing emails during major sales events. They feature relevant product categories based on past purchases and often include a coupon code or free-shipping promotion.

Buzzfeed provides another great example of a company that optimizes email marketing to reach subscribers. According to Campaign Monitor, it has created a collection of diverse and audience-catered newsletters that are tailored to the preferences of Buzzfeed's subscribers.[10] Emails feature relevant articles and funny GIFs that prompt subscribers to visit the site to read more. On average, subscribers who visit the site via email spend more time on the site than those website visitors who have come from other channels.

Regardless of their email marketing strategy, companies utilize email marketing platforms like Mailchimp to reach target audiences. Mailchimp is built for growing businesses, and in 2022 it launched a Super Bowl advertising campaign to promote its services.[11] As a martech (marketing technology) company, it offers small businesses tools for guiding consumers through a customer journey to a purchase. Mailchimp's automation tool, specifically, allows businesses to send email campaigns based on a consumer's interaction with an email message. The result is a highly personalized email conversation between the small business and the customer.

LINK TO LEARNING

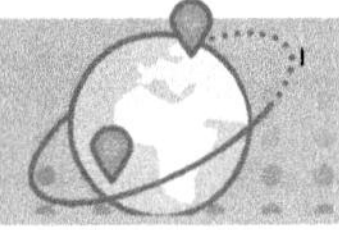

Mailchimp

Learn how Mailchimp's CEO and cofounder, Ben Chestnut, built and grew the Mailchimp email platform in this podcast: NPR's How I Built This with Guy Raz (https://openstax.org/r/benchestnut).

Check out the 2022 Super Bowl commercial with DJ Khaled here.

Click to view content (https://openstax.org/books/principles-marketing/pages/16-1-traditional-direct-marketing)

Email marketing is also known as permission-based marketing. Permission-based marketing requires that marketers get consent to send email and text messages to consumers prior to contacting them with a promotional message. Once a consumer opts in to receive an email or text message, they are given the option to opt out by clicking on an unsubscribe link or by reply texting a company to opt out of messages.

Consumers typically opt in to receiving emails when they place an online order so that they may receive order confirmation and shipping updates. In addition, consumers are also opting in to receive other value-added content, such as exclusive discounts, access to a webinar, a free trial, or some other type of value exchange.

Content Marketing

Websites, email, and other forms of online marketing are only as good as the content they carry. **Content marketing** involves creating and distributing content that is valuable and relevant to a company's target customers. New York–based Dotdash Meredith is a good example of this. The company's digital brands include Verywell, The Spruce, Byrdie, and others. Dotdash Meredith is a unit of Barry Diller's IAC. Company policy: no pop-up ads!

As with other forms of direct marketing, content is about driving customers to take some desired action. Consumers would much rather consume a funny video clip, a highlight reel of their favorite athlete, and an inspiring quote or comment than see banner ads and pop-up ads. In order for content marketing to work, it must be useful, relevant, high quality, and engaging to the targeted audience.

When content is delivered through social media, blogs, and email, consumers have the opportunity to directly engage with the company and other content consumers. They can like, share, retweet, and mark as a favorite—all examples of actions taken in response to the content. Marketers can use the data created by these actions to perform sentiment analysis and generate other metrics. The challenge with content marketing is that it is constantly changing. Companies are tasked with constantly updating their content and continuing to tell stories that their audience wants to hear and engage with.

Online Video Marketing

Online video marketing involves creating videos that tell a story about a product, company, or brand that is designed to drive consumer engagement through activities such as liking, sharing, and retweeting. Video marketing is becoming increasingly popular as a marketing tool because the cost of creating video campaigns has dropped significantly in the last decade due to technological advancements. Biteable, for example, offers marketers a cost-effective way to create brand videos that are quick, simple, and customizable.

Along with the drop in cost to produce online videos, consumer demand for videos has increased. Because of this demand, Instagram, Facebook, and Twitter have pivoted to video-first platforms. Wyzowl's annual State of Video Marketing Survey revealed in 2021 that online video watching has doubled since 2018 and that online marketers "feel positive about the return on investment offered by video more than ever as it continues to strongly influence traffic, leads, sales, and audience understanding."[12]

LINK TO LEARNING

Wyzowl's Survey Found on HubSpot

Read more about the key data points learned by Wyzowl in its 2022 survey. You might be interested to learn that 86 percent of businesses use video as a marketing tool, 94 percent of companies believe videos help customers better understand their product, and 99 percent of video marketers said they will continue using video. You can find the full report here (https://openstax.org/r/videomarketingstatistics). There's a ton of interesting information!

Blogs and Online Forums

A **blog** is an online journal of interests, beliefs, or other topics published by a person, a group of people, or an organization. In its early stages, a blog was a personal journal that someone posted to the web. It's since evolved into an online marketing tool that is typically a website or a webpage and serves a variety of purposes.

First, a blog's purpose can be to share valuable and relevant information with targeted audiences. Ultimately, the goal is to attract visitors to the page or site and convert them to customers. In addition, marketers create blog content on sometimes a weekly or even daily basis so that consumers continue to visit the site or the page to access the new content. When the blog content is good, visitors will continue to engage with the articles produced by the company. Ultimately, this helps a company's organic ranking on Google. In Google, your page or website will rank higher on the Google search results page as it grows in popularity and consumers click on it.

Blogs are also a great way to create and nurture online communities, or groups of people with similar interests connecting to one another online.

Customer relationship management company HubSpot is excellent at creating high-quality blog content for marketing and business professionals. It covers an array of professional topics, from marketing to human resources management to communicating effectively in the workplace. Its content ultimately drives visitors to its website, where they'll find a suite of programs designed for marketing, sales, customer service, and operations.

Blogging can be an integral part of a content strategy as long as marketers dedicate time and resources to continue updating the content. Visitors appreciate fresh and relevant information, and delaying the delivery of high-quality content may mean a loss of visitor interest.

LINK TO LEARNING

Content Marketing Tools

Learn more about the types of content marketing tools marketers have to work with by reading this HubSpot article (https://openstax.org/r/contentmarketingtypes). Included are the types you're probably more familiar with, like blogs and videos, but also discussed are the ones you may not have as much experience with like, white papers and case studies.

Advantages of Online Direct Marketing

There are several key advantages that make online direct marketing an attractive tool for marketers. First, online direct marketing is not restricted by geographical boundaries. The internet is readily available to most consumers globally, making it practical to market around the globe.

Second, online direct marketing is much less expensive than other forms of marketing when considering its global reach. Imagine how expensive it would be to send direct-mail catalogs to customers all over the world. Establishing an online presence by developing a website and creating video and blog content is relatively inexpensive compared to other forms of promotion.

Third, online direct marketing is easy to measure in terms of campaign performance. With advertising tools targeted to mass audiences, it's difficult to attribute a sale to a particular television or radio commercial. With online direct advertising, marketers can track the performance of their campaigns based on consumers' interaction with digital tools such as email, online videos, and a company's website. For example, when Nike creates online video content that is posted on YouTube and its website, Nike marketers can track consumers' engagement with that content, in addition to the consumer's online journey. Online direct marketing reveals real-time insights into the effectiveness of campaigns compared to more traditional forms of promotion.

Fourth, online direct marketing is highly targeted. Marketers can carefully focus promotion efforts on very specific groups of consumers based on their geography, their social media channel preferences, and other variables. Online direct marketing also allows for retargeting, which occurs when consumers visit different websites but are shown similar ads based on their online consumer behavior.

Finally, online direct marketing allows for real-time interaction between brands and consumers. Consumers may start with a Google search and end with the completion of an online purchase. Throughout the online consumer buying process, marketers have the opportunity to engage with the consumer in real time.

Traditional direct marketing and online direct marketing offer a variety of benefits in connecting marketers to targeted consumers.

CAREERS IN MARKETING

Digital Marketer

Digital marketers build and implement a company's online-related activities and sales. Review this job description (https://openstax.org/r/jobdescriptionsdigitalmarketing) and list of qualifications from Glassdoor for more details. There are several additional resources that will help you better understand the digital marketing job role and what it will take to get a job in this field:

- Ahrefs—A Source for Digital Marketing Tutorials: "How to Start a Career in Digital Marketing (Step-by-Step)"
  Click to view content (https://openstax.org/books/principles-marketing/pages/16-1-traditional-direct-marketing)
- Neil Patel: "How to Get a Digital Marketing Job with No Experience"
  Click to view content (https://openstax.org/books/principles-marketing/pages/16-1-traditional-direct-marketing)
- Digital Marketing Institute: "7 of the Hottest Digital Marketing Jobs (https://openstax.org/r/digitalmarketinginstitute)"
- Indeed: "How to Get a Job in Digital Marketing in 7 Steps (https://openstax.org/r/careeradvicefindingajob)"
- Emerson College: "5 Reasons to Choose a Career in Digital Marketing in 2022 (https://openstax.org/r/marketinganalyticsemersonedu)"

Knowledge Check

It's time to check your knowledge on the concepts presented in this section. Refer to the Answer Key at the end of the book for feedback.

1. Which of the following best describes the difference between traditional direct marketing and online direct marketing?
   a. Online direct marketing uses digital tools to individually engage with consumers and call them to take some desired action. Traditional direct marketing does not allow a quick call to action.
   b. Traditional direct marketing is more effective than online direct marketing.
   c. Online direct marketing allows marketers to target consumers based on factors such as their location, age, and income. Traditional direct marketing can also be based on demographic factors.
   d. Traditional direct marketing channels do not include a call to action, and online direct marketing channels do.

2. Which of the following best summarizes the cause for the emergence of online direct marketing as a promotion tool?
   a. The explosion of internet usage, online shopping, and smartphone usage and the advancement of digital marketing technologies best explains the emergence of online direct marketing.
   b. Consumers are spending less time watching movies and shows.
   c. Traditional direct marketing tools have gotten too expensive and are no longer effective at engaging customers.

d. Traditional direct marketing doesn't offer the same degree of message relevance that online direct marketing does.

3. Which type of marketing involves creating and distributing content that is valuable and relevant to a company's target customers?
   a. Website marketing
   b. Blog marketing
   c. Email marketing
   d. Content marketing

4. Which form of online marketing is permission-based, meaning that consumers must consent to receiving online messages?
   a. Website marketing
   b. Blog marketing
   c. Content marketing
   d. Email marketing

5. Which of the following represents an advantage of using online direct marketing tools?
   a. Online direct marketing allows marketers to target consumers globally because of worldwide access to the internet.
   b. Online direct marketing is highly targeted in that marketers can reach customers through a variety of digital channels that are inexpensive compared to other promotion tools.
   c. Online direct marketing allows for easier measurement of ROI on campaigns.
   d. All of these are advantages of online direct marketing.

16.2 | Social Media and Mobile Marketing

Learning Outcomes

By the end of this section, you will be able to:
   LO 1 Discuss social media marketing and its opportunities and challenges.
   LO 2 Discuss mobile marketing and its opportunities and challenges.

Social Media Marketing

Figure 16.6 Social media marketing has created an opportunity for marketers to reach consumers in real time through campaigns run on digital platforms such as YouTube, Instagram, and others. (credit: "Social Media Word Cloud" by cloudincome.com/flickr, CC BY 2.0)

As discussed in the previous section, internet and digital technology usage have surged across the globe, creating opportunities for marketers to engage with consumers in real time. Social media marketing has emerged as a powerful online marketing tool as consumer time spent on these platforms (see Figure 16.6) has grown substantially over the last decade. A growing share of Americans report that they use YouTube and Facebook more than any other social media platform. In segments under the age of 30, the most popular platforms are Instagram, Snapchat, and TikTok.

Social Media Marketing Defined

Social media marketing is defined as using social media platforms to deliver content that drives engagement with your brand. Companies from PepsiCo to Home Depot to the pizza restaurant located in town use social media to connect with users, share content, and, ultimately, generate sales. Marketers can create brand profiles and sponsored content that they pay for.

Warby Parker uses Instagram to create high-quality content and showcase different styles of eyeglasses based on face shape. Users may click on the post, read and reply to comments, like it, mark it as a favorite, or share it on their own feed. If they are in the market for new eyewear, the social media post may drive them to the company's website, where they can virtually try on different styles of eyeglasses and ultimately make a purchase.

Social media marketing offers some advantages and disadvantages. The advantages include that it is highly targeted, it allows for engagement with and among users, it is a great tool for driving visitors to a company's website, and it is easily measured.

Uses of Social Media Marketing

Marketers recognize that social media presents an exciting opportunity to connect with consumers across a variety of platforms. Unlike some other forms of promotion, social media marketing allows marketers to precisely target audiences. Marketers can create social media campaigns that target demographic attributes such as gender, age, and location in addition to psychographic attributes such as interests and viewing behavior.

For example, Facebook allows marketers to upload a list of customers that includes the demographic and psychographic attributes of the company's target audience. Facebook then creates what's called a "lookalike audience" that matches those customer attributes to the attributes of Facebook users so that the company's ads will show up in the feeds of the lookalike audience.

Social media marketing also creates the opportunity for users to engage with one another and company content. It's an excellent vehicle for marketers to distribute their online video and blog content in addition to communicating promotional offers. Marketers can monitor engagement and participate in ongoing conversations with users who comment, like, and share content.

Harvard Business Review (HBR) provides a great example of how to use social media marketing effectively. HBR, a business management magazine published by the Harvard Business Publishing subsidiary of Harvard University, offers paid subscribers the latest research and articles on all things related to management.

During the pandemic, HBR gave people free access to all HBR content. The campaign ran on social media and resulted in increased traffic at the HBR website. This brings us to another important advantage of social media marketing. It can create traffic or visitors that link from the social media platform directly to the company's website.

Finally, social media marketing is highly measurable. Online marketers can evaluate key engagement metrics such as clicks, likes, and shares and optimize their social media campaigns so that they achieve the goals they set. For example, posting at 1:00 p.m. EST on Facebook results in getting the most shares while posting content at 3:00 p.m. EST results in getting the most clicks.

A major disadvantage of social media marketing is that brands don't have complete control over the message. Consumers can freely write comments that are harmful to a brand's reputation. Amazon's Jeff Bezos famously wished everyone a "Happy Earth Day" in a tweet that showed him dogsledding above the Arctic Circle in Norway. He received serious backlash from Twitter users who pointed out at the time that Amazon employees were underpaid and overworked.[13]

In addition to losing control over the message, social media marketing requires a great deal of resources, including time and money. Content is key to creating engagement, and continuous creation of new and engaging content requires resources. Social media pages and posts also need to be monitored for engagement. For example, companies that are active on social media have a plan for reviewing and replying to sometimes hundreds of comments. Fortunately, there are great online tools to help automate replies to comments.

Facebook

Facebook, whose parent company was rebranded as Meta in 2021, is the largest social media platform, with over 2.9 billion monthly active users and $117.92 billion in revenue.[14] These numbers make this platform attractive for reaching a diverse, global audience. Facebook is facing the challenge that a growing percentage of its users are baby boomers (born between 1946 and 1964) while teens are using other platforms, like TikTok and YouTube, more frequently.

In addition, Facebook has been scrutinized because of how the company uses personal data. Six in ten social media users report that they've observed and temporarily believed something they've read on Facebook that turned out to be false information.[15]

In addition, there's a growing concern about the role that social media has played in dividing people. Fifty percent of users who are millennials say that Facebook fosters division, compared to only 38 percent of baby boomers.[16]

Facebook is still clearly the behemoth of social media platforms, and so long as it holds that position, marketers will continue to use it as a channel to deliver content and drive engagement with targeted customers.

Instagram

As a social media platform, Instagram's growth has exploded over the last decade. While not as large as Facebook in terms of users, it still boasts 1 billion active users every month. Instagram attracts a younger demographic, mostly people under the age of 30, which makes it attractive for brands targeting this audience.[17]

The company previously known as Facebook purchased Instagram in 2012. The union of Facebook and Instagram under one corporate entity has provided synergistic benefits to users, companies included. First, social media allows users to cross-post on the two platforms. And second, this has the advantage of increasing reach and repetition of messages more efficiently.

From a social media advertising perspective, the integration of Facebook and Instagram allows companies to manage and monitor campaigns across the two platforms easily. Furthermore, companies that have leveraged these integrative features have enjoyed stronger campaign performances in terms of clicks, views, and website conversions.

Spotify uses Instagram Stories brilliantly during its #yearwrapped campaign that drops every December. Instagram Stories lets users post photos and videos that disappear after 24 hours. It's become a very powerful sharing tool with more than 500 million users posting stories every day.

Spotify created a special webpage that presents visitors with their most listened to artists, songs, and other interesting insights related to their music habits over the year. Spotify gives visitors the option of sharing these highlights on other social platforms. This campaign has proved to be highly engaging, with more than 60 million Spotify users engaging with Spotify's Instagram Story and 3 billion #yearwrapped playlists streamed as a result of the campaign.

LinkedIn

For business professionals seeking networking, partnership, and employment opportunities, LinkedIn proves to be an excellent social media platform (see Figure 16.7). LinkedIn boasts 722 million users, who are known as members. Among social media platforms, LinkedIn is considered the most trusted, with 73 percent of members agreeing that LinkedIn protects members' privacy.[18]

Figure 16.7 LinkedIn is a business professional platform that is used by marketers to reach consumers. (credit: "LinkedIn Pen" by Sheila Scarborough/flickr, CC BY 2.0)

LinkedIn Live is the platform's live streaming feature, which allows companies to engage directly with community members. Vimeo leveraged the feature when it held a "Working Lunch" series. Using a seminar format, it brought together experts across the business, communication, and technology industries and interested members. The goal was to engage with the audience, provide relevant information, and drive use and engagement of the platform.

While not the largest social platform, LinkedIn most certainly serves as an important tool for connecting with business professionals in the B2B space.

Pinterest

With 478 million monthly users, Pinterest is a social platform that allows users to visually explore an endless array of ideas from recipes to home decor to crafts to personal style.[19] Users can use the platform's search bar to look for topics or people that interest them, which produces results related to search keywords.

For businesses, Pinterest offers a host of benefits as a social marketing tool. First, 97 percent of searches are unbranded.[20] Simply put, consumers aren't looking for brand-specific content when browsing the platform. This is music to the ears of companies that can place their ads in Pinterest feeds near relevant content. For example, a user may search for "image of vintage running shoes" on Pinterest, which would result in a host of profiles featuring content related to the search terms. A well-placed New Balance advertisement featuring its vintage 720 sneaker would be a strategic marketing move in this situation (see Figure 16.8).

Figure 16.8 A marketer could place a New Balance sneaker advertisement on Pinterest near unbranded searches. (credit: "New Balance Limited Edition Pink Ribbon 3190 Running Shoes" by slgckgc/flickr, CC BY 2.0)

Twitter

As a social platform, Twitter is a microblogging news and networking site where users typically post shorter messages known as tweets. After receiving complaints that 140 characters weren't enough room to express ideas, Twitter expanded its character limit from 140 to 270 in 2017. It has approximately 238 million daily active users, with about 14.5 million living in the United States. It has seen steady growth in international appeal.[21]

Similar to LinkedIn, Twitter is a popular B2B digital marketing tool, with 67 percent of all B2B businesses using the platform to reach business customers.[22] Twitter users have a high expectation that a company will respond to a tweet; therefore, marketers who choose this platform should be prepared to engage with users directly. Twitter's ownership and policy changes in 2022 led many people and companies to reconsider their relationship with the platform, but it will likely remain a major force in marketing and business for years to come.

Podcasts

Podcasts are often free, on-demand, downloadable audio recordings that cover a variety of topics and are typically made available on a weekly or monthly basis. Podcasts are distributed through applications such as Apple's Podcasts, Google Podcasts, Spotify, and Audible, but they can also be published on a company's website. Podcasting has been growing at a "hockey stick" rate—200 percent year-on-year growth.[23] Recognizing a huge opportunity, Spotify acquired podcasting company Megaphone in 2020.[24] The acquisition positions Spotify as the "go-to" platform for premium podcast content, which offers new opportunities for advertisers. In a world where people question information they are given, podcast hosts stand out because 52 percent of listeners trust advertising when endorsed by the host.[25] The hosts can offer brand endorsements and approvals in addition to stories that they bring to life via audio. Listeners take in what the host says and then build it out in their own minds. Podcast creators leverage social media platforms to drive traffic to applications and sites where the podcasts can be played or downloaded.

Podcasts can be an effective digital marketing tool when marketers want to hyper target a niche audience with relevant topics. They are typically created to share educational information and often result in a good return on investment because of the value they create for loyal listeners.

eLearning company Harappa Education produces the *Habits Matter* podcast, which focuses on topics about learning and personal growth. Listeners are attracted to the series because they want to learn something new without the noise of a marketing message. Podcasts are effective at creating value, building relationships, and engaging target audiences in a subtle way.

LINK TO LEARNING

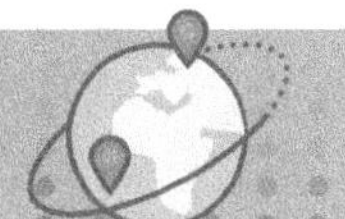

Social Media Strategy

Social media marketing can be complex because of the variety of platforms and new features being added all the time. Check out this guide from HubSpot on how to develop a social media strategy (https://openstax.org/r/marketingsocialmediastrategy).

Also, check out the *Habits Matter* podcast. Hosted by Shreyasi Singh, the *Habits Matter* podcast explores humanity at work. Check it out here at Apple (https://openstax.org/r/podcasthabitsmatter) or here at Spotify (https://openstax.org/r/openspotifyshow).

Social Media Marketing: Opportunities and Challenges

When marketers are considering social media as a digital marketing tool, they need to weigh its opportunities and its challenges in order to determine if it's the right-fit channel for reaching targeted customers.

The major opportunities of social media marketing include reaching global customers, increasing brand awareness, engaging with targeted customers, and increasing website traffic. First, social media connects companies to billions of users across the globe. Because of this reach, companies can connect with new and existing customers in profitable ways.

In addition, because of the billions of active users on social media, brands can increase awareness of their existence with targeted consumers. For example, a five-year-old swimsuit and beachwear company, Cupshe, had little to no brand recognition among US consumers until it launched campaigns on Facebook and Instagram. In 2020, the company boasted $150 million in sales without a single storefront.[26] Consumers were exposed to the brand via social media ads, which then drove them to the company's website to browse styles and make purchases.

In addition to increasing brand awareness, social platforms help brands engage directly with consumers. Mass forms of promotion such as advertising only offer one-way communication from the company to the customer. Social media platforms allow for multidirectional communication between the company and users and brand communities.

Finally, social media drives traffic to company websites. Users see a sponsored advertisement in their news feed that is highly relevant to their interests and click on the content to learn more, browse inventory, and, ultimately, make a purchase.

The major challenge facing marketers who use social media to reach target audiences is that there is a growing distrust of social media platforms in terms of what they do with our private information. In addition, social media marketing requires dedicated campaign managers who can post fresh content frequently, monitor engagement, and respond to comments. The third disadvantage is that while multidirectional dialogue between consumers and the company is an advantage, the comments cannot be controlled. Users can tarnish the company's brand name if they share negative experiences or opinions about the brand.

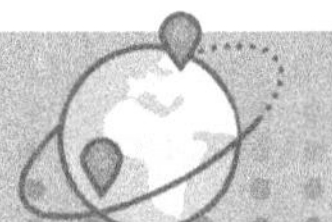

LINK TO LEARNING

What Goes Viral?

Why do some things go viral and others don't? Learn from BuzzFeed's publisher Dao Nguyen and her TED Talk on the tactics her team uses to make things go viral.

Click to view content (https://openstax.org/books/principles-marketing/pages/16-2-social-media-and-mobile-marketing)

Integrated Social Media Marketing

Integrated social media marketing involves creating a clear, consistent, and synergistic message across all social media platforms. When consumers are presented with coordinated messages across social media platforms, brand awareness and purchase intention increase.

Mobile Marketing: Definition and Strategies

Mobile marketing is defined as the use of multiple digital marketing channels that are designed to reach consumers on their smartphones and tablets. Given the variety of digital tools that marketers use to engage with consumers, it's important to discuss how mobile device use impacts digital marketing strategies. Usage of mobile devices to access the internet and applications has steadily increased over the last ten years.[27] As mobile device technology and digital technology has improved, people are doing everything from refinancing their homes to buying cars online. Mobile device usage will continue to grow, and as consumers spend more time on mobile devices, marketers must adapt their strategies to meet consumers where they are.

There are currently 6.4 billion smartphone users worldwide, and usage is expected to continue to grow over the next decade.[28] In 2022, US mobile advertising spend is expected to reach $137.13 billion, where it was $100 billion in 2021.[29] Given these compelling statistics, companies must be prepared with an effective mobile marketing strategy. Marketing for mobile devices is not the same as marketing for desktops. Consumers expect a more personalized experience when they engage with brands on their smartphones.

Elements of a successful mobile marketing strategy should include responsive design, mobile-friendly emails, app development, and memorable URLs.

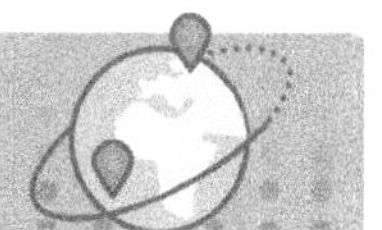

LINK TO LEARNING

US Mobile Advertising

To learn more about the predicted growth of mobile advertising in the United States, read this article from Oberlo (https://openstax.org/r/mobileadvertisinggrowth). It states that US spend is expected to grow 14 percent to $156 billion in 2023 and up to $174 billion in 2024.

Responsive Web Design

Responsive web design means that when people visit your website via their mobile device, the menus and content display in a way that is easy to read and engage with. Users don't need to pinch, expand, or scroll the screen to view content. Responsive web design became the standard in 2015 when Google announced that mobile-friendly websites would be prioritized over non-mobile-friendly designs in search results. Responsive web design is critical to ensuring that visitors have a good experience while navigating your website.

Mobile-Friendly Emails

Mobile-friendly emails are emails whose images, text, and links display in a user-friendly way when accessed via a mobile device. With 68 percent of emails being opened on mobile devices, responsive design is necessary to create a good user experience.[30] Similar to responsive web design, email content needs to display on mobile devices in a way that is simple for the user to consume.

One way that email marketers can meet mobile-friendly standards is to ensure that subject lines are between 41 and 50 characters. Subject lines should capture attention and paint a benefit for the subscriber. In addition, mobile-friendly emails often contain a pre-header, which is the first line of text in your email. It provides context for what the email contains. Finally, emails should be concise with a clear and easy-to-find call to action. Many emails contain buttons that link email viewers directly to the company's website. The button is typically rectangular and includes actionable language like "Get Started" or "Shop the Sale."

Developing an App

For some companies, developing a mobile app is an important element in their mobile strategy. Because a shocking 90 percent of people's mobile usage is on smartphone apps, marketers must consider the value in creating one.[31]

One benefit of developing a mobile app is that apps provide direct communication and engagement opportunities with customers at the touch of a button. Amazon's app, for example, makes it easy to search for and purchase products from mobile devices. The alternative is for users to open their browser on their phone, type in the Amazon URL, and search directly from the mobile site. Apps make it convenient for consumers.

Short/Memorable URLs

An internet site's address on the web is technically known as a uniform resource locator (URL). In the digital world, you could have a great website with great content and a strong social media presence, but visitors cannot reach your website without a well-constructed URL.

Having a shorter, memorable URL is an important marketing tactic for the following reasons. First, it's easy for people to remember. Second, shorter URLs are easier to share, whether it's through email, text, or social media. Finally, optimizing the length of a URL makes it much easier for Google to find and display in search results.

There are a number of applications, such as TinyURL and Bitly, that are capable of turning long URLs into shorter ones; however, the jury is still out on whether search engines perceive these URLs as trustworthy.

Mobile Marketing: Opportunities and Challenges

Mobile marketing presents clear opportunities for digital marketers. First, mobile device usage continues to grow as consumers stratify their time across various devices at once. In addition, mobile devices allow people to experience almost constant connectivity that ignores the boundaries that traditional marketing channels must observe, such as time and place. For example, Nothing Bundt Cakes' store hours of operation might be 10:00 a.m. to 6:00 p.m. However, accessing its website to place an order can happen at any time of day from any location.

The shift in mobile usage behavior provides a number of opportunities for marketers to connect with consumers in a place where they are spending more and more time. Additionally, consumers are using mobile devices to conduct product research, view customer reviews, and interact with brands on social media platforms.

In addition to mobile marketing opportunities, this channel also presents challenges to digital marketers. The first challenge is finding the right mix of mobile channels to reach your target audience. For some companies, SMS texting makes sense because customers are open to receiving promotional messages via text. If the company has a mobile application, it may consider sending push notifications that alert users to important information when they aren't engaging with the app. Understanding your target audience is key to determining which mobile tools make the most sense.

A second challenge with mobile marketing is measuring results. While companies can easily measure things like in-app purchases and emails opened and clicked, it's more difficult for marketers to see whether someone has seen a push notification or in-app message.

Knowledge Check

It's time to check your knowledge on the concepts presented in this section. Refer to the Answer Key at the end of the book for feedback.

1. Which of the following is an advantage of social media marketing?
   a. Social media is highly targeted in its ability to reach segments of consumers who share common interests and demographics.
   b. With social media, marketers have complete control of the message.
   c. Social media is very easy to manage and requires few resources.
   d. Social media is the best channel for the B2B market.

2. Which of the following is a challenge that marketers face when using social media marketing?
   a. Social media marketing does not allow companies to target multiple audiences at the same time.
   b. Social media use is unpredictable, with users only logging in once or twice per week.
   c. Companies do not have control over the message.
   d. Social media does a poor job of driving traffic to websites.

3. Which of the following is a characteristic of a good mobile strategy?
   a. Mobile websites should have a responsive design so visitors have a good user experience.
   b. Emails should be sent to consumers on a weekly basis in order to stay engaged with mobile users.
   c. Avoid using push notification features to avoid overcommunicating with your users.
   d. Measure whether or not a mobile device user has seen a push notification.

4. When a company's website adapts to whatever screen consumers are using and users don't need to pinch, expand, or scroll the screen to view content, this is known as ________.
   a. website design
   b. responsive marketing

   c. content marketing

   d. responsive web design

5. Which of the following represents a challenge for mobile marketing?

   a. Mobile device usage is on the decline.

   b. It's challenging to measure mobile marketing campaigns.

   c. Responsive design is difficult to implement.

   d. People are using email less and less.

MARKETING IN PRACTICE

National Geographic

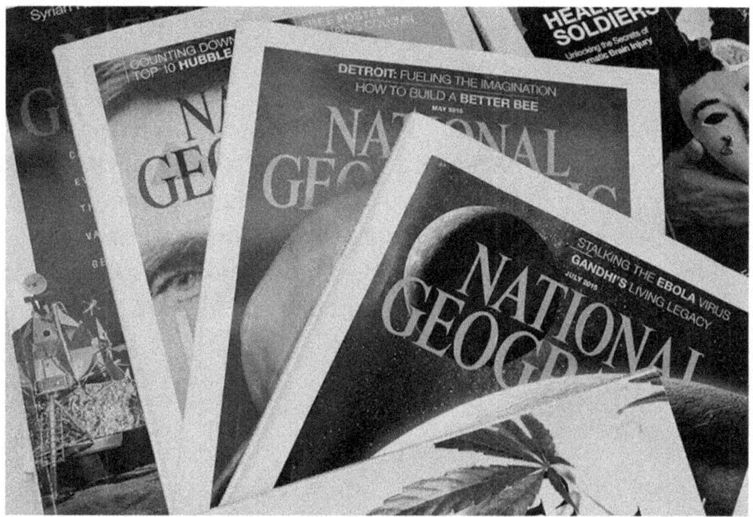

Figure 16.9 National Geographic has utilized Instagram for a promotional strategy as a way to share never-before-seen photographs. (credit: "National Geographic" by Open Grid Scheduler/Grid Engine/flickr, Public Domain)

National Geographic has over 220 million followers on Instagram, boasting the leading brand account on the site.[32] It shares stunning images of people, places, animals, and natural landscapes from all over the world. As a visual storyteller, *National Geographic* captures some of the most awe-inspiring, unfiltered images that the world has ever seen (see Figure 16.9).

Instagram has served as an effective vehicle for sharing these images globally. *National Geographic* has utilized the platform to drive engagement with followers. Its famous "Wanderlust" social media campaign invites amateur photographers from around the world to post the best photographs they've taken while traveling.[33] Followers use the #wanderlustcontest hashtag to connect with the *National Geographic* community of travelers. Its strategy to promote user-generated content was a great way to connect with followers and build continuous engagement.

In addition to its Wanderlust campaign, *National Geographic* uses Instagram and other social media platforms to share content that is central to the brand's values. For example, on "The Endangered Species Day" and "The Oceans Day," it pushes content related to wildlife and nature protection using powerful images and statistics.[34]

Through social media, *National Geographic* is able to share its passion for nature and wildlife with a community of like-minded people. As a tool, social media allows *National Geographic* to engage with followers in a personal way.

16.3 | Metrics Used to Evaluate the Success of Online Marketing

Learning Outcomes

By the end of this section, you will be able to:
- **LO** 1 Discuss the role of marketing metrics in digital, online, social media, and mobile marketing.
- **LO** 2 List and describe the metrics used to evaluate the success of online marketing.

Types of Online Marketing Metrics

While online marketing tools have numerous advantages over traditional tools, it's important for marketers to pay close attention to metrics that indicate the performance of their online marketing campaigns. Metrics are goals that marketers are trying to reach through their campaigns, and they are typically quantitative in nature. For example, companies measure the performance of their social media campaigns by measuring how many likes, shares, or comments are posted in response to the content. While each online marketing tool has its own set of metrics, we'll focus on the following tools.

Website Traffic

Website traffic is the total number of visitors to a company's website. For some companies, website traffic can help move consumers further along the sales funnel and closer to making a purchase. A **sales funnel** is a visual representation of the customer journey from product awareness to product purchase. For e-commerce sites specifically, online marketers want to increase traffic to their website, which represents the top of the sales funnel, where most consumers will stop. The number of consumers will eventually dwindle until there is an actual purchase, which represents the narrow, lower part of the funnel (see Figure 16.10).

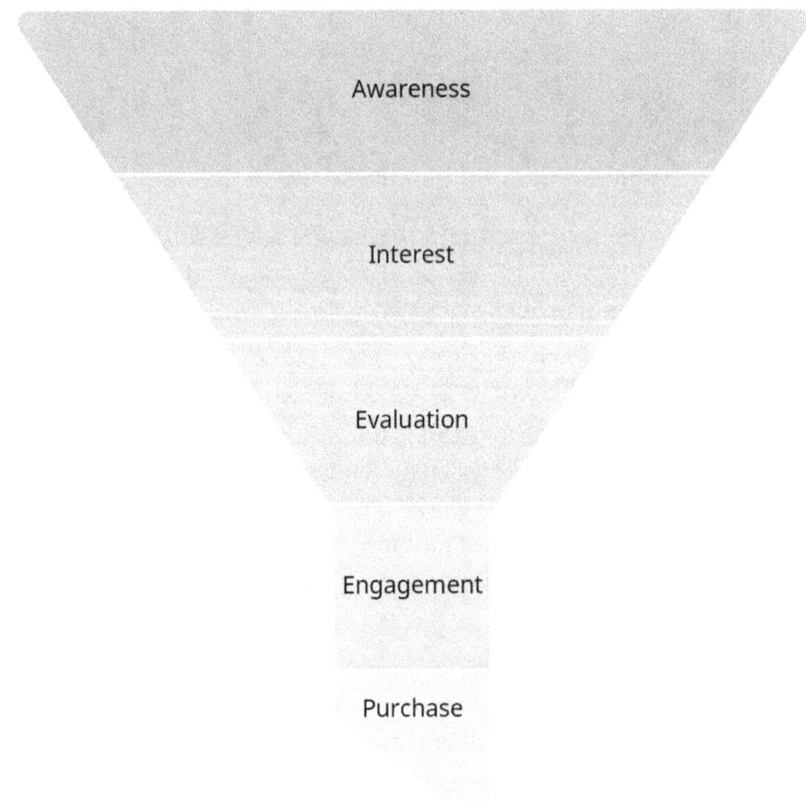

Figure 16.10 Sales Funnel from Awareness to Purchase (attribution: Copyright Rice University, OpenStax, under CC BY 4.0 license)

Traffic by Source

Monitoring website **traffic by source** means paying attention to the site from which the website traffic came.

For example, social media is famous for generating traffic to companies' websites. Online marketers can track this information by attaching a piece of tracking code to links on social media pages and other sources to assess where the visitor came from. In addition to social media, traffic sources can be email, paid search, organic search, paid social, and affiliates.

Paid search is a type of digital advertising where marketers pay search engines like Google and Bing to place their ads in sponsored spots at the top or bottom of a search engine results page (SERP). A **SERP (Search Engine Results Pages)** is the list of search results that displays on a search engine's page after someone enters key search terms into a search query box. Say, for example, a consumer is looking for a local company to investigate and fix a leak in their ceiling. That customer would likely visit Google and type in the search terms "plumbers near me." Google then displays the SERP featuring sponsored companies in top positions on the page. Companies bid on key search terms like "fix leaky roof" in an auction with competitors. If their bid is high enough, they will secure a top position on Google's search results page. In turn, when users click on that sponsored add, they are directed to the company's website or landing page.

Organic search refers to the list of websites on a search results page that have not been paid for by marketers. Search engines use algorithms to deliver search results that are relevant to the key search terms that a visitor has entered. When someone is searching for a local plumber on Google and they click on an organic search listing, the company that appears organically in those search results does not pay for the traffic that visits its website.

Paid social is similar to paid search in that marketers pay social media companies to display sponsored digital advertisements to targeted customers on their platform. Social media users who click on a sponsored social advertisement are then directed to the company's website or landing page.

Affiliates are people or companies that earn a commission for driving traffic to another person's or company's website where they make a purchase. CJ Affiliate, formerly known as Commission Junction, provides affiliate marketers with a marketplace to connect with brands who pay affiliates for driving traffic and purchases online.

Conversions

Simply put, **conversions** happen when a company turns a visitor into a customer. When a consumer purchases a LEGO set on the company's website, that's a conversion. When a new user signs up for TikTok, that's a conversion. Conversions are important in measuring the success of online marketing campaigns and the consumers' purchase experience.

Bounce Rate

Bounce rate is a metric that online marketers use to measure what percentage of visitors visit the site, view one page, and then leave. Bounce rates can be examined for each page of your website. Online marketers want to aim for a bounce rate that is lower than 40 percent. Higher bounce rates indicate issues with pages, including the time it takes for them to load in a visitor's browser.

Search Trends

Search trends are data points that indicate how frequently a term is searched. Researching search trends provides insight into who a company's customers are and what they are currently interested in. Google Trends is a free tool that online marketers can use to gather this information. Monitoring search trends has some predictive benefits to online marketers, who can recommend changes to products, advertising, and budgeting based on what consumers are searching for. For example, marketers utilize keyword tools offered by companies like Semrush to gain insights into customer search activity. Semrush provides customers with information on the value of popular search terms.

New versus Returning Visitors

New visitors, or new users, are people who are just learning about your website. A new visitor is someone who is visiting your website for the first time. **Returning visitors** are visitors or users who have been to your website before. Analyzing new and returning user metrics provides online marketers with a sense of how effective the company is in attracting new visitors compared to returning visitors. If there's an increase in new visitors, online marketers may be able to conclude that they are successfully attracting new customers via the online marketing tools they are using.

Average Session Duration

A **session** is defined as a collection of interactions that occur on a company's website. For example, if someone searches for Nike soccer cleats on Google, they'll likely click on a landing page that takes them to the Nike website's page related to soccer footwear. While on the page, the visitor may then click to browse different styles and colors and maybe watch a video of a famous athlete playing in the cleats. The visitor may then decide to make a purchase by selecting their size and clicking on a CTA (call-to-action) button such as "Add to Cart." This collection of activities equates to a session. Online marketers examine session duration as a way to measure engagement. If someone visits your shopping cart page after adding an item but then leaves within a few seconds (known as shopping cart abandonment), that may indicate issues with that page.

Page Views

Page views is a metric related to how many total pages have been viewed on your website. Websites typically have a home page, which is where visitors land when they type in your main URL. But depending on the company, its website could have many pages in addition to the home page. For example, e-commerce sites have pages that allow visitors to browse products. There might be review pages for each product and pages dedicated to blogs or articles about featured products. There's likely to be a customer support page and a terms and conditions page. The possibilities are almost endless. Online marketers use page views as a metric to gauge the success of their website pages.

Most Visited Pages

In analyzing page views, online marketers can gain important insights, such as which pages are most visited. If they identify content on their website that attracts a larger number of views, they can attribute those page views to a traffic source, such as social media or a blog.

Social Engagement

Social engagement relates to the number of actions that social media users take in direct relation to your company, brand, or product. Social engagement can be measured by the number of likes, shares, retweets, and comments made by account followers.

Click-Through Rate

When users visit Google and begin searching for something they are interested in, Google returns what are called search results. This is the list of solutions or answers to the search terms a user entered in the Google search bar. Some companies pay to appear at the very top of that search results page. As noted above, this is known as paid search. When users see the ad, this is known as an **impression**. The **click-through rate (CTR)** is the percentage of people who click on your ad. Measuring CTR indicates how successful their search advertisement is in attracting users to click. The ads are linked to a landing page, where the consumer is presented with additional information that is designed to lead them to a purchase. A high CTR leads to more traffic and ultimately conversions.

Cost per Click

Search engines like Google and Bing generate revenue by charging companies that pay for search ads to appear on search result pages. The **cost per click (CPC)** is the cost companies pay search engines for each click that a search advertisement receives. This cost is based on the keywords that a company bids on. Simply put, there are competitors in the auction who are willing to pay a certain amount to appear on the search results page when a user enters certain keywords. Depending on how competitive the auction is, CPC can fluctuate, and online marketers analyze CPC to ensure they don't overpay to have their search ads display.

Let's suppose that you wanted to purchase a Tampa Bay NFL jersey. You are interested in finding one at the lowest price possible. You're also interested in the team's home jersey. You may type in the search engine bar: Tampa Jersey in white. Retailers like Fanatics and NFLshop.com will appear at the top of the search results page next to the word "Ad." If NFLshop.com appears first, it won the auction over the search keywords you entered.

Online marketers set limits on how much they are willing to bid on certain keywords. If they bid too low, they lose the auction and may not get the impressions they need. If they bid too high, they risk overpaying for their search advertising. They should identify their goals and bid accordingly.

Cost per Acquisition

Cost per acquisition (CPA) is also known as cost per action or cost per conversion. It relates to the aggregate or cumulative cost of acquiring a customer. CPA can be measured by channel or campaign. The conversion could be a sale, a form completion, or a click.

The CPA formula is:

$$\text{Cost per Acquisiton (CPA)} = \frac{\text{Dollars Spent on Campaign}}{\text{Number of Conversions}}$$

For example, let's look at CPA for a paid search campaign. Fanatics uses paid search to reach customers interested in buying athletic apparel. Let's assume that Fanatics runs a search campaign for one month that costs the company $20,000. The campaign was responsible for driving over 1 million visits to the website and 32,000 conversions. 32,000 conversions at $20,000 would result in a CPA of $0.63, meaning that each customer conversion cost the company $0.63.

$$\text{Cost per Acquisiton (CPA)} = \frac{\$20,000}{32,000} = \$0.63$$

This calculation can be somewhat misleading, however, because it fails to account for the resources spent creating the ad and managing the search campaign. Nevertheless, online marketers monitor CPA because it helps them measure the effectiveness of their online marketing strategies. The lower the CPA, the more effective the campaign.

MARKETING DASHBOARD

Targeted Advertising

As a consumer, have you ever wondered why you see certain advertisements on social media but not others? The answer is targeted advertising. Targeted advertising allows marketing professionals to specify a target audience of their choosing. For example, you may see advertisements for winter boots if you have recently initiated a search with those terms. At the same time, a friend might see advertisements for winter tires for the same reason.

Targeted advertising can be expensive because it is tailored to a marketer's exact specifications. Therefore, marketing professionals calculate the cost every time a prospective customer clicks on a targeted ad through their website. This cost-per-click metric shows us how much the marketing professional pays every time a prospect clicks on an ad.

Cost per click has a role in search engine marketing as well. For example, if our advertisement is served up on a search engine results page (SERP) and a prospective customer clicks on that advertisement, the marketing team must pay the search provider.

As savvy marketers, we know that not every click results in a purchase. So, we have to be careful not to invest more in clicks than our profitability allows. We also need to consider the average revenue and profit per order and the customer lifetime value when determining the efficacy of a targeted advertising campaign.

The formula for cost per click is the total cost for the digital campaign/number of clicks.

$$\text{Cost per Click} = \frac{\text{Total Cost of Digital Campaign}}{\text{Number of Clicks}}$$

Give the cost-per-click calculation a try for yourself. What is the cost per click of each of the four campaigns for a pet store?

Campaign	Total Campaign Cost	Number of Clicks
Dog Food	$12,000	18,100 clicks
Cat Food	$10,000	20,200 clicks
Aquariums	$7,000	19,050 clicks
Bird Feeders	$5,500	5,000 clicks

Table 16.1

Solution
Dog food: $0.66/click

Cat food: $0.50/click

Aquariums: $0.37/click

Bird feeders: $1.10/click

What additional information would we need to know to determine whether the cost per click for each product is a good investment?

Solution
Average revenue and profit per order, percentage of people who click through who make a purchase, and/or customer lifetime value

Let's suppose that Najja found our pet store website on a targeted ad, clicked through, and placed a $70 order for bird feeders that had a 10 percent profit margin for our pet store. Was the click-through rate a good investment?

Solution
Yes. The pet store profited $7 on the single purchase at a click-through rate of just $1.10. In addition, Najja may purchase more in the future, making the click-through rate an even better investment.

Knowledge Check

It's time to check your knowledge on the concepts presented in this section. Refer to the Answer Key at the end of the book for feedback.

1. Which of the following best describes why online marketing metrics are important?
   a. Online marketing metrics help marketers understand whether or not their products and services create value for consumers.
   b. Online marketing metrics are an important part of understanding the factors that influence consumer behavior.
   c. Online marketing metrics help marketers measure the effectiveness of marketing managers.
   d. Online marketing metrics help marketers measure the performance of their online marketing campaigns.

2. An online automotive magazine is running a social media campaign to increase paid subscriptions. Which of the following would be an example of a conversion on its website given the campaign's goal?
   a. A visitor uses the search tool on the website to search "vintage European cars."
   b. A visitor enters their email address to receive updates.
   c. A visitor enters their payment information and contact information and clicks on "place order."
   d. A visitor downloads the app on their mobile phone.

3. The Warton Hotel is running an online marketing campaign and would like to measure the percentage of people who only visit its site one time. Which online marketing metric would be most helpful to the hotel in this situation?
   a. Counting new and returning customers who visit the site
   b. Counting page views
   c. Examining the bounce rate
   d. Counting unique users

4. Which of the metrics could be used to measure the performance of a social media campaign?
   a. Social engagement
   b. Page views
   c. Bounce rate
   d. Cost per click

5. Jax's Sushi House wishes to compare DoorDash's and Google's performance in driving traffic to the restaurant's website. Which of the following explains why Jax's Sushi House wants to compare sources?
   a. Measuring traffic by source provides insight to online marketers about the effectiveness of sources that best drive traffic to a company's website.
   b. Measuring traffic by source allows marketers to measure the effectiveness of the online shopping cart experience.
   c. Online marketers can determine the effectiveness of their home page by examining traffic by source.
   d. Evaluating traffic by source means looking at the total numbers of visitors to a website and comparing it to the total number of visitors from a source.

16.4   Ethical Issues in Digital Marketing and Social Media

Learning Outcomes

By the end of this section, you will be able to:
- **LO** 1 Describe ethical issues with respect to digital marketing and social media.
- **LO** 2 Explain why ethical issues exist.

Privacy, Transparency, and Awareness

While digital marketing tools and social media provide online marketers with effective ways to engage with customers, build relationships, and drive consumers toward a purchase, there are ethical issues that marketers must consider when utilizing these tools.

First, because of the highly targeted capabilities of digital and social media, companies have access to large amounts of personal data, including name, email address, phone number, as well as personal interests, social and political views, and shopping behavior. Consumers are increasingly concerned about data privacy. In a recent survey by KPMG, 86 percent of the respondents have a growing concern about data privacy, and 78 percent fear the amount of data being collected.[35]

Given this growth in distrust of how personal data is handled, some companies have responded with updated policies designed to be more transparent about how data will be used. Seventy-five percent of consumers polled reported that they want increased transparency.[36]

In 2021, Apple released features for iPhone and iPad users that allow consumers to have stronger control of how their data is used.[37] Using pop-ups, Apple device users will be able to allow or disallow companies to track their activity across apps and the websites they link to. This move by Apple resulted in some back-and-forth commentary by Meta's Mark Zuckerberg and Apple CEO Tim Cook. Tech companies like Facebook and Google depend on being able to target the advertising on their applications to users using personal data. Giving greater privacy control to iPhone users presents a threat to the core of their business models.

Social media platforms in particular mine personal data and then use it to sell advertising space on news feeds of consumers who match the demographics and psychographics of a company's target market. With nearly 71 percent of social media users taking the time to check their privacy settings on social media, it's clear that this issue is front and center for a majority of users.[38] Companies can respect the privacy of their users by being transparent about what data they collect and how they use it.

Tracking Consumer Data

The reality is that it's not just social media companies and search engines that track consumer data. A majority of companies use tracking codes to follow consumers and data about them as they navigate the web. Zoho, a productivity and collaboration app, reported that in the B2B space, about 72 percent of businesses do not inform customers that they are being tracked by third parties.[39]

The Use of Client Reviews

Client reviews involve feedback that a customer or client posts directly to a platform that can accessed by consumers during the buying process. Companies that use client or customer reviews include Amazon.com, Wayfair, and Lands' End. Customers rate their experience with the product typically by assigning stars and commenting on their satisfaction.

Reviews can be helpful to consumers during the search phase of the buying process because reviews provide a real-world glimpse into the favorability of a product. For example, Wayfair invites customers to post pictures of items like sofas and end tables once a customer has styled the room. This provides shoppers a real-life view of the product, its color, and its size, among other things.

Beyond the reviews on e-commerce sites, Google serves as a major player in the customer review space. Consumers often rely on Google reviews when deciding on whether to hire a local business. In addition to Google, consumers can find reviews for travel on Tripadvisor, restaurant reviews on Zomato, and reviews of software programs on G2.

Marketers recognize the power of customer reviews as a digital promotional tool, as consumers report that they perceive reviews as more credible than messages created by the company itself.

COMPANIES WITH A CONSCIENCE

Apple's Taking Big Steps to Protect Privacy

Figure 16.11 Apple is employing several steps to further protect consumers and their personal data. (credit: "iPhone 5s Applications" by Marco Verch/flickr, CC BY 2.0)

In January 2022, Apple took one of its most impactful steps toward protecting the privacy of iCloud users, the iCloud Private Relay (see Figure 16.11).[40] When enabled on Apple devices, this feature hides a user's IP address from the websites they visit, essentially masking a user's entire online footprint.

The privacy feature is a game changer in the digital marketing space, as companies like Meta and Google depend on seeing a consumer's online journey to learn more about who they are and what interests they have. Tracking online activity allows companies to serve users with relevant marketing messages and offerings.

In addition to the privacy relay, Apple also released "Hide My Email," which allows Apple device users to enter a unique email address on websites without sharing their actual email address.[41] Emails that are sent to a randomly generated address are then forwarded to a user's inbox, thereby hiding a user's actual email address.

Finally, Apple has updated its Mail app such that it prevents marketers from tracking whether or not someone has opened an email.[42] Email marketers measure the percentage of people who open marketing emails to determine their level of engagement and the effectiveness of the email.

Apple appears to be taking consumer privacy to another level. By offering a collection of privacy-centric features, it is equipping consumers with tools to protect their personal information and navigate the web unseen.

Check out Apple's website to learn more about iCloud Private Relay (https://openstax.org/r/abouticloud).

Also read about it in this *Wired* article (https://openstax.org/r/howappleicloud).

Chapter Summary

Direct, online, and social media marketing include a mix of useful tools that help marketers engage with targeted consumers in a way that is personalized and is designed to drive the audience to follow through on the desired marketing action. With the explosion in internet and mobile device usage coupled with advancements in digital technology, online marketing tools have been developed to help marketers meet consumers in the digital space. These tools are capable of connecting online marketers to carefully targeted individuals. With the development of these tools come ethical issues related to privacy. As consumer concern for privacy protection grows, companies will need to adapt their privacy policies to be more transparent about how they use consumer data.

Key Terms

affiliates   people or companies that earn a commission for driving traffic to another person's or company's website where they make a purchase

blog   an online journal of interests, beliefs, and other topics published by a person, a group of people, or an organization

bounce rate   a metric that online marketers use to measure what percentage of visitors who visit the site, view one page, and then leave

call center   a centralized space where agents or representatives answer inbound calls and place outbound calls

catalog marketing   also known as direct mail order and is one of the oldest forms of promotion, which typically includes a variety of products often vividly displayed in a high-gloss magazine-like format

click-through rate (CTR)   the percentage of people who click on an online ad

client reviews   involve feedback that a customer or client posts directly to a platform that can accessed by consumers during the buying process

content marketing   creating and distributing online content that is valuable and relevant to a company's target customers

conversions   happen when a company turns a visitor into a customer

cost per acquisition (CPA)   also known as cost per action or cost per conversion, relates to the aggregate or cumulative cost of acquiring a customer and can be measured by channel or campaign

cost per click (CPC)   the cost companies pay search engines for each click that a search advertisement receives, which is based on the keywords a company bids on

direct marketing   using communication tools that directly engage with individual consumers for the ultimate purpose of calling them to take some marketing action

direct-mail marketing   a type of direct marketing that involves marketers sending mail directly to people's homes or places of business; for example, catalogs and postcards

direct-response television marketing   a type of direct marketing that is designed to compel viewers to take some immediate action such, as calling a phone number or visiting a website presented during a television commercial

email marketing   a type of direct marketing that is highly personal and designed to build relationships with consumers

impression   when users see an online ad

integrated social media marketing   involves creating a clear, consistent, and synergistic message across all social media platforms

marketing emails   emails that are promotional in nature and typically involve a marketing offer

mobile marketing   using multiple digital marketing channels that are designed to reach consumers on their smartphones and tablets

mobile-friendly emails   emails whose images, text, and links display in a way that is easy to read when accessed via a mobile device

new visitors   people who are first visiting your website, also known as new users

online direct marketing   uses a rich collection of online tools, such as websites and email, to target individual consumers with an offer designed to compel consumers to take some action, such as visit a website or make an online purchase

online video marketing   involves creating videos that tell a story about a product, company, or brand that is designed to drive consumer engagement through activities such as liking, sharing, and retweeting

organic search   the list of websites on a search engine results page that have not been paid for by marketers

page views   a metric related to how many total pages have been viewed on your website

paid search   a type of digital advertising where marketers pay search engines like Google and Bing to place their ads in sponsored spots at the top or bottom of a search results page

paid social   a type of digital marketing advertising where a company pays a social media company to display a digital advertisement to targeted customers on its platform

podcasts   often free, on-demand, downloadable audio recordings that cover a variety of topics and are typically made available on a weekly or monthly basis

responsive web design   designing a website that is configured to adapt to any device, making it easy for visitors to read and interact with its features

returning visitors   visitors or users who have been to your website before

sales funnel   a visual representation of the customer journey from product awareness to product purchase

search trends   data points that indicate how frequently a term is searched

seminars   a tool that allows companies to share their expertise and knowledge related to a topic, issue, or industry; can be done in person or virtually

SERP (Search Engine Results Page)   the list of search results that displays on a search engine's page after someone enters key search terms into a search query box

session   a collection of interactions that occur on a company's website

social engagement   relates to the number of actions that social media users take in direct relation to your company, brand, or product

social media marketing   using social media platforms, such as Facebook, Instagram, LinkedIn, and Twitter, to deliver content that drives engagement with your brand

telemarketing   a type of direct marketing that involves a company representative placing or answering customer phone calls with the intention of guiding the consumer toward making a purchase

trade shows   exhibition events that provide companies the opportunity to present themselves and their products and services to industry peers

traffic by source   means paying attention to the site from which the website traffic came

website marketing   The promotion of a website that results in driving traffic or visitors to the site to learn more about the product or company or to make a purchase

website traffic   the total number of visitors to a company's website

Applied Marketing Knowledge: Discussion Questions

1. The Association of National Marketers (ANA) acquired the Data & Marketing Association (formerly the Direct Marketing Association (DMA)). This organization has several arms. One of them is the dmaconsumers.org. Visit the website, and see what services it has to aid consumers (https://openstax.org/r/dmaconsumers).

2. Choose three people that you know, each from a different generation. Explain the concept of online, social media, and mobile marketing. Ask the following questions: "Do you engage with these forms of marketing?" "Have you purchased anything from one of these forms?" "Do you have any concerns about using any of the marketing strategies discussed?" Then, explain whether anyone's answers surprised you.

3. When considering the privacy issue, where does the responsibility fall? Is it with the business, or is it with the consumer? Is it both? How can a consumer guard themselves? What can a company do to make sure it

is practicing ethical marketing?

4. The main goals of consumer protection laws and regulations are to protect consumers' privacy and identity and to protect consumers from unfair or deceitful actions. Research the following regulation and law to familiarize yourself with them: the Telemarketing Sales Rule and the CAN-SPAM Act.

Critical Thinking Exercises

1. Compose a paragraph (150–200 words) using all of the following terms as they relate to direct, online, social media, and mobile marketing. The goal is to prove you understand the meaning of each term.

2. List the positive and negative value of each of these forms of marketing: direct mail, social media, mobile, content and telemarketing. Think about products, messages, and delivery systems.

3. Now consider the target market for direct mail, social media, mobile, content marketing, and telemarketing. Does the chosen form of marketing present challenges in growing the target market? If so, how can those challenges be met and overcome?

Building Your Personal Brand

Goal-setting is the development of an action plan designed to motivate and guide an individual, group, or organization to reach a goal. There are several models of goal setting; one of the popular ones is SMART goal-setting. SMART stands for goals that are specific, measurable, action-oriented, realistic, and time-bound.

Consider a goal you might set for yourself that's SMART. For example, if your goal is to intern at a marketing firm ,you might establish the following SMART goals:

- Specific: Create a list of possible companies you want to target for an internship, and indicate why.
- Measurable: Quantify the number of contacts at each company you plan to make in a week, and map those to calendar dates.
- Action-oriented: Develop a plan for reaching out to and making appointments with those contacts.
- Realistic: Is what you're setting reasonable when you consider your work schedule, schoolwork, personal responsibilities, etc.? Set goals that are achievable.
- Time-bound: Consider all of the steps, and decide how much time it will take you to complete this goal.

Now set yourself two goals around building your personal brand. Is there a skill you wish to learn or a website you want to develop? Whatever your goals are, be sure to consider the SMART goal-setting model as you develop them.

What Do Marketers Do?

Check out the Association of National Advertisers (ANA) website (https://openstax.org/r/ananet), and scan the wealth of information available. It offers a content library, newsstand, marketing futures, blogs, and podcasts. Throughout this information, you will learn more about many aspects of current trends, future opportunities, and simply what it is that marketers are doing now. Being educated on the many associations and the information available can inspire you to look at marketing careers in a different light.

Navigate to the Content Library, then the Media Channels section. (In order to see the link to the Content Library, you need to hover over "Resources" at the top of the page.) From this section, review the various pieces of content available, and choose one to read. After reading, write a two-paragraph summary on what you learned, what you found most interesting, and why.

 Closing Company Case

Publix

Founded in 1930, supermarket chain Publix started with one store in Winter Haven, Florida. It now has over

1,200 stores throughout the Southeast. The company was founded on the promise of superior customer service. With unwavering dedication to quality and value, Publix is now one of the 10 largest-volume supermarket chains in the country.

Publix is employee-owned, and the pride and dedication of its employees shows in the daily interactions with customers and the communities it serves. Walk into any Publix grocery store, and the spacious aisles and displays provide for ease and access. The brightly lit shelves and soft music make for a pleasant shopping experience. With a wide selection of quality products and its own Publix brand, customers are typically delighted with the availability of premium and well-priced items.

A hallmark of the Publix shopping experience is the checkout. Its friendly Publix cashiers and abundance of grocery baggers make shopping a pleasure. No matter how big or small an order might be, the baggers are always eager to help customers out to the car with their groceries.

As the company worked to develop the superior in-store shopping experience, consumer preferences for grocery shopping began to change. Amazon, a leader in online shopping, bought Whole Foods. Adding to its already "everything store" approach, Amazon was now able to deliver groceries within a two-hour window.

In 2016, Publix began a pilot with Instacart. Instacart is an online ordering and delivery platform, partnering primarily with grocery and drugstore chains nationwide. Publix had plans in place to launch Instacart with all Publix locations by 2020.

When COVID-19 began raging throughout the United States and economies were shuttered, demand for grocery delivery was high. Publix and Instacart rallied to meet the need. Each Publix location was tasked with getting its merchandise uploaded on its website, and Instacart was quickly hiring employees to shop for and deliver groceries to homes across its market area.

Using a mobile app, Publix consumers continue to use Instacart to shop for grocery delivery. Through the robust Publix website, consumers are able to place orders for party trays, bakery items, and whole-meal catering solutions. Publix regularly posts updates on food recalls and highlights of its sustainability efforts. Consumers who opt in can join the Publix Club to receive emails with coupons and weekly discounts on groceries.

Publix has an active social media presence. With over 3 million Facebook followers, loyal consumers often comment on their good finds, grocery deals, and favorite products. Publix provides its followers with favorite recipes and new products.

Through Instagram, Publix shares photos of some of its food products as well as ways it supports its communities and helps with environmental sustainability issues. Customers regularly like and comment on the Instagram posts featuring Publix food items and holiday meal ideas.[43]

To learn more about these companies, visit the Publix website (https://openstax.org/r/publix) and the Instacart website (https://openstax.org/r/instacart).

Case Questions

1. Describe the ways Publix is utilizing its website to connect with customers.

2. In what ways can consumers engage with Publix through digital media?

3. What are some of the methods Publix can utilize to determine success with its digital efforts?

4. How did Publix use digital resources to respond to consumer needs during the COVID-19 pandemic?

References

1. "Number of Active Subscribers of HelloFresh and Blue Apron from 2016 to 2021," Statista, accessed February 13, 2022, https://www.statista.com/statistics/947620/meal-kit-companies-number-subscribers-worldwide/.

2. Tom Ryan, "Does Direct Mail or Email Deliver Greater Results for Retailers?," RetailWire, March 25, 2019, https://retailwire.com/discussion/does-direct-mail-or-email-deliver-greater-results-for-retailers/.

3. Jonathan Z. Zhang, "Why Catalogs Are Making a Comeback," *Harvard Business Review*, February 11, 2020, https://hbr.org/2020/02/why-catalogs-are-making-a-comeback.

4. "National Do Not Call Registry FAQs," Consumer Advice, Federal Trade Commission, May 2021, https://www.consumer.ftc.gov/articles/national-do-not-call-registry-faqs.

5. Anne Stych, "Proactiv Rebrands, Moves from Acne into Other Areas of Skincare," Bizwomen, American City Business Journals, January 21, 2022, https://www.bizjournals.com/bizwomen/news/latest-news/2022/01/proactiv-rebrands-moves-from-acne-into-other-area.html.

6. "About Us," MailCon, last modified December 21, 2021, https://mailcon.com/about/.

7. Deyan Georgiev, "67+ Revealing Smartphone Statistics for 2022," Tech Jury, October 14, 2022, https://techjury.net/blog/smartphone-usage-statistics/#gref

8. CJ Bangah, "What Is on the Horizon for Digital Advertising in 2022 and Beyond?," LinkedIn, October 22, 2021, https://www.linkedin.com/pulse/what-horizon-digital-advertising-2022-beyond-cj-bangah/.

9. Katrina Kirsch, "The Ultimate List of Email Marketing Stats for 2022," *The HubSpot Marketing Blog*, HubSpot, updated January 20, 2022, https://blog.hubspot.com/marketing/email-marketing-stats.

10. Andrea Wildt, "5 Brands Crushing It with Email Marketing and Automation," *The Digital and Email Marketing Blog*, Campaign Monitor, May 29, 2019, https://www.campaignmonitor.com/blog/email-marketing/5-brands-crushing-marketing-automation/.

11. "Watch DJ Khaled & How QuickBooks + Mailchimp Help Small Businesses in Super Bowl Campaigns," Chhattisgarh News, accessed February 13, 2022, https://world360news.com/en/watch-dj-khaled-how-quickbooks-mailchimp-help-small-businesses-super-bowl-campaigns.

12. Adam Hayes, "What Video Marketers Should Know in 2022, according to Wyzowl Research," *The HubSpot Marketing Blog*, HubSpot, January 26, 2022, https://blog.hubspot.com/marketing/state-of-video-marketing-new-data.

13. Chris Matyszczyk, "Amazon CEO Jeff Bezos Showed Off His Exciting Vacation on Twitter. What Happened Next Wasn't Pretty," *Inc.*, April 23, 2018, https://www.inc.com/chris-matyszczyk/amazon-ceo-jeff-bezos-showed-off-his-exciting-vacation-on-twitter-what-happened-next-wasnt-pretty.html.

14. Mansoor Iqbal, "Facebook Revenue and Usage Statistics (2022)," App Data, Business of Apps, updated January 19, 2022, https://www.businessofapps.com/data/facebook-statistics.

15. Chris Raymond, "So What Do You Think of Facebook Now?," Consumer Reports, March 15, 2019, https://www.consumerreports.org/social-media/what-do-you-think-of-facebook-now-survey/.

16. Raymond, "What Do You Think?"

17. Dominique Jackson, "Instagram vs. Facebook: Which Is Best for Your Brand's Strategy?," *Sprout Blog*, Sprout Social, June 30, 2019, https://sproutsocial.com/insights/instagram-vs-facebook/.

18. Christina Newberry, "38 LinkedIn Statistics Marketers Should Know in 2021," Hootsuite, January 12, 2021, https://blog.hootsuite.com/linkedin-statistics-business.

19. "All about Pinterest," Pinterest Help, Pinterest, accessed February 13, 2022, https://help.pinterest.com/en/guide/all-about-pinterest.

20. "Pinterest Demographics: Find Your Audience," Pinterest Business, Pinterest, accessed February 13, 2022, https://business.pinterest.com/en/audience/.

21. "Number of Monetizable Daily Active Twitter Users (mDAU) Worldwide from 1st Quarter 2017 to 3rd Quarter 2021," Statista, accessed February 13, 2022, https://www.statista.com/statistics/970920/monetizable-daily-active-twitter-users-worldwide/.

22. Ying Lin, "10 Twitter Statistics Every Marketer Should Know in 2021 (Infographic)," *Oberlo Blog*, Oberlo, January 25, 2021, https://www.oberlo.com/blog/twitter-statistics.

23. Damian Radcliffe, "Why Podcasting Is on the Rise: 8 Trends Publishers Cannot Ignore," What's New in Publishing, last modified December 17, 2020, https://whatsnewinpublishing.com/why-podcasting-is-on-the-rise-8-trends-publishers-cannot-ignore/.

24. "How Spotify Is Strengthening Our Investment in Podcast Advertising with Acquisition of Megaphone," For the Record, Spotify, November 10, 2020, https://newsroom.spotify.com/2020-11-10/how-spotify-is-strengthening-our-investment-in-podcast-advertising-with-acquisition-of-megaphone/.

25. "Podcasts and the Next Level of Influence," Spotify Advertising, Spotify, March 2019, https://ads.spotify.com/en-US/news-and-insights/podcasts-and-the-next-level-of-influence/.

26. Maile McCann, "How Cupshe Built a $150 Million Swimwear Business by Embracing Both DTC and Amazon," Modern Retail, Digiday Media, August 30, 2021, https://www.modernretail.co/startups/how-cupshe-built-a-150-million-swimwear-business-by-embracing-both-dtc-and-amazon/.

27. Ashley Wilson, "Top Mobile Marketing Challenges and How to Overcome Them," *CRM and Technology Blog*, Technology Advisors, June 30, 2021, https://www.techadv.com/blog/top-mobile-marketing-challenges-and-how-overcome-them.

28. Kateryna Hanko, "35+ Must-Know Phone Usage Statistics for 2022," *Clario Blog*, Clario Tech, April 8, 2022, https://clario.co/blog/phone-usage-statistics/.

29. "US Mobile Advertising Growth (2019–2024)," Statistics Library, Oberlo, updated February 2022, https://www.oberlo.com/statistics/mobile-advertising-growth.

30. "7 Essential Tips to Creating Mobile Friendly Emails," *The Digital and Email Marketing Blog*, Campaign Monitor, May 21, 2019, https://www.campaignmonitor.com/blog/email-marketing/mobile-friendly-email-tips/.

31. Pietro Saccomani, "People Spent 90% of Their Mobile Time Using Apps in 2021," *Mobiloud Blog*, MobiLoud, last modified March 1, 2022, https://www.mobiloud.com/blog/mobile-apps-vs-mobile-websites.

32. "National Geographic's Instagram Accounts Reach 200 Million Followers," National Geographic Partners, May 28, 2020, https://nationalgeographicpartners.com/2020/05/nat-geo-instagram-accounts-near-200-million-followers/.

33. Tasmin Oxford, "National Geographic Inspires Wanderlust with Its Latest UGC Campaign," Marketing, Reuters Events, September 17, 2015, https://www.reutersevents.com/marketing/brand-marketing/national-geographic-inspires-wanderlust-its-latest-ugc-campaign.

34. Nat Geo Wild (@natgeowild), "Today is #EndangeredSpeciesDay. Every year on the third Friday in May, #ESDay recognizes and support national efforts to protect our #endangeredspecies," Instagram photo, May 15, 2015, https://www.instagram.com/p/2uQN2swzXH/.

35. Lance Whitney, "Data Privacy Is a Growing Concern for More Consumers," TechRepublic, TechnologyAdvice, August 17, 2021, https://www.techrepublic.com/article/data-privacy-is-a-growing-concern-for-more-consumers/.

36. Whitney, "Data Privacy."

37. David Price, "iOS 15 Latest Version, Problems & New Features for iPhones," *Macworld*, August 18, 2022, https://www.macworld.com/article/675711/ios-15-latest-version-problems-new-features-for-iphone.html.

38. Peter Suciu, "There Isn't Enough Privacy on Social Media and That Is a Real Problem," *Forbes*, June 26, 2020, https://www.forbes.com/sites/petersuciu/2020/06/26/there-isnt-enough-privacy-on-social-media-and-that-is-a-real-problem/.

39. "Zoho Privacy Survey Finds 62% of Businesses Aren't Telling Customers about Third-Party Ad Trackers Collecting Their Data," Business Wire, December 15, 2020, https://www.businesswire.com/news/home/20201215005426/en/Zoho-Privacy-Survey-Finds-62-of-Businesses-Aren%E2%80%99t-Telling-Customers-About-Third-Party-Ad-Trackers-Collecting-Their-Data.

40. "About iCloud Private Relay," Apple Support, Apple, July 11, 2022, https://support.apple.com/en-us/HT212614.

41. "What Is Hide My Email?," Apple Support, Apple, January 31, 2022, https://support.apple.com/en-us/HT210425.

42. Rob Kaczanowski, "How Apple's Mail Privacy Changes Affect Email Open Tracking," *Postmark Blog*, Postmark, November 9, 2021, https://postmarkapp.com/blog/how-apples-mail-privacy-changes-affect-email-open-tracking.

43. Mike Miller, "Publix Supermarket Makes Shopping and Road Tripping a Pleasure," Florida Back Roads Travel, March 24, 2022, https://www.florida-backroads-travel.com/publix-supermarket.html; Todd Jones, "A Message about Coronavirus (VOVID-19) from Publix CEO Todd Jones," Publix Press Release, https://corporate.publix.com/newsroom/news-stories/covid-19-message-from-ceo; Russell Redman, "Publix Rolls Out 15-Minute Grocery Delivery via Instacart," SN Supermarket News, April 28, 2022, https://www.supermarketnews.com/online-retail/publix-rolls-out-15-minute-grocery-delivery-instacart

17

Distribution: Delivering Customer Value

Figure 17.1 Marketers need to determine distribution strategies that gets their products in the hands of consumers, like the partnership between Whole Foods and Outstanding Foods. (credit: modification of work "Whole Foods Market Full Middle Eastern Food Shelves" by Raed Mansour/flickr, CC BY 2.0)

Chapter Outline

In the Spotlight

Have you ever had a great idea for a new food product? If so, do you have any idea where you would sell it to reach your target customers? Unlike traditional grocery retailers, Whole Foods specializes in selling high-quality natural and organic foods. Getting the green light to sell through its stores requires manufacturers to follow strict quality standards, including adherence to Whole Foods' banned ingredient list.

Founders Dave Anderson and Bill Glaser of Outstanding Foods and maker of PigOut, a vegan, bacon-flavored chip snack, recognized that in order to reach vegans and nonvegans with a plant-based, bacon-flavored chip, they need to retail at outlets that would attract such consumers.[1]

After testing their product, they opted for a nationwide launch and distribution strategy. Using a broker network, they selected distribution channels that aligned with both natural and mainstream grocery stores. This strategy would help secure the national target market coverage they were looking for. The product strategy of natural ingredients gave Outstanding Foods the green light it needed to meet Whole Foods' strict food standards. Through their partnership, Whole Foods and Outstanding Foods are able to create and deliver value to their vegan customer base who appreciate access to food products that are tasty and bring delight.

17.1 | The Use and Value of Marketing Channels

Learning Outcomes

By the end of this section, you will be able to:
- **LO** 1 Describe the use of marketing channels.
- **LO** 2 Identify the different types of marketing channels.
- **LO** 3 Discuss how marketing intermediaries add value to products.

What Are Marketing Channels?

In addition to identifying ways to create value for consumers, marketers must also decide how to distribute market offerings. In this section, you'll explore the important role that marketing channels play in delivering value to targeted customers.

A **marketing channel** is a system of people, organizations, and activities that work together to make goods and services available to consumers to purchase. Along the marketing channel, ownership of these goods and services is transferred from one channel member to the next. The goal is to create and deliver value to the final consumer by distributing these goods and services. The **final consumer** is the end user of a good or service. It includes grocery store shoppers, movie stream viewers, app users, vacation-takers, and many more.

LINK TO LEARNING

Distribution

To learn more about how the distribution of products works and the decisions marketers must consider when choosing the right marketing channel, watch the Channels of Distribution in Marketing: 8 Distribution Channels to Consider video.

Click to view content (https://openstax.org/books/principles-marketing/pages/17-1-the-use-and-value-of-marketing-channels)

Marketing Channels (Distribution Channels) Defined

It's not enough for companies to create, price, and promote products and services that deliver value. A company must also decide where and how consumers can access and purchase the company's market offering. Market offerings can include tangible goods, services, experiences, digital products, ideas, and information. All market offerings require a marketing or distribution channel to reach consumers.

Think of a channel like a stream or a river that carries a market offering to the consumer. **Distribution** describes how a company makes its market offering accessible for purchase. Local companies that sell to a smaller, more geographically concentrated set of consumers have a more simplified marketing or distribution channel compared to global companies.

The film industry provides a great example of the distribution decisions that marketers must make. Before a production company releases a new movie, it must decide which channels are best for distributing the movie to consumers. In today's market, movie producers have a slew of distribution options, including Netflix, HBOMax, and YouTube, to name a few. They also have the option of distributing through traditional movie theaters, such as AMC or Regal. Regardless of the marketing channel they pursue, their goal is to distribute their movie to the right customers at the right place and at the right time. Production companies will choose the marketing channel that is most efficient at helping them achieve this goal.

Marketing Channels for Consumer Products

Companies that use intermediaries to deliver value to consumers have a variety of marketing channel options. There are four major types of intermediaries: agents or brokers, distributors, wholesalers, and retailers (see Figure 17.2).

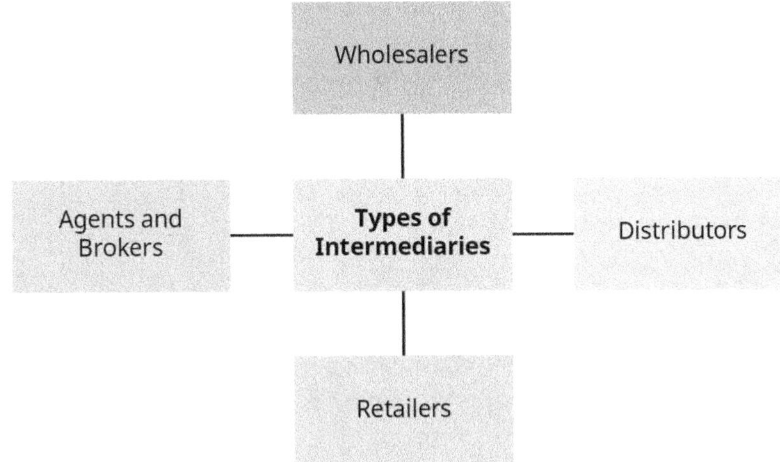

Figure 17.2 Types of Intermediaries (attribution: Copyright Rice University, OpenStax, under CC BY 4.0 license)

An **agent** or broker is someone who acts as an extension to the manufacturer. While they never take possession of the product or service they represent, they earn a commission or collect a fee for facilitating the transaction between the customer and the manufacturer. Auto insurance agents, for example, may sell Geico or Allstate auto insurance policies to consumers. The agent serves as a representative who answers questions, gathers information, and provides a quote on behalf of the insurance company.

A **distributor** takes ownership of the product and tends to align itself closely with a manufacturer. For example, Coca-Cola uses distributors who contract to distribute only Coca-Cola products, not PepsiCo products.

Wholesalers are similar to distributors in that they take ownership of products; however, they buy a variety of products in large quantities and bulk-break for the purpose of distributing an assortment of products to retailers in a quantity aimed at meeting the needs of end users or consumers. Let's examine how the different types of intermediaries depend on one another. AstraZeneca manufactures prescription medications that are made available to consumers by way of pharmacies such as CVS and Walgreens. Pharmacies are retailers in the marketing channel because they sell a wide variety of consumer products, from toothpaste to milk to medications.

Before AstraZeneca's medications reach retail pharmacies, they are purchased in bulk by wholesalers who partner directly with AstraZeneca. Wholesalers are an integral part of the marketing channel because they package and handle medications and manage the logistics of delivery to retail pharmacies. This creates value for the customer in that the right quantity of medications arrives at retail pharmacies safely and in good condition.

The fourth type of intermediary is the **retailer**. Retailers also take ownership of the product, and their sole focus is on reaching the end user or customer directly. They purchase a wide variety of products in smaller amounts that meet the wants and needs of consumers. Retailers include companies like Rite Aid, Walmart, Target, and Hallmark.

Intermediary Functions

The intermediaries' role is critical, and they perform a variety of functions (as shown in Table 17.1) that create value for other members in the marketing channel.

Intermediary Functions
Transactional: Buying, selling, and temporary risk-bearing
Logistical: Handling, packing, inventorying, and transporting
Facilitating: Financing and information sharing

Table 17.1 Intermediary Functions

Let's examine the three functions: transactional, logistical, and facilitating.

Transactional Functions

Intermediaries perform a variety of transactional functions that improve the efficiency of the channel. **Transactional functions** involve the buying, selling, and risk-bearing that accompany the movement of products along the marketing channel. Companies share the risk of ownership by temporarily possessing products before selling them to another channel member.

Imagine if a small bakery made the best oatmeal raisin cookies and decided to distribute them to consumers using local restaurants in the city. The bakery sells to the restaurant, who then sells to the customer. Temporary risk-sharing, in this scenario, means that at first the bakery assumes the risk in the making, storing, and transporting of the cookies, but that risk transfers to the restaurant once the restaurant buys the cookies. The restaurant then assumes ownership and responsibility for selling the cookies, which may involve placing them someplace customers can see them.

The transactional functions of buying, selling, and risk-bearing help add value in the marketing channel because the system allows for channel members to work together to move a product offering to consumers in an efficient and effective way.

Logistical Functions

In addition to transactional functions, intermediaries also perform **logistical functions**, which involve handling, packing, inventorying, transporting, warehousing, and ensuring the security of products as they make their way to the customer. In the earlier bakery example, the bakery must ensure the cookies are fresh and tasty in order to continue supplying restaurants with a product that consumers desire. In order to ensure that cookies meet the wants and needs of customers, both the bakery and the restaurant must ensure the product is handled safely in the marketing channel. That might mean selecting a trucking company that secures the cookies during transport to restaurants as well as packaging them so that freshness is sealed and quality is maintained.

Facilitating Functions

In addition to transactional and logistical functions, intermediaries also help in the facilitation of the purchase of products and services. **Facilitating functions** involve activities such as financing and sharing information with members of the marketing channel. Intermediaries may provide financing to one another and to the end user to help move the product along the channel. Financing involves one channel member allowing another channel member to pay over time.

In the bakery example, pretend that the restaurant purchases $12,000 in cookies each year. Instead of the bakery requiring the restaurant to pay for the order in full at the beginning of each year, it allows the restaurant to pay $1,000 a month over a 12-month period. This benefits the restaurant in that a large amount of capital isn't tied up in its cookie order payment but instead is spread out over time. While some companies require payment in full, others permit payment installments over time. The terms of payment are explicitly stated at the start of the buying and selling relationship between companies.

Intermediaries also share information that can be used to improve marketing decisions. Intermediaries often share key data such as consumer feedback on a product or service, the shopping behavior surrounding that product or service, and historical purchase trends. The facilitating functions that intermediaries perform ultimately help marketing channel members make better distribution decisions and, in some cases, financially support the movement of these products and services in the name of delivering value to customers.

How Intermediaries Add Value to Customers

Intermediaries play a critical role in adding value to customers. They specialize in aspects of distribution that manufacturers don't wish to specialize in. They create efficiencies in the marketing channel by reducing transactions, sharing important information among partners, and matching the right quantity of the right product to customer demand. While manufacturers focus on creating value for customers, intermediaries focus on delivering that value.

Dove manufactures millions of units of body wash, bar soap, dry spray antiperspirant, and hair products. In turn, it sells large quantities of these products to wholesalers, who after buying in bulk, break these large quantities down into smaller assortments that are then sold to retailers. This allows consumers to buy a variety of products in smaller amounts. They can visit a Target, a CVS, or the Amazon website and purchase three bars of soap, one bottle of shampoo, and one bottle of conditioner.

Without intermediaries, customers would need to buy directly from every manufacturer producing the desired product. Imagine grocery shopping without intermediaries. Instead of shopping at one or two grocery retailers for bread, milk, cereal, fruit, and ice cream, shoppers would need to buy from individual manufacturers, making shopping extremely time consuming and difficult.

Intermediaries add value by reducing the number of transactions between companies and customers. As illustrated in Figure 17.3, there are nine transactions without intermediaries and five transactions with the use of intermediaries. Consider the inefficiencies if companies had to directly transact with individual consumers.

Without Intermediaries—9 Transactions

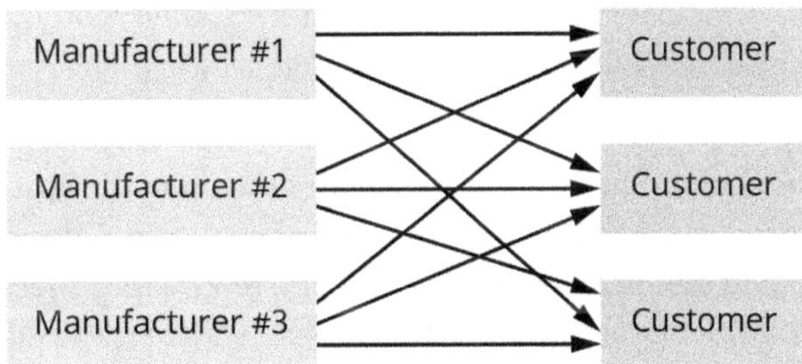

With Intermediaries—5 Transactions

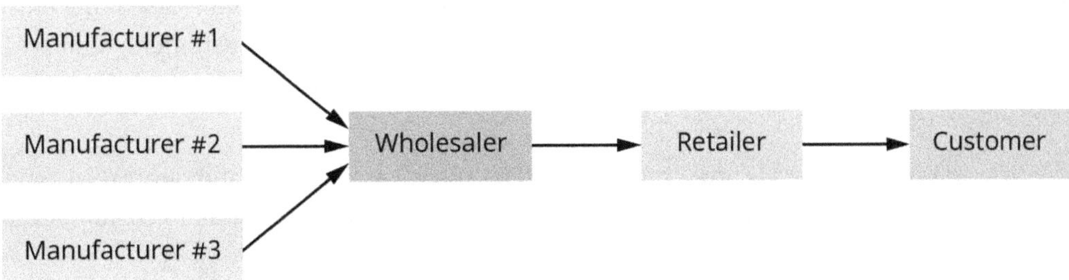

Figure 17.3 How Intermediaries Add Value by Reducing Transactions (attribution: Copyright Rice University, OpenStax, under CC BY 4.0 license)

Providing Needed Information about Products and Services

Intermediaries share pertinent information about the products and services that move through the distribution channel. More specifically, intermediaries gather, analyze, and communicate information to other distribution partners to improve the effectiveness and efficiency of the channel. This flow ultimately helps marketers plan and optimize the distribution channel so that consumers get the right products and services at the right place and at the right time.

Adjusting for Discrepancy of Quantity

As intermediaries move products and services from manufacturers to consumers, they offer the valuable service of accumulating and bulk-breaking. **Bulk-breaking** is when an intermediary takes a large quantity of a manufacturer's product and breaks it down into smaller units to be distributed to retailers based on the consumer demand. Consumers desire to purchase in smaller quantities from retailers. Wholesalers buy in bulk from producers and break the bulk into the right size quantity for retailers, who ultimately meet the needs of consumers who want an assortment of products in small quantities.

Accumulating relates to intermediaries buying in bulk from different manufacturers. When buying in bulk, it is beneficial to the manufacturers because the risk is passed from manufacturers to intermediaries. The United States produces hundreds of millions of bushels of apples, oranges, and peaches each year.[2] These types of produce require different types of climates and care and are therefore grown in different states across the country. Wholesalers play a critical role in buying an assortment of this product in bulk from these producers and ensure that they are sold to retailers in the right quantity to meet the needs of consumers.

Together these activities allow intermediaries to offer retailers the right number of products to offer consumers, based on demand.

Adjusting for Discrepancy of Assortment

Intermediaries also add value by adjusting for the discrepancies of assortment between the manufacturer and the consumer. Discrepancy of assortment is the difference between the variety of products that a manufacturer produces and the variety that consumers want to purchase. **Adjusting for discrepancy of assortment** occurs when an intermediary buys from manufacturers, then regroups products into different assortments based on what consumers are demanding from retailers.

While manufacturers generally produce large quantities of one or a few types of products, consumers demand small quantities of an assortment of products. For example, when visiting the grocery store, consumers demand an array of different products in small quantities. Depending on the size of their household, consumers are generally shopping to meet the needs of one or a few people; therefore, they value the ability to buy a variety of products in smaller quantities. Intermediaries mitigate these differences by matching supply assortment to demand assortment.

Providing Credit to Customers

Intermediaries also provide credit to customers. Consumers can hardly check out at a cash register without being asked if they would like to sign up for a credit card. By extending credit to customers, retailers from Dick's Sporting Goods to furniture retailer Wayfair give customers the chance to spend now and pay over a period of time with interest.

While providing credit to customers is often accompanied by special email offers and direct mail coupon codes, the corresponding interest rates are often high. Nevertheless, providing credit to customers can create brand loyalty and provide retailers with insight into consumer purchases.[3]

CAREERS IN MARKETING

Distribution Management

Distribution managers determine when, where, and how much of a product is distributed. Learn more about the job role and what it entails in this video.

Click to view content (https://openstax.org/books/principles-marketing/pages/17-1-the-use-and-value-of-marketing-channels)

Michigan State University provides insightful information (https://openstax.org/r/distributionmanagerdirector) on this career, including a sample job description, roles and responsibilities, salary, education, and training. When looking at your skill development and what you may need in order to obtain a job, check out ZipRecruiter's website. It indicates that while there are several skills needed in this job role, compliance and customer service are the most common. Read more about the needed skills (https://openstax.org/r/resumekeywordsandskills) on the Zip Recruiter website.

Knowledge Check

It's time to check your knowledge on the concepts presented in this section. Refer to the Answer Key at the end of the book for feedback.

1. A(n) ________ is a group of people, organizations, processes, and activities that work together to deliver products and services to the consumer.
   a. wholesaler
   b. manufacturer
   c. intermediary
   d. marketing channel

2. A(n) ________ is someone who acts as an extension of the manufacturer. While they never take possession of the product or service they represent, they earn a commission or collect a fee for facilitating the transaction between the customer and the manufacturer.
   a. retailer
   b. wholesaler
   c. distributor
   d. agent

3. Without intermediaries, the number of transactions between the total number of manufacturers and the total number of consumers would ________.
   a. decrease
   b. stay the same
   c. increase
   d. decrease temporarily

4. What do intermediaries do to add value in the marketing channel?
   a. They perform important activities that manufacturers are not experts at performing.
   b. They increase the price of products and services for customers.
   c. They increase the amount of time it takes for products and services to reach consumers.
   d. They make improvements to the product so that it functions better.

5. As intermediaries move products and services from manufacturers to consumers, what key services do

they offer?
a.   Pricing and promoting across geographical areas
b.   Surveying customers to ensure they are satisfied with their product or service experience
c.   Competing with one another to reduce prices for consumers
d.   Accumulating, bulk-breaking, adjusting for assortment discrepancies, and providing financing

17.2 | Types of Marketing Channels

Learning Outcomes

By the end of this section, you will be able to:
- **LO** 1 Identify the types of marketing channels that exist for consumer products.
- **LO** 2 Describe the types of marketing channels that exist for business/industrial products.
- **LO** 3 Discuss vertical, horizontal, multichannel, and omnichannel marketing systems.

Types of Marketing Channels

When determining the most effective and efficient way to reach consumers with products, companies have two options. Companies can either sell and distribute their products directly to consumers, known as a **direct channel**, or they can partner with intermediaries who can assist with the distribution, known as an **indirect channel**.

Direct Channel: From Producer to Consumer

In some cases, manufacturers decide that a direct marketing channel makes sense. A **direct marketing channel** does not use intermediaries but rather involves the manufacturer distributing its market offering directly to consumers. When consumers purchase pizza from their locally owned and operated pizza shop, the distribution of that pizza passes from the restaurant directly to the consumer. There are no intermediaries between the pizza shop and the customer.

Indirect Channels: From Producer to Intermediary to Consumer

An indirect channel involves the utilization of one or more intermediaries to distribute a market offering to consumers. Continuing with our pizza shop example, if a local pizza shop offered pizza that was delicious enough to package, freeze, and sell through local grocery stores in the frozen food aisle, that pizza shop would be adding an indirect channel of distribution.

In some cases, manufacturers or producers sell to retailers without the use of wholesalers or distributors, called the **producer to retailer to consumer channel**. A local Ace Hardware, for example, sells fishing lures made by the local scout troop. The troop purchases the supplies necessary to make the lures then sells them to Ace Hardware, which sells them to customers.

With producer to wholesaler to retailer to consumer—a more complex marketing channel—multiple types of intermediaries are needed. Procter & Gamble, the maker of Crest, Gillette, and Pampers, relies on an intricate network of intermediaries composed of wholesalers and retailers that work interdependently to ensure the right mix and quantity of products reach consumers. Consider all the places a consumer can purchase Procter & Gamble products all over the world.

For some industries, the distribution network is complex, and agents represent the manufacturer in marketing channel negotiations. Health insurance agents, for example, represent major insurance carriers such as Aetna and Blue Cross by providing consumers with information about health plans in their state. In these situations, the agent does not take ownership of the product like other intermediaries but rather is paid a fee by the insurance carrier.

For companies with a diverse product category that spans the globe, indirect channels of distribution make the most sense. Procter & Gamble sells hundreds of different products across many product categories worldwide. Indirect channels are necessary in such cases. Figure 17.4 illustrates the difference between a direct and indirect channel of distribution for consumer products.

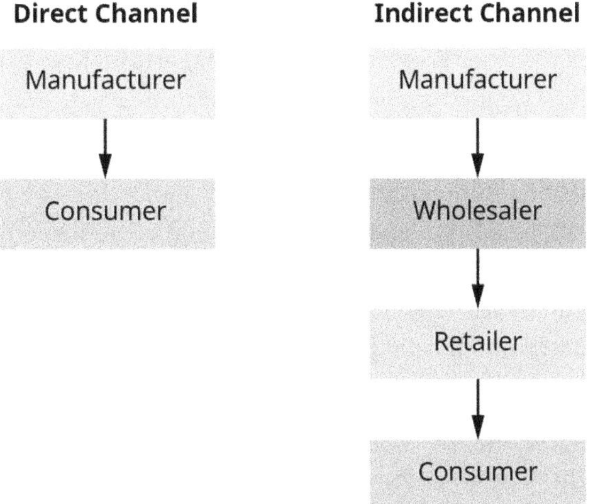

Figure 17.4 Channels of Distribution for Consumer Products (attribution: Copyright Rice University, OpenStax, under CC BY 4.0 license)

Marketing Channels for Business/Industrial Products

The **business-to-business (B2B)** market is comprised of companies who buy from and sell to other companies. In the B2B space, businesses are not distributing to final consumers but rather to other businesses. Companies in the B2B market buy, sell, and use materials, resources, and technology from one another to create products, where a business is the final consumer or destination.

Within this market, there are agents, brokers, distributors, and wholesalers who specialize in moving industrial products along the marketing channel to the final business consumer. Figure 17.5 illustrates an example of a distribution channel for business products.

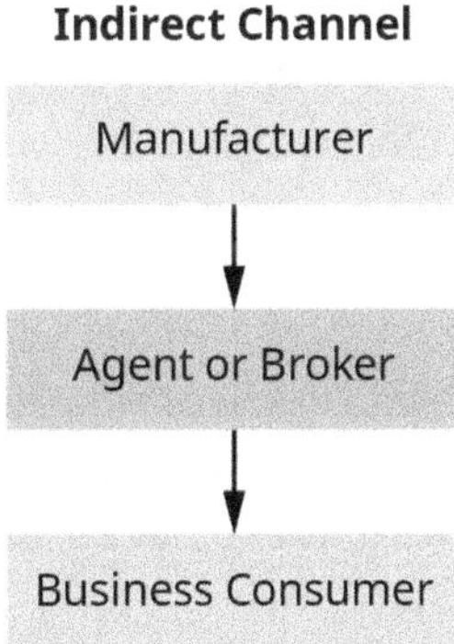

Figure 17.5 Channel of Distribution for Business (attribution: Copyright Rice University, OpenStax, under CC BY 4.0 license)

Direct Channel: From Producer to Business/Industrial User

Much like the **business-to-consumer (B2C)** space, when a company sells products or services directly to a final consumer or end user, the B2B marketing channel can be direct without the use of intermediaries. The direct channel is typically used when the nature of the product is complex, is expensive, or requires intensive resources to move the product from the manufacturer to the business customer. Airplane manufacturers like Boeing and Airbus produce and sell aircraft directly to airlines like Delta Air Lines and American Airlines, who then offer flights to consumers. Given the expense and complexity of distributing airplanes, the direct channel makes the most sense.

Industries often rely on the expertise of intermediaries to reach business users with their products and services. The advantages of the indirect channel in the business-to-business (B2B) space are similar to those in the business-to-consumer (B2C) space. For some industries, intermediaries perform important functions along the business marketing channel that they themselves are not experts in. Let's explore the different indirect marketing channels.

With producer to industrial distributor to business/industrial user channels, car manufacturers like Toyota and Honda rely on tens of thousands of different parts, which are manufactured by parts producers. **Producers** are companies that supply the raw materials that manufacturers need to create consumer products. Parts producers such as the car seating and E-Systems engineering company Lear rely on distributors to move their products and technology to automobile manufacturers. Using a distributor allows Lear to focus on its center of excellence—researching, designing, and building innovative seating technology solutions for vehicles.

Agents in the B2B space represent companies who produce industrial products and services and serve as an intermediary between the producer and the business user. The value of the agent is similar in the B2B space as it is in the B2C space. Agents add value by addressing product- or service-related questions and concerns. They typically earn a commission or a fee off the sale of the industrial product.

For more complex industrial marketing channels with global business users, producers will work with agents who partner directly with distributors to move products. For example, the automobile industry relies on agents and distributors to reach business users. According to Global Fleet, the largest fleet vehicle management company in the world, of the 313 million vehicles driven in the United States and Canada, about 9 million are corporate cars.[4] Element Fleet Management, based out of Toronto, Ontario, manages corporate vehicle fleets across the United States, Canada, and Mexico. Companies whose operations reach global markets typically rely on a much more complex channel that involves multiple layers of intermediaries to distribute products and services to business customers.

Other Marketing Systems

Manufacturers or producers along with their intermediary channel partners work in a system to move products and services to consumers. There are four major system types: a vertical marketing system, a horizontal marketing system, a multichannel marketing system, and an omnichannel marketing system. We'll explore each of these systems next.

Vertical Marketing System

A **vertical marketing system** (VMS) is a system in which companies in the marketing channel work together in a coordinated, collaborative, and customer-centric way. Unlike conventional systems, vertical marketing systems are less concerned with their profit margins and have a laser-like focus on working together to deliver value to consumers.

A VMS is unique in that all members of the marketing channel work as one unified group. Producers, wholesalers, and distributors share the common goal of creating and delivering value to consumers. In contrast, a conventional system is one in which each intermediary works as a distinct company, each trying to maximize profits at the expense of other channel members. VMS has grown in popularity over the conventional system because it results in fewer channel conflicts and increased customer value.

LINK TO LEARNING

Marketing Systems

To learn more about how marketing systems work, check out these videos:

- What Is a Channel System?
  Click to view content (https://openstax.org/books/principles-marketing/pages/17-2-types-of-marketing-channels)
- What Is a Vertical Marketing System?
  Click to view content (https://openstax.org/books/principles-marketing/pages/17-2-types-of-marketing-channels)

In Figure 17.6, observe the structural differences between the conventional marketing system (part A) and the vertical marketing system (part B). In the conventional model, the manufacturer sells to wholesalers, who then sell to retailers, who then sell to consumers. In the vertical marketing system, channel members are working together as strategic partners to distribute products to consumers.

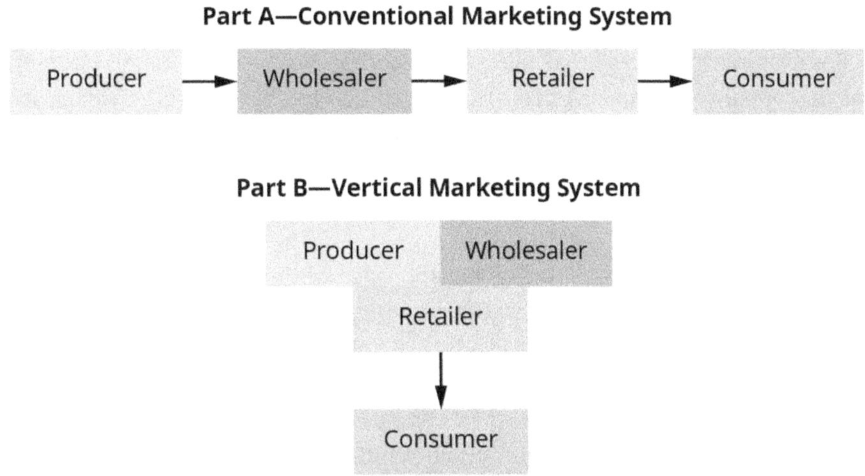

Figure 17.6 Structural Differences between Conventional and Vertical Marketing Systems (attribution: Copyright Rice University, OpenStax, under CC BY 4.0 license)

There are three types of vertical marketing systems: corporate, administered, and contractual (see Figure 17.7). In a **corporate VMS**, one member of the distribution channel owns the other members. For example, Walmart manufacturers its own private label brand of beauty and health products under the name Equate. Walmart not only controls the manufacturing of products under the brand but also owns and operate the wholesaler that distributes Equate-branded products to Walmart stores all over the world. Walmart reduces risk by owning and thus controlling the various channel members in its VMS. The corporate VMS approach allows for a unified system of creating and delivering customer value.

In an **administered VMS**, there is no ownership of channel members. However, there is one member who is large and powerful enough to coordinate and manage the distribution activities of other channels members. For example, Procter & Gamble manufacturers 65 brands in over 10 product categories. Given its size and power, it requires a high level of cooperation among wholesalers and retailers.

In a **contractual VMS**, there are independent companies that have joined together by contract for a mutually beneficial purpose. Each company operates independently of the others but integrates its activities to achieve its goals. An example of a contractual VMS is a franchise organization, such as Chipotle or McDonald's, in which the companies contract with a wholesaler to distribute products to the franchisees.

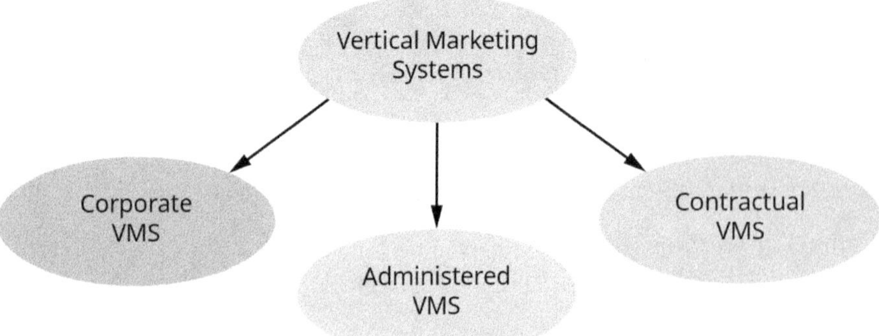

Figure 17.7 Types of Vertical Marketing Systems (attribution: Copyright Rice University, OpenStax, under CC BY 4.0 license)

Horizontal Marketing System

In a **horizontal marketing system**, unrelated companies partner to offer products and services in a shared space. For example, J.Crew and New Balance have partnered together for the last decade to sell a unique line of New Balance–branded sneakers that can only be found on J.Crew's website. In a horizontal system, companies partner to leverage the value they create for customers in a collaborative way.

Multichannel Marketing System

A **multichannel distribution system** is where a single company sets up multiple distribution channels to reach customers. For example, Nike has brick-and-mortar stores across major cities. Customers can visit the store, try on shoes and apparel, and make a purchase. In addition to physical stores, Nike also distributes its shoes and apparel through its online store Nike.com, through e-tailers like Amazon.com, and through other brick-and-mortar stores like Kohl's and Foot Locker.

Omnichannel Marketing System

An **omnichannel marketing system** is a multichannel approach whereby companies give consumers a variety of ways to purchase, receive, and return products. For example, in addition to purchasing products online and in-store, Dick's Sporting Goods offers customers a variety of options for receiving a product. Consumers can buy online and pick up in-store. They can also buy online from one of the store's kiosks and have it delivered to their home or some other location. Omnichannel marketing systems are designed to offer consumers a seamless buying experience, which further creates and delivers value.

LINK TO LEARNING

Omnichannel

To learn more about an omnichannel marketing system, check out these videos:

- Ted Talk: Omnichannel: Retail (R)evolution
  Click to view content (https://openstax.org/books/principles-marketing/pages/17-2-types-of-marketing-channels)
- Teredata: Omni-Channel Retailing
  Click to view content (https://openstax.org/books/principles-marketing/pages/17-2-types-of-marketing-channels)

Knowledge Check

It's time to check your knowledge on the concepts presented in this section. Refer to the Answer Key at the end of the book for feedback.

1. A(n) _______ marketing channel does not use intermediaries but rather involves the manufacturer distributing its market offering directly to consumers.
   a. indirect
   b. direct
   c. omnichannel
   d. multichannel

2. A(n) _______ marketing channel partners with intermediaries including distributors, wholesalers, agents, or retailers to sell and distribute its products.
   a. omnichannel
   b. indirect
   c. multichannel
   d. vertical channel

3. In the B2B or industrial space, manufacturers or producers sell products and services aimed at reaching a(n) _______ end user.
   a. consumer
   b. agent
   c. business
   d. wholesaler

4. In a(n) _______, one member of the distribution channel owns the other members.
   a. administered vertical marketing system
   b. corporate vertical marketing system
   c. horizontal marketing system
   d. multichannel marketing system

5. What is the difference between multichannel and omnichannel marketing systems?
   a. Multichannel marketing systems are designed primarily for online distribution.
   b. Omnichannel marketing systems are designed primarily for in-store distribution.
   c. Omnichannel marketing systems are more flexible and seamless in how consumers can buy and receive products and services.
   d. Multichannel marketing systems are more flexible and seamless in how consumers can buy and receive products and services.

17.3 | Factors Influencing Channel Choice

Learning Outcomes

By the end of this section, you will be able to:
- **LO** 1 Identify the factors that influence channel choice in distribution.
- **LO** 2 Describe the different types of target market coverage.
- **LO** 3 Discuss the buyer requirements influencing channel choice.
- **LO** 4 Explain the product-related factors influencing channel choice.
- **LO** 5 Describe the cost factors influencing channel choice.

Target Market Coverage

Target market coverage is defined as having the resources and capabilities to reach and serve consumers in a company's target market. Companies of all sizes must determine precisely how they will reach consumers with their products and services. Smaller companies tend to focus on smaller, more local markets, while larger companies must meet the consumer demand of larger, even global markets. A company's decision about which channel is best for meeting the needs of consumers involves a number of considerations.

The first factor that plays an important role in channel choice is target market coverage. Companies must analyze the size of their target market and their budget and ensure they have the appropriate coverage. For example, a small local bakery may only target towns in its area; therefore, its target market coverage is rather small. Kohlberg & Company, the owner of the Sara Lee and Thomas' brands, on the other hand, reaches global consumers and therefore requires far greater market coverage.

Depending on the size of their target market and the products and services they sell, companies must decide between an intensive, selective, or exclusive distribution strategy.

Intensive Distribution

Intensive distribution is a strategy that entails distributing a company's market offering through all possible intermediaries. With an intensive distribution, a consumer is able to find a company's product virtually everywhere. Intensive distribution makes sense for products that compete in a competitive market where consumers can easily choose an alternative if a company's product isn't available.

Coca-Cola and Kraft, for example, use intensive distribution so that consumers around the world can access their products everywhere and anywhere they'd shop for food and beverages.

Selective Distribution

Selective distribution is a strategy that includes choosing more than one, but fewer than all possible intermediaries to distribute a company's market offering. Companies choose selective distribution when they don't need the expansive coverage that intensive distribution provides but still need to reach their target market at specific retail outlets. Large appliance companies such as Whirlpool and General Electric use selective distribution by making their products available through their dealer networks and at selective large retailers like Lowe's and Home Depot.

Exclusive Distribution

In direct contrast to an intensive distribution strategy, some companies intentionally use an exclusive distribution strategy. **Exclusive distribution** is a strategy that involves allowing a limited number of intermediaries to distribute a company's market offering. Luxury brand Rolex, for example, allows a limited number of retailers to sell its luxury watches. The exclusivity of these retailers reinforces Rolex's distinctive position of being a luxurious, hard-to-get brand.

Fulfillment of Buyer Requirements

In addition to determining target market coverage, companies must also consider a channel's ability to fulfill the requirements of buyers. Consumers have specific product and service expectations that must be fulfilled in order to satisfy their wants and needs. For example, when consumers purchase bottled water, they expect the bottle to be filled to the top, the cap to be sealed before opening, and the water to taste fresh and clean. With these buyer requirements in mind, companies who make bottled water must ensure that they work with channel members who are able to fulfill these buyer requirements because these requirements are critical to the perception of consumer value.

Information

Companies who recognize that buyers require information to make a decision between competing products may work with channel members who can provide these services. Consumers with limited knowledge of a product, for example, may be more likely to purchase that product after an in-store demonstration, for example. Grocery retailers like Whole Foods will often host in-store demonstrations of new food products for shoppers to sample (see Figure 17.8). Providing this service makes Whole Foods a desirable channel partner for start-up food brands looking to break into a highly competitive market. In another example, Ace Hardware may be a perfect channel partner for a new brand of tools because of Ace Hardware's reputation for being "the helpful place." Working with a channel member who can provide the service of in-store demonstrations creates value for the consumer and thus is a factor in determining channel choice.

Figure 17.8 Whole Foods uses in-store demonstrations as a way to share product information with consumers. (credit: "Whole Foods Market Ann Arbor" by Andypiper/flickr, CC BY 2.0)

Convenience

In some cases, buyers demand convenience and will only purchase products and services that are in close proximity to where they live, work, or shop. Companies must consider whether their target customers value convenience. For example, buyers shopping for chewing gum likely value convenience much more than buyers shopping for skis. Companies whose buyers require convenience should choose retail outlets that are convenient and hassle-free.

Variety

Companies must also consider how their target market values variety. Imagine walking into a pet supply store and only seeing one type of pet food. Buyers generally have a desire to choose from a variety of competing products. Petco and PetSmart recognize that consumers appreciate variety in everything from pet food to pet supplies such as toys, leashes, and bedding. For companies who compete in a crowded market where buyers have many options, selecting outlets that offer a variety of similar and competing products makes the most sense.

Pre- or Post-Sale Service

Pre-sale service entails all the activities that help a buyer make a purchase decision, while **post-sale service** entails all the activities that help a buyer recognize the value of the product. A pre-sale service can be observed at a car dealership where shoppers are invited to test-drive a vehicle and apply for financing. Post-sale service in this same example would be the offering of vehicle services, such as free oil changes and tire rotations for the life of the vehicle.

For some companies, the service that's provided before and after the sale is critical to customer-perceived value. **Customer-perceived value** is the overall perception that a consumer has about a company, brand, or product and is measured by what the consumer is willing to pay in return for the features and benefits in the market offering. Companies that sell large appliances and furniture, for example, understand that consumers value haul-away services. For example, for an additional fee, Lowe's offers customers the option of having their old appliance hauled away and their new appliance installed. These complementary services are important because they add value to the customer's product experience (see Figure 17.9).

Figure 17.9 Lowe's appliance haul-away program provides a post-sales service as a value-add item to influence potential consumers. (credit: "Show-Me Green Tax" by Rachel Gleason/KOMU News/flickr, CC BY 2.0)

Product-Related Factors

In addition to target market coverage and requirements of the buyer, there are product-related factors that can influence channel decisions. Product-related factors include things like unit value, perishability, and the bulk and weight of a product. These factors can influence the distribution decisions that companies make (see Figure 17.10).

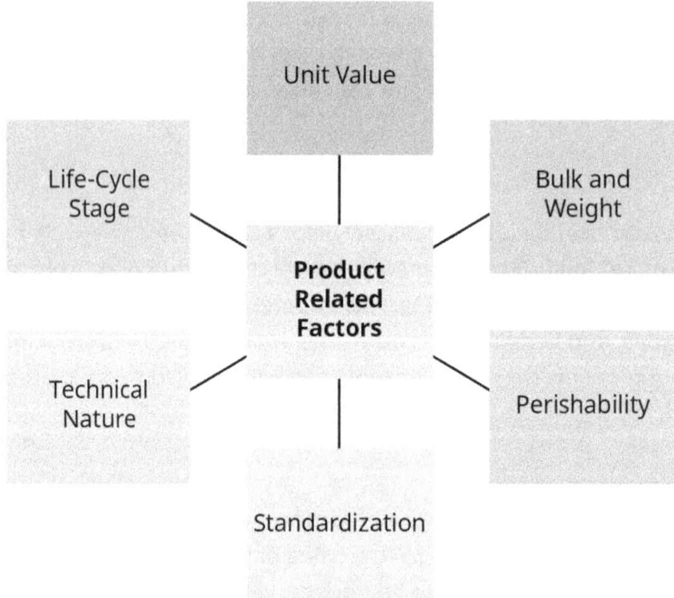

Figure 17.10 Product-Related Factors (attribution: Copyright Rice University, OpenStax, under CC BY 4.0 license)

Unit Value

A product's **unit value**, or the price that a company charges for one unit or item, can influence channel length decisions. **Channel length** relates to the number of intermediaries in the marketing channel. For example, products with high unit values, such as cars, boats, and airplanes, will have a much shorter distribution channel than nonperishable products, such as crackers, bandages, and tissues, which have a low unit value. Because of the complexities and costs of moving heavy or awkward products, companies seek a shorter distribution channel to mitigate these factors. There are companies that specialize in moving more expensive and complex products.

Perishability

Perishability relates to the likelihood that a product will spoil, decay, or expire if not used in a timely manner. A product's perishability also influences channel decisions. For example, orange-juice maker Tropicana's marketing channel looks much different than Nabisco's Ritz Crackers' channel. Because orange juice must be kept cold throughout the distribution process, Tropicana makes channel decisions that allow it to protect the integrity of the product throughout the distribution process. Working with channel partners who are experts at storing, handling, and moving perishable products is one of the most important factors for companies who manufacture perishable products.

Alongside unit value, perishability can also influence channel length. Companies marketing perishable goods such as milk, cheese, and meat products require a shorter distribution channel because these products have a limited shelf life.

Bulk and Weight

Much like a product's unit value, the bulk and weight of a product influence channel length. The **bulk and weight** of a product is the density and heaviness of one unit of product. Companies that sell larger and heavier items are more likely to use a direct or short distribution channel to avoid issues that arise when too many intermediaries handle a product. For example, because hot tubs or personal spas are bulky and heavy, they are more prone to product damage during distribution. Furthermore, there are typically fewer intermediaries between the manufacturer and the customer in order to mitigate the high costs associated with distributing hot tubs.[5]

Standardization

The standardization of a product also impacts channel decisions. Products that are **standardized** have no differences in how they are manufactured. Standardized products are uniform and consistent. Agricultural products, such as grain and corn, are standardized. Consumers are unable to tell the difference between these products because of their standardization. Standardized products have a longer channel length than customized products. Customized products are adapted depending on the customer's needs. They typically require a shorter distribution channel. Companies must consider the impact of standardization before making channel decisions.

Technical Nature of a Product

Products sold in the tech space are typically more complex and often require an onboarding process. For example, the customer-relationship management firm Salesforce offers companies a cloud-based application that allows it to manage millions of contacts or people as they move along the sales cycle from lead to prospect to customer. Products with a technical component often have a short channel length, meaning there is no intermediary between the company and the business consumer. They are distributed directly to business consumers (or B2B) because of the onboarding, implementation, training, support, and maintenance aspects of the product. Companies that use Salesforce have access to a customer relationship management expert who ensures that the program is being used and managed effectively in order for the customer to get the most out of the product.

Product Life-Cycle Stage

A product's life-cycle stage may also impact channel decisions. **Product life cycle** refers to the various stages that a product goes through from its introduction phase, to its growth and maturity phase, and in some cases to its decline phase. For example, during the introduction phase of a product's life cycle, where profits and consumer knowledge of a product are low, companies may make more conservative channel decisions. As the product enters the growth stage, companies may expand distribution to meet consumer demand. As the product enters the maturity stage and ultimately the decline state, a company must ensure that its distribution strategy aligns with its changing consumer demand.

Profitability

The profitability of a channel can also influence channel decisions. Profitability relates to the amount of money that stands to be gained after a company pays its expenses. A simple way to calculate profitability is to subtract these expenses from the revenue generated.

Companies must evaluate not just the revenue generated by working with channel partners but also the channel member's ability to operate profitably. Channels that are not able to manage distribution costs effectively are less attractive for companies seeking to earn a profit. Companies ultimately have an obligation to be profitable, and choosing channel partners that help them achieve their overarching goals is more desirable than those who cannot.

Knowledge Check

It's time to check your knowledge on the concepts presented in this section. Refer to the Answer Key at the end of the book for feedback.

1. Which of the following overarching factors can impact channel choice in the distribution of products and services?
   a. Target market coverage, fulfillment of buyer requirements, and profitability
   b. Intensive, selective, and exclusive distribution
   c. The technical nature of the product and its fixed and variable costs
   d. The profitability of the channel and its members' abilities to meet consumer needs

2. ABC Toys desires to distribute products across global markets. It is likely using what type of distribution strategy?
   a. Exclusive
   b. Selective
   c. Unlimited
   d. Intensive

3. Total Appliance offers buyers installation services for refrigerators, dishwashers, washers, and dryers for $50. In addition, it also offers buyers a free annual tune-up of any major appliance purchased through its retail outlet. Which buyer requirement does Total Appliance fulfill?
   a. Variety
   b. Post-sale service
   c. Pre-sale service
   d. Convenience

4. MilkyIce markets ice cream products through grocery retailers in the United States. Which of the following product-related factors would have the biggest impact on MilkyIce's channel choice?
   a. Standardization
   b. Bulk and weight
   c. Perishability
   d. Unit value

5. Which overarching factor involves analyzing the revenues and costs associated with a channel?
   a. Unit value
   b. Fixed costs
   c. Variable costs
   d. Profitability

17.4 | Managing the Distribution Channel

Learning Outcomes

By the end of this section, you will be able to:
- **LO** 1 Describe how channel members are selected.
- **LO** 2 Explain how channel members are managed and motivated.
- **LO** 3 Discuss how channel conflict is handled.
- **LO** 4 Summarize the metrics used for channel member evaluation.

Selecting Channel Members

After a manufacturer has evaluated its distribution channel options, it now needs to select the right channel members and manage and motivate them to operate effectively and efficiently. In addition, the manufacturer must also address any conflicts that may arise in the marketing channel. A **channel member**, also known as an intermediary, is a company that works in a network with other companies to help move products from manufacturers to final consumers. Channel members perform a variety of important tasks that collectively create value for the consumer.

The channel members that a company selects depends entirely on the company's evaluation of the channel member alternatives. Manufacturers should examine each channel member's years in business and experience carrying product lines. They should also evaluate each member's reputation and its profitability. PetVivo, maker of biomedical devices for pets, selected Vetcove to distribute a device for pets with osteoporosis. Because PetVivo needed to reach veterinary hospitals and clinics across all 50 states, Vetcove was the right choice because of its experience serving over 13,000 veterinary hospitals and clinics. Its expertise and reputation were attractive characteristics for PetVivo.[6]

Managing and Motivating Channel Members

After channel members have been selected, manufacturers must continuously manage and motivate members to work together to achieve their collective goals. It's similar to a partnership or relationship where companies depend on one another to marshal the product along the marketing channel.

The qualities of an effective channel relationship include collaboration, transparency, and cohesion. When members work together toward a common goal of delivering value to the consumer, the channel is more effective. Companies like L'Oréal and Procter & Gamble must work harmoniously to build mutually beneficial relationships with their distribution network because it's critical to meeting the needs of their consumers. Failure to do so could be detrimental to channel members if customer value declines because of conflict.

In addition to managing relationships, manufacturers must also find ways to reinforce channel member performance. Manufacturers can provide incentives, such as bonuses and other types of rewards, when channel members meet the manufacturer's goals. In addition to incentives, manufacturers can also listen to and support channel members by providing them with helpful sales materials, product samples, and the right messaging.

Evaluating Channel Members

Manufacturers must systematically evaluate channel member performance to ensure that each member is meeting standards. Failure to evaluate performance can lead to inefficiencies in the channel and a decline in customer-perceived value.

Handling Channel Conflict

Sometimes channel members experience conflict during the distribution process. **Channel conflict** is when companies in the distribution channel have disagreements due to a competitive versus collaborative mindset. For example, a channel member may cause conflict because its focus isn't on creating value but on driving down costs at the expense of the customer. This could create conflict in the channel if channel partners and ultimately consumers are impacted by an excessive profit orientation.

Vertical Conflict

A **vertical conflict** is a conflict that exists between different levels of a vertical channel. When the goals of manufacturers, wholesalers, and retailers aren't aligned in the marketing channel, the customer will ultimately suffer, either by paying more for a product or experiencing a product shortage.

Disintermediation is the process of removing an intermediary from a marketing channel. It occurs when manufacturers have discovered an opportunity to sell directly to end users or final consumers. It can also occur if a manufacturer pivots from its traditional distribution strategy to something completely different. In a classic example, the birth of Apple iTunes essentially put traditional outlets for purchasing music out of business. In another example, traditional movie theaters are experiencing disintermediation as streaming services like Netflix and HBOMax are releasing new films that 10 years ago would have been released only in theaters.

Horizontal Conflict

A **horizontal conflict** is when there is disagreement among firms at the same level in the marketing channel. For example, Holiday Inn has a variety of locations in New York City. If one Holiday Inn drives its prices down to outcompete its partners, that could cause conflict among the other Holiday Inn locations that perceive it as stealing customers through pricing tactics.

The Use of Metrics in Evaluating Channel Members

In order to evaluate channel performance, companies use key metrics including inventory turnover rate, order accuracy rate, time to ship, total units in storage, and percentage of on-time shipments. By monitoring these metrics, companies can assess their performance and make adjustments as needed. Figure 17.11 presents key metrics used in evaluating channel member performance. Let's look at each of these more closely.

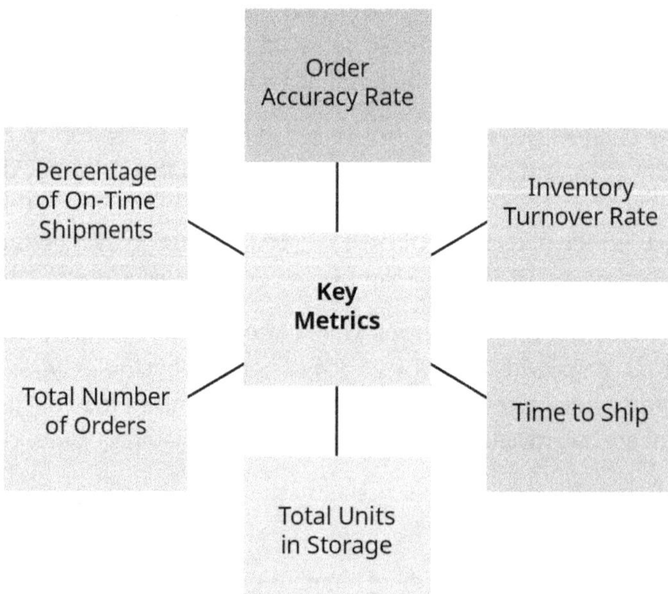

Figure 17.11 Performance Metrics (attribution: Copyright Rice University, OpenStax, under CC BY 4.0 license)

Inventory turnover rate is a metric that measures how quickly inventory is turned over or sold. Trader Joe's faced a dilemma with the COVID-19 pandemic as consumers stocked up on nonperishable goods like pasta and rice. As consumer demand increased, Trader Joe's supply warehouses were virtually empty as they waited for new inventory to come in. When metrics fall outside what a company considers normal or acceptable, it can then make adjustments, such as introduce new products to fill demand as in the case of Trader Joe's.[7]

Order accuracy rate is an important ecommerce metric. It measures the percentage of orders that are processed, fulfilled, and shipped to consumers without any errors. If you've purchased a pair of sneakers and the wrong size arrives at your home, this constitutes order inaccuracy. These errors can be costly to companies, who then need to process, fulfill, and send another order.

Time to ship, also known as order cycle time, is the length of time from when a customer places an order to when it reaches them. Amazon has redefined consumer expectations related to shipping. With high expectations that purchased items will arrive quickly, online shoppers say that delivery time influences their purchase decision. The time-to-ship metric is a useful tool to measure how quickly a manufacturer can get its products through channel members to consumers.

Total units in storage is a metric used to evaluate warehouse efficiency. This is a real-time metric that changes as items are sold and leave the warehouse and new inventory moves in. This metric also provides insight into warehousing and inventory costs as well as the number of SKUs, or stock-keeping units, a warehouse is managing at any given time. SKUs are unique numbers assigned to every single product in a warehouse.

The **total number of orders** is an important metric. The total number of orders is the sum of all orders that a company received in a given time period. It provides insight into consumer demand and helps manufacturers to plan accordingly. For seasonal products like winter coats and pumpkin-flavored cookies, the total number of orders may fluctuate throughout the year. Evaluating the total number of orders over time helps manufacturers watch for fluctuations and plan accordingly.

Percentage of on-time shipments is a metric used to evaluate how well a channel member meets its promise of delivering goods on time. This metric is especially important to industries that market perishable goods like meat and dairy. Imagine if the Greek yogurt manufacturer Chobani (see Figure 17.12) worked with an intermediary that only met its delivery date 50 percent of the time. This would directly impact the shelf life of the product at the retail level and cost everyone in the channel money.

Figure 17.12 Percentage of on-time shipments is an inventory turnover metric used by companies like Chobani to evaluate a distribution channel's effectiveness at meeting product need. (credit: "Blood Orange Yogurt" by tbiley/flickr, CC BY 2.0)

Alongside time to ship, measuring average delivery days looks at the average number of days it takes shipping carriers to deliver purchased goods to consumers. This is important to consumers who value the timely delivery of products purchased online. Manufacturers may choose to work with a company like Amazon because of its core competency of fulfilling and delivering products to consumers relatively quickly.

Knowledge Check

It's time to check your knowledge on the concepts presented in this section. Refer to the Answer Key at the end of the book for feedback.

1. XYZ Appliance is evaluating wholesalers to determine which one would be the right match for its distribution strategy. Which of the following wholesalers would be the best match for XYZ Appliance?
   a. Wholesaler A is brand new to the large appliance market.
   b. Wholesaler B has 20 years of experience in wholesaling food products and is the most expensive.
   c. Wholesaler C has five years of experience in the large appliance market, has a solid reputation, and is profitable.
   d. Wholesaler D has two years of experience in the small appliance market and is the cheapest.

2. DirectDocumentaries is a streaming service that provides subscribers with access to documentaries. It currently works with three production companies that it continuously manages to ensure timely production and delivery of new documentaries. Which of the following scenarios is an example of good channel management?
   a. Production Company A distributes its documentaries through DirectDocumentaries but has also set up an additional domain on the web to distribute directly to viewers. DirectDocumentaries does not know about this additional streaming outlet.
   b. Production Company B has only been operating for one year. DirectDocumentaries is skeptical about Production Company B's capabilities so shares limited information with it. DirectDocumentaries offers little to no support in Production Company B's development.
   c. Production Company C is a powerhouse, producing 30 to 40 documentaries a year. DirectDocumentaries and Production Company C work closely together to ensure that documentary releases occur at strategic times. They also openly share information about what's working and what's not. They have a common goal in reaching customers with innovative ideas.
   d. Production Company D is rarely happy. It feels that DirectDocumentaries favors other producers and rarely features its productions on a subscriber's homepage. Production Company D has complained several times.

3. ________ occurs when manufacturers cut out intermediaries and sell directly to end users or final buyers. It can also occur if a manufacturer pivots from its traditional distribution strategy to something completely different.
   a. Horizontal conflict
   b. Vertical conflict
   c. Intermediary conflict
   d. Disintermediation

4. Which of the following is a key metric that assesses the percentage of orders that are processed, fulfilled, and shipped to consumers without any errors?
   a. Order accuracy rate
   b. Inventory turnover rate
   c. Total number of orders
   d. Average delivery days

5. ________ measures the length of time from when a customer places an order to when it reaches them.
   a. Average delivery days
   b. Time to ship
   c. Inventory turnover rate
   d. Total number of orders

17.5 | The Supply Chain and Its Functions

Learning Outcomes

By the end of this section, you will be able to:

- **LO 1** Define supply chain management (SCM).
- **LO 2** Explain the role of marketing in supply chain management.
- **LO 3** Describe the various functions of supply chain management.

Supply Chain Management (SCM) Defined

A **supply chain** is the entire process of distribution from acquiring the raw materials needed to make products to delivering final goods to consumers. Companies with high-performing supply chains recognize that it starts with a customer-centered mindset. All activities must be managed with the end goal of creating and delivering value to the target consumer.

Supply chain management (SCM) is the process of managing all the members and activities from the procurement and transformation of raw materials into finished goods through their distribution to targeted consumers.

The Role of Marketing in Supply Chain Management

Marketing plays an integral role in the management of the supply chain. Marketing entails creating and delivering products that meet the needs of customers all while building relationships through customer engagement. Companies ensure that they deliver on their value proposition to consumers through the features and benefits of the product itself. Ensuring fulfillment of a company's value proposition starts with working with the right suppliers who provide the materials and ingredients to help companies fulfill their promise.

For example, Dave's Killer Bread (DKB) has positioned itself as the maker of "the best bread you've ever tasted, power-packed with organic whole grain nutrition." The promise to consumers starts with selecting suppliers who are certified organic and who can consistently deliver high-quality ingredients. DKB's promise to consumers starts as far back as the grains selected by DKB's suppliers.

Functions of Supply Chain Management

Supply chain management has five major functions. These include purchasing, operations, logistics, resource management, and information workflow (see Figure 17.13). Good supply chains perform these functions in a way that meets the wants and needs of final consumers efficiently.

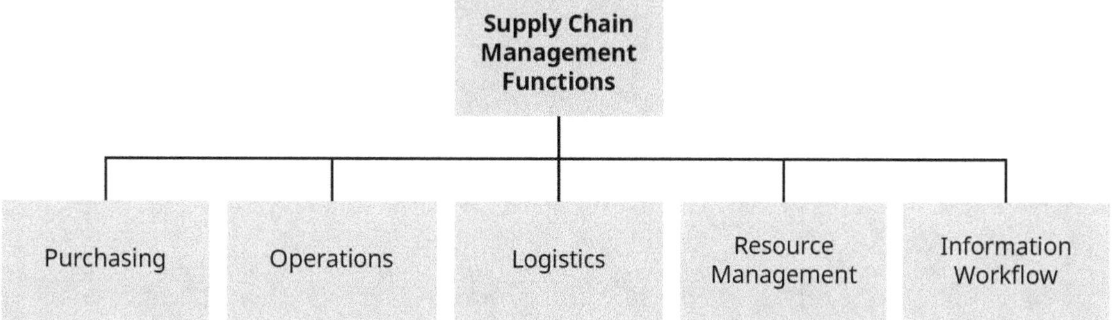

Figure 17.13 The Five Major Functions of Supply Chain Management (attribution: Copyright Rice University, OpenStax, under CC BY 4.0 license)

Purchasing

Purchasing is the process of buying materials needed to manufacture products. These materials are purchased from suppliers, who must be able to deliver them in accordance with the manufacturer's timeline.

Therefore, the manufacturer's companies and suppliers must communicate and coordinate to ensure timely delivery of materials.

For example, Ben & Jerry's ice cream flavor Mint Chocolate Chance has cream, skim milk, sugar, egg yolks, white flour, cocoa powder, soybean oil, and vanilla extract, among other ingredients. Ben and Jerry's must forecast the number of ingredients it needs to purchase so that these amounts match the demand for this particular flavor. The company, in turn, assesses things like total number of orders and inventory turnover for its Mint Chocolate Chance product to help forecast the quantity of ingredients it will need from suppliers.

Operations

Operations is everything a company does on a day-to-day basis to run a company. Before a company purchases the needed materials and begins production, it must forecast demand for its products. Forecasting involves anticipating or projecting how many units of a product will be sold during a given period. Accurate forecasting must align with inventory management and production schedules to ensure that the company is operationally positioned to manufacture the right amount of product to meet the needs of consumers.

Logistics

Logistics is a function that involves the coordination of all supply chain activities, such as warehousing, inventory management, and transportation. Companies along the supply chain must communicate effectively to ensure that products reach consumers in a timely and efficient way in the precise form that the consumer expects. For example, when consumers eat McDonald's French fries, they expect the fries to taste a certain way. Suppliers and intermediaries along the channel work together to ensure that those expectations are met. Good logistical management helps ensure this.

Resource Management

Resource management is the planning, organizing, and controlling of resources. Resources include the labor, the raw materials, and the technology that are required to move products from their raw material phase to finished goods available for consumption. Effective supply chain management requires the right allocation of these resources to the right supply chain activities to optimize the entire system.

Information Workflow

Information workflow is a supply chain management function that relates to what and how information moves between members of the supply chain. If information doesn't flow effectively or communication is poor, the entire process can suffer as a result of disruptions, delays, and mistakes. Employing a systematic approach to sharing information across the supply chain ensures that the right companies have the right data to make the right decisions at the right time.

LINK TO LEARNING

Supply Chain Management

To learn more about how supply chain management works, review the following article and video: IBM and Supply Chain Management (https://openstax.org/r/supplychainmanagement).

Knowledge Check

It's time to check your knowledge on the concepts presented in this section. Refer to the Answer Key at the end of the book for feedback.

1. _______ entails managing all the members and activities from the procurement and transformation of raw

materials into finished goods through their distribution to targeted consumers.
   a. Logistics
   b. Integrated logistics management
   c. Supply chain management
   d. Warehousing

2. Which of the following best demonstrates the role that marketing plays in supply chain management?
   a. In order for companies to deliver on their value proposition to consumers, they must ensure that the activities and members in the supply chain share the common goal of delivering value to consumers.
   b. Companies need to raise the price of their products with the supply chain in mind so that they earn a profit.
   c. Companies must market their products to supply chain members in order to win partnership with them.
   d. Companies should only work with supply chain members who can save time and money in the distribution of products. Savings are most important to customers.

3. Companies that manufacture goods rely on raw materials to produce the products they sell. This describes the function of ________.
   a. inventory management
   b. supply chain management
   c. transportation
   d. purchasing

4. ________ include(s) the labor, the raw materials, and the technology that are required to move products from their raw material phase to finished goods available for consumption.
   a. Purchasing
   b. Logistics
   c. Forecasting
   d. Resources

5. ________ is a supply chain management function that relates to what and how information moves between members of the supply chain.
   a. Information workflow
   b. Forecasting
   c. Logistics
   d. Resource management

17.6 Logistics and Its Functions

Learning Outcomes

By the end of this section, you will be able to:

   LO 1 Define and describe logistics.
   LO 2 Explain the functions of logistics.
   LO 3 Describe logistics information management.
   LO 4 Describe integrated logistics management.
   LO 5 Characterize third-party logistics (3PL) providers.

Logistics Defined

An important function of the supply is logistics, which includes all the activities involved in the flow of products from manufacturers to consumers. Logistics is the planning, organizing, and controlling of the movement of raw materials and ultimately finished goods from manufacturers to final consumers.

For example, the logistics involved in getting orange juice to consumers includes a variety of activities, such as packing and transporting. It is critical that there is a coordinated effort between all channel members involved in that process. The functions or purpose of logistics is explored next.

Functions of Logistics

Getting products from manufacturers to final consumers requires the coordinated efforts of all channel members. These efforts require an understanding of key activities that need to occur as products flow through the marketing channel. The major functions of logistics explored next include warehousing, inventory management, and transportation.

Warehousing is the stocking, maintaining, and controlling of products while they await the next step in their journey to the final consumer. Warehousing requires receiving and storing new stock, picking and packing ordered items, and shipping products off to their next destination. Depending on the product, warehousing may also involve maintaining control of the warehouse's temperature to ensure that perishable goods or food that needs to be held at a certain temperature don't spoil.

Inventory management is a function that involves identifying the type of inventory and how much a company has on hand at any given time. Managing inventory is a critical logistics function because it ensures that there isn't too much or too little on hand.

Transportation is the physical movement of products by either road, water, or air (see Figure 17.14). Companies must determine which method or methods of transportation make the most sense given the nature of the product, the location of the target market, and costs associated with each method. Transportation also involves all the activities such as the generation of shipping documents, the calculation of delivery time, and the need for additional resources like technology or special equipment. For example, an ice cream manufacturer would need to ensure that the transportation methods it selects to distribute its products are temperature controlled to maintain the integrity and safety of the products.

Figure 17.14 Shipping containers are used by transportation companies in the distribution channel to move products by ship. (credit: "LARS MAERSK" by Bernard Spragg.NZ/flickr, Public Domain)

There are three factors that companies must consider in selecting a mode of transportation. First is the product itself. Products that are hazardous, perishable, or problematic to handle may impact transportation methods. Location is a second factor that can impact the mode of transportation. Companies must consider shipping origin, which is the location where the product is shipping from. They must also consider the shipping destination, or the location where the product must land. A company transporting products from China to the United States, for example, needs to select transportation methods that allow it to move products over large bodies of water. The third factor impacting transportation methods is any special considerations related to time or urgency. Companies need to consider how quickly they need products moved from origin to destination. There are a variety of transportation methods available, including trucking, rail, water carriers, air carriers, or some combination of these.

In Table 17.2 different modes of transportation are presented along with their relative speed of delivery, cost, and accessibility. Accessibility means how readily available or convenient the mode of transportation is. For example, trucking is an accessible mode of transportation because of the strong road infrastructure in the United States. Let's compare the different modes of transportation based on these characteristics.

Trucking or road transportation makes the most sense for companies that are transporting between destinations that are connected by land. It is highly accessible, meaning that trucking is readily available to companies looking for a low-cost mode of transportation.

Rail is a second mode of transportation that is best suited for moving goods in cases where speed of delivery is not urgent and low transportation costs are important. Similar to rail, water carriers offer an even slower mode of transportation at an even lower cost than rail, making it a popular mode for moving consumer goods from China to the United States.

For some companies, more than one mode of transportation is needed. Multimodal transportation involves companies using two or more types of transportation to move goods from origin to destination. For example, Apple may use air to ship iPhones to European airports but then trucks to continue the journey in getting iPhones to warehouses or distribution centers and retailers.

Mode	Speed	Cost	Accessibility
Trucking	Moderate	Low	High
Railroads	Slow	Low	Moderate
Water Carriers	Very slow	Very low	Moderate
Air Carriers	Fast	Very high	Low
Digital	Very fast	Very low	Very High

Table 17.2 Modes of Transportation and Relative Factors

Logistics Information Management

For a supply chain to be effective, manufacturers, suppliers, channel members, and customers need useful logistical information that can help them make informed decisions. Logistics information management is the recording and reporting of useful information that channel members can analyze and validate during the process of moving products.

Channel members use a system to access and manage logistics information in real time. This information allows members to develop demand forecasts, where they predict what and how much consumers will demand in the future, which in turn helps them to make decisions about how much raw materials and other supplies they need to meet consumer demand.

Integrated Logistics Management

Integrated logistics management means that every element of logistics works cohesively to ensure that products flow from manufacturer to final consumer in an efficient and effective way. Companies must first begin by defining the objectives of logistics management. For example, in the procurement and distribution of agricultural products, the supply chain might collectively set objectives that everyone along the chain commits to. They may, for example, set objectives to minimize costs, meet delivery times 95 percent of the time, and communicate openly and honestly about product availability and product flow in a consistent and systematic way. Or they may strive cohesively to manage inventory more effectively to reduce the possibility of shortage or surplus.

Whatever objectives they set for the supply chain, each member strives to integrate its activities and information with the activities and information of other members to ensure cohesive and synergistic handling of products for the ultimate purpose of meeting the wants and needs of the consumer.

Third-Party Logistics (3PL) Providers

A **third-party logistics provider** is a company that is contracted by a channel member to handle one or more of the functional areas of logistics. 3PL providers can be warehouses, distribution centers, or fulfillment centers that have expertise in managing certain logistical activities.

The advantages of working with 3PL providers is that logistics is their core competency, it is less expensive to outsource, and they offer flexibility. Owning warehouses and trucking systems requires a great deal of capital. Companies would much rather work with a 3PL provider than assume the financial risk of owning and operating their own transportation and warehousing systems.

Imagine if pet food maker Purina had to purchase its own warehousing and trucking business to store and move its goods all over the United States. It would be very costly and require a large capital commitment. In addition, 3PL providers offer the advantage of strategic location. They often market themselves as being located in the precisely right zones that a supply chain needs to reach targeted consumers.

The downside of using 3PL providers is the loss of control. Manufacturers are essentially turning over logistics responsibilities to other companies, who assume control of communication and interaction with suppliers. To combat this, manufacturers should continuously analyze performance metrics and communicate with 3PL providers.

Knowledge Check

It's time to check your knowledge on the concepts presented in this section. Refer to the Answer Key at the end of the book for feedback.

1. _______ makes the most sense for companies who need to transport products quickly.
   a. Trucking
   b. Air transportation
   c. Rail transportation
   d. Water transportation

2. _______ is the planning, organizing, and controlling of the movement of raw materials and ultimately finished goods to end consumers.
   a. Supply chain management
   b. Logistics
   c. A marketing channel
   d. Transportation

3. Which of the following best explains the importance and use of logistics information?
   a. Companies use logistics information to sell to other companies that target similar consumers.
   b. Companies use logistics information to market additional products to consumers.
   c. Companies use logistics information to develop demand forecasts, conduct supply planning, and

    optimize supply chain effectiveness.

    d. Companies rarely use logistics information to guide decision-making.

4. _______ ensures that every element of logistics as part of the entire supply chain is part of a system that works cohesively to ensure that the wants and needs of final customers are met.

    a. A marketing channel

    b. Information management

    c. Integrated marketing communication

    d. Integrated logistics management

5. Which of the following explains why companies would use a third-party logistics (3PL) provider to distribute products?

    a. 3PL providers have the expertise, flexibility, and cost efficiencies that manufacturers do not possess in logistics.

    b. 3PL providers understand how to promote a product more effectively than a company does.

    c. 3PL providers own warehouses to help store and manage inventory.

    d. 3 PL providers own and operate their own transportation system.

17.7 | Ethical Issues in Supply Chain Management

Learning Outcomes

By the end of this section, you will be able to:

LO 1 Discuss the issue of the carbon footprint versus the speed of shipping.

LO 2 Discuss the issue of sourcing sustainably.

Carbon Footprint versus the Speed of Shipping

As companies strive to deliver the right products to the right customers at the right time, they are faced with the competing interest of protecting the environment in which they operate.

LINK TO LEARNING

Environmental Responsibility in the Supply Chain

To learn more about environmental responsibility in the supply chain, watch the following video: Value, Speed, Environmental and Societal Impact – HP's Supply Chain.

Click to view content (https://openstax.org/books/principles-marketing/pages/17-7-ethical-issues-in-supply-chain-management)

Sustainability is a company's effort to reduce its impact on the environment as products move from source procurement through production through distribution to final consumers. Companies that practice sustainability balance their goal of speedy delivery with a commitment to reducing their carbon footprint. While traditional marketing channels focus on speed and cost, a sustainable channel also factors in goals aimed at mitigating the harm the supply chain causes to both humans and the environment.

Sourcing Sustainably

Sustainable sourcing is the process of considering suppliers' social, ethical, and environmental performance. The benefits of sourcing sustainably are improved reputation, brand protection, and an opportunity to attract new consumers and reach new markets. When a company claims it sources sustainably, it means that it is both transparent and ethical regarding the raw materials it uses in its products. It is not only transparent and ethical in its sourcing of materials but also environmentally conscious about its manufacturing process.

The shoe company Allbirds has sought to use natural instead of petroleum-based synthetic materials, which is what a majority of footwear is made from. By 2025, it aims for 75 percent of its shoes to be sustainably sourced using both natural and recycled raw materials.[8]

COMPANIES WITH A CONSCIENCE

Allbirds

Figure 17.15 Sustainability is a core part of the Allbirds mission and marketing message. (credit: "Allbirds Shoes" by Guillermo Fernandes/flickr, Public Domain)

For decades, the footwear industry has missed the opportunity to look to Mother Nature for more sustainable footwear materials. Tim Brown, the founder of Allbirds, believed it was time to think differently (see Figure 17.15). With most shoe companies using petroleum-based raw materials, Brown sought to think more sustainably about offering a shoe that was both comfortable and environmentally friendly. Along with Joey Zwillinger, a product engineer and renewables guru, Brown developed a revolutionary wool fabric designed for footwear. Allbirds uses SweetFoam, a shoe sole material made from plant-based leather. To increase the durability of the shoe, it also uses recycled synthetics where needed, which helps extend the life of the product. It is continuously researching and developing ways to innovate around the sustainable sourcing of shoe materials with the goals of not only doubling the lifetime of its products but also reducing its carbon footprint related to raw materials by 25 percent in 2025.[9]

Sustainability is at the core of everything Allbirds does. While it is certainly interested in offering consumers a comfortable shoe, it also cares deeply about the process and materials involved in making that shoe comfortable.[10]

Chapter Summary

In this chapter, the functions and benefits of marketing channels are explored. Marketing channels play an important role in moving products from manufacturers to final consumers. Channel members, also known as intermediaries, specialize in specific activities that help the flow of products. They play a transactional role by bringing manufacturers and consumers together. They also help with the logistical distribution of products by sorting, storing, and bulk-breaking so consumers can purchase what they want in the desired quantity. Finally, they facilitate the flow of goods by doing things like offering consumers credit to make purchases. Channel members can include manufacturers, wholesalers, distributers, retailers, agents, brokers, and ultimately final consumers.

In addition, the types of marketing systems are also explored. Vertical marketing systems can include corporate, administered, and contractual. In addition, some companies use a horizontal, multichannel, or omnichannel marketing system. Factors that dictate the type of channel a company chooses include target market coverage and the selection of an intensive, selective, or exclusive distribution channel.

Fulfillment of buyer requirements such as information, convenience, variety, and service pre- and post-purchase are also important determining factors. In addition, product-related factors such as perishability, product life-cycle stage, value, and the technical nature of a product are also to be considered when choosing a marketing channel. Lastly, the profitability of the channel is a huge consideration given that companies aim to operate efficiently while delivering value to consumers.

Selecting, managing, and motivating channel members require a strategy to handle channel conflict. Evaluating channel members requires the use of metrics and includes inventory turnover rate, accuracy rate, the time it takes to ship, units that have to be stored, number of orders processed in a given period of time, the percentage of on-time shipments, and the average number of delivery days.

The functions of supply chain management include purchasing, operations, logistics, resource management, and information workflow. Any or all of these functions can be outsourced. The decision requires careful consideration and evaluation of the cost/benefit ratio. The functions of logistics, such as warehousing, inventory management, and transportation, can also be outsourced.

Finally, the ethical issues in supply chain management were discussed. They include carbon footprint vs. the speed of shipping and sourcing sustainably.

Key Terms

accumulating   relates to intermediaries buying in bulk from different manufacturers

adjusting for discrepancy of assortment   occurs when an intermediary buys from manufacturers, then regroups products into different assortments based on what consumers are demanding from retailers

administered VMS   one type of vertical marketing system where there is no ownership of channel members but instead one member who is large enough to coordinate and manage the distribution activities of other channels members

agent   a type of intermediary who acts as an extension to the manufacturer

bulk and weight   the density and heaviness of one unit of product

bulk-breaking   occurs when an intermediary takes a large bundling of a manufacturer's product and breaks it down into single units to be distributed to retailers based on the retailer's order

business-to-business (B2B)   a market comprised of companies who buy from and/or sell to other companies

business-to-consumer (B2C)   a market comprised of companies that manufacture and sell products or services directly to a final consumer or end user

channel conflict   disagreements between companies in the marketing channel due to a competitive versus a collaborative mindset

channel length   relates to the number of intermediaries in the marketing channel

channel member (intermediary)   a company that works in a network with other companies to help gets products from manufacturers to final consumers

contractual VMS   independent companies that have joined together by contract for a mutually beneficial purpose

corporate VMS   when one member of the distribution channel owns the other members

customer-perceived value   the overall perception that a consumer has about a company, brand, or product and is measured by what the consumer is willing to pay in return for the features and benefits in the market offering

direct channel   when companies sell and distribute their products directly to consumers

direct marketing channel   when a manufacturer does not use intermediaries but rather involves the manufacturer distributing its market offering directly to consumers

disintermediation   the process of removing an intermediary from a marketing channel

distribution   the process of making products and services available and accessible to consumers to purchase

distributor   a type of intermediary that takes ownership of the product and tends to align itself closely with a manufacturer

exclusive distribution   a strategy that involves allowing a limited number of intermediaries to distribute a company's market offering

facilitating functions   activities such as financing and information sharing in the marketing channel

final consumer   the end user of a good or service

horizontal conflict   when there is disagreement among firms at the same level in the marketing channel

horizontal marketing system   a group of unrelated companies that offer products and services in a shared space

indirect channel   involves the utilization of one or more intermediaries to distribute a market offering to consumers

intensive distribution   a distribution strategy that entails distributing a company's market offering through all possible intermediaries

inventory management   a function that involves identifying the type of inventory and how much a company has on hand at any given time

inventory turnover rate   a metric that measures how quickly inventory is turned over, or sold

logistical functions   the handling, packing, inventorying, transporting, warehousing, and ensuring the security of products as they make their way to the customer

logistics   the coordination of all supply chain activities, such as warehousing, inventory management, and transportation

marketing channel   system of people, organizations, and activities that work together to make goods and services available to consumers for use

multichannel distribution system   where a single company sets up multiple distribution channels to reach customers

omnichannel marketing system   multichannel approach whereby companies give consumers a variety of ways to purchase, receive, and return products

order accuracy rate   a metric that measures the percentage of orders that are processed, fulfilled, and shipped to consumers without any errors

percentage of on-time shipments   a metric used to evaluate how well a channel member meets its promise of delivering goods on time

perishability   relates to the likelihood that a product will spoil, decay, or expire if not used in a timely manner

post-sale service   all activities provided by a company that reinforce the value of the product or service for the buyer

pre-sale service   all activities provided by a company that help a buyer make a purchase decision

producer   a company that supplies the raw materials that manufacturers need to create consumer products

producer to retailer to consumer channel   when manufacturers or producers sell to retailers without the use of wholesalers or distributors

product life cycle   the various stages that a product goes through from its introduction phase, to its growth and maturity phase, and in some cases to its decline phase

purchasing   the process of buying materials needed to manufacture products

retailer   a type of intermediary where retailers take ownership of the product and their sole focus is on reaching the end user or customer directly

selective distribution   a strategy that includes choosing more than one, but fewer than all possible intermediaries to distribute a company's market offering

standardized   products that have no difference in how they are manufactured

supply chain   a network between a company and its suppliers to produce and distribute a specific product to the final buyer

supply chain management   all members and activities from the procurement and transformation of raw materials into finished goods through their distribution to targeted consumers

sustainability   a company's effort to reduce its impact on the environment as products move from source procurement through production through distribution to final consumers

sustainable sourcing   the process of considering suppliers' social, ethical, and environmental performance

target market coverage   resources and capabilities needed to reach consumers in a company's target market

third-party logistics (3PL) provider   a company that is contracted by a channel member to handle one or more of the functional areas of logistics; often warehouses, distribution centers, or fulfillment centers that have expertise in managing certain logistical activities

time to ship   also known as order cycle time, the length of time from when a customer places an order to when it reaches them

total number of orders   the sum of all orders that a company received in a given time period

total units in storage   a metric used to evaluate warehouse efficiency that changes as items are sold and leave the warehouse and new inventory moves in

transactional functions   buying, selling, and risk-bearing that goes along with the movement of products along the marketing channel

unit value   the price that a company charges for one unit or item

vertical conflict   a conflict that exists between different levels of a vertical channel

vertical marketing system   companies in the marketing channel that work together in a coordinated, collaborative, and customer-centric way

warehousing   the stocking, maintaining, and controlling of products while they await the next step in their journey to the final consumer

wholesaler   similar to distributors in that they take ownership of products; buys products in large quantities for the purpose of distributing an assortment of products to retailers

Applied Marketing Knowledge: Discussion Questions

1. What are the methods used to evaluate channel members? Why is this important?

2. Explain the various forms of marketing systems. What factors go into the decision regarding which system is best suited to the given organization?

3. Target market coverage is broken down into intensive, selective, and exclusive distribution. Evaluate which form of coverage works for what category of products, why, and give an example of each form.

4. List the different forms of transportation for moving goods. What are the positives and negatives for each form? Can you think of a way to reduce the risk?

Critical Thinking Exercises

1. Create a strategy for managing channel conflict within a marketing channel.

2. Considering what we have learned in the last several years about supply chain interruption, along with what we have covered in this chapter, what are some of the strategies that a company can use to reduce risk?

3. Evaluate alternatives and incentives that companies/marketers can offer customers to manage the speed of shipping while reducing the carbon footprint.

 Building Your Personal Brand

Consider what sustainability and social responsibility mean to you. How do they impact your life and your activities? Is it in a positive, negative, or neutral way?

Let this information guide you in creating your authentic self. Develop your awareness of the ways that you can support the movements that speak to you. For instance, if you have strong beliefs in helping to create a cleaner environment, find activities that support that. Think clean stream, neighborhood beautification, or teaching children recycling, all the while making sure that you are genuine in upholding those concepts in your life. The list of opportunities is multilayered and unlimited.

Write 200–400 words outlining your personal brand as it relates to sustainability and social responsibility. How is your personal brand impacted by these concepts now? With these concepts in mind, how would you like your personal brand to evolve?

 What Do Marketers Do?

Contact one of the following businesses and ask to speak to a person in the supply chain or logistics department. You might have to go through several people to actually get to the one that can best answer your questions. The goal with this exercise is to ask questions regarding the logistics in these companies to better understand the complex process. Every logistics department is involved in the movement of goods (the coming and/or going), but they vary in how they go about it.

- A local warehouse
- UPS
- FedEx
- An Amazon.com warehouse (they have multiple layers that you can contact as well as their logistics partner program)
- A trucking company

When you speak to the professional, be prepared with questions that will help you understand this position. Here are a handful of questions to get you started:

1. What is your job title and function?
2. How would you describe your department?
3. How did you obtain your position?
4. What skills, background, or degree are needed to do this type of work?
5. What are the main challenges faced by the department in the job?
6. Are you aware of differences in how you run your operations versus a similar company? If yes, can you outline examples?

Marketing Plan Exercise

Complete the following information about the company and products/services you chose to focus on as you develop the marketing plan throughout the course. You may need to conduct research in order to obtain necessary information.

Instructions: Using the Marketing Plan Template file you created from Marketing and Customer Value assignment and expanded upon in Strategic Planning in Marketing, Market Segmentation, Targeting, and Positioning, Marketing Research and Market Intelligence, Products: Consumer Offerings, Pricing Products and Services, and Integrated Marketing Communications, complete the following section of your marketing plan:

- Marketing Strategy: Distribution

Submit the marketing plan to your instructor for grading and feedback.

Closing Company Case

Global Containers & Custom Packaging Inc.

It happens without much thinking—you go online, click on the item, add it to your cart, pay for it, and then wait for it to arrive, usually in just a few days. And although you don't give it much thought, there is a lot going on when making a purchase. It may appear that the product "just arrives" at your location, but it's not quite that simple. The manufacturer must decide how to best ship the product, whether it be by truck, ship, air or some combination of all three of them. Also, depending on the size of the company that is purchasing the product and the size of the order of the product, it might make a stop at a wholesaler before ending up on retail shelves or in your mailbox.

One company that is working "behind the scenes" to ensure that your package arrives intact and on time is Global Containers and Custom Packaging (https://openstax.org/r/globalcontainers). Global Containers and Custom Packaging is a full-service logistics company. It offers logistics and warehouse management, packaging distribution, and quality inspection and sorting.[11]

Strategically headquartered along the US-Mexico border in El Paso, Texas, Global Containers and Custom Packaging offers local packaging distribution services that provide value and solutions to the retail and maquiladora market. Customers include companies like Amazon.com, Hewlett Packard, Honeywell, Align Technology (the makers of Invisalign system for straightening teeth), and ASO (a leader in consumer first-aid products).

Started in 2009, the company was founded to provide a full-service logistics solution. José Ochoa, one of the company's founders, started off as an industrial engineer and saw a need for a full-service logistics solution offering a high level of customer service. Some of the solutions that the company offers are just-in-time inventory management, report management, flexibility in hours (it will receive a truck or ship a product after hours or on the weekend with no extra cost to the client—a service that is practically unheard of in this industry), traceability of consumption behavior, and coming soon, accepting crypto payments.

Managing all of the pieces of a logistics solution can be tricky, especially in an environment with unprecedented shipping delays. Global Containers and Custom Packaging takes a proactive approach in managing its clients' business—it will advise customers on upcoming delays on products that it doesn't currently have in inventory. By staying in constant contact with the client, it has been able to keep delays and bottlenecks because of missing items to a minimum. All this is accomplished while the industry has seen shipping delays skyrocket.

It's not surprising given the company's proactive approach to managing delays, offering superior customer service and comprehensive offerings, that it has received the prestigious Bridge Accelerator Award, an award focused on businesses that are looking for ways to grow and innovate in the Paso del Norte region.[12]

Case Questions

1. Is the marketing channel a direct channel or indirect channel in this case? Why?

2. Global Containers and Custom Packaging provides trucking shipping solutions primarily between Mexico and the United States. What are the six factors impacting the choice of channel? Which have the most important impact in this case?

3. What are the main product-related factors that have an impact on the choice to ship products via truck from the United States to Mexico?

4. Name the different supply chain management levels that Global Containers and Custom Packaging provides.

References

1. "Outstanding Foods: Taking This Little Pig-Free Bacon Chip to Market," BeyondBrands, accessed March 27, 2022, https://www.beyondbrands.org/work/outstandingfoods.

2. "Apples," Agricultural Marketing Resource Center, Iowa State University, revised September 2021, https://www.agmrc.org/commodities-products/fruits/apples.

3. Latoya Irby, "How Store Credit Cards Are Different from Regular Credit Cards," The Balance, Dotdash Meredith, updated November 21, 2020, https://www.thebalance.com/store-credit-cards-are-different-from-credit-cards-960146.

4. Daniel Bland, "Largest Vehicle Fleet Management, Leasing Players in North America," Global Fleet: The Executive Network, Nexus Communications, updated July 7, 2021, https://www.globalfleet.com/en/leasing-and-rental/north-america/features/largest-vehicle-fleet-management-leasing-players-north-america.

5. Technavio, *Hot Tub Market Growth, Size, Trends, Analysis Report by Type, Application, Region and Segment Forecast 2020–2024*, August 2021, https://www.technavio.com/report/hot-tub-market-industry-analysis.

6. "Petvivo Holdings, Inc. Announces Distribution of Its Veterinary Medical Device, Spryng[TM], by Vetcove, Inc.," Yahoo! Finance, Yahoo, January 5, 2022, https://finance.yahoo.com/news/petvivo-holdings-inc-announces-distribution-123000670.html.

7. Jennifer Strailey, "Trader Joe's Talks Supply Chain, TP and a Return to Normalcy," Winsight Grocery Business, Winsight, May 4, 2020, https://www.winsightgrocerybusiness.com/retailers/trader-joes-talks-supply-chain-tp-return-normalcy.

8. "Killer Breads," Dave's Killer Bread, accessed June 1, 2022, https://www.daveskillerbread.com/products.

9. "Renewable Materials," Allbirds, accessed May 31, 2022, https://www.allbirds.com/pages/renewable-materials.

10. Allbirds, "Renewable Materials."

11. https://globalcontainers.net; https://globalcontainers.net/blog/

12. "The Bridge Accelerator—Binational Supplier Development Program," https://www.tecma.com/the-bridge-accelerator-binational-supplier-development-program/

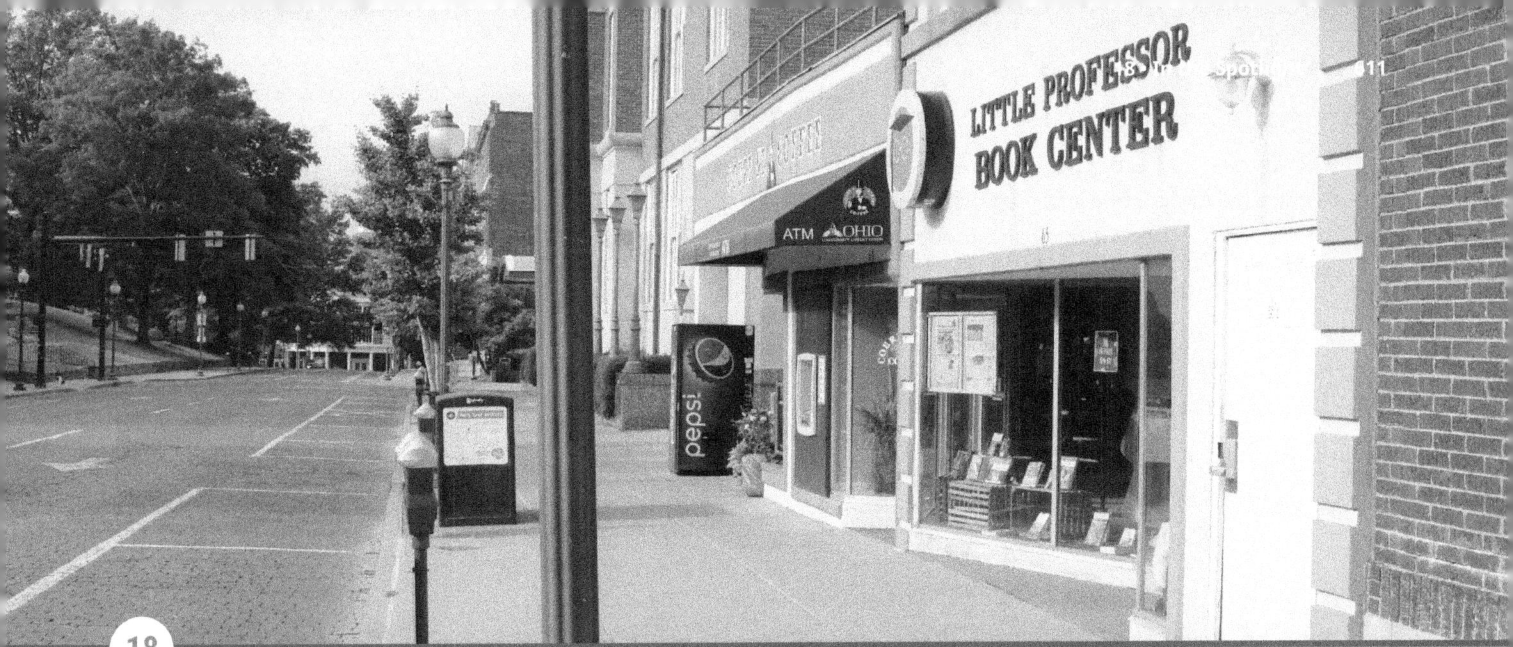

18 Retailing and Wholesaling

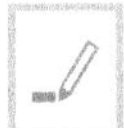

Figure 18.1 There are numerous retail and wholesale channels, including brick-and-mortar stores. (credit: modification of work "Athens, Ohio" by Dan Keck/flickr, Public Domain)

Chapter Outline

In the Spotlight

It is no surprise that retailing has changed over the years. In the 1980s and 1990s, big-box retailers such as Walmart began opening stores in small towns and forcing local mom-and-pop shops out of business. In the 2000s, with the rise of Internet shopping, more brick-and-mortar retailers closed their doors. The COVID-19 pandemic resulted in another wave of retail closures. While future prospects for a number of retail operations appear bleak, many retailers—both new and established—are finding innovative ways to attract customers back into the stores.

Precycle is a grocery store in the Bushwick neighborhood of Brooklyn, New York. In order to differentiate her store from other local shops, Precycle owner Katerina Bogatireva decided to focus her efforts on serving a niche market of consumers who are committed to protecting the environment. Shoppers at Precycle can find a wide variety of spices, fruits, grains, pastas, toothbrushes, and many household basics. But what shoppers won't find at Precycle is plastic. Bogatireva opened the store in an effort to reduce the amount of plastic that is used in retailing. All the items in Precycle are not only free from plastic and sold in bulk, they are locally sourced.[1]

Similar types of stores have been popping up throughout the United States. Consumers are more and more aware of the ongoing problem that plastic creates for our oceans and general environment. Additionally, more consumers are becoming locavores, people who purchase food that is locally grown.[2] Local and more traditional brick-and-mortar retailers are ideal to meet these consumer demands. Post-pandemic, we may see increased numbers of brick-and-mortar retailers responding to these new consumer demands. Only time will tell.

18.1   Retailing and the Role of Retailers in the Distribution Channel

Learning Outcomes

By the end of this section, you will be able to:
- **LO** 1 Define retailing.
- **LO** 2 Discuss the functions of retailers in the distribution channel.

Retailing Defined

When marketers plan their distribution strategies, they must determine which channel is best suited to get their goods and services into the hands of consumers. A distribution channel is a set of businesses that move the product or service from the manufacturer to the end user or buyer.[3] Figure 18.2 outlines the most common types of distribution channels for consumer goods. These businesses, often called intermediaries, play important roles in the distribution of goods and services. **Intermediaries** are companies that act as liaisons between the buyer and seller. These companies can take on a variety of roles to facilitate the transfer of products and services from a manufacturer to the end user. The path that a product or service takes from seller to buyer, including the intermediaries, is called the distribution or marketing channel. The length of the channel—short or long—will depend on many factors, including the product itself.

When you first glance at Figure 18.2, it might seem logical for producers to simply provide goods and services directly to the consumer. Imagine that you were thirsty and wanted a cold can of Pepsi. However, you did not have any at home, and retailers did not exist. How would you get your Pepsi? Well, without retailers, you would have to rely on either going directly to the closest Pepsi bottling plant or requesting a Pepsi employee to deliver a can to your home. Can you imagine how costly that would be for PepsiCo? Now imagine doing that for every single product you wish to purchase. Obviously, this seems implausible—and almost laughable. While many companies have traditionally utilized longer channels to distribute their products, companies today often use more direct (shorter) channels or multiple channels. When a manufacturer utilizes multiple channels to distribute its product, it's known as an **omnichannel strategy**. Amazon, for example, uses multiple distribution channels. Some products are sold directly to the consumer, while other products come from independent retailers, who then fulfill the order.

Consider another example: You are planning a trip with your friends. You have found a Marriott hotel that suits your needs. You may choose to book directly with Marriott through its website or reservation phone number. Alternatively, you may choose to book through a third party, such as Hotels.com, or even by calling your travel agent. Marriott is utilizing multiple channels for its service, so it is utilizing an omnichannel distribution approach.

Today, even social media plays a role in the distribution channel. Looking at the above example, Marriott might consider utilizing social media as yet another point of contact for the organization's employees and customers to interact. Customers can often book a room and receive customer service directly through the company's social media platforms.[4] As you will learn later, the choice of which distribution channel to use depends largely on the type of product and the manufacturer's strategy.

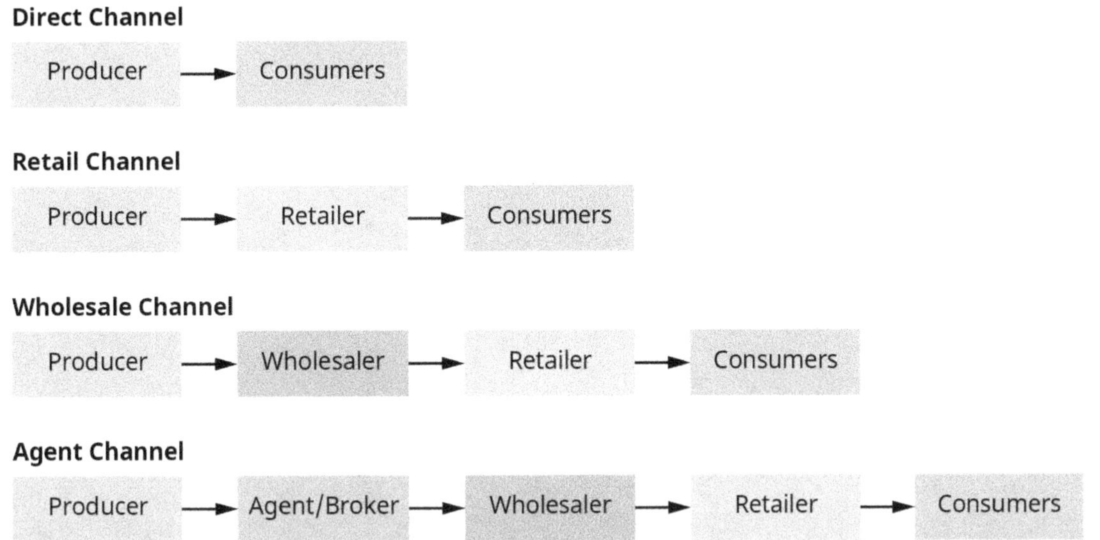

Figure 18.2 Distribution Channels for Consumer Products (attribution: Copyright Rice University, OpenStax, under CC BY 4.0 license)

Regardless of how many channel members are included in the distribution channel, retailing is the final stop in the channel before products and services reach the consumer. **Retailing** is the process of selling goods and services to consumers. As it relates to the distribution channel, retailers do not often manufacture the goods being sold. Rather, retailers buy products from the manufacturing firms or wholesalers and resell them to the consumer. While the number of traditional brick-and-mortar retail establishments has declined drastically over the past few decades, retailers remain an important part of the distribution channel. Retailing entails *all* activities involved in selling the goods and services to the consumer; in other words, retailers have their own marketing mix plan to accomplish their goals. Because retailing is the final link between the manufacturer and consumer, retailers have as much incentive to sell products as those who produce the product.

The Functions of Retailing in the Distribution Channel

Retailing has many important functions in the distribution channel. Consider Target, a general-merchandise retailer with stores in all 50 states and the District of Columbia, as well as locations across the globe.[5] Target offers a wide variety of consumer goods in each of its large brick-and-mortar locations. In addition to what we, as consumers, see when shopping at Target, there are many other important functions for Target and other retailers in the distribution channel (see Figure 18.3). Let's look at these functions in detail.

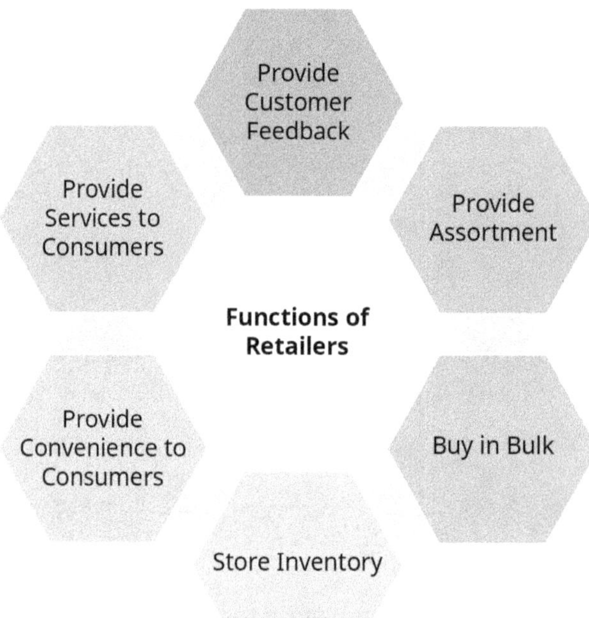

Figure 18.3 Functions of Retailers (attribution: Copyright Rice University, OpenStax, under CC BY 4.0 license)

Provide Assortment

Retailers provide assortment for consumers. Assortment simply refers to the number of options in a given product category or the number of products offered. Consider the Pepsi beverage example from earlier in the chapter. What if you weren't sure which drink you wanted? Rather than go directly to a Pepsi bottling plant, you decide to go to Target where you will find an assortment of drink varieties and brands to choose from.

Target also offers a wide variety of other products. So, while you are there, you decide to purchase your drink and some home furnishings and groceries. The assortment of brands and products in general gives the consumer options and convenience—something most consumers value in their busy lives.

Many large retailers also offer their own brand of products. This allows the company to provide competing options to consumers at different price points, typically lower than the name brands. For example, Walmart offers various name brands of acetaminophen, one being the more popular brand Tylenol and the other a lower-priced, comparable product labeled Great Value. By providing multiple purchase options, the retailer is able to target more than one consumer market.

Buy in Bulk

Because retail establishments are often large and have ample storage, they are able to purchase and sell items in bulk. Consider the quantity of one product, such as Pepsi 12-packs, that Target has on its shelves. In addition, the store has stock in the back room for when the shelves are empty. Target's ability to buy in bulk allows it to serve a large number of consumers at any given time.

From a broader standpoint, consider the number of Pepsi 12-packs that the entire Target store network purchases in a given week. Target's ability to purchase such large quantities allows it to negotiate lower prices with PepsiCo (and other channel members). In turn, retailers can provide consumers with lower prices than if the consumer purchased directly from Pepsi.

Store Inventory

The ability of retailers to hold inventory allows them to quickly restock shelves or, in the case of Internet retailers, get the product shipped quickly. This allows consumers the convenience of being able to get an item as quickly as possible.

Provide Convenience to Consumers

Retailers provide a considerable amount of convenience to consumers. Consider the distance from your home or work to your closest retailer. For most consumers, retailers are within a few miles. This proximity makes retailers convenient. The process of choosing a retail location for development has become somewhat of a science in recent decades. There are companies that specialize in partnering with retailers to determine the best locations for store placement. To determine locations, things like traffic patterns and demographics are collected and analyzed.[6]

A second service that retailers provide is convenient hours of operation. Consider Walmart, which has locations that are open 24 hours, or grocery stores that are open on Thanksgiving morning for last-minute food purchases.

Retailers also allow consumers to more closely evaluate a product for purchase. For example, some consumers would much rather purchase clothing items from a brick-and-mortar retailer rather than online because they can feel the texture of the cloth and try the item on to determine if it fits and looks good.

Providing Services to Customers

Most retailers provide services to consumers that are not a core product offering. For example, you can purchase groceries and household essentials at retailers such as Walmart or Kroger, but you can also purchase stamps, buy a lottery ticket, refill your prepaid phone minutes, drop off mail, and in some locations get a haircut or an eye exam and deposit a check at the bank.[7] With the convenience of multiple services, retailers make other tasks more convenient for consumers.

While there is an added value to the consumer to have all these services in one location, it's also a benefit to the retailers. For example, the hair salon located inside Walmart has the added benefit of the higher foot traffic inside the store. Since so many consumers are already in the store, they may be more apt to stop in for a haircut. Furthermore, while hair salon owners or individual stylists pay rent on the space inside Walmart, they don't have the overhead that might come with a standalone building. The advantage of this partnership for Walmart is that it receives additional income through the rent paid by the hair salon. The company also may build consumer loyalty since it is providing its consumers with additional convenience by offering these services.

Collecting and Providing Feedback

An important factor in any distribution channel is that of member relationships. Remember that all parties in the distribution channel have a stake in one another's success. Because retailers are the last link between the product and the consumer, they have a unique opportunity to collect feedback from customers and share that with other channel members. This can take many different forms. For example, if you use a loyalty card at your favorite grocery retailer, your purchases are tracked. The data collected is a wealth of information that informs a retailer's strategy and decisions. For example, the company may use the data to inform the type of promotions to run or coupons to offer.

Retailers also provide customer feedback to their channel partners. This feedback can let suppliers know the demand for products and if products are being offered at the right time and the right place. If products are not selling well in a retail establishment, the retailer and channel partners can look to customer feedback to determine the issue and resolve it.

CAREERS IN MARKETING

Distribution

There is much to consider with distribution channels. Learn more about the distribution channel types, impact of the digital age, and choosing a distribution channel and read examples of making distribution channels work (https://openstax.org/r/learningcentresales) in this article. Learn in this article how to use distribution (https://openstax.org/r/salesoptimizeddistribution) to a sales advantage. And while we want everything to run smoothly, it rarely does all the time. Learn about how things could go wrong (https://openstax.org/r/saleschannelpartner) and options for managing these situations.

Now that you've had a chance to understand what distributors do, does a career in distribution interest you? There are several types of jobs in distribution. Do your research and learn about the types. Start by reading this article to learn the differences between a distribution manager, industrial production manager, and a purchasing manager. (https://openstax.org/r/articlescareersindistribution) You will learn about the needed degree of study, necessary skills, potential job growth, and median salary. Run a Google search on distribution careers, and you'll be shown numerous job postings. This is a great way to gain insight into the career specifics with multiple companies.

Knowledge Check

It's time to check your knowledge on the concepts presented in this section. Refer to the Answer Key at the end of the book for feedback.

1. Channel members that generally do not manufacture goods but rather buy them from another channel member and sell them to the consumer are said to be practicing _______.
   a. manufacturing
   b. wholesaling
   c. retailing
   d. inventory

2. Which of the following is NOT a function of retailing?
   a. Buying in large quantities and selling to other businesses for the purpose of reselling them to consumers
   b. Providing assortment and variety of products
   c. Holding inventory
   d. Providing convenient location and store hours

3. As a new entrepreneur, you are deciding whether to offer your customers a loyalty card that is linked digitally to technology. Which function of retailing would you be engaged in?
   a. Providing services to consumers
   b. Holding inventory
   c. Providing convenient location and hours of operation
   d. Providing consumer communication

4. A company that utilizes more than one channel in its distribution is using which type of strategy?
   a. Direct channel
   b. Direct-to-consumer channel
   c. Omnichannel

   d.   None of the above is correct.

5. Schwan's Company prepares frozen foods to be delivered to the door of the consumer. Which of the following is the most likely distribution channel for Schwan's?
    a.   Manufacturer – Agent – Wholesaler – Retailer – Consumer
    b.   Manufacturer – Retailer
    c.   Manufacturer – Consumer
    d.   Manufacturer – Wholesaler – Retailer

18.2 | Major Types of Retailers

Learning Outcomes

By the end of this section, you will be able to:

LO 1 Characterize various store retailers.
LO 2 Characterize various non-store retailers

Retailers, in some form or another, have been around for most of human history. As early as 800 BCE in ancient Athens, Greece, businesspeople sold their goods in developed markets at the city's center.[8] Throughout history, this type of business has grown and become more specialized based on the needs of customers and the ability we now have to travel fairly easily. Today, retailers are often defined by their product lines—a group of products that are related to one another. Retailers are broken into two main categories, store or non-store retailers, which are further broken into retail types. Retail types are defined by their product lines. See Table 18.1 for a breakdown of retail types, the typical product focus for that retail type, and examples of retailers that fall into that type.

Retail Type	Product Focus	Example
Store Retailers		
Specialty Store	Single product line	AutoZone
Department store	Wide variety of product lines	JCPenney, Kohl's
Supermarket	Multiple product lines; focused mostly on grocery with limited services	Publix, Kroger, Save A Lot
Superstore	Combination of supermarket and department store	Target, Walmart
Convenience Store	Limited range of everyday items	7-Eleven, Speedway
Category killer	Very large superstores with wide product lines within a category	Best Buy, Lowe's, Home Depot, Staples, Office Depot

Table 18.1 Types of Retailers

Retail Type	Product Focus	Example
Discount store	Broad range of products with few or no services	Dollar General, Dollar Tree, Family Dollar
Off-price retailer	Brand name overstock, irregulars, and closeouts	T.J.Maxx, Ross
Factory outlet	Overstock or over-manufactured brand-name items, usually clothing; typically in a mall setting with other factory outlets	Sawgrass Mills Factory Outlet, Indiana Premium Outlets, Osage Outlets; Hanes Outlet, L.L.Bean Outlet
Warehouse club	Bulk items at discount for paid membership	Sam's Club, BJ's, Costco
Non-store retailers		Vending machines, direct-mail catalogs, television home shopping online, telemarketing, direct selling
Automatic vending	Unmanned with very limited product line located in places store retailers are not	Snack and beverage machines in a hospital waiting room
Direct mail and catalogs	Limited product lines advertised through the mail	Tiffany & Co.'s Blue Book, L.L.Bean, Fingerhut
Television home shopping	Limited product lines advertised on television	Home Shopping Network, QVC
Online retailing	Can be wide or limited product lines of products offered for sale via the Internet	Amazon
Telemarketing	Very limited product line sold via the telephone	
Direct selling	Very limited product line sold by salespeople who are very knowledgeable about the product and sell directly to a business or end user; used in B2C, but more often in B2B	Kirby Vacuums (B2C) Publishing companies (B2B) Technology companies (B2B)

Table 18.1 Types of Retailers

Store Retailers

Retailers tend to be the easiest of the channel members to identify because we see them everywhere we go, both in person and online. A **store retailer** is a traditional brick-and-mortar establishment where products are displayed for customers to purchase. Store retailers can be categorized in many ways based on their strategy mix, which includes a combination of store hours, location, product assortment, and prices.[9]

As the number of store retailers has decreased significantly over the years due to their higher operating costs, some companies have found more innovative ways to provide their products in a similar setting. For example, Amazon Go is a store retailer that allows customers to shop in-store, but has eliminated the use of cashiers (and long lines). As customers choose the products they want, the automated store keeps track of the purchase and charges the customers when they exit the store.[10]

Specialty Stores

Specialty stores focus on selling a single type of product or a single product line. The employees of specialty stores are often very knowledgeable about the products they sell and offer high levels of customer service. For example, when you need a new battery in your car, you may head straight to AutoZone, a retailer specializing in vehicle parts. When you arrive, an associate will be able to assist you in choosing the correct battery for the make and model of your car, and sometimes, they may be able to install it for you.

Department Stores

Department stores are typically larger than specialty stores and have separate areas or departments for similar product lines. For example, areas could include shoes, kids' clothing, housewares, and so on. Each compartmentalized area may mimic the look and feel of a specialty store to make for a more intimate experience, but often the sales associates are not highly trained in each area. For example, Kohl's, a department store chain in the United States, has separate departments containing women's fashion, shoes, kitchenware, and toys.

Supermarkets

A **supermarket** is defined as a store that mostly focuses on a product mix of grocery items but also carries household and personal items and offers limited services. One example is Publix, an employee-owned supermarket chain that opened in 1930 and has nearly 1,000 stores in the southeastern United States.[11] Publix's average retail size is roughly 32,000 square feet, and more than 50 percent of its shelves are dedicated to grocery items. The other 50 percent consists of cleaning items, toiletries, over-the-counter medicines, beer/liquor, and personal hygiene products. Like most supermarkets, Publix also offers a deli, a bakery, hot food bars, a pharmacy, some apparel, and sometimes even pool supplies, toys, and other nonfood items.

Convenience Stores

Named for their convenient location, a **convenience store** is a small retail business that stocks a limited range of everyday items, such as groceries, snacks, soft drinks, tobacco, toiletries, and lottery tickets (see Figure 18.4). In the United States, convenience stores are most often linked to gas stations. Convenience stores offer consumers the convenience of stopping to fill up their tank and running inside for a few essential items without having to drive to a supermarket or other retailer. The first convenience store in the United States opened in Texas in 1927 and later became known as 7-Eleven. In 2020, there were approximately 150,000 convenience stores in the United States.[12]

Figure 18.4 A convenience store is a type of retail store that is conveniently located and carries limited items. (credit: "Wawa Miami" by Phillip Pessar/flickr, CC BY 2.0)

Superstores

Superstores are very large retailers that have characteristics of both supermarkets and department stores (see Figure 18.5). Like supermarkets, they sell a wide range of grocery items. But they also have considerable space dedicated to nonfood departments, as do department stores. Target operates 1,927 retail stores in the United States. Some of its stores are considered superstores, where consumers can purchase not only (nearly) everything on their grocery list, but also clothing, household goods, electronics, toys, and sporting equipment.

Figure 18.5 Target is a type of superstore that sells a wide variety of personal and grocery items. (credit: "Target" by Mike Mozart, JeepersMedia/flickr, CC BY 2.0)

Category Killers

Category killers are large superstores or big-box retailers that are bigger, cheaper, and more convenient than other types of stores. Because of their sheer size, they have the advantage of buying products in very large quantities, which gives them a strong negotiation position for the price they pay to distributors. In turn, they can then offer discounted prices to consumers. These stores are called category killers because they often put nearby specialty stores out of business. Home Depot and Lowe's are considered category killers because of their exhaustive inventory selection and low prices. The popularity of this big-box format means that smaller hardware stores may find it difficult to compete.

Discount Stores

During the 2008 recession, many retailers began closing their doors. But Dollar General was one retailer that saw exponential growth during this time.[13] Dollar General and competitor Dollar Tree are **discount stores**—stores that sell a broad range of products at lower prices than competitors. While discount stores offer lower prices and often less variety than competitors, they often also offer fewer services and little customer service. As inflation put pressure on household budgets in 2022, shoppers from a range of income levels turned to dollar stores to save money on everyday necessities.

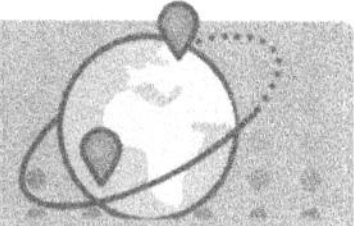

LINK TO LEARNING

Dollar Stores and the Community

Learn more about the impact dollar stores have on the community and commerce. It's not always positive. Experts speak in this video about the potential negative impact and issues.

Click to view content (https://openstax.org/books/principles-marketing/pages/18-2-major-types-of-retailers)

Off-Price Retailers

Retailers that provide high-quality, name-brand goods at deeply discounted prices are considered **off-price retailers**. These retailers often purchase brand names that are irregular, closeouts, overstock, and off-season. While these retailers offer goods within more than one product line, often consumers cannot be guaranteed to find the same brand or item(s) in a store twice. T.J.Maxx, one of the largest clothing retailers in the country, utilizes this strategy. The company's buyers purchase over-ordered or over-manufactured products from distributors at deeply discounted prices. This merchandise is then offered to the consumer at lower prices than can be found in department stores.

Factory Outlets

In some ways, **factory outlets** are similar to off-price retailers (see Figure 18.6). The goods found in factory outlets are typically over-manufactured and sold at lower prices. However, factory outlet goods are sold directly from the manufacturer rather than through a third party. Many clothing manufacturers have factory outlets, which are typically clustered together in a factory outlet mall, a space where numerous factory outlets are located. For example, you may see Coach, Gap, or Lands' End stores in outlet malls. Sawgrass Mills Factory Outlet, located in Sunrise, Florida, is the largest factory outlet mall in the United States. It houses over 350 factory outlet stores, including Adidas, LEGO, and Zales.[14]

Figure 18.6 Factory outlet stores offer lower-priced items sold directly from the manufacturer. (credit: "DSCF1532.JPG" by jkonrath/flickr, CC BY 2.0)

Warehouse Clubs

Warehouse clubs (see Figure 18.7) are a type of retailer that sells goods in bulk at discounted prices to members only. Shoppers must first become members of the warehouse club before they are allowed to purchase. Costco and Sam's Club are two of the largest warehouse clubs in the United States, and both offer a limited variety of perishable and nonperishable goods. Warehouse clubs operate out of enormous, no-frills, low-cost facilities that resemble warehouses.

Figure 18.7 Costco is a warehouse club that offers bulk items at a discount; consumers can only enter if they are paid members. (credit: "Costco (East Lyme, Connecticut)" by jjbers/flickr, CC BY 2.0)

Non-store Retailers

Non-store retailers are those retailers that operate outside of the traditional brick-and-mortar location. There are six main types of non-store retailers, and we will examine each in the following sections.

Automatic Vending

Also referred to as vending machines, **automatic vending** is the use of an electronic device that dispenses a product (see Figure 18.8). There is no direct human contact in the transaction. Traditionally, automatic vending machines would dispense items such as potato chips, candy, and soft drinks. However, more recently, companies have found automatic vending to be successful with other items, from cell phones to hot meals to automobiles. Carvana is an automatic vending non-store retailer. Using Carvana, consumers can purchase their cars online, complete with financing, and pick up their vehicles at one of its vending machines or have it delivered with little or no human interaction needed. Debuting its 27th car vending machine in Atlanta, Georgia, in 2020 Carvana now has a location that is 12 stories high and holds 43 vehicles.[15] The company unveiled its first car vending machine in 2012, taking automobile shopping—and automatic vending—to a whole new level!

Figure 18.8 Carvana features automobile vending machines that allow consumers to purchase cars online and have them delivered. (credit: "Carvana Delorean Back to the Future Time Machine" by zombieite/flickr, CC BY 2.0)

Direct Mail and Catalogs

Direct mail involves solicited or unsolicited advertising of products and services to prospective customers through the mail (Figure 18.9). Direct mail and catalogs are likely the oldest form of non-store retailing. The first mail-order catalog in the United States was Tiffany & Co.'s *Blue Book* in 1845.[16] The company still uses catalogs in addition to store retail locations, and the catalogs feature some of the rarest diamonds and jewels in the world. A more popular mail-order catalog that began in the 1800s was the Sears Roebuck and Co. catalog, the "big book," which came to feature hundreds of pages of products offered by the company; the last was published in 1993. With the rise of the Internet, catalogs and direct mail are not as prevalent in marketing today, but it is still a retailing strategy that works for many companies.

Figure 18.9 Direct mail offers products to consumers via advertisements sent through the mail. (credit: "Catalog" by Nicolás Boullosa/flickr, CC BY 2.0)

Television Home Shopping

Another example of a non-store retailer is television home shopping. **Television home shopping** primarily targets women over the age of 40 and is a business practice in which products or services are sold via television. There are some cable network stations that are dedicated solely to home shopping 24 hours a day, 7 days a week. One example is QVC, which stands for Quality, Value, and Convenience. The company was founded in 1986 and purchased its rival Home Shopping Network (HSN) in 2017. It generated $14.1 billion in profits in 2018.[17] The 2015 Hollywood movie *Joy*, starring Jennifer Lawrence, showcases real-life entrepreneur Joy Mangano and the power of QVC as a non-store retailer.

Similar to online shopping, consumers can order products directly from a company via telephone or the Internet. Unlike the Internet and direct-mail catalogs, however, viewers can see the product being demonstrated or modeled in real time. While QVC hosts are demonstrating products, control room employees are able to monitor sales in real time as they are placed.

Online Retailing

Online retailing allows consumers to search and purchase products remotely over the Internet. Although the Internet's public birthday is debatable, online retailing started shortly thereafter. Though Amazon (started by Jeff Bezos in 1995 as a book retailer) was not the first online retailer, its inception prompted thousands of companies to follow suit. In 2021, US consumers spent $5.4 trillion at online retail stores, a figure that is expected to increase. It is anticipated that, by 2023, online shopping will make up 22 percent of retail sales across the globe.[18]

Telemarketing

Telemarketing is the attempted sale or marketing of goods and services to potential customers via telephone. The telephone has been used as a sales tool since shortly after its invention. The 1970s, however, was the decade when technology became advanced enough that call centers—a centralized location or department that handles calls from customers—became an economical way of contacting potential customers. Over the next few decades, telemarketing became a staple in marketers' strategies. But this resulted in consumers being annoyed with these calls and a rise in scamming calls, particularly those targeting the elderly. In 1991, the Federal Trade Commission (FTC) addressed this problem with new rules for telemarketers, but it was not until 2003 that the Do Not Call Registry was created.[19] Even with these changes, legitimate and non-legitimate telemarketing finds its way onto phones. While many (legitimate) companies still utilize this form of non-store retailing, telemarketing is generally used (and more widely accepted) in business-to-business (B2B) settings.

Direct Selling

Direct selling is selling products and services directly to the consumer in a non-retail setting. Direct selling typically consists of a salesperson attempting to sell a product or service to a potential customer at their residence or place of employment. This practice was very popular in the 1950 and 1960s when women were often stay-at-home mothers and/or homemakers. Salespeople would bring the product—a vacuum, for example—to the consumer's home and demonstrate its benefits in an attempt to make a sale. With the rise of two-income families and the Internet, direct selling is not used frequently today in the consumer market. It is, however, still a widely used practice in B2B. However, it remains effective for some companies, such as Kirby, which still sends salespeople door-to-door to sell its vacuums.

Knowledge Check

It's time to check your knowledge on the concepts presented in this section. Refer to the Answer Key at the end of the book for feedback.

1. After class, Drue realized that the cafeteria was closed, so instead he purchased a candy bar and soft drink from a vending machine. Which type of retailing did Drue utilize?
   a. Factory outlet
   b. Automatic vending
   c. Warehouse club
   d. Direct mail

2. Of the following, which retailing strategy would be most appropriate for customers who are neither tech-savvy nor able to shop at store retailers?
   a. Automatic vending
   b. Television home shopping
   c. Warehouse clubs
   d. Online retailing

3. After school, Adrian decides to stop at the local Costco. Unfortunately, the store won't allow him in unless he first purchases a membership. Which type of retailer has Adrian entered?
   a. Factory outlet
   b. Warehouse club
   c. Discount store
   d. Superstore

4. Retailers providing high-quality goods at discounted prices are called ________
   a. superstores
   b. discount stores
   c. off-price retailers
   d. warehouse clubs

5. Some manufacturers operate their own retail locations; when they are left with excess inventory, they often provide these to what type of retail locations?
   a. Factory outlets
   b. Warehouse clubs
   c. Department stores
   d. Discount stores

18.3 | Retailing Strategy Decisions

Learning Outcomes

By the end of this section, you will be able to:
- **LO** 1 Describe how pricing affects retail strategy decisions.
- **LO** 2 Explain how location is a factor in retail strategy decisions.
- **LO** 3 Discuss the importance of retailer communications.
- **LO** 4 Explain how merchandise affects retail strategy decisions.

Retailing Strategy Decisions

Retail marketers and other retail business leaders need to determine which retail strategy will work best for the products they sell. Recall that retailers often buy in bulk, break down that bulk into smaller units, and sell to the end consumer. As you may also recall, *value* refers to a perceived worth of a product based on its service, price, and utility provided. As marketers are determining the optimal strategy for the products and services being offered, value again becomes an important factor.

The three most important items to consider in retail strategy that factor directly into value are pricing, location, and merchandise (see Figure 18.10). Because retailers sell goods and services often produced by another company, communication with channel members is another important topic. Let's look at retail strategy decisions more closely.

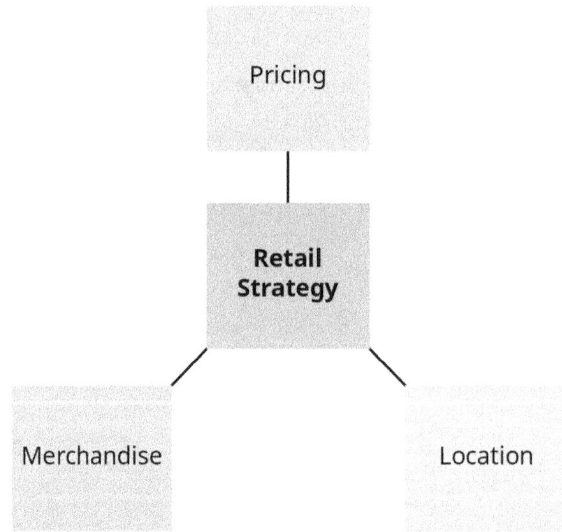

Figure 18.10 Retail Strategy Decisions (attribution: Copyright Rice University, OpenStax, under CC BY 4.0 license)

Retail Pricing

Retailers will determine the price for their product based on many factors, including their cost to purchase the product, shipping, storing, and other overhead expenses associated with the business. For store retailers, overhead expense is typically much higher than it is for online retailers considering the brick-and-mortar location, decoration of the store, storage, employee salaries, shrinkage (loss due to spoilage and theft), and other factors. The goal of the retailer, just like any for-profit business, is to make money; therefore, retailers must consider not only their own cost of doing business, but what consumers are willing to pay for the products and services they sell.

Markup

Markup is the additional amount added to the price retailers purchase goods for. Often conveyed as a percentage, markup is the retail selling price minus the initial purchase price, divided by the initial purchase price, times 100. Here is the formula:

$$\text{Markup Percentage} = \left(\frac{\text{Selling Price} - \text{Purchase Price}}{\text{Purchase Price}} \right) \times 100$$

For example, say you manage a footwear retailer. You are interested in selling a new line of tennis shoes that you purchase for $50 a pair. You decide to sell these new sneakers to consumers for $75 a pair. What is your markup?

Your markup is 50%, as shown here:

$$\text{Initial Markup} = \left(\frac{\$75 - \$50}{\$50} \right) \times 100 = 50\%$$

The easiest way many retailers choose a markup is to use a strategy that doubles the wholesale price, known as **keystone pricing**. Generally speaking, retailers tend to mark up prices somewhere around 50%. However, this can vary greatly from industry to industry. For example, retail grocers have a markup of around 15%, while clothing is generally marked up anywhere from 100% to 300%.[20]

Original and Maintained Markup

There is a difference in markup from when it's originally set to what is actually realized when the product sells. Using the shoe retail business example, you determined your markup is 50%. This is known as the **original markup**, the markup that you have decided upon at the *onset* of placing the shoes for sale, which includes the original price to purchase the shoes and the cost of the shoes to the consumer. Using the above shoe store example, your original markup percentage is 50%.

What price the product actually sells for is considered the maintained markup. In your shoe store, let's say you anticipated selling 100 pairs of shoes this month, but you only sold 75. As such, your original markup has been decreased. The **maintained markup** is the *actual* markup realized on the product that is sold to the consumer. It is the difference between the cost of goods sold and the *actual* retail price of the goods when sold. It is based on actual sales, not planned sales.

Markdowns

Maintained markup also accounts for markdowns, which were not factored into the original markup. A **markdown** is a price decrease for a product that is at the end of its life cycle or season. Markdowns assist retailers in selling through inventory by increasing temporary demand for products through a lower-price offering. If there is low demand for the 25 pairs of tennis shoes remaining in your inventory, you may consider marking them down to $60, then again to $50, and so on. Ideally, markdowns will, at the very least, cover the wholesale cost of the goods. Markdowns lower the maintained markup and the retailer's gross profit.

Gross Margin

Gross margin refers to the actual sales dollars received (net sales) minus the cost of goods sold. It is the amount of profit made before deducting selling, general, and administrative cost and is calculated as a percentage. Let's say that you sold 75 pairs of shoes at $80 but had to mark down the remaining 25 pairs to $50 a pair. To determine your gross margin, you calculate net sales and deduct the cost of goods sold. Here is the net sales formula:

$$75 \text{ pairs of shoes} \times \$80 = \$6{,}000 \text{ in net sales}$$
$$25 \text{ pairs of shoes} \times \$50 = \$1{,}250 \text{ in net sales}$$
$$\textbf{Total net sales} = \textbf{\$6{,}000} + \textbf{\$1{,}250} = \textbf{\$7{,}250}$$

The cost of goods sold (COGS) calculation is as follows:

$$\text{COGS} = 100 \text{ pair of shoes} \times \$40 = \$4{,}000$$

The gross margin calculation is as follows:

$$\text{Margin} = \$7{,}250 \text{ total net sales} - \$4{,}000 \text{ cost of goods sold} = \$3{,}250 \times 100\% = 32.5\%$$

Store Location

An age-old saying in retailing and real estate is that the three most important variables in choosing where to establish a business are location, location, and location. If consumers cannot find or easily access a store retailer, they will not spend their time looking but instead will take their business elsewhere.

Retailers will look at location selection from many angles, including how far away a competitor is located, how many of the same store (for chain stores) are within a certain driving distance, how many miles the average consumer would have to drive to reach the location, and how easy it is to access the location. For example, if you live in a smaller, rural town, there may be a regular Walmart but not a Walmart Supercenter. Why? Consider the population size of your town, the number of competitors, and how close the nearest Walmart Supercenter is located. Retailers such as Walmart know exactly the distance consumers are willing to drive to do their shopping. Perhaps there is a Walmart Supercenter within the distance they know consumers are willing to drive, so they have no need to add one to your town.

In determining location, retailers also must decide if their business is better suited to a freestanding location, a business district or strip mall, or another type of location. Let's examine several types of locations.

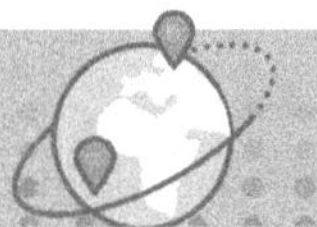

LINK TO LEARNING

Success in Small Towns

With the rise of large retailers such as Walmart, smaller mom-and-pop stores have struggled to compete in the last few decades. In small towns and rural areas, this has presented an economic problem. However, some retailers are finding new success in locating in these areas. Watch this clip on how Dollar Stores is finding its niche in towns where many other retailers have closed their doors.

Click to view content (https://openstax.org/books/principles-marketing/pages/18-3-retailing-strategy-decisions)

Central Business District

A **central business district** (CBD) is the commercial and business center of a given city or town (see Figure 18.11). While it is usually centrally located, its chief characteristic is its proximity to the largest number of people. Manhattan is the world's largest central business district. One of New York City's five boroughs, Manhattan is home to dozens of neighborhoods and hundreds of businesses, tourist attractions, and retail establishments. It has the highest retail rent in the world.[21] In smaller towns and cities, these downtown areas slowly started to decline with the growth of larger nearby cities. However, many cities are now working hard to restore their downtown and town square areas and turn central business districts into thriving areas once again.

Figure 18.11 A central business district, like downtown Chicago, is the commercial center of a city or town. (credit: "Aerial View of High-Rise Buildings in Chicago's Gold Coast and Magnificent Mile Areas" by Marco Verch/flickr, CC BY 2.0)

Regional Shopping Centers

Regional shopping centers, commonly referred to as shopping malls, offer general merchandise or fashion-oriented products and services (see Figure 18.12). They are enclosed buildings with access to retailers through a common walkway. Most regional malls have one to four anchor stores—large, well-known department stores—and numerous smaller specialty stores, as well as restaurants and activities. This blend of shopping and entertainment is sometimes known as retailtainment. For example, the Mall of America, located in Minneapolis, Minnesota, houses not only department and specialty stores, but also numerous restaurants, a cinema, an aquarium, and a theme park.[22]

Figure 18.12 Regional shopping centers, also known as shopping malls, provide access to retailers through a common walkway and often have one to four anchor stores. (credit: "Lisboa/Lisbon/Lisbon (Explore)" by Bert Kaufmann/flickr, CC BY 2.0)

Regional shopping centers typically service consumers who live anywhere from 5 to 15 miles away.[23] Regional shopping centers are becoming scarcer due to retailers moving into strip malls, an increase in Internet shopping, and the effects of the COVID-19 pandemic. It is not unusual to see regional shopping centers primarily deserted (sometimes called "zombie malls") or transformed into non-retail office space.

Strip Malls

Strip malls are classified by an attached row of retail stores offering both products and services (see Figure 18.13). Consumers enter stores from outside the building, and unlike in regional shopping centers, there is no internal walkway that links storefronts.[24] Rather, there is a sidewalk running in front of and connecting the individual stores. Strip malls often service neighborhoods within one mile of their location, and stores are generally the same size as one another.

Figure 18.13 A strip mall is a collection of retail stores that consumers enter from outside the building. (credit: "20091112_001" by jarchie/flickr, CC BY 2.0)

While strip malls are as old as regional shopping centers, they did not become more popular than regional centers until the late 1990s. The biggest draw to strip malls for consumers was that they did not have to walk through an entire regional shopping center to reach one store, yet could shop at multiple stores if desired. Department stores, factory outlets, and off-price retailers are often found in strip malls, along with specialty stores, service-oriented retail businesses, and restaurants.

Freestanding Retail Location

Freestanding retail locations are those store retailers that are not attached to any other retailer or establishment. Freestanding locations are more prevalent in smaller, less-populated areas (due to space). Gas stations, convenience stores, and superstores often occupy freestanding locations because they do not need anchors to pull consumers in. Freestanding locations are often less expensive to buy or lease as they are not anchored to established prime retail. In addition, retailers that choose a freestanding location often have fewer restrictions on design of the location, unlike those required of strip mall operators. On the other hand, these locations lack the foot traffic that may be gained from other types of retailers.[25]

Aside from the physical location of the retailer, decisions about exactly how the store is laid out and where products will be shelved is equally important. When you enter a grocery store, for example, you may note that the customer service center is often toward the front, allowing quick access to the services provided. You may also note that the milk, one of the most-purchased products in grocery stores, is often located in the back of the store. If it is purchased so frequently, why put it in the back? Most likely consumers will grab a few other items on their way to or from the back of the store, increasing the dollars spent.

Even the atmosphere of the retail location has been studied by retailers over the years. What does it smell like? What is the temperature? What music is playing? How is it decorated? Each of these considerations plays an important overall role in developing a retailing strategy based on the target market.

Omnichannel Marketing

Omnichannel marketing refers to an integrated approach and cooperation by the various channels to ensure a consistent brand message to customers.[26] Consider Starbucks and its mobile app. The Starbucks mobile rewards app is designed for customers to have a similar experience to that of walking inside the store or even visiting its website. Utilizing an omnichannel strategy provides many advantages to both the consumer and company that might be otherwise more difficult to achieve. Omnichannel marketing provides increased access to products and improved brand visibility and allows for more personalization. This provides customers with a consistent experience with the brand regardless of where they experience it.

Customers continue to look for ways to order products online, particularly as the world became more accustomed to purchasing from home during COVID-19 lockdowns. This has required the companies within distribution channels to reassess the way products and services get to the consumer. An omnichannel approach allows organizations to maximize the shopping experience for the consumer by integrating multiple delivery and engagement options.[27]

LINK TO LEARNING

Omnichannel Revolution

Consumers have high expectations of their online and in-person retailers. Learn from this TED Talk about the future of retailing from an eyewear company that is looking to revolutionize the retail experience.

Click to view content (https://openstax.org/books/principles-marketing/pages/18-3-retailing-strategy-decisions)

Also read about how you can use omnichannel experiences (https://openstax.org/r/serviceomnichannel) to create profits and the difference between omnichannel and multichannel experiences.

Retailer Communication

Retailers communicate to both their consumers and other channel members. The communication to consumers must be clear and concise to let potential customers know exactly what is being offered. While retailers develop communication strategies to directly reach their consumers, they will also collaborate on communication strategies with channel partners. For example, a Target commercial may feature a sale on Kellogg's cereal. The retailer and the manufacturer have worked together on a joint message for the consumer. Consider a second example. When you walk into a bookstore and see the latest release of a popular author's book in the front of the store display, the bookstore and the publisher have collaborated on all elements of that display: signage, how the book story is conveyed, display setup, etc.

This upward flow of communication is also important in a distribution channel. Retailers are on the front line of the exchange with consumers. Therefore, they can relay communication regarding products upward to other channel members. Assume a product that is sold primarily at retailers is being returned frequently because consumers are confused about how to use it. This information can be relayed back to the manufacturer, and the two can work together to overcome this challenge. It's important to remember that every member of the channel is in business to make money and add value to other channel members, so the more communication and cooperation the channel members have with one another, the more likely it is that they will all enjoy success.

Merchandise

Coupled with location and price, the choice of retail strategy will largely depend on the type of merchandise being offered to the consumer. **Merchandise** is simply the goods that are being offered for sale by a retailer. For large superstores, merchandise can include hundreds or thousands of pieces of merchandise, while smaller specialty stores stock narrow but deep product lines.

Retailers pay close attention to their choice of merchandise in terms of category management. **Category management** refers to a grouping of similar products into categories based upon consumer usage. The concept allows marketers to decrease competition between similar products and also buy similar product bundles at lower cost. Most retail chain stores use category management as a way to lower costs. For example, suppose a retailer has 20 stores across the country. Rather than having a buyer from each location analyze prices and find the best supplier for their location, a centralized group of people negotiates prices and contracts for all retail locations. The time and money that the retailer saves add up when done for all or most products carried.

Knowledge Check

It's time to check your knowledge on the concepts presented in this section. Refer to the Answer Key at the end of the book for feedback.

1. After trying to sell a line of clothing at your retail location, you decide to change the price from $25 to $15. Which pricing strategy have you used?
   a. Markup
   b. Original markup
   c. Maintained markup
   d. Markdown

2. A superstore chain is planning to open an establishment in the town Levi lives in. Which of the following would be the most likely location for this superstore?
   a. Central business district
   b. Strip mall
   c. Freestanding location
   d. Regional shopping district

3. You are interested in opening a small retail location that sells handmade jewelry in the small, rural town you reside in. Which of the following would be your best choice of location?
   a. Department store
   b. Regional shopping center
   c. Central business district
   d. Automatic vending

4. Pablo is trying to determine their gross margin at the end of the quarter. Which is the correct equation?
   a. Units sold times selling price
   b. Units purchased times purchase price
   c. Net sales less cost of goods sold
   d. Unit cost plus the sale price

5. Which of the following has had the most impact on a customer's access to product, brand visibility, and personalization?
   a. Omnichannel marketing
   b. Freestanding retail locations
   c. Retail communication
   d. Strip malls

18.4 | Recent Trends in Retailing

Learning Outcomes

By the end of this section, you will be able to:
   LO 1 List major trends and developments in retailing.
   LO 2 Discuss the reason for these trends and developments.

Trends in Retailing

As consumer behavior changes and as technology advances, marketers must make changes to stay relevant in the minds of their target market. During the late 1800s, the department store began the transition away from small mom-and-pop stores. In the 1920s, the first supermarket opened. In the 1950s, door-to-door selling was in full swing. In the 1980s, infomercials became mainstream. In the 1990s, online shopping got its start. In the 2000s, traditional brick-and-mortar stores began online sales. The rise of social media began in 2007, which created new selling opportunities (see Figure 18.14). Then, in 2017, the United States saw a slight shift back toward traditional store retailers. But, alas, in 2020 as the COVID-19 pandemic arose, that shift reversed again to online. These are just a few examples of how retailing has evolved with the times in the last century. As consumers get busier with their work and social lives, retailers find new ways to create value with the products they are selling. Let's take a deeper look at some of the more recent trends in retailing.

Figure 18.14 Social media created new selling opportunities for marketers. (credit: "Social Media Mix 3D Icons - Mix #1" by howtostartablogonline.net/Blogtrepreneur/flickr, CC BY 2.0)

Social Commerce

Social commerce is the blend of e-commerce and social media. With the rise of social media, brands have found new ways to engage and create lasting relationships with consumers. Many brands use social media as an additional marketing tool to engage more personally with customers. Retailers can do so in a variety of ways, from shoppable posts to influencer videos and everything in between.

Let's take a look at Macy's, an iconic American department store chain founded in 1858. Macy's has weathered many changes in the retail landscape, and today it utilizes social commerce in a variety of ways. In 2020, the company opened its ambassador program to people outside the company—influencers who would promote Macy's products through affiliate links or shoppable videos on social media.[28] The pay is 5 percent commission on sales. Why this shift to working with influencers? Simple. Consumers tend to trust the opinion of influential individuals over company-created marketing. And for Macy's and numerous other retailers, the strategy has worked because social commerce grew 30 percent from 2019 to 2020.[29]

As social media has grown since the inception of Facebook in 2004, marketers and social media apps alike have taken advantage of the ability of consumers to interact with brands and to purchase products directly in-app. For example, Instagram's Shop and Checkout feature allows consumers to purchase products immediately without ever leaving the app.[30] With the onset of the COVID-19 pandemic, the ability of consumers to purchase products while staying sheltered in place resulted in a change in behavior that is likely to endure in the coming years.

Online Stores in Offline Spaces

Have you ever purchased something online and picked it up at the store? This is what is referred to as online stores in offline spaces. While this practice was slowly gaining traction among larger retailers, the COVID-19 pandemic accelerated this trend drastically throughout nearly every industry. Retailers that already had the technology in place and/or were already testing such practices made a fairly easy transition to this new demand. Others closed their doors forever or scrambled to update their strategies to include some form of online sales.[31]

Walgreens, the second-largest pharmacy chain in the United States, was extremely successful in making such changes on the fly. In 2019, the company began allowing customers to order items online and pick them up at the drive-through window, which was previously primarily used for prescription pick up. Because the drive-through window was already established at Walgreens, it put them at a unique advantage to transition quickly to offer online orders in offline spaces.[32]

Same-Day Delivery

While most might think of Amazon Prime as the originator of same-day package delivery, the concept has actually been around for decades but was less prevalent in retail. Companies that offer legal and financial services have long had same-day delivery of their documents. In addition, restaurants have been offering guaranteed on-time delivery for some time. Florists have also offered one-day service for many years, particularly for funeral arrangements. And while Amazon Prime made the practice much more widespread throughout retailing, the now-defunct company Kozmo.com likely pioneered the practice in 1998.[33]

Kozmo was an online retailer that promised one-hour delivery of "videos, games, DVDs, music, mags, books, food, basics & more," including Starbucks coffee.[34] The company was popular with young professionals and college students, but it couldn't stay afloat and closed in 2001. The company likely inspired the US Postal Service Metro Post, which allowed Amazon to offer same-day delivery of packages in San Francisco in 2012.[35] Fast-forward to today, and many retailers, including Amazon and Walmart, offer same-day delivery in larger, well-populated areas.

The Emergence of Digital Wallets

Digital wallets are software-based systems that allow for secure transactions. Digital wallets were first used in the late 1990s, but today they offer more security and allow users to save numerous passwords and payment methods. The system allows users to quickly make online purchases without having to remember passwords or dig through their physical wallets to get cash.[36] They also allow users to pay for products and services in-store directly from their phones, allowing for touchless payments.

If you are familiar with the Apple Store or the Google Play Store, you've likely used digital wallets. When you purchase online on one of these devices, an automated display will come up asking if you would like to save your log-in and payment information. Once saved, each time you log in to the same website or begin to make a purchase, the digital wallet will auto-fill your information. While digital wallets are a huge time-saver for consumers, they also benefit retailers by capturing a sale that might have been lost due to inconvenience.

Knowledge Check

It's time to check your knowledge on the concepts presented in this section. Refer to the Answer Key at the end of the book for feedback.

1. Which of the following trends in retailing grew considerably during the COVID-19 pandemic?
    a.   Social commerce
    b.   Online stores in offline spaces
    c.   Digital wallets
    d.   All of the above trends grew considerably.

2. Cam posts numerous times on TikTok and Instagram. As a result, she is asked to work as an influencer for a major retailer. Which trend in retailing is Cam a part of?
   a. Online stores in offline spaces
   b. E-commerce
   c. Social commerce
   d. Same-day delivery

3. Software-based systems that allow for secure transactions by storing passwords and payment information are known as _______.
   a. e-commerce
   b. online stores in offline spaces
   c. social commerce
   d. digital wallets

4. Of the following, which is the most likely reason for an increase in online shopping?
   a. A pandemic
   b. The shift from two-income to one-income families
   c. More people retiring than ever before
   d. The rise in regional shopping centers

5. Which of the following is TRUE of social commerce?
   a. Social media is on the decline.
   b. Very few brands and companies utilize social media.
   c. Social media is one way to incorporate omnichannel marketing.
   d. Social media decreases personalization with customers.

18.5 Wholesaling

Learning Outcomes

By the end of this section, you will be able to:
   LO 1 Define wholesaling.
   LO 2 Identify different types of wholesalers.

Wholesaling Defined

Wholesaling is the business of buying goods in bulk at a discount from a manufacturer or other distribution channel member and selling them to retailers for a higher price. Wholesalers are often referred to as middlemen because they are the entity that links the producer to the retailer. Unlike retailers, wholesalers generally do not interact with customers or have physical locations for them to visit. Wholesalers engage in a variety of business practices including buying, storing, selling, and marketing.

Wholesalers are integral marketing intermediaries, responsible for getting the right product to the right place at the right time and creating additional value for the customer and other channel members. Furthermore, wholesalers actually make the final price for consumers less because they purchase in bulk, whereas some smaller retailers could not afford do so. There are several types of wholesalers, and each has its unique importance in the distribution channel.

Types of Wholesalers

In addition to the general importance noted above, each type of wholesaler plays a specific and integral role in getting products from a manufacturer to the end user. The decision of which type of wholesaler a retailer will utilize—or which type of wholesaling a wholesaler chooses—will largely depend on the type of product, the additional services needed, and often, the industry as a whole. The following section examines the types of merchant wholesalers (see Figure 18.15).

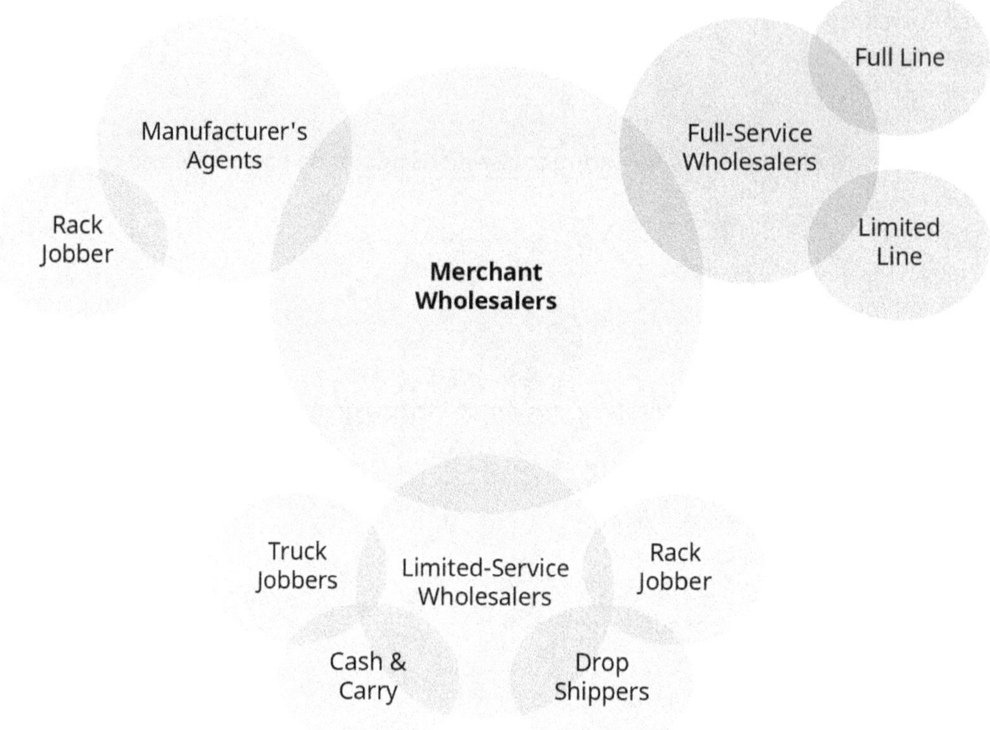

Figure 18.15 Types of Merchant Wholesalers (attribution: Copyright Rice University, OpenStax, under CC BY 4.0 license)

Merchant Wholesalers

Merchant wholesalers engage in buying, storing, and physically handling products in large quantities and selling those products in smaller quantities to retailers.[37] Merchant wholesalers are the most common form of wholesaling and can take on many responsibilities in the distribution channel to assist retailers. Merchant wholesalers are classified by the level of service they provide to retailers and include full-service wholesalers, limited-service wholesalers, and manufacturer's agents. Retailers and manufacturers will choose which type of wholesaler to work with based on their needs. Some large retailers, such as Walmart, may need fewer services from wholesalers than smaller specialty stores will need. As you continue to read, remember that wholesalers are a business—so they are in business to make money, but they also take on risk in doing so.

Full-Service Wholesalers

Wholesalers that take on the most risk are full-service wholesalers. **Full-service wholesalers** offer retailers the most complete range of services, such as buying, selling, storage, transportation, sorting, and financing. This type of wholesaler likely has its own salespeople to assist retailers, and some assist in the stocking of the products on retailers' shelves. They often provide retailers lines of credit to purchase products now and pay at a later date. Merchant wholesalers focus on either general or specialty merchandise.

Full-service wholesalers that offer an extensive list of merchandise for sale are known as **general-merchandise (full-line) wholesalers**. Retailers are able to purchase most, if not all, of their inventory from one wholesaler. For retailers, general-merchandise wholesaling is convenient because it provides for greater availability and flexibility with product quantities. However, retailers need to be cautious in utilizing only one wholesaler for all of their needs as they may find themselves in predicaments they cannot contractually be protected from—such as higher prices.

Unlike general-merchandise wholesalers, which focus on an extensive line of products, **specialty wholesalers** focus on a limited line of products. For example, Sysco, one of the country's largest food-service wholesalers, focuses on limited product lines, such as food and food-service supplies.[38] The company's target market includes hospitals and nursing homes, schools and colleges, and other entities that offer food service on a large scale. You might be surprised to learn that your high school cafeteria or college commons is served by Sysco.[39] The company offers a host of services to its customers, such as financing, consultation, menu assistance, and food production.

Limited-Service Wholesalers

As the name suggests, **limited-service wholesalers** offer a limited range of services to retailers. These wholesalers often compensate for the lack of services by offering lower prices than full-service wholesalers. For example, a limited-service wholesaler may not be able to offer retailers financing or stocking services, but it may purchase excess inventory from full-service wholesalers or manufacturers at a deeply discounted rate and in turn offer a better price to retailers. Limited-service wholesalers offer retailers many services to increase value.

Rack jobbers are companies that work with retailers to display and sell a product in-store. These items are often not products that the retailer would ordinarily stock and are budget-friendly items. For example, when you enter a gas station and see a rack of cell phone chargers and accessories, it is likely that they are from a rack jobber. The rack jobber stocks and maintains the cell phone display, and the gas station receives a portion of the sales. The advantage to the retailer is that it is not responsible for ordering products or maintaining and stocking displays; it is almost like passive income. The biggest disadvantage to retailers is that rack jobbers may over- or under-order products or fail to maintain displays as frequently as needed.

Cash-and-carry wholesalers are those that offer a limited line of fast-moving goods that they sell to retailers for cash. Because these wholesalers do not have to have massive amounts of storage space and do not offer services, they are able to offer products at lower prices. They also do not often deliver products, so they do not have overhead related to transportation. The advantage to the retailer is lower prices. But the disadvantages include no guarantee of product, the expense of transportation, and the demand for cash payment.

Drop shippers are retailers that use suppliers to ship products directly to the end consumer. In this case, retailers sell the product to the consumer, but they don't actually ever take possession (stock on a shelf, have inventory, etc.) of the product. The retailer only pays for the product after the consumer pays for and receives the order. Drop shipping is advantageous to retailers because they do not assume much risk since they do not take possession of the product. However, the profit margins for drop shippers are usually lower than utilizing other wholesalers because the wholesaler assumes all the risk.

Truck jobbers are wholesalers that make calls to retailers carrying goods on a truck. They carry a small inventory of the same product or small product lines, such as milk or bread. Because they have inventory in the truck, they can stop at a retailer, take the order, and deliver it within the same call. Truck jobbers are most often used for perishable foods that cannot sit in a warehouse waiting to be ordered.

Manufacturer's Agents or Representatives

The final, and perhaps least common, type of wholesaler is a manufacturer's agent or manufacturer's representative. Unlike the other types of wholesalers mentioned above, agents do not take possession of any product at any time. Rather, **manufacturer's agents** are independent contractors who act as salespersons for multiple manufacturers to sell similar (but not competing) products to retailers. The agent provides advantages to both to the manufacturer and the retailer. This is particularly true for smaller manufacturers where the expense and management of a sales force would likely not be feasible. Rather, an agent can take on the responsibility of working with the retailers or wholesalers to sell the product.[40]

Knowledge Check

It's time to check your knowledge on the concepts presented in this section. Refer to the Answer Key at the

end of the book for feedback.

1. Which of the following best describes wholesalers?
   a.   Businesses that buy in bulk at discounted prices and sell to retailers
   b.   Online stores in offline spaces
   c.   The final link between manufacturers and consumers
   d.   Businesses that produce goods and services

2. Your friend Jesus wants to start a retailing business but doesn't think he can afford space, nor does he wish to travel and make sales calls to retailers. Which of the following might be the best warehousing option for Jesus?
   a.   Rack jobber
   b.   Specialty wholesaler
   c.   Cash-and-carry wholesaler
   d.   Drop shipper

3. The type of wholesaler that offers the most complete range of services is known as a ________.
   a.   rack jobber
   b.   cash-and-carry wholesaler
   c.   limited-service wholesaler
   d.   general-merchandise wholesaler

4. Which type of wholesaler utilizes independent contractors as liaisons between manufacturers and retailers?
   a.   Manufacturer's agents
   b.   Rack jobbers
   c.   Truck jobbers
   d.   Full-line wholesalers

5. ________ are companies that agree with retailers to display and sell products in-store.
   a.   Rack jobbers
   b.   Cash-and-carry wholesalers
   c.   Drop shippers
   d.   Truck jobbers

18.6 Recent Trends in Wholesaling

Learning Outcomes

By the end of this section, you will be able to:

  LO 1 Explain the impact of growing competition and global dynamics.
  LO 2 Discuss the complexity of regulatory requirements.
  LO 3 Discuss the challenges of technology evolution.

Growing Competition

Prior to 2019, most of us did not give much thought to the supply chain or its channel members. We went to the store and were welcomed with endless aisles of the products we were used to purchasing. However, when the COVID-19 pandemic hit, the entire country became more in tune with channel members. Wholesalers were not unaffected by the disruption that the pandemic caused channel members, and new trends are on the horizon for wholesalers. Let's take a look at these recent trends that affect wholesaling.

Wholesalers are a central link in the economy and supply chain. The industry is facing tough competition with new as well as nontraditional wholesalers entering the market. Just as consumers are demanding more convenient shopping experiences and increased value in products and services, retailers are demanding the same from their intermediaries. Wholesalers must find innovative and competitive business models to compete.

The Impact of Global Dynamics on the Supply Chain

Globalization has been integrating global markets for the past several decades. And supply chains have had to adjust to keep up with these changes. With products available from around the world at lower costs and retailers demanding faster deliveries, many wholesalers have expanded their operations in response to the rise of the global economy. This comes with its own set of challenges, such as an expanded sales force and the need to understand other economies, cultures, and languages.

More recently, it has become apparent in the United States and around the world that supply chain participants were not prepared for disruptions such as those seen during the COVID-19 pandemic. Shortages of workers, products, containers, and long-haul truck drivers have proven to the industry that some major changes need to occur.

Regulatory Requirements and Complexity

With advancements in technology (and the need for consumer security) as well as the growing global economy, regulatory requirements also increase—and become more complex. Wholesalers must understand such requirements in order to conduct business legally. For example, wholesalers need a special license to distribute restricted goods, such as alcohol, controlled drugs, firearms, and pesticides. Depending on the type of transportation mode being used—such as tractor-trailers hauling containers—special licensing may need to be obtained.

Wholesalers also have a large responsibility when it comes to disposing of waste. More specific government regulations in regard to wholesalers include the Sale of Goods Act, which requires goods sold to be safe and include clear directions.[41] The government has also enacted various rules to protect consumers and to be able to trace products.

Consumer Protection

Caveat emptor (Latin for "let the buyer beware") was a long-standing motto in commercial transactions, one that implies the buyer purchases at their own risk. However, consumer protection laws are now woven into the fabric of the economy. Regulations help keep sellers honest and consumers protected. In general, consumer protection regulations exist to prevent unethical or dangerous business practices throughout the distribution channel. These practices range from false advertising to predatory lending to scams and frauds.[42] Some of these will be discussed later in the chapter.

Product Traceability

Product traceability refers to the ability to track all processes for a product, from the procurement of raw materials to production, consumption, and disposal. Increasing numbers of consumers want to know exactly where their products are coming from and whether they are ethically sourced.[43] Aside from consumer demand, it is a crucial part of the distribution channel as product recalls become more common.

For example, on January 6, 2022, the US Department of Agriculture (USDA) announced a recall of over 25,000 pounds of ground beef.[44] Because of product traceability, the specific ground beef under the recall was able to be traced to a specific location, production date, and lot. Without product traceability, there may have been no way of knowing where the ground beef came from, forcing consumers to discard purchases of product that was not tainted. Additionally, product traceability helps combat counterfeit products by finding the originating source.

LINK TO LEARNING

Traceability Standards

The GS1 Global Traceability Standard defines what is minimally acceptable for full supply chain traceability. It establishes a full system that traces products end to end. Read more about the standards and see how it's applied (https://openstax.org/r/howtraceability) to food.

Challenges of Technology Evolution

The advancement and increased use of technology has brought about both challenges and opportunities for wholesalers. Product traceability has become increasingly easier, for example. Orders are easier to make and track. However, technology is expensive and comes with a learning curve for new users. The increased demand of consumers and retail customers requires wholesalers to keep up with technological advancements to stay competitive.

Knowledge Check

It's time to check your knowledge on the concepts presented in this section. Refer to the Answer Key at the end of the book for feedback.

1. What does *caveat emptor* translate to in English?
   a. Buyer beware
   b. Manufacturer beware
   c. Retailer beware
   d. Consumer protection

2. Justia saw on the news that chicken was recently recalled by the US Food and Drug Administration (FDA). The news anchor specified which sell-by dates, manufacturer, and retailers were affected. Justia doesn't understand how the FDA can know, with such specificity, which chickens were affected. How would you describe to Justia this specificity?
   a. Increased competition
   b. E-commerce
   c. Caveat emptor
   d. Product traceability

3. Which of the following is NOT an advantage of product traceability?
   a. It makes it easier to trace counterfeit goods.
   b. It makes it easier to trace tainted food.
   c. It creates less work for distribution channel members.
   d. It makes it easier for consumers to know where products come from.

4. Which of the following is NOT a growing trend in wholesaling?
   a. Decreased government regulations
   b. Increased competition
   c. Increase in globalization
   d. Increase in technological advances

5. Which regulation requires goods sold to be safe and include clear directions?
   a. Sale of Goods Act

b.   Food and Drug Act
c.   Caveat Emptor
d.   Better Business Bureau

18.7 | Ethical Issues in Retailing and Wholesaling

Learning Outcomes

By the end of this section, you will be able to:

LO 1   Discuss ethical issues in retailing.
LO 2   Discuss ethical issues in wholesaling.

Ethical Issues in Retailing

As with any business entity, ethical issues arise in both retailing and wholesaling. It can be easy to find oneself in an ethical dilemma while trying to meet consumer demands and stay competitive. There are several prominent ethical issues that arise specifically with retailing and wholesaling.

Because retailers are the final link between manufacturer and consumer, ethical issues often arise in the practices used toward consumers. Common issues in retail include deceptive or misleading marketing, poor treatment of consumers, and misleading sales tactics.

Unethical Practices Used by Retailers

Although there has been a considerable rise in the number of consumers and advocacy groups calling out unethical business practices, many retailers still attempt to use tactics to sway consumers into purchasing products. Truly Organic, a retailer based in Miami Beach, Florida, came under attack by the Federal Trade Commission (FTC) in 2019 for misleading consumers into believing their products were 100 percent organic, which wasn't entirely true.[45] The case stated that Truly Organic was guilty of **false or misleading advertising**, an unethical marketing practice by which consumers are given false or misleading information about a product or service.

Misleading or manipulative sales tactics is another common unethical practice used by retailers. Misleading sales tactics involve misleading the consumer with untrue information regarding a product or service. Subscription services used to be notorious for misleading sales tactics as they offered a service or product for a free trial but did not include in the promotion that the consumer would be charged every month after a free trial. There are many regulations that require such companies to disclose this information.

Ethical Issues in Wholesaling

Just as retailers may face the temptation to be unethical toward consumers, wholesalers often find themselves in an ethical dilemma with their retail customers. Two common ethical issues that arise in wholesaling surround fairness and pricing.

Fairness and Billing

Fairness can certainly be a subjective term. What you and your sibling may each deem as fair is based on your individual perspectives and opinions. In wholesaling, and commerce in general, the government has enacted regulations to maintain fairness in business practices. You have probably heard the term "monopoly." In the United States, monopolies are considered unfair business practices and thus are largely against FTC regulations. If one or a few businesses control all of an industry, the laws of supply and demand cease to exist because one company controls both. In the wholesaling industry, the same rules apply. If a wholesaler requires a retailer to sign very specific contracts that they will use no other wholesaler, the retailer is at the mercy of the wholesaler when it comes to everything surrounding their business's livelihood.

Just as with fairness, wholesalers also need to pay close attention to their billing practices. Wholesalers and retailers agree on the billing method to be used in their contract. However, it is unethical for wholesalers to bill retailers for product never shipped or received, damaged product without recourse, or product not ordered.

COMPANIES WITH A CONSCIENCE

Trader Joe's

In 1967 in Pasadena, California, the first Trader Joe's was opened. Today, the retail grocery chain has 505 stores in over 42 states as well as an online presence. Trader Joe's has always been committed to improving sustainability in its channel. Unlike many competitors in the grocery industry, Trader Joe's donates 100 percent of its unsold products. It does not allow certain controversial products in the manufacturing of its private-label goods and continues to make organic products more accessible. Additionally, the company has removed more than 6 million pounds of plastic from packaging and continues to have high rates of employee satisfaction.[46] The ethical decisions of Trader Joe's involve relationship building throughout the supply chain to ensure that each channel member upholds the high ethical standards that help enhance the customer experience.

There are other supermarkets known for ethical practices. These include Natural Grocers, Sprouts, Costco, and Whole Foods.[47]

Chapter Summary

This chapter explores two important members of the distribution channel and value delivery system: wholesalers and retailers. Both add value to the product by ensuring assorted merchandise is available when and where customers want it and at an acceptable price. Retailers buy products from manufacturing firms or wholesalers and provide them for sale to the consumer.

Retailers buy in bulk, hold inventory, offer convenient hours for shoppers, supply services, and collect and share feedback from consumers with other members of the distribution channel. Retailers may have a storefront; non-store retailers usually sell through direct mail and catalogs, vending machines, direct selling, online sites, TV home shopping, and telemarketing. Retail strategy includes identifying target audiences, choosing location(s), providing a product assortment, and pricing.

Wholesalers buy goods in bulk at a discount from a manufacturer or other distribution channel member and sell them to retailers for a higher price. They are often called "middlemen" because they link the manufacturer to the retailer. Unlike retailers, wholesalers do not interact with the final consumer, and they do not have highly visible physical locations accessible to end consumers. Wholesalers engage in a variety of business practices including buying, storing, selling, transporting, financing, and even marketing.

Just as in all marketing strategies, retailers and wholesalers contend with changes in consumer behavior and expectations, technological advances, complex regulations, channel member availability, and international dynamics. Of the regulations, most are intended to protect consumers from unethical or dangerous products and business practices.

Key Terms

automatic vending   the use of an electronic device that dispenses a product

cash-and-carry wholesalers   wholesalers that offer a limited line of fast-moving goods that they sell to retailers for cash

category killers   large superstores, most often chains stores, that are bigger, cheaper, and more convenient than competitors

category management   grouping similar products into categories based on customer usage

central business district (CBD)   the commercial and business center of a given city or town

convenience store   a small retail business that stocks a limited range of everyday items such as groceries, snacks, soft drinks, tobacco, toiletries, and lottery tickets

department stores   larger retailers that have separated areas—or departments—for similar product lines

digital wallets   software-based systems that allow for secure transactions

direct mail   solicited or unsolicited advertising of products and services to prospective customers through the mail

direct selling   a marketing strategy that involves selling products and services directly to the consumer in a non-retail setting

discount store   retailer that sells a broad range of products at lower prices than competitors

drop shippers   a wholesaler business model where retailers use suppliers to ship products directly to the end consumer

factory outlets   retailers that offer overstocked merchandise at discounted prices

false or misleading advertising   an unethical marketing practice by which consumers are given false or misleading information about a product or service

freestanding retail locations   store retailers that are not attached to any other retailer or establishment

full-service wholesalers   wholesalers that offer retailers the most complete range of services, such as buying, selling, storage, transportation, sorting, and financing

general-merchandise (full-line) wholesalers   wholesalers that offer an extensive list of merchandise for sale

gross margin   net sales minus the cost of goods sold

intermediaries   companies that act as liaisons between the buyer and seller

keystone pricing   a pricing strategy that doubles the price from the wholesaler or manufacturer

limited-service wholesalers   wholesalers that offer a limited range of services to retailers to increase value

maintained markup   the actual markup on the merchandise that is sold to the consumer

manufacturer's agents   independent contractors who act as salespeople for multiple manufacturers to sell similar (but not competing) products to retailers

markdown   a price decrease for a product that is at the end of its life cycle or season

markup   the amount added to the cost retailers purchase goods for

merchandise   the goods that are being offered for sale by a retailer

merchant wholesalers   wholesalers that engage in buying, storing, and physically handling products in large quantities and selling those products in smaller quantities to retailers

non-store retailers   retailers that operate outside of traditional brick-and-mortar locations

off-price retailers   retailers that provide high-quality goods at lower prices

omnichannel marketing   utilization of multiple distribution channels

omnichannel strategy   manufacturer strategy that uses multiple distribution channels to distribute a product

online retailing   a business model that allows consumers to search and purchase products remotely over the Internet

original markup   the markup a business has decided upon at the onset of the offering, which includes planned sales and overhead

product traceability   the ability to track all processes for a product from the procurement of raw materials to production, consumption, and disposal

rack jobbers   wholesalers (or manufacturers) that agree with retailers to display and sell a product in a retail store

regional shopping centers   commonly referred to as "malls"; collection of stores that offer general merchandise or fashion-oriented offerings

retailing   the process of selling goods and services to consumers

social commerce   a blend of e-commerce and social media

specialty stores   retailers that focus on selling a single type of product or a single product line

specialty wholesalers   wholesalers that focus on a limited line of products but carry the line in some depth

store retailer   a traditional brick-and-mortar establishment where products are displayed for customers to purchase

strip malls   classified by an attached row of retail stores offering both products and services

supermarket   retailer that mostly focuses on a product mix of grocery items but also carries household and personal items and offers limited services

superstores   very large retailers that have characteristics of both supermarkets and department stores

telemarketing   the attempted sale, or marketing, of goods and services to potential customers via telephone

television home shopping   a business practice in which products or services are sold via television

truck jobbers   wholesalers that make calls to retailers carrying goods on a truck

warehouse clubs   retailers that sell goods in bulk at discounted prices

wholesaling   the business of buying goods in bulk at a discount from a manufacturer or other distribution channel member and selling them retailers for a higher price

Applied Marketing Knowledge: Discussion Questions

1. Define direct consumer marketing channels and indirect consumer marketing channels. List an example of each type and explain the difference between them.

2. The shift to online shopping has challenged many retailers who had only a brick-and-mortar location. One of the industries hit hardest by changes in consumer behavior is travel agencies because travelers can access much of the necessary pricing information themselves and then purchase tickets directly from the

airlines. Name two additional store retailers that have virtually disappeared because of non-store retailing.

3. *Markup* is a term used by retailers to explain how much revenue comes from the difference between the cost of acquiring a product and the price it is sold for. Why do florists usually mark up their products 80% while grocers generally mark up their products 15%?

4. How does location matter for a wholesale business?

5. Is it ethically acceptable for a jewelry store to advertise $50 diamond-studded heart necklaces for Valentine's Day and then tell customers who come to the store that the $50 necklace is out of stock but a $75 option is in stock?

Critical Thinking Exercises

1. According to PR Newswire, more than 40 percent of the overall revenue from the multimodal distribution market is due to roadway logistics. Give three reasons why retailers and wholesalers depend largely on roads—rather than rail, air, or water—to send and receive products. Why do roads create the greatest transportation-based revenue for businesses and lowest costs for consumers?

2. Thanks to retailers and wholesalers and their strategies, products may be distributed in various ways. What are two examples of consumer products that are sold by retailers, and what is the corresponding distribution strategy?

3. Most firms today take advantage of multimodal transportation, especially those that source and distribute products internationally. List three reasons why multimodal transportation makes sense financially for a retailer like Amazon that operates in a time-sensitive marketplace.

Building Your Personal Brand

Have you ever worked in a grocery store stocking shelves, worked at your campus bookstore, or waited on customers at a restaurant or drive-through? Working in retail is a fantastic resume booster. Not only have you advanced your knowledge of the business world, but you have also worked closely with demanding customers and management in a retail environment. Learning to serve customers, following training and rules, being part of a successful job interview, and holding a job outside of school are all highly coveted experiences. According to the Skills You Need website, the most important employability skills include "getting along with and working well with other people" and "being reliable and dependable: doing what you say you will by the deadline you have agreed [to] and turning up when you are meant to be there."[48] Create or revise your resume to include the applicable skills.

What Do Marketers Do?

C.H. Robinson is a third-party logistics provider headquartered in Eden Prairie, Minnesota. Many businesses outsource elements of distribution, warehousing, and fulfillment services to companies such as C.H. Robinson. Like wholesalers, logistics providers, also an intrinsic part of the value delivery system, operate largely outside of the public eye.

Reach out to one of the 297 C.H. Robinson locations and ask if you can speak to someone about recent supply chain trends for a college course assignment. Your questions may include the following:

- How does technology impact the supply chain?
- What is the biggest industry you work with that depends on supply chain partners?
- How has the COVID-19 pandemic impacted product availability and distribution efforts?
- What does a typical day at C.H. Robinson consist of?
- What special training do I need to work in supply chain logistics?
- What is a typical salary for a professional new to C.H. Robinson?

- Do you have an internship program?

Marketing Plan Exercise

Complete the following information about the company and products/services you chose to focus on as you develop the marketing plan throughout the course. You may need to conduct research in order to obtain the necessary information.

Instructions: Using the Marketing Plan Template file you created from the Marketing and Customer Value assignment and expanded upon in Strategic Planning in Marketing, Market Segmentation, Targeting, and Positioning, Marketing Research and Market Intelligence, Products: Consumer Offerings, Pricing Products and Services, Integrated Marketing Communications, and Distribution: Delivering Customer Value, complete the following section of your marketing plan:

- Budgeting
- Action Programs
- Controls to Monitor Progress

Submit the marketing plan to your instructor for grading and feedback.

Closing Company Case

Ace Hardware

With annual sales of more than $400 billion in the United States, the home improvement market has no shortage of eager shoppers. While Home Depot and Lowe's dominate the market in terms of sales, Ace Hardware dominates by number of locations and customer satisfaction.[49]

What started in 1924 as a way for the independent hardware retailer to buy inventory like the "big guys," saving money based on volume, has grown into one of the largest and most well-known retailer-owned cooperatives. Founded by a group of Chicago hardware store owners who wanted to save money and enable the smaller hardware store to compete, is now a worldwide leader in home improvement.

Ace prides itself on being the local neighborhood hardware store. Its major niche in the market is to provide the best service to customers. To this end, Ace has always hired knowledgeable staff to help answer questions, locate products, and provide advice. Ace buys inventory according to the needs and wants of its local consumers, but its real niche is in customer service. Generally, a customer isn't in the store for more than five minutes before a friendly, red-shirted Ace employee is asking if they need help.

Early on, Ace wanted to set itself apart based on its helpful and friendly service. Playing on this value proposition and looking to build brand awareness, Ace crafted a very catchy ad campaign, which has solidified the Ace brand. Back in the 1970s and 1980s, Ace became known by its famous jingle, "Ace is the place with the helpful hardware man." This jingle is still being used today, and you can see it here.

Click to view content (https://openstax.org/books/principles-marketing/pages/18-closing-company-case)
Because retailers must execute well on all the marketing mix variables, for a retailer like Ace to be successful, it needs to understand its customers in the local market. In doing so, it can also identify the best location for the store in order to meet the needs of those customers and how they travel around town. Ace knows the customers well, so it is able to set prices and provide products according to local needs.

One of the founding principles of Ace is that each store should be locally owned and operated. Because of this, Ace is embedded in the communities they serve. You will often find the local Ace team stepping in to help with community projects or sponsor local sports teams. The stores work with independent producers to stock locally made products.

Over the past decade, retailing has seen significant changes in how consumers shop. Amazon has swiftly transformed and dominated retailing. Many independent brick-and-mortar retailers have been unable to compete with the convenience of online ordering and at-home delivery.

And with the onset of the COVID-19 pandemic in 2020, retailers everywhere were scrambling to adapt. Ace quickly transformed into an online as well as in-store retailer. Through a quick revamp of its website, Ace was able to offer its customers the ability to order and pay online with options to either pick up at the store or have the product(s) delivered to their home. Home delivery was fulfilled by the local Ace Hardware employees.

Another advantage to Ace Hardware is the services it provides. Making keys, sharpening lawn mower blades and chains for chain saws, repairing screens, and mixing customer paint have allowed Ace to go the extra mile for items customers must come to the store for.[50]

Case Questions

1. Ace fulfills many of the marketing mix variables. What are some of the marketing activities of a local Ace Hardware store?

2. What is the retail classification of Ace Hardware?

3. How does Ace Hardware differentiate itself from the big-box stores like Lowe's and Home Depot?

4. How was Ace Hardware able to adapt to the digital age and work with consumers who were not shopping in-store during the height of the COVID-19 pandemic?

References

1. Precycle (website), accessed September 2, 2022, https://www.precyclenyc.com/.

2. Kim Souza, "Nielsen: Consumers Will Want More Local Foods in 2020," Talk Business & Politics, October 29, 2019, https://talkbusiness.net/2019/10/nielsen-consumers-will-want-more-local-foods-in-2020/.

3. Jason Fernando, "What Is a Distribution Channel in Business and How Does It Work?," Investopedia, Dotdash Meredith, updated May 12, 2022, https://www.investopedia.com/terms/d/distribution-channel.asp.

4. Evangelos Christou and Chryssoula Chatzigeorgiou, "Adoption of Social Media as Distribution Channels in Tourism Marketing: A Qualitative Analysis of Consumers' Experiences," *Journal of Tourism, Heritage & Services Marketing* 6, no. 1 (2020): 25–32, https://doi.org/10.5281/zenodo.3603355.

5. "Our Locations," Target Corporate, Target Brands, accessed September 2, 2022, https://corporate.target.com/about/locations.

6. Tony Hernández and David Bennison, "The Art and Science of Retail Location Decisions," *International Journal of Retail & Distribution Management* 28, no. 8 (2000): 357–367, https://doi.org/10.1108/09590550010337391.

7. "Walmart Services," Walmart.com, accessed September 2, 2022, https://www.walmart.com/services.

8. Susan Meyer, "The History and Evolution of Retail Stores: From Mom and Pop to Online Shops," *BigCommerce Blog*, BigCommerce, last modified July 15, 2022, https://www.bigcommerce.com/blog/retail/.

9. "Retail Industry Sectors: Types of Retail," Domain (Industry) Knowledgebase, TechnoFunc, accessed September 2, 2022, https://www.technofunc.com/index.php/domain-knowledge/retail-industry/item/retail-industry-sectors-types-of-retail.

10. "Amazon Go," Amazon.com, accessed September 2, 2022, https://www.amazon.com/b?ie=UTF8&node=16008589011.

11. "Company Overview," Corporate Homepage, Publix Super Markets, accessed September 2, 2022, https://corporate.publix.com/about-publix/company-overview.

12. "About NACS," NACS, accessed September 2, 2022, https://www.convenience.org/About-NACS.

13. Daniel Gross, "The Almighty Dollar (Store)," Slate, June 13, 2009, https://slate.com/business/2009/06/dollar-general-is-the-retail-store-that-figured-out-how-to-beat-the-recession.html.

14. "About Sawgrass Mills," Sawgrass Mills, Simon Property Group, accessed September 2, 2022, https://www.simon.com/mall/sawgrass-mills/about.

15. "Carvana Debuts Flagship Car Vending Machine in Atlanta," Investor Relations, Carvana, November 18, 2020, https://investors.carvana.com/news-releases/2020/11-18-2020-110046117.

16. "10 Oldest Mail Order Catalogs in the World," Oldest.org, last modified May 17, 2022, https://www.oldest.org/artliterature/mail-order-catalogs/.

17. Jake Rossen, "15 Things You Might Not Know about QVC," *Mental Floss*, August 12, 2015, https://www.mentalfloss.com/article/67266/14-things-you-might-not-know-about-qvc.

18. Carmen Ang, "Timeline: Key Events in the History of Online Shopping," Visual Capitalist, updated October 6, 2021, https://www.visualcapitalist.com/history-of-online-shopping/.

19. "Do Not Call," Federal Communications Commission, last modified June 22, 2016, https://www.fcc.gov/general/do-not-call.

20. Patrick Gleeson, "What Is a Normal Markup Percentage?," Small Business, Chron.com, updated March 8, 2019, https://smallbusiness.chron.com/normal-markup-percentage-80750.html.

21. Janette Sadik-Khan, "A Plea for Fifth Avenue," *New York Times*, January 9, 2017, https://www.nytimes.com/2017/01/09/opinion/a-plea-for-fifth-avenue.html.

22. Mall of America (website), MOAC Mall Holdings, accessed September 2, 2022, https://www.mallofamerica.com/.

23. "U.S. Shopping-Center Classification and Characteristics," ICSC, International Council of Shopping Centers, January 2017, https://www.icsc.com/uploads/research/general/US_CENTER_CLASSIFICATION.pdf.

24. International Council of Shopping Centers, "U.S. Shopping-Center Classification."

25. Shari Waters, "Pros and Cons of the Different Types of Retail Locations," LiveAbout, Dotdash Meredith, updated February 6, 2020, https://www.thebalancesmb.com/types-of-retail-locations-2890244.

26. "What Is Omnichannel Marketing: Definition, Tips, and Examples," Marketing Evolution, accessed September 2, 2022, https://www.marketingevolution.com/knowledge-center/topic/marketing-essentials/omnichannel.

27. Hokey Min, "Exploring Omni-channels for Customer-centric E-tailing," *Logistics* 5, no. 2 (2021), May 25, 2021, https://doi.org/10.3390/logistics5020031.

28. Liz Flora, "Macy's Doubles Down on Social Commerce," Glossy, Digiday Media, August 4, 2020, https://www.glossy.co/beauty/macys-doubles-down-on-social-commerce/.

29. Jessica Wong, "The Latest E-commerce Trend: What You Need to Know about Social Commerce," Forbes Communications Council, Forbes Media, December 3, 2021, https://www.forbes.com/sites/forbescommunicationscouncil/2021/12/03/the-latest-e-commerce-trend-what-you-need-to-know-about-social-commerce/.

30. "How Social Media Shopping Is Changing the Retail Game," *Floor Covering News*, February 8, 2022, https://www.fcnews.net/2022/02/how-social-media-shopping-is-changing-the-retail-game/.

31. UWorx Group, "Online Stores in Offline Spaces," LinkedIn, October 13, 2021, https://www.linkedin.com/pulse/online-stores-offline-spaces-uworx-group/.

32. "Walgreens Introduces New Digital 'Order Ahead' Drive-Thru Shopping Experience," Walgreens Newsroom, Walgreens, May 4, 2020, https://news.walgreens.com/press-center/news/walgreens-introduces-new-digital-order-ahead-drive-thru-shopping-experience.htm.

33. "The Rise of Same-Day Package Delivery," *Our Blog*, Parcel Pending, last modified September 2, 2021, https://www.parcelpending.com/blog/the-rise-of-same-day-package-delivery/.

34. Kozmo.com (website), Wayback Machine, Internet Archive, archived April 8, 2000, https://web.archive.org/web/20000408214847/http://www.kozmo.com/.

35. "MetroPost," *United States Postal Service 2014 Annual Report to Congress*, United States Postal Service, 2014, https://about.usps.com/publications/annual-report-comprehensive-statement-2014/ar2014/annualreport2014_tech_071.htm.

36. Julia Kagan, "Digital Wallet Explained: Types with Examples and How It Works," Investopedia, Dotdash Meredith, updated April 10, 2022, https://www.investopedia.com/terms/d/digital-wallet.asp.

37. "Wholesaling," Encyclopedia Table of Contents, *Inc.*, updated January 5, 2021, https://www.inc.com/encyclopedia/wholesaling.html.

38. "Our Products," Sysco, accessed September 2, 2022, https://www.sysco.com/Products/Products/Product-Categories.html.

39. "Sysco's Customers Performance," CSI Market, accessed September 2, 2022, https://csimarket.com/stocks/markets_glance.php?code=SYY.

40. "Manufacturers' Agents," Encyclopedia Table of Contents, *Inc.*, updated January 5, 2021, https://www.inc.com/encyclopedia/manufacturers-agents.html.

41. Claire Shaw, "Legal Requirements for Wholesalers and Retailers," *Everyday Law Blog UK*, Rocket Lawyer, June 9, 2021, https://www.rocketlawyer.com/gb/en/blog/legal-requirements-for-wholesalers-and-retailers/.

42. Ana Gonzalez Ribeiro, "What Are Consumer Protection Laws?," Investopedia, Dotdash Meredith, updated August 1, 2022, https://www.investopedia.com/articles/pf/10/know-your-consumer-protection-laws.asp.

43. Ash Baggott, "What Is Product Traceability?," *Holded Blog*, Holded, November 14, 2019, https://www.holded.com/blog/what-is-product-traceability.

44. "Interstate Meat Dist. Inc. Recalls Ground Beef Products due to Possible E. Coli 0157:H7 Contamination," Food Safety and Inspection Service, U.S. Department of Agriculture, January 6, 2022, https://www.fsis.usda.gov/recalls-alerts/interstate-meat-dist.-inc.-recalls-ground-beef-products-due-possible-e.-coli-o157h7.

45. "Truly Organic Inc.," Legal Library, Federal Trade Commission, updated September 19, 2019, https://www.ftc.gov/enforcement/cases-proceedings/192-3077/truly-organic-inc.

46. Heather Seely, "8 Most Ethical Supermarkets for Guilt-Free Grocery Shopping," Tamborasi, February 8, 2021, https://www.tamborasi.com/ethical-supermarkets/.

47. Seely, "8 Most Ethical Supermarkets."

48. "Employability Skills: The Skills You Need to Get a Job," Skills You Need, accessed September 2, 2022, https://www.skillsyouneed.com/Tedgeneral/employability-skills.html.

49. "DIY and Home Improvement in the U.S.: Statistics & Facts," Statista, September 12, 2022, https://www.statista.com/topics/1732/home-improvement/.

50. "Local Ace Hardware Store Services," Ace Hardware, accessed September 2, 2022, https://www.acehardware.com/store-services.

Sustainable Marketing: The New Paradigm

Figure 19.1 Sustainability marketing, which takes into account present consumers' needs without harming the future, is growing in importance as consumers shift to being more environmentally conscious in their purchasing decisions. (credit: "Hike" by Loren Kerns/flickr, CC BY 2.0)

Chapter Outline

In the Spotlight

According to Accenture, a global professional services company, "Sustainable organizations are purpose-led businesses which inspire their people and partners to deliver lasting financial performance, equitable impact, and societal value that earns and retains the trust of all stakeholders."[1] Sustainability is about doing business without negatively affecting society. Without sustainable practices, companies may negatively contribute to issues in the environment, inequality, and social injustice.[2] Consumers, employees, and other interested parties are now holding businesses to higher standards: 74 percent of consumers agree that conducting ethical practices is an important reason to support a company or brand; 65 percent of employees believe that businesses should leave their employees better off through work; and 81 percent of sustainable investment indexes outperformed comparable benchmarks in 2020.[3] According to John Streur, CEO of Calvert Research and Management, "In 2021, we see companies almost competing with one another on sustainability."[4] The proof is in the pudding. A 2021 report by the Weinreb Group found that "there were more chief sustainability officers, or CSOs, recruited in 2020 than in the previous three years combined."[5]

Barron's, a respected source on financial news, creates a 100 Most Sustainable Companies list each year. In 2021, the popular kitchen supply store Williams-Sonoma stood out above others because its board consisted of 67 percent women.[6] Williams-Sonoma, Inc.'s 2021 impact report outlined that, at the time of publication, 46 percent of the company's products supported one or more of its environmental and social initiatives, and the company aims to increase that amount to 75 percent by 2030.[7] In 2020, Williams-Sonoma joined the United Nations (UN) Global Compact and aligned its corporate goals with the UN Sustainable Development Goals.[8] To learn more about Williams-Sonoma's sustainablity efforts and plans, review its 2021 impact report (https://openstax.org/r/impactreport), its corporate responsibility web page (https://openstax.org/r/sustainabilitywilliams), and the sustainability section of its website (https://openstax.org/r/williamsonoma).

Williams-Sonoma is just one example of a company with a vision and a commitment to sustainability. Other companies known for their sustainability commitments and practices include Microsoft, VMware, Intuit, Apple, and Mastercard.[9]

In the future, all global companies must commit to, assess, and validate the goal of sustainability; as you'll learn in this chapter, it's becoming a significant factor in how businesses evaluate success. Those companies that fully embrace this commitment will stand out most to consumers and achieve business success.

19.1 | Sustainable Marketing

Learning Outcomes

By the end of this section, you will be able to:
- **LO** 1 Define sustainable marketing.
- **LO** 2 Explain the three pillars of sustainable marketing.

Environmental Sustainability

Consumers increasingly demand purpose over profits from the brands they work for, shop for, invest in, and allow within their communities. In fact, an IBM study on consumer behavior indicated that 57 percent of consumers would alter consumption habits to be more environmentally conscious, and nearly 80 percent of survey respondents indicated that sustainability is essential.[10] Therefore, sustainability is a business imperative. As defined by Philip Kotler, Professor Emeritus at Northwestern University, "the concept of sustainable marketing holds that an organization should meet the needs of its present consumers without compromising the ability of future generations to fulfill their own needs."[11] In other words, products and services consumed today should not harm consumers of tomorrow.

Sustainable marketing infuses purpose into socially conscious brands, products, and services. Marketing seeks to differentiate the brand based on mission. Sustainable brands define a purpose, orient to consumers' and related groups' values, align purpose with strategy, and reflect sustainability in marketing. This business strategy gives brands an edge with those who seek brands that align with their values.

The three pillars of sustainable marketing include environmental sustainability, social good, and economic return (see Figure 19.2). You may have heard the term "planet, people, and profits," which describes the three pillars of sustainable marketing. Businesses meet the needs of the marketplace without sacrificing the future viability of the world. Companies are increasingly following an **environmental, social, and governance strategy** and use these **ESG pillars** to guide their work. The topic extends beyond sustainability into doing what's right socially and ethically. Companies report their quantitative and qualitative results in annual disclosures to share the impact of ESG efforts.

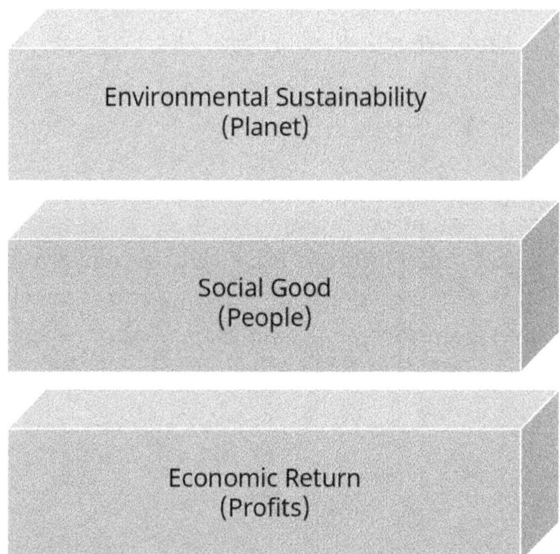

Figure 19.2 Three Pillars of Sustainable Marketing (attribution: Copyright Rice University, OpenStax, under CC BY 4.0 license)

LINK TO LEARNING

ESG

Are you interested in learning more about the elements of ESG? Here are several sources where you can read more:

- Global advisory firm, PwC (https://openstax.org/r/socialandcorporategovernance)
- Finance company, NerdWallet (https://openstax.org/r/esginvesting)
- HubSpot 2022 sustainability report (https://openstax.org/r/hubspotsustainability)
- Accenture (https://openstax.org/r/sustainabilitycreatingvalue)

The **environmental pillar** focuses on reducing a company's impact on the environment. For example, companies may reduce their environmental impact through recycling, reusing, minimizing waste, and increasing energy efficiency. Stonyfield Organic has a commitment to the environmental pillar with its plans to cut carbon emissions by 30 percent by 2030. In addition, it plans to focus on energy conservation, waste reduction, and sustainable packaging and logistics.[12] Additionally, Subaru of Indiana Automotive operates a "green lean" manufacturing facility that is designed as zero landfill. Subaru recycles or composts 98 percent of its manufacturing waste, and the remaining 2 percent is incinerated as waste to fuel.[13]

The **social pillar** considers a company's consumers and employees and creates a more inclusive environment for its community. Much of the work in the social pillar occurs through responsive programs for employees that increase well-being. However, companies can also reach beyond their walls to impact their communities.

LINK TO LEARNING

The Story behind State Bags

There are many examples of companies that work to support their communities. One example is State Bags. State Bags donates a bag filled with school supplies for each bag purchased. It also partners with nonprofits such as Seeds of Peace, Time's Up, and Bottomless Closet to support women and children from underserved communities.[14] You can learn more about State Bags and its work by visiting the company's website (https://openstax.org/r/statebagspages) or following the State Bags Instagram account (https://openstax.org/r/instagramstatebags).

Adobe is another example of a company that works inside and outside its organization to effect social change by partnering with local nonprofits in the communities in which its employees live and work. Adobe has a rich diversity, equity, and inclusion initiative within its organization that empowers diverse voices. For example, Gen Create is a digital space for diverse thinkers and creators to collaborate to change the world for the common good. Finally, Adobe provides access to its software to underserved communities to work toward greater equity regardless of location.

LINK TO LEARNING

Adobe Gen Create

Check out Adobe's Gen Create program (https://openstax.org/r/resourcefornextgeneration), a place for young creators to collaborate and effect change.

The **economic pillar (governance pillar)** of sustainability concerns profitability and business ethics. Businesses cannot be sustainable if they are not profitable, which is a clear key sustainability performance indicator. Companies can demonstrate success in the economic pillar through proper governance structures, risk management, and compliance. Proper governance over voting, legal compliance, and accounting standards shows people that companies are following their obligations. Governance also includes business ethics, anticompetitive practices, and tax transparency. At the end of the day, is the company doing the right thing for its investors and all of its interested parties?

Governance structures can be examined to ensure diversity of leadership that aligns with the company's various interested and influential groups. Fortune and Refinitiv partnered to develop a Measure Up initiative that aims to bring transparency to businesses diversity, equity, and inclusion work of the Fortune 500. The initiative reviewed measures such as policies, employee resource groups, percentage of minorities in board or leadership positions, and salary parity to determine a score for companies. Companies such as Microsoft, Target, and Gap rated highly on the criteria, demonstrating advanced diversity, equity, and inclusion.[15] Amazon publishes its representation statistics sorted by job level to illustrate how it is making progress on creating a more diverse workforce.

LINK TO LEARNING

Measure Up

Learn more about the Measure Up initiative (https://openstax.org/r/partnershipmethodology) to help businesses build fair and inclusive work spaces. In its work, it ranks companies based on their diversity, equity, and inclusion (DEI) disclosure and performance metrics.

Knowledge Check

It's time to check your knowledge on the concepts presented in this section. Refer to the Answer Key at the end of the book for feedback.

1. If a brand develops a diversity, equity, and inclusion initiative, which pillar of sustainability is addressed?
   a. Environmental
   b. Social
   c. Economic
   d. All of the above are correct.

2. How does sustainable marketing differentiate from other types of marketing?
   a. It is more expensive.
   b. It is only for people who care about the environment.
   c. It is a business imperative.
   d. It is rooted in purpose.

19.2 Traditional Marketing versus Sustainable Marketing

Learning Outcomes

By the end of this section, you will be able to:
   LO 1 Explain how the parties in traditional and sustainable marketing are different.
   LO 2 Define the different objectives in traditional and sustainable marketing.

Differences between Traditional and Sustainable Marketing

Traditional marketing takes a customer approach and focuses on product, price, place, and promotion for a target audience. Sustainable marketing takes a "stakeholder approach" and considers customers, shareholders, employees, vendors, interest groups, media, and the general public. These groups are interested in the brand's sustainability agenda, which becomes the focus of the marketing effort.

Costco is an example of a company that takes this kind of approach to its sustainability marketing. Costco describes its sustainability agenda this way: "Sustainability to us is remaining a profitable business while doing the right thing." Costco honors three sustainability principles: "For Costco to thrive, the world needs to thrive. We are committed to doing our part to help. We focus on issues related to our business and where we can contribute to real, results-driven positive impact. We do not have all of the answers, are learning as we go and seek continuous improvement."[16] These principles demonstrate a commitment to all of Costco's interested parties. For example, Costco pays its employees above market rates to honor its commitment to support its employees and communities.

LINK TO LEARNING

Costco Sustainability Commitment

Costco publishes its commitment to sustainability on its website as a way to be fully transparent about its sustainability strategy. The company shares its code of ethics, mission statement, sustainability principles and responsibilities, and development goals. You can read more about its commitment here (https://openstax.org/r/sustainabilityintroduction).

Traditional business strategy indicates that shareholder return is the primary obligation of companies. However, a sustainable business strategy suggests that companies have a **corporate social responsibility (CSR)** to use their platforms to improve the world and not cause harm. Furthermore, an environmental, social, and governance (ESG) strategy holds companies accountable for their sustainability work. An ESG strategy uses an organization's influence to make positive change and develop metrics to show how purpose is measured.

Businesses have always been required to comply with environmental laws, but sustainable companies put the environment in the center, designing for the environment. New Belgium Brewery in Fort Collins, Colorado, is a foremost example of a company designed around the environment. The brand is committed to clean energy to combat climate change. New Belgium Brewery has three principles woven into its business model to keep management accountable for its sustainability goal of becoming carbon neutral by 2030. Those principles are to

- reduce emissions by creating electricity from wastewater, collecting heat while brewing to reuse, and earning LEED certification on its properties;
- work with interest groups to advocate for improved climate policies; and
- improve recycling in the United States through its cofounded glass recycling coalition.[17]

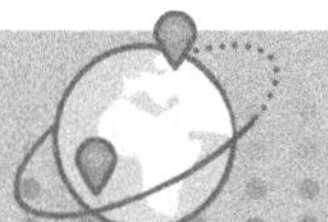

LINK TO LEARNING

New Belgium Brewery Commitment to Climate

Learn more about New Belgium Brewery sustainability strategies by reading about its commitment to climate (https://openstax.org/r/companymissionclimate).

Knowledge Check

It's time to check your knowledge on the concepts presented in this section. Refer to the Answer Key at the end of the book for feedback.

1. Traditional marketing takes a customer approach, while sustainable marketing takes a(n) _______ approach.
   a. shareholder
   b. value
   c. economic
   d. cost-savings

2. In sustainable marketing, companies innovate now and do which of the following for the future?
   a. Earn money
   b. Ensure viability
   c. Save money
   d. Earn profits

19.3 The Benefits of Sustainable Marketing

Learning Outcomes

By the end of this section, you will be able to:
  LO 1 Describe the various benefits of sustainable marketing.
  LO 2 Explain why sustainable marketing is a business imperative.

Purpose-Driven Strategy

A **purpose-driven strategy** is when companies work to make a difference in their community through their decisions and support of environmental programs. There are numerous benefits to developing a purpose-driven business strategy, including enhanced brand recognition, reduced costs, improved effectiveness, easier regulatory compliance, waste minimization, and enhanced return on investment (ROI) (see Figure 19.3).

Harvard Business School Professor Rebecca Henderson indicates that businesses must adopt a shared value orientation. Doing well and doing good are mutually dependent. Companies cannot do good if they are not doing well. Companies with strong ESG programs outperform the market long-term despite the short-term investment.[18]

PepsiCo developed its sustainability program under former CEO Indra Nooyi. Nooyi understood the benefits of purpose to planet, people, and profits. PepsiCo focuses on agriculture, water, packaging, product, climate, and people to create systemic change within PepsiCo and the broader environment. The results of this work are outlined in an annual sustainability metrics report that holds PepsiCo accountable for its purpose. The company earned over $70 billion in net revenue in 2020, illustrating the shared value opportunity.[19]

LINK TO LEARNING

PepsiCo and Its Purpose-Driven Strategy

Read more about PepsiCo and its commitment to sustainability in its 2021 ESG Report (https://openstax.org/r/sustainabilityandesgtopics) and its ESG Performance Metrics report (https://openstax.org/r/sustainabilityandesgtopics2021).

Figure 19.3 Benefits of Sustainable Marketing (attribution: Copyright Rice University, OpenStax, under CC BY 4.0 license)

Enhanced Brand Recognition

Brands that incorporate purpose earn enhanced brand recognition for that work, which can become a competitive advantage and result in higher profitability. Patagonia is a prime example of a company known for its sustainability programs. Its founder, Yvon Chouinard, envisioned the company as a pillar of sustainability and set the stage for other companies to follow. Patagonia sells outdoor wear that is durable and designed around sustainability. The brand will repair its goods to avoid customers purchasing new ones when they reuse them. It also donates 1 percent of annual sales to good causes worldwide. Finally, Patagonia facilitates an Action Works website that connects interested parties with local environmental protection groups to promote activism.[20] These sustainability activities are critical to ensuring that Patagonia is a brand with a purpose.

Reduced Costs

Sustainability practices often carry an up-front investment; however, over time, these costs typically return a cost reduction. A survey by Bain & Company indicates five times revenue growth among all brands scoring highest on sustainability.[21] This is possible because sustainability programs mean reduced materials, recycling programs, and lower use of natural resources, which are all good for the planet and reduce production costs.

For example, Ben & Jerry's stopped using plastic straws and spoons in its stores.[22] This reduction strategy was good for the planet while also decreasing expenses for the business, demonstrating that planet and profits can be mutually beneficial. Founders Ben Cohen and Jerry Greenfield set forth a product, economic, and social mission for the business. In response to the success seen from Ben & Jerry's, the "triple bottom line" mission has been adopted by many organizations that seek to align profit, planet, and people.

Improved Effectiveness

Sustainability practices can improve organization effectiveness. For example, investing in human capital is an area of importance because potential new employees consider purpose, well-being, culture, diversity, equity, and inclusion when deciding where to work. Mastercard is an organization that prioritizes its people, and it sees improved effectiveness as a result. Mastercard saw an average annual profit growth of nearly 19 percent in the 10 years it connected purpose to profits.[23]

The Anya Hindmarch company brought attention to the excessive use of plastic bags in 2007 with its "I Am Not a Plastic Bag" campaign.[24] The campaign sought to replace plastic bags with an eco-friendly alternative that reuses existing materials. Since 2007, companies have followed suit with reusable tote bags that serve as both a sustainability measure and a means of advertising their brands.

LINK TO LEARNING

Anya Hindmarch and Antidote

Anya Hindmarch's "I Am Not a Plastic Bag" campaign was a collaboration with Antidote, a creative agency, that gained loads of press coverage. That publicity contributed to the U.K. decision to charge for plastic bags. Read more about the campaign from the Anya Hindmarch website (https://openstax.org/r/imnotaplasticbag) and Antidote's website (https://openstax.org/r/antidote). When you're finished, take a moment to be inspired by Anya Hindmarch and her recent sustainability fashion product, a collection of biodegradable leather bags (https://openstax.org/r/hindmarchlaunches).

Easier Compliance with Regulators

In addition to returning value to shareholders, companies are also responsible for following international, national, and local laws. A sustainability agenda goes beyond companies' legal obligations and extends to serving the world better. This strategy eases compliance by going above and beyond what is expected by government agencies. For example, the US Environmental Protection Agency (EPA) provides regulatory information by sector to provide businesses with clear regulatory compliance criteria.

LINK TO LEARNING

EPA Regulatory Information

If you're interested in learning more about the EPA's regulatory information and its compliance criteria per industry, check out this regulatory information by business sector (https://openstax.org/r/regulatoryinformation).

Waste Minimization

Environmental measures can reduce waste, creating a healthier planet. Many organizations are focused on waste minimization to demonstrate a commitment to the Earth. For example, McDonald's has set a waste minimization goal of having 100 percent guest packaging derived from renewable, recycled, or certified sources by 2025. This is impactful because single-use plastics are a known source of waste, particularly in the oceans where plastic outnumbers fish in some regions.[25]

Enhanced Return on Investment

As with any business strategy, goals and metrics are also important with a sustainability strategy. Organizations expect a return on investment when resources are committed, even with sustainability work. Organizations can look at several factors to determine the financial return on sustainability efforts. They will evaluate the increased interest from investors, changes in brand value, and revenue. Additionally, organizations can consider the well-being of their employees, their impact on the planet, and their efforts to improve the world as another key measure of success (see Figure 19.4).

Figure 19.4 Factors to Consider in Evaluating ROI with Sustainability Strategies (attribution: Copyright Rice University, OpenStax, under CC BY 4.0 license)

Knowledge Check

It's time to check your knowledge on the concepts presented in this section. Refer to the Answer Key at the end of the book for feedback.

1. Which of the following is the sustainability strategy benefit when a company becomes known for its

sustainability efforts and it becomes a competitive advantage?
a. Increased brand recognition
b. Reduced costs
c. Waste minimization
d. Enhanced return on investment

2. Which benefit of sustainability occurs when brands show their shareholders an economic return on sustainability programs?
a. Increased brand recognition
b. Reduced costs
c. Waste minimization
d. Enhanced return on investment

19.4 Sustainable Marketing Principles

Learning Outcomes

By the end of this section, you will be able to:

LO 1 List the principles of sustainable marketing.
LO 2 Explain how these principles are put into practice.

Consumer-Oriented Marketing

Consumer-oriented marketing is a solution focused on a customer's need. The product is designed to solve a problem, distributed for convenience, and promoted as a solution to the consumer's needs. A consumer-oriented marketing strategy requires extensive marketing research to understand the consumer's needs. Organizations then must design the four Ps around those needs. Finally, a consumer-oriented marketing strategy requires customer service and feedback to ensure that consumer needs are met. Zappos is known for having a customer-oriented marketing strategy. With its strategy, it focuses heavily on customer service and has assembled an extensive team that solves any issue a consumer may face with an order.

LINK TO LEARNING

Consumer-Oriented Marketing

Numerous companies are well-known for their consumer-oriented marketing approaches. Read this succinct summary on what Starbucks, Patagonia, Zappos, Amazon, and Nordstrom are specifically doing to understand their customer's journey and build customer loyalty (https://openstax.org/r/marketingevolution).

For a deeper look into Zappos' strategy, read this article from Entrepreneur (https://openstax.org/r/entrepreneur) that outlines nine steps to Zappos' exceptional service.

Customer-Value Marketing

Customer-value marketing seeks to provide the customer with maximum utility compared to competitors. Customers make a value exchange when purchasing a product, so they naturally ask themselves whether the cost is worth the value of the transaction. This does not mean that all customer-value products and services are inexpensive. In fact, the high price of a product might be an intentional choice by the company to attract a specific target audience. For example, Tiffany & Co. has created a luxury brand around its jewelry's value to customers.

Innovative Marketing

Innovative marketing uses media as a method for capturing shoppers' attention and converting them into customers. The ever-changing digital landscape offers myriad possibilities to engage an audience in an innovative marketing strategy. For example, Shedd Aquarium in Chicago took its penguins on a field trip to meet their aquatic roommates for a virtual event in 2020. During the field trip, the Aquarium broadcasted on social media and delighted animal lovers worldwide while promoting the aquarium.

Mission Marketing

Mission-driven marketing aligns purpose and brand. With mission-driven marketing, a company uses its core mission and purpose as the focus of its marketing strategies.

A mission-driven organization can be a for-profit or nonprofit, governmental or nongovernmental, public or private, or religious entity.

Charity: Water is an outstanding example of a mission-driven organization that uses marketing to inspire its audience. Its mission is to bring clean water to communities that face a clean water crisis. The founder, Scott Harrison, has his own story that inspires the mission, and storytelling is integral to implementing charity: water's marketing strategy.

LINK TO LEARNING

Charity: Water

Charity: water has raised more than $640 million and funded more than 91,000 water projects in 29 countries. Watch this video about Scott Harrison's journey and witness his storytelling abilities as he shares his personal experience around the impact of dirty water.

Click to view content (https://openstax.org/books/principles-marketing/pages/19-4-sustainable-marketing-principles)

Societal Marketing

Societal marketing is most akin to the sustainability strategies discussed in this chapter. A societal marketing strategy fulfills social responsibility obligations while satisfying customer needs. Athleta, a Gap company, sells premium-priced performance apparel to female athletes. Its product is designed for a target audience of women in motion. Athleta launched a *Power of She* campaign to celebrate the diversity of women and serve as a societal marketing effort. Additionally, approximately 70 percent of Athleta's apparel is manufactured from recycled and sustainable materials.[26]

Knowledge Check

It's time to check your knowledge on the concepts presented in this section. Refer to the Answer Key at the end of the book for feedback.

1. ________ uses media as the lead for awareness building.
   a. Consumer-oriented marketing
   b. Customer-value marketing
   c. Innovative marketing
   d. Mission marketing

2. Which of the following puts a purpose at the center of marketing and is implemented most often using storytelling?

a. Consumer-oriented marketing
b. Customer-value marketing
c. Innovative marketing
d. Mission marketing

19.5 | Purpose-Driven Marketing

Learning Outcomes

By the end of this section, you will be able to:
LO 1 Understand issues related to purpose-driven marketing.
LO 2 Articulate best practices in purpose-driven marketing.

Brand Purpose

Brands satisfy many people, from employees to investors, to customers, to suppliers, and to the communities that they serve. These parties ask for more than a good product at a fair price. They ask for a brand to stand for something more than the product or service being offered. Brand purpose is developed deep in the DNA of an organization and should be infused in everything the brand says and does.

Accenture conducted a global survey of 30,000 consumers about brand purpose. It found that 62 percent of customers want companies to take a stand on issues such as sustainability, transparency, or fair working conditions. Furthermore, the brand purpose should align closely with the consumer's values to create an optimal purchase choice. Consumers are willing to switch brands if their values do not align.[27]

The challenge runs deep. People expect brands to connect to a deep purpose; however, they are intolerant of brands who do so inauthentically. Walmart is an example of a company that received backlash from customers because of what they felt was not authentic. In May 2022, Walmart launched an ice cream flavor for the upcoming Juneteenth holiday. Consumers felt that Walmart was trying to sell a product rather than honor an important day in history.[28] This example demonstrates the importance of holding a purpose at the center of the brand instead of using it as a means of selling a product.

Bombas knows how to build purpose into its DNA. The innovative, purpose-driven brand built its business on donating socks and underwear to homeless shelters with each purchase. As of this writing, Bombas has donated over 5 million items with the help of 3,500 impact partners in every state.[29] Its message is simple: you buy socks, they give socks. Purpose is at the heart of Bombas's organizational mission, and it will share it with anyone who will listen.

LINK TO LEARNING

More about Walmart and Bombas

There are numerous articles about Walmart and the Juneteenth backlash. Here are two worth reading so you can gain better insight into the customer's perspective:

- CNN, *Walmart Apologizes for Selling Juneteenth Ice Cream* (https://openstax.org/r/walmartjuneteenth)
- New York Daily News, *Walmart's Juneteenth Ice Cream Leaves a Bad Aftertaste* (https://openstax.org/r/icecreamcontroversy)

CNN Business interviewed the founders of Bombas to learn more about their work to provide homeless people with socks. Check out this video about how Bombas integrates purpose and business (https://openstax.org/r/bombassocksfresh).

Brands That Put Purpose First

The brands that put purpose at the center create ways for their customers to experience purpose. Dove was a pioneer in brand purpose when it developed its Campaign for Real Beauty. Marketing research uncovered that young girls were impacted by media's standards of beauty. Dove took this insight and decided to tackle a systemic societal problem. This multi-decade campaign led to a celebration of all types of beauty, redefining how we think of women and impacting self-esteem. Customers could experience purpose because the Campaign for Real Beauty was all about them. The Campaign for Real Beauty was more than just advertising; it reflected who Dove wanted to be in the world.[30]

LINK TO LEARNING

Dove's Campaign for Real Beauty

Dove's campaign included several ads and commercials. Seeing examples of how companies focus on purpose will help your creativity in future marketing jobs. Explore the commercials created by Dove:

- Real Beauty Sketches, a commercial that artistically compares the gap between self-perception with perception from others
  Click to view content (https://openstax.org/books/principles-marketing/pages/19-5-purpose-driven-marketing)
- Anti-photoshopping film *Evolution*, a very popular and viral commercial of a behind-the-scenes look at what happens with beauty ads
  Click to view content (https://openstax.org/books/principles-marketing/pages/19-5-purpose-driven-marketing)
- Reverse Selfie, a commercial about the impact of social media on young girls' self-esteem
  Click to view content (https://openstax.org/books/principles-marketing/pages/19-5-purpose-driven-marketing)

Why was this campaign so successful? There are numerous articles and opinion pieces that provide insight into its success. Read these two out for a sampling:

- Global Brands, *The Success of Dove's Real Beauty Campaign* (https://openstax.org/r/thesuccessofdoves)
- Digital Marketing Institute, *Dove: A Spotless Approach to Digital Marketing* (https://openstax.org/r/doveaspotless)

Purpose-driven brands speak up, even when it's difficult or costly to do so. If you read the news, you may see brands taking a stand on social issues. Russia's war on Ukraine in 2022 urged several American companies to cease operations in Russia. It can be costly to cease operations in a country as large and populous as Russia, but companies such as Starbucks and McDonald's decided that their purpose was more important than their profits in this case.

Brands with purpose are intentional about inclusion. While exclusivity can be an effective marketing tactic for luxury brands, purpose-driven brands know that inclusivity is paramount. Procter & Gamble is known as a company that weaves inclusion into the fabric of its organization, from its hiring practices to the use of its paid media.

LINK TO LEARNING

Procter & Gamble Prioritizes People

Visit Procter & Gamble's (P&G) "Explore Our Stories" web page (https://openstax.org/r/equalityandinclusion) to view how the company prioritizes inclusion and creates opportunities for all people. Read three to five stories and consider what P&G is saying about who and what it values. Also, look at the partners that P&G collaborates with to create change in its communities.

Knowledge Check

It's time to check your knowledge on the concepts presented in this section. Refer to the Answer Key at the end of the book for feedback.

1. Which of the following concepts are related to purpose-driven marketing?
   a. Transparency
   b. Sustainability
   c. Fair working conditions
   d. All of the above are correct.

2. Which of the following is a best practice of purpose-driven brands?
   a. Standing up for what's right
   b. Good advertising
   c. Telling everyone about their purpose
   d. Being profitable

Chapter Summary

Sustainable marketing is an effort by companies to run their business to serve the customers of today while preserving the world for the customers of tomorrow. Companies are increasingly following an ESG, or environmental, social, governance, structure to bring transparency to their sustainability efforts. Sustainable marketing uses the main drivers of traditional marketing such as customer satisfaction, but it considers a broader set of impacted groups. There are myriad benefits to sustainable marketing as it relates to brand equity, financial measures, and government compliance. Purpose-driven brands stand for something more than what they sell, and they build their organization around that stated purpose.

Key Terms

consumer-oriented marketing   marketing strategies focused on customer needs and solving their problems

corporate social responsibility (CSR)   sustainable business strategy where companies use their platform to do good, improve the world, and be socially accountable to their customers and other interested parties

customer-value marketing   marketing strategies in which a company works to provide the customer with maximum value compared to competitors

economic pillar (governance pillar)   the sustainability pillar that concerns profitability and business ethics

environmental pillar   the sustainability pillar that focuses on reducing a company's impact on the environment

environmental, social, and governance strategy   a strategy that holds companies accountable for a sustainability strategy

ESG pillars   the three pillars of environmental, social, and governance that guide corporate sustainability work

innovative marketing   marketing strategies that use media as the method for capturing prospects' attention and converting them into customers

mission-driven marketing   marketing strategies that align purpose and brand by using the corporate core mission and purpose as their focus

purpose-driven strategy   strategy in which companies work to make a difference in their communities through their decisions and support of environmental programs

social pillar   the sustainability pillar that focuses on creating an inclusive environment for the community

societal marketing   a marketing strategy focused on fulfilling social responsibility obligations while also satisfying customer needs

sustainable marketing   a marketing strategy that infuses purpose into socially conscious products and services

Applied Marketing Knowledge: Discussion Questions

1. If we agree with the notion that products and services of today should not harm people of tomorrow, how would you redesign your favorite snack food to be more sustainable?

2. The three pillars of sustainability are environmental sustainability, social good, and economic return. Why are these three pillars intertwined? What would happen if you had one without the other two?

3. Research New Belgium Brewery. How do the company's sustainability practices benefit the environment, communities, and its financial bottom line?

4. Waste minimization is a key sustainability strategy. Take a look in your kitchen cabinets and describe the products that could be made with less waste.

5. Review the trailer for "This is a True Story" on Charity: Water's website (https://openstax.org/r/charitywaterorg). How has the nonprofit gamified its mission?

Critical Thinking Exercises

1. Design a sustainability campaign. Select a product or service that is not currently sustainable and redesign it to be sustainable. Consider how you would change the form, function, packaging, distribution, and/or target audience.

2. Evaluate a purpose-driven brand. Review the website for the footwear company Allbirds (https://openstax.org/r/allbirdssustainablepractices). Describe how sustainability is at the heart of its mission as a company.

3. Review the Edelman Trust Barometer (https://openstax.org/r/2022trustbarometer). What does this research tell you about the importance of brand trust? Discuss the brands you trust and describe the actions that they take to invoke that trust.

Building Your Personal Brand

A workplace study by Blue Beyond Consulting shows that 8 in 10 employees say that it's important that their employer's values align with their values. Furthermore, more than 75 percent of respondents indicated that they expect their employer and business to be a force for good.[31]

Consider what you value and how you would like your future employer to honor those values. Research a few organizations to find an employer that closely aligns with your values. Write about how you might integrate your personal purpose with that of your employer to make the change that you wish to see in the world.

References

1. "Shaping the Sustainable Organization," Accenture, accessed September 7, 2022, https://www.accenture.com/us-en/insights/sustainability/sustainable-organization.

2. Alexandra Spiliakos, "What Does 'Sustainability' Mean in Business?," *Business Insights* (blog), Harvard Business School Online, October 10, 2018, https://online.hbs.edu/blog/post/what-is-sustainability-in-business.

3. Accenture, "Shaping."

4. Lauren Foster, "Barron's 100 Most Sustainable Companies," *Barron's*, February 11, 2022, https://www.barrons.com/articles/most-sustainable-companies-51644564600.

5. Ibid.

6. Ibid.

7. Williams-Sonoma Inc., *Good by Design: Impact Report 2021*, July 2022, https://sustainability.williams-sonomainc.com/wp-content/uploads/2022/07/WSI-2021-Impact-Report.pdf.

8. Ibid.

9. Diana Olick, "These Are the 10 Greenest Large Companies of 2022, according to Just Capital," CNBC, April 22, 2022, https://www.cnbc.com/2022/04/22/10-greenest-large-companies-of-2022-according-to-just-capital.html.

10. Karl Haller, Jim Lee, and Jane Cheung, "Meet the 2020 Consumers Driving Change," Research Insights, June 2020, https://www.ibm.com/downloads/cas/EXK4XKX8#:~:text=Nearly%206%20in%2010%20consumers,this%20jumps%20to%2077%20percent.

11. Adanma Onuoha, "What Is Sustainable Marketing?" Network for Business Sustainability, October 12, 2021, https://nbs.net/articles/what-is-sustainable-marketing/.

12. Black Morgan, "101 Companies Committed to Reducing Their Carbon Footprint," *Forbes*, August 26, 2019, https://www.forbes.com/sites/blakemorgan/2019/08/26/101-companies-committed-to-reducing-their-carbon-footprint/?sh=6c30ded6260b.

13. Roben Farzad, "Subaru of Indiana: America's Greenest Carmaker," *Business Week*, June 7, 2011, https://www.nbcnews.com/id/wbna43269332.

14. Home page, State Bags, accessed March 10, 2022, https://statebags.com/?source=pepperjam&publisherId=21181&clickId=3897953715.

15. "Measure Up Initiative: Fortune and Refinitiv Partnership (Methodology)," Fortune, accessed March 20, 2022,

https://fortune.com/franchise-list-page/measure-up-initiative-fortune-refinitiv-partnership-methodology/.

16. "Costco Wholesale Corporation Sustainability Commitment," Costco, accessed December 28, 2021, https://www.costco.com/sustainability-introduction.html?&reloaded=true.

17. "Climate: Our Commitments," New Belgium Brewing, accessed December 6, 2021, https://www.newbelgium.com/company/mission/climate/.

18. Natalie Chladek, "Why You Need Sustainability in Your Business Strategy," *Business Insights* (blog), November 6, 2019, https://online.hbs.edu/blog/post/business-sustainability-strategies.

19. PepsiCo, "2021 ESG Summary Overview," June 28, 2022, https://www.pepsico.com/docs/default-source/sustainability-and-esg-topics/2021-esg-summary/pep_csr21_summary_v5a.pdf?sfvrsn=c61afffa_0.

20. "Environmental & Social Footprint," Patagonia, accessed April 29, 2022, https://www.patagonia.com/our-footprint/.

21. Jenny Davis-Peccoud and Magali Deryckere, "How Sustainable Brands Add Value," Bain & Company, October 4, 2021, https://www.bain.com/insights/how-sustainable-brands-add-value-snap-chart/.

22. "Sustainable Packaging," Ben & Jerry's, accessed December 6, 2021, https://www.benjerry.com/values/how-we-do-business/sustainable-packaging.

23. "Resources to Change the Working World," World at Work, accessed December 6, 2021, https://worldatwork.org/workspan/articles/case-study-advancing-purpose-driven-total-rewards-at-mastercard.

24. "I'm Not a Plastic Bag," Anya Hindmarch, accessed April 29, 2022, https://us.anyahindmarch.com/pages/im-not-a-plastic-bag.

25. Sara Napolitano Matz, "Companies Working to Reduce Single-Use Plastics," U.S. Chamber of Commerce Foundation, accessed January 3, 2019, https://www.uschamberfoundation.org/blog/post/companies-working-reduce-single-use-plastics.

26. Gap, Inc., "Global Sustainability Report," 2020, https://www.gapinc.com/CMSPages/GetAzureFile.aspx?path=~\gapcorporatesite\media\images\values\sustainability\documents\gap-inc-2019-report_1.pdf&hash=62614e2d67a5330d0baca5f0bacc53f4934d652f64d85a89728509b20c7e7b64.

27. Rachel Barton, "From Me to We: The Rise of the Purpose-Led Brand," Accenture Strategy Research Report, December 5, 2018. https://www.accenture.com/us-en/insights/strategy/brand-purpose.

28. Jordan Valinsky, "Walmart Apologizes for Selling Juneteenth Ice Cream," CNN Business, updated May 24, 2022, https://www.cnn.com/2022/05/24/business-food/walmart-juneteenth-ice-cream/index.html.

29. Home page, Bombas, accessed June 7, 2022, http://www.bombas.com/.

30. "Dove Campaigns," Dove, accessed June 7, 2022, https://www.dove.com/us/en/stories/campaigns.html.

31. Beyond Blue Consulting, "'The Great Resignation': A Majority of Employees Would Quit Their Job - And Only 1 in 4 Workers Would Accept One - If Company Values Do Not Align with Personal Values." Cision PR Newswire, October 20, 2021, https://www.prnewswire.com/news-releases/the-great-resignation-a-majority-of-employees-would-quit-their-job-and-only-1-in-4-workers-would-accept-one-if-company-values-do-not-align-with-personal-values-301404919.html.

Answer Key

Chapter 1

1.1 Knowledge Check

1. c. Place utility addresses convenience in terms of where a consumer can purchase your company's product.
2. b. Marketing is a complex activity and includes creating, communicating, delivering, and exchanging offerings that have value for customers, clients, partners, and society at large.
3. a. Employees are internal parties.
4. a. Customer equity is the total potential profits a company earns from its current and potential customers.
5. d. The aim of successful customer relationship management is to produce high customer equity.

1.2 Knowledge Check

1. d. The 4Ps of marketing are product, price, place, and promotion.
2. b. Price is the amount consumers pay for a product or service.
3. c. Place—sometimes known as distribution—involves focusing on how and where to deliver the product to consumers most likely to buy it.
4. d. Place— sometimes known as distribution—involves focusing on how and where to deliver the product to consumers most likely to buy it.
5. d. In the realm of promotion advertising, direct mail, social media communications, trade shows, events, coupons, and media choices are among the many aspects considered.

1.3 Knowledge Check

1. a. Materials considers the availability of the resources needed for product. It is the element that looks at the supply.
2. b. Market intermediaries are retailers, wholesalers, and others in the distribution channel who help deliver products to the end user.
3. a. The competition has to be assessed to see how well and to what degree the need you hope to fulfill is currently being addressed.
4. b. The technological domain is responsible for emerging production technologies as well as the creation of new innovations that make possible new products.
5. d. The social and cultural domain is concern with such things as social trends, attitudes, and opinions.

1.4 Knowledge Check

1. a. The product concept is concerned most with the quality of the product a company intends to sell.
2. c. The societal marketing concept involves meeting consumers' and businesses' current needs while simultaneously being aware of the environmental impact of marketing decisions on future generations' ability to meet their needs.
3. c. The goal of the selling concept was simple: beat the competition. Customer needs and satisfaction took a back seat to beating the competition.
4. a. This order accurately represents the evolution of marketing.
5. b. During the societal era, it was recognized that society as a whole, had to be considered in all activities.

1.5 Knowledge Check

1. d. A delight need is an added value you may get from the seller without prior expectation or request for the same.
2. c. The customer is the individual or business that purchases the product or service. The consumer is the user of the product or service.
3. d. The value that a product promises to deliver is called the value proposition.
4. a. The benefit(s) to the customer or consumer relative to the cost is known as value.

5. c. The exchange process is designed to allow for the transaction to occur without either party feeling like the other has benefitted at its own cost.

1.6 Knowledge Check

1. d. All the other choices are ways of achieving customer relationship management. Offering the lowest price of all companies on the market is not.
2. b. Customer relationship management (CRM) is the means through which companies track, manage, and analyze customer interactions.
3. b. Customer loyalty is a customer's willingness to repeatedly return to a company to conduct business.
4. d. Collaborative CRM is sharing customer data with outside companies. It can give the company a fuller perspective on customers by collaborating with other companies in order to obtain data to which it would not otherwise have access.
5. a. A customer loyalty program offers rewards, discounts, and other special incentives designed to attract and retain customers.

Chapter 2

2.1 Knowledge Check

1. b. The mission statement sums up in a few sentences what the company does, who it serves, and what differentiates it from its competitors.
2. c. Corporate-level strategy covers the entire business in a complex organization in which there are multiple businesses, divisions, or operating units.
3. d. A business's overall strategy encompasses the plans, actions, objectives, and goals that outline how the business will compete in its chosen markets given its portfolio of products or services.
4. b. A gap analysis is an internal analysis of a company or business unit used to identify deficiencies that may hinder its abilities to meet its goals.
5. d. Goals should be realistic and have a reasonable chance of being met.

2.2 Knowledge Check

1. a. The fact that the health club is the only facility in the area to offer water aerobics classes would be categorized as a strength in terms of a SWOT analysis.
2. a. The BCG matrix captures the market share and market growth of products in a portfolio of offerings.
3. c. A cash cow has high market share in a low-growth industry.
4. c. Opportunities are openings for something positive to happen if you can capitalize on them.
5. d. A company that pursues a product development strategy introduces new (and/or improved) products into the market to replace existing ones in order to improve its competitive position and sales.

2.3 Knowledge Check

1. d. In this paragraph of the executive summary, you would describe the current marketplace and industry sectors in which you sell your products and/or services, the trends affecting and influencing them, and the innovations currently taking place within the market.
2. c. In a SWOT analysis, strengths and weaknesses are factors that are internal to the organization.
3. c. A perceptual map suggests where your product or service stands in relation to the competition.
4. b. A SWOT analysis identifies key internal influences (strengths and weaknesses) and external influences (threats and opportunities).
5. d. Within the current marketing situation of your marketing plan, you should include a competitive analysis and a discussion of how competitors fare in the marketplace.

2.4 Knowledge Check

1. d. KPIs consist of a very focused selection of core variables that allow us to monitor the health/

performance of the organization. We need enough indicators to evaluate the various critical aspects of the organization. We need to avoid having so many that the clutter obscures symptoms that should be highlighted.

2. a. We should always monitor KPIs on a continuous basis. Some information is only available periodically when financials are produced and production statistics are rolled up. The use of real-time dashboards can make it possible to monitor KPIs in real time. The faster we can get the data, the faster we can make adjustments (when required).

3. a. To calculate the CSAT score, take the total number of satisfied customers and divide that by the total number of responses. Then multiply that number by 100 to obtain the percentage. In this scenario, you add 500 and 300 to get 800. Then divide that by 1,825 to get .438. Multiple that by 100 for 44%.

4. d. A single data point in isolation tells us very little. However, we can compare the data point to other data points (for example, historical results, forecasts, operating tolerances, or industry averages) to judge our effectiveness.

5. d. We discussed the concept of lifetime customer value (LCV) in the text. Customer acquisition can be very expensive, especially with a missionary sell (e.g., convincing a customer that they have a need for an unknown product or service). Repeat purchases may not require any additional promotional expense. Happy customers also serve as brand ambassadors that spread the word about a company's products/services. Negative reviews from brand ambassadors can be extremely damaging—we want to uncover any problems right away.

Chapter 3

3.1 Knowledge Check

1. c. Complex buying behavior involves high involvement in the buying decision and the perception of significant differences between brands.

2. b. Marketing stimuli are those generated by the marketer and are comprised of the 4Ps of marketing—product, promotion, price, and place.

3. d. Purchase timing is the outcome of the thinking that takes place in the buyer's black box. Samantha is stimulated to buy the mattress during the holiday weekend in order to take advantage of the sale.

4. b. Habitual buying behavior has low involvement in the purchase decision and doesn't perceive much brand differentiation. If your regular brand isn't available or another brand is on sale, you'll probably buy the other brand.

5. c. Consumer buying behavior encompasses the actions you take before buying a product or service.

3.2 Knowledge Check

1. c. Situational factors influencing consumers are external factors that affect how consumers encounter and interact with a product, forming their opinions at that moment in time. Environmental factors such as aroma, lighting, music, and noise can either encourage or discourage the purchase of a product.

2. a. Culture refers to the values, ideas, and attitudes that are learned and shared among the members of a group.

3. b. The safety and security level of Maslow's hierarchy of needs reflects the need to be safe from physical and psychological harm.

4. d. Selective distortion is the tendency of people to interpret information in a way that fits their preconceived notions.

5. b. The behavioral intention aspect of an attitude is what you as a consumer plan to do—buy the brand or not buy the brand.

3.3 Knowledge Check

1. c. They are evaluating the "bundle of attributes" of each venue.

2. a. Ra'Shana has detected a difference between her actual state (not having a functional car) and her

desired state (having a car that runs).

3. c. Having identified that he needs a new laptop, Jason is searching for more information about different laptops and their capabilities.
4. b. Heuristics are types of preexisting value judgments that are used when people make purchase decisions.
5. c. It appears that Nathan and his husband have already done an information search and are now evaluating their new car alternatives.

Chapter 4

4.1 Knowledge Check

1. c. Derived demand is a market demand for a good or service that results from a demand for a related good or service.
2. a. A B2B (or "business-to-business") transaction is one that is conducted between one business and another.
3. c. B2B purchasing is more likely to involve complex negotiations concerning price, delivery schedules, technical specifications, etc., so personal selling plays a vital role.
4. c. The B2B market is more geographically concentrated in areas based on cost, access, and availability of resources.
5. d. DaVonte's purchase of the lumber in connection with his business is a B2B transaction; the purchase of batteries for the smoke detector in his house is a B2C transaction.

4.2 Knowledge Check

1. c. Government markets make up the largest single business and organizational market in the United States.
2. a. A straight rebuy is making a routine purchase of a standard product or products with no modifications from a familiar supplier.
3. c. In a modified rebuy, the purchaser is buying goods that have been purchased previously but changes either the supplier or certain elements of the previous order.
4. c. The initiator is the individual within the buying center who first suggests the idea of purchasing a new product or service.
5. d. Buyers are those who have authority within the organization to select suppliers and negotiate and arrange the purchase terms.

4.3 Knowledge Check

1. c. The goals and objectives act as a major element as to what the business purchases.
2. a. Legal factors include laws, rules, and regulations with which a business or individual must comply.
3. d. Conditional factors include the present financial condition of the organization, as well as product/service availability.
4. b. Economic factors include the level of primary demand, the economic outlook, and the cost of money (i.e., interest rates).
5. d. The availability of the product or service plays a significant role in the buying decision, and availability is a conditional factor.

4.4 Knowledge Check

1. c. The purpose of a product specification is to provide a description and statement of the requirements of a product, the components of a product, the capability or performance of a product, and/or the service or work to be performed to create a product.
2. d. Stage 5 of the B2B buying process is proposal solicitation, in which qualified vendors are asked to submit proposals.

3. b. In Stage 2: Need description, the buying center will work to put some parameters around what needs to be purchased and develop a bill of materials.
4. d. In Stage 7: Order-routine specification, the B2B buyer negotiates the order, listing the technical specifications, the quantity needed, the expected time of delivery, etc.
5. a. Similar to consumer buying, the first stage in the B2B buying decision process occurs when someone identifies a problem that can be resolved through a purchase.

Chapter 5

5.1 Knowledge Check

1. c. Starbucks researches the culture of the countries in which it operates so that beverages appeal to local tastes.
2. a. Psychographic segmentation divides consumers into different groups based on internal characteristics like personality, values, and beliefs.
3. c. Demographic segmentation groups consumers by focusing on traits such as age, gender, income, etc.
4. c. Garnier has segmented the market based upon the benefits sought by the consumer.
5. d. Just like our in-text example of Mirror, Peloton speaks to the personality of people who want to work out but can't find the time to go to the gym.

5.2 Knowledge Check

1. c. Firmographics segments customers based on sets of characteristics such as industry, location, size, legal structure, and performance.
2. a. Technographic segmentation is based on the various hardware and software used by B2B customers.
3. c. Value-based segmentation (sometimes called tiering or profitability segmentation) groups customers according to the potential value they may bring to a business.
4. c. Firmographics segments customers based on sets of characteristics such as industry, location, size, legal structure, and performance.
5. d. Needs-based segmentation is based on the premise that a marketer should focus their limited resources on those customers that need the product and have the ability to purchase it.

5.3 Knowledge Check

1. b. Societies with a high degree of uncertainty avoidance compensate for this uncertainty by establishing rules, policies, and procedures, whereas societies with low uncertainty avoidance more readily accept change.
2. a. Infrastructure is the basic physical systems of a nation, such as roads, sewage treatment, communication, water treatment, etc.
3. d. In countries with a high masculinity ranking, men are intended to lead; women are supposed to follow.
4. c. Economic factors consider things like inflation, per capita income, unemployment, etc.
5. b. Masculinity/femininity assesses "masculine" values (such as achievement, ambition, and acquisition) versus "feminine" values like quality of life and service to others.

5.4 Knowledge Check

1. d. A market segment should be measurable—that is, you should be able to accurately determine the size of the market segment in terms of sales value or number of customers so you can decide whether, how, and to what extent you should focus your efforts on that segment.
2. c. A market segment should be substantial because it's inefficient to waste resources to market the product or service to a segment too small to justify a company's time.
3. a. Accessibility refers to the ability to reach customers in the chosen segment at an affordable cost, given the strengths and abilities of your marketing department.
4. d. Accessibility refers to the ability to reach customers in the chosen segment at an affordable cost, given

the strengths and abilities of your marketing department.

5. c. A measurable market segment means that you can accurately determine the size of the segment in terms of either sales volume or number of customers.

5.5 Knowledge Check

1. c. Undifferentiated marketing treats all buyers or potential buyers as a homogenous group and creates one message for an entire audience.
2. a. A buyer persona is a semi-fictional representation of your ideal customer based on market research and real data about your existing customers.
3. c. Concentrated marketing (or niche marketing) is a subset of a market on which a particular product or service is focused. In Lefty's case, it is focusing on left-handed people.
4. c. A differentiated marketing strategy focuses on the differences between segments and designs a specific marketing mix for each segment.
5. d. A niche market (or concentrated marketing) channels all marketing actions toward one well-defined segment of the market. In this case, the subset is people over the age of 55 who are in the market for an active adult lifestyle.

5.6 Knowledge Check

1. c. A positioning statement defines where your offering fits in the marketplace and why it is better than competitors' offerings.
2. a. The STP process is an acronym for segmentation, targeting, and positioning.
3. b. Differentiated positioning is based on the differentiating characteristics or qualities that make your product/service/brand better than those of your competitors.
4. c. Determinant attributes are those attributes or factors that a customer uses in making their purchase decision.
5. d. A perceptual map is a visual diagram that shows how the average target market consumer perceives your product versus those of your competitors.

Chapter 6

6.1 Knowledge Check

1. d. Marketing research is the process of collecting information from a variety of sources in order to make a good managerial decision.
2. b. A marketing information system is a collection of data that an organization uses to make marketing decisions.
3. b. Individuals uploading personal data into social media is part of the volume, velocity, and variety of data that makes up big data.
4. a. Although marketing research is helpful in providing the data necessary for successful business ventures, there is no guarantee that it will cause customer satisfaction.
5. c. Although a competitor's information is interesting, your company would not have access to it, and therefore it would not be considered marketing research.

6.2 Knowledge Check

1. c. A response to a customer service survey by a customer would be external information.
2. a. Of the available answers, pricing of the competition would be a good source of information to have before setting Xin's price.
3. d. A marketing information system is not a source of information—it is where the information is stored within a business.
4. d. A competitor's website is an opportunity to learn more about the company and its resources, products, promotional plans, and pricing.

5. b. Internal data is data that already exists within a company's database. Internal data includes sales records, product research, pricing comparisons, and other data compiled previously.

6.3 Knowledge Check

1. d. Deciding who to include in the research study is part of designing the sample.
2. a. A mailed survey can be sent to all households easily through a postal service.
3. c. The collection of data includes both primary (focus group and survey data) and secondary (journal articles and syndicated data).
4. d. A frequency analysis shows how many people reported each answer on a survey.
5. a. A cross tabulation shows the relationship of two different variables, so the researcher can see if there is correlation between the two.

Chapter 7

7.1 Knowledge Check

1. a. Global market opportunities refer to the favorable conditions that allow companies to choose to expand globally.
2. c. Cultural barriers are a hindrance to international trade.
3. a. Cultural sensitivity involves a person's ability to be aware of and appreciate cultural differences.
4. d. This advice to Ashia could not only be offensive to her dinner guest but would also cause poor business relationships.
5. b. Business politics vary greatly across cultures. Businesspeople must decide how far they are willing to adapt to the local expectations.

7.2 Knowledge Check

1. a. An exchange rate is the rate at which one country's currency can be exchanged for that of another country
2. c. As stability increases in a country, the economy often improves.
3. a. Stereotypes are assumptions or generalizations made about an entire group of people.
4. d. An embargo is a complete halt of trading with a specific country or of a specific good.
5. b. The USMCA is a trade bloc agreement between the United States, Mexico, and Canada.

7.3 Knowledge Check

1. a. McDonald's is a franchise.
2. c. Exporting is the easiest way in which to begin an international business.
3. a. Licensing is an agreement whereby one company can legally use the copyrighted material of another for a royalty fee.
4. d. A joint venture is a business arrangement whereby two or more companies create a single enterprise or project.
5. b. An international firm has centralized decision-making, meaning decisions are made in the home country headquarters.

7.4 Knowledge Check

1. a. A standardized strategy employs the same strategy for every market.
2. c. The degree to which a promotion strategy should change depends on the market.
3. a. "Real Magic" is Coca-Cola's slogan in New Zealand.
4. d. The whole channel refers to all distribution channel members, including manufacturers, retailers, transportation, and wholesalers.
5. b. Singapore has the highest automobile prices due the country's small size and limited infrastructure.

Chapter 8

8.1 Knowledge Check

1. a. Choosing between standardization and adaptation strategies includes balancing internal capabilities like operations, sales, and customer service with external forces like competition and consumer demographic changes.
2. d. Constrained standards do not increase flexibility. Constraints, instead, limit options for companies and consumers.
3. d. A marketing adaptation strategy involves adjusting a company's efforts, as well as its marketing mix, to increase its appeal and respond to consumers' specific needs, tastes, or expectations. This must be done according to the company's abilities and resources.
4. c. Adaptation strategies can increase production costs instead of reducing them.
5. b. Increasing a company's customer base is a benefit associated with diversity marketing as an adaptation strategy.

8.2 Knowledge Check

1. d. Diversity marketing includes identifying different subsegments of consumers that share cultural and sociodemographic characteristics and creating advertisements to connect with them.
2. a. Diversity marketing is important because today's marketplace is changing dramatically everywhere.
3. c. For companies to be successful in any market, the focus of diversity marketing should be consumer centric. This means putting targeted customers first regarding any decisions about a company's goods, services, or experiences to create satisfaction and strengthen loyalty.
4. d. Diversity in market research is a good idea because it can help companies win over people from different segments of the population by providing better cultural and social information. This can reduce wrong assumptions and avert public relations missteps.
5. b. Tech-savvy and digital natives are not a sociodemographic segment; they are behavioral segments. Hispanic, Black, Asian, American Indian, and Alaskan Native people are among multicultural segments. Gen Xers, Zoomers, and consumers with disabilities are among sociodemographic segments.

8.3 Knowledge Check

1. d. Culture is described as all of these statements.
2. c. Values and attitudes are not examples of external expressions of culture. They are examples of internal expressions of culture.
3. b. Marketers must be careful using symbols as cultural expressions because they can have different meanings among different cultures.
4. c. An advertisement that speaks to personal accomplishments, independence, and assertiveness is appealing to individualism.
5. a. An advertisement that is visually appealing and emphasizes quality of life, people, and relationships is an example of femininity.

8.4 Knowledge Check

1. c. The Hispanic population is the largest multicultural segment in the United States based on 2020 US Census data.
2. b. A person from Puerto Rico or of Puerto Rican descent is both Hispanic and Latino/Latina. *Hispanic* is a language-based term describing somebody from a Spanish-speaking place, while Latino/Latina is a location-based term that identifies gendered individuals whose families originate in Latin America.
3. b. Acculturation is the process by which a person's family cultural patterns change because of direct and constant contact with a different culture.
4. d. An overwhelming majority of Black people believe that race and community engagement are a major part of the Black identity.

5. a. Success requires connecting with each demographic on a personal and intimate level. This inevitably means that one must understand the cultural identities and the context within each population segment. Being successful with diversity marketing includes various multicultural and sociodemographic segments.

8.5 Knowledge Check

1. d. Sociodemographic marketing is a subcategory of diversity marketing. It intentionally targets certain audiences with attractive advertising and promotions based on shared social and demographic variables. Overlaying these two factors has several worthwhile benefits for marketers.
2. a. For marketers, focusing on the societal experience around belonging (acceptance, welcoming, support, and inclusion) is key for reaching the growing number of LGBTQIA+ consumers.
3. d. All of these are important steps to consider to be more successful in advertising to consumers based on their generations.
4. c. Use an approach that ensures the company's efforts express humanity, authenticity, and inclusivity, which can involve consulting or hiring individuals who have a disability rather than using actors or models who do not.
5. b. It is projected that consumer spending will continued to be dominated by baby boomers. While this isn't a new trend, it is certainly a trend that will continue through the 2030s as this generation ages out.

Chapter 9

9.1 Knowledge Check

1. a. A haircut is a service because it cannot be touched, owned, or stored for later use.
2. c. An experience combines marketing, technology, and service to alter the consumer's perception.
3. a. A convenience product is widely available, has a low cost, and does not require a lot of consideration.
4. d. A bag is a supply that does not retain value on a balance sheet.
5. c. The customer seeks both the core product (the bike) and the online classes, warranty, customer service, and support (the augmented product) in order to stay fit.

9.2 Knowledge Check

1. b. Oreo's selection of flavors represents a product line because it encompasses multiple similar products.
2. c. A product mix contains all the products that a company sells.
3. a. An addition of a type of pizza would represent product line depth.
4. d. Product line depth refers to the number of products in a product line. Products must be similar or complementary to be part of the same product line.
5. b. Product line filling has the benefit of protecting a brand from competitors that might enter the market with a similar offering and utilizes the brand's capacity to produce more products.

9.3 Knowledge Check

1. d. While profitability is measured along the product life cycle, it is not a stage of the product life cycle.
2. c. The product life cycle follows a product's sales and profitability.
3. b. The growth stage is characterized by a rapid increase in sales.
4. c. Stable sales and profitability characterize the maturity stage.
5. c. Brands that are a fad are typically introduced, grow rapidly, and decline quickly.

9.4 Knowledge Check

1. b. The growth stage of the product life cycle is characterized by increasing distribution channels.
2. a. Pricing strategies are most common during the introduction stage of the product life cycle.
3. d. Harvesting and divesture are most common during the decline stage of the product life cycle.
4. c. Product and market modification are most common during the maturity stage of the product life cycle. LaToya is engaging in both product and market modification.

   5. b. Expanding distribution, improving product quality, and messaging are most common during the growth stage of the product life cycle.

9.5 Knowledge Check

1. b. Brands often evoke positive feelings that allow a company to charge more for its product or service.
2. d. Brand value is the financial asset associated with a brand.
3. c. Brand equity is the additional value that a brand has over its competitors, while values, benefits, and attributes are all associated with brand positioning.
4. b. Whole Foods uses the 365 brand as a private label for its products.
5. d. The two brands collaborated on one offering.

9.6 Knowledge Check

1. b. Domino's is leveraging its brand to a new category of products.
2. a. A line extension retains the product category and brand.
3. a. Customers who frequently change brands are switchers.
4. d. Hard-core loyal customers primarily purchase one brand in the category.
5. c. Brand preference measures intended behavior.

9.7 Knowledge Check

1. c. Colors, fonts, and logos can capture attention.
2. d. A package as product indicates usability.
3. c. Packaging can provide safety from personal harm from the product.
4. c. The package displayed value to the consumer.
5. b. Customer experience is created when the package adds to the experience of consuming the brand.

9.8 Knowledge Check

1. d. Typically, wood is not used in grocery packaging.
2. d. Natural resources are part of the biological cycle.
3. c. Companies are trying to reduce packaging to only the necessary parts in their sustainability efforts.
4. d. Discarded packaging can be found in water sources, in landfills, and on the ground.
5. d. Biodegradation turns the product back into a natural resource that becomes a nutrient for plants.

Chapter 10

10.1 Knowledge Check

1. c. With dynamically continuous innovation, some changes in consumer habits are necessary, but the changes aren't as dramatic as with discontinuous innovation and are not as insignificant as in continuous innovation.
2. b. Remember, new-to-the-firm products aren't new to the world, but they are a new product venture for the firm.
3. d. The laundry detergent is supposedly a current product made better.
4. b. With continuous innovation, the existing product undergoes only marginal changes and doesn't alter consumer habits.
5. d. Revenue streams are the different sources from which a business earns money from the sale of its goods or services.

10.2 Knowledge Check

1. c. A prototype is an early model of a new product that R&D develops in order to be able to test the design.
2. b. Concept testing is a research method that involves determining how customers feel about the new product before actually launching it.

3. d. Commercialization is where the "rubber hits the road" and the company introduces the product to the market on a full-scale basis, involving production, marketing, distribution, and customer support.
4. b. In sales-wave research, consumers are initially allowed to try the product at no cost. They are then reoffered the product (or a competitor's product) at a reduced price a number of times (i.e., sales waves). The point of this research is to see how many consumers select the new product and record their reported levels of satisfaction with the product.
5. d. The first stage in the new product development process is idea generation.

10.3 Knowledge Check

1. d. Product metrics are data measurements that businesses use to evaluate the success of a product.
2. b. Current year percentage of sales is a "quick and dirty" way to estimate the product's future value.
3. c. Return on investment (ROI) is a performance measure used to evaluate the profitability of new product development.
4. c. Time to value is a critical metric that measures how long it takes new users to recognize the value of your product.
5. d. Annual recurring revenue (ARR) is the annual value of revenue generated from subscriptions and contracts.

10.4 Knowledge Check

1. c. Technological synergy is how much of a match there is between the existing technological skills of the firm and the technological skills needed to execute the new product initiative.
2. a. The study found that new product failure rates varied among industries, ranging from 35 percent for health care products to 49 percent for consumer goods.
3. b. The prolonged delay of a new product can have many implications: changing customer needs/wants, an economic downturn, rising unemployment rates, or even the evolution of different market segments.
4. d. In an effort to bring "something new" to the market, companies often include features that make the product more costly to produce.
5. a. Products that deliver real and unique benefits to customers are typically more successful than products that have few positive points of differentiation compared to existing products on the market.

10.5 Knowledge Check

1. d. Innovators typically buy new products as soon as they hit the market.
2. a. Product awareness is the first stage in the consumer adoption process, in which a company creates awareness that the product is available.
3. d. Communicability is the extent to which the benefits of a new product are likely to be noticed and discussed by consumers.
4. c. Laggards are more in tune with the past than the future, and they are skeptical of new ideas.
5. d. Consumers in the late majority category are typically slow to catch on to the popularity of new products or services.

Chapter 11

11.1 Knowledge Check

1. c. The concept of service perishability states that services (such as airline tickets) cannot be stored in inventory for future use or sale.
2. a. Service intangibility refers to the fact that you can't see or touch a service before it is performed.
3. c. Service variability may be defined as the changes in the quality of the same service provided by different service providers.
4. c. People-based services are those in which people, rather than equipment or machinery, play the major role in delivery, and within this classification, people-based services can be broken down further into

services provided by unskilled labor (e.g., parking lot attendant), skilled labor (e.g., plumber), and professionals (e.g., attorneys and accountants).

5. d. Equipment-based services are those in which machinery or other forms of technology are used to perform the service tasks required by customers. Since there is no person involved in the parking service, the parking meter is considered an automated equipment-based service.

11.2 Knowledge Check

1. c. According to the service-profit chain model, customer loyalty drives profitability and growth.
2. a. Employee satisfaction is the extent to which employees are happy and/or content with their jobs and work environment.
3. c. According to the model, customer satisfaction (Step 5) and customer loyalty (Step 6) are related and directly linked.
4. c. Interactive marketing occurs when employees and customers interact. It is there where the promises made during external marketing are either kept, broken, or exceeded by employees.
5. d. According to the service-profit chain model, employee satisfaction is inversely related to employee turnover (i.e., an increase in employee satisfaction results in a decrease in turnover).

11.3 Knowledge Check

1. c. The knowledge gap represents the difference between what customers expect and what the company *thinks* they expect.
2. a. The policy gap is the difference between management's perception of the customer's needs and the translation of that understanding into service delivery policies and standards.
3. c. The customer gap is the difference between the customer's expectations of the service and their perception of the experience itself.
4. c. According to the model, the five dimensions that would result in service excellence and lead to higher customer loyalty are reliability, assurance, tangibles, empathy, and responsiveness.
5. d. Tangibles represent the physical facilities, employees' appearance, equipment, machinery, and information systems.

Chapter 12

12.1 Knowledge Check

1. a. Artificial time constraints tell the consumer they will miss out if they don't purchase right now.
2. c. To determine profit, total costs (fixed and variable) are subtracted from total revenue.
3. a. Perceived value is perceived benefits less perceived costs.
4. d. Price anchoring is a strategy that utilizes a psychological theory that buyers frame their price reference around the first piece of information they see.
5. b. The value that a buyer receives from an exchange takes into account the perceived benefits and costs of making the purchase.

12.2 Knowledge Check

1. c. Channels of distribution include the importance of understanding the value of a product through the lens of suppliers and retailers.
2. d. Compatibility refers to the consistency of pricing decisions with the other marketing mix elements.
3. a. Analyzing the critical Cs of pricing will help ensure the pricing strategies are set appropriately.
4. b. Cost does not only include the materials needed to produce a produce, but all other costs associated with doing business.
5. d. The five critical Cs of pricing include cost, customers, channels of distribution, competition, and compatibility.

12.3 Knowledge Check

1. c. The demand curve describes the relationship of demand and price for most goods and services.
2. b. Fixed costs do not change based on the number of units produced.
3. d. As demand declines for a product, it is generally expected that prices will also decrease.
4. a. Total costs are equal to fixed costs + variable costs.
5. d. Cross-elasticity of demand refers to the increase in demand for a substitute product when the price of a product increases.

12.4 Knowledge Check

1. c. Penetration pricing is setting an initially low price to capture as much market share as possible.
2. d. The break-even unit formula is Fixed Costs / (Unit Price + Variable Unit Cost)
3. a. $Break\ Even\ in\ Units = Fixed\ Costs/(Unit\ Price - Variable\ Unit\ Cost) = 100/(2.00 - 0.25)$
4. b. Price skimming sets an initially high price to capture the portion of the market willing to pay the price.
5. d. Penetration pricing attempts to capture the greatest market share possible when introducing a new product.

12.5 Knowledge Check

1. c. Bundle pricing is a tactic that has a lower price for a bundle of items than when those items are purchased separately.
2. a. Captive pricing is a tactic used when there is both a core and a captive product.
3. a. Odd-even pricing is a tactic used to illustrate value or quality to a customer through pricing.
4. b. Price skimming sets an initially high price for *new* products to capture the portion of the market willing to pay the price.
5. d. Economy pricing is a tactic in which products are priced much lower than their name-brand competitors.

Chapter 13

13.1 Knowledge Check

1. a. The goal of IMC is to communicate a clear and consistent message through various promotional mix methods that will reach the various segments of the target market.
2. b. The promotional mix method of advertising is a paid form of nonpersonal communication.
3. c. Advertising is a paid form of nonpersonal communications meant to reach a large audience.
4. a. Sales promotion includes coupons that help to induce sales in the short term.
5. b. Public relations encompasses nonpaid activities that promote a product, service, idea, or person.

13.2 Knowledge Check

1. a. The celebrity is the paid spokesperson of the company, and they are the sender of the message.
2. b. Noise is anything that gets in the way of the sender and the message intended for the receiver.
3. c. Television advertising is the medium through which the message is delivered.
4. a. Encoding is the process of taking ideas and information and putting them into symbolic form.
5. a. The Tennessee Department of Tourist Development sent the message, so it is the source.

13.3 Knowledge Check

1. c. The combination of product placement, paid advertising, and the screening of the film on the British Airways flights is an example of integrated marketing communications.
2. a. Integrated marketing communications seeks to have all of the promotions send a consistent and unified image to the customer.
3. c. Sally's ability to recall and think of Taco Bell to fulfill her needs is a benefit of improved brand awareness.
4. d. Because Tina is satisfied and educated on all the ways to shop at Walgreens, she is exhibiting customer

satisfaction.

5. c. Using multiple promotional methods to send a consistent message is the goal of integrated marketing communications.

13.4 Knowledge Check

1. c. The process should begin with a complete understanding of the target audience for the promotional efforts.
2. d. Jennifer is acting on the promotional method Panera Bread used to reach her in the customer journey.
3. b. With continuity scheduling, an advertiser is showing its advertisement on a continuous schedule without variation.
4. b. Nestlé Tollhouse is working to create an emotional connection with the consumer.
5. c. Wendy's would be using all that their budget could afford for the marketing promotions.

Chapter 14

14.1 Knowledge Check

1. a. One media channel used in advertising is commercials.
2. c. This is an example of institutional advertising.
3. a. Advertising has a low per-exposure cost.
4. d. Product advertisements focus on one product from an organization's product mix and/or comparing it with competitors.
5. b. Advertising is still one of the costlier elements of the promotion mix.

14.2 Knowledge Check

1. a. Posttests are utilized after a campaign has launched.
2. c. The first step in advertising planning is determining objectives.
3. a. Millennials are more likely to see advertisements in digital form, such as social media, rather than more traditional media.
4. d. *Reach* refers to the estimated number of potential customers that can be reached with an advertising campaign.
5. a. Assessment is the final step of the advertising plan.

14.3 Knowledge Check

1. a. ROAS = $500/$20 = $25
2. c. Brand recognition involves recognizing a brand based on a picture or logo.
3. a. Return on ad spend (ROAS) calculates the revenue generated for each advertising dollar spent.
4. d. KPIs, or key performance indicators, measure the effectiveness of an advertising campaign.
5. b. Impressions = Rating × Target Population × Number of Ads. In this scenario, Liam is missing the rating information.

14.4 Knowledge Check

1. a. Public relations is earned.
2. c. Lobbying involves attempts to influence public policy and law.
3. a. Events are a type of public relations in which a company participates to increase brand awareness.
4. d. Press relations is the part of public relations that creates and maintains positive relationships with the press.
5. b. Public affairs involves creating relationships with public officials.

14.5 Knowledge Check

1. a. The company's donation and the public relations surrounding it has created sales and leads.

2. c. Public relations is often not under a company's direct control.
3. a. The company had no direct control over whether the press release would be picked up by news stations.
4. d. Public relations is free, and it has no guaranteed results.
5. b. Taco Bell was hoping that the campaign would outweigh the negative brand image caused by the lawsuit (and it worked).

Chapter 15

15.1 Knowledge Check

1. d. Personal selling is used by companies when they have a product that needs explanation and education, it is higher in price, and it can be varied according to the needs of the customer.
2. c. Personal selling is the one-on-one interaction between a sales professional and the potential customer.
3. b. Personal selling allows for the sales professional to adjust the product to meet the needs and wants of the customer.
4. b. Most products in the market have a lot of competition. The level of competition has nothing to do with the use of personal selling.
5. d. Jasmine has effectively demonstrated the personal selling skills of one-on-one interaction with the customer, meeting the needs and wants of the customer, and having personal communication with the customer to satisfy their needs and wants.

15.2 Knowledge Check

1. d. When customers call into a company to place an order an inside order taker is the person answering and taking the order.
2. b. When several people within the organization are responsible for making the sale, this is considered a team selling approach
3. c. The person who is responsible for making sure the product meets the needs of the customer is the technical specialist.
4. d. Missionary sales is responsible for educating and informing while also encouraging the use of a product.
5. a. Companies often have support personnel to assist with elements of the sale. This can include checking on inventory and setting appointments for outside sales professionals.

15.3 Knowledge Check

1. d. Lucia is trying to find the qualified people to buy the products.
2. a. When customers have questions and the sales professional is ready to answer the questions, this is typically considered handling objections.
3. d. Shakira is acting more as a consultant to help her customer have the best fit for their needs.
4. c. During the approach phase, the sales professional gathers insights and seeks to contact the prospect to build rapport and gather more information on the needs and wants of the prospect.
5. c. Keith is demonstrating the product and telling about the features that are important to the prospect. Keith is doing the presentation.

15.4 Knowledge Check

1. c. Lev needs to know how many sales professionals he will need to hire.
2. d. Malika is focused on bringing in new customers.
3. b. Companies regularly need to inform and educate their sales professionals about the products they are selling.
4. c. Nestle is most likely paying Johnny a commission on the sales he makes.
5. a. Ranee needs to spend time on selling activities.

15.5 Knowledge Check

1. d. This is an example of sales promotion geared toward generating an immediate sale.
2. b. The sales promotion is structured to stimulate demand for more product.
3. c. Rolex wants to spread information about its products to the target market of customers that will be present at the events.
4. a. Sales promotion is primarily to stimulate demand in the short term.
5. a. Sally is happy and satisfied when she gets email and promotions from American Eagle.

15.6 Knowledge Check

1. b. Coupons provide a saving off of the purchase of a specific product.
2. d. Samples provide for a free amount of product.
3. b. Sweepstakes give consumers a chance to win when they purchase something or follow the rules of the sweepstakes.
4. a. Allowances and discounts are typically provided to the trade and used to push the product to the customer.
5. d. Sales promotion is a short-term incentive to consumers and the trade.

Chapter 16

16.1 Knowledge Check

1. a. Online direct marketing includes digital tools such as email, websites, online videos, and blogs to communicate and engage with individual consumers and elicit a desired consumer response or action.
2. a. As consumers are more connected to the internet via their mobile devices and digital technologies have evolved, online direct marketing has emerged as a practical promotion tool for reaching consumers.
3. d. Content marketing involves creating and distributing content that consumers find meaningful and valuable. With content marketing, marketers must anticipate what type of content their audience wants and tell their story in a way that the audience can relate to.
4. d. Email marketing is permission-based marketing. Consumers must opt in to receive messages from companies. This typically occurs when a consumer purchases a product or service and asserts that they would like to receive messages from the company from which they've purchased.
5. d. Advantages of online direct marketing are that it has global reach, is highly targeted, and can be much easier to measure ROI.

16.2 Knowledge Check

1. a. An advantage of social media marketing is that companies can concentrate their promotional efforts on very specific groups of consumers who share common interests and demographics.
2. c. Lack of control over the message is a challenge for social media marketers. Consumers who are dissatisfied with the company can use social media to make negative comments that could hurt brand reputation.
3. a. An important element of a good mobile strategy is ensuring that your website has a responsive design. Simply put, this means ensuring that menus and content are easy to read and that the user has a good experience on the site regardless of the device.
4. d. Responsive web design is a website development approach that results in a website's display dynamically changing to adapt to whatever device a consumer uses. This approach is important to ensuring that consumers have a good user experience regardless of the device they are using.
5. b. Measuring mobile campaigns can be challenging because it's difficult to measure whether a consumer has seen a push notification or in-app message.

16.3 Knowledge Check

1. d. Online marketing metrics help marketers measure the performance of their online marketing

campaigns.

2. c. Because the goal of the campaign is to increase paid subscriptions, a visitor who enters their payment information and contact information and clicks "place order" would be a conversion.
3. c. The bounce rate measures the percentage of times visitors leave your site after visiting only one page.
4. a. Social engagement relates to the actions that users take when they engage with content on social media. Online marketers measure clicks, likes, shares, and comments to help online marketers assess the quality of their content.
5. a. Jax's Sushi House will learn which source is more effective at driving traffic to the restaurant's website.

Chapter 17

17.1 Knowledge Check

1. d. A marketing channel is a collection of people, organizations, processes, and activities that work together to deliver products and services to the consumer.
2. d. Agents serve as representatives of manufacturers. While they never take possession of a product or service, they earn a commission or collect a fee for facilitating the transaction between the customers and the manufacturer.
3. c. When intermediaries are removed from the marketing channel, manufacturers must then be solely responsible for distributing products directly to all customers. Thus, the number of transactions would increase.
4. a. Intermediaries add value by performing important activities that manufacturers are not expert at performing. This helps create efficiency in the marketing channel, which helps meet the wants and needs of targeted customers.
5. d. Accumulating, bulk-breaking, adjusting for assortment discrepancies, and providing financing are the valuable services that intermediaries provide.

17.2 Knowledge Check

1. b. A direct marketing channel sells and distributes directly to the consumer without the use of intermediaries.
2. b. An indirect marketing channel relies on a partnership with intermediaries to sell and distribute its products.
3. c. In the B2B or industrial space, manufacturers or producers sell products and services aimed at reaching a business end user.
4. b. In a corporate vertical marketing system, one channel member owns one or more other channel members.
5. c. Omnichannel marketing systems allow consumers to buy and receive products and services seamlessly across a variety of channels, including online and in-store.

17.3 Knowledge Check

1. a. The three overarching factors that impact channel choice include target market coverage, fulfillment of buyer requirements, and profitability.
2. d. An intensive distribution strategy is used when a company wants to distribute through every possible retail outlet where a consumer might find its products.
3. b. A post-sale service is a buyer requirement that is fulfilled after the purchase of a product.
4. c. Perishability is an important factor in channel decisions for companies who sell products that have a short shelf life.
5. d. Profitability is a factor that companies consider when choosing a distribution channel. Companies are attracted to channels that help them maximize profits and operate more efficiently.

17.4 Knowledge Check

1. c. Manufacturers should select channel members based on years of experience, reputation, experience within the market, and profitability. In the scenario above, selecting a channel member based on experience, reputation, and profitability makes the most sense.
2. c. Production Company C and DirectDocumentaries are involved in a well-managed relationship. There is cohesion and transparency, and they share common goals.
3. d. Disintermediation occurs when a channel member is removed from the distribution channel.
4. a. Order accuracy rate is the percentage of orders that are processed, fulfilled, and shipped to consumers without any errors.
5. b. Time to ship is a metric that measures the length of time from when a customer places an order to when it reaches them.

17.5 Knowledge Check

1. c. Supply chain management entails managing all the members and activities from the procurement and transformation of raw materials into finished goods through their distribution to targeted consumers.
2. a. In order for companies to deliver on their value proposition to consumers, they must ensure that the activities and members in the supply chain share the common goal of delivering value to consumers.
3. d. Companies that manufacture goods rely on raw materials to produce the products they sell. They purchase the required materials from suppliers, who must be able to deliver them in accordance with the manufacturer's timeline.
4. d. Resources include the labor, the raw materials, and the technology that are required to move products from their raw material phase to finished goods available for consumption.
5. a. Information workflow is a supply chain management function that relates to what and how information moves between members of the supply chain.

17.6 Knowledge Check

1. b. Air transportation provides the fastest delivery speed over trucking, rail, and water transportation.
2. b. Logistics is the planning, organizing, and controlling the movement of raw materials and ultimately finished goods to end consumers
3. c. Companies use logistics information to develop demand forecasts and conduct supply planning. It can also be used to analyze and assess the effectiveness and efficiency of the supply chain to ensure optimization.
4. d. Integrated logistics management ensures that every element of logistics as part of the entire supply chain is part of a system that works cohesively to ensure that the wants and needs of final customers are met.
5. a. 3PL providers have the expertise, flexibility, and cost efficiencies in logistics that manufacturers don't possess.

Chapter 18

18.1 Knowledge Check

1. c. Retailing is the process of selling goods and services to the consumer.
2. a. Wholesalers are in business to buy in large quantities and sell to other businesses.
3. d. Loyalty cards are one way retailers can communicate with consumers.
4. c. An omnichannel strategy is one that utilizes multiple channels.
5. c. Schwan's eliminates the intermediaries and sells directly to the consumers.

18.2 Knowledge Check

1. b. Automatic vending includes vending machines, in which there is no buyer-seller interaction.
2. b. Television home shopping would be the most likely retailing strategy to reach this target market.

Consumers can call a toll-free number to place an order without ever leaving their home.

3. b. Warehouse clubs sell in bulk to consumers who purchase memberships.
4. c. Off-price retailers are those providing high-quality goods at discounted prices.
5. a. Factory outlets are retailers that are operated by manufacturers to sell overstock items at discounted prices.

18.3 Knowledge Check

1. d. A markdown is a price decrease for a product that is at the end of its life cycle or season.
2. c. Superstores generally choose a freestanding location.
3. c. A small, rural town is most likely to have a central business district, or "downtown."
4. c. Gross margin = net sales – cost of goods sold
5. a. Omnichannel marketing increases customer's access to product, brand visibility, and personalization because it utilizes multiple channels to reach the customer.

18.4 Knowledge Check

1. d. All of the trends grew considerably.
2. c. Social commerce is a blend of e-commerce and social media, where retailers often use influencers to market products.
3. d. Digital wallets store consumers' passwords and payment information for safety and ease of ordering online.
4. a. Pandemics, such as the one in COVID-19 pandemic, forced many consumers to stay home. This caused a significant rise in online shopping.
5. c. Social media is one way in which companies can utilize an omnichannel marketing strategy, one in which utilizes many different channels to reach customers.

18.5 Knowledge Check

1. a. Wholesalers are businesses that buy products in bulk and sell to retailers.
2. d. Retailers use drop shippers to ship products directly to the end consumer.
3. d. General-merchandise wholesalers offer the most complete range of services.
4. a. Manufacturer's agents are independent contractors who act as salespersons for multiple manufacturers to sell similar (but not competing) products to retailers.
5. a. Rack jobbers are companies that agree with retailers to display and sell products in-store.

18.6 Knowledge Check

1. a. Caveat emptor is Latin for "let the buyer beware."
2. d. Product traceability allows products to be traced throughout the distribution channel to the manufacturer.
3. c. Product traceability does not make less work for distribution channel members.
4. a. Government regulations are not decreasing but are increasing and becoming more complex.
5. a. The Sale of Goods Act requires the accurate, safe, and clear use of directions on goods and services sold.

Chapter 19

19.1 Knowledge Check

1. b. Diversity, equity, and inclusion support people, which makes it a social initiative.
2. d. Sustainable marketing is rooted in purpose, based on mission, and seeks to align people, planet, and profits.

19.2 Knowledge Check

1. a. Sustainable marketing considers all parties.
2. b. Sustainable marketing innovates now while ensuring a viable future.

19.3 Knowledge Check

1. a. Increased brand recognition occurs when brands are known for their sustainability efforts.
2. d. Return on investment occurs when brands can show that the sustainability investment had a positive economic return.

19.4 Knowledge Check

1. c. Innovative marketing uses the media to spur awareness and convert prospects into customers.
2. d. Mission marketing puts purpose at the center of marketing and uses storytelling to spur action.

19.5 Knowledge Check

1. d. Transparency, sustainability, and fair working conditions are all concepts related to purpose-driven marketing.
2. a. Purpose-driven brands stand up for what is right.

Index

Symbols